Nineteenth-Century Literature Criticism

Guide to Gale Literary Criticism Series

When you need to review criticism of literary works, these are the Gale series to use:

If the author's death date is:

You should turn to:

After Dec. 31, 1959
(or author is still living)

CONTEMPORARY LITERARY CRITICISM

for example: Jorge Luis Borges, Anthony Burgess,
William Faulkner, Mary Gordon,
Ernest Hemingway, Iris Murdoch

1900 through 1959

TWENTIETH-CENTURY LITERARY CRITICISM

for example: Willa Cather, F. Scott Fitzgerald,
Henry James, Mark Twain, Virginia Woolf

1800 through 1899

NINETEENTH-CENTURY LITERATURE CRITICISM

for example: Fedor Dostoevski, Nathaniel Hawthorne,
George Sand, William Wordsworth

1400 through 1799

LITERATURE CRITICISM FROM 1400 TO 1800
(excluding Shakespeare)

for example: Anne Bradstreet, Daniel Defoe,
Alexander Pope, François Rabelais,
Jonathan Swift, Phillis Wheatley

SHAKESPEAREAN CRITICISM

Shakespeare's plays and poetry

Antiquity through 1399

CLASSICAL AND MEDIEVAL LITERATURE CRITICISM

for example: Dante, Homer, Plato, Sophocles, Vergil,
the Beowulf poet

(Volume 1 forthcoming)

Gale also publishes related criticism series:

CHILDREN'S LITERATURE REVIEW

This ongoing series covers authors of all eras. Presents criticism on authors and author/illustrators who write for the preschool through high school audience.

CONTEMPORARY ISSUES CRITICISM

This two volume set presents criticism on contemporary authors writing on current issues. Topics covered include the social sciences, philosophy, economics, natural science, law, and related areas.

ISSN 0732-1864

Volume 14

Nineteenth-Century Literature Criticism

Excerpts from Criticism of the
Works of Novelists, Poets, Playwrights,
Short Story Writers, Philosophers, and Other
Creative Writers Who Died between 1800
and 1900, from the First Published Critical
Appraisals to Current Evaluations

Cherie D. Abbey
Editor

Jelena Obradovic Kronick
Janet Mullane
Associate Editors

Gale Research Company
Book Tower
Detroit, Michigan 48226

STAFF

Cherie D. Abbey, *Editor*

Jelena Obradovic Kronick, Janet Mullane, *Associate Editors*

Gail Ann Schulte, Robert Thomas Wilson, *Senior Assistant Editors*

Rachel Carlson, Vivian L. Metcalf, Mary Nelson-Pulice, *Assistant Editors*

Sheila Fitzgerald, Phyllis Carmel Mendelson, Emily B. Tennyson,
Anna C. Wallbillich, *Contributing Editors*
Melissa Reiff Hug, *Contributing Assistant Editor*

Jeanne A. Gough, *Permissions & Production Manager*
Lizbeth A. Purdy, *Production Supervisor*
Denise Michlewicz Broderick, *Production Coordinator*
Eric Berger, *Assistant Production Coordinator*
Kathleen M. Cook, Maureen Duffy, Sheila J. Nasea, *Editorial Assistants*

Victoria B. Cariappa, *Research Coordinator*
Maureen R. Richards, *Assistant Research Coordinator*
Daniel Kurt Gilbert, Kent Graham, Michele R. O'Connell,
Keith E. Schooley, Filomena Sgambati, Vincenza G. Tranchida,
Mary D. Wise, *Research Assistants*

Linda Marcella Pugliese, *Manuscript Coordinator*
Donna Craft, *Assistant Manuscript Coordinator*
Maureen A. Puhl, Rosetta Irene Simms, *Manuscript Assistants*

Janice M. Mach, *Permissions Coordinator, Text*
Patricia A. Seefelt, *Permissions Coordinator, Illustrations*
Susan D. Battista, Margaret A. Chamberlain, Sandra C. Davis, Kathy Grell, *Assistant Permissions Coordinators*
Mabel C. Gurney, Josephine M. Keene, Mary M. Matuz, *Senior Permissions Assistants*
Margaret A. Carson, H. Diane Cooper, Colleen M. Crane, *Permissions Assistants*
Eileen H. Baehr, Anita L. Ransom, Kimberly F. Smilay, *Permissions Clerks*

Frederick G. Ruffner, *Publisher*
Dedria Bryfonski, *Editorial Director*
Ellen Crowley, *Associate Editorial Director*
Laurie Lanzen Harris, *Director, Literary Criticism Division*
Dennis Poupard, *Senior Editor, Literary Criticism Series*

Copyright © 1987 by Gale Research Company

Library of Congress Catalog Card Number 81-6943
ISBN 0-8103-5814-X
ISSN 0732-1864

Computerized photocomposition by
Typographics, Incorporated
Kansas City, Missouri

Printed in the United States

Contents

Preface

The nineteenth century was a time of tremendous growth in human endeavor: in science, in social history, and particularly in literature. The era saw the development of the novel, witnessed radical changes from classicism to romanticism to realism, and contained intellectual and artistic ideas that continue to inspire authors of our own century. The importance of the writers of the nineteenth century is twofold, for they provide insight into their own time as well as into the universal nature of human experience.

The literary criticism of an era can also give us insight into the moral and intellectual atmosphere of the past, because the criteria by which a work of art is judged reflect current philosophical and social attitudes. Literary criticism takes many forms: the traditional essay, the book or play review, even the parodic poem. Criticism can also be of several types: normative, descriptive, interpretive, textual, appreciative, generic. Collectively, the range of critical response helps us to understand a work of art, an author, an era.

The Scope of the Work

The success of two of Gale's current literary series, *Contemporary Literary Criticism (CLC)* and *Twentieth-Century Literary Criticism (TCLC),* which excerpt criticism of creative writing from the twentieth century, suggested an equivalent need among students and teachers of literature of the nineteenth century. Moreover, since the analysis of this literature spans almost two hundred years, a vast amount of critical material confronts the student.

Nineteenth-Century Literature Criticism (NCLC) presents significant passages from published criticism on authors who died between 1800 and 1900. The author list for each volume of *NCLC* is carefully compiled to represent a variety of genres and nationalities and to cover authors who are currently regarded as the most important writers of their era as well as those whose contribution to literature and literary history is significant. The truly great writers are rare, and in the intervals between them lesser but genuine artists, as well as writers who enjoyed immense popularity in their own time and in their own countries, are important to the study of nineteenth-century literature. The length of each author entry is intended to reflect the amount of attention the author has received from critics writing in English and from foreign critics in translation. Articles and books that have not been translated into English are excluded. However, since many of the major foreign studies have been translated into English and are excerpted in *NCLC,* author entries reflect the viewpoints of many nationalities. Each author entry represents a historical overview of critical reaction to the author's work: early criticism is presented to indicate initial responses and later selections represent any rise or decline in the author's literary reputation. We have also attempted to identify and include excerpts from the seminal essays on each author as well as modern perspectives. Thus, *NCLC* is designed to serve as an introduction for the student of nineteenth-century literature to the authors of that period and to the most significant commentators on these authors.

NCLC entries are intended to be definitive overviews. In order to devote more attention to each writer, approximately fifteen authors are included in each 600-page volume compared with about fifty authors in a *CLC* volume of similar size. Because of the great quantity of critical material available on many authors, and because of the resurgence of criticism generated by such events as an author's centennial or anniversary celebration, the republication of an author's works, or publication of a newly translated work or volume of letters, an author may appear more than once. Usually, a few author entries in each volume of *NCLC* are devoted to single works by major authors who have appeared previously in the series. Only those individual works that have been the subject of extensive criticism and are widely studied in literature courses are selected for this in-depth treatment. Robert Louis Stevenson's *Strange Case of Dr. Jekyll and Mr. Hyde* and William Makepeace Thackeray's *Vanity Fair* are the subjects of such entries in *NCLC,* Volume 14.

The Organization of the Book

An author section consists of the following elements: author heading, biographical and critical introduction, principal works, excerpts of criticism (each preceded by explanatory notes and followed by a bibliographical citation), and an additional bibliography.

- The *author heading* consists of the author's full name, followed by birth and death dates. The unbracketed portion of the name denotes the form under which the author most commonly wrote. If an author wrote consistently under a pseudonym, the pseudonym will be listed in the author heading and the real name given in parentheses on the first line of the biographical and critical introduction. Also located at the beginning of the introduction are any name variations under which an author wrote, including transliterated forms for authors whose languages use nonroman alphabets. Uncertainty as to a birth or death date is indicated by a question mark.

- A *portrait* of the author is included when available. Many entries also feature illustrations of materials pertinent to an author's career, including manuscript pages, letters, book illustrations, and representations of important people, places, and events in an author's life.

- The *biographical and critical introduction* contains background information that elucidates the author's creative output. When applicable, biographical and critical introductions are followed by references to additional entries on the author in past volumes of *NCLC* and in other literary reference series published by Gale Research Company. These include *Dictionary of Literary Biography, Children's Literature Review,* and *Something about the Author.*

- The list of *principal works* is chronological by date of first book publication and identifies genres. In those instances where the first publication was in other than the English language, the title and date of the first English-language edition are given in brackets. Unless otherwise indicated, dramas are dated by the first performance, rather than first publication.

- *Criticism* is arranged chronologically in each author section to provide a perspective on any changes in critical evaluation over the years. In the text of each author entry, titles by the author are printed in boldface type. This allows the reader to ascertain without difficulty the works being discussed. For purposes of easier identification, the critic's name and the publication date of the essay are given at the beginning of each piece of criticism. Unsigned criticism is preceded by the title of the journal in which it appeared. For an anonymous essay later attributed to a critic, the critic's name appears in brackets at the beginning of the excerpt and in the bibliographical citation.

- Essays are prefaced with *explanatory notes* as an additional aid to students using *NCLC*. The explanatory notes provide several types of useful information, including the reputation of the critic, the importance of a work of criticism, a synopsis of the essay, the specific approach of the critic (biographical, psychoanalytic, structuralist, etc.), and the growth of critical controversy or changes in critical trends regarding an author's work. In some cases, these notes include cross-references to related criticism in the author's entry or in the additional bibliography. Dates in parentheses within the explanatory notes refer to other essays in the author entry.

- A complete *bibliographical citation* designed to facilitate the location of the original essay or book follows each piece of criticism.

- The *additional bibliography* appearing at the end of each author entry suggests further reading on the author. In some cases it includes essays for which the editors could not obtain reprint rights.

An appendix lists the sources from which material in the volume is reprinted. It does not, however, list every book or periodical consulted for the volume.

Cumulative Indexes

Each volume of *NCLC* includes a cumulative index listing all the authors who have appeared in *Contemporary Literary Criticism, Twentieth-Century Literary Criticism, Nineteenth-Century Literature Criticism,* and *Literature Criticism from 1400 to 1800,* along with cross-references to the Gale series *Children's Literature Review, Authors in the News, Contemporary Authors, Contemporary Authors Autobiography Series, Dictionary of Literary Biography, Something about the Author,* and *Yesterday's Authors of Books for Children.* Users will welcome this cumulated author index as a useful tool for locating an author within the various series. The index, which lists birth and death dates when available, will be particularly valuable for those authors who are identified with a certain period but whose death date causes them to be placed in another, or for those authors whose careers span two periods. For example, Fedor Dostoevski is found in *NCLC,* yet Leo Tolstoy, another major nineteenth-century Russian novelist, is found in *TCLC.*

NCLC also includes a cumulative nationality index to authors. Authors are listed alphabetically by nationality, followed by the volume numbers in which they appear.

A cumulative index to critics is another useful feature of *NCLC*. Under each critic's name are listed the authors on whom the critic has written and the volume and page where the criticism appears.

Acknowledgments

No work of this scope can be accomplished without the cooperation of many people. The editors especially wish to thank the copyright holders of the excerpts included in this volume, the permissions managers of the book and magazine publishing companies for assisting us in securing reprint rights, and the staffs of the Detroit Public Library, University of Michigan Library, and Wayne State University Library for making their resources available to us. We are also grateful to Anthony J. Bogucki for his assistance with copyright research. The editors also wish to acknowledge The Bettmann Archive, Inc., for the endpaper illustration of Robert Louis Stevenson.

Suggestions Are Welcome

The editors welcome the comments and suggestions of readers to expand the coverage and enhance the usefulness of the series.

Authors to Appear in Future Volumes

About, Edmond Francois 1828-1885
Aguilo I. Fuster, Maria 1825-1897
Aksakov, Konstantin 1817-1860
Aleardi, Aleadro 1812-1878
Alecsandri, Vasile 1821-1890
Alencar, Jose 1829-1877
Alfieri, Vittorio 1749-1803
Allingham, William 1824-1889
Almquist, Carl Jonas Love 1793-1866
Alorne, Leonor de Almeida 1750-1839
Alsop, Richard 1761-1815
Altimirano, Ignacio Manuel 1834-1893
Alvarenga, Manuel Inacio da Silva
  1749-1814
Alvares de Azevedo, Manuel Antonio
  1831-1852
Anzengruber, Ludwig 1839-1889
Arany, Janos 1817-1882
Arene, Paul 1843-1893
Aribau, Bonaventura Carlos 1798-1862
Arjona de Cubas, Manuel Maria de
  1771-1820
Arnault, Antoine Vincent 1766-1834
Arneth, Alfred von 1819-1897
Arnim, Bettina von 1785-1859
Arnold, Thomas 1795-1842
Arriaza y Superviela, Juan Bautista
  1770-1837
Asbjornsen, Peter Christian 1812-1885
Ascasubi, Hilario 1807-1875
Atterbom, Per Daniel Amadeus
  1790-1855
Aubanel, Theodore 1829-1886
Auerbach, Berthold 1812-1882
Augier, Guillaume V.E. 1820-1889
Azeglio, Massimo D' 1798-1866
Azevedo, Guilherme de 1839-1882
Bakin (pseud. of Takizawa Okikani)
  1767-1848
Bakunin, Mikhail Aleksandrovich
  1814-1876
Baratynski, Jewgenij Abramovich
  1800-1844
Barnes, William 1801-1886
Batyushkov, Konstantin 1778-1855
Beattie, James 1735-1803
Beckford, William 1760-1844
Becquer, Gustavo Adolfo 1836-1870
Bentham, Jeremy 1748-1832
Beranger, Jean-Pierre de 1780-1857
Berchet, Giovanni 1783-1851
Berzsenyi, Daniel 1776-1836
Black, William 1841-1898
Blair, Hugh 1718-1800
Blicher, Steen Steensen 1782-1848
Bocage, Manuel Maria Barbosa du
  1765-1805

Boratynsky, Yevgeny 1800-1844
Borel, Petrus 1809-1859
Boreman, Yokutiel 1825-1890
Borne, Ludwig 1786-1837
Botev, Hristo 1778-1842
Brinckman, John 1814-1870
Bronte, Emily 1812-1848
Brown, Charles Brockden 1777-1810
Browning, Robert 1812-1889
Buchner, Georg 1813-1837
Campbell, James Edwin 1867-1895
Campbell, Thomas 1777-1844
Carlyle, Thomas 1795-1881
Castelo Branco, Camilo 1825-1890
Castro Alves, Antonio de 1847-1871
Channing, William Ellery 1780-1842
Chatterje, Bankin Chanda 1838-1894
Chivers, Thomas Holly 1807?-1858
Claudius, Matthais 1740-1815
Clough, Arthur Hugh 1819-1861
Cobbett, William 1762-1835
Colenso, John William 1814-1883
Coleridge, Hartley 1796-1849
Collett, Camilla 1813-1895
Comte, Auguste 1798-1857
Conrad, Robert T. 1810-1858
Conscience, Hendrik 1812-1883
Cooke, Philip Pendleton 1816-1850
Corbiere, Edouard 1845-1875
Crabbe, George 1754-1832
Cruz E Sousa, Joao da 1861-1898
Desbordes-Valmore, Marceline
  1786-1859
Deschamps, Emile 1791-1871
Deus, Joao de 1830-1896
Dickinson, Emily 1830-1886
Dinis, Julio 1839-1871
Dinsmoor, Robert 1757-1836
Du Maurier, George 1834-1896
Echeverria, Esteban 1805-1851
Eminescy, Mihai 1850-1889
Engels, Friedrich 1820-1895
Espronceda, Jose 1808-1842
Ettinger, Solomon 1799-1855
Euchel, Issac 1756-1804
Ferguson, Samuel 1810-1886
Fernandez de Lizardi, Jose Joaquin
  1776-1827
Fernandez de Moratin, Leandro
  1760-1828
Fet, Afanasy 1820-1892
Feuillet, Octave 1821-1890
Fontane, Theodor 1819-1898
Freiligrath, Hermann Ferdinand
  1810-1876
Freytag, Gustav 1816-1895
Ganivet, Angel 1865-1898

Garrett, Almeida 1799-1854
Garshin, Vsevolod Mikhaylovich
  1855-1888
Gezelle, Guido 1830-1899
Ghalib, Asadullah Khan 1797-1869
Goldschmidt, Meir Aron 1819-1887
Goncalves Dias, Antonio 1823-1864
Griboyedov, Aleksander Sergeyevich
  1795-1829
Grigor'yev, Appolon Aleksandrovich
  1822-1864
Groth, Klaus 1819-1899
Grun, Anastasius (pseud. of Anton
  Alexander Graf von Auersperg)
  1806-1876
Guerrazzi, Francesco Domenico
  1804-1873
Gutierrez Najera, Manuel 1859-1895
Gutzkow, Karl Ferdinand 1811-1878
Ha-Kohen, Shalom 1772-1845
Halleck, Fitz-Greene 1790-1867
Harris, George Washington 1814-1869
Hayne, Paul Hamilton 1830-1886
Hazlitt, William 1778-1830
Hebbel, Christian Friedrich 1813-1863
Hebel, Johann Peter 1760-1826
Hegel, Georg Wilhelm Friedrich
  1770-1831
Heiberg, Johann Ludvig 1813-1863
Herculano, Alexandre 1810-1866
Hernandez, Jose 1834-1886
Hertz, Henrik 1798-1870
Herwegh, Georg 1817-1875
Hoffman, Charles Fenno 1806-1884
Holderlin, Friedrich 1770-1843
Hood, Thomas 1799-1845
Hooper, Johnson Jones 1815-1863
Hopkins, Gerard Manley 1844-1889
Horton, George Moses 1798-1880
Howitt, William 1792-1879
Hughes, Thomas 1822-1896
Imlay, Gilbert 1754?-1828?
Irwin, Thomas Caulfield 1823-1892
Issacs, Jorge 1837-1895
Jacobsen, Jens Peter 1847-1885
Jippensha, Ikku 1765-1831
Kant, Immanuel 1724-1804
Karr, Jean Baptiste Alphonse 1808-1890
Keble, John 1792-1866
Khomyakov, Alexey S. 1804-1860
Kierkegaard, Soren 1813-1855
Kinglake, Alexander W. 1809-1891
Kingsley, Charles 1819-1875
Kivi, Alexis 1834-1872
Koltsov, Alexey Vasilyevich 1809-1842
Kotzebue, August von 1761-1819
Kraszewski, Josef Ignacy 1812-1887

Kreutzwald, Friedrich Reinhold 1803-1882
Krochmal, Nahman 1785-1840
Krudener, Valeria Barbara Julia de Wietinghoff 1766-1824
Lampman, Archibald 1861-1899
Landon, Letitia Elizabeth 1802-1838
Larra y Sanchez de Castro, Mariano 1809-1837
Lebensohn, Micah Joseph 1828-1852
Leconte de Lisle, Charles-Marie-Rene 1818-1894
Lenau, Nikolaus 1802-1850
Leontyev, Konstantin 1831-1891
Leopardi, Giacoma 1798-1837
Leskov, Nikolai 1831-1895
Lever, Charles James 1806-1872
Levisohn, Solomon 1789-1822
Lewes, George Henry 1817-1878
Leyden, John 1775-1811
Lobensohn, Micah Gregory 1775-1810
Longstreet, Augustus Baldwin 1790-1870
Lopez de Ayola y Herrera, Adelardo 1819-1871
Lover, Samuel 1797-1868
Luzzato, Samuel David 1800-1865
Macedo, Joaquim Manuel de 1820-1882
Macha, Karel Hynek 1810-1836
Mackenzie, Henry 1745-1831
Malmon, Solomon 1754-1800
Mangan, James Clarence 1803-1849
Manzoni, Alessandro 1785-1873
Mapu, Abraham 1808-1868
Marii, Jose 1853-1895
Markovic, Svetozar 1846-1875
Martinez de La Rosa, Francisco 1787-1862
Mathews, Cornelius 1817-1889
McCulloch, Thomas 1776-1843
Merriman, Brian 1747-1805
Meyer, Conrad Ferdinand 1825-1898
Montgomery, James 1771-1854
Morton, Sarah Wentworth 1759-1846
Muller, Friedrich 1749-1825
Murger, Henri 1822-1861
Neruda, Jan 1834-1891
Nestroy, Johann 1801-1862
Newman, John Henry 1801-1890
Niccolini, Giambattista 1782-1861

Nievo, Ippolito 1831-1861
Nodier, Charles 1780-1844
Obradovic, Dositej 1742-1811
Oehlenschlager, Adam 1779-1850
O'Neddy, Philothee (pseud. of Theophile Dondey) 1811-1875
O'Shaughnessy, Arthur William Edgar 1844-1881
Ostrovsky, Alexander 1823-1886
Paine, Thomas 1737-1809
Peacock, Thomas Love 1785-1866
Perk, Jacques 1859-1881
Pisemsky, Alexey F. 1820-1881
Pompeia, Raul D'Avila 1863-1895
Popovic, Jovan Sterija 1806-1856
Praed, Winthrop Mackworth 1802-1839
Prati, Giovanni 1814-1884
Preseren, France 1800-1849
Pringle, Thomas 1789-1834
Procter, Adelaide Ann 1825-1864
Procter, Bryan Waller 1787-1874
Pye, Henry James 1745-1813
Quental, Antero Tarquinio de 1842-1891
Quinet, Edgar 1803-1875
Quintana, Manuel Jose 1772-1857
Radishchev, Aleksander 1749-1802
Raftery, Anthony 1784-1835
Raimund, Ferdinand 1790-1836
Reid, Mayne 1818-1883
Renan, Ernest 1823-1892
Reuter, Fritz 1810-1874
Rogers, Samuel 1763-1855
Ruckert, Friedrich 1788-1866
Runeberg, Johan 1804-1877
Rydberg, Viktor 1828-1895
Saavedra y Ramirez de Boquedano, Angel de 1791-1865
Sacher-Mosoch, Leopold von 1836-1895
Saltykov-Shchedrin, Mikhail 1826-1892
Satanov, Isaac 1732-1805
Schiller, Johann Friedrich 1759-1805
Schlegel, August 1767-1845
Schlegel, Karl 1772-1829
Scott, Sir Walter 1771-1832
Scribe, Augustin Eugene 1791-1861
Sedgwick, Catherine Maria 1789-1867
Senoa, August 1838-1881
Shelley, Percy Bysshe 1792-1822

Shulman, Kalman 1819-1899
Sigourney, Lydia Howard Huntley 1791-1856
Silva, Jose Asuncion 1865-1896
Slaveykov, Petko 1828-1895
Slowacki, Juliusz 1809-1848
Smith, Richard Penn 1799-1854
Smolenskin, Peretz 1842-1885
Stagnelius, Erik Johan 1793-1823
Staring, Antonie Christiaan Wynand 1767-1840
Stendhal (pseud. of Henri Beyle) 1783-1842
Stifter, Adalbert 1805-1868
Stone, John Augustus 1801-1834
Taine, Hippolyte 1828-1893
Taunay, Alfredo d'Ecragnole 1843-1899
Taylor, Bayard 1825-1878
Tennyson, Alfred, Lord 1809-1892
Terry, Lucy (Lucy Terry Prince) 1730-1821
Thompson, Daniel Pierce 1795-1868
Thompson, Samuel 1766-1816
Thomson, James 1834-1882
Tiedge, Christoph August 1752-1841
Timrod, Henry 1828-1867
Tommaseo, Nicolo 1802-1874
Tompa, Mihaly 1817-1888
Topelius, Zachris 1818-1898
Turgenev, Ivan 1818-1883
Tyutchev, Fedor I. 1803-1873
Uhland, Ludvig 1787-1862
Valaoritis, Aristotelis 1824-1879
Valles, Jules 1832-1885
Verde, Cesario 1855-1886
Villaverde, Cirilio 1812-1894
Vinje, Aasmund Olavsson 1818-1870
Vorosmarty, Mihaly 1800-1855
Weisse, Christian Felix 1726-1804
Welhaven, Johan S. 1807-1873
Werner, Zacharius 1768-1823
Wescott, Edward Noyes 1846-1898
Wessely, Nattali Herz 1725-1805
Whitman, Sarah Helen 1803-1878
Wieland, Christoph Martin 1733-1813
Woolson, Constance Fenimore 1840-1894
Zhukovsky, Vasily 1783-1852

Émile Gaboriau

1832-1873

French novelist and journalist.

Often credited with the creation of the first detective novel, Gaboriau introduced in his popular and sensational crime novels many now-familiar narrative methods and detective techniques. Furthermore, scholars cite the series of five books featuring the investigators Lecoq and Père Tabaret as a significant link between Edgar Allan Poe's short stories of detection and Sir Arthur Conan Doyle's Sherlock Holmes tales. Though Gaboriau's work remains largely unread today, he continues to be recognized as a key figure in the development of the detective fiction genre.

Gaboriau was born in Saujon, France, to a bourgeois family. Though his father encouraged him to pursue a career in law, Gaboriau evaded legal studies by joining the cavalry in 1851. During his seven-year term of military service he reached the rank of sergeant major, but left the army when he saw no further opportunity for advancement. After moving to Paris, he took a variety of jobs to support himself: he worked as a shipping clerk, manager of a livery stable, editor of a minor periodical, ballad-writer for street singers, and composer of poetic mottoes for cakes, wrapping paper, and shopping bags. In 1859, he began to publish anecdotes of military life and sketches of famous Parisian actresses and royal mistresses in newspapers and magazines. This writing experience led to a position as secretary to Paul Féval, a popular author of lurid sensational romances that appeared as serial supplements to daily newspapers. Known as "feuilletons," the supplements were the French equivalent of the English "penny dreadfuls" or the American "dime novels." Gaboriau's duties as Féval's secretary probably included researching city morgues, prisons, and police stations for background information as well as ghost-writing some of the daily episodes of the feuilletons.

The knowledge of the French judicial system and Parisian criminal life that Gaboriau acquired as Féval's assistant served him well when he became a feuilletonist in his own right in 1861. During the next five years, Gaboriau produced seven serialized works, but these melodramatic accounts of society and manners attracted little attention until the appearance of *L'affaire Lerouge* (*The Widow Lerouge*). This serial, based on a contemporary crime, won Gaboriau both popular and financial success. Gaboriau's feuilleton included the customary elements of intrigue, crime, and confused identity, but the work was unique in its primary emphasis on the criminal investigation process and the detectives Lecoq and Père Tabaret. Because of this innovative focus many scholars recognize *The Widow Lerouge* as the first true detective novel. Between 1867 and 1869, Gaboriau produced four more novels that featured the idiosyncratic amateur investigator, Tabaret, and the dedicated, egotistical police detective, Lecoq. *Le crime d'Orcival* (*The Mystery of Orcival*), *Le dossier no. 113* (*File No. 113*), *Les esclaves de Paris* (*The Slaves of Paris*), and *Monsieur Lecoq* follow the pattern established in *The Widow Lerouge*. Each work is composed of two volumes: the first opens with a mysterious crime and then describes the detective's efforts to solve it, while the second includes a lengthy digressive history of the characters and their motivations. Though the second vol-

umes were less popular than the action-oriented detective portions, Gaboriau's novels were avidly read, both as serials in periodicals and in book form. His popularity soon spread to England and America, where numerous translations and plagiarized versions were released. Gaboriau profited handsomely from the sale of his novels in France, but he continued writing at a frantic pace, producing five more novels that focused exclusively on society as well as a collection of shorter detective pieces. At the time of his death in 1873, he was at work on two new novels in which he hoped to escape the commercialism of the feuilleton. Some scholars conclude that these fragmentary manuscripts would have proved Gaboriau's best work, had he finished them. While his later writings are generally regarded as inferior to his detective novels, some critics consider *Le petit vieux des Batignolles* (*The Little Old Man of the Batignolles*), a novella published posthumously with a collection of short stories, equal to his best work.

Criticism of Gaboriau's work focuses almost exclusively on his detective tales. Some early critics argued that these novels were marred by inconsistencies as well as by the discursive style that Gaboriau adopted as a feuilletonist. Generally, however, contemporary reviewers assessed his works very favorably; though sensational and crime-ridden, Gaboriau's novels never glorify the criminal elements and thus could not be faulted on moral grounds. Commentators also admired Gaboriau's use of scrupulously accurate legal detail, his effective settings, and his careful plot construction. Yet following the first glow of popularity, his books were generally forgotten, and Gaboriau was cited only as an important precursor to Doyle. In the 1920s and 1930s, his reputation enjoyed a brief revival, and his reissued works drew positive commentary from such critics as Valentine Williams and Dorothy L. Sayers, who praised Gaboriau's originality, style, and characterizations. Their critiques established his historical importance to the evolution of the detective genre, a position defended by E. F. Bleiler and R. F. Stewart in the latter part of the twentieth century.

Gaboriau's original detection techniques, which dazzled nineteenth-century readers and are still widely copied, have today earned his novels the status of classics in their genre. Though Gaboriau is of interest primarily to students of the history of mystery literature, many scholars have accorded him the title "the father of the detective novel."

*PRINCIPAL WORKS

Le 13e hussards (sketches) 1861
  [*The Thirteenth Hussars*, 1888]
Les gens de bureau (novel) 1862
  [*The Men of the Bureau*, 1880]
Les mariages d'aventure (sketches) 1862
  [Published in two volumes: *A Chance Marriage*, 1878;
    Promises of Marriage, 1883]
L'affaire Lerouge (novel) 1866
  [*The Widow Lerouge*, 1873]
Le crime d'Orcival (novel) 1867
  [*The Mystery of Orcival*, 1871]
Le dossier no. 113 (novel) 1867
  [*File No. 113*, 1875]
Les esclaves de Paris (novel) 1868
  [*The Slaves of Paris*, 1882]
Monsieur Lecoq (novel) 1869
  [*Monsieur Lecoq*, 1880]
La vie infernale (novel) 1870
  [*The Count's Secret*, 1881]
La clique dorée (novel) 1871
  [*The Clique of Gold*, 1891]
La dégringolade (novel) 1872
  [*The Downward Path*, 1883]
La corde au cou (novel) 1873
  [*Within an Inch of His Life*, 1873]
L'argent des autres (novel) 1874
  [*Other People's Money*, 1874]
Le petit vieux des Batignolles (novella and short stories)
    1876
  [*The Little Old Man of the Batignolles; or, A Chapter
    from a Detective's Memoirs*, 1880]

*Most of Gaboriau's works were first published in serial form in daily newspapers.

THE SATURDAY REVIEW, LONDON (essay date 1866)

[*The following excerpt is drawn from an early review of* The Widow Lerouge.]

The story [of *L'affaire Lerouge*] is well told, and is full of those fine and delicate touches, those epigrammatic sentences and incisive phrases, so peculiarly French; the ingenuity of the evidence is very clever, and the analysis of character and motive subtle and true. It is not ghastly and immoral like Germinie Lacerteux, and some others of late production, but it is neat, careful, well sustained, and interesting; and, if criminal, is also decent. (p. 738)

> *A review of "L'affaire Lerouge," in* The Saturday Review, *London, Vol. 22, No. 581, December 15, 1866, pp. 737-38.*

THE SATURDAY REVIEW, LONDON (essay date 1867)

[*The author of the following review of* File No. 113 *finds the novel lacking in ingenuity and claims that Gaboriau's concern with minute plot details led him to commit absurdities and gross oversights.*]

It will be easy for our readers to imagine for themselves the general nature of M. Gaboriau's plot [in *Le Dossier No. 113*]. We cannot say that we perfectly understand all the dark ramifications of plots and counterplots in which his persons lead a mysterious existence. There are two or three of the crimes which are generally most interesting. There is a villain who poisons his brother, and thereby possesses himself of a fortune. There is a theft which we can only compare to the Road murder; two persons, of apparently unimpeachable honour, have keys to a banker's safe, to which no one else has any apparent means of access; and one morning it appears to have been opened, and 350,000 francs subtracted from it. There is, further, an elaborate and diabolical system of *chantage*—the French name for extorting money by threats of exposure—which tortures two amiable women to the verge of insanity. The police authorities and their spies, the villains, the honest people, and above all the wonderful amateur detective [Père Tabaret] . . . are always plunged in a series of more or less unintelligible intrigues, which the reader can scarcely follow without giddiness. There are thrilling meetings in dark corners of Paris, where terrific threats are being exchanged; and it is not without a serious effort of thought that we can realize the position in which any one of the actors stands to the others, and remember what will be the effect of any given remark at a given moment. The writer of such a story has of course no very exalted ambition. He does not seek to give us any profound analysis of character, for it is evidently quite sufficient labour to drive such a perplexing team of personages, and to keep the reins tolerably distinct. The one aim that he can propose to himself is to amuse us by the ingenuity of the story; and the great difficulty is to keep the reader just at the right pitch of attention. If he thinks too little about what he is reading, he soon gets hopelessly muddled as to the various combinations of the plot; and if he thinks too much, he sees that they are all made of moonshine. The principle upon which all such stories depend is a very simple one, and was used with remarkable skill by Poe in his ghastly fiction of the *Murders in the Rue Morgue*. The artifice is something of this kind. When a man has constructed a riddle, he has of course little trouble in finding the answer to it; and if the reader followed the writer's mental process, he would not wonder at its ingenuity. Poe started by imagining a murder by a chimpanzee, and made the beast leave just enough hints of his performance to afford grounds for a guess at his agency. But he of course began by giving the reader the riddle without the explanation, and asked him to guess it. Here, he said, are the hints; what can you make of them? When the reader gave it up, he supplied the key, which of course fitted admirably. And most people forgot to remark how easy it was, when the crime was given, to invent the necessary evidence for its discovery, and also forgot to remark that a sensible man might with equal propriety have made a different guess; for it does not follow in such cases that, because one solution explains the facts, another will not do equally well. M. Gaboriau constantly makes use of this simple artifice. Thus the only trace left upon the safe which has been opened is a certain mysterious scratch. The super-excellent detective thinks about this for three days, and at last hits upon an explanation which solves the mystery and leads ultimately to the discomfiture of the villains. This is, that whilst one person was trying to press the key into the lock, another must have suddenly drawn back his arm by a jerk. When M. Gaboriau had settled the details of the crime, it was of course easy to invent this indication, and it is equally easy to call upon us to admire the marvellous sagacity of his detective in explaining it. And yet in practice such a scratch would admit of fifty other explanations, and a detective who stuck to this one theory would be making a foolish assumption, though it might accidentally turn out that he was right. In the meantime, whilst this astonishing inference is being made, no one else has thought of the most obvious expedient of all—that of getting the numbers of the stolen notes. The detective aforesaid mentions after a time that he has hit upon this plan, and quite confounds his hearer by the wisdom which he has thereby shown; but of course M. Gaboriau is bound to find some profounder device for discomfiting the rogues, and nothing more is heard of tracing the notes. Indeed, if people took the shortest way to their ends, no one could get a sufficiently complicated plot; and, in seeking to get matters into a duly ravelled condition, M. Gaboriau inevitably commits greater oversights than this. He is so careful to raise little entanglements that he forgets some of the most obvious difficulties; if his readers look at matters from a different point of view from his own, the absurdity of some of his assumptions becomes evident. Thus, at one part of his story, it is essential that a villain should be of most attractive appearance, and act the character of a young Frenchman of fortune and birth, whilst moving in good society. At another, the same villain, in obedience to other necessities, has to be the son of an English jockey, who has been better educated than usual, but has made his living by card-sharping in London. That such a youth should enter the house of a rich banker as a native Frenchman of high social position, is, we hope, slightly improbable. Or again, a certain Marquis de Clameran has killed two men, and been sentenced to several years' imprisonment. He escapes, but calmly comes back to France—after twenty years, it is true—but under the same name, and in great wealth and comfort; and it never occurs to any one but his brother that he is the old Marquis de Clameran come back.

In short, without exposing the absurdity of a tissue of absurdities, we may say that the absurdities are really not plausible enough even for a novel. We see the strings too plainly to care about the puppets. Moreover, the complication is mainly produced by a device which is rather tiresome—that of beginning the story in the middle and turning back half way through to tell what had happened before the book began; *à propos* to which we may remark that the amateur detective is supposed to relate these pre-introductory matters, and that in the course of a week he has discovered the particulars of conversations which took place twenty years before. The method by which he obtains this surprising result is by getting copies of letters written by another person about the time of his investigation, which certainly implies that his penetration must have been

An illustration of the murder scene from The Widow Le-rouge.

enormous. We have, however, said enough to prove that *Le Dossier No. 113* is, in our opinion, wanting in the merit to which it aspires, that of being amusingly ingenious. (p. 546)

> *A review of "Le dossier no. 113," in* The Saturday Review, *London, Vol. 24, No. 626, October 26, 1867, pp. 545-46.*

THE SATURDAY REVIEW, LONDON   (essay date 1869)

[*In a survey of current French literature, this reviewer commends Gaboriau's* The Slaves of Paris *as entertaining reading.*]

If we must have sensational stories full of horrors and improbabilities, we should prefer applying to writers who, like M. Gaboriau, aim at nothing else but excitement pure and simple. *Les Esclaves de Paris* has no pretensions to teach philosophy or to recommend Red Republicanism; it does not form part of a triology destined to illustrate a grand social thought. M. Gaboriau's sole purpose is to amuse, and he does so thoroughly. It is hard to believe that what he calls *le chantage*—that is to say, the art of worming out people's secrets and trading with them—is as extensively practised in Paris as our novelist suggests; but *chantage* has afforded the groundwork for two interesting volumes.

A review of "Les esclaves de Paris," in The Saturday Review, *London, Vol. 27, No. 710, June 5, 1869, p. 758.*

THE SATURDAY REVIEW, LONDON   (essay date 1878)

[*In the following excerpt, the anonymous critic attributes Gaboriau's success to his careful attention to and consistency in plot details. The critic also dismisses moral objections to Gaboriau's novels, noting that the author demonstrated no sympathy with crime and "never failed to make his criminals utterly odious."*]

The most successful author of novels of mystery was, beyond all doubt, the late Emile Gaboriau, some of whose curious and rather ghastly stories seem to be now as widely read as when they were first produced. *L'Affaire Lerouge* and *Le Crime d'Orcival* have gone through twelve editions, and *Le Dossier No. 113* through ten. A greater success could hardly be desired for any novelist; but it might perhaps be urged that nevertheless it is not one to be envied, inasmuch as Gaboriau's works are of a demoralizing nature. The criticism would, however, be unfounded, for, though he usually dealt with crime, he was totally free from any morbid sympathy with it, and never failed to make his criminals utterly odious. The success of his books, then, was certainly not due to any degrading characteristics, and, if it was not of a very lofty kind, it can hardly be denied that it was considerable, and that some of his works are found highly interesting by a great many people.

The point to which we now desire to draw attention is that the great effect which these romances produce on the reader is due not so much to the inventive genius of the writer as to the extraordinary care given by him to the arrangement of his story, and to the thought bestowed by him on every incident down to the most minute. He had considerable inventive power, no doubt; but in this respect other novelists, both English and French, have been quite equal to him. What gave such singular force to some of his fictions was the immense trouble he took to think out every detail of his plot; and that not during the progress of the work, but apparently before he put pen to paper. (p. 619)

[*L'Affaire Lerouge*], no doubt, is an ingenious story, but at the same time it does not show any very extraordinary originality or inventive power. Some parts of it, such as the silence of a man for fear of compromising a woman, and the reappearance of a person supposed to be dead, are old enough, and must be familiar to most readers; and yet *L'Affaire Lerouge* is perhaps the most successful novel of its kind ever written, and probably few of those who have read it can say with truth that it failed to interest them. Its force is due in part, no doubt, to its well-contrived story; but in still greater degree to the careful manner in which the writer, before beginning the work as it appeared, evidently thought out, not only his main plot, but everything connected with it, the sequence of all the facts, the exits and entrances, it may almost be said, of the leading characters. The author, therefore, when writing, developed his story according to a plan considered down to its minutest detail, and, having all the threads in his hand, was able to produce exactly the effect he desired. There is nothing at first apparently to connect the advocate with the murder of Claudine Lerouge; but when the mystery is at last made clear, the fact of his being the assassin is seen to be a necessary inference from the preceding parts of the work, and all the carefully considered incidents are seen to point to the same conclusion, except in one or two cases where the writer makes slight mistakes; but it is

probably almost impossible altogether to avoid these in a novel of this kind. On the whole, the work is wonderfully consistent. The reader who desires to verify what has been said as to Gaboriau's method can easily do so by turning back to the opening chapters after finishing the work. He will then see how completely everything connected with the story must have been present to the author's mind when those were written. If it be said that the opening chapters may have been composed last, the answer is that this cannot have been the case, as the small errors which have been mentioned are in these chapters, and would certainly have been avoided if they had been written after the rest of the book was completed. Probably *L'Affaire Lerouge,* like most of Gaboriau's works, appeared in *feuilletons,* so that the opening chapters must of necessity have been written first, and, once written, could not be altered. It certainly is not to be desired that English writers should imitate Gaboriau in his fondness for describing crimes and horrors; but perhaps some of those who wish to achieve success in what may now be considered as the business of novel-writing might do well to study the method which he followed in producing the most successful of his works. (pp. 619-20)

A review of "L'affaire Lerouge," in The Saturday Review, *London, Vol. 45, No. 1177, May 18, 1878, pp. 619-20.*

[A. INNES SHAND]   (essay date 1879)

[*Calling Gaboriau a pioneer in his genre, Shand points to Gaboriau's emphasis on individualized characters and ingenious plots as his main contribution to the crime fiction model established by Poe. For another discussion by Shand, see the excerpt dated 1890.*]

It is nearly six years since the death of Emile Gaboriau, and no one has succeeded as yet in imitating him even tolerably, though he had struck into a line that was as profitable as it was popular. We are not inclined to overrate Gaboriau's genius, for genius he had of a certain sort. . . . [His] system was less difficult than it seems, since he must have worked his puzzles out *en revers,*—putting them together with an eye to pulling them to pieces. But his originality in his own *genre* is unquestionable, though in the main conception of his romances he took Edgar Poe for his model. But Gaboriau embellished and improved on the workmanship of the morbid American. The murders of the Rue Morgue and the other stories of the sort are hard and dry *procès-verbals,* where the crime is everything, and the people go for little, except in so far as their antecedents enlighten the detection. With Gaboriau, on the other hand, we have individuality in each character, and animation as well as coarser excitement in the story. The dialogue is lively, and always illustrative. Perhaps Gaboriau has had but indifferent justice done to him, because he betook himself to a style of romance which was supposed to be the speciality of police-reporters and penny-a-liners. His readers were inclined to take it for granted that his criminals were mere stage villains, and that his police-agents, apart from their infallible *flair,* were such puppets as one sets in motion in a melodrama. The fact . . . [is] that they are nothing of the kind. Extreme pains have been bestowed on the more subtle traits of the personages by which, while being tracked, examined or tried, they are compromised, condemned, or acquitted. Read Gaboriau carefully as you will, it is rarely indeed that you find a flaw in the meshes of the intricate nets he has been weaving. Or, to change the metaphor, the springs of the complicated action, packed away as they are, the one within the other, are always working in marvellous harmony towards the appointed end. The ingenuity of some of his combinations and suggestions is extraordinary; and we believe his works might be very profitable reading to public prosecutors as well as intelligent detectives. His *Maître Lecoq* and his *Père Tabaret* have ideas which would certainly not necessarily occur to the most *rusé* practitioner of the Rue Jerusalem; and they do not prove their astuteness by a single happy thought. On the contrary, the stuff of their nature is that of the heaven-born detective, who is an observer from temperament rather than from habit, and who draws his mathematical deductions from a comparison of the most trivial signs. The proof that Gaboriau's books are something more than the vulgar *feuilleton* of the 'Police News,' is that most of them will bear reading again, though the sensations of the dénouement have been anticipated. In reading for the second time, we read with a different but a higher interest. Thus in the *L'affaire Lerouge*, for example, there is an admirable mystification. The respectable and admirably conducted Noel Gerdy, who has coolly committed a brutal murder, plays the hypocrite systematically to such perfection that we can understand the famous amateur detective being his familiar intimate without entertaining a suspicion as to his nature and habits. The disclosure having been made, and Noel fatally compromised, the circumstances strike you as carrying improbability on the face of them; so you read again and are severely critical in the expectation of catching M. Gaboriau tripping. And we believe, by the way, that in that very novel we have come upon the only oversight with which we can reproach him, although it is not in the history of Noel's intimacy with Père Tabaret. It is a missing fragment of a foil, which is one of the most deadly *pièces de conviction* against the innocent Viscount de Commarin; and the fragment, so far as we can remember, is never either traced or accounted for. But exceptions of this kind only prove the rule; and when we think how the author has varied and multiplied the startling details in his criminal plots, we must admit that his fertility of invention is marvellous. The story of the *Petit Vieux des Batignolles,* the last work he wrote, though short and slight, was by no means the least clever. One unfortunate habit he had, which may perhaps be attributed to considerations of money. He almost invariably lengthened and weakened his novels by some long-winded digression, which was at least as much episodical as explanatory. When the interest was being driven along at high-pressure pace, he would blow off the steam all of a sudden, and shunt his criminals and detectives on to a siding, while, going back among his personages for perhaps a generation, he tells us how all the circumstances had come about. (pp. 698-99)

[*A. Innes Shand*], *"Contemporary Literature, VI: French Novels,"* in Blackwood's Edinburgh Magazine, *Vol. CXXV, No. DCCLXIV, June, 1879, pp. 678-703.*

ALFRED E. GATHORNE HARDY   (essay date 1884)

[*Characterizing Gaboriau's novels as entertaining, well constructed, and intellectually challenging, Gathorne Hardy maintains that they are superior to those of Poe and Wilkie Collins and recommends them to students of French legal practice.*]

To those who are desirous of becoming acquainted with the French criminal procedure, and have not the leisure or inclination to study abstruse legal text-books, I pass on the advice given me many years ago by the late Mr. Justice Willes, when I was marshal on the Northern Circuit. "Young man," he said, "you mean to practice at the Bar, and will find it useful to know the French criminal practice; you had better read Gaboriau's novels, and they will give you a thorough insight into it." Those who have shared with me the privilege of the friendship of that most learned judge and excellent man, will agree that his two distinguishing characteristics as a lawyer were accuracy and profundity, and that he himself would never have given such advice without having compared with the parent sources of code and commentary the streams which, in the form of light literature, he so recommended to others. I followed his advice at once, and have since devoured Gaboriau's works over and over again with infinite pleasure, and if it is necessary to cite more exalted critics in their favour, I believe that two men among the greatest of their generation—Prince Bismarck and Lord Beaconsfield—were great readers and admirers of these fictions. The ingenuity with which the plots are constructed, and the care and industry with which they are elaborated, even to their minutest details, in my opinion far outshine the greatest successes of Poe and Wilkie Collins in similar fields of literature, and I doubt whether anyone who is really fond of the what I may call puzzle class of novels could tear himself away from *Monsieur Lecoq* or *L'Affaire Le Rouge* until the answer to the riddle had been revealed, or the candle burnt down to the socket.

As a general rule the plan of Gaboriau's various works is uniform. A crime is committed under mysterious circumstances, and one portion of the book is devoted to detecting its author and proving the innocence of those who are wrongly suspected, while a second portion details the circumstances, often commencing at a remote date, which led to its commission. The general interest of the latter part is usually far inferior to that of the former. The reader must be prepared for murders, thefts, bigamy, and other crimes, and "moving accidents in flood and field"; but if Gaboriau wishes, like the fat boy in *Pickwick,* "to make your flesh creep," judging from my own experience he does not in the least degree succeed. My feelings are never at all harrowed by the woes of bereaved relations, plundered bankers, and betrayed damsels; who all seem to me as lay-figures constructed to set off to advantage the life-like personalities of the real heroes, the marvellous detectives whose instinctive perception of the true facts of a crime, and the motives of its perpetrators, far excel the wonders of modern thought-reading. . . . (pp. 593-94)

Alfred E. Gathorne Hardy, "The Examination of Prisoners: Emile Gaboriau," in The National Review, *London, Vol. III, July, 1884, pp. 591-604.*

SIR ARTHUR CONAN DOYLE   (essay date 1887)

[*Doyle was a late nineteenth- and early twentieth-century English novelist and short story writer who is best remembered as the creator of Sherlock Holmes. The following excerpt from Dr. Watson's recounting of a dialogue with Sherlock Holmes is taken from Doyle's* A Study in Scarlet, *which was first published in* Beeton's Christmas Annual *in November, 1887. Although Holmes here claims superiority to Lecoq, later critics often link Gaboriau's and Doyle's creations in discussions of detective fiction.*]

'Have you read Gaboriau's works?' I asked. 'Does Lecoq come up to your idea of a detective?'

Sherlock Holmes sniffed sardonically. 'Lecoq was a miserable bungler,' he said, in an angry voice; 'he had only one thing to recommend him, and that was his energy. That book made me positively ill. The question was how to identify an unknown prisoner. I could have done it in twenty-four hours. Lecoq took six months or so. It might be made a text-book for detectives to teach them what to avoid.' (pp. 31-2)

Sir Arthur Conan Doyle, "The Science of Deduction," in his A Study in Scarlet, Doubleday & Company, Inc., 1974, pp. 23-33.

[A. INNES SHAND] (essay date 1890)

[In the following excerpt, Shand praises Gaboriau's consistently accurate, detailed plots and unique "systems" of detection, but faults the novelist's characterizations and digressive explanatory passages. For further commentary by Shand, see the excerpt dated 1879.]

[Gaboriau] elaborated, if he did not invent, the romance which turns entirely on the detection of a crime. He glorifies and idealises the exploits of the élite of the handful of men who control the dangerous masses of Paris. If he is not incapable of the delineation of character—like Boisgobey, his most promising pupil—he is quite indifferent to it. The natures and temperaments of his heroes, as originally indicated, are continually contradicting themselves. He has his heroines; he is fond of arranging unequal marriages; he introduces love-affairs, but they only lead up to striking situations, and the sentimentalism and the pathos are alike fictitious. On the other hand, there are no inconsistencies in the careful construction of the plot. From the first to the final chapter it works smoothly and without a hitch. En passant, or incidentally, he lays himself out to explain away whatever seems improbable and incredible. He is inspired by the veritable genius of the detective business, and his superiority in his special department is undeniable. At the same time, he has his invariable "system," like his heroes of the Rue Jerusalem; and when we come to understand it, his successful ingenuity is less astonishing than it appears at first sight. He always works backwards: he argues backwards from prearranged and established facts; and his infallible sneers, with their instinctive flair, interpret to the ignorant the signs that are clear to them. Consequently his Père Tabaret and his Monsieur Lecoq are pure creations of the fancy, parading an intelligence they do not really possess. None the less do they serve his purpose and ours, inasmuch as we credit them with gifts approaching the miraculous. We are brought to share the blind confidence of the Père Absinthe, who, dazzled by the clairvoyance of his clever young colleague Lecoq, asks, with the best faith in the world, what the people they had been tracking said to each other.

The personages of Gaboriau's mises-en-scène are generally much the same. There is the "suspect" entangled in advance in the meshes of circumstantial evidence; there is a sulking somebody else whom sooner or later we begin to fancy may have had much to say to the atrocity; there is the juge d'instruction, always of rare sagacity, though he changes nature and methods in the different books; and there is the shrewd but kindly old surgeon, of rough or forbidding manners, who is told off for the autopsy of the corpse, and whose experience draws invaluable deductions. Above all, there is the brilliant detective, who, by the light of intuitive perception, follows out his profession as a science. He is an enthusiast, of course, whether he has taken to the pursuit in his ripe maturity like Tabaret, or in his boiling and ambitious jeunesse like Lecoq, who builds his hopes of fortune on the favour of the Prefecture. They are enthusiasts to the point that old Tabaret compromises his reputation without regret, keeping the most irregular hours; while young Lecoq is ready to sell a masure belonging to him,

that he may take his revenge on the subtle and mysterious Mai who has befooled him on several occasions at their game of blind-man's-buff. Those enthusiasts always go in terror of their lives—for sundry convicts have sworn to slay them on their return from Cayenne, or their dismissal from forced works at Melun or Fontrevault. No wonder the criminals they have hunted down owe them a bitter grudge, for the concentrated zeal they bring to the chase seems beyond the limits of fair professional business. . . . Nothing shows more the extreme care of Gaboriau's workmanship than his development of the "systems" he attributes to the Tabarets and Lecoqs. In the reflection in the fiction of the imaginary facts, the whole fabric is based on logical deduction; the minutest details must be mutually self-supporting; and the demonstration of some insignificant flaw involves the collapse of the entire structure. The demonstration of one of these mathematical problems is worked out indirectly when Tabaret throws up his hands in remorseful horror at the Vicomte de Caumarin, who is charged with an atrocious murder, but is not provided with an irrefutable alibi. Otherwise the circumstantial evidence is complete; but that fundamental omission is sufficient to invalidate it, and Tabaret is in despair because the prosecutors, clinging to the ideas he has been labouring assiduously to drive into their heads, are bent upon sending an innocent man to the guillotine. For of course the favourite trick of the criminal novelist is to send suspicion running on a false trail, as in the case of de Caumarin, or in that of Prosper Bertomy in the Dossier, No. 113. Then some detective of transcendental intelligence comes to the rescue, and the mining and countermining go briskly forward. (pp. 178-79)

Darkening the colours and accentuating details, Gaboriau has turned chantage to excellent purpose. The most thrilling sensations of Le Dossier No. 113 depend upon it; and still more exciting is La Corde au Cou, of which chantage is the theme, as it supplies the title. We follow with sympathy and indignation each new pressure of the cord, as a turn of the operator's wrist intensifies the torture. We know that the victim must live on and endure; he can never find a refuge in suicide and repose in the Morgue, since his miseries are to end in a blissful dénouement. But those novels on chantage remind us of Gaboriau's worst fault as a story-teller. Explaining the source of the secrets—and it is the same, though in a lesser degree, with his mysterious murders—he wearies us with interminable and explanatory digressions. As a clever artist he must have known it was a mistake: we can only suppose that the method paid him. An innocent suspect is under lock and key: the real offender begins to have good cause to tremble, and our interest is being wrought up to the highest pitch, when, with the "crak-crak" of some chorus in a vaudeville, a dramatic chapter closes, and in commencing the next we are stagnating in the backwaters of some episode of family history which came off in the provinces forty years before. On the whole, we prefer the plan of Monsieur Lecoq, which devotes an entire volume to the crime, and the second and succeeding volume to its causes. Perhaps for that reason we rank the short and unpretentious Petit Vieux des Batignolles among the very best of Gaboriau's books. It goes straight to the point, and is all to the purpose. (p. 180)

[A. Innes Shand], "Crime in Fiction," in Blackwood's Edinburgh Magazine, Vol. CXLVIII, No. DCCCXCVIII, August, 1890, pp. 172-89.

THE BOOKMAN, LONDON (essay date 1900)

[The author of the following excerpt asserts that Gaboriau has been unjustly ignored by critics. Though the novelist had no pre-

A climactic scene from The Widow Lerouge.

tensions to great literary style, this writer believes that he is to be commended for his creation of Lecoq and for his accurate descriptions of Parisian criminal life.]

Gaboriau is one of those writers who, while appealing strongly to thousands upon thousands of readers, are by the critics absolutely ignored as literary forces. He is, as a rule, passed by as a mere spinner of detective stories, a light and rather frivolous entertainer. Now, in his case, this seems to be particularly unjust. He made no pretension to literary style or effect. His love passages, as love passages pure and simple, are of the most conventional and threadbare. It is quite true that he was only making stories; but he wrote of a certain side of life as he knew it, and for his background he drew upon the store of experience acquired by years of watching the ebb and flow of Paris. It is said that the plots of his books were taken almost bodily from the secret archives of the Rue Jerusalem, and one may readily believe it. There is a little touch of the *Comédie Humaine* to be found in his works. He knew his Balzac and his Molière, and he made use of this knowledge. That dark under side of the criminal life of Paris with which Gaboriau deals furnished Balzac with some of his most powerful themes.

Justly or unjustly, Emile Gaboriau is regarded, first of all, as the creator of one powerful character. And yet we do not think that he himself ever wished to give such pre-eminence to Monsieur Lecoq or that he even realised the dramatic qualities of the great detective. Had he aimed to show Lecoq infallible, omniscient, would there have been a Père Tabaret? The real

Lecoq is a factor in only three books—*The Mystery of Orcival, Monsieur Lecoq* and *File No. 113*. In *Other People's Money* and *The Lerouge Case* he is a mere subordinate. Sherlock Holmes fleered at him as a bungler, a mere practical investigator, whose only merit was his patience and his capacity for hard work [see excerpt by Doyle dated 1887]. True, he was not a builder of fancy hypotheses; he did not show so well in the lime-light. But we defy any reader to take up Lecoq's arguments and evidence and be unconvinced. And his evolving a complete theory from the chance words, "It is the Prussians who are coming," let drop by the pretended May, in the first chapter of *Monsieur Lecoq,* shows an imagination of a very high order. (pp. 106-07)

> *A review of "L'affaire Lerouge" and other novels, in* The Bookman, *London, Vol. XII, No. 2, October, 1900, pp. 106-07.*

THE LIVING AGE (essay date 1901)

[*Though* Monsieur Lecoq *has many characteristics in common with sensational fiction, this critic claims that Gaboriau's craftsmanship and ingenuity raise the novel above the level of the English penny dreadful.*]

The re-issue, in a genteel *format,* of the enslaving works of Emile Gaboriau should be an event of special interest to a generation whose appetite for sensational serials surpasses that of any previous generation. For Gaboriau, besides being the chosen novelist of Bismarck, was the greatest mere sensation-monger, save one, that ever lived. His superior, of course, was Eugène Sue, author of the incomparable *Wandering Jew* and *The Mysteries of Paris.* (p. 129)

Gaboriau was a lesser figure [than Sue], but a figure not to be despised. He was more than a mechanical concoctor. In craftsmanship, though not in the amplitude of his inspiration, he excelled Sue, and he certainly had what is called "a pretty gift" of writing. The perusal of *Monsieur Lecoq,* and its sequel, "The Honor of the Name," has, we confess, impressed us with a sense of Gaboriau's sterling ability. The first book in which the afterwards famous Lecoq commences his career by a brilliant failure, begins with a murder, and is nothing more than a detective story; but it is a detective story conceived in the true romantic manner, and depending for effect more on its general atmosphere of a terrible mystery than on circumstantial ingenuities. Sherlock Holmes might have taught Lecoq many little dodges, but Lecoq was by far the greater intellect— an intellect that moved in larger curves on a higher plane. Character rather than event controls the progress of the tale, and this is clearly perceived in the sequel—an immense novel which distinctly recalls Balzac's *Les Paysans,* and is, moreover, a very tolerable imitation of that sinister drama. From "The Honor of the Name" you perceive that Gaboriau, thereby proving himself an ambitious and intrepid artist, had drawn together in the murder the threads of a vast and complicated politico-social intrigue rooted in the national life of France. "The Honor of the Name," despite its sensational aspects, is quite a serious study of history; it shows the fatal war of class against class, and it is the record, not of a few individuals, but of a society. One cannot but observe that the French novelist has, as regards material, a two-fold advantage over the English: first, in the political vicissitudes of France during the nineteenth century, and, second, in the peculiar functions of the *Juge d' Instruction* under French criminal law. France seems to have made her history for the behoof of her novelists. As for the *Juge d'Instruction,* he is simply invaluable. Take, for an instance, the long examination of May by M. Segmuller in *Monsieur Lecoq;* it is almost the best thing in the book and serves a thousand ends. But Gaboriau could have succeeded without either French history or the *Juge d' Instruction.* The entrance of Blanche into the cottage and her poisoning of Marie Anne, in "The Honor of the Name," is an excellent sample of his rich inventive faculty. And his skill in *synthetizing* the significance of multitudinous facts in one item of evidence is finely exemplified in his use of the phrase uttered by the captured murderer—"It is the Prussians who are coming" (in *Lecoq*). Before reaching the conclusion of the sequel you are made to see that the whole tragedy is wrapped up in that phrase. In fine, it was not by chance that Gaboriau acquired his reputation. We in England have rather condescended towards him, as the artificer of a gloried penny-dreadful; that is a mistake. (pp. 129-30)

> *"The Sensational Serial: An Enquiry," in* The Living Age, *Vol. CCXXX, No. 2974, July 6, 1901, pp. 129-32.*

ARTHUR BARTLETT MAURICE   (essay date 1902)

[*In this excerpt from his essay on the development of character types, Maurice briefly traces the influence of Gaboriau's Tabaret on Doyle's Sherlock Holmes.*]

If in one line we can trace the ancestry of Sherlock Holmes to Edgar Allan Poe's Dupin, in another we can work back to Gaboriau, not, however, to the great Lecoq, but to old Tabaret, better known to the official police who are introduced into the tales as Père Tirauclair. From Dupin, Holmes derived his intellectual acumen, his faculty of mentally placing himself in the position of another, and thereby divining that other's motives and plans, his raising of the observation of minute outward details to the dignity of an exact science. Père Tirauclair inspired him to that wide knowledge of criminal and contemporary history which enabled him to throw a light on the most puzzling problem and to find some analogy to the most *outré* case. With Lecoq, Holmes has absolutely nothing in common.

The deductions of Dupin and of Sherlock Holmes we are ready to accept, because we feel that it is romance, and in romance we care to refute only what seriously jars our sense of what is logical; we take those of Lecoq, because they convince beyond all question, because when one has been forced upon us, we are ready defiantly to maintain that no other is possible. (p. 235)

> *Arthur Bartlett Maurice, "The Detective in Fiction," in* The Bookman, *New York, Vol. XV, May, 1902, pp. 231-36.*

FRANK WADLEIGH CHANDLER   (essay date 1907)

[*In this excerpt from his study of the connection between picaresque and detective literature, Chandler suggests that Gaboriau's novels display characteristics of both genres.*]

[Gaboriau perfected] the literature of crime-detection in France. In a succession of novels, from *L'Affaire Lerouge* . . . to *La Corde au Cou,* . . . as well as in two posthumous tales [*L'Argent des Autres* and *La Dégringolade*], . . . this prolific author developed his famous detectives, Lecoq the professional, and Père Tabaret the amateur. Both agree in the infinite zest and patience with which they track down criminals. They are not so much analysts as blood-hounds, keen on the scent from the

first rumor of crime, and untiring in the chase. Action with them is everything. They cannot rest until their prey be found. Unlike Poe's Dupin, they indulge in no calm diagnosis of the case at home, and prepare no carefully constructed theory to be wrought out by others. And because they mix immediately with the world of crime, the account of their exploits is invariably melodramatic.

Gaboriau drew his inspiration from Vidocq, Balzac, and the Archives of the Rue de Jérusalem,—that arsenal of criminal records capable of furnishing forth a whole army of novelists. . . . Frequently Gaboriau dwells overmuch upon the intercalated history of his criminal, developing the motives that produced the crime in so great detail as to obscure the interest in crime-detection. Such passages, however, show the influence of the picaresque rather than of the detective formula, and they tacitly acknowledge the close relationship between the two. (pp. 529-30)

> *Frank Wadleigh Chandler, "The Literature of Crime-Detection," in his* The Literature of Roguery, *Vol. II, Houghton, Mifflin and Company, 1907, pp. 524-50.*

HARRY THURSTON PECK   (essay date 1909)

[*Gaboriau is the artistic link between Poe and Doyle, Peck asserts in the excerpt below. While Gaboriau's characterization of M. Lecoq is superior to Poe's detective characterizations, the French novelist lacked the human interest of Doyle's hero, Holmes.*]

[The defect in Poe's] tales lies in the fact that their author could not create a living, breathing character. His personages are nothing but abstractions. He moves them about like chessmen on a board, and we are interested, not in them, but in the problem with which they have to do.

In order that the detective story should be something more than mathematics applied to fiction—or, perhaps, fiction applied to mathematics—it was necessary that what Poe did should be combined with a sympathetic understanding of human nature. This combination was effected—imperfectly, to be sure, but still with great ability—by Émile Gaboriau in the best of his detective stories, *M. Lecoq.* (p. 262)

Gaboriau became fascinated by the thoroughness and precision of [the marvelously elaborate system of espionage established by Napoleon III in contemporary France]. He studied it in all its phases, and with the greatest care. As a result of this study, he wrote the novels which, with all their blemishes, are still read eagerly in many countries and in many languages.

Of these novels, the one best constructed and most deserving of fame is that entitled *M. Lecoq.* . . . In it is seen an ingenuity equal to that of Poe, while there is also shown a fair success in sketching character. Moreover, the author has introduced a new type of deductive reasoner which suggested to Conan Doyle the interesting Mycroft Holmes, brother of Sherlock Holmes, and that great detective's superior in the subtlety of his intellectual processes. (pp. 263-64.)

The scene of the prisoner's examination by [the] magistrate [in *M. Lecoq*] is one of thrilling interest, and it gives to us Anglo-Saxons a vivid picture of the workings of French law in its assumption that a prisoner is guilty unless he proves his innocence. The long, searching inquiry in which the judge alternately pleads with the accused and browbeats, threatens, and tortures him, hoping at last to break him down and wring from him a full confession, is wonderfully written. (pp. 265-66)

[In Gaboriau's characterization of Père Tirauclair] we find a conception more attractive even than that of [Poe's C. Auguste Dupin]; and the literary touches of Gaboriau and Doyle give us a genuine personality that far surpasses the interest of a mere calculating machine.

It is true that Gaboriau mars his story by injecting into it a long secondary narrative. Conan Doyle made precisely the same mistake in his first successful detective tale, *A Study in Scarlet;* but it was a mistake which he never repeated. Gaboriau, therefore, is a link between Edgar Allan Poe and Conan Doyle, just as Poe himself is a link between Voltaire and Gaboriau. (p. 268)

Gaboriau is superior to Poe [in characterization]. Had there been no Gaboriau, we might never have had that fascinating cycle of stories which Conan Doyle has written around the great detective who lived in Baker Street, and whose name is as well known all over the world to-day as that of Shylock, Falstaff, or any other creation of Shakespeare himself, with, perhaps, Hamlet as the one exception. (p. 270)

Gaboriau is an excellent literary artisan. His mysteries are very neatly constructed. The parts all dovetail perfectly. But they have little artistic value, and the unravelling of their complicated plots is like the dissection of a Chinese puzzle which interests by its ingenuity, but appeals neither to the intellect nor to the imagination. (p. 273)

> *Harry Thurston Peck, "The Detective Story," in his* Studies in Several Literatures, *Dodd, Mead and Company, 1909, pp. 257-78.*

BURTON EGBERT STEVENSON   (essay date 1913)

> [*Including Lecoq and Tabaret in his list of the classic characters of detective fiction, Stevenson recounts two of Tabaret's greatest scenes. He faults Gaboriau only for his overuse of coincidence and inclusion of digressive romantic subplots.*]

[Among] all the detectives, amateur and professional, who have appeared before the public and performed their little tricks, there are only four who are classic—C. Auguste Dupin, Tabaret, M. Lecoq, and Sherlock Holmes. These abide. Beside them, the others are mere shadows. And these four are memorable not because they never bungled, not because occasionally they struck home with a cleverness and certainty which makes us forgive their mistakes. Their supreme moments are moments to be remembered with delight. (p. 49)

Twenty years after Poe's death, Emile Gaboriau began [a] series of detective stories which still remain, on the whole, the best of their class. There is probably no scene more satisfying than that in which Tabaret arrives at the place of the murder in *The Lerouge Case,* and, after a short investigation, proceeds to reconstruct the crime. Here, plainly, is the genesis of Sherlock Holmes, and yet Holmes never quite rose to this height. And it is in this story that Tabaret reaches his supreme moment—the moment when, after having bound his chain about his victim, assured that there is not a single weak link in it, he sees it shiver to pieces. The accused man has been arrested, has been taken before a magistrate, and, although stunned and incoherent, has doggedly asserted his innocence, but has as doggedly refused to say where he was on the night of the crime. Finally he is led away and Tabaret enters.

"I have come," he says, "to know if any investigations are necessary to demolish the alibi pleaded by the prisoner."

"He pleaded no alibi," the magistrate replies.

"What? No alibi!" cries the detective. "He has, of course, then, confessed everything."

"No, he has confessed nothing. He acknowledges that the proofs are decisive: he cannot give an account of how he spent his time, but he protests his innocence."

Tabaret is thunderstruck—and reaches his supreme moment.

"Not an alibi!" he murmurs. "No explanations! It is inconceivable! We must then be mistaken: he cannot be the criminal. That is certain!"

The magistrate laughs at him, and Tabaret explains that the man who committed this crime, so carefully planned, so cleverly carried out, so audacious and yet so prudent, would, under no circumstances, have failed to provide himself with a convincing alibi, and that a man who has no alibi cannot possibly be the criminal. Still the magistrate laughs, and Tabaret proceeds to lay down a principle which all writers of detective fiction would do well to learn by heart:

> "Given a crime, with all the circumstances and details, I construct, bit by bit, a plan of accusation, which I do not guarantee until it is entire and perfect. If a man is found to whom this plan applies exactly in every particular, the author of the crime is found; otherwise one has laid hands upon an innocent person. It is not sufficient that such and such particulars seem to point to him; it must be all or nothing."

Those six words sum up the whole science of detection: it must be all or nothing. . . . [Writers dream] of some day writing a story in which the edifice of conviction is slowly and carefully built, four-square, like the frame of a sky-scraper, with every beam tested and every bolt rivetted, formidable and apparently impregnable, yet with a tiny hidden defect which, just as the last bolt is being placed, brings the whole structure smashing to the ground. That would be worth doing!

In the Lerouge case, Tabaret built such an edifice; but Gaboriau carries coincidence too far. It is admissible that both the real murderer and the man suspected of the crime should, on that particular evening, have been carrying an umbrella and wearing a high hat; perhaps it is admissible, since they are the same age and about the same build, that their shoes should be of the same size and shape; but when the author equips them both with lavender kid gloves he adds one coincidence too many. In his desire to strengthen the chain of evidence, he overleaps himself and loses the confidence of the reader. (pp. 51-2)

Tabaret has a worthy pupil in M. Lecoq, although it should not be forgotten that he remains a pupil, with many things unlearned, to the end of the chapter. Sherlock Holmes's gibe at him [see excerpt by Doyle dated 1887] seems to be the result of an unworthy envy. For Lecoq, though inferior to Tabaret, is far greater than Holmes—more picturesque, more subtle, more resourceful—and with a sense of humour. Probably his greatest moment occurs in *The Mystery of Orcival.* A murder has been committed and a house ransacked, the furniture upset, the clock thrown from the mantel. It has stopped at twenty minutes past three, and to every one it seems evident that it was at that hour the crime occurred. Lecoq replaces the clock on the mantel, and slowly pushes forward the minute-hand to half-past three. The clock strikes eleven.

That was a great idea—so great that no one will ever dare use it again without acknowledging its source. Sherlock Holmes came perilously near it, once, when he solved a mystery by re-winding a watch. But the honours belong to Gaboriau. And for another thing the Frenchman deserves all praise. He recognised the fact that, to hold the interest, it is not enough that a crime should be committed and the criminal in the end discovered. There must be something more than that. There must be a war of intellect, a clash of theories. There must be confronting investigators, one seeking to establish a man's guilt, the other to establish his innocence. For the reader, the real pleasure is in following, step by step, this contest.

In so far as detective work goes, Gaboriau's stories are far better than Conan Doyle's; but Gaboriau tried to do too much. He sought to add a love interest, and in that respect he failed. Every one of his tales is built upon the threadbare formula, "cherchez la femme"; every one turns back for its motive to an illicit love affair. . . . [I have] no patience with a plot which, for its explanation, must go back two or three generations; so these portions of Gaboriau's stories are to be skimmed rapidly, until Tabaret or Lecoq appears again upon the scene. Then not a word is to be missed. Amat Tabaret! (pp. 52-3)

Burton Egbert Stevenson, "Supreme Moments in Detective Fiction," in The Bookman, *New York, Vol. XXXVII, No. 7, March, 1913, pp. 49-54.*

VALENTINE WILLIAMS (essay date 1923)

[*In the following excerpt from his article commemorating the fiftieth anniversary of Gaboriau's death, Williams discusses the early critical reception and the circumstances surrounding the publication of Gaboriau's detective fiction. He also states that Gaboriau expanded the model for detective fiction established by Poe, introducing lively characterization and dramatic plots to the genre.*]

The present year will mark the fiftieth anniversary of the death of Emile Gaboriau. He has an indisputable claim to be regarded as the father of the detective novel. Poe, it is true, was his precursor and his direct inspiration: but Gaboriau was far from being a feeble imitator. [A French writer justly observes:]

> He derived from this class of story . . . a new type, and impressed his own particular quality upon it so well that, instead of being a servile and insignificant plagiarist, he stands out as an original and fertile creator. . . .

Poe was the scientist who produced the text-book; Gaboriau seized upon his exposition and dramatized it. There is no "love interest" in Poe's [Dupin] trilogy; the dialogue is stilted, and the characters are merely chessmen set out to present a problem.

In each of his five great detective novels Gaboriau also has an intricate problem, but it is the centre of a highly dramatic plot with living figures (interspersed, it is true, with many dummies of the French feuilleton), a brisk dialogue and a keen perception of "situations." He is, first and last, a journalist, drawing, as one may clearly see, upon a well-filled notebook; but a journalist equipped with a brilliant analytical brain which, as his life story shows, circumstances never permitted to find its fullest and highest expression. (p. 612)

When fame, who so often limps far behind material prosperity, reached the feuilletonist's desk, she found an empty chair. To-day, fifty years after Gaboriau was laid to rest in the family vault at Jonzac, running through the coarse woof of plot and counter-plot which the concierges demanded from his stories for their daily sou, we may discern the scarlet thread of a brilliant mind. Here, through the jostling throng of desperately wicked dukes, of incredibly noble maids, of *banquiers véreux,* Monsieur Lecoq, simple agent of the Sûreté, comes stepping, fresh as a bridegroom, *un beau gars, à l'oeil clair, à l'air résolu,* or, as casual visitors saw him in his careful disguise, a sober personage of distinguished appearance, with his gold spectacles, his white tie, and his *mince redingote.*

Against a canvas of tiresome puppets he stands out a living figure, notwithstanding the curious metamorphoses to which, in the course of the stories, the exigencies of the feuilleton subjected him. He is as French as the crowing cock, which, with its proud motto, "Semper Vigilans," he chose as his device. His limpid mind, his crystal-clear reasoning, his dazzling deductions, his fluttering *panache,* his ups and downs, his hopes and fears, all these are wholly French.

When Gaboriau died, *Le Siècle* called him "the inventor of the *roman judiciaire.*" The unknown writer, who thus shrewdly gave his dead *confrère* his due, would open his eyes to-day could he survey the large and lusty progeny of which Monsieur Lecoq is the father. But there is a hint of cold condescension in the way in which some of the contemporary newspapers dispose, in a brief *fait divers,* of "M. Emile Gaboriau, author of *romans judiciaires,* which have had the greatest success." (pp. 613-14)

[Marius Topin wrote in his *Romanciers contemporains* in 1876:]

> Gaboriau . . . has long been ranged among the facile scribes of the cheap newspapers, the hurried improvisers, the novelists who share with the police reports and the *faits divers* the breathless curiosity of the fishwives and porters. Gaboriau is classified, ticketed, numbered. There is nothing more to be said. That he is loved by so many common readers does not please the cultured. In the highly aristocratic republic of letters the innumerable suffrages of the plebs must not be confounded with the select opinions of a few delicate-minded censors.

And he proceeds to pay a warmly sincere tribute to the "scientific art" of Gaboriau's five great crime stories. (p. 614)

Monsieur Lecoq is said to be the faithful portrait of one of the highest officials in the Prefecture of Gaboriau's day; but Gévrol, nicknamed "The General," who flits in and out of the stories, the type of old-fashioned detective and a sore thorn in the side of Monsieur Lecoq; and Fanferlot (a detective in *Dossier 113*) with his "turned-up nose, thin lips, and small, round eyes of irritating mobility," are also clearly sketched from life. (p. 616)

[After] *Le Crime d'Orcival* only *La Corde au Cou,* not one of his happiest efforts, and a short tale *Le Petit Vieux des Batignolles,* which I hold to be in some respects the best detective story ever written, were in his especial vein. The rest were terrific romances of modern life with double-dyed villains and blameless heroines and mysterious love affairs. Their digressions, and digressions from digressions, are endless; the colours are laid on very thick; and to-day they possess little interest. (p. 618)

[Gaboriau] was a facile, but immensely conscientious, worker. He never sat down to write until his plot was clear in his mind, and it is recorded of him that he would fill from two to three thousand sheets of his specially prepared paper without correction or erasure. On the other hand, he devoted immense care to the revision of the proofs of his stories in book form and the galleys, as he returned them to the publisher, were almost unrecognizable.

A notebook was his constant companion. In it he would jot down such ideas as occurred to him, usually with a brief scenario. He has always on the lookout for types, and when he came across a character that seemed suitable to figure in a story he would sometimes even make a rough sketch so as to impress the salient features on his mind.

Like Charles Dickens, he took infinite trouble with the names of his personages, which, we are informed an eloquent commentary on the sublime nonchalance of French feuilleton writing!—he frequently changed in the course of publication. One of his great amusements, Alfred d'Aunay records, was to study a passer-by in the street and try to glean, by processes of reasoning and observation, his mode of life and social standing, and then to shadow his victim to see if his deductions were correct.

It is suggested that Gaboriau's five great criminal romances (*L' Affaire Lerouge, Le Crime d'Orcival, Dossier 113, Monsieur Lecoq,* and *La Corde au Cou*) were the fruition of that early impulse of his to write *Les Récits Etranges* after the manner of Poe. However that may be, what is certain is that he wished to publish the five books under the general title, *Processes of Reasoning in Judicial Affairs.* (p. 619)

[The] fetters of the feuilleton galled the genius of Gaboriau. He wrote . . . in haste, twisting his plot and modifying his characters, often, no doubt, in deference to the wishes of his editor. The result is patchwork, and, in the case of his greatest creation, Monsieur Lecoq, this immortal character, as he passes through the stories, is cluttered up with a mass of incongruities which Gaboriau, had he lived, would surely have planed away. (p. 620)

[The] first volume of *Monsieur Lecoq* is incontestably Gaboriau's masterpiece. I say advisedly "the first volume," for the second, narrating at inordinate length the life history of a wicked duke from 1815 on, is one long yawn compared to the four hundred pages of vivid, pulsating prose of its companion.

Gaboriau's scheme in this splendid story is clear. He set himself to construct a ladder between the lowest and the highest levels of society. To Lecoq he allotted the task of following up the trail of a crime that led from a squalid cabaret outside the Paris fortifications to a ducal mansion in the Faubourg St. Germain. (pp. 621-22)

It is difficult for anybody with imagination to lay down the first volume of *Monsieur Lecoq* before he has read it through to the last page. With uncanny skill Gaboriau interests his readers, not only in his central figure, the detective, and his desperate fight against the stubborn incredulity of his chiefs, but also in the mysterious prisoner whose determination to mislead the police as to his identity is reinforced by secret associates outside the prison. It culminates in that thrilling chase through Paris when Lecoq, in despair of ever identifying

the accused, having deliberately let the prisoner escape, shadows him through the streets—and loses him. (p. 622)

Valentine Williams, "Gaboriau: Father of the Detective Novel," in The National Review, *London, Vol. LXXXII, No. 490, December, 1923, pp. 611-22.*

[T. S. ELIOT]   (essay date 1929)

[*Eliot, an American-born English poet, essayist, and critic, is regarded as one of the most influential literary figures of the first half of the twentieth century. In the following excerpt from his brief note on the reissue of* The Mystery of Orcival, *Eliot praises the novel, pointing out the importance of considering it in historical perspective.*]

[The] revival of Gaboriau is fully justified by a perusal of [*The Mystery of Orcival*]. . . . [We] protest that the publishers have not provided a short note about the author . . . , for the serious critic of such fiction knows how much the *date* at which a book was written matters. The elaborate and protean disguises of the detective ended with Sherlock Holmes, but in Gaboriau's time they were not only permissible but commendable. Lecoq, when one knows the dates, does wear extremely well. One of the merits of this story is that we know the criminal very early: the only difficulty is to prove the crime and to catch the culprit. (p. 760)

[*T. S. Eliot*], *in a review of "The Mystery of Orcival," in* The Criterion, *Vol. VIII, No. XXXIII, July, 1929, pp. 760-61.*

H. DOUGLAS THOMSON   (essay date 1931)

[*Announcing that "'The Great Gaboriau Revival' is under way," Thomson commends Gaboriau's psychologically and emotionally appealing detectives and cases, but finds that his novels are unsatisfying to modern readers because the mystery is not sustained long enough.*]

Until recently Gaboriau had fallen on evil days. He was once regarded as second only to Sir Arthur Conan Doyle, and his detective, Lecoq, was as famous as Sherlock Holmes. After a time the Victorians seemed to forget him, and the younger generation knew him only as a name. (p. 94)

[Today], "The Great Gaboriau Revival" is under way. . . . There is a growing habit amongst publishers of reprinting earlier examples of the genre—an act of grace which confers on the detective story a definite literary status. (p. 95)

Gaboriau, experimentalist that he was, had quite a definite opinion of what the detective story ought to be. "The inquest of a crime," he makes Lecoq say, in *Le Crime d'Orcival,* "is nothing more nor less than the solution of a problem. Given the crime, proved, patent, you commence by seeking out all the circumstances, whether serious or superficial; the details and the particulars. When these have been carefully gathered, you classify them, and put them in their order and date. You thus know the victim, the crime and the circumstances; it remains to find the third term of the problem, that is X, the unknown quantity—the guilty party. The task is a difficult one, but not so difficult as is first imagined."

Gaboriau's novels do not, however, quite satisfy our own notions. They are not so much detective stories, as stories in which a detective has helped, but only helped, to unravel a tangled skein of events. A prolonged course of reading may have prejudiced us against Gaboriau, in much the same way as reading a sequel before the original is apt to spoil the latter. . . . [Gaboriau's novels have] no grand dénouement. The reader having read only half the book can name the guilty person. The problem is not protracted enough; and even from a grossly material point of view the detection occupies only a fraction of the whole.

Nevertheless, Gaboriau does not seem to have made up his mind as to what constituted the *ideal* construction. Experience, in a way, handicapped him; for, knowing that court proceedings bulk largely in the history of any criminal case, he felt obliged to retain the proportion. Gaboriau's court scenes are delicious entertainment. In a few bold strokes he paints the examining magistrate, the prisoner, the detective all agog with excitement. He packs his novels with axioms of criminal procedure, and that type of psychology which betokens the witty precisian.

Gaboriau leant towards realism in another particular, chiefly in his later novels. He seems to have formed a preference for a more concrete type of investigation. What is said of Lecoq in *Monsieur Lecoq* is equally true of Gaboriau himself:—

> He next had recourse to a mode of investigation which is generally the last resort of the police, but which is generally successful, because it is so sensible and simple.
>
> He determined to examine all the books in which the law compels the proprietors of hotels and lodging houses to keep a record of their guests.
>
> Rising long before daybreak and going to bed late at night, he spent all his time in visiting the hotels, furnished houses and lodgings in Paris.
>
>   (pp. 96-8)

This is one instance which shows that Gaboriau latterly tended to make his stories *romans policiers* pure and simple—chronicles of the police methods adopted to catch a known criminal.

Historically, Gaboriau is one of the pioneers. He was the father of the detective novel as opposed to the detective story. He made the way straight for Sir Arthur Conan Doyle. He was a master in the art of story telling. . . . Where Gaboriau improved on Poe was in his heightening of the interest and in the intensification of the human appeal. Gaboriau took no half measures. He decided in the first place to make the problem such that it would give rein to the emotions. Secondly, he gave the detective a personality. (pp. 98-9)

All Gaboriau's problems arise from family scandals and intrigues. A blot on the escutcheon and there was no saying to what crime it might not lead. Gaboriau saw that there is no secret so well kept as a family secret. Complication of the plot would be easier when the origin of the mystery might take one years back. (p. 99)

[Gaboriau] gave us two detectives, Père Tabaret and Lecoq. As far as reputation goes the pupil has quite eclipsed his master. Lecoq was certainly Gaboriau's favourite. His appearance is more frequent, and we are allowed to witness the development of his powers. Père Tabaret is a type of detective very much in the contemporary fashion. He took up detection, as we saw, to dispel his boredom. (There is a no more discontented class of people than the dilettante detectives, even at the present moment when unemployment and an aristocratic scorn for the dole would constitute a more cogent reason for adopting the pursuit.) Tabaret is an amateur at the game, the magnet from

time to time of the professionals' ridicule. He is also an amateur in the less flattering sense. Always liable to make mistakes, he was once actually responsible for the execution of an innocent man. He is as eccentric as Dupin, and his garrulous landlady has not got a dog's chance. His eccentricity gives comic relief, "but unlike Holmes's does not give an impression of latent genius." . . . In his use of paradox he is almost as doctrinaire as Father Brown.

Lecoq is often mentioned in the same breath as Dupin and Sherlock Holmes. He is an amusing character; *that* needs no stressing. But it must occur to one that perhaps after all his name is just a shade greater than his deserts. His is borrowed plumage. (pp. 99-100)

Gaboriau's murders and robberies are not the meticulously planned affairs with which we are now familiar. Smith Minor would turn up his nose at them. Père Tabaret himself complained that criminals were not what they used to be. "Blunderers as well as cowards," he styled them. And if they did not leave behind them their visiting-cards, they left quite enough evidence to be going on with.

Gaboriau's legacy is for all that a rich one. Many of his tricks and ruses have now become clichés. (p. 102)

Many of Gaboriau's stratagems are now hackneyed. Time stops whenever a murder is committed. The clock never escapes, and the deceitful hands play the deuce with one's calculations. . . . [Furniture] has a "physiognomy." An escritoire and overturned chairs are never absent from the scene of the crime. We note too the never failing presence of a confusing number of wine glasses or coffee cups—seldom of plates, forks or spoons. Tobacco in some form or another of disintegration is another necessary stage property. Gaboriau makes one of his careless criminals leave behind him the end of a Trabucos cigar. Then there is the undergraduate's trick of rumpling the bed clothes to make the bed appear to have been slept in. But one rumples in vain if only the bolster is removed. "A bed is one of those terrible witnesses which never misguide." Footprints are always being discovered; but at this stage they are used to trace movements, rather than for identification purposes. Lecoq once has recourse to a regular Austin Freeman expedient when he preserves the footprints in the melting snow by means of his plaster casts. Whether it is a piece of symbolism or realism, a murder is inevitably accompanied by a heavy fall of rain. Generally speaking the detection is of the familiar Sherlock Holmes variety—keen observation coupled with rapid inference. A leap of more than two yards to avoid a flower bed is assumed to prove that the man "was active and, therefore, young."

It was Gaboriau's idea to present the reader with a sketch plan of the scene of the crime. The idea is in itself a sound one; a picture may brighten a narrative as a graph may give life to tables of figures. But an excessive use of it has converted it into a mixed blessing. It is apt . . . to get on one's nerves. Gaboriau uses it properly and does not force the conscientious reader to turn back to it nor annoy the unconscientious by continual and unnecessary reference. (pp. 103-05)

L'Affaire Lerouge and *Le Crime d'Orcival* are undoubtedly Gaboriau's best novels. Of the rest the best that can be said of *Le Dossier No. 113* is that it would make an excellent film; of *Monsieur Lecoq* that the first part, "L'Enquête," falls under the less attractive category of a pure *roman policier,* while the second, "L'Honneur du Nom," as rather tedious family his-

Mascarin questions Paul in this illustration from Caught in
the Net.

tory. The majority are nothing more or less than emotional
blood and thunder novels. (p. 105)

> *H. Douglas Thomson, "The French Detective Novel,"*
> *in his* Masters of Mystery: A Study of the Detective
> Story, *1931. Reprint by Folcroft Library Editions,*
> *1973, pp. 92-121.*

[DOROTHY L. SAYERS]   (essay date 1935)

*[Sayers is acknowledged as one of the great mystery writers of
the twentieth century. As a detective novelist, she is best remembered for her creation of the aristocratic amateur sleuth Lord
Peter Wimsey, who figures prominently in many of her mysteries.
Sayers's contribution to the genre lies in her attempt to transform
the detective novel into "a novel of manners, instead of a mere
crossword puzzle." In the following excerpt, Sayers praises Gaboriau's thematic breadth and his attempt to synthesize intellectual puzzles with human drama. She observes that although later
detective novelists have perfected the techniques Gaboriau introduced, few have balanced suspense and human psychology with
Gaboriau's success.]*

Emile Gaboriau, like some other literary pioneers, is to-day
probably more venerated than read. Everybody knows that he
was a master of detective fiction and that he created Monsieur
Lecoq; but when it comes to celebrating the centenary of his

birth the younger generation of readers is apt to feel like Miss
Codger on being presented to a Pogram by a Hominy:—

> A thrilling moment is it in its impressiveness
> on what we call our feelings. But why we call
> them so, or why impressed they are, or if im-
> pressed they are at all, or if at all we are, or if
> there really is, oh gasping one! a Lecoq or a
> Gaboriau, or any active principle to which we
> give those titles, is a topic, Spirit searching,
> light abandoned, much too vast to enter on, at
> this unlooked-for crisis.

Yet the present is a very good moment at which to ask ourselves
whether impressed we are at all and whether there is, in fact,
any active principle behind the lip-homage we offer to Gaboriau. . . .

The present-day reader may well be excused [from a study of
Gaboriau] if he feels that the topic is "much too vast to enter
on." The mere reading of the books presents a formidable
difficulty, for most of them are out of print and all of them
are fat. Faced with *Monsieur Lecoq* or with *La Corde au Cou*—
each containing, in the French edition, between four and five
hundred pages of ugly and sight-destroying letterpress—one
wonders whether the palm is worth the dust. "I suppose,"
says the reader, plaintively, "I shall find him very old-fashioned." He is old-fashioned; yet perhaps he was more so yesterday than he is to-day, while to-morrow may find him back
in the fashion. Mr. H. Douglas Thomson, writing in 1931 in
Masters of Mystery [see excerpt above], said of him:—

> Gaboriau's novels do not, however, quite sat-
> isfy our own notions. They are not so much
> detective stories as stories in which a detective
> has helped, but only helped, to unravel an en-
> tangled skein of events. . . . The mystery is
> gradually cleared up. The reader having read
> half the book can name the guilty person. The
> problem is not protracted enough; and even from
> a grossly material point of view the detection
> occupies only a fraction of the whole.

There is the modern case against Gaboriau, succinctly stated;
and it resolves itself into two counts: a division of interest, and
the lack of the "surprise" element to which we have become
accustomed. To these objections we may add two more: the
enormous length of the narrative and the slow amplitude of its
development. It is easy enough to account for all these characteristics historically; but in doing so we may find also an
artistic justification for them, as valid to-day as it was seventy
years ago. . . .

[For] the police and their methods . . . Gaboriau felt . . . glamorous enthusiasm; and therefore, though Tabaret the amateur
is his earliest detective hero, though Lecoq is Tabaret's pupil
and Tabaret the final court of appeal invoked when Lecoq by
himself has failed, it is Lecoq and not Tabaret, the professional
and not the amateur, who is the better known and the more
beloved of Gaboriau's heroes. Tabaret has the benevolent eccentricities, but Lecoq the great heroic moments; and it is
significant that *Le Crime d'Orcival,* in which Lecoq acts alone,
is Gaboriau's best book. It is as though the writer, dominated
at first by Poe's notion of contrasting amateur methods favourably with those of the police, had found his admiration
for the *Sûreté* too much for him, and had conceived the idea
of developing the contrast within the framework of the police
organization itself. Tabaret and Lecoq make common cause;

they triumph, not over routine police methods but over the jealousy of Lecoq's official rivals or over the personal prejudices of some provincial *juge d'instruction*. Thus, though Gaboriau is in a very real sense the model and precursor of Conan Doyle, he is also the precursor of Freeman Wills Crofts and of that whole school of modern detective writers whose true hero is Scotland Yard.

The moment was favourable to the development of the *roman policier* on both sides of the Channel. . . . Both in England and in France the mystery fiction of the sixties had its roots in real police work; Collins and Gaboriau—both enthusiastic students of Fenimore Cooper—undoubtedly read and influenced one another (the works of Collins were all translated into French, and the works of Gaboriau stood on Collins's bookshelves); and it is probable that behind both was the American influence, not only of Fenimore Cooper but of Edgar Allan Poe.

Yet neither Collins nor Poe succeeded, at that time, in founding a school of what we should now call pure detective fiction. The works of both contained large elements both of "sensation" and of *comédie de moeurs,* and it was these elements that were taken up and elaborated by their immediate successors. Not till we come to Conan Doyle do we again get stories in which the detection forms the whole interest as in those tales of Poe which were so precociously in advance of their time. The truth is that neither Collins nor Gaboriau aimed at writing what we should call detective stories. What we look upon as their defects were due to no failure of method but rather to a difference of purpose. With all their passion for secrets and puzzles, they were novelists, and they aimed at writing novels. They can certainly never have dreamed that the detective problem could come to stand as a book by itself, cut off from the great stream of human and literary tradition. For them, the character interest was as necessary as the plot interest.

That is why, to the modern fancier of the "chessboard" type of detective fiction, their books seem to be fumbling and uncertain in construction and stuffed with extraneous material; whereas to them, the work of a Doyle, a Connington, a Crofts or a Rhode would doubtless have appeared thin, dry and lacking in emotional power. Both parties would be, to some extent, right. It is significant that, when Conan Doyle did at length set detective fiction on the road which it was to follow for four decades he took it by way of the short story. (p. 677)

[With the great technical gain of modern detective literature] there went, however, a loss: the characterization, the human story, began to disappear from detective fiction. This happened, not only because the mere physical bulk of the novel was decreasing . . . but also because the "surprise ending" by its nature imposed restrictions upon the humanity of the narrative. If the be-all and end-all of the detective story is to conceal the identity of the criminal, then the most important and moving part of the human interest has to be omitted—namely, the character and motives of the criminal himself. He is the mainspring of the whole action, yet we may never see into the works; and this, even from the intellectual point of view, is unfortunate. Moreover, this restriction in its turn restricts the handling of all the other characters; for, if all but one are intimately analysed, then that remaining one must of necessity be the criminal; so that the author, to keep his secret, must leave the majority of his characters unanalysed. . . .

Of this integral artistic difficulty the early masters of the detective novel were quite aware. . . . Gaboriau, in *L'Affaire Lerouge,* tackled it along straight-forward lines of character-draw-

ing, but at the cost of taking the reader into his confidence behind the detective's back. While Tabaret still believes Noël Gerdy to be a model of youthful sobriety, we know that he is keeping an expensive mistress and is desperate for money. We understand and sympathize with Noël, but are all the readier to believe that, if money can be got by doing murder, then Noël is the man to do it. Consequently, we solve the mystery before the detective. This defect may have been less obvious in 1866 than it is to-day; the contrast between the false nobility of the claimant Noël and the true nobility of the real vicomte, Albert de Commarin, is delicately enough done to deceive the unsophisticated. Clearly, however, the author himself was dissatisfied. No doubt he felt that he had fallen between two stools. By trying to keep his secret he had prevented himself from extracting the full juice of emotion from Noël's agonizing situation; yet, in trying to make that situation clear he had more than jeopardized the secret. In his three succeeding books, [*Le Dossier No. 113, Le Crime d'Orcival*, and *Monsieur Lecoq*] . . . , he abandoned all attempt at compromise and used an expedient which to us appears clumsy and inartistic, but which offered perhaps the best scope for his peculiar talent.

These stories are built on the scheme used subsequently by Conan Doyle in *A Study in Scarlet* and *The Valley of Fear*. A crime is committed; the police investigations are put in hand; the inquiry is brought up to the point at which the detective is able to name the murderer and discover the motive for the crime. Then, instead of jumbling the necessary data into a brief summary by the detective or confession by the criminal, the author breaks off and retells the story in detail from the beginning, showing the whole emotional and dramatic interplay of circumstance and character. Finally, in a kind of coda, the detective action is taken up again, to show us the end of the inquiry and the fate of the criminal.

It is obvious that the great drawback to this kind of construction is the sudden and violent break in continuity. At the moment when we are most excited about Monsieur Lecoq we have to forget him and interest ourselves in an entirely different set of people. But if we make the effort we are to some extent rewarded by the greatly increased richness and significance of the book as an interpretation of life. We see the passions and interests which led to a sordid murder, not foreshortened into a paragraph but spread out over a prospect as wide as life itself, and moving ineluctably through a real time and space to a predestined end behind the grisly glass cases of the Morgue and under the chill light of a police investigation. Here is the case as Lecoq sees it; there were the passions as the people felt them. We may not care to see the thing done in this way; but it is as well to bear in mind, when we read Gaboriau, that the way was deliberately chosen for a definite artistic end. It is not that he is unable to write a detective story but that he prefers to write a human drama.

His drama, it is true, is melodrama; there was probably never a writer more ingenious in wringing the last ounce of agitation from an intrigue. "Intrigue" is the right word: his plots all turn upon illicit love and the humiliations sustained by noble families at the hands of their illegitimate scions. Compared with the work of his English contemporaries, Gaboriau's novels suffer from monotony of theme; but in dealing with that theme his nationality gives him an enormous advantage. His stage is narrow, but it is intensely lit; his plot makes contact with life at one or two points only, but the contact is ringingly made. He is a ferocious moralist, pursuing the sins of youth with savage retribution, but at least he is allowed to persuade us that the sins have been committed. . . . It is true that Gaboriau's noble young men and pure maidens are puppets as dreary as the virtuous young couples in Dickens or anybody else; and here he must yield the palm to Collins, who had an unexpected talent for making decent young people interesting. It is also a pity that Gaboriau, the son of a provincial notary, should have been so romantically intoxicated by the splendours of the ancient French nobility. The lustre of a great name and great riches dazzles his eyes; in their honour as in their dishonour, his dukes and counts and viscounts tower up always a little more than lifesize, rigid with caste, insolent with ineffable *morgue,* interminable rhetoricians upon the point of honour. Yet, though he sees them magnified, he can see them justly: and in *Le Crime d'Orcival* he can ruthlessly chastise his own weakness in Mme. Sauvresy and strip off the false glitter from de Trémorel to show the cheap and ugly clay beneath. In so doing, and particularly in the scene where this pinchbeck villain sets out to commit a spectacular suicide and fails absurdly through lack of courage to pull the trigger, he lifts his melodrama, for the first and only time, to the level of genuine high comedy.

But for us, the importance of Gaboriau lies, of course, in his police work. Here his eyes are not blinded with excess of light, and all his pictures are drawn with an exact and witty realism. He knows inside out the life of the *petit fonctionnaire,* the professional jealousies of the local magistracy, the cacklings of small-town gossip, the frictions between the *procureur* and the *maire,* the pomposities of the country doctor, the rivalry between the village policeman and the man sent down from the *Sûreté,* the difficulties in which a *juge d'instruction* may find himself when trying to steer a safe course between his political allegiance and the integrity of his professional conscience. He can show us the behaviour of every kind of suspect under the brutal onslaught of the French system of interrogation, from the cringing and plausible old offender to the despairing innocent caught in a hopeless trap of circumstance; his court scenes are ruthlessly authentic in minute detail; and his acquaintance with the topography of the Paris underworld and all its unpleasing fauna is "extensive and peculiar." If Lecoq himself sometimes appears to us rather as a superman than as an ordinary being, it is not because of any miracles of intuitive inspiration (for all his deductions are careful and logical) but merely because of his nerve-shattering facility in disguise and his inability to resist what Sherlock Holmes calls "a touch of the dramatic." . . .

It is easy for us to-day to dismiss the detective exploits of Tabaret and Lecoq as interesting specimens of a primitive art. We may feel ourselves greater than Gaboriau because we stand on his shoulders. But in that central problem of effecting a synthesis of intellectual and emotional interest have we come any nearer to a solution than he did? . . .

What Gaboriau, with all his faults of construction, with all his pedestrian dryness of style, with all his artificiality and absurdity of rhetoric has, which his successors have not, is breadth of treatment and, in a large sense, seriousness of aim. Crudely and melodramatically, but with enormous energy and gusto, he is writing novels and not anecdotes, attempting a criticism of life and not filling in time with cross-word puzzles related to nothing in particular. He never quite succeeded in synthesizing intellect and emotion, but at least he made the attempt. Now that books are once more growing longer there is an opportunity for the modern detective writer to make the attempt again and, with his perfected technique, to do it better. Ga-

boriau, who died suddenly in 1873 at the early age of thirty-eight, had only seven years of full literary life, and of his thirteen or fourteen books not all are detective stories. But in those seven years he left his mark upon detective history; and one fortress at least which bears the scars of his cannon has been left by those that came after, not only unachieved but unassaulted. (p. 678)

> [*Dorothy L. Sayers*], "Emile Gaboriau, 1835-1873: The Detective Novelist's Dilemma," in The Times Literary Supplement, *No. 1761, November 2, 1935, pp. 677-78.*

HOWARD HAYCRAFT   (essay date 1941)

[*Haycraft argues that Gaboriau never realized his potential as a writer. His novels fail as detective fiction because the main characters' logical deductions are artistically incompatible with the melodramatic backgrounds and secondary characters Gaboriau uses.*]

Seven typically artificial and not very successful novels of military and fashionable life had come from Gaboriau's too facile pen before *L'Affaire Lerouge* began its serial career in a dying newspaper called *Le Pays* in 1866. In the sense that it was the first story of novel length to employ detection as an important theme, it is perhaps entitled to the appellation "the first detective novel"—though it bears little resemblance to what we mean by the term to-day. (p. 32)

When [Gaboriau] sticks to detection, it is excellent detection indeed; but . . . [rarely] did he succeed in so limiting himself. In *Monsieur Lecoq,* which many critics consider his masterpiece, he put all the detection into the first volume, devoting the entire second half to the narration of a tedious family chronicle. The family, it may be noted in passing, is the basis of most of Gaboriau's novels, as it was of most French fiction of his time. Family scandal is at the bottom of virtually all the problems investigated by his detectives, and the feuilletonist who knew his concierge and shop-girl audience missed few opportunities such a subject presented for melodramatic digression. The proportion of detection is no greater in the other novels. Furthermore, the solution by the detective is seldom the apex of the story. There is no single rise of action to a grand dénouement. We know the guilty party before the book is half through, and from that point forward we read (if we are able!) another story, or several sub-stories, about the same characters. (pp. 32-3)

[The] stories come to life when Lecoq is on the stage. The difficulty is that he is too often in the wings or hiding behind false faces.

In the conflict, described by Williams [see excerpt dated 1923], between Lecoq and his background, we find the key to Gaboriau's chief failure according to the standards of modern detective fiction. In his attempt to mix incompatible elements—the lurid unreality of the yellow-back and the cool logic of detection—he violates one of the prime requirements of the form: the semblance, at least, of plausibility. ("A sense of verisimilitude is essential to the detective novel."—Willard Huntington Wright.) The mésalliance he thus unwittingly and unfortunately began has persisted in the French detective story virtually to this day, to its undeniable detriment.

Nevertheless, Gaboriau's logic—when he does give it rein—is definitely of the better sort; it is only the backgrounds that are at fault. Many of Lecoq's devices are still in use to-day, although of course in altered and generally amplified form. His test to tell whether a bed has been slept in, the example of the striking clock to show that the hands have been set back— to mention but two—have been employed in principle at least by more fictional sleuths of a later day than one would care to estimate. There is nothing really new in Lecoq's reasoning; it stems directly from Dupin. But Gaboriau, drawing on his well-filled police-court notebooks and on Vidocq's *Mémoires,* elaborated Poe's abstractions with fresh illustrations and variations. (Sherlock Holmes, it is true, scorned Lecoq as "a miserable bungler" [see excerpt by Doyle dated 1887]. But in the same breath he dismissed Dupin as "a very inferior fellow." For all his exemplary qualities, it is to be feared that the Baker Street seer was not immune to professional jealousy!)

Because of the diverse elements in Gaboriau, it is difficult to classify the ultimate result with any degree of exactitude. He presented plot and detection virtually as separate entities. On the former side, his work was purely *physical;* on the latter, almost as elaborately *mental* as "Marie Rogêt." The issue of this mismating was a *divided* rather than a *balanced* detective story. Any final evaluation of his contribution must therefore distinguish carefully between promise and achievement. By a paradox that would have appealed to his French mind, his reputation to-day rests largely on the fact that he is so seldom read! For Gaboriau is one of those authors whom everybody talks about but whose works (if the truth be told) are virtually unknown. Few modern readers would have the patience to abide the tawdry puppetry, the fustian, the cheap sensationalism, the dull and irrelevant digressions, the dreary and artificial verbiage that are the feuilletonist at his too-frequent worst, in order to get at the few grains of highly competent detection. This is perhaps as well, for (to continue the metaphor) the greatest value of the grain was its germinal quality. (pp. 34-6)

It is for this implied rather than fulfilled promise that the world honors Gaboriau; for this, and for the impetus he gave the detective story in his own time. Had he lived to write the works that he planned, his honors on both scores would almost certainly have been greater. Even as it is, generations of later detective story writers are in his debt. He blazed no really new trails, but he tilled in honest peasant fashion a great deal of virgin soil. (p. 36)

> *Howard Haycraft, "The In-Between Years (Development)," in his* Murder for Pleasure: The Life and Times of the Detective Story, *D. Appleton-Century Company Incorporated, 1941, pp. 28-44.*

A. E. MURCH   (essay date 1958)

[*Murch recognizes Gaboriau as the originator of the French* roman policier, *or "police novel," a genre that he enriched with his creation of the likeable detective, Lecoq, and his introduction of the "red herring," or false lead. Further, Murch describes Gaboriau's struggle to combine episodic narrative structure with in-depth character study.*]

[Gaboriau's detective novels] are sensational and melodramatic, as such fiction had to be to please its public, but they differ from *romans-feuilletons* in that the reader's attention is focussed on the detection, not the commission, of crime. In them Gaboriau originated the 'roman-policier' which was to form a major part of French popular fiction for the next quarter of a century. (p. 121)

In *L'Affaire Lerouge,* the opening chapters direct the limelight upon two official detectives of established reputation, M. Daburon, *le juge d'instruction,* and the celebrated Gévrol, *chef de la police de sûreté,* and it seems as though Gaboriau's original intention was to make them the central figures in his new novel of detection. But they are quickly eclipsed by two much more interesting characters, Père Tabaret and Monsieur Lecoq. (p. 122)

On his original appearance Lecoq is introduced with scant ceremony as a comparatively unimportant figure, merely Gévrol's junior assistant for the day, and Gaboriau describes him as 'an old offender now reconciled with the law,' a particularly interesting phrase because it places Lecoq, as an ex-convict turned policeman, in the same category as Vidocq, or Balzac's Gondureau, or the typical *agent de police* of any time in the previous hundred years. The term may have been used unthinkingly, simply as a conventional description—it has that air in the text—but Gaboriau seems to have regretted the phrase later, for as Lecoq became the central figure in the novels which followed, he went to some trouble to explain away this alleged stain on his hero's good name. (p. 123)

To enable Lecoq to fill his new rôle of French police-detective hero with brilliant efficiency. Gaboriau endowed him with powers derived from all his predecessors in detection. Lecoq can follow a trail as cleverly as the Princes of Serendip or Cooper's Indian braves, and he has all Vidocq's courage and intuition, his mastery of disguise, his familiarity with criminal ways. In view of Gaboriau's admiration for Edgar Allan Poe it is not surprising to find many points of similarity between Lecoq and Dupin, and they both regard a mysterious puzzle as a challenge to their powers of perception; they reason with mathematical precision and enjoy giving little lectures on 'algebraic analysis' to their associates. But whereas Dupin was an abstract logician, an arm-chair amateur detective, Lecoq threw himself with intense energy into the physical, as well as the mental, activities of practical police work, and over and above his inherited qualities he brought fresh skills of his own to the scientific detection of crime.... No-one, before him, used plaster to preserve a record of footprints, or drew a careful sketch of the scene of the crime, to be incorporated in the text. Lecoq and Père Tabaret are the first detectives to astonish the police (and the reader) by giving a detailed description of their suspect after making a brief examination of the scene of the crime. Père Tabaret, in *L'Affaire Lerouge,* takes a quick glance around, and remarks:—

> "He is a young man, below average height, elegantly dressed and wearing a top hat. He carried an umbrella, and was smoking a Havana cigar in a holder."

Lecoq, in "L'Enquête" (the first volume of *Monsieur Lecoq)* looks at the snow-covered ground outside an inn, and at once describes the man who walked across it half-an-hour ago:—

> "He is middle-aged and very tall, wearing a soft cap and a chestnut-coloured overcoat with a fleecy surface. He is very probably married."

In precisely the same way, twenty years or so later, Sherlock Holmes staggered his associates with such comments, ... and Tabaret, Lecoq and Holmes are all alike in not revealing until some time later the simple indications that enabled them to make their dramatic pronouncements.

Lecoq is drawn as a man to be liked as a human being, not merely admired as a detective, and, clever though he is, he is not infallible. In "L'Enquête," he allowed himself to be baulked of almost certain success after a long, exhausting quest, simply because he could not credit that his missing suspect was really a Duke. A chat with old Tabaret gave him fresh heart and a new line of enquiry, and at the end of the second volume he brought his case to a triumphant conclusion.

Gaboriau further enriched detective fiction by his perception of the suspense value of the 'red herring,' and often sent suspicion running on a false trail laid by circumstantial evidence. Prosper Bertomy, in *Le Dossier No. 113* and *le vicomte de Caumarin* in *L'Affaire Lerouge,* seem almost certainly guilty until, at last, new information shows them to be wrongly suspected. The case against Caumarin is so strong that he is actually on trial for murder when Père Tabaret, learning that the prisoner has no alibi for the material time, deduces that he must therefore be innocent, and begins to reconsider the evidence against him. In *Le Crime d'Orcival* Lecoq is faced with a similar need to revise his conclusions in view of conflicting indications, and in this respect Gaboriau pointed the way to that subtle and delicately balanced see-saw of detective argument which was later brought to such perfection in the novels of Freeman Wills Crofts and Father Ronald Knox.

In view of the antipathy so long felt in France towards the police, it was a remarkable achievement to win popularity for a police-hero. Indeed, Gaboriau first followed Poe's example, and in the opening instalments of *L'Affaire Lerouge* it is the amateur detective, Père Tabaret, who shines most brightly. But as the tale developed, Gaboriau invested police affairs with a glamour that caught his readers' attention, and focussed their interest upon Monsieur Lecoq. He was so typically French, and the device of a crowing cock, which he chose for his personal symbol, so aptly expressed his high-stepping self assurance, his quick eye for trifles, his bedraggled dejection when success eluded him and his exultant bravado when he was lucky! The logical force of his soundly reasoned arguments appealed to French habits of thought, and readers could also enjoy his revelations of interdepartmental rivalries within the *Préfecture;* the jealousy of a village policeman for the man sent down by the *Sûreté;* the dilemma of a *juge d'instruction,* divided between professional duty and loyalty to personal ties; the routine of prison management; and the behaviour of various types of suspect when subjected to the gruelling French system of interrogation.

In developing his novels of Monsieur Lecoq, Gaboriau found himself faced with the artistic difficulty inherent in fiction of this type. In essence, a detective story concerns itself with an analytical enquiry into a given set of circumstances, and for that reason, though the enquiry may be protracted, the tale is really episodic. The most satisfying, the most technically perfect, examples of detective fiction—the tales of Dupin and of Sherlock Holmes, for instance—are short stories. It is difficult for a longer work to concern itself with a detective theme to the virtual exclusion of that intimate study of character which is the province of the true novelist. In writing a detective novel the author generally finds himself involved in two conflicting subjects, on one hand a complicated puzzle calling for the exercise of the reasoning powers, and on the other a human drama which appeals to the emotions.

Gaboriau attempted to overcome this difficulty in *L'Affaire Lerouge* by breaking off the thread of detection at a dramatic moment (in a manner very frustrating to a modern reader) and

A depiction of Parisian rogues from Caught in the Net.

interpolating the life-stories of the people concerned, even to the extent of taking the reader into his confidence behind the detective's back. In *Monsieur Lecoq* he went to the length of writing two separate volumes, the first setting forth the problem as Lecoq saw it, and the second relating, from the beginning, the human drama that culminated in the crime, with Lecoq completing his case in the final pages. *Le Crime d'Orcival* is much shorter, the interpolation less tedious, and Lecoq's investigations are not seriously interrupted. This book, in which Gaboriau more nearly approaches the technique of the twentieth century detective novel, is his best work by modern standards, with the possible exception of *Le Petit Vieux des Batignolles* ..., which shows a further advance towards the 'pure' detective story, and foreshadows the device of the 'trick' ending. The murderer laid a false trail with meticulous care, and was caught only because the police, in ignorance of a material fact which he assumed they would know, blundered on the truth almost by accident. (pp. 124-27)

> *A. E. Murch, "The Rise of the 'Roman-Policier',"*
> *in his* The Development of the Detective Novel, *Philosophical Library, 1958, pp. 115-32.*

E. F. BLEILER   (essay date 1975)

[Bleiler affirms Gaboriau's historical importance and the status of Monsieur Lecoq *as a "perennial classic," but concludes that*

Gaboriau was "an author with a fine lesser imagination and an excellent skill at research, hampered by a lack of large-scale insight."]

Did Gaboriau really invent the modern detective novel? The answer is a qualified "Yes," if each of the three words "modern," "detective" and "novel" is taken with precision. Generally speaking, in both English and French, there had been a considerable body of crime fiction before Gaboriau's day, and some of this contained the germs of later developments, including primitive detectives and detection. But most of this material, like Victor's *The Dead Letter,* could not be considered modern, being only curious ancestral effigies for future generations to look upon. (p. x)

Gaboriau should not be seen as a collection of influences, but as a man who crystallized and solidified what may have been in the air around him. He unified a certain grouping of characteristics and created a form. Féval may have talked about ratiocinative deduction two or three years before Gaboriau, but he apparently did not care or was unable to develop the idea. Vidocq wandered about Paris in disguise, seeking criminals, and Balzac and Sue may have written long novels that combined comedy of manners with crime motives, but Gaboriau still has the distinction, in *L'Affaire Lerouge,* of having created the first modern novel that was clearly and unmistakably and consciously and primarily a detective story. (p. xii)

Gaboriau in a vague sort of way seems to have thought of the later novels, from *L'Affaire Lerouge* on, as segments of a consistent universe, a small *comédie humaine.* As a result there is a certain carry-over of names and personalities from one novel to another. The reader often finds a familiar face among the newcomers. This situation, unfortunately, is complicated by the fact that Gaboriau was careless in his chronology and cross-references, and is inconsistent almost as often as consistent. A further complication is that Gaboriau simply liked certain names and used them over.

A common frame of mind, similarly, permeates all the novels of Gaboriau, both detective and social. The ultimate spring of all his major work is scandal of the sexual sort. Forbidden amours, illegitimacy, golddigging, adultery—all provide final motivation for action. This is in striking contrast to the British novels that are roughly contemporary. . . . Wilkie Collins, in the two great novels, *The Woman in White* and *The Moonstone,* uses financial greed to motivate the stories. The ultimate in *The Woman in White* is Fosco's wish to obtain an inheritance, and the ultimate in *The Moonstone* is the monetary value of the gem. In Doyle's work, the ultimate is usually greed, with revenge a second consideration. For the other British Victorians—LeFanu, Miss Braddon, Mrs. Wood—the motivation is sometimes economic, sometimes the passion of anger, sometimes erotic, but never scandalous.

One could say simply and flippantly, that this simply means that Gaboriau was a Frenchman, and that his novels reflect the folkways of the time. But I do not know whether this is true. The psychologies of the characters—their violent passions and hatreds, their filial devotion, their raffishness, their strange innocences and pruderies—do they represent an aspect of life in the middle classes of Gaboriau's milieu, perhaps the ideals of his own pecksniffian family, or are they a literary convention, or perhaps both?

The motivations in Gaboriau are consistent and the personalities are consistent. A high problem of the generation before Ga-

boriau, one that entered very frequently in the fiction of the 1860's, was the haughty old revanchist nobility, returning in the post-Napoleonic restoration. There was the boom and bust of the Emperor Louis Napoleon; the extravagances of inverse machismo, when a chance act or word might ruin a girl's life, even though nothing significant had happened. Did this configuration of folkways really dominate mid-Victorian bourgeois France? I do not know, any more than if British lords in the comparable English literature perpetually tried to swindle their relatives. (pp. xvi-xviii)

For reasons now forgotten, Gaboriau's work was appreciated in America before England. (p. xix)

Before the appearance of Gaboriau's novels in America, the American detective story had been on the trivial side numerically. There were prehistoric detective stories before 1840 by Charles Brockden Brown and William Leggett; there was Poe's crystallization of the form and invention of ratiocinative deduction; but only a few minor successors to Poe. Then suddenly, shortly after the appearance of Gaboriau, the country was flooded with series after series of detective novels in dime-novel format. They were not modern detective stories, it is true; but they were novels that involved a crime, a detective (usually official), and some detection. I am inclined to think that this explosion of interest is the result of two foreign influences: to a lesser extent British detective casebooks (like "Waters"), as published by Dick and Fitzgerald, and to a larger extent, the long novels of Gaboriau.

In England Gaboriau's works began to appear in *Vizetelly's Sensational Novels* from 1883 on. Some of the translations may have been taken from American piracies; others may have been British in origin. This date 1883, it will be observed, is not far removed from 1887, the date of A. C. Doyle's *Study in Scarlet.* Doyle's diary notes reveal that he read certain of Gaboriau's novels, and in later years he recalled *The Widow Lerouge,* though somewhat dimly. Yet enough of the schema and details of Gaboriau's work remained in Doyle's mind that Doyle without Gaboriau would have been quite different. If Poe's Dupin was the father of Tabaret and Lecoq, Tabaret and Lecoq are the father and godfather of Sherlock Holmes. This is not to say, of course, that there were no other elements, or to deny Doyle's own ingenious contributions. (pp. xix-xx)

Gaboriau is obviously a historical link of the utmost importance [between Poe and Doyle]. Is he more than this? Is he an author worth reading in his own right? My answer is a limited "Yes." While he has great weaknesses, he also has certain strengths that are almost unique.

Let us omit the question of Gaboriau's French style, which has been called alternately brilliant and whimsical, ironic and lyric. These qualities do not emerge in the translations, but the translations are admittedly bad. They are hastily, carelessly, insensitively prepared hackwork, which at times are neither French nor English.

Gaboriau is certainly one of the most accomplished plotters in the genre. He is capable of working out a complex group of life situations and interweaving them without boring the reader or confusing him.

Complex plots, of course, were a standby of Victorian popular literature, and in England G. W. M. Reynolds and Wilkie Collins specialized in comparable material. Yet it is safe to say that Gaboriau at his best excelled them both in ornateness.

Such erector-set stories, however, may not be the highest achievement in literature (especially since the twentieth century is likely to seek other values), but they are still achievements that demand respect.

The detective novel is a notoriously difficult form to plot, since, to express it in the lowest terms, the author must devise something to fill in the space between the crime and the revealment or detection. It is greatly to Gaboriau's credit that in what is the first modern detective novel he solved the problem as well [as] any one has done since. Where *The Widow Lerouge* has flaws, they are in other areas.

Gaboriau's second strength lies in his detailed factual backgrounds and in his criminological and legal accuracy. Strictly speaking, this is not purely a matter of literature, but the reader of one hundred years later can appreciate the care that went into the descriptions of judicial processes, quirks of law, detectional insights, and the whole philosophy of French criminal investigation. British jurists have been known to recommend Gaboriau's novels to juniors who wanted a rapid picture of French criminal procedure. Gaboriau's old chief, Féval, faked in such matters and relied on imagination to carry him through. Gaboriau was correct. If Gaboriau describes the powers of the examining magistrate, if he explains a point in the law of inheritance, if he describes a suicide by carbon monoxide from unventilated charcoal braziers, one can be sure that he has checked the point. For Gaboriau there are no giant sea anemones, no devil's foot. If a young man is sent to the war in French Indo-China, and a crime is committed there, as in *The Gilded Clique,* one can be sure that extradition and venue are correctly handled. All this mirrors a world strange to the American reader, a world where the prisoner is officially guilty unless he can prove his innocence, where police entrapment (as in the Epilogue to *Monsieur Lecoq*) is permissible.

Where does Gaboriau fail? His portrayal of people. His characters have been called cardboard, and the accusation is, for the most part, true. They do resemble the moving dummies in a shooting gallery. Yet this criticism is a little over-simple. While the various counts and barons, fake and real, that people the novels, the adulterous ladies and virtuous ingenues, the sincere young lovers with mistresses on the side—are statues or lay-figures that sustain a drapery of plot, Gaboriau did succeed in animating two major characters, Lecoq and Tabaret, the voices of realism, rather than of romance.

A little more consciousness of technique might have worked wonders for Gaboriau in this respect. When Gaboriau works through the mind of a single character, which he does to some extent with Lecoq and Tabaret, his skill at recognizing motivation and his ability to create small detail can work an animation. When Gaboriau, on the other hand, attempts to make his characters interact romantically, when he speaks remotely as a recording witness, he loses his honesty of emotion and de-sparks what might have been human. This is where melodrama comes in, and this is where disaster strikes.

Perhaps the safest judgment of Gaboriau as a whole is to call him an author with a fine lesser imagination and an excellent skill at research, hampered by a lack of large-scale insight. Too often he sets up trumpery effects that do not succeed, and too often he is false. This may seem to be a harsh judgment, but the reader can look at the works of Balzac to see what happens when a first-rate writer, even though he may lack smoothness, works on material somewhat similar to Gaboriau's.

Criticism should stay at criticism, and reading pleasure should remain reading pleasure. Despite a modern reader's occasional annoyance at Gaboriau's weaknesses, *Monsieur Lecoq,* Part One, is still very much worth reading; it is easily the most animated of Gaboriau's works. The ingenuity of the author's deductions; the piquant personality of the young man who is determined to make his way in his profession, despite obstacles of official stupidity and criminal cunning; the thrill of the psychological duel between the helpless prisoner in his cell and the imaginative detective—these are the factors that make *Monsieur Lecoq* a perennial classic. (pp. xxi-xxiii)

> *E. F. Bleiler, in an introduction to* Monsieur Lecoq
> *by Émile Gaboriau, edited by E. F. Bleiler, Dover
> Publications, Inc., 1975, pp. v-xxviii.*

R. F. STEWART   (essay date 1980)

[*Stewart emphasizes Gaboriau's significance in the development of detective fiction. Noting that Gaboriau was surprisingly acceptable to critics who generally considered sensationalistic crime fiction immoral, Stewart identifies several influences on Gaboriau's writings and concludes with the suggestion that the author has not received full credit for his impact on Doyle and succeeding detective novelists.*]

What kind of book was Gaboriau writing that it was accepted by both readers and critics and that it succeeded where English sensation novelists, treating the same topics of crime, mystery and detectives, were left far behind? In what did he differ so greatly from Miss Braddon and Collins that he overcame the critical hostility to this kind of novel and won readers in a country already well-catered for in the field of sensation?

That Gaboriau had achieved something both different and more acceptable is clear from the critics' broadly favourable reaction to him, though of course they had no reason at first to suspect that he was instituting a sub-division of sensation fiction which was to become so extensive and in some respects so apparently different as to be able in time to deny its parent. To begin with, Gaboriau's superiority and the grounds for his critical acclaim were indicated more by favourable comparisons than by positive appreciations. He was good because the rest were bad—and bad often in a moral sense. This is seen in the *Saturday's* comment . . . that *L'Affaire Lerouge* 'is not ghastly and immoral, like . . . some others of recent production', followed in haste and surprise at commending a book dealing with crime by, 'if criminal, [it] is also decent' [see excerpt dated 1866]. (pp. 237-38)

[The] tendency of sensationalists to exalt or exonerate evil was a sticking point for many critics, who saw themselves as the guardians of moral as well as of literary taste. In Gaboriau they seemed to find an author of whom they could approve even though he dealt in the hitherto reprehensible subject of crime. Black, in Gaboriau, was black, and white was white: the bad were punished and the good lived happily ever after; there were no complications except in the plot, no lessons except in detection, and analysis was confined to clues. So was born the ideology of the detective story. (p. 239)

[Gaboriau] was the first novelist deliberately, consistently and completely to swing the criminal romance away from the crime and the criminal and to focus on the detective. . . . Before Gaboriau there were novels with detectives, not novels about detectives or novels about detection. There are odd examples of works which approach Gaboriau's concentration on these themes—*The Notting Hill Mystery, Lady Audley's Secret, The Moonstone*—but even these lack that vital intention of exalting these elements. Again, none of these books was followed by others in quite the same vein or using the same characters, and their popularity was due at least as much to other factors as to their detectives and detection—the thrill of a beautiful murderess in *Lady Audley's Secret,* the interplay of character in *The Moonstone,* and even though *The Notting Hill Mystery* is presented from the investigator's point of view, the interest is centred on Baron R. But Gaboriau sets the detective in the centre of the stage, turns the limelight on him and puts him through his paces. And both author and character come through with flying colours.

In one direction Poe is Gaboriau's obvious inspiration. It may safely be assumed that he had read Poe in Baudelaire's translation which enjoyed immense success in France. (p. 240)

In another direction Gaboriau's stories have their roots firmly planted in a French tradition. Just as novels with detectives were being written in England for many years before Doyle, so too in France Gaboriau could draw on a wealth of fiction replete with mysteries and detectives, and just as Doyle fits into the English sensational tradition, so Gaboriau is part of the French. Balzac and Dumas are obvious influences, but the undergrowth was no less thick than England's—Zevaco, Decourcelle, Ponson du Terrail and Gaboriau's employer, Féval, to name but a few. (pp. 241-42)

Without the efforts of these predecessors Gaboriau might never have conceived and executed his detective stories. There is probably more of Balzac than of Poe in Gaboriau, [seen in] his habit of using the same characters over a series of novels and of modelling his aristocrats along Balzac's lines. . . .

Gaboriau's achievement was to produce something new from the old formulas, the old characters and the old plots of sensation fiction, This he did by arranging his people and events round the detective—the detective who had always been there but in the background. Nothing changed except the emphasis. (p. 242)

It is probably to his judicious intermingling of the new with the old that Gaboriau owes some of his success. In *Monsieur Lecoq,* for example, the man known as Mai, whose identity Lecoq spends most of the first part of the book trying to establish, is not the villain of the piece but the object of a plot. It is vital to Lecoq's pride that he find his answer; it is equally vital to Mai and his friends that his true identity is not established or the honour of his name will be compromised. The reader, however, is free to adopt either the interesting new angle of following with the hound—*in detail,* which had not happened before, or the edifying variation on the well-proven old angle—running with the *innocent* hare. Whichever the reader chooses, Gaboriau wins; of course the reader chooses to do both and Gaboriau doubles his winnings. (p. 245)

· · · · ·

Doyle made two well-known comments about Gaboriau. The first is in *A Study in Scarlet* [see excerpt dated 1887]. . . . The second is in his autobiography, *Memories and Adventures* . . . : 'Gaboriau had rather attracted me by the neat dove-tailing of his plots'. There is a whiff of contradiction here, but since the first was written by Doyle in his capacity as a literary agent and the second by Doyle *qua* Doyle, I think we are justified in taking the autobiographical comment as nearer his true opinion.

Doyle does not elaborate on what he means by 'neat dove-tailing', but the structure of his own long stories leaves little doubt. Thus in both *A Study in Scarlet* and *The Valley of Fear . . .* Doyle faithfully follows Gaboriau's system of a first part concerned with a crime, its investigation and virtual solution, then a second part in which time is turned back and a new story started which from remote beginnings brings the reader to the commission of the crime discovered at the opening of the book. (p. 256)

This similarity of construction is a very obvious common factor in Gaboriau and Doyle, and is generally condemned in both. (p. 257)

Doyle owed rather more to Gaboriau than the histories tell us, a suspicion borne out by another, less well-known, reference to Gaboriau in Doyle's diary. John Dickson Carr mentions it in his biography of Doyle:

> 'I have read Gaboriau's *Lecoq the Detective*', he wrote; the first reference to Gaboriau in all his papers, '*The Gilded Clique,* and a story concerning the murder of an old woman, the name of which I forget.' Looking this up, he inserted *The Lerouge Case.* 'All very good. Wilkie Collins, but more so.'
>
> (p. 259)

No absolute disparagement of Doyle is intended here; only a suggestion that the distribution of recognition within detective fiction could bear some reorganisation. Doyle freely admitted his debt to Poe. Gaboriau, I am sure, would have admitted a similar debt. Nor can we doubt Doyle's sincerity when he wrote: 'As to work which is unconsciously imitative, it is not to be expected that a man's style and mode of treatment should spring fully formed from his own brain', but it was Poe alone that he seemed to have in mind here. Given the foregoing, one feels that he owes, for his start in life, a more immediate debt to Gaboriau, not for showing him that stories about detectives and detection could be written—Poe did that—but for showing him that they could become alive. That was the achievement of both Gaboriau and Doyle, and if in the long run Doyle did it better, could he have done it at all without Gaboriau's lead? (p. 260)

In a positive and deliberate sense, Gaboriau set out to write about detectives, their successes, their failures, to have them as his centrepieces, to propose them as superior alternatives to rogues and criminals. No, he was not writing 'detective fiction', but to say this is now to quibble. What he did write was, twenty years later, considered so distinctive and influential as to be worth the invention of the term. This is where Gaboriau differs from Collins and all the other writers of the time who employed detectives. To them—and to many later writers—the detective was useful. To Gaboriau he was vital.

So fascinated was Gaboriau by detectives that he set himself to render the unacceptable attractive. Beside Gaboriau's interest, Dickens' and Collins' appears negligible. (pp. 276-77)

Up to Gaboriau, no novelist—and Poe only in the short story—had taken a detective and thrust greatness upon him. Gaboriau differs radically from all [early detective novelists] in that he starts with a detective and finishes with a detective. Even Poe ends with a dissertation, and Robert Audley is a detective in spite of himself. With his long, historical flashbacks Gaboriau gives us rather more than we have come to expect. . . . [As] twentieth-century detective stories *Monsieur Lecoq* and *Le Dos-*

sier No. 113 are too long, but the detective parts are complete in themselves. Indeed, the first part of the former, **"L'en-quête"**, is so self-contained that it has been published on its own on several occasions with no mention of its second part, **"L'honneur du nom"**. The 'digressions' in *L'Affaire Lerouge* and *Le Crime d'Orcival* are much more closely linked with the detective plot; they may seem long-winded, but they are Gaboriau's way of doing something that had never been done before. Moreover, the romances which make up the second parts of the other two books, especially that in *Le Dossier No. 113*, are entertaining in themselves if the reader can disabuse himself of the notion that the problem of who did it is necessarily central to the detective story.

Of course Gaboriau did not obey the rules. He was making them, or at least one, and that a much more basic one than anything to follow and on which all that followed depended; the rule, simply, that detective stories could be written and enjoyed. We can accept or reject, as we please, any or all of the explanations of his faults. . . . But whatever we do, we cannot deny that the intention to write novels about detectives and the achievement of that intention are Gaboriau's lasting contributions to literature. (pp. 278-79)

> *R. F. Stewart, "The Reader Learns Much That He Has Guessed" and "In Which an Important Act of Restitution Is Made," in his* . . . And Always a Detective: Chapters on the History of Detective Fiction, *David & Charles, 1980, pp. 231-52, 253-79.*

ADDITIONAL BIBLIOGRAPHY

Cambiaire, Célestin Pierre. "Poe and Émile Gaboriau." In his *The Influence of Edgar Allan Poe in France*, pp. 264-80. 1927. Reprint. St. Clair Shores, Mich.: Scholarly Press, 1971.

> Compares Poe's detective stories with Gaboriau's novels. While Cambiaire maintains that Poe was the superior artist, he grants that Gaboriau was not slavish in his imitations of Poe's technique.

Symons, Julian. "Dickens, Collins, Gaboriau: The Pattern Forms." In his *Mortal Consequences: A History—From the Detective Story to the Crime Novel*, pp. 36-53. New York: Harper & Row, Publishers, 1972.

> Claims that Gaboriau has been underrated. Symons finds that although Gaboriau's novels lack humor and skilled characterization, they display the author's analytical intelligence and thorough knowledge of French police procedures.

Wells, Carolyn. *The Technique of the Mystery Story*. Springfield, Mass.: Home Correspondence School, 1913, 336 p.

> Surveys the history and characteristics of detective fiction and credits Gaboriau, along with Poe and Doyle, with the invention of the genre.

Wright, Willard Huntington. "The Great Detective Stories." In *The Art of the Mystery Story: A Collection of Critical Essays*, edited by Howard Haycraft, pp. 33-70. New York: Simon and Schuster, 1946.

> Assesses Gaboriau's place in the history of detective fiction. Wright calls Gaboriau's *The Widow Lerouge* "the first great stride in the detective novel."

William Godwin

1756-1836

English philosopher, novelist, essayist, historian, dramatist, and biographer.

Godwin is recognized as a philosopher and author whose writings strongly influenced the English Romantic writers. His anarchistic and rationalistic beliefs are delineated in his philosophical masterpiece, *An Enquiry Concerning Political Justice and Its Influence on General Virtue and Happiness*. In this work, Godwin stated that humankind is innately good and capable of living harmoniously without laws or institutions. These tenets are dramatized in his best-known novel, *Things As They Are; or, The Adventures of Caleb Williams*, a didactic tale about the evils of government. Though Godwin wrote other novels as well as biographies and essays, critics point out that these works lack the emotional power and intellectual appeal of *Caleb Williams* and *Political Justice*. Despite his prolific career, Godwin's reputation has declined, and he is primarily known today as a figure of historical importance.

The seventh of thirteen children, Godwin was born in Wisbeach, England, to a Presbyterian minister and his wife. Raised in a strict, puritanical environment, Godwin trained for the ministry at an early age and became a Sandemanian clergyman in 1777. However, after studying the French revolutionary philosophers, he grew disenchanted with religion and eventually became an atheist. Leaving the church in 1783, Godwin moved to London, intending to make his living as an author. There he contributed to the *London Review* and wrote factual pamphlets and biographies; these writings, though intellectually rigorous, lack the philosophical content that distinguishes his subsequent work.

In 1793, Godwin published *Political Justice,* which contains the theoretical essence of all his later writings. In this work, Godwin denounced contemporary goverhments as corrupt and ineffective, hypothesizing that reason rather than law should provide the ruling force of society. Through the development of reason, he declared, humanity could become perfect. He also contended that property should not be accumulated by individuals, but should instead be held in trust for those in need. In discussing penal servitude, Godwin maintained that criminals should be reformed, not merely punished. Of all the arguments advanced in *Political Justice,* perhaps the best known is Godwin's disdain for the institution of marriage: he advocated that men and women should be united solely by a bond of mutual respect rather than a social and legal contract. Godwin was nearly prosecuted for these unconventional beliefs. However, among those who sympathized with its unorthodox tenets, *Political Justice* met with immediate acclaim, and its author was widely hailed as an influential philosopher.

Following the success of *Political Justice,* Godwin produced *Caleb Williams*, a novel inspired by his desire to disseminate the ideas of *Political Justice* through a more popular form. A tale of good triumphing over evil and an individual conquering a corrupt system, the novel tells the story of Caleb Williams, a man persecuted by his employer, Ferdinando Falkland, and jailed for a crime he did not commit. Godwin's plot combines historical events with psychological realism and Gothic and

detective elements. The original preface, in which the author defined the novel as "a study and delineation of things passing in the moral world," was considered politically subversive and was consequently suppressed for many years. *Caleb Williams* endures, however, as a record of the revolutionary spirit and as one of the first novels to successfully combine fiction and philosophy. Though undeniably propagandistic, the novel won critical praise for its synthesis of content and style. In particular, critics noted that Godwin's use of first-person narration lends an element of immediacy to *Caleb Williams*. With *Political Justice, Caleb Williams* provided Godwin with his only financial success.

Godwin was already an established and influential writer in 1796 when he met Mary Wollstonecraft, the author of *A Vindication of the Rights of Woman,* an attack on society's treatment of women. Their rapport was immediate, and soon the two began living together. When Wollstonecraft became pregnant a few months later, the two wed despite their mutual distaste for the institution of marriage because they wanted to ensure the legal rights of their child. By all accounts, both found great joy in wedlock, but their happiness was short-lived. Several days after the birth of their daughter in 1797, Wollstonecraft died of complications from the delivery. A desolate Godwin recorded his memories of their brief life together in *Memoirs of the Author of "A Vindication of the Rights of*

Woman," in which he wrote of his wife, "I honoured her intellectual powers and the nobleness and generosity of her propensities; mere tenderness would not have been adequate to produce the happiness we experienced." Left with his infant daughter as well as a stepdaughter to care for, Godwin set out to find a mother for his children. He was turned down by one woman after another before marrying Mary Jane Clairmont, a harsh, cruel woman who treated his children poorly.

Despite the sorrows of his personal life, Godwin continued to write. In 1799, shortly before his marriage to Clairmont, Godwin had published *St. Leon,* a historical novel that reflects his interest in heroic drama and his desire to modify some of his earlier radical beliefs, which were considered harsh and insensitive. A sentimental depiction of the joys of domesticity, *St. Leon* is also a tribute to his late wife. Response to the novel was mixed, and critics termed *St. Leon* more ambitious in design than Godwin's range would permit. His next novel, *Fleetwood,* which appeared six years later, is considered both a synthesis of Romantic ideals and a reconstruction of Godwin's earlier philosophy. Though some critics praised *Fleetwood*'s philosophical framework, most considered it poorly organized and overly didactic. Like *St. Leon, Fleetwood* sold poorly.

After the publication of *Fleetwood,* Godwin and his wife began publishing children's books, histories, and biographies in a desperate attempt to support their growing family. Godwin also relied heavily on the financial assistance of the young followers who sought his philosophical guidance; most notable among these was the Romantic poet Percy Bysshe Shelley. In 1814, Shelley, who was already married, eloped with Godwin's sixteen-year-old daughter, Mary. Though a furious Godwin disowned them both, he continued to demand Shelley's monetary support. Godwin's wrath diminished when the two married several years later, and he became once again extremely close to his daughter. Shelley remained a devoted disciple of his father-in-law and aided the initial reception of Godwin's *Mandeville* by writing a strongly favorable review. Inspired by the fiction of Sir Walter Scott, *Mandeville* is considered indicative of the general decline in Godwin's fiction following *Caleb Williams.* Godwin's last novels, *Cloudesly* and *Deloraine,* generated little positive response upon their publication and are today considered dull.

In addition to his fiction, Godwin published several book-length essays, including *Thoughts on Man: His Nature, Productions, and Discoveries* and *Of Population: An Enquiry Concerning the Power of Increase in the Numbers of Mankind, Being an Answer to Mr. Malthus' Essay on That Subject.* The latter work contests the political theories of Thomas Malthus as delineated in his *Essay on the Principle of Population.* While Malthus argued for a check on population growth, Godwin opposed any type of law or governing institution that would inhibit human nature. Despite his steady literary output, Godwin struggled financially until 1833, when he was appointed yeoman usher of the exchequer and was granted a government pension. Though no longer compelled by financial necessity, Godwin steadfastly continued to write until his death three years later.

At the time of his death, Godwin's contemporaries considered him a figure of historical and literary importance whose beliefs had briefly inspired such individuals as Samuel Taylor Coleridge and Robert Southey, who together created a pantisocracy, or egalitarian agricultural society, based on Godwin's theories. His revolutionary writings also influenced Shelley and

William Wordsworth, who both based their Romantic philosophies on his ideas on personal freedom. However, Godwin's works soon fell into relative obscurity, receiving attention only from such literary figures as Thomas De Quincey and Leslie Stephen, who both censured his verbosity and excessive didacticism. It was not until the turn of the century that critics began to demonstrate a renewed interest in Godwin as a philosopher and author. Early twentieth-century studies stressed the literary merits of *Political Justice* and its value as a philosophical and historical document. *Caleb Williams,* too, has enjoyed a revival. Since the 1940s, critics have analyzed various aspects of the work, including its elements of tragedy and mystery, the two endings for the novel, and the prose style. Critics differ on whether Godwin best articulated his philosophy in the essay or novel form. Nonetheless, they point out his ideological consistency: despite the variety of genres in which Godwin composed, the philosophical thread that he developed in *Political Justice* dominates every work.

Today, *Caleb Williams* continues to be read and studied widely; the profusion of articles written on the novel each year attests to its enduring popularity. Critics also regard the work as a seminal contribution to the evolution of the English novel. *Political Justice* endures as a testament to Godwin's talent at the peak of his powers and as one of the main documents of English Romantic philosophy. In addition, Godwin's importance derives from his influence on the Romantics, especially on the verse of Wordsworth and Shelley. Godwin's reputation today rests on three areas: *Caleb Williams,* his theories as expressed in *Political Justice,* and his imprint on contemporary and modern literature.

PRINCIPAL WORKS

An Account of the Seminary That Will Be Opened at Epsom (prospectus) 1783
The History of the Life of William Pitt (biography) 1783
An Enquiry Concerning Political Justice and Its Influence on General Virtue and Happiness (essay) 1793; also published in revised form as *Enquiry Concerning Political Justice and Its Influence on Morals and Happiness,* 1796
Things As They Are; or, The Adventures of Caleb Williams (novel) 1794; also published as *The Adventures of Caleb Williams; or, Things As They Are,* 1839
The Enquirer: Reflections on Education, Manners, and Literature (essays) 1797
Memoirs of the Author of "A Vindication of the Rights of Woman" (memoirs) 1798
St. Leon: A Tale of the Sixteenth Century (novel) 1799
Life of Geoffrey Chaucer (biography) 1803
Fleetwood; or, The New Man of Feeling (novel) 1805
Faulkener [first publication] (drama) 1807
Mandeville: A Tale of the Seventeenth Century in England (novel) 1817
Of Population: An Enquiry Concerning the Power of Increase in the Numbers of Mankind, Being an Answer to Mr. Malthus' Essay on That Subject (essay) 1820
Cloudesly (novel) 1830
Thoughts on Man: His Nature, Productions, and Discoveries (essay) 1831
Deloraine (novel) 1833
Lives of the Necromancers; or, An Account of the Most Eminent Persons Who Have Claimed or to Whom Has

Been Imputed the Exercise of Magical Power
(biographical sketches)   1834
Essays Never Before Published   (essays)   1873

SAMUEL TAYLOR COLERIDGE   (poem date 1793)

[*An English poet and critic, Coleridge was central to the English Romantic movement and is considered one of the greatest literary critics in the English language. His sonnet, "To William Godwin," originally appeared in the* Morning Chronicle *on January 10, 1793.*]

O form'd t'illumine a sunless world forlorn,
As o'er the chill and dusky brow of Night,
In Finland's wintry skies the Mimic Morn
   Electric pours a stream of rosy light,

Pleas'd I have mark'd OPPRESSION, terror-pale,
   Since, through the windings of her dark machine,
   Thy steady eye has shot its glances keen—
And bade th'All-lovely 'scenes at distance hail.'

Nor will I not thy holy guidance bless,
   And hymn thee, GODWIN! with an ardent lay;
   For that thy voice, in Passion's stormy day,
When wild I roam'd the bleak heath of Distress,

Bade the bright form of Justice meet my way
And told me that her name was HAPPINESS.

> Samuel Taylor Coleridge, "'To William Godwin',"
> in Godwin and the Age of Transition, *edited by A. E. Rodway, Barnes & Noble, Inc., 1952, p. 206.*

WILLIAM GODWIN   (essay date 1794)

[*Written in 1794, Godwin's preface to the first edition of* Caleb Williams *was suppressed and not published until much later. Because of the conservative political atmosphere at the time, booksellers feared that the preface might be considered traitorous.*]

The following narrative is intended to answer a purpose more general and important than immediately appears upon the face of it. The question now afloat in the world respecting THINGS AS THEY ARE is the most interesting that can be presented to the human mind. While one party pleads for reformation and change, the other extols in the warmest terms the existing constitution of society. It seemed as if something would be gained for the decision of this question, if that constitution were faithfully developed in its practical effects. What is now presented to the public is no refined and abstract speculation; it is a study and delineation of things passing in the moral world. It is but of late that the inestimable importance of political principles has been adequately apprehended. It is now known to philosophers, that the spirit and character of the government intrudes itself into every rank of society. But this is a truth highly worthy to be communicated to persons whom books of philosophy and science are never likely to reach. Accordingly it was proposed, in the invention of the following work, to comprehend, as far as the progressive nature of a single story would allow, a general review of the modes of domestic and unrecorded despotism by which man becomes the destroyer of man. If the author shall have taught a valuable lesson, without subtracting from the interest and passion by

which a performance of this sort ought to be characterised, he will have reason to congratulate himself upon the vehicle he has chosen. (pp. xix-xx)

> *William Godwin, in a preface to his* The Adventures of Caleb Williams; or, Things as They Are, *revised edition, Richard Bentley, 1849, pp. xix-xx.*

THE BRITISH CRITIC   (essay date 1794)

[*In the following excerpt, the critic harshly condemns* Caleb Williams, *stating that the novel represents "the evil use" of Godwin's talents.*]

[*Things as They Are; or, The Adventures of Caleb Williams*] is a striking example of the evil use which may be made of considerable talents, connected with such a degree of intrepidity as can inspire the author with resolution to attack religion, virtue, government, laws, and above all, the desire (hitherto accounted laudable) of leaving a good name to posterity.

In this extraordinary performance, every gentleman is a hard hearted assassin, or a prejudiced tyrant; every Judge is unjust, every Justice corrupt and blind. Sentiments of respect to Christianity are given only to the vilest wretch in the book; while the most respectable person in the drama abhors the idea of "shackling his expiring friend with the fetters of superstition."

In order to render the laws of his country odious, the author places an innocent prisoner, whose story he (avowedly) takes from the Newgate Calendar of the first George's reign, in a dungeon; the wretched, unhealthy state of which he steals (as avowedly) from one of the benevolent Howard's painful descriptions of a worse gaol than common. We will only add, that the character, on which the author seems to dwell with most pleasure, is that of a leader of robbers, one who dwells in a ruinous retreat, and dispatches felons and murderers, in parties, around the country.

When a work is so directly pointed at every band which connects society, and at every principle which renders it amiable, its very merits become noxious as they tend to cause its being known in a wider circle. (pp. 70-1)

> *A review of "Things as They Are; or, The Adventures of Caleb Williams," in* The British Critic, *Vol. IV, July, 1794, pp. 70-1.*

THE MONTHLY REVIEW, LONDON   (essay date 1794)

[*In the following excerpt from a review of* Caleb Williams, *the critic terms the plot "a whining love tale," but praises the novel as an outstanding example of philosophical fiction.*]

Between fiction and philosophy there seems to be no natural alliance:—yet philosophers, in order to obtain for their dogmata a more ready reception, have often judged it expedient to introduce them to the world in the captivating dress of fable. It was not to be supposed that the energetic mind of Mr. Godwin, long inured as it must have been to abstract speculation and sublime inquiry, would condescend to employ itself in framing a whining love tale. . . . In writing *The Adventures of Caleb Williams,* this philosopher had doubtless some higher object in view; and it is not difficult to perceive that this object has been to give an easy passport, and general circulation, to some of his favourite opinions. Having laid it down as a first principle that virtue consists in justice, or the wise and equal pursuit of general good, he thinks it necessary, in order to carry his system into effect, to investigate many sentiments which, though hitherto considered as the legitimate offspring of nature, and even as possessing some degree of moral value, are in his judgment only the creatures of error and prejudice. In this class he appears to rank that sense of honour which seeks its ultimate reward in the good opinion of mankind. Accordingly, this fictitious narrative seems to have been written chiefly for the purpose of representing, in strong colours, the fatal consequence of suffering the love of fame to become predominant.

Mr. Falkland, who ought, perhaps, rather than Caleb Williams, to be considered as the principal actor in this drama, exhibits a character wholly formed on the visionary principles of honour. Early tinctured with extravagant notions on this subject, by the heroic poets of Italy, he cherishes a romantic pride; which, notwithstanding his natural propensity toward benevolence, displayed in occasional acts of generosity, soon forms his ruling passion, and at length overwhelms him with accumulated wretchedness. He is the fool of honour; a man whom, in the pursuit of reputation, nothing could divert; who would purchase the character of a true, gallant, and undaunted hero, at the expence of worlds; and who thinks every calamity nominal except a stain on his honour. His virtue, his life, his everlasting peace of mind, are cheap sacrifices to be made at the shrine of fame; and there is no crime too horrible for him to commit in pursuit of this object. (pp. 145-46)

This visionary character is drawn with uncommon strength of conception and energy of language. The reader, while he respects and adores the virtues of Falkland, feels infinite regret that his mad passion for reputation should suppress every feeling of humanity, and become the source of unspeakable misery to himself, and of the most tragical calamity to others. The character, though original, will perhaps be admitted to be consistent; unless it should be thought difficult to reconcile the benevolence every where ascribed to Falkland, with the *deliberate* injustice and cruelty which were shewn in suffering the innocent Hawkins and his son to be executed, in preference to confessing his own guilt.—It will perhaps be said that the ruling passion of Falkland was not benevolence, but the love of fame; yet it may be questioned whether such benevolence, as is ascribed to Falkland, be not utterly incompatible with the tyrannical sway which is given in his character to the *selfish* passion of the love of fame. . . .

A farther object in this story appears to have been to exhibit an example of the danger of indulging an idle curiosity, merely for its own gratification; and the fatal consequences of this folly were perhaps never so impressively exemplified as in the story of Caleb Williams, the confidential servant of Falkland. (p. 147)

With due allowance for systematical eccentricity, (the reader will pardon the paradoxical expression,) this performance, interesting but not gratifying to the feelings and the passions, and written in a style of laboured dignity rather than of easy familiarity, is singularly entitled to be characterized as a work in which the powers of genius and philosophy are strongly united. (p. 149)

> E., *"Godwin's 'Things as They Are'," in* The Monthly Review, *London, Vol. XV, October, 1794, pp. 145-49.*

WILLIAM GODWIN (essay date 1799)

[*In the following excerpt from his 1799 preface to* St. Leon, *Godwin explains his desire to depict the joys of domestic life.*]

It has been said of Shakespeare, that he

> Exhausted worlds, and then imagined new:

but the burthen sustained by Shakespeare was too heavy for the shoulders of any other individual. I leave the first part of the task above mentioned to be divided among those celebrated novelists, living and dead, who have attempted to delineate the scenes of real life. In [*St. Leon*] I have endeavoured to gain footing in one neglected track of the latter province. The hearts and the curiosity of readers have been assailed in so many ways, that we, writers who bring up the rear of our illustrious predecessors, must be contented to arrive at novelty in whatever mode we are able. The foundation of the following tale is such as, it is not to be supposed, ever existed. But, if I have mixed human feelings and passions with incredible situations, and thus rendered them impressive and interesting, I shall entertain some hope to be pardoned the boldness and irregularity of my design.

Some readers of my graver productions will perhaps, in perusing these little volumes, accuse me of inconsistency; the affections and charities of private life being every where in this publication a topic of the warmest eulogium, while in the **Enquiry Concerning Political Justice** they seemed to be treated with no great degree of indulgence and favour. In answer to this objection, all I think it necessary to say on the present occasion is, that, for more than four years, I have been anxious for opportunity and leisure to modify some of the earlier chapters of that work in conformity to the sentiments inculcated in this. Not that I see cause to make any change respecting the principle of justice, or any thing else fundamental to the system there delivered; but that I apprehend domestic and private affections inseparable from the nature of man, and from what may be styled the culture of the heart, and am fully persuaded that they are not incompatible with a profound and active sense of justice in the mind of him that cherishes them. True wisdom will recommend to us individual attachments; for with them our minds are more thoroughly maintained in activity and life than they can be under the privation of them; and it is better that man should be a living being, than a stock or a stone. True virtue will sanction this recommendation; since it is the object of virtue to produce happiness, and since the man who lives in the midst of domestic relations will have many opportunities of conferring pleasure, minute in the detail, yet not trivial in the amount, without interfering with the purposes of general benevolence. Nay, by kindling his sensibility, and harmonising his soul, they may be expected, if he is endowed with a liberal and manly spirit, to render him more prompt in the service of strangers and the public. (pp. ix-x)

> *William Godwin, in a preface to his* St. Leon: A Tale of the Sixteenth Century, *Colburn and Bentley, 1831, pp. vii-x.*

ROBERT SOUTHEY (letter date 1800)

[*An English poet, historian, biographer, essayist, short story writer, and editor, Southey was a prominent literary figure of the late eighteenth and early nineteenth centuries and a key member of the Lake School of poetry. In the following extract from a letter to his friend Coleridge, Southey offers a mixed assessment of* St. Leon.]

How like you Godwin's novel [*St. Leon*]? It is at times powerfully written—but it is dilated or diluted. St. Leon always acts so like a fool that his conduct is the most unbelievable part of the volume, and Godwin is always exposing himself in a posture which says "come kick me!" The passage in the first volume about voluptuousness, which recommends a course of brothel studies, is very exceptionable, and Godwin ought to have recollected what allusion his enemies would immediately make. I was quite pained and irritated at the man's folly. (p. 213)

Robert Southey, in a letter to Samuel Taylor Coleridge in January, 1800, in his New Letters of Robert Southey: 1792-1810, Vol. 1, *edited by Kenneth Curry, Columbia University Press, 1965, pp. 212-14.*

T. R. MALTHUS (essay date 1806)

[*A nineteenth-century English political and economic theorist, Malthus is best known for his* Essay on the Principle of Population. *There, Malthus proposed his controversial thesis that population growth should be controlled. In the following excerpt from that work, he outlines his objections to Godwin's theories in* Political Justice. *Focusing on his ideas regarding marriage and his proposed system of providing for children "by general benevolence," Malthus argues that Godwin's social model would prove economically disastrous. Godwin later rebutted Malthus's statements in his* Of Population.]

In reading Mr. Godwin's ingenious [*An Enquiry Concerning Political Justice*], it is impossible not to be struck with the spirit and energy of his style, the force and precision of some of his reasonings, the ardent tone of his thoughts, and particularly with that impressive earnestness of manner which gives an air of truth to the whole. At the same time it must be confessed that he has not proceeded in his inquiries with the caution that sound philosophy requires. His conclusions are often unwarranted by his premises. He fails sometimes in removing objections which he himself brings forward. He relies too much on general and abstract propositions which will not admit of application. And his conjectures certainly far outstrip the modesty of nature.

The system of equality which Mr. Godwin proposes is, on a first view, the most beautiful and engaging of any that has yet appeared. A melioration of society to be produced merely by reason and conviction gives more promise of permanence than any change effected and maintained by force. The unlimited exercise of private judgment is a doctrine grand and captivating, and has a vast superiority over those systems, where every individual is in a manner the slave of the public. The substitution of benevolence, as the masterspring and moving principle of society, instead of self-love, appears at first sight to be a consummation devoutly to be wished. In short, it is impossible to contemplate the whole of this fair picture without emotions of delight and admiration, accompanied with an ardent longing for the period of its accomplishment. But alas! that moment can never arrive. The whole is little better than a dream—a phantom of the imagination. (pp. 98-9)

The great errour under which Mr. Godwin labours throughout his whole work is, the attributing of almost all the vices and misery that prevail in civil society to human institutions. Political regulations, and the established administration of property, are, with him, the fruitful sources of all evil, the hotbeds of all the crimes that degrade mankind. Were this really a true state of the case, it would not seem an absolutely hopeless task to remove evil completely from the world; and reason seems to be the proper and adequate instrument for effecting so great a purpose. But the truth is, that though human institutions appear to be the obvious and obtrusive causes of much mischief to mankind, they are, in reality, light and superficial, in comparison with those deeper-feated causes of evil which result from the laws of nature. (pp. 100-01)

Man cannot live in the midst of plenty. All cannot share alike the bounties of nature. Were there no established administration of property every man would be obliged to guard with force his little store. Selfishness would be triumphant. The subjects of contention would be perpetual. Every individual would be under a constant anxiety about corporal support, and not a single intellect would be left free to expatiate in the field of thought.

How little Mr. Godwin has turned his attention to the real state of human society will sufficiently appear, from the manner in which he endeavours to remove the difficulty of an overcharged population. He says,

> The obvious answer to this objection is, that to reason thus is to foresee difficulties at a great distance. Three fourths of the habitable globe are now uncultivated. The parts already cultivated are capable of immeasurable improvement. Myriads of centuries of still increasing population may pass away, and the earth be still found sufficient for the subsistence of its inhabitants.
>
> (pp. 102-03)

[Let] us imagine for a moment Mr. Godwin's system of equality realized in its utmost extent, and see how soon this difficulty might be expected to press, under so perfect a form of society. A theory that will not admit of application cannot possibly be just.

Let us suppose all the causes of vice and misery in this island removed. War and contention cease. Unwholesome trades and manufactories do not exist. Crowds no longer collect together in great and pestilent cities for purposes of court intrigue, of commerce, and vicious gratification. Simple, healthy, and rational amusements take place of drinking, gaming, and debauchery. There are no towns sufficiently large to have any prejudicial effects on the human constitution. The greater part of the happy inhabitants of this terrestrial Paradise live in hamlets and farm houses scattered over the face of the country. All men are equal. (pp. 103-04)

Mr. Godwin considers marriage as a fraud and a monopoly. Let us suppose the commerce of the sexes established upon principles of the most perfect freedom. Mr. Godwin does not think himself that this freedom would lead to a promiscuous intercourse; and in this I perfectly agree with him. The love of variety is a vicious, corrupt, and unnatural taste, and could not prevail in any great degree in a simple and virtuous state of society. Each man would probably select for himself a partner to whom he would adhere, as long as that adherence continued to be the choice of both parties. It would be of little consequence, according to Mr. Godwin, how many children a woman had, or to whom they belonged. Provisions and assistance would spontaneously flow from the quarter in which they abounded to the quarter in which they were deficient. And every man according to his capacity would be ready to furnish instruction to the rising generation.

I cannot conceive a form of society so favourable upon the whole to population. The irremediableness of marriage, as it is at present constituted, undoubtedly deters many from entering into this state. An unshackled intercourse on the contrary would be a most powerful incitement to early attachments; and as we are supposing no anxiety about the future support of children to exist, I do not conceive that there would be one woman in a hundred, of twenty-three years of age, without a family. (pp. 104-05)

There can be little doubt that the equalization of property which we have supposed, added to the circumstance of the labour of the whole community being directed chiefly to agriculture, would tend greatly to augment the produce of the country. But to answer the demands of a population increasing so rapidly, Mr. Godwin's calculation of half an hour a day would certainly not be sufficient. It is probable that the half of every man's time must be employed for this purpose. Yet with such or much greater exertions, a person who is acquainted with the nature of the soil in this country, and who reflects on the fertility of the lands already in cultivation, and the barrenness of those that are not cultivated, will be very much disposed to doubt whether the whole average produce could possibly be doubled in twenty-five years from the present period. (pp. 106-07)

During the next period where will the food be found to satisfy the importunate demands of the increasing numbers? Where is the fresh land to turn up? Where is the dressing necessary to improve that which is already in cultivation? There is no person with the smallest knowledge of land but would say, that it was impossible that the average produce of the country could be increased during the second twenty-five years, by a quantity equal to what it at present yields. Yet we will suppose this increase, however improbable, to take place. The exuberant strength of the argument allows of almost any concession. Even with this concession however, there would be eleven millions at the expiration of the second term unprovided for. (pp. 107-08)

Alas! what becomes of the picture, where men lived in the midst of plenty, where no man was obliged to provide with anxiety and pain for his restless wants; where the narrow principle of selfishness did not exist; where the mind was delivered from her perpetual anxiety about corporal support, and free to expatiate in the field of thought which is congenial to her. This beautiful fabric of the imagination vanishes at the severe touch of truth. (p. 108)

No human institutions here existed, to the perverseness of which Mr. Godwin ascribes the original sin of the worst men. No opposition had been produced by them between public and private good. No monopoly had been created of those advantages which reason directs to be left in common. No man had been goaded to the breach of order by unjust laws. Benevolence had established her reign in all hearts. And yet in so short a period as fifty years, violence, oppression, falsehood, misery, every hateful vice, and every form of distress which degrade and sadden the present state of society, seem to have been generated by the most imperious circumstances, by laws inherent in the nature of man, and absolutely independent of all human regulations.

If we be not yet too well convinced of the reality of this melancholy picture, let us but look for a moment into the next period of twenty-five years, and we shall see 44 millions of human beings without the means of support; and at the conclusion of the first century the population would be 176 millions, and the food only sufficient for 55 millions, leaving 121 millions unprovided for. In these ages want indeed would be triumphant, and rapine and murder must reign at large: and yet all this time we are supposing the produce of the earth absolutely unlimited, and the yearly increase greater than the boldest speculator can imagine.

This is undoubtedly a very different view of the difficulty arising from the principle of population, from that which Mr. Godwin gives, when he says, "Myriads of centuries of still increasing population may pass away, and the earth be still found sufficient for the subsistence of its inhabitants." (pp. 109-10)

It may be curious to observe in the case that we have been supposing, how some of the principal laws, which at present govern civilized society, would be successively dictated by the most imperious necessity. As man, according to Mr. Godwin, is the creature of the impressions to which he is subject, the goadings of want could not continue long before some violations of public or private stock would necessarily take place. As these violations increased in number and extent, the more active and comprehensive intellects of the society would soon perceive, that while population was fast increasing the yearly produce of the country would shortly begin to diminish. The urgency of the case would suggest the necessity of some immediate measures being taken for the general safety. Some kind of convention would then be called, and the dangerous situation of the country stated in the strongest terms. It would be observed, that while they lived in the midst of plenty it was of little consequence who laboured the least, or who possessed the least, as every man was perfectly willing and ready to supply the wants of his neighbour. But that the question was no longer whether one man should give to another that which he did not use himself; but whether he should give to his neighbour the food which was absolutely necessary to his own existence. It would be represented, that the number of those who were in want very greatly exceeded the number and means of those who should supply them; that these pressing wants, which, from the state of the produce of the country, could not all be gratified, had occasioned some flagrant violations of justice; that these violations had already checked the increase of food, and would, if they were not by some means or other prevented, throw the whole community into confusion; that imperious necessity seemed to dictate, that a yearly increase of produce should, if possible, be obtained at all events; that in order to effect this first great and indispensable purpose it would be advisable to make a more complete division of land, and to secure every man's property against violation by the most powerful sanctions. (pp. 111-13)

The next subject which would come under discussion, intimately connected with the preceding, is the commerce of the sexes. It would be urged by those who had turned their attention to the true cause of the difficulties under which the community laboured, that while every man felt secure that all his children would be well provided for by general benevolence, the powers of the earth would be absolutely inadequate to produce food for the population which would inevitably ensue; that even if the whole attention and labour of the society were directed to this sole point, and if by the most perfect security of property, and every other encouragement that could be thought of, the greatest possible increase of produce were yearly obtained; yet still the increase of food would by no means keep pace with the much more rapid increase of population; that some check to population therefore was imperiously called for; that the most natural and obvious check seemed to be to make every man provide for his own children; that this would operate in some respect as a measure and a guide in the increase of population, as it might be expected that no man would bring beings into the world for whom he could not find the means of support; that where this notwithstanding was the case, it seemed necessary for the example of others, that the disgrace and inconvenience attending such a conduct should fall upon that individual who had thus inconsiderately plunged himself and his innocent children into want and misery.

The institution of marriage, or at least of some express or implied obligation on every man to support his own children, seems to be the natural result of these reasonings in a community under the difficulties that we have supposed. (pp. 114-15)

> *T. R. Malthus, "Of Systems of Equality: Godwin," in his* An Essay on the Principle of Population; or, A View of Its Past and Present Effects on Human Happiness, Vol. II, *third edition, J. Johnson, 1806, pp. 98-133.*

PERCY BYSSHE SHELLEY   (letter date 1817)

[*Regarded as a major English poet, Shelley was a leading figure in the English Romantic movement. He was also married to Godwin's daughter Mary. Influenced and inspired by Godwin's philosophy all throughout his writing career, Shelley expresses his admiration for* Mandeville *in the following extract from a letter to Godwin. For additional commentary by Shelley, see excerpt below dated 1817.*]

I have read *Mandeville,* but I must read it again soon. For the interest is of that irresistible & overwhelming kind, that the mind in its influence is like a cloud borne on by an impetuous wind, like one breathlessly carried forward who has no time to pause, or observe the causes of his career. I think the *power* of *Mandeville* is inferior to nothing that you have done, & were it not for the character of Falkland, no instance in which you have exerted that power of *creation* which you possess beyond all contemporary writers might compare with it. Falkland is still alone: power is in Falkland not as in Mandeville. Tumult hurried onward by the tempest, but Tranquillity standing unshaken amid its fiercest rage! But *Caleb Williams* never shakes the deepest soul like *Mandeville.* It must be said that in the latter you rule with a rod of iron. The picture is never bright, & we wonder whence you drew the darkness with which its shades are deepened until the epithet of tenfold night almost ceases to be metaphor. The NOUN *smorfia* touches some cord within us with such a cold & jarring power, that I started, & for some time could scarce believe but that I was Mandeville, & that this hideous grin was stamped upon my own face.

In style & strength of expression *Mandeville* is wonderfully great, & the energy & the sweetness of the sentiments [are] scarcely to be equalled. Clifford's character as mere beauty is a divine & soothing contrast, & I do not think, if perhaps I except (& I know not if I ought to do so) the speech of Agathon in the *Symposium* of Plato that there ever was produced a moral discourse more characteristic of all that is admirable & lovely in human Nature more lovely & admirable in itself than that of Henrietta to Mandeville as he is recovering from madness— Shall I say that when I discovered that she was pleading all this time secretly for her lover, & when at last she abandoned— weakly abandoned poor Mandeville I felt an involuntary & perhaps an unreasonable pang? (pp. 573-74)

> *Percy Bysshe Shelley, in a letter to William Godwin on December 7, 1817, in his* The Letters of Percy Bysshe Shelley: Shelley in England, Vol. I, *edited by Frederick L. Jones, Oxford at the Clarendon Press, Oxford, 1964, pp. 572-74.*

ELFIN KNIGHT [PSEUDONYM OF PERCY BYSSHE SHELLEY] (letter date 1817)

[*Here, Shelley elaborates on the comments on* Mandeville *in his letter to Godwin (see excerpt above dated 1817) and additionally praises Godwin's literary, intellectual, and philosophical talents.*]

[The] author of *Mandeville* is one of the most illustrious examples of intellectual power of the present age. He has exhibited that variety and universality of talent which distinguishes him who is destined to inherit lasting renown from the possessors of temporary celebrity. If his claims were to be measured solely by the comprehension and accuracy of his researches into ethical and political science, still it would be difficult to name a contemporary competitor. Let us make a deduction of all those parts of his moral system which are liable to any possible controversy and consider simply those which only to allege is to establish, and which belong to that most important class of truths which he that announces to mankind seems less to teach than to recall.

[Godwin's] *Political Justice* is the first moral system explicitly founded upon the doctrine of the negativeness of rights and the positiveness of duties, an obscure feeling of which has been the basis of all the political liberty and private virtue in the world. But he is also the author of *Caleb Williams;* and if we had no other record of a mind but simply some fragment containing the conception of the character of Falkland, doubtless we should say, "This is an extraordinary mind, and undoubtedly was capable of the very sublimest enterprises of thought."

St. Leon and *Fleetwood* are molded, with somewhat inferior distinctness, in the same character of a union of delicacy and power. The *Essay on Sepulchres* has all the solemnity and depth of passion which belong to a mind that sympathizes, as one man with his friend, in the interests of future ages, and in the concerns of the vanished generations of mankind.

It may be said with truth that Godwin has been treated unjustly by those of his countrymen upon whose favor temporary distinction depends. If he had devoted his high accomplishments to flatter the selfishness of the rich or enforced those doctrines on which the powerful depend for power, they would no doubt have rewarded him with their countenance, and he might have been more fortunate in that sunshine than Mr. Malthus or Dr. Paley. But the difference would still have been as wide as that which must forever divide notoriety from fame. Godwin has been to the present age in moral philosophy what Wordsworth is in poetry. (pp. 308-09)

Mandeville is Godwin's last production. The interest of this novel is undoubtedly equal, in some respects superior, to that of *Caleb Williams.* Yet there is no character like Falkland, whom the author, with that sublime casuistry which is the parent of toleration and forbearance, persuades us personally to love, while his actions must forever remain the theme of our astonishment and abhorrence. Mandeville challenges our compassion, and no more. His errors arise from an immutable necessity of internal nature, and from much of a constitutional antipathy and suspicion, which soon sprang up into a hatred and contempt and barren misanthropy, which, as it had no roots in genius or virtue, produces no fruit uncongenial with the soil wherein it grew. Those of Falkland arose from a high, though perverted conception of the majesty of human nature, from a powerful sympathy with his species, and from a temper which led him to believe that the very reputation of excellence should walk among mankind, unquestioned and undefiled. So far as it was a defect to link the interest of the tale with anything inferior to Falkland, so is *Mandeville* defective. But if the varieties of human character, the depth and complexity of human motive, those sources of the union of strength and weakness, those useful occasions for pleading in favor of universal kindness and toleration are just subjects for illustration and development in a work of fiction. *Mandeville* yields in interest and importance to none of the productions of the author.

The language is more rich and various, and the expressions more eloquently sweet, without losing that energy and distinctness which characterizes *Political Justice* and *Caleb Williams*. The moral speculations have a strength and consistency and boldness which have been less clearly aimed at in his other works of fiction. The pleadings of Henrietta to Mandeville, after his recovery from madness, in favor of virtue and benevolent energy, compose in every respect the most perfect and beautiful piece of writing of modern times. It is the genuine doctrine of *Political Justice* presented in one perspicuous and impressive view, and clothed in such enchanting melody of language as seems scarcely less than the writings of Plato to realize those lines of Milton:

> How charming is divine Philosophy!
> Not harsh and crabbed, as dull fools suppose,
> But musical as is Apollo's lute.

Clifford's talk, too, about wealth has a beautiful and readily to be disentangled intermixture of truth and error. Clifford is a person who, without those characteristics which usually constitute the sublime, is sublime from the mere excess of loveliness and innocence. Henrietta's first appearance to Mandeville at Mandeville House is an occurrence resplendent with the sunrise of life; it recalls to the memory many a vision, or perhaps but one, which the delusive exhalations of unbaffled hope has invested with a rose-like luster as of morning, yet unlike morning a light which, once extinguished, never can return. Henrietta seems at first to be all that a susceptible heart imagines in the object of its earliest passion. We scarcely can see her, she is so beautiful. There is a mist of dazzling loveliness which encircles her and shuts out from the sight all that is mortal in her transcendent charms. But the veil is gradually withdrawn, and she "fades into the light of common day." Her actions and even her sentiments do not correspond with the elevation of her speculative opinions and the fearless purity which should be and is the accompaniment of truth and virtue. But she has a divided affection, and she is faithful there only where infidelity would have been self-sacrifice. Could the spotless Henrietta have subjected her love for Clifford to the vain and insulting accidents of wealth and reputation and the babbling of a miserable old woman and have proceeded unshrinkingly to her nuptial feast from the expostulations of Mandeville's impassioned and pathetic madness? It might be well in the author to show the foundations of human hope thus overturned, for his picture would otherwise have been illumined with one gleam of light; it was his skill to enforce the moral "that all things are vanity" and that "the house of mourning is better than the house of feasting"; and we are indebted to those who make us feel the instability of our nature that we may lay the knowledge which is its foundation deep and make the affections which are its cement strong. But one regrets that Henrietta, who soared far beyond her contemporaries in her opinions, who was so beautiful that she seemed a spirit among mankind should act and feel no otherwise than the least exalted of her sex; and still more that the author capable of conceiving something so admirable and lovely should have been withheld by the tenor of the fiction which he chose from executing it

to its full extent. It almost seems in the original conception of the character of Henrietta that something was imagined too vast and too uncommon to be realized; and the feeling weighs like disappointment on the mind.

But these considered with reference to the core of the story are extrinsical. The events of the tale flow on like the stream of fate, regular and irresistible, and growing at once darker and swifter in their progress; there is no surprise; there is no shock; we are prepared for the worst from the very opening scene, though we wonder whence the author drew the shadows which render the moral darkness every instant more profound and at last so appalling and complete. The interest is awfully deep and rapid. To struggle with it would be gossamer attempting to bear up against the tempest. In this respect it is more powerful than *Caleb Williams*—the interest of *Caleb Williams* being as rapid but not so profound as that of *Mandeville*. It is a wind which tears up the deepest waters of the ocean of mind. The reader's mind is hurried on, as he approaches the end, with breathless and accelerated impulse. (pp. 309-11)

> *Elfin Knight* [*pseudonym of Percy Bysshe Shelley*], *in a letter to the editor of "The Examiner," on December 28, 1817, in* Shelley's Prose; *or,* The Trumpet of a Prophecy *by Percy Bysshe Shelley, edited by David Lee Clark, The University of New Mexico Press, 1954, pp. 308-11.*

THE NORTH AMERICAN REVIEW   (essay date 1818)

[*In the following excerpt from a review of* Mandeville, *the critic faults the lugubrious tone and "forbidding air" of Godwin's writings, but acknowledges his insight into human nature.*]

Godwin is a writer of a severe and sombre cast, who seems to take a gloomy satisfaction in dwelling upon whatever is deplorable in the constitution of society, or execrable and loathsome in human nature. In many parts of each of his works, and more especially in *Caleb Williams* and *Political Justice*, he writes with the spirit of a conspirator against the moral government of the world; and seems to look upon all the order, and beauty, and harmony of the social system, as Satan contemplated the delights of Eden, when he first alighted on the Tree of Life,—as something to be blasted and spoiled.

But he has nothing of malignity in [*Mandeville*];—he every where speaks like one of benevolent dispositions; but his benevolence is ill directed; he does not, like Satan, regard mankind, as those 'whom he could pity' for the evils, his own labours are intended to bring upon them. He compassionates them for what constitutes the beauty, and dignity, and security of existence. Though he sometimes speaks in tones of condolence, he more frequently utters the language of indignation and reproach. 'Of what use,' says he, 'are talents and sentiments in the corrupt wilderness of human society? It is a rank and rotten soil, from which every finer shrub draws poison as it grows. All, that, in a happier field and purer air, would expand into virtue and germinate into usefulness, is thus converted into henbane and deadly nightshade.'

This, and a thousand other passages of a similar import, scattered through his writings, are not the occasional burstings out of a wronged and burthened mind, striving to pour off its bitterness in momentary exclamations. (p. 92)

It has been, and continues, in a degree, to be a favourite doctrine with him, that all the restraints of decorum, propriety, and law, are infringements of the inalienable liberties of man, and constitute a tyranny, that subdues and enslaves the noblest principles of our nature. One infers, from the general tenor of his speculations, that nations are only great prisons, differing, principally, in the number of prisoners and prison-keepers. (pp. 92-3)

Godwin's imagination peoples the world with an over proportion of the unfortunate good on the one hand, and, on the other, of foul and monstrous beings, bent upon mean pursuits, and in love with errour and folly—creatures, that contaminate the atmosphere they breathe, and communicate a moral pestilence by their touch. It becomes a noble mind to loathe such wretches, and show the purity and elevation of its nature by acting in opposition to the maxims of the world. Whenever domestick or social duties interfere with this high way of thinking and acting, they may be violated and spurned—the citizen may defy the government that protects him; the husband may desert his wife, and the son may brave and insult his father.

These sentiments are not always directly inculcated; they are sometimes denied; but whatever may be the letter, this is commonly the spirit of his lessons. Though they often present sound maxims of conduct to the understanding, they generally shed a pestiferous influence upon the heart. One reads, without any transports, without any of the free and expanding emotions, which the thoughts of more generous minds inspire; but not without sensations;—he presses forward eagerly, not more out of interest and curiosity, than from a desire to be relieved from an indescribable aching of the soul and suffocation of the feelings, with which the stories of Godwin invariably oppress the reader.

At the conclusion, he finds himself sickened and disgusted with the world, as a scene of misery and guilt; he is ready to exclaim against Providence, and reprobate the constitution of nature, by which it seems to be ordained, that virtue and vice, wisdom and folly, honour and meanness, shall be idle and futile qualities, and that men shall be endowed with sensibilities, only to feel more poignantly the ills to which they are born. If he adopts Godwin's notions,—that all the miseries of the world spring from the artificial system of civil society, and the influence of false prejudices,—he becomes affected with a scornful pity of his fellow beings; he has an enthusiastick desire that they should come to have new, though he hardly knows what, views of happiness, and dignity, and honour, and begin to act upon certain new and sublime principles, which, however, he can but imperfectly define; he only knows, that they are altogether opposite to what the world has been accustomed to, and something much better. (pp. 93-4)

Such are some of the leading characteristics and tendencies of Godwin's philosophy;—under which name may be comprehended the greater part of his works, for his fictions are philosophical treatises, no less than his *Political Justice*. His views of life, and his moral and political principles, are prominent parts of his thinking, and are always obtruding themselves. But notwithstanding all the absurdities, and distortions and misconceptions, with which his writings abound, they probably have not done much absolute mischief to mankind. (pp. 94-5)

Godwin is a writer of a forbidding air, arising partly from his affectation of stateliness and independence, and partly from his practice of mixing up too much of metaphysical and economical philosophy in his stories. He is violent and bold in the extreme, and sticks not to be coarse, if he can but be strong. His mind is well stored with knowledge, and he has reflected much and deeply, though not always justly, upon men and their

pursuits. He occasionally throws out great and striking thoughts upon the philosophy of the mind and the economy of society. Propriety and probability are counted for nothing with him, and he seems to pursue his eccentrick course with more energy, the further it carries him from nature. He rarely thinks in a generous, pathetick, or kindly strain, though there are not wanting touching passages in his works. The most remarkable of this sort, now in our recollection, is that, in which St. Leon is described as visiting his daughters, after he has renewed his life by drinking the elixir. But, whatever may be Godwin's faults, he has produced two masterpieces in their kind, in *St. Leon* and *Caleb Williams;* and this ought to satisfy his ambition. *Mandeville* is not likely to add to his reputation; it is indeed a falling off, and is so repulsive and hard featured a story, that not many readers, we believe, have resolution to go through it. (p. 97)

Godwin's other novels are very thin of events; this contains still fewer than those. His work has no resemblance to a dramatic representation of characters and actions, so constructed, that, in the perusal, a thousand associated images, recollections and sentiments, spontaneously spring up in the reader's mind, which are not directly expressed. It is rather the exhibition of his philosophical opinions in the form of dissertations,—a detail of the thoughts and feelings of his personages, and a consideration of the influences, which the incidents may be supposed to have, in determining their dispositions and characters. He is occupied with what passes within his persons, instead of what is taking place about them. His real actors seem to be certain principles and opinions and passions,—which are not qualities and ingredients, that go to the composition of his personages, and form a part of them, but rather make use of them as mere instruments. All this gives an abstract, metaphysical turn to his narratives, whence to readers, who flutter from novel to novel, in quest of vacant amusement, they have a rugged and forbidding aspect.

This effect is aggravated by his set, stately, inverted style of writing, and by his abundance of distant allusions, strained conceptions, and obsolete words and phrases, and forced expressions. Add to these, that his figurative expressions are violent, sometimes to absurdity. Take a few examples—his hate of Clifford hung, 'with insurmountable weight, *upon the neck of Henrietta's mind.*' . . .—'Inhuman laughter flayed and mangled my ears, like a hundred lancets.' . . .—'Doors leaped from their hinges, to give Clifford entrance.' . . .—'Henrietta entered, with triumphant wheels, into the fortress of my heart.' . . .—There were certain *muscles of my intellectual frame*, that had never been brought into play.' . . .—'These trials produced tremendous explosions and *earthquakes* in my bosom.' . . . He sometimes repeats the same thoughts in the same language, even when they are of little importance; and gives the characters of his persons again and again; and is not content with stating how things are, but must reckon up all the possibilities of their having been otherwise, and pursue these suppositions into all their consequences. It thus happens that the action is often at a stand, and the reader seems to himself as if he were on a voyage, in a vessel, which should lie by half the time, while the master might take observations and work up his reckoning.

If one is not repelled by these discouragements, he will open to himself in *Mandeville* a rich vein of sentiment and reflection. He will find in it the elevated strain of thinking, nervous eloquence and keen penetration, which are characteristic of its author. Like his other novels, it contains an important lesson, forcibly inculcated—it shows the forlornness and misery of a jealous, sullen, aspiring mind, that makes great claims on the world, without proper efforts to justify or enforce them. The author in this, as in his previous works, displays, with appalling truth, the despotic sovereignty and all searching observation of publick opinion, in so much, that one trembles with the consciousness of being subject to this tremendous power, which he cannot fly from or resist. No writer has perhaps more adequately expressed,—what every body feels,—how much of the good and ill of life is involved in reputation. The sentiments we excite in others become, in some sort, a part of ourselves; we either bear a good or an ill fame, that, like a charm, makes us invulnerable to 'the slings and arrows of fortune,' or exposes us, defenceless and sorely alive, to the shaft. The opinion of men pursues and hangs upon us like destiny, and our reputation encompasses us like a luminous atmosphere, that exhibits us, either blemished or fair, to the eyes of the world. (pp. 104-05)

"Godwin's 'Mandeville'," in The North American Review, *Vol. VII, No. 1, May, 1818, pp. 92-105.*

WILLIAM HAZLITT   (essay date 1825)

[*One of the most important commentators of the Romantic age, Hazlitt was an English critic and journalist. He is best known for his descriptive criticism in which he stressed that no abilities beyond judgment and analysis are necessary on the part of the critic. In the following excerpt, Hazlitt surveys Godwin's literary career, philosophy, and decline in popularity. For additional commentary by Hazlitt, see excerpt dated 1830.*]

The Spirit of the Age was never more fully shown than in its treatment of [William Godwin]—its love of paradox and change, its dastard submission to prejudice and to the fashion of the day. Five-and-twenty years ago he was in the very zenith of a sultry and unwholesome popularity; he blazed as a sun in the firmament of reputation; no one was more talked of, more looked up to, more sought after, and wherever liberty, truth, justice was the theme, his name was not far off. Now he has sunk below the horizon, and enjoys the serene twilight of a doubtful immortality. (p. 17)

[The] author of *Political Justice* and of *Caleb Williams* can never die; his name is an abstraction in letters; his works are standard in the history of intellect. . . .

No work in our time gave such a blow to the philosophical mind of the country as the celebrated *Enquiry Concerning Political Justice.* Tom Paine was considered for the time as a Tom Fool to him, Paley an old woman, Edmund Burke a flashy sophist. Truth, moral truth, it was supposed, had here taken up its abode; and these were the oracles of thought. . . .

Mr. Godwin indulged in extreme opinions, and carried with him all the most sanguine and fearless understandings of the time. What then? Because those opinions were overcharged, were they therefore altogether groundless? Is the very God of our idolatry all of a sudden to become an abomination and an anathema? Could so many young men of talent, of education, and of principle have been hurried away by what had neither truth nor nature, not one particle of honest feeling nor the least show of reason in it? (p. 18)

The fault . . . of Mr. Godwin's philosophy, in one word, was too much ambition—'by that sin fell the angels!' He conceived too nobly of his fellows (the most unpardonable crime against them, for there is nothing that annoys our self-love so much as being complimented on imaginary achievements, to which we are wholly unequal)—he raised the standard of morality

above the reach of humanity, and by directing virtue to the most airy and romantic heights, made her path dangerous, solitary, and impracticable. The author of the *Political Justice* took abstract reason for the rule of conduct and abstract good for its end. He places the human mind on an elevation, from which it commands a view of the whole line of moral consequences; and requires it to conform its acts to the larger and more enlightened conscience which it has thus acquired. He absolves man from the gross and narrow ties of sense, custom, authority, private and local attachment, in order that he may devote himself to the boundless pursuit of universal benevolence.

Mr. Godwin gives no quarter to the amiable weaknesses of our nature, nor does he stoop to avail himself of the supplementary aids of an imperfect virtue. Gratitude, promises, friendship, family affection give way, not that they may be merged in the opposite vices or in want of principle, but that the void may be filled up by the disinterested love of good and the dictates of inflexible justice, which is 'the law of laws, and sovereign of sovereigns.' All minor considerations yield, in his system, to the stern sense of duty, as they do, in the ordinary and established ones, to the voice of necessity. Mr. Godwin's theory, and that of more approved reasoners, differ only in this, that what are with them the exceptions, the extreme cases, he makes the every-day rule. No one denies that on great occasions, in moments of fearful excitement, or when a mighty object is at stake, the lesser and merely instrumental points of duty are to be sacrificed without remorse at the shrine of patriotism, of honour, and of conscience. (pp. 20-1)

The *Enquiry Concerning Political Justice* (it was urged by its favourers and defenders at the time, and may still be so, without either profaneness or levity) is a metaphysical and logical commentary on some of the most beautiful and striking texts of Scripture. Mr. Godwin is a mixture of the Stoic and of the Christian philosopher. To break the force of the vulgar objections and outcry that have been raised against the Modern Philosophy, as if it were a new and monstrous birth in morals, it may be worth noticing, that volumes of sermons have been written to excuse the founder of Christianity for not including friendship and private affection among its golden rules, but rather excluding them. Moreover, the answer to the question, 'Who is thy neighbour?' added to the divine precept, 'Thou shalt love thy neighbour as thyself,' is the same as in the exploded pages of our author—'he to whom we can do most good.' In determining this point, we were not to be influenced by any extrinsic or collateral considerations, by our own predilections, or the expectations of others, by our obligations to them or any services they might be able to render us, by the climate they were born in, by the house they lived in, by rank, or religion, or party, or personal ties, but by the abstract merits, the pure and unbiassed justice of the case.

The artificial helps and checks to moral conduct were set aside as spurious and unnecessary, and we came at once to the grand and simple question—'In what manner we could best contribute to the greatest possible good?' This was the paramount obligation in all cases whatever, from which we had no right to free ourselves upon any idle or formal pretext, and of which each person was to judge for himself, under the infallible authority of his own opinion and the inviolable sanction of his self-approbation. 'There was the rub that made *philosophy* of so short life!' Mr. Godwin's definition of morals was the same as the admired one of law, *reason without passion;* but with the unlimited scope of private opinion, and in a boundless field of speculation (for nothing less would satisfy the pretensions of the New School), there was danger that the unseasoned novice might substitute some pragmatical conceit of his own for the rule of right reason, and mistake a heartless indifference for a superiority to more natural and generous feelings. Our ardent and dauntless reformer followed out the moral of the parable of the Good Samaritan into its most rigid and repulsive consequences with a pen of steel, and let fall his 'trenchant blade' on every vulnerable point of human infirmity; but there is a want in his system of the mild and persuasive tone of the Gospel, where 'all is conscience and tender heart.' (pp. 21-3)

[If] it is admitted that Reason alone is not the sole and self-sufficient ground of morals, it is to Mr. Godwin that we are indebted for having settled the point. No one denied or distrusted this principle (before his time) as the absolute judge and interpreter in all questions of difficulty; and if this is no longer the case, it is because he has taken this principle, and followed it into its remotest consequences with more keenness of eye and steadiness of hand than any other expounder of ethics. His grand work is (at least) an *experimentum crucis* to show the weak sides and imperfections of human reason as the sole law of human action. (pp. 26-7)

Captain Parry would be thought to have rendered a service to navigation and his country, no less by proving that there is no North-West Passage, than if he had ascertained that there is one: so Mr. Godwin has rendered an essential service to moral science, by attempting (in vain) to pass the Arctic Circle and Frozen Regions, where the understanding is no longer warmed by the affections, nor fanned by the breeze of fancy! This is the effect of all bold, original, and powerful thinking, that it either discovers the truth or detects where error lies; and the only crime with which Mr. Godwin can be charged as a political and moral reasoner is, that he has displayed a more ardent spirit and a more independent activity of thought than others, in establishing the fallacy (if fallacy it be) of an old popular prejudice that *the Just and True were one,* by 'championing it to the Outrance,' and in the final result placing the Gothic structure of human virtue on an humbler, but a wider and safer, foundation than it had hitherto occupied in the volumes and systems of the learned.

Mr. Godwin is an inventor in the regions of romance, as well as a skilful and hardy explorer of those of moral truth. *Caleb Williams* and *St. Leon* are two of the most splendid and impressive works of the imagination that have appeared in our times. It is not merely that these novels are very well for a philosopher to have produced—they are admirable and complete in themselves, and would not lead you to suppose that the author, who is so entirely at home in human character and dramatic situation, had ever dabbled in logic or metaphysics. The first of these, particularly, is a masterpiece, both as to invention and execution. The romantic and chivalrous principle of the love of personal fame is embodied in the finest possible manner in the character of Falkland; as in Caleb Williams (who is not the first, but the second character in the piece) we see the very demon of curiosity personified. Perhaps the art, with which these two characters are contrived to relieve and set off each other, has never been surpassed in any work of fiction, with the exception of the immortal satire of Cervantes. The restless and inquisitive spirit of Caleb Williams, in search and in possession of his patron's fatal secret, haunts the latter like a second conscience, plants stings in his tortured mind, fans the flame of his jealous ambition, struggling with agonized remorse; and the hapless but noble-minded Falkland at length

falls a martyr to the persecution of that morbid and overpowering interest, of which his mingled virtues and vices have rendered him the object.

We conceive no one ever began *Caleb Williams* that did not read it through: no one that ever read it could possibly forget it, or speak of it after any length of time but with an impression as if the events and feelings had been personal to himself. This is the case also with the story of *St. Leon* which, with less dramatic interest and intensity of purpose, is set off by a more gorgeous and flowing eloquence and by a crown of preternatural imagery, that waves over it like a palm-tree! It is the beauty and the charm of Mr. Godwin's descriptions that the reader identifies himself with the author; and the secret of this is, that the author has identified himself with his personages. Indeed, he has created them. They are the proper issue of his brain, lawfully begot, not foundlings, nor the 'bastards of his art.' He is not an indifferent, callous spectator of the scenes which he himself pourtrays, but without seeming to feel them. There is no look of patch-work and plagiarism, the beggarly copiousness of borrowed wealth; no tracery-work from worm-eaten manuscripts, from forgotten chronicles, nor piecing out of vague traditions with fragments and snatches of old ballads, so that the result resembles a gaudy, staring transparency, in which you cannot distinguish the daubing of the painter from the light that shines through the flimsy colours, and gives them brilliancy.

Here all is clearly made out with strokes of the pencil, by fair, not by factitious means. Our author takes a given subject from nature or from books, and then fills it up with the ardent workings of his own mind, with the teeming and audible pulses of his own heart. The effect is entire and satisfactory in proportion. The work (so to speak) and the author are one. We are not puzzled to decide upon their respective pretensions. In reading Mr. Godwin's novels, we know what share of merit the author has in them. (pp. 27-9)

Mr. Godwin, in all his writings, dwells upon one idea or exclusive view of a subject, aggrandises a sentiment, exaggerates a character, or pushes an argument to extremes, and makes up by the force of style and continuity of feeling for what he wants in variety of incident or ease of manner. This necessary defect is observable in his best works, and is still more so in *Fleetwood* and *Mandeville;* the one of which, compared with his more admired performances, is mawkish, and the other morbid. Mr. Godwin is also an essayist, an historian—in short, what is he not, that belongs to the character of an indefatigable and accomplished author? (p. 30)

William Hazlitt, "William Godwin," in his The Spirit of the Age; or, Contemporary Portraits, *1825. Reprint by Oxford University Press, London, 1947, pp. 17-34.*

[WILLIAM HAZLITT]   (essay date 1830)

[*In the following review of* Cloudesly, *Hazlitt contends that Godwin's talents have declined markedly since the publication of* Caleb Williams. *Though he considers* Cloudesly *technically accomplished, Hazlitt deems it unoriginal and overly didactic. For additional commentary by Hazlitt, see excerpt dated 1825.*]

We find little of the author of *Caleb Williams* in [*Cloudesly*], except the name in the title-page. Either we are changed, or Mr Godwin is changed, since he wrote that masterly performance. We remember the first time of reading it well, though now long ago. In addition to the singularity and surprise occasioned by seeing a romance written by a philosopher and politician, what a quickening of the pulse,—what an interest in the progress of the story,—what an eager curiosity in divining the future,—what an individuality and contrast in the characters,—what an elevation and what a fall was that of Falkland;—how we felt for his blighted hopes, his remorse, and despair, and took part with Caleb Williams as his ordinary and unformed sentiments are brought out, and rendered more and more acute by the force of circumstances, till hurried on by an increasing and incontrollable impulse, he turns upon his proud benefactor and unrelenting persecutor, and in a mortal struggle, overthrows him on the vantage-ground of humanity and justice! There is not a moment's pause in the action or sentiments: the breath is suspended, the faculties wound up to the highest pitch, as we read. . . . Mr Godwin was thought a man of very powerful and versatile genius; and in him the understanding and the imagination reflected a mutual and dazzling light upon each other. His *St. Leon* did not lessen the wonder, nor the public admiration of him, or rather 'seemed like another morn risen on mid-noon.' But from that time he has done nothing of superlative merit. He has imitated himself, and not well. He has changed the glittering spear, which always detected truth or novelty, for a leaden foil. We cannot say of his last work (*Cloudesly*),—'Even in his ashes live his wonted fires.' The story is cast indeed something in the same moulds as *Caleb Williams;* but they are not filled and running over with molten passion, or with scalding tears. The situations and characters, though forced and extreme, are without effect from the want of juxtaposition and collision. Cloudesly (the elder) is like Caleb Williams, a person of low origin, and rebels against his patron and employer; but he remains a characterless, passive, inefficient agent to the last,—forming his plans and resolutions at a distance,—not whirled from expedient to expedient, nor driven from one sleepless hiding-place to another; and his lordly and conscience-stricken accomplice (Danvers) keeps his state in like manner, brooding over his guilt and remorse in solitude, with scarce an object or effort to vary the round of his reflections,—a lengthened paraphrase of grief. The only dramatic incidents in the coarse of the narrative are, the sudden metamorphosis of the Florentine Count Camaldoli into the robber St Elmo, and the unexpected and opportune arrival of Lord Danvers in person, carry the same prospect with you, like a map in your hand, the whole way. Mr Godwin has laid no ambuscade for the unwary reader—no picturesque group greets the eye as you pass on—no sudden turn at an angle places you on the giddy verge of a precipice. Nevertheless, our author's courage never flags. Mr Godwin is an eminent rhetorician; and he shows it in this, that he expatiates, discusses, amplifies, with equal fervour, and unabated ingenuity, on the merest accidents of the way-side, or common-places of human life. Thus, for instance, if a youth of eleven or twelve years of age is introduced upon the carpet, the author sets himself to show, with a laudable candour and communicativeness, what the peculiar features of that period of life are, and 'takes an inventory' of all the particulars,—such as sparkling eyes, roses in the cheeks, a smooth forehead, flaxen locks, elasticity of limb, lively animal spirits, and all the flush of hope,—as if he were describing a novelty, or some *terra incognita,* to the reader. . . . Every man's strength is his weakness, and turns in some way or other against himself. Mr Godwin has been so long accustomed to trust to his own powers, and to draw upon his own resources, that he comes at length to imagine that he can build a palace of words upon nothing. When he lavished the colours of style, and the exuberant strength of his fancy, on descriptions like those of the

character of Margaret, the wife of St Leon, or of his musings in the dungeon of Bethlem Gabor, or of his enthusiasm on discovering the philosopher's stone, and being restored to youth and the plenitude of joy by drinking the *Elixir Vitae;*—or when he recounts the long and lasting despair which succeeded that utter separation from his kind, and that deep solitude which followed him into crowds and cities,—deeper and more appalling than the dungeon of Bethlem Gabor,—we were never weary of being borne along by the golden tide of eloquence, supplied from the true sources of passion and feeling. But when he bestows the same elaboration of phrases, and artificial arrangement of sentences, to set off the most trite and obvious truisms, we confess it has to us a striking effect of the *bathos.* (pp. 147-49)

We have a graver charge yet to bring against Mr Godwin on the score of style, than that it leads him into useless amplification: from his desire to load and give effect to his descriptions, he runs different characters and feelings into one another. By not stopping short of excess and hyperbole, he loses the line of distinction, and 'o'ersteps the modesty of nature.' All his characters are patterns of vice or virtue. They are carried to extremes,—they are abstractions of woe, miracles of wit and gaiety,—gifted with every grace and accomplishment that can be enumerated in the same page; and they are not only prodigies in themselves, but destined to immortal renown, though we have never heard of their names before. This is not like a veteran in the art, but like the raptures of some boarding-school girl in love with every new face or dress she sees. It is difficult to say which is the most extraordinary genius,—the improvisatori Bernardino Perfetti, or his nephew, Francesco, or young Julian. Mr Godwin still sees with 'eyes of youth.' Irene is a Greek, the model of beauty and of conjugal faith. Eudocia, her maid, who marries the elder Cloudesly, is a Greek too, and nearly as handsome and as exemplary in her conduct. Again, on the same principle, the account of Irene's devotion to her father and her husband, is by no means clearly discriminated. The spiritual feeling is exaggerated till it is confounded with the passionate; and the passionate is spiritualized in the same incontinence of tropes and figures, till it loses its distinctive character. Each sentiment, by being over-done, is neutralized into a sort of platonics. It is obvious to remark, that the novel of *Cloudesly* has no hero, no principal figure. The attention is divided, and wavers between Meadows, who is a candidate for the reader's sympathy through the first half volume, and whose affairs and love adventures at St Petersburg are huddled up in haste, and broke off in the middle; Lord Danvers, who is the guilty sufferer; Cloudesly, his sullen, dilatory Mentor; and Julian, (the supposed offspring of Cloudesly, but real son of Lord Alton, and nephew of Lord Danvers,) who turns out the fortunate youth of the piece. The story is awkwardly told. Meadows begins it with an account of himself, and a topographical description of the Russian empire, which has nothing to do with the subject; and nearly through the remainder of the work, listens to a speech of Lord Danvers, recounting his own history and that of Julian, which lasts for six hundred pages without interruption or stop. It is the longest parenthesis in a narrative that ever was known. Meadows then emerges from his *incognito* once more, as if he had been hid behind a curtain, and gives the *coup-de-grace* to his own autobiography, and the lingering sufferings of his patron. The plot is borrowed from a real event that took place concerning a disputed succession in the middle of the last century, and which gave birth not long after to a novel with the title of *Annesley.* We should like to meet with a copy of this work, in order to see how a writer of less genius would get to the end of his task, and carry the reader along with him without the aid of those subtle researches and lofty declamations with which Mr Godwin has supplied the place of facts and circumstances. (pp. 150-51)

[The] fault of this and some other of the author's productions is, that the critical and didactic part overlays the narrative and dramatic part; as we see in some editions of the poets, where there are two lines of original text, and the rest of the page is heavy with the lumber and pedantry of the commentators. The writer does not call characters from the dead, or conjure them from the regions of fancy, to paint their peculiar physiognomy, or tell us their story, so much as (like the anatomist) to dissect and demonstrate on the insertion of the bones, the springs of the muscles, and those understood principles of life and motion which are common to the species. Now, in a novel, we want the individual, and not the *genus*. The tale of *Cloudesly* is a dissertation on remorse. Besides, this truth of science is often a different thing from the truth of nature, which is modified by a thousand accidents, 'subject to all the skyey influences;'— not a mechanical principle, brooding over and working every thing out of itself. (p. 152)

Mr Godwin's mind is, we conceive, essentially active, and therefore may naturally be expected to wear itself out sooner than those that are passive to external impressions, and receive continual new accessions to their stock of knowledge and acquirement:

> A fiery soul that working out its way,
> Fretted the pigmy body to decay,
> And o'er-inform'd its tenement of clay.

That some of this author's latter works are (in our judgment) comparatively feeble, is, therefore, no matter of surprise to us, and still less is it matter of reproach or triumph. We look upon it as a consequence incident to that constitution of mind and operation of the faculties. (pp. 152-53)

> [*William Hazlitt*], "Mr. Godwin," in The Edinburgh Review, *Vol. LI, No. CI, April, 1830, pp. 144-59.*

[MARY SHELLEY] (essay date 1830)

[*An English novelist, Shelley achieved great fame as the author of* Frankenstein; or, The Modern Prometheus, *a classic tale of Gothic horror. She was also the daughter of Godwin and Woll-stonecraft. In her review of* Cloudesly, *Shelley offers glowing praise for Godwin's characterization, narrative style, and didactic intent.*]

While other writers represent manners rather than passions, or passions at once vague and incomplete, [Mr. Godwin] conceives, in its entireness, the living picture of an event with all its adjuncts; he sets it down in its vivid reality: no part is dim, no part is tame. We have the clear and distinct representation of his conception, and are made to feel that his portraiture is endowed with the very essence and spirit of nature. (p. 711)

Of all modern writers, Mr. Godwin has arrived most sedulously, and most successfully, at the highest species of perfection his department of art affords. He sketches in his own mind, with a comprehensive and bold imagination, the plan of his work; he digs at the foundations, and learns all the due bearings of his position; he examines his materials, and sees exactly to what purpose each is best fitted; he makes an incident; he unerringly divines the results, both of the event and passion, which this incident will bring forth. By dint of the

mastery of thought, he transfuses himself into the very souls of his personages; he dives into their secret hearts, and lays bare, even to their anatomy, their workings; not a pulsation escapes him,—while yet all is blended into one whole, which forms the pervading impulse of the individual he brings before us. Who, remembering Falkland, but feels as if he had stood by that noble ruin, and watched its downfall! Who but writhes under the self-dejection of Mandeville, and feels the while his own heart whisper fearful oracles of the tameless and sad incongruities of our souls! Who but exulted madly with St. Leon, when he obtained his specious gifts! (p. 712)

Cloudesly is before us, a fresh example of what we have been saying. This tale contains a train of events, each naturally flowing one from the other, and each growing in importance and dignity as they proceed. We have no extraneous ornaments; no discursive flights. Comparing this book with others, we felt as if we had quitted gardens and parks, and tamer landscapes, for a scene on nature's grandest scale; that we wandered among giants' rocks, "the naked bones of the world waiting to be clothed." We use this quotation, because it suggested itself to our minds as we read these volumes, but we must guard our meaning from the idea of there being any turgidness in *Cloudesly*. Grace and dignity, joined to power, are its characteristics. The first volume is the least interesting. The author digs at the foundation, and then places the first stones; then we begin to feel the just proportions and promising beauty of the plan, till the tantalizing work of preparation finally yields to the full manifestation of the conception of the artist. If we may be permitted another metaphor, and this last is the most just, we will say that this work reminds us of the solemn strain of some cathedral organ. First, a few appropriate chords are fitfully and variously struck; a prelude succeeds to awaken our attention, and then rises the full peal, which swells upon the ear, till the air appears overcharged and overflowing with majestic harmonies. As far as an image can go, this exactly pourtrays our sensations on reading *Cloudesly*. The composer rapts us from ourselves, filling our bosoms with new and extraordinary emotions, while we sit soul-enchained by the wonders of his art. (pp. 712-13)

It is the peculiar excellence of Mr. Godwin's writing, that there is not a word too much, and curtailment of the narrative would be like displaying the unfilled-up outline of beauty; we might feel that it was there, and yet remain in ignorance of its peculiar features. The interest is imperative, but unconstrained; nature dwells paramount in every part. As it proceeds, it becomes high-wrought, without being harrowing. To the end, the tragedy is tempered by the softest spirit of humanity; it touches the verge of terror, only to bring us the more soothingly back to milder feelings. We close the book, not tantalized by a sense of the injustice of fate, nor tormented by a painful depicting of unrebuked guilt, but with a compassion for the criminal, and a love or admiration for the innocent, at once elevating and delightful. The few last pages are indeed a record of truths and sentiments, which, as coming from one who has lived so long, and, synonymous with this expression, suffered so much, inculcates a philosophy very opposite from the misanthropical one so prevalent a little while ago.

Mr. Godwin's style is at once simple and energetic; it is full, without being inflated. (p. 714)

Here is nothing harsh and crabbed, nothing morbid and disheartening: every page displays freshness and vigour, each one containing some lesson to teach us confidence, love, and hope. This philosophy, as emanating from experience, is a precious boon, such as, since the days of the philosophers of old, has seldom been bequeathed to us. Let the reader turn to the last page of the third volume, and learn thence, that a glory still remains to the earth, an attribute to our mortal natures, that must elevate and bless us while man remains; and let our hearts exult, when one of the wisest men of this or any age tells us, that "the true key of the universe is love." (p. 716)

> [*Mary Shelley*], *in a review of "Cloudesly; A Tale," in* Blackwood's Edinburgh Magazine, *Vol. XXVII, No. CLXVI, May, 1830, pp. 711-16.*

[J. A. HERAUD AND WILLIAM MAGINN]   (essay date 1830)

[*Heraud was an English poet, dramatist, and critic. Maginn, one of the most prominent journalists in England during the first half of the nineteenth century, wrote prolifically for a number of English periodicals. Here they discuss the strengths and weaknesses of Godwin's novels, terming* Cloudesly *his best production to date.*]

Mr. Godwin is a veteran author—so much so, indeed, that he is looked upon by general readers rather as one of the by-gone, than as presently existing. This has been owing as much to the infrequency of his appearance, as to the transcending excellence of his productions, which is indeed such as to associate him at once in our minds with the mighty dead. This infrequency of appearance is the cause of the transcending excellence by which he has attained a living immortality. Mr. Godwin seems to have had no ambition of being esteemed a ready writer, capable of sending out his novel and a half a year. His ambition is of a higher mark—like Ben Jonson, while inferior authors thought only of making their works, plays—he has aimed at making his plays, works. Accordingly, we find in his novels no marks of haste or inattention, though, perhaps, more than enough of elaboration. (p. 381)

Mr. Godwin's sympathies in [*Cloudesley*] were all for the distant and future; the *endless* perfectibility of the human species engages more of his affection than the welfare of the present race of mankind, who, for the generations that may exist some centuries hence, are to suffer spoliation of property, and the destruction of established institutions. Not such is the moral code of the Gospel, in which all is practicable, all virtue is founded in mercy, kindness, benevolence, and comfort, alike to him that gives and him that takes. There we find no wild supposition of an interest which cannot be described, as it does not exist; no course of actions is proposed, without a motive direct and reflected. But . . . Godwin's mind has been progressive—and he lived to outgrow much of what was erroneous in his opinions. (p. 384)

Mr. Godwin's mind is not poetical. . . . By a poetical mind, we mean, in this instance, one that exercises, by turns or together, the faculties both of the fancy and the imagination. Mr. Godwin can only be said to exert one of these. In so far as imagination is poetry, Mr. Godwin's mind is poetical. Mr. Godwin images out an *idea* better than any other man living. But the idea is given too monotonously; it is aggrandized and exaggerated; but never realized. This was the case in his philosophical work [*Political Justice*]. . . . It was the working out of one idea—pushing the argument founded on it to extremes; and sticking to an exclusive view of the subject in hand. Now, all this is very well for a trial of skill, but fails to discover truth, which is not confined in holes and corners in any such way, but is as free as the general air, as broad as the whole heavens. His novels, accordingly, want variety, because the

fancy is not exercised in aggregating poetical forms in order to the manifold exhibition of the ideal creation. The perfection of art is in the union of the ideal and the real—this is Shakspeare's excellence—it is also Sir Walter Scott's; but it is not Mr. Godwin's. Inasmuch as Mr. Godwin creates, (if he does create,) he is entitled to a high character even as a poet; but it is in the process of his work that he loses that character. He works like a mathematician, not like a poet; he demonstrates his conclusion, not suggests it. There is moreover, no surprise, in any of the incidents, no curiosity excited in the reader's mind. The reader is as much possessed, from the beginning, with the idea as the author himself; he anticipates the course of the work, he has no curiosity respecting the coming incidents, but only desires to discover how, and with what force of style they will be treated. Sometimes, also, as in the third volume of *Caleb Williams,* there is too much made of one section of the argument; but the reader feels, as well as the author, that the fault is committed to stuff the volume, and pities and forgives.

There is great want of material, such as picturesque scenery, local association, manners, and traditions, in *Caleb Williams.* The hint, as the author states, was suggested by the popular tale of *Blue Beard.* His idea was to exhibit the passion of curiosity. This he does in the person of Caleb Williams, a young man in the service of one Falkland, who feels, from some circumstances, a curiosity to know whether his master was not guilty of a murder for which other persons had been executed. The character of Falkland is constructed in the same way. The love of fame is his one principle of conduct. A brutal insult hurts his chivalrous feelings; in a moment of madness, he takes a fatal revenge, and, to preserve his character, he permits the vengeance of the law to fall upon the innocent. It is ascribing, after all, too much power to Williams's inveterate curiosity, that it should possess the fascination of extracting from such a man so important a secret. Supposing, however, that he should get possession of the secret, all the rest follows as a matter of course; that Falkland should endeavour to prevent Williams from divulging it. The means which he adopts for this purpose are so insufferable; his suspicion is so nice and extreme, that, in self-defence, his confidant is obliged to betray him. Falkland is a noble character; and, at the end, the magnificence of his nature breaks out afresh, and redeems him, through his last act of forgiveness, within the limits of human sympathy.

Throughout this work the novelist delights to shew the imperfections of our social institutions, and indulges in constant satire on the ordinary motives to conduct. All the common notions of society are set at nought, and his minor characters are made the objects of extreme contempt. Only the intellectual are represented as admirable. Now this is not true to nature, as, in the meanest specimens of humanity, some glimpses of the divinity are discernible, and moral worth frequently belongs to those who are most deficient in intellectual acquisitions.

But in the *Travels of St. Leon,* as the author has himself told us, he shews how good is individual conformity to the customs and usages of society, and how fatal to the possessor is an immunity from the common cares and anxieties of mortality. (pp. 385-86)

We have no doubt that Mr. Godwin thought that, in this novel, he was enforcing a fine moral, namely, that the possession of unlimited wealth, and the gift of immortality, were inconsistent with the present condition of the human race, and ineffectual for individual happiness.—This, however, will not be found to hold; the only moral that it inculcates is, that such a privilege bestowed on a single individual, would confer on him an invidious distinction, which would tend to his perpetual discomfort. It leaves the problem unsolved; what would be the effect of such powers, if possessed by every man?

We know not that it is necessary to allude to Mr. Godwin's novel of *Fleetwood,* as we do not recollect it ever having been brought into discussion, in any estimate of his merits, with which we are acquainted. There is in *Fleetwood,* as usual, an attempt at exhibiting the morally marvellous, which excites no illusion, and little sympathy; combined with frequent beauties of detail, striking eloquence of expression, great energy of intellect, and much to arouse and stimulate the better order of novel readers. The story acquires importance in its progress. The jealousy of the married Fleetwood is worked out with elaborate skill. This subject, however, was not sufficient to occupy the three volumes. (p. 386)

Original as his works are in construction and execution, the ideas which are the germs of each, were not the sole property of the author, but suggested by his course of reading, and determined by the degree of progression in which his mind found itself at the time of writing. His has not been the power of producing or creating ideas, but of conceiving them strongly, when presented by accident or study to his understanding. His mind is built up and edified by a certain process of self-instruction; and the force of his intellect drives on the acquired idea through all the forms of the understanding until the applicable categories are exhausted, and then ceases from its labour. This process is slow in its work of education, and its results are dependant upon the diligence of study. Besides this, Mr. Godwin has no facility in varying the form and costume of his intellectualizations. He cannot, like the Scots novelist, present a counterpart of previous characters and incidents in a new production—*"another, yet the same."* What he has once written, he has written; and another version would not only fail of interest, but be deficient in execution. Mr. Godwin dwells in an intellectual world; "a world of empty forms," as Kant would have said; not in the world of the senses. He can scarcely be said to embody, so much as to impersonate; but his persons, whatever their number, are the same in essence, and in unity of substance are but one; for they are not physical persons, but "beings of the mind." (pp. 386-87)

[It] is our opinion, that Godwin's last novel [*Cloudesley*] is his best. *Caleb Williams* has the advantage of old associations in its favour; it is the work on which the author's reputation has been established—with which his genius is identified. *Cloudesley,* also, has a strange defect. It is well-conceived—it is admirably executed—it is miserably constructed. But with all the claims of the first work on public regard, and this great drawback from the latter, we repeat, that we are of opinion, the judicious reader will decide in favour of its greater claims on permanent approbation. (p. 387)

The language of this novel is written in a less ambitious and inverted, and therefore better, style than most of Godwin's productions. In this respect, it is far superior to his *History of the Commonwealth,* which is composed in the worst species of what is called the historical style. The tone of composition in *Cloudesley* is quiet, calm, and graceful—the course of the narrative is gradual and even, not marked by any starts of passionate energy and expression, but patiently worked out to its conclusion—the doom of restitution and punition. The penitence of Lord Danvers is preferable to the unavailing remorse of Falkland—it is a more congenial representation of human

nature—shews more of the good in the evil—and is solemnly touched with the pencil of a master in his art. How fine is the idea of the retribution for his crime, in the loss, one by one, of his children, and, lastly, of his wife—so that he is left heirless, and without hope of progeny, and is, at length, fain to restore his brother's son to the heritage of his fathers. How exquisite is the description of the manner in which Cloudesley proceeded in the education of his ward, and the fatherly interest which became gradually generated in his mind towards the boy! Julian himself is a fine adumbration of a generous and ingenuous boyhood, too susceptible to temptation, with no more power of resistance than youths in general, without experience, are capable of exerting. This is much better than the subsidiary story of *Caleb Williams,* altogether descriptive as it is of the brutal parts of humanity, whether exhibited in stations of power or servility. There is "a relish of salvation in it," which is highly agreeable to a cultivated taste. To many of the readers of *Cloudesley,* perhaps, the interest of the main story and its adjuncts may be less intense—the passion less harrowing—the excitement less engrossing; but the judicious critic will perceive that the philosophy is more true, and the philanthropy more amiable, if not more profound, than in *Caleb Williams.* The intense energy characteristic of that work is a mark of inexperienced authorship—it is indicative of a state of mind in which the writer is possessed of, instead of being possessed with, an idea. We can see the enthusiast at work, watching and waiting for the inspiration, uncertain whither he shall be carried; but desirous of being rapt away, whatever the end may be. (p. 391)

Excellent, however, as this production is, and superior to every other novel published during the last season, it may, we think, be reasonably questioned, whether with novel readers it has had so much success as some of the more time-serving productions of the same kind. With this result, Mr. Godwin is no doubt well content. (p. 392)

The prime instrument employed by Mr. Godwin in his novels is analysis. In this he is . . . distinguishable from Sir Walter Scott, who proceeds synthetically; that is, by an accumulation of particulars, in which the character is presented at once in its integrity to the reader.

Mr. Godwin, however, in his preface to the present work, expresses his opinion, that

> Analysis is a science more commensurate to human faculties than synthesis.
>
> (p. 393)

We readily agree with Mr. Godwin, that to analyze is a far easier task than to synthesize. The novelist, however, would do the latter who consulted the oracle in his bosom, and *added* its responses in aid of those conclusions which he had otherwise obtained. We cannot, however, allow that this oracle is consulted by Mr. Godwin, if he intend by it what is usually meant by *the heart.* The only oracle he consults is his understanding; the process which he exercises constitutes a series of judgments.—The act of judging consists in an union of sensuous presentations in a consciousness; which union is either *analytical* by identity, or *synthetical* by the addition of such presentations to each other. But inasmuch as Mr. Godwin's personage is ideal, the origin of his judgments is not empirical, (as the Kantists would say,) but, *à priori,* as springing from the *pure* understanding and reason. And it is upon this account that, while we cannot bestow upon Mr. Godwin the highest philosophical degrees, we are willing to grant him, nevertheless, a very high diploma indeed, from the metaphysical college of which we profess ourselves to be unworthy members. Nevertheless, we cannot help regretting that Mr. Godwin's scheme of philosophy was not of the more elevated kind, because, what have we not reason to expect, in that case, might have been his success, with his philosophical tact, seeing what has already been that of Sir Walter Scott, without it, who, nevertheless, worked in the spirit of the higher philosophy, by force of that natural instinct, as it were, and that genius, which is also nature, and therefore, like nature, transcends all the results of art, with the most exquisite art, though without any appearance of it?

Would also, on another account, that his philosophy had been rather synthetical than analytical! His genius then would have attained a more elevated reach in his productions. It has been said, that Mr. Godwin is a metaphysician grafted on a dissenting preacher. Would that he had grafted again on the metaphysician the divine! The highest range of metaphysical inquiry, which the latter character implies, is only possible by means of synthesis. The understanding may overstep its limits into the mere field of intellectual beings; and Mr. Godwin has so far overstept its limits; but he has not exercised his mind in those high endeavours, in which it is no longer completely satisfied with an empirical use of the rules of understanding, this use being always conditional, but expels even the understanding itself from its sphere, to seek, entirely out of its limits, for those ideal beings, through which, by the aid of a strong imagination, it may, without any empirical conditions, complete its mighty labour. Then it rises, on the wings of the pure reason, to the contemplation of ideas, which are not only subjectively and necessarily real, but also objectively possible.

That Mr. Godwin's mind is capable of this elevated reach is, nevertheless, sufficiently evident. A passage of this kind occurs in *Mandeville.*

> Religion is the most important of all things, the great point of discrimination that divides the man from the brute. It is our special prerogative, that we can converse with that which we cannot see, and believe in that, the existence of which is reported to us by none of our senses. Such is the abstract and exalted nature of man. This it is that constitutes us intellectual, and truly entitles us to the denomination of reasonable beings. All that passes before the senses of the body, is a scenic exhibition: and he that is busied about these fantastic appearances, 'walketh in a vain shew, and disquieteth himself in vain.' Invisible things are the only realities; invisible things alone are the things that shall remain.

We say that this passage indicates power in Mr. Godwin to rise to the desired elevation so characteristic of a pure rationalist. But it is doubtful whether he speaks here in his own character or that of Mandeville. We are in doubt whether he did not intend it as a part of the attributes with which he has invested that fictitious personage, as belonging to that most repulsive form of Calvinism, which he describes as having so deleterious an effect upon his mind and character. At any rate, the principle which we are advocating exerts no practical influence upon Mr. Godwin's writings. This is a subject, with us, of great regret; not only as it has contracted the moral utility of his productions, but as it has confined the flight of his genius to a humbler quarry than that to which it was naturally destined.

The fact is, that all theological ideas are carefully excluded from this writer's compositions. He treats, ever and anon, of the subject of remorse—and he delineates it well. No man can better shew the writhings and contortions of his victims, who, in general, also, either expressly or by implication, are represented as repentant. But as this remorse is without religious consolation—so their repentance is without religious motive. It is the growth of circumstances—of dire necessity, or miserable expediency—never the result of any higher principles, than the beggarly elements of this world. (pp. 393-95)

We should be sorry, if any of our above remarks should be construed to amount to a charge either of practical or speculative atheism, whether in Mr. Godwin or in his writings; but, without scruple of any sort, we do accuse him of want of faith. We accuse Cromwell of want of faith. Such deficiency is inseparable from him who either does ill that good may come, or advocates the doing of it. Mr. Godwin has exercised all the lower faculties of his mind too long—let him rise to the exertion of that "which is the substance of things hoped for, the evidence of things not seen;" that, by which "the elders obtained a good report"—that, through which, "we understand that the worlds were framed by the word of God, so that things which are seen were not made of things which do appear."

It is not without propriety that we make this appeal to this illustrious writer, because it is not without hope. His mind, we have proved, has been progressive. From antipathy to social institutions, it has proceeded to sympathy with them; until, at length, as in his last work, his nature overflows with the spirit of charity. (p. 395)

> [*J. A. Heraud and William Maginn*], "*Mr. Godwin's Novels,*" *in* Fraser's Magazine, *Vol. II, No. X, November, 1830, pp. 381-96.*

LEIGH HUNT   (essay date 1831)

[*An English poet and essayist, Hunt is remembered as a literary critic who encouraged and influenced several Romantic poets, especially John Keats and Shelley. Here, Hunt praises* Caleb Williams *and notes that Godwin "succeeds far better in moving by pain than by pleasure." Hunt's comments were written in 1831.*]

Caleb Williams is a masterly work of absorbing interest. We do not think the character of *Falkland* a very natural one; that is to say, we do not think that any man, not under the influence of physical madness, could commit the crime that he does; and yet have been accustomed from childhood to those habits of self-restraint and the most amiable virtue. There would have been overt acts of impatience and resentfulness, many times, in such a man; or else his virtue would have set most uneasily upon him. *Falkland* is no fool of virtue, whatever the author may sometimes appear to have intended him; but he may be allowed to be a sort of *Sir Charles Grandison,* taking himself for what he was not. He is Richardson's hero in miniature, under the sad disadvantage of having committed a capital offence! The less varnished characters in this novel are admirably painted; *Tyrrel, Grimes* and all the rest, as far as we recollect them, for we have not seen the novel for many years . . . ; [recently] we sat down incontinently, and read nearly seven chapters without being able to take our eyes from the book. This is the right thing. Criticism may or may not be all in an error. We think, however, it will be conceded that Mr. Godwin succeeds far better in moving by pain than by pleasure. His works are calculated to do more good to the unimaginative, than the reverse; or at least to those whose imaginations are not cultivated, and who are willing to have the rudiments of thought and feeling thrust upon them, at as much expense as the author pleases. We confess, for our own parts, we are among those who have had wounds enough, and are willing to have a little balm. We can dispense with being poked in the fifth rib, or taking our breakfast within hearing of the cries of a surgery. We think that the list of happy books might be increased without detriment to the salutary stock of dissatisfaction. But at the same time, we allow to the full the merit of such works as *Caleb Williams;* and having neutralized our criticism by saying what we read of it again without stopping, we shall proceed to redeem our character for a masculine endurance by saying that we shall infallibly read the whole volume through. Yes: we shall submit our scalp to Mr. Godwin, so tempting is his tomahawk. (pp. 373-74)

> Leigh Hunt, ''A Review of Cooper's 'The Pilot' and Godwin's 'Caleb Williams','' in his Literary Criticism, edited by Lawrence Huston Houtchens and Carolyn Washburn Houtchens, Columbia University Press, 1956, pp. 372-75.

[WILLIAM MAGINN] (essay date 1834)

[*One of the most prominent journalists in England during the first half of the nineteenth century, Maginn wrote prolifically for a variety of English periodicals and was the founding editor of* Fraser's Magazine for Town and Country, *from which the following excerpt is drawn. Here, Maginn surveys Godwin's career, focusing on his ideas and style.*]

Yonder walks William Godwin! The marks of age press heavily upon him; but there gleams out of that strange face and above that stranger figure the eye of fire which lighted up with the conceptions of *Caleb Williams* and *St. Leon.* Wonderful books! Once read, not only ever remembered, but ever graven on the mind of those who know how to read. We can enter into the feeling of Lord Byron's exclamation, when, after asking Godwin why he did not write a new novel, his lordship received from the old man the answer, that it would kill him. ''And what matter,'' said Lord Byron; ''we should have another *St. Leon.*''

But it was not to be. There is power, and stirring thought in *Fleetwood, Mandeville,* and *Cloudesly;* but they are not what Lord Byron called for. The promised *Seven Sleepers,* which was to be the conclusion of a new series of *St. Leon,* has never come; and of Godwin the novelist we suppose there is an end. Of Godwin the politician we have little good to say. He started in opposition to the received views of the world on all the most important affairs in which that world is concerned; and it is perfectly unnecessary to add, that the world beat in the end, as indeed in his case it deserved to beat. The principles of his *Political Justice,* derived as it was pretended from the Bible, would, if they could have been acted upon, have subverted all the honourable relations of society, and destroyed all the ennobling or redeeming feelings of the heart. Godwin himself, as he confesses in his preface to *St. Leon* [see excerpt dated 1799], was sorry for having insulted, in that cold-blooded and, we must say, absurd book, those charities and duties which are the links of life: we should be much surprised if he has not since repented of all the work. In his [*Of Population*], he shewed that true feelings were prevalent in his mind, though he failed in producing the fit refutation of the desperate quackery which he opposed, and which was destined to fall to destruction before the hand of Sadler. His *Thoughts on Man,* containing much

that is eloquent, contain but little that is profound; and we are sorry to find, that though his scepticism on the most vital points is not so recklessly urged as in former days, it is scarcely abated. His historical work on the Commonwealth is a failure. . . .

He has now taken his place in our world of authors; and we incline to think, that *Caleb Williams* and *St. Leon* are the only books of his which will be remembered. His mind is not productive,—therein singularly differing from that of Sir Walter Scott, with whom alone, as a novelist of power, he of all our contemporaries can be compared. There is a want of invention even in his best books; and we can believe the current story, that *Caleb Williams* was written to illustrate a system, or to prove that a novel might be composed without reference to the passion of love. Once fairly embarked in his book, he forgot his systems; but the idea of so originating them proves that there is a deficiency in the mind. The phrenologists inform us, that the organ of veneration is wholly and most singularly absent in his head;—we do not exactly believe in phrenology; but his works prove to us, that there is some want in his intellect which operates to control the impulses of his genius.

> [*William Maginn*], ''William Godwin, Esq.,'' in Fraser's Magazine, *Vol. LVIII, No. X, October, 1834, p. 463.*

[EDGAR ALLAN POE] (essay date 1835)

[*Considered one of America's most outstanding men of letters, Poe was a distinguished poet, novelist, essayist, journalist, short story writer, editor, and critic. Poe stressed an analytical rather than emotive approach to literature and emphasized the specifics of style and construction in a work instead of concentrating solely on the importance of ideological statement. Here, he favorably reviews* Lives of the Necromancers *and praises Godwin's prose and philosophical insight.*]

The name of the author of *Caleb Williams,* and of *St. Leon,* is, with us, a word of weight, and one which we consider a guarantee for the excellence of any composition to which it may be affixed. There is about all the writings of Godwin, one peculiarity which we are not sure that we have ever seen pointed out for observation, but which, nevertheless, is his chief idiosyncrasy—setting him peculiarly apart from all other *literati* of the day. We allude to an air of mature thought—of deliberate premeditation pervading, in a remarkable degree, even his most common-place observations. He never uses a hurried expression, or hazards either an ambiguous phrase, or a premature opinion. His style therefore is highly artificial; but the extreme finish and proportion always observable about it, render this artificiality, which in less able hands would be wearisome, in him a grace inestimable. We are never tired of his terse, nervous, and sonorous periods—for their terseness, their energy, and even their melody, are made, in all cases, subservient to the sense with which they are invariably fraught. No English writer, with whom we have any acquaintance, with the single exception of Coleridge, has a fuller appreciation of the value of *words;* and none is more nicely discriminative between closely-approximating meanings.

The avowed purpose of [*Lives of the Necromancers*] is to exhibit a wide view of human credulity. ''To know''—says Mr. Godwin—''the things that are not, and cannot be, but have been imagined and believed, is the most curious chapter in the annals of man.'' *In extenso* we differ with him.

> There are more things in Heaven and Earth, Horatio,
> Than are dreamt of in thy philosophy.

There are many things, too, in the great circle of human experience, more curious than even the records of human credulity—but that they form *one* of the most curious chapters, we were at all times ready to believe, and had we been in any degree skeptical, the **Lives of the Necromancers** would have convinced us. . . .

The design, if we understand it, is to display in their widest extent, the great range and wild extravagancy of the imagination of man. It is almost superfluous to say that in this he has fully succeeded. His compilation is an invaluable work, evincing much labor and research, and full of absorbing interest. The only drawback to the great pleasure which its perusal has afforded us, is found in the author's unwelcome announcement in the Preface, that for the present he winds up his literary labors with the production of this book. The pen which wrote *Caleb Williams,* should never for a moment be idle.

[Edgar Allan Poe], ''Godwin's Necromancy,'' in The Southern Literary Messenger, Vol. II, No. 1, December, 1835, p. 65.

GEORGE GILFILLAN   (essay date 1845)

[*Gilfillan was a Scottish clergyman and poet as well as a prolific critic and biographer. In the following excerpt from his* Gallery of Literary Portraits, *Gilfillan praises the style and characterization of* Caleb Williams *and* St. Leon, *but considers Godwin's later works less successful. De Quincey disputes Gilfillan's assessment of* Caleb Williams *in the excerpt dated 1845-46.*]

While **Caleb Williams** is in every circulating library, and needs more frequently, we have heard, than almost any novel, to be replaced, the **Enquiry Concerning Political Justice,** is read only by a few hardy explorers, and reminds them, contrasting its past influence with its present neglect, of some cataract, once the terror and the glory of the wilderness, but which, by the fall of its cliff of vantage, has been robbed of its voice of thunder, shorn of its Samson-like locks of spray, dwarfed into comparative insipidity, deserted by its crowding admirers, and left to pine alone in the desert of which it was once the pride, and to sigh for the days of other years. And yet, while of *Caleb Williams* it was predicted by some sapient friend, that, if published, it would be the grave of his literary reputation, the other lifted him, as on dragon wings, into instant and dangerous popularity; the *Enquiry* was the balloon which bore him giddily up, the novel the parachute which broke his fall.

As a novelist, indeed, Godwin, apart from the accidents of opinion and popular caprice, occupies a higher place than as a philosopher. As a philosopher, he is neither altogether new nor altogether true; he is ingenious, but unsafe, and the width of the field he traverses, and the celerity with which he runs across it, and the calm dogmatism with which he announces the most extreme and startling opinions, excite suspicions as to the depth of his knowledge, and the comprehension of his views. They surround the figure of the sage with an air and edging of charlatanerie. As a novelist, on the contrary, he passes for no more than he is,—a real and robust original. He proceeds in this walk with the exulting freedom and confidence of one, who has hit on a vein entirely new. He imagines a character after his own heart; a quiet, curious, prying, philo-sophical being, with a strong underdash of the morbid, if not of the mad; and he thickens around him circumstances, which, by making him altogether a misanthrope, and nearly a maniac, bring out all the powers and the passions of his nature. The main actor in each of his tales, at first recumbent, is, at length, ere you leave him, rampant with whatever may be the pervading principle of his being. And so with the author himself; he, too, catches fire by running. At first slow, embarrassed, uninteresting, commonplace, he becomes rapid, ardent, overpowering. The general tone of his writing, however, is calm. ''In the very whirlwind of his passion, he begets a temperance which gives it smoothness.'' His heat is never that of the sun with all his beams around him; but of the round rayless orb seen shining from the summit of Mont Blanc, still and stripped in the deep black ether. He has more passion than imagination. And even his passion he has learned more by sympathy than by personal feeling. And amid his most tempestuous scenes, you see the calm and stern eye of philosophic analysis looking on. His imagery is not copious, nor always original, but its sparseness is its strength; it startles you with unexpected and momentary brilliance; the flash comes sudden as the lightning; like it, too, it comes from the cloud, and like it, it bares the breast of heaven in an instant, and in an instant is gone. No preparatory flourish or preliminary sound,—no sheets of useless splendour;—each figure is a fork of fire which strikes, and needs no second blow. Nay, often his images are singularly commonplace, and you wonder how they move you so, till you resolve this into the power of the hand which jaculates its own energy in them. His style is not the least remarkable thing about his compositions. It is a smooth succession of short and simple sentences, each clear as crystal, and none ever distracting the attention from the subject to its own construction. It is a style in which you cannot explain how the total effect rises out of the individual parts, and which is forgotten as entirely during perusal as is the pane of glass through which you gaze at a comet or a star. The *form,* too, favours the general effect. Each narrative takes the shape of an autobiography, and the incessant recurrence of the pronoun *I* transports you to a confessional, where you hear told you, in subdued tones, a tale which might ''rouse the dead to hear.'' Systematically, he rejects the use of supernatural machinery, profuse descriptions, and mere mechanical horrors. Like Brockden Brown, he despises to summon up a ghost from the grave; he invokes the ''mightier might'' of the passions of living flesh; he excites terror often, but it is the terror which dilated man wields over his fellow, colossal and crushing, but distinct; not the vague and shadowy form of fear which springs from preternatural agency. His path is not, like that of Monk Lewis and Maturin, sulphureous and slippery, as through some swart mine; it is a *terribil via,* but clear, direct, above ground—a line of light passing through dark forests, over mountains, and by the brink of tremendous precipices. . . . His novels resemble the paintings of John Martin, being a gallery, nay, a world in themselves; and it is a gloomy gallery and a strange world. In both, monotony and mannerism are incessant; but the monotony is that of the sounding deep, the mannerism that of the thunderbolts of heaven. Martin might append to his one continual flash of lightning, which is present in all his pictures, now to reveal a deluge, now to garland the brow of a fiend—now to rend the veil of a temple, and now to guide the invaders through the breach of a city—the words, ''John Martin, his mark.'' Godwin's novels are not less terribly distinguished, to those who understand their cipher—the deep scar of misery, branded, whether literally, as in **Mandeville,** or figuratively, as in all his other tales, upon the brow of the ''Victim of Society.''

We well remember our first reading of *Caleb Williams*. We commenced it about nine o'clock at night, sitting by ourselves in a lonely room—read on and on, forgetful of time, place, and of the fact, especially, that our candle was going out, till, lo! at one of the most enchaining of its situations, it suddenly dropped down, and we were in darkness! It was a most provoking position. The family were "dead asleep," not a spark of light to be got, and there were we, sitting with the book we had been devouring in our hands, pressing it in our enthusiasm to our breast, and yet unable to see a syllable of its contents. It was, we remember, in our seventeenth year, and we did not bear the disappointment so philosophically as we would now. We went to bed intensely chagrined, were long of sleeping,—when we did sleep, dreamed stupid sulky dreams about Hawkins and Tyrrell, and by earliest dawn were up and tearing out its heart. There is about it a stronger suction and swell of interest than in any novel we know, with the exception of one or two of Sir Walter's. You are in it ere you are aware. You put your hand playfully into a child's, and are surprised to find it held in the grasp of a giant. It becomes a fascination. Struggle you may, and kick—but he holds you by his glittering eye. There is no convulsion in the narrative either, few starts or spasms, no string of asterisks, (that base modern device,) to quicken your flagging curiosity; no frightful chasms yawn in your face; the stream is at once still as a mill-lead, and strong as a rapid. But it has higher merits than that of mere interest—a very subordinate kind of excellence, after all; for does not a will interest more than a *Waverley?*—the letter of a friend, more than the most sublime production of the human mind? There is a uniqueness in the whole conception of the tale, the incidents are imagined with consummate art, and succeed each other with breathless rapidity; the moral, so far as it respects the then wretched state of prison discipline and legal forms, is strongly pointed; and the writing, though far from elegant or finished, has in parts the rude power of those sentences which criminals, martyrs, and maniacs, scrawl upon their walls or windows, in the eloquence of desperation. The characters are not Englishmen, (none of Godwin's characters, indeed, seem to belong to any country; they are all, like their creator, philosophers, and citizens of the world, be they thieves or jailors, highwaymen or hags, ruffians or gentlemen,) but they are generally men. We like Falkland least of all, though we tremble at him, as the terrible incarnation of the principle of honour. He is certainly a striking creation; but resembles rather one of the fictitious beings of heraldry, than a real man. No such noble nature was ever so soured into a fiend; no such large heart was ever contracted into a scorpion-circle of fire, narrowing around its victim. Godwin's Falkland is in truth a more monstrous improbability than his daughter's Frankenstein. He is described as a paragon of benevolence and virtue, and yet to preserve, not the consciousness of honour, but, as Fuseli remarked, its mere reputation; he sets himself deliberately, by every despicable art, by every enormous energy of injustice, to blast a being whom, all the while, he respects and admires. And you are expected, throughout the whole career of the injury, to blend admiration of the inflicter, with sympathy for the victim. It is an attempt to reconcile the most glaring moral contradictions, an attempt worthy of the author of the far-famed chapter on "Necessity," and an attempt in which, strange to say, he nearly succeeds. You never altogether lose your regard for Falkland; and this chiefly because Caleb Williams himself never does. . . . Williams himself is the creation of circumstances, and has all the prominent points in his character struck out by the rude collisions he encounters. Originally he is neither more nor less than a shrewd, inquisitive youth.

He is never much more, indeed, than a foil to the power and interest of his principal. Tyrrell is a brute, nor even an English brute; but a brute proper and positive. He is drawn sternly and *con amore*. The other characters, Miss Melville, Raymond, Collins, &c. are very insipid, with the exception of Gines, the bloodhound, who is painted with the force, gusto, and almost inhuman sympathy of a Landseer; and the hag who attempts the life of Caleb in the robber's den, a dire figure, pointed into powerful relief by her butcher's cleaver, a coarser Clytemnestra, if great things may be likened to small. Such is *Caleb Williams,* a work which made an era in the fictitious writing of the age, and which has not only created a school of imitators, but coloured insensibly many works, which profess and possess independent claims; such as the Paul Cliffords, Eugene Arams, Rookwoods, and Oliver Twists, of Bulwer, Ainsworth, and Boz, which, but for it, we verily believe, had never been. Written with the care and consciousness of one who felt himself writing for immortality, it still keeps its place amid the immense fry of ordinary tales, embalmed and insulated in the rough salt of its own essential and original power.

If *Caleb Williams* be the most interesting and popular, *St. Leon* is the most pathetic and imaginative of his tales. It does not, indeed, in our judgment, do full justice to the character of an alchymist;—a character which ought to attract more interest nowadays, when chemistry has approached the verge of transformations nearly as wonderful as that which he sought by self-denial, and abstinence, and unwearied perseverance, and solemn prayer. (pp. 18-25)

This is our ideal of an alchymist: and has Godwin satisfied this ideal? We must answer, No. St. Leon is not a seeker for the philosopher's stone, nor yet its finder. He gains it by no protracted and painful process; he stumbles upon it by chance. It is not a reward; it is not a result; it drops at his feet as from the clouds. He wears, therefore, its mystic crown awkwardly, and like a *parvenu*. He never, somehow, seems satisfied that he has a proper claim to it, nor are you. What right, you say, has this broken-down moody gambler and ex-count to a gift so rare, which so many prophets and righteous men have desired in vain? Unworthy of its possession, no wonder that it avenges itself by making him the most miserable of men. The evils, too, of the successful alchymist's position are, we think, somewhat overdrawn. Money, it is true, cannot unlock every dungeon, melt every refractory element, or quench the fury of devouring flames; but it is clearly not answerable for the calamities into which his own recklessness or extravagance, or the savage superstitions of his age, plunge the Count St. Leon. Because he neglects ordinary precautions, and indulges needless expense, must the power of gold, as an engine of vast benevolence and amelioration, be reduced to a negative quantity? Indeed, the book defeats its own apparent object. As a satire upon gold, it is dull and powerless. As a picture of its princely prerogatives, it is captivating in the extreme. More successfully still, though not more justly, does he depict the misery of immortality on earth. He impresses us with the deepest sense of the dreary position of a man, whose stupendous privileges have only rendered him "alone in the world." Who does not pity St. Leon burying his noble wife, bidding farewell to his charming daughters, and setting forward on his solitary journey, "friendless, friendless, alone, alone?" Who weeps not with him as he feels that his gift has insulated him for ever; that an immortal can form no abiding connexion with "the ephemeron of an hour?" This is the impression which the author wishes to give, and he does give it; and it is most melancholy. But, perhaps, he has not brought out with due force the other side of the medal;—the consolations of such a solitude; a solitude like that of the brideless sun, diffusing, unweariedly, his tide of power and splendour; of the solitary stars; of the "childless cherubs." . . . Still, St. Leon is a magnificent romance. We all remember the grand outburst of his feelings after he knows the secret; though it rises less from the fact that the mysteries of nature are open, than that they are open to *him*. Hence, in the celebrated exclamation, "For me the wheels of the universe are made to roll backwards," we must lay the emphasis on the second word. But, better than this is that melancholy figure of the stranger, whose name is not given; whose history you must guess from the disconnected expressions of his despair; whose mysterious entrance is announced in words so significant and thrilling, like a blast of trumpets, and whom you doubt, in your perplexity, to be an incarnation of the fiend; so disastrous is the influence he sheds on the cottage by the lake, and on the destiny of its inmates. He reminds us of Coleridge's "Ancient Marinere." Like him, he is nameless; like him, he passes "like Night from land to land;" like him, he has strange power of speech; like him, he carries a deep burden of secret upon his breast, which he must disclose; like him, he has a special message to an individual, which colours all the after history of his being. Like the wedding guest, St. Leon becomes a wiser and a sadder man.

And then there is the noble Marguerite de Damville, the ideal of a matron, a mother, a wife, a woman; whose very step moves to the music of lofty purpose, and before whom her husband, even while holding the keys of nature and of immortal life, dwindles into insignificance. Blessings on thee, William Godwin, for this fine creation! a creation realising all our fondest dreams of the majesty, purity, and wisdom which gracious Nature can build up, when she pleases, in one woman's form. (pp. 27-30)

And while she is the loveliest, Bethlem Gabor is the most terrific character in this or in almost any tale. He is a "bear bereaved of his whelps." His castle has been burned; his wife and babes, "all his pretty ones," murdered; and he steps up upon their corpses into a giant of misanthropy. His figure itself proclaims his character. His stature is Titanic; his hair, a dead black; his face, all scarred and scorched with sword and flame; one eye is gone, but the other has gathered up into its solitary orb the fury which fell from it, and glares with a double portion of demoniac meaning. His voice is thunder; and as he talks in a torrent of imprecation against man, and nature, and Eternal Providence, his stature dilates, his breast swells and heaves like an angry wave, and a "supernatural eloquence seems to inspire and enshroud him." His every thought is tinctured with gall. (p. 31)

Mandeville is, like Bethlem Gabor, a misanthrope, but wants the energy and grandeur of that extraordinary character. He is not maddened into the feeling by circumstances; he hates, because he has nothing else to do. It is but in him the escape of immeasurable ennui. Godwin was probably seduced into this miscreation by the success of Gabor, forgetting that to reproduce any character is dangerous, and that what will pass, nay, tell, in a sketch, may be intolerable in a full-length portraiture. The power of this tale,—and it has great power,—lies not in story, for story there is little; nor in variety, for variety there is none; nor in characters, for character of any prominence there is but one—Mandeville himself; but in the minute and pains-taking analysis of hatred, as it roots itself in the soil of one morbid spirit, and gradually, as it grows, covers all with the blackness of darkness; and in the eloquence of certain

insulated passages, collecting the pith of the fell passion, and reminding you of those dark, soundless wells in the wilderness, into which you tremble to look down at noonday. And what an exit the hero has at length, leaving the stage with that ghastly gash upon his face, which grins out the intelligence that Clifford has set his mark on him, and that he is his for ever. (p. 33)

Fleetwood and Cloudesly, with many beauties of thought and style, are but faint, moony reflexes of the others, and we may silently drop both from the catalogue of the works, begirt by which he shall yet stand "before the dread tribunal of Tocome," to receive the verdict of immortality. . . .

[Godwin's] *Life of Chaucer* includes some ingenious dissertations, but is a total misnomer, inasmuch as it contains little or no biography. His *Essay on Sepulchres* is full of learning, and seems to have been a favourite with its author; but, crushed down under its ominous title, it is now safely deposited in the tomb of the Capulets. His *Lives of Milton's Nephews* were another still birth. He is better at writing the life of a fictitious, than a real personage. His Sermons,—called curiously *Sketches from History*,—which we glanced over, *à la* Charles Lamb, at a book-stall in Glasgow, a good many years ago, are desperately dry, and we do not wonder that he soon ceased to be a preacher. His tragedies were sins of youth, and—would it were so with all such!—are forgotten forever. His *Memoirs of the Author of "A Vindication of the Rights of Woman"* does not add to his reputation. (p. 34)

> George Gilfillan, "William Godwin," in his A Gallery of Literary Portraits, *William Tait, 1845, pp. 15-36.*

THOMAS DE QUINCEY   (essay date 1845-46)

[*An English critic and essayist, De Quincey used his own life as the subject of his best-known work,* Confessions of an English Opium Eater, *in which he chronicled his addiction to opium. De Quincey also contributed reviews to a number of London journals and earned a reputation as an insightful if occasionally long-winded literary critic. Here, he responds to Gilfillan's essay (see excerpt dated 1845), disagreeing vehemently with his estimate of the popularity of* Caleb Williams. *De Quincey's remarks were first published in* Tait's Magazine *in November-December 1845 and January-April 1846.*]

[Men] of talent have raised *Caleb Williams* to a station in the first rank of novels; whilst many more, amongst whom I am compelled to class myself, can see in it no merit of any kind. A schism, which is really perplexing, exists in this particular case. . . . (pp. 328-29)

They who vote against it are in a large majority. The Germans, whose literature offers a free port to all the eccentricities of the earth, have never welcomed *Caleb Williams*. Chenier, the ruling *littérateur* of Paris in the days of Napoleon, when reviewing the literature of his own day, dismisses Caleb contemptuously as coarse and vulgar. It is not therefore to the German taste; it is not to the French. And, as to our own country, Mr. Gilfillan is undoubtedly wrong in supposing that it "is in every circulating library, and needs more frequently than almost any novel to be replaced." If this were so, in presence of the immortal novels which for one hundred and fifty years have been gathering into the garners of our English literature, I should look next to see the race of men returning from venison and wheat to their primitive diet of acorns. But I believe that the number of editions yet published would at once discredit this account of the book's popularity. Neither is it likely, *a priori,* that such a popularity could arise even for a moment. The interest from secret and vindictive murder, though coarse, is undoubtedly deep. What would make us thrill in real life,—the case, for instance, of a neighbour lying under the suspicion of such a murder,—would make us thrill in a novel. But then it must be managed with art, and covered with mystery. For a long time it must continue doubtful both as to the fact, and the circumstances, and the motive. Whereas, in the case of Mr. Falkland, there is little mystery of any kind: not much, and only for a short time, to Caleb; and none at all to the reader, who could have relieved the curiosity of Mr. Caleb from the first, if he were placed in communication with him. (pp. 332-33)

The possibility that any individual in the minority can have regarded Godwin . . . [in a positive light] seems to argue that we of the majority must be wrong. Deep impressions seem to justify themselves. *We* may have failed to perceive things which *are* in the object; but it is not so easy for others to perceive things which are *not,*—or, at least, hardly in a case like this, where (though a minority) these "others" still exist in number sufficient to check and to confirm each other. On the other hand, Godwin's name seems sinking out of remembrance; and he is remembered less by the novels that succeeded, or by the philosophy that he abjured, than as the man that had Mary Wollstonecraft for his wife, Mrs. Shelley for his daughter, and the immortal Shelley as his son-in-law. (p. 335)

> *Thomas De Quincey, "Notes on Gilfillan's Literary Portraits: William Godwin," in his* The Collected Writings of Thomas De Quincey, *edited by David Masson, A. & C. Black, 1897, pp. 326-35.*

LESLIE STEPHEN   (essay date 1876)

[Stephen is considered one of the most important English literary critics of the late Victorian and early Edwardian eras; he also wrote extensively on Godwin. In his criticism, which is often moralistic, Stephen argues that all literature is nothing more than an imaginative rendering, in concrete terms, of a writer's philosophy or beliefs. In the following excerpt, Stephen explicates Godwin's philosophy as outlined in Political Justice *and offers a brief assessment of* St. Leon *and* Caleb Williams. *For additional commentary by Stephen, see excerpt dated 1902.]*

Godwin's [*Political Justice*] in its general design reminds us rather of French than of English models. He is what so few Englishmen are—a thorough-going "ergotist." His treatise embodies what is called inexorable logic. In other words it represents the really illogical frame of mind which refuses to be shocked by a *reductio ad absurdum.* One principle is ridden to death. That principle is the supremacy and all-sufficiency of reason. As a true prophet of the era, Godwin makes a clean sweep of all tradition. He rejects all that implicit reason which has embodied the past experience of the race in dumb, instinctive prejudices, without becoming articulate in logical demonstrations. So far his affinities are distinctly French, and, like Tom Paine, he represents the English reaction of the French movement. But it is plain that he has sat at the feet of other teachers. He ranks Hume with "the most illustrious and venerable of men" for his logical profoundness; and it is chiefly from Hume that he borrows his philosophical armoury. The influence of the great sceptic is evident throughout the book. Following Hume, he rejects the social contract and the *à priori* doctrine of the rights of man, popular with the school of Rousseau. He borrows Hume's arguments against freewill, though perhaps not thoroughly understanding them, and accepts Hume's

utilitarianism and his admission of the unselfish impulses. Godwin's philosophy, in short, is derived from Berkeley and Hume; his sentiment from the revolutionary doctrines then triumphant in France; but he gives a turn of his own to the adopted materials. The main outlines of his curious system may be briefly indicated.

All the revolutionary theories, and Godwin's among them, start from the assumption of human equality. Man, in their dialects, means the colourless unit which remains when abstraction has been made of all the peculiarities of race, government, and religion that cause one man to differ from another. This metaphysical entity, admirably fitted to be the subject-matter of beautiful mathematical demonstrations, is then identified with the concrete animal; and it is assumed that because man, stripped of all specific qualities, must be everywhere the same, therefore men, as clothed with all those qualities, must be the same. Thus all appeals to history and experience may be summarily set aside as irrelevant, because referring to the accidents instead of the essence. But how are we to determine the qualities of human nature in the abstract? for some primitive quality must be left to afford a point of adhesion for our logic. Godwin's answer is again modelled upon Hume. Man is not only devoid of innate ideas, but almost, it would seem, of innate capacities. The mind, if there be a mind, is nothing but a series of thoughts and sensations, which may or may not inhere in some hypothetical substratum. Hence the person is entirely built up of the various ideas which have somehow cohered in what may or may not be a mind. We begin life without innate principles or instincts, and though some differences of animal structure must be admitted, they are comparatively trifling. "It is the impression that makes the man, and compared with the empire of impression the mere differences of animal structure are inexpressibly unimportant and powerless." Large brains are made by many thoughts, not thoughts by the brain. It is needless to ask whether this doctrine be legitimately derived from Hume, or should not lead to a self-destructive scepticism. Godwin infers from it the indefinite modifiability of every human being. The embryo man is so nearly a zero that everything which makes the complete adult is due to the accumulation of ideas poured in since his birth. When the process takes place legitimately it is called reason. When illegitimately, we have the various forms of error which produce vice in morality, tyranny in politics, and inequality in society. We must naturally conquer error. The will is entirely determined by opinion, if the will be anything but opinion; and therefore truth is omnipotent. You have nothing to do but to exhibit to a man adequately the reasons for right conduct, and he will inevitably adopt it. The passions, even those which have been regarded as strongest, may be easily conquered, if only their nature is clearly exhibited. Man, therefore, is "perfectible, or, in other words, susceptible of perpetual improvement."

The morality founded upon this doctrine is utilitarian; but not in the ordinary sense. The weak side of the old utilitarianism was the necessary imperfection of its appeal to experience. In framing a calculus of human happiness it started from the individual, instead of the social, point of view. It tried, that is, to reckon the consequences of an action, without taking into account the history of the social organism which can alone explain its moral development. Godwin shares this weakness. But most utilitarians started also with the first principle that a man's own happiness could be the only end of his actions. Their doctrine was, therefore, identified with the doctrine of pure selfishness, whether backed or not by some reference to supernatural sanctions. The opposite school, which sought to discover the moral law in pure reason, endeavoured to dispense with any empirical test. Morality must have no reference to happiness, to save it from degenerating into mere prudence. Godwin borrows from both sides. He is an intellectual utilitarian. Morality, as he reiterates, is nothing but a calculation of consequences. It is a kind of moral arithmetic. That action is best which produces the greatest sum of happiness. Vice is a wrong calculation, and virtue a right calculation of consequences. (pp. 451-52)

Thus interpreted, utilitarianism seems to be fairly obnoxious to one of the alternative accusations generally levelled against it. It does not sanction selfishness, but it prescribes an impossible standard of heroism. I am to act as an angelic spectator, freed from all the ties and prejudices of my condition and animated only by an impartial desire for the happiness of all men, would wish me to act. Every man "is bound to consider himself a debtor in all his faculties, his opportunities, and his industry to the general welfare. This is a debt which must always be paying, never discharged." The least deviation from the path which leads to the greatest happiness of the species is a crime. Every man "should feel himself obliged to scruple" (qy. not to scruple?) "the laying out his entire strength and forfeiting his life upon any single instance of public exertion." This is in fact the creditor and debtor theory of Calvinism, translated into philosophy. When we have done all, we are unprofitable servants.

Man, then, is not merely a reasonable being, but is, so to speak, created by reason. He is hardly even the sheet of white paper, on which experience is to write its arguments. His very tissue is itself woven out of argument. Since good arguments naturally prevail over bad ones, man, could a hearing for the truth be secured, might be actually constructed of right reason. Reason should be the sole judge of truth; the sufficient sanction of morality; the sole agent in regenerating society. For somehow things have gone terribly wrong, and though man as he might be has indefinite capacities for wisdom and virtue, man as he is has been most accurately painted by Swift. He is a Yahoo, and is to be made into an angel. It has come to pass, as a matter of fact, that society is bound together by instincts, rather than by reasoned convictions. A modern utilitarian might appeal to experience as showing the paramount importance of those instincts. But with Godwin, who reasons from the nature of man considered as a colourless unit, provided only with a capacity for reason and for happiness, such an appeal is impossible. An instinct is not reason, and therefore must lead to superstition instead of science. . . . Reason, which starts from assuming the equality of mankind, must condemn monarchy and aristocracy, which imply some natural inequality. Therefore, as Godwin says, "it must be laid down as a first principle that monarchy is an imposture." But this is a trifle. "Government is nothing but regulated force;" but force is not argument, therefore all government is wrong. "That any man or body of men should impose their sense upon persons of a different opinion, is, absolutely speaking, wrong, and in all cases deeply to be regretted;" though in some cases the evil, essential to government, must be endured. The cases, however, on Godwin's showing, would be few. Association of any kind is bad, for even voluntary associations tend to suppress the free play of individual sentiment.

This simple logic makes a clean sweep of all political institutions. In an ideal country the constitution would consist of two articles; the first dividing it into equal electoral districts; the second prescribing means of electing a national assembly,

"not to say that the latter of these articles may very probably be dispensed with." Hence, he thinks, would speedily follow the breaking up of the empire into a confederacy of small republics, and another "sufficiently memorable" consequence—"the gradual extinction of law." Even criminal law, as he argues at length, is a blunder. The gallows is most illogical. It appeals to fear instead of reason. (pp. 453-54)

The good simple Godwin! After this it is a trifle to observe that he abolishes monarchy, aristocracy, churches, armies, laws, associations, inequality of property, and marriage. All promises are, in some degree, evil; for to promise is to limit in some degree the future exercise of my reason. The unalterable promise made in marriage is specially objectionable; and Godwin observes with his usual calmness that "the abolition of the present system of marriage appears to involve no evil." It is, he says, an important question whether in a reasonable state of society, the rule would be promiscuous intercourse, or an adherence of particular pairs, so long as they mutually agreed. He thinks the latter alternative the most probable, because "it is the nature of the human mind to persist for a certain length of time in its opinion or choice." Thus society is finally pulverized and reduced to a mere agglomeration of independent atoms combining and separating according to chance or the dictates of pure reason. This result itself is happily to be brought about, not by violence, but by the diffusion of sound reason. Modern worshippers of Individualism may seem to be feeble plagiarists from Godwin.

The result of applying Godwin's principles is of course to be the advent of the millennium. Everybody is to be good and happy. The labours of every man for half-an-hour a day will supply the wants of all men. The abolition of law will lead to the disappearance of crime. (p. 455)

It is one of his doctrines that a man should always be ready to revise his opinions, for how else can he be devoted to reason? and he availed himself liberally of the privilege. . . . Both volumes . . . [of *Political Justice*] contain much interesting writing. They have Godwin's characteristic merits. The style is rather too smooth, and Godwin is given to terribly trite classical illustrations after the old-fashioned model; but the style, if over smooth, is lucid, and the appropriate exponent of a mind always calm, candid, and in earnest. He argues fairly and thoughtfully; and even when he indulges in commonplaces, as, to say the truth, he indulges pretty freely, his evident conviction of their importance redeems them from contempt. The most pleasing part, to my taste at least, is that which deals with education. Godwin's sympathy with youth is always amiable, and in education we are still most in need of his favourite doctrine. The old brutal theories, which treat the infant mind as a mere receptacle into which ideas are to be crammed by main stress of birch and discipline, whether it be or be not capable of assimilating them, is not so rampant now as then; but it has left behind it some awkward legacies in various forms of scholastic pedantry. Godwin urges very forcibly that the teacher should aim at stimulating the desire for knowledge instead of injecting knowledge ready made; and should try to turn out youths of five-and-twenty with teachable minds, not with minds ready to teach the universe. A hint or two of this kind might be useful at our universities. It can hardly be said, however, that Godwin's essays have much permanent literary value. They have almost as little of Hazlitt's vigour as of Lamb's humour. (pp. 457-58)

Godwin's two successful novels, *Caleb Williams* and *St. Leon*, are of more interest than the *Essays*. They seem both to be connected with the speculations of the *Political Justice. Caleb Williams* was intended, as the original preface declared, to give a "general review of the modes of domestic and unrecorded despotism by which man becomes the destroyer of man" [see excerpt by Godwin dated 1794]. Godwin had himself explained sensibly enough, though with some queer illustrations, the obvious objection to the hybrid genus of pamphlet novels. Homer, he thinks, meant the *Iliad* as an "example of the fatal consequences of discord among political allies." In practice it has enhanced "the false lustre of military achievements." Whatever Homer meant, the efficient moral of a story is apt to differ from that intended by the author. In fact, the logical objection is as strong as the artistic. A novel can show at most what would happen if the novelist were in the place of Providence. From *Caleb Williams* it would be difficult to draw any decided inference. Falkland, the refined hero, is supposed to be a victim to the absurd superstitions of honour. This induces him, first, to murder a ruffian who has grossly insulted him; then to allow two innocent men to be hanged for the crime; and finally to carry out, for many years, a relentless persecution of poor Caleb Williams, who has divined his secret. The most obvious moral is that you ought not to have half a conscience. If Falkland had been thoroughly virtuous, he would not have committed murder; if thoroughly vicious, he would not have been tortured to death by remorse. But fortunately this childish design of enforcing a political theory did not spoil Godwin's story. The situation is impressive, and, in spite of many clumsy details, is impressively represented. The spectacle of a man of delicate sense of honour writhing under the dread of detection, and opposed by an incarnation of vulgar curiosity, moves us to forget the superfluous moral. (pp. 458-59)

Godwin has no ... mechanical skill, and little of what we should call poetical imagination. His characters do not live, and are not dexterously picked out. A love story which is intruded is commonplace and rather coarse. A rambling account of a den of thieves suggests recollections of *Gil Blas*. It is meant to be politically instructive, and is tiresome and irrelevant; and yet the story lays hold of us. The main reason is obvious. The author may not have mastered the story, but the story has mastered him. He is possessed and dominated by his characters. Though he is neither a Fielding nor a Scott, he interests us as he would have interested us by describing a real set of adventures of similar character. In the hands of a more powerful writer, Falkland and his victim might have been more alive; but few writers could have communicated to us more vividly the strong fascination by which Godwin watches the creatures of his fancy. His straightforward sincerity and the genuine interest of a moralist in the working out of an ethical problem are at the bottom of Godwin's success.

St. Leon is an inferior work. Here, too, indeed, there is a striking situation, possibly suggested by Godwin's speculations on human immortality. A ruined noble has retired to a quiet retreat to enjoy domestic happiness. He hospitably receives an old man, persecuted, broken down, and anxious to die, who slowly intimates that he is the possessor of the secret of immortality and of the philosopher's stone. St. Leon may only have it on condition of revealing it to no one. It has been a curse to its proprietor, who has learnt the folly of trying to "vary from the kindly ways of man." St. Leon's temptation, his unwillingness to possess a secret which will separate him from his family gradually yielding to the desire of boundless wealth and life, is strikingly set forth. Here Godwin has to deal with a problem to his taste; and he writes with a power reminding us of *Caleb Williams*. Enough is done to suggest

that the story might be impressive in other hands.... But Godwin makes the interest turn almost exclusively upon the difficulty felt by St. Leon in accounting for his sudden wealth. That is a difficulty which might surely have been surmounted by a man of talent with a possible eternity in front of him. The story becomes a rather commonplace romance, devoted in great part to an attack upon the Inquisition, and now barely readable. (pp. 459-61)

[Godwin's] creed deserves a word of notice, if only as greatly influencing and probably identical with the creed of Shelley. Godwin was called an Atheist, and, in a sense, may have deserved the name. We find his nephew, Charles Clairmont, lamenting pathetically that "the idea of God and a future state is so deeply rooted" in him that he fears that he will "never be able to get over it." Conscientious perseverance may do much in such matters. When, however, another disciple of Godwin boasts of having made a convert to Atheism, Godwin rebukes him, and calls his "zeal of proselytism" in such a cause unnatural. Godwin explains that he does not believe in an "intellectual God, a God made after the image of man," but that he thinks a man wrong who is without a sense of religion. From other passages it seems that Godwin was in a state of mind common enough, though not so commonly avowed. He distinctly disbelieves in the God of Christianity, and regards him as not only a fiction, but an immoral fiction. He does not "believe in God" as those words would be understood by a Deist, or even by a Pantheist. His belief, if it is to be called a belief, is too vague to be fixed in a formula. It vanishes when looked at directly. But he feels deeply the importance of those vague emotions of awful reverence which are prompted by a calm contemplation of the mysteries and infinities of the surrounding universe, and is anxious to preserve without attempting to explain or justify them. In later years he seems to have become more tolerant to the established order, and less anxious to upset existing beliefs. Yet the legacy of essays called by him *Christianity Unveiled*, after the familiar title of Holbach's essay, was meant as a destructive attack upon the popular creed, and it is significant of the change of feeling that a man so genuinely convinced of the supreme importance of a candid utterance of all opinions, did not think it a duty to fire the mine in his lifetime. (p. 461)

> *Leslie Stephen, "William Godwin," in* The Fortnightly Review, *Vol. XXVI, No. 118, October 1, 1876, pp. 444-61.*

LESLIE STEPHEN (essay date 1902)

[*Here, Stephen surveys Godwin's career and deems the author a "superlative bore" despite his numerous literary and philosophical accomplishments. This essay first appeared in the* National Review *in February 1902. For additional commentary by Stephen, see excerpt dated 1876.*]

Hazlitt has recorded a conversation in which he and his friends discussed an interesting problem: If you were able to summon from the dead any of the great men of old, whom would you select for an interview? ... One thing, I fancy, is quite clear: Nobody would ask for an hour of William Godwin. His most obvious qualities, a remorseless "ergotism," squeezing the last drops out of an argument; a frigid dogmatism, not redeemed by the fervour which half excuses fanaticism; and a singular incapacity for even suspecting the humorous or fanciful aspects of life, are qualities which go far to make the superlative bore. They may be harmless or even advantageous in a man who wishes to compose a political Euclid, but that kind of author is not likely to be attractive at a supper-party, and certainly not likely to succeed in other branches of literary work. Yet it is odd that, without too much violence to language, we might describe Godwin as one of the most versatile authors of his time. Though a dealer in the most abstract speculations, he became an industrious Dryasdust, raking in the obscurest assortments of waste paper. In spite of his priggishness, he was a writer of popular books for children, and, without the smallest claims to poetic imagination, he was the author of one tragedy which escaped failure. A more remarkable fact, however, was his success as a novelist. He wrote in a comparatively barren period. The generation which had been impressed by the novels of Richardson, Fielding, Smollett, Sterne, and Goldsmith had passed away, and the novel of the nineteenth century had not yet come to life in Miss Austen and Scott. The novels which were produced in the interval, and can still be read by any one except conscientious professors of English literature, may be counted on the fingers—perhaps of one hand. Godwin's *Caleb Williams* is one of the few. It can be read without the pressure of a sense of duty. It has lived—though in comparative obscurity—for over a century, and high authorities tell us that vitality prolonged for that period raises a presumption that a book deserves the title of classic. Three generations must have accepted it, and as each naturally condemns the taste of the old fogies, its predecessors, the agreement implies some permanent attractiveness. There has been time for a reaction and a re-reaction. Living novelists, if one may judge from their practice, will say that *Caleb Williams* offends against all manner of sound canons of criticism. I am a little sceptical as to all such canons, and rather infer that a book which can survive in spite of such incompatibility must have had some of the seeds of life. Few writers, I fear, can be confident that their works will interest their great-great-grandchildren; and only such happy persons should be quite ready to throw the first stone. (pp. 111-13)

[Godwin] reminds us of a familiar difficulty which besets writers of fiction. When they introduce a bore for the sake of the comic effect of his tediousness, the tediousness is very apt to tire the reader. . . . [Godwin] was a bore by nature. Everybody, I hold, is a bore to some people, but Godwin was one of the unlucky persons capable of boring all round. He can never be amusing taken by himself, and we have to make the effort of seeing him among his fellow-actors before we catch any glimpse of the comedy in which he played a part. (p. 114)

Godwin, in any case, might well pass for a great philosopher. He dealt in what is called "inexorable logic." That is to say, that whenever he ran his head against a lamp-post, he calmly asserted that it did not exist. If the proper way of making a science of politics be to ignore all appeals to experience, his method was irreproachable. That happened to be precisely the opinion of a good many people at the time, and Godwin's Utopia [as presented in *Political Justice*], though liable to collapse at the first touch of common-sense, appeared to enthusiasts to be solid because self-consistent. Moreover, if we consider the merits of the exposition, apart from the validity of the theory expounded, it showed remarkable literary power. The style is simple and solid; the argument is well arranged; and, in short, the logical architecture leaves nothing to be desired if we will allow the architect to use for his material what is really mere moonshine. Nor can it be denied that he is appealing to the sense of justice and humanity of his readers; and that, if he is not impassioned, there is a general glow of benevolent sentiment which commended him to the more gen-

erous impulses of the revolutionary period. I have only to say, however, that it is easy to understand that Godwin would act the part of philosopher to perfection. . . . In Godwin's days, Newnham and Girton were not even conceivable; and a philosopher might hope to be taken seriously by a circle of feminine admirers. They could revere a man, not though, but because, he was a bore. Incapacity for lighter talk proved that his thoughts were absorbed in serious topics, and the absence of romance showed that in him the emotions were under the sway of reason. (pp. 121-22)

Posterity has long ceased to hanker after *Mandeville*. I, at least, have tried in vain to discover the slightest justification for Shelley's enthusiasm [see excerpts dated 1817]. Can we discover any grounds for such enthusiasm in Godwin's masterpiece? *Caleb Williams* was published when Godwin's fame was at its zenith—just before the trial of his friends. A preface, announcing its purpose, was suppressed for the time by the fears of his publisher [see excerpt dated 1794]. "It is now known to philosophers," says this document (philosophers had just been enlightened by *Political Justice*), "that the spirit and character of government intrude into every rank of life." The novel was to illustrate this truth, and to exhibit "the modes of domestic and unrecorded despotism by which man becomes the destroyer of man." That is to say, apparently, it is to show how the wicked aristocrat carries into private life the execrable principles of kings and ministers. *Caleb Williams* was, like *Uncle Tom's Cabin,* to rouse men to a sense of the evils of slavery. The reader, unassisted by the preface, would scarcely perceive this doctrine between the lines. Falkland, the hero, is a model country gentleman; not only a benevolent and public-spirited landlord, but a man of taste and a poet. Like his predecessor, Sir Charles Grandison, he shows his high qualities under the most delicate circumstances. (pp. 130-31)

[The book] suggests the question, What has become of the moral? How about the wickedness of government? The answer must be that it has passed out of sight. Something, indeed, is made of the social abuses of the time: there is a prison of the old pattern, and an innocent man who dies in it because he is too poor to pay for legal assistance; and an impossible band of robbers—imported apparently from the region described by Schiller—whose captain argues philosophically as to the rights of property with Williams. But such matters only supply accessories. Falkland, the centre of interest, is not the typical oppressor of the poor; and, whenever he is not murdering or concealing a murder, uses his influence for the best possible purposes. His mind has been poisoned, we are told, by the "idle and groundless romances of chivalry." He suffers from Don Quixote's complaint, but has managed to mislearn his lesson. The Don would certainly have felt bound to fight instead of meanly assassinating. Falkland is a perverse monomaniac, who will guard his reputation even by deserving infamy. That, no doubt, might suggest a very interesting motive. The psychology of hypocrisy—of the transition by which the sense of honour is replaced by a desire for being honoured—might be embodied in a lifelike hero, as it is common enough in real life. With Godwin, Falkland becomes a heap of contradictory qualities. Monomaniacs are rather in favour now, and a modern novelist would, perhaps, make Falkland into an illustration of heredity or the general corruption of society. But he is so obviously unreal, and all the incidents so frankly impossible, that we scarcely feel even the interest excited by a caricature of conceivable wickedness. Why, then, are we interested? In the first place, because mysterious crimes are always interesting. The interest may be wrong, but it is natural. But, in the next place, given the situation and shutting our eyes to impossibilities, Godwin shows the kind of power manifested by the *Political Justice*. The story is developed with admirable order and lucidity—if the machinery will not bear inspection we need not inspect—and the agony is slowly and steadily piled up till the catastrophe in which the victim suddenly changes places with the oppressor. . . . Godwin's hero does not pray— it would be against his principles—he invokes the force of reason; but the result is the same, and the gradual working up of the catastrophe, the slow and steady evolution of the diabolical agency, has a fascinating power. We catch something of the writer's own profound interest in the story, and admire at least the persistence and ingenuity (perverse as its means) with which variations are performed upon the theme which is always in view. Godwin, of course, had not a trace of the peculiar skill exemplified in *Pride and Prejudice,* where every incident is both perfectly natural and conducive to the effect. Yet his incidents are so well combined that the book has the same sort of unity and co-ordination, and even the formality of the style is congenial to his own ideals. (pp. 135-37)

Caleb Williams might be compared with Mrs. Clive's very striking Paul Ferroll. Ferroll combines the murderer and the polished gentleman far more intelligibly than Falkland, and refuses to let an innocent person suffer in his place. Godwin's book has, however, a certain advantage from the fervour due to his intended moral. The moral, it is true, eludes him. It reminds one of Lowell's description of an orator who tries in vain to get his subject properly laid down. He makes desperate attempts, wanders off in many directions, and in his last contortion "sees his subjick a-nosin' round arter him ag'in." Still, the pursuit of a subject gives a certain unction to oratory, and in the same kind of perverted and anomalous fashion, Godwin's moral gives a sort of momentum and diffused energy to his mass of incongruities.

Godwin's next novel, *St. Leon,* is, I suppose, the last—in spite of Shelley—which anybody has read in modern times, and marks a stage in his development. It appeared in 1799, and shows that he had learned something from his brief married life. He announces in the preface that he has now learned that there is really some good in the ''private affections'' [see excerpt dated 1799]. He adds calmly that this opinion is perfectly consistent with the rest of his doctrines—though to most readers the alteration required in them seems to be considerable. Anyhow, his new doctrine again provided him with a really striking situation. St. Leon is a French nobleman of the seventeenth century, though, it need hardly be said, Godwin takes very little trouble to give any genuine picture of the time. . . . The purpose is to show how miserable a man would become when his exemption from mortality made him incapable of sympathy with his ephemeral companions. That is the kind of text which might have been treated effectively in the old moral tale of the Candide variety. Godwin not only expands it into a long quasi-historical novel, with all manner of impossible adventures and coincidences, but contrives to miss the moral. The point of the situation in his version comes to be the difficulty which St. Leon finds in accounting for his sudden accession to boundless wealth. He has a perfect wife, supposed to be meant for a portrait of Mary Wollstonecraft, but the poor lady is tormented by a curiosity as keen as that of Caleb Williams. . . . Godwin had got further from realities than he was in *Caleb Williams,* and makes his characters indulge in a stilted declamation which he appears to have meant for passion. (pp. 139-42)

Godwin, by the time of *St. Leon,* was forcing his vein under pressure of embarrassment, and the usual result followed. In *Caleb Williams* it was by a kind of good luck that his philosophy provided him with an effective situation, and though it did not in the least prove his moral, and though characters and incidents are simply preposterous, gave a certain power to his elbow. . . . *Caleb Williams* is a kind of literary curiosity—a monstrous hybrid between different species—which gains its interest by a fortunate confusion. But if any one should be prompted to push his study into other novels, I fear that he is destined to disappointment. (p. 143)

> Leslie Stephen, ''William Godwin's Novels,'' in his Studies of a Biographer, Vol. III, *G. P. Putnam's Sons, 1907, pp. 111-43.*

GEORGE McLEAN HARPER   (essay date 1912)

[*Harper discusses Godwin's philosophy as outlined in* Political Justice *and his reputation as a philosopher.*]

The share of Godwin's *Political Justice* in the intellectual movement of the nineteenth century was not at all considerable, if we set aside its influence on Wordsworth and Shelley and the Utilitarian school of philosophy. No other fact more strikingly illustrates the reactionary character of political theory in that century. (pp. 645-46)

Godwin has this . . . in common with Locke, that his philosophy is integral. It is rigorously deduced from a few chief principles. Thus its ethics cannot be held separately from its metaphysics, nor can its politics be detached from its psychology. The largest and the soundest parts of the *Enquiry Concerning Political Justice* are devoted to ethical and political considerations, which can, indeed, hardly be distinguished from one another, as it is his dearest purpose to show they should not be. Godwin insists that his conclusions in these departments of practical conduct depend on his doctrines of knowledge and will. He is a determinist, and the only weak element of his book is his insufficient argument for necessity. The many pleas in favor of free will which have suggested themselves to philosophers, as well as to humbler thinkers, he almost wholly fails to take into account.

Equally dogmatic, though not so audacious, because more widely shared, is his belief that experience is the source of all knowledge. 'Nothing can be more incontrovertible,' he asserts, 'than that we do not bring preëstablished ideas into the world with us.'

Justice, he contends, is the whole duty of man. And it seems that his criterion of justice is the greatest good of the greatest number; for he says, 'Utility, as it regards percipient beings, is the only basis of moral and political truth.' Reason is the only organ whereby men can discover what is just. 'To a rational being, there can,' he says, 'be but one rule of conduct, justice, and one mode of ascertaining that rule, the exercise of his understanding.' Intuition, and every form of mystical illumination, together with all authority, whether of numbers, antiquity, institutions, or 'inspired words,' are calmly set aside. Morality is a matter of knowledge: 'The most essential part of virtue consists in the incessantly seeking to inform ourselves more accurately upon the subject of utility and right.'

Godwin affirms these principles unhesitatingly, and as if they must of course be admitted by every thinking person to whom they are stated separately, each in its own strength. But he himself supplies, in his practical illustrations, difficulties which might not have occurred to a less acute mind. And it was upon these examples that his opponents seized. For instance, since man is a moral being and all his actions are either just or unjust, he has no rights, that is, no moral options, but only duties. And therefore there is no place for deeds of gratitude, for pardon, for partiality to friends or kindred, for charity, for vindictive punishment. Moreover, a promise has no sanctity, and an oath is an abomination; because 'an individual surrenders the best attribute of man the moment he resolves to adhere to certain fixed principles for reasons not now present to his mind, but which formerly were.' Marriage, accordingly, falls under his disapproval, in so far as it is a relation maintained solely in virtue of a promise. (pp. 646-47)

Some of these principles are to be found distinctly echoed— sometimes approved and sometimes painfully questioned, but certainly echoed—in Wordsworth's tragedy, *The Borderers;* and the slightly earlier poem, ''Guilt and Sorrow,'' indicates that he was imbued with Godwin's doctrine that 'under the system of necessity, the ideas of guilt, crime, desert, and accountableness have no place.' Godwin declares that since the will is not free, 'the assassin cannot help the murder he commits any more than the dagger.' Punishment, therefore, should be limited to restraining the criminal from repeating his act of injustice.

It is evident that a society holding such views must reject all but the barest essentials of government, must be reduced to the most extreme individualism. Accordingly we find Godwin insisting that 'government is an evil, an usurpation upon the private judgment and individual conscience of mankind.' . . . (p. 647)

To say that Godwin was lacking in historical feeling is putting the case too negatively. It is more correct to say that he chose not to be hampered by history. He regarded the present with keen perceptive powers and looked to the future. The absence of a background in his picture of human destiny is not due to shallowness of literary culture, but to a deliberate theory. He was one of the last of the philosophers of the Enlightenment in the eighteenth century. And his method, as regards the use of history, is precisely the method of that whole great movement.

A peculiarity of his own, however, is that he relies altogether upon his individual judgment, and not at all upon the collective judgment of his fellow men, which he mistrusts because it has been institutionally organized and thus clogged with the weight of selfish advantages. And even in his own case, he trusts, or professes to trust, only his perceptive and logical powers, and not at all his affections. He has, however, by no means succeeded in shutting out every emotional influence. To take him at his word in this respect is to do him an injustice. His principles are not cold-drawn. There is no fire more intense than the flame of pure intelligence. It is not conceivable that, without the tremor of inward burning, a man possessed, as Godwin was, with a sense of responsibility could write: 'The doctrine of the injustice of accumulated property has been the foundation of all religious morality.' The philosophy of the Enlightenment may well have been too difficult, too sheer, for minds accustomed to beaten tracks in the broad vales of thought, but it was not wanting in emotional splendor. Right or wrong, the man who could affirm that 'there must in the nature of things be one best form of government,' because 'the points in which human beings resemble are infinitely more considerable than those in which they differ,' was moved by a deep moral feeling, as well as by the perception of truths from which most men shrink. (pp. 648-49)

Godwinism soon fell into deep and undeserved disrepute. This was not due wholly to its peculiar features, some of which were beyond the comprehension of pragmatical minds, and others objectionable on the very grounds of general utility to which Godwin sought to refer his thinking. It was due chiefly to the inherent unattractiveness of the whole philosophy of the Enlightenment, and to the inauspicious character of the times. Pure rationalism can, perhaps, never be expected to win the favor of more than a small minority, even among reflective men. Its voice is in no age altogether silent, but the echoes nearly always come back mingled with alien notes, the note of classicism, the note of transcendentalism, the note of romanticism. (p. 649)

George McLean Harper, ''Rousseau, Godwin, and Wordsworth,'' in The Atlantic Monthly, *Vol. CIX, May, 1912, pp. 639-50.*

B. SPRAGUE ALLEN (essay date 1918)

[*Interpreting* St. Leon *and* Fleetwood *as sentimental works that indicate Godwin's belief in the joys of domesticity and love, Allen discusses the relationship in the two novels between the individual and society.*]

[In] his novels Godwin departed far from the rationalistic spirit of *Political Justice.* He has such an immoderate desire for emotion for its own sake, that, like many other sentimentalists, he makes no attempt to proportion the intensity of feeling to the importance of the object that excites it. The net result is extravagance, strained, ineffectual pathos, and frequently the defiance of common sense.

Two of Godwin's novels, *St. Leon* and *Fleetwood,* are deserving, I believe, of special treatment. . . . Godwin, after his marriage with Mary Wollstonecraft and in the interval between the publication of *Caleb Williams* and *St. Leon,* came to see the error of his inflexible statement that, under the guidance of his reason and without regard for the disquieting emotions of gratitude, patriotism, and love of kin, the individual is always under obligation to regulate his actions with a view to their ultimate utility to society, as it is thus only that he can achieve the ideal of justice and philanthropy. Godwin now admits the importance of feeling as a motive for conduct; instead of deprecating its influence, he grants its ethical justification, and in his Preface to *St. Leon* expresses the conviction that the cultivation of family affections is absolutely indispensable to the complete development of the individual, and, instead of checking, fosters wider social sympathy [see excerpt dated 1799]. Whether or not ''the culture of the heart'' invalidates the rationalistic theories of *Political Justice* is not the question here, and, at all events, it is a conclusion which Godwin himself denies. (pp. 16-17)

[Underneath] the forbidding exterior of *Political Justice* and more unmistakably in *Caleb Williams,* there flowed a current of sentimentalism, and Godwin's later attitude toward the tender emotions is probably not so much a complete change of front as a consistent outgrowth of existent tendencies. The upshot is that in *St. Leon* and in all his subsequent novels this new faith in domestic affection and his doctrine of love reinforce one another and gradually merge together into a sentimental gospel of love. (pp. 17-18)

In *St. Leon* Godwin shows the necessity of revising the ideals dominating the life of the individual. His method is to start his hero out in life under the guidance of false ideals, to subject him to a varied and painful experience in which his ideals, being tested, prove delusions, and, finally, to lead him by degrees to the perception of essential ethical values. St. Leon is an aristocrat, cherishing the typically false notions that wealth, display, and princely luxury, are the only means to happiness. Reduced in circumstances, he lives in retirement with his noble wife and four children what is really an idyllic existence, but he scarcely appreciates his blessings. When he learns from a stranger the secret of immortality and the philosopher's stone, all his sleeping ambitions burst into life. His imagination is inflamed by the hope of realizing splendid dreams of earthly glory and of restoring his wife and children to the position in society which was theirs by birth. With impressive, even if extravagant irony, Godwin exposes the fallacy of St. Leon's hope. His wealth increases his wants, and makes him dissatisfied with his peaceful life; and his inability to explain satisfactorily the source of his wealth estranges him from his son, breaks the heart of his wife, and entails unutterable misery upon himself.

In the terms of revolutionary philosophy what is the significance of *St. Leon*? In unmasking the hollowness of wealth, luxury, and worldly ambition Godwin meant to illuminate as truths the principle of human brotherhood and the joy and wisdom of a simple life. To these ideals St. Leon had, at first, been indifferent, but when it was too late, he realized their supreme value. The man who does not crave for the sympathy of his fellows, is abnormal, because, as Godwin insists, love is not an occasional or incidental need of man's nature, but a fundamental requirement of his soul. It quickens and, in fact, conditions the development of his whole spiritual being. Indeed, the possibilities of emotional life can be realized only in social communication; pleasurable feelings are intensified by the responsive joy of our fellows, and painful feelings are assuaged only by the sympathy of others. So the demands of his inmost being weave about the individual a network of a thousand ties which bind him inevitably and for his own good to the society in which he lives. Domestic affection is no longer selfish in its tendency and at variance with the principles of absolute morality, as Godwin had asserted in *Political Justice,* but it is a noble manifestation of a deeply rooted instinct. No wonder St. Leon, contemplating his family, cries, "What are gold and jewels and precious utensils? Mere dross and dirt. The human face and the human heart, reciprocations of kindness and love, and all the nameless sympathies of our nature, these are the only objects worth being attached to." Moreover, this affection does not blight the growth of social sympathy; rather, indeed, do the tender duties of the family circle awaken into activity a desire to help others not akin to us.

The love of wife and children does not, however, satisfy man's need for sympathy, Godwin assures us. The dependence of the individual upon society is portrayed with poignant force in St. Leon's awful realization that his superhuman powers have blasted a chasm between him and the whole human race. He perceives with anguish that, by reason of his exemption from earthly cares, his hopes and fears, joys and sorrows, all will be of another order, such as no mortal can comprehend. The very gift of immortality seems a curse, and he shrinks with loathing from the contemplation of the future to which he is doomed. It will be his cruel destiny to see the coming and going of successive generations of men, and love for him will be a futile passion because every mortal must inevitably be torn from him by death. "I can no longer cheat my fancy; I know that I am alone. The creature does not exist with whom I have any common language, or any genuine sympathy. Society is a bitter

and galling mockery to my heart; it only shows in more glaring colors my desolate condition." The philosophers of the "selfish theory" had claimed that man sought social intercourse not out of love of his kind, but merely for the sake of the personal material advantages which such an intercourse afforded. Godwin comes to the rescue of human nature, and shows that St. Leon, placed by his peculiar powers beyond all need of mortal assistance, craves, nevertheless, the society of men.

The sentimental literature of the day glorified charity. . . . But the philanthropic schemes of St. Leon outstrip them all. Filled with an ambition to achieve something commensurate with his superhuman powers, he journeys to Hungary, and, assuming the function of a god, undertakes to relieve the whole nation from the misery into which it has been plunged by the war. (pp. 18-21)

Over against St. Leon, the lover of his species, Godwin sets the Titanic misanthrope, Bethlem Gabor. Like Karl Moor of Schiller's *Robbers,* he is the embodiment of tremendous energy, his passions have superhuman violence, and in the blindness of egoism he would annihilate the whole human race for a personal wrong. But here a very definite distinction must be drawn between Godwin's attitude toward misanthropy and that of many other writers of the romantic period. The active misanthropy of Karl Moor as well as the contempt for mankind which is implied in the *Weltschmerz* of such characters as Saint-Preux and Werther, is portrayed as an expression of cynicism that is justified by the manners and insipidity of the average man; Rousseau, Goethe, and Schiller are, in reality, voicing their own discontent. Godwin, however, did not take misanthropy as his theme because he had lost faith in human nature. Far from it. To cherish bitter feelings toward mankind, he believes, is no assurance of superiority of soul, but a spiritual misfortune, cutting off the individual from all the ennobling advantages of social intercourse. The hatred of mankind is not sanctioned because evil may exist in human nature; in truth, misanthropy betokens a lamentable blindness to the excellence that is the possession of every man, woman, and child. In its origin Godwin regards misanthropy as a perversion of the inborn human craving for love. (pp. 21-2)

Had he possessed the lyrical power of Rousseau, Godwin's exaltation of [the] gospel of love would remind us more often of Jean-Jacques. At any rate, he floods his book with feeling. This excessive emotionalism has been justly struck at by the anonymous parodist of *St. Leon,* who, after burlesquing one of Godwin's domestic scenes, bursts out rapturously, "It was indeed a delicious sight, and I think I have well described it. I am but a bad hand at sublime description, but at the tender, pathetic, *homely scene,* I do not know my equal." From our point of view this ridicule seems well deserved, but the fact remains, to judge from the comments of Godwin's contemporaries, that *St. Leon* deeply impressed many of its readers. We may be assured it appealed to a host of Rousseauists who had been indifferent to the austere statement of the doctrine of benevolence in *Political Justice.* It is a book completely of its time, born of glowing optimism, and valuable as a revelation of what a revolutionary idealist thought of human nature. In its delineation of the tragedy of the individual cut off from opportunity to satisfy the longing of his being for companionship, it is in harmony with the spirit of the "Ancient Mariner" and *Frankenstein.* (pp. 22-3)

Fleetwood clarifies still further Godwin's judgment of the unhappy individual who is bound to society by no ties of sympathy, and reveals him in reaction against that particularly ignoble form of sentimentalism, the *Weltschmerz*. In so far as that is the case, the novel is interesting as Godwin's commentary on an emotional pose that many of his generation, and Byron in particular among Englishmen, regarded as distinctly "the correct thing" among fashionable swaggerers. Significantly enough, Godwin would cure this sentimental pessimism by a doctrine of optimism scarcely less sentimental in its own way.

Fleetwood is the spiritual brother of those languid epicures in feeling, Saint-Preux and Werther, Chateaubriand's René, Madame de Staël's Lord Nelvil, Sénancour's Obermann, and Lamartine's yet unborn Raphael. Nurtured among the wild Welsh mountains and in the pathetic solitude of a motherless childhood, Fleetwood has developed a most exquisite sensibility. After a period of dissipation on the continent, where he is deceived by two mistresses in turn, and after acquaintance with the insincerity of literary life and the corruption of politics, he realizes the chasm between the ideal and the actual and tastes all the bitterness of disillusionment. In his loneliness he travels for years to discover relief for his *ennui*, but all in vain. He finally arrives at the age of forty-five, hopeless of finding a true friend, contemptuous of all human interests, convinced of the insipidity of life and the spiritual emptiness of a world in which no one of his ideals comes to fruition. When we see Fleetwood in this mood, we expect that, like many another victim of impotent idealism, he will attempt to escape from hideous reality by suicide. Werther took the fatal step; Saint-Preux, René, Obermann, and Raphael contemplated it.

At this very point Godwin reacts, and reacts decisively, against the solution which most of his contemporaries would have given to Fleetwood's spiritual dilemma. He represents Fleetwood as becoming acquainted, at this crucial moment of his career, with Macneil, a disciple of Rousseau. This gentleman, who has a sublime faith in the essential goodness of humanity, quickly exposes the sophistry of Fleetwood's convictions. In protest against Fleetwood's contempt for man, Macneil assures him that almost every individual of the species is "endowed with angelic virtues," and that whenever he sees a man, he recognizes him as "something to love—not with a love of compassion, but with a love of approbation." Fleetwood's life is unnatural, because even a rapturous love of nature and of brute creation cannot satisfy man's inborn need for the society of his kind. (pp. 23-5)

What is the exact bearing of Godwin's reaction against the *Weltschmerz*? In the first place, convinced of the essential solidarity of the human race and the value of social intercourse, he rejects the notion that any individual can afford to hold himself aloof from his fellows in fancied superiority. To appreciate the importance of this protest one has only to read the literature of the romantic period to find, constantly recurring, the idea that genius is synonymous with martyrdom; to be harried by duties from which his talent should exempt him, and to be scorned by a dull, uncomprehending world is conceived as the unhappy lot of every finer spirit. In the second place, Godwin shows the utter futility of pursuing an unattainable ideal that alienates the individual from the world, and fallaciously enough, seems to relieve him of the necessity of doing what good lies in his power. The ideal is to be found in the actual; so Fleetwood discovers that in marriage he has realized the ideal of friendship for which he has sought so long. Furthermore, Godwin in this novel and elsewhere argues against sentimental passivity when he insists that it is nothing less than immoral for an individual to cherish unduly painful emotions

that will incapacitate him for useful benevolent activities. That delicacy of feeling which impairs a man's energy, is only another name for selfishness. To cure the *Weltschmerz* Godwin urges the hopeless sufferer to substitute altruistic motives for the egoistic impulses governing his life. Suicide is only a cowardly escape from every man's duty to do as much good as he can in the world. In a word, then, St. Leon wrecked his life, because he did not heed the gospel of love until it was too late; Fleetwood, after a bitter spiritual struggle, carries it into practice and enjoys the blessings which St. Leon had thrown away. Godwin should, indeed, have great credit for reacting against the peculiarly morbid form of sentimentalism that flourished more on the continent than in England, and of which the victims deserve pathological investigation no less than literary study. Without question his criticism of the pessimistic pose and his recognition of the power of social intercourse to discipline and develop character show the soundest thinking, but unfortunately his tendency to believe so well of human nature that he will not tolerate the attitude of the misanthropist, is tainted more than once by almost maudlin optimism. Curiously enough, Godwin's solution of the spiritual trouble of his age is akin to Goethe's ideal of self-renunciation; but whereas in its consummation Faust's philanthropy is purged completely of egotism, the altruism of St. Leon and Fleetwood is always associated with the delicious self-consciousness of the sentimentalist, seeking opportunities for indulging his feelings and enjoying the contemplation of his own benevolence. Godwin's doctrine of philanthropy is too deeply rooted in sentimentalism to attain to the noble dignity, the restraint, and self-forgetfulness of Goethe's ideal. (pp. 25-7)

> *B. Sprague Allen, "William Godwin as a Sentimentalist," in* PMLA, *33, n.s., Vol. XXXIII, No. XXVI, March, 1918, pp. 1-29.*

GEORGE SAINTSBURY   (essay date 1920)

[*Saintsbury was an English literary historian and critic of the late nineteenth and early twentieth centuries. In the following excerpt, Saintsbury analyzes Godwin's doctrine in* Political Justice *and deems it a highly impractical form of government, created strictly on theory without any accounting for human nature. This essay was originally published in the* New World *in November 1920.*]

[*Political Justice*] is the most remarkable example extant in its own direction of what has been called the intellect left to itself, and working out consequences from certain assumed principles, without regard to experience, or expediency, or humour, or common sense. Appearing, as it did, just at the time when the practical excesses of the French Revolution had reached their highest, *Political Justice* arranged the Anarchist theory— the theory which regards all positive law, all regular institutions, all punishments, all interferences, in short, of any kind with the individual except in the way of kindness, as things utterly unjustifiable and radically bad. The antithesis between Justice and Law is at the very root of this book, and is not much less at the root of *Caleb Williams.*

Marriage, religion, monarchy, being all restraints, have to go; though Godwin is so preternaturally serious and thorough-going that he deprecates the use of force to overthrow institutions quite as strongly as the use of force to maintain them. (pp. 368-69)

[Though] very well and clearly written, . . . [*Political Justice* conducts] its demonstrations with a relentless and stolid contempt of all sense of the ridiculous on the one hand, and on the other of those appeals by rhetoric to passion, which are most formidable when addressed to popular audiences. Its effect on the unthinking was probably next to *nil;* its fallacies were seen at once by steady heads; but its influence on young and enthusiastic persons of more wits than experience was incalculable. (p. 370)

[Grave] and grotesque absurdity . . . [also] saturates Godwin's anarchism. Despite or through the varnish of amiability abovementioned, there are germs of the worst results of Bolshevism itself. But we may find something equally amusing and suggestive in his serious proposition that "All attachments to individuals, *except in proportion to their merits,* are plainly unjust." One sees at once how extremely convenient this is, or would be, on one slight supposition—that human beings were not human beings. Attachment being a mere calculus of merits, envy, jealousy, hatred, malice and all uncharitableness would vanish at once. If my friend dropped me for another friend I should philosophically observe that the other friend's merits were no doubt superior to mine. If my wife left me in the same way, or if any young lady refused to be my wife, the same reflection would at once remove all soreness of feeling. If my father cut me off with a shilling—though indeed on Godwin's system there would be no shillings and no cutting off, with very dubious fatherhood—I should either acknowledge the paternal acuteness in perceiving my want of merit, or deplore the blindness in miscalculating my possession of it. Perhaps the following passage, which has to do with community of goods, is even funnier. Godwin was a student; and it seems to have occurred even to him that it would be rather a nuisance if another person came into his room and said: "Philosopher, I want this room to sit in and that table to work at." But his undoubting mind was never staggered long by any commonsense consideration. "Disputes," he says—and I am now quoting his very words—"would in reality be impossible. They are the offspring of a misshapen and disproportionate love of ourselves. Do you want my table? Make one for yourself; or, if I be more skilful in that respect than you, I will make one for you. Do you want it immediately? Let us compare the urgency of my wants and yours, and let justice decide." That an abstraction *can't* decide: that each disputant will be quite certain beforehand that she decides for him; and that the upshot of it will be either resort to brute force (which Godwin hated) or to that embodied Justice, to wit Law, which he perhaps hated less, but which his system compelled him to declare to be worse; that if you are perpetually to interrupt business and pleasure to discuss and compare respective claims to their implements life cannot go on for a day—these are the things which the plain man sees at once, but to which Godwin shut his eyes with that sublime, that inexpugnable, that utterly hopeless and desperately mischievous persistence which only implicit faith in theory can confer upon mankind. When a man decides, as Godwin does, that exactly half an hour's work per diem on the part of everybody will satisfy all the reasonable wants of the human race, he is beyond argument: you can only laugh at him or shut him up.

Caleb Williams—still a common enough book, not merely in libraries but in modern bookshops, ever willing to book orders—is a sort of fictitious illustration or object-lesson in the doctrines of the more abstract treatise. The hero by chance discovers the fact of a murder having been committed (under circumstances, it is true, of gross provocation) by a man of high reputation and otherwise unblemished character, and the whole story of the book, which is very ingeniously constructed, turns upon the efforts of the criminal to suppress the danger

of a revelation. Even here the indictment against society is of the most unpractical kind, and Godwin is apparently blind to the obvious retort that in his own ideal commonwealth private murder would probably be one of the most frequent of things, inasmuch as on the one hand there would be no other hope of redressing an injury, and on the other there would, on the strictest system of *Political Justice,* be no fear of punishment.

This point is of importance. It will be observed, and may be objected, that this "Bolshevism in its Cradle" lacks a good many things which are associated with the same creed, or nocreed, at the present day. There are no Soviets; there is no *special* anti-Capitalism; there is no *special* worship of the proletariat; and there *is* a special putting forward of sweet reasonableness and absence of violent methods. But then most of us in our cradles do differ considerably from our grown-up stages: even Lord Palmerston, who thought we were all "born good," certainly did not think that we all remained good. And while Godwinism was practically certain to develop all the corruptions of its maturity, that development would be as certain in some cases by reaction as in others by development proper. If Godwin did not say in so many words, *"La propriété c'est le vol,"* his own theory of temporary and readjustable property according to merit must (human nature being what human nature is) turn into Proudhon's; and it only wanted time and the Marxian miasma to spread the notion that capital is the worst form of property. (pp. 370-73)

That, as he grew older, Godwin grew in some respects wiser— not merely in the way of becoming, without the slightest regard to correlative merit, a sinecurist under Government, though he had previously held that everybody ought to work and that there ought to be no Government at all—is not surprising. The children (or indeed the parents) of Revolution generally grow wiser unless their offspring or parent devours them too soon. But he has also left very amusing letters to intending disciples who took *Political Justice* at the foot of its letter. And his last philosophical work, the *Thoughts on Man,* . . . would certainly not of itself suggest identity of authorship with his first. But this again is common, and, except to those who care only for the anecdotage of literature and history, adds nothing to the interest of *Political Justice* itself. That interest lies in the fact that the book is the first book in English, and one of the first books in any language, to advocate complete reversal, or at any rate removal, of all hitherto accepted principles of law in politics, religion, morals and everything that affects the *conduct* of men. The author's history and personality add a little to the interest of the book and supply comment, sometimes decidedly ironic, on its principles; nor is this addition, perhaps, quite accidental or uninstructive. But it is as an early gospeller of what in various modifications or developments has since been known as Anarchism, Nihilism, Communism (in the *Commune* sense), and finally Bolshevism, that Godwin most deserves attention and will best "repay perusal." (pp. 382-83)

> *George Saintsbury, "Bolshevism in Its Cradle," in his* The Collected Essays and Papers of George Saintsbury: 1875-1920, Vol. III, *E. P. Dutton & Co., 1923, pp. 365-83.*

C. H. DRIVER   (lecture date 1929-30)

[*Driver provides a detailed examination of* Political Justice, *focusing on the influences on Godwin's thought, his importance to future political movements, and the intent and consequences of his theories. Driver's comments were originally delivered as a lecture in 1929-30.*]

Political Justice is a work which holds a unique place in the history of English political theory; it is unique in doctrine and in scope. Before examining Godwin's teaching in detail it is necessary as a preliminary to stress two general features of his treatise which may help us the better to appreciate the nature of its teaching—namely, that it was written during a period of very rapid transition, wherein were mingled ideas and forces both new and old; and that its author intended it to be a comprehensive system embracing every aspect of society and essentially valid for all time. Godwin sought for the permanent beneath the flux, and found cause for unbounded hope as a result of his quest.

This book is essentially the product of the epoch which separates the old world from the new, the agricultural from the industrial. Much of the interest it has for us lies in the fact that it is thus symbolical, being both retrospective and prospective in its reference. Godwin confronts the problems of the future with intellectual preconceptions derived from the past. His work, on the one hand, is in a very real sense a synthesis of the speculation of the previous century, possessing all the general features of that speculation both as to attitude and as to method. On the other hand, it states for the future its major problems and provides the starting-point for much of its speculation.

Godwin was not an original thinker. His book is definitely the product of extensive reading (frequently acknowledged in footnotes), the results of which have been organised and integrated by a man of marked intellectual characteristics and of striking personal temperament. He sets out to build a Temple of Reason, and it is always easy to see whence he has quarried his materials; but he remains his own architect. It has been said that no single idea in *Political Justice* is original, and this is probably true. From Locke and the empiricists he borrowed his ideas of the nature and structure of mind; from Rousseau, Helvétius, and Holbach he learnt the effects which education and political institutions have on the formation of character; from Mably and others he accepted the idea of the uniformity of truth; Paine taught him the distinction between society and government; and from all these writers he took over the criticisms of monarchy and aristocracy. His criticism of private property is obviously inspired by Mably and by Wallace, and to a less extent by Plato and Sir Thomas More. Such a statement of his indebtedness could be extended to cover practically every page of his writing, but it would avail little. No catalogue of sources can explain a man. His originality is rather to be sought in the logical unity of his scheme and the intrepidity with which he pushed his system to its logical extreme, as no English philosopher had done before.

Being thus eclectic, *Political Justice* possesses all the main features associated with that line of Enlightenment speculation which derives chiefly from the Cartesian outlook. It is individualistic and atomistic in its attitude to society, regarding society as "nothing more than an aggregate of individuals." Moreover, it is uncompromisingly intellectualistic in tone, as examination of the doctrine reveals, and is completely lacking in that emotional driving power of romanticism which Rousseau introduced into political theory. If Rousseau stood for the idyllic imagination, . . . and Burke for the moral imagination, then Godwin above all stood for the rational imagination and its concomitants—the idea of progress and of human perfectibility—which resulted from the confluence of the Baconian and Cartesian influences. That rational imagination underlies all his writing, and is revealed at the beginning of *Political Justice*. (pp. 145-47)

Another characteristic of Godwin's work, which is derived from the preceding century, and which is an inevitable accompaniment of his rationalism, is its *a priori* method. Analysis will show how rigidly Godwin bases the whole of his political teaching on his doctrine of an immutable moral law from which particular deductions to meet particular exigencies can be made. (p. 148)

The importance of Godwin's work lies in the fact that he it was who first disclosed in England the essentially radical spirit inherent in the outlook of the Enlightenment. This was undoubtedly due to the influence of the French thinkers acting upon his own uncompromising Nonconformist dispositions. He turned these doctrines to account, not to make a plea for the enlightened despot who should remedy the abuses of organised society by purifying it and levelling it up through his wisdom, but to destroy social organisation entirely as something inevitably evil and opposed to reason.

But although Godwin's work is backward-looking so far as its intellectualism and its method are concerned, yet it has features which gave it marked significance for the future. For instance, his insistence on the doctrine of progress involved a *purposive* attitude to social phenomena, and that attitude—coming as it did at the beginning of the mightiest epoch of social change in our history—was destined to spread and to modify political life to an incalculable extent. . . . Godwin's entire work is a . . . vehement denunciation of the doctrine of indifference. The fact that he sought a remedy in exactly the opposite direction to that in which later generations have gone—in abolition of all restraint, instead of increasing social control—need not blind us to the essential significance of this protest. He had a keen sense of prevailing social misery and of the appalling waste of human life involved in the social system around him. . . . In the next century such an attitude of social purposiveness was to become general, instead of being the exception; and the dissemination of such an attitude was the prelude to democracy.

In a second respect, however, Godwin's work has a bearing on the future—in his realisation that the idea of property is the fundamental problem of human society. . . . Few other political philosophers in England had for a century considered it as the paramount *practical problem;* but such it was for Godwin. In this respect he shows greater detachment and more insight than most of the revolutionaries with whom he was associated. He says plainly that republicanism will not solve the social problems. Only a redistribution of property can do that. This issue had been raised during the Commonwealth period, but from the Restoration onward had fallen into the background of political speculation this side of the Channel. (pp. 148-50)

Apart from the attribute of social purposiveness and the question of property, there is another sense in which Godwin has significance for the century that followed, and that is in his emphasis on the necessity for leisure and education as the indispensable bases for the erection of democracy. This point of view—the complete antithesis of Burke's idea of the "swinish multitude"—follows from Godwin's conception of the perfectibility of man. He has a thoroughly evangelical regard for the intrinsic worth of every human being; his moral ideal involves the development of the reason latent in all men; and for him we fall short of this moral ideal so long as there remain any undeveloped potentialities in the soul of man. Adopting as he did the Socratic position that knowledge is virtue, Godwin sees in the extension of education the only medium of progress and reform. It was this fact which made him distrust violence and any form of collective endeavour such as leagues, societies, and unions; it was this fact which led him to break with Thelwall and the physical force men; and it was this fact also that led him to imply in many places in *Political Justice* that reform must come relatively slowly through the propaganda work of a small intellectual aristocracy.

Besides this double aspect of *Political Justice* as both retrospective and prospective there is another general feature of the work which needs emphasising, and that is its comprehensiveness. In one sense Godwin's book is misnamed; it is far more extensive in scope than its title at first glance would imply. But Godwin is careful to explain in what sense he is using his terms. For him politics does not mean merely the machinery of government and its construction; nor does justice mean merely a legal ideal. By politics he means rather the general science of human virtue and happiness. Politics is really a general ethical study. He tells us in the preface that he "conceived politics to be the proper vehicle of a liberal morality"; and in his first chapter he criticises the generally accepted meaning of the word "politics." He says that it has been used in too narrow a sense by writers hitherto, for they have not displayed "a consciousness of the intimate connection of the different parts of the social system, whether it relates to the intercourse of individuals or to the maxims and institutes of states and nations." . . . Godwin is accordingly at pains to show that "government is still more considerable in its incidental effects than in those intended to be produced." It is all-pervading in its influence; it "insinuates itself into our personal dispositions and insensibly communicates its own spirit to our private transactions"; it is the ever-present but invisible environment, controlling the life of every single member of the community by compelling the adaptation of the individual to itself, unconsciously, but none the less completely. No other English writer had conceived his subject in such a comprehensive way, although since Godwin's time the complexity of the issues involved in the problems of politics has been increasingly realised.

Since he adopted this viewpoint, it is not surprising that Godwin made his own work "perspicuous." It is not so much a treatise on politics as on sociology. Besides being what he himself calls a "political science," it is a treatise on ethics, on philosophy, and on individual and social psychology. It treats of education and religion; it roams from the problem of free will to the question of immortality. . . . Above all, he wrote with a practical intention. He clearly wanted to modify public opinion and to hasten the coming of the day of enlightenment. This was to be no mere academic treatise, but a work "from the perusal of which no man should rise without being strengthened in habits of sincerity, fortitude, and justice."

This last remark reveals another general trait of *Political Justice*. It was comprehensive not only in the sense that a large variety of subjects was dealt with, but also in the sense that its author was trying to look at the issues *sub specie eternitatis*. He writes on cosmic problems with a consummate self-confidence, and his political theory is in a direct sense the by-product of his cosmology. From beginning to end he is always asking what are the "general principles," not what are the facts; and he entertains no doubt in his own mind that once these general principles are found they can be applied to all concrete problems with ease. . . . He is completely convinced of the truth of his general principles; he is quite confident that they alone embody the entire truth; he is assured that his teaching is in perfect harmony with "the general scheme of things," so that even though the adventitious sin of man may postpone

the coming of the reign of reason, yet that reign must come sooner or later, and neither principalities nor powers will be able ultimately to prevent it. Godwin had dropped the specific tenets of the Calvinist creed; but his book is Calvinistic in spirit throughout, and a realisation of this fact helps us the better to appraise his teaching. For a discoverable God he substituted a discoverable universe. For grace working silently in the heart of man he substituted reason. Instead of righteousness as the principle of conduct he pleaded for enlightenment, since the mind—once awakened to the sublimity of eternal truth—must of necessity act in conformity with it. Lastly, and as a corollary of what has been said, for the need of conversion he substituted the need for education; man could attain his true status only by turning away from the intellectual errors into which he had fallen, and by contemplating the immutable laws of the universe. Godwin in more than one place seems to think that this awakening of the soul may happen suddenly, though he hopes the process may not be too sudden in the community as a whole. He prefers that the awakening should first occur among the spiritual *élite*, who should be, as it were, missionaries to their fellows. When the enlightenment has become general, then the whole political and social problem will be solved. The awakening to the truth means automatically that the calm period of reason will succeed, since "in reality the chains fall off themselves when the magic of opinion is dissolved." It is the old doctrine that the truth would make men free. (pp. 150-53)

[Godwin] reiterates his position to an almost wearisome degree, and recurs to his "first principles" with every specific problem. We will examine first, therefore, his theory of man; and next his conception of the universe, so far as he presents that as determining political theory.

His theory of man is fundamental. All men, whatever their colour and wherever they are born, are made in the same way. "All men are conscious that man is a being of one common nature, and feel the propriety of the treatment they receive from one another being measured by a common standard." The points in which human beings are alike "are infinitely more considerable than those in which they differ." This common nature has several marked features. First, all minds at birth are a *tabula rasa,* and we bring into the world with us no innate principles. Consequently at birth there is "no essential difference between the child of the lord and the porter." But in the second place man is born endowed with reason, or at least the potentiality of reason. "All men are partakers of the common faculty reason, and may be supposed to have some communication with the common preceptor truth." Godwin is always saying that man is an intellectual being; but he nowhere tells us clearly exactly what he means by reason. He appears to mean by that term the capacity, or the faculty, for discerning cause and effect in phenomena. But the strangest aspect of Godwin's doctrine is his contention that reason exerts a compulsive power over its possessor. Man always acts in accordance with such reason as he has, even though that may not be fully developed. No other faculty intervenes in action; indeed, given the perception of one or more causal relationships, action follows automatically in accordance with that perception. Hence it follows that "Man being, as we have now found him to be, a simple substance, governed by the apprehensions of his understanding, nothing further is requisite but the improvement of his reasoning faculty to make him virtuous and happy." So there can be no such thing as free will. Godwin devotes twenty pages to destroying the case for free will, and to showing that if there is to be a science of mind it must be based on the necessitarian hypothesis. The mind is itself built up of associated sequences of ideas derived from the perceptions of reason. Thus the inner world of mind, like the outer world of matter, is a causal system. Therefore "man is in reality a passive and not an active being"; "considered in himself he is merely a being capable of impression, a recipient of perceptions." This doctrine Godwin uses at almost every stage of his argument, and especially in connection with treatment of crime and punishment. Paradoxically enough, also, it is this doctrine which is going to give him his chief reason for optimism for the future.

Four important consequences follow from this conception of human beings as passive creatures without innate ideas, but endowed with a potential reasoning faculty. The first is that there is no distinction between will and intellect; action is automatic, for it is impossible to imagine, in the light of the above teaching,

> that, in the case of an intellectual faculty placed in an aptly organised body, preference can exist together with a consciousness (gained from experience) of our power to obtain the object preferred, without a certain motion of the animal frame being the necessary result. We need only attend to the obvious meaning of the terms in order to perceive that the will is merely, as it has been happily termed, the last act of the understanding.

The second consequence is the moral and intellectual equality of all human beings, at least potentially:

> From these simple principles we may deduce the moral equality of mankind. We are partakers of a common nature, and the same causes that contribute to the benefit of one contribute to the benefit of another. Our senses and faculties are of the same denomination. Our pleasures and pains will therefore be the same. We are all of us endowed with reason, able to compare, to judge, and to infer. The improvement therefore which is to be desired for the one, is to be desired for the other.

The third consequence, which again is utilised throughout *Political Justice,* is the doctrine that character is determined by environment, and by environment only:

> From these reasonings it sufficiently appears, that the moral qualities of men are the produce of the impressions made upon them, and that there is no instance of an original propensity to evil. Our virtues and vices may be traced to the incidents which make the history of our lives, and if these incidents could be divested of every improper tendency, vice would be extirpated from the world.

The fourth consequence which Godwin deduces from his view of the capacities of man is "the doctrine of benevolence." Man does not act from the impulse of self-love, for the understanding of virtue is itself a motive exciting to action; and by virtue he means conformity with the moral law, which commands the consideration of other people's needs as much as one's own. "Man is not originally vicious."

When we turn from Godwin's theories of the nature of man to his theories of the nature of the universe we find him no less explicit, and from the combination of the two doctrines

the whole of his political theory is derived. We may summarise his teaching under this head by the theorem that he conceived of the universe as a system of cause and effect, working by immutable laws, and implying a code of moral principles which are themselves rational and discernible by the human reason.

To begin with, it is a *system;* and the main purpose of *Political Justice* is to delineate that system. "I am myself part of a great whole," he says; and it is this whole that he means by the word "truth." . . . But it is a system which works by the immutable laws of cause and effect. He speaks of "the great chain of causes from which every event in the universe takes its rise." . . . These immutable laws involve a code of moral principles. Godwin is a utilitarian, and for him virtue and happiness are interchangeable terms. Virtue is thus organic to nature, in the sense that nature has ordained that all men shall pursue their own happiness; and in the attainment of that complete harmony which is real happiness they help to promote the happiness of others also. It is this harmony ordained by nature which constitutes the moral code, and which Godwin calls justice. "If truth be one," he says, "there must be one code of truths on the subject of our reciprocal duties," for "the course of nature and the course of perfect theory are the same." (pp. 154-58)

Such are Godwin's basic theories of man and the universe. Man is of one nature; the universe is one system; the moral law is one code; and necessity reigns everywhere. There follow certain consequences of great importance for politics, "leading to a bold and comprehensive view of man in society." Five such consequences have in particular to be noted.

In the first place, all doctrine of rights in the political sense completely disappears. The moral law prescribes what duty the individual owes to his neighbours and what duty they owe to him, and nothing more is necessary. The argument is simple. "By right . . . has always been understood discretion, that is, full and complete power of either doing a thing or omitting it, without the person's becoming liable to animadversion or censure from another." But

> the rights of one man cannot clash with, or be destructive of, the rights of another; for this, instead of rendering the subject an important branch of truth and morality (as the advocates of the rights of man certainly understand it to be), would be to reduce it to a heap of unintelligible jargon and inconsistency. If one man have a right to be free another man cannot have the right to make him a slave.

Nobody has a right to omit what his duty prescribes: "from hence it inevitably follows that men have no rights." Nothing is more surprising, says Godwin, than that two ideas so incompatible as man and rights should have been associated together, since either term "must be utterly exclusive and annihilatory of the other." Once posit that man is an intellectual being, it follows that he can learn from immutable justice what his duties are, and thereby all talk of rights becomes meaningless. . . . Society cannot change eternal truth. It can require of me everything that it is my duty to do, and no more (hence it cannot compel me to go to war on its behalf). Conversely, society is bound to do for its members everything that can contribute to their welfare (and on the strength of this Godwin later denies any absolute right to property).

A second consequence, no less important than the denial of inherent rights, follows from Godwin's views of man and his world, and this is the fact that there can be no such thing as legislation in any real sense. Law cannot be made, for it simply *is;* and the most venerable Senate "can only interpret and announce the law which derives its real validity from a higher and less mutable authority." And, again, legislation is

> a term not applicable to human society. Men cannot do more than declare and interpret law; nor can there be an authority so paramount as to have the prerogative of making that to be law which abstract and immutable justice had not made to be law previously to that inter-position—

though he admits that as a temporary expedient it might be found necessary to have an authority empowered to declare those general principles.

The third consequence is that no obedience is due to government as such. The object of government is the exertion of force; and the duty of man is the exercise of his reason. I am bound to submit to justice and truth, because they approve themselves to my judgment; but I submit to erroneous government only because there is no alternative.

> The compliance I yield to government independently of my approbation of its measures is of the same species as my compliance with a wild beast that forces me to run north when my judgment and inclination prompt me to go south.

So it follows that "no Government ought pertinaciously to resist the change of its own institutions," or to hinder the fullest possible discussion. The individual judgment is the only valid tribunal, and man is in all cases

> obliged to consult that judgement before he can determine whether the matter in question be of the sort provided for or no. So that from this reasoning it ultimately appears that no man is obliged to conform to any rule of conduct farther than the rule is consistent with justice.

The contrary doctrine has been the source of more calamities to mankind than all the other errors of the human understanding. "Depravity would have gained little ground in the world, if every man had been in the exercise of his independent judgement."

A fourth consequence of Godwin's general philosophical outlook is that there is one best form of government. Truth is one; and truth "cannot be so variable as to change its nature by crossing an arm of the sea"; it is at all times and in all places the same. Man's nature is everywhere the same in essentials also; therefore he always needs the same things. Hence "there must in the nature of things be one best form of government which all intellects sufficiently roused from the slumber of savage ignorance will be irresistibly incited to approve." Difference in climate need not modify political theory.

Such are the general premises of Godwin's political thinking, and such are the consequences which these premises involve for him. But if the living of a social life is part of the general problem of morality, and if on the other hand man is born morally neutral, but endowed with the potentialities of reason, the question then arises: What are the causes of moral improvement? The general nature of the answer to this question has already been implied, but Godwin examines it with considerable fullness.

There are three principal sources of moral improvement: literature, education, and political organisation. The first two are limited in their scope. Literature, although it has already "reconciled the whole thinking world respecting the great principles of the system of the universe," appeals only to a few. The bulk of the community has neither the time nor the capacity to devote to it, because of the inequitable distribution of wealth. Education, although in some respects a more powerful instrument, is also circumscribed in its influence; partly because of the difficulty of finding the sagacious and disinterested teacher, but mainly because its benefits will be neutralised by the evil environment when the youth passes into the world. The environment must first be altered before the other two instruments can be fully utilised. That is why political organisation is of such overwhelming importance. If that organisation be based on the true laws of morality, then man, being a creature passive to his environment, will himself grow moral. By creating the invisible but omnipresent social environment government has an incalculable power of suggestion, entering into every action and every thought of man. (pp. 158-62)

> C. H. Driver, "William Godwin," in The Social & Political Ideas of Some Representative Thinkers of the Revolutionary Era, *edited by F. J. C. Hearnshaw, George G. Harrap & Company Ltd., 1931, pp. 141-80.*

JOHN MIDDLETON MURRY   (essay date 1938)

[*Murry was a noted English essayist, magazine editor, and literary critic who wrote during the first half of the twentieth century. In the following excerpt, he analyzes the philosophy of* Political Justice, *emphasizing that Godwin was one of the most humane and concrete political thinkers of his time.*]

It is impossible to understand Godwin, or his curious aloofness from the political movements of his day, except we appreciate that he was no more a mere democrat than Cromwell or Rousseau. He was concerned for the integrity of the individual man. Therefore, the political revolutionary or even the moderate political reformer did not know what to make of him. Without the faintest intention of paradox, he was always springing surprises. His denunciation in *Political Justice* of the fetish of majority worship, "that intolerable insult upon all reason and justice—the deciding of truth by the counting up of numbers," is of a piece with his spirited attack, forty years later, on the viciousness of vote by ballot in his final book of essays, *Thoughts on Man.* The ballot-box would, it is true, enable a man to vote as he pleased; but what was that compared to the fact that it will encourage him in duplicity and make dissimulation a necessity? That sounds almost fantastical: quite fantastical is his serious doubt at the end of *Political Justice* whether in a true society of real individuals its members would consent to play orchestral music or act in dramas, because of the attaint to their individuality. But what underlies his extraordinary generalization: "Everything understood by the term co-operation is in some sense an evil" is an impassioned conviction of the worth and potentialities of the individual, and an endeavour to implant in men's imaginations the conception of what human integrity might mean.

It was this strain in *Political Justice* which set young men's hearts on fire. The difference between Godwin and the enthusiasts who fell by the wayside, who (as Hazlitt sardonically put it) "lost their way in Utopia, and found it in Old Sarum," was that Godwin had the power to endure. He had come to his vision first through a long and peculiar religious tradition, and secondly through hard thinking on the basis of a religious struggle of his own. He was thirty-five, and a mature and well battered man when he conceived *Political Justice:* he had fought his way to his vision. Now he rationalized it. It was really all perfectly simple, as genuine religious vision always is.

Godwin saw, quite plainly, that men could be very much better than they are—so much better, indeed, as to be virtually quite different. The means of this regeneration of man was Reason. But reason in Godwin's argument was a peculiar thing; it was inherently compulsive. Godwin's Reason was, in fact, the same as the faculty of understanding the Truth in Blake's apothegm: "Truth cannot be uttered so as to be understood and not be believed." There is no difference between that and the Godwinian axiom that "Sound reasoning and truth, when adequately communicated, must always be victorious over error." (pp. 248-50)

"Universal benevolence" was, in Godwin's system, self-evident. The only problem is to understand why it is not in operation. The answer is, of course, simple. "Positive institutions"—Monarchy, Aristocracy, the Church, the property-system—have corrupted men, and made them opaque to its illumination. The problem shifts a plane. By what means can these diabolical "positive institutions" be changed? The answer is by the propagation of "universal benevolence," in idea and act, among those who are responsive to it. The problem shifts again. What are the desirable changes in positive institutions which the disciples of universal benevolence should pursue? This, more than any other, is the question which Godwin answers in *Political Justice.* And it is intelligible that he induced in his fellow political reformers a kind of uncomprehending despair. He seemed to be answering the same question as they; but, in fact, it was a quite different one. His real answer is that all positive institutions should be abolished. That is to say, his answer is on the same plane as his problem: not political at all, as we (like his associates) understand the word, but moral and religious. And once more Godwin's creed is better summed up by Blake than by himself: "Religion is Politics, and Politics is Brotherhood." The real solution, and ultimately the only solution, is the conversion, by "adequate communication" of the truth, of a number of men to self-evident "universal benevolence." Their example will be contagious, and the process of regeneration accelerated.

But in the meantime? Godwin was only partly interested in the meantime. He did not really believe in the efficacy of transitional measures; he could do no more than allow that they were better than nothing. In practical politics he was content to be a Whig of the radical kind; but though he was ready to intervene, as he did very effectively in the trial of the twelve reformers with his brilliant pamphlet, *Cursory Strictures on Chief Justice Eyre's Charge to the Grand Jury*, he was not to be implicated in revolutionary politics. He was willing to bear his witness to the evil of the existing order, and the good that might one day be; and he bore his witness bravely: but he profoundly mistrusted political organization toward the good. Let evolution begin at home, in the hearts and minds of men; it would last longer than the enthusiasms and extravagances of the London Corresponding Society. His attitude to the politics of reform was largely colored by his deep mistrust of State action, which proceeded less from his having imbibed the English political individualism of his century than from his having absorbed the religious individualism of Independency. He imagined that he was the antithesis of Rousseau in this matter; but in fact he did not understand Rousseau, who, it must be confessed, was a much more realistic and revolutionary *polit-*

ical thinker than Godwin. Rousseau's fundamental axioms that organized society, however calamitous its original advent might be deemed, was now necessary to human existence, and that now the specifically human problem was to moralize the organization of society, so that society might become the means to a new kind of human liberty—these positions were strictly incomprehensible to Godwin. The notion that men might need to be "forced to be free" was worse than a paradox to him; it was a blasphemy. Nevertheless, the conception is essential to any positive social thinking that is not to be stultified by atomism. That men may need to be "forced to be free" is merely an extreme assertion of the necessity of obedience to Law, without which a society cannot be imagined at all. The practical problem is to determine where the power that may "force men to be free" ought to reside, how it shall be placed there, and how men may be safeguarded from its perversion to quite other ends. These problems, into the consideration of which Rousseau entered as deeply as any man has done, can hardly be said to have been real to Godwin at all. His thought was, in essence, Protestant, millennial and anarchical.

So far as Godwin's conception can be reduced to practical terms, it meant the formation of a society within society—a little nucleus of the elect, practicing universal benevolence among themselves and seeking by their example to accelerate the normal process of political development, in which they participated without illusion and without repugnance. In this form, the kinship between his thought and that of the Independents is manifest; Godwinism is secular Sandemanianism. And the much-derided "perfectibility of man" is no more, and no less, than the reassertion in secular terms of the possibility of regeneration. That this regeneration ultimately involves the abolition of all coercive government is self-evident: in so far as the regeneration actually takes place what is good in such government becomes supererogatory, what is bad, a manifest evil.

But Godwin imagined that all government was coercive government. This is no more true than that all education is coercive, or indeed all experience whatsoever. Government is justified, in the eyes of imaginative reason, as the indispensable means for the formation of beneficent social habit—the habit of well-doing; to reject government, because it has been, and is always liable to be, diabolically abused, is to reject society itself. On the other hand, to accept the necessity of government does not involve rejecting the ideal of "universal benevolence." The assumption that these positions are destructive of one another, which Godwin appears always to be making, derives partly from the difficulty of expressing a religious intuition in secular terms, and partly from the evil condition of English government in his day. (pp. 250-52)

It was not so much against coercive government, as against coercion in general that Godwin protested. He was convinced that man could not enter the reign of love by compulsion, or even by organization. Hence the apparent paradox that political association for reform was almost as repugnant to him as governmental repression. Persuasion, working from individual to individual, was the only way to achieve a regeneration of society that was not superficial and specious. Godwin's seeming extravagance should not blind us to the element of truth in this. It is more apparent today than it was during the nineteenth century that political democracy will not yield more than you put into it in the way of social and moral regeneration. The difference between Godwin and Rousseau here is that Rousseau maintained (as I believe, rightly) that the very process of moral regeneration in the individual involved the recognition that organized society is necessary. The regenerated individual, in Rousseau's vision, works definitely to make society a fitting instrument of individual regeneration: to change secular society into a religious society.

This was beyond the range of Godwin's Independent and individualistic thought. But Godwin's faith in persuasion was not really excessive. There is no other process conceivable by which men can learn to love one another. What is odd is that Godwin appears to consider no other kind of persuasion than the least persuasive form of it, namely, logical argument. But that is only appearance. He means something different. (p. 253)

Posterity owes Godwin a rehabilitation which it will yet have to perform. For the moment he still lives on "in the serene twilight of a doubtful immortality," and in that deceitful medium he looms vaguely as a sort of fabulous monster of rationality. Yet when we come to regard him closely, he appears as one of the most human figures of his time. . . . The quality that is diffused through his whole work is rare and human and tender. In the eighteen-thirties, when even Charles Lamb was showing signs of panic at the doings of "Captain Swing," but no sign of comprehension of the appalling misery of the starved farm-laborer, Godwin was writing that "the merits and demerits of the public house were very unjustly rated by the fastidious among the more favored orders of society." The country ale-house was a place where discontent was fomented and sedition talked, said the frightened interests. Let them be shut! Godwin turns the tables with a vengeance. He calls the public house the laborer's university, where men are educated into citizenship. Such a degree of imaginative sympathy and tolerance toward the laborer was almost unparalleled among his most enlightened contemporaries. "Universal benevolence" was not a remote and ideal condition to Godwin: it was the way he felt. (pp. 256-57)

Such was Godwin's ideal: that men should be, instead of automata obedient to "positive institutions," "absolute human beings and genuine individuals." It is remarkable that he finds this ideal condition realized in the boy at play. That means simply that what he believed in, and strove to propagate as the goal of education, was human spontaneity and mutual tolerance. Somehow the spontaneity of the child was to be recreated in the grown and advised man.

From his noble conception of the individual, Godwin derived a criterion for a swift and searching criticism of the State. "The only legitimate object of political institutions," he wrote in one of the final chapters of *Political Justice*, "is the advantage of individuals. All that cannot be brought home to them—national wealth, prosperity and glory—can be advantageous only to the self-interested impostors." Godwin, who is generally reckoned one of the most abstract of political thinkers, was in fact one of the most concrete; but it is to be noted that even here his phrasing is deceptive. By "individuals" he means all individuals; and he takes it for granted that he will be so understood. The "wealth of nations" is humanly meaningless, and even a sinister equivocation, unless it involves the comfort and security of the individuals who compose the nation.

As often, the visionary is the true realist. He has the innocent eye which sees things as they are. But how was the condition to be achieved in which the welfare of individuals should become the sole object of political institutions? Ultimately, only by increasing the number of those to whom this *raison d'être* of government was self-evident. And Godwin could hardly help

being fascinated by the speculation that, if this became self-evident to many men, there would be no need of government. Undoubtedly he indulged this dream overmuch and rationalized it to excess; but that was partly because he lacked an idiom and philosophy of growth in which to express his thought. In fact, no man was more patient of the slowness of political and social improvement than Godwin. He was content to work a change in the hearts of a few by putting a vision before their imaginations. Thus a new motive would be introduced into that process of necessity which to the last Godwin believed governed the world of men. "The decisions of our will are always in obedience to the strongest motive." The acceptance of this psychological determinism Godwin, like Spinoza, held to be the highest spiritual achievement of man; it was for him the sole authentic fount of true tolerance. (pp. 258-59)

John Middleton Murry, "William Godwin," in his Heroes of Thought, *Julian Messner, Inc., 1938, pp. 245-59.*

ANGUS WILSON   (essay date 1951)

[Wilson is one of the most important English novelists of the postwar years. In the following excerpt, he defends Godwin as an original and sensitive novelist.]

[As] works of art [Godwin's novels] are all, in some degree, failures—three, at least, completely so. Excuses and explanations for Godwin's failure as a novelist can be offered: *Caleb Williams* is by far the most successful work, and it alone was written before external circumstances made writing a fight against time and debt and family warfare. Much of the failure of *St. Leon, Fleetwood,* and *Mandeville* may be accounted for by the pressure of miserable hackwork; the total collapse of *Cloudesly* and *Deloraine* may be charged to old age and spent forces. The fact remains, however, that Godwin's powers as a novelist were very limited; that, with every excuse made for difficult circumstances, he never developed them, and that this artistic limitation makes even the best, the most original of his novels, at times unendurable, and renders the weaker, the less original, worthless.

That any writer of such intellectual distinction, whose style and powers were so ill adapted to this medium, should have chosen to express himself in it, must seem curious. The choice is only partly, I think, explained by the growing popularity of the novel, and the large financial returns, which he always hoped for, but never succeeded in securing, to relieve his load of debts. The deeper reason lies in the nature of the material which he put into his novels. The guilt, the horror and the tragedy of the eighteenth century lay in the hinterland of the minds of its sensitive men. For many—politicians and men of affairs, even some artists—it was so well repressed, so covered over by hard work and harder play that it could only emerge in periodic madness which no formal social life, no tea with Mrs. Unwin or Mrs. Thrale, no midnight sessions in the House, or early morning gambling or debauch, could heal. Godwin found his relief in the symbolism of the novel. (pp. 38-9)

Had he lived half a century later, Godwin might well have given utterance to his emotions in a form that would have been adequate to its content, for by that time the creative genius of Dickens had transformed the old picaresque shape of *Pickwick Papers* into the great psychological social novels like *Bleak House* or *Our Mutual Friend*. The Victorian novelists were to carry the symbolisation of personal conflict in fictitious forms to the height of art. But Godwin was, in this respect, a pioneer without creative genius. He could imitate forms; he could not create them. The eighteenth-century forms which he had at hand were the least suited for the emotions he wished to express. The picaresque novels of Le Sage or Fielding or Smollett are no happy treasure-trove for the Freudian investigator, no deep reservoir of the subconscious. Yet it was the picaresque form with its central character moving from group to group that made the outline of Godwin's six novels. In *Caleb Williams* where 'things as they are'—the primary title of the novel—formed part of the subject matter, the old Fieldingesque method, so well adapted to simple social indignation, sufficed. Godwin, in the purely descriptive scenes of this novel—the gaol, the robbers' retreat, the lodgings of the odious Mr. Spurrel—showed a gift for caricature and dialogue that never appeared elsewhere in his work. But for the fall from grace of noble Falkland, his dark, resolute pursuit of Williams, the hero's nightmare flight from omnipotent anger, his final resolution and defiance, the forms of Fielding and Smollett gave no answer. So it was with the endless flight of St. Leon before the effects of his own magic powers, or of Mandeville's inescapable corruption from pride and suspicion.

Something Godwin may have found in the works of a greater novelist than Fielding or Smollett—Richardson, though mainly one suspects through his Continental imitators. Whether, however, by direct influence, or through the enervated medium of Rousseau or of Henry Mackenzie, there is an interesting parallel between Richardson's approach to his principal characters—his portrayal of the seeming omnipotence of the guilty Mr. B. and Lovelace, his emphasis upon the final victory of the innocent Pamela and Clarissa—and Godwin's greatest successes in his novels—the psychology of Falkland, Williams or Mandeville, and the moral order they symbolise. Richardson, of course, was an artist of a different class from Godwin, but there is also a similar parallel between their principal defects. The prolixity of *St. Leon, Caleb Williams,* and *Mandeville* springs, in some degree, from lack of formal sense, but it is also, in part, the logical outcome of that same itching obsession with human motive that produces the most tedious passages of *Clarissa* and *Grandison,* as it does the most brilliant.

Godwin, it must be noted, belongs on this side to the greatest stream of eighteenth-century fiction—that of Richardson, Prévost and Sade. Their analysis of power, guilt and pursuit were expressed in sexual symbols, his in the more trite language of social melodrama and historical romance.

In this choice of expression, of course, he followed the fashionable 'Gothic' trend of his day, the course of Mrs. Radcliffe and 'Monk' Lewis, the stage convention of his successful playwright friend, Holcroft, and his less successful playwright friend, Coleridge. . . . The stately, if somewhat stilted eighteenth-century style, so well suited for *Political Justice,* sits comically upon the narration of mystery and horror, and his reverence for the decencies of language forbade him the extravagances and vulgarities in which Lewis or Mrs. Radcliffe developed their Gothic tales. In this combination of formal language and romantic narrative he is more akin to Sir Walter Scott, whose work was still unwritten when *Caleb Williams* and *St. Leon* appeared. Indeed, some of his most successful passages—the description of the battle of Pavia and of the dungeons of Bethlem Gabor in *St. Leon,* the ill-fated Royalist rising in *Mandeville,* are a foretaste of Scott at his best.

But Gothic mysteries and historical romances were alike as inadequate as the picaresque to contain the subtle, psychological pessimism of Godwin's emotions. Like so many figures of the 'Romantic movement', he was drawn to the literature of an earlier age to satisfy his needs. (pp. 39-40)

There is a frightening chasm, a nightmare dissociation between the gloomy tortured lives of Godwin's heroes and the sweet reasonableness, the universal good sense of *Political Justice,* though the horror of the novels gives full answer to the facile criticism of Godwin's anarchism on the grounds of psychological naïveté and failure to consider the problem of evil. It is true that the dichotomy is there, damaging both political treatise and romance, but Godwin was fully aware of this schizophrenic tendency. After the publication of *Caleb Williams* in which he bade defiance to the morose tyranny of his Calvinist childhood—father, God and all the powers there are—he attempted in every successive novel to suggest an answer to man's solitude, fear and isolating pride. His answers were of two kinds, both, of course, embedded in the thought of his age. In *Fleetwood* we are offered the ennobling answer of man communing with nature in the person of the sage—almost Chinese in type—M. Ruffigny, who from the majestic heights of the Alps—the El Dorado of so much eighteenth-century aspiration—gives counsels of order, decency, the nobility of man and the sublimity of the rivers and hills. The excellent family of the Macneils, in the same novel, resident among the more picturesque but still ennobling scenes of the Lake District, suggest the second solution—the simple, cultivated, busy life of domestic bliss. But it is in the almost Swiss Family Robinson happiness of St. Leon's retreat on the Swiss lakeside that we get the crown of these two escapes from the awful choice between solitude and despair or the pursuit of power and degradation. It is in St. Leon's wife, Marguerite—the image of Mary Wollstonecraft—that the highest virtues are embodied. In the sublimity of nature, in the deep communings of a solitary mind is shown the path of Wordsworth. In the simple pleasures of amiable intercourse, in the domestic fireside, in the little polite group of compatible tempers, is offered the eighteenth-century answer. It was thus with his gardening schemes and his letter-writing that Shenstone fought melancholy; it was so with his hares and his tea with Mrs. Unwin that Cowper fought the inevitability of Hell; this was the solace of Streatham's garden and Dr. Burney's drawing-room for Johnson's agonised mind. The flames of the Manichaean dilemma leapt up and licked at the sensitive mind in the eighteenth century as in our own. For all those who cannot follow Mr. Huxley into his Yogic retreat from their ardour, or escape with Mr. Graham Greene into the solace of the Church, for all those who hate the forces of power—whether of *laissez-faire* capitalism or State tyranny—and must yet find their solution in man's own natural goodness, the novels of Godwin, with all their absurdities, demand attention. (p. 40)

Angus Wilson, "The Novels of William Godwin," in World Review, *n.s. Vol. 28, June, 1951, pp. 37-40.*

P. N. FURBANK (essay date 1955)

[*Furbank surveys Godwin's novels and* Political Justice, *focusing on his "exact study and dramatization of morbid passion."*]

To read one's way through Godwin is to get more than one has bargained for. He is a richer study, there is more *to* him, than one is often given to believe; at least, this was the present writer's experience. One finds, it is true, an exploded thinker and a discredited character—a figure both comic and disreputable; but one finds also a serious artist and the absorbing history of a long intellectual development.

To understand Godwin it is necessary to take both his political writings and his novels into account, and to see the real links between them. For the novels are not reflections of the political writings; they are the complement of them, and in some ways a counterblast to them. The novels, apart from *Caleb Williams,* have a low reputation, I think certainly an unjustifiably low one. In part, this is because critics have as often as not been unwilling to accept the genre of his novels. It is one that we do not happen to have many examples of in English, though they are common in other languages: I mean the dramatized history of a state of mind, on the lines of *René, Werter, Hero of Our Own Times* etc. It is a form of confessional literature, and in France takes some of its inspiration from Rousseau's *Confessions.* (In England, so far as it exists, it derives in part from religious confessions: there is a fine example in Hogg's *Confessions of a Justified Sinner.*) It is a form which comes into being with the Romantic revival, and is, perhaps, the Romantic substitute for tragedy. Its most natural subject-matter is various forms of misanthropy. The greatest flowering of this genre is to be found in Dostoevsky: and the reader brought up on *Notes from Underground* and *The Insulted and Injured* should have no difficulty in recognizing the sort of thing Godwin is writing. It is important to point this out, however, because in the past Godwin has sometimes been linked with the 'roman philosophique' of Holcroft and Bage, which is quite a different genre—a species of picaresque novel with Voltairean dialogue, a form distinctly less important in the history of the novel.

There is a real affinity between Godwin and Dostoevsky, for all that the latter is so incomparably the greater writer. They are both truly first-hand historians of the conscience. Both are always fresh in their discoveries about the soul, because always true to their own inner experience. Godwin's later novels are almost intolerably bleak, the tract of experience that they deal with is excessively narrow and hideous in kind, but still burningly felt, and in its own way fresh—a contribution to our knowledge of psychology. The stir of life is there.—I speak of *St. Leon, Fleetwood* and *Mandeville.* It is less true of the last two novels, *Cloudesly* and *Deloraine.*

Common opinion is in the right, and *Caleb Williams* is certainly Godwin's best complete novel; and it has particular reasons for success which the later novels do not possess. All Godwin's novels are autobiographical or confessional, but *Caleb Williams* is so in a subtler and more adventurous way than the others. To put it briefly, the novel is a highly dramatized symbolical picture of Godwin himself in the act of writing *Political Justice.* I think it is important to point this out at once, for some of the brilliance and originality of the conception is missed if we fail to realize it. (pp. 214-15)

Caleb Williams is clearly Godwin himself, Falkland the *ancien régime,* and the opening of the trunk is the writing of *Political Justice.* The secret of the trunk is the secret which Godwin brings to the light of day in *Political Justice,* the guilty secret of government: and in describing Caleb's fierce glee and terror at making the discovery he is describing his own emotion at conceiving the theories of that work.

It is plain that Godwin was in a state of extreme excitement at the time of writing his famous political work. The cold-blooded rationalism of *Political Justice,* its apparently placid nihilism, was conceived in passion. It looks at first sight a paradox that the sedate anarchist and pedantic advocate of universal benevolence should also be the painter of the wild scenes of passion and mania that fill *Caleb Williams;* but the explanation is simple, it is that the emotions that fill the novel are those which Godwin himself experienced in writing the celebrated treatise. 'Show me that you are afraid of my entertaining certain opinions or learning certain principles, and you will infallibly sooner or later awaken my curiosity': so says Godwin in *Political Justice;* and to satisfy this curiosity in whatever spirit of calm inquiry is in imagination most desperate, perhaps the most guilty, of acts.

The doctrine of *Political Justice* is that truth has only to be heard to prevail. . . . Tyrannical government holds its power not by force but by imposition. It hides its tyrannies behind the plausible fallacies of marriage and property-rights and the sanctity of pledges, etc. To detect the fallacies is the whole of the battle. Touch the *secrets* of government, and, as with Falkland, you have touched the sore. In *Political Justice* Godwin talks as though the touching could be done with impunity, and seems to wish to represent the whole process of revolution as an innocent one. In *Caleb Williams* he does justice to the guilty side of the picture. The book, of course, was written under the shadow of the Terror.

What a powerful fable Godwin's plot is! And how brilliantly its implications are worked out. See for instance how much he makes of the complexity of Caleb's motives in prying into his noble master's secrets. Caleb's ruling passion is his curiosity, and it is both a good and an evil. It is this that has enabled him to improve his mind: and it is no vulgar curiosity. . . . On the other hand it has all the signs of an evil passion when it leads him to spy upon his master. . . . His most generous qualities (like Falkland's) help to precipitate him towards his fatal step. (pp. 215-17)

Falkland's tragedy is to be the victim of his own best impulses. In original character he is nobler than his servant; he has been brought up in the cult of honour and chivalry, and it is his passionate devotion to these which hurries him into the most despicable of crimes. It is a psychological law for Godwin that the best is in danger of turning into the worst. Falkland's tyrannical cruelty springs from hysteria, and not from original baseness. This is Godwin's way of doing justice to the *ancien régime.*

Godwin, in fact, has achieved something very difficult in this novel. He has found a human situation to parallel the impersonal issue of revolution: not a replica of it in miniature, but a psychological analogue. Something which, unlike the abstract issue, does not frustrate our sympathies at every turn. To do this, he depends very much on a favourite concept, the equivocalness of innocence and guilt: the book has a number of surprises, arising from this idea. (p. 218)

There is a further paradox, closely related to the guilty-innocence one, in Godwin's conception of necessity. The destiny which seems so cruel, destroying Falkland and turning Caleb into a trembling victim, turns out to have been beneficent after all. Caleb's vicious curiosity is revealed as the instrument of Providence—like the eye of God in the cautionary volume on which Godwin partly based his story, 'perpetually pursuing the guilty, and laying open their most hidden retreat to the light of day'. (pp. 218-19)

Caleb Williams . . . differs from the rest of Godwin in having symbolical applications. I have discussed the symbolical side of it, because it seems to me so interestingly conceived. It represents the writer's guilt-situation *vis-à-vis* revolution more satisfactorily than either Schiller's *Robbers* or Wordsworth's *Borderers.* (p. 219)

What *Caleb Williams* has in common with Godwin's other novels is the exact study and dramatization of morbid passion. Godwin is expert in describing the moment in which a passion first seizes upon the mind. He is the great master of *possession*. To read of Falkland's reaction to Tyrrel's insult is to know at once that something more than commonplace literary psychology is involved. . . . *St. Leon* gives us a whole series of these moments of possession. The book, indeed, is an analysis of a man's career in terms of such moments. Again, in *Fleetwood,* the newly married hero brings back his bride to his childhood home, and next morning shows her what had been his favourite room. He is about to rhapsodize about his love for it, when she innocently remarks that she thinks she will have it for her own. His 'animal spirits' are 'suddenly driven back upon his heart' by this; and a career of obsession begins for him.

Fleetwood and *Mandeville* are purely psychological studies, two case-histories of obsession. *St. Leon,* although also a case-history—in Gothic guise—has in addition some symbolical reference to contemporary political issues, and so stands nearer to *Caleb Williams.*

In his treatment of the passions, Godwin, in his own queer way, takes something from Elizabethan dramatists. The sudden madnesses of passion that attack Fleetwood and Falkland are those of Leontes and Lear: a mind hitherto immune to violent experience is suddenly swamped by it, and overset by the suddenness of the onrush. Fleetwood, in particular, is the Leontes *de nos jours. Fleetwood* is a duller work than its two predecessors, till we reach the third volume and Fleetwood's marriage: then it takes fire. (This part is probably Godwin's finest achievement outside *Caleb Williams.*) The novel is the natural history of, and also a satire on, a Man of Feeling. (pp. 219-20)

[*Fleetwood*] puts one in mind of . . . Jacobean tragedy; of Tourneur, for instance. Discovering the Elizabethan dramatists was the great intellectual event of [Godwin's] middle years. He speaks with joy of the immense new prospect of excitement it opened up to him. . . . The important likeness, of course, is in conception—in a view of the workings of passion—and not in language. When he is not vehement, Godwin is painfully prosy in language, and even his most vehement utterances often suffer in this way, though we forget the weakness in the fierceness and hurry of the sentiment. In dialogue he has a special aptitude for short, intense exchanges. . . . (p. 222)

Whilst Godwin obviously lacks certain qualities of the dramatist, he possesses some of the advantages of the novelist. He can handle relationships as well as individual psychology; and here too he has original discoveries to offer. Particularly is this true of *Fleetwood,* in which, as a change from the preceding novels, Godwin intended to deal with everyday life and manners. The story, according to Godwin, is to consist of 'such adventures, as for the most part have occurred to at least one-half of the Englishmen now existing'. . . . Many of his observations of behaviour and touches of feeling are truly original and good. He not only examines shades of feeling with great precision, he can make them play a part in the course of events. For instance, once Fleetwood has banished his wife from his house, she is inflexible to any suggestion of reconciliation. She considers that he would never have treated her so, if she had had a dowry. And on reflection, we realize she is right. Some time after Fleetwood has begun to woo her, she loses her dowry through a fraud. Fleetwood has no need of the money, and he loves her no less; but his relations with her change, notwithstanding. (pp. 223-24)

Godwin's character perhaps especially fitted him for his treatment of the passions. One seems to see him so clearly, the prosaic, argumentative prodigy of the dissenting academy, famous for his calm and unimpassioned discussion, a heart unusually unpractised in the emotions, devoted to a 'fearless tranquillity' as he calls it, suddenly infected by one great passionate excitement (I mean, at the time of writing *Political Justice*) and thereafter catching the passions, and observing himself catch them, one after one, like belated childhood diseases. . . . What often strikes one about Godwin is that he does not *want* to believe in the importance of the feelings; he is made to admit it rather against his will. Even then, he is always eager to explain their existence on mechanical lines. (p. 224)

[Few writers] have written more movingly of the pains of human existence; but fewer still at such a moment would have been so prosaically frank. He lets us down with a bump; and yet in so doing he in a way makes us admire him the more. I find this a great attraction in a character that is certainly no great shakes by ordinary standards. No doubt the cult of 'perfect sincerity' often enough turns Godwin into an object of fun, if not of contempt. He clings to the doctrine, pathetically, absurdly, often disreputably. (pp. 226-27)

P. N. Furbank, "Godwin's Novels," in Essays in Criticism, *Vol. V, No. 3, July, 1955, pp. 214-28.*

JAMES T. BOULTON   (essay date 1963)

[*Boulton discusses the didacticism and psychological analysis in Godwin's writings, as well as the influence of William Shakespeare, Samuel Johnson, Coleridge, and Wordsworth on his use of language in the novels.*]

In his novels Godwin wished to possess his readers of 'all the circumstances' bearing on an individual in any given situation, the circumstances being both material and psychological. Psychological analysis was his *forté* as he realised:

> the thing in which my imagination revelled the most freely, was the analysis of the private and internal operations of the mind, employing my metaphysical dissecting knife in tracing and laying bare the involutions of motive, and recording the gradually accumulating impulses, which led the personages I had to describe primarily to adopt the particular way of proceeding in which they afterwards embarked.

The novelist's 'dissecting knife' is both a valuable and a dangerous tool: it can lay bare motive with great vividness and clarity, it can be used to demonstrate the connection between impulse and action, and so on, but if its use becomes an end in itself the patient is reduced to the level of an 'object' and ceases to be a living creature. . . . [It] is well to remember that Godwin was, as his prefaces make clear, a didactic novelist; at his best he surmounts the obstacles this title suggests, but at other times he was obstructed by them. 'We will enlighten you', he remarks in *Political Justice* and it is when this determination takes hold of the novelist—whether the enlightenment be moral or intellectual, through an exhaustive examination of motive and intention or through the giving of information—that he becomes tedious. And even if our final judgment emphasises his creative success in, say, *Caleb Williams* or the final volume of *Fleetwood,* the first two volumes of that novel and many wearying passages in *St. Leon* among others must not be left out of account.

The experience of writing *Political Justice* must not of course be held responsible only for Godwin's failures; it also contributed significantly to his success. As in that work, so in the novels, the essence of his manner is an inexorable deliberateness; 'the chain and combination of events, that proceeds *systematically* from link to link' is what fascinates him and gives a distinctive comprehensiveness to his novels. It is this which lends to the pursuit of Caleb by the seemingly omnipresent Falkland, or to the endless frustrations of St. Leon, or the gradual and inevitable oncoming jealousy in Fleetwood, an almost nightmarish dimension of relentless inevitability. All Godwin's chief characters suffer the agony described by St. Leon—'the snare, woven and drawing close round me on all sides for my destruction'—and if this experience is to be agonising it must be slow but not ponderous; there must be a high degree of inwardness in the presentation of characters and not mere psychological 'information' given about them; and general truths deriving from specific situations should seem to arise inevitably rather than being a principal objective.

To take an example: the following passage records Caleb's decision to watch Falkland in order to discover his apparently guilty secret:

> The instant I had chosen this employment for myself, I found a strange sort of pleasure in it. To do what is forbidden always has its charms, because we have an indistinct apprehension of something arbitrary and tyrannical in the prohibition. To be a spy upon Mr. Falkland! That there was danger in the employment, served to give an alluring pungency to the choice. I remembered the stern reprimand I had received, and his terrible looks; and the recollection gave a kind of tingling sensation, not altogether unallied to enjoyment. The further I advanced, the more the sensation was irresistible. I seemed to myself perpetually upon the brink of being countermined, and perpetually roused to guard my designs. The more impenetrable Mr. Falkland was determined to be, the more uncontrollable was my curiosity. Through the whole, my alarm and apprehension of personal danger had a large mixture of frankness and simplicity, conscious of meaning no ill, that made me continually ready to say every thing that was upon my mind, and would not suffer me to believe that, when things were brought to the test, any one could be seriously angry with me.

Here Godwin's slow, deliberate analysis is at its best. His concentration is on the movement of Caleb's mind, but his own fascination in the amalgam of a curious terror and pleasure, and in the attraction of 'brinkmanship' to a mentality which is at once alert and naïve, comes strongly through. In other words, though the record of this mental state is Caleb's, the zest with which it is communicated arises from the creative pleasure Godwin experienced while writing it. His tendency to generalise is kept subservient to the interest in Caleb's state of mind; the second sentence is a general statement, but it is valid, pertinent, and so placed that we cannot forget the specific situation that gives rise to it. And, finally, there is nothing static about the prose; the analysis is not an academic exercise, but is justified because it advances the plot and records, at a significant moment, the psychological condition of a central figure.

In such a passage—and the mental torment Fleetwood suffers after his marriage provides further examples—the psychological insights are first-rate and the deliberate slowness with which they are revealed largely accounts for Godwin's success: one feels that this *is* the way in which a man's mind motivated by both honesty and self-justification would work. But when urgency and creative excitement are absent the slowness develops into tedium, pleasurable discovery into laborious informativeness; habits of thinking and writing formed while composing *Political Justice* then become deleterious. (pp. 233-35)

Between these two qualitative extremes is a mid-way level of writing which might be described as analytic 'statement'; it lacks the dramatic immediacy and inwardness of the first passage and relies on first-person statements *about* a psychological condition. It is the equivalent in Godwin's novels of the descriptive method used in *Political Justice* to disprove the optimistic philosophers; in both analysis is present but the language keeps the felt experience at arm's length. (p. 236)

Godwin frequently fails to distinguish between conceptual truth arrived at through argument and logical exposition such as is appropriate in *Political Justice,* and the imaginative truth of a novel which is embodied in the facts of a created situation and validated by the intensity and completeness of our response to it. In this connection, Godwin's generalising mode, necessary in *Political Justice,* often proves deleterious in the novels. . . . *St. Leon* frequently suffers from this defect. Having modified his views about 'the culture of the heart' by 1799, Godwin takes every opportunity in this novel to speak of sexual attachment with 'the warmest eulogium', but he does so in general terms more appropriate to *Political Justice.* (p. 237)

A similarly uneven awareness of the difference between philosophical treatise and imaginative literature accounts for Godwin's variable success in handling dialogue. . . . [For] the most part Godwin's imagination is actively engaged in creating characters whose speech idiom is alive and appropriate. Particularly in [*St. Leon*] does he score with the many low-life characters; the very fact that they lack the philosophical sophistication that Godwin was accustomed to meet with in his personal life, the fact that they live intellectually in a recognisably different world compelled him to think creatively about their idiom. This was not invariably the case. In *St. Leon,* where a negro character appears, the narrator disdains 'the mimic toil of inventing a jargon . . . suitable to the lowness of his condition'. In *Caleb Williams,* however, Godwin does not sidestep the problem in this way, nor do we feel that he has invented a 'jargon'; consequently, characters like Tyrrel and Grimes live through their spoken language. Without a living idiom they would be nothing better than properties in a horror novel. . . . [For] the most part jailers and thieves, boors and labourers in *Caleb Williams* are made convincing by means of their idiom; they, too, form part of a society organised on one central principle of tyranny which affects the behaviour of all classes—and it was the recognition of this fact that stimulated Godwin's creative imagination.

When this compulsion is inoperative he lapses too easily into an undistinguished style which responds neither to the speaker nor to the occasion; it is solely a vehicle for the communication of ideas. To give proof of this claim would be tedious; suffice it to say that Godwin is capable merely of turning into direct speech the kind of meditation already quoted (on marriage) from *St. Leon.* At such times he notably lacks what can be called a common, workaday level of style which will crisply and effectively carry him over stretches of ordinary narrative;

instead he often has recourse to a clumsy version of the language he had been accustomed to using in *Political Justice.* (pp. 238-40)

Another test of Godwin's sensitivity to appropriate style is to examine the echoes of other writers—principally Shakespeare and Johnson—that one frequently comes across in the novels. Johnson's manner . . . provided some advantages (amplitude, comprehensiveness, attention to nuances and distinctions, and the like) as a model for the writing of *Political Justice;* it is a handicap as a *general* guide for writing a novel. . . . 'Learned without ostentation, refined without foppery, elegant without effeminacy'. This description of Falkland exactly reproduces the rhythm and balance of Johnson's remarks on Addison's prose style, and it is not out of place—but St. Leon's memory of his mother's affection is less appropriately cast in a Johnsonian mould:

> I was her darling and her pride, her waking study, and her nightly dream. Yet I was not pampered into corporeal imbecility, or suffered to rust in inactivity of mind.

Once Godwin drops into the Johnsonian triad of the first sentence he is, as it were, led into the pseudo-Johnsonian pomposity of the second. . . . And it is this accumulation of verbal weight that is one of Godwin's chief failings.

But it is Shakespeare on whom Godwin most often leans. In *Caleb Williams,* where Godwin's imagination works most effectively, the source-play for the majority of his allusions is *Macbeth,* the Shakespearean tragedy that is undoubtedly closest in mood and story to his own novel. Macbeth and Falkland are both pursued and pursuing, both are inexorably caught in the net of their own making, and both are the victims of ambition. To be reminded, therefore, of the play by 'curses, deep, not loud', 'misfortune comes so thick upon me', '"sleep no more"', or 'the milk of human kindness', might be regarded as valid and purposeful. But one's conviction is weakened by looking at the contexts of these allusions. The first relates to the social reaction to Tyrrel's brutal treatment of Emily, the second is spoken by the dispossessed tenant-farmer Hawkins, the third has reference to the suffering Caleb endured from the discovery of Falkland's secret, and the last is applied to the grotesque female who cooks for the band of thieves which befriends Caleb. There is indeed no thematic consistency about the use of these allusions; Godwin does not introduce them with a full understanding of their value, but indiscriminately as they occur to him by simple association. The extreme example of an allusion used as a cliché occurs in *St. Leon,* where the hero considers the advantages of wealth: 'I contemplated the honour, love, obedience, troops of friends, which are so apt to attend upon wealth.' The words are mere counters which happen to have been strung together and remain as a unit in Godwin's mind; the fact that Macbeth was lamenting the absence of these things and that the allusion inevitably evokes a sense of tragic decline and loss does not perturb Godwin in the least. (pp. 241-42)

In the final volume of *Fleetwood* Godwin blatantly exploits the Othello-Iago-Desdemona situation: Fleetwood is driven insane with jealousy because of his wife's supposed infidelity with his nephew, the soldier Kenrick, through the machinations of Gifford, also his nephew. The reliance on Shakespeare is in itself no disgrace, and it must be said that the device produces some of Godwin's most powerful writing. He relies on a detailed memory of *Othello:* Gifford's techniques were all learnt from Iago; Fleetwood is given a letter by Gifford which seems fully to incriminate Mary; he visits her bedroom, finds her asleep, disbelieves the affectionate words she speaks to him in a dream, and steals a kiss from her; and finally he denounces her. And yet, not only does Godwin allude, not to Iago but to Hamlet when describing Gifford—'thus did this damnable calumniator lead me on, with broken sentences, and "ambiguous givings-out"'—but when Fleetwood imagines Mary to be set on calming his misgivings he remarks:

> It was thus that Cleopatra inveigled Mark Antony to his ruin, when she had determined to play him false with his confident Dolabella. As my wife left the room, I saw her apply her handkerchief to her eyes. . . .

Such evidence of insensibility is scarcely credible.

Yet this kind of literary and verbal insensitivity is frequently found. In *Caleb Williams* even Falkland at times almost degenerates into the conventional figure of a horror novel, the man who gnashes his teeth and stamps in rage. . . . (p. 243)

On the other hand, it is vital to note occasions when Godwin's choice of language and metaphor is precise and effective. Three examples must suffice. The first is a brief one from *Caleb Williams;* it occurs when Caleb establishes his initially idyllic relationship with Laura Denison:

> While our familiarity gained in duration, it equally gained in that subtlety of communication by which it seemed to shoot forth its roots in every direction.

The metaphor is unobtrusive, almost casual, but it acts exactly as it should, stressing the living yet invisible growth of a developing acquaintance. The second comes from the point at which St. Leon experiences immortality as distinct from merely contemplating the idea of it. Godwin tries to capture the sensation vividly, and does so through an exploration of the difference between the Christian, who believes in 'eternal bliss' but has only a 'faint and indistinct picture' of it in his mind, and

> the feelings of the celebrated apostles, who had been taken up into the third heaven, and had beheld the new Jerusalem with all its jaspers, its chrysolites, its emeralds, and its sapphires.

The parallel is just, it is worked out with care, and one can feel the writer's determination to think concretely about the abstract issue: 'It is so different a thing to conceive a proposition theoretically, and to experience it in practice.' And the final example, from *Fleetwood,* involves a discrimination between the man of 'simple perception' (Sir Charles Gleed) and the man of 'imagination' (Fleetwood himself). The distinction is made by contrasting the responses to a landscape of a farmer and a poet, the former seeing the detail of soil, weather, and crops, the latter seeing 'a living scene, animated by a mysterious power, whose operations he contemplated with admiration and reverence'. 'The farmer's were perceptions; his were feelings'. That the distinction was a commonplace in the late eighteenth and early nineteenth centuries is immaterial; it is important that it should be made, and Godwin makes it with great care and vividness.

This is to take only one illustration from each of three novels, but the common factor in all is significant. Each example—and they were not initially chosen with this in mind—involves an attempt by Godwin to think precisely about a feature of human character, to assess and capture imaginatively some moral perception. Behind each lies an abstract issue which had stimulated the philosopher in him—the nature of human relationships, the difference between theory and practice, or the nature of perception; the intellectual stimulus excited clear, creative thought about the characters and situations which embodied these abstractions; and the result is fresh, lucid, and fluent prose. . . . On the other hand, where Godwin is not intellectually as well as emotionally involved the outcome is unconvincing. He is not so involved for most of the first two volumes of *Fleetwood,* for example, hence their tediousness for long stretches. The rakes and mistresses with whom Fleetwood associates do not come alive, they are merely verbal forms without body; consequently, when we learn that Fleetwood had 'passed the Rubicon of vice' and had become 'hardened and brutalised' we note them as statements that mean nothing on our pulses. Indeed, at one point Godwin implicitly confesses his lack of involvement. Fleetwood visits the court of Louis XV and Godwin remarks that it would be 'superfluous' for him to describe the depravity of a court which 'the reader may find in so many volumes amply and ambitiously detailed'. In thus avoiding his responsibility he may have had in mind those 'innocent and inexperienced readers' for whose safety he is scrupulous in *St. Leon,* but the truth is that he is writing as an observer and not as a man imaginatively involved in human actions. (pp. 244-45)

A major reason for the failure of *St. Leon* lies in Godwin's design: to '"mix human feelings and passions with incredible situations, and thus render them impressive and interesting"'; *St. Leon,* in other words, is Godwin's "Ancient Mariner." The story was to be of 'the miraculous class', necessitating the constant invention of novel and surprising situations; Godwin's ingenuity is kept at full stretch, but the reader becomes wearied by an incredible sequence of events, each of which increases the hero's misfortunes. There are incidental successes within the novel; even in the improbable happenings centring on the giant, Bethlem Gabor, Godwin's amazement at the resilience of the human mind brings St. Leon alive and momentarily saves him from being a puppet of circumstance; but as a whole the novel is insufficiently pervaded by intellectual vigour and, because of its design, Godwin is too intent on manipulating events. If, however, *St. Leon* is Coleridgean, *Caleb Williams* and *Fleetwood* are Wordsworthian. In them he is concerned with '*things as they are*'; his purpose is to give the charm of novelty to things of every day. The first is a story of 'uncommon events' but 'entirely within the laws and established course of nature'; the second, even more Wordsworthian, is to give 'a certain kind of novelty' to 'common and ordinary adventures'. Thus, although inventive ingenuity was still called for, it was working on the material of ordinary life and—equally important—within a society in which operated the moral forces Godwin had examined in *Political Justice.* That *Fleetwood* does not make a forceful impact on the reader until the final volume is significant. . . . [The] novel comes to life with dramatic suddenness when a false estimate of rank and wealth distorts the moral perception of the central character, a man—as Godwin said of Burke—who was a strange mixture of 'dark and saturnine temper' with 'urbanity and a susceptibility of the kinder affections'.

This final volume of *Fleetwood* is the nearest approach both in mood and successful achievement to Godwin's best novel, *Caleb Williams.* And what most distinguishes these two among his other novels—besides a more intelligent choice of form,

A portrait of Mary Wollstonecraft shortly before her death.

the stimulus of intellectual excitement, and the concentration on 'things as they are'— is the presence in both of a powerful central figure driven to near insanity by a regard for rank and social eminence, a veneration for the values of aristocracy. He is a man in both cases whose moral vision is distorted by this obsessive veneration; he earns of the other characters and of the reader sympathy and admiration mixed with regret for misused talents; he excites a response, indeed, such as Burke aroused in Godwin. . . . [Here] was the most fearful evidence of the power of a traditional social morality to corrupt even the best human qualities, and the creative results, above all in *Caleb Williams,* are manifest. Instead of characters dissected as mere objects (as in *St. Leon* or the early volumes of *Fleetwood*), we are presented with an excited series of discoveries about the springs of human action; instead of the language of abstract speculation habitually used in *Political Justice,* we have an idiom that is generally alive and flexible; and instead of a writer who is a kind of bemused schoolmaster, we have Godwin imaginatively resolving the problem raised by a contemporary situation. (pp. 247-49)

James T. Boulton, "William Godwin, Philosopher and Novelist," in his The Language of Politics in the Age of Wilkes and Burke, *Routledge & Kegan Paul, 1963, pp. 207-49.*

WALLACE AUSTIN FLANDERS (essay date 1967)

[*Flanders interprets* St. Leon *as an elaboration of the literary techniques Godwin used in* Caleb Williams *and of his philosophical theories in* Political Justice. *He argues, in addition, that in*

St. Leon *Godwin employed "the supernatural trappings of Gothic fiction for didactic purposes."*]

Godwin employed in **St. Leon** much more directly than he did in **Caleb Williams** the characteristic techniques of Gothic fiction, and used them to illustrate and elaborate on the ideas published earlier in **Political Justice.** Thus the novel is interesting partly as it extends the range of Gothic fiction, not so much in its introduction of "'criminal' and 'alchemical' elements," but in its combination of the two dominant schools of novel writing in the 1790's: the Gothic and the "philosophical." (p. 533)

Although there is in **Caleb Williams** an interest in subjective experience much like that of the Gothic novel, there is no attempt to introduce the supernatural, either directly, as in *The Monk,* or indirectly, as in Mrs. Radcliffe's pseudo horrors. **St. Leon,** on the other hand, uses the supernatural trappings of Gothic fiction for didactic purposes. In **Caleb Williams,** the institutions representing the evils which Godwin attacks are recognizably English and contemporary; in **St. Leon** Godwin turns to the strangeness and exoticism of the supernatural, to foreign countries and remote periods of history for a setting in which to play out the consequences of his ideas.

Godwin's reputation as a sternly rational thinker would not lead one to expect him to indulge in the sensational delights of Gothic fiction; yet, much like other writers of Gothic novels, in his fiction he was always interested in abnormal states of mind issuing from corruptions of human nature and reason. Like Swift, he seems to be more fascinated with aberrations than the norm he upholds. Then there were other reasons for exploring the Gothic style; **St. Leon** was perhaps the first of Godwin's mature works to be inspired by commercial reasons. Even though Godwin never ignores his serious purpose in the novel, he adopted its mode at least in part to attract readers, having the dual aims of the professional novelist and the moralist. (p. 534)

In spite of its Gothic framework, the central purpose of the novel is to inculcate moral truths. In the first edition of **Political Justice** Godwin classed literature as one of the "three principal causes of moral improvement." He said that "few engines can be more powerful, and at the same time more salutary in their tendency, than literature. Without enquiring for the present into the cause of this phenomenon, it is sufficiently evident in fact, that the human mind is strongly infected with prejudice and mistake. The various opinions prevailing in different countries and among different classes of men upon the same subject, are most innumerable; and yet of all these opinions only one can be true. Now the effectual way of extirpating these prejudices and mistakes seems to be literature." Godwin's speaking of literature as an "engine" is typical of his attitudes; he later spoke of the novel in the Preface to **Caleb Williams** as a "vehicle" for teaching "a valuable lesson" [see excerpt dated 1794]. Many of the moral concerns prominent in **Caleb Williams** recur in **St. Leon,** often in a similar guise, and this recurrence shows the constancy of his novelistic aims. (pp. 535-36)

The supernatural elements in **St. Leon** are closely involved with the central theme. The effects of St. Leon's possession of superhuman powers is the central subject of the novel, and their appeal to his ambition is his downfall. In St. Leon's career, as in Falkland's in **Caleb Williams,** Godwin shows that power which divides man from man is a curse. St. Leon's ambition and pride make him dissatisfied with a simple but

secure life in Switzerland. . . . Godwin has much to say in **Political Justice** about the effects of bad education on the moral state of both individuals and the society they form. In St. Leon's case vicious education has produced a temperament which leads him to turn away from the principles of justice and morality, based for Godwin perhaps most firmly in the dictate of absolute sincerity, to a systematic practice of deception for the purpose of furthering his ambition.

The secrecy which St. Leon is forced to maintain is the agent of his undoing, for in hiding his resources and his action he cuts himself off from all mankind. (pp. 536-37)

In the essay **"On Awakening the Mind"** in *The Enquirer* . . . Godwin stated that "Man is a social being. In society the interests of individuals are intertwisted with each other, and cannot be separated." This belief, whose operation in Godwin's mind is very close to that of sentimental benevolence, is fundamental to his ideas on political justice, and was important in determining the idea of **St. Leon.** The novel shows the calamity resulting when a man tries to alter his social relationships by untwisting the natural bonds tying man to man. In St. Leon's hyperbolic case these bonds are the basic conditions of human existence, such as the necessity of labor and the inevitability of death. When St. Leon suffers for the first time the fear and scorn of the ignorant, with whom he would never associate on a personal level but who now join in society's suspicious rejection of him, Godwin shows that even this apparently inconsequential breaking of the social bond is a "calamity." . . . Every step St. Leon takes toward freeing himself from the common hazards and necessities of human life takes away as well a portion of the potential happiness resulting from his common humanity and leaves him more unnatural and miserable. He refrains from taking the Elixir of Life until his preservation depends on it. Its baleful effect . . . is rather to heighten his sense of isolation than to reinvigorate him. . . . (pp. 537-38)

This misery adds up to a terrible indictment of what St. Leon has done. He learns that "it is indeed absurd, it may be termed profanation, to talk of solitary pleasure." . . . The word "profanation" indicates Godwin's meaning, for he condemns St. Leon's power as a profanation of human nature and the moral order of the world—parallels to God in Godwin's atheistic universe. The implications of this condemnation extend to any powers and privileges a man may claim which are not the common property of humanity. The source of the wrong here is the same as in **Caleb Williams:** like Falkland, St. Leon uses prerogatives to wrest from life what he desires and fails to gain respect for himself naturally and honestly. This divorce from natural justice makes both characters solitary and miserable. In **St. Leon** the supernatural becomes a metaphor for what is depicted in natural terms in **Caleb Williams.**

The novel's treatment of domestic affection as a morally cultivating exercise of benevolence is closely related to the main theme of the novel and therefore to the novel's Gothic elements. The natural blessings of domestic happiness are opposed to the objects of St. Leon's ambition. The corruption of his ideas brought about through his education and his life in Paris led him to accept unnatural and antisocial powers in the place of honest labor and affection. He never regains the flawed happiness of the sojourn in Switzerland after he abandons the confidence and hence the love of his family; no benevolence or philanthropy he attempts can succeed to the extent of the limited good he could have promoted by serving them. The miscarriage of his attempts at social benevolence in Hungary illustrates his failure in trying to transcend natural limitations. The loss of the respect of all mankind follows upon his rejection of natural affection and the social bonds of family life. This emphasis clearly reveals the middle-class sentimentalist leanings of Godwin's apparently revolutionary "rationalistic" ethics, which were strongly but perhaps less evidently present in his earlier *Political Justice*.

The didactic intentions of Godwin's development of these themes is well served by the wanderings of his outcast hero. St. Leon is morally condemned because his choice of evil destroys his bonds with humanity, but in his wanderings Godwin has many opportunities to display a variety of social injustices in society's reactions to the outcast himself. This device lends sympathy to St. Leon without changing Godwin's estimation of the worth of his motives. Showing kinship to the legend of the Wandering Jew but ultimately drawn from the example of the earlier uses of picaresque literature for social commentary, it reveals the moral corruption of both St. Leon and his persecutors. Godwin never condones persecution or torture, although they follow St. Leon because of his guilt. (pp. 538-39)

The idea that the issues with which he deals in the novel should grow out of the historical circumstances of its background does not seem to have occurred to Godwin; he rather grafted contemporary concerns onto his historical setting. . . . Godwin, as concerned as he was with the revolution and personally aware of its effects, in *St. Leon* still uses history in the classical manner; he writes a novel in which "not only the psychology of the characters, but the manners depicted are entirely those of the writer's own day" and in which there is no "derivation of the individuality of characters from the historical peculiarity of their age."

In his treatment of the Inquisition, Godwin uses his historical background characteristically as a pretense for introducing moral commentary on a contemporary theme. He openly connects the Inquisition with English attempts to suppress all liberal political ideas in the face of the French revolutionary threat. (pp. 539-40)

St. Leon's flight to Spain to escape persecution is the original device which enables Godwin to enlarge his didacticism. . . . Godwin counts on the British abhorrence of Catholicism and on the current literary associations of the black mysteries of the Roman Church to make his point. St. Leon refers to the prison of the Inquisition as a "scene of Horrors" and other details of the imprisonment lend it a Gothic cast; the prisoners are described as "mere shades of men, cold, inert, glaring bodies, which the heaven born soul has long since deserted and left to themselves." . . . In this case, unlike many similar treatments of the evil of the church, the Gothic horrors are intended to emphasize the evil of religious persecution rather than merely to produce a shiver of terror.

The other Gothic elements in the novel, whether actually supernatural or only atmospheric, also lead to the enforcement of ideas. Godwin, always interested in the psychological states of his characters, creates in St. Leon a variation on the theme of the haunted wanderer which lent much Gothic feeling to *Caleb Williams* and lends romantic feeling to his basically didactic intentions. St. Leon is remorseful over his past and regrets with anguish his loss of the means of giving his family those joys he covets for them. He wanders alone through conventionally wild landscapes in which he is tormented by his emotions. . . . This misery and self-condemnation amid the sublimity of nature prepare St. Leon for the acceptance of the stranger's gift, which proves his final ruin, and thereby provide an emotional tone suitable to the magnitude of his corruption. (p. 541)

Such tormenting guilt anticipates that of the Byronic villain-hero, but Godwin's interest in states of mind is generally more "scientific" than Byron's; he often introduces little discourses on the psychology of guilt. Even though he does not admire irrationality, he shows a constant awareness that there are depths of experience not revealed in the ideal rational man who is the ultimate product and agent of political justice. His despairing creatures fascinate him and at times seem to press him to a denial of his usual belief in the efficacy of reason as a control of human behavior. . . . St. Leon leaping from rock to rock in his frenzy and secret guilt reminds us of Manfred and the guilt-haunted heroes of Byron's Oriental Tales. Godwin's treatment of St. Leon is close in feeling to the romantic conception of the persecuted, sensitive misfit of Byron and Shelley although Godwin condemns the misfit instead of exalting him. (p. 542)

[St. Leon] remains a man to be pitied but a man whose anti-social emotions are never glorified. St. Leon is not a complete villain, however, for he reveals Godwin's ambiguity of feeling. Godwin's sensibilities are perhaps inevitably more stimulated by the aberration than the norm, and therefore he emphasizes the sufferings of the culpable St. Leon much as Evans notes. Intellectually, Godwin's moral commitment to the standards of *Political Justice* never wavers in *St. Leon* and finally gives a justification to its Gothicism. . . .

The Hungarian episode provides perhaps the most striking Gothic exercise in the novel and reveals as well the aesthetic problems with which Godwin was struggling in *St. Leon*. Here Godwin serves his didactic aims by pursuing the indictment of despotism as a variety of the unjust power which divides man from man. St. Leon is shocked to find the rulers of Hungary jealous of his attempts to aid the starving populace because any alleviation of their suffering lessens the government's despotic power. He is in great danger because he dares to lessen the misery on which tyranny feeds. He meets the wild and distorted misanthrope, Bethlem Gabor, who, because of the effects of injustice, is dedicated to hatred of mankind. As the prisoners of the Inquisition become mere shadows of men through the effects of despotism, Gabor becomes through the effect of despotic cruelty a sublimely magnified type of man's malignity. (p. 543)

The exaggerated psychology is in keeping with the incredibly exaggerated drawing of Gabor's whole character. It illustrates Godwin's theses about crime and harks back to the idea in *Political Justice* that evil is imposed on man by his institutions, chiefly political ones. Gabor turns against St. Leon, not only because he is suspicious and jealous of his magic powers but also because he has been taught to hate by men, who, like St. Leon, have tried to extend their power by unnatural and unjust means. St. Leon attempts benevolent actions in Hungary but fails because his power is founded not on natural justice but on unnatural wealth.

The sources of his misery combine against St. Leon in a Gothic nightmare of oppression. Gabor imprisons him in a dungeon—this indispensable asset of the Gothic novel is played upon with relish—and he escapes only by accident. Godwin portrays the kinship between the corruption of the two men at length; Gabor, a fully developed sublime villain, is a double for the outcast St. Leon. . . . (pp. 543-44)

The symbolic power inherent in the St. Leon-Gabor relationship is not fully realized because of Godwin's lack of literary skill. He tries for Gothic effects, as in his description of St. Leon's hunger pangs: "The gnawings I now felt in my stomach were intolerable. They were at one period so severe, that I can compare them to nothing but the sensation of having swallowed a glowing ember . . . the pain was diversified with intervals of a death-like and insupportable sickness—But no; I will not attempt to describe the horrors of hunger sublimed by despair, where the torture of the mind gives new pungency and uproar to the corporeal anguish." . . . No better and no worse than most such descriptions, this passage finds its relevance to Godwin's idea in its reference to the "tortures of the mind," which, although they are perhaps the essence of all Gothic terror, take on added significance in St. Leon's consciousness of his moral guilt.

Although Godwin employs in these ways the supernatural and Gothic effects as metaphor and illustration of the unjust and unnatural possession and exercise of power, they strain his somewhat limited literary powers—as the character of Gabor amply reveals. The problem of creating an aura of probability was for Godwin a vexing one. Although St. Leon is cut off from society because his magic removes for him some of the basic cares of mankind, Godwin must, in order to gain our sympathy, portray him as a vulnerable human being, subject to anxieties and concerns such as hunger and fear of death which should not touch him very deeply. (pp. 544-45)

Godwin was not successful in handling the Gothic elements, although he was able to endow them with meaning. His rationalistic temperament made it difficult for him to lose himself in an effect. The very intellectualism which led him to give didactic meaning to the supernatural kept him from making it fully effective. Yet in consistency of idea and intellectual interest *St. Leon* is superior to most contemporary didactic novels. As a work of Gothic fiction it is interesting for what it attempts to do; its serious metaphorical use of the supernatural was a rarity in the literature of the eighteenth century. In using Gothic subjects for his purposes, Godwin foreshadows later, more successful uses of such materials after Gothicism had faded. . . . Godwin was, in spite of his weaknesses, perhaps instrumental in extending the range of prose fiction through both *Caleb Williams* and *St. Leon.* (p. 545)

Wallace Austin Flanders, "Godwin and Gothicism: 'St. Leon'," in Texas Studies in Literature and Language, *Vol. VIII, No. 4, Winter, 1967, pp. 533-45.*

ERIC ROTHSTEIN (essay date 1967)

[*Rothstein contends that* Caleb Williams *is a unified moral tale whose narrative action moves from "the egoistic portrayal of external events to the objective . . . recognition of personal morality."*]

Largely because of Godwin's own insistence on ideology, the "message" of *Caleb Williams* seems curiously detachable from its literary artistry. Critics who have tried to reconcile the two have evoked such dubious genres as the Political Novel and the Psychological Novel, and have claimed that one is the vehicle or the complement of the other in satisfying Godwin's inner conflict between reform and romance. Some see a sadomasochistic Gothicism as setting and libretto for the victory of middle-class virtue over its feudal pursuers; some find a profound anatomy of obsession carried on, half intended, beneath the white sheets of Godwin's rationalism; or some discover both, in a muddled way, going on at once. I should like to propose a different approach. I contend that *Caleb Williams* is very much of a piece, that it is primarily moral, and that its social or psychological interests serve to exemplify or to express moral terms. Furthermore, I maintain that despite his stylistic limitations, Godwin succeeded in writing a skilfully planned and formally satisfying work of art. He did so by contriving an intricate *Bildungsroman*—or spiritual autobiography—in which Caleb learns about things as they are, within him and outside him, through a flow of actual events and of psychologically symbolic events connected by analogy.

This contention implies at least three postulates. The first is that *Caleb Williams* centres upon individual recognition, not social exposure; the second, that despite Godwin's sporadic determinism, the novel insists on moral action and choice; the third, that we must consider what happens in the novel as Caleb's renderings, not as objective fact. I believe that these postulates are not so precarious as they may seem. As to the first, we should observe that neither Caleb's curiosity nor Falkland's greed for reputation, the two characteristics that are the tinder of the plot, seems to be socially determined or even socially encouraged. . . . Falkland's fatal disposition comes from reading Italian romances, not from the society in which he actually moves. "Imagination" and "fancy," according to Caleb, encourage in Falkland a "temper perpetually alive to the sentiments of birth and honour," while philosophy, which was presumably what society brought to his education, "purged" his imagination. . . . Even the despotism of Barnabas Tyrrel, about which one hears in Chapter III, comes from his having been spoiled as a child, and must therefore have been latent within him. Given that these three men, portrayed in the opening three chapters, are the most important actors in the book, one may well be sceptical about Godwin's indicting society. It seems obvious that, ideologically, social malfeasances are extensions of personal evils. At most, the social stimulus makes individual corruption plausible or feasible in terms of verisimilitude; or it palliates the faults which it approves. But these are secondary refinements. Evil in *Caleb Williams* comes from individual human beings, whom society as a whole reflects. Men must change before society can.

To throw the moral burden upon individual action forces one to assume that people can make choices and follow them. Godwin at times undeniably claimed to believe that principles of necessity bind each man, and this claim appears to run counter to the moral freedom in *Caleb Williams*. In temper, it probably does. But *Caleb Williams* is no more obliged to work in terms of necessity than *Rasselas,* say, must work in moral terms because its author was a brilliant and insistent moralist. . . . [In *Caleb Williams*] Godwin limited himself formally by setting up as narrator a young man whose mind and conscience operate in terms of moral will. However we may judge Caleb's individual responses to his world, we cannot exclude those responses from our range of understanding. Moral praise, blame, and therefore choice, are intrinsic to the novel. Furthermore, our sense of Caleb's individuality, made quite marked by the first-person narration, works against our thinking of him deterministically.

By insisting on the importance of free will in the novel, one can see why Godwin threw aside his first conclusion, in which Caleb is finally rebuffed by Falkland and by the law, so that he ends his memoir broken, delirious, and impotent. The logic of the novel leads to a conclusion that throws the onus not on society and its squires, as Godwin must have perceived on re-reading, but on the freely chosen evil of the individual. The published conclusion, as a result, shows us Caleb's inner guilt after Falkland and society have cleared his name: "it is now only," he tells us, "that I am truly miserable." . . . One can also understand, following this line of argument, the short path between *Caleb Williams* and Godwin's next two novels, *St. Leon* and *Fleetwood*, in both of which the moral act is paramount.

Such an emphasis upon the individual and his moral choice leads directly to my third postulate, that one must consider the events in the novel as Caleb's renderings rather than as objective fact. Clearly, some of the events must represent Caleb's subjective re-creations, if not distortions, of a reality that hides from the reader in ambiguity. Information about Falkland's past involvement with Tyrrel and Emily Melville, transcriptions of private conversations and still more private feelings—these appear on Caleb's pages, although by any standard of literal accuracy he could not have discovered them. Unless one is to assume that Godwin pointlessly abrogated his narrative convention at the very beginning of the novel, when one would think that he might well be establishing it, one must agree that the first third of the novel, more or less, presents Caleb the narrator as an author rather than as an objective historian. . . . Godwin must have wanted Caleb to tell the flashback story in his own way. By so doing, Caleb could provide us with various moral patterns, later picked up by analogy, and with an index of his own mind and experience through the allusory structure of the story he tells. (pp. 18-20)

Godwin's obvious interest is not in neat causal plot, of the sort that a rational social reformer might fancy, but in the effect of events on Caleb and Caleb's moral development.

If we accept this sort of reading, we can understand Godwin's letting the plot turn on a series of malign accidents that appear more suitable to the professed purpose of Hardy's novels than to any fictional exposition of *Political Justice*. Caleb happens to wander to Mr. Forester's house just at the time that Mr. Falkland happens to arrive there, and so is suspected (with some reason) of chicanery. Falkland's spy Gines happens to be the same man whom Caleb had earlier served to humiliate, and Gines' brother happens to be the very printer to whom the disguised Caleb sends his pamphlets. If events are seen as shaped by the narrator, one does not balk at Godwin's balancing the humiliation of Falkland and the humiliation of Gines against one another. One accepts his playing off the capture of real criminals (Gines' task) with the capture of fictional ones (the printer's), thereby to embellish the theme of reality and imagination that pervades the novel. . . . [Examples] of different sorts all suggest a fatalism far removed from Godwin's ideas of necessity. The fatalism here is symbolic, and exists not in the structure of William Godwin's world but in that of Caleb's spiritual voyage.

To say that Caleb is in some way the creative poet of his own history, mingling world and self, is inevitably to remind oneself that Godwin was an almost exact contemporary of Blake and that *Caleb Williams* is only four years older than "The Rime of the Ancient Mariner." . . . Godwin, the son of a dissenting minister, did not desert the tradition of Bunyan and Defoe, who brought the allegorical autobiography to its highest point at the turn of the eighteenth century. In the preface to *Caleb Williams*, Godwin mentions his reading John Reynolds' collection of providential tales, *God's Revenge Against Murder*, first published in 1635. He also was reading that most intricate of eighteenth-century spiritual journeys, *Clarissa*, while writing his own novel. Admittedly, Godwin has disembarrassed himself of the theology of these works. But he has adapted the form by keeping a kind of providential force, as the "coincidences" listed above should indicate. Caleb is driven toward truth, a recognition of his own blindness and his own egoism. That process is clarified for the reader through the systematic use of allusion and of analogous moral acts.

Caleb Williams itself begins with the flashback to the history of Falkland and Tyrrel, which presents a sort of moral lexicon for what is to happen later. When examining it closely, one finds that Caleb tells this history like a plagiarist, borrowing ideal schemes of action from several sources, most prominently from the novels of Richardson. Because Richardson was so extraordinarily popular in the late eighteenth century, close parallels with events in *Sir Charles Grandison* and *Clarissa* could not pass unnoticed: the allusions must be as intentional as they are thorough. Let me indicate how thorough they are. Falkland goes to Italy like Sir Charles Grandison, where he teaches English to a beautiful rich Italian girl, as does Sir Charles. The result in both novels is that the Englishmen must confront jealous Italian pretenders to the girl's hand—Count Belvedere in Richardson and Count Malvesi, which sounds like a negative inflected form of "belvedere," in Godwin; in both novels, the Englishman subdues the Italian by his noble behaviour. . . . Surely these duplications of Richardson's plots, compressed into ten brief chapters, cannot be coincidental. They may demonstrate Godwin's poverty of imagination, or they may be intended to characterize Caleb, who tells us the history. The latter seems more likely. Caleb can only cast his story in terms that he knows, the terms of books rather than of men. His moral knowledge in this first part of the novel is confined by romance.

"Romance," for Godwin, would have included the Bible and perhaps also English history, from which other particulars of the flashback story are drawn by the naïve Caleb. After he gets past such allegorically conceived names as "Clare" for his famous poet, and "Tyrrel" for his rural tyrant, he moves to "Barnabas," Tyrrel's Christian name, with ironic reference to the Apostle who, the Golden Legend says, "was harmonious [*ordinatus*] in his three faculties, the rational, the concupiscible, and the irascible. . . . He was harmonious with God, deferring to the authority of God, to His majesty and His goodness. . . . He nourished his flock by word, good deeds, and example." The ironic joke appears in *Joseph Andrews*, and Caleb carries it to its logical end in all respects. "Ferdinando Falkland" conflates two English Civil War heroes, the parliamentary general Ferdinando Fairfax and the great royalist Lord Falkland, both of whom appear in Clarendon's *History of the Rebellion*. (pp. 21-3)

Within this double context of Bible and patriotism, Caleb's own name is expressive. Caleb in the book of Numbers . . . stills the rebellious people, and is thereby justified by the Lord and permitted to enter the Promised Land. Our hero wills himself to be this Caleb, blessed and powerful. Eventually, the name turns out to be ironic as "Barnabas" is ironic, and for the same reasons. Just as Tyrrel tries through the law and force to make the world an adjunct of his own ego, in a wild perversion of his apostolic name, so too Caleb tries. The methods differ: Caleb treats all men only as they relate to him, a conversion of reality into self-interest that parallels and anticipates his writing subjective memoirs like objective history. Reality twists into spiritual patterns when seen only from the standpoint of the self, as Caleb sees it and as the tradition of the allegorical autobiography sees it. But the autobiography has a social function. It transforms the self into a universal by explicating a general pilgrimage of the soul, by being written for social benefit, and by stressing the metaphysical reality that it can perceive from its own partial and humble point of view. Caleb writes only as a mental diversion and to clear his name with posterity . . . ; from these facts, we immediately learn the egocentrism of his proceedings. By itself, this egocentrism might be unimportant. It becomes important when seen as a shadow of the callousness, the selfishness, the spiritual despotism that Caleb practises toward Falkland during the early part of the novel, and that overwhelms him with remorse at the end.

Caleb's egoism is established for us by the end of the first chapter, in which Godwin establishes the nature of his sympathy: "My heart bleeds at the recollection of [Falkland's] misfortunes, as if they were my own. How can it fail to do so? To his story the whole fortune of my life was linked; because he was miserable, my happiness, my name, and my existence have been irretrievably blasted." All feeling for Caleb is self-centred; compassion is at best a literary delight. . . . To Falkland's forbearance and rational rebukes, Caleb remains insensible, like Tyrrel and unlike Malvesi. And these days of spying, of goading, of merciless persecution, Caleb calls "a more favourable period of my life." . . . (pp. 24-5)

Caleb's subsequent imprisonment as a thief corresponds, as he would see it, to the unjust imprisonments of young Hawkins and Emily Melville the social underlings whom Tyrrel had arrested respectively as thief and defaulter. Ignoring his own role in corrupting Falkland to a second Tyrrel, Caleb appears partially right. But his egoism and aggrievedness keep him from pressing his analogies further and from seeing that Falkland's dishonour at Tyrrel's hands (for embezzling Tyrrel's neighbourhood reputation) places Falkland too in the list of victims along with Emily and Hawkins. If one looks at the correspondences in these terms, Caleb, who has carried on the work of dishonouring his better, is the second Tyrrel. Again and again, he catches himself up in his simplifications.

A passage from Godwin's *Enquirer* . . . reveals still another twist: "one of the most sacred principles of social life, is honour, the forbearance that man is entitled to claim from man, that a man of worth would as soon steal my purse or forge a title-deed to my estate, as read the letter he sees lying on my table." The letter from Hawkins that Caleb reads . . . has slipped to the floor, but I do not think Godwin would admit such distinctions. Caleb's being accused as a thief, his having his box pried open and Falkland's valuables thrust into it, represents a symbolically accurate punishment. . . . Godwin is guiding us to understand Caleb's actions as the moral equivalents of crime, if not literally crime itself. Caleb is properly discredited and imprisoned, since the false accusation simply lends public arms to naked moral truth.

Prison is dehumanizing, and the keepers vain tyrants. In other words, prison duplicates, on a squalidly physical level, Caleb's own personality, which has made Falkland an object to watch and fetter close. Caleb, of course, claims that the prison is quite alien to his nature—amusingly enough, he insists that the turnkey not exceed a set social function and threatens revenge for insolence . . . , not reflecting on his own relationship with his master. He tries twice to escape, and details for us his methods of doing so. His description, full of pride at his ingenuity and industry, goes on much longer than the mere narrative demands, and thus should be seen as part of his professed

rhetoric . . . , designed to impress us in his favour and to cheer himself. (pp. 25-6)

As Caleb has entered prison, the novel has moved from its earlier structure of patriotic romance to an anti-social romance or history, as Caleb senses his isolation and symbolically analogizes himself with a legendary criminal. These new terms reflect a fortunate loss of naïveté, but cannot stand up morally better than the old. Raymond's gang offers Caleb a close look at criminals, and permits him to discover for himself that they subsist on despair, self-deceit, and brutality . . . , epitomized by the old hag who attempts his life. Their violence discredits his narrow social condemnations. . . . (p. 27)

The last section of the novel proper, between Caleb's first accusation of Falkland and the "Postscript," picks up the moral, the literary, the spiritual, and the romance themes about which we have been talking. Images of divinity increase, compelling our attention to God and the Devil, those supreme imaginative creators of Truth and the Lie. The Biblical romance of the flashback story now produces a metaphysical echo. Falkland's agent Gines is "infernal" and "diabolic"; the "God-like Falkland" seems "burnt and parched by the eternal fire that burned within him," which can be compared to "the imaginary hell, which the great enemy of mankind is represented as carrying every where about with him." . . . Just as Falkland has earlier shaped a sort of objective truth from Caleb's inner condition, making him first a thief (in the eyes of society) and then a legendary villain, so now he makes Caleb's chosen disguises come true. Caleb finds himself a real beggar—"meagreness and poverty were the ordinary attendants of my course" . . .— and a real Wandering Jew. He has refused rest to Falkland, like the Jew who refused Christ rest on Calvary, and falls victim to the social lash of a retributive God. He thereby learns what reputation means; but he cannot infer from it the principle of utility, as he has not in the past, despite the warning of Collins that bare truth is no absolute . . . , despite the example of Falkland who has saved a village from total conflagration by destroying a few houses . . . , despite the implicit plea of Raymond that repentance should make past folly fade. Caleb once more resolves to create his own world of truth and to arraign the poet of his fate.

Caleb's pointless and malicious accusations against Falkland have no effect but to kill the man and tarnish his name; what is proved is Caleb's own blindness. The flashback story had warned him of this in the actions of Tyrrel—Emily and Falkland survive arrest from a sickbed three days each, in obvious parallelism—and his own story had warned him in the actions of a second Tyrrel, the corrupted Falkland. But Caleb cannot read experience morally, an exercise left for us, and through his act of will he falls unredeemable. In wresting the truth from Falkland and in revealing it, he has created his own hell about himself: now he must live within his sorry creation, newly rich with knowledge and newly powerless. . . . At this point the guilt that has been projected into symbolic action appears within the person who has exemplified its true source, Caleb himself; the narrative pattern has been completed by moving from the egoistic portrayal of external events to the objective (if not disinterested) recognition of personal morality. The memoirs that have been begun to cheer and vindicate the writer end with an unselfish zeal for expiation and a socially meaningful justice.

Caleb Williams is a novel of great polish and complexity, with obvious stylistic faults, with less obvious but far more significant imaginative virtues. It is a broader novel than its critics give it credit for. . . . I do not want to denigrate the seriousness of its social commentary—the prisons, the squirearchy, the magistracy are all as foul in Godwin's eyes as in Caleb's— but to place that social commentary in its proper moral terms. Nor would I deny . . . that *Caleb Williams* and *Political Justice* are closely related; the relation is reciprocal. From examining the two books as Godwin's thought evolves through them, one can see him moving toward the dictum that he enunciates in *Enquirer*. . . : "The first and most fundamental principle in the intercourse of man with man, is reverence." A better single motto for *Caleb Williams* would be hard to find. From its logic, Godwin moved to the overtly domestic fantasy of *St. Leon* and the overtly domestic psychometry of *Fleetwood,* both impressive but loose novels. *Caleb Williams* can by no means be called a loose novel: its matter is limited enough to be manageable and Godwin manages it brilliantly, brilliantly enough to make it one of the great artistic achievements of the late eighteenth century. (pp. 28-30)

> Eric Rothstein, "Allusion and Analogy in the Romance of 'Caleb Williams'," in University of Toronto Quarterly, *Vol. XXXVII, No. 1, October, 1967, pp. 18-30.*

JOHN PESTA (essay date 1971)

[*Interpreting* Caleb Williams *as a tragic novel, Pesta discusses Caleb and Falkland's "wasted opportunity for love."*]

Caleb Williams is a tragic novel because the possibility for love between the hero Caleb and his enemy Falkland is wasted. At the end of the novel Caleb reflects: "I thought that if Falkland were dead, I should return once again to all that makes life worth possessing. I thought that if the guilt of Falkland were established, fortune and the world would smile upon my efforts. Both these events are accomplished; and it is now only that I am truly miserable." . . . Caleb comes to realize that his long sufferings—flight from Falkland, continuous fear of capture, years of anxiety and despair—have been trivial in comparison with the intense remorse he now feels after conquering his master. The novel ends on a note of tragic desolation. . . .

The standard interpretation of Godwin's novel depicts Caleb as a helpless individual within an unjust system and Falkland as a powerful aristocrat with the legal means to persecute his victim. But the relationship between Godwin's characters is more complicated than this statement suggests. Caleb and Falkland find much to admire and praise in each other. There is strong attraction as well as hostility between them, love as well as hate. To understand the novel properly, we must see how its tragic human dimension conforms to Godwin's social and political ideas. (p. 67)

Self-love hinders Caleb and Falkland from achieving a beneficial relationship based on selfless love. Their realization that through blind selfishness and misunderstanding they have caused each other's downfall accounts for the novel's moving conclusion. Tragic suffering results from a wasted opportunity for love. (p. 68)

Ultimately tragedy happens in *Caleb Williams* because two characters who could understand and benefit each other become not "father and son" but mortal enemies. Caleb flees, and Falkland takes advantage of his superior social position to persecute him. The novel becomes a tale of terror and pursuit in the Gothic mode. In the end Caleb triumphs by forcing Falkland to make a public confession. The destruction of Falkland's

pride and Caleb's deep remorse suggest the fierceness of struggle and the guilt and loneliness of triumph in an archetypal conflict between father and son.

Several lines of evidence support the theory that a father-son relationship exists between Godwin's central characters. First, Caleb and Falkland resemble and attract each other, for though they differ in social class and experience, they share essential personality traits. Second, throughout the novel Caleb displays a need to find a parent-figure to replace his own dead parents. Besides Falkland he tries to attach himself to Collins, Forester, Spurrel, and Laura, but all these attempts end in rebuffs. Third, there is an intriguing pattern of mythopoeic imagery, in which Falkland is represented as a supernatural being whom Caleb both fears and loves. (1) Although Caleb's curiosity instigates the fatal connection with Falkland, certain personal factors reveal their spiritual affinity. Both have literary pretensions. Both are intelligent and sensitive to each other's feelings. Most importantly, both are proud and egoistic, qualities that make it difficult for them to engage in a selfless relationship. Falkland's pride involves his obsession with honor and reputation. (p. 69)

Although a development toward friendship takes place early in the novel, Caleb's probing curiosity and Falkland's sense of guilt block this. In a discussion of Alexander the Great, Caleb inadvertently strikes at the root of his master's secret by condemning Alexander's deeds as the unjustifiable murders of a madman susceptible to momentary provocations. "The instant I had uttered these words," Caleb adds, "I felt what it was that I had done. There was a magnetical sympathy between me and my patron, so that their effect was not sooner produced upon him, than my own mind reproached me with the inhumanity of the allusion." . . . The feelings of Caleb and Falkland are so closely attuned that already Caleb can blame himself for distressing his master.

(2) At various times Caleb describes or speaks to several characters as parents. One of these is Collins, an old servant of Falkland's. "My father!" Caleb says to him, "I am your son! once your little Caleb, whom you a thousand times loaded with kindness." . . . Another is Laura—"my comforter, my friend, my mother!" . . .—the admirable woman Caleb meets after fleeing to Wales. Like Collins and Laura, another parent-figure, Falkland's brother Forester, rejects Caleb because of the crimes that Falkland falsely alleges against him, after Caleb attempts to expose his guilt. Falkland seems to interpose whenever Caleb comes near finding parental security. By doing so, Falkland at once persecutes Caleb as an enemy and retains control over him, as if in spirit he alone is Caleb's true parent. (p. 70)

(3) Certain mythic images intensify the love-hate relationship. No consistent pattern exists, for at different times Falkland appears to Caleb as godlike or infernal. A key passage early in the novel, when Caleb decides to spy on Falkland, brings out Caleb's feelings toward him as a divine being: "I determined to place myself as a watch upon my patron. The instant I had chosen this employment for myself, I found a strange sort of pleasure in it. To do what is forbidden always has its charms, because we have an indistinct apprehension of something arbitrary and tyrannical in the prohibition." . . . The editorializing here is related to Godwin's political theme, but more interesting is Caleb's state of mind, his "strange sort of pleasure." The wish for forbidden knowledge goes back to the Garden of Eden, and Caleb's transgression is a sort of Original

Sin from which all his sufferings flow. The arbitrary power is not only political but, perhaps, divine. (pp. 70-1)

A suprapersonal force of evil pervades the novel. Despite the apparent contradiction, however, the representation of Falkland as both godlike and demonic is in keeping with the novel's ambivalent emotional structure. In the supercharged world of *Caleb Williams* it is appropriate that Falkland's mixed qualities of good and evil, benevolence and egoism, should be presented in a heightened manner. The major effect of mythopoeic references is to elevate the personal involvement between Caleb and Falkland and to amplify, often to the point of melodrama, the tone of the novel. The God-man imagery lends strength to the claim that on the man-to-man level the relationship between Falkland and Caleb is that of father and son.

As the preceding outline shows, it is possible to infer a spiritual kinship between Caleb and Falkland and to find many direct statements of love and esteem on Caleb's part. But it remains necessary to determine whether the concrete action of the novel supports these hints and statements, and in particular whether Falkland gives any sign of sharing Caleb's affection. One point that readers generally overlook is that Falkland is not Caleb's constant enemy. In the last volume, after Caleb has been bound over for trial on the trumped-up charge of robbing Falkland, an event takes place that sheds light on Falkland's paternalistic attitude. On the day set for trial, Falkland does not appear, and Caleb is allowed to go free. Afterwards, at a meeting at an inn, Falkland denies that he has sought to injure Caleb. Instead it was Forester, Falkland's brother, who offered a reward for Caleb's capture because he regarded Caleb as an impertinent upstart seeking to slander Falkland. Falkland insists that his sole object has been the preservation of Caleb's life and that, in all his wanderings, Caleb has never been out of his sight. (pp. 71-2)

Within the time scheme of the novel, Falkland's pursuit of Caleb lasts several years, whereas Forester's pursuit covers only a few months. But in terms of space a far greater portion of the book is devoted to Forester's efforts. Godwin's handling of Forester represents a major weakness of the novel, for this character, who plays such a crucial role in the plot, is seldom onstage, and his comings and goings seem quite contrived. For instance, his absence from Caleb's trial, after he has taken great pains to apprehend Caleb, is altogether unsatisfactory. Nonetheless, readers who disregard Forester's role as initial pursuer and who reduce the relationship between Falkland and Caleb to a simple pursuer-pursued situation will fail to appreciate the complexity of their involvement. (pp. 72-3)

In depicting the development of Caleb's character, Godwin avoids a fallacy by having Caleb bring his story up to the present toward the end of the last volume. The opening of Chapter Fourteen makes clear that the last two chapters and especially the Postscript are written with a different attitude from that of the preceding chapters. Caleb's sense of guilt and sorrow develops only in this closing section. If the entire novel were written in long retrospect instead of reaching a present moment before the end, it would be fallacious in a first-person narrative not to represent the narrator's state of mind as the same at the start as at the end. Swift's narrator in *Gulliver's Travels* exemplifies such an omission.

My interpretation of *Caleb Williams* as a tragedy of wasted love lays much emphasis on events that occur near the end of the novel. (p. 74)

Do the tragic implications of *Caleb Williams* conflict with Godwin's political themes? If we accept the standard interpretation of *Caleb Williams,* which regards Caleb and Falkland simply as enemies, quasi-symbolic representations of innocence and oppression, then the reversal of roles that takes place at the end and Caleb's guilt and self-blame make no sense. But the standard conception of Godwin's doctrine is too narrow. . . . Not Falkland but Tyrrel represents the spirit of tyranny; Falkland stands for monarchy built on the ideal of honor. Godwin considered this ideal a total failure as a social code. . . . The failure of Falkland and Caleb to overcome egoism and to reach a profitable interchange of help and understanding suggests that society also will remain unsatisfactory so long as men fail to transcend selfishness and prejudice. . . . Godwin should not be held to a narrow polemical view that simply attacks tyranny. *Caleb Williams* offers a moral and emotional solution to human problems that is at once more moving and effective: love and understanding are needed for men to achieve peace, harmony, and justice, if man is not forever to be the destroyer of man.

To read *Caleb Williams* as a tragic novel is to extend its relevance beyond eighteenth-century historical circumstances into the timeless question of the human condition. A tragedy conceived in terms of personal relations is peculiarly modern, and the central situation of the novel, Caleb's search for a father, constitutes a dominant issue in modern literature. In an age when traditional religious beliefs have been shaken, strong emphasis has been placed on the beneficial, even salvific power of personal relationships. To this extent *Caleb Williams* anticipates the modern dilemma of an alienated individual searching for order and security in an uncertain world. (pp. 75-6)

> *John Pesta, " 'Caleb Williams': A Tragedy of Wasted Love," in* Tennessee Studies in Literature, *Vol. 16, 1971, pp. 67-76.*

JOANN P. COBB (essay date 1973)

[*Cobb contends that Godwin's novels are linked by the theme of human misery caused by both the perversion of human nature and such institutions as government and religion.*]

Caleb Williams and the five novels which succeeded it—*St. Leon* . . . , *Fleetwood* . . . , *Mandeville* . . . , *Cloudesly* . . . , and *Deloraine* . . .—even though they contain a variety of character types, settings, and plots are very closely related thematically. The encompassing and pervasive theme which dominates the novels is human misery, the cause of which is two-fold: the institutions which dominate human life are a corrupting and limiting influence on human behavior, and individuals pervert human nature by actions which are contrary to reason and benevolence. Each novel involves a variation on this theme. The institution which is responsible for evil may be government, the law, aristocracy, or religion. The suffering protagonist may violate his conscience through passion, predisposition, or premeditation. The result is always the same—tragedy. It is significant that all six novels deal almost exclusively with disaster.

Caleb Williams demonstrates the iniquity which results from the perversion or denial of truth, and each succeeding novel continues the demonstration. Godwin used the novels to illustrate the validity of the basic conclusions of *Political Justice:* Political institutions coerce man, enforce prejudice, prevent enlightenment, subvert morality, and therefore produce unhappiness. "Truth is omnipotent"; if man is free to seek the truth, it will prevail and, in turn, promote rational progress and universal benevolence. To deny truth and submit to political coercion is to live in the misery depicted in Godwin's novels. He used the novels both as a proving ground for his philosophical conclusions and as a vehicle for disseminating his ideas. Because the novels were published during a forty-year period after the appearance of *Political Justice,* they also provided Godwin with the means of promulgating the emendation of his original thought. The fundamental conclusions of *Political Justice* are never denied in the fiction, but the study of each novel individually reveals a gradual modification of certain ideas. Each novel is related to *Political Justice* as the demonstration of the validity of its philosophical conclusions, as the modification or rejection of certain ideas, or both.

The 1798 edition of the *Enquiry Concerning Political Justice and Its Influence on Morals and Happiness* is considered the valid culmination of Godwin's thoughts on political justice. The title indicates that Godwin believed that the importance of politics lies in its relation to virtue and happiness, and his political philosophy is at the same time a moral philosophy. His doctrine of human perfectibility and rational progress depends upon the existence of absolute truth which becomes the standard for measuring progress. Man is capable of knowing these truths through reason which "collates" emotions and feelings, as well as ideas and apprehensions, and judges rightly the truth of a situation in relation to eternal truth.

Since man is capable of right judgment, lack of it indicates the subversion of human nature by false opinion inflicted upon man by outside force. Godwin emphasizes the importance of this conclusion in stating the corollaries of his fundamental position in regard to the power of truth: "Sound reasoning and truth, when adequately communicated, must always be victorious over error: Sound reasoning and truth are capable of being so communicated: Truth is omnipotent: The vices and moral weakness of man are not invincible: Man is perfectible, or in other words susceptible of perpetual improvement." Since truth is omnipotent, according to Godwin, he who knows the truth must act in accordance with it. Evil thus becomes only the absence of good or lack of knowledge. Vice will disappear when man gains enough knowledge, and this is the foundation for Godwin's belief in rational progress. (pp. 16-17)

The difficulty of full acceptance of Godwin's philosophy lies in his fundamental belief that man is basically good and primarily rational. The charge that Godwin ignores the problem of evil is, to a great extent, a valid criticism of *Political Justice.* A complete understanding of Godwin's thought requires an investigation of the novels which succeeded *Political Justice,* complemented it, and sometimes contradicted it. The problem of evil is fully investigated in the novels. Here it is depicted as a direct result of malevolence and error. The tortured lives of Godwin's heroes demonstrate the evil which prevails when men refuse to submit to truth or institutions enforce error. In Godwin's philosophy, pain and evil are synonymous and the aura of misery which pervades his novels gives evidence of his concern over the problem of evil.

The Preface to Godwin's first major novel, *Caleb Williams . . . ,* points out the work's intention "to comprehend, as far as the progressive nature of a single story would allow, a general review of the modes of domestic and unrecorded despotism, by which man becomes the destroyer of man" [see excerpt dated 1794]. The major emphasis in this work is on law and the corruption which results from the imposition of it. Law represents institutional society in *Caleb Williams* as government represents all institutions in *Political Justice. . . .* (pp. 17-18)

Falkland and Tyrrel represent the decadent aristocracy which government and law encourage and sustain. Falkland, apparently a refined, sensitive, and benevolent man, is reduced by a momentary submission to passion to a life of suffering; Tyrrel, who is totally degenerate, ruins not only himself, but everything and everyone he touches. Falkland, a victim of Tyrrel's injustice, is in turn moved to inflict injustice on Caleb Williams, and it is the law which permits the machinations of the privileged to oppress and corrupt the rest of society. Falkland's compulsive dedication to his reputation results in the deaths of three men, the destruction of Caleb Williams, and the loss of his own physical and mental health. He is the first of Godwin's guilty, suffering, fictional characters who demonstrate the misery which results when human beings deny the omnipotence of truth and justice. Falkland's unjust and inhuman persecution of Caleb Williams, through the manipulation of the law, demonstrates its dehumanizing effects on both guilty and innocent, as well as the absurdity of "legal justice."

In *Political Justice* Godwin denies the efficacy of punishment, which may reasonably be inflicted only when it will produce an "overbalance of good." To punish a miscreant "for what is past and irrecoverable, and for the consideration of that only, must be ranked among the most pernicious exhibitions of an untutored barbarism." Punishment requires the use of force and "coercion first annihilates the understanding of the subject upon whom it is exercised, and then of him who employs it." Falkland coerces Caleb and destroys himself. Caleb's long flight from his oppressor takes him to prison, to the hideout of a band of robbers, to the London slums, and to a remote corner of Wales. The inhumanity of man is demonstrated in each of these places. Godwin, the revolutionary, speaks through Caleb Williams to demonstrate the depth of the ignominy and misery to which man may sink. (pp. 18-19)

Caleb Williams demonstrates the corruption of mankind as a result of the political institutions which inhibit the progress of truth. If the novel does not offer a solution to the misery of society, it offers an emphatic denunciation of "things as they are." The alternative may be found in *Political Justice.*

The Preface to the first edition of *St. Leon: A Tale of the Sixteenth Century . . .* offers further evidence that Godwin himself connected the opinions expressed in *Political Justice* with those of the novels. He realizes that the conclusions about marriage in this novel are a topic "of the warmest eulogium, while in the Enquiry concerning Political Justice they seemed to be treated with no great degree of indulgence and favour" [see excerpt dated 1799]. (p. 19)

St. Leon begins Godwin's long investigation of the institution of marriage which culminates in the ideal marriage depicted in *Deloraine.* It has been suggested that St. Leon's wife, Marguerite, is the image of Godwin's first wife, Mary Wollstonecraft, but if *St. Leon* is a criticism of man "as he is," it is evident in neither the representations of Godwin's personal life nor the setting of the novel. Though the events take place in the sixteenth century, the problems which assault the characters are timeless. St. Leon's gift of immortal life and the problems this gift entails represent man's search for power and immortality at the sacrifice of justice and benevolence in this life. St. Leon sacrifices both general and private benevolence to self-interest and, in the process, loses happiness for himself, his family, and everyone he encounters. (p. 20)

It is evident in *St. Leon* and the succeeding novels that man needs sympathy and understanding, and the private affections of a wife, family, and friends in addition to his rational benevolence toward mankind in general.

Godwin's third major novel, *Fleetwood: or The New Man of Feeling* . . . , is set in contemporary society and records incidents that "multitudes of readers have themselves passed through." The author forestalls criticism from those "certain persons who condescend to make my supposed inconsistencies the favourite object of their research," by asserting that *Political Justice* recommends not "a pitiful attempt by scattered examples to rennovate the face of society," but "a grand and comprehensive improvement of its members." Godwin has already admitted in *St. Leon* that he now approves of "private affections." (p. 21)

Godwin's next novel, *Mandeville: A Tale of the Seventeenth Century in England* . . . , assumes essentially the form of the memoirs of a madman. Like his predecessor, Fleetwood, Mandeville is a madman ultimately because he cannot perceive truth, goodness, and virtue; that is, he is out of contact with reality. His mature madness is a direct result of his abnormal childhood, and Godwin presents in this novel a case-study of the effects upon the human mind of bigotry and prejudice, horror and cruelty.

One of Godwin's fundamental theories in *Political Justice* is the primacy of environment over heredity in its influence on human lives: "The actions and dispositions of men are not the offspring of an original bias that they bring into the world in favor of one sentiment or character rather than another, but flow entirely from the operation of circumstances and events acting upon a faculty of receiving sensible impressions." Godwin rejects innate principles, instincts, and prenatal influences as critically important in directing the actions of human beings and concentrates on the effects of education: "It has appeared that the characters of men are determined in all their most essential circumstances by education. By education in this place I would be understood to convey the most comprehensive sense that can possibly be annexed to that word, including every incident that produces an idea in the mind, and can give birth to a train of reflections."

The education of the infant Mandeville plausibly produced a madman. At the age of three he witnessed the murder of his mother and father, and every other English Protestant in the company, during the religious wars in Ireland. The uncle who became his guardian was a neurotic recluse who had not put on his shoes to leave his room for twenty years and who could tolerate his nephew only once a month for two minutes. The memory of his uncle's gloomy, isolated estate and the teachings of his tutor, a Protestant Divine who hated the Roman church, formed the mature Mandeville. The detailed exposition of Bradford's opposition to the Catholic church permits Godwin to demonstrate his objection to the superintendence of opinion and the enforcement of prejudice which are a necessary complement to institutional religion.

In *Political Justice,* Godwin considers religious establishments under the section which deals with the political superintendence of opinion. Godwin asserts that "the system of religious conformity, is a system of blind submission"; "the tendency of a code of religious conformity is to make men hypocrites""; and, the clergy "are fettered in the outset by having a code of propositions put into their hands, in a conformity to which all their inquiries must terminate." But the primary objection of Godwin to institutional religion is that it impedes the progress of truth: "The direct tendency of science, is to increase from

age to age, and to proceed, from the slenderest beginnings, to the most admirable conclusions. But care is taken, in the present case [religion], to anticipate these conclusions, and to bind men, by promises and penalties, not to improve upon the science of their ancestors." Rational progress depends upon the assumption that "it is the characteristic of mind to be capable of improvement." To believe that the ultimate truth has been discovered is to become static rather than progressive. According to Godwin, religious institutions, like other political and social institutions, advocate permanence and stagnation and then, worst of all, use force to achieve these ends. (pp. 23-4)

Mandeville is unique among the Godwinian protagonists in his ultimate refusal to "see" truth. Each of the others submits at last to the irresistible power of reason. Circumstances have destroyed Mandeville's ability to perceive truth—he is mad. Modern psychological theory tends to support the conclusion that abnormal childhood conditions may provoke the onset of psychotic obsession in the adult. Though Godwin's pre-scientific psychology differs somewhat from post-Freudian theory, the ultimate conclusions are basically the same: human misery is learned and therefore is not inevitable. Godwin's case-study of the effect of two distinct kinds of "education" upon a brother and sister demonstrates his belief in the possibility of human progress. Mandeville's psychological maladjustment is a result of his early learning. In the words of Mandeville: "It is the express purpose of the narrative in which I am engaged, to show how the concurrence of a variety of causes operate to form a character." Reasonable causes, on the other hand, work to produce a well-adjusted and happy man.

Cloudesly: A Tale . . . , which was published a full thirteen years after its predecessor, bears certain resemblances to both *Mandeville* and *Caleb Williams* and adumbrates *Deloraine*. Earl Danvers, who is the real protagonist of the novel since Cloudesly plays only a minor role, is like Mandeville eclipsed by a rival and like Falkland and Deloraine is made to suffer terribly from remorse and guilt. Danvers' rival is his elder brother, who receives preferential treatment, but Danvers is saved from obsessive hatred by the benevolence of the elder brother himself. One mistake, the concealing of the true heir after his brother's death, leads to a lifetime of mental suffering and demonstrates the futility of sacrificing truth to material power. Danvers' life touches many people in many countries and allows Godwin to illustrate the difference between natural good and ambition, to investigate further the problems of education, and to remind his readers once more of the power of truth. (p. 24)

Though the "voice of truth" is not featured so blatantly in the other novels, its presence in each is too obvious to be denied. The disparity among the characters who are ultimately overcome by truth and reason in *Cloudesly* emphasizes Godwin's continuing belief in its power. In this novel, truth conquers an English nobleman and an English servant, an Italian nobleman, and a Turkish military leader. Godwin's attempt to demonstrate to man the need for truth and benevolence endures until the end of his career as a novelist. His failure to convince his readers of this necessity provokes the cry of Deloraine in the last novel.

Deloraine . . . , which was published when the author was seventy-seven years of age, reiterates the conclusion of his first novel: human guilt and remorse exact a heavier penalty upon the individual than any social or political institution could possibly impose. The debilitating effects of vengeance on both pursuer and pursued, the agony of guilt and remorse which follows crime and deception, and the inhumanity of political institutions are related again, with an important addition. In the person of Catherine Deloraine, Godwin concludes his career as a novelist with a last eloquent and very moving demonstration of the power of truth. (p. 26)

Joann P. Cobb, "Godwin's Novels and 'Political Justice'," in Enlightenment Essays, *Vol. IV, No. 1, Spring, 1973, pp. 15-28.*

C. R. KROPF (essay date 1976)

[*Kropf interprets* Caleb Williams *as "a serious contribution to the ongoing controversy over the instructive purpose and method of fiction."*]

Caleb Williams contributes a statement to the continuing dispute over how fiction best fulfills its instructive intent and to the nearly related problem of the place which fiction should have in the whole educational process of the young.

Among the numerous ways in which the novel and education are related, two are of immediate relevance to *Caleb Williams.* Perhaps because of Richardson's and Fielding's examples, the novel of the eighteenth century took education as one of its major themes. Fielding uses education as an effective method of characterization, and Richardson's Pamela enters a lengthy debate over the best kind of education for her son and writes an extended commentary on Locke's *Thoughts Concerning Education.* (p. 81)

It seems fairly obvious that the phrase which acts as the title of Godwin's novel *Things as They Are* was popularly associated with the two closely related questions of how the reading audience best learns from fiction and how an author can most effectively furnish instruction, by providing vicarious experience in the manner of Fielding and the novel or by holding up models for imitation in the manner of Richardson and the romance. Readers of Godwin's works know that his interest in these and other questions concerning education is readily apparent. In *The Enquirer* he treats such standard questions as the place of the classics in education and the long disputed matter of public versus private (i.e., domestic) education, and his contemporary readers recognized that his novels were intended to instruct the public in the nature of education.... The title [*Things as They Are*] declares in very specific terms that the novel will present us with a fictional world more approximate to Fielding's than to Richardson's, a world of everyday realism and all its moral ambiguity, and that it will instruct by providing vicarious experience, not by holding up patterns of virtue and vice.

At the same time, the novel has something serious to say about the education of youth and about the educations of all three of the major characters at our first introduction to them. In each case the characters are recognizable stereotypes which had appeared repeatedly in earlier works to illustrate various facets of education. Williams is the young man who knows nothing of the world but is well acquainted with books. Falkland, with one unfortunate flaw, is a fine example of what an eighteenth-century gentleman's education should make of him, while Tyrrel is the typical boorish country squire, spoiled by his mother and fawned over by his tutor, a type which appears in *Joseph Andrews* in the person of the nameless country squire who "roasts" Parson Adams. It is reasonably accurate to say that the novel explores the consequences of the miseducation of Tyrrel and Williams. Falkland's polish contrasted to Tyrrel's

ill-mannered rusticity finally goads the latter into provoking Falkland fatally, and Williams's curiosity, undirected by worldly prudence, leads to his own tragedy.

Of more interest, however, is the related theme of how fiction instructs. Both Williams and Falkland are the victims of their reading in romance. Williams tells us that he has an "invincible attachment" to romances. "I panted for the unravelling of an adventure, with an anxiety, perhaps almost equal to that of the man whose future happiness or misery depended on the issue."... The statement, of course, is more true than Williams knows, for on the unravelling of Falkland's adventure his own happiness does indeed depend. Williams's own natural curiosity, misdirected by his reading about the world as it should be as depicted in romances and uninformed about the world as it is, is his destruction. Falkland's preoccupation with romance is no less destructive of his own happiness. (pp. 83-4)

The lives of both men are destroyed by their taking the exemplary world of the romance for a pattern to be imitated.... Falkland tries to live according to a set of values which has nothing to do with the world as it is. Somewhat less obviously Williams does the same thing. He pursues Falkland's secret with the same intensity with which he would watch a plot unwind.... Through at least the first half of the plot one gets the distinct impression that Williams is a character in the wrong novel, one used to living in the world as it should be and now floundering about in the world as it is. To survive, Williams must and does learn the devious ways of the world, but by then both he and Falkland have destroyed their own happiness because of the false ideals they have picked up from their youthful reading in romances.

To read *Caleb Williams* as an attack on romance is perhaps to discover the answer to one serious question about the novel: Why did Godwin rewrite the conclusion? In the original manuscript version the novel ends with Falkland's triumph in the final trial and Williams's subsequent defeat and madness. Apparently dissatisfied, Godwin rewrote the final few pages giving the victory to Williams and concluding with Falkland's death three days later. At first glance the new conclusion seems to be inconsistent with the internal logic of the novel, ... for in a world where injustice is presumably supreme, it gives the ultimate triumph to truth and justice. The new conclusion therefore seems to undermine the propagandistic thrust of the rest of the work. The problem is more apparent than real, however. That truth eventually triumphs does nothing to obviate the injustices which the characters have done to themselves and to each other. Indeed, the fact that truth does finally prevail gives one final and bitterly ironic twist to the novel, for all of the suffering which Falkland and Williams undergo is thereby robbed of what little meaning it may have had. Falkland dies lacking the one thing, a spotless reputation, which he had lived for, and Williams faces a future burdened with the knowledge that he is a murderer.... Godwin's point is not that truth will never prevail, but that the present state of society and its laws being what they are it will prevail only at an enormous and useless expense in human misery.

If anything it is the original conclusion which belies one major point the novel attempts to make. It will be recalled that in the dispute between the advocates of Fielding and the novel on one hand, and Richardson and romance on the other, one matter of contention is characterization. The romance is thought to perform its instructive intent by providing such exemplary characters as Sir Richard Grandison or such negative examples as Lovelace. In the novel, however, such moral oversimplification is not allowed, and the moral ambiguity of a character like Tom Jones is thought to provide useful instruction in the world as it is. The original ending of *Caleb Williams* places the work distinctly within the realm of romance according to this scheme of things. Falkland's character is thoroughly blackened, and Williams is depicted as the suffering innocent whose plight calls on our tears. But in a work which attacks the pernicious effects of romance it will not do to risk the charge of self-contradiction by employing the romance's favorite device of moral over-simplification. The revised version avoids this problem by placing the conflict in a morally ambiguous context. In the final paragraphs of his narrative Williams reflects on Falkland's death: "I have been his murderer. It was fit that he should praise my patience, who has fallen a victim, life and fame, to my precipitation! It would have been merciful in comparison, if I had planted a dagger in his heart." It is no longer very clear who has been persecuting whom.... (pp. 84-6)

Thanks to the miseducation inflicted on them by the authors of romances, Falkland and Williams are each victim and tyrant to the other. To read *Caleb Williams* in this manner is to see it as more than a fictional gloss on *Political Justice*. It presents its reader with a morally complex dilemma and makes a serious contribution to the ongoing controversy over the instructive purpose and method of fiction. (p. 86)

> C. R. Kropf, "'Caleb Williams' and the Attack on Romance," in Studies in the Novel, *Vol. VIII, No. 1, Spring, 1976, pp. 81-7.*

IAN OUSBY (essay date 1976)

[*Ousby discusses* Caleb Williams *as "a modernized version of the revenge tragedy" in which the detective and the criminal become symbiotically merged.*]

[Despite] Caleb's obvious courage, energy, and resourcefulness, the reader's view of his character is ultimately hostile. His detective activities involve, in a subtler and transmuted form, several of the themes associated with both Gines and his real-life counterparts. The characterization of Caleb thus shows how the sociologically determined suspicions of the detective manifest themselves in a complex fictional context.

In modern detective fiction the detective plays a role like that of the Duke in Shakespearean comedy: a moral hero and a figure of power, he establishes intellectual certainties and restores the order which has previously been threatened. Caleb Williams, on the contrary, is essentially a tragic figure, powerless in everything except his ability to catalyze discord. His discovery of Falkland's guilt does little good and a great deal of harm. (p. 21)

Even though Caleb is finally successful [at exposing Falkland], the import of the denouement is profoundly dissimilar from its equivalents in modern detective fiction. Superficially a moment of triumph for the detective, it is really a moment of psychological and moral defeat. It destroys even the detective's certainties about himself....

[At the beginning of the novel Caleb] is clearly no simple hayseed, but his view of life and his knowledge of the world smack distinctly of the evening class and the midnight oil; they are bookish and theoretical rather than experiential. (p. 22)

His move from the village to Falkland's manor house involves him for the first time in a world of experience and complexity.

In contrast to the world of Caleb's youth, Falkland's world is one of social power and sophistication, of intellectual and cultural refinement. Through his acquaintance with Falkland and his detective investigations, Caleb is introduced to psychological and moral complexities for which neither village life nor his books had prepared him. (p. 23)

The hero of revenge tragedy undergoes a similar development. Like Caleb, Hamlet and Vindice are scholars thrust into a world of action, a world of decisions with direct human consequences rather than of abstract problems. Again like Caleb, Bussy D'Ambois is the blunt countryman forced to cope with the complexities of court life. In both literal and symbolic terms the court of Jacobean drama and Falkland's manor house function similarly: they epitomize the world of sophistication and complexity with which the hero must deal. Moreover, the complexities presented to Caleb by Falkland's life assume a form familiar in revenge tragedy: the hidden crime or sin which gives the lie to the avowed public standards of morality.

In these circumstances the reaction of the revenge hero is a delicate balance of attraction and repulsion. He becomes a railer at corruption, fascinated by what he attacks. Caleb's reaction to Falkland hinges on a similar paradox. Initially viewing his master as an unspotted emblem of innocence and purity, he then deliberately destroys this ideal image by embarking on his detective activities. Once Caleb has discovered the truth about Falkland's murder of Tyrrel, he oscillates between continued admiration and a hatred of both Falkland and the social system he represents. (pp. 23-4)

Caleb's curiosity, the motive that makes him turn detective, corresponds to the revenger's desire for revenge. In Jacobean drama revenge has an awkward habit of recoiling upon its actor's head, and the revenger commonly dies hoist with his own petard. Caleb's detection exposes him to the same fate. With his discovery of Falkland's crime Caleb's role—to use his own terminology—switches from the "offensive" to the "defensive." ... Successful as a detective, he almost immediately finds himself in the dock rather than the witness box, and thereafter moves steadily toward social disgrace and psychological ruin. The stages of his destruction mirror his activities as a detective. (p. 24)

The revenger's fate as victim of his own machinations represents a judgment on his actions. As the dying Laertes sees, his death is an ironic stroke of justice. For revenge in Jacobean drama is a morally corrosive activity. Superficially it appears to make its actor the agent of justice; yet far from exemplifying his moral integrity, it calls into question and impairs that integrity. Corrupted by the pursuit of revenge, the revenger dies a victim of the disease he has begun by attempting to cure. Yet viewing a similar reversal in his own life, Caleb Williams can see only a grim irony of fate and an indictment of the social system. His resemblance to the revenger is completed by a nuance which eludes him: the element of punishment, of implicit judgment on the questionable morality of his own activities as a detective.

Caleb Williams, then, can be viewed as a modernized version of the revenge tragedy. The parallel serves to underline the book's essential movement and to suggest the terms by which its hero should be judged. Like the revenger, Caleb in his role as detective is subject to criticism for both his morals and his motives. The matter is complicated, however, by the fact that the entire story is told by Caleb himself: as an autobiographer, he is bent on self-vindication, not self-criticism. He distracts attention from his failings by describing his character in deceptively simple and laudatory terms. According to his own account, he is merely innocent and curious.

Caleb's protestations of innocence begin on the book's first page. "My own conscience," he declares, "witnesses in behalf of that innocence my pretensions to which are regarded in the world as incredible." . . . Indeed, he has undertaken the narrative to clear himself of the charge of theft which Falkland has used to blacken his character and render his adult life "a theatre of calamity." . . . As the narrative proceeds, however, it becomes apparent that Caleb aims at much more than a purely legal vindication.

To the word "innocence" are added other terms suggestive of broader qualities and often touching on key Godwinian concepts, terms such as "simplicity" and "sincerity." The insistence is not merely that Caleb is not a thief but also that he is innocent in more profound ways. He is, he implies, without guilt or sin. Exhibiting this purity in his youth and his early days at Falkland House, he has miraculously retained it through all the miseries and complexities of his relationship with Falkland.

In trying to seek out the precise nature of this vaunted innocence, the reader is likely to find himself in sympathy with Falkland, who at one point quotes with approval the dying words of Brutus: "O Virtue! I sought thee as a substance, but I find thee an empty name!" . . . For all the frequency with which Caleb invokes it, his innocence proves elusive and nebulous. Part of the reader's doubt arises from the very frequency with which Caleb resorts to the term to explain or justify his actions. Describing his first suspicion that Falkland is a murderer, and aware that "the reader will scarcely believe that the idea suggested itself to my mind," he immediately excuses himself on the grounds that: "It was but a passing thought; but it serves to mark the simplicity of my character." . . . The explanation is, in fact, open to objection on two counts. As the narrative makes clear, the suspicion is anything but passing. Moreover, the reader cannot lightly accept a definition of innocence or simplicity which includes such a readiness to believe evil of others; one imagines that innocence is distinguished by precisely the opposite tendency. (pp. 24-6)

[His] interviews with Falkland show not innocence but a convenient, false naiveté. Whether or not Caleb's actions are justifiable, it is clearly misleading to call them "innocent." Caleb himself admits as much when he refers to his own "air of innocence" and his "apparent want of design." . . . The effect of this admission, however, is somewhat decreased by his apparent lack of interest in drawing any distinction between the true and the false, between innocence and guile—a failing which he later insists to be one of the worst aspects of the world's opinion. (p. 26)

Caleb's use of the idea of innocence serves to draw attention to both his unreliability as narrator and his dubious moral status. Obviously he is innocent—as he claims to be—in the strictly legal sense. The substance behind his other claims seems merely to be an initial naiveté, an "ignorance of the world" . . . , which is distinguished primarily by the speed of its disappearance. (pp. 26-7)

Caleb's innocence is destroyed by his curiosity. He himself points to this quality as the mainspring of his character and the determinant of his fortunes. Listing its manifestations, he first mentions his "mechanical turn" . . . , shown later in his mastery of such diverse skills as lockpicking, carpentry, acting,

watchmaking, and writing. This vein of practical ingenuity, combined with a readiness to learn, aligns him with the tradition of sturdy Protestant heroes stemming from Robinson Crusoe. . . .

Fictional detectives are frequently characterized by pragmatism and by practical ingenuity. In Caleb's case, however, these qualities are strangely unrelated to that side of his curiosity which makes him turn detective. His resourcefulness and his willingness to learn are important primarily in helping him to resist and evade Falkland's tyranny, and are only marginally relevant to the events which provoke that tyranny. Caleb's ingenuity arises from a practical interest in the world around him and has an immediate, sometimes vital use. By contrast, his curiosity about Falkland is strictly nonutilitarian. (p. 27)

His eagerness is in response to an irrational obsession rather than a practical need. Caleb is the victim of "a kind of fatal impulse that seemed destined to hurry me to my destruction." . . . In imagery which suggests the similarity of his obsessive curiosity to Edgar Allan Poe's "imp of the perverse," Caleb speaks of the "demon" . . . which finally brings him to "the verge of the precipice." . . . (pp. 27-8)

A similar habit of self-aggrandizement characterizes the way in which Caleb describes that side of his curiosity which prompts him to become a detective. He is, he explains near the beginning of the narrative, "a sort of natural philosopher." . . . Reflecting ruefully on the causes of his misfortunes, he remarks, "My offence had merely been a mistaken thirst of knowledge." . . . Such remarks are vague in reference but have the unmistakable effect of suggesting that the reader should view Caleb as a noble Faustian overreacher or a daring speculator. (p. 28)

In fact, Caleb's curiosity is of precisely the sort that he himself had previously designated as "ignoble." . . . He develops an interest in Falkland unadorned by either moral concern or intellectual originality. Rather, his master affords him "an ample field for speculation and conjecture." . . . As if to emphasize the point that Caleb's speculation is that of the gossip rather than the moral philosopher, the reader is told that the other servants in the house regard Falkland in a strikingly similar manner. . . . Although Caleb's curiosity eventually leads him into realms of moral and intellectual complexity which a Faust or a St. Leon might well inhabit, this is essentially an accident—one that he hardly welcomes—and not the result of any intention on his part. Rather than being the overreacher which his narrative tone at times suggests, Caleb the detective is more the Peeping Tom and the gossip, a figure who invites criticism.

Caleb enters Falkland's service a young and inexperienced man, ignorant of the ways of the world. Under the pressure of curiosity about his master's life he outgrows his initial naiveté, replacing it with a feigned naiveté, an "air of innocence." Godwin's firm disapproval of the type of social manner and behavior adopted by Caleb is on record elsewhere. "Insincerity," he writes in *The Enquirer,* "corrupts and empoisons the soul of the actor, and is of pernicious example to every spectator." Indeed, sincerity—one of the terms that Caleb uses with so uncritical a liberality—is a vital concept in Godwin's vision of ideal social intercourse. However, the description of Caleb's activities as a detective does not reflect merely the social ethics of a philosopher who could on occasion take extreme positions. It also represents a specific response to contemporary issues.

In the novel Caleb is not called a "detective," for the term did not gain currency until the middle of the nineteenth century. He is called a "spy." . . . Then, as now, the term could refer simply to "one who spies upon or watches a person or persons secretly." In its more specialized sense it was applied to the professional snooper, in particular to the spy whose investigations served matters of foreign or military policy, or of internal security. (pp. 28-9)

[*Caleb Williams*] reflects not only the general hostility to spying but also the fear of the spy in its acutest form. That Caleb should be the servant of the man whose crime he uncovers is a fact of central importance to the narrative. Caleb's twin identity as servant and spy is implicit in his Christian name. . . .

Godwin, with his Calvinist upbringing and his youthful experience as a minister, would certainly have been aware of these references. Indeed, throughout the book Caleb's roles as servant and spy are continually brought into juxtaposition. The occasion on which the term "spy" is first used of Caleb also draws attention to his social status. Falkland threatens him: "You set yourself as a spy upon my actions. But bitterly shall you repent your insolence. Do you think you shall watch my privacies with impunity?" . . . Later Falkland reproves Caleb's attempts to draw him into conversation as "improper" . . . and warns him, "learn to be more respectful!" . . . In each case the criticism invokes not an abstract moral code but a code of conduct dictated by their positions as master and servant. (p. 34)

This deliberate juxtaposition is ironic. . . . A combination of faithful service and efficient surveillance is impossible, for spying requires of Caleb a violation of the duties involved in his assigned social role. The breach of fidelity takes on particular significance within the context of the master-servant relationship.

From the beginning of the narrative it is made clear that Falkland, despite the eccentricities caused by his private guilt, is in the salient respects a model employer. . . . "His manner was kind, attentive and humane" . . . , Caleb reports of their first meeting, adding: "My reception was as gracious and encouraging as I could possibly desire. Mr. Falkland questioned me respecting my learning, and my conceptions of men and things, and listened to my answers with condescension and approbation. This kindness soon restored to me a considerable part of my self-possession, though I still felt restrained by the graceful, but unaltered dignity of his carriage." . . . On the one hand, Falkland's behavior implicitly asserts the master's right to keep his servants at a respectful distance. On the other, his manner shows a kindness and sensitivity appropriate to the local squire who is offering to bring an orphaned youth under the protection of the "family." In view of this latter characteristic, Caleb's suspicions have about them an air of churlish ingratitude. They represent, as it were, a refusal to return kind attentions with kind thoughts. However, the burden of the criticism falls not so much on the suspicions themselves as on the course of conduct that they lead Caleb to pursue.

The air of frankness that he feigns in his conversations with Falkland in fact represents an exaggerated version of that "studied countenance" which Godwin noted in all servants. Inscrutability becomes supplemented by a calculated deceptiveness. From Falkland's point of view the effect is to increase the gap that separates him from his servant. From Caleb's viewpoint the gap is narrowed, for he renders himself deliberately unknowable in order to penetrate his master's privacies more successfully. On the psychological level, Caleb attempts to delve into the hidden recesses of his master's mind, to uncover the source of his private anguish. On the physical level, his activities involve a violation of his master's private possessions. (pp. 35-6)

Refusing to view his master's affairs from a respectful distance, Caleb is claiming an intimacy with Falkland to which even a social equal would have no right. By thus converting himself into Falkland's inquisitor rather than his servant, Caleb is not merely offending against the initial terms of the relationship, but threatening to reverse them. (p. 36)

Thus, although Caleb begins his detection with the interests of a gossip, he develops into a mischief-maker of a peculiarly potent sort. The magistrate's expostulation when Caleb finally presents evidence against Falkland reflects a very real fear in the contemporary audience: "There would be a speedy end to all order and good government, if fellows that trample upon ranks and distinctions in this atrocious sort, were upon any consideration suffered to get off." . . . The criticism is one that Caleb himself cannot entirely discount. Though it only serves to add spice to the adventure, he is on occasion uneasily aware of the "forbidden" . . . nature of his investigations. (pp. 36-7)

To this analysis of the judgments passed on Caleb it may be objected that they suggest a surprising degree of accord between Godwin the radical philosopher and the middle-class public of his day, as they imply an agreement between Godwin and Falkland, the epitome of the established system. The answer to the objection is that, on the issue of spying, such agreement exists. Caleb's detection involves a disregard for those basic qualities—sincerity and sensitivity—upon which Godwin's ideal social code was based. (p. 37)

Though Falkland's later treatment of Caleb is identified with that social tyranny which Godwin so hated, Caleb's actions also strongly resemble that rash revolutionism which the author criticized in his fellow radicals. Godwin's political writings look forward to the gradual evolution of a Utopian society while ruling out the desirability of revolution in the streets.

Eschewing revolution as a means of attaining his ideal goals, Godwin often adopts a stance of modified liberalism. It is perhaps unfortunate that his thought should be best known through *Political Justice,* a work which avowedly concentrates on abstract theory and favors expressions of absolute disapproval of various social institutions. As *The Enquirer* and the pamphlet writings show, Godwin had a flexible mind, and his practical response was usually to accept the fact that such institutions were here to stay for at least the foreseeable future and to suggest ways in which they might be made more liberal and humane.

To *Caleb Williams* this habit leads to a distribution of sympathy between Caleb, the assailant of the social order, and Falkland, the representative of "things as they are." Though Godwin later agrees with Caleb's fulminations against the system, he also sympathizes with Falkland's protests against the implications of Caleb's conduct as a spy. Falkland's angry dismissal of the detective as an "insolent domestic" . . . thus carries with it the endorsement of a writer who in practice often showed a cautious and pragmatic acquiescence to current institutions.

In *Caleb Williams* detection is not merely a transgression of social etiquette; it is also a complex psychological process that further renders Caleb's status as hero dubious. He achieves the intimacy with Falkland that he so passionately desires, but it proves a curse rather than a blessing. As his investigations progress, Caleb plunges deeper and deeper into moral uncertainties. Caleb and Falkland begin to resemble each other, and their fates become inextricably linked; by the end of the novel, detective and criminal appear more like symbiotic twins than antagonists.

Although Caleb's ultimate conduct toward his master smacks of churlish ingratitude, his initial response is a profound—indeed, an exaggerated—respect. In a book replete with purple rhetoric his declarations of feeling for Falkland loom especially hyperbolic. (pp. 37-8)

Caleb's assumption of the role of detective appears an act of involuntary iconoclasm against the idol he himself has created, a surrender to "the demon that possessed me." . . . Significantly, one of his first actions as a detective is to launch an oblique attack on Falkland by voicing doubts about the character of Alexander the Great, who attempted to "persuade mankind that he was the son of Jupiter Ammon." . . . Caleb cites the opinions of Fielding and Doctor Prideaux, which Falkland considers to be "Accursed blasphemy!" . . . But blasphemy is always an ambiguous activity, and disbelief does not supplant veneration in Caleb's mind. In fact, the story that originally sows the seed of suspicion also provides him with "a thousand fresh reasons to admire and love Mr. Falkland." . . .

Caleb's discovery of the truth about Falkland's past merely intensifies his emotional turbulence. He had earlier promised himself "an unknown gratification" . . . in the achievement of the secret, and he celebrated its pursuit as a means toward maturity and the expansion of his powers. It proves, however, to be an initiation into a world of frightening experience. . . . (p. 39)

In his "mistaken thirst of knowledge" . . . Caleb has encountered the problem of evil in a peculiarly complex and disturbing form. During his investigations he had been uneasily aware of their forbidden nature, if only in the most obvious sense that they went against Falkland's commands. He discovered that, despite his good intentions and his earnestness, he contained the seeds of evil within himself; he could, as he confesses to Falkland, yield to a "demon." . . . (pp. 39-40)

Expressed in abstract terms, the truth that Caleb has discovered is that good and evil, though apparently worlds apart, are in practice bedfellows. In his relationship with Falkland, Caleb enacts this truth for the rest of the novel. Rather than appearing as simple polar opposites, the detective and the criminal become inextricably connected. . . .

This close structural relationship is emphasized by the emotional bonds that develop between the detective and the criminal. Caleb eventually achieves an intimacy with Falkland, though of a type he neither expected nor welcomes. He has sympathy for Falkland. . . . (p. 40)

When apart, each is unable to rid himself of the mental presence of the other. After Caleb's departure from the manor and escape from prison, Falkland persists in remaining obsessed by his very existence. Even after his ex-master's death Caleb cannot forget him. . . . Brought together by their obsessive natures, they conclude by becoming obsessed with each other. The process involves something approaching a destruction of their separate identities. . . .

This destruction of their separate identities is aided by the manner in which Caleb progressively comes to resemble Falk-

land. The effect of detection upon Caleb is like the effect of the crime itself upon Falkland. The servant develops the master's desperate "sensibility to reputation" . . . ; this is actually his main motive for writing his memoirs. Energetic and youthful, he had initially appeared the antithesis of his decaying and neurotic master. Having become the sole sharer of Falkland's secret, unable to blot out the knowledge and reluctant to communicate it to others, Caleb ages as Falkland himself had aged after Tyrrel's death. (p. 41)

Their final confrontation, when Caleb at last publicly accuses his master of murder, brings to a climax the emotional bond and the similarity between the two men. The intimacy which Caleb's earlier detection had initiated is symbolically culminated and acknowledged. (pp. 41-2)

During one of his insinuating conversations with his master, Caleb had remarked that "innocence and guilt are too much confounded in human life." . . . He was referring to the fallibility of the world's opinion, but his remark might apply in another sense to the world to which his detective activities have introduced him. For the final effect of the relationship between the detective and the criminal is to introduce ambiguities on the psychological level similar to those on the social level. Detection begins as an activity apparently designed to establish moral and intellectual clarity. The detective, voluntarily or involuntarily, assumes the role of an agent of justice, seeking to distinguish good from evil and to identify the source of evil. Caleb's relationship with Falkland, however, progressively suggests that good and evil do not admit of so simple a polarization. Inextricably linked, the detective and the criminal are similar in their characters and in their fates. Rather than emerging as antithetical or antagonistic in their relations, they grow into symbiotic twins. (p. 42)

Ian Ousby, " 'Caleb Williams'," in his Bloodhounds of Heaven: The Detective in English Fiction from Godwin to Doyle, *Cambridge, Mass.: Harvard University Press, 1976, pp. 19-42.*

MITZI MYERS   (essay date 1981)

[*Myers argues that Godwin's biography of Wollstonecraft,* Memoirs of the Author of "A Vindication of the Rights of Woman," *reveals much about Godwin's own attitudes. According to Myers, the work can be read as "a part of Godwin's intellectual—and emotional—biography."*]

Though it has long been recognized that Wollstonecraft's effect on Godwin's later thought was complicated and profound, the *Memoirs* have received surprisingly little attention as an important document in Godwin's reformulation of *Political Justice*'s rationalistic doctrines. Yet their pervasive emphasis on feeling and their candid exploration of personal relationships epitomize philosophical issues, and Wollstonecraft is treated both as personality and as principle, at once individual woman and symbol of cultural values, even of an alternate cognitive mode. Generically, then, Godwin's memoir is an unusual hybrid, one which unites Wollstonecraft's notion of herself, Godwin's reading of her character, and his analysis of that character's impact on himself and his philosophy. Moreover, these variant species of life-writing mesh within a narrative framework structured both by Godwin's basic philosophical assumptions and his proclivities for romantic fiction.

It is not surprising that so complex a work should produce divergent responses. Its history tells much about changing conceptions of biography, as well as cultural attitudes toward women and feminism. The reception of the biography was remarkably stormy: both subject and author bore the stigmata of sans-culottic reform, and 1798 was clouded by political repression. Worse yet, Godwin's philosophical tenet of sincerity rendered him an opponent of biographical reticence and thus something of an innovator in life-writing. Indeed, his extreme frankness in publicizing his wife's sexual entanglements, suicide attempts, and unorthodox religious opinions so soon after her death still retains its power to surprise, if not to shock. The *Memoirs* spread far and wide facts which had not been generally known, juicy tidbits greedily seized by the conservative press for a brutal propaganda campaign.... Wollstonecraft became a horrible example of voracious female sexuality run wild, her life, her death, the *Memoirs* themselves warnings, intoned one pious clergyman, directly inspired by the hand of Providence. (pp. 300-01)

In their origin in crisis, in their interiorized presentation of subject and biographer alike, in their consequences for Godwin's later philosophy, the *Memoirs* are a congeries of romantic attitudes, their shaping of self and subject in terms of internal and private aspects a paradigm of romantic biography and, to some extent, of confessional autobiography as well.

The genesis and strategies of the *Memoirs* make them exemplary for the study of biography as the artistic construct resulting from the intersection of two personalities. The story of how the philosopher who pronounced marriage a pernicious institution and the feminist who had a child outside wedlock settled into satisfying if unconventional domesticity is best delineated in the almost daily notes of the lovers themselves. It is only necessary to notice here a basic pattern in their letters which clarifies Godwin's impetus in the *Memoirs:* the configuration of love as mutuality, as the reciprocal expansion of latent powers, as education in short. Godwin's confessional *disjecta membra* reiterate his "prominent vein of docility," that ductile teachability which is the constant companion of his scepticism, a willingness to learn from others that made him, thought Coleridge, almost "too persuadible a man." In this, his most stirring and deeply felt emotional relationship, Godwin, Wollstonecraft's "boy pupil," gladly learned as well as gladly taught. (pp. 303-04)

[His] portrayal of Wollstonecraft in the *Memoirs* [is] a portrayal which was further shaped by his reading and rereading of her most romantic works throughout their relationship, as his unpublished journal records; he was always a diligent student of what he wanted to understand.

Godwin's journal for their last month together suggests Wollstonecraft's tutelage and cryptically hints at self-exploration. Stimulated by immersion in such romantic texts as *Werther, Julie,* the *Confessions,* and by her example, he worked on a "Life" in early August 1797, while concurrently studying Rousseau. Such reading nicely epitomizes his attitudes toward his wife and indicates the kind of confessional models he drew on for the *Memoirs*.... On 30 August, while Wollstonecraft was in labor, Godwin settled down to reread *Mary,* her first novel, an autobiographical fiction drenched in personal feeling. His entries from that day until the tenth of September when she died are succinctly painful. 10 September reads, "20 minutes before 8," followed by three blank heavily scored lines. He could not form the words, and he could not attend the funeral. The emotions suppressed in his journal poured out in letters to friends, "more like distracted lines than any thing rational," one recipient commented.

This grief-stricken correspondence enunciates the images and themes expanded in the *Memoirs,* sketches the just-discovered order of verities, the new mode of being, Godwin is trying to take in. He describes Wollstonecraft as without equal in the world, his guide to a kind of happiness he had previously been unable to imagine, indeed "scarcely admitted the possibility of it." She is a "light," whose memory will make him "wise and more human." His only pleasure is the cultivation of melancholy: he wants to weaken his stoicism and refine his sensibility. "I love," he writes, "to tread the edge of intellectual danger ... and in this indulgence and this vigilance I place my present luxury." Godwin felt he had "half-destroyed" himself in writing such letters as these, but he soon found a more satisfactory employment. He abandoned the separate lodgings where he had always worked for his wife's study, enshrined her portrait as inspiriting muse, and steeped himself in her writings, as if he were trying to absorb her very essence. (pp. 305-06)

The *Memoirs,* then, were undertaken as a mode of self-therapy, in which the mourner seeks both to come to terms with his loss and, through empathically entering the beloved's personality, to assimilate and exemplify those emotional lessons he is conning. But the *Memoirs* are more than psychological self-help. They are also an imaginatively organized artistic construct drawing on Godwin's previous experience as thinker and novelist, a complex example of intergeneric, as well as interpersonal, reciprocity. Godwin was not a novice at biography: he had begun his literary career as a biographer, and he projected and published several lives besides the *Memoirs*. As a philosophical student of history, he had examined carefully the problems inherent in the writing of biography or individual history. In an unpublished essay from January 1797, parts of which later surfaced in the preface to his 1830 novel *Cloudesly,* Godwin considers the relationship "Of History and Romance." He finds the minute particularities and psychological details of individual history far more valuable than general historical abstractions, for the human mind naturally gravitates to "individualities." Biography leads to self-knowledge and imaginative moral enthusiasm; it instructs in motivation and the way passions operate. Significantly, Godwin pictures the student of individuals producing his collected materials to "engage in the solemn act of self-investigation ... &, by a sort of magnetism, cause those particulars to start out to view in ourselves, which might otherwise have lain for ever undetected." Yet because of man's complexity—"the folds of the human heart, the endless intermixture of motive with motive"—Godwin concludes that biography is finally only a useful guess in the dark, an attempt to "hit on that thread" which will unravel the essence of the subject. It is, paradoxically, the author of fictitious narrative, of romance, who writes real history: the biographer is but a romantic writer without the "sublime license of imagination."

"True history" Godwin defines as "a delineation of consistent, human character, in a display of the manner in which such a character acts under successive circumstances, in showing how character increases & assimilates new substances to its own, & how it decays, together with the catastrophe into which by its own gravity it naturally declines," a relevant recipe for lives feigned or real. Whether the overt fable of romance or the covert fable of history, Godwin's "first enquiry is, Can I derive instruction from it? Is it a genuine praxis upon the nature of man?" Truth to human nature, grasped through sympathetic self-projection, is his criterion. The poet or novelist, he argues, is superior to the historian because he begins his task with "a preconception of the qualities" that belong to his subject. Knowing "the principle of [that subject's] actions," he need only educe from his premises and "aid those conclusions by consulting the oracle in his bosom, the suggestions of his own heart," in order to unfold the "seeds of character" and the "modes in which they expand themselves," the organic connection of plot and character. Such is the rationale for Godwin's romances, all psychological case histories of individuals, the same approach—analytic, autobiographical—also informs his history of his wife, in which he seeks to have the best of both worlds: the historian's factual accuracy, the novelist's psychological penetration and, always his desideratum, unity of effect. Godwin's wariness of scientific truth in life-writing . . . implies a rather sophisticated awareness that the story of a life, one's own or another's, is in important ways necessarily a fiction, the artistic recreation, even creation, of a character's essence. Godwin's developing romantic aesthetic offers one solution to that "stiff" artistic problem inherent in biography: how to infuse the "granite-like solidity" of factual truth with the "rainbow-like intangibility" of personality.

In the *Memoirs,* then, Godwin is exercising the imaginative freedom of the artist, demonstrating through his selection and shaping of fact, through his empathic narrator's thematic interposition, that sensitive affectivity he finds so exemplary in Wollstonecraft herself. Indeed, in his preface, Godwin presents his wife as a moral model, the detailing of whose gifts, especially those private "virtues which discover themselves principally in personal intercourse," will promote public benefit, improvement contingent on his engaging readerly "sympathy." . . . The outraged response to this edifying purpose might have been predicted even by Godwin himself, for he was still smarting from the slights Wollstonecraft suffered when they married . . . , thus forcing her acquaintances to recognize that she had never been Gilbert Imlay's wife and that her daughter Fanny was illegitimate. Yet he proceeds to elaborate not only this tragic liaison, but also Wollstonecraft's intense and unrequited passion for the married Henry Fuseli, the fact that she became Godwin's mistress shortly after her break with Imlay, and the information that the two married only because she was again pregnant. Godwin's extraordinary candor might be explained by his philosophic sincerity or Rousseau's example, but he did not in fact tell everything he knew. He omitted, for instance, what still remains one of the most problematic episodes in Wollstonecraft's career—her leading role in engineering her sister Eliza's separation from her husband. Godwin stresses that his practice is grounded in factual accuracy: he emphasizes his first-hand knowledge, the early notes he took as a student of human nature, the inquiries for further data he made. His facts are, so far as he could discover, true, but he is willing to make significant deletions when they do not serve his thematic purpose. That purpose, however, necessitates his including even the most intimate particulars which contribute to his interpretation of Wollstonecraft as an energetic and idealistic woman of genius whose trajectory was fueled by her attempts to realize those extraordinary emotional and imaginative capabilities she possessed. She is "a lofty and undaunted spirit," a "great soul"—a real life romantic heroine. . . . Every biographer of Wollstonecraft must decide how to resolve the complexities of her character and achievement, how to adjust her rationalism and her romanticism. Godwin's decision was clearly determined by his own needs. And it is Wollstonecraft as exemplar for him with which he is ultimately most concerned, her biography entailing his autobiography. (pp. 307-09)

Feeling, imagination, and sympathy constitute both his method and his theme. Disparaging private affections, the Godwin of *Political Justice* liked to talk of disinterestedness and universal benevolence, of judging human actions as an "impartial spectator." Shifting from academic argument to palpable reality, Godwin the biographer tries hard to get inside his subject's skin, to understand how and why she developed as she did. He must feel his way into the subjective situation of a woman of "ardent imagination" who "felt herself formed for domestic affection, and all those tender charities, which men of sensibility have constantly treated as the dearest band of human society," charities he, the man of rationality, had heretofore denigrated as impediments to perfectibility. . . . Comprehending this life requires that he reassess his former position step by step, a process not thoroughly accomplished until the reworked second edition of the *Memoirs* where he emerges as a full-fledged "new man of feeling," to anticipate the subtitle of his 1805 novel *Fleetwood.* Beginning with an image to be quickened in his text, Godwin refines that image and himself in composition, as his pattern of analysis and defense, addition and revision, testifies. As his imaginative apperception of Wollstonecraft and the values she embodies matures, so his methodic efforts to become acquainted with himself mandate a change of heart, a tempering of system. Indicatively, with the draft of her biography ripening to fruition, "Life (moi-même)"—Godwin habitually couches the emotionally charged in French—reappears in his journal by 29 November.

The biographer's subtle strategies foster the thinker's conversion; the writing of the life itself is for him a further lesson in his ongoing personal and philosophical quest for what nourishes human improvement. As he elsewhere remarks, one fully understands a subject because, not before, he has written about it. The second edition of the *Memoirs* was promptly followed by a crucially important autobiographical note in which he finds *Political Justice* "essentially defective, in . . . not yielding a proper attention to the empire of feeling. The voluntary actions of men are under the direction of their feelings." Rather than the rational calculation of consequences, the spontaneity of virtue now kindles his interest. He had come to believe that man is inevitably spurred by motives peculiar to him as an individual, that domestic affections, ineradicable and infinitely powerful, are not only inseparable from the "culture of the heart," but that they are premier instigators of morality. Godwin's succeeding works and personal memoranda bear continued witness to his new-found faith in feeling, domestic affections, and marriage; that institution once "the worst of all laws," "the worst of all properties," "the worst of monopolies" is transformed into "the grand holiday of our human nature . . . the white spot, the little gleam of pure sunshine, which compensates for a thousand other hardships and calamities." Meticulously casting and recasting the audits of his mental experience, Godwin elaborated on the insights generated by Wollstonecraft and the writing of the *Memoirs* throughout his long life, his successive revisions calling to mind Nietzsche's equation of philosophy with "confession . . . a species of involuntary and unconscious autobiography."

Those biographical tactics which crystallized his conceptions Godwin blends from varied sources: his own memory and imaginative excursions into the mind of his subject, novels, essays, and autobiographies of sensibility, Wollstonecraft's fiction, the revelatory documents he was editing—a harmonious nexus resonant as the character he presents. For his is a less naive formulation than some critics allow. Like his successors (one reason Wollstonecraft lures biographers), he discovered in her transports and sorrows a ready-made tragic plot. He also found to hand in his literary models an organizing image, the paradigm of romantic genius within which Wollstonecraft's temperament and activities could be satisfyingly shaped. And it is an image consonant with his subject's view of herself, indeed explicitly sanctioned by her works. . . . Wollstonecraft is for Godwin "a female Werter," "endowed with the most exquisite and delicious sensibility," a spirit "almost of too fine a texture to encounter the vicissitudes of human affairs, to whom pleasure is transport, and disappointment is agony indescribable." . . . (pp. 310-12)

But the tenderness Godwin treasures is not the whole of his account. The concomitant of Wollstonecraft's potent sensibility is resilient strength, the decisiveness and confidence, even the quick temper and imperious resentment whose existence he does not blink. Though his focus is the private individual rather than the public reformer—he finds her two *Vindications* harsh and rugged, not wholly typical of her "essential" nature—his integrating motif of romantic genius embraces affective range and social protest, stretches to accommodate both the independent champion of her sex and the "worshipper of domestic life." . . . It also implies that remarkable intuitive gift he makes so much of in his autobiographical conclusion. Wollstonecraft filtered through such an alembic lets Godwin indulge his bent toward impressionism and psychological dissection, the latter perhaps most telling in his reconstruction of the Imlay debacle—that "ill-starred unhappy passion." . . . His characteristic accent on motivation and determining matrix dovetails nicely with Wollstonecraft's own approach to her life. Unlike many early biographers, he furnishes an etiology of genius, a personality gradually assuming its own unique form, not just a finished and mature personage. He gives full weight to her childhood remembrance—the parental tyranny, the lack of love—and his rendering of her recollections, from brief phrases to whole portraits, is demonstrably colored by literary memory. He indicates how her life and temperament shaped her work and frequently notes the autobiographical strain in her writing; he was the first to stress the influence of her personal experience on her career, a fundamental point in modern explication. He cites with artistry, marrying his text to hers, appropriating her voice to express his own loss. (pp. 312-13)

Godwin's personal situation and mental history play an increasingly prominent role as the biography unfolds. Throughout, his interpretive assessments and philosophical asides operate self-referentially. He projects his experience as journalist or radical on Wollstonecraft's past (with occasional skewed results), considers such topics as religion, gratitude, cohabitation, and suicide in line with his peculiar tenets, and periodically calls attention to his privileged knowledge and his bereavement. His comments also, especially in connection with Wollstonecraft's traumatic loves, evince self-emendation, as in this concession to the emotive: "Moral reasoning is nothing but the awakening of certain feelings." . . . But it is in the moving final chapters that he makes explicit the meaning for him of his interaction with Wollstonecraft, with, as he says, the same frank simplicity pervading the whole work. Turning from implicit to avowed autobiography, he traces minutely the growth of their affection, which he describes in terms of equality and mutual companionship: "friendship melting into love." Yet more revealingly, he delineates how one who "never loved till now" was initiated through that experience into fresh truths and new ways of knowing. . . .

Godwin's central autobiographical theme is his thwarted access to enriched perception, developed through symbiotic spiritual profiles in which "the improvement I was in the act of re-

ceiving" is equated with "the leading traits of her intellectual character from which it flowed." . . . His specialization in the fine psychological discrimination of complex and dynamic emotional states serves him well in appraising his own condition. With his customary exactitude, he sifts his nascent receptivity with analytical rigor. He and Wollstonecraft, he believes, cultivated their powers in divergent directions—logic and metaphysics versus a taste for the picturesque. But the difference between the two is not merely one of specialization. . . . Wollstonecraft . . . incarnates for Godwin intuitive imagination, the alternate cognitive mode of romantic genius. Here too he could find warrant in her works, from the *Rights of Woman* to "On Poetry" to the "Hints." Enlarging on her unwavering intuition as established early in the *Memoirs* . . . , Godwin relates how his "oscillation and skepticism were fixed by her boldness." He judges that this instantaneous insight, at once a feeling and a faculty of understanding, can be nurtured through "the daily recurrence of a striking example"; such attuned intelligence, then, is learnable through "responsive vibration" and reeducated habit. . . . Dissatisfied with this summation, however, Godwin recasts it, as well as other key passages, in the revised edition.

The second version of the *Memoirs* has received a bad press; it is usually dismissed without examination as a more discreet rendition of the first, its modifications intended merely to appease an irate public. But close collation invites a different view. Many of the variances are minor. As ever, Godwin corrected word by word; striving for precision, he rephrases, inserts new reflections. He was also clearly aware of widespread strictures. He excises some references to living people, occasional phrases which had struck a live nerve in reviewers . . . , and a very few minor details which might be open to misinterpretation. But he leaves unaltered a much attacked section on Wollstonecraft's lack of deathbed religion, and he refuses to blur his central conception of his subject or to abridge his treatment of her unconventional acts. On the contrary, he copes with the criticism by probing those acts and their rationale yet more. He is alert to justify, but he does not apologize. His additions expand on the romantic motifs which unify the work. He repeats that his history is "personal," not solely a literary biography. He renews attention to Wollstonecraft's "two most cherished conceptions, the picturesque and the affectionate." . . . His reworking of the by now notorious Imlay affair typifies his handling. Stressing that the narrow rules of vulgar morality cannot contain "the being who restlessly aspires to superior gratification," he locates Wollstonecraft's mistake not in the irregularity of the liaison, but in her misjudgment of the person. He insists that her desperate and prolonged attempts to hang on to her recalcitrant lover were the consequence of her idealism. The affectivity Godwin celebrates is not passive; he counters the reviewers' sneers at the "unresisting slave of feeling" with fresh emphasis on her native energy and elevation. Her very errors, he urges, "were connected and interwoven with the qualities most characteristic of her disposition and genius." . . . (pp. 313-15)

Godwin's most extensive reconsiderations signify his own growing preoccupation with the inner life. In the interval between editions, he had worked out new views on marriage and solidified the philosophical underpinning of his solicitude for the affective. Selection of the beloved becomes the most important choice of private life, and he now terms prejudice his earlier support for individual nonconformity with marital custom, though he still believes that current laws demand reform. . . . Too, the wholly rewritten section on Wollstonecraft's relationship with Fuseli says even more about Godwin than his subject. The first edition dilates on Wollstonecraft's ideal of love as the principal solace of life; the second offers no timid toning down, but a position paper on domestic affections as vivifiers of sensibility and social sympathy which stands as Godwin's *locus classicus* on the topic, quoted and requoted in subsequent works. Such changes are not recantations, but expansions of his vision of human possibility. Nor does his remodeled conclusion betray the closet chauvinist, as some argue. His musing on the acculturated approaches of male and female discloses less sexism than self-exploration. In emblemizing himself and Wollstonecraft as representatives of the discursive and the intuitive, Godwin is trying both to grasp that quality in her cast of mind so superior to his own in valued ways and to ground more firmly his marital idyll of complementary reciprocity, mutual interdependence. Indeed, his marriage signifies for him the now desired fusion of reason and feeling, intellect wedding imagination. Intent on clarifying his new mental set and Wollstonecraft's role as catalyst, Godwin discards hazy wording for a sharper contrast between her imaginative strength and emotional spontaneity and his own diffident skepticism that anxiously examines and reexamines, a self-portrait he sketches again and again. Wollstonecraft as the guiding "light of my steps" suffuses both endings, but, revealingly, he adds to the second version a manifesto: "her sensibility determined me to a careful development of my feelings," a promise of personal evolution faithfully kept. . . . If Godwin's romantic heroine is not the whole of Wollstonecraft's complex nature, his portrayal is the generous artistic tribute of a diligent student to a gifted teacher, a light refracted through biographical involvement. (pp. 315-16)

> Mitzi Myers, "Godwin's 'Memoirs' of Wollstonecraft: The Shaping of Self and Subject," in Studies in Romanticism, *Vol. 20, No. 3, Fall, 1981, pp. 299-316.*

DAVID MORSE (essay date 1982)

[*Morse suggests that Godwin's use of the Gothic form in* Caleb Williams *enabled him to combine psychological exploration with social criticism.*]

The correlation between a radical political vision and a Gothic mode of presentation characterises all the major novelists of the 1790s, but it was William Godwin . . . , in his *Caleb Williams* . . . , which bears the provocative alternative title 'Things as They Are'—a clear-enough indication that the domination that Godwin describes is not to be taken as mere fiction—who produced the most powerful articulation of the social nightmare of a class society. Indeed, in reading this novel we can scarcely avoid the connection between religious and political dissent, for Godwin was brought up in a Sandemanian environment and his novel is offered not as mere entertainment but as a discourse that is directly relevant to real life, a translation into more immediate terms of the principles of his *Political Justice*— though it is, of course, not simply to be regarded as a political-philosophical comic strip. In his Preface [see excerpt dated 1794] Godwin insisted that his purpose was both didactic and down-to-earth. . . . (p. 41)

Godwin's formulation is far from crude. It indicates a new type of fictional purpose: the delineation of a particular type of value system and a representation of the ways in which domination becomes institutionalised, legitimised and endlessly extended so that it reaches into the remotest corners of society, carrying its contagion everywhere with the relentless thoroughness of a plague. So provocative did this intention appear that Godwin was forced to withdraw it for the first edition of 1794. In *Caleb Williams* we find a more complex social vision and social critique than in any other Gothic novel, or in the other works of Godwin himself. For Godwin's criticism is not directed purely and simply at individuals, but is also directed at the social circumstances that determine the pattern of their actions. *Caleb Williams* is thus a determinist novel, but this term is not to be construed in any fatalist sense: for Godwin, determining circumstances can also generate a sense of freedom, as his description of the psychological processes of Caleb Williams testifies. But Godwin did believe that men were deeply influenced by their environment and the values and pressures by which they were surrounded. For this reason his thought, though characterised by great optimism about the possibility of human progress, to which he assigns no limit, is often unexpectedly pessimistic when it comes to a more immediate prognosis. In the section of *Political Justice* in which Godwin shows how men are influenced by their environment, and, in particular by the nature of political organisation, he writes,

> Political institution, by the consequences with which it is pregnant, strongly suggests to everyone who enters within its sphere, what is the path he should avoid, as well as what he should pursue. Under a government fundamentally erroneous he will see intrepid virtue proscribed, and a servile and corrupt spirit uniformly encouraged. But morality itself is nothing but the calculation of consequences. What strange confusion will the spectacle of that knavery which is universally practised through all the existing classes of society produce in the mind? The preceptor cannot go out of the world, or prevent the intercourse of his pupil with human beings of a character different from his own.

The connection between a social and political system where manipulation, intimidation and the brutal exercise of power are not the exception but the rule and the circumstances that affect the lives of every single individual is a constant if largely implicit thread running through the narrative of *Caleb Williams*. . . . The argument of the novel is . . . generalised through a series of parallels and analogies: Caleb's fate mirrors and is directly connected with that of Hawkins; while even the apparently kindly and well disposed Falkland comes to echo both the tyranny of Tyrrel and that of powerful rulers. Justice is therefore shown to be not an objective quality but a function of class position: 'justice' is used against *some* (the weak and poor) by *others* (the rich and powerful). For this reason also, Caleb Williams's period of imprisonment is far more than a transitory moment in the narrative. For Godwin and for his Romantic contemporaries the prison, though a place which few voluntarily visit and whose operations remain obscure to the majority, is nevertheless a crucial focus of moral indignation, because it simultaneously exemplifies both the torments to which one man can subject another and the heartless manner in which a man can be deprived of the use of the very faculties and abilities that make him what he is. (pp. 42-4)

[It] is patent that religious imperatives help to formulate and give edge to Godwin's social criticism. Man has been formed for freedom, and therefore to imprison him and to deprive him of his capacity for action is not simply gratuitous, immoral and cruel: it is a violation of the pattern of divine providence. The prison embodies the truth of modern culture and parodies all dreams of social justice and progress. . . . (p. 45)

But the prison also has a further significance for Godwin. Godwin belongs to the intellectual tradition of Shaftesbury, which laid great stress on man's social impulses, which are the source both of his moral capacity and of his disposition to expand and develop that capacity. But, when a prisoner is placed in solitary confinement in order to 'educate' and 're-form' him, the methods by which this is to be achieved are, in fact, calculated to achieve exactly the reverse:

> Shall we be most effectively formed to justice, benevolence and prudence in our intercourse with each other, in a state of solitude? Will not our selfish and unsocial dispositions be perpetually increased? What temptation has he to think of benevolence or justice, who has no opportunity to exercise it? The true soil in which atrocious crimes are found to germinate, is a gloomy and morose disposition. Will his heart become much either softened or expanded, who breathes the atmosphere of a dungeon?

This cascade of rhetorical questions from *Political Justice* makes it indisputably clear how great an evil imprisonment is for Godwin. But in *Caleb Williams* the notion of imprisonment is vastly expanded. For Godwin shows that in their different ways both Falkland and Caleb Williams become prisoners, because they are cut off from free communication of their thoughts and feelings to others. Falkland, because of the crime that he has committed and because of his failure to confess it, is locked up within himself in an agonising interior solitude that places him beyond the beneficent sphere of human communication. And, even when he is finally brought to the point where he has to reveal the whole story to Caleb Williams, his decision loses its virtue, because he insists on binding Caleb at one and the same moment to an oath never to disclose what his master has told him. From this action many evils flow. Falkland himself continues to be tortured by guilt, remorse and, above all, anxiety that at some point or another Caleb will eventually reveal everything to persons who may be inclined to believe him. Consequently he employs the sinister and implacable Gines to pursue Caleb and to watch and observe his every action. Caleb's own existence becomes equally intolerable, since he is forced to adopt a variety of disguises and to flee from place to place; like Falkland before him, he cannot afford to open his heart to others, since any such action would only be one step towards his downfall. Disguise, for Godwin, heir to a puritan tradition, is a false mode of being, a dangerous step into inauthenticity and deceitful seeming. . . . (pp. 45-6)

But, in fairness, it must be added that Godwin has already shown the price that Caleb has paid for his various subterfuges and the torment of his continual loneliness and distrust. The point is that Caleb, like Falkland, forces himself to go *against nature* (to invoke the phrase that in French symbolism was later to acquire such resonance, though with more positive connotations), for at every moment when he yields to ordinary and normal human feelings he finds himself betrayed. . . . Indeed, perhaps the most interesting part of the novel is [the] depiction of Caleb Williams's frantic inner world in the closing stages of the narrative, which, while designed to show the agonies of internal isolation, has the paradoxical side-effect of showing the very processes of consciousness as a form of torture. This may well be Godwin's deepest and most enduring

fictional legacy. After Godwin it was scarcely possible to show men thinking calm, lucid and appropriate thoughts: the representation of consciousness from Poe to Dostoevsky and Kafka became rather a matter of frenzied leaps, switches and jumps, of thought doubling and redoubling upon itself, of ideas flooding recklessly and pell-mell into the mind, the revelation of a chaotic inner world. This is all of a piece with Godwin's views on the changeableness of human nature. (pp. 46-7)

In *Caleb Williams* there is no necessity that Falkland or Caleb Williams play the part of hypocrite or of false seemer; there is nothing inherent in the role or the position. It is rather society that creates it through the possibility it affords for one man to dominate and oppress another; because in the absence of a spirit of freedom and equality between all men there is also necessarily lacking an openness and sincerity in their mutual dealings. The doubling of Falkland and Caleb Williams has the effect of generalising the theme of the novel and of showing that the issue is not one of an unchangeable human nature that makes one man a hypocrite and another a miser, but rather of a particular form of social organisation which has the effect of isolating men from one another and of rendering their attempts to communicate with one another dubious and unstable, even destructive. But in this novel Godwin opened a fictional Pandora's box, which was to have repercussions spreading far beyond his own particular philosophy. For he initiated a whole series of novels in which men enter into mutual confidences and are oppressed by mysterious and enigmatic others, in which hypocrisy and an appearance of public righteousness are exposed by the mechanism of the double. The couple of the hypocrite and the double haunts Romantic and post-Romantic literature because of the very facility with which these fictional devices can speak the unspoken or unspeakable. These motifs are so popular because they lend themselves to a spirit of irreverence and bitter mockery: they expose the falsity and the hollowness of man in his public and social roles and point to deeper and more complex psychological realities which society cannot permit, and which even the individual may be reluctant to scrutinise too closely. At the same time the whole tradition of the examined self of the individual's scrutiny of his own motives becomes more and more problematic. The mind offers no certainties. As Godwin points out in *Political Justice,*

> Self-deception is of all things the most easy. Whoever ardently wishes to find a proposition true, may be expected insensibly to veer towards the opinion that suits his inclination. It cannot be wondered at, by him who considers the subtlety of the human mind, that belief should scarcely ever rest upon the mere basis of evidence, and that arguments are always viewed through a delusive medium, magnifying them into Alps, or diminishing them to nothing.

The Gothic becomes, *par excellence,* the genre of uncertainty: devoted not simply to an epistemological scepticism at a parade of fantastic and delusionary appearances, leaving the spectator baffled and bemused by puzzling and contradictory evidences; but, far more significantly, throwing into question the very reliability of the mind that scrutinises those appearances, and displaying the mind itself as fraught with division and contradiction. Freudianism is simply the inheritor of this Gothic legacy—retaining, as did the nineteenth century, the fascination with unconscious and subconscious mental processes, but shedding the social critique to which the Gothic once emphatically gestured. (pp. 47-9)

*David Morse, "The Social Novel and the Gothic,"
in his* Romanticism: A Structural Analysis, *Barnes
& Noble Books, 1982, pp. 13-49.*

ADDITIONAL BIBLIOGRAPHY

Allen, B. Sprague. "William Godwin and the Stage." *PMLA* XXXV,
n.s. XXVIII, No. 3 (1920): 358-74.
    Explores the relationship between several of Godwin's novels and
various English, French, and American dramas. In addition, Allen
discusses Godwin's friendship with the American playwright
Thomas Cooper.

Baker, Ernest A. "The Novel of Doctrine." In his *The History of the
English Novel: The Novel of Sentiment and the Gothic Romance*, pp.
228-55. London: H. F. & G. Witherby, 1934.
    Contains an overview of Godwin's career. Baker describes God-
win's works as possessing "an express purpose; they all set forth
his judgments on existing society in the light of his intellectualist
philosophy, and in each case their particular object is defined at
the outset."

Barker, Gerard A. "Justice to Caleb Williams." *Studies in the Novel*
VI, No. 4 (Winter 1974): 377-88.
    An analysis of the ending of *Caleb Williams*. Barker praises God-
win's conclusion, contending that "it turns Caleb's final confrontation into a moral triumph."

Brailsford, H. N. *Shelley, Godwin, and Their Circle*. London: Williams and Norgate, 1913, 256 p.
    Describes the intellectual and political atmosphere in which God-
win lived.

Brown, Ford K. *The Life of William Godwin*. London: J. M. Dent &
Sons, 1926, 387 p.
    A biography of Godwin.

Clark, John P. *The Philosophical Anarchism of William Godwin*.
Princeton: Princeton University Press, 1977, 343 p.
    Examines Godwin's moral philosophy and his approach to social
and political problems.

Dowden, Edward. "Theorists of Revolution." In his *The French Revolution and English Literature: Lectures Delivered in Connection with
the Sesquicentennial Celebration of Princeton University*, pp. 47-89.
1897. Reprint. Port Washington, N.Y.: Kennikat Press, 1967.
    A biographical study of Godwin and Wollstonecraft. Dowden also
examines Godwin's presentation of his doctrine of revolution in
Political Justice.

Dumas, D. Gilbert. "Things As They Were: The Original Ending of
Caleb Williams." *Studies in English Literature 1500-1900* VI (1966):
575-97.
    A discussion of the original, unpublished ending to *Caleb Wil-
liams*, discovered in the holograph manuscript of the novel. Dumas analyzes how the alternate ending—had it been published—
would have affected the novel.

Fleisher, David. *William Godwin: A Study in Liberalism*. New York:
Augustus Kelly, 1951, 155 p.
    A detailed study of Godwin's ideas and themes, interspersed with
biographical details. Fleisher considers Godwin primarily as a
philosopher rather than as an author.

Gold, Alex, Jr. "It's Only Love: The Politics of Passion in Godwin's
Caleb Williams." *Texas Studies in Literature and Language* 19, No.
2 (Summer 1977): 135-60.
    Considers the influence of government upon Caleb's character.

Gross, Harvey. "The Pursuer and the Pursued: A Study of *Caleb
Williams*." *Texas Studies in Literature and Language* I, No. 3 (Autumn
1959): 401-11.
    An analysis of the historical and literary influences on *Caleb
Williams*.

Grylls, Rosalie Glynn. *William Godwin and His World*. London: Od-
hams Press, 1953, 256 p.
    A biography of Godwin that emphasizes the social and political
environment of the late Enlightenment.

Harvey, A. D. "The Nightmare of *Caleb Williams*." *Essays in Criticism* XXVI, No. 3 (July 1976): 236-49.
    Interprets *Caleb Williams* as an analysis of "the corrupting influ-
ence of society."

Hogle, Jerrold E. "The Texture of the Self in Godwin's *Things As
They Are*." *Boundary 2* VII, No. 2 (Winter 1979): 261-81.
    A semiotic study of *Caleb Williams*.

Locke, Don. *A Fantasy of Reason: The Life and Thought of William
Godwin*. London: Routledge & Kegan Paul, 1980, 398 p.
    A detailed study of Godwin's life and philosophical development.

Marshall, Peter H. *William Godwin*. New Haven: Yale University
Press, 1984, 497 p.
    A recent biographical study.

Monro, D. H. *Godwin's Moral Philosophy: An Interpretation of William Godwin*. London: Oxford University Press, 1953, 205 p.
    Presents Godwin as a moralist rather than as a political reformer.

Murry, John Middleton. "William Godwin." In his *Countries of the
Mind: Essays in Literary Criticism, second series*, pp. 181-87. London:
Oxford University Press, 1931.
    A discussion of Godwin's relationship with Wollstonecraft and
his son-in-law, Shelley.

Paul, C. Kegan. *William Godwin: His Friends and Contemporaries*.
2 vols. London: Henry S. King and Co., 1876.
    A biography based on Godwin's diaries, letters, and autobio-
graphical fragments.

Pollin, Burton Ralph. *Education and Enlightenment in the Works of
William Godwin*. New York: Las Americas Publishing Co., 1962,
293 p.
    An analysis of the role of education in Godwin's literary and
philosophical development.

————. *Godwin Criticism: A Synoptic Bibliography*. Toronto: University of Toronto Press, 1967, 659 p.
    A bibliography of works by and about Godwin published between
1783 and 1966.

Priestley, F. E. L. "Platonism in William Godwin's *Political Justice*."
Modern Language Quarterly 4, No. 1 (March 1943): 63-9.
    Interprets *Political Justice* as a document influenced more by
eighteenth-century Platonism than by the tradition of empirical
philosophy.

Scheuermann, Mona. "Outside the Human Circle: Views from Hawthorne and Godwin." *The Nathaniel Hawthorne Journal* (1975): 182-91.
    Studies the psychology of alienation as evidenced in the works
of Godwin and Nathaniel Hawthorne.

Sherburn, George. "Godwin's Later Novels." *Studies in Romanticism*
I, No. 2 (Winter 1962): 65-82.
    An overview of Godwin's literary career following the publication
of *Caleb Williams*.

Tysdahl, B. J. *William Godwin As Novelist*. London: Athlone, 1981,
205 p.
    The first book-length study of Godwin's novels. Tysdahl assesses
the novels in light of Godwin's philosophical writings and discusses the relationship between the two genres.

Uphaus, Robert W. "Moral and Tendency in *Caleb Williams*." In his
*The Impossible Observer: Reason and the Reader in Eighteenth-Cen-
tury Prose*, pp. 123-36. Lexington: University Press of Kentucky,
1979.
    Considers *Caleb Williams* as a "psychological encounter with
fears and desires."

Willey, Basil. "'Nature' in Revolution and Reaction." In his *The Eighteenth Century Background: Studies on the Idea of Nature in the Thought of the Period,* pp. 205-52. New York: Columbia University Press, 1941.
   Assesses Godwin as a representative of eighteenth-century rationalism at its conclusion.

Woodcock, George. *William Godwin: A Biographical Study.* London: Porcupine Press, 1946, 266 p.
   A study of Godwin's life and philosophy.

————. "The Man of Reason." In his *Anarchism: A History of Libertarian Ideas and Movements,* pp. 60-93. Cleveland: World Publishing Co., Meridian Books, 1967.
   A discussion of Godwin's libertarian philosophy in the context of nineteenth-century anarchism.

Oliver Wendell Holmes

1809-1894

American essayist, poet, novelist, and biographer.

Holmes is considered one of the most versatile American authors of the nineteenth century. Though he wrote in a wide variety of genres, he is best known for his popular collection of essays *The Autocrat of the Breakfast-Table*. Critics believe that these fictional conversations provided Holmes with the ideal medium for expressing his views on humankind and its institutions and for acting, in his own words, as "his own Boswell." Holmes's novels, too, have attracted the interest of scholars. In these, most notably in *Elsie Venner*, he incorporated his pioneering theories of psychology and clarified his arguments against Calvinism and the concept of original sin. In addition to his literary works, Holmes was respected for his controversial scientific essays and for his brilliant skill as a conversationalist. Holmes's reputation has diminished considerably in recent years; perhaps the most famous and important figure in Boston intellectual circles during the second half of the nineteenth century, he is now remembered chiefly for the sparkling wit of *The Autocrat* and the spirit of free inquiry demonstrated by the wide range of his interests.

Holmes was born in Cambridge, Massachusetts, in 1809 to Sarah Wendell Holmes and the Reverend Abiel Holmes. A Calvinist minister, the Reverend Holmes was forced out of his parish in 1829 as a result of a conflict between the conservative and liberal factions within his congregation. For the younger Holmes, this event, as well as his early religious training, engendered a lifelong antagonism toward the Puritan strictures of Calvinism, which critics trace throughout his literary and scientific writings. Holmes attended Phillips Academy at Andover from 1824 to 1825 and then entered Harvard University. When he lost interest in his law studies, he transferred to medicine. After taking advanced courses in Paris in 1833, he returned to Harvard and completed the requirements for his medical degree in 1836. Holmes then practiced as a personal physician until 1839, when he was appointed to a professorship at Dartmouth College. The following year, he married Amelia Lee Jackson, with whom he had three children.

Holmes achieved distinction during the 1840s and 1850s as a teacher and scientific writer, and he later won great respect as Dean of the Harvard Medical School. He was also active on the lecture circuit, speaking on a wide variety of medical topics. In his 1842 essay, *Homeopathy and Its Kindred Delusions*, Holmes demonstrated the futility and danger of some existing medical treatments; in *The Contagiousness of Puerperal Fever*, written in 1843, he suggested that physicians themselves could be the carriers of disease. Despite the uproar of criticism that his essays elicited, he held his ground. Holmes retired from Harvard in 1882, yet remained active as a writer and public speaker. He once wrote that "life is a fatal complaint and an eminently contagious one," and having outlived most of his family and friends, he died at the age of eighty-five.

While his medical career was flourishing, Holmes was also gaining respect as a poet. His first public notice came in 1830 with the publication in a Boston newspaper of "Old Ironsides," a poem protesting the government's plans to dismantle the

frigate *U.S.S. Constitution*. The poem touched a patriotic nerve, and the ensuing public outcry saved the ship for its role as an historical relic. Buoyed by his early popular success, Holmes published *Poems* in 1836; expanded and revised editions of the collection followed in 1846, 1848, and 1849. Holmes wrote much serious poetry, but his output also included a large number of occasional verses composed in either heroic and octosyllabic couplets or in the meter of the folk ballad. Most of Holmes's poems express his views about the human condition and his hopes for its improvement. In "The Chambered Nautilus," for example, Holmes speculated on the growth of the soul; in "The Last Leaf," he depicted the problems of old age. Holmes is generally considered neither an innovator nor an influence on the development of American poetry, and many commentators point out that his style derives from the neoclassicism of the Augustan age of eighteenth-century England. Nevertheless, critics consistently note that he successfully used poetry as a forum for expressing his philosophy, particularly in such pieces as "The Deacon's Masterpiece; or, The Wonderful 'One-Hoss Shay'," his strongest poetic statement against Calvinism. Holmes's approach to writing also demonstrates his scientific bent of mind: he claimed that his meter was modeled on the pulse and respiration rate of a speaker reading poetry aloud. Scholars affirm that his many later collections, including *Songs in Many Keys*, *Soundings from the Atlantic*, *Songs of*

Many Seasons, and *The Last Leaf*, attest to the endurance of Holmes's poetic gift.

Already an established poet, Holmes began writing prose pieces in 1858 for the *Atlantic Monthly* at the invitation of its editor, James Russell Lowell. Holmes's first contributions, which were later collected as *The Autocrat*, present the breakfast-table conversations of a fictional group of boarding-house residents, narrated by a member nicknamed "the autocrat." Complete with well-developed characters and plot, this work is difficult to place within a genre, but is most often classified as a collection of essays. *The Autocrat* achieved enormous popular and critical success and helped to establish the *Atlantic Monthly's* reputation. While some pieces were humorous, others contained Holmes's ideas for changing society, and still others satirized various aspects of Calvinism. Holmes especially delighted in debunking "any logical system . . . supposed by its authors to be perfect, uncorrectable, and therefore, everlasting." *The Autocrat* was followed by *The Professor at the Breakfast-Table* in 1860, *The Poet at the Breakfast-Table* in 1872, and *Over the Teacups* in 1891. These four collections comprise what is usually referred to as the Breakfast-Table series.

Just as he had used the Breakfast-Table books to present his views on society, Holmes utilized his so-called "medicated novels" to explore the causes and treatment of aberrant behavior. *Elsie Venner*, *The Guardian Angel*, and *A Mortal Antipathy* strongly attest to Holmes's scientific interest. Critics are divided in their views of these works: some consider them novels concerned with psychology, others regard them as scientific treatises presented in a fictional framework, while still others claim that Holmes's novels are not about science, but about morality. In the first, *Elsie Venner*, which originally appeared serially in the *Atlantic Monthly* as *The Professor's Story*, Holmes created a protagonist who is believed to be part human and part serpent as a result of a prenatal snakebite. In this novel, Holmes discourses on such topics as prejudice, the Calvinist concept of original sin, and human psychology and sexuality. Most critics contend that *Elsie Venner* lacks artistic merit, though they argue that Holmes's perceptive character studies anticipate the psychological theories of Sigmund Freud and Carl Jung. In *The Guardian Angel*, Holmes discussed the influences of heredity and environment on mental and physical health. The novel also warns against a Puritan upbringing for children. *A Mortal Antipathy*, which ran serially in the *Atlantic Monthly* as *The New Portfolio*, deals with the causes and cures of childhood trauma. Commentators stress that the issues in these "medicated novels" derive from their author's background as a scientist; indeed, in each the characters seek out doctors and professors for help—suggesting that Holmes looked to science, not theology, to provide the answers for humanity's complex problems.

Criticism of Holmes's literary efforts is as varied as his fields of expertise, and a consensus of opinion is difficult to obtain. Scholars have debated whether he is predominantly a literary figure or a scientist, focusing on the frequent incorporation of medical themes and terminology into his works. The critics S. I. Hayakawa and Howard Mumford Jones argued that those who view Holmes primarily as an artist overlook his most important quality: his scientific interest. They also point out that his essays on medical topics exhibit his best prose, free of Victorian constraints. Yet other commentators, both in the nineteenth and twentieth centuries, have chosen not to acknowledge as primary Holmes's scientific career, emphasizing instead his role as an author.

In assessments of Holmes as a writer, scholarly emphasis has shifted over time from his poetry to his fictional essays and then to his novels. While early critics of his verse stressed his humor, wit, and patriotism, some also stated that his poetry was shallow and dilettantish, and Holmes himself noted in a preface to an 1862 collection that his poetic promise remained unfulfilled. After he published *The Autocrat*, critics transferred their attention to his prose. Some reviewers praised his versatility and wit, yet others denounced the provincialism, elitism, and political conservatism of his sketches. Holmes's privileged financial and social position, in addition, led to charges of insularity: many critics faulted his failure to support the abolitionist and women's rights movements. Conversely, his sympathizers point out that despite his limited contact with persons and ideas outside of New England, Holmes was expansive in his interests and expertise, and the didactic tone of much of his writing can be read as his concern for the welfare of others. However, it is Holmes's novels that have proven most interesting to twentieth-century critics. Controversial when published because of their intimate look at human physiology and psychology, they remain so today. While *The Autocrat* is still considered his best work, Holmes's novels have attracted attention from modern critics, who praise them as important early psychological studies.

Though still valued for his contributions to literature, science, theology, and psychology, Holmes is no longer as popular with readers as he once was. Yet despite this diminution of his reputation, which many critics attribute to the decline of New England's influence on American culture, Holmes and his writings still attract considerable commentary. Today, *The Autocrat*, likened by Virginia Woolf to the taste of "champagne after breakfast cups of weak tea," continues to occupy an important place in American literature.

(See also *Dictionary of Literary Biography*, Vol. 1: *The American Renaissance in New England*.)

---

*PRINCIPAL WORKS

Poems (poetry) 1836; also published in revised form as
    Poems, 1846, 1848, 1849
Homeopathy and Its Kindred Delusions (essay) 1842
The Contagiousness of Puerperal Fever (essay) 1843
Urania: A Rhymed Lesson (poetry) 1846
Astraea: The Balance of Illusions (poetry) 1850
The Autocrat of the Breakfast-Table (essays) 1858
The Professor at the Breakfast-Table (essays) 1860
Currents and Counter-Currents in Medical Science (essays)
    1861
Elsie Venner: A Romance of Destiny (novel) 1861
Songs in Many Keys (poetry) 1862
Soundings from the Atlantic (poetry) 1864
The Guardian Angel (novel) 1867
Mechanism in Thought and Morals (essay) 1871
The Poet at the Breakfast-Table (essays) 1872
"Crime and Automatism" (essay) 1875; published in
    periodical *Atlantic Monthly*
Songs of Many Seasons (poetry) 1875
John Lothrop Motley (memoir) 1879
The School-Boy (poetry) 1879
The Iron Gate, and Other Poems (poetry) 1880
Medical Essays, 1842-1882 (essays) 1883

*Many of Holmes's works were first published in the *Atlantic Monthly*.

THE NORTH AMERICAN REVIEW   (essay date 1837)

[*This critic praises Holmes's entertaining and humorous collection,* Poems.]

We have seldom had more genuine enjoyment in the course of our critical labors, than in examining [Mr. Holmes's *Poems*]. (p. 275)

Mr. Holmes does not write in [a] mezzotinto style; he reminds us more of the clear strong lines of the ancient engravers. His manner is entirely his own, manly and unaffected; generally easy and playful, and sinking at times into 'a most humorous sadness.' The latter is evidently his favorite style, and we think his best. . . . [All] poetry which has any relation to humanity, will deal in smiles as well as tears. The critic may demonstrate that it is undignified in the poet to entertain his readers; but, an appeal being open from criticism to nature, whoever makes us laugh in this care-worn world will always be sustained by the common gratitude of mankind.

The first of these poems, called [**"Poetry: A Metrical Essay"**] . . . , was recited at the last anniversary of the Phi Beta Kappa Society, at Cambridge. As it was pronounced, it seemed to us more like inspiration than most any thing which ever came our way. As readers, we find it finished with much care, and abounding in striking thoughts and illustrations; but we apprehend that it was not so great a favorite with the writer as some of the lyrical pieces, which were struck off with less labor, but more power. One or two fine specimens of the latter are inserted in the larger poem by way of illustration; and with most readers these will be regarded as the pearls, and the poem as the string. We would not, however, do it injustice; the chief defect is the want of clearness, in expressing the truths in relation to poetical materials and inspirations which it contains. Some passages in it require to be read twice, before the reader is sure of their meaning. This occasional obscurity is strongly contrasted with the easy and natural flow of the lyrical poems. Nothing need be more beautiful than the lines on the Cambridge Church-yard, a place to which many hearts are bound by strong associations; and [**"Old Ironsides,"**] the strain upon the plan proposed by the Navy Department for breaking up the Frigate Constitution, an unhappy suggestion of some one who was probably more familiar with national ship-yards than national feelings, will rank with the best martial songs of England.

We think that the comic pieces in this little collection are decidedly the best, or rather we should say those in which a quiet humor is blended with the pathetic so as to heighten the effect of the grotesque without destroying the plaintive character of the whole. An example of this is afforded in **"The Last Reader"**; it is evidently the kind of writing in which the author takes most pleasure; and if he should find room for poetical pursuits in the cares of his profession, we hope that this graceful style will be his choice. At the same time we must allow that his more comic pieces are exceedingly entertaining; particularly the lines upon the Comet, which is irresistible for its humor, and at the same time contains one or two passages of great power. The incident so well related in **"The Height of the Ridiculous"** might be fact, not fable.

We have not time to give an acount of the work in detail, nor is it necessary; a book so entertaining is by this time in the hands of a great proportion of our readers. They will agree with us in the opinion that the author is a man of genius, and in the hope that the favor with which his work has been received may induce him to come before the public again. (pp. 276-77)

> "Holmes's 'Poems'," *in* The North American Review, *Vol. XLIV, No. 94, January, 1837, pp. 275-77.*

THE YALE LITERARY MAGAZINE   (essay date 1837)

[*This anonymous critic praises Holmes's "humor and manly sentiment" in* Poems, *but censures the uneven quality of individual pieces.*]

The distinguishing characteristics of Mr. Holmes' [*Poems*] are manliness and humor. We say of his *book*, we shall give our notions on what we think are the true elements of his character (*id est* his poetic character) in the course of our article. The first thing that strikes is, that the writer has a way of saying a thing which is his own way, and that this is always manly. He casts his thoughts in a mould that shows his familiarity with the best writers; that he has been to the very fountain head for instruction, and come away benefitted by it. He knows how to be sentimental without silliness, and vigorous without violence; and in such situations as we would think him most likely to fail, he has contrived to acquit himself with credit. He does not for the sake of a thought let himself down to it, but if he must have it he brings it up to his own station. Neither does he seem to have yielded to that most besetting sin of all clever writers, a disposition to run as near to mawkishness as possible without falling into it, and by a delicacy and a mastery of good language produce something which we can't call bad, and yet for the life of us cannot give them credit for. We see nothing of this. On the contrary, there is too little sentimentality; and we could wish he had allowed himself more latitude where he shows himself so capable. He stops as if he were afraid of cloying us, and contents himself with saying a little less than just enough. Now though we honor the motive here we could wish it otherwise. We would have Mr. Holmes indulge himself in that delicate vein of simple melancholy which is so full of pathos, which is always found in every genuine poet, and which he himself possesses in an eminent degree; and though we know advice of this kind would let a host of evils on us if taken indiscriminately, yet we have no fears in giving it to a man like him whose good sense will surely never let him overstep the bounds of modesty.

The other characteristic of this book is, its playfulness. We don't recollect ever to have met before, in any one book and written by one person, so many pieces of sparkling humor.

Some of them are conceived in the happiest vein, and executed in the most felicitous manner. They have the advantage of being finished without the appearance of study—in fact seem to have dropped from the pen without effort. They open sly and soberly, about the middle you begin to suspect something, at last you lay aside the gentleman and literally roar. We notice also that there rarely or never recurs the same thought. . . . The thoughts in this book are rarely or never diluted; every line seems to have its business there, and the conclusion you come to after reading it is, that the thing is 'about done up.' Now this is saying a great deal. The art of writing a playful poem, easy yet vigorous, familiar yet original, and then to know just when to leave off, is the highest art of poetry. When we try to be natural, and select smooth and musical words to make the rhythm melodious, there is danger of letting the thought go *for* the word; and while we are chasing after this phrase or that, twisting it about and trying to knock the corners off that it may fit into the structure, the spirit is gone. Any one at all familiar with writing knows also, that the thoughts suggested in the heat of composition seem original often when they are not; and we take up many a manuscript after laying it by to cool, and find a work valueless which cost us a deal of labor. Mr. Holmes has steered clear of all this. Dean Swift's definition of a good style fits him exactly, 'proper words in proper places.' His words are well chosen, the rhythm is smooth, and in most cases the thought apparent at a glance. In his hands the language is made to twist itself many ways; yet the collocation is always natural and the spirit preserved. The conclusion we come to is, that Mr. Holmes is a poet of very fine powers, and that he deems his art of importance enough to be studied and studied well. His book has delighted us. . . . (pp. 116-18)

But we have not done with him. The reader will perceive we have all along carried the impression, of humor and manly sentiment being his chief characteristics. This is true of his book, in which, with one or two exceptions, these qualities are mostly prominent. But we said something back, of some different notions entertained by us about the true character of his genius—which we now return to. Nothing is more glaringly apparent in literary history, than the wonderful discrepancy we sometimes find, when we compare the *works* with the *ways* of literary men. An author before the public is like a belle in a drawing-room, in his very best; every thing offensive is put out of sight, out of compliment to the company. But this supposes the author's character bad—let us change the illustration. An author before the public is like a well educated lady, who out of favor to certain prejudices of the company avoids certain topics of conversation which are offensive to them. This suits our purpose better, and it is here we believe where our poet is. There is a delicate vein of the most melancholy witchery in him, which so far as we can judge he keeps aiming to suppress, and his reason is doubtless the fact, that the common mass of mankind speak coldly of or do not understand it. We believe we can understand him here; we believe that poetry with him is a sacred feeling; and if he ever brings it up and lets it gush forth in the full freshness of its own deep melody, he feels very much as the ancients did when strangers laid hands on their household gods, it seems to him like a kind of desecration. We believe this the secret of our poet's not indulging himself in this kind of writing, and yet in this vein we believe lies his power. We are strengthened in this by the fact, that the very finest specimens of real poetry in the book are of this character; and, also, that in the humorous pieces there is an under current of simple pathos, the more fascinating perhaps from the stinted quantities dealt out to us. (p. 118)

["**The Last Reader**"] is exquisite poetry. It melts into the heart like the melody of a dream when that heart is aching; and had our author written nothing else we should not soon forget him. The verse beginning:

> And when my name no more is heard,

is perfect; and what Coleridge says of Shakspeare, that you cannot add or diminish by a word to advantage, is true here. Would any one believe after reading [this] beautiful poem, that the same pen could trace the following, speaking of an old man—

> My grandmamma has said,—
> Poor old lady, she is dead,
>   Long ago,—
> That he had a Roman nose,
> And his cheek was like a rose
>   In the snow . . .

or this, of a girl's losing her lover:

> Down fell that pretty innocent as falls a snow white
>   lamb,
> *Her hair drooped round her pallid cheeks like sea-weed*
>   *on a clam;*

or this, entitled ["**The Height of the Ridiculous**":] . . .

> He read the next; the grin grew broad,
>   And shot from ear to ear;
> He read the third; a chuckling noise
>   I now began to hear.
>
> The fourth; he broke into a roar;
>   The fifth; his waistband split;
> The sixth; he burst five buttons off,
>   And tumbled in a fit. . . .

Ye ghosts of Momus! look at it. The fellow holding his sides, frothing like a puppy got the hydrophobia, and the breeches flying. There's a scene for you to give tragedy the hysterics, or set the carved face on a brass door-knocker grinning. Well done, Mr. Holmes. (pp. 120-21)

We come now to the most disagreeable part of our work, viz. to censure; but, by the way, we think the 'why and wherefore' of our fault-finding will be that which reviews generally have passed over. We shall not stop to point out certain obscurities we have heard urged, though they may be urged perhaps with some propriety. There are a few passages which require to be re-read to be understood clearly; but when the reader will explain certain passages in Milton, and hundreds of them in Byron we can point him to, why then let him blame Mr. Holmes if he chooses. Nor shall we stop to mention an evident failure, in the winding up of one or two of the humorous pieces. A humorous composition, one that hits, one that gets hold of you, one that makes you laugh 'in resolution's spite;' such a poem must open ambiguously, begin to smoke in the middle, and go off with a flash. As a general thing he is very successful. As a specimen of genuine English humor we instance "**The Music Grinders**," and the "**Oysterman**," and for one evincing the true Elian spirit, we instance "**The Song of the Tread-mill**." In fact this little *morceau* gave us as much pleasure as some of Lamb's finest. We wish the last verse was better however— still, it is tart, pithy, and gloriously humorous. But the conclusion of the "**Mysterious Visitor**" is altogether unworthy of the body of that poem; and, as we understand it, the lines to the "**Portrait of a Lady**," are but little better. But for all this we are well compensated on the whole by the rest of the book, so we let it go. But what we *have* to blame our poet for is, a fault which himself has confessed, viz. the admission of certain confessedly *mediocre* poems, to fill out the volume. Our remarks shall be rather severe here, as the thing particularly offends us. In the preface he says, 'having written comparatively little, and nothing of late years until within a few months, I could ill afford to be over nice in my selection.' Now this is a most odious confession—odious because a man of his genius has no business to make it, and odious because the last part of the statement is false. He *can* afford to be nice in his selection: however, if he cannot, he has no business to select at all. The thought appendaged, also, that the publisher must be gratified, is abominable—just as if, in building up the cause of literature, the object is to well line the pockets of booksellers. This is twisting things about with a vengeance. We always thought, that the supporting of publishers was a matter altogether incidental to the great work of advancing intelligence, and that the credit of *writing* a sound book took the precedence of the printing it. However it is one of the improvements of the age. We'll wager our poet any thing that we can pick out the very pieces inserted to swell the volume. What right have "**La Grisette**," "**A Souvenir**," "**My Companions**," "**The proud Pedestrian**," and "**Evening, by a tailor**"—what right have these by the side of the splendid opening on the fourth page, "**The last Reader**," "**The last Leaf**," "**To a Katydid**," "**The dying Seneca**," and twenty others we could mention? There never was such a coupling since the days of Job. It may be said, a man has a right to do what he likes with his own—we deny it totally and forever. A man who *can* write good poetry, has no more business to write bad, than a man whose character is up for truth telling, gets a charter thereby to lie when he chooses.... The truth of it is, we like Mr. Holmes; like his manner and method, and that too exceedingly, therefore we don't like to see him make himself unlikeable. (pp. 122-23)

Mr. Holmes has done well in this—his first volume we believe—and we hope soon to see him in another. His fresh and manly style of writing, we hesitate not in saying is very creditable to our literature, and will help refute the notion so vigorously cried up by a class of us, that this country is no place for poetry. (p. 123)

> *A review of "Poems," in* The Yale Literary Magazine, *Vol. II, No. 4, February, 1837, pp. 113-24.*

THE NORTH AMERICAN REVIEW (essay date 1847)

[*In the following excerpt from a largely favorable review of* Urania, *the anonymous critic remarks on Holmes's mastery of style.*]

[*Urania*] is the modest and rather enigmatical title of a very lively and beautiful poem. (p. 208)

Though [Dr. Holmes] has published very little, he is one of the most popular of American poets, [and] . . . he deserves all his reputation. Some may object, that much of his popularity is to be ascribed to the exuberance of his wit, in which he easily surpasses all his contemporaries excepting Hood. To this we answer, that wit may justly be considered as one of the brightest ornaments of poetry; and in his case, as well as in that of his English predecessor to whom we have just alluded, it is by no means unattended by the higher and more characteristic excellences of his profession. His fancy teems with bright and appropriate images, and these are woven into his plan usually with exquisite finish and grace. His artistic merits are very great; his versification is never slovenly, nor his diction

meagre or coarse; and many of his shorter pieces are inwrought with so much fire and imagination as to rank among our best lyrics.

This is high praise, and in order to justify it, we should find it necessary to quote rather from the volume of his [*Poems*] . . . than from the brief "rhymed lesson," quite local and occasional in character, which is now before us. But we must not make citations from a work which is in the hands of nearly all our readers, while the choicer portions of it are as familiar to them as the songs of their childhood. *Urania*—a title which for some inexplicable reason he has chosen to annex to this later publication—has some striking faults; but it has also characteristic passages enough to support our high estimate of the writer's powers. It is a mere medley of bright thoughts and laughing satire, with here and there a momentary expression of deep feeling, which betrays a spirit that may be touched to nobler issues. The poet glances about like a butterfly from one topic to another, hardly resting on any one long enough to obtain more than a sip of its honey. The versification is uniformly flowing and harmonious, and the lines are never bolstered out with feeble or unmeaning expressions. (pp. 212-13)

[The description of a Sabbath morning in the city contains] vigorous and striking lines, which no living poet certainly need be ashamed to own. The deep and holy sentiment which pervades the latter portion of [those lines] may suffice to convince those of their error who have hitherto regarded Dr. Holmes only as a rhyming Momus. There are many felicities of expression in them which show great mastery of style, and perfect familiarity with the well of English undefiled. This, indeed, is one of the characteristic merits of our bard. His diction is uniformly terse, precise, and vigorous, never cheating the ear with sound that veils an ambiguity of meaning, nor violating by a hair's breadth the established usages of language. His words ring clear and shrill, like good coin tried on the counter. He has entire command of Anglo-Saxon phraseology, and the most familiar turns of speech, without ever sinking into baldness or vulgarity; and he often adapts colloquial expressions to his purpose with a felicity of setting which reminds one of Dean Swift.... There is much good sense, as well as pungent wit [in the poem].... (p. 215)

[Dr. Holmes] has shown much versatility of power, and we hope, on greeting him again, to find that he has been wandering in some of the higher walks of poesy. Let him not seek excuse for keeping his wings folded, on the ground that his daily pursuits confine him to the prosaic side of life. He gives a laughing sketch, indeed, of the incongruity between the subjects of thought that are commended to him by his profession, and these furtive offerings to the Muse. But Aesculapius was the favorite son of Apollo, and the two deities were often worshipped at the same shrine. They will not quarrel with each other, if our author's homage is divided between them; nor can he be said to abandon the healing art who worships also the god of the silver bow, the slayer of the Python, and the author of the oracular responses given at Delphi. There are golden hours of leisure even in the practice of a successful physician, and these at least may be consecrated to more ambitious uses. (p. 216)

> *"Holmes's 'Urania'," in* The North American Review, *Vol. LXIV, No. 134, January, 1847, pp. 208-16.*

[JAMES RUSSELL LOWELL] (poem date 1848)

[*Lowell was a celebrated nineteenth-century American poet, critic, essayist, and editor of two leading journals, the* Atlantic Monthly *and the* North American Review. *He is noted today for his satirical and critical writings, including* A Fable for Critics, *a book-length poem featuring witty critical portraits of his contemporaries. In the following excerpt from that work, Lowell playfully describes Holmes's poetic style.*]

There's Holmes, who is matchless among you for wit;
A Leyden-jar always full-charged, from which flit
The electrical tingles of hit after hit;
In long poems 'tis painful sometimes and invites
A thought of the way the new Telegraph writes,
Which pricks down its little sharp sentences spitefully
As if you got more than you'd title to rightfully,
And if it were hoping its wild father Lightning
Would flame in for a second and give you a fright'ning.
He has perfect sway of what *I* call a sham metre,
But many admire it, the English hexameter,
And Campbell, I think, wrote most commonly worse,
With less nerve, swing, and fire in the same kind of
    verse,
Nor e'er achieved aught in't so worthy of praise
As the tribute of Holmes to the grand *Marseillaise.*
You went crazy last year over Bulwer's New Timon;—
Why, if B., to the day of his dying, should rhyme on,
Heaping verses on verses and tomes upon tomes,
He could ne'er reach the best point and vigor of
    Holmes.
His are just the fine hands, too, to weave you a lyric
Full of fancy, fun, feeling, or spiced with satyric
In so kindly a measure, that nobody knows
What to do but e'en join in the laugh, friends and foes.

                                                    (pp. 69-70)

[*James Russell Lowell*], *in his* A Fable for Critics;
or, A Glance at a Few of Our Literary Progenies,
second edition, G. P. Putnam, 1848, 80 p.

JOHN GREENLEAF WHITTIER   (essay date 1849)

[*Whittier was a noted American poet, abolitionist, journalist, and critic who encouraged the idea of American literary nationalism. In the following excerpt, he admires the wit and humor in* Poems, *but also values Holmes's ability to touch "the deeper chords of the heart."*]

If any of our readers (and at times we fear it is the case with all) need amusement, and the wholesome alterative of a hearty laugh, we commend them not to Dr. Holmes the physician, but to Dr. Holmes the scholar, the wit, and the humorist; not to the scientific medical professor's barbarous Latin, but to his poetical prescriptions, given in choice old Saxon. We have tried them, and are ready to give the doctor certificates of their efficacy....

The volume [*Poems*] now before us gives, in addition to the poems and lyrics contained in the two previous editions, some hundred or more pages of the later productions of the author, in the sprightly vein, and marked by the brilliant fancy and felicitous diction for which the former were noteworthy.... **"Terpsichore,"** read at an annual dinner of the Phi Beta Kappa Society at Cambridge, sparkles throughout with keen wit, quaint conceits, and satire so good-natured that the subjects of it can enjoy it as heartily as their neighbors. (p. 516)

There are, as might be expected, some common-place pieces in the volume—a few failures in the line of humor. **"The Spectre Pig,"** the **"Dorchester Giant,"** **"The Height of the Ridiculous,"** and one or two others, might be omitted in the

next edition without detriment. They would do well enough for an amateur humorist, but are scarcely worthy of one who stands at the head of the profession.

It was said of James Smith, of the "Rejected Addresses," that "if he had not been a witty man, he would have been a *great* man." Hood's humor and drollery kept in the back-ground the pathos and beauty of his soberer productions; and Dr. Holmes, we suspect, might have ranked higher, among a large class of readers, than he now does, had he never written his **"Ballad of the Oysterman,"** his **"Comet,"** and his **"September Gale."** Such lyrics as **"La Grisette," "The Puritan's Vision,"** and that unique compound of humor and pathos, **"The Last Leaf,"** show that he possesses the power of touching the deeper chords of the heart, and of calling forth tears as well as smiles. (p. 517)

Dr. Holmes has been likened to Thomas Hood; but there is little in common between them, save the power of combining fancy and sentiment with grotesque drollery and humor.... Holmes writes simply for the amusement of himself and his readers; he deals only with the vanity, the foibles, and the minor faults of mankind, good-naturedly and almost sympathizingly suggesting excuses for the folly which he tosses about on the horns of his ridicule. In this respect he differs widely from his fellow-townsman, Russell Lowell, whose keen wit and scathing sarcasm, in the famous *Biglow Papers,* and the notes of Parson Wilbur, strike at the great evils of society, and deal with the rank offences of church and state. Hosea Biglow, in his way, is as earnest a preacher as Habakkuk Mucklewrath, or Obadiah Bind-their-kings-in-chains-and-their-nobles-in-fetters-of-iron. His verse smacks of the old Puritan flavor. Holmes

A portrait of Holmes as a young man. The Granger Collection, New York.

has a gentler mission. His careless, genial humor reminds us of James Smith in his *Rejected Addresses* and "Horace in London." Long may he live to make broader the face of our care-ridden generation, and to realize for himself the truth of the wise man's declaration, that "a merry heart is a continual feast." (p. 518)

John Greenleaf Whittier, "Mirth and Medicine," in Littell's Living Age, *Vol. XX, No. 251, March 10, 1849, pp. 516-18.*

MARY RUSSELL MITFORD   (essay date 1852)

[*Mitford was an English sketch writer, dramatist, poet, novelist, and critic whose legacy to nineteenth-century literature includes some of the most endearing sketches of English country life. Here, Mitford praises Holmes's originality and his descriptions in* As-traea.]

Among the strange events of these strange days of ours, when revolutions and counter-revolutions, constitutions changed one week and rechanged the next, seem to crowd into a fortnight the work of a century, annihilating time, just as railways and electric telegraphs annihilate space,—in these days of curious novelty, nothing has taken me more pleasantly by surprise than the school of true and original poetry that has sprung up among our blood relations (I had well nigh called them our fellow-countrymen) across the Atlantic; they who speak the same tongue and inherit the same literature. And of all this flight of genuine poets, I hardly know any one so original as Dr. Holmes. For him we can find no living prototype; to track his footsteps, we must travel back as far as Pope or Dryden; and to my mind it would be well if some of our own bards would take the same journey—provided always, it produced the same result. Lofty, poignant, graceful, grand, high of thought, and clear of word, we could fancy ourselves reading some pungent page of "Absalom and Achitophel," or of the "Moral Epistles," if it were not for the pervading nationality, which, excepting Whittier, American poets have generally wanted, and for that true reflection of the manners and the follies of the age, without which satire would fail alike of its purpose and its name. (p. 399)

The grace and pathos of [Dr. Holmes's] introduction [to *Astraea*] must be felt by every one. It has all the sweetness of Goldsmith, with more force and less obviousness of thought.

The poem opens with a description of an American spring, equally true to general nature and to the locality where it is written. The truth is so evident in the one case, that we take it for granted in the other. The couplet on the crocus for instance, a couplet so far as I know unmatched in flower painting, gives us most exquisitely expressed an image that meets our eye every March. The "shy turtles ranging their platoons," we never have seen, and probably never shall see, and yet the accuracy of the picture is as clear to us as that of the most familiar flower of our border. (p. 402)

After this we are introduced to a winter room, delineated with equal taste and fidelity;—the very home of lettered comfort. . . . (p. 403)

Such is the opening of the *Astraea*. It speaks much for the man whose affluence of intellect could afford such an outpouring for a single occasion, the recitation of one solitary evening; and hardly less for the audience that prompted and welcomed such an effort. (p. 406)

Mary Russell Mitford, "American Poets," in her Recollections of a Literary Life; or, Books, Places,

and People, *1852. Reprint by Harper & Brothers, Publishers, 1855, pp. 399-410.*

[FRANK H. HILL]   (essay date 1861)

[*In addition to criticizing Holmes's provincialism and lack of originality, Hill questions the propriety of his treatment of abnormality in* Elsie Venner, *commenting that the heroine's story "illustrates the fantastic extravagance, that lack of a controlling good taste, which mark American literature."*]

Dr. Holmes is indisputably and above all an entertaining writer. He thinks, and he can express his thought articulately. He flashes upon you an ingenious suggestion, or a whimsical paradox, clothed in fantastic guise, and without giving you time to pause upon the truth it contains, or to reflect even whether what seems so plausible is true, presents you with another and another in endless sequence. The general effect is somewhat kaleidoscopic. It suits, we suppose, the rapid hurry of the American mind, which cannot delay upon any thing, but which glances quickly over a thousand things; which is curious, but has its curiosity easily sated; which propounds countless questions, and is contented with the first plausible reply. Another source of Dr. Holmes's American popularity lies, no doubt, in the circumstance that he is a man of varied culture, accomplished in no ordinary degree; and that he addresses a people among whom a certain low average of education is universal, but among whom a high order of cultivation is rare. His writings abound in pleasant hints, stimulative to curiosity, of regions of thought and literature into which his readers have never penetrated; and they agreeably enlarge, though by fitful glimpses, which rapidly close in, the mental horizon of the great body of subscribers to the *Atlantic Monthly*. But though enriched with European culture, Dr. Holmes is essentially an American. Rub the varnish off the Russian, and the Tartar is seen beneath. There is the exaggerated provincialism of sentiment, the confusion of extent of territory with national greatness, of democratic equality with personal freedom, which characterise the typical American. (p. 363)

So far from admitting with [Dr. Holmes], however, that "America is the only place where man is full-grown," we contend that in America we have not the full-grown man, but only the over-grown boy. There is the boastful self-exaggeration, the inability of taking fair measure of its capacities and attainments as compared with those of its contemporaries and predecessors, which mark a people that has not yet cut its wisdom-teeth. The products of the American mind have no mellowness; there is a crude acidity about them. With all his intensely American feeling, however, Dr. Holmes is unable to make any advance towards the creation of a specifically American literature. He no sooner puts pen to paper than he becomes imitative. As in Washington Irving we have the revivication of the *Spectator* school of literature, as in Cooper we see only the pale and watery reflexion of Walter Scott, so in Dr. Holmes we have an American edition (expurgated) of Montaigne and Rabelais and Sterne. The modern work of English literature which the *Autocrat* and the *Professor* at the breakfast-table at once call to mind,—as much, perhaps, in the way of contrast as in the way of resemblance,—is the *Noctes Ambrosianæ*. The broad rollicking humour and strong sense of the Scotch professor, however, are in contrast as remarkable with the somewhat thin intellectual wit of the American, as the dry toast and tea of a Boston boarding-house are to the "strong waters" and meat-suppers of Ambrose's. The divinity student and school-dame and vexed female in bombazine are the proper hearers of the wisdom of the Autocrat, as the Shepherd and Tickler are the fitting interlocutors of North. The entire absence of dramatic powers in Holmes is, however, what chiefly differentiates him from Wilson. The boarders at his breakfast-table are only so many points to which the Autocrat attaches the threads of his conversation, so many mirrors in which he is variously reflected. They exist only as they are shone upon by him. We are sorry to speak in what appears disparagement of a writer for whom we entertain a very sincere admiration; from whom the reader is sure of entertainment and of a certain amount of mental stimulus; in whom we acknowledge wit, humour, fancy—real, if not of the highest order, shrewd observations of life, if not deep insight into character, ingenious if somewhat superficial criticism on art, literature, and philosophy. We are glad to add, without any qualification, that Dr. Holmes's sympathies are always large and humane; and that the most odious of tyrannies,—always associated in those who indulge it with a deep underlying scepticism, which suspects its own truth of being a cunningly disguised lie that may be found out, the tyranny which would suppress free thought on the most stupendous of all themes,—is thoroughly hated and despised by him. Seeing life by snatches rather than seeing it whole, apprehensive of the salient points of a character rather than grasping it in its living unity, endowed, in a word, with susceptible fancy rather than with a sterling imagination, Dr. Holmes's vocation would appear not to be towards fiction. It is in fragmentary "guesses at truth," rather than in completed delineations of life and character, that his strength hitherto has seemed to lie. Whether *Elsie Venner* confirms this pre-supposition, or rather the author's doctrine, that every man has at least one novel in him, and "that he (Dr. Holmes), as an individual of the human race, could write one novel, or story, at any rate, if he would;"—which of these alternatives is true remains to be seen. If he has succeeded, he has furnished the best refutation of Mr. Hawthorne's notion that American life and manners do not afford materials for a romance, by doing what was pronounced impossible. *Solvitur ambulando.*

The "destiny" which is referred to in the title-page is not, we may premise, the "manifest destiny" of which we used to hear so much in connexion with America,—romance though that appears now to have become. It refers to the doctrine, very prominent in all Dr. Holmes's writings, that character, mental and moral, is largely dependent on organization; that transmitted and congenital qualities form a determining force in life. This opinion is not peculiar to Dr. Holmes. Every man, not only of science, but of sense, holds it, with more or less limitation; and Dr. Holmes himself does not hold it altogether without limitation. In many cases, however, the limitation is held so strongly as practically to reduce the original truth to nothing; in others so slight a limitation is admitted as virtually to leave the doctrine unchecked, to drift into a materialistic fatalism. Apart from the nicely-balanced judgments of physiologists and psychologists, in the matter of truths admitted into any mind, there are some which, from a natural affinity, become operative in it, and are always present with it; they form the key by which it unlocks the secrets of character, the light in which it views nature and life, the interpretation of all mysteries. There are other truths, different of course in different persons, which, admitted in words, are practically ignored. To the former class, in the case of Dr. Holmes, belongs the doctrine of congenital qualities, coming to us by hereditary transmission. It is the clue by which he finds his way through the labyrinth. He deduces from it, as he well may, many lessons of practical wisdom, and of tender and enlarged charity. Not denying, occasionally in a sort of moral compulsion conceding,

that the mind has a self-determining power, operative under fixed conditions, he soon loses sight of the self-determining power, and remembers only the fixed conditions. Character, he allows, is destiny; but organisation is character, and organisation is an affair of race and parentage and external influences, moulding the individual as clay is moulded. This is the "destiny," the "romance" of which is told in *Elsie Venner*. It is there put in a very bold and startling, and what will be to some minds repulsive, shape. (pp. 365-67)

The conception of a literally brute nature in a human form is in itself by no means attractive. The idea of a reptile semi-parentage is still more repulsive. (p. 370)

We are quite incompetent to discuss the physiological basis of the story. We demur, however, to the propriety of illustrating a "grave scientific doctrine" by what may possibly be a wild and unscientific delusion; and still more to the artistic suitability of introducing into a story of prosaic modern life, abounding in Yankee vulgarisms, an incident so abnormal and unverified as that on which *Elsie Venner* hinges. Granting for the moment its possibility, granting its actuality, it still is out of place. The scenery and events, the tone and colouring of the tale, are not in keeping with it. The conception illustrates the fantastic extravagance, that lack of a controlling good taste, which mark American literature. It is "sensation writing;" the object is to startle. The best proof of this is that Dr. Holmes's serpent-woman does not excite awe, pity, or terror, but simply incredulity. *Elsie Venner,* so far as the heroine's character is concerned, has neither the verisimilitude of a story of real life, nor the instructiveness of avowed parable or allegory. Dr. Holmes is by no means the first to describe the gradual humanising of a character in which a nature lower than human predominates. Mr. Hawthorne has done so in his romance of *Transformation*. The stories of Undines and of Neckars are other instances. But these are avowedly only the mere play of a graceful or pathetic fancy, or the symbolical utterance of truths which we can detach from their exterior form. A case like that of Elsie Venner belongs to the morbid pathologist, and not to the novelist. To be treated with effect in fiction, it should be transferred to an age or country—to Egypt or Greece—where, in the strangeness of the surrounding scenery and costume, rites and beliefs, it would lose something of the monstrosity which attaches to it as actually presented.

The secondary characters in *Elsie Venner* are, to our mind, more happily conceived than that of the heroine. The work derives its chief value not from the "romance of destiny" which it contains, but from the glimpses which it affords us of ordinary American life in a provincial town of New England. The two ministers, Liberal and Calvinist, the Rev. Chauncy Fairweather and the Rev. Dr. Honeywood, each covertly leaning to the other's faith; Deacon Sloper and Colonel Sprowle and Mr. Silas Peckham, are, we dare say, faithful portraitures. The picture, if it be a correct one, is by no means flattering. It leaves an impression that over American society there is diffused an incurable vulgarity of speech, sentiment, and language, hard to define, but perceptible in every word and gesture. We do not pretend that in the middle classes of an English town we should find any remarkable degree of refinement. But here there is a pervading atmosphere of good breeding, which extends to those who do not themselves possess access to the immediate sources of cultivation. Even more conclusive, however, than the genuine vulgarity of the characters whom Dr. Holmes intends to paint as vulgar, is the real vulgarity of those whom he would represent to us as well-taught and highly-bred gentlemen, of whom Mr. Bernard Langdon is the type. His utter failure in this character would seem as if the model on which it was founded was not over common. His success in delineating the Slopers and Sprowles is in remarkable contrast. In the one, probably he draws from experience, in the other, from imagination. Be this as it may, the latter have an air of reality which is entirely wanting to the former. The inference which is suggested by this, as to the condition of American society outside of the great centres of intelligence, may be unjust, but it is not unnatural. (pp. 371-72)

> *[Frank H. Hill], in "Dr. Oliver Wendell Holmes and 'Elsie Venner',"* in The National Review, *London, Vol. XIII, No. XXVI, October, 1861, pp. 359-72.*

OLIVER WENDELL HOLMES   (poem date 1862)

[In the following excerpt from his "To My Readers," written to introduce an 1862 edition of his collected poems, Holmes admits that his promise remains, as yet, unfulfilled.]

> Nay, blame me not; I might have spared
>   Your patience many a trivial verse,
> Yet these my earlier welcome shared,
>   So, let the better shield the worse.
>
> And some might say, "Those ruder songs
>   Had freshness which the new have lost;
> To spring the opening leaf belongs,
>   The chestnut-burs await the frost." ...
>
> Deal gently with us, ye who read!
>   Our largest hope is unfulfilled,—
> The promise still outruns the deed,—
>   The tower, but not the spire, we build.
>
> Our whitest pearl we never find;
>   Our ripest fruit we never reach;
> The flowering moments of the mind
>   Drop half their petals in our speech.
>
> These are my blossoms; if they wear
>   One streak of morn or evening's glow,
> Accept them; but to me more fair
>   The buds of song that never blow.

(pp. 1-2)

> *Oliver Wendell Holmes, "To My Readers," in his* The Complete Poetical Works of Oliver Wendell Holmes, *edited by Horace E. Scudder, Houghton Mifflin Company, 1895, pp. 1-2.*

[GERALD MASSEY]   (essay date 1867)

[Massey praises the manner in which Holmes uses humor to tell Americans "a few truths," thereby counteracting their provincialism.]

Oliver Wendell Holmes is ... doing his best to tell his countrymen a few truths it was well they should learn, especially from their own writers. He can say the most unpalatable things in the pleasantest possible way. He does not appeal to the pride and pugnacity of his countrymen, or tell them that America is the only place in which a man can stand upright and draw free breath. He thinks there is 'no sufficient flavour of humanity in the soil' out of which they grow, and that it makes a man humane to 'live on the old humanized soil' of Europe. He will not deny the past for the sake of glorifying the present. 'They say a dead man's hand cures swellings if laid on them; nothing

like the dead cold hand of the past to take down our tumid egotism.' He is equally the enemy of 'high-falutin,' and spread-eagleism, and social slang. 'First-rate,' 'prime,' 'a prime article,' 'a superior piece of goods,' 'a gent in a flowered vest;' all such expressions are final. They blast the lineage of him or her who utters them, for generations up and down. He tells them that 'good breeding is surface Christianity.' He slyly consoles them with the thought that 'good Americans when they die go to Paris.' He is thoroughly national himself, and would have American patriotism large and liberal, not a narrow provincial conceit. The 'autocrat' is assuredly one of the pleasantest specimens of the American gentleman, and one of the most charming of all chatty companions; genial, witty, and wise; never wearisome. We fancy the *Autocrat of the Breakfast Table* is not so well known or widely read in this country as it deserves to be. A more delightful book has not come over the Atlantic. (pp. 233-34)

[Holmes] brings American humour to its finest point, and is, in fact, the first of American *Wits*. ...

[A] speciality of Holmes's wit [is] the kind of *badinage* with which he quizzes common sense so successfully, by his happy paradox of serious straightforward statement, and quiet qualifying afterwards by which he tapers his point. (p. 234)

> *[Gerald Massey], "Yankee Humour," in* The Quarterly Review, *Vol. CXXII, No. CCXLIII, January, 1867, pp. 212-37.*

THE NATION   (essay date 1867)

[This anonymous reviewer identifies several faults in The Guardian Angel, *contending that it contributed to the decline in Holmes's reputation as a novelist.]*

What "goes without saying," as the French put it, Dr. Holmes is very apt to say; that, we believe, is the thing which chiefly interferes with our enjoyment of his works. The third page of *The Guardian Angel* gives an example of what we mean. Is there any one who refuses to admit that his "local paper" is seldom to be called an admirable thing? No one, we are fully persuaded. So it is a little—or not a little—unpleasing when a ponderous, much-creaking piece of machinery is dragged out, and that somewhat aged truth—painfully true, we may call it—is violently driven into us, with every appearance of triumph on the part of the engineer. Surely it had several times before sunk through all our minds of its own weight. ... [It] may have been a stroke of art in Dr. Holmes's work—his making his professor, when his lead-pencil is in hand, so stupid as he is. But it has not the appearance of being intended for stupidity. Thus Mr. Gridley goes on through his *Banner and Oracle*, advertisements and all; and with something of the same manner Dr. Holmes, as it appears to us, goes through his story—too often bearing on hard when only the lightest touch would have been pleasing, not to say sufferable; sternly breaking on his wheel the deadest of bugs and butterflies. For example, is a man "really *so* satirical" when he does this sort of thing? It is about Gifted Hopkins, the typical newspaper poet and village bard—a figure which has come to be, perhaps, the very least mirth-provoking of all with which satire deals. Satirists in kittenhood have played with it till the breath is long gone out of it. ... (p. 390)

Of this fault of bearing on too hard, we repeat, the book itself, taken as a whole, is an example. When he had written the *Autocrat of the Breakfast Table,* Dr. Holmes would have done

Holmes's gambrel-roofed house in Cambridge.

well, as it has since appeared, had he ceased from satire. That series of papers gave him a brilliant reputation which from that time forward he has gone on damaging, diminishing it by each new book; diminishing the brilliance of it, at any rate, though it may well enough be that he has extended it among more people. He has never stopped hammering at the same nail which he hit on the head when he first struck. *The Professor* took away something from the estimation in which we had been holding the *Autocrat; Elsie Venner* took away a little more; and *The Guardian Angel* takes away a larger portion than was removed by either of the others.

We speak of the author as a satirist. That he is, mainly; he is hardly to be called a novelist. His characters are figures labelled and set up to be fired at, or are names about which a love story is told, or they embody some physiologico-psychological theory; but they are never to be called characters in any true sense of the word. Never is rather a large word, perhaps. We can remember "the young man called John"; and we remember him as almost entirely and always human. But this can be said of no other of the personages—boarding-house keepers, young lovers, artists, soldiers, ministers, boarding-school girls—with whose names Doctor Holmes's books are filled. The incidents of his stories and their arrangement into a plot are generally better invented than the characters, and answer well enough the main purpose of the book, which is always essentially an attack on some theological dogma, an attack made sometimes directly and sometimes by the setting forth of some such theory as this, for example—the one on which is built the novel before us: "It was the strife of her 'Vision,' only in another form— the contest of two lives her blood inherited, for the conquest of her soul." But the humorist and man of wit and satirist

leads the novelist astray. Most of his incidents, invented or borrowed, are of no special importance to his subject, and he is often compelled to come forward in his own person and tell us what he intends by them.

Of *The Guardian Angel* as a novel, then, it is hardly worth while to talk. The theory above quoted is well enough illustrated by the incidents which the author has used in *The Guardian Angel;* the narrative part of the novel is at any rate as good as the narrative part of *Elsie Venner* or *The Autocrat* or *The Professor,* and in all these novels the narrative part is good enough for the satirist's purpose. As to the doctrine which is put forward in all these works—the limitations of human moral responsibility, the effect on the soul of the bad company of the body—we profess ourselves believers in it as Dr. Holmes states it; as doctors generally state it, when they are not doctors of divinity, without humanity. He simply asks us to accept the facts of human nature instead of kicking against the pricks, in the fashion of the divines of a hundred years ago. If his persistence in preaching a doctrine now for a long time pretty generally accepted is going to be serviceable, we are not going to find fault with him in his capacity of preacher. Only, if it is permitted, we doubt whether his anxiety to preach is justified by the state of things around him; and very certainly we do not feel called on to say that his sermon is very new—in fact, we do feel called on to say that it is old, and old sermons have been said to be tiresome. It frequently happens to people to believe in a preacher's text, and even to accept the discourse of a preacher, without thinking the text the most valuable of texts, or the discourse extremely edifying to the hearer or creditable to the preacher.

Witty, Dr. Holmes is pretty sure to be; and the bright things in *The Guardian Angel* are numerous. (pp. 390-91)

On the whole, *The Guardian Angel* is far from being unreadable, unless one is too fastidious. Each reader of this notice can, we think, judge fairly for himself. For our own part, . . . we found in the volume [passages] worth reading, and we may say that we found enough of them and found them fresh enough to repay us tolerably for going through a good deal of triteness and dulness and flippancy. (p. 391)

> A review of "The Guardian Angel," in The Nation, Vol. V, No. 124, November 24, 1867, pp. 390-91.

EDWIN P. WHIPPLE (essay date 1876)

[*Whipple assesses Holmes as a vigorous, witty writer whose poetic talents can be seen in all of his writings.*]

Oliver Wendell Holmes—wit, satirist, humorist, novelist, scholar, scientist—is, above every thing, a poet, for the qualities of the poet pervade all the operations of his variously gifted mind. His sense of the ludicrous is not keener than his sense of the beautiful; his wit and humor are but the sportive exercise of a fancy and imagination which he has abundantly exercised on serious topics; and the extensive learning and acute logic of the man of science are none the less solid in substance because in expression they are accompanied by a throng of images and illustrations which endow erudition with life, and give a charm to the most closely linked chain of reasoning. The first thing which strikes a reader of Holmes is the vigor and elasticity of his nature. He is incapable of weakness. He is fresh and manly even when he securely treads the scarcely marked line which separates sentiment from sentimentality. This prevailing vigor proceeds from a strength of individuality which is often pushed to dogmatic self-assertion. It is felt as much in his airy, fleering mockeries of folly and pretension, as in his almost Juvenalian invectives against baseness and fraud—in the pleasant way in which he stretches a coxcomb on the rack of wit, as in the energy with which he grapples an opponent in the tussle of argumentation. He never seems to imagine that he can be inferior to the thinker whose position he assails, any more than to the noodle whose nonsense he jeers at. In argument he is sometimes the victor, in virtue of scornfully excluding what another reasoner would include, and thus seems to make his own intellect the measure of the whole subject in discussion. When in his *Autocrat,* or his *Professor,* or his *Poet, at the Breakfast Table,* he touches theological themes, he is peculiarly exasperating to theological opponents, not only for the effectiveness of his direct hits, but for the easy way in which he gayly overlooks considerations which their whole culture has induced them to deem of vital moment. The truth is that Holmes's dogmatism comes rather from the vividness and rapidity of his perceptions than from the arrogance of his personality. "This," he seems to say, "is not my opinion; it is a demonstrated law which you willfully ignore while pretending to be scholars." The indomitable courage of the man carries him through all the exciting controversies he scornfully invites. Holmes, for the last forty years, has been expressing this inexhaustible vitality of nature in various ways, and to-day he appears as vigorous as he was in his prime, more vigorous than he was in his youth. His early poems sparkled with thought and abounded in energy; but still they can not be compared in wit, in humor, in depth of sentiment, in beauty of diction, in thoughtfulness, in lyrical force, with the poems of the past twenty-five years of his life. It is needless to give

even the titles of the many pieces which are fixed in the memory of all cultivated readers among his countrymen. His novels, *Elsie Venner* and *The Guardian Angel,* rank high among original American contributions to the domain of romance. In prose, as in verse, his fecundity and vigor of thought have found adequate expression in a corresponding point and compactness of style. (p. 516)

> Edwin P. Whipple, "The First Century of the Republic (Seventeenth Paper)," in Harper's New Monthly Magazine, Vol. LII, No. CCCX, March, 1876, pp. 514-33.

OLIVER WENDELL HOLMES (essay date 1883)

[*In this excerpt from his preface to an 1883 edition of* Elsie Venner, *Holmes defends the premise of the novel, explaining that his aim "was to test the doctrine of 'original sin' and human responsibility."*]

[*Elsie Venner*] is the story which a dear old lady, my very good friend, spoke of as "a medicated novel," and quite properly refused to read. I was always pleased with her discriminating criticism. It *is* a medicated novel, and if she wished to read for mere amusement and helpful recreation there was no need of troubling herself with a story written with a different end in view.

This story has called forth so many curious inquiries that it seems worth while to answer the more important questions which have occurred to its readers.

In the first place, it is not based on any well-ascertained physiological fact. There are old fables about patients who have barked like dogs or crowed like cocks, after being bitten or wounded by those animals. There is nothing impossible in the idea that Romulus and Remus may have imbibed wolfish traits of character from the wet nurse the legend assigned them, but the legend is not sound history, and the supposition is nothing more than a speculative fancy. Still, there is a limbo of curious evidence bearing on the subject of pre-natal influences sufficient to form the starting-point of an imaginative composition.

The real aim of the story was to test the doctrine of "original sin" and human responsibility for the disordered volition coming under that technical denomination. Was Elsie Venner, poisoned by the venom of a crotalus before she was born, morally responsible for the "volitional" aberrations, which translated into acts become what is known as sin, and, it may be, what is punished as crime? If, on presentation of the evidence, she becomes by the verdict of the human conscience a proper object of divine pity and not of divine wrath, as a subject of moral poisoning, wherein lies the difference between her position at the bar of judgment, human or divine, and that of the unfortunate victim who received a moral poison from a remote ancestor before he drew his first breath?

It might be supposed that the character of Elsie Venner was suggested by some of the fabulous personages of classical or mediæval story. I remember that a French critic spoke of her as *cette pauvre Mélusine.* I ought to have been ashamed, perhaps, but I had not the slightest idea who Melusina was until I hunted up the story, and found that she was a fairy, who for some offence was changed every Saturday to a serpent from her waist downward. I was of course familiar with Keats's Lamia, another imaginary being, the subject of magical transformation into a serpent. My story was well advanced before Hawthorne's wonderful *Marble Faun,* which might be thought to have furnished me with the hint of a mixed nature,—human, with an alien element,—was published or known to me. So that my poor heroine found her origin, not in fable or romance, but in a physiological conception fertilized by a theological dogma. (pp. ix-x)

The story has won the attention and enjoyed the favor of a limited class of readers, and if it still continues to interest others of the same tastes and habits of thought I can ask nothing more of it. (p. xi)

> *Oliver Wendell Holmes, ''A Second Preface,'' in his* Elsie Venner: A Romance of Destiny, *Houghton, Mifflin and Company, 1892, pp. ix-xi.*

THE NATION (essay date 1885)

[*This reviewer of Holmes's biography of Ralph Waldo Emerson insists that it contains little new material and points out "conspicuous deficiencies" in Holmes's research, yet praises its wit and intrinsic interest.*]

[In Doctor Holmes's **Ralph Waldo Emerson,**] very little is . . . added to what we before knew of Emerson's career, while the greater part of what others have gathered is . . . omitted. Viewing the book merely as a memoir, the reader is disappointed; but taking it for what it is, a detailed review of the *opera omnia* of one man of genius by another, with running annotations, grave, gay, learned, and witty, it becomes both valuable and attractive. This is the form, evidently, in which Doctor Holmes has conceived his work—two-thirds of the pages (roughly estimating) being made of this sort of commentary. This is evidently done, to some extent, as task-work, though in a loyal spirit. There is a good deal that suggests the scissors and paste; and sometimes in the later pages, when the annotator comes back to the charge for the hundredth time, and says of an essay, ''If I must select any of its wise words, I will choose,'' etc . . . , the reader is disposed to recall little Alice's answer when Humpty Dumpty says, ''If it comes to that, I can repeat poetry as well as any one''; and he is tempted to reply hastily with Alice, ''O, but it needn't come to that.'' And yet, when we think how many capital sayings, how many delicious *obiter dicta,* are scattered through these four hundred pages—how many single phrases here occur that we should recognize as the Autocrat's if we came upon them in the desert of Sahara or the Congressional Debates—we are ready to pardon everything to the inexhaustible lapidary who thus fills our hands with gems.

Such phrases occur, for instance, when he compares Thoreau to one who insists on ''nibbling his asparagus at the wrong end'' . . . , and Bowen reviewing Emerson to ''a sagacious pointer making the acquaintance of a box-tortoise.'' . . .

It is among the most conspicuous deficiencies of this memoir that it leaves us almost wholly uninformed as to two of the most important aspects of Emerson's earlier life—his relations to the anti-slavery agitation and to the so-called transcendental movement. In both cases there is an obvious lack of personal knowledge, not filled by any assiduous inquiry. In the days when Emerson was in his prime, Holmes was but lately returned from Europe, full of zeal for his profession and his art—medicine and poetry; the latter then belonging almost wholly to the department of *vers de société*. It is pretty evident from some of his verses of that period—for instance, those on Jean Paul, whom he called ''a German-silver spoon''—that transcendentalism simply bored him; while toward the anti-slavery agitation he probably had the usual prejudices of his social and

professional circle, though not in any acrid form. On these two important and almost controlling aspects of Emerson's life, therefore, he was as unsympathetic as Ticknor or Everett; and though he makes some slight effort to describe that part of Emerson's environment, the sketch has neither amplitude nor life. He deals with Emerson as literature alone, and scarcely alludes to his surroundings. Where he does he is often in error: for instance, he utterly underrates Emerson's relations to the abolitionists, with whom he says that he ''had never been identified.'' . . . It is impossible to say what Doctor Holmes means by being identified; Emerson no more merged himself in any anti-slavery society than in the ''Saturday Club.'' But there is no doubt that from the day when his great address on West India Emancipation was delivered at Concord (August 1, 1844), the abolitionists, who were not at all given to claiming or even recognizing any half-converts, always accounted Emerson as their own. Doctor Holmes says of the Concord oration: ''This discourse would not have satisfied the abolitionists'' . . . , but he could easily have ascertained whether it actually did satisfy them or not by stepping into the Boston Public Library and looking at a file of the *Liberator* for 1844. He would then have perceived at once that the mere fact of Emerson's speaking at that time and place and on that subject was an act of self-identification with the unpopular party. . . .

Something of the same deficiency that mars Doctor Holmes's treatment of Emerson's anti-slavery attitude is likewise found when he comes to treat the ''transcendental'' movement. There is a disproportion almost absurd in giving six pages to the *Monthly Anthology,* because it was edited by Emerson's father, and only five pages to the *Dial,* into which Emerson put so much of his own intellectual life. Even of those five pages, nearly four are taken bodily from the Emerson-Carlyle correspondence, which is in everybody's hands. It is possible that the omission may be due to the fact that this period has already been well delineated in other volumes of the series. It is certainly a proof of the still living interest in that particular intellectual movement that four of the eight volumes of the ''American Men of Letters'' series have been devoted to its leaders; but, after all, each volume in the list should have a certain completeness in itself, even at the risk of some repetition. As a result of this want, we have Emerson isolated, whereas he can only be fitly viewed as the centre of a group.

As we go through the book, we find here and there some minor misapprehensions. Thus Doctor Holmes, like Matthew Arnold, makes the mistake of quoting in full . . . Emerson's characterization of the Whig and Democratic parties of forty years ago, and assuming it as still valid of the Democratic and Republican parties of today; the fact being not only that the lines are changed, but the positions almost reversed. (p. 99)

But all these deficiencies may be regarded as minor matters, since the main interest which will attract most readers to the book will lie in those literary estimates of which it chiefly consists. The very fact of the great difference in quality, if not in grade, of genius between the author and the subject will enhance this interest to the highest point. So remote, in truth, are the two men, that the book might almost be entitled 'Contributions to the Natural History of the Wood-Thrush, by a Canary Bird.' Sometimes, to our amazement, we find the two very dissimilar warblers singing the same note, as when Holmes endorses, with evident heartiness, Emerson's famous Divinity Hall address. Yet the divergence soon appears when the mystic bird of the woods sounds a note too high. Thus, Emerson's essay on ''The Over-soul,'' in which so many have found, or thought they found, a jubilant delight, is to Holmes only a "rhapsody" . . . ; and he speaks with what can only be called contempt of the "Essay on Immortality." . . . But we must take a man, or a bird, for the notes that he can reach, not for those which do not properly belong to his genus or sub-order. On the whole, the criticisms on Emerson's prose, though they sometimes appear tame or perfunctory, are sympathetic as to the matter, and not unappreciative in respect to the manner; but it is when the critic comes to the poetry that we see how two fine minds may meet, despite all variations of temperament. Even here we find some criticism that is merely academical, as where Holmes complains of the redundant syllable in Emerson's line—

By his own meek and incorruptible will—

and calls it a "span-worm line," lifting up its back in the middle. . . . One is led to suspect the critic of being rather led away and captured by his own stroke of wit, as will sometimes happen. . . .

It is a satisfaction to find, after this specimen, that when the same style of academical treatment is carried still further by Mr. Matthew Arnold, Doctor Holmes is all ready to protest against it, and declines, as it were, to allow any one else to prescribe for his venerated patient. . . .

[It] is the supreme merit of Holmes's criticism that he shows himself able to go beyond the limitations of his own school,

Dr. Holmes in 1860.

and do honor to a poet utterly dissimilar to himself. The reader can well forgive many a fault of omission and commission in a book that leaves to us the bequest of such generous praise for another. It is a fine act of self-abnegation when one who has so successfully cultivated his own well-defined field of genius expresses cordial admiration for a domain more vast. . . . (p. 100)

"Holmes's 'Emerson'," in The Nation, *Vol. XL, No. 1022, January 29, 1885, pp. 99-100.*

EDMUND C. STEDMAN (essay date 1885)

[*A major nineteenth-century American critic and anthologist, Stedman gained wide critical influence as the author of* Victorian Poets *and* Poets of America, *published in 1875 and 1895, respectively. In conjunction with his popular* American Anthology, *the latter work helped to establish a greater interest in and appreciation for American literature. Reviewing Holmes's long career as a poet, novelist, and essayist, Stedman notes the author's proficiency in several different genres, examines the reasons for his endurance as an artist, and suggests that Holmes's success owes much to his personality.*]

The distinction between [Holmes's] poetry and that of the new makers of society-verse is that his is a survival, theirs the attempted revival, of something that has gone before. He wears the seal of "that past Georgian day" by direct inheritance, not from the old time in England, but from that time in England's lettered colonies, whose inner sections still preserve the hereditary language and customs as they are scarcely to be found elsewhere. His work is as emblematic of the past as are the stairways and hand-carvings in various houses of Cambridge, Portsmouth, and Norwich. . . . Among living old-style poets, Dr. Holmes, the least complex and various, seems most nearly to the manner born; his work, as I say, being a survival, and not an experiment. It is freshened, however, by the animation which, haplessly for compilers of provincial literature, was wanting in the good Old Colony days. The maker wears the ancestral garb, and is a poet in spite of it. His verses have the courtesy and wit, without the pedagogy, of the knee-buckle time, and a flavor that is really their own. There are other eighteenth-century survivors, whose sponsors are formality and dullness; but Holmes has the modern vivacity, and adjusts without effort even the most hackneyed measures to a new occasion. Throughout the changes of fifty years he has practiced the method familiar to his youth, thinking it fit and natural, and one to which he would do well to cling. The conservative persistency of his muse is as notable in matter as in manner. On the whole, so far as we can classify him, he is at the head of his class, and in other respects a class by himself. (p. 503)

What one does easily is apt to be his forte, though years may pass before he finds this out. Holmes's early pieces, mostly college-verse, were better of their kind than those of a better kind written in youth by some of his contemporaries. The humbler the type, the sooner the development. The young poet had the aid of a suitable habitat; life at Harvard was the precise thing to bring out his talent. There was nothing of the hermit-thrush in him; his temper was not of the withdrawing and reflective kind, nor moodily introspective,—it throve on fellowship, and he looked to his mates for an audience as readily as they to him for a toast-master. He seems to have escaped the poetic measles altogether; if not, he hid his disorder with rare good sense, for his verse nowhere shows that he felt himself "among men, but not of them"; on the contrary, he fairly might plume himself on reversing the Childe's boast, and declare "I have loved the world, and the world me." (pp. 503-04)

As a versifier, he started with the advantage of hitting the public by buffo-pieces, and with the disadvantage of being expected to make his after-hits in the same manner,—to write for popular amusement in the major rather than the minor key. His verses, with the measured drum-beat of their natural rhythm, were easily understood; he bothered his audience with no accidental effects, no philandering after the finer lyrical distinctions. It is not hard to surmise what "standard" poets had been found on his father's book-shelves. Eloquence was a feature of his lyrics,—such as broke out in the line, "Ay, tear her tattered ensign down!" and the simple force of **"Old Ironsides"** is indeed worth noting as it culminates in the last stanza. The making of verse that is seized upon by school-day spokesmen barely outlived the influence of Croly, of Drake and Halleck, of Pierpont with his "Stand! the ground's your own, my braves!" and Holmes himself would scarcely write in this way now. Yet one who sees, looming up by the Portsmouth docks, a fine old hulk to which these lines secured half a century of preservation will find them coming again to mind. **"The Meeting of the Dryads,"** another early poem, is marked by so much grace that it seems as if the youth who wrote its quatrains might in time have added a companion-piece to **"The Talking Oak."** The things which he turned off with purely comic aim were neatly finished, and the merriment of a new writer, who dared not be "as funny" as he could, did quite as much for him as his poems of a higher class. The fashion of the latter, however, we see returning again. There is the pathetic silhouette of the old man, who so

> Shakes his feeble head,
> That it seems as if he said,
> 'They are gone.'

This equals the best recent knee-buckle verse, and excels most of it in simplicity. It taught a lesson to Locker and Saxe, and more than one among younger favorites look up to Holmes affectionately, conscious that the author of **"The Last Leaf,"** **"My Aunt,"** **"The Dilemma,"** and of later trifles still more refined, like **"Dorothy Q.,"** is the Nestor of their light-armed holiday encampment.

A poet so full of zest is wont to live his life, rather than to scorn delights in service of the thankless muse. Dr. Holmes's easy-going method, and a sensible estimate of his own powers, have defined the limits of his zeal. His poetry was and is, like his humor, the overflow of a nervous, original, decidedly intellectual nature; of a sparkling life, no less, in which he gathered the full worth of hey-day experiences. See that glimpse of Paris, a student's penciled sketch, with Clemence tripping down the Rue de Seine. It is but a bit, yet through its atmosphere we make out a poet who cared as much for the sweets of the poetic life as for the work that was its product. He had through it all a Puritan sense of duty, and the worldly wisdom that goes with a due perception of values, and he never lost sight of his practical career. His profession, after all, was what he took most seriously. Accepting, then, with hearty thanks, his care-dispelling rhyme and reason, pleased often by the fancies which he tendered in lieu of imagination and power,— we go through the collection of his verse, and see that it has amounted to a great deal in the course of a bustling fifty years. These numerous pieces divide themselves, as to form, into two classes,—lyrics and poetic essays in solid couplet-verse; as to purpose, into the lighter songs that may be sung, and the nobler

numbers, part lyrical, part the poems, both gay and sober, delivered at frequent intervals during his pleasant career. (p. 505)

His pieces light and wise—**"Contentment,"** the **"Epilogue to the Breakfast-table Series,"** **"At the Pantomime,"** **"A Familiar Letter,"** etc.—are always enjoyable. One or two are exquisite in treatment of the past. **"Dorothy Q.,"** that sprightly capture of a portrait's maiden soul, has given, like **"The Last Leaf,"** lessons to admiring pupils of our time. For sheer humor, **"The One-hoss Shay"** and **"Parson Turell's Legacy"** are memorable,—extravagances, but full of character, almost as purely Yankee as "Tam O'Shanter" is purely Scotch. In various whimsicalities, Holmes sets the key for Harte and others to follow. **"The First Fan,"** read at a bric-à-brac festival in 1877, proves him an adept in the latest mode. There is also a conceit of showing the youngsters a trick or two, in the story **"How the Old Horse Won the Bet,"** told to the class of '71 by the minstrel of the class of '29, and pointed with the moral that "A horse *can* trot, for all he's old."

Good and bright as these things are, some of his graver work excels them. Where most in earnest he is most imaginative; this, of course, is where he is most interested, and this again, in moods the results of his scientific bent and experience. Here he shows himself akin to those who have both lightness and strength. Thackeray's reverential mood, that was so beautiful, is matched by the feeling which Holmes, having the familiarity with Nature that breeds contempt in graver men, exhibits in his thoughts upon **"The Living Temple."** The stanzas thus named, in measure and reverent effect, are not unworthy to be read with Addison's lofty paraphrase of the Nineteenth Psalm. Humility in presence of recognized law is the spirit of the flings at cant and half-truth in his rhymed essays. There are charity and tenderness in **"The Voiceless,"** **"Avis,"** **"Iris,"** and **"The Silent Melody."** Another little poem, **"Under the Violets,"** reveals the lover of Collins. But **"The Living Temple"** and **"The Chambered Nautilus"** doubtless show us their writer's finest qualities, and are not soon to be forgotten. There is a group of his "Vignettes," in recollection of Wordsworth, Moore, Keats, and Shelley, whose cadence is due to that gift of sympathetic vibration which poets seem to possess. These pieces are as good as any to furnish examples of the sudden fancies peculiar to Holmes's genius, whose glint, if not imagination, is like that of the sparks struck off from it. (pp. 506-07)

The things which, after all, sharply distinguish Holmes from other poets, and constitute the bulk of his work, are the lyrics and metrical essays composed for special audiences or occasions. Starting without much creative ambition, and as a bard of mirth and sentiment, it is plain that he was subject to faults which an easy standard entails. His aptitude for writing, with entire correctness, in familiar measures, has been such that nothing but an equal mental aptness could make up for the frequent padding, the inevitably thin passages, of his longer efforts, and for the conceits to which, like Moore and Hood, he has been tempted to sacrifice the spirit of many a graceful poem. To this day there is no telling whither a fancy, once caught and mounted, will bear this lively rider. Poetry at times has seemed his diversion, rather than a high endeavor; yet perhaps this very seeming is essential to the frolic and careless temper of society-verse. The charm that is instant, the triumph of the passing hour,—these are captured by song that often is transitory as the night which listens to it. In Holmes we have an attractive voice devoted to a secondary order of expression. Yet many of his notes survive, and are worthy of a rehearing. A true faculty is requisite to insure this result, and it is but just to say that with his own growth his brilliant occasional pieces strengthened in thought, wit, and feeling.

With respect to his style, there is no one more free from structural whims and vagaries. He has an ear for the "classical" forms of English verse, the academic measures which still bid fair to hold their own—those confirmed by Pope and Goldsmith, and here in vogue long after German dreams, Italian languors, and the French rataplan had their effect upon the poets of our motherland across the sea. His way of thought, like his style, is straightforward and sententious; both are the reverse of what is called transcendental. When he has sustained work to do, and braces himself for a great occasion, nothing will suit but the rhymed pentameter; his heaviest roadster, sixteen hands high, for a long journey. It has served him well, is his by use and possession, and he sturdily will trust it to the end. . . . (p. 507)

The mechanism of Holmes's briefer occasional poems is fully as trite and simple. Whether this may be from choice or limitation, he has accumulated a unique series of pieces, vivacious as those of Tom Moore, but with the brain of New England in them, and notions and instances without end. How sure their author's sense of the fitness of things, his gift of adaptability to the occasion,—to how many occasions, and what different things! . . . The half of his early collections is made up from efforts of this sort, and they constitute nine-tenths of his verse during the last thirty years. Now, what has carried Holmes so bravely through all this, if not a kind of special masterhood, an individuality, humor, touch, that we shall not see again? Thus we come, in fine, to be sensible of the distinctive gift of this poet. The achievement for which he must be noted is, that in a field the most arduous and least attractive he should bear himself with such zest and fitness as to be numbered among poets, and should do honor to an office which they chiefly dread or mistrust, and which is little calculated to excite their inspiration. (p. 508)

At forty-eight he began a new career, as if it were granted him to live life over, with the wisdom of middle-age in his favor at the start. Coming, in a sense, like an author's first book, *The Autocrat of the Breakfast-Table* naturally was twice as clever as any "first book" of the period. It appears that this work was planned in his youth; but we owe to his maturity the experience, drollery, proverbial humor, and suggestion that flow at ease through its pages. Little is too high or too low for the comment of this down-east philosopher. A kind of attenuated Franklin, he views things and folks with the less robustness, but with keener distinction and insight. His pertinent maxims are so frequent that it seems, as it was said of Emerson, as if he had jotted them down from time to time and here first brought them to application; they are apothegms of common life and action, often of mental experience, strung together by a device so original as to make the work quite a novelty in literature. The Autocrat holds an intellectual tourney at a boarding-house table; there jousts against humbug and stupidity, gives light touches of knowledge, sentiment, illustration, coins here and there a phrase destined to be long current, nor forgets the poetic duty of providing a little idyl of human love and interest. Here, also, we find his best lyrical pieces,—on the side of beauty, **"The Chambered Nautilus"** and **"The Living Temple"**; on that of mirth, **"The One-Hoss Shay."** . . . (pp. 508-09)

Two later books, completing the Autocrat series, follow in a similar vein, their scene the same boarding-house, their slight plots varied by new personages and by-play, the conductor of the Yankee symposia the same Autocrat, through the aid of a Professor and a Poet successively. The best comment on these works is made by their sagacious author, who likens them to the wine of grapes that are squeezed in the press after the first juice that runs of itself from the heart of the fruit has been drawn off. (p. 509)

The Professor is written somewhat in the manner of Sterne, yet without much artifice. The story of Iris is an interwoven thread of gold. The poems in this book are inferior to those of the *Autocrat,* but its author here and there shows a gift of drawing real characters; the episode of the Little Gentleman is itself a poem,—its close very touching, though imitated from the death-scene in Tristram Shandy. *The Poet at the Breakfast-Table,* written some years after, is of a more serious cast than its predecessors, chiefly devoted to Holmes's peculiar mental speculations and his fluent gossip on books and learning. He makes his rare old pundit a liberal thinker, clearly of the notion that a high scholarship leads to broader views. I do not think he would banish Greek from a college curriculum; but if he should, the Old Master would cry out upon him. Between the second and third works of this series, his [*Elsie Venner* and *The Guardian Angel*] had appeared,—curious examples of what a clever observer can do by way of fiction in the afternoon of life. As conceptions, these were definite and original, as much so as Hawthorne's; but that great romancer would have presented in a far more dramatic and imaginative fashion an Elsie Venner, tainted with the ophidian madness that so vexed her human soul,—a Myrtle Hazard, inheriting the trace of Indian savagery at war with her higher organization. The somewhat crude handling of these tales betrays the fact that the author was not trained by practice in the novelist's art. But they have the merit of coming down to fact with an exhibition of common, often vulgar, everyday life in the country towns of Massachusetts. This, and realistic drawings of sundry provincial types, Holmes produces in a manner directly on the way to the subsequent evolution of more finished works like Howells's *A Modern Instance* and *The Undiscovered Country.* Meanwhile he verifies his birthright by adapting these narratives to the debate on inherited tendency, limited responsibility, and freedom of the will. On the whole, the novels and the Autocrat volumes were indigenous works, in plot and style behind the deft creations of our day, but with their writer's acumen everywhere conspicuous. If their science and suggestion now seem trite, it must be owned that the case was opposite when they were written, and that ideas now familiar were set afloat in this way. Little of our recent literature is so fresh, relatively to our period, as these books were in consideration of their own. As Holmes's humor had relaxed the grimness of a Puritan constituency, so his prose satire did much to liberalize their clerical system. This was not without some wrath and objurgation on the part of the more rigid clergy and laity alike, and at times worked to the disadvantage of the satirist and his publishers. The situation now seems far away and amusing: equally so, the queer audacity of his off-hand pronunciamentos upon the gravest themes. He was responsible, I fear, for a very airy settlement of distracting social problems, to his own satisfaction and that of a generation of half-informed readers; for getting ready sanction to his postulate of a Brahmin caste, and leading many a Gifted Hopkins to set up for its representative. Yet his dialogues and stories are in every way the expression of a stimulating personage, their author,—a frank display of the Autocrat himself. If one would learn how to be his own Boswell, these five books are naïve examples of a successful American method.

Holmes's mental fiber, sturdier with use, shows to advantage in a few poems, speeches, and prose essays of his later years. These illustrate the benefits to an author of having, in Quaker diction, a concern upon him; each, like the speech **"On the Inevitable Crisis,"** is the outflow of personal conviction, or like **"Homeopathy vs. Allopathy," "The Physiology of Versification,"** etc., the discussion of a topic in which he takes a special interest. (pp. 509-10)

The notable prose essay on Edwards excites a wish that he oftener had found occasion to indulge his talent for analytic characterization. He has few superiors in discernment of a man's individuality, however distinct that individuality may be from his own. Emerson, for example, was a thinker and poet whose chartered disciples scarcely would have selected Holmes as likely to proffer a sympathetic or even objective transcript of him. Yet, when the time came, Holmes was equal to the effort. He presented with singular clearness, and with an epigrammatic genius at white heat, if not the esoteric view of the Concord Plotinus, at least what could enable an audience to get at the mold of that serene teacher and make some fortunate surmise of the spirit that ennobled it. I do not recall a more faithful and graphic *outside* portrait. (p. 510)

Holmes, among our poets, is . . . [an] original writer, but his prose is a setting for brilliants of a different kind; his shrewd sayings are bright with native metaphor; he is a proverb-maker, some of whose words are not without wings. When he ranges along the line of his tastes and studies, we find him honestly bred. Plato and the Stagirite, the Elzevir classics, the English essayists, the fathers of the healing art, must be in sight on his shelves. . . . (pp. 510-11)

But his proper study is man, the regard of people and movements close at hand. Somewhat distrustful of the "inner light," he stands squarely upon observation, experience, induction; yet at times is so volatile a theorist that one asks how much of his saying is conviction, and how much mirth or whim. His profession has put him on the alert for natural tendency, in the belief that fortune goes by inheritance. Crime and virtue are physically foreordained. He takes unkindly to sentimental attempts at reform. His temper and training so largely affect his writings that the latter scarcely can be criticised from the merely literary point of view. Holmes's conservatism, then, goes well enough with a poet of the old régime, and with the maker of light satires and well-bred verse. (p. 511)

If the question is asked, Would the verse of Doctor Holmes be held in so much favor if he had not confirmed his reputation by prose replete with poetic humor and analogy? the fairest answer may be in the negative. Together, his writings surely owe their main success to an approximate exhibition of the author himself. Where the man is even more lively than his work, the public takes kindly to the one and the other. The jester is privileged even in the court of art and letters; yet if one could apply to Holmes—the jester, homilist, and man of feeling—his own process, we should have analysis indeed. Were the theme assigned to himself, we should have an inimitably honest setting forth of his merits and foibles, from this keen anatomist of mind and body, this smile-begetter, this purveyor to so many feasts. As a New Englander he long ago was awarded the highest sectional praise,—that of being, among all his tribe, the cutest. His cleverness and versatility bewilder outside judges. Is he a genius? By all means. And in what degree? His prose, for the most part, is peculiarly original. His serious poetry scarcely has been the serious work of his life; but in his specialty, verse suited to the frolic or pathos of

occasions, he has given us much of the best-delivered in his own time, and has excelled all others in delivery. Both his strength and weakness lie in his genial temper and his brisk, speculative habit of mind. For, though almost the only modern poet who has infused enough spirit into table and rostrum verse to make it worth recording, his poetry has appealed to the present rather than the future; and, again, he has too curious and analytic a brain for purely artistic work. Of Holmes as a satirist, which it is not unusual to call him, I have said but little. His metrical satires are of the amiable sort that debars him from kinsmanship with the Juvenals of old, or the Popes and Churchills of more recent times. There is more real satire in one of Hosea Biglow's lyrics than in all our laughing philosopher's irony, rhymed and unrhymed. Yet he is a keen observer of the follies and chances which satire makes its food. Give him personages, reminiscences, manners, to touch upon, and he is quite at home. He may not reproduce these imaginatively, in their stronger combinations; but the Autocrat makes no unseemly boast when he says: "It was in teaching of Life that we came together. I thought I knew something about that, that I could speak or write about it to some purpose." Let us consider then, that if Holmes had died young, we should have missed a choice example of the New England fiber which strengthens while it lasts; that he has lived to round a personality that will be traditional for at least the time granted to one or two less characteristic worthies of revolutionary days; that—"'twas all he wished"—a few of his lyrics already belong to our select anthology, and one or two of his books must be counted as factors in what twentieth-century chroniclers will term (and here is matter for reflection) the development of "early" American literature. (p. 512)

> *Edmund C. Stedman, "Oliver Wendell Holmes," in* The Century, *Vol. XXIX, No. 4, February, 1885, pp. 502-12.*

EDWARD DELILLE   (essay date 1886)

[*Surveying Holmes's literary career, Delille argues that much of the author's work was superficial and finds in his writing "a certain general suggestion of great powers not exerted to the full."*]

With an aptitude for pure literature rarely if ever surpassed; with a technical training such as falls to the lot of very few men, and for the want of which many an aspiring spirit has sunk by the way; with, in a word, the finest gifts developed by the highest culture, what has Dr. Holmes accomplished? Has he written any pages which will remain as if graven in bronze? Has he struck out any such pregnant, irresistibly penetrating thoughts as those which render the names of Rochefoucauld and Chamfort immortal? Has he introduced any new formula of literary art, has he even achieved any searching general study of social life?

Dr. Holmes's sole work, in reality, has been to present in a graceful, able, and amusing way philosophy not transcending the bounds of the ordinarily intelligent mind, psychology which, however just and acute, is never especially profound, and objective observation wonderfully vivid and gay, but on the whole somewhat slight. His thought is not in the highest sense original, albeit originality is the quality of all others which his admirers claim for him. Precisely those views for which Dr. Holmes obtains the most credit have been condensed by other men into formulas more definite than his. His merit has consisted less in the conception of his ideas than in the concoction of the *sauce piquante* wherewith he serves them up.

Of course the maxim that nothing under the sun is new applies more completely to literature than to any other intellectual exercise. And it cannot fairly be contended, for the mere reason that every one of his clever little aphorisms and theories (that of the "depolarization of ideas," for instance, or that of the "triple mental strata") may be met with in various French psychologists and moralists, from Montaigne downwards: it cannot on these grounds be contended that the author of *The Autocrat of the Breakfast-Table* lacks originality of thought. Most of these metaphysical subtleties and conceits, could they but be traced to their absolute source, would be found to belong to the very first philosopher that set sail on the sea of introspection; ideas must perforce be drawn from a common stock, and he is the best literary artist who can dress them in the most attractive garb. It is in Dr. Holmes's general attitude towards the weighty truths with which he loves lightly to deal that he reveals the want of that higher moral power which, in default of a better word, may be termed "originality." (pp. 235-36)

[Judging] from the general tenor of his works, Dr. Holmes has always considered art and culture as being at least as essential to human welfare as universal suffrage. Indeed, in his own amiable way, he has occasionally laughed at his countrymen's "new-wordly" pretensions. The flapping of the American eagle's wings has never quite reconciled him to the harshness of the American peacock's scream, if a simile may be adapted from Emerson—himself a religious believer in all things American. But the spectacle of a great Government becoming an example when expected to remain a model might have inspired a *littérateur* so highly authorised as Dr. Holmes with comments somewhat more vigorous, were not his satiric pen dipped in *eau sucréc* instead of aquafortis. There was very little danger indeed of such a study as *Democracy* coming from the "dean" of American letters.

Dr. Holmes is too genial, it will be said, too tolerant, too kindly, to play the part of censor or polemical writer. He prefers agreeable pleasantry to denunciation. Very true; but then tolerance is a quality hardly compatible with high genius. Tolerance has never had much effect in redressing wrong. No reformer or moralist or satirist has ever been conspicuously "tolerant." Can the deeper shades of feeling, in a word such as this, be supposed to exist without some admixture of passion? And have many of the world's great literary spirits succeeded in suppressing that strain of sensitive bitterness, generally called "cynicism" by the majority of the public who neither think nor feel? Perhaps, on the whole, it may be justly assumed that a writer so successful as is Dr. Holmes in escaping any similar charge owes this enviable result to a certain lack of profundity as well as to the "sunniness" of his humour. (p. 237)

It is rather in his poetry than his prose that Dr. Holmes's limitations stand revealed: and that a writer's faults and merits both appear thc morc plainly in his vcrse is probably a gcncral rule, supposing, of course, he can handle verse quite freely, which is assuredly the case with Dr. Holmes. In the best of Dr. Holmes's poetry there is much delicacy of feeling, vivacity of observation, and literary elegance and ease; but his strain of song never rises so high or flows so strongly as that of poets born. There is always about his metrical achievements a hint of the somewhat paltry product called *vers de société*, to which true poets rarely condescend; nor would any true poet have fallen to the low level occupied so contentedly by much—by

perhaps the major part—of Dr. Holmes's verse. His would-be humorous pieces are often lamentably trivial. Witness the following stanza:

> Know old Cambridge? Hope you do.
> Born there! Don't say so! I was too;
> Born in a house with a gambrel roof—
> Standing still, if you must have proof—
> ('Gambrel? Gambrel?' Let me beg
> You'll look at a horse's hinder leg—
> First great angle above the hoof,
> That's the gambrel; hence gambrel roof.)

No, Dr. Holmes, not gambrel; doggerel.

To cite such rhymes as these in estimating, howsoever slightly, the poetical genius of a writer like Dr. Holmes, would scarcely be justifiable were they not a fair sample of a good many others by the same facile pen. To mistake wretched jingle for smartness; and to be merely "chirpy" when designing to be cheerful are tendencies in Dr. Holmes which all except his out-and-out-admirers will regret. (pp. 238-39)

The fact that Dr. Holmes is a versifier rather than a poet is emphasised by two particulars; one being his strong and perhaps personal consciousness of the tinkering mechanical side of rhyme-making (which has inspired him with several of his most entertaining prose passages), and the other his instinctive fondness for the graceful and highly-cultured but artificial and non-poetical manner of Pope. As an instance of Dr. Holmes's great proficiency in the latter style, and as a set-off against the nonsense-rhymes quoted above, some lines may now be given from the Prologue to *The Autocrat of the Breakfast-Table:*— . . .

> The victim knelt, still waiting for the blow.
> 'Why strikest not? perform thy murderous act,'
> The prisoner said (his voice was slightly cracked).
> 'Friend, I *have* struck,' the artist straight replied;
> 'Wait but one moment, and yourself decide,'
> He held his snuff-box—'now, then, if you please'—
> The prisoner sniffed, and with a crashing sneeze,
> Off his head tumbled—bowled along the floor—
> Bounced down the steps—the prisoner said no more.
>
> 'Woman! thy falchion is a glittering eye;
> If death lurks in it, oh how sweet to die!
> Thou takest hearts as Rudolph took the head;
> We die of love, and never dream we're dead.'

Words are not needed to point out the humour and literary grace of this delightful little *jeu d'esprit*, not unworthy in its elegance and spirit of the Augustan age. One could wish that throughout Dr. Holmes's poetic work there were more lines in the vein of the headsman Rudolph, with somewhat less of patter about "gambrels" and the like.

While there seems, on the whole, reason to conclude that Dr. Holmes is devoid of the higher poetical faculty, it must be recognised that many of his pieces gain a distinct value both from their clever execution, and from the tender affectionate sentiment, which . . . is the real keynote of the Bostonian humourist's nature.

There is in Dr. Holmes himself, as in most persons of keen sensibilities and quick intelligence, a certain suggestion of childhood, and his sympathy with, his love for, all that is childlike, is one of his finest traits. His tone in writing of children—whether in prose or in verse—is always delicately *ému*, to use an expressive French term without a parallel in

English. Thus, nothing could be more affecting than his description of the thrush-like thrill in the voice of a poor little girl, lying crushed by a cruel accident on a cot in a hospital in Paris. The feeling with which he speaks of this "blessed angel's" quietude in the arms of death is of the kind that wins on the instant the reader's affection to the writer. (pp. 239-40)

Dr. Holmes's three novels, *Elsie Venner, The Guardian Angel,* and *A Mortal Antipathy* (his latest production), are not only delightful reading, but afford palpable evidence of what their author might have, yet has not, done. It is indeed surprising that a writer capable of weaving tales thus brimful of human interest, and of portraying with such consummate skill the most idiosyncratic aspects of American life, should have been content, as it were, to sample the rich mine lying open at his feet, instead of exploring it fully—impossible, after reading *Elsie Venner,* to doubt that Dr. Holmes could have been (had he but wished it) *the* American novelist of the century. Hawthorne, unsurpassed as an artist and psychologist, was hardly the man to treat that every-day existence from which his dreamy soul recoiled. Mr. Howells, at the present day, is somewhat lacking in vigour and in breadth. But Dr. Oliver Wendell Holmes possesses in the highest degree the power of depicting characters; this is, among his various literary gifts, the most genuine and the foremost. (p. 241)

Dr. Holmes's works of fiction—taking *The Guardian Angel* and *Elsie Venner* for chief examples—are compounded of three principal elements namely, physiology, religion, and New England life. No praise could be too high for the manner in which Dr. Holmes treats the first and the last of these themes. Medical science has had few keener students than he, and who has ever discoursed on medical affairs so suggestively, so acutely, altogether so delightfully? His delineation of American provincial existence—indeed of American existence in general—is so excellently good, that the world ought to have had a dozen volumes full of it instead of only three. But in the matter of New England dogmatism Dr. Holmes has not done as much as was possible.

Having spent the almost entirety of a long life in New England, and being by training and taste a man of liberal ideas, Dr. Wendell Holmes has had every reason to know Puritanic orthodoxy for what it really is. (p. 242)

[He] has been enabled to perceive through his own daily experience to what extremes the spirit of creed may go in circles devoid of culture and art; and having had these things, as it were, within reach of hand, it would seem that he might have assailed them more effectually than by the means of witty innuedo and metaphysical discussion. Surely a little outspoken statement of opinion would have gone further—in the mouth of a great intellectual leader—than all the epigrammatic sayings about "oaks being out of their place in flower-pots," and "healthy people not needing to take the air in closed carriages," while the pages of brilliant hair-splitting were not needed to prove the dangerous and extraordinary facts that black is not blue nor the human heart a block of wood. One is convinced upon reading Dr. Holmes that his sentiments on the subject of dogmatism are far stronger than he ventures to express, which but renders one the more impatient at his constantly approaching, and never openly discussing, the theme of all others as to which frank speaking is most desirable. In short, one realises that this playing at fence with a question so vital as that of religious belief argues either a degree of indifference or else some lack of moral courage.

As matters now stand with Dr. Holmes, the three "Breakfast-Table" books constitute his greatest contribution to literature, and are those on which his fame chiefly depends. Few English or American readers are unacquainted with these admirable works. A very thesaurus might be drawn up from the pages of *The Autocrat, The Professor,* and *The Poet,* of wit and wisdom by Dr. Holmes. The Schoolmistress and Iris, Little Boston and the young man called John, the Model of all the Virtues, the Koh i-Noor, *et tutti quanti,* are familiar to most mouths as household words. The humour, the wit, the sentiment with which these characters are drawn no longer call for comment or for praise.

To seek the weakest link of a chain implies not weakness, but strength, in all the other links. Stress has been laid, above, on certain elements in Dr. Holmes's work which are conceived to be inferior to the rest. Perhaps this has mainly been because the rest is excellent beyond discussion. And yet not quite so either, for there seems to arise from these fascinating novels, delightful studies, sparkling essays and clever verses, a certain general suggestion of great powers not exerted to the full.

Dr. Oliver Wendell Holmes is a *bel esprit* of the finest water, a humourist of a high type, a ripe scholar, a brilliant stylist, an accomplished *gentilhomme de lettres.* But his possession of all these gifts rather enhances than diminishes the regret that they should be, to a certain extent, impaired by the spirit of a *dilettante.* (pp. 242-43)

Members of the Saturday Club, clockwise from top: Emerson, Hawthorne, Lowell, Longfellow, Whittier, Motley, and Holmes (center).

Edward Delille, "Oliver Wendell Holmes," *in* The
Fortnightly Review, *n.s. Vol. XL, No. CCXXXVI,
August, 1886, pp. 235-43.*

[A. INNES SHAND]   (essay date 1892)

[*Shand asserts that while all Holmes's writings have the ability
to surprise the reader and to combat dogmatism, the author is at
his best in his novels, particularly* Elsie Venner.]

[Dr. Holmes] wrote—we were going to say at random—on
anything and everything; he expressed his views and ideas with
American frankness.... He was brimming over with the exuberance of animal spirits; instinctively he treated his subjects
satirically, and he was overflowing with wit and fun and drollery. It was his nature to be logically or paradoxically aggressive, and when he had once fairly established his footing as
the Autocrat, as he admits himself, he gave the rein to his
aggressiveness in the *Professor,* and afterwards as *The Poet at
the Breakfast-Table.* He expressed himself on the gravest questions of Time and Eternity, with a licence of speculation and
a liberty of language which must often have shocked or scan-
dalised New Englanders of the stricter sects. To much of his
heterodoxy, whether outspoken or suggested, although it was
based upon benevolence and broad philanthropy, we altogether
take exception. We believe that, like some of the most respectable characters in his own novels, he was driven to extremes in the necessary reaction against the dogmatic Calvinism
and the cruelly eclectic Predestinarianism, which revolted ...
his moral sense. On many minor matters, and especially on
those concerning the orthodox practice of medicine, he had his
prejudices, antipathies, and strong prepossessions. But we are
persuaded that he always wrote according to his convictions;
those convictions generally appear to have been abiding; and
although he was intellectually emotional and impulsive, he was
essentially a fair-minded man. So his essays, although desultory in the extreme, show, nevertheless, consistency in principles and thought. Their fascinations are infinite; but perhaps
their principal attraction is that they are a self-revelation and
a running commentary on the writer, whose personality is always conspicuous. They are full of the versatile individuality
which gives them the changing colours of the chameleon—of
instruction, of information, of entertainment.... [When] at
his lightest he is essentially reflective and philosophic. A vein
of introspective or subjective analysis runs under everything,
even the drollery. As for his humour, it is dry and quaint, and
has distinctly a piquant Transatlantic flavour, although it differs
as widely from the humour of the Wild West as the sanctified
and strait-laced capital of Massachusetts from the last-born
mining township in Nebraska or Colorado. (pp. 194-96)

[Holmes's miscellaneous work has a distinct] American character. He lays the scenes of his monologues and colloquies in
a society which is somewhat novel and unfamiliar to us. The
characters and interlocutors he introduces to play their parts,
as his puppets, are all of them genuinely Transatlantic types,
and they were fresh when not distinctly original. His analogies,
his illustrations, his metaphors, his inexhaustible and happily
applicable reminiscences are drawn for the most part from the
settled States in New England. There our English habits may
have been modified by the soil, the climate, the circumstances,
and republican institutions; but they still perpetuate the English
traditions and memories which were affectionately cherished
by the descendants of the patriotic Pilgrims. (p. 197)

He made his reputation in Europe by the *Autocrat of the Breakfast-Table,* and it is probably on the 'Autocrat' that his reputation may rest. But in our opinion he shows himself and his
genius most characteristically in the novels, which have scarcely
been sufficiently appreciated; and the most characteristic and
the most striking is *Elsie Venner.* The conception is extremely
original. We find a parallel, perhaps—although no plagiarism,
for the two were conceived almost contemporaneously—in the
Transformation of his countryman Hawthorne. In the prefaces
to each of his novels he is apologetic, and that to *Elsie* is no
exception. In the guise of fiction he has put forward some
"grave scientific doctrine," but one of those doctrines born
of a morbidly lively imagination, which more prosaically minded
practitioners were disposed to ridicule. It underlies the delineation of the leading personalities, but it is evolved, insidiously, as it were, and with wonderful art, so as to give dramatic
interest and power to the characters and situations. Nor is
"insidious" an inappropriate term to employ, considering that
this story turns on the venom of a serpent infused in the veins
of a beautiful maiden, and tainting the fresh springs of her
nature with the guile and cruelty of the rattlesnake. It is a wild
fancy, given by the theorist for what it is worth, and mystery
envelops the whole matter. From the beginning Holmes has
made the most of the romantic materials to be found in New
England. There is no lack in the back-settlements of striking
and even of savage scenery, and the ancestral mansion of the
house of Venner is environed by terrors and horrors.... [El-
sie's] sad story is worked out with equal strength and pathos.
That she is predestined to misery we know and feel: the question
is, whether the magic of her magnetic attractions may not
involve the life of some man doomed to love her more dearly
than her father. The end is brought about and the spell is
dissolved by natural and logical means, if we subscribe to the
scientific theory. She sickens, she droops, and she dies at the
period which nature has mercifully assigned to the venomous
mortality of the rattlesnake. (pp. 198-99)

There is a great deal of the dramatic, too, in the career of the
scapegrace who comes from the Wild West, claiming near
kindred with the Venners. Cousin Richard has led a reckless
life; with his callous conscience he is indifferent to crime, and
only cares for its consequences. But the man of blood never
went in for a more reckless venture than when he dreams of
marrying his cousin, the snake-maiden, and that he soon realises. Nevertheless he still perseveres, and he sticks at nothing—
not even, in defiance of Massachusetts law, at strangling the
man he believes his rival. Like the frowning rattlesnake ledge,
Cousin Richard is all the more effective that he comes into the
peaceful society of Rockland like a raving wolf descending on
the sheepfolds. But this fantastic and sensational novel has
another side, and one which, as in Holmes's other pictures,
makes it delightful reading to the humourist and the student of
quaint manners in New England. Like Washington Irving, he
seems to delight in lovingly satirising the simple characters
and the odd fashions and customs which still linger in se-
questered agricultural communities. It is literally a new world
from our own into which we are introduced. The educational
institutions, in particular, would appear to indicate primitive
simplicity, if not primeval purity.... [The schoolmaster, Ber-
nard] Langdon, with his susceptible heart, reminds us of Ulysses among the sirens. But he was assailed through the eyes
rather than the ears, although he taught in a home of melodious
voices. We should say that the strain was too severe upon
mortal manhood, save that there was a certain security in the
multiplicity of attractions. It was there he made the acquaintance of the passionate Elsie, but he might have been in the

harem of an occidental voluptuary. The maidens of New England are always blooming and often beautiful. . . . (pp. 199-200)

The description of the great village or little township, like that of so many others in his novels, reminds us of an English Selborne. It still retains its rural character; it has never been approached by the speculative builder; its peaceful dulness warns away the enriched stock-jobber and the plutocrat of the petroleum springs. It reverences a local aristocracy like that of the Venners, who can trace their ancestry back for half-a-dozen of generations. But the select oligarchy of the place consists of the divines and the doctor, and one or two men who have made a comfortable independence in retail trade or any other respectable way. It boasts several of those venerable mansions which are the pride of Conservative New England—mansions like the old gambrel-house in which Holmes was born, and on which he dwells with loving minuteness of detail. . . . With their steep roofs and multifarious gables, and their old-fashioned gardens, with their bowers and carefully clipped hedges, they much resemble such English parsonages of Queen Anne's time as we see in the frontispiece to White's *Selborne*. And, like Selborne Rectory, they are surrounded by the secular elms which are always the pride of a New England village. One of these mansions was occupied by Colonel Sprowle, and it was in that mansion the Colonel gave his memorable party, which is admirably illustrative of the manners of the place, and an excellent specimen, moreover, of the dry and somewhat saturnine New England humour. It might have been a reminiscence by our old Nova Scotian friend Sam Slick [Thomas C. Haliburton]. (pp. 200-01)

In his monologues, in his essays, or in his novels, there are no characters whom Holmes analyses with greater enjoyment and subtlety—we may add, with more delicate humour—than that of the benevolent divine who has been bred a truculent Calvinist. The creed in which he has been educated, and which he feels bound to preach, is always clashing with his experiences, and still more often with his feelings. Waiving the doctrines of original sin and universal corruption, it is without conviction that he warns his tolerably decent-living flock that five-sixths of them are doomed to everlasting perdition. That was a matter on which Holmes felt very deeply, and in the reaction from the stern Calvinistic training of his youth he was driven latterly into the opposite extreme. (p. 202)

The Guardian Angel is also far-fetched and fantastic in its *motif*; but though there is a much more carefully constructed plot, it is also more conventional and commonplace in its treatment. There is the good old idea of the missing will, appropriately produced towards the *dénouement* to confound rascality and redress injustice. The story promulgates the moral notion of limited responsibility, founded on the scientific principle of heredity. We have the same sombre and romantic old houses as in *Elsie;* the same types of old characters who have been superannuated or shunted in a society which is progressing elsewhere at railway pace; the same austerity of dogmatic Calvinism, which casts gloomy clouds over sunny natures and repels the disciples it endeavours to enlist. But there is likewise the same agreeable relief in the undercurrent of quaint or sparkling humour, which is none the less pleasant that it is sometimes tinged with pathos. . . .

As for *A Mortal Antipathy*, the author may well avow in his preface that it was a very hazardous experiment. It is so ingeniously wrought out, with natural or possible details, that Holmes seems to have steered pretty wide of absurdity. But it is founded on a problematical case that might occur once in a

millennium, and the victim of a catastrophe is cured by a counter-shock which is less medical than melodramatic. (p. 203)

The Autocrat, and the kindred volumes which succeeded, demand intellectual congeniality or sympathy. We suspect that all who love them, love them almost to excess, and have fallen in love with them at first sight. Holmes is original, analytical, pathetical, satirical and sprightly, diffusive, desultory and discursive, without pretending to any great profundity. The range of his studies and reading has been extraordinarily wide; his tastes, or at least his interests, are endless; he is always striking unexpected attitudes or seeking for unfamiliar points of view. . . . [His] cynicism is assumed, and lies always on the surface; and his satire only stings when he is in solemn earnest, and rebelling against the gratuitous burdens which humanity imposes upon itself. (pp. 203-04)

The *Professor* and the *Poet* are in similar style, as is *Over the Teacups*, which closes the series. In the last there are still the old freshness and quaintness of thought, but they are tinged, like many of the later poems, with the melancholy of declining maturity. The old man speaks of accumulating years in the spirit of the philosopher; but with all its drawbacks he loves life well, and is very loath to leave it. He has known little or nothing of the sufferings of broken health; his strength has been more than sufficient for each day; he looks forward with vague hopes to a blissful futurity, but he shrinks from exchanging certainty for uncertainty. Holmes . . . is far from orthodox; and with less than Johnson's depth of well-reasoned and pious confidence, he really has Johnson's horror of death. He does not discourse "de Senectute," in the optimistic vein of the eloquent heathen sage. He is inclined to indulge in melancholy metaphor; sometimes he mocks his apprehensions, and seeks to console himself with grimly amusing satire. He is glad to remember that age is infinitely more cheerful in this nineteenth century than it used to be some two thousand years ago. . . . What he cannot away with is the modern writers who will make life out to be worse than it is, who paint the monstrosities of humanity as the normal state of mankind, or delight in dilating on actual horrors. Their realism, or rather their hyper-realism, is horribly unwholesome. . . . And as Holmes says indignantly, with great truth, the responsibility of immoral writers is terrible, for there are stains there is no possibility of effacing. "One who has had the mischance to soil his mind by reading certain poems of Swift, will never cleanse it to its original whiteness." As for the old 'Autocrat' himself, if his theology be somewhat broad, there is no question about the invariable purity of his morality; and his works, without exception, are absolutely free from the suggestion of vice or the suspicion of evil. (pp. 206-07)

[Holmes's] poetry is more diffuse and less emphatic than his prose. He shines most in such humorous satire and comical *vers de société Americaine* as "The Deacon's Masterpiece," "Parson Turell's Legacy," or "How the old horse won the bet"—which, by the way, although Holmes had a predilection for racing, is the record of a physically impossible feat, and flies in the face of all the canons of race-riding. His many songs of the War show that he was no Tyrtaeus, and among the most touching are those inspired by his innermost and abiding feelings, dealing with declining years and the inevitable decay of man. (p. 207)

[*A. Innes Shand*], "Oliver Wendell Holmes," in Blackwood's Edinburgh Magazine, *Vol. CLII, No. DCCCCXXII, August, 1892, pp. 194-207.*

Build thee more stately mansions, O my soul
As the swift seasons roll!
Leave thy low-vaulted past
Let each new temple, nobler than the last,
Shut thee from heaven with a dome more vast
Till thou at length art free,
Leaving thine outgrown shell by life's unresting sea!

1858

1892

Oliver Wendell Holmes

Boston, March 1st 1892.

Holmes's handwritten lines from "The Chambered Nautilus."

HENRY CABOT LODGE   (essay date 1894)

[*Henry Cabot Lodge, a member of the U.S. House of Representatives (1887-93) and a U.S. senator from Massachusetts (1893-1924), is remembered for his biographies of George Cabot, Alexander Hamilton, Daniel Webster, and George Washington, as well as for his* The Story of the Revolution *and* The Senate and the League of Nations. *In the following excerpt from an essay written several weeks after Holmes's death, Lodge discusses Holmes's literary career, deeming* The Autocrat *his best work and commending his patriotism.*]

Dr. Holmes is perhaps most often thought of as the poet of occasion, and certainly no one has ever surpassed him in this field. He was always apt, always happy, always had the essential lightness of touch, and the right mingling of wit and sentiment. But he was very much more than a writer of occasional poems, and his extraordinary success in this direction has tended to obscure his much higher successes, and to cause men to overlook the fact that he was a true poet in the best sense. The brilliant occasional poems were only the glitter on the surface, and behind them lay depths of feeling and beauties of imagery and thought to which full justice has not yet been, but surely will be, done. He felt this a little himself; and he never wrote a truer line than when he said:

> While my gay stanza pleased the banquet's lords,
> My soul within was tuned to deeper chords.

In his poetry and in his mastery of all the forms of verse, he showed the variety of talent which was perhaps his most characteristic quality. He had a strong bent toward the kind of poetry of which Pope is the best example, and possessed much in common with the author of the *Essay on Man*. He had the same easy flow in his verse, the same finish, wit of a kindlier sort, the same wisdom without any attempt at rhymed meta-physics, and the same power of saying, in smooth and perfect lines,

> What oft was thought,
> But ne'er so well expressed.

The metrical form which is so identified with Pope always seemed to appeal to Dr. Holmes, and, when he employed it, it lost nothing in his hands. But this was only one of many instruments which he used. He was admirable in narrative and ballad poetry, the poetry of energy and movement and incident, of which **"Bunker Hill Battle"** is as good an example as any. He ventured often into the dangerous domain of comic poetry, where so few have succeeded and so many failed, and he always came out successful, saved by the sanity and balance which one always feels in everything he wrote. Of a much higher order were the poems of dry humor, where a kindly satire and homely wisdom pointed the moral, as in the **"One Hoss Shay."** But he did work far finer and better than all this, excellent as this was in its kind. He was not one of

> The bards sublime,
> Whose distant footsteps echo through the corridors of time.

Nor was he one of those who seem to have sounded all the depths and shoals of passion. I do not think he thought so himself or ever was under the least misapprehension as to the nature of his own work, and in this freedom from illusions lay one secret of his success and of the tact which never failed. . . . [The] aspiring note is often heard in his verse, and there are many poems by Dr. Holmes filled with the purest and tenderest sentiment. Such are the lines on the death of his classmate and friend, Professor Peirce; such is the **"Iron Gate,"** the tender and beautiful poem which he read at the breakfast given him on his seventieth birthday. Such, too, are his lyrics, which include much of his best work, and which have in a high degree the fervor and the concentration which the best lyric ought always to possess.

People generally link his name with a memory of wit and humor, for he had both in large measure, and the world is very grateful to any one who can make it laugh. But the sentiment and aspiration, which are of higher quality than wit and humor can ever be and which are felt oftenest in the poems that love of man or love of country inspired, as well as the perfection of the poet's workmanship, and the originality of his thought, are too often overlooked. This perfection of form and felicity of imagery never left him. In the poem on the death of Francis Parkman, written only a year before his own death, when he was well past eighty, there is neither weakness nor falling off. The sentiment is as true and simple as ever, the flow of the verse as easy, and when he puts England's conquest of France in Canada into the single line

> The Lilies withered where the Lion trod,

we need no critic to tell us that the old happiness of phrase and power of imagery remained undimmed to the last.

Yet when all is said of his poetry, of which he left so much fixed in our language to be prized and loved and remembered, I think it cannot be doubted that the work of Dr. Holmes, which will be most lasting is the *Autocrat of the Breakfast Table* and its successors.

The novel of *Elsie Venner* is a strong and interesting book. The story holds us fast, and the study of a strange and morbid state of mind has the fascination given to the snakes themselves. Such a book would have made the fame and fortune of a lesser man. But as lasting literature in the highest sense, it falls behind the *Autocrat*. There the whole man spoke. There he found full scope for his wit, and humor and mirth, his keen observation, his varied learning, his worldly wisdom, his indignation with wrong, and his tenderest sentiment. To attempt to analyze the *Autocrat* and its successors would be impossible. It is not the kind of work that lends itself to analysis or criticism. It is the study of many-sided humanity in the form of the essay rather than the novel, although the creation and development of character play in it a large part. Such books with life in them are few and rare, although many have attempted them, but when they have the great vital qualities they are not of the fashion of the day which passeth away but for all time, because they open to us the pages of the great book of human nature. Montaigne and Addison, Goldsmith and Sterne, and Charles Lamb are the best, perhaps the only ones really in this field, for the exact combination of wit and humor, of pathos and wisdom, of sense and sentiment, where the lesson of life runs close beneath the jest and the realities tread hard upon the fancies, is as essential as it is hard to find. To this small and chosen company Dr. Holmes belongs, and in it holds high place. All the qualities, all the diversities are there, and, most important of all, the perfect balance among them is there too. The style runs with the theme, always easy but never slovenly, always pure and good but never labored, like talk by the fireside, without either affection or carelessness, while over it all (and this is stronger in Dr. Holmes than in anyone else) hangs an atmosphere of friendliness which draws us nearer to the writer than any other quality. (pp. 673-76)

[Dr. Holmes] had one personal quality which ought not to be passed over without mention anywhere or at any time. He was a thorough American and always a patriot, always national and independent, and never colonial or subservient to foreign opinion. In the war of the rebellion no one was a stronger upholder of the national cause than he. In his earliest verse we catch constantly the flutter of the flag, and in his war poems we feel the rush and life of the great uprising which saved the nation. He was in the best sense a citizen of the world, of broad and catholic sympathies. But he was first and before that an American and a citizen of the United States, and this fact is at once proof and reason that he was able to do work which has carried delight to many people of many tongues, and which has won him a high and lasting place in the great literature of the English-speaking people. (p. 677)

> Henry Cabot Lodge, "Dr. Holmes," in The North American Review, *Vol. CLIV, No. 457, December, 1894, pp. 669-77.*

[ROWLAND E. PROTHERO]   (essay date 1895)

[*Contending that Holmes was "above all, an American patriot," Prothero discusses the various influences on Holmes's style and sums up his contributions to American literature.*]

The parentage, childhood, and early surroundings of a man of genius must always be matters of biographical interest. But in the case of Oliver Wendell Holmes they possess a special value for the literary critic. They imparted to his works a characteristic flavour; they shaped his views of literature and society; they dictated his choice of the audience to which he appealed; they directed his mind into the particular groove of thought that partially explains the welcome which his writings have always received in the Old World. Above all, they implanted and fostered those refined instincts, which led him to oppose the premature effort of his contemporaries to force originality, and to condemn as unreasonable the demand, made half a century ago, that Transatlantic literature should appear in a new shape, 'shaggy and unshorn, shaking the earth like a herd of buffaloes.' Nurtured in the best traditions of Old-World scholarship, he felt no sympathy with the young American movement for the assertion of literary independence. Bred upon English models, and living among cultivated men in an University town, he did not, like some of his contemporaries, revolt against the established canons of art, or push the principle of Republicanism into the world of letters. Careful in his choice of poetical subjects, and conservative in his adherence to accepted rules of rhyme or rhythm, he never echoed the impatience of Judge Story, who grew 'tired,' as he told his son, 'of the endless imitations of the forms and figures and topics of British poetry.'

To his ancestry and his early training Holmes owed, as we think, some of the most prominent features in the peculiar position that he occupied in the literary life of his country. From first to last he was a sturdy opponent of the lawless independence which at one time threatened to vulgarise the literature of the New World, and thence to extend its influence to England. Another reason for laying stress on the parentage of Holmes is supplied by two of his best-known novels. Though *Elsie Venner* and *The Guardian Angel* had the object of demonstrating the cruelty of the most extreme doctrine of original sin, they were also both written to illustrate the limits set to human responsibility by inherited tendencies. The theory was a favourite one with their author. It reappears, again and again, in his writings; it supplies the main argument to his essay on **"Crime and Automatism."** He would have said himself that in his mental equipments he was what his forefathers had made him. He compares the body in which we travel over the isthmus of life, not to a private carriage, but to an omnibus, filled inside and out with our ancestors. On his father's side he was descended from a Puritan family of importance which settled in Connecticut in the seventeenth century. Thus his paternal ancestors were those sturdy Roundheads who formed the aristocracy of New England, and he inherited blood

> Such as warmed the pilgrim sons of toil
> Who held from God the charter of the soil.
>
> (pp. 189-90)

From one point of view Holmes is a product of the leisured Augustan age, a cultured survival of the Georgian era of colonial history. From another he has all the alertness of the busy-brained enquiring man of science who adorns the present century. He is at once skilled in the conduct of the 'clouded cane,' and an adept in the use of the stethoscope. He excels in the patrician art of light *vers de société,* and delights in the 'straight-backed measure' which 'sheathed the steel-bright epigrams of Pope.' But he is also essentially a modern American in the nimbleness, vivacity, and concreteness of his mind, in the versatility that achieves success in widely different fields, and in the rapid intuition with which he links together incongruities by their hidden resemblances. It is the union of the two ages which gives a peculiar flavour to his writings. His manner and his general attitude towards men and things carry us back to the days when Pope was regarded as greater than Homer, when Bryant sate in Arctic isolation as the Dean of American poets, when Halleck was considered a rival to Byron, when Miss Sedgwick was the Miss Edgeworth of the New world, when Lydia Sigourney was a Transatlantic Felicia Hemans, and when Whittier seemed 'destined for the tar-pot, rather than the tripod.' His matter, on the other hand, transports us into an active bustling world of steam-engines and electricity, surrounds us with an atmosphere of polemics and controversies which was alien to the previous century, and keeps us abreast with, sometimes in advance of, the latest developments of modern thought. The shrewd observation and the strong practical sense of a nineteenth-century Franklin are tempered by the sympathies and expressed with the epigrammatic polish of an aristocratic age. He is at once master of the revels among the polished wits of the coffee-house, and the representative of the sagacious, alert, enterprising men of business who have made modern America.

Holmes's conservatism was strong. Republican though he was, he was essentially an aristocrat. . . . He ridiculed the appetite of his fellow-countrymen for high-sounding titles; he satirised the American love of superlatives; he laughed at the exaggeration of modesty which sometimes bordered perilously near to pruriency. (pp. 198-200)

The debt which the best American literature, and all who in the Old World and the New appreciate its mixture of freshness and refinement, owe to Holmes is very great. How great the debt was has not yet been fully recognized by his countrymen. When young America demanded that the political revolution which separated the Old and New Worlds should have its literary counterpart in a similar revolt, Holmes threw all his influence into the opposite scale. He urged, with keen satire as well as with the force of example, that even a Republic must recognize the laws of conventional decorum, and that those who enter the Temple of the Muses outrage propriety if they ostentatiously flaunt their working dress. To him, as much as to any other man, we owe it, that the Versailles of American

literature has not been invaded to a greater extent than it has by the vocabulary and manners of the 'Halles.' (p. 201)

Patrician in his tastes, aristocratic in his sympathies, Conservative in his opinions, anti-democratic but not anti-Republican, he was, above all, an American patriot. His war-songs ring true with loyalty to the nation; and his **"Hunt after my Captain"** is full of eager sympathy with the cause of the star-spangled banner.

As a poet Holmes is greater in equipment than in achievement. He is the master of a terse pointed style, at once clear and condensed: his versification is easy and simple; his choice of epithets is often felicitous; his works, whether grave or gay, have the clear-cut crispness and the brilliant sparkle of high polish. He blends comedy and seriousness, humour and pathos, wit and sentiment with the admirable dexterity that heightens their effect by harmonious contrast. His wildest freaks of humour are yet allied with manly feeling, shrewd observation, sound sense, and genial wisdom. (pp. 201-02)

But, *Figaro-ci, Figaro-lá,* in an evil hour for the full development of his gifts, Holmes has been called upon to write verses on every possible occasion. Stanzas to be read at banquets, addresses to distinguished visitors, panegyrics on dead friends, and songs in praise of good fellowship constitute the bulk of his work. In this department of literature he was unrivalled. His society-verse stands by itself in America. It is not merely that his work has the neat finish of a cultured leisured age, that despises the rough approximations of a century content with ready-made goods. Fastidious polish marks the product of all writers of his school. But Holmes was, as it were, born to the patrician industry which, since he began to write, others have cultivated assiduously. The art that they sought to revive was with him a survival, and, as a consequence, his lines ring true and genuine, while those of his successors necessarily bear the stamp of artificiality. Brilliant writers of occasional verses rarely reach the highest rank among poets; the careless ease which such poetry demands is generally incompatible with strength of feeling or massiveness of intellect. Holmes is no exception to the rule. His lively versatility, nimble wit, tender feeling, and eloquent rhetoric imposed upon his efforts limits that his extraordinary facility of composition and light-hearted gaiety only rendered more insurmountable. For power he substitutes refined taste. For imagination he offers us a fancy which, however light, sportive, and charming it may be, is rarely creative. Instead of ideality he gives us conceits that are often apt, often graceful, and often, it must be added, pushed too far. With him poetry seems to have been a diversion rather than a serious pursuit, a distraction but not a passion, and his compositions impress us as the work of a clever man of literary talent, not as the utterances of the man of genius. Holmes has, however, written many poems which suggest that, under other circumstances, his achievement might have been greater. Had he not been called upon to be the Scheherezade of American feasts, he might have given us more poems like **"The Chambered Nautilus"** and **"Dorothy Q.,"** or written ballads with the true ring of

> Come hither, God-be-Glorified,
>   And sit upon my knee;
> Behold the dream unfolding
>   Whereof I spake to thee,
> By the winter's hearth in Leyden,
>   And on the stormy sea.

Holmes has somewhere expressed the belief that 'every articulately speaking human being has in him stuff for *one* novel in three volumes.' 'All, after that,' he adds, 'are with some persons failures.' He has himself written three novels, none of which can, in our opinion, be called successful. They abound in homely wisdom and caustic humour; they contain shrewdly observed pictures of New England life; they are filled with thrilling incidents. But in constructive skill they are singularly deficient, and they show little dramatic power. The author is always on the stage directing the movements of his puppets, and bringing with him a 'medicated atmosphere.' The minor figures are coarsely drawn and harshly coloured; the chief actors are anatomical puzzles, concrete problems in heredity, examples of mental states, psychological instances scientifically, but not dramatically, constructed. No one can read *Elsie Venner* without feeling how differently the heroine would have fared in the hands of Hawthorne.

Wanting in the serious purpose of a poet, lacking the constructive and dramatic genius of the novelist, Holmes discovered in the *Autocrat* the form of expression which was most perfectly fitted for the display of his gifts. In 1857 the *Atlantic Monthly* was founded, and to its pages he contributed the rambling discursive series which established the reputation of the new review and his own best title to immortality. In table-talk we do not want the imaginative genius, the prophetic spirit, the reflective brooding of the poet. Its charm lies in the lightness and ease of its flow, the crispness and pungency of its reflections, the freshness and pertinence of its observations. Good conversation is, like occasional verse, a patrician art which Holmes inherited. In his hands it is the instrument by which he can teach without being didactic, preach without sermonising, and amuse without offending the most fastidious taste. Here the want of constructive power is not seriously felt, and the perpetual presence of the author's personality is a positive advantage. The figures on the stage of the boarding-house require no individuality, for they are only the puppets with which the Autocrat plays at his pleasure. Holmes did not wait till the age of forty-eight to discover the best means of displaying his brilliant gifts. More than a quarter of a century before, he had printed in the *New England Magazine* the first of two papers called **"The Autocrat of the Breakfast Table."** They attracted no attention; they were, as he himself says, 'the crude products of his uncombed literary boyhood.' But the idea of table-talk was not forgotten by their author. When he returned to his early experiment of 1831, he had gained the reflective maturity, the varied experience, the ripeness of judgment which are essential to the success of the essayist. The best work of a Lamb, a Sterne, or a Montaigne is the ripe fruit of middle life.

It is by the Autocrat that, in our opinion, the name of Holmes will live. The three volumes of table-talk which form the series are unequal in merit. They are neither narratives nor dramas; but collectively they form a treasure-house of practical philosophy. Incomparably the best is the first of the series, and it also contains two poems which, in very different styles, are two of the best representatives of his poetic gifts,—**"The Chambered Nautilus"** and **"The One-Hoss Shay."** The simple movement, the easy play, the frankness of the whole give it the appearance and the charm of a spoken soliloquy. We see the thought first as it appears in the rough clay, then pinched and patted here and there, till it is moulded into the shape of aphorism, or epigram, or apophthegm. Out of the medley of unexpected thoughts and quaint satire shine gleams of deeper feeling, sparks of brilliant fancy, penetrating rays of insight into men and things. It is full of earnest purpose; but the fight for the conditions of healthy national existence, the pursuit of

mental truth, the effort to enforce the laws of common sense and experience are conveyed by humorous suggestions, condensed into proverbs of homely wisdom, enforced by grotesque contrasts, drollery, and pathos. His nimbleness of wit and his keen appreciation of the resemblances which underlie apparent incongruities enable him to expound his subject by a variety of ingenius images, to decorate it with novel suggestions, and to illustrate it by a succession of fresh sidelights gathered from the maturity of his practical and reflective experience.

The whole of the series is replete with a homour which in America is rare, if not peculiar to Holmes. One set of circumstances checked, another fostered the growth of humour in the New World. Out of the shock of the opposing tides emerged the matter-of-fact, dry, sarcastic character of the national product. Puritan grimness restrained the flow of animal spirits, enforced the duty of concealing ridiculous ideas, and so determined its demure, covert character. At the same time the meeting of savagery and civilization sharpened to their keenest edge the sense of incongruities, the perception of concealed analogies, the appreciation of hidden resemblances. The native wit bears upon it the stamp of the influences of two contending forces. The broad buffoonery which often does duty for it is not a national product, though the attempt to obtain the sanction of Biblical phraseology undoubtedly represents one effect, and not always the most pleasing one, of this union of natural laughter and inherited sternness.

Holmes's humour was not the lean, joyless, silent laugh of the Puritan. It need scarcely be added that he is never a mere buffoon, and never attempts to eke out the poverty of his jest by flavouring it with the language of the Bible. His humour is not dry, sarcastic, rasping, cynical. It is the expression of a nature neither stoical nor ascetic, but cheerful, genial, and optimistic. It has the slyness of natural gaiety rathen than the demureness of conscious self-repression. It is sweet, wholesome, sympathetic, kindly, at once enjoying and enjoyable. It recognizes no moral evil in that happiness and delight of existence which Puritanism placed under so severe an interdict. It rests on a deeper basis than mere intellectual quickness or the keen perception of whimsical contrasts and absurd resemblances. It does not depend for its effect on the shock of surprise, on the raciness of exaggeration, or on the irony of understatement. There is in it something of the large humanity without the playful yet pathetic wistfulness of Thackeray. Both men approach their subject through the heart as well as through the head. There is neither cynical scorn nor ungenerous contempt in the humour of either. But the American is more confident in the progress of the world, more hopeful of society, more convinced of the natural goodness of his fellow-men. The one is, as it were, the product of the saddened experiences of an Old World, the other of the buoyant optimism that belongs to a society which is still in its youth. Holmes's humour bears re-reading, because it draws its inspiration from a deep but tender insight into human character and from the genial interest of life of a kindly-hearted, generous-natured man. No writer did more in his generation to soften the harshness of the Puritan temper, or to disperse with the cheerful warmth of innocent enjoyment the chilling gloom of its austere rule in New England. For this, even more than for his purely literary influences, he deserved, and gained, the affection of his fellow-countrymen. (pp. 202-06)

[*Rowland E. Prothero*], in a review of "The Writings of Oliver Wendell Holmes," in The Quarterly Review, *Vol. CLXXIX, No. CCCLIX, January, 1895, pp. 189-206.*

LESLIE STEPHEN   (essay date 1896)

[Stephen is considered one of the most important English literary critics of the late Victorian and early Edwardian eras. In his criticism, which is often moralistic, Stephen argues that all literature is nothing more than an imaginative rendering, in concrete terms, of a writer's philosophy or beliefs. In the following excerpt, Stephen comments on The Autocrat, Elsie Venner, *and Holmes's later poetry, concluding with particular admiration for his freedom from the "mawkishness which sometimes makes good morality terribly insipid."]*

Few modern writers have roused a stronger feeling of personal affection than O. W. Holmes. (p. 626)

His works are not voluminous; and, though he had published some of his best verses before he was thirty, he was nearly fifty before he began the series of essays which really made him famous. Few popular authors have had a narrower escape from obscurity. He would, in any case, have been remembered in his own circle as a brilliant talker, and there would have been some curiosity as to the writer of the **"Last Leaf"** and two or three other poems. But had it not been for the judicious impulse given by his friend Lowell which induced him to make his appearance as the "autocrat," his reputation would have resembled that of Wolfe, of "not a drum was beat" celebrity. Who, it would have been asked, was the author of the few lines which we all know by heart? and we should have turned up the article devoted to him in a biographical dictionary. But he would not have revealed himself with that curious completeness upon which all his critics have remarked. He often heard, as he says in an interesting letter, that he "had unlocked the secret of some heart which others, infinitely more famous, infinitely more entitled to claim the freedom, have failed to find opening for them." He cannot help believing that "there is some human tone in his written voice which sometimes finds a chord not often set vibrating." The secret of this gift is not hard to penetrate. . . . He remarks in the same letter that his life was "rather solitary than social"; and the society which he did frequent was not in one of the greatest centres of intellectual movement. In certain ways, too, even Bostonians must admit that the social atmosphere was of a kind to nip some of the luxuriant growths congenial to older abodes of art and letters. Holmes' attachment to his surroundings was as keen as if the conditions had been of the most genial. . . . So Holmes cherished whatever could be called historically interesting in his own country, because the supply of the appropriate material was so limited. Men who live in the shadow of Westminster Abbey or go to universities which the great men of many centuries have filled with associations, are apt to become a little bored with the topic. . . . As he grew up his patriotism did not diminish in intensity. All that happened was that he became qualified to catch its comic aspects. When the "young fellow they call John" laid down the famous proposition that "Boston State House is the hub of the solar system," and adds that "you couldn't pry that out of a Boston man if you had the tire of all creation straightened out for a crowbar," the autocrat accepts the "satire of the remark," and admits that the "axis of the earth sticks out visibly through the centre of each and every town and city." But he does not pretend to conceal that the sentiment, outrageous if literally accepted, tickles his fancy agreeably. . . . Holmes as a man shares the young fellow's enthusiasm, though he wishes us to understand that he is aware in cold blood that it is not quite the whole truth. The little deformed gentleman in the *Professor* gives a still more vigorous mouthpiece of the same sentiment. "A new race, and a whole new world for the newborn human soul to

work in! And Boston is the brain of it, and has been any time these hundred years! That's all I claim for Boston, that it is the thinking centre of the continent and therefore of the planet!"—in which respect its superiority to Philadelphia and New York is easily demonstrated. The little gentleman is one of Holmes' most spirited characters, and makes a very convenient organ for the utterance of opinions not to be turned into serious dogmas—but also not to be overlooked. Boston is an ideal as well as a real city; it represents "the American principle," whatever that may precisely be. It is the three-hilled city as opposed to the seven-hilled city or reason against Rome. Democratic America has a different humanity from feudal Europe "and so must have a new divinity." Religion has to be "Americanized," and Boston is in the van of the struggle.

This might suggest a good many remarks for which Holmes would, perhaps, leave his deformed gentleman to reply. He has not committed himself to an unreserved support of a personage who reflects only one of his moods. One point, however, has to be noticed. Holmes, like others, had revolted against Calvinism as represented by the Westminster Confession. Many pages in his essays are directed against the old-fashioned creed; and, as we are told, made him the object of warm denunciations by the orthodox. Young people . . . were forbidden to read the *Autocrat,* and *Elsie Venner* was regarded as a dangerous manifesto. This, it must be admitted, sounds strange at the present day. Were any books ever more obviously harmless? People who remember certain English controversies about [theologian Frederick Denison] Maurice, which happened a little before the appearance of the *Autocrat,* may succeed in understanding why, in the country of the Puritans, Holmes should have passed for a heresiarch. Yet it now requires an effort to put oneself in that position, and certainly Holmes' remarks would now hardly excite a shudder in the best regulated families. Still they represented what seems to have been the most important passage of his mental history. The old Puritanism, one may guess, appeared to him in a new light when he had sat at the feet of Parisian professors. The old Boston, at any rate, was not quite the "hub of the universe" in the physiologist's point of view; and he fancied, when the old and the new currents met, a good deal of the sediment of old-fashioned dogma would be precipitated. Still, the old problem which Calvinism had answered in its own way came up in a new form. The doctrine of hereditary sin might be abandoned, but the problems of scientific "heredity" took its place. Jonathan Edwards' discussions of moral responsibility have a serious meaning when they are dissociated from the ghastly visions of hell-fire. Holmes gave more place to these controversies than some of his readers liked; and I need say nothing as to the merit of his own conclusions. They interest us chiefly because they gave rise to that provoking book, *Elsie Venner.* I call it "provoking" merely because it will not square nicely with any orthodox canons of criticism. In the first place, it has an air of being didactic, or is a book with a tendency, or, in the old-fashioned phrase, is a novel with a purpose. I confess that I should have no objection to it upon that ground. I always found *Sandford and Merton* a delightful work in my childhood, and I partly preserve that degrading taste. I like books with a moral. Some authors, it is true, are cramped by their morals, and occasionally tripped up into flat absurdity. Still, a writer often gets a certain unction from the delusion that he is preaching as well as story-telling; and so long as anyone is working with a will, and defying the critics and all their ways, he has the root of the matter in him. Holmes, it must be remarked, did not suppose that he was proving anything in *Elsie Venner;* he recognized the truth of the axiom propounded in the *Rose and the Ring* that blank verse is not argument; and the imaginary behaviour of an impossible being cannot possibly lead to any conclusion. When we meet a being who is half woman and half a snake it will be time to settle the moral code for judging her. Holmes, in fact, says in his prefaces that he only took an imaginary case in order to call attention to the same difficulty in the common course of things. To that I can see no objection. Clearly, every great tragedy involves some interesting question of casuistry; and casuistry may repay the debt by suggesting a good plot for a novel. The only question is, whether the extravagant hypothesis, be it purely fantastic or contrived to illustrate a point in ethics, has really been turned to good account. Here I confess to a conflict of feeling which, I suspect, is shared by others. The book makes me read it just whenever I take it up, and yet I am never satisfied. Perhaps it is that I want more rattlesnake; I want to have the thrill which my ancestors felt when they told legends of werewolves; I wish the snake-woman to be as poetical as Coleridge's Geraldine, to tremble while I read, and to be encouraged in my belief by such an infusion of science as will reconcile me to the surroundings of the nineteenth century in New England. That is, no doubt, to wish at the lowest that Holmes could have been combined with Hawthorne—not to suggest the creator of Caliban—and that their qualities could have coalesced with as little interference as those of Elsie and the snake. So much is suggested that one wants a more complete achievement. The fact is simply, I suppose, that Holmes had not the essential quality of the inspired novelist. He did not get fairly absorbed in his story and feel as though he were watching, instead of contriving, the development of a situation. That, for example, is the way in which Richardson declares himself to have written, and which partly explains the fascination to our forefathers of his moralizing and long-winded narratives. Holmes is distinctly a spectator from outside, and his attention is too easily distracted. I do not, in the least object to a novelist discoursing or supplying comments if it be his natural vein; I am not simple-minded enough to care for the loss of the illusion. But the novelist should not give an analysis in place of a concrete picture, or wander into irrelevant remarks. Now, Holmes' intellect is so lively and unruly that the poor snake-lady gets too often squeezed into the background. He is struck by the peculiarities of New England villages, their houses, or their "collations," or their "hired men," and is immediately plunged into vivacious descriptions and disquisitions. We have to change moods too rapidly; to feel on one page a shudder at the uncanny being, with something not human looking out of her eyes; and, on the next, to be laughing at the queer social jumble of a village gathering. If, in spite of these artistic defects, the book somehow takes so firm a grasp of one's memory, it is the stronger proof of the excellence of the materials which form so curious a mosaic. After all, the writer never goes to sleep, and that is a merit which redeems a good many faults of design.

One condition of the excellence of the *Autocrat* and its successors is of course that in them this irrepressible vivacity and versatility finds in him a thoroughly appropriate field. They have, as we see at once, the merits of the best conversation. (pp. 629-33)

Talk, said Holmes, is "to me only spading up the ground for crops of thought." He was half the time "interviewing himself" and looking for his own thoughts, "as a school-boy turns his pockets inside out to find what is in them." The *Autocrat* is the outcome of this investigation. . . . The *Autocrat* might suggest a series of riddles or problems for some future examiner in English literature. Why is controversy like the Hydrostatic

Paradox? Why is a poem like a meerschaum? What is the "very obvious" resemblance between the pupil of the eye and the mind of the bigot? In what respects may truths be properly compared to dice and lies to marbles? Why should a trustworthy friend be like a cheap watch? How does the proper treatment for Guinea-worm illustrate the best mode of treating habitual drunkards? The answers to these and many equally ingenious parallels illustrate Holmes' power of perceiving analogies; and show, too, how his talent had been polished in the conversational arena. (pp. 634-35)

It is Holmes' special peculiarity that the childish buoyancy remains almost to the end, unbroken and irrepressible. He could hardly indeed have sympathized with the doctrine that heaven lies about us in our infancy, for we do not cherish that—illusion is it? or faith, till we are forced to admit that we can only see the light of common day. Holmes never seems to have lost the early buoyancy—only to have acquired new toys; even physiology which he studied seriously enough, and which is not generally regarded as amusing, supplies him with intellectual playthings, quaint fancies, and startling analogies to be tossed about like balls by a skilful juggler. The early poems, written in the pure extravagance of boyish fun, like the **"Spectre Pig"** and **"The Mysterious Visitor,"** show characteristics which may be overlaid but are never obliterated. I don't know that any of his poems are more thoroughly himself than the early lines on a portrait:—

> That thing thou fondly deem'st a nose,
>   Unsightly though it be,—
> In spite of all the world's cold scorn,
>   It may be much to thee.

The inimitable **"One-Horse Shay"** was written when he was near fifty, and the **"Broomstick Train,"** almost equally full of fun, when he was over eighty, and had sorrows enough to quench most men's last sparkles of vivacity. No human being ever fought more gallantly with the old enemy who defeats us all in the end. (pp. 639-40)

[**"The Last Leaf"**], I humbly confess, does not quite touch me as it should, because it seems too ingenious. Like Blanco White's famous sonnet, it rather tempts me, at least, to think what reply I could make to the argument. But the **"Last Leaf"** might be made into the text of all that I wish to say. The exquisite pathos of the verse about the mossy marbles linked to the fun of the irresistible though sinful "grin" is the typical instance of Holmes' special combination of qualities. He is one of the writers who is destined to live long—longer, it may be, than some of greater intellectual force and higher imagination, because he succeeds so admirably in flavouring the milk of human kindness with an element which is not acid and yet gets rid of the mawkishness which sometimes makes good morality terribly insipid. (p. 641)

Leslie Stephen, "Oliver Wendell Holmes," in The National Review, *London, Vol. XXVII, No. 161, July, 1896, pp. 626-41.*

VIRGINIA WOOLF (essay date 1909)

[A British novelist, essayist, and short story writer, Woolf is one of the most prominent literary figures of the twentieth century. Like her contemporary James Joyce, with whom she is often compared, Woolf is remembered as one of the most innovative of the stream of consciousness novelists, and her critical writings, covering almost the entire range of literature, contain some of her finest prose. In her discussion of Holmes's work, Woolf praises

the gusto of The Autocrat *and observes that "it tastes like champagne after breakfast cups of weak tea." Woolf's essay, which was occasioned by the 1909 publication of Lewis W. Townsend's biography of Holmes, first appeared in the* Times Literary Supplement *on August 26 of that year.*]

Let us own at once that Dr. Holmes's works can hardly be said to survive in the sense that they still play any part in our lives; nor is he among the writers who live on without any message to deliver because of the sheer delight that we take in their art. The fact that there is someone who will write a centenary biography for a public that reads the *Autocrat* cannot be set down to either of these causes; and yet, if we seek it on a lower plane, we shall surely find reason enough. There is, to begin with, the reason that our own experience affords us. When we take it up at a tender age—for it is one of the first books that one reads for oneself—it tastes like champagne after breakfast cups of weak tea. The miraculous ease with which the talk flows on, the richness of simile and anecdote, the humour and the pathos, the astonishing maturity of the style, and, above all, some quality less easy to define, as though fruits just beyond our reach were being dropped plump into our hands and proving deliciously firm and bright—these sensations make it impossible to think of the *Autocrat* save as an elderly relative who has pressed half-sovereigns into one's palm and at the same time flattered one's self-esteem. Later, if some of the charm is gone, one is able to appraise these virtues more soberly. They have, curiously enough, far more of the useful than of the ornamental in their composition. We are more impressed, that is, by the honesty and the common sense of the *Autocrat*'s remarks, and by the fact that they are the fruit of wide observation, than by the devices with which they are decked out.

The pages of the book abound with passages like the following:

Two men are walking by the polyphloesboean ocean, one of them having a small tin cup with which he can scoop up a gill of sea-water when he will, and the other nothing but his hands, which will hardly hold water at all—and you call the tin cup a miraculous possession! It is the ocean that is the miracle, my infant apostle! . . . Nothing is clearer than that all things are in all things, and that just according to the intensity and extension of our mental being we shall see the many in the one and the one in the many. Did Sir Isaac think what he was saying when he made *his* speech about the ocean—the child and the pebbles, you know? Did he mean to speak slightingly of a pebble? Of a spherical solid which stood sentinel over its compartment of space before the stone that became the pyramids had grown solid, and has watched it until now! A body which knows all the currents of force that traverse the globe; which holds by invisible threads to the ring of Saturn and the belt of Orion! A body from the contemplation of which an archangel could infer the entire inorganic universe as the simplest of corollaries! A throne of the all-pervading Deity, who has guided its very atom since the rosary of heaven was strung with beaded stars!

This is sufficiently plausible and yet light in weight; the style shares what we are apt to think the typical American defect of over-ingenuity and an uneasy love of decoration; as though

they had not yet learnt the art of sitting still. The universe to [Dr. Holmes], as he says, 'swam in an ocean of similitudes and analogies'; but the imaginative power which is thus implied is often more simply and more happily displayed. The sight of old things inspires him, or memories of boyhood.

Now, the sloop-of-war the Wasp, Captain Blakely, after gloriously capturing the Reindeer and the Avon, had disappeared from the face of the ocean, and was supposed to be lost. But there was no proof of it, and, of course, for a time, hopes were entertained that she might be heard from. . . . This was one of those dreams that I nursed and never told. Let me make a clean breast of it now, and say that, so late as to have outgrown childhood, perhaps to have got far on towards manhood, when the roar of the cannon has struck suddenly on my ear, I have started with a thrill of vague expectation and tremulous delight, and the long-unspoken words have articulated themselves in the mind's dumb whisper, *The Wasp has come!*

The useful virtues are there, nevertheless. The love of joy, in the first place, which raced in his blood from the cradle was even more of a virtue when the *Autocrat* was published than

The autocrat holding forth at the head of the breakfast-table.

it is now. There were strict parents who forbade their children to read the book because it made free with the gloomy morality of the time. His sincerity, too, which would show itself in an acrid humour as a young man, gives an air of pugnacity to the kindly pages of the *Autocrat.* He hated pomp, and stupidity, and disease. It may not be due to the presence of high virtues, and yet how briskly his writing moves along! We can almost hear him talk, 'taking the words out of one's mouth', in his eagerness to get them said. Much of this animation is due to the easy and almost incessant play of the *Autocrat*'s humour; and yet we doubt whether Dr. Holmes can be called a humourist in the true sense of the word. There is something that paralyses the will in humour, and Dr. Holmes was primarily a medical man who valued sanity above all things. Laughter is good, as fresh air is good, but he retracts instinctively if there is any fear that he has gone too deep:

> I know it is a sin
> For me to sit and grin—

that is the kindly spirit that gives his humour its lightness, and, it must be added, its shallowness. For, when the range is so scrupulously limited, only a superficial insight is possible; if the world is only moderately ridiculous it can never be very sublime. But it is easy enough to account for the fact that his characters have little hold upon our sympathies by reflecting that Dr. Holmes did not write in order to create men and women, but in order to state the opinions which a lifetime of observation had taught him. We feel this even in the book which has at least the form of a novel. In *Elsie Venner* he wished to answer the question which he had asked as a child; can we be justly punished for an hereditary sin? The result is that we watch a skilful experiment; all Dr. Holmes's humour and learning (he kept a live rattlesnake for months, and read 'all printed knowledge' about poison) play round the subject, and he makes us perceive how curious and interesting the case is. But—for this is the sum of our objections—we are not interested in the heroine; and the novel so far as it seeks to convince us emotionally is a failure. Even so, Dr. Holmes succeeds, as he nearly always does succeed, in making us think; he presents so many facts about rattlesnakes and provincial life, so many reflections upon human life in general, with such briskness and such a lively interest in his own ideas, that the portentous 'physiological conception, fertilized by a theological idea' [see excerpt dated 1883], is as fresh and almost as amusing as the *Autocrat* or *The Professor*. The likeness to these works, which no disguise of fiction will obscure, proves again that he could not, as he puts it, 'get out of his personality', but by that we only mean to define his powers in certain respects, for 'personality' limits Shakespeare himself. We mean that he is one of those writers who do not see much more than other people see, and yet they see it with some indescribable turn of vision, which reveals their own character and serves to form their views into a coherent creed. Thus it is that his readers always talk of their 'intimacy' with Dr. Holmes; they know what kind of person he was as well as what he taught. They know that he loved rowing and horses and great trees; that he was full of sentiment for his childhood; that he liked men to be strong and sanguine, and honoured the weakness of women; that he loathed all gloom and unhealthiness; that charity and tolerance were the virtues he loved, and if one could combine them with wit it was so much to the good. Above all, one must enjoy life and live to the utmost of one's powers. It reads something like a medical prescription, and one does not want health alone. Nevertheless, when the obvious objections are made, we need not doubt that it will benefit thousands in the future, and they will love the man who lived as he wrote. (pp. 235-40)

> Virginia Woolf, ''Oliver Wendell Holmes,'' in her Granite and Rainbow: Essays, *Harcourt, Brace & World, Inc., 1958, pp. 232-40.*

JOHN MACY (essay date 1913)

[*Macy was an American literary critic and an editor of the* Boston Herald *and the* Nation. *His most important work is* The Spirit of American Literature, *which denounces the genteel tradition and calls for realism and the use of native materials in American literature. Macy argues that* ''Holmes is the single great discursive essayist that America has bound in its slender sheaf of literary harvest,'' *but maintains that he viewed life from his comfortable place on* ''the sunny side of a clean street.'']

Holmes's views have been familiar for fifty years, and he now seems on the whole a witty, finely bred old gentleman, expressing over the teacups ideas that are mild and respectable, certainly not dynamitical. It is to-day a little difficult to realize that he, too, was a revolter, that the first numbers of the *Atlantic Monthly*, made precious by *The Autocrat*, encountered opposition among some of the conventional religious barbarians who were a dull majority in our free and independent country. Holmes is the unsuperstitious man of the world, the rationalist, the spokesman of what in his time is radical science, protesting against the theological attitude toward life. His mind is inquisitive, discursive, fanciful, but very solidly sane. His manner is consciously well-bred, conciliatory, even elegant—a very innocent mask for some loaded guns that he fires while looking unconcernedly at something else. Having inspected the world and found it out, he does not attack it at full cry like a reformer; but in perfectly modulated tones, in a voice twinkling with laughter, though seldom yielding to the full chest tones of mirth, he discourses urbanely of men and their ways. Without quite knowing whence the shot came, the enemy has received a blow fairly amidships. Holmes touches profundities with an assumption of amateurish inquiry, which with him is a method of humour, and not, as with Matthew Arnold, a dodging, unconvincing modesty.

Because of Holmes's rationalism and urbanity, and also because his verse has a carven finish and intellectual glitter, he has been often referred to the eighteenth century which is preëminent for its town-bred essayists and witty versifiers. . . . Holmes is the single great discursive essayist that America has bound in its slender sheaf of literary harvest. It is easy, but not profoundly critical to say, ''Holmes—essayist, and witty poet—eighteenth century, noted for essays and witty poems— ah, yes, Holmes had a belated eighteenth-century mind.'' The truth is he was a very modern man, wholly of his time and place. In form, in substance he is no closer to the eighteenth century than is Emerson or Thoreau. In the topics he discusses, in the nervous eclectic variety of his mind, he is characteristic of his day and generation. (pp. 155-57)

Holmes is a well-stored modern man. Moreover his is a foreward-looking, not a backward-looking mind. Despite all recent rapid changes of ideas and the silencing, if not the disappearance, of some prejudices that he attacked, he is closer to us than to any time before him. His old-fashioned garment is a dramatic costume, as was Lamb's. *The Autocrat* is a fresh, day-lit, life-lit book, tingling with present day issues, though we have lost the sense of stir which it made in the obdurate bosom of Calvinism. We do not recognize ourselves in the breakfast-eaters to whom Mr. Addison condescended so charmingly; indeed, it were better on some mornings to go back to bed if there were nothing more vital in the world than the *Spectator* brings. But the Autocrat is our neighbour. He can keep one up at night. Here is a champion of our kind of thought, a spirited, though half-disguised controversialist, a believer in intellectual courage, in which our world, Holmes's Boston especially, is, at this advanced date, deplorably lacking. "You never need think you can turn over any old falsehood without a terrible squirming and scattering of the horrid little population that dwells under it." So speaks Doctor Holmes of Beacon Street, our contemporary, though not the contemporary of the intellectual decadence of Beacon Street. "Do I think that the particular form of lying often seen in newspapers, under the title 'From Our Foreign Correspondent' does any harm? Why, no, I don't know that it does. I suppose it doesn't really deceive people any more than the *Arabian Nights* or *Gulliver's Travels* do." There speaks our contemporary, though not the contemporary of the men who edited the newspapers that the boy brought this morning.

The Autocrat came full-blooded and shapely of limb from the brow of humour, a new form, a new manner. There is nothing like it in the whole range of *causerie*. (pp. 158-59)

He belongs with the classic few . . . because the classic is a man who does something that other classics have not done. He joins them by writing a book in his own way without too much regard for established immortals. *The Autocrat* is a new mode of essay, "every man his own Boswell." It pretends to be a record of talk, and thereby gains the privileges of talk without sacrificing the advantages of literary phrasing when that is needed to put the thought in order. It is free from the rigours of the formal essay and secures a natural right to circle over the universe, alighting when it will and soaring when it will. (Holmes's grotesque delicious image is "putting his straw in the bung of the universe.") The table-talkers, Selden, Hazlitt, Coleridge have left fine fragments, epigrammatic, witty; sententious, poetical, of the conversational man or rather of the monologuizing man. Holmes, with an instinctive dramatic sense, favours a broader idea of human talk. He embodies himself in a variety of mouthpieces. The characters afford him opportunity to say things that he really means but which a Brahmin physician might not care to express *propria voce*. He enjoys in himself and others the habit of the human mind of jumping from topic to topic, and his table-talk form enables him to indulge the enjoyment. He drops with apparent casualness the conclusion of a life-long reflection on a pet idea, and then turns lightly to something else, so that the favourite thought does not betray how much the author thinks of it. Holmes was nearly fifty when he wrote *The Autocrat* and he had written little prose before; he drew on the untouched treasures of a mind at vigorous maturity, stocked full of experience.

It is from experience that he dips oftenest and deepest. He is a reader, an amateur of books, but not a bookish man. . . . Whenever he speaks of books, in *The Autocrat* or *The Professor,* he speaks with unerring perspicacity and individuality of judgment. . . . Holmes makes you close his book, with your finger between the pages, and let your fancy run on what he has been saying. He stands on his own feet thinking about life and does not sit on the shoulders of the literary giants of the ages.

Yet few of his more bookish contemporaries, devoted to purely literary questions, write so well as he does; only Hawthorne, of the New Englanders, equals him in unbroken perfection of style. Holmes is one of the masters of style in whose phrasing

there is no technical flaw, no expression blurred and but loosely approximate to the thought. His prose and his verse are free from false verbal notes. There is in his work not one of those sentences that somehow get neglected in the practical business of making manuscript, and which suffer for the healing touch of proofreader or editor. This is the more remarkable in view of the range of Holmes's thought. He expresses a great many kinds of idea. (The very index to *The Autocrat* is a work of humour.) He leaps from witty fooling and whimsicalities to some puzzling problem of psychology which he fetches into the light of his transparent logical style; then with an instinctive avoidance of tedium and long explanation, he leaves the problem and passes to a bit of sentiment, often on a high plane of feeling, where he is equally sure and in command of the resources of language. (pp. 161-62)

His thoughts on love in *The Professor* are beautiful, at once speculative and humane. He slips once or twice into the mists of poetical metaphysics (on the verge of the region where Emerson wanders in his essay on Love), but comes swiftly back to the persons at the table. He seldom quite lets go his moorings in life.

The Autocrat is the cream of a man's mind at fifty. Had he said the best that he had to say, and would the next book be a limping sequel unable to keep the pace of its predecessor? There are those who find *The Professor* even better than *The Autocrat*. Indeed it is a deepening and ripening of the Autocrat's method and quality of thought. The Professor argues a little more at length, moves more steadily in one subject, with less fantastic flitting, fewer wayward excursions in pursuit of lateral analogies. The old verve is there, with an admixture of a sharper satire. There is a reason why *The Autocrat* should have had a sequel. That gentle old fellow had, to his surprise, started some controversies by the fresh candour of his thoughts on life and religion. These controversies suggested new ideas, but they were not for the Autocrat to take up; they would have been out of character. (pp. 162-63)

The Poet and *Over the Teacups* are written in the Doctor's inimitable manner, or perhaps it would be fair to say in the manner that only Holmes could imitate. They suffer in comparison with himself alone. The sources of good talk are by no means run dry, though the stream is a little thinner. (p. 164)

His success in portraying characters and making them talk in the true idioms of life encouraged him to write a novel. *Elsie Venner* is an ingenious story, and it needs not to be said that it is well written; Holmes did not know how otherwise to write. But he had not the gifts of the genuine novelist. He might have discovered them in himself if he had begun to look for them at thirty instead of at fifty. The manager of *Elsie Venner* is the Professor; he shows through delightfully at times, in spite of the shivery tale. Perhaps we do not shiver now; for we have lived through Ibsen and other men of tragic genius, whose "problems" are more intense and harrowing than any idea of the Doctor's. *Elsie Venner* excites in us intellectual interest and gives the pleasure which a fine mind always offers even in some form of literature to which it is not best adapted. *The Guardian Angel,* another tale strung on a curious thesis, is more delightful than *Elsie Venner*. It is written in a lower key. If the Professor is stage manager of *Elsie Venner,* the director of *The Guardian Angel* is the Autocrat. The first half of the book, where the problems of the plot have not begun to close in and demand of the author a skill that he does not quite possess, is as full of wise fun as so many pages of the breakfast-table series.

From the time when Holmes, at twenty-one, struck the public fancy with his stirring, boyish verses, **"Old Ironsides,"** he was known as a writer of occasional poetry; he is perhaps the most uniformly skilful and delightful maker of rhymes in commemoration of local events to be found in English literature. He was ambitious to be known as a poet, as is every man of letters who has tasted at all of the divinest spring. His verses are among the most graceful pages of *The Autocrat,* and in their kind they are perfect. As he never wrote poor prose, so he never wrote bad poetry. And yet—he is not a poet of lofty rank. He is a neat versifier of humour, sentiment, and friendship, fundamentally sincere and dexterous in touching his modest lyre.... Holmes's most ambitious poem, the one which he was most eager to have remembered as poetry, is **"The Chambered Nautilus."** To me it seems an elaborated conceit, pretty but not moving. The best of his poems is **"The Last Leaf,"** which touches with a fine tenderness, through a playfully turned stanza, the true pathos of age. **"Wind-Clouds and Star Drifts,"** elevated in thought and well done in its way, is cold as prose. As the Poet at the Breakfast Table himself says of the verses: "They were evidently written honestly, and with feeling, and no doubt meant to be reverential." But the inexplicable inspiration never descended upon the Autocrat-Poet-Professor. The prose passage in *The Autocrat* about the sea and the mountains is essentially better poetry than any of Holmes's verse.... (pp. 164-66)

In the poetry of light sentiment, of humour and sparkling word-play Holmes is perfectly successful. He is the best possible maker of after-dinner verses. The spirit of college festivals and friendly reunions he caught and spun into cunning rhymes, not once but in fifty pieces. **"The Deacon's Masterpiece"** and **"The Broomstick Train"** possess that unquestionable merit which is settled once for all by the fact that no one else ever did anything like them. The Brahmin Doctor had only one peer in the versifying of Yankee humour and that was his neighbour across the river, Mr. Hosea Biglow.

Holmes belonged to the prosperous comfortable classes. He took very much to heart some of the problems of his time, the intellectual and religious problems. He was a very keen and advanced investigator of some questions of psychology, and no man ever phrased scientific knowledge more perspicuously for the layman. But life for him was easy, and he saw things from the sunny side of a clean street.... He writes for the few, not the many; he addresses those who can catch an idea as it flies. His odd combination of logic and fantasy makes his work a continuous delight; the process of his thought as he unfolds it is fascinating, and he himself watches it with a delighted sense of surprise. He is the most modest of egotists, and, except when he is attacking an enemy (always a generalized intellectual enemy, never a personal one), he suggests rather than asserts. His intellectual curiosity warily eludes closed final statements; to him the universe is going on all the time and was not concluded with the last remark that any of us happened to regard as ultimate. Every imagination that meets his is stimulated to go on thinking about a world that is so full of a number of things. (pp. 167-69)

> *John Macy, "Holmes," in his* The Spirit of American Literature, *Doubleday, Page & Company, 1913, pp. 155-70.*

HENRY JAMES   (essay date 1915)

[*James was an American-born English novelist, short story writer, critic, and essayist of the late nineteenth and early twentieth*

centuries. He is regarded as one of the greatest novelists of the English language and admired as a lucid and insightful critic. James was a frequent contributor to several prominent American journals, including the North American Review, the Nation, *and the* Atlantic Monthly. *James here praises* The Autocrat *as a classic and claims that Holmes was instrumental in the development of the American novel.*]

The *Atlantic* was for years practically the sole organ of that admirable writer and wit, that master of almost every form of observational, of meditational, and of humorous ingenuity, the author of *The Autocrat of the Breakfast Table* and of *Elsie Venner.... The Autocrat of the Breakfast Table,* the American contribution to literature, that I can recall, most nearly meeting the conditions and enjoying the fortune of a classic, quite sufficiently accounts, I think, for our sense not only at the time, but during a long stretch of the subsequent, that we had there the most precious of the metals in the very finest fusion. Such perhaps was not entirely the air in which we saw *Elsie Venner* bathed—since if this too was a case of the shining substance of the author's mind, so extraordinarily agile within its own circle of content, the application of the admirable engine was yet not perhaps so happy; in spite of all of which nothing would induce me now to lower our then claim for this fiction as the charmingest of the 'old' American group, the romances of Hawthorne of course always excepted.

The new American novel—for that was preparing—had at the season I refer to scarce glimmered into view; but its first seeds were to be sown very exactly in *Atlantic* soil.... (pp. 25-6)

> *Henry James, "Mr. and Mrs. James T. Fields," in* The Atlantic Monthly, *Vol. 116, No. 1, July, 1915, pp. 21-31.*

VERNON LOUIS PARRINGTON   (essay date 1927)

[*An American historian, biographer, and critic, Parrington is best known for his unfinished literary history of the United States,* Main Currents in American Thought, *written from the point of view of a Jeffersonian liberal. In the excerpt below, Parrington views Holmes as a spokesman for the Boston Brahmins.*]

Since the death of Holmes in 1894, his reputation has shrunk and dwindled with that of his group. With the rise of other literary schools, New England standards have been submitted to a somewhat rude overhauling, and Brahmin ideals are no longer reckoned so authoritative as they were once believed to be, nor the supremacy of Boston genius so indisputable. Concord has risen as Cambridge and Beacon Street have declined, and in the shadow of Emerson and Thoreau, the wit of Back Bay is in danger of being obscured. Unsupported by his physical presence, his writings seem far less vital than they did when the echoes of his clever talk were still sounding through them. Certain intellectual shortcomings are more obvious when his works are brought together in a library edition: in the mass his prose seems far more discursive and his verse thinner and more jingly than when the several bits appeared singly, personally sponsored by the author in whose cleverness everybody delighted. Read with sprightly vivacity to a group of sympathetic listeners at the mellowest hour of the dinner, his occasional verse must have sparkled brightly and have gone off with such a crackle of laughter as to convince the Back Bay that the asthmatic little gentleman with bubbling spirits was a veritable poet, on the same friendly footing with the muse that he was with Beacon Street. (p. 442)

[Though] a full-blown Victorian in manners and tastes, Holmes was something of a child of the eighteenth century at heart. The situation in which he found himself might have proved disconcerting if he had chosen to speculate upon it. By nature a thoroughgoing rationalist, he lived in a romantic age. A gentleman of "parts and learning," with a quick and lively fancy that blossomed in the pat phrase and neat couplet, he loved wit and hated dullness with true Augustan zeal. The great days of Queen Anne were a perennial inspiration to him. He clung to the heroic couplet through all the changes of romantic styles. He moralized in rime with the fluency if not the finish of Pope. He satirized Calvinism with an honest wrath that he might have learned of Swift. He commented in his table-talk on the manners of the times with the chatty discursiveness of Addison. Like the earlier wits, he discovered a deep sympathy for the maturity and ripe wisdom of the classics. (pp. 443-44)

Romantic garments fitted him ill, yet he persisted in trying them on. He even got to like them, and came finally to prefer **"The Chambered Nautilus"** above his other poems—a strange perversion of taste for a rationalist. **"The One-Hoss Shay"** is worth a volume of such pretty moralizing. **"Parson Turell's Legacy"** and **"The Moral Bully"** are in better vein—witty, lucid, critical—than any half-hearted ventures in romanticism. The eighteenth-century wit does not appear to advantage patched with Victorian sentiment, and he should have been rationalist enough to know it.

As a Beacon Street Victorian Holmes was as full of virtuous prejudices as an egg is full of meat; but as a rationalist, with a modest scientific equipment that came from his professional training, he kept the windows of his mind open to the winds of scientific inquiry that were blowing briskly to the concern of orthodox souls. Many a barnacled craft was foundering in those gales, and Holmes watched their going-down with visible satisfaction. He was perhaps the most militant Unitarian amongst Boston laymen. Hatred of Calvinistic dogma was an obsession with him; it dominated his thought and colored much of his work, *Elsie Venner* and his table-talk as frankly as **"The One-Hoss Shay."** The criticism to which he subjected the old-school dogmas was always vehement, often vindictive. Long after the battle had been won he kept annoying the retreating enemy. (p. 445)

On . . . [Calvinism] he was militantly radical, never shirking debate, but whetting the edge of his satire and impaling his victim neatly with his logic. He took sardonic delight in turning Calvinism against itself, in the clever *reductio ad absurdum* of the Edwardean argument. Perhaps this major intellectual interest appears most adequately in his picture of the Master, the autobiographical rationalist whom he introduces into *The Poet at the Breakfast Table*. A dabbler in the law, theology and medicine, a philosophic contemplator of the Order of Things, who refused to permit "the territory of a man's mind" to be "fenced in," who agreed with the Poet in thinking somewhat ill of the specialist who dedicated his life to the study of beetles, preferring to range widely through time and eternity, who followed Darwin and was deep in bacteriology, trying "curious experiments in spontaneous generation"—this was Holmes on the intellectual side, a genial disseminator of the latest scientific speculations, a tolerant amateur of the things of the mind, a friendly dabbler in absolute moralities, who hoped "to do some sound thinking in heaven" if he ever got there, but who was too pleasantly engaged with Beacon Street to settle things now. (p. 446)

In his literary work Holmes was always the talker rather than the writer. The charm of the vivid and racy colloquial marks every page. A clever aphorism or telling pun is the objective of every paragraph, and it explodes with a brilliant shower of sparks. But like every talker his discursiveness is inveterate; he wanders far in pursuit of his point and sometimes returns empty-handed. He was always an amateur; life was too agreeable for him to take the trouble to become an artist. The essay was his most congenial form—his novels are to be taken no more seriously than his occasional verse. *Elsie Venner* wraps up the familiar problem of moral determinism in pleasantly discursive chat of Yankee bumpkinism in contrast with Yankee Brahminism, and he returns his impeccable hero to Beacon Street, after his sojourn in the provinces, to reward him with the Brahmin rewards—a munificent practice, a charming wife, and an exalted social position. What richer reward could be desired by one who had tasted to the full the mellow flavor of that society? Staid, delightful, self-satisfied, righteous little Beacon Street! Last refuge and citadel of the old Brahmin respectability; basking in the afternoon sunshine of its culture, not realizing that its sun is already well past the meridian; in love with its own virtues and unaware that the morrow will see the invasion of the Huns and Vandals of plutocracy, to whose plethoric bank books Brahmin culture must eventually bow—who would not have liked it? It was something after all

A depiction of the professor and John from The Professor at the Breakfast-Table.

to have been its favorite wit, its ready oracle, its clever poet, who in praising his fellow Brahmins was well aware that he discreetly praised his own admirable qualities. Kindly, delightful, fortunate Dr. Holmes! chief citizen of the Hub of the Universe! He was born and lived with a silver spoon in his mouth, and if a grudging posterity inclines to rate him and his little world somewhat lower than he rated them, what difference can that make to him? Tolerant himself, we should perhaps emulate his example, and not insist too rudely that he is only a minor figure in American literature. (pp. 450-51)

> *Vernon Louis Parrington, "The Authentic Brahmin," in his* Main Currents in American Thought, an Interpretation of American Literature from the Beginnings to 1920: The Romantic Revolution in America, 1800-1860, Vol. 2, *1927. Reprint by Harcourt Brace Jovanovich, Inc., 1954, pp. 442-63.*

GAY WILSON ALLEN (essay date 1935)

[*In the following excerpt, Allen provides a detailed analysis of Holmes's poetry and concludes that he had little influence on American versification.*]

There is almost every reason for us not to expect a prosodic system from Holmes, or even much prosodic thinking at all. He was first of all a physician and professor of anatomy, and most of his poetry is colored to some extent by the scientist, directly in subject-matter and idiom and indirectly in the scientific reserve that always held in check his poetic imagination.

In the second place, he was a "throw back," as most critics have pointed out (though they often over-emphasize it). He says in his note to ["**Poetry, A Metrical Essay**"] ... that, "This Academic Poem presents the simple and partial views of a young person trained after the schools of classical English verse as represented by Pope, Goldsmith, and Campbell, with whose lines his memory was early stocked." And in many respects, he remained an eighteenth-century neo-classicist all of his life. But even in this confession we must remember Holmes's statement that the poem, which would of course include the versification, represents only his "partial views." It is plain, however, that this young poet was not headed toward any sort of prosodic revolution.

In the third place, Holmes was always primarily an "occasional" poet, despite the fact that he did write some fine poetry for more serious purposes; and the occasional poet, like the journalistic versifier, may be counted upon to follow the conventions. For new forms divert attention to technique, whereas the "occasional" poet wants all attention focused on what he has to say. So long, therefore, as Holmes remained the writer of after-dinner verse (and such he did remain until the end of his days), he was practically compelled to continue using the familiar octosyllabic couplet, the heroic couplet, ballad meter, and other simple and accepted forms.

Nevertheless, we do find Holmes now and then speculating on prosodic questions. The most widely known instance, of course, is **"The Physiology of Versification,"** which is typical of Holmes the scientist, and which proclaims that there is a vital and necessary connection between the laws of versification and the respiration and the pulse, "the true time-keepers of the body." (pp. 193-94)

On the same grounds, Holmes argues that the "heroic line" is more difficult to read because only about fourteen verses are pronounced in a minute; so that, "If a breath is allowed to each line the respiration will be longer and slower than natural, and a sense of effort and fatigue will soon be the consequence." Though the caesura is a "breathing-place," it "entirely breaks up the natural rhythm of breathing." The twelve- and the fourteen-syllable lines are also found difficult for the same reasons.

Now this argument is ingenious and interesting, but it is so "scientific" that it fails to take into account all the facts. Holmes admits that different persons have different respiratory rhythms, and hence his argument may not hold for all people. Moreover, he does not consider the fact that in enjambed octosyllabics, two, three, or several lines are read at one breath-sweep. And in blank verse, which is undoubtedly the most "natural" speaking verse (as Shakespeare's dramas are sufficient to prove), the irregular variation of short and long breath-sweeps gives us the most pleasing effects. But still more important is the fact that this theory is an attempt to explain conventional, classical, accepted prosody, in which end-stopped lines predominate. It is more physiological than prosodic. The attempt to explain prosody on physiological principles is commendable, yet the chief value of the essay for the student of prosody lies in the fact that it is the best proof we could ask that Holmes took conventional prosody for granted. (pp. 194-95)

And yet, strangely enough, there is in his 1836 preface [to *Poems*] a doctrine which sounds curiously "modern," even "modernistic" or "cubistic." In defending the "extravagant" in poetry, he says:

> A series of hyperbolical images is considered beneath criticism by the same judges who would write treatises upon the sculptured satyrs and painted arabesques of antiquity, which are only hyperbole in stone and colors. As material objects in different lights repeat themselves in shadows variously elongated, contracted, or exaggerated, so our solid and sober thoughts caricature themselves in fantastic shapes inseparable from their originals, and having a unity in their extravagance, which proves them to have retained their proportions in certain respects, however differing in outline from their prototypes.

But this preface is apparently a defence of the poems in the 1836 volume, all of which obey the conventional rules of versification. Apparently Holmes never thought of trying to convey his "hyperbolical images" and "caricature" by a "fantastic" or "exaggerated" technique.

Holmes did make valuable contributions to the practice of American versification, and exerted a powerful influence toward reinstating the French polish and perfection of eighteenth-century English ideals; yet we must study him as a versifier and not as a conscious prosodist.

Though Holmes early began to use practically all the verse forms that he ever used, the ballad measure seems to be most characteristic of his earlier period. He never surpassed **"The Spectre Pig,"** for instance, in his imitations of the genuine folk ballad, despite the fact that he insisted on placing it in the last section of his collected poems under the heading of "Verses from the Oldest Portfolio." It is difficult to find anywhere a more subtle, ironical, and satirical parody of the thought, diction, and rhythm of the ballad.

> It was the stalwart butcher man,
>   That knit his swarthy brow,
> And said the gentle Pig must die,
>   And sealed it with a vow.

> And oh! it was the gentle Pig
> Lay stretched upon the ground,
> And ah! it was the cruel knife
> His little heart that found.

These inversions and parataxes are not awkward, as we might expect, but produce a rhythm which is an unmistakable folk ballad tune. We also find the same "tune" in **"The Mysterious Visitor."**

"Old Ironsides" . . . is in the same ballad measure, yet is different in several details. The eight-line stanzas are fairly regular in meter and have a two-line thought-movement, as in **"The Spectre Pig"** and the genuine folk ballads; but only four of the twenty-four lines are enjambed, there are comparatively few metrical stresses, and the diction and syntactical constructions are more natural than in **"The Spectre Pig."** (pp. 196-97)

"The Star and the Water-Lily" . . . contains a generous sprinkling of anapestic feet, a variation which Holmes continued to use intermittently during his whole poetic career. . . .

"To an Insect" and **"My Aunt"** . . . , however, are more typical of Holmes's ballad measure, being straight iambic, 4 + 3. **"The Cambridge Churchyard"** is in precisely the same meter, but is less regular and inclined to singsong because of a skilful variation of stresses, including initial accented syllables, secondary accents, and spondees. (p. 198)

• • • • •

Holmes used the four-stress iambic line extensively from his college days (*cf.* **"The Meeting of the Dryads"**) until very near the end of his life. His four-stress verse includes simple stanza forms, such as the *abab* quatrain, octosyllabic couplets, and "clipped" four-stress iambic. No new, eccentric, or irregular versification is found in the handling of these forms, and since they are so common anyway, a full discussion of them should not be necessary.

His juvenile **"The Meeting of the Dryads"** is characteristic of much of Holmes's regular octosyllabic lines, with its inversions, smooth and regular beats, and couplet movement (even with alternate rime):

> In every julep that he drinks,
> May gout, and bile, and headache be;
> And when he strives to calm his pain,
> May colic mingle with his tea.

"Under the Violets" . . . is different in its versification only in the greater enjambment of its third stanza, the first four lines being read at one sweep. Rarely are more than two lines enjambed in Holmes's four-stress verse. (p. 199)

Holmes's most famous four-stress couplets are those of **"The Deacon's Masterpiece, or The Wonderful 'One-Hoss Shay'."** . . . The monotonous rime and absurd rhythm are part of the humor of this piece, but the versification is little better than doggerel. . . .

"Parson Turell's Legacy" . . . , written in the same year as the **"One-Hoss Shay"** . . . , is, on the whole, more regular, though the rhythm in some passages is broken by short, elliptical sentences, resulting in a colloquialism very characteristic of Holmes's humorous verse:

> Facts respecting an old arm-chair.
> At Cambridge. Is kept in the College there.
> Seems but little the worse for wear.

(p. 201)

Another colloquial device is the use of abbreviations, with a consequent eccentricity of rhythm, as in **"How the Old Horse Won the Bet"**:

> The swift g. m., old Hiram's nag,
> The fleet s. h., Dan Pfeiffer's brag,
> With these a third—and who is he
> That stands beside his fast b. g.?

On the whole, **"Dorothy Q,"** with its very sparing enjambment and monotonous singsong rhythm, is characteristic of Holmes's four-stress couplets. Like Whittier's *Snow-Bound*, it is important for its description, not for its versification, though it is a much smoother and less awkward poem than Whittier's. **"At the Pantomime"** has greater enjambment, with more skilfully varied pauses, and contains some of Holmes's most pleasing octosyllabic couplets. (p. 202)

• • • • •

Holmes admitted his eighteenth-century prosodic background, and . . . he seemed to resent Lowell's laughing "at the old square-toed heroic." In **"Poem Read at the Dinner Given to the Author by the Medical Profession,"** he proudly admits his allegiance to this measure:

> And so the hand that takes the lyre for you
> Plays the old tune on strings that once were new. . . .
> I smile to listen while the critic's scorn
> Flouts the proud purple kings have nobly worn;

This passage is also a good illustration of the metrical regularity of Holmes's heroics. Each line has exactly ten syllables, inverted feet are used sparingly, spondees rarely (but *cf.* "proud purple"), and each couplet is closed or "couplet moulded" in the eighteenth-century manner. (p. 204)

Holmes used this measure extensively, both for serious and "familiar" verse. Most of his long poems are in this form. His "Five Stories and a Sequel," which he collected under the heading of "Readings Over the Teacups," are all in heroic couplets. They include **"To My Old Readers," "The Banker's Secret," "The Exile's Secret," "The Lover's Secret," "The Statesman's Secret," "The Mother's Secret,"** and **"The Secret of the Stars."** These poems are not so well known as Holmes's four-stress couplets of the **"One-Hoss Shay,"** yet they contain some good versification, such as **"The Secret of the Stars,"** which has some beautiful cadences, held in check only by the rime and a corresponding tendency toward the full stop after the completion of the rime. Many of the first lines of couplets, though, are enjambed:

> In vain the sweeping equatorial pries
> Through every world-sown corner of the skies,
> To the far orb that so remotely strays
> Our midnight darkness is its noonday blaze;
> In vain the climbing soul of creeping man
> Metes out the heavenly concave with a span,

These lines are less "couplet moulded" than the average eighteenth-century English heroics, but the neo-classical model is apparent. It is in this measure, however, that the eighteenth-century influence on Holmes's versification is strongest. (pp. 205-06)

• • • • •

Holmes wrote comparatively little blank verse, probably because it is not a very convenient form for "occasional" poems; and his few attempts are perhaps less known than any other poetic form that he used. But the little blank verse that he did write is, so far as versification goes, unusually good. The 1864 **"A Sea Dialogue"** contains some awkward lines, the worst being:

> Friend, you seem thoughtful. I not wonder much
> That he who sails the ocean should be sad.

Yet the 1872 **"Wind-Cloud and Star-Drifts"** shows complete mastery of the form. Especially commendable are the long breath-sweeps, permitting sustained cadences in the best blank verse tradition. (p. 206)

However much Holmes's heroic couplets may be in the eighteenth-century tradition, his blank verse is certainly not, for it shows scarcely a trace of the couplet influence. Yet it is more in the tradition of Freneau than of Bryant, since it echoes the good workmanship of Freneau (*cf. The Rising Glory of America*) and lacks the sonority of Bryant's *Thanatopsis*.

*   *   *   *   *

The popularity of **"The Chambered Nautilus"** and the poet's own undisguised pride in this poem make a discussion of it almost imperative. In a letter to George Ticknor, Holmes declares, "I am as willing to submit this [poem] to criticism as any I have written, in form as well as substance, and I have not seen any English verse of just the same pattern."

In none of his other poems do we find Holmes using such freely varied accents as in **"The Chambered Nautilus."** There are, in fact, so many reversed feet and interpolated spondees that no one stanza accurately indicates the underlying rhythmical pattern. (pp. 206-07)

It is probably unsafe to press very far a search for symbolism in the form of this poem, yet one wonders whether the rhythms (including the combinations of pentameter, trimeter, and alexandrine in the novel stanzaic arrangement) were not intended to symbolize the crenulated and scalloped shell of the chambered nautilus. At any rate, the form is, as Holmes himself believed, very unusual, and perhaps unique.

*   *   *   *   *

Next to **"The Chambered Nautilus,"** Holmes perhaps took most pride in **"The Last Leaf,"** at least among his stanzaic poems. Certainly it is the only other poem which he believed he had written on an original model. His own explanation of why he happened to use the "somewhat singular measure" is amusing. "I had become a little known as a versifier, and I thought that one or two other young writers were following my efforts with imitations. . . . I determined to write in a measure which would at once betray any copyist." He mentions Campbell's *Battle of the Baltic* as having probably suggested the form, "But I do not remember any poem in the same measure, except such as have been written since its publication."

It is a little puzzling why Holmes took so much pride in the form of this poem, but his handling of it is easy and dexterous. (pp. 208-09)

The rhythm does have a lilt which is more musical than anything else Holmes ever wrote. The only trouble is that it is almost too musical, the "tune" obtruding itself into the reading so much that the poem is mostly sound. Still, it is a competent lyric. And its music is reminiscent of the seventeenth-century English lyrics.

Holmes's most peculiar stanza is the unrimed trochaic quatrain of **"De Sauty,"** composed of three six-stress and one three-stress lines. This is unique in his poetry, for his only other unrimed verse is regular blank verse, and no other poem of his is so predominantly trochaic. (pp. 209-10)

The **"Two Sonnets: Harvard"** . . . and the sonnet sequence to Longfellow, **"Our Dead Singer"** . . . , show that Holmes could handle the Italian form with ease and facility, and it is surprising and regrettable that he did not write more sonnets. . . .

To judge by Holmes's random stanzas, his sonnets, his blank verse, and his few excellent lyrics, he could have achieved success in almost any conventional meter; yet as we have seen, he always remained essentially a poet of octosyllabics and the heroic couplet. . . .

While Holmes won considerable fame and distinction in his day, it is doubtful whether he has had much influence on American versification, (1) because he used the old measures without contributing anything new to their handling except an urbane unself-consciousness and an epigrammatic polish, and (2), and consequently, because his method called attention to content rather than technique. (p. 211)

> *Gay Wilson Allen, "Oliver Wendell Holmes," in his* American Prosody, *American Book Company, 1935, pp. 193-216.*

VAN WYCK BROOKS   (essay date 1936)

[*Brooks was an American critic, biographer, editor, and translator who is best known as a chronicler of America's cultural history. In the following excerpt, he contends that Holmes used* The Autocrat *and* Elsie Venner *as vehicles to unsettle his readers and to encourage them to question their beliefs. For further commentary by Brooks, see Additional Bibliography.*]

In his diplomatic way, the Autocrat attacked all the mental habits of his hearers. What was this "logical mind," the fruit of generations of preachers and lawyers, but the One-Hoss Shay of Calvinism? The doctor had no use for Calvinism, and he knew that, while they laughed at the one-hoss shay in Boston and at Harvard, it was no laughing matter in the country. He was determined to break it up,—if laughter failed, by other means, by quoting half a dozen sciences, by the use of analogies and comparisons, by every method but controversy, since controversy equalized the foolish and the wise and no one knew this better than the fools. For what was the "logical mind" of Calvinism but the parent of all injustice, the *a priori* and the *parti pris,* narrow judgment, rigid condemnation, all those moral plagues, in other words, from which the American mind so patently suffered? Did he mean to weaken moral obligations by drawing up the blinds of this dark chamber and letting in the light? His object was merely to define them; for the light he let into the dark chamber was the light of common sense, a doctor's view of the problem of cause and effect as it really expressed itself in human nature. Was some question of crime involved? The "logical mind" spoke of original sin and anathematized the doctor. The rational mind spoke of the effect and anathematized the cause. As for the fruits of the old religion, many of the minister's patients were fools and cowards, and all too many of them were also liars. (Immense sensation at the table.)

The Autocrat was prepared for the sensation. The religious weeklies and monthlies, all over the country, began to throw brickbats at him. The doctor was imperturbable. One cannot turn over any old falsehood without a terrible squirming and scattering of the unpleasant little population that dwells under it. No one can ever say anything to make his neighbors wiser or better without being abused for doing so; and, if there is one thing that people detest, it is to have their little mistakes made fun of. The Autocrat continued, with calm good humor, always ready to talk as long as a few boarders remained at the table, twirling their knives, perhaps, balancing their spoons on the edge of their tea-cups or tilting on their chairs against the wall. (pp. 3-4)

Everybody listened to the Autocrat, except a little group of thinkers who also described themselves as Humanists. Perhaps they were not in the room when [the Autocrat] remarked: ''Beware of making your moral staple consist of the negative virtues. It is good to abstain, and teach others to abstain, from all that is sinful and harmful. But making a business of it leads to emaciation of character, unless one feeds largely also on the more nutritious diet of active sympathetic benevolence.'' Perhaps this little group considered the doctor frivolous, with his marked distaste for a ''soul-subduing decorum.'' But everyone else was prepared to listen when he wrote a novel, *Elsie Venner;* for he had long believed that every intelligent man had the stuff of a novel in him, and therefore why not he? ... His novels were ''medicated novels''; and, as the doctor was always a talker, he strolled about from page to page, airing his views about his characters, dismissing them at times with a turn of the hand as if they were so many cases at a medical meeting. His composition was very untidy. But he always had a new story even when it was only a ghost of a story, as in the breakfast-table series, and he always had a problem to deal with,—hysteria in a young girl, a young man's gynophobia, morbid religious excitement and its effects. There were happy streaks in all his writings, and striking applications of modern science; and his essay on *Mechanism in Thought and Morals,* the ''underground workshop of thought,''—the unconscious,—was a brilliant anticipation of Dr. Freud. In fact, although *Elsie Venner,* of all [his] later books, was the only one that seriously counted, the doctor knew so much about human nature, and had such a tang of his own, that one could read him at his worst with pleasure. (pp. 13-14)

[With *Elsie Venner*] the doctor cast a bombshell into the circle of his fellow-boarders. Every breakfast-table in the country resounded with *Elsie Venner.* Were you a Unitarian or a Calvinist, or any other variety of Jew or Christian, were you interested in the recent theories about heredity and environment, in medical and therapeutic questions, philosophy, criminology, education? Then *Elsie Venner* had something to say to you, and sometimes it was not a pleasant message. If, as a good Unitarian, you liked to think of the soul as an ''unstained white tablet,'' then Elsie with her wicked little powders was an awkward nut to crack. The question whether Elsie could help herself was even more of a dose for the Orthodox. If you were a Pharisee, you fared still worse; for if Elsie was not responsible, if she could not be accused of sin,—however one might punish her for crime,—what became of your own pretensions? Were you not obliged to see that your valor and justice, your strength, truth, and virtue were merely the result of your happy fortune? What was your aristocracy but a sum that began with a one in tar and a two in tallow, and perhaps a three in whale-oil, however maintained by pluck? Your elevated type of face and figure were due not to you and your father's virtue, beyond a certain measure, but to the money made from the tar and the tallow that bought the air and sunshine, the healthy, happy summers, the good nursing and doc-

Iris at the Little Gentleman's sickbed, from The Professor at the Breakfast-Table.

toring, the best cuts of the best beef and mutton, which enabled your father, and his father and his, to grow up in such a kindly fashion and, when they were grown, to afford the costly luxury of beauty and marry the finest specimens of the other sex. This train of reasoning went a long way when the valor and the truth, strength and virtue were so obviously poisoned *out* of a race by the food of the bushman in his forest, by the foul air and darkness of the tenement-houses where half one's fellow-Christians were constrained to live. Just how far it went, the doctor might not have cared to think, for the ''sunny street that holds the sifted few,'' the ''swell-fronts and south-exposure houses'' had a singular charm for him, as for other mortals, and the people who lived inside these houses were not only just as good as other people but the pleasantest for a doctor to take care of. ''Why not take the tops of your sparrowgrass? Somebody must have 'em,—why shouldn't you?'' Such was the doctor's advice to a young disciple; and, in fact, he never pretended to be a sage, too lofty for these trifles. He knew that a certain amount of glass was mingled with the bricks in the house he lived in, a knowledge that disarmed the caster of pebbles; and meanwhile he had discharged a thunderbolt that fairly rocked the walls of Philistinism. Who, after reading *Elsie Venner,* could talk about ''total depravity''? Who was to condemn? Who to judge? Or pride himself too much on his family portraits? Or think that God had given him his lands and chattels in recognition of his Christian virtue? Dr. Holmes, perhaps unwittingly, had played into the hands of Dr. Darwin. He had played into the hands of Dr. Freud. He had played into the hands of another doctor of whom he had never heard, Dr. Marx. One never knows how far a doctor's table-talk may carry him. (p. 15)

Van Wyck Brooks, "Dr. Holmes: Forerunner of the Moderns," in The Saturday Review of Literature, *Vol. XIV, No. 9, June 27, 1936, pp. 3-4, 13-15.*

S. I. HAYAKAWA AND HOWARD MUMFORD JONES (essay date 1939)

[*Hayakawa, an American semanticist, educator, and critic, is best known for his* Language in Thought and Action. *Jones, a twentieth-century American critic, humanist, and literary scholar, is noted for his illuminating commentary on the development of American culture and literature. In the following excerpt, Hayakawa and Jones stress that Holmes was an amateur in literature who "knew that the bardic gift had been denied him." Discussing Holmes's novels, verse, essays, and intellectual outlook, the critics conclude that he was "one of the most winsome characters in literary history." For additional commentary by Jones, see excerpt dated 1964; for further criticism by Hayakawa, see Additional Bibliography.*]

The casualness with which Holmes's medical career has been treated by literary critics, while natural, has had one unfortunate result: sufficient consideration has never been given by students of his literary writings to the fact that to him literature was never more than a sideline. The usual accounts of Holmes as the charming representative of the "silver age" of America, the "typical Brahmin," the fashionable after-dinner speaker and wit, the sentimental and kindly old gentleman, are true enough; but they fail to do justice to an important aspect of his character. Few writers have shown more kindliness and consideration in dealing with opinions they despise; it is frequently thought, therefore, that he was a social hot-house product, superficially brilliant, but lacking in robustness and vigor. Such an interpretation, of course, has been especially attractive to the opponents of the "genteel tradition," the admirers of the brawny, muscular, and untamed in American literature and life. But, while it is true that in his literary writings Holmes was all too scrupulous lest he offend the chaste ear of maidens or shock the decent piety of elderly spinsters, in his professional writings he reveals an altogether different personality—a sinewy and aggressive fighter, conscious of his strength, proud of the great scientific spirit he represented, exulting in his polemical cunning. His was a time when eloquence counted for more in the medical profession than it does today. Taking advantage, therefore, of every weapon at his hand, he sailed into his controversies with incisiveness, irony, and vigor. His medical papers sometimes make much better reading than his literary prose. (pp. xxxix-xl)

In literature, . . . Holmes was an amateur, in the sense of one whose real vocation was elsewhere. To compare Holmes even cursorily with writers who have taken themselves seriously as writers is to see that he is of a different order of being as a literary man. Shelley, Milton, Pope, Swift, Emerson, D. H. Lawrence—or even lesser men like Rupert Brooke—have in common a kind of artistic seriousness, a bardic or prophetic urge which has impelled them to write. Holmes, on the contrary, with neither a tragic nor a profoundly comic view of life, with none of the impassioned concern with ultimate realities which Matthew Arnold has called "high seriousness,"

with no deep sense of pathos, or even of melodrama, with no interest in advancing the technique of poetry, is distinctly an amateur in letters. His literary writings, on the whole, are partly the leisure-hour meditations of the physician, partly a means of spreading certain items of professional propaganda, partly a distillation of his social life. The mere fact that he employs the novel in the crudely didactic fashion of *Elsie Venner, The Guardian Angel,* and *A Mortal Antipathy,* shows how remote from him is the point of view of the genuine artist; these novels are, in the very motives that gave them birth, the novels of an amateur. If further proof were needed, one has only to point to the perfunctory admiration and easy generalities that usually characterize his criticism of other authors, as in his essays on Washington Irving and Nathaniel Hawthorne. No thoroughgoing artist would ever have contented himself with such offhand remarks about other artists.

From his literary writings alone, therefore, we cannot understand the whole personality of Holmes. If he deals rarely or not at all with problems deeply tragical or pathetic, if he never discloses the grandeurs of inner spiritual conflict, if nothing he writes seems to be of the nature of an inspired *aperçu* into the nature of man or things, we need have no reason to conclude that he failed to recognize the importance of such attainments, or that his notions concerning literature were unsound. Holmes himself knew that the genuine artist is always in a sense a seer. He also knew that the bardic gift had been denied him. (pp. xli-xlii)

The main trouble with all three of [Holmes's] "medicated" novels is that the avowed purpose is always sacrificed in order to make a good-natured concession to the reader's supposed desire for a happy ending. The problem of moral responsibility, especially when treated in order to enlist the reader's sympathy for those unfortunates who sin or err through no fault of their own, should be a tragic and not a sentimental theme. Holmes's failure in these novels is that he arouses neither terror nor pity, nor even a strong sense of the pathetic. In *Elsie Venner,* the strongest of the three, there are moments of power, as when Elsie flattens her forehead in anger and fixes her cold, snake-like eyes on an enemy, or stares down a real rattlesnake in the mountains so that it crawls off abashed. But in the course of the novel, which has striking melodramatic possibilities, she leads a singularly blameless life, and dies conveniently before she has done any harm. The moral of the story, therefore, misses fire. The weight of his moral argument is carried, however, not by the story, but by the long, discursive conversations between the physician, Dr. Kittredge, and the Calvinist clergyman, the Reverend Dr. Honeywood. But these conversations (and the similar devices which carry the argument in the other two novels) show such skill in the presentation of his point of view that it is easy to forget the defects of the novel as a novel. Naturally, however, a point of view that can be presented in such a form as he uses—that is, permitting the opposition to present its opinions and drawing the opposing views closer by tact and ingenuity—is not an uncompromising one. Regarding himself as a devout Christian, Holmes is able to keep what he values in Calvinism at the same time that he propounds his anti-Calvinistic doctrines.

The boundaries to Holmes's determinism are set not simply by a reluctance to carry out a theory to its logical end, but by his sense that an attempt to establish complete determinism would require his going too far beyond the knowledge then available to medical science. . . . Although emphatically asserting that people who enjoy moral health have freedom of the will, he shows by many case studies that there is a class of unfortunates (as Holmes said, "out of health, morally") who have no freedom, being so unhappily situated or physiologically ill-constructed, that they must undergo some kind of *"traitement morale palliatif et curatif"* before they can overcome their deficiencies and achieve moral freedom.

What then was the realm in which Holmes believed that man could be morally "free"? Despine solved the problem sufficiently for his own purposes by saying that anyone who was conscious of making a moral choice was free. Holmes accepted this position in **"Crime and Automatism,"** but elsewhere he shows that as a determinist he is a great deal farther advanced than Despine, in that he saw how much of the action of perfectly normal human beings is governed not by moral choice but by mechanical principles. His essay *Mechanism in Thought and Morals* . . . , which represents his farthest advance in deterministic thought, reveals an intimate acquaintance with the medical knowledge then available on the relations between thought and physiological chemistry, between thought and anatomical structure; in fact, he foreshadows accurately the direction which physiology, experimental psychology, and neurological anatomy were to take in ensuing years. He shows no religious or superstitious fear of investigation in this direction—in fact, in **"Crime and Automatism"** he goes so far as to say that an illusory belief in the power of self-determination is sufficient for practical moral purposes—but he nevertheless maintained that "we do not find Hamlet and Faust, right and wrong, the valor of men and the purity of women, by testing for albumen, or examining fibres in microscopes." If, of course, these "spiritual" attainments of man are not to be found in the material conditions where they have their birth, where are they to be sought? This is a question never quite answered by Holmes, so that the complaints about the ambiguity of his position made by some of his contemporaries were not without justification. (pp. l-liii)

Science . . . is conceived humanistically in Holmes—that is, it is regarded as a part of, and not an enemy of, humane knowledge. . . . Perhaps his own triumph in the puerperal-fever controversy served to enliven his interest in the struggles others had in getting their views accepted. At any rate, he took the side of science in every controversy against popular prejudice or theological opposition. This is not to say that Holmes was contumacious. He devoted little space to the great Darwinian controversy: his conclusions about Darwinism are succinctly summarized in *The Professor at the Breakfast-Table* . . . , and in *The Poet at the Breakfast-Table* . . . the matter is touched upon again, but in no argumentative way. By the time Holmes got to writing about Darwin at all, the controversy was, to him, settled and won, and he accepted Darwinism complacently. The effect of Darwinism on his philosophy was that of reinforcing views arrived at earlier, such as his conviction that "Nature" is a "true divine manifestation," and that "development upward is the general law of the race." The basic optimism upon which such an attitude is founded is general throughout his work, and is even hinted at as early as 1831 in the juvenile **"Autocrat of the Breakfast-Table"** papers published in Buckingham's *New England Magazine*.

Holmes was fortunate in that the faith he put in science was one which the many great scientific discoveries of his time kept constantly alive and fresh. Science was proceeding triumphantly towards a better understanding of man and his universe; there was a beneficent order in nature which Divine Providence had provided; the Calvinist bogeys of hell-fire and torment had

been driven out of all but the more backward intellectual communities. America, the cradle of freedom, was reaching higher and higher levels of humane and scientific achievement, and his beloved city of Boston was contributing more than her share to the nation's glory in every line of laudable activity. The vulgarities of America, such as the daughters of the *nouveaux riches* satirized in **Elsie Venner,** and literary insurgents like Whitman, were the temporary aberrations of a growing civilization, and could be regarded humorously. It was a pleasant and hopeful world that Holmes inhabited. (pp. lvi-lviii)

[So] far as his familiar verse is concerned, Holmes appears to have been always in his prime. There was a period prior to 1831 in which he stumbled around for certainty of expression. Then from **"The Last Leaf"** to **"The Broomstick Train,"** that is to say, for a period of almost sixty years, his talents did not abate, but enabled him to turn out, in a great quantity though intermittently, familiar verse of high finish and perfection. (p. lxxxvi)

Holmes is . . . the best familiar verse writer in classic American letters, and the first American to devote himself to any great extent to this type of art. His only predecessor in this is Irving, who, however, produced only a little, and that at rare intervals. His successors, on the other hand, have maintained a strong tradition of familiar verse in America—so strong, indeed, that it seems almost to be the only American literary tradition that has a reasonable continuity, unaffected by fads and movements and social convulsions, to the present day. (pp. lxxxvii-lxxxviii)

The bulk of Oliver Wendell Holmes's [occasional] poetry, because it celebrates such fugitive events, is destined to be forgotten. It already has few readers left. But since it is a rare example of its kind in American literature, it deserves at least a kindly and sympathetic farewell before it fades into complete oblivion. (p. xc)

Perhaps nothing contributed so much to the charm of Holmes's occasional verses as his childlike and happy acceptance of the pleasures of society and the admiration and love of his friends. . . . Slight as the themes of many of these verses are, and easy as are their sentiments, it does not appear that he ever contented himself with a slovenly or hasty piece of work. (pp. xciv-xcv)

It goes almost without saying that the qualities which made Holmes an excellent occasional poet make his serious poetry unsatisfying. . . . The triteness of sentiment that makes his verses appropriate to occasions makes his serious lyrics commonplace and undistinguished. For certain shades of delicate pathos, as in **"Under the Violets,"** Holmes was capable of tender and appropriate expression, the competence and sincerity of which no one would question; but this poem is far from being great poetry, although it is one of his best. Its most striking fault to a reader today is its diffuseness. (pp. xcv-xcvi)

Amid all the third-rate prettiness that is to be found in the collected edition of Holmes's works, there are a few poems, however, that stand out as distinctly better than the rest. **"The Voiceless,"** though by no means a great poem, is not third-rate. In it Holmes celebrates the pathos of those who have deep emotions but cannot express them.

On this subject of poetic inarticulateness, Holmes always manages to be genuinely tender and sympathetic, as the poem **"To the Poets Who Only Read and Listen"** further indicates. A deep sense of the mediocrity of his own verses and a fear that his poetic reputation was transitory made Holmes increasingly uneasy as he grew older. (p. xcviii)

Holmes was himself, in a sense, one of these inarticulate poets with whom he sympathized—he wrote enough, but had expressed few sentiments that rose from the depths of his being. It is not without significance that much of his better work, such as "Musa" . . . , expresses sympathy with inarticulateness.

"**The Chambered Nautilus**" is a real exception among Holmes's poems. We can readily believe what he has said about the feeling of exaltation he experienced when writing it. Short as it is, it states his most profound beliefs, his humanistic, non-religious, ethical idealism. (p. xcix)

With his amazing aptitude for daring similes that are the spice of his prose, with his quick intellectual curiosity, with his love of analysis which the romantic fashions of poetry in his time rarely permitted him to indulge except in prose, there seems to be more than a possibility that Holmes's poetic gifts might have flourished more richly had he lived in a time when metaphysical poetry was popular. Although not as complex in its intellectual convolutions as metaphysical poetry usually is, "**The Chambered Nautilus**" is an excellent example of the typically metaphysical "conceit" worked out with complete sureness of taste and judgment. (p. c)

Holmes's temper, capable of no sustained passion, but readily moved to quick bursts of tenderness, humor, sympathy, and raillery—his mind, erudite in many odd ways but pedantic in none—found complete expression in the new kind of essay form he evolved [in *The Autocrat of the Breakfast-Table*]. He was a brilliant conversationalist, and was not unconscious of his powers. Like every conversationalist, he probably had wished at one time or another for a Boswell to record his best remarks. (p. ci)

Now, no less than when they first appeared, it is the element of surprise . . . that constitutes the greatest charm of Holmes's papers in *The Autocrat,* in its sequels, *The Professor at the Breakfast-Table* . . . , *The Poet at the Breakfast-Table* . . . , and even in the more subdued product of his old age, *Over the Teacups.* . . . This element of surprise is due, first of all, to his close and reflective observation of even the most trivial matters with a view to discovering their larger implications. . . . (p. cii)

A second source of this surprise is his lively erudition, which he uses with startling ingenuity for purposes of metaphor, simile, and illustrative analogy. . . . His scientific knowledge is wide and deep, but the vast number of little things he knows about life—the speech habits of various classes of people, the peculiarities of men in various occupations, the records of racing-horses, the mannerisms of men and women in every kind of social situation—his sum of general knowledge is so great that it is in itself a kind of erudition. And all this varied information is not a dead mass of facts, but it is like a myriad of flying atoms in an electrical tube, ready to light up at the slightest current of thought in the obscurest corners of human experience. His figures of speech are drawn from every imaginable source, chemical, anatomical, commercial, social, natural, pugilistical, nautical, "reportorial" or "newspaporial" (as he called it), historical, and physiological. (p. ciii)

A third reason for the element of surprise in Holmes's writings is the unconventionality of his thought. He was fond of paradoxes, not of the perverse kind such as Wilde and Shaw and Noel Coward delight in, but of the kind which owe their paradoxical character to the fact that they are startling to conventionality while being undeniably true. (p. civ)

The fourth reason for the surprise is Holmes's extraordinary ability to change his moods swiftly, even suddenly and abruptly, without destroying his design, or producing in the reader any sense of a lack of connection. . . . As everybody who has tried must know, to execute gracefully such swift changes of mood requires real technical virtuosity in the prose writer. (p. cv)

For litheness, for richness, for zest, for occasional blunt speaking, and above all, for adaptability, Holmes's style is perhaps without equal in American literature. Emerson has written a loftier prose; Lowell, a capricious, more analytical one. Melville, in spite of bad lapses, has epic qualities, and Hawthorne, magic—both beyond Holmes's reach. None of these, however, has a prose so various in its powers. Holmes's style is the best example that can be found in American letters of the lucidity, brilliance, ease, and flexible accuracy which we are accustomed to regard as the crowning ornaments of French prose. (p. cvii)

The conversations of [*The Autocrat* and its sequels] are united by a tiny filament of narrative. While Holmes was by no means alone in introducing narrative into the essay, he has approached a good deal closer to the novel than other essayists, especially by bringing events to a mildly dramatic close at the end of each series: the marriage of the Autocrat; the death of the Little Gentleman and the marriages of Iris and "the young fellow called John" in *The Professor;* the breaking up of the boardinghouse and the happy settlement of all the residents in *The Poet.* Charming as the narrative element is, however, these works are not novels, because the principal interest lies not in actions, not in the discussion of actions, but in opinions. The characters are not there for their own sake, but to provide the varieties of points of view that are necessary to conversation, and to create openings so that the Autocrat (Professor, Poet) may make his pronouncements. (p. cviii)

How perfectly this breakfast-table form suited Holmes's talents is indicated not only by his success with it, but by the fact that even when he tries to leave it temporarily, he unconsciously turns back to it. *Elsie Venner* and *The Guardian Angel,* while they cannot be taken seriously as triumphs of the novelist's art, are redeemed from artistic disgrace by their excellence as essays. In *Elsie Venner,* some of the most interesting passages are provided by Dr. Honeywood and Dr. Kittredge, who, sharing the function of the Autocrat between them, comment in conversation on the events; furthermore, such conversational episodes as Widow Rowen's tea party are the high points of the book. (Holmes never writes with so much gusto as when describing a social event: preparations for a party, the making out of invitation lists, the gathering of the guests, the surreptitious examination by guests of the quality of the silverware, etc.) *The Guardian Angel* is even more reminiscent of the Breakfast-Table series. Byles Gridley, Esq., is Holmes's own flattering self-portrait, and all the events revolve around him just as they do around the Autocrat in the essays. These two novels are not without their claims to an honorable mention in the history of American fiction—first, for their accurate observation of New England manners, speech, and scenery, which entitles them to a distinguished place in our regionalist literature; secondly, for their contribution to the development of the novel of purpose in America. If they are rarely given the credit due them, it is because their conspicuous excellences are those of the essayist, rather than of the novelist. It is more than a coincidence that the book least reminiscent of the Breakfast-Table series, *A Mortal Antipathy,* is his least successful work. (pp. cx-cxi)

The only fault that can be found with his method is that the concessions to the intellectual infirmities of the backward, the prejudiced, and the uninformed which his form so admirably enables him to make, are sometimes a trifle humiliating to a modern reader, whose backwardness, prejudice, and ignorance lie in other directions. (In making this objection, however, we should only be complaining of a trait in Holmes that at all other times we find delightful—his profound courteousness.) With a personality such as Holmes had—sentimental, excessively sociable, incapable of vehemence except in matters strictly relating to his profession, so even-tempered that he missed both the great heights and the great depths—it is perhaps to be wondered at that he became an artist at all. But in finding the perfect medium for imparting his attitude towards life, Holmes, without genius, or even an artistic temperament (if that is a help), succeeded in becoming a genuine artist. He established his own rules, evolved his own form. No one else can hope to do anything with the form he created, so peculiarly adapted is it to his own individuality. But he has form, and he has substance, and a perfect reconciliation of the one with the other. There are greater artists and greater men of whom this cannot be said. (p. cxi)

Holmes's main shortcomings—the narrowness of his universe, his blindness . . . to the heterogeneous America that was growing up around him—make some of his views seem hopelessly limited and provincial. Few poets have lived who have had so much faith in the better things of the society they lived in. (p. cxii)

But his optimism is by no means a sad commentary on the quality of his mind, as our more disillusioned contemporaries have hastened to conclude. It is merely the expression of Holmes's temperament: the childlike simplicity of a candid heart, which believes eternally (if it can be said without superciliousness or disrespect) in Santa Claus. His age was not without its skepticisms, but he escaped them or solved them. All the industrial vandalism of the post-Civil-War period disturbed him, . . . but he serenely continued on his way, believing in the "tolerable certainty of human averages," which was empirical evidence of the benevolence of God. Had he less charm, we might well be tempted to dismiss him . . . for what we cannot help regarding as his naïveté. But we cannot, because he is one of the most winsome characters in literary history. It is impossible not to be impressed by the richness of his humane and scientific culture, and by the minuteness and sensitivity of his social perceptions. It is impossible, too, to resist the appeal of his central intellectual principle: "I don't want you to believe anything I say; I only want you to see what makes me believe it." (pp. cxii-cxiii)

S. I. Hayakawa and Howard Mumford Jones, "Oliver Wendell Holmes," in Oliver Wendell Holmes: Representative Selections *by Oliver Wendell Holmes, edited by S. I. Hayakawa and Howard Mumford Jones, American Book Company, 1939, pp. ix-cxiii.*

CLARENCE P. OBERNDORF   (essay date 1943)

[*Oberndorf, a professor of clinical psychiatry, analyzes Holmes's "medicated novels," emphasizing that the author's thinking was dominated by his training in medicine.*]

[Holmes's *Elsie Venner, The Guardian Angel,* and *A Mortal Antipathy*] present essentially in fictional form complex psychiatric situations made more vivid by backgrounds reflecting the standards, customs, and ideology of the last half of the

An illustration of the heroine from Elsie Venner.

nineteenth century. The family relationships portrayed not only helped to produce the neurotic manifestations but at the same time kept them alive. (p. v)

It is small wonder that the novels of Holmes, especially *The Guardian Angel* and *A Mortal Antipathy,* found little acclaim when they appeared. The average reader discovered in their melodramatic qualities the commonplaces of the second-rate fiction writers of the period—very likely he skipped over the heavier philosophical and psychological paragraphs. If these passages received any of his attention they must have appeared as technical and uninteresting as clinical case reports. Many portions of Holmes's stories make dull reading, with their wordy, stereotyped and old-fashioned dialogue and the repetition of certain character types almost unchanged in each of the novels. To add to the monotony, in each story Holmes has followed a similar plan of treatment and resorted to well-worn models for the introduction of the setting and the erection of the plots.

Nevertheless these dated novels seemed of sufficient importance as psychiatric and analytic studies of neuroses to warrant their re-presentation to sociologists and physicians. (pp. v-vi)

· · · · ·

Holmes, for all his preferential social background and academic training, could not escape in his home and in his subsequent contacts the impact of repressive environmental influences. Holmes's father was a Calvinist minister; from all account, an exceptionally genial Calvinist. Nevertheless he believed firmly in predestation and preordination. Holmes's reaction to the fatalist religious principles of his father was in an escape, an eminently respectable escape, into science and scholarship. A horror of the depressing damnation theology of his childhood aroused in Holmes a bitter antipathy and lifelong rebellion against its crippling influences and manifestations.

The drive to counteract and correct the hopeless Calvinist philosophy appears time and again in his essays and in his three novels written late in life. A contemporary critic dubbed them "medicated novels." The term is appropriate, for in each the main character presents a psychiatric problem and is under the care of a doctor of skill and experience, who serves as an interpreter of the sickness.

Of course Holmes would not have regarded himself as a psychiatrist because this specialty was not to develop as an extramural practice for another fifty years. The most advanced psychiatrists of his day were concerned almost exclusively with the abolition of forcible restraint and punishment of the insane and the introduction of more humane attitudes and methods in custodial asylums. Even the problems of psychiatric classification and prognosis, which so engrossed the attention and encouraged the debating skill of psychiatrists from approximately 1885 to 1910, had been barely broached. Nevertheless, those tense psychiatric situations which destroy individuals, disrupt families, and disturb social groups were quite as prevalent then as today, and the physician was increasingly displacing the pastor in these cases as the counselor and authority.

To be a truly great physician in any but a purely technical specialty, or even a successful one, the medical practitioner must possess what are sometimes called "intuitive" gifts as a psychiatrist. This quality depends upon his experience as a clinician supplemented by his sympathy and consideration for people whose minds and bodies are distorted by physical pain or disappointments in life. The social import of these psychiatric situations impressed Holmes to such a degree that he assumed the same fighting radicalism in regard to their recognition and treatment as he had toward the control of the contagiousness of childbed fever, the value of scientific dentistry, the folly of overmedication, and the fallacies of homeopathy.

Holmes tried his talents in poetry, essays, and fiction but he continued first, last, and forever, the physician, his thinking dominated by his medical training and his daily scientific work. He was also a theological reformer, a philosopher, and, as indicated above, according to the present concept of this specialty, a psychiatrist many of whose ideas fell in line with the most advanced of this present day. In certain essentials Holmes's theory and philosophy of approach to psychological problems is prophetic of psychoanalysis and anticipated Freud's formulations and the psychoanalytic psychiatry which grew out of it. (pp. 4-7)

· · · · ·

Holmes wrote his earlier psychiatric novels with the direct purpose of demonstrating that there is no inherited guilt. In the *Mechanism in Thought and Morals,* he has much to say on processes which might account for personal guilt. He expounds his ideas clearly, forcefully, and unequivocally. The object of his thesis is now never in doubt—namely, that such a thing as absolute freedom of the will cannot exist because of uncon-

scious processes which are affecting the individual's conscious activity all the time. If for this reason alone, Holmes affirms that we must regard with charity and understanding many deviations in conduct which are asocial and antisocial. He says: "Do we ever think without knowing that we are thinking? The question may be disguised so as to look a little less paradoxical: Are there any mental processes of which we are unconscious at the time, but which we recognize as having taken place by finding certain results in our minds?" (pp. 8-9)

All the reflections in *Mechanism in Thought and Morals* constitute a recapitulation of thoughts which Holmes had confirmed in psychopathological conditions during his career as a practicing and consulting physician. But Holmes did not put them in the form of a medical essay. He may have felt that his medical colleagues would be unreceptive and antagonistic, and probably was smarter than he knew. At all events here again he was prophetic of Freud, whose original presentations before the Vienna Medical Society met with a humiliating reception. (p. 13)

Holmes at the time his novels appeared was a professor of anatomy, a subject of dry bones and dead bodies, and as an anatomist his opinions on psychiatric disorders would not have been considered important to the practicing physicians and psychiatrists. He therefore deliberately and probably shrewdly chose narrative as a medium through which to bring his views before the public. His three stories are poor fiction when judged by modern criteria or compared with the masters of his time— Poe, Thackeray, Balzac, or even Hawthorne of his own literary group. . . . Their plots are simple, almost juvenile and, in two of them, the reader is not disappointed in the customary thwarting of the villain and the coming of true love to its own.

Although *Elsie Venner* enjoyed something of a popular success, literary critics dealt none too kindly with this or with Holmes's subsequent psychological works of fiction that were "tainted with the physiological." Surely Holmes, far more sensitive concerning his literary reputation both as a poet and novelist than about his clinical ability, would not have been pleased that these studies of abnormal characters should be regarded as case histories. In the light of the development of modern psychiatry they remain as testimony to his medical acuity, his knowledge, and his profound psychiatric understanding.

There can be slight doubt that the doctors who play such a prominent role in these social dramas and employ a similar technique in handling them are none other than a composite picture of Holmes himself. There also should be included in this class the crusty, warm-hearted, old Professor Byles Gridley who plays the part of amateur detective in *Guardian Angel.*

If one were to translate into psychoanalytic parlance the receptive and understanding method of these doctors with their patients it would follow the lines of the "passive technique" generally preferred in psychoanalytic practice today. Certainly it was defiantly at variance with the bad-tasting drug therapy of the time for the treatment of hysteria and other nervous symptoms.

In terms of professional conduct, the doctors' approach combines those qualities so desirable in every physician but indispensable in a psychiatrist—namely, patience, forbearance, tolerance, equanimity, accurate observation of the patient's actions and utterances, and unremitting consideration for the patient's psychological and environmental handicaps.

These psychiatric and psychoanalytic principles were not merely philosophical musing with Holmes. They rested upon clinical orientation and, because of this fact, his observations have a directness, reality, and cogency which other novelists have been able to portray with greater vividness and emotional appeal. A dozen years intervened between the writing of *Elsie Venner* . . . and *Mechanism in Thought and Morals*. During that time Holmes had gathered together his ideas and beliefs supporting the doctrine of limited responsibility and had developed for the treatment of mental disorders principles of theory and practice which are considered modern today.

Holmes saw with unusual clearness the far-reaching effects of mental disorder in the home and in intrafamilial relationships, especially the power of such disorders to restrict and distort the lives of the well—this was the effect of Elsie Venner's illness upon her father, and of the psychically determined invalidism of Mrs. Stoker, the minister's wife, upon her young daughter in *The Guardian Angel*.

Novels must have the element of love. This is not lacking in Holmes's stories. Here it takes the form not of violent, passionate or sensuous love, but of spiritual love, with its vital influence as an agency in molding character and establishing emotional balance. In *Elsie Venner* the love affect had been immobilized and became blocked; in *The Guardian Angel* Myrtle Hazard's capacity to love had been turned into resentment and rebellion; in *A Mortal Antipathy* Maurice Kirkwood's normal tendencies had been held in check by a morbid fear of young women.

All of these characters have one quality in common—they lost their mothers before the age of two, and during infancy and childhood had mother substitutes who were deficient in one way or another. From certain aspects the emotional disorder of each may be regarded as a reaction to a lack of love and to frustration in their unconscious search for the missing parent. Elsie Venner made an awkward attempt to free herself by falling in love but was unsuccessful and the rebuff and denial made her die. In *The Guardian Angel* and *A Mortal Antipathy* the principal characters achieve love through a symbolic rebirth (rescue from death by a person of the opposite sex who is an appropriate partner for marriage).

In *Elsie Venner* the circumstance that her mother was bitten by a snake during pregnancy is held responsible for the reptilian traits which Elsie showed. This is not psychoanalytic thinking. Yet few would dispute that the case is interpreted with the insight of analytic psychiatry. Moreover, the interesting question of the influence of very early, even antenatal, damage on later anxiety has recently been reëxamined in the light of observations made during the psychoanalysis of patients.

The second novel, *The Guardian Angel,* is a study of hereditary influences on the mind of one individual and on the development of hysterical symptoms. Written during the mellowness of Holmes's advancing years it is a final and unsparing thrust at meddling by the clergy in situations where emotional disturbance is threatening the very existence of the patient.

Holmes maintains that "this body in which we journey across the isthmus between the oceans is not a private carriage but an omnibus." In Myrtle Hazard of *The Guardian Angel,* the traits and experiences of antecedents reappear and produce strange and unaccountable actions (hysteria), seemingly belonging to the personalities of several ancestors. An analogous concept has received wide attention under the term "collective unconscious," as used by the Swiss psychiatrist, Carl Jung,

at one time closely associated with Freud. However, in the collective (archaic) unconscious as conceived by Jung, integral figures of remote ancestors as described in Myrtle Hazard are not generally presumed to exist.

The final novel, *A Mortal Antipathy,* is the study, by a fine psychiatrist, of a compulsion type of morbid fear. The preface, like the prefaces of the two previous novels, defends the validity of the actual framework of the story from a medical standpoint. In it Holmes approaches more significantly the psychoanalytic position of Freud—namely, that a personal shock or trauma in very early infancy may cause a conditioning which the individual sometimes does not outgrow.

The theory of bisexuality and the importance of bisexual components in influencing the characters of the individuals is more than implied in the description of each one of the abnormal personalities. The masculine traits in childhood of both Elsie Venner, the man-hater, and Myrtle Hazard, something of a tomboy, are unmistakable. The bisexual theme becomes even clearer in *A Mortal Antipathy,* when Holmes repeatedly contrasts the femininity of Euthymia Tower with the masculinity of Lurida Vincent—and it is apparent that he has little sympathy with the latter. The illness of Myrtle Hazard is typical of the hysterias described by Charcot, but which are not so often seen today.

The theme of determinism with its variations—whether antenatal, directly inherited, or psychic—is repeated in all the novels. It seems as though Holmes may have been under a compulsion to write off his father's Calvinism and predestination, but never quite succeeded. As he advanced in years, the determinism, as in *A Mortal Antipathy,* assumed individualistic and personal aspects—conditions which fitted a type of causation more in harmony with scientific criteria. But it is not my intention here to interpret these novels psychoanalytically as a reflection of any personal unconscious conflicts which their author may have had. Certainly, whatever these conflicts were and however deep they may have been, they were transformed into the highest type of human productivity and helpful coöperation.

The harsh New England predestinistic morality produced many a dismal domestic drama like those so effectively portrayed by Hawthorne in *The House of the Seven Gables* and by Edith Wharton in *Ethan Frome*. The mystifying physiological manifestations of self-denial and self-restraint Holmes grasped at the bedside. This repressive cultural attitude lingered on after his death. But the scientific spirit continued to grow great and strong in Cambridge and Boston. (pp. 13-18)

One wonders why Holmes's ideas did not receive greater attention when they were written. Probably society at large was far less prepared to entertain them in 1870 than it was to accept Freud reluctantly in 1910. But this does not explain why Holmes's theories were not more critically tested by two truly distinguished scientists of the Boston group who immediately followed him—William James, the philosopher, and Morton Prince, the psychiatrist. This is especially true of Prince, whose work on multiple personality is his outstanding contribution to psychiatry.

Psychiatry had remained in the sterile stage of description and classification. The social significance of mental deviation, so stressed by Holmes, had not been grasped by science or society. Neither James nor Prince could give heed to dynamism of thought or appreciate its correlation to the masterly clinical descriptions sketched by Holmes. . . . (p. 19)

Clarence P. Oberndorf, "Foreword" and "Intro-
duction: Dynamic Psychiatry and Holmes," in The
Psychiatric Novels of Oliver Wendell Holmes *by Oliver
Wendell Holmes, edited by Clarence P. Oberndorf,
Columbia University Press, 1943, pp. v-viii, 1-19.*

CHARLES BOEWE (essay date 1954)

[*Boewe examines Holmes's use of the theory of reflex action in*
Elsie Venner, The Guardian Angel, *and* A Mortal Antipathy.]

The nimbus of science that surrounds the three novels of Oliver
Wendell Holmes has often been found to be more impressive
than their literary merit. William Dean Howells recalled that
"a faint, faint odor of the pharmacopoeia clung to their pages;
their magic was scientific," and more recent commentators
have pointed out that much of their power of persuasion owes
something to science. Holmes's own statement that *Elsie Venner* is intended to attack Calvinism—that the "real aim of the
story was to test the doctrine of 'original sin' and human responsibility for the disordered volition coming under that technical denomination" [see excerpt dated 1883]—has tended too
often to throw the emphasis in discussions of the novels wholly
toward theological concerns, slighting the science that provides
the foundation for their arguments. To the extent that all three
are concerned with disordered volition, all are attacks on Calvinism. Each is a study of a different kind of limitation of the
will, and all aim to persuade the reader that rational people
cannot hold others accountable for acts over which they have
no control.

Even in his own time Holmes seemed to some of his readers
to be flaying dead horses; surely today the theological issue of
the novels is less arresting than the scientific element, especially when it is seen how advanced the science really was.
That there is a single scientific theory underlying all three books
and that Holmes made bold speculative use of this theory has
not been generally recognized. It is my intention to show here
that they have a common indebtedness to the physiological
theory of reflex action, and that awareness of this debt can
give us an added respect for Holmes's excursions into fiction.

Holmes's Phi Beta Kappa address, *Mechanism in Thought and
Morals,* which was delivered almost at the mid-point of his
career as professor of anatomy, is "a brilliant anticipation of
Dr. Freud," says Van Wyck Brooks [see excerpt dated 1936].
Indeed, in that essay Holmes does recognize the existence of
a kind of unconscious mental action, automatic and beyond
the control of the will, when he asks, "What happens when
one idea brings up another? Some internal movement, of which
we are wholly unconscious, and which we only know by its
effect." Ten years earlier, in *The Professor at the Breakfast-
Table* . . . , he had also alluded to a sensation we all have
experienced: "that a deep layer of thought sometimes makes
itself felt through the superincumbent strata. . . ." However,
the unconscious mental actions which he noted seemed to him
to be nothing new or astonishing—"that there are such," he
said, "is laid down in the strongest terms by Leibnitz, whose
doctrine reverses the axiom of Descartes into *sum, ergo cogito.*" While we may acknowledge that Holmes anticipated Freud
in the recognition of the unconscious, still we cannot say that
his psychology was Freudian. As is so often true, Holmes
himself provides the best terminology. In 1874, in his essay
"Crime and Automatism," he said that the prison reforms
which he advocated—"these newer modes of thought," as he
called them—"are to a large extent outgrowths of what we

may call physiological psychology." "Physiological" is the
correct qualifier for his psychology. He clearly saw that "the
foundations of this [science] were laid in those studies of individual character made by the phrenologists, much in the same
way that the foundations of chemistry were laid by the alchemists." This is the psychology which supports the plots of
Holmes's three novels, a physiological psychology based on
the concept of mechanical reflex action.

Holmes was primarily indebted for his theory of reflex action
to the experiments of the English physician and physiologist
Marshall Hall . . . , though it had been at least partly implied
in the theory of mechanical animal action of Descartes and in
David Hartley's psychology of association. (pp. 303-05)

As Holmes was to describe it, reflex action is "the mechanical
sympathy . . . of distant parts. . . ." Surely what made the
discovery attractive to Holmes was that Hall "furnished the
basis for that conception of the reflex as a neural arc which
functions independently of the brain. . . ." Thus Holmes learned
that the cause for action may sidestep the brain, and consequently sidestep volition; here was scientific justification for
his cherished belief that man's free will is no freer than a drop
of water imprisoned in a crystal: "One little fluid particle in
the crystalline prism of the solid universe!" (p. 306)

The study of reflex function in its higher sphere of course is
its application to morality. But, one asks, did Holmes think
morality depends upon nothing more than the well-oiled automatic functioning of the mechanisms Marshall Hall had called
reflex arcs? Holmes was not prepared to say. Though he was
one of America's first serious microscopists, the study of microscopic neuroanatomy, which would one day show the actual
neural arcs, was still in its infancy. He had only Hall's theory
to go on, a theory which satisfactorily explained certain experimental data that had been collected about the behavior of
mutilated turtles and hedgehogs, a theory which he confidently
assumed should apply equally to human beings—one which
fitted nicely with his preconceived idea of free will. The study
of reflex action seemed to him to offer a fruitful method in the
exploration of human behavior, but he realized how much
remained to be done. In *Elsie Venner,* the Professor, like the
Autocrat, Holmes's thinly disguised self, says that "the limitations of human responsibility have never been properly studied. . . ." Marshall Hall had shown how that sort of study could
be conducted by means of relatively simple physiological experiments in the realm of animal life; it remained for someone
else to do a similar thing for man, in the much more complicated regions of psychology. Such a study would give morality
a scientific footing. "Automatic action in the moral world,"
the Professor muses, "the *reflex movement* which *seems* to be
self-determination, and has been hanged and howled at as such
(metaphorically) for nobody knows how many centuries: until
somebody shall study this as Marshall Hall has studied reflex
nervous action in the bodily system, I would not give much
for men's judgments of each others' characters." Meanwhile
he could speculate, and the speculation could be safely expressed in novels, which no one supposed to be true anyway.

Holmes suggests, then, that his first two novels, *Elsie Venner*
. . . and *The Guardian Angel,* . . . may be considered studies
of reflex action in the sphere of morality. The third, *A Mortal
Antipathy* . . . , is even more concerned with reflex action. The
method of his studies, however, is less demonstration than
persuasion.

Hence it is that the characters of his protagonists in all three
novels are drawn to make the reader as sympathetic with them

as possible. Elsie Venner in the novel which bears her name, Myrtle Hazard in *The Guardian Angel,* and Maurice Kirkwood in *A Mortal Antipathy* all had lost their mothers before the age of two. All are withdrawn from society. All are strange people whom society, though it tolerates them, is unwilling to accept without reservations; and, to hammer home the point of each story more convincingly, all are provided with limitations unlikely to be met with in the ordinary drawing room. Since their moral actions have not been explained by a Marshall Hall, how can anyone judge them harshly? Or more particularly, how can anyone judge a normal person harshly?

The important element of *Elsie Venner* is the prearranged restriction of Elsie's will. Her personality illustrates the theory of reflex action, as Holmes understood it, on its most physiological level. Since the "reflex movement which seems to be self-determination" operates in all of us, Holmes was able, by providing Elsie with a special physiological constitution, to contrast her unique reflexes with the normal. Elsie's mother had been bitten by a rattlesnake while her daughter was *in utero,* the rattlesnake poison causing the child to be part snake and part girl. It makes little difference whether or not Holmes believed in such prenatal conditioning; he said in the preface to the novel that he used "this doctrine as a part of the machinery . . . without pledging his absolute belief in it to the extent to which it is asserted or implied." But having committed himself to such a proposition, he did determine to have his account of Elsie as scientifically probable as he could. He kept a live rattlesnake in a glass jar to study its habits while he was writing the novel, and, as he always followed the reports of his fellow Boston physicians, he may have remembered reading an article on "A Case of Destitution of the Moral Feelings" which described a person who had snakelike characteristics.

Elsie is depicted quite convincingly in terms of a snake: she has a sinuous neck and diamond-shaped eyes; her clothing suggests snakelike qualities; she has compulsions to writhe in orgiastic dances, even her ordinary walk is slithering; she experiences torpor in the winter; her unblinking eyes have a hypnotic ability; and she is literally cold-blooded. She does not suffer from the delusion that she is part snake; she actually *is* part snake. She becomes ill when the rattlesnake side of her nature suppresses the human, and she dies when the natural term of the snake's existence is done.

Elsie's story is a study of the will limited by chemical agents. It becomes apparent as the novel unfolds that she cannot be held responsible for behavior that depends upon venom introduced into her blood stream before her birth, though the mechanism of her reflexes is left unexplained—no Marshall Hall had yet studied reflex actions in the moral world. Yet, how Elsie's sad history disproves the doctrine of original sin is still a little confusing, for she cannot be said to sin at all, in the ordinary sense of the word. Her "sin" is her unconventional behavior. Holmes, always an optimist, assumes that people tend naturally toward goodness and that they tend naturally toward the conventional in social behavior; a deviation from goodness correlates with a deviation from correct behavior. If carefully reared young ladies do not customarily go about acting like serpents, when we find one like Elsie deviating from the normal we must explain her aberrations in terms of forces over which her will has no control. Likewise, we must explain deviations from the normal in moral behavior in similar terms. So, near the end of the novel, Holmes presents this challenge to his readers: "if, while the will lies sealed in its fountain, it

Myrtle Hazard reading about her ancestors in The Guardian Angel.

may be poisoned at its very source, so that it shall flow dark and deadly through its whole course, who are we that we should judge our fellow-creatures by ourselves?"

As an anatomist and poet, Holmes had no reluctance to celebrate the human body's magnificent mechanics:

> Look in upon thy wondrous frame,—
> Eternal wisdom still the same!

But as a physician called upon to treat the body's multitude of ills, he readily saw its shortcomings. He argued that as one has no right to expect to find a perfect body in this imperfect world, he has no right to expect to find a perfect moral nature. "'Sin,' or the failure of an imperfectly made and imperfectly guided being to keep a perfect law," he wrote to Harriet Beecher Stowe, "seems to me to be given in the mere statement of the conditions of humanity, and could not be a surprise or a disappointment to a Creator with reasoning powers no greater than those of a human being of ordinary wisdom."

In *The Guardian Angel* Holmes came closer to the higher sphere of reflex action which he claimed both it and *Elsie Venner* dealt with. No chemical agent controls Myrtle Hazard's will; rather, her destiny is determined by inherited traits from four female ancestors. The first of these is Ann Holyoake, a sixteenth-century martyr. The next, though we do not have Myrtle's genealogy complete, is Ruth Bradford, who was accused of sorcery during the New England witchcraft delusion. She is of less importance than the others. Then comes Judith Pride, a great beauty, who was Myrtle's great-grandmother. And last, Myrtle's grandmother, Virginia Wild, who was part Indian. All of these women exercise varying degrees of influence on the growing heroine of the novel, and these influences are made to illustrate the author's somewhat hesitantly put thesis: "It is by no means certain that our individual personality is the single inhabitant of these our corporeal frames." Of course it is by no means certain that we do share our corporeal frames with guests, and Holmes makes no great effort to contradict common sense; again he had chosen a biological hypothesis—and rather a wild one at that, suggested perhaps by Francis Galton's "composite portraits"—as part of the machinery of the novel, "without pledging his absolute belief in it." (pp. 307-11)

Myrtle is made to believe that sometimes the spirits of her departed ancestors take actual possession of her material body; at other times they merely guide her conduct. For the rationalist reader there is sufficient evidence in the story to explain her visions (in which the ancestors enter her body) entirely in terms of hysteria. Holmes never commits himself to anything that is scientifically disreputable; he skates carefully on the thin ice between the unlikely and the improbable, letting the reader choose his own interpretation. The author's concern, after all, is to persuade his reader to believe that reflex functions operate in the higher sphere—that is, that his heroine is not responsible for her actions; and the method he chooses to relieve her of responsibility is to have her subject to uncontrollable hereditary influences. Near the middle of the novel he stops his narrative to admonish that "the reader, if such there be, who believes in the absolute independence and self-determination of the will, and the consequent total responsibility of every human being for every irregular nervous action and ill-governed muscular contraction, may as well lay down this narrative, or he may lose all faith in poor Myrtle Hazard, and all patience with the writer who tells her story."

It may be that one begins to lose patience with a novelist who takes the simple twitching of a frog's hind leg, magnifies it to explain the abnormal twitching of a snake-girl, and then asks his readers to believe the baby inherited its grandmother's blue eyes according to the same principle. The fact is that once Holmes started using the reflex-action theory for fictional purposes his conception of it entirely outgrew the bounds of Marshall Hall's unpretentious discovery; by this time it stood for any kind of force beyond human control—for anything for which we cannot hold ourselves responsible. (pp. 312-13)

Holmes is not especially concerned with the manner in which characteristics are transmitted by heredity; he only demands freedom to explore the consequences of this kind of automatic action, even if his exploration takes him into dangerous territory. . . . (p. 313)

A Mortal Antipathy uses the theory more in the spirit of Marshall Hall's actual accomplishments than the others, and less as a catch-all for uncontrollable biological forces. It is Holmes's only attempt to use reflex action as the sole supporting framework of a novel, and it is the only place where he tries to give an explanation for the mechanism of the reflex involved. That the novel is an unsatisfactory artistic performance cannot be argued away; but as a serious attempt to utilize and extend the fringe of exact knowledge in a work of fiction, it deserves to be understood on its own terms.

Though the novel rambles like the *Autocrat,* essentially it is the story of Maurice Kirkwood, who has an antipathy to beau-

tiful young women because, as a baby, he was accidentally dropped into a thorn bush by his beautiful cousin Laura. (p. 314)

When he grows up, Maurice reads all he can about antipathies, and he comes to understand the nature of his malady. He writes an account of his life "for the instruction of others, and especially for the light it throws on certain peculiarities of human character often wrongly interpreted as due to moral perversion, when they are in reality the results of misdirected or reversed actions in some of the closely connected nervous centres." This autobiography, one notes, is written only to instruct others; it serves no cathartic function for the writer, for Holmes's psychology is still a physiological psychology—in no way does he anticipate the psychiatric couch.

In his autobiographical sketch, Maurice is given the use of the facts of reflex action as Holmes himself understood them; the explanation is reserved for the savants of the Royal Academy of the Biological Sciences, the speculation for Dr. Butts, Maurice's physician. Maurice, as a layman, is permitted to remark that:

> It is enough to say here, without entering into the explanation of the fact, which will be found simple enough as seen by the light of modern physiological science, that the "nervous disturbance" which the presence of a woman in the flower of her age produced in my system was *a sense of impending death,* sudden, overwhelming, unconquerable, appalling. It was a reversed action of the nervous centres,—the opposite of that which flushes the young lover's cheek and hurries his bounding pulses as he comes into the presence of the object of his passion.

In *A Mortal Antipathy,* Holmes wisely foresaw and correctly described the conditioned reflex in a human being; his description leaves little to be asked. It is only when he lets his speculation run unchecked that he goes farther than available knowledge warranted. . . . Maurice recovers from his antipathy when he is saved from a burning house by a young and beautiful woman, Euthymia Tower. "The change which had taken place in the vital currents of Maurice Kirkwood's system was as simple and solid a fact as the change in a magnetic needle when the boreal becomes the austral pole, and the austral the boreal." Too simple, in the light of what we now know about psychology, but wholly consistent with the terms of the problem as Holmes had set them up.

It is ironic that in his medicated novels Dr. Holmes could not sufficiently sugar-coat the medicine to make it palatable to his readers. Miss Tilton is surely right when she says of *Elsie Venner* that Holmes failed to make his characters more than academic illustrations, either from the point of view of aesthetics or physiology [see Additional Bibliography]. This failure is true of all the novels. Yet they have the distinction of being founded in common on a theory of behavior until then unexploited in fiction . . . and all are sincere pleas for sympathy with unfortunates whose bodily constitutions make them irresponsible for their acts. It is to be hoped that as interest in the relation between science and literature continues to grow, Holmes's novels will not be neglected. (pp. 318-19)

Charles Boewe, "Reflex Action in the Novels of Oliver Wendell Holmes," in American Literature, *Vol. 26, November, 1954, pp. 303-19.*

R. W. B. LEWIS (essay date 1955)

[Lewis, an American literary critic and historian of ideas, maintains that Holmes used his novels as vehicles for dramatizing his ideas about science and history.]

"If for the Fall of man, science comes to substitute the Rise of man, sir, it means the utter disintegration of all the spiritual pessimisms which have been like a spasm in the heart and a cramp in the intellect of man for so many centuries." The operative word in that utterance of Oliver Wendell Holmes, with its Johnsonian stance and its thoroughly Holmesian metaphor, is "science." For Holmes was not merely echoing the current Unitarian resentment against orthodoxy's picture of fallen nature: he was advocating a new picture of man and indicating the sources of his evidence.

"Science" meant many things, but in the ethical discussion it meant primarily the pre-Darwinian evolutionary hypothesis of Lamarck, a hypothesis about the steady development of the human species which happily coincided with and could be taken as a kind of proof of the contemporary high estimate of human nature. Holmes took the Lamarckian theory as the basis for his best-known (though not at all his most attractive) poem, **"The Chambered Nautilus"** . . . , in which the soul is compared to the shellfish and enjoined, like it, to build itself ever more stately mansions, "each new temple nobler than the last."

What science was replacing, according to Holmes, was a view of life ordered by the moralism of a desiccated Calvinist theology. He saw orthodoxy as embodying a set of beliefs and precepts inherited from a remote Asiatic epoch: tradition in its most paralyzing form. "Our dwellings are built on shell-heaps," he said; "the kitchen-midden of the age of stone. Inherited beliefs, as obscure in their origin as the parentage of the cave-dwellers, are stronger with many minds than the evidence of the senses and the simplest deductions of the intelligence." Holmes bent his energies to removing ancient ideas from the head and an ancient anxiety from the heart of living man. His motivation was that of his fellow-Unitarians; but his special weapon was empirical science: the evidence of the senses.

Holmes is an instructive guide for us, as we leave the wastelands of orthodoxy and approach the new Eden of Walt Whitman, for he himself made almost the entire journey. He went to school at orthodox Andover, where a whipping he received evidently produced a sort of traumatic experience. He came on to Harvard, in 1825, when Unitarianism was in the ascendancy, and became its wittiest exponent. He moved on to be one of America's leading men of science. In fact, Oliver Wendell Holmes, whose long life . . . spanned the century, ought to have been a most arresting figure, perhaps the representative man of his age; it is not easy to say why he so often disappoints us. Perhaps it is because he was at the center of so many tendencies and managed to occupy the middle only by achieving a consistent mediocrity.

Holmes stood midway between the vanishing virility of his father's Calvinism and the emerging vitality of his son's militant humanism; what seems to have been available to him from either direction was frequently only the secondary or illusory. The suspicions which clouded his kindly view of human nature lacked the terrible strength which his father, Abiel Holmes, brought to his Calvinist ministry, while his enlightened repudiation of the divine elect took him only as far as the socially eligible, and his replacement of the visible saints by the Boston quality had little of the astringent social philosophy of his son, the Justice. Holmes stood at the heart of his own time. He

was, of course, a Harvard man forever, and the class poet par excellence; he was also a respected colleague and friend of the Swiss zoölogist, Louis Agassiz. Holmes could listen attentively to the Swedenborgian mystifyings by which the elder James mapped the way of regeneration; he could equally grasp and expound the therapeutic methods by which clinical psychology hoped to accomplish the same thing. He led the attack on the old theology; but he was a competent critic and a great lover of the old literature. His interests were rich and varied; yet what we are apt to find in him is less a synthesis of these interests than a good-humored shrewdness about them all, a solid common sense not deep enough for skepticism, not large enough for faith.

At the same time, it is probably misleading to say of him, in the phrase which has clung, that he was an "authentic Brahmin"—unless Brahminism is a more complex state of mind than is commonly allowed. For Holmes, like his partially autobiographical character Byles Gridley in *The Guardian Angel,* was "a strange union of trampling radicalism in some directions and high-stepping conservatism in others." The traditionalist side is better known and remembered; it included familiar traits of the party of Memory, and it has helped to associate him with that party far more than Holmes would have wanted. . . . When he began to talk about the nature and function of science, he had something new to say and a resonant vocabulary in which to say it: "The attitude of modern science is erect, her aspect serene, her determination inflexible, her onward movement unflinching; because she believes herself, in the order of providence, the true successor of the men of old who brought down the light of heaven to men."

Almost all of the Holmes that interests us here is in that sentence. The qualities that Holmes attributes to science could be attributed with the same buoyant confidence to the individual in America. As the profile of the new Adam emerges, we can notice that he too is erect, serene, inflexible, unflinching: and, according to Dr. Holmes, exactly because "modern science" had liberated him, explained him to himself, and imparted to him science's own stalwart nature. For science would provide the new religion and the new prophets and mediators; science would write the new testament and invent the new metaphors. If Dr. Holmes, as one of the first champions of science, did very well at this game, it was largely because he understood to a remarkable extent what the game was about. Perhaps the most succinct statement of Holmes's achievement was that he recast traditional religious concepts in scientific and humanistic terms, that he extracted what he saw as the *facts* of the human situation from the metaphors of myth and posited them anew in the language of psychology and anthropology.

Holmes's artful and sometimes even compelling transpositions are illustrated best in two of his scientific or "medicated" novels, *Elsie Venner* and *The Guardian Angel.* The very genre to which Holmes ascribed these books was a sign of his enterprise; for while Emerson and Whitman were trying their best to convert medical facts into inspirational poetry, Holmes was converting a literary form into a vehicle for a medical case history. Each of the books also enacts the crucial shift in the long arguments between minister and doctor, with the doctor getting the final word in every discussion. Holmes's "novels" are suggestive if, out of fairness to their author, we do not ask of them any questions prompted by a literary bias.

In *Elsie Venner* . . . , Holmes tested the dreary theories which George Ellis and his Unitarian associates imputed to orthodoxy: that a living individual could be "a partaker in a sin committed before his birth''; that he can consequently suffer punishment ''for the offence of another.'' Holmes said in the Introduction that he had attempted ''to illustrate the doctrine of inherited moral responsibility for other people's misbehavior.'' This way of formulating or loading the question indicates the extent to which Holmes conceived of his work as an exercise in scientific history. Holmes took Hawthorne's *The Marble Faun* (written later than *Elsie Venner,* but published a year before) as giving the same answer to the same question: though Hawthorne was testing innocence rather than its opposite, and the similarity of the two novels is essentially the similarity of ethics to medicine. For Holmes, that similarity was close: how close, he demonstrated in his narrative of the hapless Elsie, whose case emerged as an analogy to what Holmes took to be the doctrine of original sin. (pp. 32-5)

Holmes never pretended that there was nothing wrong with the world or with individual human beings; he was not innocent, he was merely kind. The defense of Elsie Venner sprang from Holmes's awareness of and his compassion for human failings, and it communicated his warming belief that to understand is to forgive. But he was sure that theology, or at least the only theology he knew much about, would not help anyone to understand. That was to be the function of science. Science could teach a man to search for the origins and causes of bad actions; and if it discovered them to lie in ''external influences,'' in ''bad ancestors, abuse in childhood, bad company,'' science was prepared to argue that the actions themselves were not in any moral sense bad after all.

What he wanted, in short, was a renovation of the moral vocabulary. In order to get it, Holmes felt the necessity of rejecting the entire traditional scheme of thought, replacing it with those studies by which his friend President Eliot was simultaneously revamping the Harvard curriculum: ''The truth is,'' wrote Holmes in an essay on Jonathan Edwards, ''that the whole system of beliefs which came in with the story of the 'fall of man,' the curse of the father conveyed by natural descent to his posterity . . . is gently fading out of enlightened intelligence. . . . Astronomy, Geology, Ethnology, and a comparative study of Oriental religions have opened the way; and now Anthropology has taken hold of the matter.''

Holmes's own renovated vocabulary—his chosen symbols for describing renovated human nature—consisted of a series of medical metaphors. ''Like a spasm in the heart and a cramp in the intellect''; ''our tumid egotism''; ''treat bad men as if they were insane'': these are examples of Holmes's favorite device, and one which he managed with uncommon dexterity. He shared the prevalent belief in the doctrine of correspondences, or likeness in the elements of the physical and the spiritual world, but in his own peculiar way. For while Emerson, Thoreau, and Melville found gleams of spiritual meaning in the physical scene, a dim outline of the ideal in the actual, Holmes pointed to the operation in the ideal realm of actual or physical functions. Emerson thought that science (as he said in *Nature* and in other essays) should be completed and validated by his own brand of metaphysics; Holmes thought that the realm of spirit could be overhauled by going about it in a scientific manner. ''For what we want in the religious and political organisms,'' he wrote, ''is just that kind of vital change which takes place in our bodies,—interstitial disintegration and reintegration.''

If the bad habits of Elsie Venner were pardoned because they sprang from a bad ancestry, the self-destructive instinct of Myrtle Hazard, the heroine of Holmes's second medicated novel,

The Guardian Angel . . . , was overcome by the gracious influence of a good ancestor. The books are not at all contradictory in theme; indeed, they serve to resolve the apparent contradictions in their author; and the second novel is a valuable complement to the volume published six years earlier. (pp. 37-8)

In Myrtle's departure from the orthodox environment and her regeneration in the doctor's home, there is a symbolism, almost stiffening into allegory, of the succession by science of the dried-up moralism of ''religion.'' But in *The Guardian Angel* Holmes is less interested in continuing the battle against a moldering theology than in describing the anatomy of the mental personality and in exposing the scientific bases of the rebirth ritual. The experience of Myrtle's immersion in water, for example, though projected with slight dramatic effectiveness (much less, say, than the comparable experience of the young hero at the end of Melville's *White-Jacket* . . .), is handled with an acute consciousness of its psychic significance. Holmes is careful to introduce images of her dimly remembered mother into the girl's disturbed imagination, just before she makes the plunge—which is explicitly intended to be what later psychologists would call a return to the womb. Holmes knew what he was about, to the extent that it scarcely measures his awareness to say only that he ''anticipated'' some of the insights of Freud and Jung. On this ground, Holmes may be admired in his own right. He centered his story on a genuine mental illness, revealed its causes in austerity and repression, and suggested a therapy which much later practice would not seriously dispute.

We may recognize in the domination of the young heroine by Aunt Silence what Freud would call the repression of the ego by the superego. An excessive control by the superego—the repository of conventional moral attitudes—results, according to Freud, in a melancholy which can lead toward self-destruction; and that was precisely the effect of Aunt Silence. Perhaps more striking yet was Holmes's exposure, in a pre-Jungian manner, of the presence within the recesses of the mind of personality types filtered down from the past. The theme of *The Guardian Angel* and its title are derived from this notion, as Holmes explains in the opening pages: ''There is recorded an experience of one of the living persons mentioned in this narrative which tends to show that some, at least, who have long been dead, may enjoy a kind of secondary and imperfect, yet self-conscious life in these bodily tenements which we are in the habit of considering exclusively our own.'' And Myrtle Hazard's habit, during moments of stress, of revealing in her features the welling-up of ancestral influence permits Dr. Hurlbut, the Tiresias of this novel, to utter the book's message: ''Live folks are just dead folks warmed over.'' The theme is more persuasively stated than it is dramatized; but Holmes's awkward technique for showing in action what he meant in theory was a failure of narrative art (to which he hardly aspired) rather than of psychological insight.

Holmes did succeed, moreover, in distinguishing between those remote influences, treating them, the way Jung would do, as dramatis personae encountered on the psychic journey. Among them, in Myrtle's case, we find an Indian forebear, who appears in the girl's occasional gestures of violence; and the guardian angel, the ''guide'' who shepherds Myrtle through a variety of perils, an ancestor named Anne Holyoake, a sixteenth-century Puritan martyr. It is her image that Myrtle confuses with that of her mother. Holmes's story thus follows the symbolic pattern later proposed by Jung as the myth of psychic reinte-

A depiction of the infant Maurice's traumatizing accident in A Mortal Antipathy.

gration: the escape, the plunge, the journey, the dangerous and the saving encounters, the magical guidance to the journey's end, and the final healing of the personality.

The Guardian Angel, though without merit as literature, is a telling contribution toward resolving the tensions between Memory and Hope. Ancestry was the point of intersection for Holmes. Both of his novels and most of his essays make it plain that he sought, with the hopeful, to rid the living of the oppressive misdirection of "bad ancestors," and to stand the present on its own feet. But Holmes had a Brahmin's respect for family and good breeding; and he was able to see how the past might nourish as well as stifle. The conservatism in him was peculiarly reinforced by his advanced psychiatric understanding of the value of the past as directive. The example of Oliver Wendell Holmes might support a contention that the renewed persuasion about the necessity of tradition could best emerge not in theological but in psychological terms: by demonstrating the powerful stabilizing and energizing effect which the past may have upon the isolated personality.

The pathos of such isolation was felt and expressed even by that archetypal man of good hope, Emerson, who captured the sense of confusion and aimlessness which afflicted his more sensitive contemporaries with the words: "Here we drift. . . . To what port are we bound? Who knows!" Those wistful questions illustrated the point which, a century later, Thomas Mann would discover from the psychology of Freud and Jung:

the point that the individual "would be confused, helpless, unstable" if his career "consisted merely in the unique and the present." Mann would argue that experience took on meaning and purpose only when it was regarded as typical, not unique—the re-enactment of the past, not the pure event in the present. Holmes hinted at much the same thing, as he set about answering those Emersonian questions by turning to psychotherapy. The question for him was, How had the lost child—Myrtle Hazard, for example—arrived at her condition? And the cure required an adjustment in the working relations between the present and the past.

But the genuinely hopeful were not really interested in either Holmes's analysis or his proposals. Emerson, with total assurance, referred his own questions for answer to the Oversoul; and a moment later could rejoice in the very adventurousness of the uncharted journey. Every tendency in the age which Holmes himself most admired was pushing toward a total neglect of the past rather than a last-minute attempt to restore some of its value. The dominant emotion was exhilaration, not wistfulness. "The expansive future is our arena," declaimed that hopeful organ, the *Democratic Review*. "We are entering on its untrodden ways . . . with a clear conscience unsullied by the past." The excitement of life, for the hopeful, lay exactly in its present uniqueness; the burden of doubt and guilt had been disposed of when the whole range of European experience had been repudiated, for the burden was the chief product of that experience. The individual moral course was thus to be plotted—not in terms of readjustment or of identification with any portion of the past, and much less in terms of redemption—but simply in terms of the healthy cultivation of natural, unimpaired faculties. (pp. 38-41)

> *R. W. B. Lewis, "The New Adam: Holmes and Whitman," in his* The American Adam: Innocence, Tragedy, and Tradition in the Nineteenth Century, *The University of Chicago Press, 1955, pp. 28-53.*

HOWARD MUMFORD JONES (essay date 1964)

[Jones considers the literary merit of Holmes's works, focusing on his theories of psychology. For additional commentary by Jones, see excerpt dated 1939.]

[Holmes's] mundane spirit is a limited spirit; and Holmes works within its limitations. His collected works contain no instance of passion whether intellectual or emotional. Elsie Venner, his only attempt at sexuality in the novel of that name, though she suffers, suffers in a distant, smothered, and indirect way. His other women are out of *Godey's Lady's Book*. Over some of these genteel wraiths, the Iris's and the Avis's of the Breakfast Table series, he occasionally grows maudlin as only the late eighteenth century could grow maudlin. He has no knowledge of, no interest in, economics, politics, sociology, save as the Civil War roused him to eloquence; and though Boston was changing under his eyes, though he claimed he had bored that ancient city through and through as if it were a cheese, he knows little or nothing of filthy slums, metropolitan degradation, or laissez-faire immorality. Racial snobbery once or twice pained him, and he has an honorable passage and an honorable poem against anti-Semitism, but, in general, American treatment of immigrants, Indians, and slaves drew from him either mild reproof or none. He was neither Wendell Phillips nor William Lloyd Garrison. He knows nothing of Emerson's over-soul, nor of Melville's white whale, nor of Hawthorne's *Scarlet Letter*. . . . As a medical man he must have seen a good deal of suffering and evil . . .; yet in his kindly universe there are no dark Satanic mills, and we are some light years away from the darkness of William Faulkner, the cold cruelty of Robinson Jeffers, the taciturn Prometheanism of Hemingway.

What, then, do we have? We cannot all be giant-like; and what one finds in Oliver Wendell Holmes is a striking example of the free play of lucid and honest intelligence in limited surroundings over a few great problems of life—the relation of God to man, the relation of heredity to responsibility, the relation of truth to tradition. These are important themes which Holmes, a man of eighteenth-century inheritance living and working in the American equivalent of the Victorian world, treated with eloquence, with humor, with sarcasm, with denunciation; and in doing so he freed a great number of his countrymen from fear and ignorance. If Heinrich Heine asked to be remembered as a soldier in the war of humanity for liberation, Oliver Wendell Holmes—and how prim and proper he seems along side the mercurial and fascinating Jew!—enlisted in the same army and fought with some of the same weapons. A distance separates **"The One-Hoss Shay"** . . . from Heine's "Atta Troll," but the distance is not as great as at first it seems. A man who could write as Holmes did of "one more example of the methods of wringing a dry cloth for drops of evidence," or describe homeopathy as "a mingled mass of perverse ingenuity, of tinsel erudition, of imbecile credulity, and of artful misrepresentation, too often mingled in practice, if we may trust the authority of its founder, with heartless and shameless imposition," is not very remote from the savagery or the wit of the German poet. (pp. 89-91)

I find . . . on re-reading Holmes, that his interest for moderns lies . . . in his anticipations, often startling, of some of the doctrines of psychology. His medicated fiction has been considered by some historians to anticipate the theories of Freud and Jung. Dr. Clarence P. Oberndorf, for example, has published a study called *The Psychiatric Novels of Oliver Wendell Holmes* [see excerpt dated 1943]. In each of the three tales we are presented with a child left motherless at an early age and subjected to some sort of austere and unsympathetic force; in each we deal with an obsession developed in childhood; in each there is a sympathetic physician who watches over the central personage; and in each the narrative carries hero or heroine to cure or to destruction. The first and third stories—*Elsie Venner* and *A Mortal Antipathy*—focus upon infantile shock. *The Guardian Angel* vaguely foreshadows the collective unconscious of Jung and deals with the problem of multiple personality. All this is true enough, but we do not have to go to Europe to ascertain the originality of Holmes. We have only to turn to the masterpiece of another son of Harvard, *The Principles of Psychology,* of William James, published in 1890, four years before the death of Holmes and one year before the appearance of *Over the Teacups* in volume form. One of the central doctrines in James appears in the great chapter on the nature of consciousness. In *Over the Teacups,* one finds Holmes' tribute to James for his "full exposition of the doctrine of plural personality."

The culture of Federalist Boston, for all its worldliness and its urbanity, was an inward-looking, a brooding consciousness, concerned for the attributes of personality. If I were called upon to define the most "modern" theme in the twelve volumes of Holmes' complete works, I think I should select the nature of consciousness in its relation to personality. The entire Breakfast Table series, from *The Autocrat* to *Over the Teacups,* is,

in a sense, nothing more than the expression of the author's multifaceted personality—autocrat, professor, poet, sage. The novels are quasi-laboratory reports on personality problems. The two biographies are patient attempts at the analysis of striking personalities, and the remaining volumes (including the poetry) contain many passages concerning the development of personality, the relation of personality and freedom, and the meaning of consciousness.

His work as an anatomist possibly focussed Holmes' attention upon the leading role heredity plays in psychic life. When Harriet Beecher Stowe inquired what he really meant in *Elsie Venner,* he wrote that he wanted to "stir up" the question of automatic agency in relation to self-determination and that he used the rattlesnake to dramatize the truth that personality may be shaped by an "unconscious, intuitive tendency, dating from a powerful ante-natal influence which modifies the whole organization." He thought no malformed character wholly shapes (or mis-shapes) itself, as this trenchant passage from *The Poet at the Breakfast-Table* makes clear: "People hold up their hands at a moral monster as if there was no reason for his existence but his own choice . . . ; study . . . will teach you that you do not get such a malformed character . . . without a long chain of causes to account for it; and, if you only knew these causes, you would know perfectly well what to expect." Hang him, if it is for the good of society, he continued, but "recognize the fact that what you hate in him is chiefly misfortune, and that if you had been born with his villainous low forehead and poisoned instincts . . . you would not have been sitting there in your gold-bowed spectacles . . . passing judgment on the peccadilloes of your fellow creatures." Waiving the question whether the actions of a character like Popeye in Faulkner's *Sanctuary* are peccadilloes, one notes to what an astonishing degree Holmes' doctrine anticipates the assumptions of many modern novelists.

If many components of personality are for him inheritances, Holmes was equally impressed by the influence of environment in shaping consciousness, as the famous passages about the Brahmin caste and about quality and equality exist to prove. The Americans, he wrote, are touchy about social distinctions, but it is as impossible to avoid them as to avoid recognizing the facts of natural history. Environment shapes personality. Changes in our manner of existence, he wrote in 1861, imply that "we have experienced some very profound impression which will sooner or later betray itself in permanent effects on the minds and bodies of many among us"; and he noted the increase of what we would call psychosomatic symptoms in New England during the first months of the Civil War. His explanation might have been written by William James: "The same trains of thought go tramping round in one circle through the brain, like the supernumeraries that make up the grand army of a stage-show. Now, if a thought goes round through the brain a thousand times a day, it will have worn as deep a track as one which has passed through it once a week for twenty years."

In such passages Holmes is talking about matters external to consciousness; what of the operations of consciousness itself? The more Holmes studied the matter, the more unpredictable, the more complicated he found the matter to be. He compares the operations of men's minds to the varied moves in chess; he returns again and again to the idea that when two persons converse, multiple personalities may be engaged in talking— John and Thomas as they are each to himself, John and Thomas as they are to each other, John and Thomas as they are in the eyes of God. He was more and more fascinated by both the unconscious operations of the mind and by what we, following James and others, call the stream of consciousness. The Poet says in *The Poet at the Breakfast-Table*: "Some kinds of thoughts breed in the dark of one's mind like the blind fishes in the Mammoth Cave. We can't see them and they can't see us; but sooner or later the daylight gets in and we find that some cold, fishy little negative has been spawning over our beliefs, and the brood of blind questions it has given birth to are burrowing round and under and butting their blunt noses against the pillars of faith . . . some of our old beliefs are dying out every year, and others feed on them and grow fat." "My thoughts," observes the Professor, "flow in layers, or strata, at least three deep. I follow a slow person's talk, and keep a perfectly clear under-current of my own beneath it. Under both runs obscurely a consciousness belonging to a third train of reflections, independent of the two others." And the same personage sagely observes: "We shall probably never have the least idea of the enormous number of impressions which pass through our consciousness, until in some future life we see the photographic record of our thoughts and the stereoscopic picture of our actions. There go more pieces to make up a conscious life or a living body than you think for."

A long autobiographical passage in the volume is a proleptic example of what James was to call the blooming, buzzing confusion of conscious life—Holmes talking about a "keyboard of nerve-pulps, not as yet tanned or ossified, to the finger-touch of all outward agencies . . . the filmy threads of this web of life in which we insects buzz a while." The creative consciousness of the poet was, he thought, of this nature; and there is poignancy in reading the many passages in which Holmes, who longed for poetical fame more than he longed for anything else, broods over the psychology of art, alternating between the romantic concept of God-given genius and the late eighteenth-century idea of decorum, craftmanship, and imitation.

In a psychic universe of this sort, the idea of conscious control, of choice, of freedom of the will more and more diminished. A footnote to the standard edition of *The Professor at the Breakfast-Table* gives us Holmes' final estimate:

> The more I have observed and reflected, the more limited seems to me the field of action of the human will. Every act of choice involves a special relation between the *ego* and the conditions before it. But no man knows what forces are at work in the determination of his *ego*. The bias which decides his choice between two or more motives may come from some unsuspected ancestral source, of which he knows nothing at all. He is automatic in virtue of that hidden feeling that he is self-determining.

This, oddly enough, approaches the very doctrine of Jonathan Edwards that he denounced, but Holmes cannot shake off his cultural inheritance, he cannot think of men as machines walking, he had to keep God and vitalism in the universe, he had to retain an ideal end for science. And the same essay which proclaims that "the more we study the will in the way of analysis, the more strictly does it appear to be determined by the infinitely varied conditions of the individual," also declares that men are free and responsible agents in proportion as they feel themselves to be free! Here is the passage:

> In spite of the strongest-motive necessitarian doctrine, we do certainly have a feeling,

amounting to a working belief, that we are free to choose before we have made our choice. We have a sense of difficulty overcome by effort in many acts of choice. We have a feeling in retrospect, amounting to a practical belief, that we could have left undone the things that we have done and that we could have done the things that we ought to have done and did not do, and we accuse or else excuse ourselves accordingly.

Doubtless a logician can reconcile these statements with Holmes' belief that the laws of human nature are generalizations of the fact that every organ obeys its proper stimulus, but the lay mind finds a certain difficulty in the task. (pp. 96-101)

[Holmes's] firm rootage in the traditions of Boston prevented his ever approximating the vagaries of a genius like Strindberg or D. H. Lawrence, but at the same time it limited him. In *The Autocrat* he says that "the fluent, self-determining power of human beings is a very strictly limited agency in the universe," and he defined the chief planes of its limitation as organization, education, and condition. The same thing is true of Holmes in actuality. The logic of his thinking about the limits of responsibility should have led him to endorse nineteenth-century naturalism, but he read the death-bed scene in *Madame Bovary* with horror and charged the naturalists with being obsessed by filth. His explorations of the stream of consciousness should have led him in the direction of the association of ideas as a mode of poetry; his culture kept him within the confines of the late Augustan poetic manner modified by Regency wit. His medical doctrine was essentially democratic, inasmuch as all men are equally imperfect, equally the products of heredity; his social training kept him to an elegant republicanism. He hovered on the edge of philosophical determinism, but his urbanity rebuked his pessimism, and, child of a hopeful era, he thought that God and science would ever move from more to more, so that his most famous serious poem could conclude with a promise of perfect freedom:

> Build thee more stately mansions, O my soul,
>   As the swift seasons roll!
>   Leave thy low-vaulted past!
> Let each new temple, nobler than the last,
>   Shut thee from heaven with a dome more vast,
>   Till thou at length are free,
> Leaving thine outgrown shell by life's unresting sea!

Here is the incorrigible optimism of much American thought, and I think it significant that Holmes, whose biography of Emerson is commonly said to be inadequate because of the lack of sympathetic understanding between Cambridge manners and Concord dreams, comes in fact thus to parallel the poetic epigraph for Emerson's *Nature*:

> A subtle chain of countless rings
> The next unto the farthest brings;
> The eye reads omens where it goes,
> And speaks all languages the rose;
> And, striving to be man, the worm
> Mounts through all the spires of form.

Holmes found Emerson's book a poetic anticipation of evolution—"evolution of the best and elimination of the worst as the law of being," he said. Perhaps the unity of New England thought in the nineteenth century was greater than we had supposed. (pp. 101-02)

Dr. Holmes in front of his Beacon Street house in Boston.

Howard Mumford Jones, "Oliver Wendell Holmes (1809-1894)," in his History and the Contemporary: Essays in Nineteenth-Century Literature, *The University of Wisconsin Press, 1964, pp. 84-102.*

BRIGID BROPHY, MICHAEL LEVEY, AND CHARLES OSBORNE (essay date 1967)

[Brophy, Levey, and Osborne contend that The Autocrat *is wholly underserving of attention.]*

Naturally it was the breakfast table: his facetiousness, his bounce, his sententiousness [in *The Autocrat of the Breakfast Table*] accost you with precisely the effect of funny stories before 9 a.m. Not that Holmes runs much to *stories;* he's incapable of making even blunt points; he meanders, but at the pace of a torrent. In the paragraphs of classical allusion and quotation one might surmise a motive (showing off). Otherwise he seems to talk on and on through sheer wanton aggressiveness. The book might be someone's rough notes for a set of very full footnotes to something, what the something is being unguessable. Only Holmes would have actually supplied such a book with footnotes.

His manner suggests (can it be because he was a doctor?) that he's constantly pressed for time: 'Immense sensation at the table—sudden retirement of the angular female in oxydated

bombazine. Movement of adhesion—as they say in the Chamber of Deputies—on the part of the young fellow they call John . . .' But what is he hurrying *for*? Perhaps to leave himself space for his sentimental passages: 'Ah, but I must not forget that dear little child I saw and heard in a French hospital. Between two and three years old. . . . Lying in bed, patient, gentle. Rough students round her . . . but the child placid, perfectly still. I spoke to her, and the blessed little creature answered me in a voice of such heavenly sweetness, with the reedy thrill in it which you have heard in the thrush's evensong, that I seem to hear it at this moment, while I am writing, so many, many years afterwards.' No wonder Mark Twain used *The Autocrat of the Breakfast Table* as a 'courting-book' and that his wife kept it in a box 'with the love letters'. It might *be* Huck Finn's love-talk.

The Autocrat is in current print as a 'classic', in a paperback series professing to be 'a timeless treasury of the world's great writings'. Since none of Holmes's remarks has point or relevance in the internal context of his book, it is a kindness to apply one of them to his book's situation in a treasury of great writings: 'Literary life is full of curious phenomena. I don't know that there is anything more noticeable than what we may call *conventional reputations*. There is a tacit understanding in every community of men of letters that they will not disturb the popular fallacy respecting this or that electro-gilded celebrity.' It's time to admit the electro-gilt has worn away and there's nothing beneath. (pp. 57-8)

> *Brigid Brophy, Michael Levey, and Charles Osborne, " 'The Autocrat of the Breakfast Table'," in their* Fifty Works of English and American Literature We Could Do Without, *1967. Reprint by Stein and Day Publishers, 1968, pp. 57-8.*

LEWIS LEARY (essay date 1974)

[Leary identifies the characteristics of Holmes's humor.]

Oliver Wendell Holmes probably possessed more minor literary virtues than any writer of his generation. . . . His essays were read and admired by almost every literary compatriot. His novels, now almost forgotten, were filled with good talk and wittily turned character sketches, all strung upon plots only loosely knitted together. For Oliver Wendell Holmes was a miniaturist in literature, better at the small thing, intricately wrought, than on a larger canvas. (p. 117)

[Holmes] flit lightly over surfaces. His laughter was a pleasant protection against the vagaries of mad reformers, misguided clergymen, and poets like Walt Whitman and Edgar Allan Poe, both of whom seemed to most proper Bostonians undisciplined in taste and lacking in judgment. Though Dr. Holmes admired much in Ralph Waldo Emerson, and in some respects echoed in lighter vein some of his more prominent ideas, he did make playful fun of what he called the more "cobwebby" notions of the Transcendentalists. Reformers of any kind were victims, he said, of "inflammation of the conscience." He insisted that

> The ludicrous has its place in the universe; it is not a human invention, but one of the Divine ideas, illustrated in the practical jokes of kittens and monkeys long before Aristophanes and Shakespeare. How curious it is that we always consider solemnity and the absence of all gay surpluses and encounter of wits as essential to the idea of the future life of those whom we

thus deprive of half their faculties and then call
blessed!

(p. 119)

[Much] of Holmes's humor is so topical that, unlike his one-horse shay, it failed even to outlive its century. (p. 120)

In [*The Autocrat of the Breakfast-Table, The Professor at the Breakfast-Table, The Poet at the Breakfast-Table,* and *Over the Teacups*] the genial irascibility of Oliver Wendell Holmes found most effective and most exuberant expression. They were conversation pieces in which people sitting around a table engaged in sprightly good talk. If it tended often to become a monologue in which the Autocrat, the Professor, the Poet, or the aging Dr. Holmes himself monopolized most of the conversation, so much the better. Almost everything he said was worth a chortle or a gasp.

Most of these essays are colored with rambling, quiet humor, often reciting an incident, much as Mark Twain later would, with apparent great seriousness, with the humorous point, what Mark Twain would call the "nub," concealed until just the right moment, so that, when recognized, it would draw, in Holmes's writing, a quiet chuckle from the reader, never a boisterous guffaw. There was little boisterous in Holmes's quiet fun. Like Thoreau, he often approached what he thought to be a truth indirectly. For, he said,

> Every person's feelings have a front-door and a side-door by which they may be entered. The front-door is on the street. Some keep it always open; some keep it latched; some locked; some bolted,—with a chain that will let you peep in, but not get in; and some nail it up, so that nothing can pass its threshold. This front-door leads into a passage which opens into an ante-room and this into the interior apartments. The side-door opens at once into the sacred chambers.

But, he continued, be careful to whom you entrust a key to your side-door:

> If nature or accident has put one of these keys into the hands of a person who has the torturing instinct, I can solemnly pronounce the words that Justice utters over its doomed victim,— *The Lord have mercy on your soul!* . . .

It is easy, that is, to avoid people who approach directly, but those—like poets or humorists—who insinuate themselves and their thoughts indirectly, to make you think or feel, these are the enemy, the torturers.

At other times he is more direct, dwelling on commonplaces of almost everyone's experience.

> Don't you know how hard it is for some people to get out of a room after their visit is over? They want to be off, and you want them off, but they don't know how to manage it. One would think they had been built into your parlor or study, and were waiting to be launched. I have contrived a sort of ceremonial inclined plane for such visitors, which being lubricated with certain smooth phrases, I back them down, metaphorically speaking, stern-foremost into their "native element," the great ocean of out-of-doors.

Then, somewhat deviously, he turns in analogue to the subject of literature, of bad poetry which lingers on as tenaciously as do unwanted guests: "Well, now," he went on,

> there are some poems as hard to get rid of as these rural visitors. They come in glibly, use up all the serviceable rhymes, *say, ray, beauty, duty, eyes, skies, other, brother, mountain, fountain,* and the like; and so they go on until you think that it's time for a wind-up, and the wind-up doesn't come on any terms. So they lie about until you get sick of them, and end by thrusting some cold scrap of a final couplet upon them, and turning them out of doors.

This is quiet Yankee humor, nourished on understatement, innuendo, and gracious prose. It does not translate easily in time or space. Sometimes it was gently, but, oh, so gently, ribald, and when it was Holmes, like the early Mark Twain, was careful to put it into the mouth of someone else, as when he suggested:

> All thought, my friend, the Professor, says, is of the nature of an excretion. . . . A man instinctively tries to get rid of his thought in conversation or in print as soon as it is matured; but it is hard to get at as it lies embedded, a mere potentiality, the germ of a germ, in his intellect.

But a healthy man will get rid of his thoughts, not only to avoid intellectual indigestion, but in self-protection and as a service to his fellow men. "Every real thought," he reminded his readers at another time, "knocks the wind out of somebody."

And knock the wind out of people Holmes did, but genially with quietly familiar entrance through the side-door as a welcome friend whose scolding was as well-meaning as well-phrased. People in New England still occasionally chuckle over the sometimes innocuously naughty strictures of these essays. (pp. 121-23)

Holmes [kept] youthful and laughing and gay to the end. His humor was in many respects different from that of his contemporaries. It derived more from the jovial spirit of the coffee houses in Augustan England, or of convivial, aristocratic clubmen of any time, or from the epigrammatic wit of Horace at his frolicsome best than from the boisterous American frontier. It played more often on words than on vulgar risibilities. It was often bookishly intellectual. Though genial, it was perhaps at root snobbish, well-dressed, well-mannered, excellently contrived to delight a cultivated mind. (p. 127)

He preferred to toy with ideas and to toy with words, teasing them to more expressive meaning. Though himself an irredeemable punster, he pretended great distaste for the pun; people who pun should be punished. "Let me lay down the law on the subject," he said. "Life and language are alike sacred. Homicide and *verbicide*—that is, violent treatment of a word with fatal results to its legitimate meaning, which is its life— are alike forbidden." And then he proceeded in his argument, he who disliked argument, with one of the most telling and outrageous puns of all: Manslaughter, he explained is what homicide is about; man's laughter (which is spelled exactly the same) is the end of verbicide. He pretended dislike of people who might ask whether the deluge through which Noah is said to have piloted his Ark—whether this *deluge* was not a *deal*

146

huger than any other flood. "People who make puns," he said, "are like wanton boys who put coppers on the railroad tracks. They amuse themselves and other children, but their little trick may upset a freight train of conversation for the sake of a battered witticism."

Yet it may be that Oliver Wendell Holmes's epigrammatic witticisms, so like those of Benjamin Franklin's "Poor Richard," will most surely survive. "Sin," he explained, "has many tools, but a lie is the handle that fits them all." Or again: "Habit is a labor saving device which enables man to get along with less fuel." He was sure that "We are all tattooed in our cradles with the beliefs of our tribes," that "We are all sentenced to capital punishment for the crime of living." With age, he rejoiced that "To be seventy years young is sometimes more cheerful and hopeful than to be forty years old." He was sure that "stupidity often saves a man from going mad," and that "The young man knows the rules, but the old man knows the exceptions."

As a physician, he observed that "Among the gentlemen that I have known, few, if any, are ruined by drinking. My few drunken acquaintances were generally ruined before they became drunkards. The habit of drinking is often a vice, no doubt, sometimes a misfortune, . . . but oftenest a punishment." As a man whose writings were greatly admired, but most often only by a small coterie of like-minded friends, he could muse on "How small a matter literature is to the great, seething, toiling, struggling, love-making, bread-winning, child-rearing, death-waiting men and women who fill this huge, palpitating world of ours." As a lecturer who livened his own talk with sprightly and entertaining learning, he could nonetheless assert that "All lecturers, all professors, all schoolmasters, have ruts and grooves in their minds into which their conversation is always sliding."

Unlike his Boston friend James Russell Lowell who sometimes frolicked in good, robust, common vernacular, and unlike Mark Twain and the Southwestern humorists, Dr. Holmes's drolleries were most often most effectively dressed in sophisticated, learned, polite, even "literary" language. But he could accommodate himself when he had to, as he did in talking about "the wonderful one-hoss shay," to the language of the people. (pp. 127-29)

So light and bright and good-natured was his humor that he made no enemies. His wit more often traveled delightfully over surfaces than penetrated to depths. His pinwheel mind darted exuberantly, hovering over serious thought as if afraid to alight. It was a native trait perhaps, the kind of comic coloration often taken on in self-defense, the rapier wit which pierces quickly to put an adversary off guard. He is closer to Washington Irving, whom he admired, than to Mark Twain, who puzzled and troubled him. But, if not in the main channel of American humor, Oliver Wendell Holmes at least bubbles brightly through tributary streams which continue occasionally to refresh. He would, I think, have liked it that way. (p. 130)

> *Lewis Leary, "Oliver Wendell Holmes," in* The Comic Imagination in American Literature, *edited by Louis D. Rubin, Jr., Voice of America, 1974, pp. 117-30.*

MARGARET HALLISSY (essay date 1985)

[*Hallissy analyzes* Elsie Venner *within the context of the serpent woman, or lamia, myth in literature.*]

Dr. Holmes in 1892.

"Women are for the most part poisonous creatures," wrote Arnaldus of Villanova, a medical writer of the Middle Ages. Although seldom expressed so blatantly, this attitude has an impressive pedigree in Scripture, folklore, and literature. In mythology, the serpent-woman Lamia is the other woman in the stormy marriage of Hera and Zeus. Hera's revenge is to deform Lamia so that Lamia has the face and breasts of a woman and the body of a snake. In retaliation Lamia preys on other women's children and also on young men, whom she lures to her lair and eats. In iconography, the serpent of Eden was often depicted as having a woman's head, and the sin committed there as a sexual sin, to emphasize Eve's and her daughters' seductiveness. The logical culmination of the identification of sin, snakes and women is the serpentine woman, whose venomous flesh kills physically or spiritually. The serpent with a woman's face becomes the serpentine woman.

In folklore and in later literature, the lamia retains her status as a supernatural being. She operates through fascination and witchcraft. As her story comes down through the centuries, variations are made, some of them sympathetic. A major development in the lamia tradition is that it provoked a most distinguished group of nineteenth-century writers on both sides of the Atlantic—John Keats, Nathaniel Hawthorne, and Oliver Wendell Holmes—to explore the problem of good and evil as it manifests itself in human sexuality. For these three writers, the lamia story crystallizes the problem of reconciling the ancient dichotomies which her dual nature represents: passion and reason, individual and society. They use the story as an exploration of the paradoxes and ambiguities surrounding the love of the hero for the lamia. In these writers, and for the heroes of their stories, the simple equation between women and sin is insufficient; the hero must examine himself as well. Most difficult, he must come to terms with his own sexuality as well as hers. This involves ignoring the warnings of older mentors who advise him to avoid the risk she represents. While Keats's *Lamia* and Hawthorne's "Rappaccini's Daughter" have been thoroughly analyzed, Oliver Wendell Holmes's novel *Elsie Venner* has been neglected. This novel deserves a new reading, for not only is it an important contribution to the lamia tradition in literature, but it is also significant for the study of the portrayal of women in literature. Holmes clearly wanted Elsie to be considered in relationship to the lamia tradition; but he also develops her character with enough ambiguity so that by the novel's end the reader is forced to doubt the applicability of the tradition to Elsie. The serpent-woman metaphor is imposed on Elsie by the other characters as a punishment for being too unusual in general, and too sensual in particular.

The lamia story echoes folk motifs such as the animal paramour, as in the tale of Beauty and the Beast; she is kin to mermaids, *striges* or witches, and vampires; Hecate is her mythological, and Eve her theological, mother. Because she metamorphoses, she embodies male fears of women's changeability. (pp. 406-07)

The lamia's unpleasant traits make her a poor marriage risk. A man has to be careful that the woman he is marrying is not a lamia in disguise. Such a marriage usually involves a pact in which the husband promises not to take certain steps which would uncover her true identity. When the lamia is truly known, she vanishes, and with her whatever goods she has brought to her marriage. In the more specific folk tale variants, the plot structure is strikingly similar to that found in Holmes's novel. A young man visiting the country meets a beautiful girl. She appears to be virtuous and to come from a respectable background. He falls in love with her. But alas! she is a snake-woman. An older man with special powers discovers this. The plot outcome is that "the youth becomes or remains a disciple of his deliverer, and presumably stays away thenceforth from sexual pleasures." The lamia, even if she harms no one, is always punished, as if to suppress thoroughly the evil which she represents.

In folk versions, then, the lamia story is unambiguously misogynistic. But in the literary development of the lamia story a change occurs "when the lamia began to be regarded as a symbol not of lust, but of love." The effect is a more positive portrayal of the lamia, and this change influences Holmes. His adventurousness in exploring female sexuality is all the more remarkable in view of what has been called the then-current cult of "passionlessness," glorifying the appearance of asexuality in women. Through downplaying her sexuality and emphasizing her spirituality, by deception if necessary, the typical woman could "assert control in the sexual arena," call the sexual shots and get a better husband besides. The obviously passionate woman—the phallic serpent woman—was a particularly difficult problem. If it was better to marry than to burn, one should marry a passionless woman to control the burning, not the very symbol of lust, the lamia. But when the hero fails to give himself totally to the lamia, he is seen in the context of the fiction as a failure.

Keats's poem, written in 1819, began the nineteenth-century modification of the interrelated themes of sin, snakes, and sex. Later in the century, first Hawthorne . . . , then Holmes . . . ,

published venemous-woman stories. Both Holmes and Hawthorne are linked in a relationship of mutual influence with Melville, who, in *The Confidence-Man* . . . , explores the question of the moral responsibility of the serpent. While "clinking the social glass," the cosmopolitan and the stranger discuss the coexistence of beauty and evil in creatures, particularly the serpent. They agree that the serpent, being beautiful, is not evil, indeed has a " 'latent benignity.' " (pp. 407-08)

In thinking about this dilemma in connection with *Elsie Venner,* Holmes may well have drawn a comparison between Melville's snake and his own snake-woman. How can a being be beautiful, yet evil? The question defies a simple answer. If one could have compassion for that maligned being, greater comprehension would result, but not from the action of reason. It is as impossible for a man to be a woman as for a man to be a snake, and hardly more desirable from the man's viewpoint, since to be a woman would mean bearing the weight of the intellectual constructs describing femaleness, and consequently enduring isolation, loneliness, and misery. Like the rattle of the serpent or the label of the poison, the voices of religion and culture warn men that women are dangerous. So, if a woman leads a man into ruin, it is no more than he deserves: " 'He should have respected the label.' " And yet if the bitten snake charmer is worth pity, so is the man who risks compassion. To be dispassionate, reasonable and methodological is to risk loss of the experience which can only be achieved when the judgment is suspended. This is risky; but the cautious life is ignoble. The accountability of the woman for the evil she seems to represent is for a higher court to judge.

Holmes's *Elsie Venner* explores this mystery in his story of an envenomed woman and the young man she loves. The old wives' tale of prenatal influences was still taken seriously in Holmes's day, and discussed at medical meetings and in medical journals. So Holmes, himself a physician, could with some scientific respectability describe his Elsie as having been envenomed *in utero,* because her mother was bitten by a serpent, from which wound the mother dies after Elsie's birth. This influence leaves Elsie with serpentine characteristics and moods: she could "lie . . . basking for whole hours in the sunshine"; her strength waxes and wanes with "the juices of all the poison-plants and the blood of all the creatures that feed upon them" . . . ; she even dresses in serpentine patterns and wears jewelry that resembles the rings on snakes' skin. A necklace, which she wears always, is believed to conceal telltale markings.

The legend of the poisoned maiden is ancient. It dates back at least to the pseudo-Aristotelian work *Secreta Secretorum,* and is connected with Alexander the Great in most versions. According to the legend, a beautiful girl had been " 'fed upon poison from infancy, until she was of the nature of a snake.' " After proving her mettle by poisoning many lovers, she was called upon by the enemies of Alexander as an assassination weapon, the plan being that she should seduce him and poison him too. In varying accounts, certainly her embrace, but even her breath, saliva and perspiration were deadly poisons. The author of the *Secreta Secretorum* claims to have discovered her true nature " 'by tests' " and thus saved Alexander.

Combining esoteric pseudoscience with simple misogyny, this story captured the imagination of writers on poison for hundreds of years. Any reader on the subject of poison will find repeated debates on the possibility of being envenomed through physical contact with another person; in such cases the victim is always male and perpetrator female. Since the way to "truth" in medical writing was for centuries deduction from the principles laid down by the great authorities, or by deducing from other treatises deducing from them, once this story got into the medical lore it took a long time for it to get out. Medical writers convey the same information for centuries, unscathed by experimentation.

With Andrea Bacci's treatise *De venenis et antidotis* (Rome, 1586), a new angle of reasoning is added to the story: "He denies that the maiden fed on poison would have poisoned Alexander the Great, had he lain with her, because what she ate would have been transformed into nutrition." It is this crucial change, the idea of transformation by incorporation into the self, which affects the depiction of the venomous woman in Holmes. In *Elsie Venner,* it is the protagonist Bernard Langdon's misfortune that the physician whom he consults for advice on Elsie seems not to know this newer theory. Elsie Venner, venomous though she is, may be nourishment as well. The serpent woman may be morally superior to the people around her who are defined as normal; more importantly, she offers Bernard a chance to participate in that superiority.

In fact, in *Elsie Venner* the townspeople surrounding Elsie, by whom and in relation to whom she is judged, are relentlessly normal. Rockland is populated by a sensitive but overworked schoolmarm, a pious and dedicated black servant woman, an equally dedicated but somewhat uppity Yankee manservant, socially ambitious bourgeoises, Brahmin gentry, wise, concerned and learned authority figures (fathers, professors, doctors, and clergymen), and even a black sheep of the family. To this hypertypical town comes Bernard Langdon, a young medical student interrupting his education because of his family's diminished fortunes. He is an excellent student and shows promise as a teacher as well, according to his medical school professor, who is the narrator of the novel. All the events of the novel are seen through the consciousness of this professor, who also serves as advisor to Bernard.

In the typical lamia story, as we have seen, the young man needs a mentor; but it becomes increasingly clear that Bernard has allowed his professor to guide him too much. To depend on a former teacher is no unusual phenomenon; but at some point this dependence can become harmful, as even the best-intentioned advisor has his own inadequacies. But Bernard is not yet at the point of maturity necessary to realize this. He needs his old teacher, and so the question is, what kind of man is this professor?

The answer: smug, self-assured, and opinionated, like many an academic before and since. He has no name; he is always "the professor"—a typical example of his calling. His bias is rationalistic, his stance detached. He judges from afar, and has no qualms about issuing authoritative opinions about any subject. Unlike Dr. Kittredge, a practitioner whose sympathies are exercised by daily patient contact, the narrator is an ivory-tower theoretician who judges people according to ideas found in books. As a medical student and physician himself, Holmes must have known both types.

Teachers who influence the lives of their students beyond the classroom typically have nothing material to gain from the interaction, but enjoy the psychological power, and this is the case with the relationship in the novel. Each intrusion into the life of Bernard Langdon is motivated by sincere concern. The professor has high hopes that, after "ten brilliant years of spirited, unflagging labor" . . . Bernard can stand at the top of his profession. Therefore Bernard must be cautioned to avoid "love and all that nonsense" . . . , and, when the time arrives,

to marry with an eye to professional and social advancement. This common-sense life plan, coming as it does from a seemingly wise and unselfish source, impresses the young man. Bernard does not see that the plan leaves no room for the fortuitous accident of falling in love.

Another bias which the professor passes along to Bernard is again endemic to his calling: the intellectual tradition of rationalism. For one thing, the professor assumes all problems can be solved if one keeps a cool head, and he reinforces a tendency to emotional detachment in the chilly Bernard. For another thing, the professor is an adherent of an elaborate theory of human responsibility, which he communicates to Bernard at a crucial point in Bernard's relationship with Elsie. Like the docile student who would naturally be a favorite of a professor like this, Bernard accepts his mentor's ideas.

Elsie then is set in contrast both with the ordinariness of the town and the rationality of the professor's theories. Her and Bernard's first meetings occur in situations which stress Elsie's nonconformity. They first meet as teacher and student at the Apollinean Female Institute, where young ladies are brought into conformity with the rules of reason. Then they meet again at a party given by the socially-aspiring Sprowles as a showcase for their marriageable Matilda. In each group, fellow students and fellow eligibles, Elsie differs from the ordinary girls of Rockland. To the basic situation, then, young male teacher and nubile female student, alluring enough in itself, is added Elsie's too-drastic difference from the other girls: she is extremely attractive, and she is venomous.

Who is Elsie, what is she? "By what demon is she haunted, by what taint is she blighted, by what curse is she followed, by what destiny is she marked, that her strange beauty has such a terror in it, and that hardly one shall dare to love her, and her eye glitters always, but warms for none?" . . . Over the peaceful little town hovers the shadow of Rattlesnake Ledge, where snakes breed. Into the careful, rational life of Bernard Langdon comes Elsie Venner, challenging every presupposition. She is dangerous. From early childhood her envenoming was threatening: as soon as Elsie cuts teeth, her wet-nurse sickens and dies; as a child, she bit her cousin Dick Venner so that he retains the scars as an adult; at fifteen, she rids herself of an objectionable governess by inducing in her a mysterious illness. Throughout her life she is perceived as so intractable that Dr. Kittredge advises her father to let her have her way. She wanders off, an odd behavior for a girl anyway, but made odder still by her preferred destination: trees, caves, Rattlesnake Ledge. (pp. 409-12)

In the fictional present, she is seventeen. The problem child has become an even more problematic young woman. What is to be done with a female like Elsie at sexual maturity? She cannot just be married off like any young girl. She is a maze of contradictions. Snake-like, she is cold: the light in her eyes is like the "lustre of ice" . . . , her expression is that of "remoteness, of utter isolation." . . . Yet she is also passionate: her mother was a Spaniard, and this influence (perceived by the xenophobic narrator as venomous in itself) makes for wild blood. Dancing to Spanish music, she whips herself into a frenzy, "undulating with flexuous grace." . . . Clearly she is nothing at all like the other girls.

The good citizens of Rockland chorus their disapproval of Elsie. She is possessed of "ungovernable anger" and "an irritable state of mind and body." . . . Clearly the sexual maturation of such a woman presents a problem. As her father,

Dudley Venner, puts it, "'Who would *dare* to marry Elsie?'" . . . (pp. 412-13)

There are two candidates for that honor, Bernard and also Dick Venner, Elsie's cousin. The conflict between the two (a new element in the lamia story) further adumbrates the reason/passion conflict. As we have seen, Bernard represents the intellectual achievements made possible by taming the passions. As a class, the Brahmins have been remarkably successful in producing intellectuals, but not without paying a price. The trade-off has been a loss of the vigor of the "animal nature," a decrease in "vital energy" . . . ; the Brahmins are slender, pallid, smooth-faced, delicate of feature. In short, they are cerebral and asexual. In contrast, his rival, Elsie's cousin Dick Venner, is, like Elsie herself, a "'half-breed'" . . . , with "Southern impulses in [his] wild blood," . . . which conflict with and overpower the "cunning and calculating" rationality of his "New-England side." . . . He is given to such symbolic gestures as riding his "half-tamed horse" when the "savage passion of his young blood came over him." . . . He is a bit of an outlaw; he has a dark past; and, because he is Elsie's cousin, there is a subdued incest motif. Dick Venner would seem to be a proper mate for Elsie, but she does not love him. Nor does he love her; although he is attracted to her, stronger still is the lure of her father's money. He is blood, Bernard brain, and Elsie seems attracted to what she lacks. So Dick Venner can be eliminated fairly early in the novel, to leave Bernard as the only candidate for Elsie's venomous hand.

Bernard is simultaneously attracted to and repelled by the danger Elsie represents. (p. 413)

Yet he is too much the intellectual simply to respond to Elsie naturally. He must perforce cerebralize her. Ever the attentive student, he sees her as an interesting case. He muses on the concept of fascination as a manifestation of man's affinity for the serpent, his inherited tendency to evil, the "fruit of the curse" . . . , original sin. He is able to test this theory when, himself fascinated by a snake on Rattlesnake Ledge, the spell is broken by Elsie's superior power. His medical/theological speculations are furthered when, one morning, a "dark, gypsy-looking woman" brings him a *crotalus,* a breed of snake living in the neighborhood, a creature which he desires to investigate. Alarmed, Bernard warns her of their deadliness, but the gypsy-looking woman reassures him of her immunity: "'rattlers never touches our folks.'" Bernard has never heard of the "possession of a power by certain persons, which enables them to handle these frightful reptiles with perfect impunity." . . . However, he should have. In the New Testament the followers of Christ are given the power to handle serpents and drink poison with impunity, and this is a sign of goodness. Does this mean that if he were good enough, Elsie would not be venomous for him, would perhaps even be beneficial? Rather than apply the implied moral lesson to himself, Bernard muses on the general topic of serpents and evil.

Again, the subject debated by Melville's stranger and the cosmopolitan [in *The Confidence Man*] returns: is the serpent, symbol of evil, itself evil? Bernard cannot take the question further, but, although he never knows it, Elsie has. Mr. Fairweather, the minister, recalls an incident from Elsie's childhood. He had sent a religious book to Elsie for her edification. From the book she tore out and kept the frontispiece—a picture of Eve's temptation—and threw the rest of the book out the window. For Elsie, Eve is the only important figure in religion. She said that "Eve was a good woman—and she'd have done just so if she'd been there." Mr. Fairweather sees this as

evidence of her "natural obliquity" and in fact the "'congenital sinfulness of human nature.'" . . . But Elsie's instinctive identification with Eve can also be seen as a rejection of the concept of sinfulness imposed on Eve. Eve sinned because the serpent deceived her. If she was deceived, then she is victim, not perpetrator. Like Eve, Elsie has been singled out to be a symbol, to represent a theory.

In fact, everyone around Bernard is devising theories—medical, philosophical, theological. Her own father, Dudley Venner, sees her as a victim of hysteria: Elsie is deadly because she is a woman. The long-suffering schoolmarm Helen Darley blames "'the force of transmitted tendencies.'" . . . Rev. Dr. Honeywood cites a "visitation of God" which "impairs the intellectual or the moral perceptions" but renders the person thus afflicted exempt from "common working standards of right and wrong." . . . All agree that Elsie's problem is not her fault; but none agree on what should be done about the fact that Elsie cannot marry. As Old Sophy tells Dr. Kittredge, Elsie's husband would die. Confused, Bernard consults his old professor.

The questions he asks of his medical/philosophical advisor bear on the health of body and soul. First, he wants to know if envenoming is physically possible; then, if it is, he wants to know whether a person thus envenomed is morally dangerous as well. He writes: "Is there any evidence that human beings can be wrought upon by poisons, or otherwise, so that they shall manifest any of the peculiarities belonging to beings of a lower nature?" . . . The professor replies at great length and with many citations from academic authorities. And along comes, here in the nineteenth century in America, the hoary story of Alexander the Great and his poisoned lady, cited "upon pretty good authority" . . . as medical evidence by a medical school professor. . . . The professor goes on, citing more recent stories, including the "malignant witch-woman" in Coleridge's *Christabel* and the "serpent transformed" in Keats's *Lamia.* . . . (pp. 414-15)

Bernard has also brought up the related question about the serpent-women raised by Melville in reference to the actual serpent: is the venomous being responsible for its own venomousness? Can people in this condition be "as free from moral responsibility as the instincts of the lower animals? Do you think there may be a *crime* which is not a *sin?*" . . . The professor replies with a discourse on the "limitations of human responsibility." . . . Some people are less responsible for their actions because of predisposing conditions, heredity being one, reflex or involuntary action another, and both applying to Elsie. The "moral insanity" defense in criminal trials, an innovation in Holmes's day, is based on the postulate that there exist people who are not morally responsible for their legal crimes. Holmes defended the theory of unconscious and mechanical mental action which limits human will, a theory he summarized in his Phi Beta Kappa address, *Mechanism in Thought and Morals.* The theory is obviously an early version of our "not guilty by reason of insanity" plea, and like that plea, it is not likely to inspire confidence in the person so absolved. In practice, according to the professor, the distinction between sin and crime is irrelevant: "*Treat bad men exactly as if they were insane.* They are *in-sane,* out of health, morally. Reason, which is food to sound minds, is not tolerated, still less assimilated . . . ." Although the professor does not know he is advising on Elsie, his message is to avoid the dangerous being.

Bernard Langdon is thus influenced by many theories—theological, medical, philosophical, psychological. Elsie is Eve, the channel through whom primordial guilt is transmitted. She is Circe, the enchantress whose sexual potency can distract a man from the goal of his life-journey. She is amorality, irresponsibility, madness. All these ideas stand between Elsie Venner and Bernard Langdon. The only character in the novel who can respond to Elsie without the barrier of ideas is the simple servant, Old Sophy. In fact, *Elsie Venner* is unusual as a lamia story in that there is a woman character to respond to Elsie. Usually the lamia is alone, a woman in a man's world, seen through men's perceptions. Here Old Sophy is the only person unjudgmentally sympathetic. Being black, female, nurturing, and instinctual, in a white, male and intellectually judgmental world, Sophy's influence is weak. What self-respecting young man would think of going to such a person for advice? Instead he follows the voices of reason, and it is their influence which determines his fateful reaction at the novel's climax.

Elsie, distressed, approaches Bernard. He is sympathetic but distant. "'Tell me what I can do to render your life happier,'" he asks. Elsie replies, "'*Love me!*'" This is the one thing she needs, and the one thing he cannot give her. He offers the handshake of friendship, a tepid substitute for the embrace of love. To Bernard the coldness seems to emanate from Elsie's hand: "a cold *aura* shot from it along his arm and chilled the blood running through his heart." . . . But the cold really emanates from Bernard's passionless nature—his attribution of it to Elsie is a classic case of projection. He has previously told Dr. Kittredge that he does not love Elsie; if he helps her, it would be "'in cold blood.'" . . . This stance of professional detachment is the reason that, after this crucial encounter, "it was all over with poor Elsie." . . . Deprived of the warmth of love which would have kept her alive, she sickens. The explicit offer of her virginity—"'*Love me!*'"—and Bernard's rejection of it are expressed in the imagery of flowers so often connected in literature with the young maiden. Earlier in the novel Elsie puts a flower in Bernard's copy of the *Aeneid,* at the point of the story which describes Dido's suicide after Aeneas's betrayal, to remind Bernard of the consequences of refusing passionate love. In her final illness Bernard places a sprig of white ash in a basket of flowers sent to her by her fellow students, as if giving the offer of her maidenhood back to her. Its purple leaves, an antidote to others, are poison to her. Chastity is no healthful remedy to Elsie. Bernard's prescription for her, and the flower which represents it, kills her.

So it is clear that the serpent in Elsie is her sexuality. Dr. Kittredge points out that serpents have shorter life spans than humans, and perhaps the human in Elsie can outlive the serpent. Dudley Venner regards the prenatal influence as a "blight." His hope had been that "the lower nature which had become engrafted on the higher would die out and leave the real woman's life she inherited to outlive this accidental principle which had so poisoned her childhood and youth." . . . These ideas have a dual significance. If she can be gotten safely through her peak sexual years, she will eventually become less powerful and consequently less threatening. But this is a counsel of despair. On the other hand, her sexuality might also be regarded less negatively and stripped of its association with evil. For this to happen, she needs a man who is not only emotionally responsive but also brave. Even on Elsie's deathbed, he looks at her "with almost scientific closeness of observation." . . . The lover's gaze, so crucial to the love tradition in literature, is here perverted by the spirit of dispassionate science. "Needing a Heathcliff, she has found only a proper Bostonian." He is too cold and cerebral to bring Elsie to sexual maturity.

At the funeral, before closing Elsie's coffin, Sophy takes off the gold cord Elsie had always worn around her neck. Everyone, even Sophy, thought that Elsie wore this cord to conceal serpentine marks. But "there was no shade nor blemish where the ring of gold had encircled her throat." Sophy attributes this to a miracle—the Lord taking away the mark of evil so Elsie would be fit to join the "'holy angels.'" . . . But this event at the novel's conclusion leaves a drastic ambiguity. Was Elsie really envenomed, or was she merely unusual?

Elsie's life violates several sacred norms. An undercurrent in the novel is the "idealised view of the daughter." Elsie is the only child of a widowed father. The nineteenth-century unmarried woman in her father's house has a special set of responsibilities, summarized in the telling phrase "Angel in the House." She is often raised in the image and likeness of her father, to be a companion to him in all ways save sexual. She is supposed to be a gentle, cheerful, smiling "'sunbeam,'" who can "adorn the household" with "ladylike accomplishments," provide "rest and amusement," attention, affection, and understanding for her father. She should be in no way independent; a "strong-minded girl" who is "'self-willed and arrogant, eccentric in dress and disagreeable in manner'" is a blight on her father's household. Even in the crucial process of achieving maturity by moving out of her father's house into another man's house, she is supposed to give no trouble. But Elsie Venner is a source of lifelong pain and suffering to her father. As a daughter, she is a disaster.

In an ordinary town, too, Elsie's beauty and sensuality are aberrant. Early in the novel, the narrator muses on beauty. While "in the abstract we all love beauty," to be beautiful also "carries an atmosphere of repulsion." Many people are "too poor, too ordinary, too humble, too busy, too proud" . . . to pay the price for loving an unusually beautiful person. Most people are, like Bernard, ordinary, and avoid the extraordinary. In the novel, Elsie is regarded as extraordinary by all, but she is seldom depicted as doing anything very unusual. There is little objective correlative to the fictional judgments. This could be a flaw in the narrative technique, but it could also reflect the fact that everything the narrator knows about her is filtered through the perceptions of conventional people.

These ordinary people live happily and bloodlessly ever after: Bernard finishes medical school, sets up a successful practice, and marries a "safe little lass." Even Dudley Venner remarries, allying himself with the soothing schoolmarm Helen Darley. For Elsie, who loved someone not up to the challenge of loving her, the eulogy is spoken by Dr. Honeywood: "From the life and the death of this our dear sister we should learn a lesson of patience with our fellow-creatures in their inborn peculiarities, of charity in judging what seems to us wilful faults of character. . . ." Judge not, lest you be judged; approach your fellow creatures with charity, all the more needed when dealing with the unusual person. Because the evidence of Elsie's venomousness is inconclusive, venom becomes, in addition to a symbol of female sexuality, also a symbol of divergence from socially imposed norms.

And so she may not marry. The unusual woman cannot reproduce herself without a courageous male to accept her in all her fearful complexity. For Bernard to respond to Elsie, he would have to ignore the voices of his upbringing which encourage him to quell the stirrings of passion and take the safe and intelligent path through life. Retreating from the challenge, Bernard never completes the psychic work of confronting his own sexual nature. Back in medical school, he reads a paper

significantly titled "Unresolved Nebulae in Vital Science."
. . . He has learned nothing from his unresolved relationship
with Elsie. For him, there will always be areas of darkness in
his understanding of life, because he approaches life as a science.

His marriage follows the chastity prescription, taming once
and for all the dangerous emotions connected with Elsie. But
when one marries so as not to burn, much is lost. In Bernard,
all passion is buried. His dead sexuality is like the "terrible
Rattlesnake Ledge" itself, which, after the earthquake, "with
all its envenomed reptiles, its dark fissures and black caverns,
was buried forever beneath a mighty incumbent mass of ruin."
. . . Lost forever too is Bernard's opportunity to be extraordinary, like Elsie. (pp. 415-18)

> *Margaret Hallissy, "Poisonous Creature: Holmes's
> 'Elsie Venner',"* in Studies in the Novel, *Vol. XVII,
> No. 4, Winter, 1985, pp. 406-19.*

ADDITIONAL BIBLIOGRAPHY

Brenner, Rica. "Oliver Wendell Holmes." In her *Twelve American
Poets before 1900*, pp. 169-98. New York: Harcourt, Brace and Co.,
1933.
  Assesses Holmes's literary career and claims that his works help
  to illuminate his life.

Brooks, Van Wyck. "Dr. Holmes." In his *The Flowering of New
England, 1815-1865*, pp. 478-98. New York: E. P. Dutton & Co.,
1936.
  A biographical sketch.

———. "Dr. Holmes's Boston." In his *New England: Indian Summer, 1865-1915*, pp. 1-22. New York: E. P. Dutton & Co., 1940.
  A view of Boston culture during Holmes's lifetime.

Clark, Harry Hayden. "Dr. Holmes: A Re-Interpretation." *The New
England Quarterly* XII, No. 1 (March 1939): 19-34.
  Examines Holmes's literary, social, and political views and states
  that, though they were conservative, they were "offset" by his
  radical religious and philosophical ideas.

Currier, Thomas Franklin. *A Bibliography of Oliver Wendell Holmes*.
Edited by Eleanor M. Tilton. New York: New York University Press,
1953, 707 p.
  An extensive bibliography of writings about Holmes that includes
  citations from English and foreign-language studies.

Doubleday, Neal Frank. "Dr. Holmes and the Faith in the Future."
College English 4, No. 5 (February 1943): 281-88.
  An analysis of Holmes's religious attitudes, which Doubleday
  terms "remarkably characteristic of the American mind."

Emerson, Edward Waldo. "Oliver Wendell Holmes." In his *The Early
Years of the Saturday Club, 1855-1870*, pp. 145-58. Boston: Houghton
Mifflin Co., 1918.
  A discussion of Holmes and his associates in the Saturday Club.

Fields, Annie. "Oliver Wendell Holmes: Personal Recollections and
Unpublished Letters." In her *Authors and Friends*, pp. 107-55. 1897.
Reprint. Grosse Pointe, Mich.: Scholarly Press, 1969.
  A friend's memories of Holmes.

Fuller, Harold de Wolf. "Holmes." In *American Writers on American
Literature*, edited by John Macy, pp. 153-63. New York: Horace
Liveright, 1931.
  A sketch of Holmes's life and work. Fuller contends that science
  and poetry were the strongest influences in the author's life.

Garner, Stanton. "*Elsie Venner*: Holmes's Deadly 'Book of Life'."
Huntington Library Quarterly XXXVII, No. 3 (May 1974): 283-98.
  Uses *Elsie Venner* as a paradigm for a discussion of Holmes's
  criticism of the intellectual and Brahmin society of nineteenth-
  century New England.

Grattan, C. Hartley. "Oliver Wendell Holmes." *The American Mercury* IV, No. 13 (January 1925): 37-41.
  Proposes reducing Holmes's literary fame to a "footnote," contending that most of his poetry is "dusty" and his prose work
  barren.

Hayakawa, Samuel I. "Holmes's Lowell Institute Lectures." *American Literature* 8, No. 3 (November 1936): 281-90.
  Contains brief discussions of each of the twelve lectures on English
  poets that Holmes delivered in 1853.

Howe, M. A. DeWolfe. *Holmes of the Breakfast-Table*. London: Oxford University Press, 1939, 172 p.
  An illustrated biography. Howe also traces the creation and reception of Holmes's literary works.

Howells, William Dean. "Oliver Wendell Holmes." *Harper's Magazine* XCIV, No. DLIX (December 1896): 120-34.
  An intimate recollection of Howells's personal and professional
  association with Holmes.

Hoyt, Edwin P. *The Improper Bostonian: Dr. Oliver Wendell Holmes*.
New York: William Morrow and Co., 1979, 319 p.
  A detailed, anecdotal, and fully illustrated biography of Holmes.

Kern, Alexander C. "Dr. Oliver Wendell Holmes Today." *The University of Kansas City Review* XIV, No. 3 (Spring 1948): 191-99.
  A survey that assesses the value of Holmes's literary works and
  posits some reasons for the decline in his reputation.

Knickerbocker, William S. "His Own Boswell: A Note on the Poetry
of Oliver Wendell Holmes." *The Sewanee Review* XLI, No. 1 (January-March 1933): 454-66.
  An examination of Holmes's poetry.

Kreymborg, Alfred. "Dr. Holmes and the New England Decline." In
his *Our Singing Strength: An Outline of American Poetry (1620-1930)*,
pp. 134-50. New York: Coward-McCann, 1929.
  Claims that Holmes's "wittiest warfare" was directed against
  Calvinism and adds that the author was an intellectual whose
  poetical style was reminiscent of the eighteenth century.

[Ludlow, J. M.]. "*Elsie Venner* and *Silas Marner*: A Few Words on
Two Noteworthy Novels." *Macmillan's Magazine* IV, No. 22 (August
1861): 305-09.
  A comparison that finds George Eliot's novel a study in ethics,
  and Holmes's a study of physiology.

Martin, John Stephen. "The Novels of Oliver Wendell Holmes: A Re-
Interpretation." In *Literature and Ideas in America: Essays in Memory
of Harry Hayden Clark*, edited by Robert Falk, pp. 111-27. Athens:
Ohio University Press, 1975.
  Contends that Holmes's literary reputation has remained constant
  and interprets the novels as works involved not with psychology
  but with moral issues.

Morse, John T., Jr. *Life and Letters of Oliver Wendell Holmes.*, 2
vols. Boston: Houghton, Mifflin & Co., Riverside Press, 1896.
  A detailed and illustrated biography of Holmes. Morse discusses
  Holmes's careers in medicine and literature and includes excerpts
  from the author's notes and correspondence.

Roditi, Edouard. "Oliver Wendell Holmes as Novelist." *Arizona
Quarterly* 1, No. 4 (Winter 1945): 23-33.
  Argues that Holmes used scientific terminology to give authenticity to his stories. Roditi claims that Holmes's plots are actually
  provincial Victorian romances concerned with morality rather than
  psychology.

Scudder, H. E. "Biographical Sketch." In *The Complete Poetical
Works of Oliver Wendell Holmes*, pp. xi-xxi. Boston: Houghton, Mifflin and Co., Riverside Press, 1895.
  An introduction to Holmes's poetical works that includes biographical material and critical commentary.

Sears, Lorenzo. "Oliver Wendell Holmes." In his *American Literature in the Colonial and National Periods*, pp. 327-37. 1902. Reprint. New York: Burt Franklin, 1970.

> Reviews Holmes's work and his place in American literature, praising the wit of the Breakfast-Table series.

Small, Miriam Rossiter. *Oliver Wendell Holmes*. Twayne's United States Authors Series, edited by Sylvia E. Bowman, no. 29. New York: Twayne Publishers, 1962, 176 p.

> A biography covering all facets of Holmes's life. Small also includes critical discussions of the author's works.

Strong, Augustus Hopkins. "Oliver Wendell Holmes." In his *American Poets and Their Theology*, pp. 319-67. Philadelphia: Griffith and Rowland Press, 1916.

> Argues that Holmes failed to adequately challenge Calvinism because he misunderstood its true nature.

Tilton, Eleanor M. *Amiable Autocrat: A Biography of Dr. Oliver Wendell Holmes*. New York: Henry Schuman, 1947, 470 p.

> A detailed biography that includes critical discussions of Holmes's works.

———. "Introduction." In *The Poetical Works of Oliver Wendell Holmes*, edited by Eleanor M. Tilton, pp. xvii-xxxv. Boston: Houghton Mifflin Co., 1975.

Studies Holmes's use of language, voice, and subject matter in his verse and prose.

Trent, W. P. and Erskine, John. "The New England Poets." In their *Great American Writers*, pp. 134-68. Home University Library of Modern Knowledge, edited by Herbert Fisher and others, no. 48. New York: Henry Holt & Co., 1912.

> An assessment of Holmes as a minor novelist and poet, but an accomplished essayist.

Wendell, Barrett. "Oliver Wendell Holmes." In his *A Literary History of America*, pp. 407-24. New York: Charles Scribner's Sons, 1920.

> A biographical sketch that includes a discussion of the themes of Holmes's works and the occasions for which his poems were written.

Wentersdorf, Karl P. "The Underground Workshop of Oliver Wendell Holmes." *American Literature* XXXV, No. 1 (March 1963): 1-12.

> Calls Holmes a pioneer who deserves recognition for his theories about the role of the unconscious in the creative process.

Wolfe, Don M. "Of Crime and Responsibility: Oliver Wendell Holmes." In his *The Image of Man in America*, pp. 119-28. New York: Thomas Y. Crowell Co., 1970.

> A discussion of Holmes's views on the relationship between heredity, environment, and will as expressed in both his fiction and non-fiction.

Walter Savage Landor

1775-1864

English poet, prose writer, and literary critic.

Landor is considered a master prose stylist and a significant poet of the nineteenth century. Although a contemporary of the Romantic writers, Landor was distinguished from them by his interest in classical themes and forms. Today, he is known primarily for his series entitled *Imaginary Conversations* and numerous elegant epigrams.

Born in Warwick, England, Landor was educated at the Rugby School and Trinity College, Oxford, where he received a classical education and excelled in writing Latin verse. Conflicts with the authorities and other students led to his expulsion from both schools, and Landor's formal education ended when he was nineteen. In 1795, he published his first work, *The Poems of Walter Savage Landor*. But these satiric verses on college personalities found a limited audience, and only thirty-six copies were sold. On his father's death in 1805, Landor inherited a sizable fortune. Intending to establish an estate in Wales, he purchased Llanthony Abbey in Monmouthshire and began extensive renovations. In 1808, he spent three months in Spain as a volunteer in the war against Napoleon, financing a troop himself. Landor married Julia Thuillier in 1811 and resumed work on his estate, but the Landors' years at Llanthony were marked by financial, legal, and marital disputes, and a lawsuit forced them to leave Wales in 1814. After a bitter separation of several months, they reconciled and settled in Florence, Italy, where Landor composed many of his works. They remained in Florence until 1835 when Landor, then sixty, found his marriage unendurable and moved to Bath, leaving most of his income to his wife and children. Living in England once again, Landor enjoyed friendships with Lady Blessington, Charles Dickens, John Forster, and Thomas Carlyle, among other authors and literary figures. Yet not all Landor's relationships in Bath proved so pleasant. In 1858, Landor was charged with libel when he misguidedly championed a young woman whom he believed had been wronged by a minister's wife, Mrs. Yescombe. In retaliation, Landor wrote vulgar and defamatory anonymous letters to the Yescombe household. To avoid the legal penalties and scandal resulting from the affair, Landor returned to Florence, where he unsuccessfully attempted to reconcile with his family. He was destitute, aimlessly roaming the streets of Florence, when Robert and Elizabeth Browning took him in and acted for him in financial matters. Landor spent his last years in Florence and Siena in the company of the Brownings and their American friends. Though his creative powers declined with age, he continued to write and maintain friendships with literary figures until a few months before his death in 1864.

In summarizing his opinion of his own work, Landor once stated, "Poetry was always my amusement, prose my study and work." His major prose writings, contained in the series entitled *Imaginary Conversations,* number over one hundred fifty. In addition, Landor's significant prose works include *The Pentameron and Pentalogia*, fictional dialogues between Boccaccio and Petrarch, *Pericles and Aspasia*, a series of imaginary letters describing life in the golden age of Athens, and *Citation and Examination of William Shakespeare*, an imaginary critical

discussion. In all these works, Landor depicted classical characters and literary and political figures discussing a wide variety of topics. Although Landor's prose style is often praised for its variety, restraint, and finish, his descriptions of characters and their views have frequently evoked negative reactions. Landor often deviated from historical record and accepted traditions, and the opinions expressed by his characters have been faulted as mere projections of his own attitudes toward classical republicanism and ideals of beauty and clarity.

Although Landor considered his poetry an "amusement" and therefore less important than his prose works, his early poem *Gebir,* and the parallel Latin version, *Gebirus,* were serious endeavors. Based on an Oriental myth, both of these elaborate blank verse works reflected Landor's attempt to return to the classical ideals of simplicity and severity of form. The poems, never widely read, have been regarded as insignificant and obscure by many scholars, but individual passages from *Gebir* have been highly valued for their beauty of expression. Landor also attempted to write dramas in poetic form, first in *Count Julian*, a heroic closet drama that drew on his experiences in Spain, and later in his historical trilogy, *Andrea of Hungary, Giovanna of Naples,* and *Fra Rupert*. Critics generally agree that these works merit attention as poetry but fail as drama because they lack unity and plot development. As in *Gebir*, in *The Hellenics of Walter Savage Landor* and *Heroic Idylls, with*

Additional Poems, Landor again displayed his interest in classical and mythological themes. In these collections of poetry, he employed a variety of verse forms in presenting brief, simple tales and dialogues. The shorter poems proved effective vehicles for Landor's talent. Indeed, many critics have remarked that his greatness lies in individual sentences rather than in complete works; they consider Landor a gifted epigrammatist. His Latin and English epigrams are cited as classics of the form, and his frequently anthologized lines addressed to Rose Aylmer and Ianthe are considered definitive examples. The poetic works of Landor's old age, *The Last Fruit off an Old Tree* and *Dry Sticks, Fagoted by W.S.L.,* are generally considered inferior in taste and originality.

Landor neither expected nor received widespread recognition in his lifetime; as he prophesied, "I shall dine late; but the dining room will be well-lighted, the guests few and select." Consciously writing for a limited and discerning audience, Landor shunned popular forms and topics: his Latin compositions, classical concerns, and erudite style have discouraged most readers. But the poet's poet, and the critic's critic, as Forster characterized him, has never failed to generate interest. Among the Romantics, Percy Bysshe Shelley, Charles Lamb, Thomas De Quincey, and Robert Southey praised Landor's work. In addition, Ralph Waldo Emerson, Charles Algernon Swinburne, Robert Browning, and Dickens revered the eccentric poet. While he drew such distinguished admirers, the majority of readers and critics have found his works difficult, unemotional, and uninteresting. This diversity has characterized the history of Landor criticism. In 1878, Leslie Stephen remarked, "Landor is perhaps the most striking instance in modern literature of a radical divergence of opinion between the connoisseurs and the mass of readers." Stephen's evaluation remains valid in the twentieth century: the "few and select," including T. S. Eliot, Ezra Pound, and W. B. Yeats, have respected Landor as a poet, yet his works are not widely read. Recent critics have frequently focused on the reasons for Landor's lack of popularity, though some have studied his qualities as a prose stylist and his classical sources and modes of expression. Ultimately, Landor is remembered as the author of the *Imaginary Conversations* and numerous epigrams, as a classicist in the Romantic and Victorian ages, and as an idiosyncratic, independent figure in English literary history.

PRINCIPAL WORKS

The Poems of Walter Savage Landor (poetry) 1795
Gebir (poetry) 1798
Poetry (poetry) 1802
Gebirus (poetry) 1803
Count Julian (closet drama) 1812
Idyllia Heroica Decem, Librum Phaleuciorum Unum
   (poetry) 1814
Imaginary Conversations of Literary Men and Statesmen,
   first series. 3 vols. (fictional conversations) 1824-28
Imaginary Conversations of Literary Men and Statesmen,
   second series. 2 vols. (fictional conversations) 1829
Citation and Examination of William Shakespeare before Sir
   T. Lucy, Touching Deer-Steeling (fictional
   conversation) 1834
Pericles and Aspasia (fictional letters) 1836
The Pentameron and Pentalogia (fictional conversations)
   1837
Andrea of Hungary. Giovanna of Naples (closet dramas)
   1839

Fra Rupert (closet drama) 1840
The Works of Walter Savage Landor. 2 vols. (fictional
   conversations, poetry, closet dramas, and prose) 1846
The Hellenics of Walter Savage Landor (poetry) 1847
Poemeta et Inscriptiones (poetry) 1847
The Italics of Walter Savage Landor (poetry) 1848
The Last Fruit off an Old Tree (poetry and prose) 1853
Antony and Octavius (closet drama) 1856
Dry Sticks, Fagoted by W.S.L. (poetry and translations)
   1858
Heroic Idylls, with Additional Poems (poetry) 1863
*The Works and Life of Walter Savage Landor. 8 vols.
   (fictional conversations, poetry, prose, fictional letters,
   and criticism) 1876
Letters and Other Unpublished Writings of Walter Savage
   Landor (letters, fictional conversation, fragments, and
   poetry) 1897
Letters of Walter Savage Landor, Private and Public
   (letters) 1899
Complete Works of Walter Savage Landor. 16 vols.
   (fictional conversations, poetry, prose, and letters)
   1927-36

**This work includes *Walter Savage Landor: A Biography,* by John Forster.

WALTER SAVAGE LANDOR   (essay date 1798)

[*In his preface to* Gebir, *from which the following excerpt is taken, Landor briefly discusses the origin and form of his lengthy poem. For additional commentary by Landor, see excerpts dated 1800 and 1847.*]

It may possibly save some trouble, and obviate some errors, if I take a cursory review of my own performance [in *Gebir*]. Not that I would prevent others from criticising it, but that I may explain at large, and state distinctly, its origin and design. This Poem, the fruit of Idleness and Ignorance—for had I been a botanist or mineralogist it never had been written—was principally written in Wales. The subject was taken, or rather the shadow of the subject, from a wild and incoherent, but fanciful, Arabian Romance. On the shelf of a circulating library, I met with a Critique on the various Novels of our Country. Though the work itself had nothing remarkable in it, . . . yet it presented to me, at the conclusion, the story of 'Gebirus and Charoba'. A Poem, like mine, descriptive of men and manners, should never be founded totally on fiction. But that which is originally fiction may cease in effect to be so:—the tears of Andromache are as precious as those of Sapphira. (p. 40)

I have availed myself merely of the names, and taken but few bare circumstances. I have followed no man closely; nor have I turned from my road because another stood in it: though perhaps I have momentarily, in passing, caught the object that attracted him. I have written in blank verse, because there never was a poem in rhyme that grew not tedious in a thousand lines. My choice is undoubtedly the most difficult of the two: for how many have succeeded in rhyme, in the structure at least; how few comparatively in blank verse. . . . [In most] we meet with stiffness instead of strength, and weakness instead of ease. I am aware how much I myself stand in need of favor. I demand some little from Justice; I entreat much more from Candor. If there are, now in England, ten men of taste and genius who will applaud my Poem, I declare myself fully content: I will call for a division; I shall count a majority. (pp. 40-1)

> *Walter Savage Landor, "Preface to 'Gebir' (1798),"*
> in Landor as Critic, *edited by Charles L. Proudfit,*
> *University of Nebraska Press, 1979, pp. 39-41.*

[ROBERT SOUTHEY]   (essay date 1799)

[*An English poet, historian, biographer, essayist, short story writer, and editor, Southey was a prominent literary figure of the late eighteenth and early nineteenth centuries and a key member of the Lake School of poetry. Southey's praise of* Gebir, *excerpted below, led to a lasting friendship with Landor. For additional criticism by Southey, see the excerpt dated 1812.*]

[The story of *Gebir* is] strange indeed and told in language sometimes uncouth, but abounding with such beauties as it is rarely our good fortune to discover. (p. 29)

The story of this poem is certainly ill chosen and not sufficiently whole; and the language is frequently deficient in perspicuity. These are the faults of *Gebir.* Of its beauties, our readers must already be sensible. They are of the first order; every circumstance is displayed with a force and accuracy which painting can not exceed.

> I am aware, [says the author], how much I myself stand in need of favor. I demand some little from Justice; I entreat much more from candor. If there are, now in England, ten men of taste and genius who will applaud my poem, I declare myself fully content: I will call for a division; I shall count a majority [see excerpt dated 1798].
>
> (pp. 38-9)

It is not our business to examine whether he has underrated the number of men of taste and genius in England; but we have read his poem repeatedly with more than common attention, and with far more than common delight. (p. 39)

> [*Robert Southey*], *in a review of "Gebir: A Poem,"*
> in The Critical Review, *n.s. Vol. XXVII, September,*
> *1799, pp. 29-39.*

THE MONTHLY REVIEW, LONDON   (essay date 1800)

[*The following excerpt is taken from a negative review of* Gebir.]

An unpractised author has attempted, in [*Gebir*], the difficult task of relating a romantic story in blank-verse. His performance betrays all the incorrectness and abruptness of inexperience, but it manifests occasionally some talent for description. He has fallen into the common error of those who aspire to the composition of blank-verse, by borrowing too many phrases and epithets from our incomparable Milton. (pp. 206-07)

We must observe that the story is told very obscurely, and should have been assisted by an *Argument* in prose. Young writers are often astonished to find that passages, which seem very clear to their own heated imaginations, appear very dark to their readers.—The author of the poem before us may produce something worthy of more approbation, if he will labour hard, and delay for a few years the publication of his next performance. (p. 208)

> *A review of "Gebir: A Poem," in* The Monthly Review, *London, Vol. XXXI, February, 1800, pp. 206-08.*

WALTER SAVAGE LANDOR   (essay date 1800)

[*Landor's "Post-Script to* Gebir*" was written in 1800 in response to Southey's positive assessment in the* Critical Review *(see the excerpt dated 1799) and the harsher critique in the* Monthly Review *(see the excerpt dated 1800). This piece was suppressed by Landor on the advice of his publisher and friends and did not appear in full until 1933. For additional commentary by Landor, see excerpts dated 1798 and 1847.*]

The *Critical* and *Monthly,* as being of the old establishment, are those on which at present I would fix attention. In respect to *Gebir,* the one perhaps is conducted by a partial, but certainly by a masterly, hand. It objects, and indeed with reason, to a temporary and local obscurity, which I have not been able, or I have not been willing, or I have not been bold enough, to remove: but never on the whole, since it's first institution, has a poem been more warmly praised. The other's account is short: containing one quotation and two mis-statements. "That the poem was nothing more than the version of an Arabic tale; and that the author, not content with borrowing the expressions, had made the most awkward attempts to imitate the phraseology of Milton."

The Review is not before me. I believe I have softened, but I have not perverted, nor have I deteriorated his style. No man would make or meditate so rash indefensible an attack, unless he were certain that, if not already stationed there, he could speedily drop into obscurity. I repeat to him in answer, what I before asserted in my preface, that, so far from a *translation,* there is not a single sentence, nor a single sentiment, in common with the tale. Some characters are drawn more at large, some are brought out more prominent, and several are added. I have not changed the scene, which would have distorted the piece, but every line of appropriate description, and every shade of peculiar manners, is originally and entirely my own.

Now, whether this gentleman has or has not read the poem, whether he has or has not read the romance, his account is equally false and equally malicious. For the romance is in English, therefor he could have read it; the poem is in English, and therefor he could have compared it. There is no disgrace in omitting to read them: the disgrace is, either in pretending to have done what he had not done, or in assuming a part which he was incompetent to support. But there *is* a disgrace in omitting to read Milton; there is a disgrace in forgetting him. The critic has not perused or not remembered him: it would be impossible, if he had, that he should accuse me of borrowing his expressions. I challenge him to produce them. If indeed I *had* borrowed them, so little should I have realized by the dangerous and wild speculation, that I might have composed a better poem and not have been a better poet. But I feared to break open, for the supply of my games or for the maintenance of my veteran heroes, the sacred treasury of the great republican. Although I might enjoy, not indeed the extorted, but the unguarded praise of an enemy, if my vanity could stoop so low and could live on so little,—of an enemy who, throughout so long a journey, and after so many speeches, and those on such various occasions, pertinaciously took me for Milton—I will add, for the information of my young opponent, what a more careful man would conceal, but what in his present distress will relieve him greatly, that this, which amongst the vulgar and thoughtless might currently pass for praise, is really none at all. For, the language of *Paradise Lost* ought not to be the language of *Gebir*. There should be the softened air of remote antiquity, not the severe air of unapproachable sanctity. I devoutly offer up my incence at the shrine of Milton. Woe betide the intruder that would steal it's jewels! It requires no miracle to detect the sacrilege. The crime will be found it's punishment. The venerable saints, and still more holy personages, of Raphael or Michael-Angelo, might as consistently be placed among the Bacchanals and Satyrs, bestriding the goats and bearing the vases of Poussin, as the resemblance of that poem, or any of it's component parts, could be introduced in mine.

I have avoided high-sounding words. I have attempted to throw back the gross materials, and to bring the figures forward. I knew beforehand the blame that I should incur. I knew that people would cry out "your burden was so light, we could hardly hear you breathe, pray where is your merit". For, there are few who seem thoroughly acquainted with this plain and simple truth, that it is easier to elevate the empty than to support the full. I also knew the *body* of my wine, and that years must pass over it, before it would reach it's relish. Some will think me intoxicated, and most will misconstrue my good-nature, if I invite the Reviewer, or any other friend that he will introduce,—but himself the most earnestly, as I suspect from his manner that he *poetizes*—to an amicable trial of skill.—I will subject myself to any penalty, either of writing or of ceasing to write, if the author, who criticizes with the flightiness of a poet, will assume that character at once, and, taking in series my twenty worst verses, write better an equal number, in the period of twenty years. I shall be rejoiced if he will open to me any poem of my contemporaries, of my English contemporaries I mean, and point out three pages more spirited, I will venture to add more classical than the three least happy and least accurate in *Gebir*.

In challenging a comparison the discriminating will remark, that more expertness is used than bravery. They will certainly acquit me of presumption, altogether, and judge from the character of the person thus addressed, that the champion opposed to me will not be the stoutest or most dexterous, but the heaviest or most shewy, and will readily agree that I have little cause to tremble, when probably I shall find in array against me the *Sovereign* of Mr. Pybus, or a work no less patriotic, the labor of a worthy clergyman, and in praise of better things,—to wit— *bank-notes and strong-beer*.

Many will think that I should have suppressed what I have said; but let them recollect that, amongst those ancient poets who contended for the public prize, each must not only have formed the same determination, (for defects are not usually compared with defects, but are generally contrasted with beauties) but have actually engaged, and that too more openly and personally, in a still more strenuous competition. If my rights had not been refused me, I should not have asserted my claims. Rambling by the side of the sea, or resting on the top of a mountain, and interlining with verses the letters of my friends, I sometimes thought how a Grecian would have written, but never what methods he would take to compass popularity. The nearer I approached him, tho' distant still, the more was I delighted. (pp. 350-52)

Several of these sketches were obliterated, still more laid aside and lost; various ideas I permitted to pass away, unwilling to disturb, by the slightest action, the dreams of reposing fancy. So little was I anxious to publish my rhapsodies, that I never sate down in the house, an hour at once, for the purpose of composition. Instead of making, or inviting, courtship, I declared with how little I should rest contented. Far from soliciting the attention of those who are passing by, *Gebir* is confined, I believe, to the shop of one bookseller, and I never heard that he had even made his appearance at the window. I understand not the management of these matters, but I find that the writing of a book is the least that an author has to do. My experience has not been great; and the caution which it has taught me lies entirely on the other side of publication. Before I was twenty years of age I had imprudently sent into the world a volume [*The Poems of Walter Savage Landor*], of which I was soon ashamed. It every-where met with as much commendation as was proper, and generally more. For, tho' the structure was feeble, the lines were fluent: the rhymes shewed habitual ease, and the personifications fashionable taste. I suffered any of my heroes, the greater part of whom were of a gentle kind, to look on one side thro' the eye of Pity, on the other thro' that of Love; and it was with great delight, for I could not foresee the consequences, that I heard them speak or sing with the lips of soft Persuasion. . . . I was then in raptures with what I now despise. I am far from the expectation, or the hope, that these deciduous shoots will be supported by the ivy of my maturer years. But, without any boast of prudence, I have hung up a motley and paultry skin for my puppies in their snarling playfulness to pull at, that they may not tear in pieces a better and costlier one on which I desire to rest.

After all, I do not wonder that they barked at *Gebir*—he came disguised and in tatters. Still there was nothing to authorize the impertinence with which the publication was treated by the *Monthly Review*er. These are not the faults which he complains of; tho' these might, without his consciousness, have first occasioned his ill-humour. I pity his want of abilities, and I pardon his excess of insolence. The merit is by no means small of a critic who speaks with modesty. For, his time being chiefly occupied, at first, in works fundamentally critical, at least if we suppose him desirous to *learn* before he is ambitious to *teach*, he thinks when he has attained their expressions and brevity, he has attained their solidity and profoundness. He must surely be above what he measures, else how can he measure with exactness? He must be greater, *ex officio*, than the person he brings before him; else how can he stigmatize with censure, or even dismiss with praise? (pp. 352-53)

> *Walter Savage Landor, "Post-Script to 'Gebir'," in his* The Complete Works of Walter Savage Landor: Poems, Vol. XIII, *edited by Stephen Wheeler, Chapman and Hall Ltd., 1933, pp. 350-63.*

[ROBERT SOUTHEY] (essay date 1812)

[*The following excerpt, taken from Southey's review of the anonymously published* Count Julian, *offers mixed criticism of the drama. For additional criticism by Southey, see the excerpt dated 1799.*]

The author of the drama before us [*Count Julian*], has taken a very different view of Count Julian's character from that in which the Spanish writers represent him. He is not

> El injuriado Conde, a la venganza
> Atento, y no a la fama.

as Luis de Leon describes him, a man sacrificing his country and his faith to the gratification of his revenge: the Julian of the tragedy is a hero and a patriot, seeking as much to redress the wrongs of his country as his own peculiar grievances; but unhappily attempting to effect it by the assistance of a foreign power. Repugnant as this representation of Julian is to the feelings of a Spaniard, and to those which are drawn from Spanish history, it is less so than the liberty which has been taken of ennobling Opas, the archbishop of Seville, a renegado and a traitor, whose name is detested in the peninsula. The author does not seem to be sensible that this can produce an unpleasant effect. 'It is remarkable,' he says, 'that the most important era in Spanish history should be the most obscure. This is propitious to the poet, and, above all, to the tragedian. Few characters of such an era can be glaringly misrepresented, few facts offensively perverted.' The purposes of the dramatist have certainly been served by this departure from historical verity and received tradition. (p. 86)

As a drama, it is evident that [*Count Julian*] has not been intended for representation,—so little is it addressed either to the eyes or the ears of the multitude. The fable is not always sufficiently clear; in a few instances the language, which is occasionally laboured into stiffness, borders on obscurity, and the verse is every where epic rather than dramatic.

We should have no hesitation in ascribing *Count Julian* to the author of a narrative poem of which the story is strange and unprepossessing, and the diction obscure, but in which the higher requisites of poetry are incidentally displayed in an eminent degree. The same powers are exhibited here so strikingly, and the defects which exist partake so much of the same character, that the internal evidence secures decision; but when an author has not thought proper to affix his name, the critic who gives it publicity assumes an authority to which neither the laws of courtesy nor of his profession entitle him. (p. 92)

> [*Robert Southey*], *in a review of "Count Julian: A Tragedy," in* The Quarterly Review, *Vol. VIII, No. XV, September, 1812, pp. 86-92.*

[HENRY TAYLOR AND WILLIAM GIFFORD]   (essay date 1824)

[*The following excerpt is taken from a mixed review that identifies the strengths and weaknesses of the* Imaginary Conversations.]

The nature of [*Imaginary Conversations of Literary Men and Statesmen*] is sufficiently explained by its title, to which we have only to add, that it is distributed into thirty-five conversations, maintained by distinguished personages of various ages and countries, under whose names Mr. Landor enjoys the opportunity of inculcating the most violent opinions of all parties; protesting of course against any of them being attributed to himself. The work being of a very desultory character, our remarks must be equally so.

The reader who is attracted by the names of Southey and Porson, . . . and told to expect a specimen of their conversation, must have prepared himself for no scanty exhibition of wit, for much astute criticism, and deep erudition. How will he then be surprised to find, that these eminent individuals meet only to agree upon the merits of Mr. Wordsworth's poetry! that they talk as if they were writing commentaries and tired of it, and that their dialogue is carried on with about the same speed of alternation, and vigour of contention, as the celebrated game at chess between the Spanish and Persian monarchs, each of whom resumed his deliberations in his own palace, as soon as the courier had arrived to announce his other majesty's last move! We protest against Mr. Landor's dialogue being supposed to furnish a specimen of Mr. Southey's conversation, and we will not consent to receive a sarcasm elaborately got

up, and forced on the attention in all the importunity of italics, as representing Professor Porson's style of wit. Neither can we allow our Northern contemporary, though a much smaller personage than these, to be represented, in the space of half a dozen lines, in the several characters of an ant and a serpent; and though it is doubtless with the best intentions that Mr. Wordsworth is figured in the same fruitful allegory, first as Adam, (or Eve, we do not clearly make out which,) and secondly as an elephant, yet we know enough of that gentleman's modesty to assure ourselves that he would be satisfied with appearing in one of those characters. (pp. 509-10)

In noticing the absurdities and perversities of this author, we are far from denying that he is a man of knowledge and abilities, which nothing but his singular deficiency of judgment could have rendered useless. In the absence of any rational or consistent design, these volumes display many random thoughts forcibly expressed, pointed invective thrown out as chance directed, a few reflections which are just and valuable, and a lively imagination, though it be rather exuberant than select. Others may be more fastidious, but we have been able to get over much bad taste, many elaborate epigrams, strange prose-metaphors, and politics in verse, to find entertainment in the easier and better parts of the book. (pp. 513-14)

[The] volumes in general are characterized by a spirit of pugnacity which, while it takes all its tenderness from criticism, satisfies us that rebuke is wholesome. The objects of this spirit are sufficiently multifarious, but the nearest are the most trampled upon. (p. 515)

Mr. Landor's mind is a self-constituted court of oyer and terminer, ready to try all causes which may come before it; and this court being composed of the most heterogeneous elements, and profoundly ignorant of the extent of its proper jurisdiction, passes upon each and every matter at issue, and upon all parties litigant, a sudden, peremptory, and unqualified sentence. (p. 518)

In conclusion, whatever measure of absurdity there may be in Mr. Landor's work, we desire to do him full justice: there is also in it a good deal to be admired, and some little to be approved. (p. 519)

> [*Henry Taylor and William Gifford*], "*Landor— 'Imaginary Conversations'*," *in* The Quarterly Review, *Vol. XXX, No. LX, January, 1824, pp. 508-19.*

[WILLIAM HAZLITT]   (essay date 1824)

[*One of the most important commentators of the Romantic age, Hazlitt was an English critic and journalist. Characterized by a tough, independent view of the world, by his political liberalism, and by the influence of Samuel Taylor Coleridge and Charles Lamb, Hazlitt's criticism is particularly admired for its wide range of reference and catholicity. Here, Hazlitt ridicules the* Imaginary Conversations, *attacking Landor's inconsistencies and his deviations from historical facts.*]

[Mr Landor's *Imaginary Conversations of Literary Men and Statesmen*] is as remarkable an instance as we have lately met with of the strength and weakness of the human intellect. It displays considerable originality, learning, acuteness, terseness of style, and force of invective—but it is spoiled and rendered abortive throughout by an utter want of temper, of self-knowledge, and decorum. Mr Landor's mind is far from barren in feeling or in resources; but over the natural, and (what might be) the useful growth of these, there every where springs up a luxuriant crop of caprice, dogmatism, extravagance, intolerance, quaintness, and most ludicrous arrogance,—like the red and blue flowers in corn, that, however they may dazzle the passenger's eye, choke up the harvest, and mock the hopes of the husbandman. We are not ignorant of the school to which our author belongs; and could name other writers who, in the course of a laborious life, and in productions numerous and multiform—some recent and suited to the times, some long and luckily forgotten,—in odes, inscriptions, madrigals, epics,—in essays, histories and reviews,—have run into as many absurdities, and as many extremes: But never did we see, bound up in the same volume, close-packed, and pointed with all the significance of style, the same number of contradictions, staring one another in the face, and quarrelling for the precedence. Mr Landor's book is a perfect 'institute and digest' of inconsistency: it is made up of mere antipathies in nature and in reasoning. It is a *chef-d'oeuvre* of self-opinion and self-will, strangling whatever is otherwise sound and excellent in principle, defacing whatever is beautiful in style and matter.

If it be true (as has been said) that

> Great wits to madness nearly are allied,

we know few writers that have higher or more unequivocal pretensions in this way than the author of the *Imaginary Conversations*. Would it be believed, that, trampling manfully on all history and tradition, he speaks of Tiberius as a *man of sentiment*, who retired to Capri merely to indulge a tender melancholy on the death of a beloved wife: and will have it that Nero was a most humane, amiable, and deservedly popular character—not arguing the points as doubtful or susceptible of question, but assuming them, *en passant*, as most absolute and peremptory conclusions—as if whatever was contrary to common sense and common feeling carried conviction on the face of it? In the same page he assures us, with the same oracular tranquillity, that the conflagration of Rome, and the great fire of London, were both wise and voluntary measures, arising from the necessity of purifying the cities after sickness, and leaving no narrow streets in their centres! and on turning the leaf, it is revealed to us, that there is nothing in Rome, *or in the world*, equal to—the circus in Bath! He spells the words *foreign* and *sovereign*, 'foren' and 'sovran,' and would go to the stake, or send others there, to prove the genuineness of these orthographies, which he adopts on the authority of Milton; and yet he abuses Buonaparte for being the ape of Antiquity, and talking about Miltiades. He cries up Mr Locke as 'the most *elegant* of English prose writers,' for no other reason (as we apprehend) than that he has often been considered as the least so; and compares Dr Johnson's style to 'that article of dress which the French have lately made peace with,' (a pair of pantaloons), 'divided into two parts, equal in length, breadth, and substance, with a protuberance before and behind.' He pronounces sentence upon the lost works of two ancient writers, Democritus and Menander, that the former would be worth all the philosophical remains of antiquity, and the latter not be worth having,—precisely because he can know nothing about the matter; the will to decide superseding the necessity of any positive ground of opinion, and the spirit of contradiction standing him in lieu of all other conviction. (pp. 67-9)

> [*William Hazlitt*], *"Landor's 'Imaginary Conversations',"* in *The Edinburgh Review, Vol. XL, No. LXXIX, March, 1824, pp. 67-92.*

[PEREGRINE BINGHAM?] (essay date 1824)

> [*Bingham points to minor anachronisms and errors of fact in the* Imaginary Conversations, *but otherwise commends the work as interesting and valuable.*]

[*Imaginary Conversations of Literary Men and Statesmen*] is the work of a man of no ordinary genius, benevolence, and courage: genius,—to apprehend, almost intuitively, and to express felicitously, many of the profoundest principles of morals and legislation;—benevolence,—to side and sympathize with the mass of his species, rather than with that detached and favoured portion of them who require and possess the power of applying to their own purposes the property of the people at large;—and courage,—to expose whatever is mischievous in the conduct or pretensions of this favourite few.

In the light form of conversations, the author has contrived to convey to his readers much that is instructive in politics, much that is amusing in literature:—in conversations, not carried on by Doctor and Student, Venator and Piscator, Philalethes and Eleutherus, or any such dull and unfashionable society, but by real personages with whom most of us have for some time been more or less acquainted, and whose characters, whether for good or for evil, we are pretty well able to appreciate. (pp. 431-32)

The announcement in the preface that "the peculiarities of some celebrated authors, both in style and sentiment," had been "imitated in these dialogues," tends rather to mislead the reader's expectation. The author has too much mind for a mimic, and is too proper a man to play the monkey amusingly. Here is no caricature, no burlesque, none of the fun of Tickell's "Anticipation" nor of the farce of "the Rejected Addresses," those mirth-inspiring little books which would have cured Heraclitus, and made the cave of Trophonius echo shouts of laughter:—Dr. Johnson is very sparing in the use of *verba sesquipedalia*, Milton's sentences are neither long nor latinized; and Franklin is not distinguished by short speeches, parables, and proverbs. Instead of throwing out the peculiarities of his *personae* Mr. Landor keeps them down. Undoubtedly there is in the most excentric man more that is like other folks than there is that is unlike; but he is characterized by the latter, and on that the imitator ought chiefly to fix, if he intends to produce a striking likeness. We should scarcely have suspected that imitation was any part of our author's design, had it not been so declared by himself. There is just so much of it as was unavoidable in selecting certain persons as vehicles for the utterance of appropriate opinions, and no more. The thoughts are not (as might be expected of a professed imitator) strongly coloured; but only just tinged by the media through which they pass to the reader. The identification of the author with his imagined speakers seems never complete. They do not talk of themselves, but he talks through them. They are but puppets, and his is the only voice, though it may be a little varied. He does not employ the real dramatic magic of transforming himself into the character of his selection or creation; he only produces a compound being of which a tenth may be Milton or Marvel, and the remaining nine-tenths are Walter Savage Landor. The result, however, is far more valuable than it would have been had even the most successful imitation been the distinguishing merit of the book. A number of well-known names are employed, and they are, in general, fairly and effectively employed, to give additional interest to the discussion of important questions, and to the exposure of vile sophisms and viler practices. We may never lose sight of the author, but then we never wish to lose sight of him; nay, we like the company into which he leads us all the better for their bearing evident marks of being animated by his spirit.

In a work of this description, the author cannot be held responsible for the truth of any particular opinion, or the validity of any particular argument; all that is required, being, that such opinion or argument become the speaker to whom it is ascribed. But if it happens, that in a series of imaginary dialogues, some opinions are more frequently advanced, more impressively recommended, more plausibly supported, than others, so that the effect of the whole work is, to produce a prejudice or a conviction in their favour; the author may, without injustice, be considered as the advocate of those opinions. What is the writer's own opinion? is a question which rises in every reader's mind, and Mr. Landor has furnished materials for the answer, on a tolerably comprehensive list of topics.

Undesignedly, he has fallen into some mistakes in the way of anachronism, some errors in matters of fact, and designedly, into a good deal of affectation on the score of orthography, for which affectation he adduces, as it seems to us, very insufficient reasons in a conversation between Dr. Johnson and Horne Tooke; this, however, is as much notice as we choose to bestow on points so comparatively unimportant, and having thus far discussed the manner of the work, we shall now proceed to the matter.

With regard to this, in disquisitions so purely conversational, there is little on which the critic can fasten: partly, because the author has always a retreat under the dramatic character of his interlocutors; partly, because a work so constructed consists mainly of a series of desultory observations, neither presenting nor professing to present any complete system or any exposition of principles which will admit the process of detailed examination. (pp. 432-34)

From the general tone of his language and sentiments, it is clear to us, that Mr. Landor is a man of highly poetical imagination; we collect also from the whole complexion of his book, that he has devoted no small portion of his time and labour to Belles Lettres in every shape, ancient and modern, poetry and history. But from the errors we have already mentioned, as well as from various expressions which he has employed, we are equally convinced, either that he has not had access to the great and only sources of moral and political science—those few and recent writers who have developed the only principles which can produce the greatest happiness of the greatest number—or, that having had access to them, he has bestowed very little labour on the subject. If this be so, the wonder is, not that he should have fallen into the errors in question, or should occasionally wander in the mists of vague generalities, but rather that he should have discovered and adopted so many bold truths, and so many admirable sentiments as he has himself presented for our consideration. It is true, that an intellect unshackled as his, might have discovered of itself, and with ten or twenty years' labour and practice, might have developed, and have been able to apply, consistently, the great principle of general utility. But Mr. Landor has been engaged in other pursuits; he probably has neither had the time nor the inclination to make the discovery, or pursue the application of it unassisted; and he furnishes another and a striking example of the difficulties which beset even a searching and unprejudiced intellect, in handling the great problems of morals and legislation, unless by its own exertions, or those of others, it has been furnished with the only sure key to precision and truth.

Of the mischiefs attending many established institutions—of the sinister interests which support those institutions, and wage war against all public improvement, Mr. Landor has a ready and an accurate conception: in detecting the haunts, and exposing the fallacies of all the creatures of corruption, he is as quick as lightning; but when this has been accomplished, when the ground is cleared of the enemy, and the great question comes, *quid faciendum?* he is directly at fault, and gropes about in the mists of metaphor and generalities, just as a school-boy who quotes Cicero, or as Cicero himself did two thousand years ago. (pp. 434-35)

> [*Peregrine Bingham?*], ''Landor's 'Imaginary Conversations','' in The Westminster Review, *Vol. 1, April, 1824, pp. 431-53.*

SAMUEL TAYLOR COLERIDGE   (conversation date 1834)

[*An English poet and critic, Coleridge was central to the English Romantic movement and is considered one of the greatest literary critics in the English language. In this extract, Coleridge remarks that Landor lacks imagination, consistency, and the ability to write "simple and lucid English."*]

What is it that Mr. Landor wants, to make him a poet? His powers are certainly very considerable, but he seems to be totally deficient in that modifying faculty, which compresses several units into one whole. The truth is, he does not possess imagination in its highest form—that of stamping *il più nell' uno*. Hence his poems, taken as wholes, are unintelligible; you have eminences excessively bright, and all the ground around and between them in darkness. Besides which, he has never learned, with all his energy, how to write simple and lucid English.

> *Samuel Taylor Coleridge, in a conversation on January 1, 1834, in his* The Table Talk and Omniana of Samuel Taylor Coleridge, *Oxford University Press, London, 1917, p. 286.*

[JOHN FORSTER]   (essay date 1836)

[*Forster was an English biographer, historian, critic, and editor. He had a significant impact on Landor's career and reputation as his editor and biographer. In the excerpt that follows, Forster evaluates Landor's strengths and failings as a poet, drawing instances from Landor's early dramatic poetry. For further criticism by Forster, see the excerpt dated 1846 and the Additional Bibliography.*]

[We characterize] Mr. Walter Savage Landor, as ''a poet for poets.'' In this phrase, we would have it understood, we desire to include not only the highest tribute we can pay to his genius, but also the strongest detraction we can make from it. The power, the variety, and the rapidly-associating thought, which belong alone to the poetical perceptions, and by a combination of which it is that the eye of the poet is enabled to glance in an instant from heaven to earth, and from earth to heaven,—these are in some sort necessary to him who would understand Mr. Landor's poetry as a whole. That masterly connexion of the remotest analogies which is constantly to be met with there, and never with the help of any of those long intermediate processes which are requisite to the perceptions of ordinary readers, demands, for its entire and proper appreciation, the creative, scarcely less than the percipient faculty.

While this, however, is, on the one hand, an evidence of the most vivid conception and the most perfect faith to which a poet can attain, it is no less, on the other hand, open to very serious objections. So subtle a principle of association must frequently refine itself into a fault, and it may happen, at times, with the most docile disciple of Mr. Landor, that he shall recognize nothing but a series of thoughts or feelings, each evidently in some way dependent on the other, but according to some system which he is unable clearly to ascertain. The association, in fact, is liable to spring too hastily from a non-essential quality, rather than from the acknowledged and inseparate aggregate;—as sometimes, we venture to think, and more particularly in his minor poems, from the word rather than from the thought it expresses.

It is then a necessary result, from the nature of Mr. Landor's genius, that he can never become a popular poet. A writer of verse, after Sir Walter Scott's mode, who, acting under the broadest and most obvious law of association, merely reproduces, in a higher and illustrated form, the ordinary impressions, will as surely never be unpopular. It would be curious, indeed, to take one of the grandest passages from *Gebir,* and observe the running and connecting commentary that would be required to make it continuous and intelligible to a reader very capable of mastering the mysteries of *Marmion.* When Mr. Coleridge said,—as he is reported to have alleged, in explanation of the circumstance of Mr. Landor's poems not being popular,—that "Landor had not, after all, the power of expressing his thoughts in lucid and perspicuous English" [see excerpt dated 1834]; he seems to us to have exactly mistaken the cause. We hold, on the contrary, . . . that it is more likely to be found in Mr. Landor's too thorough sensitiveness on the subject of language—in his too precise apprehension of the vehicle of his thoughts. His light is diverted, and glances excentrically off from the facettes of his gem-like words. This is his grand fault in the midst of enormous beauties.

How different from Shelley's, with whose "obscurity" it has been the fashion to class the "puzzling verses" of Landor! Shelley's error was that of presenting a vast array of synchronous images relating to the same thing. (pp. 200-01)

All Mr. Landor's reflections and images are, on the other hand, successive. . . . [Each] one of them has a body and distinctness of its own. Each one of them is also obviously dependent on the other, though at times somewhat inexplicably so—"far-fetched" we might say. And how pregnant with meaning, and in what a dress of words—*splendidior vitro,* is each in itself! For, in the most apparently obscure parts of Landor's poetry, the sections, the passages, that bewilder the reader most *in succession,* are, when viewed abstractedly, as "one entire and perfect chrysolite." Nobody's single lines are nearly so good as Landor's. How grand is this from the *Count Julian—*

> Guilt hath pavillions, but no privacy!
>
> (p. 201)

In *Gebir,* all the splendour and all the peculiarities of Mr. Landor's genius have scope. Its successions of wondrous imagery, and of sweet and delicate fancies, are set down without pause or doubt, and as though the very objects were at hand to be referred to by any gainsayer. (p. 202)

[The poem itself] is a masterpiece. Through all its wonderful imagery there is not a pause or a doubt. Why should there be? The poet speaks of *existing* marvels. He does not call them up in the reader's presence. The task of creating is already accomplished, and his office is simply to describe. It may be said, at the same time, that all optics are not sufficiently acute to bear this sort of sudden exhibition; and it may admit of a reasonable doubt whether, in all cases, such tardiness of vision should be unprovided against. These questions, it will be seen, connect themselves with what we have said of the exacting nature of Mr. Landor's poetry, and of its continual demand on the imagination, almost creative, of its readers.

But what has all this to do, we may be asked, with a "GENIUS FOR DRAMATIC POETRY" in especial? We have just come to that. The questions suggested by *Gebir* cease to be questions here. There can be no doubt that the broad characteristics we have attributed to that great poem are those that belong to the true art of dramatic composition. In the drama all that is *material* is already upon the scene and actually present to the eye. We, the audience and spectators, have the passion bodily before us; we pursue its living progress, and watch its palpable results. It follows, therefore, for these reasons, that in the drama all which is *etherial* should be absolutely discharged from the task of setting forth what is, or ought to be, already visible. We do not want words, for instance, to assure us that this passion, and all its results, do exist. Virtually indeed words assure us of it, and that in the highest degree, because it is from the existence in question that they have at once flowed. But, as words, they are there because of the passion, not the passion because of them; and it is in this *effluence* of words, as a pure effect of passion, that the genuine art of dramatic writing consists.

Now—disjoin such an effect from the material agents that have produced it, from the actors, from the scene, from the very audience, and it instantly becomes as "obscure" and "unintelligible" as Mr. Landor's general poetry, to all but those who are capable of supplying those materials from their own imagination. (p. 203)

[Is] any elaborate commentary necessary to indicate the persons and the action that belong to these few intensely dramatic lines—?

> "Stay! spare him! save the last!
> Medea! . . . is that blood? again! it drops
> From my imploring hand upon my feet . . .
> I will invoke the Eumenides no more . . .
> I will forgive thee . . . bless thee . . . bend to thee
> In all thy wishes . . . do but thou, Medea,
> Tell me, one lives.
>   "And shall I too deceive?"
> Cries from the firy car an angry voice;
> And swifter than two falling stars descend
> Two breathless bodies . . . warm, soft, motionless,
> As flowers in stillest noon before the sun,
> They lie three paces from him . . ."

This is from one of Mr. Landor's minor poems, addressed **"To Corinth."** But let us now introduce the reader to some of those full and splendid embodiments of what dramatic writing ought to be, which will justify our special and emphatic connexion of Mr. Landor's name with this great subject. . . .

[The following extract is from the dramatic poem **"Ines de Castro"**]:

> IN.   Now tell me.
> Pedro! your hand and brow are sadly parcht,
> And you are out of breath, altho' you walked
> These twenty paces, more than I who ran . . .
> And yet you always caught me when we tried.
> What would you tell me now, my faithful Pedro?
>   PED. In one word, Ines! I have ceased to love thee.
> Loose me and let me go.
> IN.   Is this your greeting?
> This your first morning salutation? turn . . .
> Can it be? must I (look at me) believe it?
>   PED. Yes, my sweet . . . yes, my Ines . . . yes, yes,
>   Ines!

IN. And are you still so generous, O my love,
As to be sorry you have ceased to love me?
To sigh, almost to weep, bending your face
Away from me, lest I should grieve to see
A change in it, and in a change a loss?
Take off that hand from above mine then! take it!
I dare not move it from me . . . 'tis the prince's,
And not my Pedro's.
    PED.   I must go.
    IN.   I once
Might ask you why. Let *me* go.
    PED.   Wouldst thou? whither?
Unfortunate! So, thou resignest me,
Light heartless girl!

Every line here is absolutely perfect. Mark, above all, the struggle of the soul in those few words—"Yes, my sweet . . . yes, my Ines . . . yes, yes, Ines!"—and the breathless haste with which, in the last passage, the prince catches at the slightest shadow of excuse to himself for his proposed desertion. (pp. 204-05)

Add to [this a] . . . transcendent scene from **"Ippolito di Este."** Ferrante and Giulio were brothers, by the father's side, to the Duke Alfonso and the Cardinal Ippolito di Este. The Cardinal deprived Ferrante of his eyes for loving the same object as his Eminence, and because she had praised the beauty of them. . . . [Ippolito] carries the Duke's sentence to Ferrante, who is attended in his prison by Giulio. After a terrible interview, Ippolito stalks out of the prison, having handed the sentence to Giulio with these words—"Take you the sentence, *and God be with both!*" Is it necessary to ask the reader's admiration for *every word* in the scene which follows? . . .

    FER. O my true brother, Giulio, *why thus hang*
Around my neck and pour forth prayers for me?
Where there are priests and kinsmen such as ours,
God hears not, nor is heard. I am prepared
For death.
    GIU. Ah! worse than death may come upon you,
Unless Heaven interpose.
    FER.   I know the worst,
And bear one comfort in my breast that fire
And steel can ne'er force from it: she I love
Will not be his, but die as she hath lived.
Doubt you? that thus you shake the head, and sigh.
    GIU. Far other doubt was mine: even this shall cease.
    FER. Speak it.
    GIU. I must: God pardon me!
    FER.   Speak on.
    GIU. Have we not dwelt in friendship from our birth,
Told the same courtier the same tale of joy,
And pointed where life's earliest thorn had pierced
Amid the sports of boyhood, ere the heart
Hath aught of bitter or unsound within?
    FER. We have indeed.
    GIU.   Has my advice been ill?
    FER. Too often ill-observed, but always good.
    GIU. *Brother, my words are not what better men*
Would speak to you; and yet my love, I think,
Must be more warm than theirs can ever be. . . .
    FER. Brother's, friend's, father's, when was it like
      yours!
    GIU. Which of them ever said what I shall say!

    FER. Speak; my desires are kindled, my fears
    quencht.
    GIU. DO NOT DELAY TO DIE, LEST CRUELLER
THAN COMMON DEATH BEFALL YOU. . . .
    GIU. Hark! hear you not the people? to the window!
They shout and clap their hands when they first meet
    you
After short absence; what shall they now do?
Up! seize the moment; shew yourself.
    FER.   Stay, Giulio!
Draw me not thither! speak not of my wrongs . . .
I would await but not arouse their vengeance,
And would deserve but court not their applause.
Little of good shall good men hope from them,
Nothing shall wiser.
         (Aside). *O were he away!*
But if I fail, he must die too, being here.
    GIU. Let me call out: they are below the grate.
They would deliver you: try this one chance.
Obdurate! would you hold me down! They're gone!
    FER. *Giulio! for shame! weep not,* or here I stay
And let vile hands deform me.

                            (pp. 207-08)

Is there any *writing in* of the action here? Are any stage-directions wanted? Does the actor of Giulio require to be told what to do, or how to do it? Are not the very words a KEAN in action? With what heart-rending earnestness do we not hear a Voice tremble, as it recalls the affection of the past, to excuse the terrible advice of the present! Does the actor of Ferrante need to know in what tones that commonplace excuse of his must be spoken, where he resigns the hope of release from the people, rather than endanger his brother,—or does he require a clue to the quiet accents of agonized resolve in which that "*aside*" must be expressed,—or to the action with which he may convey the keenness of the dagger's point? Truly we want no—*stabs himself and falls*—*right hand*—*prompt: side*—or any of those ingenious and elaborate details which abound in the books of the players. (p. 208)

[*John Forster*], "*Evidences of Genius for Dramatic Poetry,*" *in* The New Monthly Magazine, *Vol. XLVIII, No. CXC, October, 1836, pp. 200-08.*

[RALPH WALDO EMERSON]   (essay date 1841)

[*Emerson was one of the most influential figures of the nineteenth century. An American essayist and poet, he founded the Transcendentalist movement and shaped a distinctly American philosophy that embraces optimism, individuality, and mysticism. Emerson here praises the unique artistry of the* Imaginary Conversations *as seen in Landor's characterizations and astute critical perception. Yet he finds that the work lacks unity and that its value rests on the merit of individual sentences.*]

[For] twenty years we have . . . found [Landor's] *Imaginary Conversations* a sure resource in solitude, and it seems to us as original in its form as in its matter. Nay, when we remember his rich and ample page, wherein we are always sure to find free and sustained thought, a keen and precise understanding, an affluent and ready memory familiar with all chosen books, an industrious observation in every department of life, an experience to which nothing has occurred in vain, honor for every just and generous sentiment, and a scourge like that of the Furies for every oppressor, whether public or private, we feel how dignified is this perpetual Censor in his curule chair, and we wish to thank a benefactor of the reading world.

Mr. Landor is one of the foremost of that small class who make good in the nineteenth century the claims of pure literature. In these busy days of avarice and ambition, when there is so little disposition to profound thought, or to any but the most superficial intellectual entertainments, a faithful scholar receiving from past ages the treasures of wit, and enlarging them by his own love, is a friend and consoler of mankind. (pp. 263-64)

Whoever writes for the love of truth and beauty, and not with ulterior ends, belongs to [a] sacred class, and among these, few men of the present age, have a better claim to be numbered than Mr. Landor. Wherever genius or taste has existed, wherever freedom and justice are threatened, which he values as the element in which genius may work, his interest is sure to be commanded. His love of beauty is passionate, and betrays itself in all petulant and contemptuous expressions.

But beyond his delight in genius, and his love of individual and civil liberty, Mr. Landor has a perception that is much more rare, the appreciation of character. This is the more remarkable considered with his intense nationality. . . . He is buttoned in English broadcloth to the chin. He hates the Austrians, the Italians, the French, the Scotch, and the Irish. He has the common prejudices of an English landholder; values his pedigree, his acres, and the syllables of his name; loves all his advantages, is not insensible to the beauty of his watch-seal, or the Turk's head on his umbrella; yet with all this miscellaneous pride, there is a noble nature within him, which instructs him that he is so rich that he can well spare all his trappings, and, leaving to others the painting of circumstance, aspire to the office of delineating character. He draws his own portrait in the costume of a village schoolmaster, and a sailor, and serenely enjoys the victory of nature over fortune. Not only the elaborated story of Normanby, but the whimsical selection of his heads prove this taste. He draws with evident pleasure the portrait of a man, who never said anything right, and never did anything wrong. But in the character of Pericles, he has found full play for beauty and greatness of behavior, where the circumstances are in harmony with the man. These portraits, though mere sketches, must be valued as attempts in the very highest kind of narrative, which not only has very few examples to exhibit of any success, but very few competitors in the attempt. The word Character is in all mouths; it is a force which we all feel; yet who has analyzed it? What is the nature of that subtle, and majestic principle which attaches us to a few persons, not so much by personal as by the most spiritual ties? What is the quality of the persons who, without being public men, or literary men, or rich men, or active men, or (in the popular sense) religious men, have a certain salutary omnipresence in all our life's history, almost giving their own quality to the atmosphere and the landscape? A moral force, yet wholly unmindful of creed and catechism, intellectual, but scornful of books, it works directly and without means, and though it may be resisted at any time, yet resistance to it is a suicide. For the person who stands in this lofty relation to his fellow men is always the impersonation to them of their conscience. It is a sufficient proof of the extreme delicacy of this element, evanescing before any but the most sympathetic vision, that it has so seldom been employed in the drama and in novels. Mr. Landor, almost alone among living English writers, has indicated his perception of it.

These merits make Mr. Landor's position in the republic of letters one of great mark and dignity. He exercises with a grandeur of spirit the office of writer, and carries it with an air of old and unquestionable nobility. We do not recollect an example of more complete independence in literary history. He has no clanship, no friendships, that warp him. He was one of the first to pronounce Wordsworth the great poet of the age, yet he discriminates his faults with the greater freedom. He loves Pindar, Aeschylus, Euripides, Aristophanes, Demosthenes, Virgil, yet with open eyes. His position is by no means the highest in literature; he is not a poet or a philosopher. He is a man full of thoughts, but not, like Coleridge, a man of ideas. Only from a mind conversant with the First Philosophy can definitions be expected. Coleridge has contributed many valuable ones to modern literature. Mr. Landor's definitions are only enumerations of particulars; the generic law is not seized. But as it is not from the highest Alps or Andes, but from less elevated summits, that the most attractive landscape is commanded, so is Mr. Landor the most useful and agreeable of critics. He has commented on a wide variety of writers, with a closeness and an extent of view, which has enhanced the value of those authors to his readers. His Dialogue on the Epicurean philosophy is a theory of the genius of Epicurus. The Dialogue between Barrow and Newton is the best of all criticisms on the Essays of Bacon. His picture of Demosthenes in three several Dialogues is new and adequate. He has illustrated the genius of Homer, Aeschylus, Pindar, Euripides, Thucydides. Then he has examined before he expatiated, and the minuteness of his verbal criticism gives a confidence in his fidelity, when he speaks the language of meditation or of passion. His acquaintance with the English tongue is unsurpassed. He "hates false words, and seeks with care, difficulty, and moroseness, those that fit the thing." He knows the value of his own words. "They are not," he says, "written on slate." He never stoops to explanation, nor uses seven words where one will do. He is a master of condensation and suppression, and that in no vulgar way. He knows the wide difference between compression and an obscure elliptical style. The dense writer has yet ample room and choice of phrase, and even a gamesome mood often between his valid words. There is no inadequacy or disagreeable contraction in his sentence, any more than in a human face, where in a square space of a few inches is found room for every possible variety of expression.

Yet it is not as an artist, that Mr. Landor commends himself to us. He is not epic or dramatic, he has not the high, overpowering method, by which the master gives unity and integrity to a work of many parts. He is too wilful, and never abandons himself to his genius. His books are a strange mixture of politics, etymology, allegory, sentiment, and personal history, and what skill of transition he may possess is superficial, not spiritual. His merit must rest at last, not on the spirit of the dialogue, or the symmetry of any of his historical portraits, but on the value of his sentences. Many of these will secure their own immortality in English literature; and this, rightly considered, is no mean merit. These are not plants and animals, but the genetical atoms, of which both are composed. . . . Of many of Mr. Landor's sentences we are fain to remember what was said of those of Socrates, that they are cubes, which will stand firm, place them how or where you will. (pp. 265-68)

> [*Ralph Waldo Emerson*], *"Walter Savage Landor," in* The Dial, *Vol. II, No. II, October, 1841, pp. 262-71.*

ELIZABETH BARRETT with RICHARD HENGIST HORNE (essay date 1844)

[*A leading poet in Victorian England, Barrett (later Elizabeth Barrett Browning) is best known for her cycle of love poetry,*

Sonnets from the Portuguese. *In the following excerpt, she decries her contemporaries' unenthusiastic reception of Landor's works and discusses his status in literature and his qualities as a writer.*]

Mr. Landor is a man of genius and learning, who stands in a position unlike that of any other eminent individual of his time. He has received no apparent influence from any one of his contemporaries; nor have they or the public received any apparent influence from him. The absence of any fixed and definite influence upon the public is actually as it seems; but that he has exercised a considerable influence upon the minds of many of his contemporaries is inevitable, because so fine a spirit could never have passed through any competent medium without communicating its electric forces, although from the very fineness of its elements, the effect, like the cause, has been of too subtle a nature to leave a tangible or visible impress. (pp. 109-10)

Of the difference between the partialities of the public, and the eventual judgements of the people; between a deeply-founded fame and an ephemeral interest, few more striking examples will perhaps be discovered in future years than in the solitary course of Walter Savage Landor amidst the various 'lights of his day'. He has incontestably displayed original genius as a writer; the highest critical faculty—that sympathy with genius and knowledge which can only result from imagination and generous love of truth—and also a fine scholarship in the spirit as well as the letter of classical attainments. But the public, tacitly, has denied his claims, or worse—admitted them with total indifference,—letting fall from its benumbed fingers, work after work, not because any one ventured to say, or perhaps even to think, the books were unworthy, but because the hands were cold. . . . [As] a general rule, the originality of a man, say and do what he may, is necessarily in itself an argument against his rapid popularity. In the case of Mr. Landor, however, other causes than the originality of his faculty have opposed his favour with the public. He has the most select audience perhaps,—the fittest, fewest,—of any distinguished author of the day; and this of his choice. 'Give me', he said in one of his prefaces, 'ten accomplished men for readers, and I am content' [see excerpt dated 1798];—and the event does not by any means so far as we could desire, outstrip the modesty, or despair, or disdain, of this aspiration. He writes criticism for critics, and poetry for poets: his drama, when he is dramatic, will suppose neither pit nor gallery, nor critics, nor dramatic laws. He is not a publican among poets—he does not sell his Amreeta cups upon the highway. He delivers them rather with the dignity of a giver, to ticketed persons; analysing their flavour and fragrance with a learned delicacy, and an appeal to the esoteric. His very spelling of English is uncommon and theoretic. He has a vein of humour which by its own nature is peculiarly subtle and evasive; he therefore refines upon it, by his art, in order to prevent anybody discovering it without a grave, solicitous, and courtly approach, which is unspeakably ridiculous to all the parties concerned, and which no doubt the author secretly enjoys. And as if poetry were not, in English, a sufficiently unpopular dead language, he has had recourse to writing poetry in Latin; with dissertations on the Latin tongue, to fence it out doubly from the populace. *'Odi profanum vulgus, et arceo.'*

Whether Mr. Landor writes Latin or English, poetry or prose, he does it all with a certain artistic composure, as if he knew what he was doing, and respected the cunning of his right hand. At times he displays an equal respect for his wilfulness. In poetry, his *Gebir,* the **"Phocaeans"** and some other performances take a high classic rank. He can put out extraordinary

power both in description and situation; but the vitality, comprehended in the power, does not overflow along the inferior portions of the work, so as to sustain them to the level of the reader's continued attention. The poet rather builds up to his own elevations than carries them out and on; and the reader passes from admiration to admiration, by separate states or shocks, and not by a continuity of interest through the intervals of emotion. Thus it happens that his best dramatic works,—those, the impression of which on the mind is most definite and excellent,—are fragmentary; and that his complete dramas are not often read through twice, even by readers who applaud them, but for the sake of a particular act or scene.

A remark should be made on Mr. Landor's blank verse, in which the poems just named, and several others, are written. It is the very best of the regular-syllable class, the versification of 'numbers', as they have been characteristically called by the schools. His blank verse is not only the most regular that ever was written, but it is the most sweet, and far less monotonous than we should expect of a musical system which excluded occasional discords. It has all the effect of the most melodious rhyming heroic verse; indeed, it often gives the impression of elegiac verses in rhyme. As blank verse it is a very bad model. There is more freedom in his dramatic verse, and always the purest style.

His dramatic works (except the compact little scenes entitled *Pentalogia,* which are admirable) are written upon an essentially undramatic principle; or, more probably, on no principle at all. Mr. Landor well knows 'all the laws', and they seem to provoke his will to be lawless. In this species of drama-looking composition he displays at times the finest passion, the most pure and perfect style of dramatic dialogue, and an intensity of mental movements, with their invisible, undeclared, yet necessarily tragic results; all of which proves him to possess the most wonderful three-fourths of a great dramatic genius which ever appeared in the world. But the fourth part is certainly wanting by way of making good his ground to the eyes, and ears, and understanding of the masses. (pp. 115-18)

In whatever Mr. Landor writes, his power, when he puts it forth, is of the first order. He is classical in the highest sense. His conceptions stand out, clearly cut and fine, in a magnitude and nobility as far as possible removed from the small and sickly vagueness common to this century of letters. If he seems obscure at times, it is from no infirmity or inadequacy of thought or word, but from extreme concentration, and involution in brevity—for a short string can be tied in a knot, as well as a long one. He can be tender, as the strong can best be; and his pathos, when it comes, is profound. His descriptions are full and startling; his thoughts, self-produced and bold; and he has the art of taking a commonplace under a new aspect, and of leaving the Roman brick, marble. In marble indeed, he seems to work; for there is an angularity in the workmanship, whether of prose or verse, which the very exquisiteness of the polish renders more conspicuous. You may complain too of hearing the chisel; but after all, you applaud the work—it is a work well done. The elaboration produces no sense of heaviness,—the severity of the outline does not militate against beauty;—if it is cold, it is also noble—if not impulsive, it is suggestive. As a writer of Latin poems, he ranks with our most successful scholars and poets; having less harmony and majesty than Milton had,—when he aspired to the species of 'Life in Death',—but more variety and freedom of utterance. Mr. Landor's English prose writings possess most of the characteristics of his poetry; only they are more perfect in their class. His

Pericles and Aspasia, and *Pentameron,* are books for the world and for all time, whenever the world and time shall come to their senses about them; complete in beauty of sentiment and subtlety of criticism. His general style is highly scholastic and elegant,—his sentences have articulations, if such an expression may be permitted, of very excellent proportions. And, abounding in striking images and thoughts, he is remarkable for making clear the ground around them, and for lifting them, like statues to pedestals, where they may be seen most distinctly, and strike with the most enduring though often the most gradual impression. This is the case both in his prose works and his poetry. It is more conspicuously true of some of his smaller poems, which for quiet classic grace and tenderness, and exquisite care in their polish, may best be compared with beautiful cameos and vases of the antique. (pp. 118-19)

Mr. Landor's wit and humour are of a very original kind, as previously remarked. Perhaps in none of his writings does their peculiarity occur so continuously as in a series of Letters, entitled "**High and Low Life in Italy**". Every sarcasm, irony, jest, or touch of humour, is secreted beneath the skin of each tingling member of his sentences. His wit and his humour are alike covered up amidst various things, apparently intended to lead the reader astray, as certain birds are wont to do when you approach the nests that contain their broods. Or, the main jests and knotty points of a paragraph are planed down to the smooth level of the rest of the sentences, so that the reader may walk over them without knowing anything of the matter. All this may be natural to his genius; it may also result from pride, or perversity. So far from seeking the public, his genius has displayed a sort of apathy, if not antipathy, to popularity; *therefore,* the public must court it, if they would enjoy it; to possess yourself of his wit you must scrutinize; to be let into the secret of his humour you must advance 'pointing the toe'. (p. 120)

The imagination of Mr. Landor is richly graphic, classical, and subtly refined. In portraying a character, his imagination identifies itself with the mentality and the emotions of its inner being, and all those idiosyncracies which may be said to exist between a man and himself, but with which few, if anybody else, have any business. In other respects, most of his characters—especially those of his own invention—might live, think, move, and have their being in space, so little does their author trouble himself with their corporeal conditions. Whether it be that their author feels his own *physique* so strongly that it does not occur to him that any one else can need such a thing—*he* will find all that for them—or that it is the habit of his genius to abstract itself from corporeal realities (partly from the perverse love a man continually has of being his own 'opposite'), and ascend into a more subtle element of existence,—certain it is that many of his characters are totally without material or definite *form;* appear to live nowhere, and upon nothing, and to be very independent agents, to whom practical action seldom or never occurs. 'They think, therefore they are'. They feel, and know (they are apt too often to know as much as their author) therefore they are characters. But they are usually without bodily substance; and such form as they seem to have, is an abstraction which plays round them, but might go off in air at any time, and the loss be scarcely apparent. The designs of his larger works, as wholes, are also deficient in compactness of form, precision of outline, and condensation. They often seem wild, not at all intellectually, but from ungoverned will. It is difficult not to arrive at conclusions of this kind—though different minds will, of course, see differently—after a careful study of the dramas of *Andrea of Hungary, Giovanna of Naples,*

and *Fra Rupert;* the *Pericles and Aspasia,* the *Pentameron and Pentalogia,* &c. The very title of the *Imaginary Conversations* gives a strong foretaste of Mr. Landor's predominating ideality, and dismissal of mortal bonds and conditions. The extraordinary productions last named are as though their author had been rarified while listening to the conversation, or the double soliloquies, of august Shades; all of which he had carefully written down on resuming his corporeality, and where his memory failed him he had supplied the deficiency with some sterling stuff of his own. The Landorean 'peeps' seen through these ethereal dialogues and soliloquies of the mighty dead, are seldom to be mistaken; and though hardly at times in accordance with their company, are seldom unworthy of the highest.

As a partial exception to some of the foregoing remarks should be mentioned the *Examination of William Shakespeare before Sir Thomas Lucy, Knt., touching Deer-stealing.* Of all the thousands of books that have been issued from the press about Shakespeare, this one of Mr. Landor's is by far the most admirable. It is worth them all. There is the high-water mark of genius upon every page, lit by as true a sun as ever the ocean mirrored. Perfect and inimitable from beginning to end, that it has not become the most popular of all the books relating to Shakespeare, is only to be accounted for by some perversity or dullness of the public. The book is, certainly, not read. There is great love and reading bestowed upon every cant about Shakespeare, and much interest has been shown in all the hoaxes. (pp. 121-22)

Mr. Landor is not at all the product of the present age; he scarcely belongs to it; he has no direct influence upon it: but he has been an influence to some of its best teachers, and to some of the most refined illustrators of its vigorous spirit. For the rest—for the duty, the taste, or the favour of posterity—when a succession of publics shall have slowly accumulated a residuum of 'golden opinions' in the shape of pure admiring verdicts of competent minds, then only, if ever, will he attain his just estimation in the not altogether impartial roll of Fame. (p. 124)

> *Elizabeth Barrett with Richard Hengist Horne,* "*Walter Savage Landor,*" *in* A New Spirit of the Age, *edited by Richard Hengist Horne, 1844. Reprint by Oxford University Press, 1907, pp. 107-24.*

[JOHN FORSTER]   (essay date 1846)

[*The following excerpt is taken from a review of a revised edition of the* Imaginary Conversations, *which Forster assisted Landor in editing. Here, Forster comments on Landor's changes and additions to the new collection. For further criticism by Forster, see the excerpt dated 1836 and the Additional Bibliography.*]

When this Journal formerly spoke of the *Imaginary Conversations* [see excerpt by Hazlitt dated 1824], it was pointed out how exquisite the discrimination of character was in many cases, and how strange and wilful the indifference to it in others: How imperfect the dramatic appreciation of the intellect of the speakers, and of the literary tone of the age. . . . We might again take up and pursue this contrast. We might show how subtle and exact the art which sets before us the colloquy of "**Marvel and Parker,**" of the "**Emperor of China and his Minister,**" of "**Rochefoucault and La Fontaine,**" of "**Melancthon and Calvin,**" of "**Steele and Addison,**" of "**Lucian and Timotheus**"; and of other and grander Voices from the graves of Greece and Rome—while we condemned, for mere wilful singularity and want of keeping, the hearty, instead of dry tone of his **"Washington"**; the odd retinence of his **"Abbé Delille,"** who, being the most talkative Frenchman on record, lets the Englishman have almost all the talk to himself; the mere self-ventriloquizing of his **"Franklins," "Southeys," "Romillys," "Sheridans," "Talleyrands,"** and even his **"Galileos"** and **"Miltons"**;—his well-educated language, where no such advantage could possibly have been heard of; and his high reasoning powers, where nothing of the kind existed. In one of the many additions to the old Dialogues which we observe in this Collection, there is indeed an answer attempted on the latter point. Mr Landor intimates that no one would care for his statesmen and kingly interlocutors of the inferior class, if he were to show them as they show themselves,—encrusted with all the dirtiness they contract in public life, in the debility of ignorance, in the distortion of prejudice, or in the trickery of partisanship. He reasons that, principles and ideas being his objects, they must not only be reflected from high and low, but must also be exhibited where people can see them best, and are most inclined to look at them; and he implies that if this is a blemish in his book, it is one his book would be worse without.

We doubt this. We have great faith for what is exact and true in every thing, and would for the most part leave it to tell for what it simply is. And we suspect the secret of these perverse departures from obvious character, to lie no deeper than Mr Landor's substitution of his own caprice and pleasure for all other considerations. It is very clear to us in such cases, that it is Mr Landor himself who is too plainly visible throughout, whomsoever he makes the organ of his opinions; and with all our hearty admiration of him,—we must own that in the special instances adverted to, we are obstructed and thrown back by an amount of this personal wilfulness, far from becoming such an arbiter and universalist as we otherwise gladly recognize in him. His opinions are then greatly too much at the command of his predilections;—sometimes of his momentary humours. He has capricious enmities, and unreasonable likings. You see assent and dissent occasioned by mere regard for one speaker, and dislike for another. He runs into violent hyperboles both of praise and blame; is a great deal too fond, for a demonstrative critic, of sweeping preferences of this and that, to 'all' that 'ever' was written in 'any' age or country; is apt to have more images than arguments, owing to the same exuberance of fancy; sometimes allows his robust animal spirits to swell to insolence, or to degenerate into coarseness; is often too prolix in his jokes and stories; and (to get rid as fast as we can of these objections on limited points) is too much tempted, by the nicety and exactness of his scholarship, to substitute verbal criticism for spiritual; and to tire his readers with accumulated objections to people whom the world have long ceased to make gods of.

But, these drawbacks stated, how little in reality they affect the great bulk of these Conversations. What a weighty book they make! How rich in scholarship; how correct, concise, and pure in style; how full of imagination, wit, and humour; how well informed, how bold in speculation, how various in interest, how universal in sympathy! In these hundred and twenty-five Dialogues, making allowance for every shortcoming or excess, the most familiar and the most august shapes of the Past are reanimated with vigour, grace, and beauty. Its long dead ashes rekindle suddenly their wonted fires, and again shoot up into warmth and brightness. 'Large utterances,' musical and varied voices, 'thoughts that breathe' for the world's advancement, 'words that burn' against the world's oppression, sound on throughout these lofty and earnest pages. We are in the high and goodly company of Wits and Men of Letters; of

Churchmen, Lawyers, and Statesmen; of Party men, Soldiers, and Kings; of the most tender, delicate, and noble Women; and of Figures that seem this instant to have left for us the Agora or the Schools of Athens,—the Forum or the Senate of Rome. At one moment we have politicians discussing the deepest questions of state; at another, philosophers still more largely philosophizing;—poets talking of poetry, men of the world of worldly matters, Italians and French of their respective Literatures and Manners. Whether such a book obtains its meed now or hereafter, will be the least part of its writer's concern: whether it is to be read in the present age or the next, may occupy his thought no more than whether in the morning or the afternoon of the present day. . . . Mr Landor's genius has a wonderfully suggestive quality. Even where he most offends against taste or judgment, he rarely fails to stimulate thought and reflection. Paradoxes, in him simply wilful and preposterous, will often be found to contain very profound truths for us. We may assent or we may oppose, but we must *think* when in company with him; and we shall always find ourselves the wealthier for what thought germinates within us. How much the more when, in his higher and nobler compositions, we see Suggestion drop its richest fruit in perfected and consummate Truths; and when every thought and feeling are such, as he who writes must have been the better for having entertained and uttered, and we who read are certainly the better and the happier for being permitted to partake. There are differences in the Dialogues as striking, as between the summer air on a mountain top, and the crowded atmosphere of a busy city. But the reader will make his choice according to his temper; for in both . . . there is 'much matter to be heard and learn'd.'

Nor need he fear that his temper will be ruffled, here, by the eccentric spelling which prevailed in former editions of the *Imaginary Conversations*. In the book before us, to reverse a reproach we have heard levelled against his orthographic infidelities, Mr Landor spells like a Christian. It would be difficult to guess why, unless some friend has been at the pains to assure him that a popular appreciation of his writings had been somewhat intercepted, by a prevalent notion that he had not been taught spelling. A conversion it certainly is not. It is a mere tribute to fashion, a kind of sacrifice to ignorance; for we observe evidence in the additions to the old dialogue of **"Johnson and Horne Tooke,"** of even the strengthening and deepening of his orthographic heresy. . . . (pp. 487-90)

It would be too curious a labour to indicate all the additions and interpolations to the old Dialogues that have been made in this collection. In amount, we imagine, they would form little less than a sixth or seventh of the original; yet so skilfully are they interwoven, that to track and follow them is difficult. We find them in no case, for instance, interfere with that remarkable tact in the conduct of the Dialogues, by which a singular variety of topics is always sustained in each, without undue or violent transition; or any thing more of abruptness than should characterise the freedom and strength of conversation, and convey that mingled tone of study and society, which David Hume lays down to be the master-art of this style of composition. (p. 491)

[The conversations that have not before been collected] show, in undiminished force and vivacity, every characteristic of Mr Landor's genius. Any writer might have built, upon these compositions alone, an enduring reputation. The same beauties and the same faults recur; but the latter in diminished intensity. They have matter as various, and character as opposite and enlivening;—as much to occupy the intellect of the thoughtful, and as much to satisfy the imagination of the lively. They form an after-course, in short, worthy of the original banquet;—spread with the same solid viands, the same delicate rarities, and sparkling wines; the like vases of burnished gold on the board, the like statues of antique marble gracing the chamber;—but the very richness of the vases showing dark to imperfect vision, and the pure Greek on the plinths of the marble not easy to common appreciation.

Four of these new Dialogues seem to us to stand out preeminently from the rest. These are **"Lucian and Timotheus,"** **"Marvel and Parker,"** **"Emperor of China and his Minister,"** and **"Melancthon and Calvin."** In these the dramatic tone is as perfect as every other quality in the composition; and we may doubt if, in any other equal portion of Mr Landor's writings, there will be found so much beauty and fitness, so much point and gusto, so much condensation and strength. We have heard his friend Southey characterize his style, as uniting the poignancy of Champagne to the body of old English October; and nowhere, assuredly, but in Bacon or in Jeremy Taylor, do we find Prose-Poetry to compare with his,—in weight and brilliancy, or in wonderful suggestiveness. What Lucian says of Aristotle in the latter respect, we may apply to him. Whenever he presents to his readers one full-blown thought, there are several buds about it which are to open in the cool of the study. He makes us learn even more than he teaches. Without hesitation we say of these four Dialogues, and eminently of that between **"Marvel and Parker,"** that they contain a subtle discrimination of character, and passages of feeling and philosophy, pathetic, lofty, and profound, which we should not know where to equal in any living writer, and in very few of those who are immortal. (pp. 500-01)

The author and outpourer of [these works], stands apart from ordinary writers, and will be known, esteemed, and listened to, when all the rubbish of light and fashionable reading, which has so choked up our generation, shall have passed away. He has himself somewhere finely said, that the voice comes deepest from the sepulchre, and a great name has its root in the dead body. He is doubtless, for himself, well content to obey that law. But this Collection of his Writings has reminded us, for our own part, not to wait until 'deaf the praised ear, and mute the tuneful tongue.' Others, let us hope, will follow our example. And thus, while Mr Landor yet lives, he may hear what is violent and brief in his writings forgiven—what is wise, tranquil, and continuous, gratefully accepted—and may know that he has not vainly striven for those high rewards which he has so frequently and fully challenged. 'Fame, they tell you, is air; but without air there is no life for any—without fame there is none for the best.' (p. 511)

[*John Forster*], *"Landor's 'Collected Writings—New Imaginary Conversations',"* in The Edinburgh Review, *Vol. LXXXIII, No. CLXVIII, April, 1846, pp. 486-511.*

THOMAS DE QUINCEY (essay date 1847)

[*An English critic and essayist, De Quincey used his own life as the subject of his best-known work,* Confessions of an English Opium Eater, *in which he chronicled his addiction to opium. De Quincey contributed reviews to a number of London journals and earned a reputation as an insightful if occasionally long-winded literary critic. In this excerpt from his commentary on* Gebir, *De Quincey admires the "sculpturesque" qualities of the little-read poem. For further criticism by De Quincey, see the Additional Bibliography.*]

[Mr. Landor] is a man of great genius, and, as such, he *ought* to interest the public. More than enough appears of his strong, eccentric nature, through every page of his now extensive writings, to win, amongst those who have read him, a corresponding interest in all that concerns him personally: in his social relations, in his biography, in his manners, in his appearance. Out of two conditions for attracting a *personal* interest, he has powerfully realised one. His moral nature, shining with coloured light through the crystal shrine of his thoughts, will not allow of your forgetting it. A sunset of Claude, or a dying dolphin, *can* be forgotten, and generally *is* forgotten; but not the fiery radiations of a human spirit, built by nature to animate a leader in storms, a martyr, a national reformer, an arch-rebel, as circumstances might dictate, but whom too much wealth, and the accidents of education, have turned aside into a contemplative recluse. Had Mr. Landor, therefore, been read in any extent answering to his merits, he must have become, for the English public, an object of prodigious personal interest. We should have had novels upon him, lampoons upon him, libels upon him; he would have been shown up dramatically on the stage; he would, according to the old joke, have been "traduced" in French, and also "overset" in Dutch. Meantime he has *not* been read. It would be an affectation to think it. Many a writer is, by the sycophancy of literature, reputed to be read, whom in all Europe not six eyes settle upon through the revolving year. Literature, with its cowardly falsehoods, exhibits the largest field of conscious Phrygian adulation that human life has ever exposed to the derision of the heavens. Demosthenes, for instance, or Plato, is not read to the extent of twenty pages annually by ten people in Europe. The sale of their works would not account for three readers; the other six or seven are generously conceded as possibilities furnished by the great public libraries. But, then, Walter Savage Landor, though writing a little in Latin, and a very little in Italian, does not write at all in Greek. So far he has some advantage over Plato; and, if he writes chiefly in dialogue, which few people love to read any more than novels in the shape of letters, *that* is a crime common to both. So that he has the 'd—l's luck and his own, all Plato's chances, and one of his own beside—viz. his English. Still it is no use counting chances; facts are the thing. And printing-presses, whether of Europe or of England, bear witness that neither Plato nor Landor is a marketable commodity. In fact, these two men resemble each other in more particulars than it is at present necessary to say. Especially they were both inclined to be luxurious: both had a hankering after purple and fine linen; both hated "filthy dowlas" with the hatred of Falstaff, whether in appareling themselves or their diction; and both bestowed pains as elaborate upon the secret *art* of a dialogue as a lapidary would upon the cutting of a sultan's rubies.

But might not a man build a reputation on the basis of *not* being read? To be read is undoubtedly something; to be read by an odd million or so, is a sort of feather in a man's cap; but it is also a distinction that he has been read absolutely by nobody at all. . . . [However] it can be proved against Mr. Landor, that he has been read by at least a score of people, all wide awake; and if any treason is buried in a page of *his*, thank Heaven, by this time it must have been found out and reported to the authorities. So that neither can Landor plead the unlimited popularity of a novelist, aided by the interest of a tale, and by an artist, nor the total observation of a German metaphysician. Neither do mobs read him, as they do M. Sue; nor do all men turn away their eyes from him, as they do from Hegel.

This, however, is true only of Mr. Landor's prose works. His first work was a poem, vis. *Gebir;* and it had the sublime distinction, for some time, of having enjoyed only two readers; which two were Southey and myself. . . . Not knowing Southey at that time, I vainly conceited myself to be the one sole purchaser and reader of this poem. I even fancied myself to have been pointed out in the streets of Oxford, where the Landors had been well known in times preceding my own, as the one inexplicable man authentically known to possess *Gebir,* or even (it might be whispered mysteriously) to have read *Gebir.* It was not clear but this reputation might stand in lieu of any independent fame, and might raise me to literary distinction. (pp. 18-19)

By the way, the propensity to *scandalum magnatum* in Aroar was one of the things that fixed my youthful attention, and perhaps my admiration, upon *Gebir.* For myself, as perhaps the reader may have heard, I was and am a Tory; and in some remote geological era, my bones may be dug up by some future Buckland as a specimen of the fossil Tory. Yet, for all that, I loved audacity; and I gazed with some indefinite shade of approbation upon a poet whom the attorney-general might have occasion to speak with.

This, however, was a mere condiment to the main attraction of the poem. *That* lay in the picturesqueness of the images, attitudes, groups, dispersed everywhere. The eye seemed to rest everywhere upon festal processions, upon the panels of Theban gates, or upon sculptured vases. . . . [In *Gebir* there are many] striking illustrations of this sculpturesque faculty in Mr. Landor; and for this faculty it was that both Southey and myself separately and independently had named him the English Valerius Flaccus. (p. 21)

> *Thomas De Quincey, "Notes on Walter Savage Landor," in* Tait's Edinburgh Magazine, *Vol. XIV, No. CLVII, January, 1847, pp. 18-23.*

WALTER SAVAGE LANDOR   (essay date 1847)

[*In his preface to* The Hellenics, *Landor contrasts the clarity of his poetry with the "prismatic" works of his contemporaries. For additional commentary by Landor, see excerpts dated 1798 and 1800.*]

Prefixing a preface is like keeping an invited friend at the hall-door, instead of conducting him at once into the house.

Little in these pages [*The Hellenics*] will gratify the generality of readers. Poetry, in our day, is oftener prismatic than diaphanous: this is not so: they who look into it may see through. If there be anywhere a few small air-bubbles, it yet leaves to the clear vision a wide expanse of varied scenery. (p. i)

> *Walter Savage Landor, in a preface to his* The Hellenics of Walter Savage Landor: Comprising Heroic Idyls, &c., *revised edition, 1847. Reprint by R. Griffin and Co., 1859, pp. i-ii.*

[AUBREY DE VERE]   (essay date 1850)

[*De Vere, a prolific Anglo-Irish poet, critic, and essayist, here reviews* The Hellenics, *noting the influence of classical Greek literature on the poems.*]

[*The Hellenics*] cannot be better described than by saying that the name has not been ill-chosen. The subject of nearly all the poems it contains is supplied by Greece, and the treatment is in accordance with that subject. . . .

The Hellenics have all the clear outline, the definite grace, and the sunny expansiveness of Greek poetry, and not less its aversion to the mysterious and the spiritual. Above all they are classical in their peculiar mode of dealing with outward nature. (p. 409)

[The merit of Landor's poem "**The Hamadryad**"] consists chiefly in the art with which the mythological idea is blended with a human interest. (p. 413)

It is in delineating the least pronounced part of the Greek mythology that a clear discernment of its meaning is most required. In ["**The Hamadryad**"], . . . the shadowy nature of a being not so much elevated above our mortal nature as standing at one side of it, seems to us most happily indicated. Such discrimination has long been rare, both in French and in English poetry. (p. 415)

The merit of Mr. Landor's poetry consists . . . more in the grace of his narratives, the skill with which they are worked out, and the perfection of their proportions, than in particular passages. . . . (p. 417)

The most deeply-toned and perhaps the most beautiful of Mr. Landor's Hellenics is that one which bears the name of Corythos, the son of Paris and of Oenone. . . .

The reader will linger over and return to many passages of this poem; especially to the description of Helen, and the lamentation of Oenone, as—the tears dried on her cheek by the bitter wind—she stands among the cones and the whirling pine-leaves with which the Idean hill is strewn, and watches her son descending to the city. (p. 419)

Mr. Landor's poetry has sometimes been charged with a deficiency of pathos. It is true that in general he loves rather to exhibit human life in the exhilarating and equable light of day, than tinged with the lights of a low horizon, and clouded with those extended shadows which belong especially to the declining eventide of literature. His pathos has, notwithstanding, a peculiar depth and tenderness; and though unostentatious, is very far from being infrequent. (p. 420)

If Mr. Landor's various dramas were braced and animated by such a spirit as sustains the [tragic scene entitled the "**Madness of Orestes**"], . . . few modern dramatists would stand on his level. Such, however, is not the fact. Many dramatic gifts are fatally marred by one deficiency. He has not, apparently, the faculty of devising a plot in which incident not only follows, but results from, incident; while each and all, instead of being connected merely by the chain of phenomenal causation, rest on a moral support, and illustrate character. Mr. Landor is accordingly more successful in his fragmentary dramatic scenes than in his dramas, none of which appear to us written with the same power, either in the delineation of character or of passion, which is to be found in many of his *Imaginary Conversations;* as, for instance, in that true prose poem, the dialogue between Tiberius and Vipsania; or that one between Peleus and Thetis, in which a mournful passion is so marvellously introduced into a subject belonging, it might seem, exclusively to the imagination. (p. 421)

It is in Mr. Landor's minor poems that we find most abundantly that delicacy, propriety, sweetness, and concise precision, which so eminently distinguish his poetry, and remind us of the Greek anthology. (p. 428)

Mr. Landor seems to turn with aversion from many forms of composition to which recent poetry has habituated us. A ballad is not to be found among his works; nor a didactic poem; nor a sonnet; nor, we might say, a song, using the term in its stricter sense. The temperament of his poetry, buoyant at once and serene, lacks apparently that vehement excitability which precipitates itself into fragmentary snatches of music, such as the songs of our early dramatists. Among his poems, on the other hand, we find many species with which we are familiarised in ancient poetry. The Idyl, especially that larger and graver kind for which, in his Latin volume, he claims the title of "Idyllia Heroica," appears to be his favourite; but he is also attached to the elegiac commemoration, to the brief but pregnant inscription, and to the epigram, especially to that species of epigram which embodies poetry not wit, and which can dispense with a sting in the last line. These poems are frequently marked by a playful tenderness, and as often by a tender pathos. (p. 429)

The unobtrusiveness of true poetry, a quality not sufficiently valued and but infrequently exemplified of late, is among the higher characteristics of Mr. Landor's. He is wholly free from exaggeration, and he never transgresses the Delphic precept . . . 'not too much of anything.' Nothing is inserted for effect; and his best passages, contented often to lurk in shadow, are never rendered more salient by a sprinkling of 'barbaric pearl and gold.' Thus, in his pages, heroism never struts, and sorrow never wails. Seldom, indeed, has fine poetry more ascetically renounced finery, or passion more religiously abstained from bluster. It is these qualities which impart to his verse that gentlemanly character which is observed to belong to it. Unobtrusiveness is not, however, likely to conduce to the popularity of a poet in these days. An object must sparkle to catch immediate attention when seen through the dust of the thoroughfare; and in the press and crush of modern literature, the thought which is not forward to claim a place, is likely to wait long without one. The music which is music only will be heard but in the still gallery or lonely grove; while the louder instrument, that sounds of wood and wire also, flings its noisy peal across the clamour of the throng.

Mr. Landor's poetry has not been popular. Warmly as the admiration of not a few among our first poets as well as scholars has been expressed with regard to it, that sentiment has not, as yet, made its way to the mass of readers. From our remarks upon that poetry, it may not unreasonably be inferred that the absence of popularity has proceeded from the peculiar character at once of its merits and of its defects. Refinement, grace, and condensed thought are not the qualities which most immediately recommend themselves to the public; and, on the other hand, there are few faults which a reader finds it more difficult to forgive than that obscurity which makes him discontented with himself as well as with the author. Mr. Landor's prose works also have in some measure merged his poetical in his literary fame, representing, as they do, a larger portion of his mind, and embodying the stronger, though not the higher part of his genius. (p. 430)

Mr. Landor's genius, not only does not sympathise with the present age, but has been, from first to last, in ardent sympathy with the imaginative and social associations of a remote era. To the Ideal as distinguished from the National school of English poetry, his poetry belongs exclusively and without admixture, being in this respect homogeneous. The question, then, as to his future popularity is part of a much larger inquiry. It is this: Do the poets of antiquity obtain the popular sym-

pathies of our countrymen, or must we admit that they lived in the hearts of those only for whom, and among whom, they wrote, and that they can but delight the imagination of the studious at this distant day? (p. 431)

[*Aubrey De Vere*], *"Landor's Poetry," in* The Edinburgh Review, *Vol. XCI, No. CLXXXIV, April, 1850, pp. 408-43.*

THE LONDON QUARTERLY REVIEW   (essay date 1854)

[*In the excerpt below, the anonymous critic praises the literary quality and varied genres found in* The Last Fruit off an Old Tree.]

The poetic prefix of Mr. Landor's last volume [*The Last Fruit off an Old Tree*] is highly characteristic of his genius, and furnishes in brief the sum of his career. It is also a good example of his style; a style remarkable for strength and terseness, and, if somewhat hard, yet, at the same time, picturesque and pure:—

I strove with none, for none was worth my strife;
    Nature I loved, and, next to nature, art:
I warm'd both hands before the fire of life;
    It sinks, and I am ready to depart.

Here we have the bold independence and self-assertion which have always distinguished him, marking him out from men of feebler mould, like Coriolanus among degenerate Romans, and urging him, sometimes to "flutter the Volsces" in a hostile camp, and sometimes, with petulant haste, to join the forces of an enemy, and pour scorn and contumely on his own "countrymen and lovers." Here, too, his love of nature, surviving youth and riper manhood, and crowning his old age with a second spring; his delight in all the miracles of art; his joyous welcome of all that life affords, and keen relish for its thousand blessings; and, not less prominent than his epicurean gladness in the intellectual past and sensuous present, his stoical indifference to all that may await him in the mysterious and impending future. If you would figure to yourself how a heathen of the classic age would demean himself, if suddenly transported into our present era, make intimate acquaintance with the writings of Walter Landor. To our minds, the single quatrain we have quoted awakens so many recollections of their beauty, that we seem to realize the conception at once, and hail him as a grand antique,—a living representative, but not a marble image. The firm grip of his friendly hand; the occasional disdain of his haughty head; the smile with which he greets the simple beauty of a field-flower, or the matchless grace of infancy; his passion for ideal liberty and natural beauty; his impatience of all meanness, servility, and fraud; his warm and generous friendships, and his hasty and more general enmities; his soft pity for the slave, and his fierce hatred of the tyrant;—these are all marks of his peculiar greatness. But, while his intellectual character is almost purely classic, it was not possible that in all things he should resist the influence of a Christian age, and be entirely Pagan in his soul. In literature and art and politics, he is a Grecian of the age of Pericles; but, in the higher humanities,—in all but its spiritual and evangelic type,—he is a Christian of the Protestant and English Church. And now we have Walter Landor gathering the last fruits of his genius, and sending them to market for the benefit of two humble and persecuted Christians; turning from the contemplation of "the physiognomies of Solon and Pericles, of Phocion and Epicurus," and fixing an admiring regard on Francesca and Rosa Madiai.

Homely, [says he,] very homely, are the countenances and the figures of the Madiai. But they also have their heroism: they took the same choice as Hercules, preferring virtue to pleasure, labour to ease, rectitude to obliquity; patient of imprisonment, and worshipping God with unfaltering devotion, unterrified by the menaces of death. May they awaken, if not enthusiasm, at least benevolence! In which hope, on their behalf, and for their sole emolument, I edit this volume.

Let us not quarrel with Mr. Landor because the grounds of his sympathy with this persecuted pair are haply lower than ours,—that he feels admiration for their fortitude, but professes no share in the sublime convictions to which, in them at least, such fortitude is due. Be it his to refer to the choice of Hercules, the type and parable of heathen virtue; but this, too, is included in another reference, surely far more appropriate, which a thousand hearts will instinctively make,—to the humble martyrs of our faith in the early ages of the Church.

Not its charitable object only, but its literary excellence also, will commend this volume of *Last Fruit*. It contains something in every species of composition to which our author has devoted himself; and, if not equal to the best of his former writings,—which it would be unreasonable to expect from a volume published in the author's eightieth year,—they indicate, at least, no positive declension of his powers. Of the *Conversations* he says, in allusion to the living interlocutors, "No sculptor can work in sandstone so artistically or effectively as in alabaster and marble." Yet some of these are fine examples of a class of writing, not, indeed, invented by Mr. Landor, yet stamped by his genius with a new and higher charm. None of the present series could have been written by a pen less pointed or less firm than his. Three admirable papers—on Theocritus, Catullus, and Petrarca respectively—show that his critical power is no way abated. His Letters on Popery are less to our liking; and those to Cardinal Wiseman are too full of obscure irony for popular and pleasant reading. Of poem and epigram there is great variety; and his peculiar style of dramatic composition—full of pregnant and picturesque expressions, and pervaded by a certain quiet brooding interest, and thus uniting, as it seems to us, the chaste and solemn spirit of antiquity with the free handling and the fruitful character of the romantic school—is finely exhibited in the **"Five Scenes"** which bring this varied volume to a close. (pp. 289-90)

A review of "Imaginary Conversations of Greeks and Romans" and "The Last Fruit off an Old Tree," in The London Quarterly Review, *Vol. II, No. III, March, 1854, pp. 289-91.*

THE LONDON QUARTERLY REVIEW (essay date 1858)

[*This brief excerpt is gleaned from a negative review of* Dry Sticks, Fagoted by W.S.L.]

We were present with our readers when the *Last Fruits* were gathered from this sturdy and prolific tree [see excerpt dated 1854]. It is now stript from lowest branch to utmost twig, and the relics are before us [in *Dry Sticks, Fagoted by W.S.L.*]. We are not disposed to bewail a destruction which is in no sense premature. Let us own, without suspicion of ingratitude, that we never thoroughly depended on the produce of this wild fruit-tree,—wayward in growth and rude in flavour as it often proved, and never quite ripened even on the sunny side. No

wonder, then, if these lopped branches have an acrid bitterness. Indeed, they are only offered as a fagot of old sticks; and it is just to say that blossoms on not a few of them testify to the presence of a vital moisture in the stem, still sensitive of such a spring as that which is now bursting on every side, and making every hedgerow in England more fragrant than the gardens of Stamboul or Cashmere.

All the characteristics of Mr. Landor's genius survive in these last effusions. His epigrams are as bitter if not as biting as ever; his love versicles are light and trivial as before. His prejudices seem to suffer no abatement; his charities still disport themselves in a narrow circle of love and friendship. We may well doubt the real greatness of a spirit which refuses to mellow and improve; and this reflection, often forced upon the reader of the present volume, makes it but a melancholy bequest. . . .

The volume closes with some translations from the Persian, Latin verses, and tributary poems on our author. It is a little surprising to find Walter Savage Landor publishing encomiums on himself; but we cannot grudge them to a man whose faults have found more eager recognition than his genius or his virtues.

A review of "Dry Sticks, Fagoted by Walter Savage Landor," in The London Quarterly Review, *Vol. X, No. XIX, April, 1858, p. 283.*

THE TIMES, LONDON   (essay date 1858)

[*The following excerpt, taken from an editorial regarding the* Yescombe v. Landor *libel suit, reflects the impact of the scandal on Landor's reputation.*]

What a strange and scandalous story it is that we published yesterday about the old age of Walter Savage Landor! He must be so old that one is almost afraid to talk about his age. He has been so famous a writer in his time that it would have been pleasant to think of him, if still alive, as surrounded by troops of friends who were smoothing the last furlong of his long pilgrimage. He should have outlived the ill-will of others, and the animosities of his own heart. It is with unfeigned reluctance that we perform the duty which has been cast upon us of saying a few words about the trial which took place at Bristol on Monday last, in which Mr. Landor was defendant. . . . Who can read the report of the proceedings without saying that it served him right? The old poet can scarcely lay claim to impunity on the ground of failing intellect. It must be admitted that in their own nasty way—and it is a very nasty way—the verses of Landor's old age are quite equal in point and vigour to the golden produce of his prime. But it is such filthy point—such dirty vigour! Take Jonathan Swift's impurest productions, when he sat down for a regular innings at dirt—take the obscenest off-scourings of Martial, when the Roman poet was wallowing in the very cesspool of the Muses, and you will have an idea of the nature of Landor's recent literary diversions. So far we have spoken of the old man's offence as of one against decency and morality. To describe it technically, according to the form in which it was brought the other day before the Court, we must, however, speak of it as the publication of a libel; and a fouler libel than the one brought home to him was never written by man. What made the case worse was that he had selected as the object of his attack a lady whose only fault seems to have been that she had been for many years on intimate terms with her unmanly traducer. . . .

Walter Savage Landor, the poet, the man of letters, the gentleman, just tottering on the verge of the grave, actually condescended to have recourse to the expedient of anonymous letters, and these letters contained such filth that one may well wonder how the ideas could occur to a human brain. . . .

How ineffable is the disgrace to a man of Mr. Landor's ability and reputation at the close of a long life to be mixed up with so disgraceful a transaction! A slanderer, and the slanderer of a lady—a writer of anonymous letters, and these letters reeking with the foulest odours of the dirtiest stews—a violator of his pledged word—who is it to whom these words must now be applied?—

Who would not weep if Atticus were he?

> *"Walter Savage Landor," in* The Times, *London, August 25, 1858, p. 6.*

ROBERT BROWNING   (letter date 1864)

[Browning was a major poet of the Victorian age. He befriended Landor when the author, exiled from England and rejected by his wife and children, was found wandering in the streets of Florence "like an old King Lear." In this excerpt from a letter written at the time of Landor's death, Browning recalls the "grand old solitary man."]

Yes, poor Landor is off and away at last—I wish him well with all my heart: he wrote to me a month ago,—"probably about to die in a few weeks or days," but he had cried "Wolf!" so often. Five years care about him, and now he is past me. He has written passages not exceeded in beauty and subtlety by any literature that I am acquainted with; that is my opinion, other people have theirs; he was followed to the grave by two of his sons, and nobody else—the grand old solitary man, beset by weaknesses just as, in his own words, "the elephant is devoured by ants in his inaccessible solitudes." Bless us, if he had let the world tame him and strap a tower on his broad back, what havoc he would have made in the enemy's ranks!—as it was, they let off squibbs at him and he got into a rage and ran off, topsey-turveying his friends right and left. I'll tell you how he talked—the rather that I might not be impudent enough to tell you, if it occurred to me on next edifying Sunday morning's colloquy. "Mrs Landor called today" said I. "Ha—why, you did not let her in—never surely let *her* in?"—"Oh, I should let a dog in, even, bearing your name on the collar!"—"Oh, ay, a *dog*—good! but a—?"

Methinks I have a pleasure in remembering that he "gave her her own," now that the dead lion is being appraised as "worth" so much to the living Landors. (pp. 78-9)

> *Robert Browning, in a letter to Julia Wedgwood on October 3, 1864, in* Robert Browning and Julia Wedgwood: A Broken Friendship as Revealed by Their Letters, *edited by Richard Curle, Frederick A. Stokes Company, 1937, pp. 75-9.*

[ELIZA LYNN LINTON]   (essay date 1869)

[Linton claims that the merits of the Imaginary Conversations *compensate for the serious defects in the works of Landor's old age.]*

[Landor's] genius was the man. What he wrote when at his best, what he thought and felt when most inspired, was more himself than were his mere tempers; his *Imaginary Conver-*

sations were the real and permanent Landor, his passionate outbursts of violence and coarseness were only the outward and temporary man. The one will live for ever, the other will die out of the world's memory in another fifty years or so. . . . No man since Shakespeare's time has written so much wisdom or so much beauty; in no other man's works is there such exquisite tenderness, so much subtlety of thought, such wealth of imagery yet all chaste and nothing glaring, so much suggestiveness and yet such ample fulness. Not a page but contains the most deathless beauty; though also, we confess it sadly, his later volumes are disfigured by coarseness which we wish Landor had died before he had written. But these were his madnesses; we look upon them as the sorrowful ravings of insanity, and so pass them by with solemn pity, lamenting rather than condemning. It is not just to bring them too prominently forward; for he was better than these worst parts of him, and he must not be judged by them. (p. 566)

> *[Eliza Lynn Linton], "Walter Savage Landor," in* The North British Review, *Vol. L, No. C, July, 1869, pp. 550-67.*

[LESLIE STEPHEN]   (essay date 1878)

[Stephen is considered one of the most important English literary critics of the late Victorian and early Edwardian eras. In his criticism, which is often moralistic, Stephen argues that all literature is nothing more than an imaginative rendering, in concrete terms, of a writer's philosophy or beliefs. His analyses often include biographical judgments of the writer as well as the work. In the following excerpt, Stephen admits that he, like many readers, finds Landor's works dull; he then considers the reasons for Landor's failure to earn widespread, lasting fame.]

Landor is perhaps the most striking instance in modern literature of a radical divergence of opinion between the connoisseurs and the mass of readers. The general public have never been induced to read him, in spite of the lavish applauses of some self-constituted authorities. One may go further. It is doubtful whether those who aspire to a finer literary palate than is possessed by the vulgar herd are really so keenly appreciative as the innocent reader of published remarks might suppose. Hypocrisy in matters of taste—whether of the literal or metaphorical kind—is the commonest of vices. There are vintages, both material and intellectual, which are more frequently praised than heartily enjoyed. I have heard very good judges whisper in private that they have found Landor dull; and the rare citations made from his works often betray a very perfunctory study of them. (p. 667)

Southey and Wordsworth had a simple method of explaining the neglect of a great author. According to them contemporary neglect affords a negative presumption in favour of permanent reputation. No lofty poet has honour in his own generation. . . . Landor accepted and defended [this theory] with characteristic vigour. "I have published," he says, in the conversation with Hare, "five volumes of *Imaginary Conversations:* cut the worst of them through the middle, and there will remain in the decimal fraction enough to satisfy my appetite for fame. I shall dine late; but the dining-room will be well-lighted, the guests few and select." He recurs frequently to the doctrine. "Be patient!" he says, in another character. "From the higher heavens of poetry, it is long before the radiance of the brightest star can reach the world below. We hear that one man finds out one beauty, another man finds out another, placing his observatory and instruments on the poet's grave. The worms must have eaten us before we rightly know what we are. It is only when we are skeletons that we are boxed and ticketed and prized and shown. Be it so! I shall not be tired of waiting." Conscious, as he says in his own person, that in 2,000 years there have not been five volumes of prose (the work of one author) equal to his *Conversations,* he could indeed afford to wait: if conscious of earthly things, he must be waiting still. (p. 668)

Wordsworth's fame was for a long time confined to a narrow sect, and he did all in his power to hinder its spread by wilful disregard of the established canons—even when founded in reason. A reformer who will not court the prejudices even of his friends is likely to be slow in making converts. But it is one thing to be slow in getting a hearing, and another in attracting men who are quite prepared to hear. Wordsworth resembled a man coming into a drawing-room with muddy boots and a smock-frock. He courted disgust, and such courtship is pretty sure of success. But Landor made his bow in full court-dress. In spite of the difficulty of his poetry, he had all the natural graces which are apt to propitiate cultivated readers. His prose has merits so conspicuous and so dear to the critical mind, that one might have expected his welcome from the connoisseurs to be warm even beyond the limit of sincerity. To praise him was to announce one's own possession of a fine classical taste, and there can be no greater stimulus to critical enthusiasm. One might have guessed that he would be a favourite with all who set up for a discernment superior to that of the vulgar; though the causes which must obstruct a wide recognition of his merits are sufficiently obvious. It may be interesting to consider the cause of his ill success with some fulness; and it is a comfort to the critic to reflect that in such a case even obtuseness is in some sort a qualification; for it will enable one to sympathise with the vulgar insensibility to the offered delicacy, if only to substitute articulate rejection for simple stolid silence. (pp. 669-70)

Landor very frequently bores me. So do a good many writers whom I thoroughly admire. If any courage be wanted for such a confession, it is certainly not when writing upon Landor that one should be reticent for want of example. Nobody ever spoke his mind more freely about great expectations. He is, for example, almost the only poet who ever admitted that he could not read Spenser continuously.... "There is scarcely a poet of the same eminence," says Porson, obviously representing Landor in this case, "whom I have found it so delightful to read in, and so hard to read through." What Landor here says of Spenser, I should venture to say of Landor. There are few books of the kind into which one may dip with so great a certainty of finding much to admire as the *Imaginary Conversations,* and few of any high reputation which are so certain to become wearisome after a time.... But I must also admit, that on thinking of the whole five volumes, so emphatically extolled by their author, I feel certain twinges of remorse. There is a vigour of feeling, an originality of character, a fineness of style which makes one understand, if not quite agree to, the audacious self-commendation. Part of the effect is due simply to the sheer quantity of good writing. Take any essay separately, and one must admit that—to speak only of his contemporaries—there is a greater charm in passages of equal length by Lamb, De Quincey, or even Hazlitt. None of them gets upon such stilts, or seems so anxious to keep the reader at arm's length. But, on the other hand, there is something imposing in so continuous a flow of stately and generally faultless English, with so many weighty aphorisms rising spontaneously, and without a splashing or disturbance, to the surface of talk, and such an easy felicity of theme unmarred by the

flash and glitter of the modern epigrammatic style. Lamb is both sweeter and more profound, to say nothing of his incomparable humour; but then Lamb's flight is short and uncertain. De Quincey's passages of splendid rhetoric are too often succeeded by dead levels of verbosity and laboured puerilities which make annoyance alternate with enthusiasm. Hazlitt is often spasmodic, and his intrusive egotism is pettish and undignified. But so far at least as his style is concerned, Landor's unruffled stream of continuous harmony excites one's admiration the more the longer one reads. Hardly any one who has written so much has kept so uniformly to a high level, and so seldom descended to empty verbosity or to downright slipshod. It is true that the substance does not always correspond to the perfection of the form. There are frequent discontinuities of thought where the style is smoothest. He reminds one at times of those Alpine glaciers where an exquisitely rounded surface of snow conceals yawning crevasses beneath; and if one stops for a moment to think, one is apt to break through the crust with an abrupt and annoying jerk.

The excellence of Landor's style has, of course, been universally acknowledged, and it is natural that it should be more appreciated by his fellow-craftsmen than by general readers less interested in technical questions. The defects are the natural complements of its merits. When accused of being too figurative, he had a ready reply. "Wordsworth," he says in one of his *Conversations,* "slithers on the soft mud, and cannot stop himself until he comes down. In his poetry there is as much of prose as there is of poetry in the prose of Milton. But prose on certain occasions can bear a great deal of poetry; on the other hand, poetry sinks and swoons under a moderate weight of prose, and neither fan nor burnt feather can bring her to herself again." The remark about the relations of prose and poetry was originally made in a real conversation with Wordsworth in defence of Landor's own luxuriance. Wordsworth, it is said, took it to himself, and not without reason, as appears by its insertion in this *Conversation.* The retort, however happy, is no more conclusive than other cases of the *tu quoque.* We are too often inclined to say to Landor as Southey says to Porson in another place: "Pray leave these tropes and metaphors." His sense suffers from a superfetation of figures, or from the undue pursuit of a figure, till the "wind of the poor phrase is cracked." In the phrase just quoted, for example, we could dispense with the "fan and burnt feather," which have very little relation to the thought. (pp. 670-71)

[Lapses] into the inflated are of course exceptional with Landor. There can be no question of the fineness of his perception in all matters of literary form. To say that his standard of style is classical is to repeat a commonplace too obvious for repetition, except to add a doubt whether he is not often too ostentatious and self-conscious in his classicism.... Landor aims, like Bacon, at rich imagery, at giving to thoughts which appear plain more value by fineness of expression, and at compressing shrewd judgments into weighty aphorisms. He would equally rival Cicero in fulness and perspicuity; whilst a severe rejection of everything slovenly or superfluous would save him from ever deviating into the merely florid. So far as style can be really separated from thought, we may admit unreservedly that he has succeeded in his aim, and has attained a rare harmony of tone and colouring.

There may, indeed, be some doubt as to his perspicuity. Southey said that Landor was obscure, whilst adding that he could not explain the cause of the obscurity. Causes enough may be suggested. Besides his incoherency his love of figures which sometimes become half detached from the underlying thought, and an over-anxiety to avoid mere smartness which sometimes leads to real vagueness, he expects too much from his readers, or perhaps despises them too much. He will not condescend to explanation if you do not catch his drift at half a word. He is so desirous to round off his transitions gracefully, that he obliterates the necessary indications of the main divisions of the subject. When criticising Milton or Dante, he can hardly keep his hand off the finest passages in his desire to pare away superfluities. Treating himself in the same fashion, he leaves none of those little signs which, like the typographical hand prefixed to a notice, are extremely convenient, though strictly superfluous. It is doubtless unpleasant to have the hard framework of logical divisions showing too distinctly in an argument, or to have a too elaborate statement of dates and places and external relations in a romance. But such aids to the memory may be removed too freely. The building may be injured in taking away the scaffolding. . . . [However, writers] of far greater obscurity and much more repellent blemishes of style to set against much lower merits, have gained a far wider popularity. The want of sympathy between so eminent a literary artist and his time must rest upon some deeper divergence of sentiment. Landor's writings present the same kind of problem as his life. We are told, and we can see for ourselves, that he was a man of many very high, and many very amiable qualities. . . . But . . . he could never live long at peace with anybody. He was the most impracticable of men, and every turning-point in his career was decided by some vehement quarrel. (pp. 672-74)

His work was marred by the unreasonableness of a nature so impetuous and so absorbed by any momentary gust of passion that he could never bring his thoughts or his plans to a focus, or conform them to a general scheme. His prejudices master him both in speculation and practice. He cannot fairly rise above them or govern them by reference to general principles, or the permanent interests of his life. In the vulgar phrase, he is always ready to cut off his nose to spite his face. . . . With such a temperament, reasoning, which implies patient contemplation and painful liberation from prejudice, has no fair chance; his principles are not the growth of thought, but the translation into dogmas of intense likes and dislikes, which have grown up in his mind he scarcely knows how, and gathered strength by sheer force of repetition instead of deliberate examination.

His writings reflect—and in some ways only too faithfully— these idiosyncrasies. . . . The *Conversations* give much that Landor's friends would have been glad to ignore; and yet they present such a full-length portrait of the man, that it is better to dwell upon them than upon his poetry, which, moreover, with all its fine qualities, is (in my opinion) of far less intrinsic value. The ordinary reader, however, is repelled from the *Conversations* not only by mere inherent difficulties, but by comments which raise a false expectation. An easy-going critic is apt to assume of any book that it exactly fulfils the ostensible aim of the author. So we are told of *Shakspeare's Examination* (and on the high authority of Charles Lamb), that no one could have written it except Landor or Shakspeare himself. When Bacon is introduced, we are assured that the aphorisms introduced are worthy of Bacon himself. What Cicero is made to say is exactly what he would have said, "if he could;" and the dialogue between Walton, Cotton, and Oldways is, of course, as good as a passage from the *Complete Angler*. In the same spirit we are told that the dialogues were to be "one-act dramas;" and we are informed how the great philosophers, statesmen, poets, and artists of all ages did in fact pass across the stage, each represented to the life, and discoursing in his most admirable style.

All this is easy to say; but unluckily represents what the *Conversations* would have been had they been perfect. To say that they are very far from perfect is only to say that they were the compositions of a man; but Landor was also a man to whom his best friends would hardly attribute a remarkable immunity from fault. The dialogue, it need hardly be remarked, is one of the most difficult of all forms of composition. One rule, however, would be generally admitted. Landor defends his digressions on the ground that they always occur in real conversations. If we "adhere to one point," he says (in Southey's person), "it is a disquisition, not a conversation." And he adds, with one of his wilful backhanded blows at Plato, that most writers of dialogue plunge into abstruse questions, and "collect a heap of arguments to be blown away by the bloated whiff of some rhetorical charlatan, tricked out in a multiplicity of ribbons for the occasion." Possibly! but for all that, the perfect dialogue ought not, we should say, to be really incoherent. It should include digressions, but the digressions ought to return upon the main subject. The art consists in preserving real unity in the midst of the superficial deviations rendered easy by this form of conversation. . . . So far as Landor used his facilities as an excuse for rambling, instead of so skilfully subordinating them to the main purpose as to reproduce new variations on the central theme, he is clearly in error, or is at least aiming at a lower kind of excellence. And this, it may be said at once, seems to be the most radical defect in the composition of Landor's *Conversations*. They have the fault which his real talk is said to have exemplified. We are told that his temperament "disqualified him for anything like sustained reasoning, and he instinctively backed away from discussion or argument." Many of the written dialogues are a prolonged series of explosions; when one expects a continuous development of a theme, they are monotonous thunder-growls. Landor undoubtedly had a sufficient share of dramatic power to write short dialogues expressing a single situation with most admirable power, delicacy, and firmness of touch. Nor, again, does the criticism just made refer to those longer dialogues which are in reality a mere string of notes upon poems or proposals for reforms in spelling. . . . But the more elaborate dialogues suffer grievously from this absence of a true unity. There is not that skilful evolution of a central idea without the rigid formality of scientific discussion which we admire in the real masterpieces of the art. We have a conglomerate not an organic growth; a series of observations set forth with never-failing elegance of style, and often with singular keenness of perception; but they do not take us beyond the starting-point. . . . After many digressions and ramblings we find ourselves back on the same side of the original question. We are marking time with admirable gracefulness, but somehow we are not advancing. Naturally flesh and blood grow weary when there is no apparent end to a discussion, except that the author must in time be wearied of performing variations upon a single theme.

We are more easily reconciled to some other faults which are rather due to expectations raised by his critics than to positive errors. No one, for example, would care to notice an anachronism, if Landor did not occasionally put in a claim for accuracy. . . . Were it not that critics have asserted the opposite, it would be hardly worth while to say that Landor's style seldom condescends to adapt itself to the mouth of the speaker, and that from Demosthenes to Porson every interlocutor has palpably the true Landorian trick of speech. Here and there, it is true, the effect is rather unpleasant. Pericles and Aspasia are apt to indulge in criticism of English customs, and no weak regard for time and place prevents Eubulides from denouncing Canning to Demosthenes. The classical dress becomes so thin on such occasions, that even the small degree of illusion which one may fairly desiderate is too rudely interrupted. The actor does not disguise his voice enough for theatrical purposes. It is perhaps a more serious fault that the dialogue constantly lapses into monologue. We might often remove the names of the talkers as useless interruptions. Some conversations might as well be headed, in legal phraseology, Landor *v*. Landor, or at most Landor *v*. Landor and another—the other being some wretched man of straw or Guy Faux effigy dragged in to be belaboured with weighty aphorisms and talk obtrusive nonsense. Hence sometimes we resent a little the taking in vain of the name of some old friend. It is rather too hard upon Sam Johnson to be made a mere "passive bucket" into which Horne Tooke may pump his philological notions, with scarcely a feeble sputter or two to represent his smashing retorts.

There is yet another criticism or two to be added. The extreme scrupulosity with which Landor polishes his style and removes superfluities from poetical narrative, smoothing them at times till we can hardly grasp them, might have been applied to some of the wanton digressions in which the dialogues abound. We should have been glad if he had ruthlessly cut out two-thirds of the conversation between Richelieu and others, in which some charming English pastorals are mixed up with a quantity of unmistakable rubbish. But, for the most part, we can console ourselves by a smile. When Landor lowers his head and charges bull-like at the phantom of some king or priest, we are prepared for, and amused by, his impetuosity. Malesherbes discourses with great point and vigour upon French literature, and may fairly diverge into a little politics; but it is certainly comic when he suddenly remembers one of Landor's pet grievances, and the unlucky Rousseau has to discuss a question for which few people could be more ludicrously unfit—the details of a plan for reforming the institution of English justices of the peace. The grave dignity with which the subject is introduced gives additional piquancy to the absurdity. An occasional laugh at Landor is the more valuable because, to say the truth, one is not very likely to laugh with him. Nothing is more difficult for an author—as he here observes in reference to Milton—than to decide upon his own merits as a wit or humourist. I am not quite sure that this is true; for I have certainly found authors distinctly fallible in judging of their own merits as poets and philosophers. But it is undeniable that many a man laughs at his own wit who has to laugh alone. I will not take upon myself to say that Landor was without humour; he has certainly a delicate gracefulness which may be classed with the finer kinds of humour; but if anybody (to take one instance) will read the story which Chaucer tells to Boccaccio and Petrarch and pronounce it to be amusing, I can only say that his notions of humour differ materially from mine. Landor often sins as distinctly, if not as heavily.

Blemishes such as these go some way perhaps to account for Landor's unpopularity. But they are such as might be amply redeemed by his vigour, his fulness, and unflagging energy of style. There is no equally voluminous author of great power who does not fall short of his own highest achievements in a large part of his work, and who is not open to the remark that his achievements are not all that we could have wished. It is doubtless best to take what we can get, and not to repine if we do not get something better, the possibility of which is suggested by the actual accomplishment. (pp. 675-79)

Is he a man whom we can take to our hearts, treating his vagaries and ill-humours as we do the testiness of a valued friend? Or do we feel that he is one whom it is better to have for an acquaintance than for an intimate? The problem seems to have exercised those who knew him best in life. Many, like Southey or Napier, thought him a man of true nobility and tenderness of character, and looked upon his defects as mere superficial blemishes. If some who came closer seem to have had a rather different opinion, we must allow that a man's personal defects are often unimportant in his literary capacity. (pp. 679-80)

Landor, undoubtedly, may be loved; but I fancy that he can be loved unreservedly only by a very narrow circle. For when we pass from the form to the substance—from the manner in which his message is delivered to the message itself—we find that the superficial defects rise from very deep roots. Whenever we penetrate to the underlying character we find something harsh and uncongenial mixed with very high qualities. He has pronounced himself upon a wide range of subjects; there is much criticism, some of it of a very rare and admirable order; much theological and political disquisition; and much exposition, in various forms, of the practical philosophy which every man imbibes according to his faculties in his passage through the world. It would be undesirable to discuss seriously his political or religious notions. To say the truth, they are not really worth discussing; they are little more than vehement explosions of unreasoning prejudice. (p. 680)

The reason for our not producing more Landors is indeed pretty simple. Men of real poetic genius are exceedingly rare at all times, and it is still rarer to find such a man who remains a schoolboy all his life. Landor is precisely a glorified and sublime edition of the model sixth-form lad, only with an unusually strong infusion of schoolboy perversion. Perverse lads, indeed, generally kick over the traces at an earlier point: refuse to learn anything. Boys who take kindly to the classical are generally good, that is to say, docile. They develop into tutors and professors; or, when the cares of life begin to press, they start their cargo of classical lumber and fill the void with law or politics. Landor's peculiar temperament led him to kick against authority, while he yet imbibed the spirit of the teaching fully, and in some respects rather too fully.

The impatient and indomitable temper which made quiet or continuous meditation impossible, and the accidental circumstances of his life, left him in possession of qualities which are in most men subdued or expelled by the hard discipline of life. Brought into impulsive collision with all kinds of authorities, he set up a kind of schoolboy republicanism, and used all his poetic eloquence to give it an air of reality. But he never cared to bring it into harmony with any definite system of thought, or let his outbursts of temper transport him into settled antagonism with accepted principles. His aristocratic feeling lay deeper than his quarrels with aristocrats. He troubled himself just as little about theological as about political theories: he was as utterly impervious as the dullest of squires to the mystic philosophy imported by Coleridge, and found the world quite rich enough in sources of enjoyment without tormenting himself about the unseen and the ugly superstitions which thrive in mental twilight. But he had quarrelled with parsons as much as with lawyers, and could not stand the thought of a priest interfering with his affairs or limiting his amusements. And so he set up as a tolerant and hearty disciple of Epicurus. Chivalrous sentiment and an exquisite perception of the beautiful saved him from any gross interpretation of his master's principles; although, to say the truth, he shows an occasional laxity on some points which savours of the easy-going pagan, or perhaps of the noble of the old school. As he grew up he drank deep of English literature, and sympathised with the grand republican pride of Milton—as sturdy a rebel as himself, and a still nobler because more serious rhetorician. He went to Italy, and as he imbibed Italian literature, sympathised with the joyous spirit of Boccaccio and the eternal boyishness of classical art. Mediaevalism and all mystic philosophies remained unintelligible to this true-born Englishman. Irritated rather than humbled by his incapacity, he cast them aside, pretty much as a schoolboy might throw a Plato at the head of a pedantic master.

The best and most attractive dialogues are those in which he can give free play to this Epicurean sentiment; forget his political mouthing, and inoculate us for the moment with the spirit of youthful enjoyment. Nothing can be more perfectly charming in its way than Epicurus in his exquisite garden, discoursing, on his pleasant knoll, where, with violets, cyclamens, and convolvuluses clustering round, he talks to his lovely girl-disciples upon the true theory of life—temperate enjoyment of all refined pleasures, forgetfulness of all cares, and converse with true chosen spirits far from the noise of the profane vulgar: of the art, in short, by which a man of fine cultivation may make the most of this life, and learn to take death as a calm and happy subsidence into oblivion. (pp. 684-85)

[The *Pentameron*], and many of the shorter and more dramatic dialogues, have a rare charm, and the critic will return to analyse, if he can, their technical qualities. But little explanation can be needed, after reading them, of Landor's want of

popularity. If he had applied half as much literary skill to expand commonplace sentiment; if he had talked that kind of gentle twaddle by which some recent essayists edify their readers, he might have succeeded in gaining a wide popularity. Or if he had been really, as some writers seem to fancy, a deep and systematic thinker as well as a most admirable artist, he would have extorted a hearing even while provoking dissent. But his boyish waywardness has disqualified him from reaching the deeper sympathies of either class. We feel that the most superhuman of schoolboys has really a rather shallow view of life. His various outbursts of wrath amuse us at best when they do not bore, even though they take the outward form of philosophy or statesmanship. He has really no answer or vestige of answer for any problems of his, nor indeed of any other time, for he has no basis of serious thought. All he can say is, ultimately, that he feels himself in a very uncongenial atmosphere, from which it is delightful to retire, in imagination, to the society of Epicurus, or the study of a few literary masterpieces. That may be very true, but it can be interesting only to a few men of similar taste; and men of profound insight, whether of the poetic or the philosophic temperament, are apt to be vexed by his hasty dogmatism and irritable rejection of much which deserved his sympathy. His wanton quarrel with the world has been avenged by the world's indifference. We may regret the result, when we see what rare qualities have been cruelly wasted, but we cannot fairly shut our eyes to the fact that the world has a very strong case. (p. 686)

[*Leslie Stephen*], ''*Landor's 'Imaginary Conversations*',' in The Cornhill Magazine, *Vol. XXXVIII, No. 228, December, 1878, pp. 667-86.*

ALGERNON CHARLES SWINBURNE　(essay date 1882)

[*Swinburne was an English poet, dramatist, and critic. Though renowned during his lifetime for his lyric poetry, he is remembered today for his rejection of Victorian mores. In the following excerpt from an essay originally published in the ninth edition of* Encyclopaedia Britannica *in 1882, Swinburne expresses his profound admiration for Landor's works.*]

In the course of this long life [Walter Savage Landor] . . . won for himself such a double crown of glory in verse and in prose as has been worn by no other Englishman but Milton. And with that special object of his lifelong veneration he had likewise in common other claims upon our reverence to which no third competitor among English poets can equally pretend. He had the same constancy to the same principles, the same devotion to the same ideal of civic and heroic life; the same love, the same loyalty, the same wrath, scorn, and hatred, for the same several objects respectively; the same faith in the example and kinship to the spirit of the republican Romans, the same natural enjoyment and mastery of their tongue. Not accident merely but attraction must in any case have drawn them to enlist in the ranks and serve under the standard of the ancient Latin army of patriots and poets. But to Landor even more than to Milton the service of the Roman Muse was a natural and necessary expression of his genius, a spontaneous and just direction of its full and exuberant forces. . . . No poet at the age of twenty ever had more vigour of style and fluency of verse [than is evident in *The Poems of Walter Savage Landor* and his anonymous pamphlet, *Moral Epistle, Respectfully Dedicated to Earl Stanhope*]; nor perhaps has any ever shown such masterly command of epigram and satire, made vivid and vital by the purest enthusiasm and most generous indignation. Three years later appeared the first edition of the first great work

A portrait of Landor in 1804.

which was to inscribe his name for ever among the great names in English poetry. The second edition of *Gebir* appeared in 1803, with a text corrected of grave errors and improved by magnificent additions. About the same time the whole poem was also published in a Latin form, which for might and melody of line, for power and perfection of language, must always dispute the palm of precedence with the English version. . . . [Landor's experiences with the Spanish revolutionary army provided material] for the sublimest poem published in our language between the last masterpiece of Milton and the first masterpiece of Shelley—one equally worthy to stand unchallenged beside either for poetic perfection as well as moral majesty—the lofty tragedy of *Count Julian*. . . . No comparable work is to be found in English poetry between the date of *Samson Agonistes* and the date of *Prometheus Unbound;* and with both these great works it has some points of greatness in common. The superhuman isolation of agony and endurance which encircles and exalts the hero is in each case expressed with equally appropriate magnificence of effect. The style of *Count Julian,* if somewhat deficient in dramatic ease and the fluency of natural dialogue, has such might and purity and majesty of speech as elsewhere we find only in Milton so long and so steadily sustained. (pp. 201-03)

From nineteen almost to ninety his intellectual and literary activity was indefatigably incessant; but . . . he could not write a note of three lines which did not bear the mark of his 'Roman hand' in its matchless and inimitable command of a style at once the most powerful and the purest of his age. The one charge which can ever seriously be brought and maintained against it is that of such occasional obscurity or difficulty as may arise from excessive strictness in condensation of phrase and expurgation of matter not always superfluous, and sometimes almost indispensable. His English prose and his Latin verse are perhaps more frequently and more gravely liable to this charge than either his English verse or his Latin prose. At times it is wellnigh impossible for an eye less keen and swift, a scholarship less exquisite and ready than his own, to catch the precise direction and follow the perfect course of his rapid thought and radiant utterance. This apparently studious pursuit and preference of the most terse and elliptic expression which could be found for anything he might have to say could not but occasionally make even so sovereign a master of two great languages appear 'dark with excess of light;' but from no former master of either tongue in prose or verse was ever the quality of real obscurity, of loose and nebulous incertitude, more utterly alien or more naturally remote. There is nothing of cloud or fog about the path on which he leads us; but we feel now and then the want of a bridge or a handrail; we have to leap from point to point of narrative or argument without the usual help of a connecting plank. Even in his dramatic works, where least of all it should have been found, this lack of visible connection or sequence in details of thought or action is too often a source of sensible perplexity. In his noble trilogy on the history of Giovanna Queen of Naples it is sometimes actually difficult to realize on a first reading what has happened or is happening, or how, or why, or by what agency—a defect alone sufficient, but unhappily sufficient in itself, to explain the too general ignorance of a work so rich in subtle and noble treatment of character, so sure and strong in its grasp and rendering of 'high actions and high passions,' so rich in humour and in pathos, so royally serene in its commanding power upon the tragic mainsprings of terror and of pity. As a poet, he may be said on the whole to stand midway between Byron and Shelley,—about as far above the former as below the latter. If we except Catullus and Simonides, it might be hard to match

and it would be impossible to overmatch the flawless and blameless yet living and breathing beauty of his most perfect elegies, epigrams, or epitaphs. . . . His passionate compassion, his bitter and burning pity for all wrongs endured in all the world, found only their natural and inevitable outlet in his lifelong defence or advocacy of tyrannicide as the last resource of baffled justice, the last discharge of heroic duty. . . . He was a classic, and no formalist; the wide range of his just and loyal admiration had room for a genius so far from classical as Blake's. Nor in his own highest mood or method of creative as of critical work was he a classic only, in any narrow or exclusive sense of the term. On either side, immediately or hardly below his mighty masterpiece of *Pericles and Aspasia,* stand the two scarcely less beautiful and vivid studies of mediaeval Italy and Shakespearean England. The very finest flower of his immortal dialogues is probably to be found in the single volume comprising only *Imaginary Conversations of Greeks and Romans;* his utmost command of passion and pathos may be tested by its transcendent success in the distilled and concentrated tragedy of **"Tiberius and Vipsania,"** where for once he shows a quality more proper to romantic than classical imagination—the subtle and sublime and terrible power to enter the dark vestibule of distraction, to throw the whole force of his fancy, the whole fire of his spirit, into the 'shadowing passion' (as Shakespeare calls it) of gradually imminent insanity. Yet, if this and all other studies from ancient history or legend could be subtracted from the volume of his work, enough would be left whereon to rest the foundation of a fame which time could not sensibly impair. (pp. 205-09)

Algernon Charles Swinburne, "Landor," in his Miscellanies, *Worthington Company, 1886, pp. 201-09.*

GEORGE SAINTSBURY   (essay date 1893)

[*Saintsbury was an English literary historian and critic of the late nineteenth and early twentieth centuries. A prolific writer, he composed several histories of English and European literature as well as numerous critical works on individual authors, styles, and periods. In the following excerpt from his study of Landor's poetry, epigrams, and conversations, Saintsbury describes the merits and defects that characterize these works.*]

It is not easy, in reading over again Landor's voluminous poetical work, to decide on the exact reasons which have, with the large majority of readers, relegated it to the upper shelf. It is almost never bad; it is at times extremely good. The famous passages which lighten the darkness of *Gebir* and *Count Julian* are unstaled in their attraction by any custom. You may read **"Rose Aylmer"** for the hundredth time with the certain effect of that "divine despair" which inspires, and is inspired by only, the greatest poetry. **"Dirce,"** and the companion passage which Aspasia sent to Cleone, are equally sure of their own effect. But Landor is by no means obliged to rely on half a dozen purple passages like these. His enormous total of verse . . . never for long fails to yield something altogether out of the common. From the unequal and motelike crowd of the Ianthe trifles to the long "Hellenic" and dramatic or semi-dramatic pieces, the same rule holds good. With Landor you can never read long before coming to the "flashing words, the words of light"; and the light of the flash is always distinct and not like that of any other poetical star. If he is too "classical," he is not more so than many poets of the seventeenth century, especially Jonson, whom he most resembles, and whom, perhaps from a vague sense of likeness, he rather undervalues and belittles. His quality, from its intense peculiarity, is exactly the quality which bribes the literary student. His passion is not unreal; his sense of beauty is exquisite; his power of expressing it is consummate; and yet he is not, at least to some readers, interesting as a whole. They have to gird themselves up to him; to get into training for him; or else to turn basely to the well-known pieces and re-read . . . these only.

The reasons of this are probably reasons of combination. Landor has accumulated different and even contradictory claims to the honour of remaining unread, in a fashion which might seem to be allowable in one whose quest after unpopularity was so ostentatiously intentional. The very scholarly poets are usually rather scant producers; he is enormously voluminous. The dealers in epigrams and short lyrics rarely attempt long-breathed poems; Landor by turns rains epigram (using that word in its proper sense) with the copiousness of a whole anthology, and pours out a steady stream of narrative or dramatic stuff with the ceaseless flow of Spenser. Those two stout volumes [*Poems, Dialogues in Verse, and Epigrams*], crammed with poems of all sorts and sizes, are full of delight for the few who really like to read poetry. Let us permit ourselves *Sortes Landorianae* and open one of the pair without even looking to see which it is. We open on *Dry Sticks*, certainly not a promising place to open, and find these verses:

> 'Tis pleasant to behold
> The little leaves unfold
> Day after day, still pouting at the sun,
> Until at last they dare
> Lay their pure bosoms bare
> Of all these flowers, I know the sweetest one.

Quite trifling verses perhaps, but assuredly not written in a quite trifling style. You may open a hundred volumes of verse as they come fresh from the press and not find one with that style-mark on it. Yet somehow the stoutest devotee of style may be smitten with hideous moments of scepticism when reading Landor. Few men in our days, or in any days at all near them, have had such a faculty of embalming in the self-same amber beautiful things, things presentable, and things absolutely trivial and null. All the defects of the classical and "marmoreal" style are perceived when we come to such a thing as this,

> Better to praise too largely small deserts
> Than censure too severely great defects.

That has most eminently the fault of phrase-making. It is a great question whether even what is true in it is worth saying, and it is a greater question still whether the larger part of it is not false. . . . Why not,

> Better to praise too largely great deserts
> Than censure too severely small defects?

Or,

> Better to praise too scantly great deserts
> Than censure over mildly small defects?

Or in short a dozen other truisms or paradoxes or what not of the same easy kind? It is the inevitable penalty of the "classical" form that it adapts itself with the most delusive submissiveness to almost any matter. (pp. 269-70)

If we turn from Landor's shorter poems to his longer we shall find, in different matter and in different measure, the same merits and the same defects. The poet with whom it is perhaps most natural to compare him is Mr. William Morris. It is indeed almost impossible for any one who knows the two not to think

of the *Hellenics* and the **"Acts and Scenes"** when he reads the *Life and Death of Jason* and the *Earthly Paradise*. Nor is it a very difficult thing to separate the comparative merits and defects of the two. Mr. Morris cannot pretend to Landor's dignity, precision, and lasting certainty of touch. He abounds in surplusage; he is often, if not exactly slipshod, loose and fluid; his singing robe is not girt up quite tight enough, and he tends to the garrulous. But he is always interesting; he has the gift of story, he carries us along with him, and the journey is always easy and sometimes exciting. Landor, though nearly if not quite as voluble as the later poet, has an air of the utmost economy, proportion, and rigour. His phrase, if sometimes rather long, is screwed to concert pitch; he never apparently babbles; there is a show, however modern his subject, of classical severity about him. Yet Landor can be exceedingly longwinded, and does not often succeed in being very interesting. (pp. 270-71)

The merits and defects of Landor's voluminous prose, are much the same; especially in the chief division of that prose, the vast aggregate of the Conversations, into which he preferred to throw such work of his as was not verse, while as has been seen even his verse-work had a tendency to assume the same guise. He seems indeed never to have been quite at home in any other. Perhaps he cannot in any case be ranked high as a critic; but his exercises in that kind, when couched in conversational form, are at any rate much more readable than the so-called criticisms in the eighth volume of his Works, which are either desultory jottings in the nature of annotations, or else worked into a continuous form which is stiff and lifeless. (p. 271)

[Landor] has probably left us the largest, most varied and most elaborate collection of [Conversations] in existence. . . . In some respects Plato of course stands alone; and it is not a favourable symptom of Landor's own capacities that he evidently did not like him. Plato at any rate is the first of all those who have written or ever will write conversations. The only counter claim which Landor can put in against his superiority in dignity of matter and in mastery of style, is the greater variety of his own subjects. There is indeed one other claim which he might urge, though it is an illegitimate one at best, the fuller revelation of personality. We know from the works that go under his name very little, hardly anything, of Plato. . . . [But] we know almost everything of Landor. Given the Conversations as the authentic data, and such things as early troubles at college, an unsatisfactory marriage, ample means, uncongenial surroundings, foreign residence, and the like for conjectural assistance, any novelist who knew his business could depict the life of Walter Savage Landor almost exactly as it happened.

The caution of the author to the reader, "Avoid a mistake in attributing to the writer any opinions in this book but what are spoken under his own name," is interesting but infantile. We always know, we always should know if we knew nothing else about him, from the constant presence of a common and unmistakable form, when Landor is putting Landor's opinions in the mouth of no matter who it may be. If this to some extent communicates a charm to the various and voluminous work concerned, it must be admitted that it also imparts a certain monotony to it. Greek or Roman, medieval or modern, political or amatory, literary or miscellaneous, the Conversations simply convey in stately English, the soon well known and not exceedingly fresh or wide ranging opinions of the author on mundane things, with occasional and not particularly happy excursions into things divine. (pp. 271-72)

The Conversations are full of delightful things, and it is impossible for any fit reader to attempt them without discovering these things. Let the subject admit of any description of natural scenery, any dream-scene (Landor's dreams are very nearly if not quite unapproached), any passage dealing with the greater and simpler emotions, any reflection on the sublime commonplaces of life, and Landor is almost entirely to be depended upon. It does not matter, it never with him matters much, what the nominal subject is; the best things written in connection with it are sure to be fine and may very likely be superb. In the *Pericles and Aspasia* (which indeed is not conversation in form but is hardly distinguishable from it), in *The Pentameron,* in many of the classical dialogues, and in not a few of the Literary Men the author will be found quite at his best. The famous "**Epicurus, Leontium, and Ternissa**" probably shows him at almost his very best, and at very nearly his very worst. In the dialogues of Sovereigns and Statesmen I should say (and not in the least because I generally disagree with the political views there expressed) that he is at his very worst. For politics is after all an eminently practical science, and of the practical spirit Landor had literally nothing. His only plan was to put more or less odious or ridiculous statements in the mouths of persons with whom he does not agree, to mop and mow at them, or to denounce them in Ciceronian strains of invective. The infallible test of a political writer, I think, is the reflection, "Should I like to have this man on my side or not?" For my part whenever I read Landor's political utterances I say, "Thank Heaven! he is on the other."

The dialogues of Famous Women are in the same way flawed by [an] artificial and namby-pamby conception of the female character . . . ; while the Miscellaneous Conversations obviously defy analysis as a whole. The author has left nothing better than some of them, such as the long, curious, unequal, but admirable "**Penn and Peterborough;**" while in others he sinks almost below the level of rational thought. "**Lord Coleraine, Rev. Mr. Bloombury, and Rev. Mr. Swan**" is fully worthy of the author of the *Examination.* It would be difficult to say of whom "**The Duke de Richelieu, Sir Firebrace Cotes, Lady G—, and Mr. Normanby**" is worthy. "**The Emperor of China and Tsing-ti**" is probably the very worst of all the imitations of Montesquieu; and on at least some others as harsh a judgment would have to be passed if they were critically judged at all. (pp. 272-73)

On all happy occasions when his hand is in, when the right subject is before him, and when he is not tempted away from it into the indulgence of some whim, into the memory of some petty wrong, into the repetition of some tiresome crotchet, he manages language literally as a great musician manages the human voice or some other organ of sound. The meaning, though it is often noble, is never the first thing in Landor, and in particular it is quite useless to go to him for any profound, any novel, any far-reaching thought. The thought is at best sufficient, and it very frequently is that; but it seldom makes any tax upon even the most moderate understanding, and it never by any chance averts attention from the beauty and the finish of the vesture in which it is clothed. The famous dreams which close *The Pentameron* are things of which it is almost impossible to tire. Nowhere else perhaps in English does prose style, while never trespassing into that which is not prose, accompany itself with such an exquisite harmony of varied sound; nowhere is there such a complicated and yet such an easily appreciable scheme of verbal music. The sense is, as has been said, just sufficient; it is no more; it is not in itself peculiarly arresting. Although the sentiment is heartfelt, it is not extremely passionate. But it is perfectly and exactly married to the verbal music, and the verbal music is perfectly and

exactly married to it. Again, it is a whole; if not perhaps quite flawless, yet with flaws which are comparatively unimportant. It does not consist, as "fine" writing too often does, of a certain number of more or less happy phrases, notes, or passages strung together. It is, as I have called it a "scheme"; a thing really deserving those terms from the science of actual music which have been so frequently and tediously abused in literary criticism. Moreover the qualities which exist pre-eminently in this and other great passages of Landor appear everywhere on smaller scales in his prose. It is never safe, except when he attempts the comic, to skip a single page. Anywhere you may come across, in five words or in five hundred, the great Landorian phrase, the sentence cunningly balanced or intentionally and deftly broken, the paragraph built with a full knowledge of the fact that a paragraph is a structure and not a heap, the adjective wedded to its proper substantive, not indulging in unseemly promiscuity, the clause proceeding clearly and steadily to the expression of the thought assigned to it. Whatever deficiencies there may be in Landor (and, as has been and will be seen, they are not few) he is seldom if ever guilty of the worst and the commonest fault of the ornate writer, a superabundance of ornament. Of his two contemporaries who tried styles somewhat similar in point of ornateness, Wilson constantly becomes tawdry, while De Quincey sometimes approaches tawdriness. Of this, nearly the worst of literary vices, Landor was constitutionally almost incapable; and his models and methods had converted his natural inaptitude into a complete and absolute immunity. He is sometimes, especially in his fits of personal dignity and scorn, a little too stately for the subject. . . . He is alas! when he unbends this pride, too often clumsily and even indecently gamesome. But with tawdriness, even with indulgence in literary frippery, he cannot for one moment be charged. In this respect, and perhaps in this respect only, his taste was infallible. His good angel was fatally remiss in its warnings on many points wherein such taste is concerned, but in this never.

If we set ourselves to discover the particular note in Landor which occasions these discords we shall find it I believe in a quality which I can only call, as I have called it, silliness. There are other great men of letters who have as much or even more of the quality of childishness; but that is a different thing. Lafontaine and Goldsmith are the two stock examples of childishness in literary history; and childish enough they were, almost inexcusably so in life. But when we find them with pen in hand we never think of them as of anything but very clever men. Landor alone, or almost alone, has written like an angel *and* like poor Poll, and written like both at once. Hazlitt was quite as wrongheaded as Landor, and much more bad-blooded. Peacock was, at any rate in his earlier years, as much the slave of whimsical crazes. Coleridge was as unpractical. His own dear friend Southey had almost as great a difficulty in adjusting the things and estimates of the study to the estimates and the things of the forum. De Quincey was even more bookish and unworldly. But even in passages of these men with which we least agree we do not find positive silliness, a positive incapacity to take the standpoint and the view of a full-grown man who has or ought to have mingled with and jostled against the things of the world and of life. We do find this in Landor. His apologists have admitted that he was always more or less of a schoolboy; I should say that he was always more or less of a baby.

The time-honoured Norman definition of a man is "One who fights and counsels." Landor had in almost superabundant measure that part of man which fights; he was abnormally deficient in the part which counsels. In some cases where taste (of certain, not of all kinds), scholarship, poetic inspiration, chivalry (again of certain kinds), and the like could supply the place of judgment and ratiocinative faculty, he has done nobly, even without taking into account that matchless gift of expression which never deserts him for long together. But in any kind of reasoning proper he is as an infant in arms; and in that faculty which (though sometimes it be divorced from it) comes nearest to the ratiocinative, the faculty of humour, he is almost as defective. Here I know there is great difference and discrepancy between those who should agree; but I shall boldly avow that I think Landor's attempts both at humour and at wit for the most part simply deplorable, as deplorable as his idol Milton's. Some persons whom I respect, as well as others whom I do not, have professed to see a masterpiece of humour in *The Examination of William Shakespeare.* If by a majority of competent critics it is admitted that it is such, I must be a heretic.... [The] entire absence of proportion in matter, so strangely contrasted with his excellent sense of proportion in style, which characterised Landor appears in this matter of the humorous, not perhaps more strongly but, more eminently than anywhere else. It was not that humorous ideas did not visit him, for they did; but he did not in the least know how to deal with them. He mumbles a jest as a bull-dog worries or attempts to worry a rat when he is set to that alien art. His three sets of models, the classics, the English writers of the seventeenth century, and the Italians ... had each in them certain evil precedent suggestions for a jester. Landor with unerring infelicity seized on these, combined them, worked them fully out, and produced things very terrible, things which range from the concentrated dreariness of the *Examination* and the Conversation between Pitt and Canning to the smaller flashes-in-the-pan of joking dulness which are scattered about his writings *passim.*

Another thing which is extremely noticeable about Landor is the marvellously small difference between his poetry and his prose. Except again Milton (an instance ominous and full of fear) and perhaps Wordsworth, I know no other English writer of the first class of which this can be said. But Landor has versified, or almost versified, some of his actual conversations, and has left explicit declaration that not a few of his poems are simply conversations in verse.... The sententious, intense, rhythmical phrase is the same in both; the poetical intuition of sights and sounds, and other delights of sense, is not more obvious in one than in the other. The absence of continuous logical thought is not greater here than there; the remoteness from what may be called the sense of business is always the same, whether the syllables in a line be limited to ten at most, or may run on to as many as the limits of the page will admit. Although he was conscious of, and generally avoided the mistake of introducing definitely poetic rhythm into prose, it is astonishing how close is the resemblance of a short stave of his verse to a sentence of his prose. It is owing to this, among other things, that his form of verse is as compared with that of others a rather severe form, while his prose is, compared with that of others, rather florid. It is owing to this that, while some of the very happiest efforts of his verse have the simplicity and directness of the ancient epigram, some of the most agreeable efforts of his prose have in the proper sense an idyllic character.

And so we have in Landor an almost unmatched example of the merits and the defects of style by itself. To attempt once more to narrow down the reasons of both, I should say that they lie in his having had nothing particular to say with a matchless faculty for saying anything. When the latter faculty is exercised sparingly on the former defect, we often get some of the finest things in literature.... But when the thing is administered in larger and ever larger doses the intensity of the flavour palls and the absence of anything else, besides and behind the flavour, begins to tell. Yet at his very best, and taken in not too large quantities, Landor is the equal of all but the greatest, perhaps of the greatest themselves. And if, according to a natural but rather foolish fashion, we feel at any time inclined to regret that he lived so long and had so much time to accumulate indifferent as well as good work, let us remember on the other hand that his best work is scattered over almost every period of his life, except the very last and the very first, and that the best of it is of a kind worth wading through volumes of inferior work to secure. The true critical question with every writer is, "Could we spare him? Could we do without him?" Most assuredly, if we tried to do without Landor, we should lose something with which no one else could supply us. (pp. 273-76)

> *George Saintsbury, "Landor," in* Macmillan's Magazine, *Vol. 67, No. 400, February, 1893, pp. 267-76.*

FRANCIS THOMPSON   (essay date 1897)

[*Thompson was one of the most important poets of the Catholic Revival in nineteenth-century English literature. Often compared to the seventeenth-century metaphysical poets, Thompson wrote poetry and prose noted for rich verbal effects and a devotion to the values of aestheticism. In this excerpt from an article that was first published in the* Academy *in 1897, Thompson claims that Landor's prose ranks with the best written in the English language, for his classical style and strong expression of personality compensate for his lack of profound subject matter.*]

[Landor's prose] is not, as a rule, imaginative, nor distinguished by any other extra-prose qualities; it gives one no thrill, no "shock of sweet surprise": it is most absolute prose, but also most admirable prose; lucid, structural, with an unclamorous rightness of phrase. Sometimes he goes out of his way for an epithet, with self-justifying result, as when he speaks about "the omnigenous imagery of Shakespeare." The adjective is exactly and felicitously apt, a sentence-saving adjective. But this is rare. He has, in fact, described his own style— probably not unawares.

> Elegance in prose composition is mainly this: a just admission of topics and of words, neither too many nor too few of either; enough of sweetness in the sound to induce us to enter and sit still; enough of illustration and reflection to change the posture of our minds when they would tire; and enough of sound matter in the complex to repay us for our attention.

This does not describe a profound writer, nor is Landor profound. The "sound matter in the complex" is a variable quality with him. He loves paradox and paradoxical satire—for if we have called his writing "absolute prose," we by no means meant to call it prosaic. But the paradox is as likely as not to be more startling than deep; and perhaps one of the circumstances which keep the reader alert in attention is, that you never know whether the next paradox will be convincing or maddeningly perverse. He upholds, for example, the unexpected proposition that Locke is the most elegant of English writers; and to the question why Plato is so much more applauded, answers most Landorianly that it is because he is so much less read. (p. 179)

By what careful study Landor gained his command of English is to be seen in the dialogue between Horne Tooke and Johnson. It deserves to be read for its acute criticism of language—mixed, of course, with Landorian crotchets and obstinacies.

> Since we are become a learned nation . . . , not only the words we have cast aside, but also those we have substituted in the place of them, are mostly injudicious; and such others as we have taken the trouble to construct are unskilful botches.

Landor slips in expression: he does not mean that the words we have cast aside are injudicious, but that it was injudicious to cast them aside. The substance, however, is the view of all those—chiefly poets—who have striven in modern days, against a chorus of facile censure, to revive some of those cast-off pieces of the English tongue. Yet in the midst of his criticism of others he himself uses the horrible comparative "frequenter"—by way, we suppose, of being still a mutineer, and Landor he always is: the *Imaginary Conversations,* which are his classical work in prose, if (as De Quincey insists) they have many points of skilful dialogue, are not dramatic; Chatham, for instance, is not Chatham, but Landor without the smallest of masks. Mr. Coventry Patmore drew a distinction between two kinds of dogmatism: the dogmatism of the seer, and the dogmatism of the man who opines. "By their fruits ye shall know them"—which means that to discern between the two the hearer must himself have the gift of recognising, though not of divining, truth. Landor belonged emphatically to the second class. He is stiff in opinion, not because his vision of truth is so dazzling, but because he has the bull-dog's instinct of hanging-on to whatever comes between his teeth. "Mamma says so," remarked the once famous child in *Punch;* "and if Mamma says so, it *is* so, even if it isn't!" That was the opinion of Walter Savage Landor about Walter Savage Landor's opinions—even when he recommended the Greeks to fight the Turks with bows and arrows instead of firearms. Let us be thankful that a certain genius makes them not too seldom right, and that a classical style allied with a strong personality makes them always interesting. In no intellectual quality, perhaps, can he be called great; but he has written some of the best prose in the English language. (pp. 180-81)

> *Francis Thompson, "Victorian Age: Landor," in his* Literary Criticisms: Newly Discovered and Collected, *edited by Rev. Terence L. Connolly, S. J., E. P. Dutton and Company Inc., 1948, pp. 177-81.*

ARTHUR SYMONS　(essay date 1906)

[*Symons was an English critic, poet, dramatist, short story writer, and editor who first gained notoriety in the 1890s as an English decadent. Eventually, he established himself as one of the most important critics of the modern era. Symons here reviews Landor's poetry. He states that the prose works were Landor's greater achievement, but that his genius, which permeated all his writing, was primarily poetic.*]

[Landor] remains alone in English literature, to which he brought, in verse and prose, qualities of order and vehemence, of impassioned thinking and passionless feeling, not to be found combined except in his own work. And in the man there was a like mingling of opposites: nobility and tenderness, haste and magnanimity, courtesy and irresponsible self-will, whatever is characteristically English and whatever is characteristically Roman, with the defects of every quality. Landor is monumental by the excess of his virtues, which are apt to seem, at times, a little too large for the stage and scenery of his life. He desired to live with grandeur; and there is grandeur in the outlines of his character and actions. But some gust of the will, some flurry of the nerves, was always at hand, to trouble or overturn this comely order. The ancient Roman becomes an unruly child, the scholar flings aside cap and gown and leaps into the arena.

Landor began to write verse when he was a schoolboy, and it is characteristic of him that poetry came to him first as a school exercise, taken for once seriously. Latin was to him, it has been well said, "like the language of some prior state of existence, rather remembered than learned." His first book, published at the age of twenty, contains both Latin and English verse, together with a defense, in Latin, of the modern use of that language. When, a few years later, he began to work upon his first serious poem, *Gebir,* he attempted it both in Latin and in English, finally decided to write it in English, and, later on, turned it also into Latin.

Gebir was published in 1798, the year of the *Lyrical Ballads,* and, in its individual way, it marks an epoch almost as distinctly. No blank verse of comparable calibre had appeared since the death of Milton, and, though the form was at times actually reminiscent both of Milton and of the Latin structure of some of the portions as they were originally composed, it has a quality which still remains entirely its own. Cold, sensitive, splendid, so precise, so restrained, keeping step with such a stately music, scarcely any verse in English has a more individual harmony, more equable, more refreshingly calm to the ear. It contains those unforgettable lines, which can never be too often repeated:—

> But I have sinuous shells of pearly hue
> Within, and they that lustre have imbibed
> In the sun's palace-porch, where when unyoked
> His chariot-wheel stands midway in the wave:
> Shake one and it awakens, then apply
> Its polisht lips to your attentive ear,
> And it remembers its august abodes,
> And murmurs as the ocean murmurs there.

There are in it single lines like,—

> The sweet and honest avarice of love;

and there are lines marching like these:

> 　　　　　　the feast
> Was like the feast of Cepheus, when the sword
> Of Phineus, white with wonder, shook restrain'd,
> And the hilt rattled in his marble hand.

Has not that the tread of the Commander in *Don Juan?* And there are experiments in a kind of naïveté:—

> Compared with youth
> Age has a something like repose.

Tennyson is anticipated here:—

> On the soft inward pillow of her arm
> Rested her burning cheek;

Mr. Swinburne here:—

> The silent oars now dip their level wings,
> And weary with strong stroke the whitening wave.

But where the most intimately personal quality of Landor is seen is in the lofty homeliness of speech which is always definite, tangible, and about definite, tangible things. The Gadites are building, and Landor, remembering the workmen he has seen in the streets of Warwick, notes:—

> Dull falls the mallet with long labour fringed.

Gebir is wrestling with the nymph, who sweats like any mortal; Landor does not say so, but he sets her visibly before us,—

> now holding in her breath constrain'd,
> Now pushing with quick impulse and by starts,
> Till the dust blackened upon every pore.

We are far enough from Milton here; not so far, perhaps, from the Latin precision of statement; but certainly close to reality. And it is reality of a kind new to English poetry,—painter's, sculptor's, reality,—discovered, as we have seen, at precisely the moment when Wordsworth was discovering for himself the reality of simple feeling, and Coleridge the reality of imaginative wonder.

A few years after *Gebir,* Landor published two poems, "**Chrysaor**" and "**The Phocaeans**," and then, for many years, at long intervals, wrote, and occasionally published, other poems, in Latin and English, which were eventually to make up the *Idyllia Heroica* and the *Hellenics.* They are, to use a word which Browning was to invent (having learned the thing, perhaps, from Landor), dramatic idyls. The most perfect of them, "**The Death of Artemidora**," is only nineteen lines long; "**The Last of Ulysses**" fills fifty-five pages in the edition of 1847. Landor never ceased to shift their places, and to add, reject, and, above all, rewrite. The two essentially different texts are those of 1847 and 1859; and it is necessary to compare these with each other, and both with such as exist also in Latin, if we would trace with any care the diligent and never quite final labor which Landor gave to his verse.

In the poems which Landor twice translated from his own Latin, it is not often that either form of the English is quite as good as the Latin, and it is not always easy to choose between the two versions, of which the first is usually more easy and fluent, while the second, though more Latin, is often more personal to Landor. Often the second version is nearer to the original. . . . Sometimes the earlier version is the more literal, but the later one gains by condensation. (pp. 808-10)

Alike from what is gained and from what is lost in this recasting we see how uncertain, with all his care, was Landor's touch on English verse, how a Latin sound dominated his ears when he was writing English, and how his final choice of form was almost invariably of the nature of a compromise, like that of one to whom his native tongue was foreign. Compare the two versions of lines 30-34 of "**Veneris Pueri:**"—

> At neque propositum neque verba superba remittit,
> Ut Chaos antiquum flamma radiante subegit,
> Ut tenebras pepulit coelo, luctantiaque astra
> Stare, vel aeterno jussit prodire meatu,
> Ut pelago imposuit domito confinia rupes.

In 1847 "**The Children of Venus**" reads:—

> But neither his proud words did he remit
> Nor resolution: he began to boast
> How with his radiant fire he had reduced
> The ancient Chaos; how from heaven he drove
> The darkness that surrounded it, and drew
> Into their places the reluctant stars,

> And made some stand before him, others go
> Beyond illimitable space; then curb'd
> The raging sea and chain'd with rocks around.

In 1859 "**The Boys of Venus**" reads:—

> Still neither would he his intent forego
> Nor moderate his claim, nor cease to boast
> How Chaos he subdued with radiant fire,
> How from the sky its darkness he dispell'd,
> And how the struggling planets he coerced,
> Telling them to what distance they might go,
> And chain'd the raging Ocean down with rocks.

Both versions are fine, though the second, trying to follow the Latin more closely line for line, abandons the freer cadences of the first; but is either wholly without a certain constraint, which we do not feel in even those passages of Milton most like Latin? And is there not, when we read the lines in Latin, a sense, not due to mere knowledge of the fact, that we are reading an original after a translation?

Yet it is to this fact, partly, to this Latin savor in English, that not only those poems of Landor which were first written in Latin, but others also, never written in anything but English, owe their exceptional, evasive, almost illegitimate charm. What, we find ourselves saying, is this unknown, exquisite thing, which yet seems to be not quite poetry, or is certainly unlike anything else in English poetry? A perfume clings about it, as if it had been stored for centuries in cedar chests, and among spices. Nor does it fail to respond to its own appeal:—

> We are what suns and winds and waters make us.

I have read the *Hellenics,* lying by the seashore, on warm, quiet days when I heard nothing but the monotonous repetition of the sea at my feet, and they have not seemed out of key. The music is never full-throated or organ music, but picked out note by note on a reed-pipe, a slender sound with few intervals. And it is with truth that Landor says, in the preface to the edition of 1859, "Poetry, in our day, is oftener prismatic than diaphanous: this is not so: they who look into it may see through. If there be anywhere a few small air-bubbles, it yet leaves to the clear vision a wide expanse of varied scenery." (pp. 810-11)

The *Hellenics* are all in low relief; you can touch their surface, but not walk round them. Some are moulded in clay, some carved in marble; all with the same dispassionate and energetic skill of hand, the same austere sense of visible beauty. They do not imitate the variety and movement of life; they resemble the work of Flaxman rather than the work of Greek sculpture, and have the careful charm of the one rather than the restrained abundance of the other. They wish to be taken for what they are, figures in relief, harmoniously arranged, not without a reasonable decorative likeness to nature. The contours which have arrested them are suave, but a trifle rigid; the design has proportion, purity, rarely breadth or intensity. The planes are never obscured or unduly heightened; no figure, suddenly starting into life, throws disarray among the firmly stationed or sedately posed figures around.

With all his care, Landor rarely succeeds in seeming spontaneous; the fastidiousness of the choice is too conspicuous, and wounds the susceptibilities of the mind, as one who too obviously "picks and chooses" wounds the susceptibilities of a host or a friend. His touch, above all things sensitive, sometimes misses the note; in evading the brutality of statement, he sometimes leaves his meaning half expressed.

> The shore was won; the fields markt out; and roofs
> Collected the dun wings that seek house-fare;
> And presently the ruddy-bosom'd guest
> Of winter knew the doors; then infant cries
> Were heard within; and lastly, tottering steps
> Pattered along the image-stationed hall.

It is not without some intent deciphering that any one will realize from these hints that the passage of three years is meant to be indicated in them. Landor prefers to give you a sort of key, which he expects you to fit in the lock, and turn there; there is disdain in his way of stopping short, as with a half courteous and half contemptuous gesture. For the most part he hints at what has happened by mentioning an unimportant, but visible, consequence of it.

Landor's chief quality is sensitiveness; and this is seen equally in his touch on verse and in the temper of his daily life. (p. 811)

And sensitiveness makes his verse shrink away from any apparent self-assertion, all in little shivers, like the nymph's body at the first cold touch of the river. He heard a music which seemed to beat with too definite a measure, and he often draws back his finger from the string before he has quite sounded the note, so fearful is he lest the full twang should be heard. The words pause half-uttered; what they say is never more than a part of what they mean, as the tune to which they say it always supposes a more ample melody completing it behind the silence. In that familiar ending of **"The Death of Artemidora,"**—

> and now a loud deep sob
> Swell'd thro' the darken'd chamber: 't was not hers,—

we find this shy reticence, which from an idiosyncrasy has become almost a method.

Landor was a scholar of beauty, and it was with almost too disinterested an homage, too assured at once and too shy, that he approached the Muses. "The kingdom of heaven suffereth violence," and poetry wants to be wooed by life. Landor was not a strong man; he was a loud weak man; in his life we see the tumult, and only in his verse "the depth and not the tumult of the soul." His work is weakness made marmoreal; the explosive force tamed, indeed, but tamed too well, showing the lack of inner fire, so busy with rocks and lava on the surface. That is why it becomes tedious after a little; because life comes and goes in it but capriciously, like the shooting flames of his life; it is not warmed steadily throughout.

Something of this may have been in Coleridge's mind when he said, . . . "The truth is, he does not possess imagination in its highest form" [see excerpt dated 1834]. . . .

[But is] it, really, imagination which he lacks? In some lines addressed to Barry Cornwall, Landor states his own theory:

> Imagination's paper kite,
> Unless the string is held in tight,
> Whatever fits and starts it takes,
> Soon bounces on the ground, and breaks.

Landor holds in the string so tight that the kite never soars to the end of its tether. In one of his many fits of "the pride that apes humility," he writes:—

> And yet, perhaps, if some should tire
> Of too much froth or too much fire,
> There is an ear that may incline
> Even to words so dull as mine.

He was, indeed, averse to both froth and fire, and there is nothing of either in his temperate and lofty work. . . .

It is in Landor's dramatic work that we see, perhaps more clearly than elsewhere, the point beyond which he could not go, though nowhere else in his work do we see more clearly his nobility of attitude and his command of grave and splendid verse. Landor's method in dialogue is a logical method; the speeches are linked by a too definite and a too visible chain; they do not spring up out of those profound, subconscious affinities, which, in the work of the great dramatists, mimic nature with all her own apparent irregularity. (p. 812)

Landor, to forestall criticism, tells us that *Count Julian* is "rather a dialogue than a drama;" but it adopts the dramatic form, and even the form of French drama, in which the entrance of a new speaker begins a new scene. It could very well be presented by marionettes with sonorous voices, speaking behind the scenes. Landor never sees his people; they talk unmoved, or enunciate a sudden emotion with unnatural abruptness. The verse is too strict and stern, within measured Miltonic limits, for dramatic speech, or even for lifelike dialogue; thus:—

> If strength be wanted for security,
> Mountains the guard, forbidding all approach
> With iron-pointed and uplifted gates,
> Thou wilt be welcome too in Aguilar,
> Impenetrable, marble-turreted.

Yet there are moments when the Miltonic speech becomes, as it can become, nakedly dramatic:—

> Heaven will inflict it, and not I . . . but I
> Neither will fall alone nor live despised.

To Landor his own people were very real; and he says, "I brought before me the various characters, their forms, complexions, and step. In the daytime I laboured, and at night unburdened my mind, shedding many tears." But between this consciousness of a step heard in the mind, and a working knowledge of the movement of an actor across the stage, there is a great gulf; and Landor never crossed it. He aimed at producing the lofty effect of Greek tragedy, but in reading Sophocles he seems never to have realized the unerring, the infinitely ingenious playwright, to whom speech is first of all the most direct means of setting his characters to make his plot. Landor endows each of his characters with a few unvarying sentiments, and when several characters meet in action they do but give dignified expression, each as if speaking by himself, to those sentiments. The clash of wills, which makes drama, may be loud enough somewhere off the stage, but here it is but "recollected in tranquillity."

Landor is a great master of imagery, and in *Count Julian* there are many lines like these:—

> Gryphens and eagles, ivory and gold,
> Can add no clearness to the lamp above;
> Yet many look for them in palaces
> Who have them not, and want them not, at home.

Note how precise, how visual (in his own remote, sumptuous way), is the image; and how scrupulous the exactitude of the thought rendered by the image. But the image is, after all, no more than just such an ornamentation of "gryphens and eagles, ivory and gold" to a thought separately clear in itself. The image is not itself the most vital part of the speech. Take, again, the speech of Julian to Roderigo, in which an image is used with more direct aim at dramatic effect:—

> I swerve not from my purpose: thou art mine,
> Conquer'd; and I have sworn to dedicate,
> Like a torn banner on my chapel's roof,
> Thee to the power from whom thou hast rebelled.
>
> (pp. 813-14)

In the later plays and scenes, in **"The Siege of Ancona,"** and in the **"Beatrice Cenci,"** most notably, Landor seems to have more nearly mastered the dramatic method, partly by limiting himself to briefer and less complicated action; and he has finally adopted a style which is at once more flexible and more beautiful. (p. 814)

In some of the briefer scenes, those single conversations in which Landor could be so much more himself than in anything moving forward from scene to scene, there are lines that bite as well as shine; such lines as those of the drunken woman who has drowned her child:—

> *Febe.* I sometimes wish 't were back again.
> *Griselda.*   To cry?
> *Febe.* Ah! it *does* cry ere the first sea-mew cries;
> It wakes me many mornings, many nights,
> And fields of poppies could not quiet it.

It is, after all, for their single lines, single speeches, separate indications of character (the boy Caesarion in **"Antony and Octavius,"** the girl Erminia in **"The Siege of Ancona,"** a strain of nobility in the Consul, of honesty in Gallus, Inez de Castro at the moment of her death), that we remember these scenes. If we could wholly forget much of the rest, the "rhetoric-roses," not always "supremely sweet," though "the jar is full," the levity without humor, and, for the most part, without grace, the "giggling" women . . . , the placid arguing about emotions, his own loss of interest, it would seem, in some of these pages as he wrote them, we might make for ourselves in Landor what Browning in a friendly dedication calls him, "a great dramatic poet," and the master of a great and flawless dramatic style.

There is another whole section of Landor's work, consisting of epigrams and small poems, more numerous, perhaps, than any English poet since Herrick has left us. Throughout his life he persistently versified trifles, as persistently as Wordsworth, but with a very different intention. Wordsworth tries to give them a place in life, so to speak, talking them, as anecdotes or as records of definite feelings; while Landor snatches at the feeling or the incident as something which may be cunningly embalmed in verse, with almost a funereal care. Among these poems which he thus wrote there are immortal successes, such as **"Dirce"** or **"Rose Aylmer,"** with many memorable epitaphs and epitomes, and some notable satires. By their side there is no inconsiderable number of petty trivialities, graceful nothings, jocose or sentimental trifles. With a far less instinctive sense of the capacities of his own language than Herrick, Landor refused to admit that what might make a poem in Latin could fail to be a poem in English. He won over many secrets from that close language; but the ultimate secrets of his own language he never discovered. Blake, Shelley, Keats, Coleridge, Wordsworth, among his contemporaries, could all do something that he could not do, something more native, more organically English, and therefore of a more absolute beauty as poetry. (pp. 814-15)

No poet has ever been a bad prose writer, whenever he has cared to drop from poetry into prose; but it is doubtful whether any poet has been quite so fine, accomplished, and persistent a prose-writer as Landor. . . . Without his prose Landor is indeed but half, if he is half, himself. His verse at its best has an austere nobility, a delicate sensitiveness, the qualities of marble or of onyx. But there is much also which is no more than a graceful trifling, the verse of a courtly gentleman, who, as he grows older, takes more and more assiduous pains in the shaping and polishing of compliments. It is at its best when it is most personal, and no one has written more nobly of himself, more calmly, with a more lofty tenderness for humanity seen in one's small, private looking-glass. But the whole man never comes alive into the verse, body and soul, but only as a stately presence.

He has put more of himself into his prose, and it is in the prose mainly that we must seek the individual features of his soul and temperament. Every phrase comes to us with the composure and solemnity of verse, but with an easier carriage under restraint. And now he is talking, with what for him is an eagerness and straightforwardness in saying what he has to say,—the "beautiful thoughts" never "disdainful of sonorous epithets." And you discover that he has much more to say than the verse has quite fully hinted at: a whole new hemisphere of the mind becomes visible, completing the sphere. And in all his prose, though only in part of his verse, he has the qualities which he attributes to Pindar: "rejection of what is light and minute, disdain of what is trivial, and selection of those blocks from the quarry which will bear strong strokes of the hammer and retain all the marks of the chisel." He wrote far more prose than verse, concentrating his maturest years upon the writing of prose. Was it, then, that his genius was essentially a prose genius, and that it was only when he turned to prose that, in the fullest sense, he found himself? I do not think it can be said that the few finest things in Landor's verse are excelled by the best of the many fine things in his prose; but the level is higher. His genius was essentially that of the poet, and it is to this quality that he owes the greater among the excellencies of his prose. In the expression of his genius he was ambidextrous, but neither in prose nor in verse was he able to create life in his own image. No one in prose or in verse has written more finely about things; but he writes about them, he does not write them. (pp. 815-16)

Arthur Symons, *"The Poetry of Landor," in* The Atlantic Monthly, *Vol. 97, No. 6, June, 1906, pp. 808-16.*

WILLIAM BRADLEY (essay date 1914)

[In this excerpt from his book-length study of Landor's early poetry, Bradley suggests that Landor's use of theme and language in "Chrysaor" was influenced by Milton's Paradise Lost.*]*

["Chrysaor"] is unfortunately too short to do more than indicate what might have been the outcome of [Landor's] genius, had that continued to manifest itself along the same lines of thought and in the same forms. The advertisement to [**"Chrysaor"**] describes the poem as a sketch, and ther is evidence in the work itself that the original plan contemplated something larger, of which the part published was only the introduction giving an outline of the whole. Colvin judges it to be 'Landor's finest piece of narrative writing in blank verse, less monotonous in its movement than *Gebir*, more lofty and impassioned than any of the later "Hellenics" with which it was afterwards incorporated' [see Additional Bibliography].

Few seem to have either appreciated or even understood it. . . . Its importance in this study lies in the strong evidence it affords of the influence of Milton, which seems to have determined to a great extent both its form and substance. (p. 94)

The nearest approach [in classical mythology] to the incident described by Landor [in "**Chrysaor**"] is in the story of the defiance of Ajax and his destruction by Neptune, as told by Homer. . . . It is very probable that this may have suggested the chief incident of the poem, but there are indications that Milton's account of the rebellion of Satan and the Fall of Man contributed most to its spirit and form. Like its two predecessors, the "**Phocaeans**" and *Gebir*, "**Chrysaor**" is an attack upon kingship, which is here represented as associated with the slave trade. In a note on the lines,

> Man for one moment hath engaged his lord,
> Henceforth let merchants value him, not kings. . . .

there is a discussion on some forms of slavery. The inner meaning and application of the poem can hardly be understood without its help. There is, for instance, a comparison between 'the petty princes of Hesse and Hanover,' and 'their brethren the petty princes of Negroland' in favour of the latter, since they sold their subjects into a gentler and less degrading servitude. The poem, according to the same note, describes a period when tyranny was at its worst, which could only be when men were the slaves and merchandise of their rulers. At such a time their duty is to remove the common enemy—a plea for tyrannicide—since by submission they incur the enmity of the gods.

The contents of the poem, which contains only 209 lines, may be briefly summarised thus: After the overthrow of the Titans, one of them, Chrysaor, survives, and rules over Spain. He hurls defiance at Jupiter, and, refusing to adore, declares that henceforth the sacrifices of men shall be for the Titans, not for the gods. He demands that the curse upon him be removed, or he will wage war on his oppressor. Jupiter is roused to indignation against mankind for submitting to the tyranny of the Giant, and calls upon Neptune to destroy him. At one blow Gades is severed from the main, and the rebellious Titan perishes. But the nations of fair Hesperia, who had for thrice twelve years endured his yoke, must suffer the penalty. One of the fallen giants has given birth to a daughter, who, as Superstition, is permitted for ages to oppress them.

Brief as it is, the theme is presented in such a way as to form a parallel to that of *Paradise Lost*. The powers and persons in Landor's sketch play much the same part as the chief of those in Milton's epic. This is seen from the following comparison:

God the Father.	Jupiter.
God the Son.	Neptune.
Angels.	Tritons and Nymphs.
Adam and Eve.	Mankind.
Satan.	Chrysaor.
Fallen Angels.	Fallen Titans.
Sin (born of Satan).	Superstition (born of a Titan).

The resemblance in subject extends also to the language, which has . . . , as in *Gebir,* taken on something of the splendour of Milton in *Paradise Lost*. . . . It is not of course suggested that Landor has borrowed from, or consciously imitated, *Paradise Lost*; he was, however, so much under the influence of Milton

that his thoughts and style naturally drew their inspiration from that source. (pp. 97-8)

Landor's "**Chrysaor**" may be fairly described as a poetic treatment, in terms of Greek mythology, of a theme parallel to that of Milton's epic. The crime of man which brings about his fall is that of submitting to kings who usurp the authority of the gods. His punishment consists in the age-long reign of Superstition. (p. 103)

> *William Bradley, in his* The Early Poems of Walter Savage Landor: A Study of His Development and Debt to Milton, *Bradbury, Agnes & Co., 1914, 121 p.*

ERNEST DE SÉLINCOURT   (essay date 1914)

[*In this excerpt, originally printed in 1914 as an introduction to Landor's* Imaginary Conversations, *De Sélincourt demonstrates that the imaginary conversation was the form best suited to display Landor's genius and minimize his shortcomings. De Sélincourt also examines Landor's characterizations, view of history, classicism, choice of scene, and his grand, classical style.*]

Landor's outlook on life, his taste in art, and his manner of utterance are alike his own. He is remote from the literary current of his time. In an age when romanticism was in full flood he kept steadily before him the ideals and the temper of classic art. By the ideas let loose upon the world at the French Revolution he was as deeply moved as Wordsworth or as Shelley, but from their realization he hoped not for a new heaven and a new earth, but rather for a return to the noblest traditions of Athens and of Rome. He was as passionately idealistic as any poet or dreamer of the day, and the art in which he sought both refuge and expression was the product of hours of tense excitement, of deep emotional sympathy with his subject. Yet it bears no traces of the throes of its creation; its pervading characteristics are simplicity of design, a careful finish in execution, and a serenity of spirit that proclaims him its master and not its slave. The wide field of subjects over which his writings range gives evidence enough of breadth of reading, possible only to a long and leisured life. But whatever theme he handled he handled in the same severe manner. His intellectual and artistic sympathies were fixed in boyhood by a passion for classical antiquity which other interests could never shake. (pp. 79-80)

Landor's literary reputation rests most securely upon his prose. But though he realized from the first that prose was his 'study and business', he was in no hurry to establish his pre-eminence. He was a poet of rare distinction, if not of fame, at twenty-five years old; he was nearly fifty when, in 1824, he produced the first series of his *Imaginary Conversations*. 'All strong and generous wine', he tells us, 'must deposit its crust before it gratifies the palate', and in his earlier prose, discursively critical of politics, literature, and society, still more perhaps in his verse, his experience of life and his command over the resources of language can alike be seen attaining to mellowness and maturity. The Imaginary Conversation was a form of art most clearly suited to bring out the best elements in his genius and to minimize the worst. He had not that feeling for construction, that supple, quick-moving style, necessary to a writer of good narrative or complete drama. When he takes upon himself to tell a story in prose he often tells it badly; when he should keep to one point he is liable to wander from it. A striking image, a stirring reflection such as may come to him at any moment from some side-light upon his subject, is apt, when the emotion is not tense, to take him off his chosen track into some alluring by-way. But such is the way of conversation, which is most fruitful when its course is least rigorously controlled. Landor loved dialogue for its 'facility of turning the cycle of our thoughts to whatever aspect we wish'. Moreover, it responded to a distinctive quality in his genius. He was constitutionally incapable of clear abstract thinking; but when, in the manner of the dramatist, he could merge his personality in that of other men, thoughts would flash upon him, like sparks struck out, from the contact of mind with mind, of character with character. 'It has always appeared to me', he says, 'that conversation brings forth ideas readily and plenteously, and that the ideas of one person no sooner come out than another's follow them, whether upon the same side or the opposite.' Landor drew out his own thoughts upon the same principle. (pp. 88-9)

The range of characters whom Landor reveals, and through whom he reveals himself, is unrivalled by any other author. Most felicitous, perhaps, in his delineation of ancient Greece and Rome, of the Italy of the Renaissance, and of his native land from Plantagenet times down to his own day, he hardly leaves a country or a civilization unrepresented in his gallery of illustrious portraits. 'The noble mansion', he held, 'is most distinguished by the beautiful images it retains of beings passed away, and so is the noble mind.' With the heroes of the past he loved to commune in that solitude that was to him best society. . . . History was to Landor a succession of vivid personalities, whose actions and whose thoughts revealed not only themselves, but the characteristics of the time which produced them. To know them was to know their age. In his presentation of them he was quite careless of historical accuracy, of date, place, or situation. He is full of anachronisms and discrepancies in literal fact. It was not the letter but the spirit as he conceived it that he wished to reproduce, and he felt quite free to take any liberties with historical fact which tended to bring out the essential qualities of his dramatis personae. For he was artist primarily, not historian. Thus, in a conversation of exquisite beauty, *The Lady Lisle and Elizabeth Gaunt,* two heroic women judicially murdered by Judge Jeffreys for harbouring rebels are brought together by Landor in the hour before their execution. As a matter of fact they never met. But the fiction is justified by the opportunity it affords for revealing to us the inner springs of their natures. And similarly, in no way could the character of Catharine of Russia be more vividly presented to us than at the very moment when the murder of her husband, long and eagerly planned, is at last executed, and when in transports of suppressed excitement she stands with her more timid confidante at the door of the palace, and hears his blood dripping upon the floor, and the patter of the dogs' feet as they carry the marks over the palace stairs. To this dialogue Landor added a note significant beyond its actual context. 'It is unnecessary to inform the generality of readers that Catharine was not present at the murder of her husband. Nor is it easy to believe that Clytemnestra was at the murder of hers. Our business (i.e. the business of Aeschylus and all true dramatic writers) is character.' His practice is the same when his object is less obviously dramatic, and his conversation interesting rather from its ideas than from the tensity of the situation. Thus Bacon talks with Hooker at a date when Hooker had already been in the grave some ten years. Machiavelli refers to the Spanish Armada and the wars in the Netherlands. Landor does not even scruple to put into the mouths of Greeks or Romans allusions to characters and events of his own day. But he is always true to his conception of character and nationality, representing in his dramatis personae those qualities in which, as it seemed to him, not only the individuality of the speaker, but also the

genius of his nation and the peculiar spirit of his age, found clear and forcible illustration. (pp. 90-2)

But Landor is most successful with characters of more heroic build, pre-eminent either in noble action or in their capacity for suffering, great by a courage that is not merely physical, but is the index of moral and spiritual grandeur—by love that triumphs even in its apparent defeat, or by that submission to cruel destiny or unjust doom which is a proof not of man's cowering will, but of his unconquerable mind. Like the true classic artist in his outlook upon life, he is always arrested by the greatness of the soul of man. His modern sentiment is revealed by the larger emphasis he lays upon the element of tenderness with which for him greatness is ever associated. Of what passes in the world for greatness—the power of a tyrant with brutal lusts or low selfish desires—he has given many pictures; but bold and striking as they are, they tend to be exaggerated, and lack the true psychological insight with which he penetrates into those whom he can view with less bias. They are indeed dangerously like stage tyrants. Such characters, though they dominate the stage on which they act, as indeed they dominate the stage of life, are of interest to Landor chiefly as dramatic foils. Thus, Peter the Great, with his total lack of natural human feeling, throws into relief his highly strung, susceptible son, Alexis, who is swayed by emotions and inspired by ideals incomprehensible to his father, and yearns for a love of which his brutal parent is wholly incapable. In a scene conceived on similar lines, Henry VIII visits Anne Boleyn on the night before her execution. He is half-drunk, and wholly oblivious of her tender love for him and for her child—now boisterously jocose, now hurling at her shameful charges which he half-knows to be false. He laughs at her memories of a happier past, and taunts her as she pleads not for forgiveness for what she has not committed, but rather for some return of the Henry that she still loves. These portraits of Peter and of Henry are undoubtedly overdrawn, but their very exaggeration serves an obvious artistic purpose. It strengthens our sense of pathos at the sight of an exquisite fragile beauty, 'beauty that is no stronger than a flower', trodden under a wanton and muddy heel. (pp. 92-4)

Landor's art is at its finest when his characters are less fiercely contrasted, and when the tyrant has some redeeming qualities, even if he is incapable of entering into the subtler emotions of the heroine. So it is in *Leofric and Godiva,* perhaps Landor's most famous dialogue, as it was certainly among his own favourites. Leofric's love, after its own boisterous fashion, is perfectly genuine, and we are made to feel that through it his redemption may ultimately come; but at present it is entirely selfish, and thrives by the side of a callous indifference to the suffering and the starvation of his thralls. There is nothing exaggerated, nothing even unusual in the character, yet its contrast is vivid enough with the sublime figure of Godiva, whose newly awakened love for her lord has awakened also all the finer possibilities of her being. It is inseparable from her joy in the beauty of nature—'Sad is the day, and worse must follow, when we hear the blackbird in the garden and do not throb with joy'—it quickens, instead of stifling, her sympathy with the poorest of her subjects, and inspires her to an act of self-sacrifice in which she stakes more than life itself.

It is indeed to be noted that the closer the sympathy between the characters presented, the subtler is Landor's presentation of them and the more delicate his psychological insight. (pp. 94-5)

[If these scenes] are to yield up to us their full secret, they must be read not with the eye alone, but with an intensity of thought and feeling sufficient to call them up before our minds alive and moving as Landor saw them. Their high artistic concentration can only appeal to the reader whose imagination is awake to their central emotion, and is readily responsive to the subtle transitions of feeling through which the characters pass. They are classical, not only in their reserve and in their emphasis upon the heroic in character and situation, but also in a certain statuesque quality in their conception. (pp. 95-6)

The moment that he delights in depicting is that preceding the climax of the action, when some great resolution has been taken, but has yet to be fulfilled, as in the *Leofric and Godiva,* or when, as with Catharine of Russia, some great action long planned has at last been executed, and now that the climax is over, the character, as it were, recoils upon itself, and is revealed in all its complexity. He is at his greatest when some heroic soul is faced with death, and, freed at last from the trivialities that tended to obscure its true proportions, it stands out in clear outline, the light of eternity behind it. Landor does not present the death, but what might be called the emotional pose that precedes it. But in every case what he exhibits is some pause in the action, a moment when nothing is done, but much has to be endured. And in this moment of tragic suspense we feel, as it were by contrast, the passionate storm of life from which for an instant the actors have emerged. The action is all about us, through our own lively sense of the immediate past or the immediate future; it is present with us in the cries of battle which die away into the distance as we listen to the last words of Marcellus to Hannibal, in the forebodings of Godiva when the people crowd about her as she enters the city on the eve of her sacrifice—'I hope they will not crowd about me so to-morrow.' But the scene before us has the impressive stillness of arrested movement, giving opportunity for that revelation of spirit which in the tumult of action would escape observation. It is the supreme function of Landor's art, like that of painting or of sculpture, to give

> To one brief moment caught from fleeting time
> The appropriate calm of blest Eternity.

The attainment of this effect depends no more upon the careful choice of the scene to be presented than upon the manner of its presentation. Landor never gives a full statement, he never exhausts his emotion; he leaves much to be overheard by sensitive ears, relying throughout upon his elaborate and studied use of literary irony. Of irony, in the popular sense of the word, Landor was a master, and his satire is most effective, either when it is Socratic, or when he puts into the mouth of his characters words which, unconsciously to them, reveal to us their own weaknesses. But literary irony is put to higher purpose than satire. It is based not so much on the different construction put upon words by their speaker and by their audience as upon the general inadequacy of words altogether to express what we wish them to convey. Like all successful devices of art, it has its foundation in nature and the experience of life. (pp. 96-7)

In the style of his *Imaginary Conversations* there is no attempt at dramatic realism. All the dramatis personae speak Landorian English, which is far different both in rhythm and structure from the language of ordinary conversation. Landor justifies this, as was his wont, by analogy with the practice of the greatest dramatic writers.

> No man in pain . . . ever used the best part of
> the language used by Sophocles in his delinea-

tion of Philoctetes. We admit it, and willingly; and are at least as much illuded by it as by anything else we hear or see upon the stage. Poets and statuaries and painters give us an adorned imitation of the object, so skilfully treated that we receive it for a correct one. This is the only illusion that they aim at; this is the perfection of their arts.

Now, in verse dialogue most people are prepared to accept this as a recognized artistic convention. They do not call *Hamlet* unnatural because in real life Hamlet would not have spoken in blank verse. They judge of the language by its adequacy to express the ideas and emotions of the speaker, and recognize that through the beauty of the words they are attuned to sympathy with his emotion. The music of Landor's prose, as different from ordinary speech as that of Shakespeare's verse, is employed by him for the same purpose. It has its own beauty, beauty of a kind that creates the atmosphere in which his scenes have been conceived. Landor's prose is careless of what is falsely called realism. It is in 'the grand style', which arises here, as in poetry, when a serious subject is treated 'with simplicity and severity'. For if the object of art be to give immortality to great human passion, if it is its function to make

> Sorrow more beautiful than beauty's self,

it can best be achieved by some kind of idealization, and in a form which lowers that element that is painful and distressing in order to emphasize the hidden emotion of which the physical is often an imperfect manifestation. (pp. 99-100)

In that emotional prose which never overreaches itself, yet has a beauty of melody and rhythm comparable to great poetry, Landor is one of our supreme masters. Prose, he said, may be infinitely varied in modulation, it is an extension of metres, an amplification of harmonies, of which even the best and most varied poetry admits but few; certainly his own prose has a more varied and a subtler cadence than his verse. But this does not imply either that he indulged in extraneous ornament, or that he over-emphasized musical effect. The first duty of a writer, he tells us, is to be clear and concise. Obscurity is the worst fault in writing—worse to him than a flaw in the grammar, 'for we may discover a truth through such a defect which we cannot through an obscurity'. And when he is obscure himself, it is because of transitions too abrupt, through over-conciseness—never through a lack of clearness in his own mind. Next to lucidity, he delighted in fullness of sound and sense. It has often been thought that his vocabulary is too much Latinized, but though he loved Latin words for their sonority he used none that had not been fully anglicized. In diction he is always conservative, and speaks his word against slang or slovenly attempts at picturesqueness of phrase. His English is that of a scholar, but it is never pedantic, it remains essentially English in idiom and in lucidity. And the harmony of cadence that he gives it is not far-sought at the expense of the logical or intellectual elements in the style. It is the blending of proportion and force. 'Natural sequences and right subordination of thoughts and that just proportion of numbers in the sentences which follow a strong conception, are the constituents of a true harmony.' And again, 'Whatever is rightly said, sounds rightly.' His desire for a fullness of sense as well as sound makes him an intensely pictorial and imaginative writer. He often speaks in metaphor. But metaphor with him is not ornament, it is illumination. It arises inevitably from his artistic conception of his subject. 'Never look abroad for ornament' is his advice. 'Apollo, either as the god of day or the slayer of the Python, had nothing to obscure his clearness or impede his strength.' Many writers use simile and metaphor either because they do not see clearly or because they see double, because they cannot express their meaning in plain language and strive to hide their confusion of thought in a heap of glowing words. Landor is poetic in style when he sees a thing imaginatively, when his appeal is to the emotions as well as to the intellect. (pp. 101-02)

[In] simple lucid prose Landor could attain imaginative effects after which the more lyrical prose romanticists strove, often in vain, with an elaborate magnificence, or a strangeness of phrase and cadence approximating to the style of poetry. This is best exemplified in the three allegories, **"Apologue of Critobulus,"** **"The Dream of Boccaccio,"** and **"The Dream of Petrarca."** Allegory was a form of art which Landor held in no high esteem. It seemed to him a foggy way of presenting what ought to be presented clearly. He saw how most allegorists either think too much of their meaning and spoil their artistic picture, or think too much of their picture and put in details that are irrelevant to their meaning. But these short fables of Landor's are among the few perfect allegories in the language, each of them artistically beautiful, and yet with every detail of the presentation adding force and vividness to the truth he would present.

The limitations of Landor's art will be obvious enough. . . . He exacts a heavy tax from his readers, assuming that they will bring to their reading a greater knowledge of his dramatis personae and their circumstances than can fairly be expected, whilst the very clearness with which he saw them imaged in his own mind, in their movements and gestures, and in the expression on their countenances, often prevented him from leaving a sufficient clue by which we can follow his drift. At his best he demands much concentration from us; and when he is not at his best he lacks the supreme Hellenic quality of clarity. It is true of him, as of all great writers, that we must read him many times before his full meaning reaches us; it is true also, that for even an attentive mind the first reading is not so fruitful as it should be. And his style and method, suited as it is to present the heroic, the tender, and the pathetic—for all indeed that moves upon clear and simple lines—is unfitted to present the more complex and the evanescent. An uncontrollable passion, a rapid interchange of emotion, are as much outside his scope as are all the lighter forms of comedy. His art could have fashioned a Desdemona but not an Othello, a Lady Macbeth but not a Cleopatra, a Perdita or Miranda but not a Beatrice or a Rosalind. His style, always graceful and dignified, often majestic, often tender, is not flexible, and when it trespasses beyond its proper sphere it easily becomes stiff and ponderous. And those who are not willing to follow him to the heights on which his mind and passions move will find even in his noblest writing something strained and remote. Yet perhaps for this very reason he is more precious to his little clan. (pp. 102-04)

Ernest De Sélincourt, "Landor's Prose," in his Wordsworthian and Other Studies, *1947. Reprint by Russell & Russell, 1964, pp. 77-104.*

ELIZABETH NITCHIE   (essay date 1918)

[Nitchie asserts that Landor was "more truly an artist in his classicism than any of his contemporaries, except possibly Keats," for his life and works consistently demonstrated his sympathy with Greek and Roman literary and philosophical ideals.]

[In] order to understand fully the classicism of the nineteenth century, including that of Landor, we must consider how sharp was the contrast between it and that of the age of Pope. To Dryden and Pope and Johnson it was the form, the technique, and the style of the Latin authors which appealed. A dead, imitative sort of classicism was the result. . . . But Landor and Shelley and Keats were inspired with the true Hellenic spirit, and ancient Greece was reincarnated in their work. Shelley created a new Prometheus, Keats gave new meaning to the myth of Endymion, and Landor has made Aspasia live again before our eyes.

Yet Landor, strong as is his affinity with the spirit of the age in his love for the classics, seems not to be in any sense a product of the age. It is almost as if he had been born in a period to which he did not belong. For his Hellenism is of a very different stamp from that of poets like Shelley or Byron, or of antiquarian scholars like Parr or Porson, or even of an artist like Keats. To Byron, Greece typified liberty, and his interest in her was his enthusiasm for a free people. To Shelley the literature and myth of Hellas furnished material for allegory whereby he could impress the truths of Godwinism upon others. But whereas we must look in *Prometheus Unbound* for the moral purpose, the significance underlying the Hellenic machinery of the drama, we need not trouble ourselves with such a search in reading *Pericles and Aspasia* or the dialogues between Epicurus and his pupils or between Marcellus and Hannibal. It is true that occasionally Landor spoils a dialogue by introducing allusions to contemporary politics, but in the main the words of the Greeks and Romans whom he reanimates are free from modern moral or political propaganda. An intimate sympathy with the life and spirit of the characters imbues them with a reality which no other modern has succeeded in producing. The impression conveyed is that Landor is for the time being Cicero, Tiberius, Aesop, or Lucian. True, he often voices his own opinions through the mouths of his speakers. What earnest poet, novelist, or dramatist does not? But he is speaking in the terms of the theories and ideals of the golden age of classical antiquity, not the Romantic period of England. He does not make these old Greeks and Romans argue the cause of the perfectibility of man, or fulminate against the policies of the British crown. When Landor wishes to express his sympathies with Greece in her struggle for liberty he does so in his own person in an **"Ode to Corinth"** or an open letter on the **"Revolution at Athens"** contributed to the *Examiner*.

Landor was more truly an artist in his classicism than any of his contemporaries, except possibly Keats. While he felt, as did Shelley or Wordsworth, the call to be a poet, he felt none to be a prophet. He is singularly free from dogma. Although in this respect he most closely resembles Keats, yet he differs from him in that the younger poet felt more keenly the sense appeal of the external beauty of Greek myth and Greek art, and used them to spread his gospel of beauty and truth, whereas Landor, while fully appreciating this, was influenced more by the life and ideals of the actual men and women of past ages, their significance as a part of the universal scheme of existence. Keats, like a bee, gathered from the flowers of antiquity a sweetness wherewith to make his own honey; Landor, like a spring rain, sank into the classic soil and helped to make the flowers grow and blossom for the eyes of men, even becoming a part of them, the sap which flowed through their veins. No one could imagine *Endymion* to be the work of a Greek or Roman, but Elton has well said that the three dialogues from the Agamemnon story might be thought of as fragments translated from some lost old drama, dug up in a papyrus [see Additional Bibliography].

This may be due partly to the fact that Landor's scholarship was far greater than that of Keats, who had to get all his knowledge of Greek at second hand. Not that Landor is always consistently classic in thought and spirit, or always archaeologically correct. He was not a scholar . . . , nor an antiquarian. There are some anachronisms and improbabilities in his work. His knowledge of Latin was wide and accurate, but his Greek scholarship was less unexceptionable. It was secured mainly through the Latin, and his judgment, which was never influenced by the opinions of others, was sometimes prejudiced and one-sided. (pp. 149-51)

Not only was he sometimes at fault in his judgments, but often inaccurate in details. This was due to his method of work. As was said before, he was not an antiquarian. . . . Landor did not write in a library stocked with books of reference to which he could turn at need. He did not even study extensively about a person or period before writing. In fact his library was remarkably small for a man of letters. He gave away a book almost as soon as he had read it. But he did have an astonishingly retentive memory, and an unusually sympathetic intimacy with the past, which enabled him to reproduce the society of Greece and Rome with a vividness and reality which make any criticisms of inaccuracies in detail seem captious. After all it is not possible for the majority of writers to be infallible about the details even of modern life. It is the spirit which is the important part of any reanimation of past times, that which enlivens and vivifies the mass, rather than the dead letter of form and technique.

Landor said himself that he was particularly careful not to put into the mouths of his characters anything that history had assigned to them. The result is a new and individual interpretation of Greek or Roman thought, yet always one that is in harmony with the time which is represented. So harmonious are speaker and language that one constantly finds himself wondering how a certain phrase was expressed in the original. Nor in the main is this effect produced by Latinisms or Grecisms in the English. Though he is fonder of long Latin derivatives than of short Anglo-Saxon words, these usually impart a dignity and sonorousness to his style suited to the subject which is being treated or to the character who is speaking. In *Gebir,* it is true, where he is imitating Vergil in style and manner, he introduces many awkward Latinistic expressions and clauses which are almost unintelligible to one who does not know the language, and in any case are a blemish in his lines. He errs chiefly in participial constructions such as, for example,

> Lamented they their toil each night o'erthrown,

or

> He spake, and indignation sank in woe,
> Which she perceiving, pride refreshed her heart,

or

> Him overcome, her serious voice bespake.

At times there occurs a use of a verb or phrase with a significance which is characteristically Latin and which therefore causes a feeling of difficulty, as, "I should rather have *conceived from you* that the wand ought to designate those who merit the hatred of their species," or "if you had not dropped something out of which I *collect* that you think me too indif-

ferent." The use of "collect" in the sense of "understand" is marked archaic in the dictionary, but it is a very common meaning of the Latin verb *colligo,* especially in Quintilian. Again, we have such an expression as "the crown of laurel *badly cool'd* his brow," which is a clear echo of the idiomatic Latin use of *male;* or an instance of the Roman love of litotes, as in "no few," which recalls the common *non pauci,* or "Some, *nor the wealthier* of her suitors." He is somewhat too fond of Latin derivatives which are now considered rare, archaic, or obsolete, such as "propense," "discinct," "incondite," "intempestive," or "libant"; and when such a collocation of them meets the eye as "thy versicolored and cloudlike vestiary, puffed and effuse," it seems imperative to pause for breath. But with a list like this and the mention of a certain obscurity in language due to his effort after classic brevity and compression, we come to the end of the faults due to Landor's command of the ancient languages. For often the phrases, especially such as are essentially Greek, add to the classic spirit of the dialogue. (pp. 151-53)

Among all the things that he wrote Landor's own favorites were his Latin poems. These are of course the least read today, but they are worthy of notice and admiration. They are as varied in subject as in meter and show skill in the handling of both. It is remarkable that the work of a modern should be so independent and individual, yet so essentially Latin. There are reminiscences at times of Horace, as in the phrase, "Felix sorte tua," or of Vergil, as in "satque superque dedit." But he is more free from such echoes than are the Latins themselves, a considerable portion of the commentaries on whom are occupied with references to parallel passages in other authors. Though not entirely free from slips in grammar and prosody he is in general careful and accurate in the handling of his meter. He is, for instance, quite Ovidian in the management of the elegiac distich, observing almost invariably the rules for the dissyllabic ending of the pentameter and the penthimeral caesura. Quite in the style of Ovid too are his little tricks of balance of the two halves of the lines, as for example,

> Arripite arma, duces! arripite arma, viri!

or

> Quod pueri discent, discere vellet avus.

But aside from this correctness of form, his Latin verse has the merits of vigor, spontaneity, and sincerity. It is more subjective than his English verse, for he preferred the Latin for the expression of his most intimate thoughts and emotions. Latin was in reality a second mother-tongue to him, and he was as much at home with it as with English. Late in life he said, "I am sometimes at a loss for an English word, never for a Latin." In his prose essays he pleaded strongly for the use of Latin in modern times and showed by his own style how noble a vehicle of expression it could be made. His Latin prose is dignified, forceful, and varied. A good example of it is to be found in a sentence from the "Quaestio quamobrem poetae Latini recentiores minus legantur," which at the same time expresses his attitude toward the modern use of the language: "Leves homines ille sermo Romanus noster arcebit severitate sua, comprimet vi feroces, garrulos compescet maiestate: caveamus ne langueat, obtorpescat, conticiscat."

The English poems are quite different from those of his contemporaries. It has already been said that he was the least subjective of the Romantic poets. This is probably due to his manner of looking at life, which was essentially Greek and therefore objective, for the Greeks regarded the problems of existence in a singularly impersonal fashion. This is undoubtedly the reason for the contradiction between his passionate nature and his poetry, which expresses the charm of a placid life. It is not insincerity or affectation, but merely a result of his ideals, which are aesthetic rather than moral. Some of the lyrics remind us of Catullus, others of Horace, with their lesson of "aurea mediocritas," and the ode addressed to Joseph Ablett is in tone and manner very similar to the Horatian epistles. One little poem is so strikingly like a lyric by Sappho that the first four lines of it will bear quoting for the sake of comparison. Landor's lines are as follows:

> Mother, I can not mind my wheel;
> My fingers ache, my lips are dry.
> Oh! if you felt the pain I feel!
> But oh, who ever felt as I!

This lovesick maiden recalls at once the girl whom Sappho makes to say,

> Oh, my sweet mother, 'tis in vain,
> I cannot weave as once I wove,
> So 'wildered is my heart and brain
> With thinking of that youth I love.

Landor was a master, especially in his poems to Ianthe, of these "exquisite eidyllia, those carvings, as it were, in ivory or gems, which are modestly called Epigrams by the Greeks."

Although an ardent admirer of Milton, Landor's classicism is not at all like that of the author of *L'Allegro*. In the first place Landor never mingled Christian and pagan elements so inextricably as Milton did in *Comus*. Classic myth to Landor was not a part of a man's everyday vocabulary, clamoring to be used whether it sorted with the subject that was being discussed or not. He reserved it for the themes to which it belonged, for the *Hellenics* and *Heroic Idylls,* and kept his English poems remarkably free from the classic jargon which had been so popular in England in the eighteenth century. Even in the short lyrics scattered through *Pericles and Aspasia* he shows his understanding of how unsuitable classical allusions would be. For the pages of the melic poets of Greece are almost as lacking in references to mythology as those of a modern poet, save for the simplest and most natural mention of Zeus or Aphrodite. It was the Alexandrians and their Roman imitators who packed their lines with the most obscure kind of references. Landor fittingly makes no attempt to copy them, but takes for his examples Sappho or Anacreon.

Although *Gebir* is neither Greek nor Roman in theme, it clearly shows in its form and phraseology the effect of Landor's Latin affinities. It begins in true epic fashion, "I sing the fates of Gebir," and the hero seems a reflection of Aeneas, and his visit to the underworld is undoubtedly a reminiscence of the sixth book of the *Aeneid*. The Latin constructions which occur have already been spoken of, and there is also a striving after Latin brevity. Notice, for instance, the compression of the lines,

> Whate'er it be
> That grieves thee, I will pity, thou but speak,
> And I can tell thee, Tamar, pang for pang.

Sometimes the result of this compression is confusion and obscurity, especially in regard to the antecedents of the personal pronouns. One feels that if he had been writing in Latin the explicit *ille* or *hic* would have made all clear. The poem, however, with all its faults has dignity and power and has found favor with critics like Shelley and Southey. (pp. 156-58)

In the unpublished lines entitled "**An Apology for the Hellenics**," Landor wrote,

> None had yet tried to make men speak
> In English as they would in Greek.

This seems to be exactly what he has tried to do and succeeded in doing in the *Classical Dialogues*.... His usual fault of a compression too great for clarity is to be found, but nowhere is there better expression of the glory of Greece than in the dialogue between Pericles and Sophocles, or of Roman pride and the spirit of conquest than in "**Marcellus and Hannibal**" and "**Metellus and Marius**." In the dialogue with his brother, Marcus Tullius, Cicero says,

> If wiser men than those who appear at present to have spoken against my dialogues should undertake the same business, I would inform them that the most severe way of judging these works, with any plea or appearance of fairness, is to select the best passages from the best writers I may have introduced, and to place my pages in opposition to theirs in equal quantities.... Take a whole conversation, examine the quality, the quantity, the variety, the intensity, of mental power exerted. I myself would arm my adversaries, and teach them how to fight me.

It is impossible not to feel that in these words Landor is sounding a challenge to the critics. It is good and safe advice for him to give, for in general his dialogues would not suffer by comparison. It is impossible to make any word for word, line for line, or thought for thought comparison, but we can set opposite in our minds the picture that Landor draws and that which we gain from ancient sources, critical or autobiographical. We feel sure that we are listening to the Cicero who wrote on "Friendship" and "Old Age," the Cicero of the letters and the dialogues. We recognize in the Tibullus who greets his patron Messala the calm, generous, kindly poet who voiced in his elegies his love for simplicity of life and sincerity of worship. Only in Plato do we find a portrait not in harmony with that which he paints of himself.

Pericles and Aspasia is different in type and quite unique in plan. It has been called "an extended Imaginary Conversation," but it is more than that. In the reconstruction of the society of the Age of Pericles, in the portrayal of the characters of Aspasia and Cleone, in the intimate tone of their correspondence, and in the criticism of Greek authors and the imitation of them in the lyrics, epigrams, and dramatic fragments which are scattered through the letters, Landor found room to express all he had ever known or imagined about the golden age of Greece. Nowhere in modern literature can we find anything to equal it in sympathetic interpretation of antiquity. Upon laying down the book we feel that we have been reading a real correspondence between real persons—humor, personalities, comment on current literature, dull passages, and all. Especially is this true of the earlier letters, which are remarkably spontaneous and natural. At times the wits and sages of Athens do speak rather too much like Landor himself or with the pomposity of Dr. Johnson, and the attempt to reproduce the public speeches of Pericles in the style of Thucydides is the least successful portion of the book. Occasionally we hear the modern speak, as in the passages that purport to be prophecies of achievements of future ages, as for example when Pericles speaks of the future of astronomy:

We none of us know, but Anaxagoras hopes that, in a future age, human knowledge will be more extensive and more correct; and Meton has encouraged us in our speculations. The heavenly bodies may keep their secrets two or three thousand years yet; but one or other will betray them to some wakeful favorite, some Endymion beyond Latmos, perhaps in regions undiscovered, certainly in uncalculated times. Men will know more of them than they will ever know of Homer.

But the very shock that a passage like this causes is a proof that usually Landor has caught the true Hellenic spirit. The impetuous Alcibiades, the noble and generous Anaxagoras, the clever and quixotic Socrates, as well as many other men great in history and literature, appear in these pages against a background of Greek life which in its details—though, as has been said, some inaccuracies may be found by the patient archaeological delver—is remarkably real and vivid.

But the gems of the whole book are the three dramatic fragments which Aspasia writes on the story of Agamemnon for the perusal of her friend Cleone. They show Landor's classicism at its best, in the fulness of their Greek spirit and in their independence and individuality of treatment. They may profitably be put beside the work of the great Greek dramatists and compared with it. The differences in the actual course of events are not important, for Landor simply adopts the custom of the Greek dramatists, who felt at liberty to alter the story to suit their own dramatic purposes. The change in character portrayal is also an aspect of this same thing, for the Electra of Aeschylus is entirely different from the Electra of Sophocles or of Euripides. In the *Coephoroi* she is represented as urging at first the death of her mother, and thus addressing her father's spirit,

> I, father, ask this prayer, that I may work
> Aegisthos' death, and then acquittal gain.

But she is comparatively colorless, and after the recognition scene with Orestes she disappears from the action entirely. In the *Electra* of Sophocles, on the other hand, she is a woman of strongly marked character, possessed by no thought save that of revenge. Through the whole action of the drama she remains the foremost character, eager at first when she thinks her brother is dead to carry out the scheme of vengeance upon Clytemnaestra and Aegisthos herself, urging on Orestes to the murder, pitiless and unsoftened by her mother's cries, sending Aegisthos to meet his fate with the exhortation to Orestes, "Slay him outright."

The Electra of Landor is no such spirit of vengeance. Although the delineation is thoroughly in accordance with classic ideals, she is more of a true flesh-and-blood heroine than those of Aeschylus or Sophocles, or even of "Euripides the human." (pp. 159-62)

[Landor's] classicism finds expression in another form in the **Hellenics** and **Heroic Idylls**. Some of the latter, and the least spontaneous of them, are translations of his Latin **Idyllia Heroica;** the others were written originally in English. They are of various kinds, some in the shape of dialogues in verse, some blank-verse narratives, some in rhymed tetrameters, and there is one which tells no story but is a plea to mankind to aid in bringing about the liberty of Greece. Each is a jewel perfect in itself, some, like **"Chrysaor"** or the **"Hamadryad,"** marvelously cut and flashing with a thousand lights; some, like the **"Death of Artemidora,"** gleaming with the rich yet simple

luster of a pearl. They again follow no models, ancient or modern, yet the spirit of them is that of the idyllic charm which breathes from the poetry of Theocritus, Moschus, and Bion. In their restraint and severity of beauty, as well as in the graceful flow of the language, they are thoroughly Greek. We see recurring again and again Landor's favorite themes—the Trojan cycle, the story of Iphigenia. Though **"Chrysaor"** is something quite different from the others, a poem on political liberty in the style of Shelley or Keats, the rest have no modern touch. (p. 163)

Landor's classicism was not confined to things literary. His ideals, philosophy, and attitude toward life were largely those of antiquity, partly Greek and partly Roman. It was his constant effort to harmonize duty and desire that was essentially Hellenic, and his high, stern standards of nobility of character which caused Carlyle to exclaim, "The unsubduable old Roman!" I have already spoken of his purely objective attitude toward the problems of existence that was so typical of the ancient mind. Quite pagan were his ideas of personal righteousness and high-mindedness, which were almost totally unconnected with any thought of Christian service or devotion to others. And these old Roman virtues he not only practiced himself but expected to find in everyone with whom he came in contact; according to his ideal everyone should be a Scipio or a Brutus. It was his expressed aim to walk "with Epicurus on the right hand and Epictetus on the left." And there are touches of Epicureanism in his poems and elsewhere. The poem and greeting sent by Cleone to Aspasia on her birthday contain the essence of this philosophy, especially in the last sentence, "Sweetest Aspasia, live on! live on! but rather live back the past!"

To take this last from its surroundings and use it as the text of this paper is too great a temptation to be resisted. For this is exactly what Landor did; he lived on, but lived back the past and made others live it back as well—not the past of his own life, but the past of the life of the world. Nor is this confined to antiquity. His historic imagination is just as vivid when applied to the Middle Ages or to more recent conditions in England itself as when at work on the scenes of ancient Greece or Rome. He was not an antiquarian, turning back to the fifth century before Christ from the nineteenth century after, but he belonged to the time of which he wrote; his life began, not in 1775 A.D., but in the Homeric age, growing and developing with the growth and development of the world and taking a vital and active part in the life of every period in every land. He is something more than a scholar, more than a historian, or more than a writer of drama or fiction. In him the living qualities of them all were fused and molded by the spirit of Rome on her seven hills and of Athens, the violet-crowned.

Doubtless he was more of a Roman in knowledge and scholarship but more of a Greek at heart. His Hellenism was a part of his inmost nature, a species of worship, and "in the very heat and fury of romantic predominance, Landor kept a cool chamber apart, where incense was burned to the ancient gods."

> And through the trumpet of a child of Rome
> Rang the pure music of the flutes of Greece.
>
> (pp. 165-66)

Elizabeth Nitchie, "The Classicism of Walter Savage Landor," in The Classical Journal, *Vol. 14, No. 3, December, 1918, pp. 147-66.*

WALTER RALEIGH   (lecture date 1918)

[*A renowned lecturer and literary critic, Raleigh was appointed in 1904 the first professor of English literature at Oxford. His critical approach to literature was that of a highly perceptive, urbane commentator whose literary exegesis served to facilitate the nonspecialist's understanding of English literature through concise textual commentary. Raleigh's comments, originally notes for a lecture on Landor given in 1918, touch on the author's personality, the style of his poetry, his diction, his restraint, and his critical judgments.*]

Landor has many admirers, but few diligent readers. "I shall dine late; but the dining-room will be well lighted, the guests few and select." He did not add, perhaps he did not guess, that even those few guests would eat daintily and sparingly of what was provided, and would send away half the dishes untasted. I confess the extraordinary difficulty of reading Landor. One can lay him down at any time. His own coolness, quietude, selectiveness, infect his readers. They pick and choose. (p. 138)

Landor could not throw himself wholly or for long into the interests, passions, and minds of others. His *Imaginary Conversations* are not in the least dramatic. How many people have been excited by the names, and disappointed by the talk! It ends by being like a bad dream; we are always back in Landor's library, and someone is always *prosing*.

Yet, in prose or verse, he is a Master, and I think may be called a great Teacher. It is a special talent in some. How it would have pleased Landor to have a little circle and be called "The Master!" How his affectionate nature would have blossomed! What a sad thing it is to find him alone in a foreign country during his later years, companioned by a yellow dog! He had a loving heart, and was born to tyrannise. He was kind and jealous, wilful and sensitive—an unhappy blend. Such people are dreaded by their fellows, and unless they are fortunate in acquiring slaves, lead a thwarted life. As slave owners they are happy, magnanimous and humane.

I am in doubt how far an Academic School of Literature can serve the interests of creation. The live stuff won't grow in the pots. But I cannot help wishing that there had been such a school, for Landor to be made head of it. How he would have basked on the throne! And how helpful he would have been! To anyone who acknowledged his loftiness he was all courtesy, tenderness, and consideration.

His doctrine is the best you can get. A School of Literature exists to follow his teaching—so far as it attempts the real work. Simplicity, parsimony, accuracy, gravity: these make a wonderful prose.

I love Landor even when he is as haughty and stuck-up as a child, and I love his short poems best of all his works. The *Heroic Idylls,* the *Hellenics* are written in a noble style, but they are Culture poems, they breathe of the study. It is in extract that the longer poems have lived. . . . It is quite odd how Landor's people slip out of the mind. Yet some of their speeches are long remembered. The short, gem-like poems might be made the test of a lecture on style. They are single (trivial) occasions celebrated in lapidary verse. (pp. 139-41)

Landor will not raise his voice. If he feels strongly he is careful to choose words—I was going to say, no stronger than his feelings, but the truth is, a good deal weaker, or at least quieter, than his feelings. He never works up to a point, in verse or prose. He makes his point (tells the truth nakedly and severely), and then restores quiet by suggesting more peaceful considerations. This is so fixed a habit of his, that it is a mark of his style in verse or prose: his "dying fall." (p. 141)

[His] poems have the stately good manners of pride; they are not poems of passion, not for a moment self-forgetful, yet their charm (to me at least) is irresistible. They culminate in a four-lined poem as beautiful as his best:—

> Death stands above me, whispering low
> I know not what into my ear:
> Of his strange language all I know
> Is, there is not a word of fear.

The same dying fall is used in **"The Death of Artemidora"** in the *Hellenics,* and very beautifully in the prose account of the death of Acciaioli given by Boccaccio in the *Pentameron.* If you come to taste writing like that it makes coarser effects vulgar. There is a ceremonial gravity about it. Landor has an unerring feeling for impressions that the marble will take. He seems almost incapable of being deceived by pleasure or passion or anything but pride.

"What I write is not written on slate; and no finger, not that of Time himself, who dips it in the mist of years, can efface it."

> Well I remember how you smiled
> To see me write your name upon
> The soft sea-sand. *"O! what a child!*
> *You think you're writing upon stone!"*
>
> I have since written what no tide
> Shall ever wash away; what men
> Unborn shall read o'er ocean wide
> And find Ianthe's name again.

Landor always thought he was writing on stone, because he wrote nothing extravagant, excessive, exuberant. In that sense it will endure; it is pure English carefully graved, and will take long to grow old. But his work is as immortal as a graveyard.

Landor cared little for philosophy and much for history, which he saw as a great and stately pageant. He liked the great *shapes* of historical events.

A large number of his *Conversations* deal with literary criticism, and it crops up everywhere in others. Some have complained of the minuteness of his criticism, but this is what makes Landor so good a teacher. In these minute criticisms he always excels.

Landor's greatest prose passages might be collected in an anthology—"The Four Last Things." There is nothing new in what he has to say, and nothing subtle; his mind is not swift or alert. But give him a grave theme where there is nothing new to tell, and he surpasses himself. (pp. 143-45)

Landor, then, belongs to that very small company of English men of letters who are born Academicians; like Ben Jonson and Gray. Their works are stiff with scholarship. They are not congenial to our soil. The English doctrine is wider:—

> There are five and thirty ways
> Of constructing tribal lays,
> And every single one of them is right.

Landor's is one way, and not the worst. If you take him for a master the weakest passage in the worst thing you write will be immeasurably better than the poorest things in Shakespeare. (p. 145)

Walter Raleigh, "On Some Writers and Critics of the Nineteenth Century: Landor," in his On Writing and Writers, *edited by George Gordon, Edward Arnold & Co., 1926, pp. 138-45.*

The ruins of Landor's house on his estate in Llanthony. Illustration by James Wood.

STANLEY T. WILLIAMS (essay date 1921)

[*In assessing Landor's role in English literature, Williams asserts that while Landor is not important in the twentieth century, he was influential in Romantic and Victorian literary circles. For further criticism by Williams, see the excerpt dated 1923 and the Additional Bibliography.*]

Mr. Sidney Colvin says that Landorians may be counted on the fingers of two hands [see Additional Bibliography]. It is true. Most of us read the *Imaginary Conversations* with a feeling of suffocation, even though we are amazed by their author's learning. . . . The heroes of these endless dialogues come straight from the dead . . . ; they are as dusty as the mummies of the first dynasty. But—alas!—more talkative: they bicker, denounce, and harangue: they are the apotheosis of boring discussion; they are veritable ghosts on stilts. . . . [Although] modern dialogues owe something to the *Imaginary Conversations,* the fact remains that they are not read. Who in this century has performed the feat of reading them, every word? Let him speak out boldly.

As for Landor's lyrics, they are the icicles of nineteenth century literature, as those monstrous epics, *Gebir* and *Count Julian,* are the icebergs. To read Landor's poetry after Byron's or Shelley's is like leaping into the Arctic current. It seems impossible to believe that this artificial verse was written when the Romantic Movement in poetry was at its height. Yet such was the case. We of the twentieth century who are nurtured on a hundred varieties of Romanticism can hardly care much for this "marmoreal" verse. In its memory Swinburne and William Watson may write odes; nevertheless it will not be read.

Meanwhile Landor is frequently mentioned, and seriously, as a reputable poet. It is even insinuated that he is one of the nineteenth century hierarchy with a position as secure as those of the poets he seldom noticed,—Byron and Shelley. The implication is that Landor's writings have perished but his personality survives. People are fond of alluding to "the exiled Landor at Fiesole," or they refer knowingly to his temper. . . . Something is known too, of the old Roman's *hauteur;* of his litigations; of his resemblance to Lawrence Boythorn in *Bleak House.*

So they speak, the literary by-standers, but these remarks are merely echoes. Landor's personality will not save him. He dies hard, but dying he is, together with all his writings. Landor is not to be one of those immortals, whose books pass, but whose souls live on. He can never be compared, in respect to personality, as some would have us think, with Dr. Johnson. For this sort of immortality more is needed than a temper, a hearty laugh, and classical learning. No groups will be formed for the study of "Landor and His Circle." This condition may be partly because Landor spoke to "the few," but it is chiefly due to the fact that he communicated intellectual ideas whose significance today is precious little. (pp. 43-4)

[However], Landor's personality *was* great; great in a variety of ways. It is fading because of its strange quality and consequent unimportance to "modern literature." One fatal flaw this tragic hero had: his writings and sayings do not reach the hearts of men. Wise he is, wise with deep learning; brilliant as the cold sparkle on a sunny field of snow; morally lofty, also. But human he is not, and we'll have none of him today. To approach Landor, as Dr. Johnson is approached, through conversations and letters, is a chilling experience.

Landor was like the oracle which prefaced its remarks by a blast of cold air. His manner of pronouncement is like Jove's on Olympus. Inexorable. Moreover, these edicts are likely to be concerned with such popular topics as "Lycophron as a Poet", or the Greek word for violet. These are handicaps to an appreciation of Landor, but the greatest is that already mentioned. We are always forgiving assurance—and even learning—in writers. But out of their dead ages they must speak to us directly. They must entice our spirits, allure our souls. *Cor ad cor loquitur,* though the ages pass. But Landor never speaks to us; he addresses us, and talks down to us. His notions on life may be true, but we receive them without enthusiasm. His *ideas* seem to echo faintly in our own experience, but somewhere *en route* to us the emotion has been frozen. To recognize one's own feelings done in plaster of paris, read some of Landor's apothegms. (pp. 44-5)

Landor is read less and less every day; his name is becoming a reference for the prudent student to look up. Even "the few" guests show signs of an early leave-taking. Although Landor did not realize the fact, his influence was greatest during the first decades of the nineteenth century. Why? As Landor's influence disappears today a natural question is: Why was it great during his own life-time? Why did Southey, Shelley, Browning, and Swinburne think him not merely great but among the very greatest of his era?

In answer it may be stated that in general Landor's prose and poetry and personality were all powerful influences upon his contemporaries. It is evident, however, that the least influential of these three factors in Landor's reputation was his prose. Mr. Howitt says that "his *Imaginary Conversations* . . . eclipsed his verse." The eclipse has rather been mutual, resulting in complete darkness in respect to Landor's fame. At all events, in his own day, Landor influenced poets more than prose-writers; this was accomplished, naturally enough, through his poetry. As the *Conversations* appeared in ever-increasing numbers, they incited interest and respect for Landor's learning; but in all the gossip of the period, there is no evidence that they stirred writers deeply, or that they were regarded as the deepest source of Landor's influence. The *Conversations* and the *Pentameron* were simply mausoleums of learning. (p. 46)

[Vagaries] abound in the *Imaginary Conversations,* and they extend to all phases of life,—economics, politics, and religion. In addition, the reader is lost in a labyrinth of learning, for which Landor's pompous manner is a poor guide. Then, as now, the chief emotion aroused by Landor's prose must have been that of amazed respect. The style itself was damning. "He never learned," says Coleridge, "how to write simple and lucid English" [see excerpt dated 1834].

The influence of Landor's poetry, though more evident than that of his prose, was, nevertheless, limited. The lyrics and the narrative poems won over only a tiny audience. Landor founded no school, nor had he, like other nineteenth century poets, any group of imitators. The younger poets copied Rossetti, and Wordsworth, and Tennyson, but it did not occur to them to copy Landor—any more than Pindar. Classical poetry was a fad of the period, but Landor was inimitable, both in his obscure themes and in his austere manner. Compared to his the classical poems of Arnold and Tennyson were fairy-tales of Greece. Landor, as a poet, was almost as much apart, as if he had written in Persian.

Apart, and yet near. For we are approaching now the secret of Landor's influence in his own time. Imitators there were

not, but worshippers there were, and the notable thing is that these were of the best. I hope to show that Landor's instinctive doctrine . . . in literature, while it kept off the facile, the commonplace, the sensational among writers, affected deeply the very best. Moreover, though this influence of Landor's was most vital upon his coevals, through his personality, . . . it was also manifest in some degree through his poetry. Thus Shelley reads Landor unceasingly; Lamb, drunk or sober, is forever quoting "**Rose Aylmer**"; and Southey's worship of the narrative poems is fantastic.

It is, indeed, difficult to explain the devotion of some like Southey and De Quincey to Landor's poetry. . . . Possibly Southey's judgment was impaired by his friendship with Landor. But, Shelley, who had no such attachment, could not let *Gebir* alone. His biographer, Hogg, tells the story: "I often found Shelley reading *Gebir.* There was something in that poem which caught his fancy. He would read it aloud, or to himself, with a tiresome pertinacity. One morning I went to his rooms to tell him something of importance, but he would attend to nothing but *Gebir.*" And years later Swinburne bows down to *Count Julian*: "The sublimest poem published in our language between the last masterpiece of Milton and the first masterpiece of Shelley. . . . No comparable work is to be found in English poetry between the date of *Samson Agonistes* and the date of *Prometheus Unbound*" [see excerpt dated 1875-79]. And De Quincey declares the poem: "Aeschylean!" Here is a real influence directed towards some of the best minds of Landor's generation.

No one, surely, could read the lyrics which moved Shelley and Lamb, and fancy that their author was famous throughout Europe for litigations, quarrels, and violence of temper. . . . Yet it was this personality together with Landor's unflinching ideals for poetry that gave him his greatest influence over his contemporaries,—an influence greater than this achieved merely through his poetry. The picturesqueness of Landor's genius served him well. Extreme eccentricity, like extreme ugliness, may be an asset. Had Landor's temper been as unruffled as his poetry perhaps Fiesole would not have been such a Mecca for nineteenth century men of letters. Here was this venerable Prometheus of literature, stealing for nearly a century his fire from heaven, writing literally the style of gods, scorning his fellow-poets, laughing at them endlessly, pronouncing unreasonable, but strangely stimulating opinions on literature and life. . . . Why, Landor was a national character! (pp. 47-9)

That so eccentric a man should have interested is not strange. The significant thing is that he became in literature a constructive force. In spite of insane literary verdicts, Landor's praise of new books was eagerly desired. He is, Southey said, "the only man living of whose praise I was ambitious, or whose censure would have humbled me." And Robert Browning wrote to Mrs. Browning: "Landor's praise is altogether a different gift; a gold vase from King Hiram." (pp. 51-2)

So in the renewed study of Victorian literature it is well to notice the very special gifts of Walter Savage Landor and to reflect on the special task which he performed. Such an appraisal must begin, it seems to me, with the realization that little can be expected of Landor's influence now or in the future. His work is finished. Soon his devotees may be counted on the fingers of *one* hand. In 1890 W. B. Clymer wrote of Landor's influence: "His chance in the struggle for existence rests on the likelihood of there being in future generations a few men with Emerson's unjaded taste for 'pure literature.'" Perhaps. "Pure learning" would be nearer the truth. Margaret

Oliphant may speak of *Count Julian* as "worthy of the hand which showed us Hamlet and Othello." Steadman may compare *Gebir* to Keats' *Hyperion*. But Mrs. Mitford is nearer fact when she speaks, with curious juxtaposition, of "out-of-the-way writers . . . like Colley Cibber and W. S. Landor." The tendency is to think with Francis Thompson of "such minor men as Landor" [see excerpt dated 1897].

"Minor" he is now, but minor in his own day he was not. It is difficult to state in a few words the exact character of Landor's influence among his contemporaries. Certainly its essence lay in his austere idealism. In an age in which poets were introspective, Landor was objective. When others were expressing moods of unrest, reflecting the confused thought of the century, Landor was calmly imitating Pindar. When others were exhibiting the pageants of their bleeding hearts, Landor was concerned in his poetry, with subtle and delicate emotional values,—most of them Greek in origin. Landor never relinquished the ideal that poetry should be restrained, intellectual, and architectonic. Such maintenance had its effect. It is not too much to presume that Landor had an ennobling influence upon a few poets whom he definitely inspired. "Consider," says Steadman, "the names of those who, having met him and known his works, perceive in him something great and worshipful." (p. 53)

> Stanley T. Williams, "Echoes of Walter Savage Landor," in The Texas Review, Vol. VII, No. 1, October, 1921, pp. 43-53.

STANLEY T. WILLIAMS (essay date 1923)

[*Williams faults the subjective nature and undisciplined form of Landor's criticism. He suggests that Landor's critical principles are little more than common sense and that his judgments are not supported by sustained analysis. For further commentary on Landor's work by Williams, see the excerpt dated 1921 and the Additional Bibliography.*]

As a critic of literature Walter Savage Landor had ideals but few principles. Such a statement is not another paradox in the life of the old lion. It means simply that we look in vain in Landor's numerous judgments on literature for a method or a body of criteria. He never formulated a system, like Coleridge; or standards, like Arnold; nor even consistent prejudices, like Carlyle. The evolution of English criticism between Dryden and Coleridge he disregarded, as indeed he seemed to disregard all consecutive philosophical thought. He did not look into the new worlds of psychological and social criticism. He was not interested in the relations of things, but rather in the things themselves. Such statements are never truer of Landor than when he studies a piece of literature, or a writer. As a critic he never saw literature in perspective—so marvellously increased in his own day—but as something directly before him,—foreshortened. Thus he judged Pindar and Wordsworth each *per se*; one would think he was a contemporary of both. In all his criticisms we cannot find a body of guiding principles. Personal ideals are the determinants. It need scarcely be added that these are austere and high.

The few scattered principles which Landor himself expressed are less peculiar to literature than to common sense: the critic should be just; he should be learned; and, like the poet, he should write not for the many, but for the few and the discerning. This is practically all. The allusions to critics and criticism in the *Imaginary Conversations,* the *Pentameron,* and *Pericles and Aspasia* amount to this only. Such "principles"

are obvious, but Landor states them nobly, and as no one else could. Thus of justice in criticism:

> The critic walks in a garden which is not his own; and he neither must gather the blossoms to embellish his discourse, nor break the branches to display his strength. Rather let him point to what is out of order, and help to raise what is lying on the ground.

Or of knowledge this, with its grave irony:

> I would seriously recommend to the employer of our critics, young and old, that he oblige them to pursue a course of study such as this: that under the superintendence of some respectable student from the university, they first read and examine the contents of the book; a thing generally more useful in criticism than is generally thought; secondly, that they carefully write them down, number them, and range them under their several heads; thirdly that they mark every beautiful, every faulty, every ambiguous, every uncommon expression. Which being completed, that they inquire what author, ancient or modern, has treated the same subject, first in smaller, afterward in larger portions, noting every defect in precision and its causes, every excellence and its nature; that they graduate these, fixing *plus* and *minus,* and designating them more accurately and discriminately by means of colours, stronger or paler. For instance, purple might express grandeur and majesty of thought; scarlet vigour of expression; pink, liveliness; green, elegant and equable composition.

The passage suggests Landor's thoroughness in his verbal and textual criticisms, and also his contempt for the casual critic. Landor lived through the days of the Quarterlies, that period of sword-and-buckler criticism. His own works were sadly cut to pieces. [The imaginary conversation entitled] **"Southey and Porson"** was partly an outlet for his rage against the swarm of flies that were busy with him, with Southey, and with Wordsworth. But, apart from his own wounds, it was natural for one who was beyond the arrows, views, and shouts of men to have the same attitude towards criticism as towards poetry. Criticism, like poetry, to be worth anything should be for the best, and, consequently unintelligible to the common rout of men. (pp. 906-08)

His literary criticisms are characteristic offshoots of his unique aims in literature. He tried, as everyone knows, to present concepts of the intellect or of the soul unadorned, in white light. His poems are like fragments of beautifully chiselled marble; not reproductions in the manner of the Greeks, but by a miracle, original creations done in the spirit of Greece. The medium is English, severe, self-sustained, integral. The means to this end was an erudition without parallel among nineteenth century poets. This type of creative art was Landor's goal; from it he never swerved. And it is not too much to say that in many instances his literary judgments may be referred to it. From his lofty and somewhat strange ideals come his wayward opinions in criticism.

Wayward in form as in substance, Landor did not write critical essays. In no writer of the nineteenth century may be found so many critical judgments on writers without the accompanying formal essay. His really memorable opinions float about in letters and diaries, and in the notes and journals of pilgrims to Fiesole. A small anthology might be made of his notions on Byron, Shelley, or the ancients. The bulk of his literary criticism may be found in the *Imaginary Conversations*. In his letters Landor protests again and again that the opinions of these characters cannot be regarded as his own. The reader, however, vetoes this pretension. Their creator is a rather awkward Proteus; under the disguises we detect the well-known features of W. S. Landor. The reader is justified in taking the literary criticism to be Landor's though it happens to come from the lips of Petrarch or Porson. If we examine the *Conversations* minutely (which it has been my misfortune to do) we encounter everywhere brilliant epigrams on literature. Even in the political and religious subjects Landor is never very far from literary themes. His enormous knowledge of the classics must not make us, by comparison, undervalue his acquaintance with other literatures. He read less than Carlyle, and remembered less than Macaulay, but his reading was wide, and often, as in his study of Milton, concentrated. Aside from chance references, the substance of Landor's criticism is in those dialogues which he himself classified as "Conversations of Literary Men." These are reflective; there is little need to consider the circumstances or action, as in the historical conversations; and if the names of the speakers are mentally deleted, there remains in effect literary criticism. To these the reader should turn to estimate Landor as a critic of literature; to **"Southey and Porson"** (both conversations), **"The Abbe Delille and Walter Landor," "Landor," "English Visiter and Florentine Visiter,"** [sic], **"Boccaccio and Petrarch," "Archdeacon Hare and Walter Landor"**; and to others similar in character. Nor must we forget, as we consider where Landor's criticism occurs, his unusual amount of critical verse. Some of this is doggerel, like the invitation to Tennyson; some is humourous epigram, as in the fugitive lines to Dickens; and some is in Landor's noblest mood, as in the lines to Browning. Altogether this verse totals hundreds of lines, and cannot be neglected in an estimate of Landor's critical opinions.

If all such fragments were placed within the bounds of a single volume, the main characteristics of Landor as a critic would be nearly as obvious as his characteristics as a man. The first of these was a tendency to eccentric enthusiasms. Landor's judgments were arbitrary. He had, as has been indicated, no set of critical principles, and his criticism was at the mercy of high but eccentric ideals. His opinions were not based wholly on intellectual conviction, nor on emotion, but sometimes on the former, sometimes on the latter. Thus Landor praised Milton because of Milton's lofty intellectual ideals for poetry; he worshipped Southey chiefly because, I believe, he loved the man. (pp. 908-10)

As we look further into our imaginary edition of Landor's criticism we see how characteristic [his] sweeping judgments are. Their fault is that they are unsupported by critical analysis. Landor uses the critic's *faute de mieux,*—comparison and contrast. Like Macaulay he loves to classify writers. He compares Ovid to Virgil, and Spenser to Chaucer. The following is typical of this method: "Scott superseded Wordsworth, and Byron superseded Scott. . . . Scott had a wider range than either, and excelled in more qualities." Instances might be multiplied. Instead of critical analysis with reference to unifying principles, there are arbitrary judgments, and for confirmation other arbitrary judgments.

Exception must be made in respect to one or two writers in English towards whom Landor manifests a more precise critical attitude. These are the objects of his especial devotion, and receive the same scrutiny as the classical writers. Such notable examples of critical study are Dante and Milton. Landor cannot say enough of the Francesca episode, and he studies *Paradise Lost* and *Paradise Regained* with meticulous care. It may be said that he concentrates in much the same way upon Wordsworth. The conversations of **"Southey and Porson"** and **"Southey and Landor"** exhibit particularly this sort of criticism, as well as certain passages in the *Pentameron*. But even here our exception itself must be qualified. Landor makes no study of Milton historically; and there is no testing of the epics by the theories and principles of poetry. What Landor does is to examine the text and comment learnedly upon it. (pp. 911-12)

[Many of his observations are close to his] hobbies of orthography and spelling. Many pages of this sort of "criticism" weigh down the *Imaginary Conversations*. It is hardly critical analysis. It is rather the examination of a text. Whenever Landor abandons his broad, general preferences he is apt to fall into a bog of annotation. Here is obviously a transference of the scholia of classical criticism to English literature. Landor's analysis resolves itself into learned notes. And even in such appraisal of literature, which has some scholarly value, Landor is likely to be transported to whimsical verdicts. After all, of what real worth is the following? "Milton is more correct than Addison, but less correct than Hooker." Or: "Such stupendous genius, so much fancy, so much eloquence, so much vigour of intellect, never were united as in *Paradise Lost*." . . . Moreover, Landor contrives to add a certain opaque quality to his generalizations which make them no happier. "Where," he queries, "excepting in Milton, where among all the moderns, is energy always to be found in the right place?" And sometimes the epigrams are grotesque: "A rib of Shakespeare," he declares, "would have made a Milton: the same portion of Milton, all poets born ever since."

In this Landorian *mot,* however, is the suggestion of the writer's greatest power as a critic of literature, his capacity for epigrammatic criticism. . . . This power was joined to a broad vision of literature. . . . Landor wrote striking apothegms about *all* men of letters. "Roscoe's works are a feather-bed of words." We find in Addison "a sweet temperature of thought." "Young is too often fantastical and frivolous; he pins butterflies to the pulpit cushion." "Johnson had somewhat of the medlar in his nature; one side hard and austere, the other unsound." Such sententious phrases Landor threw off by hundreds; they are remarkable not only in quality, but in scope. Each stands alone, as final as an oracle from Delphi, and often, unfortunately, not less cryptic. Perhaps they can never be regarded as real literary criticism; they are too fragmentary, too reticent. But the fact that Landor left an aphorism of this sort concerning almost every writer who has ever lived demands respect. He is a critic of literature, even if a somewhat eccentric one. (pp. 912-14)

To what Matthew Arnold liked to call "the main current" of criticism Landor contributed nothing. He was no less isolated as a critic than as a poet. His method, if he can be said to own a method, is archaic and peculiar to himself. He lacked, in the highest sense, the analytical faculty. But he had great resources of knowledge, and his lapidary criticism is enriched by many striking apothegms. His literary criticism is a series of fragmentary paragraphs on literature as brilliant, as terse, and as finished as his poetical *inscriptiones* and epigrams. (p. 928)

Stanley T. Williams, "Walter Savage Landor as a Critic of Literature," in PMLA, *38, Vol. XXXVIII, No. 4, December, 1923, pp. 906-28.*

RICHARD ALDINGTON (essay date 1924)

[*Aldington is perhaps best remembered as the editor of the Imagist periodical the* Egoist *and as an influential member of that movement. The major goal of the Imagists was to free poetry from excessive verbiage and vague generalities and to utilize precise imagery. As a literary critic and biographer, Aldington combined his skills as a poet and his perceptiveness as an extremely sensitive reader to produce criticism that is creative as well as informative. Here, Aldington explores the artistic implications of Landor's preface to* The Hellenics *(see excerpt dated 1847). The critic asserts that an understanding of the "diaphanous" quality in Landor's poetry, as opposed to the "prismatic" style of the Romantic poets, is requisite to an appreciation of* The Hellenics.]

Like his friend, Southey, [Landor] is often little more than a name as a poet. Of course there is no exact method of discovering how much the *Hellenics* are read and admired; Landor may be intensely appreciated by a large, silent audience, but he is certainly not fashionable, and probably never will be. The true cause of this comparative obscurity is . . . Landor's poetic style itself, the ideal of poetry he deliberately set himself, in opposition to the tendencies of eighteenth-century moralizing poetry and nineteenth-century decorative poetry. In the preface to the *Hellenics,* written with that brusque terseness he affected towards the public, he says: "Little in these pages will gratify the generality of readers. Poetry, in our day, is oftner prismatic than diaphanous: this is not so: they who look into it may see through" [see excerpt dated 1847]. The phrase "oftner prismatic than diaphanous"—a fine terse criticism of the Romantic movement—gives a first clue to a correct appreciation of Landor's poems. The poetry of the great Romantics and their successors is so often merely "prismatic"; deficient in architectural qualities but abounding in picturesque details and irridescent language. Matthew Arnold's criticism of *Isabella* marks a cardinal weakness of Romantic poetry. . . . Now the style of Landor is deliberately architectural and "classic," perhaps the most classic (in intention) of all our poets; Landor is the most determined to reproduce in English the effects of earlier Greek poetry, the most consistent in his poetical ideal and the most ruthless expunger of every tendency and influence foreign to his ideal. Most people will admit that Arnold had a lofty ideal of the poetic art, and that he also attempted to make English some of the "classic" qualities of Greek poetry. A comparison is interesting.

> Far, far from here
> The Adriatic breaks in a warm bay
> Among the green Illyrian hills; and there
> The sunshine in the happy glens is fair,
> And by the sea, and in the brakse.
> The grass is cool, the sea-side air
> Buoyant and fresh, the mountain flowers
> As virginal and sweet as ours.

That is "prismatic" poetry. Now turn from that romantic nostalgia to the "diaphanous" lines which open Landor's poem **"To Corinth"**—

> Queen of the double sea, beloved of him
> Who shakes the world's foundations, thou hast seen
> Glory in all her beauty, all her forms;
> Seen her walk back with Theseus when he left
> The bones of Sciron bleaching to the wind,
> Above the ocean's roar and cormorant's flight,
> So high that vastest billows from above
> Show but like herbage waving in the mead;
> Seen generations throng the Isthmian games,
> And pass away; . . .

Note Arnold's weak adjectives: "warm, green, happy, fair, cool, buoyant, fresh, virginal, sweet"—so many of them "literary" and unnecessary; and then look at Landor's: "double, high, vastest, Isthmian." Does not that mark the difference between a weak, emotional poet and a strong "classic" poet. (pp. 143-45)

To use the word "classic" in describing a style is to invite misapprehension and dissent. And yet "Hellenic" alone does not define the quality of Landor's poetry at its best. He is the most deliberately Hellenic of English poets; even his quaint-sounding laconisms are an attempt to achieve Greek brevity. But however Greek his mind and tastes, Landor himself was a choleric English gentleman with tremendous pride, a manner at once violent and courteous, blustering and dignified, and above all, a heart of the most tender delicacy and generosity; and this English character is continually invading his Hellenism, even in the most objective of his poems. . . . Landor's Hellenism has a double aspect: it comes chiefly from his affinity with the spirit of Greek thought, from his understanding of the Greek ideal, from his possessing a "Greek soul"—as we say sentimentally; but it comes also from an instinctive checking of his English emotionalism. He lived in a series of emotional explosions; of wrath, pride, generosity, tenderness, indignation. How natural that he should turn for discipline to the pure serenity of Attic Greek; and knowing him as we do, how natural that Walter Savage Landor, fuming with rage over some trifle, should invest his indignation (at some local squire) with the Jovian dignity of Pericles or the cynic indifference of Diogenes. The English Landor is always visible through the Greek Landor, even in the *Hellenics*; the matter, the form, almost the very speech is Greek, but the voice is English. One suspects that his chaste Hellenic maidens wore corkscrew curls; certainly his Agamemnons and Ptolemys, Hyperbions and Rhaicos have all been christened "Walter Savage" while the republican, or rather oligarchic, sentiment is too violent, the generosity too open and quixotic to fit a nation of genial liars and unscrupulous intriguers like the Athenians. Moreover, Landor's culture, though primarily, was not exclusively Hellenic. He was very extensively read in Latin, with an exceptionally wide knowledge of neo-Latin authors; he was nourished on the best in the literatures of Italy, France, and England. And he was one of our great critics. If he was not learned in any cumbersome or pejorative sense, he possessed a culture as choice and as enthusiastic as that of Goethe, if not so extensive. (pp. 145-47)

It would be impossible for Landor's style to be purely Hellenic—he would have had to be born Greek for that—and so the much-abused "classic" still seems the correct work. After all, "classic" implies many of the qualities Landor most admired; and it implies also the opposite of all "prismatic" and all turgidly unplastic poetry. But the Greeks were Landor's masters. Unlike Keats, he did not get his Hellenism at second hand through the kaleidoscope of Jacobean English poetry. . . . Perhaps a nice discrimination could detect Milton's influence in the *Hellenics,* but in general their style is modelled on the sententious brevity of poets like Simonides, with a certain alloy of Latinisms. Notice in the following lines the rather excessive attempt at Greek simplicity and brevity—

> The sea shines bright before us. What white sail
> Plays yonder? What pursues it? Like two hawks
> Away they fly. Let us away in time
> To overtake them. Are they menaces

We hear? And shall the strong repulse the weak
Enraged at her defender? Hippias!
Art thou the man? 'Twas Hippias. He had found
His sister borne from the Cecropian port
By Thrasymedes. And reluctantly?
Ask, ask the maiden; I have no reply.

Imagine that passage re-written in the "prismatic" style of Shelley; it would occupy at least a page. Observe that this is not the Gallic classicism of Pope nor the moralized and over-formal classicism of Johnson nor verbalized Hellenism like that of "Balaustion's Adventure"; it represents an almost unique and not very successful attempt to force into English classic density and terseness. The result is sometimes more strange than beautiful, for, to achieve it, Landor boggles at no obscurity, no allusiveness, no awkward Latinism. The mere reconditeness of his allusions is sufficient to daunt some readers who will need the classical dictionary nearly as much for the *Hellenics* as for the Metamorphoses. A timid reader is not encouraged by lines like these—

> The proud Aemonian shook Aëtion's towers.
> Alpheios and Spercheios heard the shout
> Of Maenalos; Cyllenè, Pholoë,
> Parthenos, Tegea, and Lycaios, called. . . .

These, if not defects in an English poem, can hardly be called beauties; still less the frequent Latinisms, like "*illuded* into love," "with light he *irrigates* the earth," "*pubescent* flower," "*lustral* water" and "*radiant* nod." The search for brevity and simplicity, the avoidance of the "prismatic" lead to some queer banalities when (as rarely happens) Landor loses his dignity—

> Thou hadst *evinced the madness of thy passion* . . .
> Whatever is most *laudable and manly* . . .
> *Flapping* the while with laurel-rose
> The honey-gathering tribes away. . . .

Yet when all these difficulties and defects have been recorded, when we add to them the peculiar spelling Landor affected and the occasional lack of spontaneity in the language (due perhaps to some of the poems having been written in Latin and then translated into English), then we have simply cleared away the obstacles which prevent enjoyment of the poetry of the *Hellenics*. When the reader perceives Landor's ideals and method, the difficulties begin to vanish, the defects become insignificant. Those whose taste is chiefly formed on romantic poetry, those who are entirely seduced by modern impressionism, will probably not enjoy the *Hellenics*. You cannot find witty or pointed couplets or lovely suave phrases (so abundant in Keats and Tennyson) nor any of the coloured fumes of mysticism in Landor's poetry. Landor is never verbose. Harsh, over rapid, too condensed, too allusive, too "diaphanous," perhaps; but never dull, never diffuse, never ignoble, never turgid and vague.

Because the poet worked for the architectural qualities of poetry, the *Hellenics* are not easily quotable. Landor's unit is not the line, not the passage, but the poem. To quote fragments of the *Hellenics* is to show a limb or a torso instead of the whole statue. (pp. 148-51)

Landor's poetic genius was not lyric; it lay rather in dialogue and narrative. English taste insists that all poetry shall sing; without reflecting that nobody would sing a narrative. But because Landor did not sacrifice everything to sound and "prismatic" conceits it does not follow that he is lacking in richness. When for a while he relaxes from his Attic severity into a more Sicilian mood, few poets are capable of such richness. . . . (pp. 151-52)

Is it only a romantic fancy which makes one feel that no poets were ever so sensitive to the crisp outlines and clear tints of flowers and fruits as the Greeks? Landor shared that exquisite plastic feeling. Only a poet who is so gifted with the love and understanding of their beauty can so evoke their essential form and colour and scent. The demi-gods whom the Greek poets invented as the spirits of flowers and trees and windy rocks were a projection of this sensitiveness. And Landor, the tender old Englishman, understood so well that delicate respect for beauty. (pp. 152-53)

The idylls which compose the *Hellenics* are chiefly *heroic*. Landor can express the finest emotions of the lover of beauty and understand wild flowers like a sensitive woman; but he can also express fortitude with vehement eloquence. (p. 153)

It is hardly possible that the *Hellenics* could become popular. Many, whose taste is formed on less august models, will never feel the pure heroic beauty of the *Hellenics*. Yet Landor will always find some enthusiasts to prefer the "diaphanous" beauties of the *Hellenics* to the more dazzling but less satisfying attractions of "prismatic" poetry. (p. 154)

> *Richard Aldington, "Landor's 'Hellenics',"* in his Literary Studies and Reviews, The Dial Press Incorporated, 1924, pp. 141-54.

T. S. ELIOT   (lecture date 1933)

[*Eliot, an American-born English poet, essayist, and critic, is regarded as one of the most influential literary figures of the first half of the twentieth century. As a critic, he introduced a number of terms and concepts that strongly affected critical thought in his lifetime. In the following brief excerpt, taken from a lecture originally delivered at Harvard University in 1933, Eliot contrasts the importance of Landor and Wordsworth as poets.*]

[Consider] one of the very finest poets of the first part of the nineteenth century: Landor. He is an undoubted master of verse and prose; he is the author of at least one long poem which deserves to be much more read than it is; but his reputation has never been such as to bring him into comparison with Wordsworth or with either [Shelley or Keats]. . . . It is not only by reason of a handful of poems or a number of isolated lines expressive of deeper emotion than that of which Landor was capable, that we give Wordsworth his place; there is something integral about such greatness, and something significant in his place in the pattern of history, with which we have to reckon. And in estimating for ourselves the greatness of a poet we have to take into account also the *history* of his greatness. Wordsworth is an essential part of history; Landor only a magnificent by-product. (p. 88)

> *T. S. Eliot, "Shelley and Keats,"* in his The Use of Poetry and the Use of Criticism: Studies in the Relation of Criticism to Poetry in England, *Faber and Faber Limited, 1933, pp. 87-102.*

DONALD A. DAVIE   (essay date 1951)

[*An English poet, critic, educator, and translator, Davie is well respected for both his creative and critical contributions to literature. In his critical work* The Purity of Diction in English Verse, *he argued for a return to the prose-like syntax, formal structures, and conservative metaphors of the eighteenth-century Augustan poets. During the 1950s Davie was associated with the*]

Movement, a group of poets who emphasized restrained language, traditional syntax, and the moral and social implications of poetic content. In his examination of Landor's short poems and epigrams, excerpted below, Davie discusses their structure, form, and language. He declares that unevenness in diction and tone is "the besetting sin of Landor's writing, something which cancels out all his other virtues." For further commentary by Davie, see the excerpt dated 1984 and the Additional Bibliography.]

To C. H. Herford, in 1897, it seemed that 'Landor was . . . on the whole the greatest prose-writer of the age of Wordsworth; and, after Wordsworth, Coleridge, Byron, Shelley and Keats, he was its greatest poet' [see Additional Bibliography]. Whatever may be thought of Landor's prose, it would be hard to find anyone today to endorse the claim that, as a poet, he was greater than Scott, Clare, Crabbe, Hogg or Darley—all poets with whom Herford deals. I find him inferior to every one of these poets; but my intention here is not to gird at Herford or to sneer at Landor. For the latter has an importance out of proportion with his meagre achievement. At a crucial stage in the English poetic tradition he struck out alone a path of interesting and sensible experiment; and in deciding what chance there was of success, and where and how the experiment failed, we touch upon matters of importance for the writing of poetry at any time.

What Landor stood for in the writing of poetry can be seen from one of his more distinguished poems, **"To Wordsworth"**:

> He who would build his fame up high,
> The rule and plummet must apply,
> Nor say, 'I'll do what I have plann'd',
> Before he try if loam or sand
> Be still remaining in the place
> Delved for each polish't pillar's base.
> With skilful eye and fit device
> Thou raisest every edifice,
> Whether in sheltered vale it stand
> Or overlook the Dardan strand,
> Amid the cypresses that mourn
> Laodameia's love forlorn.

The advice is sufficiently trite. It appears less so, in the rather better verse of the **"Epistle to the Author of 'Festus'"**:

> Some see but sunshine, others see but gloom,
> Others confound them strangely, furiously;
> Most have an eye for colour, few for form.
> Imperfect is the glory to *create*,
> Unless on our creation we can look
> And see that all is good; we then may rest.
> In every poem train the leading shoot;
> Break off the suckers. Thought erases thought,
> As numerous sheep erase each other's print
> When spungy moss they press or sterile sand.
> Blades thickly sown want nutriment and droop,
> Although the seed be sound, and rich the soil;
> Thus healthy-born ideas, bedded close,
> By dreaming fondness perish overlain.

This is far more provocative, challenging, as it does, that other precept of the period, to 'load every rift with ore'. And yet the principle applied in the lines to Wordsworth and in these to Bailey is identical. We find it more provocative here, because, in addressing Wordsworth, Landor uses a trite architectural metaphor for quite commonplace ideas about the need for structure in longer poems; whereas in the lines to Bailey he seems to imply that a short poem requires structure no less. And we are more willing, I think, to consider the structure of

an ode or an epic than of a lyric or epigram. Just for that reason, perhaps, it is more salutary to examine Landor's theory and practice in his shorter poems. (pp. 345-46)

To begin with, it is not hard to see why we fight shy of Landor's theories about the structure of short poems. For when Landor insists that 'ideas' must be disposed carefully about the poem, not crowded one upon another, he raises at once the question of a staple language in which those 'ideas' may be set. The staple of a poem, in this sense, is the diction of the poem. And problems of poetic diction are particularly difficult in the period of the preface to *Lyrical Ballads*. . . . Landor's principles of disposition seem to me self-evidently right; and it follows that poetic diction, in the sense of a staple language for the poet, is a burning question for poets and readers in any age.

Landor's practice is another matter. The very lines in which he expounds his theory show how far he was from putting it into practice. To begin with, his word 'ideas' is peculiar, since any logical arrangement of words has meaning, and in that sense contains ideas. He cannot mean what he seems to say, that the staple, the gold ring in which the gems are set, shall be devoid of ideas, hence meaningless. And I infer that by 'ideas' Landor means rather what older critics called 'figures'. In other words, we are to find 'ideas' in this sense wherever we find in a poem any conscious rhetoric, any attempt to be striking, concentrated, or elaborate beyond what we expect from conversational prose. As a matter of fact, the lines from the **"Epistle to the Author of 'Festus'"** are themselves highly figurative, in the way they seem to condemn. And only four of them can be said to contain no images:

> Most have an eye for colour, few for form.
> Imperfect is the glory to *create*,
> Unless on our creation we can look
> And see that all is good; we then may rest.

Here, then, if anywhere, we should find the staple language, that poetic diction which Landor seems to demand, in which figures ('ideas') shall be disposed. Yet here the language is quite indiscriminate. The first line is notably conversational, the second, with its italic, even more so. But the third and fourth, with their presumptuous echo from Genesis, are elaborate, rhetorical and literary. How can this be a staple language, or a pure diction, when in the space of four lines it veers so giddily from high to low? It betrays in particular a bewildering insecurity of *tone*. At one moment the poet is addressing us amicably in the study; at the next, he is thundering from a rostrum. How can we know how to take him? What tone can we adopt in reading the poem aloud? The golden ring is cracked; and, however fine the brilliants, we can only be distressed.

This seems to me the besetting sin of all Landor's writing, something which cancels out all his other virtues. And nearly always Landor courts disaster, as here by the italic, so elsewhere by passages of direct speech. . . . The truth is that Landor merely takes no care for any consistent tone of discourse.

As a matter of fact, despite his advice to 'train the leading shoot', Landor was always prone to lose the thread of his poems, even in more obvious ways. In a poem addressed to satire, which contains some promising lines (for, like Shelley, Landor had satirical talent, but despised it), the failure with direct speech only aggravates a trailing-off into obscurity:

> Byron was not *all* Byron; one small part
> Bore the impression of a human heart.
> Guided by no clear love-star's panting light,
> Thro' the sharp surges of a northern night,

In Satire's narrow strait he swam the best,
Scattering the foam that hist about his breast.
He who might else have been more tender, first
From Scottish saltness caught his rabid thirst.
Praise Keats . . .
          'I think I've heard of him'
                       'With you
Shelley stands foremost'
           . . . And his lip was blue . . .
'I hear with pleasure any one commend
So good a soul; for Shelley is my friend.'
One leaf from Southey's laurel made explode
All his combustibles . . .
                     'An ass! by
  God!'

This is mere doodling. It would be hard to find anything less classical, in Landor's or any other sense.

It is unfair perhaps, to recall it. For we can adopt Herford's verdict on *Gebir* and say of its author that 'though hardly a great poet, he is full of the symptoms of greatness'. Nothing could be much more damaging or sadder; for, as Herford also says, 'It is characteristic of Landor that he is great in detail rather than in mass' [see Additional Bibliography]. In other words, the poet who tried above all things for the poem as an artifact, a whole thing cut loose from its maker, emerges as a true poet only in fragments and snatches. It is for this reason that one turns back through Landor's poems, coming across distinguished phrases by the way, and thinking, 'Surely I have misjudged him'. But one never has. On re-reading, the poem does not improve; it is still disastrously uneven, in the rough, unshaped. The fine writing remains irrelevant; it never adds up to an effect.

This difficulty should not arise so sharply with the epigrams. And the best of these are very good. . . . But this, it will be said, is to miss the point. His epigrams are important—the argument runs—because they retrieve the epigram from flippancy and make it once again a serious vehicle, as in the Greek Anthology. Well, I should like to think so. But in the first place flippancy can be serious in one sense where a solemn triviality is not. Such graceful marginalia as the lines **"With Petrarca's Sonnets"** or **"On Catullus"** are all very well in their way, but not serious in the sense that posterity need remember them. There are other epigrams that offer to be serious in the sense that they are momentous statements, and these that are serious in every sense often fail of their effect in the same way as the longer poems, on the score of diction.

Leaving aside the marginalia, Landor's epigrams can be divided for convenience into three classes. There are in the first place the compliments (**"Dirce"**, for instance, and most of the poems to Ianthe). Then there are traditional commonplaces, to be expressed in novel ways, with a seeming finality (**"Rose Aylmer"**, **"The leaves are falling; so am I"**). And finally there are poems which offer to be 'discoveries', original in theme but expressed in traditional form. (pp. 346-51)

The most famous example of the first class is the epigram on **"Dirce"**:

    Stand close around, ye Stygian set,
      With Dirce in one boat conveyed!
    Or Charon, seeing, may forget
      That he is old, and she a shade.

In the classical examples of such compliments, from the seventeenth and eighteenth centuries, we find the effect depends upon combining daring hyperbole with imperturbable urbanity:

    To her, whose beauty doth excell
      Stories, wee tosse theis cupps, and fill
      Sobrietie, a sacrifice
    To the bright lustre of her eyes.
    Each soule that sipps this is divine:
    Her beauty deifies the wine.

'Urbanity' begs at once the question of diction. For to explain how these trivia seem momentous, we have to give to 'urbanity' the meaning that Arnold gave to it, in "The Influence of Literary Academies", when he spoke of it as the tone or spirit of the centre, embodying the best of a civilization. There, of course, he spoke of such urbanity as an attribute of the best prose, and thought it no business of the poet. But such centrality seems the virtue of a pure diction in poetry, as of an Attic style in prose. . . . One has to say that by Landor's day to turn an elegant compliment and make momentous poetry of it was no longer a possibility: and of course it has never been possible since.

The same is true of the second class of Landor's epigrams, his attempts at 'what oft was thought but ne'er so well expressed'. To make poetry out of moral commonplace, a poet has to make it clear that he speaks not in his own voice (that would be impertinent) but as the spokesman of a social tradition. Hence the importance of the Horatian imitation for Pope, or the imitation of Juvenal by Johnson. By employing those forms and modes, the poets spoke out of a tradition which was not merely literary; for the reading of Horace and Juvenal was a tradition of social habit in the audience they addressed, which was also the society for which they spoke. The Greek epigram was no substitute. And when Landor treats a traditional commonplace ('Past ruin'd Ilion Helen lives', 'The Leaves are falling; so am I', 'There is a mountain and a wood between us') his achievement seems frail and marginal, chiefly because he does not show, in the form he chooses, how traditional, how far from original, is what he wants to say. (pp. 351-52)

There remains the third sort of epigram, which I have called 'Discoveries'. . . . Landor occasionally makes discoveries of the Wordsworthian sort, not 'what oft was thought but ne'er so well expressed', but what was never consciously thought before, nor ever expressed. Even here, I think, he tries more often than he succeeds. But sometimes he can make genuine discoveries, especially about movements of the mind:

    Something (ah! tell me what) there is
      To cause that melting tone.
    I fear a thought has gone amiss
      Returning quite alone.

[The] diction of the first two lines is faded and decadent, but this is important only because it leads us to expect something quite different from what we are given thereafter. In other words it makes the discovery more sudden and surprising. Perhaps for this reason, the lines have been found obscure, but their bearing is plain enough. Landor catches in a touching metaphor the experience of breaking off a line of thought, surprised by a melancholy reflection. He explains the shadow falling across the face of his companion by the supposition that a thought has 'gone amiss' (i.e. broken off the train of thought of which it was a link) and 'returned alone', or, as the common metaphor has it, 'brought home' to the thinker a melancholy truth. The poem, one could say, is an exploration and a discovery of what we mean when we say 'The truth was brought home to me'. To give form to an experience so fugitive yet so permanently human seems to me an achievement of a high order. Unfortunately I can think of only one other case in which Landor does something comparable, in his poem **"For an Urn in Thoresby Park"**.

There is considerable pathos in the story of Landor's life, so devoted, so disinterested, and to so little end. It is interesting and important chiefly because his attempt to put the clock back shows how inevitable was the Romantic revolution in poetic method and the conception of the poet's function. The poets had to undertake to make discoveries of truth, in some sense novel, because the poetry of truths already acknowledged depended upon conditions which no longer obtained. To make poetry out of traditional commonplace or personal compliment the poet had to write in and for a homogeneous society acknowledging strong and precise traditions of literature and manners. His awareness of such a society as his audience gave the poet the sureness of tone which comes out of a pure diction and achieves urbanity. When Landor attempted this, all the odds were against him. No such society and no such audience existed. And as a result, the great poets of the age were great in quite novel ways. Wordsworth, for instance, eschewed urbanity and made a virtue of provincialism. Shelley set out to be the discoverer in an absolute sense. Keats, when he was not the discoverer, evaded the question of a staple language by figurative luxury. And when the poets needed to be urbane . . . they sought no longer an impossible purity of diction, but a sort of calculated impurity; so that urbanity since has always been ironical. Landor is the type of the poet who refuses to acknowledge the temper of his age. There is a certain magnificence in his obstinate wrong-headedness; but it did not go to produce important poems. (pp. 353-55)

> *Donald A. Davie, "The Shorter Poems of Walter Savage Landor," in* Essays in Criticism, *Vol. I, No. 4, October, 1951, pp. 345-55.*

DOUGLAS BUSH   (essay date 1952)

[*Bush examines Landor's technical and literary ideals, concluding that he "cherished a pseudo-classical notion of form and style as ends in themselves."*]

[We] must take the briefest glance at a figure whose turbulence, unlike Byron's, shook only those in his immediate vicinity, and whose literary presence we are apt to forget, that is, Walter Savage Landor. . . . Landor's writings in verse and prose, English and Latin, covered nearly seventy years. He published *Gebir,* an epic of rather cryptic density, in the year of *Lyrical Ballads,* and lived to receive, as an aged libertarian and neo-pagan, the excited homage of Swinburne. As a person and an author, Landor belonged to the eighteenth century, the romantic age, and the Victorian age, and in all three periods he was a lion who walked by himself. He was an eighteenth-century aristocrat and a republican; a romantic poet whose theory and practice were classical; a man of explosive personality and opinions whose poetry was austerely impersonal and almost sufficiently detached from life and ideas to be called 'pure poetry' or Imagism.

But these and other paradoxes are resolved in the central fact that Landor's highest and most compelling ideal was literary and technical. While the romantic and early Victorian poets wrote with Elizabethan prodigality and colour, Landor, setting before himself such models as Pindar, strove for the compact

and 'diaphanous'—not, however, because he believed, with the young Arnold, that the high and heavy spiritual responsibility of poetry required bare strength, but because he felt no such responsibility and cherished a pseudo-classical notion of form and style as ends in themselves. Many of Landor's poems treat classical myths, but whereas for the other poets myths are symbols charged with meaning, Landor is usually content to retell the stories, and usually without much human interest. The craftsmanship that shuns the realities of experience, and concentrates on expression when there is little to express, is not even facing the problems of the craftsman. Thus, though critics periodically deplore the neglect of Landor, we cannot really say, in spite of a few fine poems, that neglect is unjustified. (pp. 150-52)

> *Douglas Bush, "Romanticism," in his* English Poetry: The Main Currents from Chaucer to the Present, *Methuen & Co. Ltd., 1952, pp. 112-52.*

LAURENCE PERRINE   (essay date 1964)

[*Landor's attitude toward immortality in his poetry suggests to Perrine that the poet rejected traditional views of life after death yet accepted death with serenity, recognizing that nature, art, and love can bring meaning to life.*]

The theme of immortality is one on which Walter Savage Landor rings many changes in his verse. He treats it in a variety of contexts and a variety of moods, sometimes seriously, sometimes lightly, almost always gracefully. As one might expect, he turns to it with increasing frequency as he grows older. His attitude toward it, however, is not one of belief. . . . [The] main evidence, both of his verse and his recorded utterances, indicates that Landor was agnostic on the question of immortality but on the whole had very little expectation of it. (p. 50)

The most direct evidence of Landor's attitude toward immortality . . . is found in his statement to Swinburne, made during the last year of his life, as reported in Gosse's *Life of Swinburne:*

> Landor talked to his young visitor with great freedom, and, in relation to the approach of death at his own advanced age, remarked that he had no belief in immortality of the soul nor opinion about it, but "was sure of one thing, that whatever was to come was best—the right thing, or the thing that ought to come."

The attitude expressed here is reflected exactly in a poem, published eleven years earlier, when Landor was 79:

> Death stands above me, whispering low
> I know not what into my ear:
> Of his strange language all I know
> Is, there is not a word of fear. . . .

In this statement and this poem seems to be summed up Landor's most considered opinion on the subject of death. Death speaks to him in a foreign tongue—i.e., one of which Landor cannot understand the *words* (which reveal whether or not there is any life to follow) but of which he *can* understand the *tone* (in which there is nothing fearful). The attitude is very much like that of Socrates in the *Apology.* There is nothing to be feared in death, for either it will give Socrates a chance to converse with the souls of the good and the great who have preceded him, or else it will be simply like a long sleep—and when was not sleep gratefully received at the end of a full day?

The note that death is not to be feared or lamented, and that Landor is ready for it when it comes, is sounded again and again through Landor's work, but not accompanied—as it would be, say, in Browning—by the notion of a life to come. More generally it is accompanied in Landor by the profession, metaphorically expressed, that this life has been a good one, and that one should be grateful for it. . . . The sentiment is repeated in a lyric published when he was 84:

> Fast fall the leaves: this never says
> To that, "Alas! how brief our days!"
> All have alike enjoy'd the sun,
> And each repeats, "*So much is won:*
> Where we are falling, millions more
> Have dropt, nor weep that life is o'er." . . .

The idea that man should make no more protest over dying than a leaf makes in leaving the tree appealed to Landor. . . . Implicit in the analogy is a rejection of immortality, for what after-life has a leaf? (pp. 52-4)

Nature and Art Landor loved, and these made life worthwhile to him without the complement of an after-life. But the term which Landor most frequently opposed to death was neither Nature nor Art, but Love—Love not in the large sense of universal brotherhood, nor of affection for friend or kin, but in the more specific sense of an emotional and physical relationship with the opposite sex. "Whatever he may profess," said Robert Browning of Landor, "the thing he really loves is a pretty girl to talk nonsense with." Browning's judgment is borne out by Landor's poetry. Though what Landor means by love may vary from a deep and enduring feeling, such as he felt for Ianthe, to a more temporary fancy, love is always the hottest flame in that fire of life before which Landor warmed his hands:

> Soon, O Ianthe! life is o'er,
>   And sooner beauty's heavenly smile:
> Grant only (and I ask no more),
>   Let love remain that little while. . . .

If Landor asks no more than this, he does not ask for immortality, and so he explicitly declares in a poem which he titled **"What is *really* my belief?"**:

> My faith is this. I do believe
> That ladies never would deceive,
> And that the little fault of Eve
> Is very easy to retrieve.
>
> She lost us immortality,
> But in good earnest what care I,
> If *you* receive my latest sigh
> And give me one—*before* I die. . . .

"Make me immortal with a kiss!" So said Faustus to Helen of Troy, and so says Landor. The tone here is playful, of course, and the poem is not to be taken very seriously; but the basic idea—that love justifies life, and does not last beyond death—is one frequently repeated in Landor's poetry. . . . (p. 54)

The immortality conferred on a lover by a kiss is figurative, but there was another kind of immortality with which Landor was frequently and literally concerned—the immortality of poetry, and the immortality of fame poetry confers on the poet and his subject. . . . Occasionally Landor has doubts of the worth or reality of even this kind of immortality:

> O immortality of fame!
> What art thou? even Shakespeare's name
> Reaches not Shakespeare in his grave.
> The wise, the virtuous, and the brave,

> Resume ere long their common clay,
> And worms are longer lived than they.
> At last some gilded letters show
> What those were call'd who lie below. . . .

But in general Landor is confident that good poetry will last, if not forever, at least for a very long time. He assures a young poet,

> Worms revel in the slime of kings,
> But perish where the laurel springs. . . .

The point is relevant because an immortality of fame is likely to be most ardently embraced by those who have given up belief in a more personal immortality. (pp. 55-6)

Landor, all critics agree, was no orthodox believer. He undoubtedly believed . . . in a benign First Cause, but he had no use for the dogmas of the sects, he continually waxed satirical against priests, and he had nothing but contempt for what he regarded as religious superstitions. His religious ideal was centered in the idea of service rather than in a ritual of worship, a system of beliefs in the supernatural, or concern for the salvation of the soul. This ideal he summed up in a letter to Southey: "To increase the sum of happiness and to diminish the sum of misery, is the only right aim both of reason and of religion." As for immortality, the argument ends where it began—in affection for this life and serene uncertainty about the next, unattended by expectation. Credulous and pious as he is, he says in one poem, he would not change "certainties for uncertainties"; and besides, he adds, his soul is "only soul enough" for one existence. . . . (p. 57)

> *Laurence Perrine, "Landor and Immortality," in* Victorian Poetry, *Vol. II, No. 1, Winter, 1964, pp. 50-7.*

GEOFFREY GRIGSON   (essay date 1964)

[*Grigson is an English poet, critic, editor, and journalist whose direct style characterizes both his criticism and his poetry. As founder and editor of the short-lived periodical* New Verse, *a forum for avant-garde poetry, Grigson distinguished himself as a strongly principled and sometimes polemical critic. In the following excerpt, Grigson views the epigram "The Dying Speech of an Old Philosopher" as a key to understanding Landor's classical ideals. He further suggests that critics have unjustly neglected Landor's poems which, though counter to the flow of the Romantic age, are creative, varied, and well-formed.*]

Something of value may be discovered about Landor's poems from our understanding, or rather our common misunderstanding, of his most famous epigram, which he called **"The Dying Speech of an Old Philosopher,"** and which he composed on the evening of his seventy-fourth birthday, after entertaining Charles Dickens and John Forster, who wrote his biography. Landor, we all know, was a hefty egotist with a loud laugh and a quick and at times violent temper; and we laugh ourselves, when we recall the first line of this birthday poem, in which he looked back over life and accepted death: we think how singular that of all men, Landor should say

> *I strove with none, for none was worth my strife,*

when his existence seems to have been an intermittent strife from childhood, and school, and university, to his extreme old age in Bath and Florence. But we are wrong, and Landor was right: Landor wrote his epigram, not as the subject of a known biography, but as a poet and as the prose-master of his *Imag-*

inary Conversations; in that role, though as a man he might be moiled in law suits and libel actions, and might end as a King Lear rejected by his children, this striving with no one, or no other writer, as writer himself, was firmly at the centre of Landor's creed, stated by him again and again. When his friend Southey died, the praise Landor accorded him, in a prose epitaph, was the praise he accorded himself in the epigram: 'Rarely hath any author been so exempt from the maladies of emulation.' To push, to scramble, to emulate, to compete, and lose independence—that was the sin of authorship, the betrayal of talent. 'Authors are like cattle going to a fair;' he makes a character say in one of the *Imaginary Conversations*, 'those of the same field can never move on without butting one another.' He butted no one for self-advancement (to criticize or despise is something else). He wrote neither for acclaim nor for money; and he realized that for this and for other reasons his situation in literature was a lonely one, and would continue to be lonely after his death. (p. xvii)

[Every] statement Landor makes in [**"The Dying Speech of an Old Philosopher"**], his life and his writings confirm explicitly. It is Landor's true biography, setting him both in and apart from his time, as our one eminent neo-classic. 'Nature I loved'— if he loved nature, that marked him as a man of his time, whether neo-classic or romantic (not that one would divorce neo-classic and romantic too absolutely), and one may recall Landor's delight—for a while—in the red sandstone valley of his Llanthony estates: 'I have made a discovery, which is, that there are both nightingales and glowworms in my valley. I would give two or three thousand less for a place that was without them'; or—for a while—in his villa garden on the slopes of Fiesole. (pp. xviii-xix)

'Nature I loved, and, next to Nature, Art': art, composure, moderation—'What is there lovely in poetry,' asked Landor, through the mouth of Boccaccio, in the *Pentameron* . . . , 'unless there be moderation and composure? Are they not better than the hot, uncontrollable harlotry of a flaunting dishevelled enthusiasm? Whoever has the power of creating, has likewise the inferior power of keeping his creation in order. The best poets are most impressive because their steps are regular; for without regularity there is neither strength nor state.'

As for the last two lines of the epigram—that he warmed 'both hands before the fire of Life,' that the fire was sinking and that Landor was ready to depart, they are a true summary of Landor's acceptance of life and death; of the fact that he neither evaded, nor substituted, preferring, for example, Wordsworth to Byron . . . , nature and natural language to seraglio and seraglio talk, or faeries and faery talk, or mists, or infinity; preferring objectivity to autotoxication or autoblabbery, *here and now* to *somewhere else and then*—

> Some see but sunshine, others see but gloom,
> Others confound them strangely, furiously;
> Most have an eye for colour, few for form.
> Imperfect is the glory to *create*,
> Unless on our creation we can look
> And see that all is good; we then may rest.

It could be argued, of course, that Landor's classicism was as much a substitution or an ideal evasion of here and now as another writer's liking for an ideal mediaevalism or an aery-faeryism derived from Drayton or *A Midsummer Night's Dream*, or border ballads; to which Landor's reply was that his ideal classic ground—Greek rather than Roman—and classic principles, demanded height, depth, severity, clarity, and grace.

In long poems his power to construct, and tell, and hold, is seldom sufficient, and his pressure does fall too low; in his short poems he sometimes goes soft, in the manner of other neo-classic poets, architects, and sculptors (such as Flaxman or Thorwaldsen, whom Landor admired). But Landor, like the Greek style architects of his time, wanted, and frequently achieved, what he considered a Greek stiffening of neo-classic sentimentality: the clear and determinate world of Greece was not the misty, indeterminate chaos of the Gothic. There were poets, Landor said, whose books in half a century would be enquired after only for 'cutting out an illuminated letter from the title-page' (Gothicizing poets) 'or of transplanting the willow at the end, that hangs so prettily over the tomb of Amaryllis' (neo-classically sentimental poets). 'If they wish to be healthy and vigorous, let them open their bosoms to the breezes of Sunium; for the air of Latium is heavy and overcharged.'

The Attic, temple-crowned, sun-clear promontory of Sunium was the ideal ground for Landor. . . . [As] Landor expressed it . . . in his poem on the Classick and the Romantick, in the grave, slow line of this poet reflecting, this poet considering ultimates:

> The ancients see us under them, and grieve
> That we are parted by a rank morass,
> Wishing its flowers more delicate and fewer.
> Abstemious were the Greeks; they never strove
> To look so fierce: their Muses were sedate,
> Never obstreperous: you heard no breath
> Outside the flute; each sound ran clear within.
> The Fauns might dance, might clap their hands, might shout,
> Might revel and run riotous; the Nymphs
> Furtively glanced, and fear'd, or seem'd to fear:
> Descended on the lightest of light wings,
> The graceful son of Maia mused apart,
> Graceful, but strong; he listen'd; he drew nigh;
> And now with his own lyre and now with voice
> Temper'd the strain; Apollo calmly smiled.

When Landor writes—and ends a poem—'Apollo calmly smiled', the three words are fact and metaphor; but fact all through. The god Apollo calmly smiled, the narrow-waisted, almond-eyed god whom we know in marble, and who is beauty, youth, composure, strength, civilization. The clear-edged congruence of word and object in Landor is one of his virtues, more acceptable, since language allows of less mannerism than stone and stucco, than the clear-edged 'Greek' architecture of Landor's time, Doric, Ionic, Corinthian, which we now value in the buildings of London and elsewhere. But it does not exhaust Landor's value as a poet to say that there is more of that clear congruence in his longer poems than we commonly admit, and to emphasize its creativity in his epigrams and shorter pieces. He is master especially of a calm line which often begins with short emphatic accented words, and then lightens; he makes poetry a matter of rhythm and language and objectivity, not of imagery and metaphysics; and he would certainly have rejected ambiguity as an evil. He is various, like his own large personality. He offers occasional perfection; he offers gravity, strength, delicacy, wit, comedy. He is lyrical, elegiacal, critical; but convinced also of pleasure—

> The narrow mind is the discontented one.
> There is pleasure in wisdom, there is wisdom in pleasure
> If thou findest no honey in thy cake,
> Put thy cake into honey with thine own right-hand,
> Nor think it defiled thereby.

He can make flickering fun, or knock down a bullock of stupidity. Criticism, perhaps with interference from the history of literature, has inclined to make less than it should have done of poems which are counter, in so many ways, to the 'romantic' flow of poetry and the other arts during Landor's extremely long, always active career. In the past many critics and readers seemed unsure or sure in the wrong way of the voluminous work of a man at times so boisterous and in some ways so uninhibited, who survived into a mealy age (when he died in 1864 he was in his nineteenth year). What was to be thought in such an age of a *poet*—better to think of the prose-writer—whose appetites and moral taste were suspect, who could write as he did about Ianthe's shell or red Priapus rearing his club among the junipers, who could deliver himself of an epigram so indecorous as

Exhausted now her sighs, and dry her tears,
For twenty youths these more than twenty years,
Anne, turning nun, swears God alone shall have her . . .
God ought to bow profoundly for the favour;

who was able to contrive poems with as much ease in outmoded Latin as in English. . . . (pp. xix-xxi)

In the present, criticism and reading have not caught up. 'Poetry was always my amusement, prose my study and business': take Landor's word for it, continue to insist that the poems are mostly occasional—(however: 'Regarding the occasional in poetry; is there less merit in taking and treating what is before us, than in seeking and wandering through an open field as we would for mushrooms?')—and use Landor's prose as an excuse for neglecting the poet (and the verse perhaps as an excuse for neglecting the prose). At any rate, a glance at the third and supplementary volumes of the *Cambridge Bibliography of English Literature* (which places Landor unfortunately among the essayists, and not the poets) shows that no English writer—no English poet—of equal size and quality has been less attended to in the last fifty years; which is a loss.

'I stand out a rude rock in the middle of a river, with no exotic or parasitical plant on it, and few others. Eddies and dimples and froth and bubbles pass rapidly by, without shaking me. Here indeed is little room for pic-nic and polka.'

Not a bad account of himself, as a poet; though Walter Landor was less a rock, and rough, than a finely shaped structure, graceful, but strong, like his Hermes in the poem, who invented the lyre and was the son of Zeus as well as of Maia. Landor himself had some of the attributes of the herm, he was more of a whole and healthy poet than many of his time; in justified pride he thought of himself in a high eagle's sunshine, as in his poem which begins

Ye who have toil'd uphill to reach the haunt
Of other men who lived in other days

and which ends (after he has established that they found nothing but owls hooting and shaking the ivy berries on their heads, and vipers hissing at them, as they crawled down)

Now, was it worth your while to mount so high
Merely to say ye did it, and to ask
If those about ye ever did the like?
Believe me, O my friends, 'twere better far

To stretch your limbs along the level sand
As they do, where small children scoop the drift,
Thinking it must be gold, where curlews soar
And scales drop glistening from the prey above.

(p. xxii)

Geoffrey Grigson, in an introduction to Poems *by Walter Savage Landor, edited by Geoffrey Grigson, Centaur Press Ltd. (England), 1964, pp. xvii-xxii.*

PIERRE VITOUX (essay date 1976)

[*In his assessment of* Gebir, *Vitoux describes Landor's style as a deliberate rejection of the poetic forms of his time in favor of a synthetic compression of language inspired by the ancients. He also finds that the poem's tragic theme represents a stage in the regeneration of humanity and expresses Landor's Romantic political ideals.*]

Gebir was published in 1798, when Landor was twenty-three. The composition of parts of the poem had begun, however, some two years before, during long rambling walks in the woods and along the sandy coast near Swansea, in Wales. Landor's attention had been arrested by a story he had found in the appendix of a book lent to him by his friend Rose Aylmer: *The Progress of Romance* . . . , by Clara Reeve, including the story of Charoba, Queen of Egypt, an adaptation from Vattier. He found it "lacking in simplicity, coherence, and argument—but there was something magnificent veiled in the twilight of antiquity." So he used it as the subject of *Gebir,* a poem which remains to this day fascinating for both its poetic diction and the originality of its conception.

The common reaction of the contemporary readers of the poem, even of the very few who received it with admiration, was the charge of excessive obscurity. Southey was delighted by its "beauties of the first order," but found the language "sometimes uncouth" and "frequently deficient in perspicuity" [see excerpt dated 1799]—and his commentary shows that he failed to grasp the essential connection between the pastoral and the heroic theme. (p. 51)

In fact, this obscurity was the result of Landor's deliberate reaction against the fluent facilities of the poetic style of his time, which was the style of his more youthful verse of 1795. His Latin epistle to his brother Robert, prefixed to *Gebirus,* includes strictures against the contemporary poets who "polish but do not sculpt," in whom every conception that is not frigid or childish "is dissolved in an over-abundance of words." In his **"Post-Script to Gebir"** [see excerpt dated 1800], he remarks of his own earlier poems that "the lines were fluent: the rhymes showed habitual ease, and the personifications fashionable taste"; and, of contemporary poetry, that it often shows "an even tenor of language, by courtesy and common acception held poetic, and an equal dilation of appropriate thoughts, hardly anywhere trivial and no-where exquisite." *Gebir* is for him a new departure; and, like Wordsworth, he starts from a rejection of a dead form, of an empty and facile poetic diction.

This rejection, however, makes him turn for a model, not to "the language really spoken by men" around him, but to the Ancients. "When I began to write *Gebir,* . . . I had just read Pindar a second time and understood him. What I admired was what nobody else had ever noticed—his proud complacency and scornful strength. If I could resemble him in nothing else, I was resolved to be as compendious and exclusive." Although *Paradise Lost* was also one of his favorite readings at the time, it has been conclusively shown that the influence of Milton is slight and limited to a few passages. What fashioned Landor's terse new style was the ideal defined in the abstract with reference to Pindar, but more concretely his attempt to experiment in English with an adaptation of the poetic medium he was using in his own Latin poetry.

This was made easier by the fact that *Gebir* and its Latin counterpart *Gebirus* were growing side by side. . . . [The] poem was taking shape in two languages simultaneously, and . . . in both, Landor's verbal imagination was striving to achieve a concentrated and expressive form, which, classical as it was in inspiration, took him as far as could be from the stereotypes of a conventionally latinized diction.

What is indeed striking, when one compares the two versions of some outstanding passages, is that the massive compression which is the keynote of the English verse reflects what is more spontaneously achieved in the synthetic language. This is apparent in the brief description of the panting serpent . . . , or in the famous Shell passage . . . which Landor invites us to compare with a similar passage in Wordsworth. Landor's description is characteristic in its strict and rounded perfection; it is also purely objective and self-sufficient, whereas that of Wordsworth, admittedly more loosely written, reaches further and opens out on the mystery of the unity of all life. The last two lines echo the Latin text without loss of harmony in conciseness:

> And it remembers its august abodes,
> And murmurs as the Ocean murmurs there.

In other places, however, the challenge of synthetic compactness is met at some cost. Many of the notes of 1803 have to make explicit what was quite clear in the Latin. The note of the adultress who "bays body," . . . explaining that "she looks up with unavailing desire to the corporeal state," develops what was implicit in "Corporeis formis illatrat." . . . Similarly, the syntactical ambiguity of "even her love thy strength was to disclose" is not present in the inflected language. Too many details of that kind contribute to make the text difficult to read. Although the difficulty is far from being an insuperable obstacle to enjoyment for a modern reader, more prepared than his predecessors to let the meaning form itself slowly, the result remains that he is jerked from one arresting scene to another instead of being carried away by the flow of the narrative. Landor's style, for all its distilled excellence, remains immature and unsuited for the sustained development of a "long poem."

The Latin element, derived from the Virgilian epic and Ovid, is also present in the treatment of the original story, but as part of a complex general design. *Gebir* is a strange poem, which defies classification, and this, as we shall see, raises more than a problem of literary genre and takes us to the center of its inspiration. Landor has several times insisted on the absurdity of affixing the label "epic" to his poem. . . . The most precise discussion of the nature of the epic poem occurs in the Preface to *Gebirus*. "It is a poem drawn from history, whether authentic or fictitious, carried by written or oral tradition; it requires various heroes, sudden changes of fortune, with mainly the hazards of war and extreme perils born by a leader; the issue must be fortunate, for it teaches that all things human yield to valour and perseverance." Landor is thus undoubtedly justified to conclude: "Not so ours." *Gebirus* was later republished by him . . . as one of his *Idyllia Heroica*. . . . It is wrong to consider an "idyll" as being exclusively pastoral in character, for it means, properly speaking, "an image in reduction of a larger

image"; the better part of Theocritus (and Moschus) is not pastoral, and there are many "idylls" in this sense in Ovid, who would have been a better poet if he had "restricted each scene to its limits" instead of "drawing out a continuous series of prodigies." But there is a great difference between Landor's later Idylls and *Gebir,* which is much more extended . . . as well as more complex in point of action. What fits it best would be the looser title of "Heroic Fable," . . . but even this would fail to cover all its aspects.

Its mixed character is at least suggested in the Prelude. The framework ("When Old Silenus called the Satyrs home . . . with Bacchus and the Nymphs . . .") is pastoral, reminiscent of a Virgilian eclogue; but Silenus "sometimes rose / Amidst the tale or pastoral, and shewed / The light of purest wisdom." Similarly, the poet's invocation is addressed to the "woody vales of Cambria," but also to its "famous hills" in an appeal to raise him from lowly subjects ("the force / Of high example influence my lay"). And the narrative is launched by means of a phrase with epic associations: "I sing the fates of Gebir" (in the Latin, "great Gebir"). In brief, the subject is the heroic story of Gebir, even though the hero's destiny implies, according to Landor's own definitions, tragic rather than epic greatness; but it will be treated in "the light of wisdom," which has its source closer to the pastoral world, and this will be achieved by means of the narrative section including Tamar, the shepherd-king, and his nymph, a pastoral episode ending in historic prophecy.

Landor's source was an unambiguous tale of violence and cunning. Gebir, the invader of Egypt, was strong and ruthless; his design was to become king of the country by forcing Charoba to marry him. But the Queen's nurse was "an artful woman . . . and a great Enchantress." Her first stratagem was to force Gebir to rebuild the ruined city, while at night the demons of the sea pulled down the buildings. But Gebir, taking the place of his chief shepherd (not here his brother) wrestled with a nymph, defeated her, and obtained from her the secret of the rites that would break the spell. Still, the nurse succeeded in her second trick, that of the poisoned garment, and Gebir died, with Charoba exclaiming: "This is the fate of such men as would compel queens to marry them"—a very limited moral lesson, indeed.

Landor took over the bare facts, but also modified them to make them meaningful. Gebir's original plans of military conquest are quickly altered. He is softened by pity, and soon love, for the young Queen. The passion of love is by no means excluded from the traditional epic, but here the tone is definitely modern. The hero is turned into a brooding man of feeling and Charoba into a modest maid who does not dare to look fully into her own heart. And although Charoba's reticence is finely described (and well used for the plot, since it will help the nurse's plotting), the sentimental parts are not the strongest ones in the poem. But Gebir's change of heart has a deeper cause. A revelation is vouchsafed to him in the course of a Descent into Hell (in Book III). This very classical episode is clearly fashioned with the sixth book of the *Aeneid* as a model: the setting, the guide (here named Aroar), the hero's meeting with his father, his vain attempt to return the unsubstantial shade's embrace, and a vision of the future. What Gebir sees, however, is not the glorious future of his race (that vision will later fall to the lot of Tamar), but the punishment of the evil deeds of tyrants. Landor does not resist the temptation of direct political satire, with George III suffering in afterlife the beheading his life had deserved. But what is even more relevant to the legendary theme is that Gebir's own father is among the sufferers, and he explains that his sin is to have exacted from his son the oath to reconquer Egypt, which had once been a possession of their dynasty. . . . [This detail] serves Landor's design to transform the spirit of the traditional epic, based on the conception of heroism fostered by a military civilization, to carry further an evolution already perceptible in Virgil's constructive national epic by infusing his poem with the modern values derived from a humanitarian and liberal inspiration. Gebir, on his return to earth, is no longer a conqueror; his aim is to unite two peoples in the bonds of brotherhood.

His new plan is doomed to failure, for in spite of the change within him he still finds himself inextricably in a false position; he is caught in the vicious circle of violence answering to violence, and he will fall a victim to the forces his military expedition has unleashed. Clearly, what Landor is here transposing into the legend is the ambiguous role of the armies of the French Revolution, carrying the ideal of freedom and imposing it by force on the nations around them. Although the mass of the people is in favor of Gebir, and of peace through reconciliation, Dalica, the Queen's nurse, still sees the man from Gades as an enemy. Dalica is a powerful development of the sorceress barely sketched in the original story. She has the initiative of the plot, for Charoba is made passive by the growing love she hesitates to acknowledge, so that it looks to her nurse as if her strength of mind has been destroyed by an evil spell. But what makes Dalica significant as a character is that she embodies and gathers around her all the reactions that work against the invader: religious bigotry, respect for custom, chauvinistic prejudices, interests vested in the political establishment—all the forms of an ignoble resistance to progress and freedom, but amounting to a real force in history intensified by the presence of the invading army. She prepares the poisoned tunic in a scene which carries reminiscences of Medea's magic rites in Ovid's Book VII of the *Metamorphoses,* and Gebir dies a helpless victim in a finale of pure, if restrained, pathos, happy to know at the last from Charoba's despair that she had no hand in his death.

Gebir's failure is underlined by the subplot. The beginning of it is steeped in an atmosphere of mythological pastoral. Tamar meets the nymph disguised as a sailor, they wrestle for a wager (his sheep against her shell), and he is defeated not so much on account of her strength as because he feels suddenly weak and trembling from an unknown cause. We are in the world of Theocritus (with eroticism somewhat toned down, but unmistakable). But this episode is further developed to counterpoint the main theme. The major scene in it is the marriage of the two lovers. . . . [The] nymph after the marriage urges Tamar to leave his brother to his destiny, and during their flight she shows him Corsica, where "From Tamar shall arise, 'tis Fate's decree, / A mortal man above all mortal praise." . . . But the promised hero of modern times, Bonaparte, is to be the liberator of mankind and represents a new ideal; he differs from the Achilles of Catullus who is to be great because his illustrious virtues and high actions will be "confessed by mothers burying their sons." . . . Here, the prophetic Book VI ends on a vision of Time redeemed from nationalism, violence and slavery. It is a passage still burdened with some allegorical obscurity (Time's "motley garb" thrown off is that of the names for the months and the days, suppressed by the French Convention), but its movement and inspiration clearly anticipate Shelley's conclusion to the third act of *Prometheus Unbound.*

> Captivity led captive, War o'erthrown,
> They shall o'er Europe, shall o'er Earth extend

> Empire that seas alone and skies confine,
> And glory that shall strike the crystal stars.

The tragedy of Gebir represents one stage, and not the end, in the process that leads to this regeneration of humanity. The hero is not only unfortunate in being entangled in the consequences of the past he has renounced, but he is also guilty because he remains king. As the nymph discerns "Gebir—tho' generous, just, humane—inhaled / Rank venom from these mansions," . . . his palace at Calpe. She wants to save Tamar from all craving for power. Landor wrote his poem in an optimistic mood, with confidence in the imminence of a new era of freedom and universal brotherhood. But he also shows himself aware of all the difficulties created by the permanence of the past and by the temptation for all men to use force and obtain power. He does not here qualify his praise of the Republican general, the "mortal man above all mortal praise," which shocked his political enemies so much. But a note in 1803 will soon register disappointment:

> Bonaparte might have been so. . . . But unhappily he thinks, that to produce great changes, is to perform great actions: to annihilate antient freedom and to substitute new, to give republics a monarchichal government, and the provinces of monarchs a republican one; in short, to overthrow by violence all the institutions and to tear from the heart all the social habits of men, has been the tenor of his politics to the present hour. . . .

There is very little Tom-Painish radicalism, by the way, in this condemnation not so much of the Consul rising to absolute power as of the subverter of traditions and natural identities, but it makes clear that Landor feels his confidence betrayed. And the Latin text only places Bonaparte above all mortal praise conditionally: "if at least he protects Justice and Liberty," introducing, rather oddly, an element of doubt at the core of the prophecy.

The doubt about the possibility of a new era for mankind is in fact at the center of the second theme. In her more-than-human wisdom, the nymph persuades Tamar to escape with her to a pleasant retreat, and the panoramic vision of the happier future is conveyed by her to the man she has just removed from the turmoil of history in the making. The theme of her exhortation is that private happiness must be placed above the strife of politics, that *otium* is better than a public life. Gebir, then, is guilty not only because he remains king, but because he is not wise enough to realize the vanity of all action. The central ambiguity of **Gebir** is that in its final development the pastoral subplot undercuts rather than supports or counterpoints the heroic theme. And this reflects (for the first and not the last time) the duality of Landor's inspiration: political involvement on the side of liberalism, embraced with passionate hopefulness, and then disillusionment and the fear of political chaos leading him to the refuge of nature and art, from which his former hopes appear as a Utopian dream rather than a goal accessible to human efforts. The two tendencies are part of the creative impulse behind **Gebir,** and they give life to the poem, even if they prevent it from being unified.

Landor has taken over an obscure Oriental tale (obscure enough to give him a free hand), and has also managed, as we have seen, to bring it within the pale of the classical tradition through the insertion of scenes or details that belong to the Greco-Latin epic. But, beyond the pleasures of imagination and transposition, he has another goal: to interpret and present his legendary plot in the light of the modern spirit of liberalism and humanitarianism. This brings him to grips with the essential problem of Romantic myth-making (illustrated in different ways by *Prometheus Unbound* and *Hyperion*): the technical difficulty of re-handling intractable material, which is, in fact, the formal aspect of the struggle to reconcile new values with the cultural past, progress with tradition, and more generally the dream of the ideal with the reality of nature and history. It is clear that *Gebir* does not quite bear up under the strain. The writer indulges in political allegorizing, escapes into irrelevant classical details, and fails to achieve complete clarity or unity. But there is a greatness in the fragments of this early ambitious design which is not to be found in Landor's later poetry. The personal lyrical poems, for which he is best known, are beautiful, and minor. As to the later Heroic Idylls, they are more limited in scope: self-contained scenes (real ''idylls''), polished verse, the erotic or domestic side-aspects of the great heroic legends— the voice of private feelings, no longer a public utterance. The Victorian poetry of Landor has accepted as final the defeat, dramatized in *Gebir,* of Romantic political idealism. (pp. 51-6)

> Pierre Vitoux, '''Gebir' as an Heroic Poem,'' in The Wordsworth Circle, *Vol. VII, No. 1, Winter, 1976, pp. 51-7.*

CHARLES L. PROUDFIT   (essay date 1979)

[*Proudfit seeks to enhance Landor's reputation as a literary critic. He finds that Landor's critical views, often faulted as digressive, inconsistent, and subjective, are redeemed by the visual imagery, metaphorical comparisons, and personal point of view he incorporated into his impressionistic judgments.*]

Walter Savage Landor has not attracted much attention as a nineteenth-century literary critic. This would not surprise him. He neither wrote as a professional critic for a specific audience; nor did he, like his contemporaries Coleridge, De Quincey, Hazlitt, Hunt, and Lamb, seek the usual critical forums of the day—the periodical review, the formal essay, and the lecture platform. 'I shall have as many readers as I desire to have in other times than ours', wrote the seventy-five-year-old Walter Savage Landor in 1850 to his friend and biographer, John Forster. 'I shall dine late; but the dining-room will be well-lighted, the guests few and select. I neither am, nor ever shall be, popular. Such never was my ambition'. . . . Devotees of Landor's poetry and prose have never been numerous, and those who have articulated their praise compose as select a company as Landor could have wished. In our own century T. S. Eliot, Ezra Pound, and W. B. Yeats have acknowledged Landor's literary achievement [see excerpt by Eliot dated 1933 and Additional Bibliography]. . . . Yet in the midst of all these laudatory remarks lavished upon Landor's poetry and prose, similar praise of Landor's literary criticism is noticeably absent.

There is reason for this. Readers who have turned to Landor's works to find a consistent application of a set of carefully determined critical principles have been disappointed. . . . Landor was a private man endowed with an income sufficient to free him to become one of the most erudite and well-read literary men of the first half of the nineteenth century. He wrote out of enjoyment rather than necessity, and his lifetime devotion to ancient and modern authors left behind him a body of critical commentary that demands our respect and repays our attention. This commentary, however, has never been eas-

ily available to readers. It has remained essentially to be discovered within his personal correspondence, suppressed or cancelled prose pieces, Latin essays, poetry, the diaries and memoirs of those who knew him, and that species of composition upon which rests his reputation as a prose writer, the *Imaginary Conversations of Literary Men and Statesmen.* On those few occasions when reviews were solicited from him, late in life, he expressed himself in a form of personal essay uniquely his own.

It is perhaps this very individuality of expression which has distinguished Landor among his contemporaries, has found him friends and enemies, and has prevented the unlearned from following along with him. The singularity of his pronouncements characterized his conversation as much as it does his writings. His acquaintances all mark the Landorian voice. . . . This Landorian voice expresses the man, his confidence in his own judgment, his vast knowledge of literature and painting, his extremes in temperament and disposition, and his ability to convey his thoughts in words and images which are memorable. (pp. 1-2)

The Landorian voice repels as well as attracts, and his critics have varied in their susceptibility to its charm. When Landor's judgments and opinions emerged in dramatized and objectified form in the *Imaginary Conversations* of 1824, his early reviewers were not swayed by the force of his personality into accepting his unorthodox opinions and pronouncements. (p. 4)

[There are certain] qualities which render Landor as critic both fascinating and frustrating. He does not merely read books; he lives them. In doing so he brings with him all of his likes and dislikes, loves and hates, strengths and weaknesses, perceptions and blind spots. He answers to no one except himself; he cares for no one's criticism but his own; he is his own ideal critic. It is little wonder that criticism of Landor's criticism has seemed so unsatisfying. Those literary historians who have endeavoured to know enough of his works even to generalize about them have had enormous difficulties. They are attempting to cope with a man who was born into a literary age that included Dr. Johnson, was educated during the exciting years of the American and French Revolutions, and was friend of two generations of Romantic writers and of many eminent Victorians. They are attempting to cope with a man responding singularly to a life spent reading, writing, or talking about reading and writing. We see the effect of this in the general and insubstantial comments they make. (p. 5)

To approach Landor in search of a method or guiding principles can only detract from the pleasure of reading him. There are critical procedures and principles, but they emerge through acquaintance, through the gradual submission to the Landorian voice as it leads one arbitrarily, often quixotically, through a library in which nothing is more meaningless than the dates on books. . . .

As the Landorian voice accompanies us through this library, making pronouncements on ancients and contemporaries, on poets loved and poets despised, on critical issues past and present, we are forced to consider whether this is the voice of an opinionated eccentric or a voice which echoes his time. It was a very long time, 1775-1864. One hardly knows whether to view him as a Neo-Classic, a Romantic, or a Victorian; and he gives the lie, perhaps more than any single figure, to the periodization of English literature. Landor not only lived in all three eras, but he also belongs within and without each of them. (p. 6)

The critic of Landor as critic soon finds himself in conflict with traditional expectations. If Landor is to be justified as a literary critic, then it seems that one ought to be able to identify his basic principles, describe his method, and place him in a historical critical tradition. Landor, however, was a unique literary man, not a professional literary critic; and his method for approaching literature is so much an extension of Landor the man that attempts to describe it in the usual ways are doomed either to superficiality or to failure. Our final view of him as a convincing literary critic must be determined by the force and substance of his personality and the enthusiasm and intellectual vigour he brought to his reading of literature. To describe his method is to describe his mental behaviour with all of its singular turns and twists and tastes. How does Landor behave as a critic? He behaves as a highly-trained reader of literature for whom the past and present are one, who respects his own judgment completely, and who considers himself especially endowed to judge since he, too, is a practising poet and prose writer. He is his own ideal poet-critic, and he has extraordinary self-confidence. Thus, he makes pronouncements; he makes a-historical comparisons; he offers opinions sustained by his likes and dislikes; and his sensitivity and temperament are such that he is susceptible to what we might call sentimental but he would call the pathetic. If his love for literature had a rival, it was painting. Thus, his imagination is visual. He thinks in images and metaphors, and his criticism binds together for us all of the senses as he entices our imaginations either with the pictures he himself creates or those of artists he chooses to compare. We may not agree with his opinions, but we can never read Boccaccio, Petrarch, Milton, Dante, or Spenser again in quite the same way after reading Landor. (p. 16)

The submission of the text to verbal analysis is fundamental to Landor's approach to the reading and criticism of literature, but this in itself presents a problem in methodology. When does Landor's verbal criticism cease to be that and become marginalia? The two do seem to overlap for him. He seems more to participate in a text than merely to read it. Consequently, much of his criticism exists in the form of marginalia: some in books he once owned, some in his personal correspondence and public letters, most notably his *Letter to Emerson* . . . ; and some in his *Imaginary Conversations* where we would honorifically label it digression. Such marginalia preserves Landor's wit and humour for us more than his formal writings, as for instance when he finds Dryden's prose 'vigorous and natural' but his poetry partly 'composed in a brothel, the remainder in a gin-shop'. . . . Such is the highly individualized personal taste of Landor. However much he may desire critics to list faults and beauties and to make formal comparisons, Landor's own criticism is frequently marked by an enthusiasm which links him with the impressionistic Romantic critics Hazlitt and Lamb. This tendency can be endearing in him, as for instance when he says: 'I love Goldsmith. The poet never transgresses into the province of the historian. There is nothing profound or important in him; but his language is gracefully familiar, everything about him is sufficiently correct and well-placed, his style is polished enough, and he invites us by an ingenious and frank simplicity'. . . . Such personal enthusiasm did sometimes mislead Landor, especially in his later years when he would lavish praise indiscriminately on writers as different as Robert Browning and Felicia Dorthea Hemans.

A certain tension is established in Landor's criticism between his concept of himself as an ideal critic, his eighteenth-century notions about how a textual critic ought to proceed, and his energetic, enthusiastic, imaginative, voracious habit of mind. Even his most successful literary form, the Imaginary Conversation, in which he attempts to re-create the natural movement of actual conversation, precludes the failure for him of the consistent application of the kind of thorough and extended critical analysis suggested in the Porson plan. Landor's thought is consistently interrupted by numerous digressions. His success rests in fulfilling the task of the critic as he describes it in *The Pentameron*:

> *Boccaccio* . . . To be useful to as many as possible is the especial duty of a critic, and his utility can only be attained by rectitude and precision. He walks in a garden which is not his own; and he neither must gather the blossoms to embellish his discourse, nor break the branches to display his strength. Rather let him point to what is out of order, and help to raise what is lying on the ground. . . .

This metaphor of the literary work as a garden in which the critic as gardener must remove the weeds and briars without disturbing the 'blossoms' and 'branches' and must 'raise' those beautiful plants that lie 'on the ground' is a favourite of Landor and figuratively describes his view that the critic's primary attention should be devoted to pointing out faults and to praising the beauties of literary works.

Landor's own practice often involves a greater concern for faults than for beauties. Yet it develops naturally from the high standards he demanded of himself as a creative artist and the high esteem in which he held verbal criticism. . . . (pp. 19-20)

One of the most unique and characteristic features of Landor's practice as a literary critic is his use of metaphorical criticism. . . . Landor's use of imagery in his literary criticism is functional rather than decorative; that is, his images, similes, and metaphors are integral to his critical thinking and are not window-dressing. Furthermore, his metaphorical criticism is given an extra dimension when one realizes that his approach to literature is not unlike his approach to representational art. . . .

When Landor wishes to blame or praise an author, he often turns to painting and sculpture for his imagery. Thus, Dryden is not 'a great poet' because 'there is not throughout his works one stroke of the sublime or one touch of the pathetic'. . . . Similarly: 'In Chaucer, . . . we recognize the strong homely strokes, the broad and negligent facility, of a great master'. . . . And the 'chief qualities' of Pindar's poetry are 'rejection of what is light and minute, disdain of what is trivial, and selection of those blocks from the quarry which will bear strong strokes of the hammer and retain all the marks of the chisel'. . . . (p. 21)

On some occasions his choice of imagery is either grotesque or realistic in the extreme. For example, Landor closes the first Conversation between Southey and himself with this grotesque image: 'A rib of Shakespeare would have made a Milton: the same portion of Milton, all poets born ever since'. . . . One of Landor's most successful realistic descriptions appropriately suggests the poetry of Crabbe: '[He] wrote with a twopenny nail, and scratched rough truths and rogues' facts on mud walls. . . . Young moralized at a distance on some external appearances of the human heart; Crabbe entered it *on all fours*, and told the people what an ugly thing it is inside'. . . . (pp. 21-2)

Landor is particularly fond of similes and extended comparisons, and he employs them in a variety of ways. He may use a simple comparison to praise a certain quality of a writer: '[Theocritus'] reflections are frequent, but seasonable; soon over, like the shadows of spring clouds on flowery meadows, and not hanging heavily upon the scene, nor depressing the vivacity of the blythe antagonists'.... Or he may use a simile to excuse a fault in a favourite author, such as the licentious tales in Boccaccio's *Decameron*: 'Their levities and gaieties are like the harmless lightnings of a summer sky in the delightful regions they were written in'.... Sometimes he suggests the difference between two writers by comparing the styles of two painters. For example, Landor says of Catullus: 'In relation to Virgil, he [Catullus] stands as Correggio in relation to Raffael: a richer colourist, a less accurate draftsman; less capable of executing grand designs, more exquisite in the working out of smaller'.... (p. 22)

Just as Landor is more successful in pointing out faults than in noting beauties, so is he especially effective in using simile and metaphor to negative ends, ranging from mild displeasure to fierce indignation. In a letter to his friend Southey, Landor writes that Wordsworth's *Lyrical Ballads* have 'sometimes disappointed me, just as an Aeolian harp has done when I expected a note more'.... When Landor wishes to convey his view that Tasso's characters are more 'vivid', 'distinct', and 'interesting' than Virgil's, he creates an extended comparison: 'The heroes of the *Aeneid* are like the half-extinct frescoes of Raphael; but what is wanting in the frescoes of the painter is effaced by time, what is wanting in the figures of the poet was wanting to his genius'.... Landor's extended comparisons can also be effective as a weapon of attack in critical discussion, as demonstrated in his strictures on Voltaire's criticism of Milton and Shakespeare in the Conversation between the Abbé Delille and himself: 'He stuck to them as a woodpecker to an old forest-tree, only for the purposes of picking out what was rotten: he has made the holes deeper than he found them, and, after all his cries and chatter, has brought home but scanty sustenance to his starveling nest'.... (pp. 22-3)

[In] order to gain an understanding of how [Landor's] method functions in conjunction with his basic criteria for determining great poetry from mediocre, we must look to those poets whom he chose most often to discuss and whose works he has celebrated in extended prose pieces. Among them we find Boccaccio, Dante, Petrarch, Spenser, Shakespeare, and Milton. Although he constantly refers to the classics, to Homer, Aeschylus, Pindar, Sophocles, Virgil, Horace, and Ovid for his touchstones in comparing poets, to only Catullus and Theocritus does he give full studies.... Wordsworth and Southey among his contemporaries receive detailed criticism; and Southey he overvalues through the sentiments of friendship, and Wordsworth he treats unjustly in his later criticism through personal dislike. Landor does not ignore the other poets of his period. Indeed, he says of them 'our field of poetry at the present time is both wider and better cultivated than it has ever been'.... (pp. 24-5)

Landor's interest in literature is that of an epicure, and quite properly one of his favourite Imaginary Conversations is that between Epicurus, the Greek philosopher, and two of his female disciples, Leontion and Ternissa. Epicurus is an idealized portrait of Landor himself, and it is Landor who speaks when Epicurus informs his young friends: 'All the imitative arts have delight for the principal object: the first of these is poetry: the highest of poetry is tragic'.... Literature is life to Landor,

and the characters of Achilles and Priam, Dido and Aeneas, Satan and Eve, and Othello and Desdemona were as real to him as the paintings that hung on his walls in his villa outside Florence and the deep and abiding friendships he formed with such men and women as Robert Southey, John Forster, Charles Dickens, Robert and Elizabeth Barrett Browning, and the Countess of Blessington. The very restrained and classical quality of his verse and short dramatic Imaginary Conversations suggests the emotional man behind them, and perhaps the poet Yeats's great admiration for Landor is partly due to his recognition of the battle between the emotional artist and the suggestive though impersonal work of art; the man and the mask....

We do not turn to Landor today in search of a new approach to literature which will foster volumes of reevaluations. We turn to Landor for his living appreciation of all he read and contemplated. So long as we cherish learning; so long as harmony in poetry is important to us; so long as we expect poetry to express the greatest ideas and the most sincere emotions; and so long as we value singularity of response, confidence in informed opinion, and an epigrammatical, imagistic turn of mind; so long will Landor have an important place for us in literary criticism, not as a professional literary critic, but as a most unique and impressive literary man. (p. 31)

Charles L. Proudfit, in an introduction to Landor as Critic, *edited by Charles L. Proudfit, Routledge & Kegan Paul, 1979, pp. 1-33.*

DONALD DAVIE (essay date 1984)

[*Davie explores the relationship between poetry and sculpture in Landor's poems and epigrams, focusing on the poet's use of "lapidary" or "chiselled" effects. Davie also compares the formal poetic ideals of Yeats and Landor and reflects on Landor's "immortality." See the excerpt dated 1951 and the Additional Bibliography for further commentary by Davie.*]

[Walter Savage Landor] was sometimes a bigot, sometimes a bully. But there are many places in his *Imaginary Conversations* where he is neither. In one such place, he has Diogenes maintain:

> There is no mass of sincerity in any place. What there is must be picked up patiently, a grain or two at a time; and the season for it is after a storm, after the overflowing of banks, and bursting of mounds, and sweeping away of landmarks. Men will always hold something back: they must be shaken and loosened a little, to make them let go what is deepest in them, and weightiest and purest.

We can set this beside something that Izaak Walton is made to say, about the love poems of Donne ...:

> So ingenious are men when the spring torrent of passion shakes up and carries away their thoughts, covering (as it were) the green meadow of still homely life with pebbles and shingle, some colourless and obtuse, some sharp and sparkling.

Taken together, these passages seem to say that the lapidary or "chiselled" effect, as in the epigram or epitaph, so far from witnessing to lack of feeling, on the contrary is the aftermath and proof of very strong and tumultuous feeling. This is what I have always believed, not on the authority of Landor or any

Landor in his later years.

one else (for instance not Yeats nor Pound, who can both be shown to have endorsed Landor on this point [see Additional Bibliography]), but from my experience of how my own emotional experience was or was not convertible into poetry. And the principal sorrow or frustration of my life in poetry has been my inability to persuade others of this to me self-evident truth. On the contrary, so entrenched among us are the associations between the marmoreal and the cold, between the stony and the dry, between the firm contour and the rigid, between the chisel and the scalpel, that any attempt to envisage poetry by analogy with the sister-art of sculpture at once arouses bristling suspicions. (p. 103)

[The] compositional habits of poets of the present day in high favour among us, though they are often declared to be "Romantic" or "post-Romantic," are very hard to relate to the Romantic Movement as an international phenomenon known to literary history. When people claim to find such a connection, it usually turns out that what they are pointing to is an aversion on the part of the poet to anything predetermined or pre-planned. But as a mode of composition, improvisation, the feeling forward from one verse-line to the next in the presence of an actual or imagined audience, was known to the Ancient World as well as to the nineteenth century. Landor wrote (1828):

> . . . No *improvisatore* ever rose above mediocrity; few have reached it. Poetry, like wine, requires a gentle and regular and long fermen-

tation. What is it if it can buoy up no wisdom, no reflection? if we can throw into it none of our experience? if no repository is to be found in it for the gems we have collected, at the price sometimes of our fortunes, of our health, and of our peace? Your *improvisatori* let drop their verses as a string of mules their morning oats, for miles together . . . The first thing a young person who wishes to be a poet has to do, is, to conquer his volubility; to compress in three verses what he had easily thrown off in twelve; and to be an hour about what had cost him a minute. If he has a *knack* for verses, he must break it and forget it. Both the poet and the painter should acquire facility and frankness; but they must be exercised with discretion; they must be sternly regulated, and in great part suppressed. The young poet will remonstrate, and more often scoff: he will appall you by placing before you the *deep mouth* of Pindar and his mountain-torrents. Tell him, and tell older ones too, that Pindar of all poets is the most accurate and the most laborious.

"Gems," in Landor's usage, is no empty figure; it means *stones,* some precious and some not, "some colourless and obtuse, some sharp and sparkling." Only by entering into the metaphor with all seriousness can we regain access to the climate of ideas familiar from past centuries, in which it was high praise of a poet to say that he was "laborious," and of his poetry that it was "laboured." From within that climate of ideas we may recover what Landor intended by "mediocrity": not something run-of-the-mill, boring, of no account; but rather a standard of accomplishment which, though relatively many attain it, many more never do. I suspect we sell it short by thinking of it as what a devoted and gifted student in an excellent Creative Writing school may attain to. It is not in itself good enough to amount to anything; but it is the serviceable platform from which a few may lift themselves to do something that matters, having learned (the first lesson) to suppress in themselves whatever they may have by way of "knack," of "facility." As for what is needed to lift off further, Landor is quite specific; it is not anything to do with technique, with diligence, with the history of the art—it is "wisdom," it is "reflection," it is "experience," accumulated "at the price sometimes of our fortunes, of our health, and of our peace." This is what composition by way of improvisation can never attain to. On the contrary, we are invited to think, wisdom and passionate experience in poetry are often to be apprehended as an effect dryly conclusive, mournful or sardonic, *closed.* (pp. 104-05)

Thinking of poetry as like sculpture—something that Landor's verse-practice invites us to, more than any of his declarations in prose—can prompt many reflections, some of them profound and a few of them topical. It invites us for instance to envisage the inherited language, the poet's medium as the poet apprehends it in the act of composing, as something no less bleakly confronting, no more negotiable, than the cliff of Carrara marble that faced Michelangelo when he went to the quarry looking for a block that should excite his sculptor's imagination. Nothing could be further from the sense of language that French theorists and their Anglo-American followers have lately pressed upon us: language seen as a band of nebulous haze, infinitely malleable and protean according as the needs or whims of speaker and of auditor impinge upon it. The question is not what language *is* (that question which so delightfully exercises philosophers and semioticians), but what language *is taken to be* by those who use it, either those who carve it or those who respond to the shapes it takes at the carver's hands. If we choose to think of the inherited language as a cliff of Carrara or Parian marble, its veins and lines of fracture imperfectly but still usefully traced by the better lexicographers, no voice out of Paris or Geneva can or should persuade us otherwise. Landor was boringly pedantic, in many of the *Imaginary Conversations,* about the etymology of English words; and he was a crank about how to spell them. But remote as all this rightly seems, in an age when English has become the *lingua franca* of airline-pilots and ground-controllers, still we cannot impugn the principle that Landor proceeded on: English is still an artistic medium, if we choose to think of it so; and indeed nothing but our so thinking of it is needed to ensure that, as an artistic medium, it shall persist. (pp. 107-08)

We should, when we write, think that we are *sculpting* language. Let no one think that this is only a fancy way of saying what we all painlessly subscribe to: the need for craftsmanship. On the contrary, the verb "to craft," nowadays much in favour among us, is one that we can do without. The sculptor—whether he works on the small scale of medal, medallion and coin, or on portrait-busts, or else monumentally, and whether "figurative" or "abstract"—is not a craftsman nor a technician, but an artist, laying on the line (as Landor says) his fortune, perhaps his health, certainly his peace of mind. In a late *Conversation* . . . Landor speaks in his own person with a sort of cracked defiance:

> Poetry was always my amusement, prose my study and business. I have published five volumes of *Imaginary Conversations*: cut the worst of them thro the middle, and there will remain in this decimal fraction quite enough to satisfy my appetite for fame. I shall dine late; but the dining-room will be well lighted, the guests few and select.

This passage, or rather the last sentence, was remodelled momentously by Yeats, in a poem of his middle years, "To a Young Beauty":

> There is not a fool can call me friend,
> And I may dine at journey's end
> With Landor and with Donne.

The coupling of Landor with Donne has seemed unaccountable to some readers; but as we have seen, Yeats had warrant for it. Yeats's confidence in posterity sounds much more ringingly than Landor's, and with good reason, for Yeats enjoyed far more fame and esteem in his lifetime than Landor did. Indeed it's not easy to say whether Landor's gamble on posterity has paid off even now; for he's represented in the standard anthologies but his name is seldom on any one's lip, and *Imaginary Conversations* is one of those works remembered more often than they are read. The point of these reflections is that, if our perspectives on the past are foreshortened, our perspectives on the future are even more so, and for reasons beyond our control. Under the threat of nuclear Armageddon no poet can appeal to posterity as confidently as Yeats or Landor did. If fame does not come in the poet's lifetime, he can have no confidence that it will come hereafter, from a posterity which, if it exists at all, may well take a form quite unimaginable. This means inevitably that the poet, stubbornly proud as he may be, is in our day dependent on his public in the here and

now, compelled to adjust to the public's expectations and preferences, in a way that Landor and Yeats could not envisage.

A little later in the same Conversation with Archdeacon Hare, Landor made another prophecy about his posthumous reputation, and one that events have shown to be more accurate:

> I stand out a rude rock in the middle of a river,
> with no exotic or parasitical plant on it, and
> few others. Eddies and dimples and froth and
> bubbles pass rapidly by, without shaking me.
> Here indeed is little room for pic-nic and polka.

From this passage too Yeats seems to have taken a hint, if no more, for a poem with the sardonic title, "Men Improve With The Years." . . . (pp. 108-10)

[Though] Yeats from time to time dallied with the lapidary aspirations of poetry, beguiled by them, he is much less firmly committed to those aspirations than Landor is. Because of Landor's constancy to that ideal, these few sentences of his may prompt the reflection that the true immortality of the poet lies in his having become, he and his works, one more stratum in that cliff, the inherited language, which future poets will apprehend as the raw material they have to work, and to work with. This is a sort of immortality which, not quite logically and yet reasonably, we can envisage as more plausibly surviving some future cataclysm than any one poet's life-record and body of work; for we all know that there are languages, long "dead," which survive in fragmentary texts only dubiously attributed to named individuals. Landor's "rude rock in the middle of a river," the craggily inscrutable island that the pleasure-craft pass by, makes that sort of sense in the nuclear age. . . . (pp. 110-11)

> *Donald Davie, "Attending to Landor," in* Ironwood,
> *Vol. 12, No. 2, Fall, 1984, pp. 103-11.*

ADDITIONAL BIBLIOGRAPHY

Becker, George J. "Landor's Political Purpose." *Studies in Philology* XXXV, No. 3 (July 1938): 446-55.
> Examines the role of politics in Landor's writings and suggests that he considered himself a "political prophet."

Buxton, John. "Walter Savage Landor (1775-1864)." In his *The Grecian Taste: Literature in the Age of Neo-Classicism, 1740-1820,* pp. 105-27. New York: Harper & Row Publishers, Barnes & Noble Books, 1978.
> Characterizes Landor's poems as presentations of classical themes in a simple, clear, classical style.

Chambers, E. K. Introduction to *Landor: Poetry and Prose* by Walter Savage Landor, pp. v-xvii. 1946. Reprint. New York: AMS Press, 1978.
> A brief survey of Landor's life and major works.

Colvin, Sidney. *Landor*. English Men of Letters, edited by John Morley. New York: Harper & Brothers, Publishers, 1881, 224 p.
> A biographical and critical study based on Forster's *Walter Savage Landor* (see entry below), but including some additional sources. Though Colvin's work is praised for its "readability," modern scholars fault it for biographical inaccuracies.

Craig, Maurice James. "Landor and Ireland." *The Dublin Magazine* n.s. XVIII, No. 3 (July-September 1943): 35-41.
> Investigates the importance of Ireland to Landor's life and thought.

Davie, Donald. "Landor as Poet." *Shenandoah* IV, Nos. 2-3 (Summer-Autumn 1953): 93-105.

Identifies the classical models for Landor's *Hellenics*, heroic poems, epigrams, and dramas.

De Quincey, Thomas. "Orthographic Mutineers." *Tait's Edinburgh Magazine* XIV, No. CLIX (March 1847): 157-62.
Pronounces Landor "outrageously crazy upon the one subject of spelling." Though De Quincey lampoons Landor's attempted spelling reforms, he admits that Landor is more scholarly and consistent in his revisions than other orthographers.

Dickens, Charles. *Bleak House*. London: Bradbury & Evans, 1853, 629 p.
Includes a caricature of Landor in the character of Lawrence Boythorn.

Dilworth, Ernest. *Walter Savage Landor*. Twayne's English Author Series, edited by Sylvia E. Bowman, no. 125. New York: Twayne Publishers, 1971, 172 p.
Includes biographical information and an examination of the style and content of Landor's verse and prose.

Elton, Oliver. "Southey and Landor." In his *A Survey of English Literature, 1780-1880*, Vol. 2, pp. 1-48. New York: Macmillan Co., 1920.
Surveys Landor's career, devoting attention to the poems, dramatic scenes, epigrams, *Hellenics, Imaginary Conversations*, and the longer prose works.

Elwin, Malcolm. *Savage Landor*. New York: Macmillan Co., 1941, 498 p.
A respected biography.

———. *Landor: A Replevin*. London: Macdonald, 1958, 502 p.
Presents a more "sympathetic" commentary on Landor's life than other biographers. Elwin attempts to "recover Landor's character from misrepresentation and his works from neglect."

Evans, Edward Waterman, Jr. *Walter Savage Landor: A Critical Study*. New York: G. P. Putnam's Sons, Knickerbocker Press, 1892, 209 p.
An early critical overview. Evans attempts to define Landor's place in literary history.

[Field, Kate]. "Last Days of Walter Savage Landor: Parts I, II, and III." *The Atlantic Monthly* XVII, Nos. CII-CIV (April, May, June, 1866): 385-95, 684-705, 540-51.
Reminiscences of Landor's later years, chronicling his habits and personality.

Forster, John. *Walter Savage Landor: A Biography*. 2 vols. London: Chapman & Hall, 1869.
The earliest biography. Forster's work is faulted by later critics and biographers as disorganized and inexact.

Gossman, Ann. "Landor and the 'Higher Fountains'." *The Classical Journal* 50, No. 7 (April 1955): 303-07.
Highlights Landor's use of the characters, themes, and sentiments of classical antiquity.

Gregory, Horace. "The Elegiac Art of Walter Savage Landor." In his *Spirit of Time and Place*, pp. 62-72. New York: W. W. Norton & Co., 1973.
Suggests that the appeal of the *Imaginary Conversations* was limited to the nineteenth century. Gregory finds that Landor's elegies and love lyrics deserve continued admiration, however.

Hare, Julius C. "On Walter Savage Landor's *Imaginary Conversations*." *The London Magazine* IX (May 1824): 523-41.
An "imaginary conversation" between Hare and a fictional critic, in which they evaluate Landor's work.

Henderson, W. Brooks Drayton. *Swinburne and Landor: A Study of Their Spiritual Relationship and Its Effect on Swinburne's Moral and Poetic Development*. London: Macmillan & Co., 1918, 304 p.
Presents Landor as "the great spiritual force" who molded Swinburne's artistic ideals and political thought. Henderson bases his study on Swinburne's expressions of admiration for Landor and examines the works of both authors to show their similarities.

Herford, C. H. "The Shelley Group." In his *The Age of Wordsworth*, pp. 216-84. 1897. Reprint. London: G. Bell & Sons, 1930.
Surveys Landor's works. Herford considers Landor the greatest prose writer of his age, and after Wordsworth, Coleridge, Byron, Shelley, and Keats, the greatest poet.

Kestner, Joseph. "The Genre of Landor's *Gebir*: 'Eminences Excessively Bright'." *The Wordsworth Circle* V, No. 1 (Winter 1974): 41-9.
Assesses *Gebir* and *Gebirus* as epyllion, or "miniaturized epics." Kestner examines the formal and thematic unity of the two poems.

Larrabee, Stephen A. "Landor and Hunt." In his *English Bards and Grecian Marbles: The Relationship between Sculpture and Poetry, Especially in the Romantic Period*, pp. 233-56. New York: Columbia University Press, 1943.
Suggests that Greek sculptures inspired Landor's poetry.

Lee, Vernon [pseudonym of Violet Paget]. "The Rhetoric of Landor." In her *The Handling of Words and Other Studies in Literary Psychology*, pp. 157-74. London: John Lane, The Bodley Head, 1923.
Concludes that Landor's lack of feeling in his writings counterbalances his powers of technique. Lee states that Landor's classicism is "indicative not of the great talent he really possessed, but of his melancholy limitations of soul."

Linton, E. Lynn. "Reminiscences of Walter Savage Landor." *Fraser's Magazine* II, No. VII (July 1870): 113-20.
Includes reminiscences of Landor's years in Bath.

Megally, Shafik H. "Landor's Dramatic Dialogues." *Cairo Studies in English* (1966): 167-80.
Focuses on the dramatic elements and lyric qualities of the *Imaginary Conversations*.

Mercier, Vivian. "The Future of Landor Criticism." In *Some British Romantics: A Collection of Essays*, pp. 43-85. Edited by James V. Logan, John E. Jordan, and Northrop Frye. Ohio State University Press, 1966.
Suggests topics for future studies on Landor.

Minchin, H. C., ed. *Walter Savage Landor: Last Days, Letters, and Conversations*, by Walter Savage Landor. London: Methuen & Co., 1934, 174 p.
Recounts the last five years of Landor's life using his letters to Browning as a primary source. Later scholars question Minchin's accuracy in dating the letters.

Morgan, Charles. "The Independence of Landor." In his *Reflections in a Mirror, second series*, pp. 122-30. London: Macmillan & Co., 1946.
Extols Landor's independent, courageous character and his unique literary expression.

Pinsky, Robert. *Landor's Poetry*. Chicago: University of Chicago Press, 1968, 179 p.
Examines the genres and themes Landor employed in his poetry, relating his work to that of the modern poet-critics Pound and Davie.

Pound, Ezra. *A B C of Reading*. New Directions Paperbook No. 89. New York: James Laughlin, 1960.
A "text book" guide to literature, with scattered references to Landor. Pound cites him in a list of authors through whom the history of English poetry may be traced.

Quillinan, E. "Imaginary Conversation, between Mr Walter Savage Landor and the Editor of *Blackwood's Magazine*." *Blackwood's Edinburgh Magazine* LIII, No. CCCXXX (April 1843): 518-36.
A criticism of Landor's *Imaginary Conversations* and political opinions in the form of an imaginary conversation.

Richards, I. A. "Fifteen Lines from Landor." *The Criterion* XII, No. XLVIII (April 1933): 355-70.
Uses a passage from *Gebir* in studying the process of understanding poetry.

Ruoff, A. LaVonne. "Walter Savage Landor's Criticism of Horace: The Odes and Epodes." *Arion* 9, Nos. 2-3 (Summer-Autumn 1970): 189-204.
> Presents Landor's criticism of Horace. This study is based on Landor's critical essays on classical poets and on the marginalia in his copy of Horace.

Saintsbury, George. "The Revival of Rhythmical Elaboration." In his *A History of English Prose Rhythm*, pp. 293-346. 1912. Reprint. Bloomington: Indiana University Press, 1965.
> Calls Landor's prose style faultless but uninspired.

———. "The First Romantic Group (The Lake Poets, Scott, Moore, Landor, etc.)." In his *A History of English Prosody: From the Twelfth Century to the Present Day*. Vol. III, *From Blake to Mr. Swinburne*. 2nd ed., pp. 47-92. London: Macmillan & Co., 1923.
> Demonstrates Landor's mastery of polyphonic prose. Saintsbury describes Landor's "Grand Style" as magnificent yet simple, severe yet opulent, frigid yet charming.

Super, R. H. "Landor and the 'Satanic School'." *Studies in Philology* XLII, No. 4 (October 1945): 793-810.
> Details Landor's literary and personal relationships with Southey, Byron, Shelley, and Leigh Hunt.

———. "Landor's American Publications." *Modern Language Quarterly* 14, No. 4 (December 1953): 360-74.
> Traces Landor's attempts to reach American readers.

———. *Walter Savage Landor*. New York: New York University Press, 1954, 654 p.
> A comprehensive, thoroughly documented biography.

Van Thal, Herbert, ed. *Landor: A Biographical Anthology*. London: George Allen & Unwin, 1973, 392 p.
> Includes an outline of Landor's life with selections from his *Imaginary Conversations* and other works.

Williams, Stanley T. "The Story of Gebir." *PMLA* XXXVI, No. 3 (September 1921): 615-31.
> Explores the origins of the obscure history of Gebir, on which Landor based his poem.

The Wordsworth Circle, Special Issue: Walter Savage Landor VII, No. 1 (Winter 1976): 3-57.
> Contains essays on Landor by such critics as Proudfit, Pinsky, Joukovsky, Mariani, Super, and Ruoff.

Yeats, W. B. *A Vision*. Rev. ed. New York: Macmillan Co., 1956.
> Contains scattered references to Landor.

Susanna (Strickland) Moodie

1803-1885

(Born Susanna Strickland) English-Canadian sketch and short story writer, poet, novelist, and author of children's books.

Regarded by many critics as one of the finest nineteenth-century Canadian immigrant writers, Moodie is best known for her *Roughing It in the Bush; or, Life in Canada* and *Life in the Clearings versus the Bush*. These collections of autobiographical sketches and poetry are noted for their humor, vivid descriptions of scenery, and realistic portrayal of life on the Canadian frontier. *Roughing It in the Bush* and *Life in the Clearings* are not well known, yet they have, since the late 1950s, enjoyed a resurgence of critical interest, with many commentators focusing on their value as both artistic and historical works. Although Moodie also published numerous short stories and novels as well as other poems and sketches throughout her career, these largely sentimental and didactic works have attracted little critical notice.

Moodie was born in Bungay, Suffolk, but moved in 1808 to Reydon Hall, a mansion near Southwold on the Suffolk coast. With ready access to the estate's well-stocked library, Moodie, her brother, and five sisters were rigorously instructed by their father in foreign languages, history, literature, and mathematics. All but one of Moodie's siblings went on to literary careers, publishing works of historical biography, fiction, poetry, and natural history. The best known of their works include Agnes and Elizabeth Strickland's *Lives of the Queens of England* and Catharine Parr Traill's *The Backwoods of Canada*.

Following the death of their father in 1818, Moodie and her sisters started contributing poems and children's stories to periodicals in order to help with the family finances. Moodie also published a juvenile work entitled *Spartacus: A Roman Story* during this period. In the late 1820s, she contributed to the journal *La belle assemblée*, publishing sketches of Suffolk life reminiscent of Mary Russell Mitford's *Our Village*. Around this time, she joined the Anti-Slavery Society and became a frequent visitor at the home of the society's secretary, the poet Thomas Pringle. During one of these visits, she met John Dunbar Moodie, whom she married in 1831. That same year she published *Enthusiasm, and Other Poems*, a collection of didactic, sentimental verses that had appeared previously in periodicals.

In 1832, after the birth of the first of their six children, the Moodies left England because of financial difficulties and immigrated to Canada. Although she had heard positive reports about the opportunities in Canada and considered the move an economic necessity, Moodie was devastated by the prospect of leaving her native land. The Moodies' life in Canada was marked by financial hardship, due in part to several failed attempts at farming, and they repeatedly relocated in hopes of improving their circumstances. The family first purchased a cleared farm in Hamilton Township, in what is now Ontario. Here Moodie encountered "Yankee" neighbors whose brash familiarity frustrated her sense of class propriety and who later became the subject of many sketches in *Roughing It in the Bush*. In 1834, the Moodies moved to the backwoods settlement of Duoro, near Peterborough, where Moodie's sister Catharine

and her brother, Samuel, lived. After another unsuccessful attempt at farming, Moodie's husband accepted a position as sheriff of Victoria District and in 1840 the family relocated to Belleville.

During her years in the backwoods Moodie published several poems and sketches in such periodicals as the *Canadian Literary Magazine*, the *New York Albion*, and the Montreal-based journal the *Literary Garland*, but it was not until after the family settled in Belleville that she devoted herself fully to writing. She then became one of the leading contributors to the *Garland*, writing new sketches and poems as well as expanding previously written pieces into novels for serialization. Among these writings published in the *Garland* were the six Canadian sketches later included in *Roughing It in the Bush*. During 1847 and 1848, Moodie and her husband also edited and wrote most of the material for the *Victoria Magazine*, a journal intended to educate Canada's growing working class.

In 1852, Moodie signed a lucrative contract with the London publisher Richard Bentley. Within three years, Bentley published *Roughing It in the Bush, Life in the Clearings*, and the autobiographical novel *Flora Lyndsay*, Moodie's three works describing her immigration and settlement in Canada. During this time he also published three of her other novels, including *Mark Hurdlestone*, and a collection of short stories entitled

Matrimonial Speculations, all of which are set in England. After this successful period, Moodie quit writing for more than a decade for reasons that are unknown. When in the 1860s she again submitted work to Bentley's firm, it was deemed inferior to her earlier writings; the only piece accepted was *The World before Them,* a novel published in 1868. She continued to write, but few of her subsequent pieces were published. Moodie's last years were marked by illness and poverty, and she died in Toronto in 1885.

Moodie's three works dealing with immigration are considered her best. *Roughing It in the Bush,* the first of the three, was intended to discourage unsuited members of the English middle class from immigrating and thus dwells on such negative aspects of frontier life as illness, danger, and death. Yet this work also contains many humorous sketches of the people, customs, and daily life of the Upper-Canadian backwoods, as well as passages and poems that reflect Moodie's romantic response to nature. Unlike *Roughing It in the Bush,* which Moodie wrote of her own accord, *Life in the Clearings* was written after Bentley's request for an account of life in the developing Canadian towns. Using a trip to Niagara Falls as its focal point, the work consists of sketches of town life and observations on colonial society. Moodie's autobiographical novel *Flora Lyndsay* deals with a young couple's decision to immigrate to Canada and includes a novel-within-a-novel ostensibly written by Flora en route to Canada. Considered the weakest of Moodie's three major works, *Flora Lyndsay* has inspired little commentary.

Until the mid-twentieth century, *Roughing It in the Bush* was regarded primarily as an important record of immigrant life in the Canadian backwoods. Then, in 1959, Carl F. Klinck called for an examination of Moodie's artistic techniques, maintaining that *Roughing It in the Bush* and *Life in the Clearings* should be studied as literary works rather than as purely historical accounts. Although *Life in the Clearings* is still valued principally as an important document of the early cultural and social development of Canada, *Roughing It in the Bush* has since become the subject of numerous interpretations. During the 1960s, critics began to examine Moodie's treatment of herself in *Roughing It in the Bush,* with some commentators arguing that she did not give a strictly autobiographical account of her experiences as had been previously assumed, but rather, as Klinck maintained, that she "dramatized her vision of herself." Critics have also studied the work's design, theme, and intent, as well as the manner in which the intensity of Moodie's personal experience allowed her to transcend what A. Charles von Guttenberg called her "sheltered middle-class veneer and sentimentality." In addition, Moodie's role in the development of Canadian literature has continued to figure prominently in modern assessments of *Roughing It in the Bush* and *Life in the Clearings.*

Though critics have all but dismissed most of Moodie's writings, the diverse examinations of *Roughing It in the Bush* that have appeared since 1959 stand as a collective testament to the many-faceted nature of this work. Whether they consider *Roughing It in the Bush* an important record of immigrant life or, as Margot Northey argued in 1984, the expression of Moodie's "long-standing, inward-looking response to her vision of herself as artist," most critics agree that Moodie is a significant though minor figure in the developing literature of nineteenth-century Canada.

PRINCIPAL WORKS

Spartacus: A Roman Story (novel) 1822
Enthusiasm, and Other Poems (poetry) 1831

Roughing It in the Bush; or, Life in Canada (sketches and poetry) 1852
Life in the Clearings versus the Bush (sketches and poetry) 1853
Mark Hurdlestone, the Gold Worshipper (novel) 1853
Flora Lyndsay; or, Passages in an Eventful Life (novel) 1854
Matrimonial Speculations (short stories) 1854
The World before Them (novel) 1868

*This work contains a chapter and several poems by John Dunbar Moodie.

SUSANNA MOODIE (essay date 1852)

[*In the following excerpt from her introduction to the first edition of* Roughing It in the Bush, *Moodie discusses the reasons that compelled certain people to immigrate to Canada. Though speaking generally, her words reveal her personal bitterness against the land sellers and others who lured the English to Canada with tales of plenty while concealing the hardships inherent in life in the Canadian backwoods.*]

In most instances, emigration is a matter of necessity, not of choice; and this is more especially true of the emigration of persons of respectable connections, or of any station or position in the world. Few educated persons, accustomed to the refinements and luxuries of European society, ever willingly relinquish those advantages, and place themselves beyond the protective influence of the wise and revered institutions of their native land, without the pressure of some urgent cause. Emigration may, indeed, generally be regarded as an act of severe duty, performed at the expense of personal enjoyment, and accompanied by the sacrifice of those local attachments which stamp the scenes amid which our childhood grew, in imperishable characters upon the heart. Nor is it until adversity has pressed sorely upon the proud and wounded spirit of the well-educated sons and daughters of old but impoverished families, that they gird up the loins of the mind, and arm themselves with fortitude to meet and dare the heart-breaking conflict.

The ordinary motives for the emigration of such persons may be summed up in a few brief words—the emigrant's hope of bettering his condition, and of escaping from the vulgar sarcasms too often hurled at the less wealthy by the purse-proud, commonplace people of the world. But there is a higher motive still, which has its origin in that love of independence which springs up spontaneously in the breasts of the high-souled children of a glorious land. They cannot labour in a menial capacity in the country where they were born and educated to command. They can trace no difference between themselves and the more fortunate individuals of a race whose blood warms their veins, and whose name they bear. The want of wealth alone places an impassable barrier between them and the more favoured offspring of the same parent stock; and they go forth to make for themselves a new name and to find another country, to forget the past and to live in the future, to exult in the prospect of their children being free and the land of their adoption great.

The choice of the country to which they devote their talents and energies depends less upon their pecuniary means than upon the fancy of the emigrant or the popularity of a name. . . . In 1830, the great tide of emigration flowed westward. Canada became the great landmark for the rich in hope and poor in purse. Public newspapers and private letters teemed with the unheard-of advantages to be derived from a settlement in this highly favoured region.

Its salubrious climate, its fertile soil, commercial advantages, great water privileges, its proximity to the mother country, and last, not least, its almost total exemption from taxation—that bugbear which keeps honest John Bull in a state of constant ferment—were the theme of every tongue, and lauded beyond all praise. The general interest, once excited, was industriously kept alive by pamphlets, published by interested parties, which prominently set forth all the *good* to be derived from a settlement in the Backwoods of Canada; while they carefully concealed the toil and hardship to be endured in order to secure these advantages. They told of lands yielding forty bushels to the acre, but they said nothing of the years when these lands, with the most careful cultivation, would barely return fifteen; when rust and smut, engendered by the vicinity of damp overhanging woods, would blast the fruits of the poor emigrant's labour, and almost deprive him of bread. They talked of log houses to be raised in a single day, by the generous exertions of friends and neighbours, but they never ventured upon a picture of the disgusting scenes of riot and low debauchery exhibited during the raising, or upon a description of the dwellings when raised—dens of dirt and misery, which would, in many instances, be shamed by an English pig-sty. The necessaries of life were described as inestimably cheap; but they forgot to add that in remote bush settlements, often twenty miles from a market town, and some of them even that distance from the nearest dwelling, the necessaries of life which would be deemed indispensable to the European, could not be procured at all, or, if obtained, could only be so by sending a man and team through a blazed forest road—a process far too expensive for frequent repetition.

Oh, ye dealers in wild lands—ye speculators in the folly and credulity of your fellow-men—what a mass of misery, and of misrepresentation productive of that misery, have ye not to answer for! You had your acres to sell, and what to you were the worn-down frames and broken hearts of the infatuated purchasers? The public believed the plausible statements you made with such earnestness, and men of all grades rushed to hear your hired orators declaim upon the blessings to be obtained by the clearers of the wilderness.

Men who had been hopeless of supporting their families in comfort and independence at home, thought that they had only to come out to Canada to make their fortunes; almost even to realize the story told in the nursery, of the sheep and oxen that ran about the streets, ready roasted, and with knives and forks upon their backs. They were made to believe that if it did not actually rain gold, that precious metal could be obtained, as is now stated of California and Australia, by stooping to pick it up.

The infection became general. A Canada mania pervaded the middle ranks of British society; thousands and tens of thousands, for the space of three or four years, landed upon these shores. A large majority of the higher class were officers of the army and navy, with their families—a class perfectly unfitted by their previous habits and education for contending with the stern realities of emigrant life. The hand that has long held the sword, and been accustomed to receive implicit obedience from those under its control, is seldom adapted to wield the spade and guide the plough, or try its strength against the stubborn trees of the forest. Nor will such persons submit cheerfully to the saucy familiarity of servants, who, republicans

in spirit, think themselves as good as their employers. Too many of these brave and honourable men were easy dupes to the designing land-speculators. Not having counted the cost, but only looked upon the bright side of the picture held up to their admiring gaze, they fell easily into the snares of their artful seducers.

To prove their zeal as colonists, they were induced to purchase large tracts of wild land in remote and unfavourable situations. This, while it impoverished and often proved the ruin of the unfortunate immigrant, possessed a double advantage to the seller. He obtained an exorbitant price for the land which he actually sold, while the residence of a respectable settler upon the spot greatly enhanced the value and price of all other lands in the neighbourhood.

It is not by such instruments as those I have just mentioned, that Providence works when it would reclaim the waste places of the earth, and make them subservient to the wants and happiness of its creatures. The Great Father of the souls and bodies of men knows the arm which wholesome labour from infancy has made strong, the nerves which have become iron by patient endurance, by exposure to weather, coarse fare, and rude shelter; and He chooses such, to send forth into the forest to hew out the rough paths for the advance of civilization. These men become wealthy and prosperous, and form the bones and sinews of a great and rising country. Their labour is wealth, not exhaustion; it produces independence and content, not homesickness and despair. What the Backwoods of Canada are to the industrious and ever-to-be-honoured sons of honest poverty, and what they are to the refined and accomplished gentleman, these simple sketches will endeavour to portray. They are drawn principally from my own experience, during a sojourn of nineteen years in the colony. (pp. xv-xviii)

> *Susanna Moodie, in an introduction to her* Roughing It in the Bush; or, Forest Life in Canada, *1852. Reprint by McClelland and Stewart Limited, 1962, pp. xv-xviii.*

THE INTERNATIONAL MONTHLY MAGAZINE   (essay date 1852)

[*The following excerpt is from a positive review of* Roughing It in the Bush.]

If there be one of life's affairs in which woman has a peculiar right to have her wishes considered and her veto respected, it is that of emigration. For, in the arduous task of establishing a new home in a half-settled country, let man do what he will to alleviate, on her fall the burthen and heat of the day. Hers are the menial toils, the frequent anxieties, the lingering homesickness, the craving after dear friends' faces and a beloved native land. Hers, too, the self-imposed duty and unselfish effort to hide regret under cheerful smiles, when the weary brother or husband returns at evening from toil in field and forest. Blessed and beautiful are the smiles of the sad-hearted, worn to wile away another's cares!

Love in a cottage has long been jeered at, and depicted as flying out of the window. It seems miraculous to behold [in Mrs. Moodie's ***Roughing It in the Bush***] the capricious little deity steadfastly braving, for many a long year, the chilly atmosphere of a log-hut in an American forest. In the year 1832, Mrs. Moodie . . . accompanied her husband, a half-pay subaltern, to the backwoods of Canada. Many were her misgivings, and they did not prove unfounded. Long and cruel was the probation she underwent, before finding comparative

Reydon Hall, where the author lived as a young girl. Photograph by Elizabeth Hopkins.

comfort and prosperity in the rugged land where at first she found so much to embitter her existence. Nobly did she bear up under countless difficulties and sufferings, supported by an energy rare in woman, and by her devoted attachment to the husband of her choice. For some years her troubles were not occasional, but continual and increasing. (p. 470)

[The Moodies' first winter in the backwoods] was a winter of painful instruction for the inexperienced young woman, and her not very prudent husband. We might fill columns with a bare list of their vexations and disasters. Amongst the former, not the least arose from the borrowing propensities of their neighbors. They had 'located' in a bad neighborhood, in the vicinity of a number of low Yankee squatters, "ignorant as savages, without their courtesy and kindness." These people walked unceremoniously at all hours into their wretched dwelling, to criticise their proceedings, make impertinent remarks, and to borrow—or rather to beg or steal, for what they borrowed they rarely returned. The most extraordinary loans were daily solicited or demanded; and Mrs. Moodie, strange and timid in her new home, and amongst these semi-barbarians—her husband, too, being much away at the farm—for some time dared not refuse to acquiesce in their impudent extortions. (p. 471)

[The anecdotes in *Roughing It in the Bush* about these neighbors] exhibit, more vividly than volumes of description, the sort of savages amongst whom poor Mrs. Moodie's lot was cast. They had all the worst qualities of Yankee and Indian— the good ones of neither. They had neither manners, heart, nor honesty. The basest selfishness, cunning, and malignity were their prominent characteristics. (p. 472)

Mrs. Moodie's work, unaffectedly and naturally written, though a little coarse, will delight ladies, please men, and even amuse

children. . . . The book is one of great originality and interest. (p. 474)

"Life in Canada," in The International Monthly Magazine, *Vol. V, No. 4, April 1, 1852, pp. 470-74.*

SUSANNA MOODIE   (essay date 1852)

[*This excerpt is from Moodie's 1852 introduction to* Life in the Clearings. *While she defends her attempt in* Roughing It in the Bush *to discourage unsuited British immigrants from settling in rural Canada, Moodie also praises the opportunities available in the colonial settlements.*]

In our work of **Roughing It in the Bush,** I endeavoured to draw a picture of Canadian life, as I found it twenty years ago, in the Backwoods. My motive in giving such a melancholy narrative to the British public was prompted by the hope of deterring well-educated people, about to settle in this colony, from entering upon a life for which they were totally unfitted by their previous pursuits and habits.

To persons unaccustomed to hard labour, and used to the comforts and luxuries deemed indispensable to those moving in the middle classes at home, a settlement in the bush can offer few advantages. It has proved the ruin of hundreds and thousands who have ventured their all in this hazardous experiment; nor can I recollect a single family of the higher class, that have come under my own personal knowledge, that ever realized an independence, or bettered their condition, by taking up wild lands in remote localities; while volumes might be filled with failures, even more disastrous than our own, to prove the truth of my former statements.

But while I have endeavoured to point out the error of gentlemen bringing delicate women and helpless children to toil in the woods, and by so doing excluding them from all social intercourse with persons in their own rank, and depriving the younger branches of the family of the advantages of education, which, in the vicinity of towns and villages, can be enjoyed by the children of the poorest emigrant, I have never said anything against the REAL benefits to be derived from a judicious choice of settlement in this great and rising country.

God forbid that any representations of mine should deter one of my countrymen from making this noble and prosperous colony his future home. But let him leave to the hardy labourer the place assigned to him by Providence, nor undertake, upon limited means, the task of pioneer in the great wilderness. Men of independent fortune can live anywhere. If such prefer a life in the woods, to the woods let them go; but they will soon find out that they could have employed the means in their power in a far more profitable manner than in chopping down trees in the bush.

There are a thousand more advantageous ways in which a man of property may invest his capital than by burying himself and his family in the woods. There never was a period in the history of the colony that offered greater inducements to men of moderate means to emigrate to Canada than the present. (pp. xxix-xxx)

Why gentlemen from Britain should obstinately crowd to the Backwoods, and prefer the coarse, hard life of an axeman to that of a respectable landed proprietor in a civilized part of the country, has always been to me a matter of surprise; for a farm under cultivation can always be purchased for less money than must necessarily be expended upon clearing and raising buildings upon a wild lot. (p. xxx)

At the period when the greatest portion of *Roughing it in the Bush* was written, I was totally ignorant of life in Canada, as it existed in the towns and villages. Thirteen years' residence in one of the most thriving districts in the Upper Province has given me many opportunities of becoming better acquainted with the manners and habits of her busy, bustling population than it was possible for me ever to obtain in the green prison of the woods.

Since my residence in a settled part of the country, I have enjoyed as much domestic peace and happiness as ever falls to the lot of poor humanity. Canada has become almost as dear to me as my native land; and the home-sickness that constantly preyed upon me in the Backwoods has long ago yielded to the deepest and most heartfelt interest in the rapidly increasing prosperity and greatness of the country of my adoption—the great foster-mother of that portion of the human family whose fatherland, however dear to them, is unable to supply them with bread.

To the honest sons of labour Canada is, indeed, an El Dorado—a land flowing with milk and honey; for they soon obtain that independence which the poor gentleman struggles in vain to realize by his own labour in the woods.

The conventional prejudices that shackle the movements of members of the higher classes in Britain are scarcely recognised in Canada; and a man is at liberty to choose the most profitable manner of acquiring wealth, without the fear of ridicule and the loss of caste. (pp. xxxi-xxxii)

I have been repeatedly asked, since the publication of *Roughing it in the Bush,* to give an account of the present state of society in the colony, and to point out its increasing prosperity and

commercial advantages; but statistics are not my forte, nor do I feel myself qualified for such an arduous and important task. My knowledge of the colony is too limited to enable me to write a comprehensive work on a subject of vital consequence, which might involve the happiness of others. But what I do know I will endeavour to sketch with a light pencil; and if I cannot convey much useful information, I will try to amuse the reader; and by a mixture of prose and poetry compile a small volume which may help to while away an idle hour, or fill up the blanks of a wet day. (p. xxxiii)

> *Susanna Moodie, in an introduction to her* Life in the Clearings, *edited by Robert L. McDougall, Macmillan of Canada, 1959, pp. xxix-xxxiii.*

THE NEW QUARTERLY REVIEW   (essay date 1853)

[*The following excerpt is from a negative review of* Mark Hurdlestone, the Gold Worshipper.]

We cannot highly congratulate the authoress of **Mark Hurdlestone** upon her success in the present instance. The tale is somewhat feeble, the characters are dull and commonplace, and the whole affair lacks spirit, incident, and life.

The preface, however, is interesting . . . [and] conveys an useful moral. . . . (p. 251)

The reader will perceive from this preface under what untoward circumstances the writer laboured when she first endeavoured to derive emolument from her pen. Her productions must therefore be perused with a more lenient eye than if they had emanated from one whose vocation is authorship. For that reason, therefore, we forbear to criticise, as we should, had we under review, the work of a professed novelist. (p. 252)

> *A review of "Mark Hurdlestone, the Gold Worshipper," in* The New Quarterly Review, *Vol. II, No. VI, 1853, pp. 251-52.*

ARCHIBALD MacMURCHY   (essay date 1906)

[*MacMurchy favorably reviews Moodie's novels about immigration and life in Canada.*]

In *Flora Lyndsay* and *Roughing It in the Bush* the authoress relates the details about leaving one's native land, the uncertainties in regard to a new country, the sorrows of leave-taking, the yearning for the homeland and all it contains. The writer does not omit to tell of the long voyage across the Atlantic, with its inconveniences, mishaps, and sufferings; the journey into the new, strange land, so extensive and so rude in comparison to the land left behind, yet, with all its disadvantages, recognized to be the land of promise for every one seeking a home and independence.

In *Life in the Clearings versus the Bush,* Mrs. Moodie gives historic sketches of cities and towns in Canada West, as they appeared in 1852. Very interesting she makes these sketches, combining with them many anecdotes and tales about residents and travellers. Let no reader miss her description of the Falls of Niagara. There is fiction in these books (perhaps more correct to say exaggeration), but the future historian of Canada, when he comes, will find in these volumes fit material ready for the writing of Canadian history.

Her work affords a good example of the style of a worthy class of fiction-writers of the early nineteenth century, with its large interest in human life, its marriages, family connections, births, and deaths, its stories of ghosts, its odd people, incredible feats of strength and endurance, the sweet home life, simple and humane. The reader of Mrs. Moodie's work receives the impression that she was of an amiable, sensible, refined, religious character. She has the additional honor of being one of the early pioneers of Canadian literature. (pp. 22-3)

> *Archibald MacMurchy, "Mrs. Susanna Moodie," in his* Handbook of Canadian Literature (English), *William Briggs, 1906, pp. 21-4.*

RAY PALMER BAKER   (essay date 1920)

[In his survey of English-Canadian literature, Baker briefly discusses the nationalistic sentiments and attitudes toward nature expressed by Moodie in her poetry and Roughing It in the Bush.*]*

[Susanna Moodie's] hopes and disappointments . . . are graphically described in her *Roughing It in the Bush; or Life in Canada* . . ., which has been equally popular in Great Britain, the United States, and Canada. Its value lies in the fact that her experiences were those of hundreds of other delicately reared gentlewomen who courageously obeyed the call of duty. From Quebec and Montreal, with their plague-infected streets, she takes her readers into the taverns of the "Front," as the counties on the Lakes were then designated, and into the offices of the despicable speculators who preyed on the ignorant immigrants. Were it not for her powers of characterization, her narrative would be as tedious as many that I have discarded. It is her ability to depict the flotsam of a raw community, the self-importance of the newly liberated serf, the vanity of the impecunious matron who boasts of her high connections at "Home," that gives her preëminence among the writers of memoirs.

Quite as fascinating as her references to the people whom she meets is the unconscious revelation of personality in her dependence on the conventional formulae of an English gentlewoman; in her surprise that the titles of "Sir" and "Madam" are "very rarely applied by inferiors," and in her little vanity of authorship. Yet, in spite of the narrowness of her sex and of her age, she emerges as a bright heroic spirit that anxiety and suffering could neither darken nor intimidate.

In her pages it is possible to trace her homesickness for the English countryside, her repugnance at her lot in the Canadian wilds, and her final contentment with her adopted home. . . . Howe, with his memorable phrases lit by the clear white flame of his imagination never uttered a higher prophecy of future greatness than this quiet, reserved Englishwoman of the Trent Valley. "You feel at every step," she writes, "that Canada must become a great nation." Its people "possess capabilities and talents which . . . will render them second to no people in the world."

Though Mrs. Moodie came to understand, and to appreciate, her neighbors, she never closed her eyes to their imperfections. Against the harshness and vulgarity of the satiric tradition she never ceased to battle. As one of the leaders in the romantic impulse, which has done much to widen the horizon of the Canadian people, she is worthy of remembrance. From childhood she had been peculiarly susceptible to natural beauty. Coming down the St. Lawrence, she tells her readers in *Roughing It,* she broke into tears at the sight of Quebec. "Next to the love of God," she asseverates, "the love of Nature may be regarded as the purest and holiest of the human heart."

Though not entirely above the aristocratic pastime of ridiculing the United States, she devoted her energies to the nobler task of arousing her neighbors to the glories of their environment. Into their narrow, unimaginative minds, warped by prejudice, she brought new images and new delights. (pp. 118-20)

[Moodie's other novels] are mere echoes of *Roughing It* on which her reputation rests. This, her most vital work, is far from perfect. The intermediate chapter, "The Land Jobber," by her husband, who also wrote a volume of reminiscences, destroys what little continuity the narrative possesses. The descriptions of the Indians, who appealed to her sense of the picturesque, lack proportion. Worst of all, the moral that no gentleman ever succeeds in the bush detracts from the matter-of-fact transcription which gives the memoir its charm. The fact that Mrs. Moodie had a "negative mind"—to borrow a phrase from the *Athenaeum*—increases her skill at portraiture. That she was willing, in general, to tell what she saw, without offering suggestions for improvement, heightens the power of her sketches. The naturalness of her manner at once invites confidence. The easy, limpid, almost slipshod style, with no pretense of force, is peculiarly ingratiating. (pp. 120-21)

In [the *Literary Garland*] and in the *Victoria Magazine*, afterwards conducted by Mrs. Moodie and her husband, most of her poems were given to the public. Though few of her lyrics were issued in book form, they speedily sang their way from periodicals and newspapers into the homes of Ontario and Quebec. Some like the **"Snow Song"** were widely popular in the United States. Although many of these ditties are entirely worthless, they brought a touch of cheer into many an unlovely settlement, and directed the attention of Canadian writers to Canadian subjects. However pernicious has become the theory that a national literature must be provincial in material, there is no gainsaying the fact that, when first promulgated by the *Literary Garland,* it stimulated independent effort and counteracted, in a small way, the influence of Byron, whose cynicism found a ready echo on this side of the Atlantic. Though it is undoubtedly true that Mrs. Moodie is indebted to the English Romanticists, it is also true that in treatment as well as in subject matter she occasionally attains to something approaching independence. Verses like **"The Canadian Herd Boy"** show how gracefully she can invest the dull routine of the backwoods with a poetic coloring. . . . (pp. 121-22)

I have referred to Mrs. Moodie's poetry because it cannot be separated from her prose: in most of her books they go hand in hand. Together they show the growing sense of national unity and the emergence of a new attitude towards Nature and the ordinary concerns of life. (p. 122)

> *Ray Palmer Baker, "Memoirs," in his* A History of English-Canadian Literature to the Confederation: Its Relation to the Literature of Great Britain and the United States, *Cambridge, Mass.: Harvard University Press, 1920, pp. 117-24.*

V. B. RHODENIZER   (essay date 1930)

[Rhodenizer praises Moodie's descriptions of the life of the early English settlers in Canada.]

Both Mrs. Moodie's prose and her verse show that she was influenced by the attitude of the English romanticists toward nature and the common life. At first, it is true, the contrast between the new and the old is to her a source of pain, but her writings reveal the gradual growth of a sympathetic attitude toward Canadian scenes and life. This attitude, combined with skill in description and in characterization of pioneer types, produced not only the best transcript we have of the conditions under which the early English settlers lived, but also a clear record of the emotional change that transformed cultured English men and women, homesick for their mother land, into loyal citizens with a strong sense of nationality and unbounded faith in the future of Canada. In *Roughing It in the Bush,* her best work, there are vivid descriptions of the journey up the St. Lawrence, of the environment of their new home, and of various kinds of new neighbours, and vivid narratives of adventures with fire, storms, and wild beasts. (p. 61)

> V. B. Rhodenizer, *"Travel, Exploration, and Memoirs," in his* A Handbook of Canadian Literature, *Graphic Publishers Limited, 1930, pp. 55-62.*

EDWARD A. McCOURT (essay date 1945)

[*McCourt maintains that* Roughing It in the Bush *provides "the best picture of life in an early Canadian backwoods settlement" in Canadian literature.*]

Since history is written mostly by men, it is inevitable that the building of Canada should be represented in our textbooks as a man's job. . . . It is the more unfortunate that our pioneer women were themselves largely inarticulate, being too much occupied with the business of looking after their husbands and rearing their numerous progeny to think of recording their struggles for posterity. But there is one notable exception. In the spare time which making a home in the wilderness and bringing up five children allowed her, Mrs. Susanna Moodie wrote a series of sketches describing the day-to-day existence which she led in the backwoods of Ontario between the years 1832 and 1840. These sketches, first published in *The Literary Garland* and later expanded into a volume of reminiscences under the title of *Roughing It in the Bush,* provide the best picture of life in an early Canadian backwoods settlement which our literature affords. (p. 77)

Apart from serving as an admirable record of life in a backwoods community, *Roughing It in the Bush* is worth reading as an antidote to the highly-coloured, sentimental accounts of pioneer life which constitute much of our romantic fiction. (p. 83)

Almost without emotion, with what in a more sophisticated writer might be regarded as deviceful understatement, [Mrs. Moodie] relates how for months at a time the family subsisted on a diet of bread, frozen potatoes, an occasional piece of bear meat, and coffee made from the roots of the ubiquitous dandelion. (p. 84)

But in spite of extravagant claims that have been made for it by over-zealous champions of our native literature, *Roughing It* is not a classic, even in the loosest sense of the term. It is an unpretentious, highly literate account of an heroic if not always intelligent struggle against a hostile environment. Such a struggle always possesses a strong element of interest in itself; and Mrs. Moodie's simple, unadorned style is well suited to her subject-matter. Only occasionally, as when she writes of the homeland, does she appropriate the manner and sentiments of her female contemporaries. *Roughing It* is for the most part a plain tale plainly told.

But the chief charm of the book derives from its characterizations. In sketching the individuals whom she encountered during her years in the bush, Mrs. Moodie shows talent of a high order. (pp. 87-8)

Mrs. Moodie suffered much during her years in the bush, but, unlike many of her compatriots, she was sustained by a never-flagging interest in the odd characters whom she encountered, and by a love of the Canadian scene which grew stronger with the passing years. Thus, in the preface to the 1871 edition of *Roughing It,* Mrs. Moodie, then in her sixty-third year, writes of Canada not as the disciple of Mrs. Hemans pining for her childhood home on the banks of the Waveney, but as the loyal and enthusiastic citizen of a country in which she has found happiness and peace. . . . (pp. 88-9)

[She] writes, in words which are a high prophecy of the future greatness of her adopted country: "You feel at every step that Canada must become a great nation." Its people "possess capabilities and talents which will render them second to no people in the world". (p. 89)

> Edward A. McCourt, *"Roughing It with the Moodies," in* Queen's Quarterly, *Vol. LII, No. 1, Spring, 1945, pp. 77-89.*

R. E. RASHLEY (essay date 1958)

[*Rashley argues that* Roughing It in the Bush *is representative of nineteenth-century Canadian immigrants' transition from initial dislike of, to eventual affection and loyalty toward, their new country.*]

With most of the [Canadian] immigrants, the gradual change from immigrant to settler which occurred as the homeland memories faded and the urgent necessity of the moment forced a coming to grips at least with the new physical world entailed two simple and necessary adjustments. One of these reflects the change from foreigner to settler which shows itself in the many early volumes as an emotional adjustment to the new world. Most of those who disliked the country in their early experiences eventually arrived at affection for it and finally developed strong local loyalties. This is an elementary adjustment which is well represented by Mrs. Susannah Moodie. (p. 17)

Mrs. Moodie's life in the Ontario backwoods was difficult in proportion to the strength of her cultural resources. Highly class conscious, educated, accustomed to the separation of military castes, and in every way the epitome of qualities unvalued in pioneer life, she found that the culture which she represented invited critical response wherever she went. (p. 18)

A good deal of Mrs. Moodie's difficulty was caused by her failure to realize, until it was forced upon her, the fact that this culture was alien and hostile to the life to which she was committed. Ignorant of life outside of her sphere, she encountered better success with the Indians than with some of her Loyalist neighbours because she was aware of a difference in their lives and made allowance for it. Her book [*Roughing It in the Bush*] reflects no bitterness, however; her adversities are recorded with good humour, and the sensibilities which made pioneer life harsh made its good things so much the better. Her distaste for the life is perhaps best stated in her quiet survey when the opportunity of change presents itself:

> For seven long years I had lived out of the world
> entirely; my person had been rendered coarse
> by hard work and exposure to the weather. I
> looked double the age I really was, and my hair

was already thickly sprinkled with grey. I clung to my solitude. I did not like to be dragged from it to mingle in gay scenes, in a busy town, and with gaily dressed people. I was no longer fit for the world; I had lost all relish for the pursuits and pleasures which are so essential to its votaries; I was contented to live and die in obscurity.

Mrs. Moodie's presentation of the picture is false to the extent that it does not give us the effects of her way of life upon the other, the pioneer picture which *includes* her type, nor tell us of the continued effort which she made through local magazines, to give substance to an indigenous literature. *Roughing It in the Bush* is a prose record of her experience, but it contains fifty-two poems. . . . Early in her narrative she writes:

In the depths of dark forests my soul droops her wings;
In tall boughs above me no merry bird sings.
The sigh of the wild winds—rush of the Floods—
Is the only sad music that wakens the moods.

Toward the end, on leaving the backwoods for the settlements, she finds that these songless boughs have won their way into her affections and she writes an "Adieu to the Woods":

Adieu! adieu!—when grieving lips refuse
   The bitter pangs of parting to declare;
And the full bosom feels that it must lose
   Friends who were wont its inmost thoughts to share.

"Now," as she says, "when not only reconciled to Canada, but loving it, and feeling a deep interest in its present welfare, and the fair prospect of its future greatness, I often look back and laugh at the feelings with which I then regarded this noble country." It is this progression from dislike to love of the country which allows Mrs. Moodie to speak for a type of reaction. It is elementary enough and inevitable in the second generation if not in the first, but worth recording as a necessary step from the old world to the new. (pp. 18-19)

The poems of Mrs. Moodie . . . are successful neither as specimens of the old world art nor as expressions, however rough, of the new world experience, but their techniques are a partial bridging of the gap. They do use the native material in part, and, in doing so, make possible a further use of the material in a mode suited to the use. The best that could be said of them is that they allow the techniques of English versification to continue so that native poetry, when it does appear, is less gauche than it might otherwise have been. (p. 21)

> *R. E. Rashley, "Immigrant Poetry, Its Nature and Significance," in his* Poetry in Canada: The First Three Steps, *The Ryerson Press, 1958, pp. 1-22.*

ROBERT L. McDOUGALL   (essay date 1959)

[*In this excerpt from his introduction to the 1959 edition of* Life in the Clearings, *McDougall emphasizes the importance of this work as a record of the early cultural and social development of Canada.*]

As its title suggests, with its hint of axe and spade, *Roughing It in the Bush* is a book about pioneering in the common sense of the term. Substantially, it is a first-hand account of an attempt made by a family of English emigrants to establish a homestead on the frontiers of Upper Canada in the early part of the nineteenth century, an undertaking which obviously meant for the author a trying physical and spiritual experience. . . .

The whole is a narrative which, though not strictly chronological, has all the immediacy of a pioneering journal. Its principal component is the sure-fire drama of man's primitive struggle against drought, storm, pestilence, fire and sickness.

Life in the Clearings, on the other hand, though written by a pioneer in pioneering times, has little about it that suggests, either in subject matter or manner of treatment, the elemental conflicts of settlement. Indeed one's first thought, and a quite natural one, is that this is a very civilized book. Mrs. Moodie was of course a very civilized person both by birth and upbringing, and practically everything she wrote bore the marks of a tradition of refinement in writing which she inherited from the eighteenth century. The vein was that of the "elegant trifle", the pointedly amateur piece of writing which was nevertheless designed to exhibit all the best graces of literary and social convention. Her novels show this kind of sophistication to a marked degree; and *Roughing It in the Bush* shows it too, for that matter, though fortunately in this case the immediacy of the material puts a ceiling on the author's usual elevation of style. In the case of *Life in the Clearings,* however, circumstances combined to encourage a formal literary manner.

The book is both less autobiographical and more self-conscious than its forerunner. Following the publication of *Roughing It in the Bush* serially in the *Literary Garland* in 1847, Mrs. Moodie was asked, as she tells us, "to give an account of the present state of society in the colony. . . ." She complied—though not, she is careful to point out, in the role of statistician or official guide to immigrants. And in taking up the task she looked, not back to her six years solitary in "the green prison of the woods", but around her at the relatively complex society which had grown up along the "front" of the St. Lawrence River and Lake Ontario in the course of two or three decades of settlement and of which she herself had by this time been a member for many years. To her private life and the life of her family, always to be dealt with reticently and now no longer particularly dramatic or made up of experiences different from those of a score of her neighbours, she gives little attention. She sketches men and women, for she liked to do this and could do it well; but since the people she was now concerned with were members of close-knit communities, she does not create the frank and vigorous character studies which are a strong point of *Roughing It in the Bush.* Especially she writes about Orange Societies, religious sects, Mechanics' Institutes, and fire-fighting co-operatives—about social rather than solitary man. (pp. vii-ix)

Mrs. Moodie herself was by this time widely known as "the woman that writes", and a more select group recognized her as a prominent contributor of fiction and poetry to the *Literary Garland.* She was Canada's challenge to Mrs. Lydia Howard Sigourney—a hollow compliment to pay her today, but one of some substance to an earlier public.

And so, naturally enough, when Mrs. Moodie wrote *Life in the Clearings* she tried to do what was expected of her: that is, write a civilized book about society. Though in a sense she was to take her readers on a journey, this was to be no pioneering journey but a tourist trip to Niagara Falls undertaken by a cultured and romantically languid author in search of better health; and its chief purpose was to be to provide a peg on which to hang anecdotes, mostly anonymous and second-hand (which was a good way of playing safe with reputations), and a series of observations about society. What remains to be said here is that the book which was the outgrowth of all these conditions can hardly be expected to reproduce the confessional strength of *Roughing It in the Bush,* any more than it can be expected to reproduce the dramatic appeal of the earlier narrative of primitive struggle. And of course it does not.

What are the compensations? Mrs. Moodie is a good reporter and she has a good subject. Remembering one of the lessons of romanticism which she forgot too often in writing her novels, she keeps her eye (and ours) upon the object. The reader will find this eye an excellent one for detail, and he will experience the pleasure that comes from exact description when Mrs. Moodie distinguishes between the colours of the waters of the St. Lawrence, the Ottawa, and the Otonabee. He will find it also an eye sensitive to pictorial effect, and he will watch with interest the dignified progress of that lone cow down the stream of the flooded Moira. Beyond this area of intellectual free-wheeling there is good value again. Honouring the terms of her assignment, Mrs. Moodie inspects with a lively curiosity the social scene—the behaviour and dress of young ladies at a ball, the fare at a picnic, the programme of a travelling circus, the ritual at a village funeral, the proceedings at a religious camp-meeting, and the life of inmates in prison and asylum of the time. It is an impressive record which the student of institutions and ways of life in early Ontario will do well to consult. And, to return to less utilitarian values, one senses always that what permeates the record is the important literary virtue of an engaging personality. The reader is hard to please who does not like Mrs. Moodie's bird-like alertness, her good sense, her tolerance, her genial and gracious manner. If he expects pretentiousness to follow from the formal literary style, he will also be gratified to discover that this writer is "but a humly body after all", and no blue-stocking.

These qualities are perhaps in themselves a sufficient recommendation to reading enjoyment. Should one go on to speak of Mrs. Moodie's handling of dialogue, of her rendering of the sensational story of Grace Marks, and of other things she does well in the present text? I think not, for there is a danger of creating the impression that we are dealing with a first-rate writer, and this is far from being the case. On the other hand, there is a good deal more to be said about *Life in the Clearings* if we come at the book from another point of view. The fact is that this is a valuable document for special reasons which have little to do with literary skills and the sharpness of a photographic eye.

An account of how an Eskimo kills seals and keeps himself warm in winter is likely to make good reading; but it will make better reading if it tells us something also about the Eskimo's concepts of time and how they compare with our own. Similarly, Mrs. Moodie has a good story to tell about pioneering it in the bush, and another good one which sketches the features of everyday life known to early Canadian settlers. But she offers still another story, which is in a way the best of the lot. This is a story whose characters are ideas and values, and it shows us how and on what terms Canadian society was being built in the days when the Moodies lived on West Bridge Street in Belleville. Considering the principles of conduct and social organization which seem to her characteristic of the society growing up around her, Mrs. Moodie makes it plain in *Life in the Clearings* that these are not exactly the principles she or others had known in England. She notes the distinguishing marks of the new society, and to some extent accounts for them. Such a record, sifted from much else that is in the book, is an early chapter in the long account of our cultural evolution. And I believe it is a chapter we can read profitably in the present crucial stage of our national development; for by re-

minding us of the nature of our cultural origins and of the kind of influences which from the beginning have been at work to modify our inheritance it can help us to form a correct notion of our national identity. Here is an aspect of Mrs. Moodie's work which can be described as important without reservation. (pp. ix-xi)

Since I shall wish to argue in a moment that the Mrs. Moodie of *Life in the Clearings* is to a considerable extent removed in her social outlook from the . . . dominant conservatism [of the Canadian pioneers], it is perhaps advisable to emphasize here her initial and essential conformity to the pattern. There is in fact ample evidence in the present text to make clear this conformity, despite the colouring of that evidence by the presence of social values of a different or at least modified sort. But if we turn back to the period covered by *Roughing It in the Bush* and beyond, the clues are unmistakable. . . . Everything about [Mrs. Moodie] bespoke respectability, refinement, and a deep sense of propriety in all matters relating to morality and the smooth functioning of the social order to which she was accustomed. Her accounts of her early experiences in the colony, as recorded in *Roughing It in the Bush,* reveal in particular her acute consciousness of class distinctions and her broadly conservative temper of mind. (p. xiv)

It was not in the nature of things . . . that the immigrants settling on the new frontiers should produce in the place they had come to an exact duplicate of the society they had left behind. To some extent, in an instinctive bid for survival in the face of their removal to a new environment, they fought to conserve the values they had brought with them. But the new environment was to prove an irresistible modifier—at least, up to a point. Specifically, ideals of social democracy were abroad in this new environment, and the immigrant soon felt the force they exerted. Thus from an early date an essentially radical force was brought to bear against the essentially conservative cast of British colonial society.

The first source of this radical influence was what may be called the frontier situation. American historians, particularly Parrington and Turner, have made much of the theory that the frontiers are almost by definition the spawning-grounds of social democracy. Their argument, which is sound for at least a limited period or part of American history, has been that the expansion of settlement into new territory is a process which constantly attracts and rewards those who have least patience with authority, and which is therefore an enemy of traditional class distinctions. . . . [The] frontier theory obviously does not fit the Canadian case as snugly as it does the American. Nevertheless, the potential of radicalism inherent in the frontier situation was a force known to Mrs. Moodie and her kind, both in their life in the bush and in the more formal social order of their life in the clearings. And the basis of its strength was the fact that life in both these areas, by setting a high premium on practicality and native industry, encouraged a spirit of independence and undermined Old World conceptions of class.

The second source of radical influence was specifically American. Undoubtedly nourished by the frontier situation, American democratic ideals assumed in the decade following 1825 what was to be historically their most vigorous political form. This was coonskin democracy, and its hero was perhaps as much Davy Crockett as it was Andrew Jackson. . . . Its adherents were ruled by a desire to give practical effect to the doctrine of social equality. For a time they raised a spirited clamour in the agrarian states beyond the Alleghenies; and because they were mobile as well as vocal their influence was felt both directly and indirectly in the British colonies to the north. They spilled over the border as part of the backwash of a nation on the move, with its main guard headed west. . . . [Their] ideas and values spread like a quick infection amongst the legions of the lower classes now pouring into the colonies. Servants were saucy with a phrase about Jack being as good as his master; and pauper immigrants, from the moment of their landing at Grosse Isle, raised the Scots equivalent for this in the cry, ''We shall a' be lairds here!''

If this was the effect of democratization on the pauper immigrant scarcely off his ship, what happened later as the new social values, gaining strength from the naturally democratic thrust of frontier life, began to press in upon the values held by the dominant group of colonial society? It is Mrs. Moodie, of course, who supplies my reference to the behaviour of pauper immigrants at Grosse Isle, and it is clear from the account she gives of this scene in *Roughing It in the Bush* that she considered their behaviour scandalously democratic. Significantly, when she refers again to the scene at the close of *Life in the Clearings,* she is thinking by this time less about subversion of the social order than about immorality. But the point at the moment is that one comes to rely on Mrs. Moodie for this kind of information. And it is precisely for this reason that *Life in the Clearings* is a very valuable book. Though there is certainly a more complete answer than Mrs. Moodie's to the question of the later course of democratic influences, this answer is scattered throughout a large number of documents (mostly periodicals) which are hard to come by and often hard to read. In the present text, on the other hand, amidst much that is interesting on other accounts, we are given a concentrated view of Old World social values reacting to pressure from the New. It is simply our good fortune, and no threat to the general validity of the testimony, that this writer shows herself to be a little more sensitive to social climate than most of her fellow-colonists.

There are two aspects to Mrs. Moodie's answer. The first is that democratic influences produced a change in her social values. The second, which is of much greater importance from the point of view of the present argument, is that these influences were resisted beyond a certain point. Mrs. Moodie's way, in other words, became characteristically a way of compromise.

Numerous comments in *Life in the Clearings* show how the tree is being bent and by what wind. Submitting her report on ''the present state of society in the colony'', Mrs. Moodie is emphatic on one point: this society is in a much healthier condition than the one she had known in England. And she associates the improvement unhesitatingly with the mixing of the classes in the new society and the absence of convention and prejudice in the relations between various occupational groups—effects which she describes frankly as being due in part at least to a ''friendly'' American influence. She likes the greater liveliness in social intercourse which is a product of this new freedom; better still, she likes the way in which the stripping away of old preconceptions about class makes possible a true estimate of a man's worth. This real worth of a man, as distinct from the special gifts which rank and wealth may bestow on him, she sees simply as the sum of his native ability, his industry, his moral training, and his education. (pp. xiv-xvii)

On the other hand, it is certainly fruitless to try to see in this writer a republican or a thorough-going democrat. Mrs. Moodie would have none of such imputations in her day, and for good reasons. Her roots in the parent culture were deep, and there

was in addition much already written into the short record of North American history (most pointedly, the bitter strife brought on by the revolt of the New England states) to urge that the lifelines to the mother country be kept clear. She therefore accepted from the new environment only what she considered fundamentally reconcilable with the monarchical principle and with the already established values of British colonial society. Despite her satisfaction at the weakening of the old class barriers, she is no leveller. She is confident that society will always be made up of those who serve and those who command, of those who carry out the ordinary duties of life and those who see visions and create. ''Equality of mind'' is therefore the extent of her egalitarian philosophy; and by this she means that she looks to education to establish a commonwealth of intellect in which all classes will mingle and communicate harmoniously. Unlike the rigorous democrat, who is inclined to mistrust the intellectual (the ''egg-head'', as he is now called) and to level downwards to mediocrity, Mrs. Moodie prizes intellect and accepts as a main goal the raising of the intellectual powers of all men to the highest point consistent with native ability. Education so conceived, moreover, she sees as a protection against the danger already apparent in her day that a new class structure will arise in which social position will go simply to those who grab most in a scramble for the spoils liberally offered by the new environment. And there are other compromises. Her liking for the amenities of freer social intercourse is tempered by her strong sense of propriety, which is in turn rooted in her feeling for tradition. Nor does her acceptance of the ideal of practicality lead to full-scale utilitarianism; for she remains an enthusiastic supporter of the arts and a champion of spiritual values. Finally, against the potentially corrosive effects of democratic ideals on ethical standards, she is the guardian of an orthodox morality and, as her comments on novel-writing in the present text show, sturdily didactic.

To these clues, which lie wholly within *Life in the Clearings,* must be added another, which lies partly within and partly beyond the book. Mrs. Moodie's response to the crucial political events of the time provides perhaps the plainest evidence available of her willingness and her ability to find a new position between opposing influences. When the Upper Canadian rebellion broke out at Montgomery's Tavern in the winter of 1837, Mr. Moodie was among the first of the ''loyal gentlemen'' of the province to volunteer his services in putting down the rebels. Mrs. Moodie, for her part, promptly wrote a poem called **''The Oath of the Canadian Volunteers''** , in which she raised a ''Huzza'' for England and spoke bitterly of the rebels as those ''whose crimes pollute our injured land''. Within a few years, however, she had modified her position, and in *Life in the Clearings* she speaks sympathetically of the rebel cause and represents William Lyon Mackenzie, its fiery leader, as a much maligned man. Yet this change took Mrs. Moodie no further than a position of compromise. On the political front, those who sympathized with Mackenzie's quarrel but refused to back the extreme ''republican'' measures he eventually proposed were known as the Moderate Reformers; and it is the views of these and of their leader, the Hon. Robert Baldwin, that are reflected when the rebellion is touched upon in *Life in the Clearings*. The symbol of the response is a biographical detail: a son born to Mrs. Moodie in 1843 was christened Robert Baldwin.

This much understood, it is no wild fancy to see in *Life in the Clearings* a kind of prophecy. The way of compromise between the Old World and the New, which was Mrs. Moodie's way, was to become the Canadian way. The evidence I have produced is not intended to suggest that this was exclusively a political way or that it invariably meant a simple arithmetical mediation between conservative and radical poles of thought— or, for that matter, that where compromise occurred the conservative pole was invariably British and the radical invariably American. Certainly the way of compromise was to be familiar to the Fathers of Confederation, just as it was to be familiar much later to the ministers of government who were to shape Canada's foreign policy in the twentieth century. . . . But in the sense of a ready-reckoning made between British and American spheres of influence, it was also a way which was to enter into the kind of language spoken by Canadians, the kind (and number) of Royal Commissions they set up, the kind of universities they established, the kind of books they wrote—in fact, into all those aspects of national life which are broadly called cultural. (pp. xviii-xx)

One point remains. To those who ask, as many have done and still do, how a sense of national identity can emerge from a process that seems to be largely a matter of borrowing and imitation, *Life in the Clearings* again has something to say. Granted that the way of compromise points in one direction to dullness, to a lack of enterprise and originality; and granted that this is a direction in which a part of the Canadian character has travelled. Yet it is worth recalling that Susanna Moodie's response was neither passive nor negative. A shift in terms and another glance at *Life in the Clearings* will indicate the more dynamic possibilities contained in this writer's adjustment to a new situation. (pp. xx-xxi)

By 1853 Mrs. Moodie had made some progress towards defining her position as a member of British colonial society on the North American continent. She had taken her bearings back across the Atlantic to the parent culture, and south across the border to American civilization; and through an intelligent use of these bearings, much more reliably than through exposure to a particular physical environment, she had begun to know where she was. It is the first stirrings of a sense of location and identity that sponsor her attack upon the condescending attitude of the British to their colonies, her rejection of the mere thought of annexation to the United States, and her repeated predictions of the future greatness of her new homeland. Patriotic sentiments are numerous in *Life in the Clearings*— many of them, as was to be expected, in praise of the mother country. But a surprising number are linked with the country of Mrs. Moodie's adoption. Here is an early version of Canadian self-determination, a form of nationalism taking shape twenty years before Confederation at a time when nationalism could be little more than a congenial idea. (p. xxi)

> Robert L. McDougall, "Editor's Introduction," in
> Life in the Clearings by Susanna Moodie, edited by
> Robert L. McDougall, 1959. Reprint by Macmillan
> of Canada, 1976, pp. vii-xxiii.

LLOYD M. SCOTT   (essay date 1959)

[*Scott maintains that Moodie's* Roughing It in the Bush *and Traill's* The Backwoods of Canada *constitute "the finest products of the [Canadian] immigrant writers."*]

The genteel class . . . made substantial contributions to [Canada's] early cultural development. The memoirs of Mrs. Moodie and her sister, Mrs. Traill—daughters of a well-to-do Suffolk family—represent the finest products of the immigrant writers. . . . Both wrote hoping to deter others from making like sacrifices in the backwoods, but their homely style and powers

of characterization and description have earned them a far different and more enduring place in Canadian letters than such a narrow purpose would suggest. The two books on which their reputations chiefly rest are now regarded as classic accounts of pioneer life. (p. 57)

Both of these immigrant writers were unconsciously answering Canada's need for a literature, a need of which they often spoke: "Here there are no historical associations, no legendary tales of those that came before us." Of course, Susanna Moodie and Catharine Traill were not conscious artists; they possessed no great genius. Nevertheless their keen observations, their insight into human problems and, perhaps most important of all, their frank self-portraits, have bequeathed us a valuable historical perspective. (p. 68)

> Lloyd M. Scott, "The English Gentlefolk in the Back-
> woods of Canada," in The Dalhousie Review, *Vol.
> 39, No. 1, Spring, 1959, pp. 56-69.*

CARL F. KLINCK   (essay date 1959)

[*In the following excerpt from his review of the 1959 edition of* Life in the Clearings, *Klinck assesses* Roughing It in the Bush *and* Life in the Clearings *as literary works rather than as purely historical accounts.*]

Life in the Clearings is described as a "companion-piece" to *Roughing It in the Bush* because it shows Mrs. Moodie's desire to add her record of the clearings, or growing towns and villages, to her earlier one about the bush, or backwoods. Is it, however, the same kind of book? Is *Roughing It in the Bush* a novel, and is *Life in the Clearings* something else?

These books owe their preservation to public interest in the social life of the pioneers, and Mrs. Moodie is established as typical of the gentlewoman of Upper Canada. Her historical worth has thus obscured her literary position, and her individuality has not been sufficiently recognized, although her curiosity, prejudices, circumstances, and especially her characterization of herself among her neighbours make her readily distinguishable even from her sister, Mrs. Traill. Her book, *Roughing It in the Bush,* has also been regarded as representative of colonial history rather than of colonial literature. Yet it is both unique and illustrative of the practices in writing which prevailed in the Canadas during the first half of the nineteenth century. Mrs. Moodie wrote within the current fashions, as she knew them in the colonies, and, in doing so, found her own way, shaping a form of fiction which incorporated and transcended the raw facts and ideas drawn from life around her. (p. 76)

Although chronologically later in Mrs Moodie's life, and in some ways more mature or "civilized," the *Clearings* looks like a trial effort, not like a sequel. It is made of similar stuff, including remainders from the earlier volume. But it is not self-contained; it proceeds without imaginative cohesion, the lack of which is felt in spite of a mechanical scheme of travel through towns from Belleville to Niagara and in spite of the predictable flow of Mrs. Moodie's admirable convictions. She has put on a one-man show of the various materials and tendencies out of which her masterpiece grew. But the prize exhibit hangs in another gallery.

The personal and sociological values of *Life in the Clearings* will not be reviewed here; they can be found on page after page of the text with genuinely entertaining illustrations drawn from experience and gossip. Professor McDougall's introductory essay is an excellent guide to this book and to Mrs. Moodie herself [see excerpt dated 1959]. He has brought us to the point, we think, where a study of this author's literary theory and practice, and a critical biography are not only possible, but are urgently required. (p. 77)

> *Carl F. Klinck, "A Gentlewoman of Upper Canada," in* Canadian Literature, *No. 1, Summer, 1959, pp. 75-7.*

CARL F. KLINCK (essay date 1962)

[*Klinck examines Moodie's use of both fictional and autobiographical elements in* Roughing It in the Bush, *claiming that she "dramatized her vision of herself."*]

[Mrs Moodie's] procedure in compiling her material for **Roughing It** and her positive intentions with regard to this book have not been fully determined. Professor Robert L. McDougall, in an excellent introduction to a recent reprint of the **Clearings**, observes that the first (the Cobourg farm) chapters of **Roughing It** deal with "the shock to Mrs Moodie's sensibilities of living in a shack" and coping with her Yankee neighbours [see excerpt dated 1959]. The later (the Otonabee) chapters deal with "man's primitive struggle against drought, storm, pestilence, fire and sickness." If any chapters are to be regarded as expendable, the second portion may be curtailed, for here the direct force of experience is not as powerfully conveyed. One does not know how Mrs Moodie would have reduced the size of her book—if, indeed, she would have consented to do so. Some of her chapters were the result of recollection in tranquillity; perhaps all of them were. There is no way of telling how much in any given chapter is due to experienced fact and how much to literary artifice. She did not pour out her confessions; she dramatized her vision of herself.

This involved more fictional latitude and a closer approach to fictional form than one would have found in the travel and immigrant literature of the 1820's, 1830's, and 1840's. In **Roughing It,** the Upper Canadian development of such literature toward stable literary forms reaches one of its plateaus. On the primitive levels there were "statistical" accounts and running narratives making a bid for the reader's interest because of apparent accuracy in reporting facts—in this case, basic data about Upper Canada. Added attractions were to be found in descriptions, brief essays, and anecdotes. All of these involved interpretation, and interpretation could go to the very borders of fanciful invention. As a later refinement, anecdotes could be fashioned into sketches, and a book like **Roughing It** might be made entirely of sketches.

Such an indigenous development undoubtedly occurred; and, within it, **Roughing It** represented a level beyond Mrs Traill's *The Backwoods of Canada.* . . . Superficially these books were similar. . . . Mrs Traill's presentation was natural, original, and skilful; the autobiographical elements were not obtrusive; the author seemed helpful, unassuming, unimpassioned, devoted to life and nature as she found it. Her style resembled the unaffected conversation of a truly well bred woman. She was on her way to fame as a naturalist; but her sister, Mrs Moodie, practising a less admirable style wavering between plain speaking and rhetoric, was on her way to fiction, a further stage in the growth of immigrant literature in the Upper Canadian environment.

The sketches in **Roughing It in the Bush** were written by a novelist. . . . Mrs Moodie, as a contributor to the Canadian

Literary Garland, was a professional writer of instalment fiction. From 1839 to 1851 she was the *Garland*'s principal author, who turned out novels of English middle-class manners and exhibited a flair for eccentricities, Dickensian humour, excursions into pathos, hosts of minor characters, and heroines of rank and sensitivity sharing some of her own qualities. (pp. xi-xiii)

Roughing It in the Bush was not officially one of her *Garland* novels, but it bore on its title page these lines:

> I sketch from Nature, and the picture's true;
> Whate'er the subject, whether grave or gay,
> Painful experience in a distant land
> Made it mine own.

The early editors of **Roughing It** saw the book in this context—in spite of Mrs Moodie's underlining of its utility as a warning to gentlefolk. The London publisher called it a "glowing narrative of personal incident and suffering," interesting and "pathetic" in its "delineations of fortitude under privation." The New York reviser, "C. F. B.," praised it for "scenes and adventures . . . so full of freshness, truth, and humour"; for the "healthy tone . . . that pervades its entertaining pages"; and for its profitable lessons. His judgement was summarized in one sentence. "Mrs. Moodie is a true heroine, and her simple narrative is a genuine romance, which has all the interest of an imaginative creation."

This shrewd observation provides an explanation of the book's nature, its enduring interest, and its essential canon. Its unity is found in terms satisfactory in its own time and allowable in ours—one character is central, and that character is the author herself. "Genuine romance" is a controversial classification, and an alternative phrase like "apprenticeship novel" may not be better; but a certain core of meaning is there. Middle-class England and America had found a substitute for chivalric romances: the modern knight could be any person seeking a way to live in the midst of social dislocation, philosophical nullity, economic slavery, decline of wealth, or impending deterioration. Through long practice Mrs Moodie knew how to put a piece of herself into such stories of adjustment to life. **Roughing It** was wholly autobiographical, her own book; she was the author-apprentice-heroine. Everything pointed to her trials and her (partial) salvation. The amusing imperfect people around her were "touched up" to be foils, revealing the central figure who could bear comparison with impunity. Sharing in all the actions, and progressively enlarging the image of herself, she gave a pattern of movement to the whole book. The principal structural force was anticipation, the reader's knowledge that she had a large fund of ironic observations—the certainty that she would soon come up with new characters and more anecdotes. Limitations of space alone would cut them short. Through them, as through fiction, there would be a lively re-creation of the past. (pp. xiii-xiv)

> *Carl F. Klinck, "Editor's Introduction," in* Roughing It in the Bush; or, Forest Life in Canada *by Susanna Moodie, McClelland and Stewart Limited, 1962, pp. ix-xiv.*

CLARA THOMAS (essay date 1966)

[*Noting Moodie's frequent and varied use of humor, Thomas praises* Roughing It in the Bush *and* Life in the Clearings, *but laments Moodie's failure to develop her talents in her later works.*]

Susanna was, in fact, not a diarist, not a writer of calm expository prose, certainly not an instructress of prospective emigrants, but a gifted recorder of character, dialogue and incident, especially of a humorous nature. Her early life in Canada made a great impact on her creative powers, extending talents that she had exercised before—character drawing and the record of incident—and releasing another that she had scarcely practised—the ability to see with a humorist's slant and to communicate her amusement to others. She never lived comfortably with her comic vision, however, or rightly estimated its potential in her writing. In *Life in the Clearings* . . . , she confesses embarrassment at her life-long tendency to laughter: "I wish nature had not given me such a quick perception of the ridiculous—such a perverse inclination to laugh in the wrong place; for though one cannot help deriving from it a wicked enjoyment, it is a very troublesome gift, and very difficult to conceal." (p. 58)

Susanna had written much fiction before coming to Canada. It had always been conventional, moral, sentimental, having to do with heroes, heroines, and villains of her own or higher social rank. In Canada she was thrust into the company of all sorts of people, few of whom were of her own social class and all of whom seemed different, often totally reprehensible, but almost always amusing. These people she could write of without inhibition and she captured a whole gallery of them, in the very accents in which she heard them speak. From the ship's captain to "the little stumpy Man," *Roughing it* is made memorable by these people and by their reported talk. Old Satan, Tom Wilson, Betty Fye, John Monaghan, Jacob and Malcolm come alive and occupy centre stage for a time; many others are recorded, as are the workers at the logging-bee, in vignettes only. In total, the book is alive with their many presences. There are a few persons she meets whose stories seem to demand her well-practised sentimental vein: the dying girl, Phoebe, is one of these, as is the strange, melancholy hunter, Brian. Even in these tales, however, she transcends her own sentimental convention as she sketches from the life.

In the service of her sketches, Susanna is recklessly self-revealing. It was natural for her to be the centre of her narrative, as Catharine is the narrator and centre of [*The Backwoods of Canada*]. But unlike her sister, Susanna, centre stage, becomes one of her own "characters": a prejudiced, class-conscious, ill-equipped pioneer, sometimes the butt of her own stories, sometimes the heroine, passionately revolting against her circumstances while slowly and uncomfortably adapting to them. Catharine quietly states the achievement, whether it be confidence in an assured social position or satisfactory relations with servants; Susanna dramatizes the struggle, with herself a storm centre. (pp. 58-9)

Roughing it in the Bush, as we know it, is an uneasy amalgam of Susanna's fictional talent, her keenly felt and humorously observed experiences, and her cautionary admonitions. On publication it was deservedly enjoyed; it was also resented by those who felt that the conditions which Mrs. Moodie described had passed away, and that, therefore, her representations were misleading, or, at the least, snobbish. It must certainly be admitted that Susanna had not been careful enough in editing her earlier work before its collected publication. She made amends, however, by the speedy preparation and publication of *Life in the Clearings* . . . , with an introduction which is both an apology for offence given and an explanation of the position taken [see excerpt dated 1852]. She reiterates her warning to the gentleman-emigrant: "let him leave to the hardy labourer

the place assigned to him by Providence, now undertaken, upon limited means, the task of pioneer in the great wilderness." But she balances this with an admission of the great gaps in her experience at the time of writing the sketches for *Roughing it in the Bush,* and with a statement of gratitude to Canada, the "country of my adoption—the great foster-mother of that portion of the human family whose fatherland, however dear to them, is unable to supply them with bread." Her earlier portraits of the rascally Yankee settlers who were at once the bane of her pioneer days and the source for some of her best sketches are now balanced by a tribute to "our enterprising, intelligent American neighbours." Their influence, she admits, has helped to produce a successful amalgamation of classes in Canada which she now finds desirable.

She based her sketches in *Life in the Clearings* on the framework of a travel narrative, a trip from Belleville to Niagara Falls. This structural device is not strong enough to support and dominate the sketches, and the book is memorable for the assembling of its parts rather than for the totality of its whole. Catharine Traill's powers of observing and reporting were predominantly exercised on her natural environment: Susanna's eye was always on individuals, and from them to their, and to her, social environment. Her descriptions of the trip itself read like romantic and sentimental "set pieces": the blue water glides by, the wooded hills recede in the distance, at the Falls "the wide world of tumbling waters are flashing and foaming in the sunlight." But the people she meets, the conversations she reports, the humorous anecdotes she tells, with herself as the central figure, are as vivid and persuasively "real" as the best of the Bush sketches, though marked by a more tolerant and less satiric tone.

Much of *Life in the Clearings* is, from our standpoint, social history, enlivened and authenticated by the presence of Susanna Moodie as its narrator. The chapters on "Camp Meetings," "Education," the "Lunatic Asylum" and the "Provincial Agricultural Show," the forerunner of the Toronto Exhibition, are documentary accounts of aspects of Ontario life in the mid-nineteenth century and as such alone are to be valued. That they were recorded by a contemporary, a practised observer, and a writer with twenty years' experience of Canada is a large bonus of good fortune. Furthermore, in this work Susanna is determinedly positive and factual in her approach, at the same time offering us the interest and vigour of her opinions. She now speaks, not from a position of passionate reaction to a new and shocking environment, but confidently, secure in her status as a Canadian, the wife of an official of the courts, and a professional woman of letters; in none of these rôles does she wish to be misunderstood.

She believed that all writing, and particularly fiction, the work of "the despised and reprobated novelist," must and will subserve a moral purpose. "I look upon these authors as heaven-inspired teachers," she proclaims, thereby establishing a didactic purpose for her own work and explaining to us the inhibiting of certain of her own talents. She deprecates her own tendency to laughter, and takes care to announce in this book that certain anecdotes she reports, in a tone of humorous satire against the pretensions of the ignorant, were "told her by another." On the other hand, her admiration for the work of nineteenth-century novelists, particularly Dickens and Thomas Hood, the "humane men" who command the reader to "step with them into these dirty abodes of guilt and wretchedness, and see what crime really is" encouraged the development of her own talent toward realistic writing. The chapters on the

A portrait of Moodie by Thomas Cheesman.

prison and its inmates, the lunatic asylum and its patients, and particularly her story of Grace Marks the murderess, are blood-chilling in their effect. Her talent toward the realistic-naturalistic portrayal of the suffering and degradation she deplored was a formidable one; its lack of development in her later writing is, like the lack of development of her comic and anecdotal veins, regrettable to us. To Susanna Moodie, however, both what she wrote and the way she wrote were dictated by her time and place in society, her reading public, and her own conception of her function as an authoress.

After *Life in the Clearings,* she wrote many novels, but in them she reverted to the romantic and sentimental vein that she had practised even before coming to Canada, and that had been the style of much of her *Literary Garland* work. *Flora Lyndsay, Mark Hurdlestone, The World Before Them, Matrimonial Speculations,* and *Dorothy Chance* are among her later works; most of them were first published in England by Bentley; some were reprinted in the United States. . . . All were directed toward an English reader—the polite young lady and her eminently Victorian mother. There was in Canada, as Susanna Moodie well knew, little or no possibility of publication and an extremely small reading public. She was never without the necessity of writing to augment a small family income and in general her readers concurred in the admonition she reports from one English lady: "Don't fill your letters home with descriptions of Canada. Who, in *England,* thinks anything of *Canada?*" Prudently, she complied. (pp. 70-2)

Clara Thomas, "The Strickland Sisters," in The Clear Spirit: Twenty Canadian Women and Their Times, *edited by Mary Quayle Innis, University of Toronto Press, 1966. pp. 42-73.*

A. CHARLES von GUTTENBERG (essay date 1969)

[*In this assessment of the merits and flaws of* Roughing It in the Bush *and* Life in the Clearings, *Guttenberg attempts to define Moodie's place in nineteenth-century Canadian literature.*]

Despite her tolerance and perseverance in the face of countless disappointments, and those largely stemming from the contrast between a comparatively barbarous way of life and the ordered social pattern from which she had removed, [Mrs. Moodie] was too much the narrow provincial gentlewoman of early nineteenth-century England. She owned too many prejudices to record her history of the new undertaking with the fully impartial eye and deeply discerning sensibility necessary to fix a perpetual memorial of this new kind of social experiment. To put it quite simply, she lacked the vision to glean all the relevant particulars, the greater majority she did observe having obvious reference to the amenities of her class in England. Such commentary is not intended to frighten readers away from what is obviously one of the better works of Canadian literature of the nineteenth century; it is intended, however, as an introduction to the serious treatment of Canadian writing, an attempt to regard Canadian authorship with no gentler or less firm an eye than one would allow any other work of art. (p. 108)

The advantages of deciding on one's genre before writing are illustrated by the failure of *Roughing it in the Bush* to be any of history, memoir, autobiography, travel book, anthropology or sociology. It is not the first because of the omission of many necessary items—a discussion of political issues, for example; as anthropology or sociology it lacks the wide and painstaking scientific treatment of details, and a full enough view of cultural phenomena—as the chapter on the Indians shows. It is not autobiography because it too often deviates into incidental sketches to the forfeit of great parts of her own story, and there is little attempt at self-analysis of mental and emotional character. And there is not enough travelling done for a travel book. So far, these are not defects, since they were not part of Mrs. Moodie's intention; we can take it that if she had any genre specifically in mind it was that of a memoir.

It comes closest, in fact, to a memoir, a sketch of events without a pressing need for their consistent examination from certain specific points of view other than that of the idiosyncracy of the author. Yet for one thing, it lacks the consistent literary style of a memoir, both in the intrusion of her husband's two chapters, and in the absence of a highly individualised approach to events. One suspects that she lacked the literary force of personality necessary to colour all she saw with her own human light; it is coloured instead with the light of a unit—an exceptional one, to be sure—of a social class. The literary quality of the work as a whole is affected by these disadvantages: it is a highly competent piece of realistic writing—except where her educated sense of propriety skirts certain essential aspects of the life she is observing—set off by a few powerful passages of romantic nature description. Her talent was much less for analytic enquiry than for surface description, yet even the latter loses power to some extent through a lack of form. All writing is, or should be initiated for some purpose, and purpose demands form. Mrs. Moodie, by compounding a series of chronologically arranged sketches, sacrifices through lack of structural integration any marked literary distinction. There is a psychological reason for this, for her domestic memoir divides attention between the mind of a middle-class English gentlewoman of that time, and the conditions of life in the colony. She has been caught between the two stools of realistic reportage of settler life and psychological self-portraiture, based in this case on a radical change in the individual due to altered environment. Not that she had any idea of the latter as a literary purpose for her work: did she not use an injunction to realism as a motto for the book: 'I sketch from Nature, and the picture's true'—and, in *Life in the Clearings,* defend novel writing on realistic and didactic grounds?

But the divided treatment is there, to add to the charm of a literary curiosity and to detract from the formal perfection. We must also remember her declared intention in writing the book: to deter 'well-educated people, about to settle in this colony, from entering upon a life for which they were totally unfitted by their previous pursuits and habits'. Fortunately Mrs. Moodie was not completely successful in this latter respect, having underestimated the hunger of the spirit for personal freedom and a 'second chance'; and she had allowed that a judicious choice of location (i.e. not in the backwoods) could lead to material and social blessings. (pp. 108-10)

[*Life in the Clearings*] was purposely written to picture 'the present state of society in the colony, and to point out its increasing prosperity and commercial advantages'. *Roughing it* had sufficiently counteracted the false stories which had been circulated in Britain to encourage emigration to Canada, and the new book was much lighter in tone, if not as stirring as that dealing with isolated bush life. (p. 117)

But *Life in the Clearings* is not the book that *Roughing it* . . . was, and the explanation is to be found in the given degree of talent and in the early upbringing of the author. There were several long and very bad novels which followed, none of them readable today, although unfortunately parts of them were relished by readers of the *Literary Garland.* Mrs. Moodie is, in fact, illustrative of a paradox obtaining in many writers of her day: the combination of the pious didactic wish to 'sketch from Nature' with a patent unreality of sentiment. It runs through all her work in varying degrees, and with the exception of her writings on Canada the unreality of sentiment vitiates almost everything she wrote. In those two works, however, and especially in the earlier, we can only suppose that the soul-shaking shock of adverse and primitive conditions such as drove her to night-long tears over an extended period, cracked her sheltered middle-class veneer and sentimentality to such an extent that, in combination with sensitive nature appreciation under ideal conditions, reality was directly apprehended. Aware that serious criticisms had been levelled at her by various newspaper critics for her adverse account of settler life in *Roughing it,* she reasserted her realistic purpose and what had been her intention there, to uphold the idea of a 'Commonwealth of intellect' while affirming that equality of station is an unreal dream. She managed, too, to make a finally reiterated point of desired British sovereignty for Canada. These were typical views held by the average, enlightened, formerly middle-class British settler in the Canadas, and it is this very representativeness of Mrs. Moodie's work that constitutes one of its important values. (pp. 117-18)

Mrs. Moodie was a tireless supporter of Imperial sovereignty, and it was doubtless well nourished through the desperate years of homesickness when she wrote so many of the 'exile' poems of *Roughing it in the Bush.* Subtitled ''**A Canadian Song**'', and set to music by her flautist husband, the following must represent the many scattered throughout her work voicing the painful nostalgia of those who, at least during their early years on the land, could only regard themselves as unwilling exiles:

> Oh! can you leave your native land
> An exile's bride to be;
> Your mother's home, and cheerful hearth
> To tempt the main with me;

Across the wide and stormy sea
To trace our foaming track,
And know the wave that bears us on
Will ne'er convey us back?
And can you in Canadian woods
With me the harvest bind,
Nor feel one lingering, sad regret
For all you leave behind?

That is the authentic note of the pre-Confederation exile, a ballad note, simple, stark, yearning, possessing a quiet plaintive beauty of its own only possible in a direct transcription of experience. Reminiscence is a dominant characteristic of nineteenth century Canadian literature to Confederation; as there was little social integration of groups or even families, so their lives were fragmentary and they therefore nostalgically orientated themselves towards an earlier period of wholeness in the home country. Mrs. Moodie's Canadian writing is in the main stream of this tradition, but she enriches that tradition—and this is her considerable additional strength—in her loving depiction of the Canadian scene, character, and way of life. (pp. 118-19)

> *A. Charles von Guttenberg, "Susanna Moodie," in his* Early Canadian Art and Literature, Europe Printing Estb., *1969, pp. 99-119.*

MARGARET ATWOOD   (essay date 1970)

[*Atwood is a contemporary Canadian poet and novelist known for her spare, direct, and controlled style. Atwood often acts as spokesperson for her native Canada, and many of her writings feature a search for identity coupled with a journey motif, especially a journey into the wilderness. These elements figure prominently in her* The Journals of Susanna Moodie, *a collection of poems that recreates scenes from Moodie's life. In the following excerpt from the afterword to that work, Atwood sketches her response to Moodie's writings.*]

These poems were generated by a dream. I dreamt I was watching an opera I had written about Susanna Moodie. I was alone in the theatre; on the empty white stage, a single figure was singing.

Although I had heard of Susanna Moodie I had never read her two books about Canada, *Roughing It in the Bush* and *Life in the Clearings.* When I did read them I was disappointed. The prose was discursive and ornamental and the books had little shape: they were collections of disconnected anecdotes. The only thing that held them together was the personality of Mrs Moodie, and what struck me most about this personality was the way in which it reflects many of the obsessions still with us.

If the national mental illness of the United States is megalomania, that of Canada is paranoid schizophrenia. Mrs Moodie is divided down the middle: she praises the Canadian landscape but accuses it of destroying her; she dislikes the people already in Canada but finds in people her only refuge from the land itself; she preaches progress and the march of civilization while brooding elegiacally upon the destruction of the wilderness; she delivers optimistic sermons while showing herself to be fascinated with deaths, murders, the criminals in Kingston Penitentiary and the incurably insane in the Toronto lunatic asylum. She claims to be an ardent Canadian patriot while all the time she is standing back from the country and criticizing it as though she were a detached observer, a stranger. Perhaps that is the way we still live. We are all immigrants to this place even if we were born here: the country is too big for anyone to inhabit completely, and in the parts unknown to us we move in fear, exiles and invaders. This country is something that must be chosen—it is so easy to leave—and if we do choose it we are still choosing a violent duality. (p. 62)

> Margaret Atwood, in an afterword in her The Journals of Susanna Moodie, *Oxford University Press, Canadian Branch, 1970, pp. 62-4.*

RONALD SUTHERLAND (essay date 1971)

[*Sutherland detects a "disconcerting . . . undertone of racism" in Moodie's writings.*]

Mrs. Moodie was manifestly convinced of the superiority of the particular class of English gentlefolk to which she belonged, and she makes the idea clear in passages such as the following in her book *Roughing It in the Bush:*

> The hand that has long held the sword, and been accustomed to receive implicit obedience from those under its control, is seldom adapted to wield the spade and guide the plough, or try its strength against the stubborn trees of the forest. Nor will such persons submit cheerfully to the saucy familiarity of servants, who, republicans in spirit, think themselves as good as their employers.
>
> (p. 35)

Moodie makes the same point many times, always carefully differentiating between "superiors" and "inferiors". She speaks of the "vicious, uneducated barbarians, who form the surplus of over-populated European countries." At one point she observes: "The semi-barbarous Yankee squatters, who had 'left their country for their country's good,' and by whom we were surrounded in our first settlement, detested us. . . ." And to this last remark of Susanna Moodie's, one is tempted to reply "No Wonder." In many respects her classification of people is reminiscent of Samuel Richardson in *Sir Charles Grandison,* where he divided his characters into three categories: men, women and Italians. Only for Moodie the classes would be English gentlemen, English ladies and barbarians.

Of course, her standards for herself were exceedingly high. Here she is admitting to an "unpardonable weakness":

> In spite of my boasted fortitude—and I think my powers of endurance have been tried to the utmost since my sojourn in this country—the rigour of the climate subdued my proud, independent English spirit, and I actually shamed my womanhood, and cried with the cold. Yes, I ought to blush at confessing such unpardonable weakness; but I was foolish and inexperienced, and unaccustomed to the yoke.
>
> (pp. 35-6)

After having read the works of Susanna Moodie, one is left with the undeniable impression that everybody—Irish, French-Canadian, Scottish, Indian, lowborn English and especially American—who is not of her particular caste has been hopelessly predestined to insignificance, *ipso facto.* Moreover, her attitude, which appears to be essentially unconscious and without malicious intent, led her to remarkable conclusions on occasion. Speaking of the cholera doctor Stephen Ayres, for instance, she comments: "A friend of mine, in this town, has

an original portrait of this notable empiric—this man sent from heaven. The face is rather handsome, but has a keen, designing expression, and is evidently that of an American from its complexion and features." (p. 36)

Now it may appear to some that I have been looking at the writings of Susanna Moodie with a magnifying glass, considering that she did no more than echo the accepted English spirit of her time, but certainly through a magnifying glass is the way Mrs. Moodie consistently looked at herself. I do not deny the merits of her literary achievement—her keen eye for appropriate detail, her ear for dialect, her capacity to capture scenes and moods. Nevertheless, throughout her work, as throughout the works of Ralph Connor, to name one other obvious example, there is always the disconcerting body-odour of race, the undertone of racism. Not the screeching, messianic racism of a Houston Stewart Chamberlain, the man who talked with demons and who sowed the field which Adolf Hitler was to harvest, but something perhaps almost as malignant in the long run, because it is in the form of a deeply ingrained pattern of thought, a conviction which may even be unconsciously held. Furthermore, it is the very conviction which in various guises has haunted and continues to haunt a nation which, if it is going to survive, must perforce develop a *modus vivendi* for people of different ethnic origins.

Moodie herself, it should be pointed out, merely chanted a common tendency of many nations, a tendency which was perhaps an inevitable adjunct to strong cultural identification, a tendency which in most circumstances was probably not of great harm or consequence. What is important to us here is that the Moodie attitude has not died a natural death, but continues to infect the thinking of many English Canadians, and that in the particular circumstances of modern Canada it could be of vital consequence. (pp. 36-7)

> Ronald Sutherland, "The Body-Odour of Race," in his Second Image: Comparative Studies in Québec/Canadian Literature, *New Press, 1971, pp. 28-59.*

R. D. MacDONALD (essay date 1972)

[*MacDonald examines the underlying design and purpose of* Roughing It in the Bush. *While highlighting the superficial contradictions in the work's style, MacDonald argues that* Roughing It in the Bush *is unified by its representations of nature.*]

Since few readers have seriously considered Susanna Moodie's *Roughing it in the Bush* as a work of art, I have had misgivings about my own exploration of the design underlying this work. Moreover, I have had to admit that Mrs. Moodie herself seems oblivious of her own purpose or of the pattern developing within her work. Says she: "It is not my intention to give a regular history of our residence in the bush, but merely to present to my readers such events as may serve to illustrate a life in the woods." A modest intention indeed! All that she seemingly requires of herself is to make her experience real. Notice that she has freed herself from the requirements of a single thesis and from the demands of a single chronology.

As Mrs. Moodie recounts the years of 1836 and 37, her purpose shifts to "illustrate the necessity of a perfect and childlike reliance upon the mercies of God. . . ." But after she has descended from her experience of the sublime and from theological speculation, she becomes wholly absorbed in the particulars of pioneer life; her book begins to read more and more like a handyman's guide, a how-to-make-do book. Her purpose now seems that of the seasoned guide who would show potential emigrants how to adapt to the bush.... In the last chapter, however, after having asserted her own contentment in the bush ("I was contented to live and die in obscurity"), after having nostalgically described the pleasantness of their leavetaking, the cordial hospitality afforded them while on the road, the beauty and good humour of their ride itself—after all this, Mrs. Moodie suddenly ends the story and then reverts to the purpose expressed in her preface:

> To the poor, industrious working man it presents many advantages; to the poor gentleman, *none!* The former works hard, puts up with coarse, scanty fare, and submits, with good grace, to hardships that would kill a domesticated animal at home. . . .

In her last words the bush is named a "prison-house" and the life there simply one of "toil" and "suffering".

How is one to read such a contradictory work? Is it best simply to use *Roughing it in the Bush* as a historian might, i.e. by looking through Susanna Moodie's book on to the 1830's of Upper Canada or of the British empire? Is it best, if one is to look at the work itself, simply to touch and go, to point out Mrs. Moodie's ironic narrative voice and then slide away from the book by comparing this voice to Jane Austen's? Or is it best finally, simply to accept *Roughing it in the Bush* as a work roughly hewn, an anecdotal travelogue, a work in which experience is half digested, a work digressive and discontinuous, a work filled with vigorous, humorous but rather pointless character sketches?

To answer these questions, I will argue first that Mrs. Moodie's representation of nature does unify *Roughing it in the Bush,* and secondly that the design of the chapters emphasizes this representation of nature. Even here the book may appear confused: it is easy to construe Susanna Moodie carrying across the Atlantic romantic notions of nature which are inappropriate to her new setting. It becomes clear quickly, however, that her romantic ecstasies are not singleminded, or naive, at least in so far as Moodie-the-writer re-creates her earlier experience. In her first description of the serene and silent beauty of the shores of the St. Lawrence, it is obvious that the writer in retrospect has so framed the scene that the reader must suspect ironic implication: picturesque beauty, one is led to believe, is not reality.... As the ship's party approaches Grosse Isle, the pastoral view of nature begins to dissipate: "It was four o'clock when we landed on the rocks, which the rays of an intensely scorching sun had rendered so hot that I could scarcely place my foot upon them." Moreover the unpleasant effect of the place upon emigrants is suddenly made clear:

> The people who covered the island appeared perfectly destitute of shame, or even a sense of common decency. Many were almost naked, still more but partially clothed. We turned in disgust from the revolting scene, but were unable to leave the spot until the captain had satisfied a noisy group of his people, who were demanding a supply of stores.

The spirit of the place becomes a disease: even Scots "who while on board ship had conducted themselves with the greatest propriety, and appeared the most quiet, orderly set of people in the world, no sooner set foot upon the island than they became infected by the same spirit of insubordination and misrule, and were just as insolent and noisy as the rest."

Again, as Mrs. Moodie describes Quebec, the same bursting of the romantic dream occurs. The "grandeur" and the "picture perfect" quality of the landscape, and the sense that this landscape is the work of a "Divine Originator" so affects her that she reports:

> my spirit fell prostrate before it, and I melted involuntarily into tears. Yes, regardless of the eager crowds around me, I leant upon the side of the vessel and cried like a child—not tears of sorrow, but a gush from the heart of pure and unalloyed delight. I heard not the many voices murmuring in my ears—I saw not the anxious beings that thronged our narrow deck—my soul at the moment was alone with God.

If this passage is not bathetic, the one following closely upon it is, as Mrs. Moodie chauvinistically prophesies that only a great nation could rise from such a great landscape. Then to make matters worse, after apparently coming back to herself, she abruptly states: "But I have wandered away from my subject into the regions of thought and must again descend to common workaday realities." On this lower level, what follows is a satirical account of the vainglorious expectations of the working class immigrants. Moreover from the first hand accounts of those who have visited Quebec, Moodie suggests that man destroys the perfection of nature—a view not entirely contrary to the Wordsworthian or romantic notions which she has carried across the Atlantic. (pp. 20-3)

Romantic anticipation and disenchantment, high style and low, continue to alternate. But this anticipation and high style become a smaller and smaller part of the book. In part, anticipation is replaced by nostalgia for the idyllic British countryside.... Nature is remembered as the "indulgent mother, holding out her living arms to enfold to her bosom her erring but devoted child." By what seems a sheer effort of will, however, Mrs. Moodie turns from her lament for things past. Still avoiding the present, she prophesies a glorious future for Canada, the land now of her future, her children's future and the land of her children's graves. Typically, however, this chapter falls away from this "high style" to the ludicrous incongruities of Tom Wilson remembered, to the low reality of the crowded immigrant boat, and finally to the droll but foreboding grumbling of Tom Wilson, who has preceded the Moodies to the New World. (p. 23)

This alternation of the high and low may lead the reader to assert that Susanna Moodie's vision was contradictory, her style uneven. But as I have said, the low is usually implied in the high or else the low frames the high. Moreover, the high mimetic mode becomes a smaller and smaller part of the book as the story becomes more and more a catalogue of narrowly averted disasters and as the story implies that in Canada, at least, nature is a heartless tyrant who grinds down the fine edges of the British gentleman. The plot itself, (as it moves in circular fashion from British village, to the Lower St. Lawrence, to Lake Ontario, to the deep bush, and finally back to the Canadian counterpart of British civilization, the village) implies surely that the Canadian bush or Canadian nature is not suitable to the Moodie family.

On a smaller scale, the arrangement of chapters, especially the alternation of episodic chapters and chapters of character sketch, again suggest a single significant pattern within *Roughing it in the Bush:* the character sketches may seem at first to have no function, beyond merely presenting interesting personalities, but these chapters act as watersheds between the flows of action, and more importantly they imply failure, if the Moodies stay in the bush. (p. 24)

One might argue that *Roughing it in the Bush* is nicely rounded off, as in the last two chapters the circle of events is completed: the Moodies have left civilization, settled in the bush and now return to civilization. . . . But the last two chapters move in an uneven fashion, beginning with elevated speculations about intuition and then shifting abruptly to the raw chunks of Mrs. Moodie's undigested experience of the bush. This first paragraph is in her high speculative style:

> The holy and mysterious nature of man is yet hidden from himself; he is still a stranger to the movements of that inner life, and knows little of its capabilities and powers. A purer religion, a higher standard of moral and intellectual training, may in time reveal all this. Man still remains a half-reclaimed savage; the leaven of Christianity is slowly and surely working its way, but it has not yet changed the whole lump, or transformed the deformed into the beauteous child of God. Oh, for that glorious day! It is coming. The dark clouds of humanity are already tinged with the golden radiance of the dawn, but the sun of righteousness has not yet arisen upon the world with healing on his wings: the light of truth still struggles in the womb of darkness, and man stumbles on to the fulfilment of his sublime and mysterious destiny.

The very next paragraph reads like the diary of an Ontario farmer totally absorbed in the particulars of his life:

> This spring I was not a little puzzled how to get in the crops. I still continued so weak that I was quite unable to assist in the field, and my good old Jenny was sorely troubled with inflamed feet, which required constant care. At this juncture, a neighbouring settler, who had recently come among us, offered to put in my small crop of peas, potatoes, and oats, in all not comprising more than eight acres, if I would lend him my oxen to log-up a large fallow of ten acres and put in his own crops. Trusting to his fair dealing, I consented to this arrangement; but he took advantage of my isolated position, and not only logged-up his fallow, but put in all his spring crops before he sowed an acre of mine. The oxen were worked down so low that they were almost unfit for use, and my crops were put in so late, and with such little care, that they all proved a failure. I should have felt this loss more severely had it happened in any previous year; but I had ceased to feel that deep interest in the affairs of the farm from a sort of conviction in my own mind that it would not long remain my home.

Perhaps this kind of unevenness is to be excused in travel or frontier literature, but as I have already suggested, the very last paragraph of the book follows illogically from the previous paragraphs. Mrs. Moodie warns the emigrant gentleman to avoid settling in the bush, yet just before this, she has been describing the beauty of the winter sleigh ride, the pleasant

leavetaking from their neighbours, and the warm hospitality of the innkeepers who shelter the Moodies on their trip to Belleville. Thus though the reader is perhaps prepared for the closing of a circular plot, he is startled at the sudden and contradictory warning which ends the book.

Recognizing the discontinuity within these last paragraphs, one should not forget the pattern that does integrate the book—the catalogue of narrowly averted disasters which increasingly imply failure for the Moodies if they do not leave the bush, and the cyclical plot (village, bush, village) which suggests that they cannot continue living in the bush. The book is also significantly tied together by those transitional chapters, those watershed chapters, which are comprised of character sketches. Each sketch is an ominous picture of the British gentleman who fails in the bush.

Tom Wilson may be seen merely as a humorous eccentric, but he really serves a larger purpose, for the impractical, absent-minded Tom, a caricature of the British gentleman, is totally incapable of coping with the bush. He fails, and his failure foreshadows Moodie's failure. (pp. 26-8)

At first reading, Brian the Still Hunter, may appear as no more than an interesting character, a Canadian counterpart of the American Natty Bumpo, the isolated gentleman of the woods who sees the woods as God's temple and who in his theological musings seems as much mystic as woodsman. But Mrs. Moodie's sketch of Brian is not a comforting one. How can one man be so violent and so gentle? This seems to be the question she is asking. . . . In his eccentricity, Brian is a mad version of the British gentleman who has gone native, who has been swallowed up by the bush, while somehow retaining the courtesy of a gentleman. His madness surely is an extension of Tom Wilson's eccentricity, and his failure a foreshadowing of the Moodies' possible end. (pp. 28-9)

Thus, despite the unevenness of Susanna Moodie's style, her contradictory set of purposes, and the anecdotal fragmentation of her story, a basic pattern unfolds in *Roughing it in the Bush*. The movement is from romantic anticipation to disillusionment, from nature as beautiful and benevolent to nature as a dangerous taskmaster. The story moves from her experience of the sublime to her catalogue of near disasters. What remains constant is Mrs. Moodie's viewpoint, an ironic and skeptical retrospection, which from the first pages brings into question the heady optimism of the emigrant. The character sketches are constant too as they imply that the British gentleman must fail in the bush. Susanna Moodie's basic fable warns "Beware!" (p. 30)

> *R. D. MacDonald, "Design and Purpose," in Ca-
> nadian Literature, No. 51, Winter, 1972, pp. 20-31.*

CARL BALLSTADT (essay date 1972)

[*Using as his starting point a series of sketches entitled "Sketches from the Country" that Moodie contributed to the journal* La belle assemblée *in 1827-29, Ballstadt examines the influence of Mary Russell Mitford's works on Moodie's sketches, including those that comprise* Roughing It in the Bush.]

Susanna Moodie's *Roughing It in the Bush* has long been recognized as a significant and valuable account of pioneer life in Upper Canada in the mid-nineteenth century. From among a host of journals, diaries, and travelogues, it is surely safe to say, her book is the one most often quoted when the historian, literary or social, needs commentary on backwoods people, frontier living conditions, or the difficulty of adjustment experienced by such upper middle-class immigrants as Mrs. Moodie and her husband.

The reasons for the pre-eminence of *Roughing It in the Bush* have also long been recognized. Mrs. Moodie's lively and humorous style, the vividness and dramatic quality of her characterization, the strength and good humour of her own personality as she encountered people and events have contributed to make her book a very readable one. For these reasons it enjoys a prominent position in any survey of our literary history, and, indeed, it has become a "touchstone" of our literary development. (p. 32)

Except for passing reference, Susanna Moodie's literary practice and acquaintanceships in England have not been considered in relationship to the form and techniques of her most successful book. As a member of a literary family which drew some attention to itself amongst minor English literary circles, Susanna Strickland sought and established literary friendships, and as a writer she followed an established pattern which, even had she remained in England, would very probably have led her to produce a book similar in many respects to *Roughing It in the Bush*. At the very least, however, when Susanna emigrated to Canada, she brought with her an awareness of models for a book of sketches about a region and its people. (p. 33)

During the years 1827-1829, Susanna Strickland contributed a series of prose sketches to a London periodical for ladies entitled *La Belle Assemblée* which was edited by a Suffolk native and friend of the Strickland family, Thomas Harral. The series, "**Sketches from the Country**", consists of five pieces: "**The Witch of East Cliff**", "**The Two Fishermen**", "**Naomi**", "**The Dead Man's Grave**", and "**Old Hannah, or, the Charm**". The first four involve Suffolk legends told to the author by elderly natives of the region. Unfortunately, they are marred by an excessively metaphorical style and are without restraint on sentiment. Only in the introduction does the author exercise economy and limit her pen to what she really knows. The fifth sketch is Susanna's personal recollection of a maid-servant at Reydon Hall, the Strickland home in Suffolk, near Southwold. It reflects warmth and good humour, and, perhaps because it is personal, is characterized by a greater directness and simplicity of style than the preceding sketches.

The importance of this series of sketches is that it represents Susanna's early attempt to emulate the writing of Mary Russell Mitford and to do for Suffolk what Miss Mitford did so prolifically and so well for Berkshire. (pp. 33-4)

Such emulation is indicated in the titles and contents of Susanna's country sketches. In the *Our Village* sketches, Miss Mitford was wont to include portraits of rural characters, accounts of country walks, and tributes to rural institutions. . . . The style is familiar and direct, exhibiting a fine attention to detail; the tone is delicate and quiet. They are sketches of ordinary life and the emphasis is upon the colour and charm of rural living. The introduction to "Hannah Bint" is a good example of her loving attention to nature, as a prelude to the character and situation of a country friend. . . . (p. 35)

The same kind of introduction is employed by Susanna in her country scenes, particularly in "**Old Hannah**" and "**The Dead Man's Grave**". The latter is characterized by the similar attention to the particulars of a locale related to a specific history or event. . . . In the introductions to four of her sketches and throughout her reminiscence of Old Hannah, Susanna Strick-

land's series reminds one of Mitford's attention to a region and its people; it is local colour fiction.

It seems very likely, then, that when Susanna Moodie decided to write of her Canadian experiences near Cobourg and Peterborough, she would have thought of Miss Mitford's books on rural life and scenery. A connection seems indicated not only by her early interest in *Our Village,* but by the fact that parts of *Roughing It in the Bush* were first published as a series of "**Canadian Sketches**" in the *Literary Garland.* That series of six sketches includes a country walk, a backwoods custom, and portraits of eccentric or peculiar characters, all categories used by Mary Mitford, and all assuming an important place in *Roughing It in the Bush* when it was published in 1852. For the British reader of the mid-nineteenth century, large sections of "**Uncle Joe and his Family**", "**Brian the Still Hunter**", "**The Charivari**", "**The Wilderness and Our Indian Friends**", and "**The Walk to Dummer**" would satisfy an appetite for impressions of the peculiarities of custom and character in British North America.

Of course, *Roughing It* was conditioned by other important factors and, therefore, has different components and tones than *Our Village.* Mrs. Moodie had more functions than one to fulfil in writing her book. She wished to convey information to prospective immigrants, to tell her personal story of fortunes and misfortunes, and to create impressions and descriptions. She is, therefore, the essayist as well as the story-teller, and *Roughing It* is both a didactic book, an autobiography, and a sketch-book of pioneer life.

In *Our Village* the author's personality as a unifying factor is much less important. Although the sketches which are entirely devoted to seasonal country walks express Mitford's personal delight in nature, she is generally objective and does not obtrude with her personal fortunes.

Differences in the tone and flavour of the two books are largely due to the landscape which each writer focuses on. While Miss Mitford's sketches take on the gentle and fertile character of the Berkshire countryside, Mrs. Moodie's reflect the larger dimensions of the Canadian scene and the sense of challenge which the bold extremes of Canadian climate and landscape demanded. (pp. 35-7)

> *Carl Ballstadt, "Susanna Moodie and the English Sketch," in* Canadian Literature, *No. 51, Winter, 1972, pp. 32-8.*

DAVID STOUCK (essay date 1974)

[*Stouck discusses the conflict in* Roughing It in the Bush *between Moodie's romantic descriptions of nature and her accounts of the harsh reality of daily pioneer life. He concludes that Moodie's "personal drama of rejection and exile and her search for a refuge from an uncaring world" are central to the Canadian imaginative experience.*]

As we struggle in Canada to define our national identity in terms of a literary tradition, we repeatedly come up against Susanna Moodie's *Roughing It in the Bush,* a conceded classic, but a book which has resisted definition and critical assimilation. Part of the reason for this is formal. *Roughing It* is generically a collection of sketches, and this loose narrative form admits the inclusion of almost any kind of literary expression: landscape description, character portraits, legends and anecdotes, philosophical reflection. Mrs. Moodie accordingly lets the Crusoe-like interest of the book (her account of survival in the backwoods) be diverted for long stretches at a time by other preoccupations. But perhaps the greater reason for our confused and dislocated responses to this book lies in our learned cultural expectations. As North Americans we have been conditioned to view the pioneer experience as the heroic period of our history, as a simpler and more affirmative era in which our ancestors made creative sacrifices to ensure and enhance the lives of future generations. But *Roughing It* is no splendid celebration of pioneer life such as we find in the classic texts of American literature, no Franklinesque account of how to rise in the world; rather it is a tale of hardship and misery which culminates in withdrawal and defeat. Above all it is a book which denies the myths of renaissance and individual power in a new land. As Canadians we are now making many reversals in our thinking, and if we are willing to relinquish what ideally might have been our first account of heroic pioneer life, we will be rewarded in turn with a book which is imaginatively much richer than we might have guessed, a book more subtle, complex, devious.

A collection of sketches (and Thoreau's *Walden* is a good example of this form developed to its highest literary and philosophical end) achieves its unity and interest from the personality of the writer, and it is with this aspect of *Roughing It* that I am most concerned. Formally speaking, Mrs. Moodie's journal is not a work of art; however, the personality of the narrator has an imaginative numinousness which has caught a sympathetic reflection in the contemporary sensibility (witness the collection of poems by Margaret Atwood, *The Journals of Susanna Moodie* [see excerpt dated 1970]) and which is often paralleled in the work of Canadian artists in the past. What is initially so fascinating in the journals is the way Mrs. Moodie's public statements continually belie the drift of her unconscious feelings. As Margaret Atwood has put it, Mrs. Moodie speaks with two voices: with one, her public voice, she attempts to affirm the myths of the pioneer experience and lauds Canada as the land of future promise; but with the other, her private voice, she inadvertently expresses negative, inadmissable feelings which invalidate her patriotic rhetoric. The fundamental opposition or tension between these two voices (between what is socially acceptable and desired and what is privately felt) gives the book an imaginative dimension which other accounts of life in the Canadian backwoods do not have.

Mrs. Moodie's imaginative conflict is most strikingly apparent in the book's style—in the contrast, for example, between the Wordsworthian response to the Canadian landscape and the writer's detailed, day-to-day observations. Nurtured on the romantic myths of early nineteenth-century England, Mrs. Moodie, on first viewing the rugged scenery along the St. Lawrence, responds in a rhapsodic manner:

> The previous day had been dark and stormy, and a heavy fog had concealed the mountain chain, which forms the stupendous background to this sublime view, entirely from our sight. As the clouds rolled away from their grey, bald brows, and cast into denser shadow the vast forest belt that girdled them round, they loomed out like mighty giants—Titans of the earth, in all their rugged and awful beauty—a thrill of wonder and delight pervaded my mind. The spectacle floated dimly on my sight—my eyes were blinded with tears—blinded by the excess of beauty. I turned to the right and to the left, I looked up and down the glorious river, never

had I beheld so many striking objects blended into one mighty whole! Nature had lavished all her noblest features in producing that enchanting scene.

The landscape in this passage is scarcely described; the distant panorama yields to an idea and correspondent emotion which blinds the narrator to the actual scene itself. The idea of nature as an unfailing source of inspiration persists throughout the journal, and in her public-spirited, affirmative mood, Mrs. Moodie asserts that "Nature ever did, and I hope ever will, continue: *'To shoot marvellous strength into my heart.'''* . . . But that very passage is followed by a confession that her feeling for Canada was like the feeling of a condemned criminal whose only hope for escape is through the grave. In the accounts of day-to-day life there are descriptions of nature which, far from Wordsworthian rhapsody, direct us to an undercurrent of negative feeling about the country and the conditions of pioneer life:

> A thaw in the middle of winter is the most disagreeable change that can be imagined. After several weeks of clear, bright, bracing, frosty weather, with a serene atmosphere and cloudless sky, you awake one morning surprised at the change in the temperature; and, upon looking out of the window, behold the woods obscured by a murky haze—not so dense as an English November fog, but more black and lowering—and the heavens shrouded in a uniform covering of leaden-coloured clouds, deepening into a livid indigo at the edge of the horizon. The snow, no longer hard and glittering, has become soft and spongy, and the foot slips into a wet and insidiously-yielding mass at every step. From the roof pours down a continuous stream of water, and the branches of the trees, collecting the moisture of the reeking atmosphere, shower it upon the earth from every dripping twig. . . .

In this mood the author describes not just the horizon, but the details in the foreground in a realistic, documentary style which is closer to the style of F. P. Grove than to her contemporaries. This is the mood in which the author explores her genuinely imaginative feelings about Canada, though at the same time never allowing herself to abandon the nineteenth-century myths of nature, mother country and pioneer.

The conflict of styles, however, involves much more than simply a literary manner unevenly executed. The Wordsworthian stance was for Mrs. Moodie not just a learned set of attitudes or an affected literary pose, but something integral to her personality—a definition of self fundamental to survival in the backwoods. What emerges in the author's account of her rude experiences is a deep-seated fear of social contact, and her *role* as a gentlewoman in the wilderness is clearly a vital defence against what she fears most. By defining herself as both a gentlewoman and a woman of letters she is able to evade a reflexive relationship with the other settlers in the area. Even more to the point she is able to evade the social failure such relationships might precipitate. Likely our first opinion of Mrs. Moodie is that she is an intolerable prude, that she is proud and affected beyond endurance. She defines her Canadian neighbours as her inferiors, both socially and intellectually, and thus explains her reluctance to participate in their society. . . . But it is a simple truth that pride invariably has its source in feelings of self-doubt, and in order to read Mrs. Moodie's journal with any sympathy we must recognize that her role playing throughout is a bulwark against a profound sense of inadequacy. (pp. 463-66)

Mrs. Moodie's sense of failure and inadequacy, which she in part cloaks under her role of gentlewoman in the backwoods, extends further than ineptitude at frontier tasks; it is rooted deeply in her nature and finds direct expression when she reflects on her separation from England. In outbursts of homesickness she upbraids herself as a guilty, unworthy creature whose exile in Canada is a form of punishment for an unspecified crime.... Her sense of failure is reinforced by her anomolous presence in the backwoods, and she retreats into her role as a gentlewoman in exile. Nor is there escape for Mrs. Moodie through her husband, for he is a weak, unsuccessful man and during moments of crisis is invariably absent. Only through her writing can Mrs. Moodie salvage something of her life, and here she significantly evades self-confrontation and dramatizes herself as a martyr figure—a victim of unjust social conditions in England and a heroic pioneer, sacrificing personal happiness so that a new country can be formed. (pp. 466-67)

In lieu of personal achievements her narrative focuses on an impersonal image of growth—the idea of Canada, "a noble, free, and rising country" . . . and the idea of mankind in general slowly but surely moving toward the fulfilment of a sublime and mysterious destiny (a sentimental vision accommodating both Victorian Christianity and something like Social Darwinism). Such statements throughout the book project an idealized and dramatic sense of self in relation to society, but one which fails to convince as a total self-image. More revealing and suggestive is the way random vignettes in the narrative—the character sketches and anecdotes—fall together to form a pattern of social aversion and a preoccupation with failure and death. All the characters that Mrs. Moodie describes at any length are, like herself, totally out of place in the backwoods. (p. 468)

Perhaps the most vivid of the character sketches is the portrait of Malcolm, "the Little Stumpy Man", who, uninvited, stays with the Moodies for nine months. Mrs. Moodie's unyielding social manner is nowhere as omnipresent and oppressive. One critic [R. D. MacDonald] has suggested that Mrs. Moodie's fear of Malcolm and his ill temper is actually sexual in origin, that she is at a fundamental level attracted to him physically. Typically, Mrs. Moodie deflects the reader's attention from herself to the unscrupulous character of her visitor (as she does in describing her borrowing neighbours) and thereby covers her true feelings. She was writing, of course, in a prohibitive, genteel tradition, so that sex is limited to such innocent vignettes as the courtship of the servants, Jacob and Mary. But when sex does appear (and sex does represent the most complete form of social communion possible) violence and death are its corollary. When Malcolm, left alone one day with Mrs. Moodie, tells his story, he reveals that he is a murderer (he once shot a man in South America) and is haunted by guilt. The same unrecognized equation is more blatantly operative in the charivari stories where sex is invariably a cause for violence and, in the case of the Negro who marries a white woman, the occasion for death.

We do not know the exact process by which the journals took final shape (whether extracted from diaries or written as sketches entirely from memory), but in the reshaping of the original experience Mrs. Moodie selects and omits detail in response

to the unconscious drift of her feelings and in accord with a dramatic sense of self. Though not a work of art *Roughing It* has a definite imaginative shape in both the structure of its events and its patterns of imagery. The picture of Canada as a land of failure and death is present from the beginning with the ship of emigrants journeying into a country laid waste by cholera.... Mrs. Moodie's final stance in the book is not unlike that of the Ancient Mariner who tells of his voyage through guilt, despair and death and who reemerges to warn those who might follow in his path.

The important question remains to be asked: in what ways do Mrs. Moodie and her journal represent the origins of a Canadian imaginative tradition? At least three definable aspects of her experience seem to be continuous in Canadian life. First, the Moodies, like the United Empire Loyalists before them and like great numbers of people since, came to Canada not with a dream of carving individual empires, but with the modest hope of salvaging a way of life threatened at home. In the Moodies' case poverty was the specific ill which caused them to emigrate, although political and religious reasons were also common. Like so many of the genteel poor from England and Scotland the Moodies sought in Canada a refuge, a way of saving pride in the face of ever dwindling economic and social circumstances. The contrast to the creative and forward-looking American experience in the eighteenth and nineteenth centuries is absolutely crucial to understanding a distinctively Canadian imaginative tradition. Seeking a haven in which to preserve customs threatened at home is imaginatively at the opposite pole from rejecting the old order and emigrating in order to begin life anew. The backward-looking nature of the Canadian experience is reflected in Mrs. Moodie's nostalgia for the daisy-covered fields of her England home. The original sense in Canada of being nowhere, or in exile, has left an indelible print on the Canadian psyche.... (pp. 469-71)

Secondly, the image of one of our first settlers as a self-pitying failure rather than a bouyant pioneer characterizes a literary tradition in which fictional protagonists more likely lose than win, or are, at best, sorely compromised by their situation in life. The hard, intractable landscape seems to breed a conviction of inescapable defeat in the Canadian hero, a feeling which also colours his social relations. (p. 471)

Thirdly, the curious affection Mrs. Moodie feels for her forest home at the time of departure is an ascetic form of imaginative pleasure which recurs with significant frequency in Canadian art. Through suffering and self-denial Mrs. Moodie has become attached to her way of life in the backwoods and to her home which she describes as "consecrated by the memory of a thousand sorrows." In a harsh, punitive landscape life is imaginatively conducted with a heightened sense of formidable odds and an almost pleasurable certainty of ultimate defeat.... Mrs. Moodie's *Roughing It in the Bush* is not a work of art, but the narrator's personal drama of rejection and exile and her search for a refuge from an uncaring world is very central to what is imaginative in the Canadian experience. (pp. 471-72)

David Stouck, "'Secrets of the Prison-House': Mrs. Moodie and the Canadian Imagination," in The Dalhousie Review, *Vol. 54, No. 3, Autumn, 1974, pp. 463-72.*

ROBIN MATHEWS   (essay date 1975)

[*Mathews considers the political orientation of* Roughing It in the Bush *and* Life in the Clearings. *Examining in particular Moodie's stance toward individualism, republicanism, and capitalism, Mathews then relates these issues to her depiction of nature and society.*]

Roughing It in the Bush has a classic shape, almost a quality of pre-destination about it, seen in retrospect. It is about the arrival of an immigrant to Canada. It is about her expectations, her surprises, and the day to day reality of life in Canada. It is about the hard task of settling, of discovering the people already present. It takes Mrs. Moodie through isolation, physical discomfort, bad and good neighbours, work in the fields, storm, fire, frost and the beginning of family. It is about evaluation and adaptation and a final move from the bush to Belleville. Mrs. Moodie reveals the genuine feelings of homesickness, uncertainty, discomfort that afflict the immigrant. She shows the forces at work to mould society in Canada—the Canadian dialectic becomes plain in her work. The book was written, some critics tell us repeatedly, by an English "aristocrat"(?) who rejects "democracy" and believes in the class system. Susanna Moodie did believe in the inevitability of social stratification, but the other claims against her are nonsense. She was, in fact, a pink tory, historical precursor to the Red Tory in Canada. . . . Susanna Moodie supported meritocracy. She moved towards breakdown of class as it was defined in Europe. She rejected individualism and—in a not fully articulated way—capitalist exploitation. She saw the threat to Canadian survival and development of community in the differences based on anything other than morals and education. And she saw the danger of uninhibited individualism. In *The Victoria Magazine*, December, 1847, Mrs. Moodie wrote that "The want of education and moral training, is the only *real* barrier that exists between the different classes of man. Nature, reason, and Christianity, recognize no other." That does not mean she was an equalitarian, because she wasn't. Ideas of total equality in her day were expressed in terms of political republicanism and social individualism. She rejected both. "Perfect unadulterated republicanism, is a beautiful but fallacious chimera, which never did exist on earth, and which . . . will not exist in heaven." (p. 4)

Individualism in **Roughing It in the Bush,** under the guise of egalitarianism, becomes the right to exploit, the right to invade. The individualistic Yankees have a real feeling of superiority, of wounded superiority, usually. Mrs. Moodie attacks the levelling pressure they exert. (p. 6)

Mrs. Moodie rejects the individualism of the Yankee; she struggles against it. But she loses much of her sense of hierarchy and belief in class superiority in Canada. She was a "progressive" thinker before she left England, and the terms of life in Canada developed the pinkness of her toryism. The Yankee is a small part of her training and provides, for the most part, a negative example. The Yankee and the U.S.A. are credited by some with teaching Mrs. Moodie about equality. But the Yankees she meets in **Roughing It in the Bush**— the majority of them—exploit her, reject her, and deny the possibility of a community based on trust. She learns cooperation partly because of the threat of the Yankee. Experience among Canadians cooperating and moving by merit brings her to a sense that class definitions of worth don't work. At one level, her advice to most gentry to stay out of Canada and her praise of people used to hard work make that point clear enough.

Mrs. Moodie is a democrat in the Canadian sense, but she abhors the individualist "democracy" of the U.S. She makes a great plea to Canadians to build their own community in gentle evolution from the mother country. (p. 7)

Near the close of **Life in the Clearings,** Mrs. Moodie is writing about the sublimity of Niagara Falls and its evocation of religious feeling. She writes that the U.S. intends to harness its side for industry:

> Ye Gods, what next will the love of gain suggest to these gold-worshippers. The whole earth should enter into a protest against such an act of sacrilege—such a shameless desecration of one of the noblest works of God.

Mrs. Moodie's apostrophe to 'the whole earth' sounds very modern in the light of recent, apparently new, concerns about nature and pollution. But in relation to a major theme in Canadian imaginative development her comment is only partly metaphorical.

Like many other Canadian writers she sees mankind's interrelation with what is called the "external world" as organic. Her move is away from the conservative view of a hierarchical, organically related society to a feeling of the possibility that society can be cooperative and egalitarian in organically continuous terms. (pp. 7-8)

Mrs. Moodie is deeply affected by the grandeur, majesty, stupendousness, sublimity, the excess of beauty, and the titanic aspects of the physical world. The experience is described in particularly Christian terms by her. But landscape and the elements become, for some later writers, an expression of the powers larger than self which may be historical, geological, cosmic—but not necessarily idealistic in an anti-materialist sense. They represent the extension and complication of real forces. They represent, therefore, an expression of reality which is comprehended by the 'native' and is integral with the values of the settlers and community builders. The experience, according to Mrs. Moodie, was unique. That would mean that the form of reality created here would also be unique. "Never," she says, "had I beheld so many striking objects blended into one mighty whole." (p. 8)

The enormity of the new experience of the physical environment is clearly connected to religious feelings for Mrs. Moodie. . . . Her experience of the physical world in Canada does not alienate her, nor does it make her despair at an apparent insignificance and absurdity of human life. Rather, it transforms her view of herself; it rearranges meaning for her. . . . Mrs. Moodie responds to her experience of the sublime with a reaffirmation of human meaning. (pp. 8-9)

Mrs. Moodie does not delude herself that Canada is Eden or that she is in the moral condition of our first parents. Canadian landscape, for her, connects her soul with God. There is a presiding power that gives her strength in the task of building civil society. . . .

The struggle necessary to make Canada a civilized society is insisted upon throughout **Roughing It in the Bush** and throughout Canadian literature. (p. 10)

In case there should be argument about Mrs. Moodie's sense of the moral condition of the Canadian new world, she defines it unequivocally. Nature is there as God made it; man must struggle *against himself* for perfected community:

> The unpeopled wastes of Canada must present the same aspect to the new settler that the world did to our first parents after their expulsion from the Garden of Eden; all the sin which could defile the spot, or haunt it with the association

of departed persons concentrated in their own persons.

In those terms *Roughing It in the Bush* has a larger life. For Mrs. Moodie is saying that the social, religious, and political philosophy of the perceiver decides his or her view of place. (p. 11)

Mrs. Moodie sees herself as part of a human network that is historically significant. . . . She moves in a complex way through what might be called one of the first steps in the Canadian experience, for she is at once *ingenue* and sophisticate. She is also *voyager*. As *ingenue* she can expose herself totally to the abuse of others in order to reveal their characters fully. . . . She is from an old world of ordered values and hierarchy, and so she can judge, or provide imaginative room for the reader to judge, the differences, failings and strengths of the new society and particular types in it. As a character typical of Canadian immigrants, in her mixture of ingenuousness and sophistication, she can involve the reader in her own character and in its growth and transformation.

Both *Roughing It in the Bush* and *Life in the Clearings* are voyages of discovery. The first is a voyage into the deeps of new settlements to discover what the terms of survival and community will be. There is a physical struggle in the material environment. But the primary struggle is with the definition of human kind in the new community, growing from the types of settlers, the effects of the physical environment, the clash of ideologies, the struggle within people of the old values and the new terms. (pp. 11-12)

The voyage structure of Mrs. Moodie's two works allows her to deal both widely and deeply with the definition of human kind in the Canadian new world. *Roughing It in the Bush* deals with ecstatic religious experience, attempted suicide and suicide, murder, madness, rejection, personal cruelty, and physical struggle to survive the extremes of frost and fire. *Life in the Clearings* is presented as a voyage to Niagara Falls, already in 1853 a place of social recourse and, fittingly, the destination of the voyage, a destination which Mrs. Moodie knows about, this time, in advance. . . . Mrs. Moodie was asked, as a kind of sequel to *Roughing It in the Bush* to tell about the state of society in the colony. The atmosphere of *Life in the Clearings* is the atmosphere of an achieved society. The battle, in a sense, has been won within the terms that she set as the dialectic. Canada is developing more slowly than the U. S. A. industrially and technologically. . . . She can believe that the cultural values in British North America are better and will be more powerful than the force of individualist capitalism in the U. S. A. But, of course, economics in Canada is also based on a structure of individualist capitalism, too. But Mrs. Moodie does not, and need not see that.

Yankee power is present, is an assumption of British North American consciousness. In fact, Mrs. Moodie includes two sketches entitled, **"Trials of a Travelling Musician,"** published first in her *Victoria Magazine* in 1847 and employing the techniques of Thomas C. Haliburton's *The Clockmaker*. Mrs. Moodie turns the coin over, however, and tells tales of a Canadian travelling in the U. S. In that way she can present a picture of U. S. society, employing the gentle satire of Haliburton for the purpose she has in *Life in the Clearings,* a gentler examination of the dialectic of forces than in *Roughing It in the Bush.* In that book she spends some time depicting the Yankee in Canada. In *Life in the Clearings* she uses the travelling musician to show something of the society the Yankees have come from.

Using the sketch popular in the England she knew and leaning a little on Haliburton's techniques of humour, Mrs. Moodie creates work in *Roughing It in the Bush* and in its sequel that treats questions and subjects that we shall not be free of in Canada for a long time, employing techniques and archetypes that describe both the Canadian fact and the ways in which Canadians deal with it, or try to.

Mrs. Moodie moves a long way through the immigrant transformation. She wants a government that is "liberal," but not U. S. What she did not know was to become of fundamental importance. She did not know that the cultural, humane, Christian values she espoused could not transform capitalist values. She could not know that the conservatism she expressed could only become North American free enterprise individualism, whatever other name it was given. Conservatism in the hands of free enterprise capitalism could only be a class ideology alienated from the land and the people, abusive of the material world and people. Mrs. Moodie's final paragraphs in *Life in the Clearings* seek to find a balance between a genuine idea of conservative organic class interdependence and the potential in Canada to release individual and group energy in an increasingly egalitarian system. She cannot forbear to make clear that she does *not* see the U. S. as having achieved a kind of life Canadians should seek. . . . (pp. 12-13)

Mrs. Moodie was a tory, but she was a pink tory. She did not believe in the supremacy of the individual. She combined a sense of the past and a sense of community with a clear sense of what needed to be changed. That means she recognized the importance of past experience to present community, at the same time as she perceived the new and peculiar demands of Canadian conditions on the life of the society and the individual. . . . She did not believe the individual was supreme; she believed in the *inalienable responsibility* of the individual to a concept of community and to the actual social order. . . .

Mrs. Moodie dealt greatly with the first steps towards Canadian society. She understood the rejection of the U. S., the necessary connection of Canadians with nature, the role of woman as community builder, the role of merit, and the place of education in the new Canadian place. But she was unaware—she almost could not be aware—of the ways in which the U. S. State would use economic techniques and technological novelty as soldiers in an army of political, cultural, and economic invasion. She could not see that Canadians of wealth would become the office

The Moodies' cottage at Belleville. Photograph by Michael Peterman.

clerks of U. S. expansionism as well as the individual exploiters of Canada themselves. That realization—and the understanding of the steps necessary to change our condition—have come late in the day. The next step—le prochain episode—has been left to Canadians of our time. (p. 14)

Robin Mathews, "Susanna Moodie, Pink Toryism, and Nineteenth Century Ideas of Canadian Identity," in Journal of Canadian Studies/Revue d'études canadiennes, *Vol. X, No. 3, August, 1975, pp. 3-15.*

CAROL SHIELDS (essay date 1977)

[*In her study of Moodie's prose works, Shields traces three recurring major themes: complex personalities, sexual reversal, and social structure. The following excerpt presents Shields's comments on the complex characterizations in Moodie's novels, short stories, and autobiographical sketches.*]

Flora Lyndsay, Mrs. Moodie writes of one of her heroines, "delighted in the study of human character." . . . And in speaking of Flora she might just as easily have been speaking of herself. Despite the fact that she often hid her absorption in personality behind the screen of nature and religion, the power and mystery of personality emerges as her overriding concern. Personality in all forms—amusing, ironic, or tragic—appears to have been her greatest diversion, and it is by examples of human personality that she attempts to divert her readers. (p. 11)

Personality, individual or collective, is her major theme; but what frees her work from the commonplaceness of the character sketch is her concern with enigma, the extreme personality, the unfathomable, the complex, the personality which refuses to break down under analysis. (p. 12)

Compared to the characters in Mrs. Moodie's Canadian books, the personalities in her fiction are often mere instruments in a plot. Uncle Beaumont in the story **"Waiting For Dead Men's Shoes,"** *(Matrimonial Speculations . . .)* is vulnerable, comic, and picturesque with his fortune, his gout, and his love of food, but he never exhibits any of the complexity with which Mrs. Moodie describes those in her Canadian books. In her Canadian characters, Brian and Malcolm, for instance, there are blurred edges, the suggestion that it is not always possible to sum up human personality. Brian and Malcolm are not part of a story but are stories in themselves.

Many of the personalities she describes have the sketchy offbeat quality of newspaper stories or local scandals. Random and pointless, they clutter her narrative, and even Mrs. Moodie seems to sense that they are inappropriate. (pp. 12-13)

It is relatively easy to separate those stories which are hearsay from those which Mrs. Moodie has experienced firsthand. Obeying her autobiographical urge, she intrudes into many of her own stories, gladly taking a part and often the most important part. Even when she stands in the background, the reader is aware of a rush of sympathy toward the character she is describing. (p. 13)

In those stories which she has obviously collected second-hand, she frequently signifies distance by assigning another narrator or by devising a dialogue which excludes herself. Physical details are strikingly absent, and so is the almost cinematic quality she evokes when she has actually witnessed such a scene as the prison of Kingston or the lunatic asylum at Toronto. But most telling of all is her plunge from the salty, almost colloquial descriptions of human activity to the conventional rhetoric which is the mark of her fiction. *Life in the Clearings* with its much greater second-hand content is a more subdued and formal book than the lively and autobiographical *Roughing It in the Bush.*

Perhaps the most appealing aspect of Mrs. Moodie's descriptions of human personality is her all-embracing acceptance of human variety and the infrequency of her moral judgments. Criminals, the most deviant of human beings, fill her with exhilaration rather than disgust. The "study" of human behaviour, as she calls it, includes all extremes of humanity, even the simple and the insane. The inmates of the asylum amuse her by their ironic self-misrepresentations, and she sees madness not as a horror, but as an alternative human response. (pp. 13-14)

It is indicative of Mrs. Moodie's overriding concern with the complexities of human personality that she is unable to sustain an abstract argument without illustrating it, frequently to the point of imbalance. For instance, in *Life in the Clearings* . . . she launches into an attack on the social custom of wearing mourning, beginning with a brief discussion of the foolishness of mourning from a religious standpoint. "It is not a reproach to Him" . . . , she asks, when all nature is in a perpetual state of change? From the religious reference she hastens through the philosophical arguments to the social argument which interests her far more and which she illustrates with a total of eleven anecdotes. These stories, some of them fragmentary and some of them crisply detailed, over-argue the case so emphatically that the reader suspects they exist for their entertainment value alone. Her best anecdotes are those in which irony is the controlling mood as in the story about a woman who orders her mourning clothes before the expected death of her brother and then is disappointed when he lives through his illness. . . . (pp. 14-15)

Human detail outweighs the literary framework in Mrs. Moodie's Canadian books; the framework, in fact, can be accommodated to hold any number of stories. . . . Her transitions tend to be either fragile or crude, and sometimes even nonexistent, but she seems not in the least reluctant to interrupt her design with a sketch from human nature.

The chapter on work bees in *Roughing It in the Bush* . . . is typical of a series of short, disjointed human anecdotes grouped under a chapter theme. Mrs. Moodie disliked bees, considering them a necessary evil in frontier life. The only redeeming feature was the opportunity they afforded to view an odd assortment of humanity at a glance and to study the interaction of personality. Temperance men such as her brother and husband are dismissed quickly. It is the more offbeat guests who engage her: old Wittals who combined a speech defect with a gross appetite; an illiterate but amazingly successful revival preacher; John who is unrivaled at the art of swearing; the slightly but not obnoxiously drunken Malachi Chroak who foolishly pretends to force one of the maids into marriage. All these sketches are slight; they seem to have been written from notes and suggest an awe for human variability rather than individuality.

But Mrs. Moodie's curiosity is also excited by characters viewed in isolation; she is detached, almost scientific at times, offering little which might be considered judgmental on individual human irregularities. (p. 15)

Eccentricity, which Mrs. Moodie not only tolerated but relished, is most frequently attached to the upper-class and appears in her work to be, almost without exception, a male indulgence; women were too occupied, apparently, to stray from the conventional path for long, and as for the poor, such deviations in behaviour were more likely to be viewed as barbarous and ignorant than tolerably eccentric. Some of the eccentric personalities described by Mrs. Moodie are so extraordinary that she feels compelled to supply a supporting footnote. (p. 16)

Gentleness usually accompanies the variety of eccentricity she describes, and her human oddities are often kind to the point of aberration. Wilhelmina Carr in *Flora Lyndsay* is expansively generous, and Tom Wilson in *Roughing It in the Bush* betrays a curious sweetness beneath his eccentricity. Even Malcolm, who was irritable and rude most of the time, was fond of children and gentle on occasion. And in almost every case of rampant eccentricity, Mrs. Moodie outlines her personalities with loneliness and suffering. Eccentrics such as Brian, Tom, and Malcolm in *Roughing It in the Bush* are not reduced by Mrs. Moodie to comic size; instead they contain their separate afflictions like species of private pain.

In her Canadian books Mrs. Moodie describes countless acts of eccentric and ironic behaviour. But her novels and tales, on the other hand, contain far more interchangeable characters, and personality is more likely to hinge on gender than on personal anomalies. Occasionally, though, her fictitious characters show complexities beyond their role type, and Mrs. Moodie herself, in a discussion of fiction, states her belief that a writer must blend qualities of good and evil in a character in order to make him believable.... (pp. 16-17)

William Mathews, for instance, who is a minor character in Mrs. Moodie's novel *Mark Hurdlestone,* is a fairly generalized representation of criminal low life. But he has periods of complexity in which he lapses into feelings of guilt. Mrs. Moodie even supplies him with something like a psychological explanation for his behaviour: the loss of his mother, Mathews says at one point, has flawed his life. Cruel and uneducated, he has strange pockets of sensitivity. When his father dies he says, "Something is gone—a string is loosened from the heart...." Unlike Godfrey, his partner in crime, William is haunted by conscience. Dark, frightening visions torment him, a voice from the "shut up depths" of his heart.... Pursued by the law, he is also pursued by "blue devils that pinch and freeze my heart." ... William speaks with a kind of dark poetry which places him in contrast to Godfrey, but, disappointingly, Mrs. Moodie does not develop his personality further; instead she allows him to harden along criminal lines. (p. 17)

In *Mark Hurdlestone,* the leading character is greatly simplified by Mrs. Moodie at first. He is the unmitigated consummation of evil: "There was not a drop of human kindness in his composition" ..., Mrs. Moodie tells her readers. He "never" mingled; he had "no" friends; "no one" had ever shaken his hand. But later his character receives some psychological shading: he is not the personification of wickedness; instead he is mad. He hates women. He is cold and unresponsive. He has a fetish about cleanliness and a mania about gold. He has distinct paranoic symptoms: he believes people are trying to poison him or gain knowledge of his wealth. And he has what Mrs. Moodie hints might be an unnatural relationship with Grenard Pike, a being just as strange in his own way as Hurdlestone.

The Green sisters in the story **"The Miss Greens"** ... are introduced as highly stereotyped spinster sisters, and one of them, Lydia, never becomes more than a vain, weak creature,

an indolent sipper of brandy. But Polly Green, obviously Mrs. Moodie's favourite just as she is the favourite of the suitor, develops into someone more recognizably human. She even has stirrings of wit; she makes her prayers short, she says, to repay the stinginess of Providence. And though she claims to be no philosopher, in her limited way she is. "Love," she says, "at the best is but a weakness, that the fondest grows ashamed of." ... John Andrews, returning from his midnight courtship, admits to being half-captivated by Polly. But she never progresses beyond this interesting and contradictory point, and Mrs. Moodie leaves her as a bride, shamefully abandoned at the altar. The whole story, in fact, is marred by a viciousness on the one hand and a heavy-footed irony on the other.

The characters in **"Richard Redpath"** ... are mainly stylized and conventional. Joshua Baynes, a foolish gourmand, and his daughter Betsey (who grieves when her fiance is drowned because her wedding clothes will be out of fashion before another groom is found) are both without real substance; even Mrs. Moodie doesn't pretend to take them seriously. But the character of Benjamin Levi is confusing, incomplete, and mysterious. Levi is a Jew, but even this status is confused for he terms himself a convert. His profession is not clearly defined either; he is both an editor and a seller of second-hand clothing.... Popularly considered to be sly and cunning, Levi is a natural philosopher, a cynic in the Shylock manner, given to such paradoxical declarations as "I never vouch for the truth of a story ... until I know it to be a lie." ... It may be that Mrs. Moodie had originally conceived a more ambitious role for Levi, but in a weak conclusion she has him suffer an absurd humiliation and death while her less interesting characters crow with glee. Obviously fascinated with Levi's contradictory personality, Mrs. Moodie has difficulty assimilating him into her fictional world; Levi, like Hurdlestone and William Mathews, is a human oddity who exists on another level of reality.

The reader gets the impression that Mrs. Moodie is unconscious of the contradictory natures of some of her characters. Aunt Dorothy in *Mark Hurdlestone* is one of these unwittingly complex people; she has all the standard equipment of a tart and a witty spinster, but her hatred of men and her contempt for romance have an edge which goes beyond the limits of her conventional role.

Mrs. Moodie's interest in personality is more than passive. She is, by her own frequent admission, a student of human behaviour, and it goes without saying that she interests herself in the motivation behind behaviour. Not surprisingly, she often demonstrates the pre-Freudian prejudices of her time. She is content to dismiss the crime of Grace Marks ... as an inexplicable visitation of sin. And she takes careful note of the phrenological evidence she sees at the prison in Kingston. She has, in addition, a strong romantic belief in the human countenance as an "index" to the mind. (pp. 17-19)

Mrs. Moodie is a woman of her times who quite naturally reflects current ideas about personality, but often she suggests psychological motivation as well. Brian, the still-hunter, she speculates, has a retarded son whose affliction may be the root of Brian's melancholia. Malcolm, her unwelcome guest, may have acquired his irascible disposition from uncaring parents. In the novel *Flora Lyndsay,* one of her later works, Mrs. Moodie frequently takes the trouble to supply causative factors for personality aberration. Captain Kitson, a neighbour of Flora's, has accumulated his eccentricity through a lifetime of social non-acceptance. Mrs. Ready owes her aggressive vulgarity to a too rapid shift from lower to middle class. Wilhelmina Carr, one of Mrs. Moodie's most extraordinary characters, provides a rapid oral sketch of her life in which many of the seeds of her later bizarre behaviour can be found; her mother had died at her birth, and her stern absentee father had been a figure of fear and dislike. Her stepmother, herself a victim of class dislocation, had indulged her, and her schoolmates had jeered at her physical oddities. Furthermore, the only man she had ever loved had refused her offer of marriage, and the only child she had been drawn to had abandoned her.

Early influences, Mrs. Moodie seems to feel, are permanent and almost impossible to overcome. (p. 20)

Her random and off-hand psychological speculations are sometimes startlingly modern and sound. When Marcella DeTrueba in the story **"Richard Redpath"** contemplates suicide, she is advised by an old seaman that suicide is no more than a means of punishing someone else; this piece of wisdom is reinforced by a story he tells of his own daughter's suicide. Clearly Mrs. Moodie subscribes to this theory because Marcella instantly recognizes the truth of it.

Aside from describing the motivation behind personality, Mrs. Moodie reveals her characters through combinations of physical description, use of incident and dialogue, shifts in narration, and direct comparison through the mechanical pairing of characters.

Her fictional characters are described in a formulaic manner, but those characters she introduces in her Canadian books are frequently brought to life in a few words. (p. 21)

As in her chapter on bees in *Roughing It in the Bush,* Mrs. Moodie frequently gathers together a number of related anecdotes, interspersing them with comments on society. Writing about the charivari or the Yankee custom of borrowing, she clusters several stories together, each one forming a single snapshot image of a group attitude. The looseness of the form permits her to shift the narration when she chooses: sometimes she tells the story herself, sometimes a friend relates it, and sometimes the story is overheard. . . .

Many of these grouped stories give only the slightest insight into human behaviour, but occasionally Mrs. Moodie is able to encapsulate a personality in a rapid series of incidents. (p. 22)

In revealing personality, Mrs. Moodie has a modern interviewer's knack for asking the right question, inquiring of Brian "what made him so fond of hunting?" . . . She quotes his reply quickly and simply, using the verb "said" in these dialogues, a device Hemingway used much later to focus the reader's attention on the words of the reply. (p. 23)

It is Mrs. Moodie's use of dialogue which does more than anything to relieve her discursive heaviness. When she attempts dialect, which she does frequently in her Canadian books, there is more than a suggestion of condescension, but when she catches regional expressions or subtle class differences, she conveys character concisely and accurately. (pp. 23-4)

In instances where personality is not clearly marked, particularly in her fiction, Mrs. Moodie employs a traditional means of revelation, that of comparing paired personalities. When male characters are being compared in this manner, the twinning is both frequent and fairly rigidly adhered to. The two brothers theme in **"Jane Redgrave"** is typical: Armyn and Edward Sternfield are brothers competing for their mother's

attention. In true Cain-Abel pattern, Armyn is eventually responsible for Edward's death. (p. 24)

The use of pairing of characters to point up personality is less rigid when women are concerned. Women are usually seen in larger groupings, confusing the comparison, and, furthermore, they relate to each other in more subtle ways, sometimes even crossing class lines and forming a flank. (p. 25)

Most of Mrs. Moodie's character revelations seem to be consciously formed from a combination of description, incident, dialogue, and comparison; but in the case of John Lyndsay, the husband of Flora Lyndsay, the personality is revealed, seemingly unconsciously, in his actions and speeches. Indeed, the narrator ironically insists that John Lyndsay is a perfect gentleman. His strength and talents are praised repeatedly, but, in contradiction, his essential heartlessness is revealed again and again. He can't be bothered taking Flora's old nurse to Canada, and even as he is kissing Flora's tears away, he is turning her to his advantage. When she "begged . . . entreated . . . coaxed" him to go on an outing with her, he bluntly refused. . . . Mrs. Moodie puts into his mouth speeches which make him a cruel manipulator. He wins his wife to his side in the argument over immigration by shaming her and making her feel she has been ungrateful. His attitudes are fixed and brutal and he has no tolerance for eccentricity; he is a relentless realist in combat with Flora's romantic nature. "I hate mystery in any shape" he tells Flora with finality. . . . (pp. 25-6)

Flora, on the other hand, even as the narrator insists that she is an obedient wife, shows a willingness to experiment; she has an easy relaxed tolerance and an active curiosity. She is also more intuitive; had the Lyndsays followed Flora's plan of not taking a servant to Canada they would have been better off. Flora's decision on which ship to take was also, in the end, the wiser course.

Flora and John are compared in their attitudes and reactions, but one senses that, though Mrs. Moodie may be consciously making a heroine of Flora, her vilification of John Lyndsay is unconscious. And it is interesting and tempting at this point to make biographical conclusions, for if Flora is a simplified extension of the author, John is almost certainly a counterpart of John Moodie, Mrs. Moodie's difficult husband, a stubborn man who was not particularly likeable or fortunate in personal dealings.

Indeed the character sketches in *Roughing It in the Bush* have one common link: most of them, at least the best of them, are of failed upper-class Englishmen—Tom, Brian, Malcolm, and always, hovering in the background, the shadow of Mr. Moodie himself. They constitute a type which Mrs. Moodie is able to represent dramatically, for in each case there is a sense of inevitability. Goodness is defeated, intelligence is scorned, sensitivity is clouted. The proper equipment for life in the bush, Mrs. Moodie seems to be saying, is ignorance, brute strength, and an absence of preconceptions. (p. 26)

Of all Mrs. Moodie's personality sketches none is more shapely than the portrait of Brian, the still-hunter. . . . The reader senses that the unsolved riddle of Brian's madness forms an exceptional attraction for her. Brian's story begins with a sudden dramatic meeting; there is a flashback about his life narrated by another visitor, and then there are several incidents concerning Brian, each a miniature portrait, each more fully illustrative of his complexity. There is even a monologue in which Brian attempts to explain his life.

Mrs. Moodie is less interested in the cause of his malady than she is in the effect, although she does once suggest that Brian's son's disability may be partially responsible. Brian is a man who is torn apart by ironies: he has several times attempted suicide but is afraid to cross the ocean for fear of drowning. He loves life but finds pleasure in killing. He has caused many of the settlers to fear for their lives, but he brings a message of comfort to Mrs. Moodie. He himself is capable of responding to irony, marvelling that a visiting naturalist should prefer the simple weeds to the lovely flowers. Brian says of the naturalist, "Well he was an innocent man . . . a very little made him happy. . . ." Mrs. Moodie repeats this statement as a double irony, for this is the way she actually sees Brian himself. The chapter on Brian ends a little too rapidly with a hasty note on Brian's later suicide and an equally hasty tribute to his goodness, but one senses that the unfinished edge to the sketch proceeds from Mrs. Moodie's own inability to comprehend the most thrilling and impenetrable of her characters.

"Human nature," Mrs. Moodie writes in *Roughing It in the Bush,* "has more strange varieties than any other menagerie can contain, and Malcolm was one of the oddest of his species." . . . Malcolm, the stranger who forced himself on the Moodies for a period of nine months, is described in the chapter "The Little Stumpy Man." He may be the most complex of all the characters Mrs. Moodie describes. The chapter about him is even more fragmented than her usual writing; she jumps from episode to episode in her frustration with him. She is plainly baffled. The string of anecdotes succeeds in forming a multi-lensed portrait of him, but the portrait is never finished; even Malcolm's eventual disappearance is clouded in mystery.

Usually razor-sharp in her physical descriptions, Mrs. Moodie falters with Malcolm. She is self-contradicting, calling him unpleasant looking, but testifying to his regular features and good colour. His voice is low and mysterious, and she senses that "the current of his feelings seemed to flow in a deep sluggish channel. . . ." The cumulative effect of the description suggests sexuality, and this impression is strengthened as Mrs. Moodie circles around Malcolm, drawing sometimes closer, sometimes further away.

Malcolm's tendency is to be unkind and rude, but in odd moments of intimacy he confesses to self-hatred and perpetual melancholy. In one extraordinary exchange he confesses to Mrs. Moodie that he has murdered a man. Mrs. Moodie receives this confidence with remarkable calm. Suggesting neither trauma nor untruth, she simply adds the murder episode on top of the pile of mysteries. When Malcolm mentions a miserable boyhood, an ill-natured mother, and a brother who was insane, she makes no link between these revelations and Malcolm, the misanthropic adult.

But she herself is more clearly revealed in this chapter than in any other place. Malcolm does not hesitate to tell her she is a prude, and Mrs. Moodie does not hesitate to repeat the charge. He also tells her that he is a man who thinks with his head, not his heart, implying perhaps that she is just the reverse. These personal exchanges between Malcolm and Mrs. Moodie are a real departure from her usual pattern; she is neither the shrewd interviewer nor the unseen observer, but a participating human being who has let her persona slip. She is often angry with her guest, petulant, bored, fascinated, exasperated, wounded, and, in the end, mystified, perhaps as much by herself as with Malcolm.

Margaret Atwood sees Mrs. Moodie as a woman divided down her Victorian middle, all manners and ladylike art forms on one side, and on the other a consciousness of sweat, dirt, disease, and mosquitoes [see excerpt dated 1970]. But it is possible that the dichotomy is not rooted in Mrs. Moodie's personality; it may be only a surface splintering, a division which exists for literary purposes, namely the division between person and persona. Her real and vulnerable self is only occasionally glimpsed. . . . She once refers briefly to the tragic drowning of her son, and there are oblique, scattered references to anxiety, weakness, and ennui, what may have been a nervous collapse near the end of her sojourn in the woods. But these are exceptions, slips of the pen, holes in the persona which she constructed for herself. (pp. 28-31)

Her persona in her early works is that of romantic heroine, the adventurous, felicitous spirit which reached fulfilment in the person of Flora Lyndsay. Mrs. Moodie likes to show herself counselling servant girls, healing the sick, teaching the infidel; she is the generous, humourous, resourceful deliverer as in the chapter **"The Walk to Dummer"** in *Roughing It in the Bush.* She is proud of her ability to be resourceful and she expresses that pride in ironic terms, the irony being that she, a woman of gentle breeding and education, should now be making coffee with dandelion roots and producing rows of well-hoed potatoes. When she fails in her first bread baking, Tom Wilson says, "I hope you make better books than bread." . . . She replies that she would rather fail as a writer than as a baker, but she is really suggesting the opposite: she is a gentlewoman to whom the mysteries of the household are unknown. Her exploration of domesticity is deliberately childlike, a pose which reinforces the image of herself as a woman of culture.

Her sensitivity to nature, she frequently points out, separates her from other people. . . . Her initial homesickness in Canada is lifted when she encounters the countryside. "It won me from my melancholy and I began to look around me with considerable interest." . . . But her English servant, she points out, does not have the ability to be lifted from sadness by scenery. A positive response to nature signified for Mrs. Moodie a delicacy of taste, an educated sensitivity.

In meeting her new countrymen she contrasts the paucity of their knowledge with her endless fund of facts. She believes that her health is nourished by fresh air, and she eats fresh apples although others tell her not to. She is the keeper of knowledge and the foe of ignorant superstition. Her persona is expanded and reinforced by the fact that she is often victimized by rude borrowing neighbours or scorned by the illiterate for her bookishness. Her uniqueness is stressed by her isolation, and her isolation is increasingly insisted upon as she moves from *Roughing It in the Bush* to the more reflective *Life in the Clearings.*

Her vision of herself as a heroine in an ongoing drama is stated most openly in the chapter "The Burning of the Fallow." In this episode she and her family have narrowly escaped death by fire; at the very moment before destruction a thundershower saves them. Later she learns that the scene has had one chance witness, an Irishman who had watched from a distant canoe. For reasons which she doesn't even attempt to explain, she finds the fact of having had a witness "comforting." It is as though her role-playing is reinforced by the existence of an audience. Her own persona, so patently constructed and so elaborately expanded, would otherwise have dissolved, unwitnessed and unverified, in the backwoods of Canada. From this innocent disclosure, one arrives at the conclusion that all of Mrs. Moodie's writing may have represented an attempt to find confirmation of her existence, an existence which was hidden in an alien wilderness and all but buried alive. (pp. 31-2)

Carol Shields, in her Susanna Moodie: Voice and Vision, Borealis Press, 1977, 81 p.

JANET GILTROW (essay date 1981)

[Giltrow treats Roughing It in the Bush and Life in the Clearings as travel narratives. She claims that Moodie's choice of the travel genre demonstrates both her unwillingness to accept her permanent status as an immigrant and her desire to return to England.]

Frances Trollope's Domestic Manners of the Americans is clearly a travel book: it begins with the writer's embarkation from England; it includes large, discursive, informational units comparing life in the New World to life in the Old; it concludes with the writer's departure from the foreign scene. Susanna Moodie's Roughing It in the Bush also begins with her departure from home; it includes substantial information on Canadian life, organized for the benefit of European readers. In contrast to Trollope, however, Moodie never made the return trip: her book ends with the family's move from the bush to Belleville, which was a more congenial site but still no asylum on this cheerless continent. But although Moodie's book thus fails to conform to the classic structure of the genre, Roughing It is a travel book and the generic values of the text are those of travel narrative. In her rhetorical stance, Moodie is a travel writer; in Canada, she is a watchful visitor—a tourist and sightseer—and her observations are directed toward a European audience.

She arrives in the New World with a ready command of the expressive sentiments of nature description, bringing with her a diction and perspective in tune with the literary habits of eighteenth- and nineteenth-century Grand Tourists. (pp. 132-33)

Moodie's pious pleasure in landscape does not easily anticipate her own incorporation into the scene. In contrast, Catharine Parr Traill's more analytic observations in The Backwoods of Canada . . . do look forward to settling down. Where Traill's prose stops at small particulars, Moodie's rides on, along an abstract plane of diffuse enthusiasm. Her high excitement at panoramic vistas and her neglect of concrete details belong to genteel sightseeing—and a quick, unimplicating view of foreign sites.

The ruling conflict in Roughing It lies between this travel esthetic and the settler's destiny. In this book and its sequel, Life in the Clearings, it seems that Moodie never learned, temperamentally, that the journey was done and travel concluded. She expects, at least unconsciously, that there has been some mistake and that she must finally turn back and resume her route. Obviously, she was pinioned by manifest evidence to the contrary, and the distance between these two poles of mind—the imagination of travel and the realization of stasis—is sometimes resolved in Roughing It by the idea of death. Morbidity alleviates the emotional stress of homesickness by suggesting a mystic return-trip, a homing of the spirit to an earthly paradise. Thus Moodie addresses "dear, dear England": "Oh that I might be permitted to return and die upon your wave-encircled shores, and rest my weary head and heart beneath your daisy-covered sod at last!" . . . After a residence of nearly twenty years in Canada, Moodie uses the exclamatory present tense to express the anguish and helplessness of a newcomer.

Her reflections on letters from home, and on the gradual diminishment of their numbers, suggest that for a long while she did not believe she was here to stay. . . . (p. 133)

The "hope of return" is a durable one, on both sides of the breach, but its dissolution is finally inevitable, and emigration is a type of death for the settler. Return and homecoming are privileges of the traveler but not of the emigrant, and in Moodie's view the anticipation of homecoming is the basis for communication between the New World and the Old. To give up hope of return is to suffer the exchange of letters to dwindle and end: a grievous silence marks the irrevocable separation. Communication from the New World to the Old sustains the emigrant in her foreign exile, and maintains her attachment, however attenuated or unrealistic, to the society where she is "known" and from which she derives her identity. The interruption of this vital communication cuts a life-line and sentences the settler to fatal anonymity: "it is as if the grave had closed over you, and the hearts that once knew and loved you know you no more." If we can see this connecting, epistolary current as a survival mechanism, we can see the importance of the larger verbal enterprise—Roughing It or Life in the Clearings—in maintaining overseas connections. That "hope of return" may disappear in reality, but it can be renewed rhetorically by a literary communication with an Old World audience. By taking up travel narrative, Moodie revives the conceit of travel.

In dispatching a successful communication to English readers, the writer cultivates her original cultural and social values, and resists the New World attitudes which might dispossess her of these imported assets. Only a peculiar strength of mind can assure the emigrant's successful resistance. In her introduction to Roughing It, Moodie describes the determination with which the settlers depart: "they gird up the loins of the mind, and arm themselves with fortitude to meet and dare the heart-breaking conflict." . . . Refusing to capitulate to Canadian society, the displaced Englishwoman internalizes all those native institutions which had once supported her. She thus remains a traveler, never adopting the ways of the foreign place.

But this is only one view of the "heart-breaking conflict." There are alternatives to it which permit the immobilized traveler some relief from traumatic restlessness and death-wishing. Moodie suggests that the settler give up making comparisons between the New World and the Old, and get rid of one aspect of the traveler's mentality: "But, oh! beware of drawing disparaging contrasts between the colony and its illustrious parent." . . . With this warning she temporarily modifies her rhetorical stance to address "British mothers of Canadian sons" and instruct them in the process of settling down and learning to love Canada. Although Moodie is herself never innocent of suggesting contrasts which disparage the colony, she does at least reach a position where she no longer wants to die. Expressions of Canadian nationalism help her a little in this, but much more helpful and vivifying is her satire. Her comic vision effaces some of her morbidity, but without rupturing her essential connection with her English audience. The laugh is on the North American, even when Moodie is the apparent victim of the incidents she reports. The objects of her wit are patently too ignorant and morally inexperienced to see the joke, which is told for the entertainment of a European reader who shares her sense of humor.

In Roughing It in the Bush life is most hilarious when it is most dreadful. At Cobourg the Moodies find themselves in an insanely inhospitable neighborhood. Moodie is surrounded by unregenerate "savages"—Yankee squatters who harass her with outrageous rudeness. So exaggerated are these characters in their outlandish greed and unscrupulousness that the Cobourg episodes create a lunatic, lawless world at the center of which is the sane, astonished Moodie. She is culturally and economically disoriented; all social and moral principles are inverted in an antic parody of the life she has known. As she was respected and regarded in England, here she is reviled and loathed. In an alien land where she is "the stranger whom they hated and despised" . . . , she is powerless to alter her circumstances, and can only laugh and submit. Rebuke is futile in this desert of "ignorance and sin" where the moral voice echoes emptily. So Susanna Moodie learns to be quiet at Cobourg but vociferous in her literary life. (pp. 134-35)

Moodie's comedy is social comedy, arising from the serious travel issue of social insubordination and disorientation. Comedy defends the insulted immigrant and her offended values by ridiculing the hostile society which discounts her. Without the perpetual comparison of the New World to the Old there would be no joke, for the fun lies in the application of a superior intelligence which knows both the true shape of society and its ludicrous mutation in Upper Canada. The narrative voice of *Life in the Clearings* speaks, for the most part, in this knowing, wry tone. (p. 135)

In *Life in the Clearings* Moodie is especially concerned, as many European travelers in North America were, with analysis of class and of distribution of power and status in this new society. She identifies the materialism of colonial culture as the most influential factor in the corruption of traditional values, and she complains that the "educated man" belongs to a socially disenfranchised minority in the colony. But Moodie is convinced that a universal cultural hierarchy underlies even the most adverse conditions: "There is no mistaking the superiority that mental cultivation bestows," even when the local economic structure promotes illiterate, unrefined citizens.

Armed with this conviction, Moodie can withstand even the most blatant disparagements conferred on a woman of letters by an illiterate society: "The idea that some country people form of an author is highly amusing. One of my boys was tauntingly told by another lad at school, 'that his ma' said that Mrs. M—invented lies and got money for them.' This was her estimation of works of mere fiction." . . . (pp. 135-36)

But, even if she can shrug off such taunts, Moodie's art cannot address such a population and must revert to an audience which shares her own idea of literature and her own vision of society. Fortunately, she has recourse to another public. . . .

With the artist's physical as well as psychological survival at issue, Moodie chooses to ignore the philistine and materialistic Canadians and go abroad for her audience.

The travel structure of *Life in the Clearings* permits a type of social satire which expresses its author's estrangement from the country through which she journeys and from the community where she resides. . . . Moodie is an unimplicated sightseer, observing the exotic assortment of curiosities which comprises Upper Canadian society, and her narrative form is so elastic as to accommodate the social observations of other, similarly detached reporters. These reporters are outsiders— travelers or guests—who witness instances of cultural depravity and then tell their stories in such a way as to recover a sense of their own station and perspective. Always, this recovery involves a satiric exaggeration of North American folly. (p. 136)

Sometimes whole chapters are necessary to formalize anecdotal or digressive impulses, but *Clearings* always, sooner or later, recovers its direction. (p. 137)

Susanna Moodie, . . . with her melancholy lament for what she had lost and her sly satire of colonial manners, is central to the Canadian literary tradition. In the structure and expression of her attitudes—her reference to a distant point of origin, her homing tendencies and her feelings of literary and cultural isolation—are patterns recognizable to Canadian readers and artists. For Susanna Moodie, the true audience is elsewhere. (p. 142)

> *Janet Giltrow, "'Painful Experience in a Distant Land': Mrs. Moodie in Canada and Mrs. Trollope in America," in* Mosaic: A Journal for the Interdisciplinary Study of Literature, *Vol. XIV, No. 2, (Spring, 1981), pp. 131-44.*

MARGOT NORTHEY   (essay date 1984)

[*Northey probes the relationship between* Roughing It in the Bush *and* Rachel Wilde; or, Trifles from the Burthen of a Life, *a serialized autobiographical novel. She concludes that Moodie's feelings of isolation and misinterpretation are the result of her "long-standing, inward-looking response to her vision of herself as artist."*]

[In *Roughing It in the Bush*], Moodie clearly uses some of the techniques of fiction to heighten the characterizations and narrative drama. Moreover, the self has a special role in this partial autobiography in which fact is not always the whole truth. (p. 117)

Roughing It in the Bush in part presents Susanna Moodie as the romantic centre of the story. Yet because the book is also partially a collection of sketches about other characters and their experiences, the picture of the heroine that emerges is not as clear or complete as if she were the continuous focus. Moodie keeps one eye turned inward toward the self and the other fixed on those odd acquaintances who reveal and represent life in the New World. The outward-turned eye is observant, analytic, and humorous; the inward-turned eye is emotional, idealistic, and sentimental. One of the reasons the book is so disjointed and abruptly shifting in tone is that while Moodie's explicit purpose is to give the outward view—to present a typical picture of immigration life useful for others—the romantic ego keeps overruling it. The sense of a uniquely long-suffering heroine counteracts that of the representative immigrant. Thus while some critics perceive the conflict in the book as arising from Moodie's attempt to impress her upper-class English values on a patently unsuited new society, or from the distance between her romantic illusions and the rough reality she finds, or even from a kind of schizophrenic split in her responses—partly admiring and partly hating the country—the conflict also arises at a more basic level from her conflicting motives as author. She wants to tell a story of this strange land and its strange people, but she also has an urge to explain and magnify herself.

This desire for self-revelation and self-justification is better understood if one turns to one of Moodie's little-known works, *Rachel Wilde; or, Trifles from the Burthen of a Life.* Moodie wrote it in serialized form for *The Victoria Magazine*, an enterprising but unprofitable publication which she and her husband created and edited while living in Belleville. The story appeared in segments from 1847 to 1848—the life of the magazine. Although ostensibly about a girl called Rachel, it is obviously an autobiography of Moodie in her childhood years. . . . In *Rachel Wilde,* despite the fictitious name, the story is continuously autobiographical; with one small exception it concentrates entirely on the child. Moreover, if one considers romantic ideas about the nature of childhood, then these recollections of the early years have more import as a key to Susanna Moodie's perception of herself than do the recollections of her later life.

Although autobiography had become popular in the eighteenth century, Rousseau's *Confessions* (1782) fostered romantic introspection and the pursuit of self-knowledge as the source of knowledge about the world. Believing in the uniqueness of each individual, the romantics gave childhood new status. Rather than seeing the personality as static, they began to see it as a developing entity; the child was not a miniature adult, but a dynamic, malleable being whose experiences and perceptions would shape the personality of the adult. Wordsworth's belief that "the Child is father of the Man" was widely shared, and thus autobiographical accounts of childhood proliferated and became a key to the author's adult perspectives. (pp. 117-19)

Seen within this romantic pattern of thinking, *Rachel Wilde* becomes the obvious natural vehicle for Susanna Moodie to use for self-revelation and justification. Certainly as a literary work it has its shortcomings, many of them the same as in Moodie's better-known books. In places, the language is stilted and conventional; the episodic structure has many jerky transitions and changes in point of view. But as a guide to Moodie's sensibility it is revealing.

Moodie begins her story with the statement that "We are all more or less, the creatures of circumstance. . . . No one ever did, or could live for himself alone. We talk of originality of thought. Can such a thing in this stage of the world's history exist? Our very thoughts are not our own." . . . Such an opening hardly suggests romantic introspection and the inward-turned eye. In fact, she seems closer to the modern stress on environmental determinism when in the second and third paragraphs she illustrates how the physical surroundings of the early years "often determine the future character of the individuals." Moodie thus leads the reader to expect that she will trace those external environmental influences on the young child—that she will tell us about society by showing those critical areas of experience where the child intersected with it and was thus shaped by it. She proceeds in the first chapter to do just that. She gives the exact details of her family in the years of her infancy. (p. 119)

After this introduction, Moodie begins to narrate the first of a series of experiences which mark Rachel's years from the time of this happy infancy to the end of her childhood. As in all autobiographies, the memory selects—and the author shapes—those incidents which reinforce the pattern that the retrospective adult has created of past experience. To some extent Moodie does try to show how the events influenced the developing character and personality. . . . But overshadowing the theme of external influences is another, a stronger theme—that of an exceptional spirit, driven by her own imagination, emotion, and spiritual sensibility. In short, the picture which emerges is that of the romantic artist, isolated and misunderstood.

This portrait is developed in three stages. The first stage is of the infant in her happy home. But even here we find a prefiguring of the struggle of the visionary artist. Rachel enlists her younger brother and older sister Dorothy (a replica of the rational, patient, Catharine Parr Strickland) in a drama she has created in which the boy is to be carried off by a wood demon. But Rachel's fantasy is misinterpreted by an alarmed older sister, and the budding artist receives a cuff for her efforts. The motif of the misunderstood artist is developed further in the second stage of the portrait when the young child is sent off for an extended period to live with the Long family. She is disliked and frequently abused by Miss Betsy Long, but the ultimate humiliation, which leads her to run away, comes after she has joyfully decorated the newly painted window frames by scraping designs on them with the scissors. To her surprise, and without explanation, she is given a severe beating with the hated rod.

In the third stage, when Rachel is home again and in the later years of childhood, she is still the object of scorn. Pronounced "bad" and "crazy-pated" by her governess, she, "like many an unfortunate, misunderstood child of genius, remains unteachable, untaught." Only her sister Dorothea is able to heal "the wounds which the daily friction of uncongenial minds, stamped into the unfortunate girl's too sensitive heart." A solitary person, since "other children felt no sympathy with her—they could not comprehend her fantastic notions" . . . , her main solace, like that of other romantic souls, is "the 'Eden' of nature" where the "Divine Mother" gives inspiration. Thus the romantic visionary is born, one who comes to believe that her "lofty visions" are "inspirations direct from heaven." (pp. 120-21)

An outcast in her own mind, Rachel is sympathetic to other outcasts, especially those of genius. She falls in love with the devil depicted in Milton's *Paradise Lost* and later is punished for her unrelenting devotion to the defeated and exiled Napoleon. The final blow comes in the last chapter when Rachel labours in secret—since her eldest sister disapproves—to write a story. When the "sacred Manuscript" is discovered, the sister wants only to use it to cover the roasting pig. (p. 121)

It would be a distortion to imply that this overdrawn portrait of the artist as a young girl is all there is to *Rachel Wilde.* Clearly Moodie is not one of those modern autobiographers who lets the childish perceptions speak for themselves. She wants to guide our understanding. At times she forces the reader to stand back and see the child in a more dispassionate way, by pointing to the stubborn wilfulness and spoilt behaviour of young Rachel; she insists that the child brought on some of her own misfortunes by her ignorance of her own weaknesses and errors. . . . Yet these critical comments are not entirely a deflation of the romantic spirit and a return for the author to the analytic observer role. Moodie's mention of Rachel's faults adheres to the romantic belief that awareness of one's own irrational weaknesses is a sign of strength. By showing she knows herself—even, or perhaps especially, as a child—she becomes a reliable adult guide to experience in general.

Many of Moodie's reflections are a gloss upon the common romantic theme of a child's growing awareness of the mystery of evil and injustice in society and the consequent separation from the infant state of innocent bliss. A few times in the story she points out the representative rather than unique nature of Rachel. Commenting on the child's propensity to ask indiscreet questions or to figure out the answers to forbidden ones, she says, "This is human nature, and Rachel, at that period, was a child of nature, and listened to no other teacher." . . . Later she apostrophises, "Ah, blessed, thrice blessed season of youth and innocence—when earth is still the paradise of God, and its crimes and sorrows are veiled from the eyes of the undefiled." . . . This remark is part of the chapter in which Rachel encounters the treachery of the servant girl, Nancy, who accuses Rachel of stealing the treacle when she herself had eaten it. Rachel is unjustly thrashed. In the most extensive comment about society in the entire story, Moodie returns to her initial thesis about the effect of environment on character:

> If [Nancy] was an artful, dishonest creature, she had been rendered so by circumstances over which she had no control. . . . her whole existence was a life-long agony. She never got a kind word from anyone; . . . and can we wonder, that to secure herself from blame, she falsely accused an innocent child. . . .

But Moodie really does not sustain this thesis with the other characters in the tale or even with Rachel. We learn less about how circumstances shape Rachel's character than about how Rachel's temperament and innate sensibilities lead her to act and react as she does. . . . Even when Moodie takes up such social issues as injustice, the focus is less on injustice in the world than on Rachel's receipt of it. The injustice of Rachel's wrongful punishment in the treacle incident and the injustice of the scorn she receives from her eldest sister on the discovery of the manuscript are but precursors, we are led to believe, for the unjust scorn she will receive as an adult artist. In the final episode, as she and her sister set out to write their manuscripts, Moodie remarks:

> Alas! poor children, they little knew the troubles and trials that beset the dangerous path they were about to tread. The love and approbation of the few, and the envy and hatred of the many. To resign the joys of the present, and to live alone for the future. To be the scorn of vulgar and common minds; the dread of the weak and sensitive, to stand alone and without sympathy, misunderstood and maligned by most of their species. . . .

Such rhetoric may seem hopelessly overblown in relation to the incident that apparently sparked it, but it is really a summation of the underlying primary theme—the artist as outcast. Coming as it does in the last chapter, and reflecting as it does the adult wisdom of the author rather than the feelings of the child, it has an extra resonance.

Following this outburst, the conclusion to the story is curious. In the penultimate paragraph Moodie abruptly informs us that after a passage of years, "The world, as umpire, decided the question of her capacity, and gave the meed of praise so long denied." Yet Rachel throws it all up in order to go off with the man she loves. In the final paragraph we learn that she "resigned the tempting wreath [the world] offered her, to follow the adverse fortunes of the beloved—to toil in poverty and sorrow by his side—a stranger and an exile in a foreign land." . . . What are we to make of this tacked-on finale? The simplest answer, of course, is that Moodie wanted to finish off the story and provide a quick accounting of what happened to the child—the roll-call of years common in many nineteenth-century stories. The contradictory tone of the final two paragraphs suggests another answer, that the author's wish to justify herself gets in the way of artistic consistency. Related to this answer is the possibility that Moodie wrote *Rachel Wilde* as a kind of explanation or supporting piece for the partial self-portrait she was creating in *Roughing It in the Bush.*

A look at dates supports this notion of linkage. *Rachel Wilde* was likely written not much prior to its appearance in the

1847-48 issues of *The Victoria Magazine*. Two of Moodie's "Scenes in Canada" (which were to become the first chapters of *Roughing It in the Bush*), "A Visit to Grosse Isle" and "First Impressions—Quebec," were also published in the 1847 issues; and it was likely not much afterwards that Moodie set her mind to finishing the rest of the book, since it was published in 1852. However, six other chapters had first appeared in *The Literary Garland* of 1847, and some of them may have been written several years before that, since Moodie was a regular contributor from 1839 onward. . . . They have that outward vision and half-humorous tone mentioned earlier in this discussion, qualities which are also found in the beginning and at occasional intervals in *Rachel Wilde*. It appears that when Moodie began to write for the public in Canada, she attempted a more uninvolved, dispassionate, observer role. But when she got into her stride in her own magazine, and pulled the early sketches together into a framework with more narrative continuity, the romantic notion of self took over.

With *Rachel Wilde,* Moodie fills in the portrait of self only partially revealed in the narratives of *Roughing It in the Bush.* Despite the initial attempt to distance herself from the material by using a fictitious name for the child and the third person voice, she quickly moves to dramatize the self. The fictional cover is so transparent that she sometimes disregards it; in several sections she switches to the first-person voice. The first time she does this, she makes a quick explanation in the following chapter, no doubt sensing the reader's confusion.

If we think of *Rachel Wilde* and the framing chapters of *Roughing It in the Bush* as linked writings, then the mention of exile at the end of the story of the child ties in nicely with the story of the later years in Canada. More importantly, the autobiography of childhood adds another dimension to the motif of exile which appears in *Roughing It in the Bush.* It shows that Moodie saw herself as a kind of outcast most of her life, first isolated from the family when she went to the Longs', later exiled from the circle of teachables run by the governess, and finally cut off from the friendship of peers and elders who misunderstood her creative nature. It can be argued, therefore, that the feelings of isolation, misinterpretation, and exile she expresses in *Roughing It in the Bush* are not simply a reaction to her particular physical circumstances but also a long-standing, inward-looking response to her vision of herself as artist. She was little appreciated as a child writer and little appreciated as an adult, whether in the bush or at the time of writing these pieces. That she yearned for recognition is also evident in *Rachel Wilde,* not only from descriptions of the hurt she felt but from the recurring image in which she fancies herself a queen. . . . Clearly the misunderstood outsider had intimations of superiority.

Linking the two works helps explain not only the ending of *Rachel Wilde* but also why Susanna's husband is such a shadowy figure in *Roughing It in the Bush.* Love is a leitmotif in the childhood story. Towards the beginning, the incident of the young soldier with his fickle sweetheart introduces the child to the notion of false love. By contrast, the maturing outcast finds partial satisfaction in her own deeper love, whether for Milton's Satan or for Napoleon. The desire for worldly admiration is only superseded by the romantic union of love. In the end, therefore, Rachel opts for a future of love despite artistic exile. Following this pattern, Susanna's husband is really less an actual personality to be carefully described than a fulfilment of this romantic ideal. In *Roughing It in the Bush* he is not a part of the outward view that perceives character sketches but a completion of the inward vision of herself as a romantic spirit.

Rachel Wilde reveals how fully Susanna Moodie saw herself as a romantic figure. Whether she grafted this mature perception of herself onto the depiction of her childhood, or whether she always had it, is difficult to prove; but the vivid, concrete descriptions of many of the experiences felt by the child suggest the latter. In any case, read as a companion piece to *Roughing It in the Bush*, *Rachel Wilde* shows how the child is mother of the woman who lives in the bush. It helps explain the persona who pushes forth insistently, if intermittently, in the story of the backwoods. Thus, the Susanna Moodie who leaves the bush, having been often abused and scorned by her neighbours, is not in her own eyes an unsuccessful settler or failed immigrant, but a sensitive artist in unsympathetic surroundings. Moreover the suffering she describes in both works has a common didactic base rooted in romantic vision. Whether she endured it in the harsh wilds of Canada or in the pleasant countryside of England, Moodie saw in her suffering, and wanted readers to see, a source of the wisdom that was her claim to respect. (pp. 121-26)

> *Margot Northey, "Completing the Self-Portrait: Moodie's 'Rachel Wilde',"* in Essays on Canadian Writing, *No. 29, Summer, 1984, pp. 117-27.*

ADDITIONAL BIBLIOGRAPHY

Ballstadt, Carl; Peterman, Michael; and Hopkins, Elizabeth. "'A Glorious Madness': Susanna Moodie and the Spiritualist Movement." *Journal of Canadian Studies* 17, No. 4 (Winter 1982-83): 88-100.
  Traces Moodie's interest and involvement in the spiritualist movement.

Davies, Robertson. *"At My Heart's Core"; "Overlaid."* Toronto: Clarke, Irwin & Co., 1966, 124 p.
  Contains *At My Heart's Core*, a drama that depicts Canadian pioneer life and features Moodie as one of its characters.

Gairdner, William D. "Traill and Moodie: The Two Realities." *Journal of Canadian Fiction* 1, No. 2 (Spring 1972): 35-42.

Portrays Moodie as a mystic who rejected rationalism in favor of the emotionalism and individualism characteristic of the European Romantic movement.

Kröller, Eva-Marie. "Resurrections: Susanna Moodie, Catharine Parr Traill, and Emily Carr in Contemporary Canadian Literature." *Journal of Popular Culture* 15, No. 3 (Winter 1981): 39-46.
  Examines recent Canadian writers' use of the works of Moodie, Traill, and Emily Carr in their own writings. Kröller focuses on Carol Shields's inclusion of Moodie in her novel *Small Ceremonies* and Atwood's recreation of Moodie in her collection of poetry entitled *The Journals of Susanna Moodie* (see excerpt dated 1970).

Lande, Lawrence M. "The Strickland Sisters." In his *Old Lamps Aglow: An Appreciation of Early Canadian Poetry,* pp. 301-07. Montreal: Fiat Lux, 1957.
  Briefly discusses the contributions made by Moodie and Traill to early Canadian poetry.

MacLulich, T. D. "Crusoe in the Backwoods: A Canadian Fable?" *Mosaic* IX, No. 2 (Winter 1976): 115-26.
  Analyzes *Roughing It in the Bush* in relation to several common interpretations of Daniel Defoe's *Robinson Crusoe*.

Noonan, G. "Susanna and Her Critics: A Strategy of Fiction for *Roughing It in the Bush*." *Studies in Canadian Literature* (Fall 1980): 280-89.
  Examines various recent critics' views of *Roughing It in the Bush*.

Pacey, Desmond. "The Colonial Period (1750-1867)." In his *Creative Writing in Canada: A Short History of English-Canadian Literature,* rev. ed., pp. 8-34. Toronto: Ryerson Press, 1961.
  A brief, laudatory comparison of Moodie's *Roughing It in the Bush* and Traill's *The Backwoods of Canada*.

Thomas, Clara. "Journeys to Freedom." *Canadian Literature* No. 51 (Winter 1972): 11-19.
  Profiles Moodie, Traill, and Anna Murphy Jameson as notable nineteenth-century Canadian frontier writers.

Tinkler, John F. "Canadian Cultural Norms and Australian Social Rules: Susanna Moodie's *Roughing It in the Bush* and Marcus Clarke's *His Natural Life*." *Canadian Literature* No. 94 (Autumn 1982): 10-22.
  Discusses the cultivation of both the Canadian wilderness and the developing Canadian society as the controlling theme of *Roughing It in the Bush*.

Weaver, Emily P. "Mrs. Traill and Mrs. Moodie: Pioneers in Literature." *The Canadian Magazine* XLVIII, No. 5 (March 1917): 473-76.
  A short biographical sketch of Moodie and Traill.

Mary Wollstonecraft Godwin Shelley

1797-1851

English novelist, editor, critic, short story and travel writer.

Shelley is best known for her novel *Frankenstein; or, The Modern Prometheus,* which has transcended the Gothic and horror genres and is now recognized as a work of philosophical and psychological resonance. Critics agree that with the depiction of a seemingly godless universe where science and technology have gone awry, Shelley created a powerful metaphor for the modern age; indeed, the *Frankenstein* myth, which has been adapted to stage, film, and television, has pervaded modern culture. Shelley's achievement is considered remarkable, moreover, because she completed the book before her twentieth birthday. In addition to *Frankenstein,* Shelley's literary works include several novels that were mildly successful in their time but are little known today and an edition of poetry by her husband, the Romantic poet Percy Bysshe Shelley, which she issued with notes that are now regarded as indispensable. Her reputation rests, however, on what she once called her "hideous progeny," *Frankenstein.*

Shelley's personal life has sometimes overshadowed her literary work. She was the wife of Percy Shelley and the daughter of Mary Wollstonecraft, the early feminist and author of *A Vindication of the Rights of Woman,* and William Godwin, the political philosopher and novelist. Her parents' wedding, which occurred when Wollstonecraft was five months pregnant with Mary, was the marriage of two of the day's most noted freethinkers. While they both objected to the institution of matrimony, they agreed to marry to ensure their child's legitimacy. Ten days after Mary's birth, Wollstonecraft died from complications, leaving Godwin, an undemonstrative and self-absorbed intellectual, to care for both Mary and Fanny Imlay, Wollstonecraft's daughter from an earlier liaison. Mary's home life improved little with the arrival four years later of a stepmother and her two children. The new Mrs. Godwin, whom contemporaries described as petty and disagreeable, favored her own offspring over the daughters of the celebrated Wollstonecraft, and Mary was often solitary and unhappy. She was not formally educated, but absorbed the intellectual atmosphere created by her father and such visitors as Samuel Taylor Coleridge. She read a wide variety of books, notably those of her mother, whom she idolized. Young Mary's favorite retreat was Wollstonecraft's grave in the St. Pancras churchyard, where she went to read and write and eventually to meet her lover, Shelley.

An admirer of Godwin, Percy Shelley visited the author's home and briefly met Mary when she was fourteen, but their attraction did not take hold until a subsequent meeting two years later. Shelley, twenty-two, was married and his wife was expecting their second child, but he and Mary, like Godwin and Wollstonecraft, believed that ties of the heart superseded legal ones. In July 1814, one month before her seventeenth birthday, Mary eloped with Percy to the continent, where, apart from two interludes in England, they spent the next several years traveling in Switzerland, Germany, and Italy. These years were characterized by financial difficulty and personal tragedy. Percy's father, Sir Timothy Shelley, a wealthy baronet, cut off his son's substantial allowance after his elopement. In 1816,

Mary's half-sister Fanny committed suicide; just weeks later, Percy's wife, Harriet, drowned herself. Mary and Percy were married in London, in part because they hoped to gain custody of his two children by Harriet, but custody was denied. Three of their own children died in infancy, and Mary fell into a deep depression that was barely dispelled by the birth in 1819 of Percy Florence, her only surviving child. The Shelleys' marriage suffered, too, in the wake of their children's deaths, and Percy formed romantic attachments to other women. Despite these trying circumstances, both Mary and Percy maintained a schedule of rigorous study—including classical and European literature, Greek, Latin, and Italian language, music and art—and ambitious writing; during this period Mary completed *Frankenstein* and another novel, *Valperga.* The two also enjoyed a coterie of stimulating friends, notably Lord Byron and Leigh Hunt. The Shelleys were settled near Lenci, Italy, on the Gulf of Spezzia in 1822 when Percy drowned during a storm while sailing to meet Leigh and Marianne Hunt. After one mournful year in Italy, Mary returned permanently to England with her son.

Shelley's life after Percy's death was marked by melancholy and hardship as she struggled to support herself and her child. Sir Timothy Shelley offered her a meager stipend, but ordered that she keep the Shelley name out of print; thus, all her works were published anonymously. In addition to producing four novels in the years after Percy's death, Mary contributed a series of biographical and critical sketches to *Chamber's Cabinet Cyclopedia,* as well as occasional short stories, which she considered potboilers, to the literary annuals of the day. The Shelleys' financial situation improved when Sir Timothy increased Percy Florence's allowance with his coming of age in 1840, which enabled mother and son to travel in Italy and Germany; their journeys are recounted in *Rambles in Germany and Italy in 1840, 1842, and 1843.* Too ill in her last few years to complete her most cherished project, a biography of her husband, Shelley died at fifty-four.

Although *Frankenstein* has consistently dominated critical discussions of Shelley's oeuvre, she also composed several other novels in addition to critical and biographical writings. Her five later novels attracted little notice, and critics generally agree that they share the faults of verbosity and awkward plotting. After *Frankenstein, The Last Man* is her best-known work. This novel, in which Shelley describes the destruction of the human race in the twenty-first century, is noted as an inventive depiction of the future and an early prototype of science fiction. *Valperga* and *The Fortunes of Perkin Warbeck* are historical novels that have received scant attention from literary critics, while *Lodore* and *Falkner,* thought by many to be autobiographical, are often examined for clues to the lives of the Shelleys and their circle. Shelley's stories were collected and published posthumously, as was *Mathilda,* a novella that appeared for the first time in the 1950s. The story of a father and daughter's incestuous attraction, it has been viewed as a fictional treatment—or distortion—of Shelley's relationship with Godwin. The posthumously published verse dramas, *Proserpine and Midas,* were written to complement one of Percy Shelley's works and have garnered mild praise for their poetry. Apart from *Frankenstein,* critics most often admire Shelley's non-fiction: the readable, though now dated, travel volumes, the essays for *Chamber's Cabinet Cyclopedia,* which are considered vigorous and erudite, and her illuminating notes on her husband's poetry.

Shelley's most famous novel was conceived in 1816 at Lake Leman, Switzerland, where she and Percy had settled near Byron and his companion, John Polidori. As Mary described in her preface to the 1831 edition of the novel, one evening after reading Gothic stories, the four challenged each other to create their own tales of horror. Mary waited several days in vain for an idea until she heard a discussion between Byron and Shelley about galvanism and the notion of creating life via electricity. That night she awoke mesmerized by a vision of a creature animated by such means. She began to write the monster's narrative, which forms the book's central section. Shelley urged her to expand the tale into a novel, and Mary subsequently added the narratives of Captain Walton and Dr. Frankenstein.

Since Shelley's death, critics have devoted little attention to her other works, focusing instead on *Frankenstein.* Early critics, generally with some dismay, usually relegated the novel to the Gothic genre then practiced by such popular authors as Ann Radcliffe and Matthew Gregory "Monk" Lewis. While most early Victorian reviewers reviled what they considered the sensationalist and gruesome elements in *Frankenstein,* many praised the anonymous author's imagination and powers of description. In the later nineteenth century and throughout *Frankenstein* criticism, commentators have focused on Prometheanism in the novel, an aspect that Shelley herself highlighted in the book's subtitle. This line of enquiry, which continues to engage critics, likens Dr. Frankenstein to the Greek mythic figure who wreaks his own destruction through abuse of power. Percy Shelley treated the same mythic-philosophic theme in his poetry, most notably in *Prometheus Unbound,* and critics have searched for his influence on *Frankenstein,* particularly in the expression of Romantic ideals and attitudes. Scholars have also debated the value of the additional narratives that he encouraged her to write. While some have praised the novel's resulting three-part structure, others have argued that these additions detract from and merely pad the story, although most have valued the other-worldly Arctic scenes. Commentators have also frequently noted the influence of Shelley's father, tracing strains of Godwin's humanitarian social views; in addition, some critics have found direct thematic links to his fiction, particularly to his novel, *Caleb Williams.* Other literary allusions often noted in *Frankenstein* include those to John Milton's *Paradise Lost,* the source of the book's epigraph, as well as Johann Wolfgang von Goethe's *Faust* and Coleridge's "The Rime of the Ancient Mariner."

Frankenstein criticism has proliferated since the 1950s, encompassing a wide variety of themes and approaches. The monster, who is often the focus of commentary, has been interpreted as representing ideas ranging from the alienation of modern humanity to the repression of women. Many commentators have viewed the monster as Dr. Frankenstein's double, an example of the doppelgänger archetype. In a similar vein, critics have discussed Dr. Frankenstein and the monster as embodying Sigmund Freud's theory of id and ego. Students of the Gothic, supernatural horror, and science fiction novel have adopted *Frankenstein* as a venerable forebear and have approached it from a historical slant. Alternately, Shelley's life has served as a starting point for those who perceive in the novel expressions of the author's feelings toward her parents, husband, children, and friends. Recent feminist critics, in particular, have found Shelley and *Frankenstein* a rich source for study, describing it, for example, as a manifestation of the author's ambivalent feelings toward motherhood.

Shelley's friend Leigh Hunt once characterized her as "four-famed—for her parents, her lord / And the poor lone impossible monster abhorr'd." Today, Shelley has emerged from the shadow of her parents and husband as an artist in her own right. The volume and variety of *Frankenstein* criticism attests to the endurance of her vision.

PRINCIPAL WORKS

*History of a Six Weeks' Tour through a Part of France,
    Switzerland, Germany, and Holland, with Letters
    Descriptive of a Sail Round the Lake of Geneva and the
    Glaciers of Chamouni* [with Percy Bysshe Shelley]
    (travel essay)   1817
Frankenstein; or, The Modern Prometheus   (novel)   1818
*Valperga; or, The Life and Adventures of Castruccio, Prince
    of Lucca*   (novel)   1823
Posthumous Poems [editor]   (poetry)   1824
The Last Man   (novel)   1826
The Fortunes of Perkin Warbeck   (novel)   1830
Lodore   (novel)   1835
Falkner   (novel)   1837
The Poetical Works of Percy Shelley [editor]   (poetry)
    1839
Rambles in Germany and Italy in 1840, 1842, and 1843
    (travel essay)   1844
The Choice: A Poem on Shelley's Death   (poetry)   1876

Tales and Stories by Mary Wollstonecraft Shelley (short stories) 1891
Proserpine and Midas [first publication] (dramas) 1922
Mathilda (novella) 1959

PERCY BYSSHE SHELLEY (poem date 1817)

[*Regarded as a major English poet, Shelley was a leading figure in the English Romantic movement. His so-called "defense of poetry," in which he investigated poetry's relation to the history of civilization, was an important contribution to nineteenth-century aesthetics. Influenced by the French philosopher Jean-Jacques Rousseau and the German poet and pre-Romanticist Johann Gottfried von Herder, Shelley viewed poetry, as he did human society, as a continuing evolution of ideas. He argued that poetry was like a mirror to its age, the history of its manners, and as such he labeled all poets "legislators and prophets" who contributed to the spiritual and political evolution of mankind. In the following excerpt, Shelley dedicates his poem* The Revolt of Islam *to Mary. He alludes to their elopement and life together and evokes her illustrious parents, particularly Mary Wollstonecraft. This dedication was written in 1817. For additional commentary by Percy Shelley, see excerpts dated 1817 and 1818.*]

Thou Friend, whose presence on my wintry heart
  Fell, like bright Spring upon some herbless plain;
How beautiful and calm and free thou wert
  In thy young wisdom, when the mortal chain
  Of Custom thou didst burst and rend in twain,
And walked as free as light the clouds among,
  Which many an envious slave then breathed in vain
From his dim dungeon, and my spirit sprung
To meet thee from the woes which had begirt it long!

No more alone through the world's wilderness,
  Although I trod the paths of high intent,
I journeyed now: no more companionless,
  Where solitude is like despair, I went.—
  There is the wisdom of a stern content
When Poverty can blight the just and good,
  When Infamy dares mock the innocent,
And cherished friends turn with the multitude
To trample: this was ours, and we unshaken stood!

Now has descended a serener hour,
  And with inconstant fortune, friends return;
Though suffering leaves the knowledge and the power
  Which says:—Let scorn be not repaid with scorn.
  And from thy side two gentle babes are born
To fill our home with smiles, and thus we are
  Most fortunate beneath life's beaming morn;
And these delights, and thou, have been to me
The parents of the Song I consecrate to thee.

Is it, that now my inexperienced fingers
  But strike the prelude of a loftier strain?
Or, must the lyre on which my spirit lingers
  Soon pause in silence, ne'er to sound again,
  Though it might shake the Anarch Custom's reign,
And charm the minds of men to Truth's own sway
  Holier than was Amphion's? I would fain
Reply in hope—but I am worn away,
And Death and Love are yet contending for their prey.

And what art thou? I know, but dare not speak:
  Time may interpret to his silent years.
Yet in the paleness of thy thoughtful cheek,
  And in the light thine ample forehead wears,
  And in thy sweetest smiles, and in thy tears,
And in thy gentle speech, a prophecy
  Is whispered, to subdue my fondest fears:
And through thine eyes, even in thy soul I see
A lamp of vestal fire burning internally.

They say that thou wert lovely from thy birth,
  Of glorious parents, thou aspiring Child.
I wonder not—for One then left this earth
  Whose life was like a setting planet mild,
  Which clothed thee in the radiance undefiled
Of its departing glory; still her fame
  Shines on thee, through the tempests dark and wild
Which shake these latter days; and thou canst claim
The shelter, from thy Sire, of an immortal name.

(pp. 38-40)

> *Percy Bysshe Shelley, "'The Revolt of Islam'," in his* Poetical Works, *edited by Thomas Hutchinson with G. M. Matthews, Oxford University Press, London, 1970, pp. 31-158.*

PERCY BYSSHE SHELLEY (essay date 1817)

[*Shelley wrote the following highly favorable review of* Frankenstein *in 1817, but it was not published until 1832. In contrast with most early reviewers, Shelley emphasizes the novel's inherent moral aspects. He also acknowledges the similarity of* Frankenstein's *style and characterizations to those of William Godwin. For additional commentary by Percy Shelley, see excerpts dated 1817 and 1818.*]

The Novel of *Frankenstein; or, the Modern Prometheus,* is undoubtedly, as a mere story, one of the most original and complete productions of the day. We debate with ourselves in wonder, as we read it, what could have been the series of thoughts—what could have been the peculiar experiences that awakened them—which conduced, in the author's mind, to the astonishing combinations of motives and incidents, and the startling catastrophe, which compose this tale. There are, perhaps, some points of subordinate importance, which prove that it is the author's first attempt. But in this judgment, which requires a very nice discrimination, we may be mistaken; for it is conducted throughout with a firm and steady hand. The interest gradually accumulates and advances towards the conclusion with the accelerated rapidity of a rock rolled down a mountain. We are led breathless with suspense and sympathy, and the heaping up of incident on incident, and the working of passion out of passion. We cry "hold, hold! enough!"—but there is yet something to come; and, like the victim whose history it relates, we think we can bear no more, and yet more is to be borne. Pelion is heapen on Ossa, and Ossa on Olympus. We climb Alp after Alp, until the horizon is seen blank, vacant, and limitless; and the head turns giddy, and the ground seems to fail under our feet.

This novel rests its claim on being a source of powerful and profound emotion. The elementary feelings of the human mind are exposed to view; and those who are accustomed to reason deeply on their origin and tendency will, perhaps, be the only persons who can sympathize, to the full extent, in the interest of the actions which are their result. But, founded on nature as they are, there is perhaps no reader, who can endure anything beside a new love story, who will not feel a responsive string touched in his inmost soul. The sentiments are so affectionate and so innocent—the characters of the subordinate agents in this strange drama are clothed in the light of such a mild and gentle mind—the pictures of domestic manners are of the most simple and attaching character: the father's is irresistible and deep. Nor are the crimes and malevolence of the single Being, though indeed withering and tremendous, the offspring of any unaccountable propensity to evil, but flow irresistibly from certain causes fully adequate to their production. They are the children, as it were, of Necessity and Human Nature. In this the direct moral of the book consists; and it is perhaps the most important, and of the most universal application, of any moral that can be enforced by example. Treat a person ill, and he will become wicked. Requite affection with scorn;—let one being be selected, for whatever cause, as the refuse of his kind—divide him, a social being, from society, and you impose upon him the irresistible obligations—malevolence and selfishness. It is thus that, too often in society, those who are best qualified to be its benefactors and its ornaments, are branded by some accident with scorn, and changed, by neglect and solitude of heart, into a scourge and a curse.

The Being in *Frankenstein* is, no doubt, a tremendous creature. It was impossible that he should not have received among men that treatment which led to the consequences of his being a social nature. He was an abortion and an anomaly; and though his mind was such as its first impressions framed it, affectionate and full of moral sensibility, yet the circumstances of his existence are so monstrous and uncommon, that, when the consequences of them became developed in action, his original goodness was gradually turned into inextinguishable misanthropy and revenge. The scene between the Being and the blind De Lacey in the cottage, is one of the most profound and extraordinary instances of pathos that we ever recollect. It is impossible to read this dialogue,—and indeed many others of a somewhat similar character,—without feeling the heart suspend its pulsations with wonder, and the "tears stream down the cheeks." The encounter and argument between Frankenstein and the Being on the sea of ice, almost approaches, in effect, to the expostulations of Caleb Williams with Falkland. It reminds us, indeed, somewhat of the style and character of that admirable writer, to whom the author has dedicated his work, and whose productions he seems to have studied.

There is only one instance, however, in which we detect the least approach to imitation; and that is the conduct of the incident of Frankenstein's landing in Ireland. The general character of the tale, indeed, resembles nothing that ever preceded it. After the death of Elizabeth, the story, like a stream which grows at once more rapid and profound as it proceeds, assumes an irresistible solemnity, and the magnificent energy and swiftness of a tempest.

The churchyard scene, in which Frankenstein visits the tombs of his family, his quitting Geneva, and his journey through Tartary to the shores of the Frozen Ocean, resemble at once the terrible reanimation of a corpse and the supernatural career of a spirit. The scene in the cabin of Walton's ship—the more than mortal enthusiasm and grandeur of the Being's speech over the dead body of his victim—is an exhibition of intellectual and imaginative power, which we think the reader will acknowledge has seldom been surpassed.

> *Percy Bysshe Shelley, "On Frankenstein," in* The Athenaeum, *No. 263, November 10, 1832, p. 730.*

PERCY BYSSHE SHELLEY   (essay date 1818)

[*The "Preface" to the first edition of* Frankenstein, *published in 1818 and excerpted below, was presented as the work of Mary Shelley. She revealed, however, in a later preface (see excerpt dated 1831) that her husband actually wrote it. Here, Percy Shelley stresses that in spite of its supernatural bases,* Frankenstein *is intended to "preserve the truth of the elementary principles of human nature" and to demonstrate the primacy of human affection and virtue. For additional commentary by Percy Shelley, see excerpts dated 1817.*]

The event on which [*Frankenstein*] is founded, has been supposed, by Dr. [Erasmus] Darwin, and some of the physiological writers of Germany, as not of impossible occurrence. I shall not be supposed as recording the remotest degree of serious faith to such an imagination; yet, assuming it as the basis of a work of fancy, I have not considered myself as merely weaving a series of supernatural terrors. The event on which the interest of the story depends is exempt from the disadvantages of a mere tale of spectres or enchantment. It was recommended by the novelty of the situations which it developes; and, however impossible as a physical fact, affords a point of view to the imagination for the delineating of human passions more comprehensive and commanding than any which the ordinary relations of existing events can yield.

I have thus endeavored to preserve the truth of the elementary principles of human nature, while I have not scrupled to innovate upon their combinations. The *Illiad*, the tragic poetry of Greece—Shakspeare, in the *Tempest*, and *Midsummer Night's Dream*—and most especially Milton, in *Paradise Lost*, conform to this rule; and the most humble novelist, who seeks to confer or receive amusement from his labors, may, without presumption, apply to prose fiction a license, or rather a rule, from the adoption of which so many exquisite combinations of human feeling have resulted in the highest specimens of poetry.

The circumstance on which my story rests was suggested in casual conversation. It was commenced, partly as a source of amusement, and partly as an expedient for exercising any untried resources of mind. Other motives were mingled with these, as the work proceeded. I am by no means indifferent to the manner in which whatever moral tendencies exist in the sentiments or characters it contains shall affect the reader; yet my chief concern in this respect has been limited to the avoiding the enervating effects of the novels of the present day, and to the exhibition of the amiableness of domestic affection, and the excellence of universal virtue. The opinions which naturally spring from the character and situation of the hero are by no means to be conceived as existing always in my own conviction; nor is any inference justly to be drawn from the following pages as prejudicing any philosophical doctrine of whatever kind. (pp. v-vi)

> *Percy Bysshe Shelley, in an extract in* Frankenstein; or, The Modern Prometheus *by Mary W. Shelley, H. G. Daggers, 1845, pp. v-vi.*

[JOHN WILSON CROKER]   (essay date 1818)

[*Croker, a principal contributor to the conservative journal the* Quarterly Review, *was nicknamed the "slashing critic" for his vitriolic literary reviews. Here, Croker acknowledges the literary powers displayed in* Frankenstein, *yet he denounces the horrific effect to which they are employed.*]

Our readers will guess . . . what a tissue of horrible and disgusting absurdity [*Frankenstein*] presents.—It is piously dedicated to Mr. Godwin, and is written in the spirit of his school. The dreams of insanity are embodied in the strong and striking language of the insane, and the author, notwithstanding the rationality of his preface [see excerpt dated 1818 by Percy Bysshe Shelley], often leaves us in doubt whether he is not as mad as his hero. Mr. Godwin is the patriarch of a literary family, whose chief skill is in delineating the wanderings of the intellect, and which strangely delights in the most afflicting and humiliating of human miseries. His disciples are a kind of *out-pensioners of Bedlam*, and, like 'Mad Bess' or 'Mad Tom,' are occasionally visited with paroxysms of genius and fits of expression, which make sober-minded people wonder and shudder. (p. 382)

It cannot be denied that [it] is nonsense—but it is nonsense decked out with circumstances and clothed in language highly terrific: it is, indeed,

———————————a tale
Told by an ideot, full of sound and fury,
Signifying nothing—

but still there is something tremendous in the unmeaning hollowness of its sound, and the vague obscurity of its images.

But when we have thus admitted that *Frankenstein* has passages which appal the mind and make the flesh creep, we have given it all the praise (if praise it can be called) which we dare to bestow. Our taste and our judgment alike revolt at this kind of writing, and the greater the ability with which it may be executed the worse it is—it inculcates no lesson of conduct, manners, or morality; it cannot mend, and will not even amuse its readers, unless their taste have been deplorably vitiated—it fatigues the feelings without interesting the understanding; it gratuitously harasses the heart, and wantonly adds to the store, already too great, of painful sensations. The author has powers, both of conception and language, which employed in a happier direction might, perhaps, (we speak dubiously,) give him a name among those whose writings amuse or amend their fellow-creatures; but we take the liberty of assuring him, and hope that he may be in a temper to listen to us, that the style which he has adopted in the present publication merely tends to defeat his own purpose, if he really had any other object in view than that of leaving the wearied reader, after a struggle between laughter and loathing, in doubt whether the head or the heart of the author be the most diseased. (p. 385)

> [*John Wilson Croker*], *in a review of "Frankenstein; or, The Modern Prometheus," in* The Quarterly Review, *Vol. XVIII, No. XXXVI, January, 1818, pp. 379-85.*

[SIR WALTER SCOTT]   (essay date 1818)

[*Scott was a Scottish novelist, poet, historian, biographer, and critic of the Romantic period who is best known for his novels, which were great popular successes. In the excerpt below, Scott places* Frankenstein *in the philosophical rather than merely sensational school of supernatural fiction, terming it a work of creative and poetic genius, despite its implausible plot.*]

[*Frankenstein*] is a novel, or more properly a romantic fiction, of a nature so peculiar, that we ought to describe the species before attempting any account of the individual production. . . .

[The] class of marvellous romances admits of several subdivisions. In the earlier productions of imagination, the poet or tale-teller does not, in his own opinion, transgress the laws of credibility, when he introduces into his narration the witches, goblins, and magicians, in the existence of which he himself, as well as his hearers, is a firm believer. This good faith, however, passes away, and works turning upon the marvellous are written and read merely on account of the exercise which they afford to the imagination of those who, like the poet Collins, love to riot in the luxuriance of oriental fiction, to rove through the meanders of enchantment, to gaze on the magnificence of golden palaces, and to repose by the waterfalls of Elysian gardens. In this species of composition, the marvellous is itself the principal and most important object both to the author and reader. (p. 613)

A more philosophical and refined use of the supernatural in works of fiction, is proper to that class in which the laws of nature are represented as altered, not for the purpose of pampering the imagination with wonders, but in order to shew the probable effect which the supposed miracles would produce on those who witnessed them. In this case, the pleasure ordinarily derived from the marvellous incidents is secondary to that which we extract from observing how mortals like ourselves would be affected,

> By scenes like these which, daring to depart
> From sober truth, are still to nature true.

Even in the description of his marvels, however, the author, who manages this style of composition with address, gives them an indirect importance with the reader, when he is able to describe, with nature and with truth, the effects which they are calculated to produce upon his dramatis personæ. . . . But success in this point is still subordinate to the author's principal object, which is less to produce an effect by means of the marvels of the narrations, than to open new trains and channels of thought, by placing men in supposed situations of an extraordinary and preternatural character, and then describing the mode of feeling and conduct which they are most likely to adopt. (pp. 613-14)

In the class of fictitious narrations to which we allude, the author opens a sort of account-current with the reader; drawing upon him, in the first place, for credit to that degree of the marvellous which he proposes to employ; and becoming virtually bound, in consequence of this indulgence, that his personages shall conduct themselves, in the extraordinary circumstances in which they are placed, according to the rules of probability, and the nature of the human heart. In this view, the *probable* is far from being laid out of sight even amid the wildest freaks of imagination; on the contrary, we grant the extraordinary postulates which the author demands as the foundation of his narrative, only on condition of his deducing the consequences with logical precision.

We have only to add, that this class of fiction has been sometimes applied to the purposes of political satire, and sometimes to the general illustration of the powers and workings of the human mind. Swift, Bergerac, and others, have employed it for the former purpose, and a good illustration of the latter is the well known *Saint Leon* of William Godwin. In this latter work, assuming the possibility of the transmutation of metals and of the *elixir vitæ*, the author has deduced, in the course of his narrative, the probable consequences of the possession of such secrets upon the fortunes and mind of him who might enjoy them. *Frankenstein* is a novel upon the same plan with *Saint Leon;* it is said to be written by Mr Percy Bysshe Shelley, who, if we are rightly informed, is son-in-law to Mr Godwin; and it is inscribed to that ingenious author. (p. 614)

[In *Frankenstein*] the author seems to us to disclose uncommon powers of poetic imagination. The feeling with which we perused the unexpected and fearful, yet, allowing the possibility of the event, very natural conclusion of Frankenstein's experiment, shook a little even our firm nerves; although such, and so numerous have been the expedients for exciting terror employed by the romantic writers of the age, that the reader may adopt Macbeth's words with a slight alteration:

> We have supp'd full with horrors:
> Direness, familiar to our "callous" thoughts,
> Cannot once startle us.

It is no slight merit in our eyes, that the tale, though wild in incident, is written in plain and forcible English, without exhibiting that mixture of hyperbolical Germanisms with which tales of wonder are usually told, as if it were necessary that the language should be as extravagant as the fiction. The ideas of the author are always clearly as well as forcibly expressed; and his descriptions of landscape have in them the choice requisites of truth, freshness, precision, and beauty. The self-education of the monster, considering the slender opportunities of acquiring knowledge he possessed, . . . [is] improbable and overstrained. That he should have not only learned to speak, but to read, and, for aught we know, to write—that he should have become acquainted with *Werter*, with Plutarch's *Lives*, and with *Paradise Lost*, by listening through a hole in a wall, seems as unlikely as that he should have acquired, in the same way, the problems of Euclid, or the art of book-keeping by single and double entry. . . . We should also be disposed, in support of the principles with which we set out, to question whether the monster, how tall, agile, and strong however, could have perpetrated so much mischief undiscovered; or passed through so many countries without being secured, either on account of his crimes, or for the benefit of some such speculator as Mr Polito, who would have been happy to have added to his museum so curious a specimen of natural history. But as we have consented to admit the leading incident of the work, perhaps some of our readers may be of opinion, that to stickle upon lesser improbabilities, is to incur the censure bestowed by the Scottish proverb on those who start at straws after swallowing *windlings*.

The following lines, which occur in the second volume, mark, we think, that the author possesses the same facility in expressing himself in verse as in prose.

> We rest; a dream has power to poison sleep.
> We rise; one wand'ring thought pollutes the day.
> We feel, conceive, or reason; laugh, or weep,
> Embrace fond woe, or cast our cares away;
> It is the same; for, be it joy or sorrow,
> The path of its departure still is free.
> Man's yesterday may ne'er be like his morrow;
> Nought may endure but mutability!

Upon the whole, the work impresses us with a high idea of the author's original genius and happy power of expression. We shall be delighted to hear that he has aspired to the *paullo majora;* and, in the meantime, congratulate our readers upon a novel which excites new reflections and untried sources of emotion. If Gray's definition of Paradise, to lie on a couch, namely, and read new novels, come any thing near truth, no small praise is due to him, who, like the author of *Frankenstein,*

has enlarged the sphere of that fascinating enjoyment. (pp. 619-20)

> [*Sir Walter Scott*], "Remarks on 'Frankenstein; or, The Modern Prometheus: A Novel'," in Blackwood's Edinburgh Magazine, Vol. II, No. XII, March, 1818, pp. 613-20.

THE EDINBURGH MAGAZINE AND LITERARY MISCELLANY (essay date 1818)

[*In the following excerpt, the critic faults the exaggerated, somewhat impious, and decidedly "Godwinian" premises of* Frankenstein.]

[*Frankenstein*] is one of the productions of the modern school in its highest style of caricature and exaggeration. It is formed on the Godwinian manner, and has all the faults, but many likewise of the beauties, of that model. In dark and gloomy views of nature and of man, bordering too closely on impiety,—in the most outrageous improbability,—in sacrificing every thing to effect,—it even goes beyond its great prototype; but in return, it possesses a similar power of fascination, something of the same mastery in harsh and savage delineations of passion, relieved in like manner by the gentler features of domestic and simple feelings. There never was a wilder story imagined, yet, like most of the fictions of this age, it has an air of reality attached to it, by being connected with the favourite projects and passions of the times. The real events of the world have, in our day, too, been of so wondrous and gigantic a kind,—the shiftings of the scenes in our stupendous drama have been so rapid and various, that Shakespeare himself, in his wildest flights, has been completely distanced by the eccentricities of actual existence. . . . [The public] can be satisfied with nothing in fiction that is not highly coloured and exaggerated; we even like a story the better that it is disjointed and irregular, and our greatest inventors, accordingly, have been obliged to accommodate themselves to the taste of the age, more, we believe, than their own judgment can, at all times, have approved of. The very extravagance of the present production will now, therefore, be, perhaps, in its favour. . . . (p. 249)

[In] this singular performance, . . . there is much power and beauty, both of thought and expression, though, in many parts, the execution is imperfect, and bearing the marks of an unpractised hand. It is one of those works, however, which, when we have read, we do not well see why it should have been written;—for a *jeu d'esprit* it is somewhat too long, grave, and laborious,—and some of our highest and most reverential feelings receive a shock from the conception on which it turns, so as to produce a painful and bewildered state of mind while we peruse it. We are accustomed, happily, to look upon the creation of a living and intelligent being as a work that is fitted only to inspire a religious emotion, and there is an impropriety, to say no worse, in placing it in any other light. It might, indeed, be the author's view to shew that the powers of man have been wisely limited, and that misery would follow their extension,—but still the expression "Creator," applied to a mere human being, gives us the same sort of shock with the phrase, "the Man Almighty," and others of the same kind, in Mr Southey's *Curse of Kehama*. All these monstrous conceptions are the consequences of the wild and irregular theories of the age; though we do not at all mean to infer that the authors who give into such freedoms have done so with any bad intentions. This incongruity, however, with our established and most sacred notions, is the chief fault in such fictions, regarding them merely in a critical point of view. Shakespeare's Caliban (though his simplicity and suitableness to the place where he is found are very delightful) is, perhaps, a more *hateful* being than our good friend in this book. But Caliban comes into existence in the received way which common superstition had pointed out; we should not have endured him if Prospero had created him. Getting over this original absurdity, the character of our monster is in good keeping;—there is a grandeur, too, in the scenery in which he makes his appearances,—the ice-mountains of the Pole, or the glaciers of the Alps;—his natural tendency to kind feelings, and the manner in which they were blighted,—and all the domestic picture of the cottage, are very interesting and beautiful. We hope yet to have more productions, both from this author and his great model, Mr. Godwin; but they would make a great improvement in their writings, if they would rather study the established order of nature as it appears, both in the world of matter and of mind, than continue to revolt our feelings by hazardous innovations in either of these departments. (pp. 252-53)

> *A review of "Frankenstein; or, The Modern Prometheus," in* The Edinburgh Magazine and Literary Miscellany, *n.s.Vol. II, March, 1818, pp. 249-53.*

THE BRITISH CRITIC   (essay date 1818)

[*This critic pronounces* Frankenstein *absurd and unnatural, but admits that the novel evinces powers that "might be disciplined into something better." Judging from references to Godwin's* Mandeville *and to a female author, the reviewer was aware of the author's true identity.*]

[*Frankenstein*] is another anomalous story of the same race and family as *Mandeville;* and, if we are not misinformed, it is intimately connected with that strange performance, by more ties than one. In the present instance, it is true, we are presented with the mysteries of equivocal generation, instead of the metaphysics of a bedlamite; but he who runs as he reads, might pronounce both novels to be *similis farinæ*. We are in doubt to what class we shall refer writings of this extravagant character; that they bear marks of considerable power, it is impossible to deny; but this power is so abused and perverted, that we should almost prefer imbecility; however much, of late years, we have been wearied and ennuied by the languid whispers of gentle sentimentality, they at least had the comfortable property of provoking no uneasy slumber; but we must protest against the waking dreams of horror excited by the unnatural stimulants of this later school; and we feel ourselves as much harassed, after rising from the perusal of these three spirit-wearing volumes, as if we had been over-dosed with laudanum, or hag-ridden by the night-mare. (p. 432)

We need scarcely say, that these volumes have neither principle, object, nor moral; the horror which abounds in them is too grotesque and *bizarre* ever to approach near the sublime, and when we did not hurry over the pages in disgust, we sometimes paused to laugh outright; and yet we suspect, that the diseased and wandering imagination, which has stepped out of all legitimate bounds, to frame these disjointed combinations and unnatural adventures, might be disciplined into something better. We heartily wish it were so, for there are occasional symptoms of no common powers of mind, struggling through a mass of absurdity, which well nigh overwhelms them; but it is a sort of absurdity that approaches so often the confines of what is wicked and immoral, that we dare hardly

The first illustration of Frankenstein's monster, from the 1831 Standard Novels edition.

trust ourselves to bestow even this qualified praise. The writer of it is, we understand, a female; this is an aggravation of that which is the prevailing fault of the novel; but if our authoress can forget the gentleness of her sex, it is no reason why we should; and we shall therefore dismiss the novel without further comment. (p. 438)

> *A review of "Frankenstein; or, The Modern Prometheus," in* The British Critic, *n.s. Vol. IX, April, 1818, pp. 432-38.*

BLACKWOOD'S EDINBURGH MAGAZINE   (essay date 1818)

[*The following excerpt is from a brief review that praises the lively, unpretentious style of Shelley's travel volume,* A Six Weeks' Tour.]

There is little information, no reflection, and very few incidents, in [*History of a Six Weeks' Tour through a Part of France, Switzerland, Germany, and Holland*], and yet it somehow or other produces considerable amusement and interest. It is the simplest and most unambitious journal imaginable of a Continental Tour; and probably in that simplicity consists its principal attraction. There is no formal appearance of a largely-promising preface; none of that assumed stateliness of intellect so ludicrous in your modern imbecil tourist; none of those common-places which, like so much dead luggage, impede the motion of the vehicle; no steeple-hunting in large towns—no talk of antiquities in every paltry village. When we lay down the volume, we are not much the wiser; but we are wholly free from that drowsiness that steals so imperceptibly from most journals, and the perusal of it rather produces the same effect as a smart walk before breakfast, in company with a lively friend who hates long stories.

The writer of this little volume, too, is a Lady, and writes like one,—with ease, gracefulness, and vivacity. Above all, there is something truly delightful in the colour of her stockings; they are of the purest white, and much more becoming than the brightest blue. She prattles away very prettily in the true English idiom, and has evidently learned her language from living lips, rather than from dead dictionaries. Though a travelling lady, and therefore entitled to understand all tongues, she very modestly confines herself to the English; and we are not the less disposed to believe, that she understands the languages of other countries, from observing that she writes well that of her own. Now and then a French phrase drops sweetly enough from her fair mouth, but the fear of bad grammar is before her eyes, and she has never ventured on a whole sentence. . . . There is also something original in the plan of travelling adopted by the fair Tourist. She is not . . . a sour, solitary spinster—she is a sweet-blooded wedded wife. Her youth has, she says, been chiefly past in pursuing, like the swallow, the inconstant summer of delight and beauty which invests this visible world. And, on the present occasion, with her husband (there is no travelling companion like a husband,) and her sister, she passes *on foot* through part of France and Switzerland, and sails down the castled magnificence of the Rhine. Her heart is at all times open to gladness and kindly feeling; and we think that no one will part with so amiable and agreeable a companion, without regret, and sincere wishes for her future happiness. (p. 412)

> *A review of "History of a Six Weeks' Tour through a Part of France, Switzerland, Germany, and Holland,"* in Blackwood's Edinburgh Magazine, *Vol. III, No. XVI, July, 1818, pp. 412-16.*

WILLIAM GODWIN   (letter date 1822)

[*An English philosopher, novelist, and essayist, Godwin is remembered as an author whose writings strongly influenced the English Romantic writers. His anarchistic and rationalistic beliefs were first delineated in his philosophical masterpiece,* An Enquiry Concerning Political Justice and Its Influence on General Virtue and Happiness, *and later dramatized in his well-known novel,* Things As They Are; or, The Adventures of Caleb Williams. *The following excerpt is from Godwin's critique of Shelley's* Valperga.]

Perhaps it may be of some use to you if I give you my opinion of [*Valperga*]. I think there are parts of high genius, and that your two females are exceedingly interesting; but I am not satisfied. *Frankenstein* was a fine thing; it was compressed, muscular, and firm; nothing relaxed and weak; no proud flesh. [*Valperga*] is a work of more genius; but it appears, in reading, that the first rule you prescribed to yourself was, I will let it be long. It contains the quantity of four volumes of *Waverley*. No hard blow was ever hit with a woolsack! (p. 52)

> *William Godwin, in a letter to Mary Wollstonecraft Shelley on November 15, 1822, in* The Life & Letters of Mary Wollstonecraft Shelley, *Vol. II by Julian Marshall, Richard Bentley & Son, 1889, pp. 50-2.*

BLACKWOOD'S EDINBURGH MAGAZINE   (essay date 1823)

[*In this excerpt from a review of* Valperga, *the critic states that while the novel possesses certain beauties, it fails to live up to the promise displayed in* Frankenstein.]

Frankenstein, at the time of its appearance, we certainly did not suspect to be the work of a female hand; the name of Shelley was whispered, and we did not hesitate to attribute the book to *Mr* Shelley. Soon, however, we were set right. We learned that *Frankenstein* was written by *Mrs* Shelley; and then we most undoubtedly said to ourselves, "For a man it was excellent, but for a woman it is wonderful." What we chiefly admired, in that wild production, was vigour of imagination and strength of language; these were unquestionable attributes, and they redeemed the defects of an absurd groundwork and an incoherent fable; and, moreover, they tempted us, and every body else, to forgive the many long passages of feeble conception and feeble execution, with which the vigorous scenes were interwoven.

The history of Castruccio Castracani [recounted in **Valperga**], on the other hand, had been long familiar to us in the glowing and energetic sketch of Machiavelli. Perhaps, on the whole, we should have been more rejoiced in the prospect of meeting Mrs Shelley again on the same dark territory, where she had first displayed so many striking powers; but the story of Castruccio we were willing to consider as not unlikely to furnish, in such hands, the basis and materials of a most romantic fiction. . . . We must confess, that in much of what we looked for, we have been disappointed; but yet, even here at the outset, we do not hesitate to say, that if we have not met with what we expected, we have met with other things almost as good.

Our chief objection, indeed, may be summed up in one word— Mrs Shelley has not done justice to the character of Castruccio. The life of him, by Machiavel, does not cover more than twenty or thirty duodecimo pages; yet, one rises from that brief sketch with a much more lively and perfect notion of the man, than from the perusal of the three closely printed volumes now on our table. There is not one spark of wit in all this book, and yet the keen Italian wit of Castruccio was one of the most striking features in his real character, and ought to have been among the most prominent in a work representing him throughout, in action and conversation. Machiavel, in two or three pages, tells stories enough to have suggested the true "*Castruccio vein.*" Who does not remember that famous one of his rebuking a young man, whom he met coming out of a house of ill fame, and who blushed on being recognized? "It was when you went in that you should have coloured," said Castruccio, "not when you come out." (p. 283)

Of all this sort of thing we have no trace in Mrs Shelley's book; and yet she appears to have contemplated a very full development of Castruccio's character. She gives us his infancy, his boyhood, his manhood, all in complete detail. The attempt, whether successful or not, certainly is made to depict the slow and gradual formation of a crafty and bloody Italian tyrant of the middle ages, out of an innocent, open-hearted and deeply-feeling youth. We suspect, that in the whole of this portraiture, far too much reliance has been laid on thoughts and feelings, not only modern, but modern and feminine at once. Perhaps we might say more; nay, perhaps we should not be saying too much, if we plainly expressed the opinion, that a very great part of Mrs Shelley's book has no inspiration, but that of a certain *school*, which is certainly a very modern, as well as a very mischievous one, and which ought never, of all things, to have numbered ladies among its disciples. But, in spite even of this, we have closed the book with no feelings but those of perfect kindness—and we shall say no more of matters that will, perhaps, suggest themselves to our readers quite strongly enough, without our giving ourselves any trouble.

Laying out of view Antehminelli's real life and character, we can have no hesitation in saying, that Mrs Shelley has given us a clever and amusing romance. Not doubting, that she will in due time make more attempts in the same way, we would fain point out, to so clever a person, faults which she might easily avoid in future, and which here, even more, perhaps, than in *Frankenstein,* neutralize much of her power. But, on further reflection, we believe the best way will be to leave all this to the working of experience. A very little consideration must be enough to shew such a writer the absurdity of introducing so many pure episodes. The framer of an historical romance should not be reminding us at every turn, that his *principal* object is to shew off his own knowledge of strange manners, or power of fine writing. If quaint manners are to be quaintly and strongly represented, the incidents, with which these are connected, ought to have a strict connexion with, and influence over, the progress of the fable, or at least the development of the principal characters of the fable. We cannot stand the stepping aside for ten pages, *merely* for the purpose of letting us see, that the writer knows the way in which the *Mysteries* of the middle ages were represented, either on, or off the Arno—we cannot spare four days of the life of Castruccio Castraccani to singers and tale-tellers, and so forth, with whom he and his story have nothing to do—we abhor all unnecessary prosing about religious sects, and we are mortally sick of "orange-tinted skies," "dirges," and "Dante." (p. 284)

The work . . . undoubtedly reflects no *discredit* even on the authoress of *Frankenstein*—although we must once more repeat our opinion, that *Valperga* is, for a second romance, by no means what its predecessor was for a first one. (p. 293)

> *A review of "Valperga; or, The Life and Adventures of Castruccio, Prince of Lucca," in* Blackwood's Edinburgh Magazine, *Vol. XII, No. LXXIV, March, 1823, pp. 283-93.*

THE LONDON LITERARY GAZETTE   (essay date 1823)

[*The reviewer favorably compares* Valperga *with* Frankenstein.]

In [*Valperga*] the most powerful passions are called into action; and love, enthusiasm, and ambition, appear on the canvass, stamped with the same wild imagination that characterized *Frankenstein.* Energetic language, landscapes worthy of poet or painter, feelings strong in their truth, are to be found in every chapter. . . . The period, that of the struggle between the Guelphs and Ghibbelines, in which it is laid, is above all favourable for display and delineation of character. . . . In this Novel it is not the events that interest us so much as the actors; and we shall give a better idea of *Valperga* by sketching the characters than by detailing the plot.

At the head of the list stands Castruccio. We see him first a gentle and affectionate child, an exile in his infancy, and his earliest impressions those of blood and fear. Next he is a spirited, generous boy, who then becomes the very model of a young warrior, brave, beautiful, and in love; but even then the evil germ is in his heart, though as yet bearing no fruit. The ambitious soldier adds the lessons of craft to those of courage,

and craft is soon followed by its shadow, cruelty; the darker outlines of the picture are gradually filled up; and in the cold-blooded, intriguing, suspicious leader of the Ghibbelines, we lose almost all trace of the once light, frank-hearted, noble Castruccio. There is truth, there is power in the portrait, yet we feel unsatisfied in gazing on it; we mark the ravages of ambition on the once fresh and affectionate heart with the same repugnance that we watch on a beautiful face the encroachments of disease. The Lord of Lucca has too much interest at first to admit of our cordially hating his worthlessness; we do not like to see our bright idol prove but a thing of human dust and dross. No other male character occupies a conspicuous place. The subtle Galeazzo, the gentle Arigo, the Bishop, Buondelmonte, though well coloured, are but mere sketches; and Pepi seems to us solely introduced to gratify a family taste for monsters. This same remark may apply to Bindo the Albinois, and the witch of the forest—sheer mummery, unworthy the other parts. Indeed the most prevailing fault through the work is the multiplicity of those introduced, from whom we are led to expect much, yet who are afterwards, as it were, forgotten by the author. But the two female pictures are exquisite, both from their contrast and in themselves. Pure, beautiful, high-minded, generous, Euthanasia is an emanation of female loveliness and female delicacy; perfect without being insipid, her superiority is forgotten and forgiven in her gentleness and her sorrow. But with all the admiration we have conceded, we must think her character ideal: it scarcely seems in woman's nature for patriotism to be a stronger feeling than love; and we could have forgiven Euthanasia for marrying Castruccio, even though he had declared war against Florence. Beatrice is the very creation of fancy and poetry: young, beautiful, enthusiastic, yielding to love as to the dictates of Heaven; taking the wild impulses of an ungoverned imagination for inspiration; passionate, yet timid; pity is almost pain when we find the innocent and radiant girl withered in her fiery hour of insanity, dying of a broken heart: it is like a relief to have Castruccio to hate for it. (p. 132)

We recommend the readers of this work to skim the commencement of the first volume, dwell on the history of Euthanasia, for its feeling; the history of her court, held four days, for its vivid picture of the manners of the age; read the whole of the second, skim again the beginning of the third, and we will leave the end to speak for itself. (p. 133)

> *A review of "Valperga; or, The Life and Adventures of Castruccio, Prince of Lucca," in* The London Literary Gazette, *No. 319, March 1, 1823, pp. 132-33.*

THE LONDON LITERARY GAZETTE   (essay date 1826)

[*In the following excerpt from a review of* The Last Man, *the critic commends Shelley's ambitious subject, but finds the novel generally unsuccessful due to plot implausibilities and too many "horrors."*]

This is a novel [*The Last Man*], of which the subject is sufficiently extraordinary. Two of the most successful poets of the day, Byron and Campbell, have dared only just to touch upon it in a few detached lines; and yet here we have three volumes of prose devoted to it by a female writer. Whether the bards were wise in their restricted flights, or whether this bolder undertaking could possibly succeed, we will not here inquire. The author, suffice it to say, is not unknown to the reading world, for her scarcely less bold, and certainly not altogether unsuccessful attempt under the title of *Frankenstein.*

We shall, therefore, merely glance at the plan and conduct of the fable. . . . There is an Introduction, not very skilfully imagined, which gives us to understand that the work is to be looked upon as a sort of free translation of certain "Sibylline Leaves," picked up by a party of modern travellers in the (so called) cave of the Cumaean Sibyl, on the shores of the Bay of Naples: and the story (as its name indicates) relates to the life and fortunes of "the Last Man," who remains on the face of the earth after it has been desolated of its human inhabitants by a great plague, which rages during the last two or three years of the twenty-first century of our present era. The story, however, commences about the year 2073—thus affording scope for much matter not connected with the catastrophe, and enabling the writer to indulge in every possible (and impossible) flight of her anticipative imagination, touching the nature of human society, and of all other mundane matters, a hundred and fifty years hence! . . .

Were this not written by a woman, it would be sad, vapid impertinence: as it is written by a woman, we male critics do not know what it is. We wish we did! Who will teach us? (p. 102)

When we repeat that these volumes are the production of a female pen, and that we have not ceased to consider Mrs. Shelley as a woman and a widow, we shall have given the clue to our abstinence from remarks upon them. That we must deem the tale altogether to be an instance of the strange misapplication of considerable talent, is most true. After the first volume, it is a sickening repetition of horrors, and a struggle after the display of morbid feelings which could not exist under the circumstances, nor even in the world as it now exists, with good and evil, joys and woes, mingled together. To hear a *last man* talking of having his "sensitive nerves anatomised" by any thing, is sheer nonsense: by the time a man had outlived his kind, Mrs. S. might be assured that the nervous system too was pretty nearly abolished. . . . Really these are sad doings. We confess that we cannot get so seriously through the world in its last convulsions as we could wish; but there may be readers who can enter into the spirit of the thing, and to them the perusal of Mrs. Shelley's book may afford gratification. We will add, that there are some strong imaginings in it; and not the least cruel of these flights appears to us to be, the author's making the last human being an unfortunate gentleman. Why not *the last Woman?* she would have known better how to paint her distress at having nobody left to talk to: we are sure the tale would have been more interesting. (p. 103)

> *A review of* "*The Last Man,*" *in* The London Literary Gazette, *No. 474, February 18, 1826, pp. 102-03.*

THE MONTHLY REVIEW, LONDON   (essay date 1826)

[*According to the author of this excerpt from a brief, unfavorable review,* The Last Man *is excessively extravagant and morbid, "the offspring of a diseased imagination, and of a most polluted taste."*]

Mrs. Shelley, true to the genius of her family, has found this breathing world and the operations and scenes which enliven it, so little worthy of her soaring fancy, that [in *The Last Man*] she once more ventures to create a world of her own, to people it with beings modelled by her own hand, and to govern it by laws drawn from the visionary theories which she has been so long taught to admire as the perfection of wisdom. She seems herself to belong to a sphere different from that with which we are conversant. Her imagination appears to delight in in-

ventions which have no foundation in ordinary occurrences, and no charm for the common sympathies of mankind. (p. 333)

This idea of *The Last Man* has already tempted the genius of more than one of our poets, and, in truth, it is a theme which appears to open a magnificent and boundless field to the imagination. But we have only to consider it for a moment, in order to be convinced that the mind of man might as well endeavour to describe the transactions which are taking place in any of the countless planets that are suspended beyond our own, as to anticipate the horrors of the day which shall see the dissolution of our system. The utmost efforts of thought are absolutely childish, when they seek to fathom the abyss of ruin, to number the accumulation of disasters, to paint the dreadful confusion, which await that final scene. Every writer who has hitherto ventured on the theme, has fallen infinitely beneath it. Mrs. Shelley, in following their example, has merely made herself ridiculous. (p. 334)

There is nothing in the conduct, in the characters, in the incidents, or in the descriptive matter of this work, to which we feel any pleasure in referring. The whole appears to us to be the offspring of a diseased imagination, and of a most polluted taste. We must observe, however, that the powers of composition displayed in this production, are by no means of an ordinary character. They are indeed uncontrolled by any of the rules of good writing; but they certainly bear the impress of genius, though perverted and spoiled by morbid affectation. Mrs. Shelley frequently attempts to give her style a rythmical conciseness, and a poetical colouring, which we take to have been the main causes of the bombast that disfigures almost every chapter of this unamiable romance.

The descriptions of the operations of the pestilence are particularly objectionable for their minuteness. It is not a picture which she gives us, but a lecture in anatomy, in which every part of the human frame is laid bare to the eye, in its most putrid state of corruption. In this part of her subject, as indeed in every other, she amplifies beyond all the bounds of moderation. We are reluctantly obliged to pronounce the work a decided failure. (p. 335)

> *A review of* "*The Last Man,*" *in* The Monthly Review, *London, Vol. I, No. III, March, 1826, pp. 333-35.*

[SIR WALTER SCOTT]   (essay date 1827)

[*Here, Scott places* Frankenstein *in the tradition of "fantastic" literature.*]

[There is a] FANTASTIC mode of writing,—in which the most wild and unbounded license is given to an irregular fancy, and all species of combination, however ludicrous, or however shocking, are attempted and executed without scruple. In the other modes of treating the supernatural, even that mystic region is subjected to some laws, however slight; and fancy, in wandering through it, is regulated by some probabilities in the wildest flight. Not so in the fantastic style of composition, which has no restraint save that which it may ultimately find in the exhausted imagination of the author. (p. 72)

Our English severity of taste will not easily adopt this wild and fantastic tone into our own literature; nay, perhaps will scarce tolerate it in translations. The only composition which approaches to it is the powerful romance of *Frankenstein,* and there, although the formation of a thinking and sentient being by scientific skill is an incident of the fantastic character, still the interest of the work does not turn upon the marvellous creation of Frankenstein's monster, but upon the feelings and sentiments which that creature is supposed to express as most natural—if we may use the phrase—to his unnatural condition and origin. In other words, the miracle is not wrought for the mere wonder, but is designed to give rise to a train of acting and reasoning in itself just and probable, although the *postulatum* on which it is grounded is in the highest degree extravagant. So far *Frankenstein,* therefore, resembles the *Travels of Gulliver,* which suppose the existence of the most extravagant fictions, in order to extract from them philosophical reasoning and moral truth. In such cases the admission of the marvellous expressly resembles a sort of entry-money paid at the door of a lecture-room,—it is a concession which must be made to the author, and for which the reader is to receive value in moral instruction. But the *fantastic* of which we are now treating encumbers itself with no such conditions, and claims no further object than to surprise the public by the wonder itself. (pp. 72-3)

[Sir Walter Scott], "On the Supernatural in Fictitious Composition: And Particularly on the Works of Hoffmann," in The Foreign Quarterly Review, *Vol. 1, No. 1, July, 1827, pp. 60-98.*

THE ATHENAEUM   (essay date 1830)

[*The following excerpt is from a favorable notice of* The Fortunes of Perkin Warbeck.]

[The] volumes before us [*The Fortunes of Perkin Warbeck*] are the productions of no ordinary pen. It is manifest that a richly-endowed and vigorous intellect has directed the hand which traced them. They are written with a noble energy of thought—a deep concentration of feeling—a fervid glow of expression, and sweet purity of sentiment, which display in their author the very highest capabilities. The reader is hurried on from action to action with a spirit-stirring impulse, which never for a moment allows his excitement to abate; and the scenes which follow each other in such rapid succession, are wrought out with all the distinctness of a present reality. The characters are drawn with great vividness, and in some of them, especially, there is an originality which strikingly marks the powerfully-creative mind of the author of *Frankenstein.*

Clifford, Frion, and Herman de Faro, we take to be very noble conceptions. The two first stand before us in the darkest hues of reckless depravity, whilst the latter is endowed with a dignity, which a peculiar mental idiosyncrasy often superadds to the natural elevation of virtue.

Mrs. Shelley's work contains simply what its title indicates—the fortunes of Perkin Warbeck, (whom our fair author presumes to be no impostor, but the true Plantagenet,) from his rescue from the Tower, when a child, to the sad termination of his career upon the scaffold.

The great defect in this romance appears to us to be the painful anticipation of disaster which is continually forced upon the reader, and which the mind cannot escape from, so that no pleasurable emotions are excited. It is painful to hurry through a succession of events which we know beforehand will all terminate unhappily. Warbeck's marriage with Lady Catherine Gordon is the only oasis amid the wilderness of misfortune through which he is doomed to wander. The interest of the reader is necessarily vastly diminished by his unavoidable

knowledge, that every effort of the hero will fail, and that destruction must overtake him at the last. (p. 323)

A review of "The Fortunes of Perkin Warbeck: A Romance," in The Athenaeum, *No. 135, May 29, 1830, pp. 323-25.*

THE EDINBURGH LITERARY JOURNAL   (essay date 1830)

[*This critic assesses the merits and faults of* The Fortunes of Perkin Warbeck, *noting particularly its excessive detail.*]

[*The Fortunes of Perkin Warbeck*] is a talented work, but, at the same time, a little tedious and heavy. Mrs Shelley informs us in the preface, that she studied the subject originally with a view towards historical detail, but that, becoming aware of its romance, she determined not to confine herself to the mere incorporation of facts narrated by the old Chroniclers. A good deal of the leaven of history, however, still remains; and though several fictitious characters have been introduced, a calm straight-forwardness of style characterises the whole book. The authoress sets out on the assumption that Perkin Warbeck was really the Duke of York, and consequently entitled to the throne of England upon the death of his elder brother Edward the Fifth. Upon this disputed question it is unnecessary for us to enter farther, than to remark that sufficient plausibility attaches to Mrs Shelley's theory, to authorise her as a novelist to avail herself of it, although we are afraid that, in order to carry it through, she has been obliged, in more instances than one, to twist to her own interpretation the established facts of history. The chief fault we have to find with her production is, that it does not blend together with sufficient skill what is fictitious and what is true. The great use of an intermixture of fiction in an historical romance, is to relieve the reader from many dry details, and agreeably to fill up the interstices between those events which rivet the attention the more powerfully that they stand forth in bold and prominent contrast to the no less important occurrences of everyday life. Mrs Shelley, however, is contented to follow her hero's fortunes through thick and thin; and instead of fixing, as we should have advised her to do, on a few circumstances of acknowledged interest and moment, and contriving that all the narrative should tend towards them, she rather prefers patiently to act the part of a biographer, and with the utmost perseverance follows Warbeck through all his fortunes, whether his adventures be brilliant or stupid, fortunate or disastrous. Could every reader enter into the fate and character of her hero with the same enthusiasm as our authoress, there would be nothing tiresome in this minuteness of detail; but even though we were to grant that he was the veritable heir to England's crown, we fear that, with one or two exceptions, there was little in his career to warrant our devoting undivided attention to it through three long volumes. (pp. 350-51)

It is therefore to be regretted, we think, that Mrs Shelley has, in the present work, indefatigably gone through the whole of Perkin Warbeck's life. Many of the smaller adventures and unsuccessful attempts at rebellion should have been omitted, because they lead to nothing, and wear out without satisfying the mind; and because, moreover, they tend to diminish our respect for her hero, pointing him out as one continually borne down by adversity, and consequently one more to be pitied than admired. Had she, on the contrary, confined her story to one or two of the more striking parts of his career,—such as his residence and marriage in Scotland, and subsequent fate,— she would have greatly strengthened her narrative; and by contracting her details into a narrower compass, given a solidity and compactness to them, in which they are at present deficient. To speak in the language of painters, her novel has not a sufficiently powerful middle-distance and foreground. The objects introduced are too much diffused and scattered. She has taken us to the top of a hill, and when we expected a broad and beautiful lake to burst upon us at once, we see nothing but the long line of a canal, which is equally broad at the one end as it is at the other.

Though we have thus stated, pretty plainly, our objection to Mrs Shelley's novel, we must at the same time state, no less plainly, that it unquestionably bears the stamp of a powerful mind, and that no one can read it without feeling a conviction that the authoress need not fear a comparison with even the most talented of her sex. It is certain that Mrs Shelley is apt at times to be heavy, and assuredly her *Last Man* is, in many parts, abundantly so, yet we entertain a high respect for her abilities, and believe her worthy to have been the wife of the author of the "Cenci." There is much powerful writing in her *Perkin Warbeck,* and several of the characters introduced—especially those of Sir Robert Clifford, Monina de Faro, and Catherine Gordon—are sketched with bold vigour and fine discrimination. It is not, however, in a facility of giving an intense individuality to the persons of her story that Mrs Shelley chiefly excels. We like her better in the narrative parts, interspersed as these always are with her own observations on men and manners, and coloured by her own peculiar imagination, feelings, and associations. (p. 351)

> *A review of "The Fortunes of Perkin Warbeck: A Romance," in* The Edinburgh Literary Journal, *No. 84, June 19, 1830, pp. 350-52.*

MARY W. SHELLEY (essay date 1831)

[*In her preface to the 1831 edition of* Frankenstein, *excerpted below, Shelley recounts the famous circumstances surrounding the conception and composition of the novel. She concludes the account with an allusion to the monster: "I bid my hideous progeny go forth and prosper."*]

The Publishers of the Standard Novels, in selecting *Frankenstein* for one of their series, expressed a wish that I should furnish them with some account of the origin of the story. I am the more willing to comply because I shall thus give a general answer to the question so very frequently asked me—"How I, then a young girl, came to think of, and to dilate upon so very hideous an idea?" It is true that I am very averse to bringing myself forward in print; but as my account will only appear as an appendage to a former production, and as it will be confined to such topics as have connection with my authorship alone I can scarcely accuse myself of a personal intrusion.

It is not singular, that, as the daughter of two persons of distinguished literary celebrity, I should very early in life have thought of writing. As a child, I scribbled; and my favorite pastime, during the hours given me for recreation, was "to write stories." Still I had a dearer pleasure than this, which was the formation of castles in the air—the indulging in waking dreams—the following up trains of thought; which had for their subject the formation of a succession of imaginary incidents. My dreams were at once more fantastic and agreeable than my writings. In the latter I was a close imitator—rather doing as others had done than putting down the suggestions of my own mind. What I wrote was intended at least for one other eye—my childhood's companion and friend—but my dreams were

all my own; I accounted for them to nobody; they were my refuge when annoyed—my dearest pleasure when free.

I lived principally in the country as a girl, and passed a considerable time in Scotland. I made occasional visits to the more picturesque parts; but my habitual residence was on the blank and dreary northern shores of the Tay, near Dundee. Blank and dreary, on retrospection, I call them; they were not so to me then. They were the cry of freedom, and the pleasant region where unheeded I could commune with the creatures of my fancy. I wrote then—but in a most common-place style. It was beneath the trees of the grounds belonging to our house, or on the bleak sides of the woodless mountains near, that my true compositions, the airy flights of my imagination, were born and fostered. I did not make myself the heroine of my tales. Life appeared to me too common-place an affair as regarded myself. I could not figure to myself that romantic woes or wonderful events would ever be my lot; but I was not confined to my own identity; and I could people the hours with creations far more interesting to me at that age, than my own sensations.

After this, my life became busier, and reality stood in place of fiction. My husband, however, was from the first very anxious that I should prove myself worthy of my parentage, and enrol myself on the page of fame. He was for ever inciting me to obtain literary reputation, which, even on my own part, I cared for then, though since I have become infinitely indifferent to it. At this time he desired that I should write, not so much with the idea that I could produce any thing worthy of notice, but that he might himself judge how far I possessed the promise of better things hereafter. Still I did nothing. Travelling, and the cares of a family, occupied my time; and study, in the way of reading, or improving my ideas in communication with his far more cultivated mind, was all of literary employment that engaged my attention.

In the summer of 1816, we visited Switzerland, and became the neighbors of Lord Byron. At first we spent our pleasant hours on the lake, or wandering on its shores; and Lord Byron, who was writing his third canto of *Childe Harold,* was the only one among us who put his thoughts upon paper. These, as he brought them successively to us, clothed in all the light and harmony of poetry, seemed to stamp as divine the glories of heaven and earth, whose influences we partook with him.

But it proved a wet, ungenial summer, and incessant rain often confined us for days to the house. Some volumes of ghost stories, translated from the German and French, fell into our hands. There was the *History of the Inconstant Lover,* who, when he thought to clasp the bride to whom he had pledged his vows, found himself in the arms of the pale ghost of her whom he had deserted. There was the tale of the sinful founder of his race, whose miserable doom it was to bestow the kiss of death on all the younger sons of his ill-fated house, just when they reached the age of promise. His gigantic, shadowy form, clothed like the ghost in Hamlet, in complete armor, but with the beaver up, was seen at midnight by the moon's fitful beams, to advance slowly along the gloomy avenue. The shape was lost beneath the shadow of the castle walls: but soon a gate swung back, a step was heard, the door of the chamber opened, and he advanced to the couch of the blooming youths, cradled in healthy sleep. Eternal sorrow sat upon his face as he bent down and kissed the forehead of the boys, who from that hour withered like flowers snapped upon the stalk. I have not seen these stories since then; but their incidents are as fresh in my mind as if I had read them yesterday.

"We will each write a ghost-story," said Lord Byron; and his proposition was acceded to. (pp. vii-viii)

I busied myself *to think of a story*—a story to rival those which had excited us to this task. One which would speak to the mysterious fears of our nature, and awaking thrilling horror—one to make the reader dread to look round, to curdle the blood, and quicken the beatings of the heart. If I did not accomplish these things, my ghost story would be unworthy of its name. I thought and pondered—vainly. I felt that blank incapability of invention which is the greatest misery of authorship, when dull Nothing replies to our anxious invocations. *Have you thought of a story?* I was asked each morning, and each morning I was forced to reply with a mortifying negative. (pp. viii-ix)

Many and long were the conversations between Lord Byron and Shelley, to which I was a devout, but nearly silent listener. During one of these, various philosophical doctrines were discussed, and among others, the nature of the principle of life, and whether there was any probability of its ever being discovered and communicated. They talked of the experiments of Dr. Darwin. (I speak not of what the Doctor really did, or said he did, but, as more to my purpose, of what was then spoken of as having been done by him,) who preserved a piece of vermicelli in a glass cage, till by some extraordinary means it began to move with voluntary motion. Not thus, after all, would life be given. Perhaps a corpse would be re-animated; galvanism had given token of such things; perhaps the component parts of a creature might be manufactured, brought together, and endued with vital warmth.

Night waned upon this talk, and even the witching hour had gone by, before we retired to rest. When I had placed my head on my pillow, I did not sleep, nor could I be said to think. My imagination, unbidden, possessed and guided me, gifting the successive images that arose in my mind with a vividness far beyond the usual bound of reverie. I saw—with shut eyes, but acute mental vision—I saw the pale student of unhallowed arts kneeling beside the thing he had put together. I saw the hideous phantasm of a man stretched out, and then, on the working of some powerful engine, show signs of life, and stir with an uneasy, half vital motion. Frightful must it be; for supremely frightful would be the effect of any human endeavor to mock the stupendous mechanism of the Creator of the world. His success would terrify the artist; he would rush away from his odious handywork, horror-stricken. He would hope that, left to itself, the slight spark of life which he had communicated, would fade; that this thing which had received such imperfect animation, would subside into dead matter; and he might sleep in the belief that the silence of the grave would quench for ever the transient existence of the hideous corps which he had looked upon as the cradle of life. He sleeps: but he is awakened; he opens his eyes: behold the horrid thing stands at his bedside, opening his curtains, and looking on him with yellow, watery, but speculative eyes.

I opened mine in terror. The idea so possessed my mind, that a thrill of fear ran through me and I wished to exchange the ghastly image of my fancy for the realities around. I see them still; the very room, the dark *parquet*, the closed shutters, with the moonlight struggling through, and the sense I had that the glassy lake and white high Alps were beyond. I could not so easily get rid of my hideous phantom; still it haunted me. I must try to think of something else. I recurred to my ghost story—my tiresome, unlucky ghost story! O! if I could only contrive one which would frighten my reader as I myself had been frightened that night!

Swift as light, and as cheering, was the idea that broke in upon me. "I have found it! What terrified me will terrify others; and I need only describe the spectre which had haunted my midnight pillow." On the morrow I announced that I had *thought of a story*. I began that day with the words, *It was on a dreary night in November,* making only a transcript of the grim terrors of my waking dream.

At first I thought but of a few pages—of a short tale; but Shelley urged me to develope the idea at greater length. I certainly did not owe the suggestion of one incident, nor scarcely of one train of feeling, to my husband, and yet, but for his incitement, it would never have taken the form in which it was presented to the world. From this declaration I must except the preface. As far as I can recollect, it was entirely written by him.

And now, once again, I bid my hideous progeny go forth and prosper. I have an affection for it, for it was the offspring of happy days, when death and grief were but words, which found no true echo in my heart. Its several pages speak of many a walk, many a drive, and many a conversation, when I was not alone; and my companion was one who, in this world, I shall never see more. But this is for myself; my readers have nothing to do with these associations. (pp. ix-x)

> *Mary W. Shelley, in an extract in her* Frankenstein; or, The Modern Prometheus, *H. G. Daggers, 1845, pp. vi-x.*

Mary Shelley at the age she wrote Frankenstein.

THE NEW-YORK MIRROR   (essay date 1833)

[*The author of the following excerpt offers a sardonic assessment of* Frankenstein's *plot implausibilities, particularly those regarding the education and development of the monster.*]

The remark applied to Shakspeare, that he not only exhausted ordinary characters, but imagined new, is not altogether inapplicable to Mrs. Shelley. She has not, like the great bard, penetrated into all the variety of human nature, but the demon, created by Frankenstein, stands as much alone as Caliban, and, like that, takes a powerful hold on the imagination. We do not, however, assume the pen to praise a work [like *Frankenstein*], so well known and justly admired by every reader of romance; we mean only to enumerate several of its defects and improbabilities. We say *improbabilities*, because, notwithstanding that the tale itself is founded on a wild superstition, yet an author, although he may create impossible characters, may not make them do impossible things. There is a probability in their actions independent of the probability of their existence. Caliban, however exclusively a creation of the poet, is, nevertheless, always kept within the bounds of probability, bating the pardonable, and, indeed, necessary absurdity of rendering the uncouth savage thoughts of his glimmering intellect in verse. The monster has a certain character to sustain, certain powers of mind to lead him, certain peculiarities of body, and he has passed through a certain series of events which have formed his mind and disposition. He exhibits no knowledge but such as he had an opportunity to acquire. He speaks only of things with which he may be supposed to have been familiar. Shakspeare does not make him write, or read, or comprehend metaphysics. If Homer had fallen into his hands, he would not have conceived it. . . .

The probabilities of Frankenstein's demon are not so well preserved. The author soon found herself in a dilemma respecting the creature at length endowed with the vital spark, and she must have been as much in doubt what to do with him, as was the poor student himself, when blasted with the fatal success of his tremendous experiment. He must eat, drink, talk, understand, think, and act. He requires, too, extraordinary cunning to elude vigilance, and yet to procure the necessaries of existence. With a gigantic form, he has only an infant's mind—no knowledge, no experience. The author has, indeed, although at some expense or probability, adroitly managed to extricate him from so many difficulties.

Here, for instance, is one absurdity in her delineation of his thoughts. It occurs almost immediately after his creation, and while his mind is yet in its unenlightened state. It was very cold in the woods where he was wandering, and having found a fire which had been left by some beggars, he was overcome with delight at the warmth, thrust his hand into the embers, "and quickly drew it out again, with a cry of pain." Thus far it is natural. It is just what the creature might have done. But when he observes, (in his subsequent narrative,) "how strange, I thought, that the same cause should produce such opposite effects," and this too before he had acquired any language, you feel at once, that, being what he was, such a philosophical reflection never could have occurred to him. The whole account of his residence by the hut of the old man, Felix &c., is exceedingly pretty, but also exceedingly improbable. His reflections, previously to his knowledge, are such as no one, without that knowledge, could possess. How could he come to the conclusion, from the noise which the family made with their lips, that they were communicating ideas, that this was a godlike science, that, in reading, they found in the paper signs for speech which they understood, and that he would have been pleased to understand those signs, but despaired, because he did not understand the sounds which they represented? All these are philosophical conclusions, which, however apparently self-evident to the enlightened, yet imply long previous study and observation. All his mental operations here are of the same inconsistent and incredible nature. By looking through a hole in the wall, and listening alone, he learns not only to understand the language, but to read it and speak it so well, that he comprehends and remembers a complicated story of considerable length and full of allusions to the institutions, character and events of a state of civilized society. What could he know of grated windows—different languages—Paris—an execution—passports—treachery—exile? &c. After having learned what he could through the chink in the cottage wall, he became accidentally possessed of *Paradise Lost*, Plutarch's *Lives*, and the *Sorrows of Werter*, which he read with intelligence and criticized with force and precision. When, at length, he decides on entering the cottage to address the blind man, his language is so correct, that his hearer holds a long conversation with him, and discovers nothing extraordinary in his pronunciation and method of speaking. . . .

One of the most improbable things in the book, is the obtuseness of Frankenstein in reference to the nature of the demon's threat, "remember, I shall be with you on your wedding night." The wretch had already murdered one of his friends, and subsequently ended the life of another, thus plainly proving that his revenge sought to wound the creator of his misery through his affections; yet Frankenstein, with the most improbable want of common sense, continues to the period of his wedding, to tremble for his own life only, without once suspecting that any harm could befall his bride. Yet which of the two would such a diabolical foe slay? So completely is he blinded on this subject, that he actually leaves Elizabeth unguarded, when any other man would have locked her, if possible, in an inaccessible castle. . . .

It is not impossible, that the author was aware of these inconsistencies, and presumed upon the license necessary to the illustration of so poetical a story; but as many of them, and especially the last, might have been obviated by a little ingenuity, and without impairing the interest of the narration, it is a matter of regret that they have not been corrected.

The reader must not suppose, from these remarks, that we intend any thing derogatory to the high reputation of the tale. Indeed it merits strong commendation. There never yet, within the pages of a romance, was a plot more startling and wildly and intensely interesting. The imagination is immediately aroused, and hurried on impetuously toward the conclusion. The style of the writer also is easy, artless, and graceful. The most stupendous events and sublimest scenes are narrated and described in unaffected yet powerful language; and, indeed, one of the most striking merits of the author, independent of the invention of the story, is the total absence of verbiage and bathos, when a more elevated and turgid style would not, by any critics, be considered as inappropriate to the lofty and exciting character of the subject. The tale is doubtless destined to immortalize the accomplished writer, and quite sanctions the remark of Mr. Moore, that it is "one of those original conceptions that take hold of the public mind at once and for ever."

A review of "Frankenstein," in The New-York Mirror, *Vol. X, No. 49, June 8, 1833, p. 390.*

THE ATHENAEUM (essay date 1835)

[*In this excerpt from a favorable review of* Lodore, *the critic praises its pleasing "feminine" attributes.*]

Mrs. Shelley's novels always possess a character of their own, which renders them acceptable to us; yet, when we sit down to consider wherein the charm of this their individuality consists, we frankly confess, that we find a difficulty in satisfying ourselves, or explaining our thoughts to others. Delicacy in conception of character, earnestness of purpose, such as draws the reader along, though, to quote an old *concetto,* "the rein be merely a string of roses"—and a gentle harmony of language, may all be mentioned as among their attributes: they are essentially feminine too in their strength as well as their sweetness, and singularly free from the soil and tinsel of this world's trick-wisdom. If, in all courtesy, we might, for once, be personal—we should not find it difficult to point out from what source the authoress of *Lodore* has derived her turn for investigating those springs and secrets of the human heart, which are least open to the eye of the superficial and vulgar gazer—whence she has inherited her conception of—

> How divine a thing
> A woman may be made,

and from whom she has caught a felicity of epithet, and a skillful ease of cadence, which make her style at times positively melodious.

It will be easy for our readers to perceive, that we have been pleased with *Lodore,* and we think, that all who can appreciate what is refined, and breathes of the affections rather than the passions, will share our pleasure. As the authoress has a style of her own, so also are her plots unlike any others with which we are acquainted. The tale of *Lodore* is consistent in its own peculiar colouring, so that we do not feel that it contains unsolved improbabilities, and difficulties and hindrances too finely drawn for reality. Without destroying any of the reader's interest, we may say that it turns upon the estrangement of Lord Lodore and his wife, which leads to the exile of the former, and afterwards to the yet more painful separation of daughter and mother. The characters of both of these are fascinating—the one softening in her resentment, and being purified from her worldliness by the lapse of time; the other, in the hour of vicissitude, strengthened by her affections, and becoming from a simple and innocent child, a faithful and noble-spirited wife—there are few creations in modern fiction, sweeter than Ethel Villiers. The incidental sketches of Miss Fitzhenry, the lonely day-dreaming old maid, and of Clorinda Saville, the violent jealous Italian wife, are also clear and *new.* The gentlemen are cast in a less decided mould, but strong enough to sustain the interest of the story, which never flags, and ends just as we would have it. . . . [Having] said so much in favour of our authoress, we may likewise tell her that she is too fond of expatiating upon the feelings of her characters, instead of letting them be shown in dialogue or action; her story, too, flows on so continuously, that it is difficult to detach a scene. . . . (pp. 238-39)

We had marked . . . passages for extract, as, for instance, those in which the simple and delightful heroine of the story comes in upon her husband in the midst of his distresses, and by her cheerful devotedness, makes their poverty not only endurable, but happy. The squalidity and meanness of narrow circumstances, may be, perhaps, too entirely left out of the picture, for the authoress has thrown the poetry of her own spirit over her story—but we like her book all the better, because, for that very reason, it resembles so much the less, the bargain-driving world we live in. (p. 239)

> *A review of "Lodore," in* The Athenaeum, *No. 387, March 28, 1835, pp. 238-39.*

[WILLIAM MAGINN] (essay date 1835)

[*One of the most prominent journalists in England during the first half of the nineteenth century, Maginn wrote articles ranging from burlesques in verse to literary criticism. In his extremely laudatory review of* Lodore, *excerpted below, Maginn praises the work's style, execution, and characterization.*]

The publication of *Lodore* has gone a considerable way towards convincing us that Mrs. Shelley might have indeed been the author of *Frankenstein*—a work which we once believed could not possibly owe its existence to a female novelist; and this, not because there is a similitude between the structure and development of *Frankenstein,* that fearful and fantastic dream of genius, and the love-story before us, which is of the every-day world—its doings and its sufferings, but because there is common to both a depth and sweep of thought—a knowledge of human kind, in its manifold relations with this earth—and a boldness and *directness* in penetrating to the recesses and displaying the motives and workings of the heart, its feelings and passions—not in woman only, but in man also—which we certainly should have imagined to be far beyond the scope and power of a lady. Yet is there, at the same time, nothing in these volumes which a lady might not have known, and felt, and written; nor can there be the slightest doubt that they are the production of a feminine mind, albeit one of robust culture and extraordinary vigour. In the form and course of thought, if not actually in the style of expression in many passages, and in the downright, unaffected, noble simplicity, with which, in *Lodore,* subjects are treated, in which the heart and senses play a subtly mingled part, we were oftentimes reminded of the confessions of that charming enthusiast, Madame Roland—the only politician and philosopher in petticoats we could ever bring ourselves to regard with affectionate respect. Like her, too, Mrs. Shelley has shewn, not only that she can unveil the soul of woman to its very uttermost recesses, but that she can divine, appreciate, and depict the character of men. The work is very unlike the generality of our modern novels; it does not contain a sweeping together of incidents from a long suite of stories, historic, romantic, and burlesque; it does not present a faded anthology of *effeté* jests, of shrivelled gallantries, and impassible sentimentalities. There is not a constant succession of the startling events, the outrageous griefs, the bloody battles, the atrocious catastrophes, which form the staple commodity of that farrago of elongated melodramas which so frequently constitutes a modern novel. Nor is that ingenious device resorted to, which was originally borrowed by our novel-spinners from the festival scene in the pantomimes, of having a number of persons, bedecked in the costume of great names, to stand by and assist at the multifarious performances of the regular actors in the scene—the pseudo-representatives of kings and Caesars, beauties and heroes, wits and sages—to witness, as it were, the vigour of Harlequin and the agility of Columbine, to say nothing of the parts of the Clown and Pantaloon. Nor is that vile expedient put in use, of pretending to gratify the prurient curiosity of the vulgar by the introduction of real characters, who have rendered themselves either distinguished or notorious on the stage of life. No! nor is the plot "perplexed in the extreme;" nor are the characters multitudinous, like the waves of the sea; nor are they ever suffered, in obedience to some immediate necessity of the author, to obey the magical injunction,

> Come like shadows,
> So depart;

nor, moreover, do we, from first to last, find a single being who is absolutely exalted above, or depressed below humanity.

The story is simple—its theme is

> Love, still love!

It treats of the hopes and fears, the joys and sorrows, the delights and dangers, the blessings and the evils, of the fierce and tender passion. A healthy moral pervades her whole treatment of the subject. (pp. 600-01)

The execution of the work is, upon the whole, extremely good—it is quite worthy of the design. The impress of an original and thoughtful mind is visible throughout, and there are many passages of exceeding gracefulness, of touching eloquence, and of intense feeling. Her most obvious faults are that of occasionally introducing, by way of illustration, wild and quaint imagery—we might say, in some instances, imagery which is quite incongruous with that it is intended to illustrate; and, secondly, that of analysing and detailing too minutely each and every one of the sensations, intermingled or successive, which, when operating in mass (so to speak), constitute a feeling or a passion. The result of this extreme elaborateness is often to weary, and always, by refining away, to injure the general effect. These faults, however, we apprehend, may be with her either the results of education, or the pious faults of imitation; for her husband has fallen into the first in several of his poems, her father is remarkable for the other.

Mrs. Shelley has not, like a weak and ambitious artist, crowded her canvass with figures. Her characters are few—they are well-considered, perfectly individualised, and in happy contrast. There is no attempt at a violent opposition of colours to produce startling effects. In the calm consciousness of power, she has dispensed altogether with a villain who, in many a grand modern novel, is made to serve the same purpose as a daub of black in one of Martin's monster-pictures. All the characters are excellently drawn: the greater number are very elaborately wrought forth, the rest are firmly sketched. (pp. 601-02)

Lodore [is] one of the best novels it has been of late years our fortune to read. We are very happy in being able to confer this praise on Mrs. Shelley, whose name is dear to us (as we doubt not, from ''the late remorse of love,'' it is to the public), for the sake alike of the dead and living—her illustrious husband, and her living son, who was born in his image. (p. 605)

> [William Maginn], in a review of "Lodore," in Fraser's Magazine, Vol. XI, No. LXV, May, 1835, pp. 600-05.

THE MONTHLY REVIEW, LONDON   (essay date 1837)

[*The following commentary on* Falkner *offers high praise for Shelley's characterization, noble sentiments, and skillful structure.*]

Falkner, is perhaps the finest and most powerful, in regard to sentiment, of Mrs. Shelley's novels. Tenderness, pathos, and romantic elevation of feeling characterize all her productions. There is not much of real life in her stories, but a vast amount of thought and pensive meditation. Her colouring is for the most part sombre, but yet refining, and when she probes to

the source of human action, though it be with much of her father's discernment, it is not with his misanthropic tendency, but with a generous sympathy with and for her kind. . . . She seems also to have imbibed much of her husband's poetic temperament, its singular loveliness and delicacy, but to have shorn it of those extravagant visions and emotions which led him beyond the province of truth, and the dictates of a well-regulated judgment, which certainly are as essential to poetic excellence, as are the flights of an ardent or sensitive imagination.

We have said that Mrs. Shelley's colouring is for the most part sombre; but it should rather, perhaps, be asserted that her themes being gloomy, and her characters closely connected with some mystery of extraordinary weight and depth, there is necessarily established very early in the story over the mind of the reader, that brooding foreboding of evil and of terrible things, that cannot be playfully dealt with. But it is to the honour of her genius, and to the force as well as delicate beauty of her minute delineations, that this gloominess is never felt to be unwelcome, but of a soft and melancholy cast. *Falkner,* for example, is a tale in which crime, dark deeds, and remorse, form prominent parts. There is great suffering also entailed upon the innocent. And yet not only is the story one of arresting power, but the chief criminal himself, who is the hero, engages the heart, and fain would we see him restored to mental comfort, and hear of him being forgiven. Along with this absorbing interest in behalf of Falkner—(which is established by nothing like meretricious or morbid sentiments, but by an acute and delicate dissection of motives and temptations, and an unmitigating picture of the consequences of crime, even in this world, as also the penitent's desire to atone for his great offences, were it but by enduring the punishment which his guilt has incurred)—there are so many charming characters, incidents, and feelings portrayed as to render this romantic story rather pathetic than gloomy, rather the vehicle of melancholy reflections than of horror. (pp. 376-77)

> A review of "Falkner," in The Monthly Review, London, n.s. Vol. I, No. III, March, 1837, pp. 376-80.

TAIT'S EDINBURGH MAGAZINE   (essay date 1844)

[*In a mixed review of Shelley's* Rambles in Germany and Italy, *this critic suggests that the book reveals too many personal details and too few factual and philosophical observations.*]

Any work must have strong claims to attention that comes before the world as the avowed production of the author of *Frankenstein,* the chosen wife of Shelley, and the daughter of William Godwin and Mary Wollstonecraft. Whether [*Rambles in Germany and Italy*] will fulfil the expectations raised by these extraordinary claims is more than doubtful. They possess many beauties of the highest kind, and, as some may think, one or two deep blemishes. Among the latter is a too frequent obtrusion of the Pantheistic or poetical religion of Shelley. Yet these form the most ambitious and eloquent passages of the series. The poetic faith is in them expounded with great eloquence and felicity, as if a Corinne were pouring forth her rapt spirit, though we miss throughout the earnestness, the impulsive movement which dictated Mary Wollstonecraft's *Letters from Norway.* Another blemish will be judged according to the temperament of the reader's own mind. Some will be touched as by a sympathetic charm from Mrs. Shelley's frequent allusions to the death of her children, and the master calamity of her life, the awful catastrophe which bereaved her of her husband; while others may feel that the sacred fount of sorrow has been too often laid bare to cold or careless eyes. These allusions are no doubt made with great delicacy; but they recur so often as to mar their own effect, if not to beget an unpleasant sensation in the reader's mind, though he may neither be indifferent nor hard of heart. To some readers it may be an objection that beyond beauty of style and sentiment, and a few scattered profound thoughts, the work does not contain much of either the precise information or philosophical disquisition which one would have expected from a writer of Mrs. Shelley's compass of mind. This holds especially of France and Germany,—not only her enthusiasm and love, but her space being monopolized by beautiful Italy. (p. 729)

> *"Mrs. Shelley's 'Rambles in Germany and Italy',"* in Tait's Edinburgh Magazine, Vol. XI, No. CXXXI, November, 1844, pp. 729-40.

RICHARD HENGIST HORNE (essay date 1844)

[*Horne, a minor English poet and critic, places* Frankenstein *among the finest romantic fiction of the day and discusses the analogies suggested by the monster. The critic also comments briefly on* Valperga *and* Falkner.]

The imaginative romance, as distinguished from the historical romance, and the actual or social life fiction, is of very rare occurrence in the literature of the present day. Whether the cause lies with the writers or the public, or the character of events and influences now operating on society, certain it is that the imaginative romance is almost extinct among us.

We had outgrown the curdling horrors and breathless apprehensions of Mrs. Radcliffe, and the roseate pomps of Miss Jane Porter. But why have we no *Frankenstein,* for that fine work is in advance of the age?

Perhaps we ought to seek the cause of the scarcity in the difficulty of the production. A mere fruitless, purposeless excitement of the imagination will not do *now.* The imaginative romance is required to be a sort of epic—a power to advance— a something to propel the frame of things. Such is Bulwer's *Zanoni,* a profound and beautiful work of fiction, which has been reviewed in its place, and in which Godwin's *St. Leon* found a worthy successor. With this single exception, the first place among the romances of our day belongs to the *Frankenstein* of Mrs. Shelley. (p. 409)

The Monster in *Frankenstein,* sublime in his ugliness, his simplicity, his passions, his wrongs, and his strength, physical and mental, embodies in the wild narrative more than one distinct and important moral theory or proposition. In himself he is the type of a class deeply and cruelly aggrieved by nature—the Deformed or hideous in figure or countenance, whose sympathies and passions are as strong as their bodily deformity renders them repulsive. An amount of human woe, great beyond reckoning, have such experienced. When the Monster pleads his cause against cruel man, and when he finally disappears on his raft on the icy sea to build his own funeral pile, he pleads the cause of all that class who have so strong a claim on the help and sympathy of the world, yet find little else but disgust or, at best, neglect.

The Monster created by Frankenstein is also an illustration of the embodied consequences of our actions. As he, when formed and endowed with life, became to his imaginary creator an everlasting, ever-present curse, so may one single action, nay a word, or it may be a thought, thrown upon the tide of time, become to its originator a curse, never to be recovered, never to be shaken off.

Frankenstein suggests yet another analogy. It teaches the tragic results of attainment when an impetuous irresistible passion hurries on the soul to its doom. Such tragic results are the sacrificial fires out of which humanity rises purified. They constitute one form of the great ministry of Pain. The conception of *Frankenstein* is the converse of that of the delightful German fiction of Peter Schlemihl, in which the *loss* of his shadow (reputation or honour) leads on the hero through several griefs and troubles to the great simplicity of nature and truth; while in *Frankenstein* the *attainment* of a gigantic reality leads through crime and desolation to the same goal, but it is only reached in the moment of death. (pp. 410-11)

Mrs. Shelley's romance entitled *Valperga* is of high merit. She exhibits in her hero a brave and successful warrior, arriving at the height of his ambition, endowed with uncommon beauty and strength, and with many good qualities, yet causes him to excite emotions of reprobation and pity, because he is cruel and a tyrant, and because in the truth of things he is unhappy. This is doing a good work, taking the false glory from the eyes and showing things as they are. There are two female characters of wonderful power and beauty. The heroine is a lovely and noble creation. Perhaps Mrs. Shelley's *Falkner* ranks next in power to *Frankenstein.* The chief character, in especial, is worked out with subtle truth and force; and the same may be said, though with different degrees and modes of working, of all the personages of the story. Mrs. Shelley's plots are always of deep interest. These works taken as wholes, if below *Fran-*

Percy Bysshe Shelley, painted by Amelia Curran in Rome in 1819, the year of his marriage to Mary Wollstonecraft Godwin.

kenstein in genius, are yet worthy of their author and of her high rank in the aristocracy of genius, as the daughter of Godwin and Mary Wollstonecraft, and the widow of Shelley. (pp. 413-14)

> Richard Hengist Horne, "Mrs. Shelley," in A New Spirit of the Age, edited by Richard Hengist Horne, 1844. Reprint by Oxford University Press, 1907, pp. 407-14.

GEORGE GILFILLAN   (essay date 1847)

[Gilfillan unfavorably compares Mary Shelley's talent with her husband's, but praises Frankenstein as "one distinct addition to our original creations."]

[Despite] Mrs. Shelley's similarity in genius to her husband—we by no means think her his equal. She has not his subtlety, swiftness, wealth of imagination, and is never caught up (like Ezekiel by his lock of hair) into the same rushing whirlwind of inspiration. She has much, however, of his imaginative and of his speculative qualities—her tendency, like his, is to the romantic, the ethereal, and the terrible. The tie detaining her, as well as him, to the earth, is slender—her protest against society is his, copied out in a fine female hand—her style is carefully and successfully modelled upon his—she bears, in brief, to him, the resemblance which Laone did to Laon, which Astarte did to Manfred. Perhaps, indeed, intercourse with a being so peculiar, that those who came in contact with, either withdrew from him in hatred, or fell into the current of his being; vanquished and enthralled, has somewhat affected the originality, and narrowed the extent of her own genius. Indian widows used to fling themselves upon the funeral pyre of their husbands: she has thrown upon that of hers her mode of thought, her mould of style, her creed, her heart, her all. Her admiration of Shelley was, and is, an idolatry. (pp. 852-53)

Mrs. Shelley's genius, though true and powerful, is monotonous and circumscribed—more so than even her father's—and, in this point, presents a strong contrast to her husband's, which could run along every note of the gamut—be witty or wise, satirical or sentimental, didactic or dramatic, epic or lyrical, as it pleased him. She has no wit, nor humour—little dramatic talent. Strong clear description of the gloomier scenes of nature, or the darker passions of the mind, or of those supernatural objects which her fancy, except in her first work, somewhat laboriously creates, is her forte. Hence her reputation still rests upon Frankenstein; for her Last Man, Perkin Warbeck, &c., are far inferior, if not entirely unworthy of her talents. She unquestionably made him; but, like a mule or a monster, he has had no progeny. . . .

The theme [of Frankenstein] is morbid and disgusting enough. . . . Nothing more preposterous than the meagre outline of the story exists in literature. But Mrs. Shelley deserves great credit, nevertheless. In the first place, she has succeeded in her delineation; she has painted this shapeless being upon the imagination of the world for ever; and beside Caliban, and Hecate, and Death in Life, and all other weird and gloomy creations, this nameless, unfortunate, involuntary, gigantic unit stands. To succeed in an attempt so daring, proves at once the power of the author, and a certain value even in the original conception. To keep verging perpetually on the limit of the absurd, and to produce the while all the effects of the sublime, this takes and tasks very high faculties indeed. Occasionally, we admit, she does overstep the mark. Thus the whole scene of the monster's education in the cottage, his overhearing the

reading of the Paradise Lost, the Sorrows of Werter, &c., and in this way acquiring knowledge and refined sentiments, seems unspeakably ridiculous. A Caco-demon weeping in concert with Eve or Werter is too ludicrous an idea—as absurd as though he had been represented as boarded at Capsicum Hall. But it is wonderful how delicately and gracefully Mrs. Shelley has managed the whole prodigious business. She touches pitch with a lady's glove, and is not defiled. From a whole forest of the "nettle danger" she extracts a sweet and plentiful supply of the "flower safety." With a fine female footing, she preserves the narrow path which divides the terrible from the disgusting. She unites, not in a junction of words alone, but in effect, the "horribly beautiful." Her monster is not only as Caliban appeared to Trinculo—a very pretty monster—but somewhat poetical and pathetic withal. You almost weep for him in his utter insulation. . . .

He is not only alone, but alone because he has no being like him throughout the whole universe. What a solitude within a solitude!—solitude comparable only to that of the Alchemist in St. Leon, when he buries his last tie to humanity in his wife's grave, and goes on his way, "friendless, friendless, alone, alone." (p. 853)

Altogether, the work is wonderful as the work of a girl of eighteen. She has never since fully equalled or approached its power, nor do we ever expect that she shall. One distinct addition to our original creations must be conceded her—and it is no little praise; for there are few writers of fiction who have done so much out of Germany. (p. 854)

> George Gilfillan, "Female Authors, No. III: Mrs. Shelley," in Tait's Edinburgh Magazine, Vol. XIV, No. CLXVIII, December, 1847, pp. 850-54.

HELEN MOORE   (essay date 1886)

[The author of the first full-length biography of Shelley, Moore demonstrates an attitude that persisted until recently: that Shelley's chief significance derived from her relationship with her husband. Moore essentially dismisses all Shelley's writings except Frankenstein, which she singles out because it "alone reflected Mrs. Shelley's true self."]

While it is true that Mrs. Shelley's place among eminent women does not rest upon the circumstance that she was Shelley's wife, it is in every sense due to the fact that she was his companion. The nature and quality of this companionship is at once an index and a test of her character. It was not that an erratic genius had made her the object of his wayward passion, or even that she was the recipient of his genuine tenderness. It was very much more than this. Think how different Mrs. Shelley's place from that held by any of the various loves of Goethe or Byron. It may not be overstating it to say that one of the chief interests we have in her, arises from a worthy curiosity to know what manner of woman it was who could be so completely the companion, who could hold such close fellowship with so marked a genius as Shelley. It is for this reason that his character must ever be a prominent element in the life of Mrs. Shelley. For the same reason, due prominence must be given to the nature of that union which welded these twain together in a spiritual oneness so instant, an intellectual harmony so complete,—in fine, a union so unlike those ordinarily made on earth, and so like those which we are told are made in Heaven, that an inconsequential world promptly decided that it had been made in Hell.

Certainly, Mrs. Shelley does not owe her fame to the extent of her literary labors. Of these we shall do more than merely speak, finding in one of them—*Frankenstein*—a peculiar literary faculty. But she must be ranked among those literary women whose true province is to influence and stimulate others; who are receptive, appreciative, and incentive, rather than productive. . . . (pp. 11-12)

[Women] possessed of the intellectual *timbre,* styled literary, fall naturally into two classes, one possessed of a power to produce beyond the scope made apparent by their personal influence, which may even give no promise of such power; the other owning and wielding a far greater influence over men about them, which gives richer promise, but which fails to transmute itself into a permanent literary yield. Of the former class are George Eliot, Charlotte Brontë, Mrs. Browning, Miss Austin, while in the latter class are Margaret Fuller, Mary Wollstonecraft, Madame de Stael, Madame Recamier, and a host of French women, of whom Madame Du Deffend may be taken as the type.

Without doubt it is to this latter class that Mrs. Shelley must be assigned; so that in proportion as her permanent contribution to the literary stock of the world is small, must we the more earnestly seek in her private life and its reflected lights, for those qualities which have made her unquestionably eminent among women. (pp. 12-13)

[Mrs. Shelley's] literary productions were few and disproportionate to her intellectual force; disappointing when viewed side by side with her peculiar gift of evoking the most artistic literary work in others. (p. 244)

Of Mrs. Shelley's writings, *Frankenstein* is without question the most noteworthy. From the day of its first appearance in print down to the present, it has had accorded to it a position as a unique and remarkable production. (pp. 244-45)

Regarded as a mere tale, it is difficult to account for the hold this story has always had upon the minds of the reading world. As a story it does not justify its own success. To say that it is remarkable as a work of imagination does not meet the difficulty. By a work of the imagination, as used in the current criticism of *Frankenstein,* is simply meant that it is a fantastic romance, such as we find in the "Arabian Nights," or in the prose tales of Poe. But a position utterly different from these is accorded to *Frankenstein.* (pp. 248-49)

[There was a dual quality in *Frankenstein*] to which it owed its singular power and place in literature. One element is doubtless the horror of the tale and the weird fancy of the author's imagination in the ordinary acceptation of the word. But it is to an entirely different department of mental conception that we must look for the secret of its peculiar influence. The faculty of imagination is something more than the recalling and rearrangements of past impressions. Profoundly considered, it is that function of the mind which formulates, as though real, a state of things which if present would so appear. It is the power of projecting the mind into unhappened realities. It is the faculty of picturing unseen verities. There is thus in it a prophetic element, not at all miraculous, but dependent upon subtile laws of association and suggestion. It is to this element that *Frankenstein* owes its power over thoughtful minds. It is by virtue of the allegorical element in it that it holds its high position as a work of the imagination. (p. 249)

[The] chief allegorical interest in the narrative concerns itself about that tendency in the human being to discard the established order of things and to create for itself a new and independent existence. In the simple story, Frankenstein made a being responsible to him alone for its creation,—a being not produced by the ordinary course of life, not amenable or even adaptable to the existing world of men. Right or wrong, better or worse, the creature may be, but different certainly, and this irreconcilable disparity points back ever to its origin, which had been anomalous and strange.

The whole story is but the elaboration of the embarrassment and dangers which flow from departure from the ordinary course of nature; this forced attempt to invade society from within. What strong existence in real life of this same tendency Mary Shelley had seen in those nearest and dearest to her! She has not failed to learn the lesson of her mother's history; time analyzes rather than destroys. And the life of Mary Wollstonecraft was doubtless seen by the clear-minded daughter in stronger contrast of light and shade than it had been by its contemporaries. Who knew so well the glories of that life? Its successes as well as its miseries had sprung from the self-same causes as those of Frankenstein,—from the breach of the conventional; from overstepping the limits; from creating an individuality and a sphere of existence denied it by Nomos, and consequently sure of the hostility of society. (pp. 255-56)

The world, by its acknowledgment of the coercive quality of *Frankenstein,* has given silent acceptance of its genius. The other works, novels, critiques, biographies, while they have had literary merit, feeling, even power, have not shown genius. *Frankenstein* alone was personal, it alone reflected Mrs. Shelley's true self. Her other books contain simply what she wrote in them: this alone contains what was written in her. (pp. 257-58)

Helen Moore, in her Mary Wollstonecraft Shelley, *J. B. Lippincott Company, 1886, 346 p.*

LUCY MADOX ROSSETTI (essay date 1890)

[*Rossetti states that the* raison d'être *of her biography of Shelley, from which the following excerpt is drawn, is to discuss Shelley's literary work. However, Rossetti offers only scant biographical criticism of the novels, granting nearly equal attention to Shelley's* Lives of Eminent Literary Men, *which is reviewed below.*]

[*Lives of Eminent Literary Men*] are a most interesting series of biographies written by a woman who could appreciate the poet's character, and enter into the injustices and sorrows from which few poets have been exempt. They show careful study, her knowledge of various countries gives local colour to her descriptions, and her love of poetry makes her an admirable critic. (p. 206)

Freedom from affectation, and a genuine love of her subject, make her biographies most readable, and for the ordinary reader there is a fund of information. (p. 207)

You feel [her sketch of Dante] is written from the heart of the woman who herself felt as she wrote. We would fain go through her different biographies, tracing her feelings, her appreciation, and poetic enthusiasm throughout, but that is impossible. She takes us through Boccaccio's life, and, as by the reflection of a sunset from a mirror, we are warmed with the glow and mirth from distant and long-past times in Italy. One feels through her works the innate delicacy of her mind. (p. 208)

Mary's studies in Spanish enabled her to treat equally well the poets of Spain and of Portugal. Her introduction is a good essay on the poetry and poets of Spain, and some of the translations, which are her own, are very happily given. The poetic impulse in Spain is traced from the Iberians through the Romans, Visigoths, Moors, and the early unknown Spanish poets, among whom there were many fine examples. (p. 211)

> *Lucy Madox Rossetti, in her* Mrs. Shelley, *1890. Reprint by The Folcroft Press, Inc., 1969, 238 p.*

THE ATHENAEUM   (essay date 1891)

[*The author of the following excerpt deems Shelley's* Tales and Stories *outdated and superficial, but occasionally intriguing.*]

[Mrs. Shelley's stories collected in *Tales and Stories by Mary Wollstonecraft Shelley*] have until now been hidden away in what Charles Lamb would have designated as books that are no books—namely, keepsakes, annuals, and, if we remember rightly, even ladies' pocket-books—volumes which are now never visited unless it be by some worshipper of Turner who is searching for his handiwork in the shape of illustrations. This is the first time that her stories have been collected, and it is as trying an ordeal to the fame of an author to have the scattered productions of a lifetime gathered together in one volume as to a painter to have a large collection of his drawings or pictures exhibited in one room. A taste of the producer's quality is obtained that goes far towards fixing his rank for ever.

It is difficult, however, to fix Mrs. Shelley's, for most of the stories are written in a style that is now as completely out of fashion as the annuals in which they first saw the light. The heroines are "children of light and love," they are liable to be addressed as "lovely and deceived one," they "speak in terms of soft silver tenderness," their "tresses are heavy with their own rich beauty," their complexions are of "marmoreal whiteness," they tread on "carpets inwoven with silk," and we even find a maiden who reminds us of Mrs. Radcliffe's heroines, who never stir out for pleasure nor fly from their prisons without taking their lutes with them. Mrs. Shelley's heroine carries her harp into the woods with her. There is no introspection in these stories, no searching study of character, but there is some imaginative power and generous sympathy with all that is noble. Their merit, of course, varies; the romantic stories are much the best; but perhaps that which will be the most interesting to all will be **"The Parvenue,"** in which, under a very sufficient disguise, we find what we have long wished to find—proof of the irritation with which Mrs. Shelley regarded her father's habit of making incessant and exorbitant demands on Shelley's pocket. It might have been well to make some corrections in this volume; they are frequently needed. (pp. 12-13)

> *A review of "Tales and Stories by Mary Wollstonecraft Shelley," in* The Athenaeum, *No. 3297, January 3, 1891, pp. 12-13.*

THE SPECTATOR   (essay date 1891)

[*The* Spectator *critic offers a mixed review of* Tales and Stories, *finding them occasionally powerful but generally of interest only as the work of the author of* Frankenstein.]

Of the seventeen tales [in *Tales and Stories by Mary Wollstonecraft Shelley*] which may be considered as fairly representative of the writer's taste in the selection of imaginative material, only two deal with a preternatural motive, and in neither is

there any violence, morbidness, or repulsiveness of treatment. **"The Mortal Immortal"** is a not specially striking handling of the often-used theme of a magically prolonged life, and it is curious to note that Mrs. Shelley seemed unable to turn to profitable imaginative account the one really original idea in the story,—that is, the mistake made by the hero, who drinks the *elixir vitae* supposing it to be merely a philtre which will destroy his love for the girl who has flouted him. **"Transformation"** is more fantastic, but not more striking. . . . Neither story is exactly poor, but both are wanting in distinction: they are just good enough to suggest what might have been made of them by such an artist as Hawthorne, Poe, or Théophile Gautier.

As a matter of fact, they were out of the line of Mrs. Shelley, who was most at home in the region of romantic picturesqueness and pathetic sentiment. The majority of her stories are of the usual "Annual" type, and they are distinguished from their companions, which have been kindly left to oblivion, only by the superiority of their general style and the artistic truthfulness of their elaborate backgrounds. The annualists as a body liked Italy, for an Italian story allowed the use of high-sounding names and wonderful incidents, the lifelikeness of which few English readers of the time were able to impeach; but Mrs. Shelley turned frequently to the much-favoured country because she knew and loved it, and her lavish descriptions have the sunlight of Claude or the sombreness of Salvator Rosa. Mrs. Shelley's imaginative gifts were not great, but they were genuine, and when she allowed herself to be dominated either by the influence of her father or her husband, her work was, as a rule, the poorer instead of the richer for the submission. We say as a rule, for here and there we find evidences of a feeling for natural beauty and a power of rendering it, which are both beautiful and Shelley-like. "The domes and turrets of the far town flashed and gleamed, the trees were dyed in splendour; two or three slight *clouds, which had drunk the radiance till it became their essence,* floated golden islets in the lustrous empyrean." We might almost fancy that the italicised words were a quotation from that wonderful poem, "To a Skylark;" and this is by no means a solitary example of a power of expression which has been learned rather than inherited. In the story of **"The Mourner,"** the writer has evidently utilised Shelley's reminiscences of his schooldays; but elsewhere we have failed to find any of these references to real persons or actual incidents which are not infrequent in her novels. That these stories will attract the general reader of to-day, is unlikely. They are interesting mainly as the work of the author of *Frankenstein.* (pp. 18-19)

> *"Mrs. Shelley's Shorter Tales," in* The Spectator, *Vol. LXVI, No. 3262, January 3, 1891, pp. 18-19.*

CLARA H. WHITMORE   (essay date 1910)

[*In a general overview of Shelley's fiction, Whitmore discusses* Frankenstein, Valperga, *and* Lodore *as the author's only noteworthy novels.*]

Frankenstein is one of those novels that defy the critic. Everyone recognises that the letters written by Captain Walton to his sister in which he tells of his meeting with Frankenstein, and repeats to her the story he has just heard from his guest, makes an awkward introduction to the real narrative. Yet all this part about Captain Walton and his crew was added at the suggestion of Shelley after the rest of the story had been written.

But the narrative of Frankenstein is so powerful, so real, that, once read, it can never be forgotten. (p. 206)

The monster created by Frankenstein is closely related to our own human nature. "My heart was fashioned to be susceptible of love and sympathy," he says, "and, when wrenched by misery to vice and hatred, it did not endure the violence of the change without torture, such as you cannot even imagine." There is a wonderful blending of good and evil in this demon, and, while the magnitude of his crimes makes us shudder, his wrongs and his loneliness awaken our pity. . . . Perhaps sadder than the story of the monster is that of Frankenstein, who, led by a desire to widen human knowledge, finds that the fulfilment of his lofty ambition has brought only a curse to mankind. (p. 207)

The interest [of *Valperga*] centres in the two heroines, Euthanasia, Countess of Valperga, and Beatrice, Prophetess of Ferrara. Strong, intellectual, and passionate, not until the time of George Eliot did women of this type become prominent in fiction. (p. 208)

[More] beautiful than the intellectual character of Euthanasia, is the spiritual one of Beatrice, the adopted daughter of the bishop of Ferrara, who is regarded with feelings of reverence by her countrymen, because of her prophetic powers. Pure and deeply religious, she accepted all the suggestions of her mind as a message from God. When Castruccio came to Ferrara and was entertained by the bishop as the prince and liberator of his country, she believed that together they could accomplish much for her beloved country: "She prayed to the Virgin to inspire her; and, again giving herself up to reverie, she wove a subtle web, whose materials she believed heavenly, but which were indeed stolen from the glowing wings of love." No wonder she believed the dictates of her own heart, she whose words the superstition of the age had so often declared miraculous. She was barely seventeen and she loved for the first time. How pathetic is her disillusionment when Castruccio bade her farewell for a season, as he was about to leave Ferrara. She had believed that the Holy Spirit had brought Castruccio to her that by the union of his manly qualities and her divine attributes some great work might be fulfilled. But as he left her, he spoke only of earthly happiness. . . . (pp. 208-09)

The daughter of Mary Wollstonecraft could fully sympathise with Beatrice. In the grief, almost madness, with which Beatrice realises her self-deception, there are traces of Frankenstein. Perhaps no problem plucked from the tree of good and evil was so ever-present to Mary Shelley as why misery so often follows an obedience to the highest dictates of the soul. Both her father and mother had experienced this; and she and Shelley had tasted of the same bitter fruit. In the analysis of Beatrice's emotions Mrs. Shelley shows herself akin to Charlotte Brontë.

Three years after the death of Shelley, she published *The Last Man*. . . . The plot is clumsy; the characters are abstractions. (p. 210)

Mrs. Shelley made the great mistake of writing this novel in the first person. *The Last Man*, who is telling the story, although he has the name of Lionel, is most assuredly of the female sex. The friendship between him and Adrian is not the friendship of man for man, but rather the love of man and woman.

Mrs. Shelley's next novel, *Lodore*, . . . had a better outlined plot and more definite characters. (pp. 212-13)

Besides two other novels of no value, *Perkin Warbeck* and *Falkner*, Mrs. Shelley wrote numerous short stories for the annuals. . . . Many of them have the intensity and sustained interest of *Frankenstein*.

After the death of her husband, grief and trouble dimmed Mrs. Shelley's imagination. But the pale student Frankenstein, the monster he created, and the beautiful priestess, Beatrice, three strong conceptions, testify to the genius of Mary Shelley. (pp. 214-15)

> Clara H. Whitmore, "Lady Caroline Lamb (1785-1828)—Mary Shelley (1797-1851)," in her Woman's Work in English Fiction: From the Restoration to the Mid-Victorian Period, G. P. Putnam's Sons, 1910, pp. 200-15.

EDITH BIRKHEAD   (essay date 1921)

[*Birkhead's* The Tale of Terror, *from which the following excerpt is drawn, is considered one of the first significant studies of the Gothic movement. Here, she offers a thoughtful overview of the virtues and flaws of* Frankenstein, *in addition to briefer considerations of* Valperga, The Last Man, *and some of Shelley's short stories.*]

It is indeed remarkable that so young and inexperienced a writer as Mary Shelley, who was only nineteen when she wrote *Frankenstein*, should betray so slight a dependence on her predecessors. It is evident from the records of her reading that the novel of terror in all its guises was familiar to her. She had beheld the majestic horror of the halls of Eblis; she had threaded her way through Mrs. Radcliffe's artfully constructed Gothic castles; she had braved the terrors of the German Ritter-, Räuber- und Schauer-Romane; she had assisted, fearful, at Lewis's midnight diablerie; she had patiently unravelled the "mystery" novels of Godwin and of Charles Brockden Brown. Yet, despite this intimate knowledge of the terrible and supernatural in fiction, Mrs. Shelley's theme and her way of handling it are completely her own. In an "acute mental vision," as real as the visions of Blake and of Shelley, she beheld her monster and the "pale student of unhallowed arts" who had created him, and then set herself to reproduce the thrill of horror inspired by her waking dream. *Frankenstein* has, indeed, been compared to Godwin's *St. Leon*, but the resemblance is so vague and superficial, and *Frankenstein* so immeasurably superior, that Mrs. Shelley's debt to her father is negligible. St. Leon accepts the gift of immortality, Frankenstein creates a new life, and in both novels the main interest lies in tracing the effect of the experiment on the soul of the man, who has pursued scientific inquiry beyond legitimate limits. But apart from this, there is little resemblance. Godwin chose the supernatural, because it chanced to be popular, and laboriously built up a cumbrous edifice, completing it by a sheer effort of will-power. His daughter, with an imagination naturally more attuned to the gruesome and fantastic, writes, when once she has wound her way into the heart of the story, in a mood of breathless excitement that drives the reader forward with feverish apprehension.

The name of Mrs. Shelley's *Frankenstein* is far-famed; but the book itself, overshadowed perhaps by its literary associations, seems to have withdrawn into the vast library of famous works that are more often mentioned than read. The very fact that the name is often bestowed on the monster instead of his creator seems to suggest that many are content to accept Mrs. Shelley's "hideous phantom" on hearsay evidence rather than encounter for themselves the terrors of his presence. The story deserves a happier fate, for, if it be read in the spirit of willing surrender that a theme so impossible demands, it has still power momentarily "to make the reader dread to look round, to curdle the blood and to quicken the beatings of the heart." (pp. 158-60)

Mrs. Shelley has been censured for setting her tale in a clumsy framework, but she tells us in her preface that she began with the words: "It was on a dreary night of November." This sentence now stands at the opening of Chapter V., where the plot begins to grip our imagination; and it seems not unfair to assume that the introductory letters and the first four chapters, which contain a tedious and largely unnecessary account of Frankenstein's early life, were written in deference to Shelley's plea that the idea should be developed at greater length, and did not form part of her original plan. The uninteresting student, Robert Walton, to whom Frankenstein, discovered dying among icebergs, tells his story, is obviously an afterthought. If Mrs. Shelley had abandoned the awkward contrivance of putting the narrative into the form of a dying man's confession, reported verbatim in a series of letters, and had opened her story, as she apparently intended, at the point where Frankenstein, after weary years of research, succeeds in creating a living being, her novel would have gained in force and intensity. From that moment it holds us fascinated. It is true that the tension relaxes from time to time, that the monster's strange education and the Godwinian precepts that fall so incongruously from his lips tend to excite our mirth, but, though we are mildly amused, we are no longer merely bored. Even the protracted descriptions of domestic life assume a new and deeper meaning, for the shadow of the monster broods over them. One by one those whom Frankenstein loves fall victims to the malice of the being he has endowed with life. Unceasingly and unrelentingly the loathsome creature dogs our imagination, more awful when he lurks unseen than when he stands actually before us. With hideous malignity he slays Frankenstein's young brother, and by a fiendish device causes Justine, an innocent girl, to be executed for the crime. Yet ere long our sympathy, which has hitherto been entirely with Frankenstein, is unexpectedly diverted to the monster who, it would seem, is wicked only because he is eternally divorced from human society. (pp. 161-62)

He describes how his physical ugliness repels human beings, who fail to realise his benevolent intentions. A father snatches from his arms the child he has rescued from death; the virtuous family, whom he admires and would fain serve, flee affrighted from his presence. To educate the monster, so that his thoughts and emotions may become articulate, and, incidentally, to accentuate his isolation from society, Mrs. Shelley inserts a complicated story about an Arabian girl, Sofie, whose lover teaches her to read from Plutarch's *Lives*, Volney's *Ruins of Empire*, *The Sorrows of Werther*, and *Paradise Lost*. The monster overhears the lessons, and ponders on this unique library, but, as he pleads his own cause the more eloquently because he knows Satan's passionate outbursts of defiance and self-pity, who would cavil at the method by which he is made to acquire his knowledge? "The cold stars shone in mockery, and the bare trees waved their branches above me; now and then the sweet voice of a bird burst forth amidst the universal stillness. All save I were at rest or in enjoyment. I, like the arch fiend, bore a hell within me." And later, near the close of the book: "The fallen angel becomes a malignant devil. Yet even that enemy of God and man had friends and associates in his desolation;

I am alone." His fate reminds us of that of *Alastor, the Spirit of Solitude,* who:

> Over the world wanders for ever
> Lone as incarnate death.

(pp. 162-63)

Like *Alastor, Frankenstein* was a plea for human sympathy, and was, according to Shelley's preface, intended "to exhibit the amiableness of domestic affection and the excellence of universal virtue." The monster has the perception and desire of goodness, but, by the circumstances of his abnormal existence, is delivered over to evil. It is this dual nature that prevents him from being a mere automaton. The monster indeed is far more real than the shadowy beings whom he pursues. Frankenstein is less an individual than a type, and only interests us through the emotions which his conflict with the monster arouses. Clerval, Elizabeth and Frankenstein's relatives are passive sufferers whose psychology does not concern us. Mrs. Shelley rightly lavishes her skill on the central figure of the book, and succeeds, as effectually as Frankenstein himself, in infusing into him the spark of life. Mrs. Shelley's aim is to "awaken thrilling horror," and, incidentally, to "exhibit the excellence of domestic virtue," and for her purpose the demon is of paramount importance. The involved, complex plot of a novel seemed to pass beyond Mrs. Shelley's control. A short tale she could handle successfully, and Shelley was unwise in inciting her to expand **Frankenstein** into a long narrative. So long as she is completely carried away by her subject Mrs. Shelley writes clearly, but when she pauses to regard the progress of her story dispassionately, she seems to be overwhelmed by the wealth of her resources and to have no power of selecting the relevant details. The laborious introductory letters, the meticulous record of Frankenstein's education, the story of Felix and Sofie, the description of the tour through England before the creation of the second monster is attempted, are all connected with the main theme by very frail links and serve to distract our attention in an irritating fashion from what really interests us. In the novel of mystery a tantalising delay may be singularly effective. In a novel which depends chiefly for its effect on sheer horror, delays are merely dangerous. By resting her terrors on a pseudo-scientific basis and by placing her story in a definite locality, Mrs. Shelley waives her right to an entire suspension of disbelief. If it be reduced to its lowest terms, the plot of Frankenstein, with its bewildering confusion of the prosaic and the fantastic, sounds as crude, disjointed and inconsequent as that of a nightmare. Mrs. Shelley's timid hesitation between imagination and reality, her attempt to reconcile incompatible things and to place a creature who belongs to no earthly land in familiar surroundings, prevents **Frankenstein** from being a wholly satisfactory and alarming novel of terror. She loves the fantastic, but she also fears it. She is weighted down by commonsense, and so flutters instead of soaring, unwilling to trust herself far from the material world. But the fact that she was able to vivify her grotesque skeleton of a plot with some degree of success is no mean tribute to her gifts. The energy and vigour of her style, her complete and serious absorption in her subject, carry us safely over many an absurdity. It is only in the duller stretches of the narrative, when her heart is not in her work, that her language becomes vague, indeterminate and blurred, and that she muffles her thoughts in words like "ascertain," "commencement," "peruse," "diffuse," instead of using their simpler Saxon equivalents. Stirred by the excitement of the events she describes, she can write forcibly in simple, direct language. She often frames short, hurried sentences such as a man would naturally utter when breathless with terror or with recollections of terror. The final impression that *Frankenstein* leaves with us is not easy to define, because the book is so uneven in quality. It is obviously the shapeless work of an immature writer who has had no experience in evolving a plot. Sometimes it is genuinely moving and impressive, but it continually falls abruptly and ludicrously short of its aim. Yet when all its faults have been laid bare, the fact remains that few readers would abandon the story half-way through. Mrs. Shelley is so thoroughly engrossed in her theme that she impels her readers onward, even though they may think but meanly of her story as a work of art.

Mrs. Shelley's second novel, *Valperga, or the Life and Adventures of Castruccio, Prince of Lucca,* . . . was a work on which she bestowed much care and labour, but the result proves that she writes best when the urgency of her imagination leaves her no leisure either to display her learning or adorn her style. She herself calls *Valperga* a "child of mighty slow growth," and Shelley adds that it was "raked out of fifty old books." Mrs. Shelley, always an industrious student, made a conscientious survey of original sources before fashioning her story of mediaeval Italy, and she is hampered by the exuberance of her knowledge. The novel is not a romance of terror; but Castruccio, though his character is sketched from authentic documents, seems towards the end of the story to resemble the picturesque villain who numbered among his ancestry Milton's Satan. He has "a majestic figure and a countenance beautiful but sad, and tarnished by the expression of pride that animated it." Beatrice, the gifted prophetess who falls deep in love with Castruccio ends her days in the dungeons of the Inquisition. Mrs. Shelley's aim, however, is not to arouse fear, but to trace the gradual deterioration of Castruccio's character from an open-hearted youth to a crafty tyrant. The blunt remarks of Godwin, who revised the manuscript, are not unjust, but fall with an ill grace from the pen of the author of *St. Leon:* "It appears in reading, that the first rule you prescribed was: 'I will let it be long.' It contains the quantity of four volumes of *Waverley.* No hard blow was ever hit with a woodsaw."

In *The Last Man,* . . . Mrs. Shelley attempted a stupendous theme, no less than a picture of the devastation of the human race by plague and pestilence. She casts her imagination forward into the twenty-first century, when the last king of England has abdicated the throne and a republic is established. Very wisely, she narrows the interest by concentrating on the pathetic fate of a group of friends who are among the last survivors, and the story becomes an idealised record of her own sufferings. The description of the loneliness of the bereft has a personal note, and reminds us of her journal, where she expresses the sorrow of being herself the last survivor, and of feeling like a "cloud from which the light of sunset has passed." Raymond, who dies in an attempt to place the standard of Greece in Stamboul, is a portrait of Byron; and Adrian, the late king's son, who finally becomes Protector, is clearly modelled on Shelley. Yet in spite of these personal reminiscences, their characters lack distinctness. Idris, Clara and Perdita are faintly etched, but Evadne, the Greek artist, who cherishes a passion for Raymond, and dies fighting against the Turks, has more colour and body than the other women, though she is somewhat theatrical. Mrs. Shelley conveys emotion more faithfully than character, and the overwrought sensibilities and dark forebodings of the diminished party of survivors who leave England to distract their minds by foreign travel are artfully suggested. The leaping, gesticulating figure, whom their jaded nerves and morbid fancy transform into a phantom, is a delir-

ious ballet-dancer; and the Black Spectre, mistaken for Death Incarnate, proves only to be a plague-stricken noble, who lurks near the party for the sake of human society. These "reasonable" solutions of the apparently supernatural remind us of Mrs. Radcliffe's method, and Mrs. Shelley shows keen psychological insight in her delineation of the state of mind which readily conjures up imaginary terrors. When Lionel Verney is left alone in the universe, her power seems to flag, and instead of the final crescendo of horror, which we expect at the end of the book, we are left with an ineffective picture of the last man in Rome in 2095 deciding to explore the countries he has not yet viewed. As he wanders amid the ruins he recalls not only "the buried Caesars," but also the monk in *The Italian,* of whom he had read in childhood—a striking proof of Mrs. Shelley's faith in the permanence of Mrs. Radcliffe's fame.

Though the style of *The Last Man* is often tediously prolix and is disfigured by patches of florid rhetoric and by inappropriate similes scattered broadcast, occasional passages of wonderful beauty recall Shelley's imagery; and, in conveying the pathos of loneliness, personal feeling lends nobility and eloquence to her style. With so ambitious a subject, it was natural that she should only partially succeed in carrying her readers with her. Though there are oases, the story is a somewhat tedious and dreary stretch of narrative that can only be traversed with considerable effort.

Mrs. Shelley's later works—*Perkin Warbeck* . . . , a historical novel; *Lodore* . . . , which describes the early life of Shelley and Harriet; *Falkner* . . . , which was influenced by *Caleb Williams*—do not belong to the history of the novel of terror; but some of her short tales, contributed to periodicals and collected in 1891, have gruesome and supernatural themes. "**A Tale of the Passions, or the Death of Despina,**" a story based on the struggles of the Guelphs and the Ghibellines, contains a perfect specimen of the traditional villain of the novel of terror:

> Every feature of his countenance spoke of the struggle of passions and the terrible egotism of one who would sacrifice himself to the establishment of his will: his black eyebrows were scattered, his grey eyes deep-set and scowling, his look at once stern and haggard. A smile seemed never to have disturbed the settled scorn which his lips expressed; his high forehead was marked by a thousand contradictory lines.

This terrific personage spends the last years of his life in orthodox fashion as an austere saint in a monastery.

"**The Mortal Immortal,**" a variation on the theme of *St. Leon,* is the record of a pupil of Cornelius Agrippa, who drank half of the elixir his master had compounded in the belief that it was a potion to destroy love. It is written on his three hundred and twenty-third birthday.

"**Transformation,**" like *Frankenstein,* dwells on the pathos of ugliness and deformity, but the subject is treated rather in the spirit of an eastern fairy tale than in that of a novel of terror. The dwarf, in return for a chest of treasure, borrows a beautiful body, and, thus disguised, wins the love of Juliet, and all ends happily. Mrs. Shelley's short stories reveal a stronger sense of proportion than her novels, and are written in a more graceful, fluent style than the books on which she expended great labour. (pp. 163-69)

Edith Birkhead, "Later Developments of the Tale of Terror," in her The Tale of Terror: A Study of the

Boris Karloff as Frankenstein's monster in the 1931 film Frankenstein. *The Granger Collection, New York.*

Gothic Romance, *1921. Reprint by Russell & Russell, Inc., 1963, pp. 157-84.*

J. MIDDLETON MURRY   (essay date 1922)

[*Murry was a noted English essayist, magazine editor, and literary critic during the first half of the twentieth century. In his review of Shelley's verse dramas,* Proserpine *and* Midas, *he praises her poetic gift as minor but true.*]

The beauty of these little pieces [*Proserpine* and *Midas*], we are sure, will come as a surprise to many, who, though they may have had no doubt of Mary Shelley's talent, can scarcely have believed that her talent was poetic. We think of her chiefly as the author of *Frankenstein,* and it has always seemed hard to reconcile the brilliant novelist of extravagant, romantic sensation with the restrained and measured commentator on her husband's poetry. These little dramas supply the connecting link between the two manifestations. Their restraint, their purity is unmistakable; and it is a natural restraint. It seems to come less from an imitation of classical models than from an experience of life itself. The Mary whose rapturous cry of ''Shelley!'' has echoed once at least in the recesses of all our hearts, has grown into a woman who has borne children and seen them die. There is a grave and delicate sadness in her

Proserpine; and even in her *Midas,* where the fable could scarcely lend itself to austerity of treatment, the same instinctive restraint is felt in her touch. She cannot laugh; she smiles, and she smiles rather sadly.

Let us not exaggerate. These dramas are in miniature. Perhaps it is a mistake to call them dramas at all. They are more truly idylls cast, as the classical idyllists so often cast them, into dramatic form. And, though we believe that they very definitely are *poems* and that they prove that Mary Shelley had her portion of the true gift, we must admit that they are small. They are small; but they are nearly perfect. Perhaps their quality can be best defined by saying that there is hardly a line of Mary Shelley's writing in these composite idylls which could be improved. . . .

It is surely not extravagantly biographical to imagine that Mary Shelley's loss of her little girl Clara in September, 1818, and the yet more bitter loss of her little boy William at Rome in June, 1819—losses whose poignancy she set herself to combat by a return to original composition—may have guided her in her choice of the story of Proserpine. It is one of the profoundest and most inspiring of classical themes, and although when Mary Shelley took it up it had not yet been handled, as it was to be, by Tennyson and Swinburne and Meredith, it had already been the occasion of some of the greatest lines in English poetry—greater lines by far than were struck out of the theme by any of these three epigoni. It is as well to have them in mind in order to judge of Mary Shelley's quality. Shakespeare's—

> O Proserpina!
> For the flowers now that frighted thou let'st fall
> From Dis's waggon . . .

and Milton's

>   Not that fair field
> Of *Enna,* where Proserpin gath'ring flowers,
> Herself a fairer flower, by gloomy Dis
> Was gather'd, which cost Ceres all that pain
> To seek her through the world:

these are two of the most magical movements of English poetry. Here is Mary Shelley:—

> Ceres for ever weeps, seeking her child,
> And in her rage has struck the land with blight;
> Trinacria mourns with her; its fertile fields
> Are dry and barren, and all little brooks
> Struggling scarce creep within their altered banks;
> The flowers that erst were wont with bended heads
> To gaze within the clear and glassy wave,
> Have died, unwatered by the failing stream—
> And yet their hue but mocks the deeper grief
> Which is the fountain of these bitter tears.

Certainly we can see the difference here between great poetry and another kind. But surely the striking thing is not so much the difference as the quiet, unobtrusive certainty with which Mary Shelley's lines hold their ground in such prodigious company. The speedwell lifts its head before the rose, and it is not abashed, for it knows that Solomon in all his glory was less beautifully arrayed.

This passage of pure and delicate poetry is not isolated in Mary Shelley's *Proserpine*. There are at least a dozen others of the same order, and one where she suddenly touches a more sombre note with equal mastery. Consider the closing line in these—

> Then you descend to deepest night, and reign
> Great Queen of Tartarus, 'mid shadows dire,
> Offspring of Hell—or in the silent groves
> Of fair Elysium through which Lethe runs,
> The sleepy river; where the windless air
> Is never struck by flight or song of bird—
> But all is calm and clear, bestowing rest,
> After the toil of life, on wretched men
> Whom thus the Gods reward for sufferings
> Gods cannot know.

It may be that the thought of the last line is Shelley's, though there is no reason to believe that Mary could not think, and think cogently, for herself; but the firm conciseness of the expression is all her own. Shelley's method of saying such a thing was quite different; it was never better.

If we are to disentangle any thread of influence at all in Mary Shelley's *Proserpine,* it is Miltonic. But if she was in fact influenced by Milton—we should not care to insist upon it— she displayed a rare discrimination in what she accepted or rejected. There is no classicism in her verse; if she has absorbed something of Milton's purity, she is on her guard against the risk of imitating Milton's triumphant mannerisms. Even when her lines most clearly ring with tones reminiscent of his, the simple music is still essentially her own. . . .

The only possible criticism of a poem which is complete with its own quiet beauty is that something of the deeper spiritual significance of the Proserpine myth escaped Mary Shelley. Had it not escaped her, she would have been different, and her poem, instead of a lovely miniature, would have been a masterpiece. That it is not; but it is a true and precious addition to the corpus of English poetry, as well as a new and shining illumination thrown upon Mary Shelley's character.

> *J. Middleton Murry, "Mary Shelley's Poetry," in* The Nation and The Athenaeum, *Vol. XXXII, No. 11, December 16, 1922, p. 461.*

HOWARD PHILLIPS LOVECRAFT   (essay date 1927)

[*Lovecraft is considered one of the foremost modern authors of supernatural horror fiction, as well as one of its most notable critics. In the following brief excerpt from his* Supernatural Horror in Literature, *which is regarded as one of the earliest and most comprehensive studies of that genre, Lovecraft praises* Frankenstein. *Lovecraft's remarks were written in 1927.*]

[Mary Shelley's] inimitable *Frankenstein; or, the Modern Prometheus* . . . is one of the horror-classics of all time. Composed in competition with her husband, Lord Byron, and Dr. John William Polidori in an effort to prove supremacy in horror-making, Mrs. Shelley's *Frankenstein* was the only one of the rival narratives to be brought to an elaborate completion; and criticism has failed to prove that the best parts are due to Shelley rather than to her. The novel, somewhat tinged but scarcely marred by moral didacticism, tells of the artificial human being molded from charnel fragments by Victor Frankenstein. . . . Some of the scenes in *Frankenstein* are unforgettable, as when the newly animated monster enters its creator's room, parts the curtains of his bed, and gazes at him in the yellow moonlight with watery eyes—"if eyes they may be called." Mrs. Shelley wrote other novels, including the fairly notable *Last Man;* but never duplicated the success of her first effort. It has the true

touch of cosmic fear, no matter how much the movement may lag in places. (pp. 38-9)

> *Howard Phillips Lovecraft, "The Aftermath of Gothic Fiction," in his* Supernatural Horror in Literature, *Ben Abramson Publisher, 1945, pp. 36-44.*

R. GLYNN GRYLLS   (essay date 1938)

[*In her biography of Shelley, from which the following excerpt is drawn, Grylls terms* Frankenstein *a "period piece" important chiefly as a forerunner of science fiction, finding* The Last Man *more relevant and worthy of attention.*]

[*Frankenstein*] is of interest as a considerable *tour de force,* for Mary was only nineteen when she wrote it, but its importance in the history of the novel depends primarily on the originality of the plot and on the descendants for which it has been responsible.

In its erection of a superstructure of fantasy on a foundation of circumstantial 'scientific' fact . . . it is the first of the Scientific Romances that have culminated in our day in the work of Mr. H. G. Wells; in this, as in its suggestion of deeper psychological and sociological implications underlying the story, *Frankenstein* marks an advance on the crude horror of the Radcliffe-Monk Lewis school. But in other respects, in style and in characterization in particular, it is badly 'dated'; the digressions and the description of scenery that delay the unfolding of the story proper are not only obvious devices to pad out the story to the dimensions of a novel (on Shelley's advice), but are conventions of the time with little to recommend them. It is not for nothing that *The Sorrows of Werther* is among the first three books that the monster came across. Frankenstein's fastidiousness and hesitancy, in debt more to German sentimentality than to *Hamlet,* make the modern reader as impatient with him as he is incredulous of the blameless beauty of the heroine. It is not the monster who is unreal in *Frankenstein,* but the human beings. The heavy Gothic diet, that Shelley was strong enough to assimilate and survive, permanently impaired Mary's weaker literary digestion.

If she had developed in *Frankenstein* and in the later novels the subtler psychology which she touched upon in the monster's *apologia* for his malignity, she would have taken a far higher rank as an artist; she would have been a novelist and not a 'fictioneer'; but she was content to deal in the stock-in-trade of her generation, and consequently her high gifts of imagination and her command over language, worthy of better things, are lost in a neglect not wholly undeserved. *Frankenstein* remains a 'period piece', of not very good date; historically interesting, but not one of the living novels of the world.

I have dealt at length with *Frankenstein* as it is the only novel of Mary Shelley's whose reputation has survived, and criticism of it applies in general to her other work.

Lodore is valuable now as veiled biography, but as a novel is not as intrinsically interesting as *The Last Man,* which, in the present writer's opinion, has not received its deserts. Her imaginative powers in it, concentrated on achieving one effect, that of utter desolation, are more successfully employed than when they range more diffusely and stray into the grandiose and the sentimental. Her description of the devastation wrought by a plague which sweeps the world and brings in its train a breakdown, more nightmarish than death itself, of the organization on which civilized existence depends takes on a heightened reality to a generation threatened by an extinction as complete from the man-made plague of war: there seems nothing fanciful in the wanderings of the surviving hero over a wrecked and deserted Europe. (pp. 319-21)

> *R. Glynn Grylls, in her* Mary Shelley: A Biography, *Oxford University Press, London, 1938, 345 p.*

SYLVA NORMAN   (essay date 1938)

[*In this excerpt from a survey of Shelley's novels, journalistic pieces, short stories, verse dramas, and poetry, Norman identifies her as a romantic and traces those qualities in many of her works. Although she credits the author with talent and inspiration, Norman essentially dismisses much of Shelley's creative writing because she was unable to devise plot and character. Norman does praise some of Shelley's nonfiction pieces, pronouncing* Lives of Eminent Men *"her soundest, most scholarly and efficient writing."*]

On June 18, 1824, Mary Shelley broke away from despondency in her journal, to be stimulated by the thrill of a 'divine night'.

> I have just returned from Kentish Town; a calm twilight pervades the clear sky; the lamp-like moon is hung out in heaven, and the bright west retains the dye of sunset. If such weather would continue, I should write again; the lamp of thought is again illumined in my heart, and the fire descends from heaven that kindles it. . . . I shall again feel the enthusiastic glow of composition, again, as I pour forth my soul upon paper, feel the winged ideas arise, and enjoy the delight of expressing them. Study and occupation will be a pleasure, and not a task, and this I shall owe to sight and companionship of trees and meadows, flowers and sunshine.

The passage reveals several small points about our authoress. First, it establishes the certainty—not without importance—that Mary was, or had been, capable of losing herself delightedly in the intimate process of creation. Such an attitude cannot be induced by advice or suggestion on the part of another, and we may take it that Mary Godwin would have been a writer if there had been no Shelley or Byron to startle her into the nightmare of *Frankenstein*. It hints further, when we consider its date, that the joy of composition could be all-sufficing, removing her from the need of Shelley's presence, and filling the desolate gap after his death. (pp. 55-6)

Further, the quotation gives a clue to her literary mentality by displaying the sources of her inspiration. They are those of the romantic—moonlight, trees and meadows, flowers and sunshine. A revolutionary would have been inspired by politics and ideas, a satirist by men. (p. 56)

[It is] the romantic period that must be borne in mind when we consider [Mary Shelley], if we are not to confuse the fashions of an age with the faults of an individual. Genius carves its own way through all conventions without being independent of its period; but average talent exists to be moulded by the current fashion, not only because escape is difficult, but also because the question of popularity is involved. The early nineteenth century favoured melancholy. Its feelings were harrowed most pleasantly by a tale of ill-starred love, and death, and deserted souls who grieved eternally. Its drama must be tragic, its lyrics despairing, its lengthy novels stuffed out with disasters and bespattered with the bleeding fragments of warm hearts.

Naturally those who wrote for a living tuned themselves in to this popular note. . . . (p. 57)

In one respect, at least, the three-volume novel presented no difficulty to Mary: she could fill it up. Words slipped easily from her pen, and, the situation once given, she found little trouble in prolonging it. But the situation was another matter, so were the characters. Genuine imaginative fertility was denied her, nor was she a keen, detached observer of men and women. Plot, in both novel and short story, was an initial bugbear that had to be overcome by a desperate search into memory or history. Even when established, the narrative was pushed along by devices that strike us now as being clumsy and tiresome, though probably acceptable to the taste of her public. Each new character is linked to the plot by a chain of information about his own past life and circumstances; he comes, as it seems, from an infinite distance—a distance the more deplorable when we find him eventually hooked tight to the plot by a past coincidence of time and presence, or a concealed identity. Far too often Mary's idea of a firmly constructed novel is to reveal the blood-relationships of apparent strangers, kinsman becoming painfully entangled with kinsman in the dark. The 'Hold, hold! he cried,—I tell thee 'tis her brother!' of [P. B. Shelley's] "Rosalind and Helen" was comfortably installed, with all its box of tricks, in Mary's mind, to be brought out less sensationally and at greater length. Again the taste of her readers is to blame; without these artificial disclosures they would have been as disappointed as Edwardian children at a pantomime that lacked its transformation scene.

As for her characters, the rule of snobbery appeared to prevail; they must be highborn, whether they were the medieval Italian chieftains of *Valperga,* the English princes of *Perkin Warbeck,* the society nobles of *Lodore* and *Falkner,* or the imaginary king's sons of *The Last Man.* There was never again so humble a hero as the student 'Frankenstein'. Yet how often are these distinguished folk incognito, even to themselves! They are brought up in peasants' huts, performing menial tasks, far in thought and mileage from the ancestral mansion. This suggests prudence on the novelist's part; some of her readers were liable to a closer acquaintance with great houses than the Whig baronet's runaway daughter-in-law, who was denied Field Place and knew the Lord of Newstead only as an exile. But the picturesque Shelley and Byron she did know, and for an authoress they were godsends. Again and again she snatched at such of their features as she might readily reproduce, so that hollow semblances and distortions of them drift through her thousands of pages, despoiled of their keen features and smothered, by the end of their pilgrimage, under fictitious clothes. . . . Almost unreal in reality, Byron fitted astonishingly well into the period novel, and if his image and identity had not been preserved for us, we could have sworn that in every case this wilful charmer was a projection of the writer's sentiment. Shelley, whose portrait required some discussion of philosophy and reform, was more difficult to catch. When Mary attempts it he becomes [scarcely recognizable]. . . . But he is useful to her, if only to bring in a train of ghostly associates and incidents which, as in *Lodore,* can be shuffled and shaped into a story.

Mary's first novel [*Frankenstein*] has become a classic, and needs no discussion here. Its popularity was fortunate for her, since all her subsequent novels, and most of her short stories, were compelled by Sir Timothy's ban to appear with 'the author of *Frankenstein*' as sole signature. The first of them, *Valperga, or the Life and Adventures of Castruccio, Prince of Lucca,* had been written during Shelley's lifetime, and the reward promised to Godwin before Mary knew how eagerly she would want it herself. If the devoted parent is to be believed, his drastic cuts and alterations were responsible for its seeing the light of publication. He had deplored its length, although two of the 'females' were 'exceedingly interesting' and to his thinking there were 'parts of high genius'. The last was a kindly estimate, and any one having the persistence to read through *Valperga,* which harbours some of Mary's dreariest writing, must thank Godwin for the liberties he took with it. And yet, at one point an echo of Shelleyan boldness enters the story, to remind us that she still had his backing.

[In *Valperga*], popularity enters in with the romantical nightmare machinery of witches, miracles, and inquisition. It is not all fustian; occasional subtleties creep into the analysis of motive and character, and the Italian landscape, being of the essence of her inspiration, is vividly and convincingly described. (pp. 60-5)

[The subject of *The Last Man*], which might have seemed almost as original as that of *Frankenstein* had it been Mary's own invention, was going the literary rounds when she seized on it to supply her need of a plot. She might, one feels, have allowed it to supply the *whole* plot; yet there is some merit in her suggestion that the end of the world, when it does come, will alarm a population fully occupied with its own absorbing activities. It certainly takes an unconscionable time to get under way. (p. 66)

The Last Man having lived and died, its author turned with decision into English History, read up her Yorkist and Lancastrian annals, received pedestrian information from her father, even begged Sir Walter Scott the expert for help with obscurer references, and produced *The Fortunes of Perkin Warbeck*. . . . There was only one romantic way of treating Perkin Warbeck; Mary believed firmly, in her preface, that records in the Tower proved him, almost beyond doubt, to be the Duke of York. Her favourite subject of nobility in disguise was thus available, giving her, as she naïvely put it, 'a hero to ennoble the pages of a humble tale'. It gave her in addition such a surfeit of material about kings and princes, royal relationships, political plans, and movements of conspirators, that she was hard pressed nearly all the way through by the necessity of embodying and arranging it while she kept the Duke's horse trotting to its doom. If the predominant note is an echo of Scott, she deserves a word of praise for her successful obstacle race. Besides, it prevented her most healthily from overindulgence in the woeful situation, simply through lack of time for it. (pp. 70-1)

It was a quiet story in that Mary decided to procure no plot for it beyond a medley of happenings based on the lives of her own circle, broken up, transplanted, fertilized (or sterilized) with fiction. *Lodore,* . . . with no claims but as a society novel, proved nearer than the historical ventures had been to the public taste. It has since been used as a competition ground for Shelleyans, who go through it neatly labelling the characters and incidents until all is docketed. . . . [In *Lodore*], Mary has skilfully split the personalities, reduced the interest, and abstracted the tragedy of her own life and circumstances. She has added intrigue and a measure of tedium to fill the gap. (pp. 72-4)

Besides her enormous novels, a good body of journalistic writing lies at Mary's door. She was anything but lazy. Her journalism—not quite of the modern miscellaneous order—falls into two sections. One comprises the *Lives of Eminent Men* written for Lardner's *Cabinet Cyclopaedia,* the other consists of stories and sketches contributed to the fashionable Annuals. They make a fair contrast, the first containing her soundest, most scholarly and efficient writing, the second being all bubble and baseless fabrication.

The full title of the Lardner volumes was *Lives of the Most Eminent Literary and Scientific Men of Italy, Spain and Portugal.* The first appeared in February 1835. Mary wrote to Mrs. Gisborne, 'The Lives of Dante and Ariosto are by Mr. [James] Montgomery, the rest are mine.' Those others, which had been 'a source of interest and pleasure' to her, were those of Petrarch, Boccaccio, Lorenzo de Medici, Bojardo, Berni, and Machiavelli, besides an article on half a dozen minor figures. In the autumn a second volume was published, in which Mary had lost Galileo and Tasso to Montgomery, but wrote on Metastasio, Goldoni, Alfieri, Guicciardini, Vittoria Colonna, Guarini, Chiabrera, Tassoni, Marini, Ugo Foscolo, and Monti— this last being pronounced as 'without question, the greatest Italian poet that has appeared since the golden days of its poetry'. (pp. 79-80)

The *Lives* were not intended to contain original research. Enough that they were accurate, readable, sympathetic, and concise. Looking through them we seem at last to have a picture of that Mary who sat studying and reading for long hours with Shelley, sparing only a moment at the end of the day to record a line in her diary. As Godwin had said of *Frankenstein,* the biographical writing was 'compressed, muscular, and firm; nothing relaxed and weak; no proud flesh'. Mary was performing a healthy, honest task imposed from without; her mind, rather than her heart, was in it, and she performed it competently.

The stories belong to another world, being written to grace those graceful Annuals—the *Keepsake,* the *Book of Beauty,* the *Forget-me-Not*—which were produced so elegantly at Christmas time, bound in rose-coloured silk covers and embellished with steel engravings of romantic subjects to illustrate the text. . . . Every fashionable lady probably had a *Keepsake* in her boudoir, so that it was worth while for the socially ambitious to contribute. Only she must suit her surroundings. A love lyric, a sketch of sunset, a romance of the East (to be illustrated by scimitars and turbans), any story of colourful heroism or sweet sacrifice, of love in mourning or rescue from villainy, for preference set amongst foreign vines and olives, rugged gorges, and torrential mountain streams. Humour was not encouraged. Obviously, Mary could write for the Annuals without much schooling. Her past dwellings lay up and down the landscapes of Italy, her connexions led her farther east to Greece, her pen was facile and her heart romantic. (pp. 81-3)

All the features we have noticed about Mary's conduct of a novel apply equally—often more disastrously—to her stories. The two were not then such different forms of art. No implicit rule laid down a limit to the scope of the short story; the 'single episode', 'the continuous mood'—such unities were unheard of, for Maupassant, Tchehov, and their disciples were yet to come. Mary's tales had as many and gaudy trimmings as a well-hung Christmas tree. In their confined space they still presented story within story, to an irritating extent. One of the worst offenders is **"Euphrasia."** . . . This story begins with a party caught in a Sussex snowdrift, waiting in such cold tedium to be rescued that a gentleman is induced to tell of his adventures in revolutionary Greece. . . . Richard Garnett, collecting Mary's tales into a volume in 1891, improved the case by cutting out the snowdrift altogether, without a word of his surgery. But he could not cover Mary's lapse of memory, whereby the adventurer's story is begun in the third person and finished in the first.

To be sure, in this Arabian Night kind of production we should not be too particular. A few genii, flying palaces, and revengeful auks might have improved their weaving; it is the attempt at realism in an artificial frame that makes them so irksome. For instance, in **"The Mourner"** one of Mary's young Nevilles goes to Eton in a Shelleyan way. 'I will not attempt to dwell on my sufferings there. . . . I was a fag to a hard taskmaster', and West Indian slavery was light compared with that bondage. After this hyperbolical indictment the young man lives a fairy tale with one of those high-born ladies who take to polite rusticity. The entire story is glitter and tinsel, ending in a tragedy. . . . (pp. 83-5)

There is no need to dwell longer on these baubles, except to mourn the wasted talent and the fragments of true observation that lie embalmed in them. In his preface to *St. Leon,* Godwin wrote in 1799: 'I have mixed human feelings and passions with incredible situations, and thus rendered them impressive and interesting.' Mary, whose work is in the Godwin tradition, tries to do the same, even borrowing her father's Wandering Jew theme for her tale of **"The Mortal Immortal"**; but her passions are as incredible as her situations. She could never leave her castles and cottages, her runaway girls and truculent pursuers, her disguised identities, funereal smiles and flower-decked tears—not though she was richer than most women of her time in keen experience. There is strength in her intellect, but it bows to her truly feminine invention which prefers to dive into a glade of detached fancy rather than face the responsibility of truth and living portraiture.

Setting aside editorship and travel notes, one more aspect of Mary's literary work remains—her poetry and drama. There is not much of it. Her longest poem, *The Choice,* written a few months after Shelley's death, mourned her lover and her own shortcomings, and doubtless raised her spirits towards exaltation, though it has no such effect now on the reader. (pp. 85-6)

Perhaps Mary's ambition did not really envisage the limited field of the lyric. For many years after her bereavement she dreamed of writing tragedy in the grand style. She had always been attracted by the glamour of the stage and the personalities of actors, and believed now that out of this personal sorrow some magnificent drama would be born. Godwin, seeing more clearly the difference between feeling and ability, dissuaded his daughter in round terms, and she gave up the idea with a sigh. However, she had already written some dramatic scenes in verse, at a time when Shelley and Byron were composing dramas. Her two mythological verse scenes, *Proserpine* and *Midas,* were written, according to their modern editor, in 1820. (pp. 88-9)

One must in honesty admit that Mary Shelley's verse dramas, pretty and sometimes poetical as they are, do not really call for analytical and comparative study. In the altering of lines and phrases [between the first and second versions] we find no great mind at work, but only, as in the case of her occasional lyrics, a musical intonation and simple command of rhythm grafted on to the usual facility of her prose language.

It is not to be wondered at that her 'poetical works' are few; those who live in permanent close contact with a poet (as Mary did mentally, even after Shelley's death) must be conceited or hard of hearing if they insist on adding their small tinkle to the sonorous note. Mary had sense and judgement enough to

leave the poetry in Shelley's hands, and to concentrate on fiction, which financial returns and a genuine if unexalted gift both served to justify. (pp. 98-9)

> *Sylva Norman, "Mary Shelley: Novelist and Dramatist," in* On Shelley *by Edmund Blunden, Gavin de Beer, and Sylva Norman, Oxford University Press, London, 1938, pp. 55-99.*

MILTON MILLHAUSER (essay date 1946)

[*Millhauser considers* Frankenstein'*s monster in relation to the tradition of the "noble savage" in literature.*]

The estimate of Mary Shelley's **Frankenstein** familiar to us from literary handbooks and popular impression emphasizes its macabre and pseudo-scientific sensationalism: properly enough, so far as either its primary conception or realized qualities are concerned. But it has the effect of obscuring from notice certain secondary aspects of the work which did, after all, figure in its history and weigh with its contemporary audience, and which must, therefore, be taken into consideration before either the book or the young mind that composed it has been properly assayed. One such minor strain, not too well recognised in criticism, is a thin vein of social speculation: a stereotyped, irrelevant, and apparently automatic repetition of the lessons of that school of liberal thought which was then termed "philosophical."

In the work of Godwin's daughter and Shelley's bride, some reflection of contemporary social radicalism—crude, second-hand, very earnest, already a little out of date—occurs almost as a matter of course; what deserves comment is just that this element entered the author's notion of her plot so late and remained so decidedly an alien in it; for it governs the story only temporarily and, so to speak, extraneously, and confuses as much as it promotes the development of the character of the central figure, the monster itself. Where one might have expected, from Mary's character, that it would prove a main *motif* of the narrative, it is actually both detrimental thereto and ill-assimilated, and must be discarded altogether before the story can advance to its principal effect.

For, throughout a considerable part of the book—roughly speaking, the first half of the middle section, beginning with chapter xi—the monster is so far from being the moral horror he presently becomes that it is hardly credible he should ever be guilty of wanton brutality at all. (The transformation, by the way, is effected most abruptly, without even the degree of psychological consistency appropriate to fantasy; two violent rebuffs and an astonishingly rigid logicality of temperament turn the monster from his lonely and contemplative benevolence to a course of harsh, melodramatic vengefulness.) Rather, in the solitary student of Volney, musing on the pageant of human history, or on the contrast between man's accomplishments and his failures—"Was man, indeed, at once so powerful, so virtuous and magnificent, yet so vicious and base?"—it is not hard to recognise that gentle lay-figure of late eighteenth century social criticism, the "natural man," bringing his innocence into forceful and oversimplified contrast with the complexities and contradictions of our civilisation. Or, more precisely, may we not see in him (because of his strange origin and untutored state) something approximating to that variation of the general "child of nature" pattern to which Professor Fairchild has attached the name of Noble Savage? Like the savage, the monster approaches our society as an outsider, tests it by natural impulse and unsophisticated reason, and responds to it with a mixture of bewilderment and dismay.

Now, this aspect of the monster's character is basically unnecessary to the horror-plot; he need not pass by this road to ferocity and misery. (There might, for instance, as easily have been an original moral flaw in his constitution, paralleling the physical one; he might, as in the vulgar imagination, have been *created* bestial.) Indeed, the more this phase of his development is dwelt upon, the less consistent with the later stages does it appear. Nor is his experience as a Noble Savage too closely integrated into the story; it is connected rather arbitrarily to his education in language, but the social reflections, as well as the narrative which is their more immediate occasion, are pure interpolation, and lead to nothing. This is a real flaw in the story, felt by the reader as expectation disappointed; the author fails to *make use* of all her speculative preparation. When, for instance, the monster is hurt—brutally attacked—by those he trusted, it is because of their human ignorance and natural terror, not society's injustice; so that his radical observations are irrelevant to his own fate. Before long, indeed, the author is able to forget that the monster was ever a "natural man" (and consequently gentle and just by inclination) at all, without apparent loss to the dramatic values of the story. Everything points to the whole idea's having been an afterthought, arising, perhaps, before the full detail of the book had been worked out, but well after the general mood and drift and structure of the plot had been decided. The chance for it was offered by the story, and Mary Shelley could not decline it, but it was not an essential part of her idea, and could only be fitted in as a disproportioned and almost pointless interpolation.

The temptation seems to have been offered by the problem of the monster's intellectual development. The effort to make her creature psychologically credible must have troubled Mrs. Shelley most in his early days. What the difficulty was appears as one writes of it; how is one to speak of the "youth," the "childhood," of a being that appeared upon the earth full-grown, and yet how else is one to speak of his period of elementary ignorance and basic learning? The author cannot allow him the normal protracted human infancy and gradual education, for the plot demands that he escape from his creator and fend for himself at once; yet both plot and probability demand that he escape unformed, that he be confused and ignorant in the world into which he has blundered. As a result, the author bestows upon him a curious apprenticeship (to call it that), an amalgam of two quite different rates of development: for he is at the same time both child and man, and learns alternately like each. Thus he can walk and clothe himself from the moment of his creation, yet, infant-like, has trouble for a long while in separating the effects of the various senses; he learns the use of fire (by strict inductive reasoning!) in a few minutes, yet it is years before he can teach himself to speak or read. For the most part, however, his story is that of an adult in the state of nature, with faculties full-grown but almost literally without experience, and therefore making the acquaintance of the most primitive social facts by toilsome and unguided individual endeavour. If one distinguishes the difficulties (possible to an adult) of ignorance from those (peculiar to a child) of incapacity, there is really only a single effort to make him behave like one new-born—the confusion of the senses; thereafter he is a full-grown and decidedly intelligent but extraordinarily inexperienced man.

Now this comes close to being a description of the Noble Savage: an adult, but an alien to our world. If at this point

Mary Shelley's mother, Mary Wollstonecraft, painted by John Opie circa 1797.

(that is, chapters xi through xv) he differs markedly from the average of the type, it is only in being not an average but an extreme; the actual savage has his own commendable if elementary civilisation that he can compare with ours, but Frankenstein's monster has only the impulses of his nature—which are, to start with, absolutely good. But this mixture of innocence with ignorance was the very point to be exhibited by the Noble Savage or the "natural man"—"man as he is not"— both forms familiar to tediousness in the literature upon which early nineteenth century ingenuous radicalism fed its mind. So that, having brought her monster, untutored and uncorrupted, into the wilderness, there to spy upon and so study civilised ways (all of which was demanded anyhow by the plot), Mrs. Shelley would have found it hard not to fall into what must have been a very familiar habit of thought. She must surely have recognised that she was straying from the plotted path, whether she identified the new influence or not; but she was trying to write a full-length novel on the basis of a rather slim idea, and in those days interpolation was not yet a sin. So, not deliberately and yet not unwillingly, she permitted the assimilation of her story and her creature into the well-worn patterns they had skirted; none the less gratefully, perhaps, because they gave the young rebel an opportunity to utter a little of what was seething in her environment—the Shelley atmosphere, crossed by Byron's sulphureous trail—and in her own eager mind.

But if the temptation was strong enough to attract her into a rather long and somewhat incongruous philosophical digression, it was still subsidiary to her initial impulse. If Godwin's daughter could not help philosophising, Shelley's wife knew also the eerie charms of the morbid, the occult, the scientifically bizarre. Her first purpose, which was melodrama, stood. Therefore the alien figure appears in the novel only momentarily—so long as, with a little effort, the plot accommodates itself to him; when he really threatens to interfere with it, he is abandoned. But if he never dominates the story, he does figure in it, and should be reckoned with. However relentlessly the first lurid vision is finally pursued to its end, the familiar lineaments of the Noble Savage, the child of nature, did come for a little while to be visible in Frankenstein's impious creation; however sharply his hideous features and terrible career may have distinguished him from the brooding islander or haughty Indian sachem, the central theme, the uncongeniality of our actual world with a certain ideal and touchingly beautiful simplicity, served to associate his history, in some degree, with theirs, and so attract him temporarily into their form. (pp. 248-50)

> *Milton Millhauser, "The Noble Savage in Mary Shelley's 'Frankenstein'," in* Notes and Queries, *Vol. 190, No. 12, June 15, 1946, pp. 248-50.*

ELIZABETH NITCHIE (essay date 1953)

[*In the following excerpt from her well-regarded critical biography of Shelley, Nitchie focuses on structure, style, and characterization in Shelley's fiction.*]

[Mary Shelley] left only two works that have survived as wholes on their own merits: the notes to Shelley's works largely because of their subject matter, *Frankenstein* because of the strange, imaginative conception and compelling writing. It is easy to dispose of her as the unworthy companion of a great poet, the progressively worsening author of sentimental fiction. Such a judgment, however, neglects the strength of her nonfiction and the positive merits of her novels and tales. (p. 179)

Mary's writing has many faults, most of which were obvious even to her contemporary admirers: lack of humor, monotony, verbosity, overwriting, sentimentality of plot and character, fondness for beautiful, blameless heroines, reliance on analysis of character at the expense of dramatic action and dialogue. With all these faults there are still positive merits that even a modern critic must allow. The charges against her as a writer can be, not refuted, perhaps, but modified, some of them considerably, some of them at least by the exception that proves the rule. The charge of impiety brought against *Frankenstein* obviously need not be considered. And that of wild imagination in *Frankenstein* and *The Last Man* seems rather absurd in an age of robots, of air-borne travel, and of a socialized Britain— and of Aldous Huxley and George Orwell. But other—and serious—literary sins must be examined.

Except for *Frankenstein* Mary's fiction reveals little originality and invention in plotting. She depended too much either on actual events or on stereotyped situations. She repeated devices, such as the riding accident which she used many times in her novels and tales in order to throw a character where she wanted him, frequently at the feet of the heroine. The endings of her stories, though not always conventionally happy and sometimes even tragic are usually contrived and foreseeable. . . . She included too much in her plots, too many incidents that were merely incidental. Godwin cut *Valperga* drastically, and yet the reviewers thought it still burdened by episodes and minor characters. She had difficulty in sustaining a long, involved plot; her use of the flash-back too often results in confusion and diffusion rather than in clarity and conciseness;

occasionally, as in one hastily written short story, she herself loses track of her plot.

Yet she had a sense of dramatic structure. Even in *Falkner* the basic irony of the situation, though marred by over-emphasis and repetition, is striking. Gerard Neville, having vowed to seek out and punish his mother's destroyer, falls in love with Elizabeth, not knowing that her foster-father Falkner is the man he seeks. He even helps Elizabeth to nurse Falkner back to life after a severe illness. The plot of *Frankenstein* is tightly knit, with contrasts creating dramatic tensions. Two main ideas, loneliness and scientific curiosity with its hopes and fears and pains, are foreshadowed in the introductory letters of Walton to his sister and developed throughout the novel.

This entire story is set in strangeness: Walton and Frankenstein meet in the mysterious white world of the ice-bound Arctic— Coleridge's "land of mist and snow." Consciously or unconsciously, Mary owed much to *The Rime of the Ancient Mariner*. In Walton's letters to his sister there are several references to the poem. Indeed he attributes his passionate enthusiasm for "the dangerous mysteries of the ocean, to that production of the most imaginative of modern poets." And the loneliness of the Mariner appealed to the lonely creator of the lonely Monster.

And as was said of Coleridge, it is not in the invention of wonders that Mary excelled—striking as her central invention is—but in the extraordinary skill with which she "paints the passions they excite." Frankenstein's exaltation and terror, his doubt and dread and remorse, his wild grief and his passion for revenge are the chief means by which we are impressed with the frightfulness of his unhallowed creation. Just as in *The Ancient Mariner* we see and feel the horrors first with the Mariner and second with the Wedding Guest, so in *Frankenstein* the wonder is twice removed from the reality. Frankenstein's horror is told in his own words, like the Mariner's story, to Walton, a man who has no personal connection with the supernatural events but who "cannot choose but hear." And there is another layer of narrative: the Monster tells his story to Frankenstein, who tells it to Walton. Yet at the end, with Frankenstein's death, the middle layer disappears and reality meets wonder—Walton comes face to face with the Monster.

There are bright fragments of reality within the inner layers: Clerval's normalcy, the idyllic home of Felix (yet broken in upon by the strange girl from the East), Elizabeth's first letter with news of their happy family life. They serve only to thicken the strange darkness that surrounds and engulfs them. The words *strange* and *unnatural* become key words, appearing and reappearing on page after page.

Thus the structure of the novel is an ingenious, strangely wrought nest of boxes, reality on the outside and horror at the core. The chief persons in this story too are both real and strange. Walton combines practical, painstaking industry with "a love for the marvellous, a belief in the marvellous" which hurries him away from normal living to exploration of the "wild sea and unvisited regions." Frankenstein goes away to the university like any other young man but is caught by the magic of modern science until he is driven into experiments unhallowed and presumptuous in their invasion of the power of the Creator. The Monster himself is non-human in his origin, his physical frame and appearance, but human in his longings and desires and even in that passion for revenge which leads him to commit inhuman crimes.

In *The Last Man* there are dramatic foreshadowings and contrasts. Raymond, foreseeing his death, looks upon the earth as a tomb, each man he meets as a corpse; thus, as the story progresses, Verney and the reader come to look upon mankind. The beauty of nature and the gaiety or the idyllic happiness of man are broken in upon by word of the progress of the plague. Adrian's dream of a paradise on earth, Merrival's prediction of eternal spring to come a hundred thousand years in the future, little Alfred's birthday party, a service at Westminster Abbey are interrupted by news of fresh victims or the actual presence of Pestilence. A sense of dramatic fitness animates the account of a performance of *Macbeth* at Drury Lane Theatre in plague-stricken London:

> A shudder like the swift passing of an electric shock ran through the house, when Rosse exclaimed, in answer to "Stands Scotland where it did?"

> Alas, poor country;
> Almost afraid to know itself! It cannot
> Be called our mother, but our grave: where nothing,
> But who knows nothing, is once seen to smile;
> Where sighs, and groans, and shrieks that rent the air,
> Are made, not marked; where violent sorrow seems
> A modern extasy: the dead man's knell
> Is there scarce asked, for who; and good men's lives
> Expire before the flowers in their caps,
> Dying, or ere they sicken.

> Each word struck the scene, as our life's passing bell; we feared to look at each other, but bent our gaze on the stage, as if our eyes could fall innocuous on that alone.

(pp. 180-84)

These moments of dramatic tension, however, do not save most of Mary's stories from prolixity and confusion.

As she had difficulty in sustaining an involved plot, so she could rarely sustain the drawing of an important character. Her heroes and heroines are usually two-dimensional, cut out like paper dolls from a pattern of Byronic gentleman or beautiful and virtuous maiden. She lacked skill in presenting the mingling of good and bad—although she had known it well in her friends. The faults in the fundamentally noble persons are of the grand sort, due to strong passions or to bad bringing up. The villains are either idle, profligate spendthrifts or tyrannical and prejudiced old men, cold of heart. It is in minor characters seen comparatively briefly or in flashes of insight into personality that Mary is successful and impressive. Mrs. Elizabeth Fitzhenry, good-natured, simple, stupid, adoring but not understanding her brother Lodore, doing her duty by Ethel in the great city of London but never dreaming that a love affair is going on under her nose, retiring with thankfulness to her quiet country life after Ethel's marriage—here is a real "character," drawn, as far as anyone knows, from Mary's own imagination. Miss Jervis, Elizabeth Falkner's governess, in her crispness and primness, her intellectual limitations and her professional conscientiousness, is a real person. (pp. 185-86)

Not all of the principal characters are flat. Adrian in *The Last Man,* though shadowy when compared with his living model, is drawn with delicate sympathy and with the rounded knowledge which his creator had of his original. Beatrice, the strange, dark, passionate girl in *Valperga,* deserves the praise she received from Shelley, Godwin, and the reviewers. Euthanasia, except for her typical extreme beauty, is an interesting woman

Mary Shelley's father, William Godwin, painted by James Northcote in 1802.

because of the conflict within her between her love for Castruccio and her love for her own people. Her gradual disenchantment is convincing in its clarity and logic.

Mary Shelley frequently used characters confused by mixed emotions and motives. The most interesting person in *Lodore* is Cornelia, whose pride is always at war with her affections and keeps her for a long time from both her daughter and her lover. In *Falkner* most of the characters are thoroughly wound up in mixed motives: Falkner in his wish for death and his love and sense of responsibility for Elizabeth; Neville in his honorable desire to vindicate his mother and his love for Elizabeth to whom such vindication would bring sorrow; Elizabeth in her own involved loyalties to Neville and to Falkner. Even when Falkner has been acquitted, he and Neville are still hampered by conflicting delicacies of feeling that delay the conclusion. Part of the drama and the tragedy of *Frankenstein* lies in the conflicts in the young scientist's own soul: his glory and his horror at his scientific achievement; his pity and his hatred of the Monster.

The Monster himself, that earliest creation of Mary's, is probably her best, most subtle, most perceptive characterization. [In] his loneliness he is a projection of Mary herself. It is that which makes him human, which is responsible for the changes in his character, which makes him tragic. Improbable as are the circumstances of his creation—why, asked one reviewer, did Frankenstein make him so huge and so hideous—and of his self-education, he becomes a real and convincing person, viewed in the round, whose motives are clear and valid. He runs through an arc of experience and of feeling for others, from love through fear and hatred to a final compassion for mankind and even for his creator. To the last he justifies his crimes by the fact that he is alone and that every man's hand has been against him. "Robbed of its romantic form," said Bertrand Russell, "there is nothing unreal in this psychology.... To an English visitor, the ex-Kaiser, at Doorn, lamented that the English no longer loved him. Dr. Burtt, in his book on the juvenile delinquent, mentions a boy of seven who drowned another boy in the Regent Canal; his reason was that neither his family nor his contemporaries showed him affection. Dr. Burtt was kind to him, and he became a respectable citizen; but no Dr. Burtt undertook the reformation of Frankenstein's monster" [see Additional Bibliography].

Vague and diffuse as Mary's characterizations sometimes are, she often presents an attitude, a characteristic, or a whole character in a concise and telling comment that shows her observant and ironic eye. "She satisfied her conscience . . . by cherishing a little quiet stock of family hate." "My aunt . . . was as a plant beneath a thick covering of ice; my hands would have been frozen in any attempt to get at it." Castruccio, the man of war, was accustomed "to count men as the numerals of a military arithmetic." And with a turn of phrase that gives fresh meaning to a cliché Mary sums up the character of Miss Jervis: "She has a heart of gold, though it does not shine." (pp. 186-88)

Her comments on the morality of society or the vanity of human wishes, her wistful reflections on life and death, on youth and age may not be original in thought. But often she finds for them a turn of phrase that stamps them with interest and individuality. "We never do what we wish when we wish it, and when we desire a thing earnestly, and it does arrive, that or we are changed, so that we slide from the summit of our wishes and find ourselves where we were." . . .

Mary's descriptive style, generalized and elaborate as much of it seems today, was considered vigorous, clear, and nervous by her contemporaries. Individual words are often precise and expressive: "the light waves coursed one another," "dusky manuscripts," "the snowdrift, whirring past the lattice." Figures of speech are often fresh and vivid. Verney speaks of "the inch and barley-corn growth of my life." Of the small remnant of English waiting on the Dover cliffs to cross to the hoped-for safety of the continent, he says, "Death had hunted us through the course of many months, even to the narrow strip of time on which we now stood." (p. 190)

In longer passages of description, although they are often colored and weakened by romantic diction, Mary can sustain a mood and create a distinct picture. She can describe scenery, especially that which she had known herself: the landscape of Tuscany through which she passed on her return to England and of which she wrote to Hunt; the streets and houses of Geneva; the country around Albano; the peaks and valleys and glaciers of the Alps. In *Frankenstein* Walton's "land of mist and snow," which she had never seen, owes much to her reading of Coleridge. But the journey of Frankenstein and Clerval down the Rhine is lively and full of detail like that in Mary's own *History of a Six Weeks' Tour*. And her vivid pictures of the grand scenes among which she began to write *Frankenstein*—the thunderstorm in the Alps, the valleys of Servox and Chamounix, the glacier and the precipitous sides of Montanvert, and the smoke of rushing avalanches, the "tremendous dome" of Mont Blanc—are not shamed by comparison with the poems written in the same months and on the same ground, Byron's third canto of *Childe Harold* and Shelley's "Mont Blanc." (p. 191)

[Darkly] dramatic moments stand out against the flatter narrative in her novels: the Monster's drawing back of the curtains on Frankenstein's bed; the collapse of the bridge of Carraia at the Spectacle of Hell in Florence; the exhumation of the body of Falkner's Alithea; Lodore's fatal duel with the American, their figures silhouetted against a moonlit sky; the discovery of Raymond's body in the ruins of Constantinople guarded by his dying dog; the climax of Mathilda's search for her father; the portentous setting for doomed humanity in *The Last Man*. . . . (p. 193)

Mary's style had considerable range. It is at its most elaborate in *The Last Man*. Here she uses the romantic poetic devices of alliteration and assonance, echo and repetition, question and apostrophe to heighten the mood. "Who was there indeed to save? What troop had we brought fit to stand at bay, and combat with the conqueror? We were a failing remnant, tamed to mere submission to the coming blow. A train half dead, through fear of death. . . . Like a few furrows of unreaped corn. . . . Like a few straggling swallows. . . . Like a stray sheep. . . . Like a cloud. . . . Such were we." The threnody of coming destruction and solitude mounts as the novel draws to its emotional close: "Thus around the shores of deserted earth, while the sun is high, and the moon waxes or wanes, angels, the spirits of the dead, and the ever-open eye of the Supreme, will behold the tiny bark, freighted with Verney—the LAST MAN."

Mary could also write simply and directly.

> Early, therefore, on Monday, August 8th, Sxxx and Cxxx went to the ass market, and purchased an ass, and the rest of the day, until four in the afternoon, was spent in preparations for our departure. . . . Packing up a few necessaries, leaving the rest to go by diligence, we departed in a fiacre from the door of the hotel, our little ass following.
>
> (p. 194)

This account, "unpresuming," as Mary calls it in her preface, gives a bright, clear picture of the "six weeks' tour" of the three light-hearted young runaways. It can be matched by direct and simple writing in the narrative of her travels with her son and his friends nearly thirty years later. (p. 195)

There is little reward for a reader of Mary Shelley's poems. . . . Her [verse] was not unmusical—she had a sense of rhythm and harmony. But except for an occasional phrase or line—

> The bride of Time no more, I wed Eternity—

> She is immortal—yet unusual fear
> Runs through my veins—

the diction is obvious, commonplace, imitative and sentimental.

Against her work as a whole so harsh a charge cannot be brought. Although the general reader would hardly care to peruse Mary Shelley's works, yet there is reward for so doing. There are familiar people to be met again, disguised and perhaps distorted, but always seen, however myopically, through the eyes of Shelley's wife. There are lesser persons, new and interesting, flashing momentarily from the pages. There are tales of power and scenes of horror to take permanent hold on the imagination. There are landscapes of beauty and of association to remain in the memory. There is writing to be admired—lucid and moving. . . . There is the woman herself, to be seen in a fuller, truer light than that cast upon her by the words of worshippers or detractors or even by her own letters and journals. It is a woman neither angel nor devil, full of faults, full of merits: brave in spite of her self-pity, liberal in her views in spite of her compromises with society, endowed with intellectual powers that command respect in spite of their limitations and with imagination capable of creative achievement in spite of her later taming of it to meet the taste of the reading public. There is in all her work, however dulled and diluted, the young author of *Frankenstein*. (pp. 199-200)

> *Elizabeth Nitchie, in her* Mary Shelley: Author of "Frankenstein", *Rutgers University Press, 1953, 255 p.*

M. A. GOLDBERG (essay date 1959)

[*Goldberg's investigation of the themes of isolation and knowledge in* Frankenstein *is considered one of the first comprehensive assessments of the novel and a milestone in* Frankenstein *studies.*]

In the central pages of Mary Shelley's *Frankenstein or, The Modern Prometheus* the reader encounters for some six chapters a personal narrative of the monster. For the first time since his creation, he is approaching his maker who sits sad and pensive near the awful majesty of Mont Blanc. Conscious of his "duties as a creator towards his creature," Frankenstein agrees to listen to the tale of this blighted being who has developed from a *tabula rasa,* experiencing in true Lockean fashion first confused, then distinct sensations, and developing in turn social affections, then moral and intellectual judgments. Crucial to his learning, we discover, has been a leather portmanteau, found one day in the forest where he has hidden himself from the eyes of mankind, and in which are contained, together with some articles of dress, a volume of Plutarch's *Lives,* the *Sorrows of Werter,* and Milton's *Paradise Lost.* The latter, he explains, has had a most profound effect upon him:

> I read it [*Paradise Lost*], as I had read the other volumes which had fallen into my hands, as a true history. . . . I often referred the several situations, as their similarity struck me, to my own. Like Adam, I was apparently united by no link to any other being in existence; but his state was far different from mine in every other respect. He had come forth from the hands of God a perfect creature, happy and prosperous, guarded by the especial care of his Creator; he was allowed to converse with, and acquire knowledge from, beings of a superior nature: but I was wretched, helpless, and alone. Many times I considered Satan as the fitter emblem of my condition; for often, like him, when I viewed the bliss of my protectors, the bitter gall of envy rose within me.

This is no idle image which the creature evokes here, comparing his own situation with Satan's, and with Adam's paradisaic state in Eden. The confusion apparent in his own consciousness—whether he is an Adam, destined ultimately for eternal grace, or a Satan, doomed to eternal darkness—is a motif crucial to the entire novel. It is crucial to the monster's tale, embedded as the innermost circle of the text. It is crucial to Frankenstein's narrative, which, unfolded to Captain Walton, encircles the monster's tale like the middle ring of a vast inferno. And it is crucial to Walton's letters, which hover about the outermost fringes of these depths. Indeed, these three circles—their relationship to one another and to the Miltonic motif—form the basic structure of the novel, a structure from which Mrs. Shelley has spun a moral web, with consistency and with precision. (pp. 27-8)

To examine [*Frankenstein*] for the terror it evokes, without perceiving its relationship to the moral context of early nineteenth-century England, is, in reality, to distort the essence of the tale.

We encounter the first indications of this moral context in the letters of Captain Walton, who has been inspired since early youth to satiate an ardent curiosity about the unknown regions of the earth. . . .

One major failing seems to threaten Walton's relentless pursuit: the lack of compassionate society, "intimate sympathy with a fellow mind." Significantly, Walton regards this want as "a most severe evil" and he readily acknowledges that "a man could boast of little happiness, who did not enjoy this blessing."

Once he encounters Victor Frankenstein amid the ice floes of the north, this conflict—between his thirst for knowledge which increasingly carries him away from society and a thirst for social love which is frustrated by this pursuit of knowledge—appears happily reconciled. His newly-found friend reminds him, however, "You seek for knowledge and wisdom, as I once did," and hopes that Walton's temptation "may not be a serpent to sting you, as mine has been." In order that Walton might "deduce an apt moral" from his own experience, Frankenstein consents to disclose the secret of his life.

Frankenstein's tale, forming the middle circle of the novel, is clearly intended, then, as an *exemplum,* aimed at weaning the captain from his obsession. Just as Walton's opening letters sound this didactic note, so do his closing epistles. "Learn my miseries, and do not seek to increase your own," Walton is cautioned at the close of Frankenstein's narrative, just as he has been previously warned: "Learn from me, if not from my precepts, at least by my example, how dangerous is the acquirement of knowledge." (p. 29)

An examination of Frankenstein's central narrative reveals that this opening motif, the temptation of knowledge and the punishment of estrangement, is echoed with consistency and clarity.

From the beginning Frankenstein is "deeply smitten with the thirst for knowledge." He too is tempted by the forbidden fruit, and his earliest sensations are "curiosity, earnest research to learn the hidden laws of nature." For him "the world was . . . a secret which I desired to divine," and even in his youth his "inquiries were directed to the metaphysical, or, in its highest sense, the physical secrets of the world." (p. 30)

Like Prometheus—whom Apollodorus describes as having first created man out of clay, then instilled into his bosom a sacred spark of fire, stolen from the heavens—Frankenstein, his nineteenth-century disciple, succeeds in infusing "a spark of being into the lifeless being" that lies before him in his laboratory. . . . What is glory for the omnipotent deity of *Genesis* or the Babylonian god Bel, for the Egyptian father-of-gods Khnoumou or the Australian creator Pund-jel, is for lesser gods, like Frankenstein, the "modern Prometheus," a crime. The apple of knowledge bears within it the acrid seeds of punishment. As with Satan and Beëlzebub, this passion to

Colin Clive as Dr. Frankenstein in James Whale's 1931 film. The Granger Collection, New York.

usurp divine prerogatives casts the new creator into a burning cauldron of his own making. (pp. 30-1)

Like Coleridge's guilt-ridden mariner, Frankenstein has a deadly weight hanging round his neck, bowing him to the ground. . . . His father had wished him "to seek amusement in society [but] I abhorred the face of man," Frankenstein admits. "I felt that I had no right to share their intercourse." Now, he reveals only the "desire to avoid society" and fly "to solitude, from the society of every creature." . . . He is "immersed in solitude," for he perceives "an insurmountable barrier" between him and his fellow-man. "I felt as if I had committed some great crime, the consciousness of which haunted me. I was guiltless, but I had indeed drawn down a horrible curse upon my head, as mortal as that of crime," . . . he confesses. Though his inner-being longs for the compassion and sympathy that society affords, his guilt has already driven him out of love's garden. He dares not even whisper "paradisaical dreams of love and joy" to Elizabeth, for, as he readily concedes, "the apple was already eaten, and the angel's arm bared to drive me from all hope." . . . (pp. 31-2)

[In] his final hours of life, he confesses to Robert Walton the sin he shares with Milton's archangel:

> All my speculations and hopes are as nothing; and, like the archangel who aspired to omni-

potence, I am chained in an eternal hell. . . . I conceived the idea and executed the creation of a man. Even now I cannot recollect without passion my reveries while the work was incomplete. I trod heaven in my thoughts, now exulting in my powers, now burning with the idea of their effects. From my infancy I was imbued with high hopes and a lofty ambition; but how am I sunk! . . .

(p. 32)

Although parallels between the temptations of Frankenstein or Walton and those of Adam or Satan are clearly delineated, it would be a grave distortion to force the analogy without noting pertinent differences. Milton's is a seventeenth-century reinterpretation of the Fall described by the Jehovistic writer of *Genesis;* but Milton's narrative also parallels to no small degree the Hellenic myth of Prometheus who having usurped the powers of the higher gods, is alienated forever from both men and gods, and chained to the frozen top of the Caucasus. This is an allusion of which Mrs. Shelley was certainly conscious, since she refers to Frankenstein as a "Modern Prometheus" in her sub-title. Also, Shelley himself was obviously aware of the structural similarity between Milton's narrative and the Greek myth, for in his preface to *Prometheus Unbound* he remarks that "the only imaginary being resembling in any degree Prometheus, is Satan." Parallels for Mrs. Shelley's handling of the guilt-theme, however, can also be found in Dostoyevsky and Kafka, or in Jung who suggests that "every step towards greater consciousness is a kind of Promethean guilt: through knowledge, the gods are as it were robbed of their fire, that is, something that was the property of the unconscious powers is torn out of its natural context and subordinated to the whims of the conscious mind."

But Frankenstein's guilt is not the psychological and mystic soul-searching of Kafka or Dostoyevsky, just as it is never completely the crime of *hubris* manifested in Aeschylus or the failure to recognize derivation which we discern in Milton. Frankenstein's crime, like Walton's, is social. Both sin against society. In syncretizing the Miltonic and Promethean motif Mrs. Shelley has clearly translated her materials into early nineteenth-century terms, just as Keats revised the myth of Endymion, and as Shelley transformed the story of Prometheus within his own contemporary framework.

Walton and Frankenstein both sin, not against self or God, but against the moral and social order. Though both begin their pursuit with benevolent intentions, each discovers his error in assuming that knowledge is a higher good than love or sympathy, and that it can be independent of the fellow-feeling afforded by a compassionate society. As a result, what had appeared initially as a benevolent intention becomes in the final analysis misguided pride, a selfish pursuit aimed at self-glory, because it evades the fulfillment of higher duties toward the social community, the brotherhood of man which forms the highest good. Understandably, then, Mrs. Shelley's book is paralleled most significantly, not by Aeschylus or Milton, but by her own contemporaries. In Byron's *Manfred,* for example, an analogous "quest of hidden knowledge" leads the hero increasingly toward a "solitude . . . peopled with the Furies." Manfred's avowed flaw ("though I wore the form, / I had no sympathy with breathing flesh") rises from the same ethical assumptions implicit in the guilt-ridden consciousness of Victor Frankenstein. Similarly, Shelley's prefatory remarks on *Alastor or, The Spirit of Solitude* indicate that "the Poet's self-centred seclusion was avenged by the furies of an irresistible passion pursuing him to speedy ruin." Shelley's supposition, that "the intellectual faculties, the imagination, the functions of sense, have their respective requisitions on the sympathy of corresponding powers in other human beings," is obviously engendered from the same general principle which has ordered the materials of *Frankenstein.*

Mrs. Shelley offers in her novel—as does Byron in *Manfred* and Shelley in *Alastor*—a theme which is clearly in the tradition of Cudworth and Price, the seventeenth-century Platonists. This is a conception inherited in the eighteenth century by Shaftesbury and Hutcheson; later, by the Scottish Common-Sense School, as represented by Adam Smith; and finally by William Godwin, who had assumed as basic to his doctrine of political justice that virtue is essentially social. Insistent that reason and free will, as developed in an enlightened society, would naturally result in the subordination of individual pleasures for the good of society as a whole, Godwin set himself in opposition to La Rochefoucauld, Hobbes, and Mandeville, for whom man was basically selfish and non-social, and to Rousseau, who had seen society as a force destructive to natural benevolence. "No being can be either virtuous, or vicious, who has no opportunity of influencing the happiness of others," Godwin had contended in his *Enquiry concerning Political Justice,* insistent that "the true solitaire cannot be considered as a moral being. . . . His conduct is vicious, because it has a tendency to render him miserable." Explaining that "virtue consists in a desire of the happiness of the species. . . . It must begin with a collective idea of the human species," Godwin argues that true knowledge is also dependent upon the social structure. "Even knowledge, and the enlargement of intellect, are poor, when unmixed with sentiments of benevolence and sympathy," he points out; ". . . and science and abstraction will soon become cold, unless they derive new attractions from ideas of society."

Similarly, Thomas Paine develops the relationship between happiness and social virtues in *The Rights of Man.* Since nature created man for social life, Paine writes, "no one man is capable, without the aid of society, of supplying his own wants; and those wants, acting upon every individual, impel the whole of them into society, as naturally as gravitation acts to a centre." Nature has gone even further than this, Paine continues. "She has implanted in him a system of social affections, which, though not necessary to his existence, are essential to his happiness. There is no period in life when this love of society ceases to act. It begins and ends with our being." (pp. 32-4)

Through Mrs. Shelley's journal entries we know that during 1816-1817, when *Frankenstein* was conceived, she and Shelley discussed the work many times. We know, too, through the *Journal,* that in these years she and Shelley both read Milton's *Paradise Lost,* and that Shelley was immersed at this same time in Godwin's *Political Justice* and Paine's *The Rights of Man,* as well as in the *Prometheus Bound* of Aeschylus. I do not mean to imply that Mary Shelley borrowed her social and moral conceptions from Paine, or from Shelley or Godwin, then deliberately embodied them within her mythological framework. It is perfectly understandable that she shared the social thought of her father and her husband, and that she wove these ideas, which were shared also by many of the enlightened English public during those decades, into an esthetic pattern of her own making.

The consistency of her social and moral theme is certainly nowhere more apparent than in the narrative of the monster, whose experience forms an essential parallel with that of Frankenstein and Walton. Like the latter, whose original intentions were directed at benevolence and sympathy, the creature initially bears the seeds of virtue. The sympathies of Walton and Frankenstein have been rendered torpid by their monomaniacal pursuit of knowledge which removes them increasingly from a compassionate society; similarly, the creature discovers that his sympathies are perpetually blunted by the misery of loneliness and isolation, estranged as he must be from human kind. At first, he views "crime as a distant evil; benevolence and generosity were ever present" in the persons of the DeLaceys, behind whose cottage he has hidden. "My heart yearned to be known and loved by these amiable creatures: to see their sweet looks directed towards me with affection was the utmost limit of my ambition," he confesses. His readings only reinforce this natural propensity for social love, so that before long he feels "the greatest ardour for virtue . . . and abhorrence for vice." . . . (pp. 35-6)

Like his maker, and like Captain Walton, the creature soon comes to realize that "sorrow only increased with knowledge," . . . for the more he learns about the nature of good and its dependence upon social intercourse, the more he recognizes the impossibility of immersing himself in it. . . .

Alternating between the role of Adam and Satan, hoping he might still be lifted to the glories of love and sympathy, but fearing that he might be forced into the depths of malevolence and depravity because of his isolation, the creature soon finds his fate determined, once the DeLaceys reject his friendly advances, just as all mankind has rejected him beforehand. "From that moment I declared everlasting war against the species," he admits. "I, like the arch-fiend, bore a hell within me; and, finding myself unsympathized with, wished to . . . spread havoc and destruction." . . . Natural proclivities toward virtue compel the creature to approach his maker and urge him to create a mate "with whom I can live in the interchange of those sympathies necessary for my being. . . . I am malicious because I am miserable," he explains, as he begs for the happiness which is his right. "Let me feel gratitude towards you for one benefit! Let me see that I excite the sympathy of some existing thing; do not deny me my request." . . . With an understanding strikingly analogous to that revealed in Godwin, Shelley, Byron, and Paine, the monster describes his moral state:

> If I have no ties and no affections, hatred and vice must be my portion; the love of another will destroy the cause of my crimes, and I shall become a thing of whose existence every one will be ignorant. My vices are the children of a forced solitude that I abhor; and my virtues will necessarily arise when I live in communion with an equal. I shall feel the affections of a sensitive being, and become linked to the chain of existence and events, from which I am now excluded.
>
> (p. 36)

In an 1817 review which has generally been ignored [see excerpt above], Shelley draws some interesting parallels between Godwin's *Caleb Williams* and *Frankenstein,* and summarizes thematic development in Mary Shelley's book with penetrating incisiveness:

> . . . The crimes and malevolence of the single Being, though indeed withering and tremendous, [are not] the offspring of any unaccount-

able propensity to evil, but flow irresistibly from certain causes fully adequate to their production. They are the children, as it were, of Necessity and Human Nature. In this the direct moral of the book consists. . . . Treat a person ill, and he will become wicked. Requite affection with scorn;—let one being be selected, for whatever cause, as the refuse of his kind—divide him, a social being, from society, and you impose upon him the irresistible obligations—malevolence and selfishness. It is thus that, too often in society, those who are best qualified to be its benefactors and its ornaments, are branded by some accident with scorn, and changed, by neglect and solitude of heart, into a scourge and a curse.

The distinction which Shelley draws here between an "unaccountable propensity to evil" and that necessitated by external social forces which isolate the individual, thus causing selfishness and malevolence, points indeed to the "direct moral of the book." Although a recent biographer [Elizabeth Nitchie; see excerpt dated 1953], noting this theme of estrangement throughout Mrs. Shelley's novels, interprets this as the author's "symbol of her own loneliness," it is apparent in any close examination of the text that "loneliness" assumes its fullest meaning relative only to the social and moral context of early nineteenth-century England. This is the context of Godwin and Paine, as well as Byron and Shelley, and certainly the context of the woman who came to be known as "the author of *Frankenstein*." (pp. 37-8)

> *M. A. Goldberg, "Moral and Myth in Mrs. Shelley's 'Frankenstein'," in* Keats-Shelley Journal, *Vol. 8, Winter, 1959, pp. 27-38.*

KINGSLEY AMIS   (essay date 1960)

[*A distinguished English novelist, poet, essayist, and editor, Amis is also the author of* New Maps in Hell, *one of the first major critical surveys of science fiction. In the following brief consideration of* Frankenstein *as a precursor of that genre, Amis identifies three popular science fiction themes that Shelley initiated in the novel. Amis's remarks were first published in* New Maps in Hell *in 1960.*]

[With] one large exception, [the Gothic novel and its successors], while all-important in the ancestry of modern fantasy, scarcely prefigure science fiction. The exception can hardly help being *Frankenstein,* which, albeit in a distorted form, has had a posthumous career of unparalleled vigour; even old Dracula has less often been exhumed in cinematic form and has never been mated or allowed to re-galvanise himself. (I had better explain at this point that the contemporary trade-term applying to the monster is "android," a synthetic being roughly resembling a man, as opposed to a robot, which is a mere peripatetic machine.) The notable thing about Frankenstein the character is that, far from being possessed of supernatural powers, he is a physiologist with academic training, a feature he has retained in his modern incarnations, while altogether losing the sentimental Shelleyan quality that marked his original appearance. Frankenstein, in the popular mind, when not confused with his monster, is easily the most outstanding representative of the generic mad scientist who plagued bad early-modern science fiction and has now been fined down into the better-adjusted but still unsociable and eccentric scientist who, often with a Miranda-like daughter-secretary in attendance,

continues to head an occasional research project and figure in the hero's thoughts as the Old Man. More important science-fiction themes than this, however, have radiated from the original book. It is true that, as L. Sprague de Camp observes [see Additional Bibliography], "all the shambling horde of modern robots and androids are descendants of Frankenstein's sadly malevolent monster," but beyond this lies the whole notion of the artificial creation which turns and rends its master. Capek's *R. U. R.* (1920) was perhaps the first modern treatment of this notion, which still regularly reappears, a recent instance being Robert Sheckley's story "Watchbird." Here an airborne device, programmed to detect and forestall aggressive intentions, ends by prohibiting most kinds of human action. This idea generalises into innumerable fictionalised sermons on the dangers of overgrown technology. . . . Before leaving *Frankenstein,* it is worth observing that a third aspect of the scientific character descends from it, that of the morally irresponsible researcher indifferent to the damage he may cause or render possible, a kind of person consciously described by Wells in *The Island of Dr. Moreau,* where animals are vivisected in an attempt to humanise them, and to all appearance unconsciously in *The Food of the Gods,* where Herakleophorbia IV, the growth-inducing compound, is thrown on to the rubbish dump and swilled down the drains and generally scattered over the countryside in a fantastically light-hearted spirit. (pp. 255-56)

> *Kingsley Amis, "Starting Points," in* Science Fiction: The Future, *edited by Dick Allen, Harcourt Brace Jovanovich, Inc., 1971, pp. 245-62.*

HAROLD BLOOM   (essay date 1965)

[*Bloom, an American critic and editor, is best known as the formulator of "revisionism," a controversial theory of literary creation based on the concept that all poets are subject to the influence of earlier poets, and that to develop their own voices, they attempt to overcome this influence through a deliberate process of "creative correction," which Bloom calls "misreading." His theories are largely based on his readings of English poetry from the Romantic period to the present. In his influential study of* Frankenstein, *excerpted below, Bloom focuses on solipsism and Prometheanism in the work, which he regards as an extreme example of "the Romantic mythology of the self."*]

The motion picture viewer who carries his obscure but still authentic taste for the sublime to the neighborhood theater, there to see the latest in an unending series of *Frankensteins,* participates in a Romantic terror now nearly one hundred and fifty years old. The terror is a familiar and a pleasing one, and few figures in contemporary mythology are as universally loved as Frankenstein's once pathetic monster, now a star beaconing from the abode of television, comic strips and the sweatshirts of the young.

"Frankenstein," to most of us, is the name of a monster rather than of a monster's creator, for the common reader and the common viewer have worked together, in their apparent confusion, to create a myth soundly based on a central duality in Mary Shelley's novel. As Richard Church [see Additional Bibliography] and Muriel Spark [see excerpt dated 1951] were the first to record, the monster and his creator are the antithetical halves of a single being. Miss Spark states the antithesis too cleanly; for her, Victor Frankenstein represents the feelings, and his nameless creature the intellect. In her view, the monster has no emotion, and "what passes for emotion . . . are really intellectual passions arrived at through rational channels." Miss Spark carries this argument far enough to insist that the monster is asexual, and that he demands a bride from Frankenstein only for companionship, a conclusion evidently at variance with the novel's text.

The antithesis between the scientist and his creature in Frankenstein is a very complex one, and to be described more fully it must be placed in the larger context of Romantic literature and its characteristic mythology. The shadow or double of the self is a constant conceptual image in Blake and Shelley, and a frequent image, more random and descriptive, in the other major Romantics, especially in Byron. In *Frankenstein,* it is the dominant and recurrent image, and accounts for much of the latent power the novel possesses. (pp. 611-12)

No Romantic writer employed the Prometheus archetype without a full awareness of its equivocal potentialities. The Prometheus of the ancients had been for the most part a spiritually reprehensible figure, though frequently a sympathetic one, both in terms of his dramatic situation and in his close alliance with mankind against the gods. But this alliance had been ruinous for man, in most versions of the myth, and the Titan's benevolence toward humanity was hardly sufficient recompense for the alienation of man from heaven that he had brought about. Both sides of Titanism are evident in earlier Christian references to the story. The same Prometheus who is taken as an analogue of the crucified Christ is regarded also as a type of Lucifer, a son of light justly cast out by an offended heaven.

In the Romantic readings of Milton's *Paradise Lost* (and *Frankenstein* is implicitly one such reading), this double identity of Prometheus is a vital element. Blake, whose mythic revolutionary named Orc is another version of Prometheus, saw Milton's Satan as a Prometheus gone wrong, as desire restrained until it became only the shadow of desire, a diminished double of creative energy. Shelley went further in judging Milton's Satan as an imperfect Prometheus, inadequate because his mixture of heroic and base qualities engendered in the reader's mind a "pernicious casuistry" inimical to the spirit of art.

Blake, more systematic a poet than Shelley, worked out an antithesis between symbolic figures he named Spectre and Emanation, the shadow of desire and the total form of desire, respectively. A reader of *Frankenstein,* recalling the novel's extraordinary conclusion with its scenes of obsessional pursuit through the Arctic wastes, can recognize the same imagery applied to a similar symbolic situation in Blake's lyric on the strife of Spectre and Emanation:

> My Spectre around me night and day
> Like a Wild beast guards my way.
> My Emanation far within
> Weeps incessantly for my Sin.
>
> A Fathomless and boundless deep,
> There we wander, there we weep;
> On the hungry craving wind
> My Spectre follows thee behind.
>
> He scents thy footsteps in the snow,
> Wheresoever thou dost go
> Thro' the wintry hail and rain . . .

Frankenstein's monster, tempting his revengeful creator on through a world of ice, is another Emanation pursued by a Spectre, with the enormous difference that he is an Emanation flawed, a nightmare of actuality, rather than a dream of desire.

Though abhorred rather than loved, the monster is the total form of Frankenstein's creative power, and is *more imaginative* than his creator. The monster is at once more intellectual *and* more emotional than his maker, indeed he excels Frankenstein as much (and in the same ways) as Milton's Adam excels Milton's God in *Paradise Lost*. The greatest paradox, and most astonishing achievement, of Mary Shelley's novel is that the monster is *more human* than his creator. This nameless being, as much a Modern Adam as his creator is a Modern Prometheus, is more lovable than his creator and more hateful, more to be pitied and more to be feared, and above all more able to give the attentive reader that shock of added consciousness which compels a heightened realization of the self. For, like Blake's Spectre and Emanation, or Shelley's Alastor and Epipsyche, Frankenstein and his monster are the solipsistic and generous halves of the one self. Frankenstein is the mind and emotions turned in upon themselves, and his creature is the mind and emotions turned imaginatively outward, seeking a greater humanization through a confrontation of other selves.

I am suggesting that what makes *Frankenstein* an important book, though it is only a strong, flawed, frequently clumsy novel is that it vividly projects a version of the Romantic mythology of the self, found, among other places, in Blake's *Book of Urizen*, Shelley's *Prometheus Unbound* and Byron's *Manfred*. It lacks the sophistication and imaginative complexity of such works but precisely because of that *Frankenstein* affords a unique introduction to the archetypal world of the Romantics. (pp. 612-13)

There are two paradoxes at the center of Mrs. Shelley's novel, and each illuminates a dilemma of the Promethean imagination. The first is that Frankenstein *was* successful: he *did* create Natural Man, not as he was, but as the meliorists saw him. Indeed, Frankenstein did better than this, since his creature was more imaginative even than himself. Frankenstein's tragedy stems, not from his Promethean excess, but from his own moral error, his failure to love. He *abhorred his creature,* became terrified of it, and fled his responsibilities.

The second paradox is the more ironic. This disaster either would not have happened, or would not have mattered anyway, if Frankenstein had been an esthetically successful maker; a beautiful "monster," or even a passable one, would not have been a monster. The creature himself bitterly observes:

> Shall I respect man when he contemns me? Let him live with me in the interchange of kindness; and, instead of injury, I would bestow every benefit upon him with tears of gratitude at his acceptance. But that cannot be; the human senses are insurmountable barriers to our union.

As the sensuous horror of his creature was no part of Victor Frankenstein's intention, it is worth noticing how this came about. It would not be unjust to characterize Victor Frankenstein, in his act of creation, as being momentarily a moral idiot. There is an indeliberate humor, to which readers since 1945 are doubtless more sensitive than earlier ones, in the contrast between the enormity of the scientist's discovery, and the mundane emotions of the discoverer. Finding that "the minuteness of the parts" slows him down, he resolves to make his creature "about eight feet in height, and proportionably large." As he works on, he allows himself to dream that "a new species would bless me as its creator and source; many happy and excellent natures would owe their being to me." Yet he knows his is a "workshop of filthy creation," and he fails the fundamental test of his own creativity. When the "dull yellow eye" of his creature opens, this creator falls from the autonomy of a supreme artificer to the terror of a child of earth: "breathless horror and disgust filled my heart." He flees his responsibility, and sets in motion the events that will lead to his own Arctic immolation, a fit end for a being (rather like Lawrence's Gerald in *Women in Love*) who has never achieved a full sense of another's existence.

It is part of Mary Shelley's insight into her mythological theme that all the monster's victims are innocents. The monster not only refuses actively to slay his guilty creator; he *mourns* for him, though with the equivocal tribute of terming the scientist a "generous and self-devoted being." Frankenstein, the Modern Prometheus who has violated nature, receives his epitaph from the ruined second nature he has made, the God-abandoned, who consciously echoes the ruined Satan of *Paradise Lost,* and proclaims "Evil thenceforth became my good." It is imaginatively fitting that the greater and more interesting consciousness of the creature should survive his creator, for he alone in Mrs. Shelley's novel possesses character. Frankenstein, like Coleridge's Ancient Mariner, has no character in his own right; both figures win a claim to our attention only by their primordial crimes against original nature.

The monster is of course Mary Shelley's finest invention, and his narrative (Chapters XI through XVI) forms the highest achievement of the novel, more absorbing even than the magnificent and almost surrealistic pursuit of the climax. In an age so given to remarkable depictions of the dignity of natural man, an age including the shepherds and beggars of Wordsworth, Frankenstein's hapless creature stands out as a sublime embodiment of heroic pathos. Though Frankenstein lacks the moral imagination to understand him, the daemon's appeal is to what is most compassionate in us:

> "Oh, Frankenstein, be not equitable to every other, and trample upon me alone, to whom thy justice, and even thy clemency and affection, is most due. Remember, that I am thy creature; *I ought to be thy Adam; but I am rather the fallen angel, whom thou drivest from joy for no misdeed.* Everywhere I see bliss, from which I alone am irrevocably excluded. I was benevolent and good; misery made me a fiend. Make me happy, and I shall again be virtuous."

The passage I have italicized is the imaginative kernel of the novel, a reminder of the novel's epigraph:

> Did I request thee, Maker, from my clay
> To mould me man? Did I solicit thee
> From darkness to promote me?
> —*Paradise Lost,* Book X, 743-5

That desperate plangency of the fallen Adam becomes the characteristic accent of the daemon's lamentations, with the influence of Milton cunningly built into the novel's narrative by the happy device of Frankenstein's creature receiving his education through reading *Paradise Lost* "as a true history." Already doomed because his standards are human, which makes him an outcast even to himself, his Miltonic education completes his fatal growth in self-consciousness. (pp. 614-16)

If we stand back from Mary Shelley's novel, in order better to view its archetypal shape, we see it as the quest of a solitary and ravaged consciousness first for consolation, then for revenge, and finally for a self-destruction that will be apocalyp-

tic, that will bring down the creator with his creature. Though Mary Shelley may not have intended it, her novel's prime theme is a necessary counterpoise to Prometheanism, for Prometheanism exalts the increase in consciousness despite all cost. Frankenstein breaks through the barrier that separates man from God, and apparently becomes the giver of life, but all he actually can give is death-in-life. The profound dejection endemic in Mary Shelley's novel is fundamental to the Romantic mythology of the self, for all Romantic horrors are diseases of excessive consciousness, of the self unable to bear the self. Kierkegaard remarks that Satan's despair is absolute, because Satan as pure spirit is pure consciousness, and for Satan (and all men in his predicament) every increase in consciousness is an increase in despair. Frankenstein's desperate creature attains the state of pure spirit through his extraordinary situation, and is racked by a consciousness in which every thought is a fresh disease.

A Romantic poet fought against self-consciousness through the strength of what he called imagination, a more than rational energy, by which thought could seek to heal itself. But Frankenstein's daemon, though he is in the archetypal situation of the Romantic Wanderer or Solitary, who sometimes was a poet, can win no release from his own story by telling it. His desperate desire for a mate is clearly an attempt to find a Shelleyan Epipsyche or Blakean Emanation for himself, a self within the self. But as he is the nightmare actualization of Frankenstein's desire, he is himself an emanation of Promethean yearnings, and his only double is his creator and denier.

When Coleridge's Ancient Mariner progressed from the purgatory of consciousness to his very minimal control of imagination, he failed to save himself. He remained in a cycle of remorse. But he at least became a salutary warning to others, and made of the Wedding Guest a wiser and a better man. Frankenstein's creature can help neither himself nor others, for he has no natural ground to which he can return. Romantic poets liked to return to the imagery of the ocean of life and immortality; in the eddying to and fro of the healing waters they could picture a hoped-for process of restoration, of a survival of consciousness despite all its agonies. Mary Shelley, with marvelous appropriateness, brings her Romantic novel to a demonic conclusion in a world of ice. The frozen sea is the inevitable emblem for both the wretched daemon and his obsessed creator, but the daemon is allowed a final image of reversed Prometheanism. There is a heroism fully earned in the being who cries farewell in a claim of sad triumph: "I shall ascend my funeral pyre triumphantly, and exult in the agony of the torturing flames." (pp. 617-18)

There is something both Godwinian and Shelleyan about the final utterance of Victor Frankenstein, which is properly made to Walton, the failed Promethean, whose ship has just turned back. Though chastened, the Modern Prometheus ends with a last word true, not to his accomplishment, but to his desire:

> "Farewell, Walton! Seek happiness in tranquility and avoid ambition, even if it be only the apparently innocent one of distinguishing yourself in science and discoveries. Yet why do I say this? I have myself been blasted in these hopes, yet another may succeed."

Shelley's Prometheus, crucified on his icy precipice, found his ultimate torment in a Fury's taunt: "And all best things are thus confused to ill." It seems a fitting summation for all the work done by Modern Prometheanism, and might have served

Boris Karloff in his third portrayal of Frankenstein's monster, from the 1939 film Son of Frankenstein. *Forrest J. Ackerman Sci-Fi CinemArchives, Hollywood.*

as an alternate epigraph for Mary Shelley's disturbing novel. (p. 618)

> Harold Bloom, ''Frankenstein; or, The New Prometheus,'' in Partisan Review, *Vol. XXXII, No. 4, Fall, 1965, pp. 611-18.*

STEPHEN CRAFTS   (essay date 1967)

[*Crafts bases his explication of* Frankenstein's monster *on the theory of ''one-dimensional'' man set forth by Herbert Marcuse, the contemporary German-American philosopher. Crafts asserts that the creature's dilemma foreshadows that of modern humanity.*]

Today the figure of Frankenstein has been relegated to the camp late show and plastic models for children. This phenomenon indicates that the original prophecy of one-dimensionality by Mary Shelley's novel has been largely subsumed in the increasing totality of advanced industrial society. Hence the irony of **Frankenstein**'s contemporary reception: Mary Shelley's very accuracy has prophesied the agent of its present neglect as social commentary. A further irony lies in the common confusion of the creator and the creature, for it was Victor Frankenstein who created a monster. The figure of horror has

been projected by man to a product, a process repeated from the novel. It is Frankenstein who deserts his monster and thus brings about the rampage which has become synonomous with the figure of the monster. A similar tendency exists today in the one-dimensional bias to distinguish between subject and object in such a way that ''value-free inquiry'' establishes evasion of responsibility as technological *modus operandi*. The same mentality fails to take seriously those works of social criticism, like **Frankenstein,** which do not seem objective or one-dimensionally real.

The term ''one-dimensional'' owes its origins to the common empirical data of social totality considered by Herbert Marcuse in his definitive work, *One-Dimensional Man*. I intend to use Marcuse's term in a limited sense as the conclusion of a process within industrial societies to stifle human sensibility within the all-inclusive context of abstraction. The distinction made by Herbert Read will prove helpful in defining the issue:

> Intellect begins with the observation of nature, proceeds to memorize and classify the facts thus observed, and by logical deduction builds up that edifice of knowledge properly called science. Sensibility, on the other hand, is a direct and particular reaction to the separate and individual nature of things.

In **Frankenstein,** Mary Shelley explores metaphorically the usurpation of sensibility by intellect and the concomitant human relationships the perversion produces. The berserk actions of Frankenstein's monster are not those of an inherently evil creature but the desperate gropings of a sensitive being attempting to assert a form of humanity following its objectification within a technological context. The cliché concerning atomic energy—that it can be used for either good or evil—however true, rests upon the assumption that we have at our disposal the critical sensibility to know which is which. Read again defines the issue:

> . . . to neglect the senses, either through ignorance of their epistemological significance, or from mere puritanical prejudice is to neglect one half of our being.

Yet in the act of creating his monster, Frankenstein extirpates a good part of his existence by avowing the technological reality of one-dimensionality. Marcuse has described this reality as follows:

> As a technological universe, advanced industrial society is a *political* universe, the latest stage in the realization of a specific historical *project*—namely, the experience, transformation, and organization of nature as the mere stuff of domination.

Domination of nature in its entirety is the professed project of Frankenstein, a latterday Faust. He defines reality for his creature and thus makes of him an object of oppression. It is the monster's reactions to his situation which form the basis of the book, for one-dimensionality reworks the grotesque as reality in its brutalization of the objectified oppressed. Rather than hunt down Frankenstein's monster today, we would be more likely to rehabilitate him for life in the ''real world'' or pacify him in furthering the aims of *pax americana*.

Another indication of the totalism which the book predicts lies in the unintentional tendency of Mrs. Shelley to abet one-dimensionality in a form of cultural imperialism: the perpetuation of the romantic myth of the Noble Savage. In this process, the objectification of human beings forms a social mentality which "kills with kindness." That is, the social frame of reference becomes so pervasive as to even order attempts to create meaningful human relationships. Thus, in creating an ideal state of being as embodied by the Noble Savage, Mary Shelley has, with good intention, perpetuated the suppression of humanity which makes Frankenstein's monster "an object for the scorn and horror of mankind." The psychic tendency to project one's own inadequacies, fantasies, etc. upon another finds its perfect example in the objectification of Frankenstein's monster. On the one hand, he becomes the technologist's projection of the horror of his own atrocity; on the other, the monster furnishes a nostalgic urge to innocence as a Noble Savage figure. In either case the monster has been objectified. The totality of one-dimensional thought thus places the burden of asserting humanity upon the technologically oppressed: it is only the oppressed who can reject the definition of reality placed upon them as objects through active rebellion. The monster's attempt to assert his humanity finds a remarkable contemporary counterpart in the Third World movement.

Frankenstein is subtitled "The Modern Prometheus" and thus involves romantic mythology, which need not concern us here beyond a consideration of Frankenstein as a Faust figure. In literature, Faust represents the ambiguity of knowledge. He is a later manifestation of Prometheus, who extended man's dominion over nature. Faust seeks to extend that dominion further and yet concomitantly brings man closer to self-destruction. The Mad Scientist has become the modern Faust figure, although he has lost this quality of ambiguity. The change lies, I think, in the increasing predominance in industrially advanced societies of intellect over sensibility. Earlier Faust figures (notably Marlowe's Dr. Faustus and Goethe's Faust) attempt, through alchemy, to reconcile religion with science or, in a sense, sensibility with intellect. The gradual assumption of religious function by science leads inexorably to one-dimensionality with its rejection of significant experience of the non-intellect. (pp. 96-8)

With his grotesque obsession with creating life wedded to the most modern means, Frankenstein resolves with Faustian incantation:

> So much has been done, . . . more, far more, will I achieve; treading in the steps already marked, I will pioneer a new way, explore unknown powers, and unfold to the world the deepest mysteries of creation. . . .

So from the beginning, Frankenstein's scientific enterprise involves the means and ends dichotomy which produces: 1) the fallacious distinction between subject and object enabling him to dominate nature; and 2) the mechanism for evading responsibility for his work.

The most remarkable feature of *Frankenstein* is the vitality of the monster in comparison to the human characters of the book. The force of the figure lies in its sense of suppressed humanity which: 1) has been victimized by technological and mythic objectification; and 2) attempts to assert its humanity through rebellion in the face of this objectification. The monster appeals to us, as he appealed to a romantic generation as the embodiment of a dream, the Noble Savage. The Noble Savage acts within a nostalgic frame of reference in that he combines both intellect and sensibility, the supposed reconciliation of innocence. Yet the monster's condemnation of Frankenstein—

"Unfeeling, heartless creature! You had endowed me with perceptions and passions and then cast me abroad an object for the scorn and horror of mankind." . . .—applies as well to the objectification of primitive life as an ideal state of being, for both creations are objectified. Thus the mentality of one-dimensionality perpetuates a system of subject-object relationships so pervasive that not even artists escape its influence. (pp. 98-9)

As the embodiment of an ideal state of being, the monster serves as a nostalgic frame of reference to an earlier day of innocence. The process involves the perhaps unconscious manipulation of primitive humanity as an abstraction. No matter how well-intentioned the Noble Savage as the embodiment of an ideal state of existence, the figure represents a species of cultural imperialism. The objectification of a group of human beings makes economic, social, and political exploitation possible. It cannot be mere coincidence that the Noble Savage first appealed to those nations in the process of colonial development. (p. 99)

It is doubtful that Mary Shelley intended to be an accomplice of colonialism, but the evolution of the monster from Noble Savage to ravager of mankind in the novel finds a similar historical development in the figure of the Happy Native of colonialization turning revolutionary in the attempt to assert his humanity, much to the chagrin of the colonialist who knows him only as an object of his own definition. The monster's self-immolation at the end of the novel is the act of a man proudly removing *himself* from the world of men who so despise him rather than allowing himself to be killed by the man, Frankenstein, who has created him as an object. The assertion of humanity on the part of the monster assumes the proportions of rebellion because humanity cannot be bestowed as edict by the oppressing party. The monster has been defined by both Frankenstein and within the context of romantic mythology as an object; he does not possess, in this sense, the humanity to assert. He must, in effect, recreate himself. (p. 100)

The monster's form of rebellion takes the peculiarly romantic form noticed by Camus: "The romantic hero . . . considers himself compelled to do evil by his nostalgia for an unrealizable good." The monster begins the classic terrorism of guerrilla warfare and even indulges in selective killing of his oppressor's immediate family. Sartre comments upon the redemptive nature of violence in his preface to Fanon's *The Wretched of the Earth:*

> . . . this irrepressible violence is neither sound and fury, nor the resurrection of savage instincts, nor even the effect of resentment: it is man re-creating himself . . . no gentleness can efface the marks of violence; only violence itself can destroy them. The native cures himself of colonial neurosis by thrusting out the settler through force of arms. When his rage boils over, he rediscovers his lost innocence and he comes to know himself in that he himself creates himself.

By espousing evil (i.e., the opposite of what his definer considers good), the monster emerges, from beneath the onus of objectification, a man. Through his terrorist activities, the monster asserts his humanity; in the assumption of depravity, he becomes a monster of his own making.

Frankenstein pursues his former creation, appropriately enough, to the Arctic wastes, fails to kill him, and dies in the effort. The *raison d'être* of the monster dies with him. Walton tells the monster, "It is not pity that you feel [after the monster has attempted to explain his situation]; you lament only because the victim of your malignity is withdrawn from your power." . . . It is the only really intelligent thing a human character has said throughout the book, for it places the causes of rebellion squarely on the oppressor. Frankenstein passes his necessity to see the monster die onto Walton, but the monster chooses to end his life on his own terms:

> I shall collect my funeral pile and consume to ashes this miserable frame. . . . I shall die. I shall no longer feel the agonies which now consume me or be the prey of feelings unsatisfied, yet unquenched. . . .

Thus, however wretched, the monster collects what dignity he retains in creating himself anew and immolates himself.

Early in the Nineteenth Century, *Frankenstein* presages one-dimensional existence. With its irrational assumptions about the rational, technological reality rejects by its very nature the necessity for human sensibility. Bereft of this basis for critical thought, an uncontrolled technology threatens to annihilate the world. At the same time, the objectification of human beings as grist for the technological mill has produced widespread alienation in advanced industrial societies as well as the movement of the Third World toward an assertion of humanity independent of that of the defining oppressor. The oppressor has himself been brutalized by his one-dimensional existence and tends to project the inadequacies of his own thwarted life upon the oppressed whom he has defined in such a way as to ease their exploitation for him. The oppressor and the oppressed, the definer and the defined, must sometime face each other. One-dimensionality seems to deny that they can do so as human beings. Mary Shelley's novel indicates that master and monster will kill each other, and so far it seems terribly accurate. (pp. 102-03)

> *Stephen Crafts, "'Frankenstein': Camp Curiosity or Premonition?" in* Catalyst, *No. 3, Summer, 1967, pp. 96-103.*

R. H. W. DILLARD (essay date 1967)

[*In the following discussion of the cinematic myth of* Frankenstein, *Dillard suggests that through the medium of film, Shelley's "minor philosophical novel" has been transformed into a major work of art.*]

We are sitting, you and I, in the plush (if somewhat worn) seats of a darkened movie house—featureless, all of us seated in rows, hearing the first dark chords of a somber score, waiting for the hard grin of death's skull to chill us all to the bone that will outlast our flesh and set on end our hair that legend says will grow long after we are dead.

And on the screen, dark figures move among the mists and tilting stones of a Central European graveyard—a hunchbacked dwarf, a tall young man. There is the clank of shovels under a full moon. High scudding clouds. The action is unclear. A body is raised from its rest, and heavy clods thump on the empty coffin lid. And somehow, a stone tower, the fury of a storm, the mad harmony of thunder, lightning, and the buzzing of machines that spit and crackle life into the shrouded figure on the table. It moves, first a hand, an arm; it rises and lurches unsteadily on sewn and cumbrous limbs. And its face is the face of death, the pain and incomprehensibility of death, the death that waits for us all. (pp. 60-1)

[The cinematic myth of Frankenstein] speaks of the darkness of being a fallen and flawed thing, alone in a world of hate and misunderstanding, out of harmony with the design of his creator and an offense to himself and to nature in that creator's eyes, doomed by the very flesh of his body to sin and separation and a long suffering unto death. The Frankenstein story speaks of the darkness of man in a fallen state, separated from God and seeking communion and understanding.

Certainly a simpler reading, and a valid one, is to consider the story of Dr. Frankenstein and his monster to be completely medieval in its moral basis, to understand it as the cautionary tale of a man who tampers with the laws of nature beyond the bounds set him by God and who suffers the sad consequences of his sin. Like Marlowe's Faustus, Frankenstein does seek too much knowledge and pays for his arrogance; but the story is something more than that, for it is as much the monster's as his creator's, and their relationship is the center of the story, dramatically and morally. As Mary Shelley wrote [*Frankenstein*] originally, it is the completely Romantic story of "The Modern Prometheus," and, although the film manages successfully to avoid most of her Shelleian philosophical lectures, it does adhere to the complexity of that central relationship. The monster defines that relationship himself in the novel, as he pleads for Frankenstein to make him a wife, and offers a clearly Romantic interpretation of his fall and of his responsibilities to his creator and his creators' responsibilities to him:

> I am thy creature, and I will be even mild and docile to my natural lord and king, if thou wilt also perform thy part, the which thou owest me. Oh, Frankenstein, be not equitable to every other, and trample upon me alone, to whom thy justice, and even thy clemency and affection, is most due. Remember that I am thy creature, I ought to be thy Adam; but I am rather the fallen angel, whom thou drivest from joy for no misdeed. Everywhere I see bliss, from which I alone am irrevocably excluded. I was benevolent and good; misery made me a fiend. Make me happy, and I shall again be virtuous.

But is his fall so simple? And what of his creator's relationship to his Creator in turn? Mary Shelley developed her story thoroughly and skillfully, and the films follow it to some degree, especially *The Bride of Frankenstein* [1935], but they have changed her rational and argumentative monster substantially and succeeded in transmuting a minor philosophical novel into a cinematic myth which carries the full emotional and moral impact of a major work of art. This is, unfortunately, not the place for a discussion of the similarities and differences between the novel and the film, but I should like to use one difference to serve as a starting point for my discussion of the films.

Mary Shelley's monster is in many ways the superior of his creator, morally as well as physically, but they can never gain an understanding because of Frankenstein's repugnance for that creature's ugliness and the misdeeds resulting from his ugliness and his isolation from human society. Frankenstein agrees to make the monster a mate but finally cannot because of that repugnance and the consequent strain on his conscience; he destroys her before she may live, and the monster loses his chance to begin a new life (and perhaps a new race) because of his creator's moral nature. In *The Bride of Frankenstein* the monster makes similar demands, for he has learned what it is to love and to be loved. Frankenstein agrees and creates a bride for his Adam, but the new Eve, impelled by whatever remains in her brain of her former human life, shrinks from her intended mate and shrieks in absolute disgust and terror. The monster, who has been driven away from every human contact and driven to violence and murder by his mistreatment, surrenders to despair and destroys himself and his bride.

Mary Shelley's monster dies, too, by his own hand when, after the death of his creator and the end of their long vendetta, he steps onto an ice floe and is "borne away by the waves and lost in darkness and distance." But he also dies a Romantic hero, morally superior to Frankenstein in his suffering and his refusal to yield his identity and life while his creator still lived. He speaks to the corpse of Frankenstein: "Blasted as thou wert, my agony was still superior to thine; for the bitter sting of remorse will not cease to rankle in my wounds until death shall close them forever"; he dies secure in the knowledge that his "spirit will sleep in peace; or if it thinks, it will not surely think thus."

The film monster does not die a hero's death, nor can he be sure of anything but death itself. He dies in a moment of total despair, rejected by even a creature of his own kind, driven to destroy not only himself but everything he is. His is a plunge into violent death, peaceful in contrast to his life but blacker by infinities than that quiet spiritual assurance of the novel's hero. The monster of the films is the ultimate victim, the final image of lost and suffering man, all illusions stripped away, naked in his own damnation. The horror of his death may be the most intense of all . . . cinematic myths, and the Frankenstein story is the most complex and, for all its darkness, finally enlightening. (pp. 82-5)

[The] monster never achieves his humanity, and his death is only a blotting out, a leap from unnatural life into nothing. Where, then, is the moral lesson, the accommodation to death in this myth? It is, I think, involved in an act of love, a feeling of sympathy with the ugliest and most outcast of living creatures, an act which no human in the films is capable of making but one which each member of the audience should make. We give our feelings to the monster, suffer and die with him. . . .

There is the power of the Frankenstein myth, the power to inspire love for the untouchable, feeling for the violent and murderous beast, love and fear involved as they seldom are but always should be. The Frankenstein myth teaches us how fallen we are and, at the same time, how we must love one another, despite all our sins and crimes, in order to live through that world and maintain the humanity which the monster could not only not find in himself, but which he smothered in those around him with their fear and violence. If the film can rouse our sympathy for the monster and his downward path to death, it has shown us the possibility of a life which, even with death as its inevitable end, can be rich with love and alive with the human spirit. (p. 90)

> R. H. W. Dillard, "Even a Man Who Is Pure at Heart: Poetry and Danger in the Horror Film," in Man and the Movies, *edited by W. R. Robinson with George Garrett, Louisiana State University Press, 1967, pp. 60-96.*

MARIO PRAZ (essay date 1968)

[*In a general consideration of* Frankenstein, *Praz surveys the novel's sources and literary descendants.*]

[Despite] its capacity of stirring our sense of horror, [Mary Shelley's *Frankenstein*] has a fundamental weakness which seriously hampers the suspense of disbelief. In the fourth chapter we read that 'after days and nights of incredible labour and fatigue', the narrator has 'succeeded in discovering the cause of generation and life', nay more, he has become himself 'capable of bestowing animation upon lifeless matter'. He then addresses his friend thus:

> I see by your eagerness, and the wonder and hope which your eyes express, my friend, that you expect to be informed of the secret with which I am acquainted; that cannot be: listen patiently until the end of my story, and you will easily perceive why I am reserved upon that subject. I will not lead you on, unguarded and ardent as I then was, to your destruction and infallible misery. Learn from me, if not by my precepts, at least by my example, how dangerous is the acquirement of knowledge.

Thus the manner of animating lifeless matter must be kept secret, but is the reader content with this blunt statement? Generally authors of pseudo-scientific novels try to lift the veil, be it only for a moment. (p. 25)

The artificial creation of a human being had been the dream of centuries, but the problem was particularly alive in the eighteenth century and Goethe voiced it in the Homunculus in the second part of *Faust* which, however, was begun only in 1826, whereas *Frankenstein* was published in 1818. Sources have been pointed out, in Godwin's novels, in Madame De Genlis's *Pygmalion et Galatée,* not to speak of *Paradise Lost;* Condillac may have contributed his psychological sensationalism, Locke was meticulously read by Mrs Shelley through December 1816 and January 1817. (pp. 27-8)

There are in *Frankenstein* echoes of Coleridge's *Rime of the Ancient Mariner,* witness the very appearance of the narrator ('his lustrous eyes dwell on me with all their melancholy sweetness', says Walton in the fourth preliminary letter), and the polar regions through which the last mad pursuit takes place; and certainly the image of the wounded deer in Chapter IX was inspired by William Cowper's famous passage (*The Task,* III, 108-20). There are also anticipations of Poe's Imp of the Perverse ('Chance or rather the evil influence, the Angel of Destruction, which asserted omnipotent sway over me from the moment I turned my reluctant steps from my father's door— led me first to Mr Kempe, professor of natural philosophy'), and even of Ahab's pursuit of Moby Dick in Frankenstein's relentless, Heaven-assigned chase of the monster. So that for the far-reaching implications of the main theme and for the grandiose scenery through which the mad chase takes place, Mrs Shelley's novel ranks as the greatest achievement of the Gothic school notwithstanding its frequent clichés of phrasing and situation and the occasionally disarming naïveté. Because the way in which the monster acquires a remarkable degree of education, to the point of reading *Paradise Lost,* Plutarch's *Lives,* and the *Sorrows of Werther,* and of quoting Milton in his speeches ('Evil thenceforth became my good', 'It presented to me as exquisite and divine a retreat as Pandaemonium appeared to the daemons of hell after their suffering in the lake of fire', etc.), is a no less serious obstacle to the suspension of disbelief than the manner in which the monster is contrived by Frankenstein out of dead limbs.

There are in the novel all the elements of a good film, whatever one thinks of the one which was actually made; witness the very spectacular end, which reads like the script for a regular Hollywood finale:

> He sprang from the cabin-window, as he said this, upon the ice-raft which lay close to the vessel. He was soon borne away by the waves and lost in darkness and distance.

Indeed, it was reserved for the film of our day to realize successfully effects that the horror novelists tried to achieve, but crudely, so crudely indeed that they easily lent themselves to Jane Austen's and Thomas Love Peacock's satires. (pp. 31-2)

> *Mario Praz, in an introduction to* Three Gothic Novels, *edited by Peter Fairclough, Penguin Books, 1968, pp. 7-34.*

MASAO MIYOSHI (essay date 1969)

[*Miyoshi's* The Divided Self, *from which the following excerpt is drawn, is a study of self-duplication and self-division in nineteenth-century literature. Here the critic suggests that the characters Walton, Clerval, and the Monster serve to illuminate various aspects of Frankenstein's personality. According to Miyoshi, Walton mirrors Frankenstein in his Faustian striving, while Clerval and the Monster represent the good and evil extremes, respectively, of the scientist's nature.*]

The Faustian theme of thirst for knowledge [in *Frankenstein*] is expressed particularly in the use of the laboratory. Not only Frankenstein but Captain Walton as well is engaged in scientific experiment. Walton's expedition parallels Frankenstein's Fausto-Promethean adventures. Nor is the Monster any different in this respect: His long tale within a tale, covering six chapters (eleventh to sixteenth), might well be called "The Education of a 'Natural' Man" (albeit an "artificial" natural man), the author's assumption being man's innate goodness and, voicing Godwin and Shelley, the failure of existing institutions to sustain him. With the Monster, too, it is an insatiable thirst for knowledge—in particular, knowledge of his origin and identity—that motivates him: "Who was I? What was I? Whence did I come? What was my destination?" (p. 80)

Godwin's daughter moved freely in the circle of the foremost poets and writers of the time, and it was unlikely that she could allow *Frankenstein* to become just another horror story. As a small child, she had heard "The Ancient Mariner" recited by Coleridge himself, and by the time she had finished her own story in May of 1817, she had come to know Thomas Peacock, "Monk" Lewis, Leigh Hunt, Byron, and, of course, Shelley. With this background, *Frankenstein* could scarcely avoid reflecting a great many serious concerns of the Romantics: the dualism of poetry and science, of the individual and society, and of faith and humanistic rationalism.

The story opens with Walton's rescue of Frankenstein. Sensing somewhere in the dark gloom of his bearing a "double existence," composed of great suffering and great glory too, Walton understands Frankenstein's dreams of retiring within, where he can preside "like a celestial spirit," . . . for Walton, too, is pulled between his thirst for "a more intimate sympathy with a fellow mind" and his longing for more inward "knowledge and wisdom." . . . The two immediately recognize these poles in each other. At the end of the story, when the ship is halted by mountains of ice on all sides, the crew urge the captain to sacrifice the expedition and return home straightaway with the first sign of the thaw. However, the dying Frankenstein, wanting desperately to track down his Monster, insists

they push on. There is here a remarkable resemblance to Conrad's *The Secret Sharer,* in which Leggatt and the captain meet and become by their identical quest indistinguishable. In *Frankenstein,* the encounter functions as more than a mere narrative convention, acting to reinforce the Faustian theme by mirroring it—Frankenstein in Walton and vice versa—and in a paradoxical way universalizing their common solitude. There are hints here too of the Mariner's meeting with the Wedding Guest, although comparison with Coleridge's poem brings out something else of interest. For a while, the Frankenstein-Mariner parallel is strongly suggested at several points. Walton, too, resembles the Coleridge hero (for example, "I am going to unexplored regions, to 'the land of mist and snow'; but I shall kill no albatross. . . .") It is only after Walton decides to terminate the voyage that Frankenstein, released at last from his monomaniacal chase, dies. Walton, then, is a kind of other possibility for Frankenstein, a life which he might have had, and it is with this in mind that the Faustian motive should be looked into.

Against this, it would be natural to insist that Frankenstein's friendship with Clerval anticipates the later one with Walton. However there the relationship was not one of identity, but of contrast; Clerval was "a being formed in the 'very poetry of nature'," . . . and occupied with "the moral relations of things." . . . Frankenstein with his scientific interests, Clerval with his poetry, the two complemented each other: "Harmony was the soul of [their] companionship." . . . Had this balance prevailed, there would have been no Frankenstein creation and consequently no tragedy to tell. However, in the world of this work, friction and discord prevail. In Frankenstein's career, first science and then poetry occupies his interest, until the possibility of either is destroyed by the Monster's vengeful reappearance.

The subtitle, *Or, The Modern Prometheus,* certainly suggests it is Frankenstein who in the creation of life has defied God and become Prometheus, but it is nonetheless the Monster's rebellion that dominates the story. The epitaph taken from *Paradise Lost*— "Did I request thee, Maker, from clay / To mould me man? Did I solicit thee / From darkness to promote me?"—points to the essential identity between Monster and maker. They are both Promethean figures and both finally return to that one clay that was their common origin.

If we treated Frankenstein's life experiment purely as the outgrowth of his rationalistic obsession the Monster would fit well into the pattern of a being who is, rather limitedly, "reason in isolation." As it happens he does not develop so straightforwardly as an embodiment of rational man. Faustian, yes, but his initial thrust of existence is toward development of his total being, moral and emotional as well as intellectual. From the De Laceys and his readings in Milton, Plutarch, and Goethe, he forms the notion, for one, of service to humanity. But there is no response to his earnest and generous efforts; on the contrary, people are horrified with his appearance and fear and hate him. He reasons that a child might be different, that he might mold a little one into a friend, but it turns out badly. The boy—Frankenstein's little brother—abuses him for his hideous appearance and the Monster strangles him. The period of Frankenstein's mastery is over; the Monster, discovering that he, too, can "create desolation," becomes a second Frankenstein. As he says to the scientist, recalling the ambiguous Master-Slave relationship so well understood by Hegel, "You are my creator, but I am your master." . . . (pp. 80-3)

At the same time, Frankenstein's enormous creative effort seems to have completely exhausted him. Henceforth rejecting his scientific pursuits, he devotes himself to Clerval's world of poetry and emotion. "A serene sky and verdant fields filled me wih ecstasy. The present season was indeed divine; the flowers of spring bloomed in the hedges, while those of summer were already in bud. I was undisturbed by thoughts which during the preceding year had pressed upon me, notwithstanding my endeavors to throw them off, with an invincible burden." . . . Frankenstein the intellectual purges the intellect through Nature.

Only with the reappearance of the Monster in his life, with his program of revenge and destruction, is this balance shaken. He can no longer take delight in the beauties of Nature and is driven back once again to a tormenting sense of his great guilt. Like many of the Gothic heroes, he is utterly at a loss over what course to take next, and his indecisiveness, which, in a sense, allows the murder of Justine, Clerval, Elizabeth, and M. Frankenstein himself, only intensifies his remorse unbearably. The disintegration of his personality is now complete.

As though to mirror his creator's cycle of guilt and remorse, the Monster too finds himself agonized. The two voice an identical feeling of bearing a "hell within" them. . . . The Monster has certainly systematically destroyed Frankenstein's family in retribution for not having been provided with a spouse. However, it may not be too far afield to propose that these murders are at the same time a projection of Frankenstein's own suppressed urge to destroy what he loves—a negative impulse lurking in the depths of rationalism. Indeed, it is only the absence of a carefully conceived plan that distinguishes Frankenstein's creation of the Monster from Dr. Jekyll's of Mr. Hyde, who is turned loose solely as a means by which the creator realizes his secret and abominable desires. The common error of calling the Monster "Frankenstein" has considerable justification. He is the scientist's deviant self.

The essential oneness of the two is manifest in still another way. Frankenstein and the Monster, engrossed with each other, are soon completely inseparable in their mutual hatred and common misery. The facts surrounding the Monster's origin, existence, and subsequent culpability are too strange to be believed, and as a result people around them lose interest in the two and their far-ranging wanderings—pursuer and pursued, creator and creature, maker and destroyer, trekking over Europe from the Alps to the Mediterranean, and from there to the North Sea. In a narrative recalling aspects of her father's *Caleb Williams,* Mary Shelley unfolds this tale of a great chase which, with society receding in significance, gradually takes on the only meaning, the only existence even, for both pursuer and pursued. We see the fugitive posting a landmark here and there that the search might continue, and when death claims the hunter, the fugitive too must die—the chase has been his life.

The Monster is an all too real nightmare for his maker, yet there is some semblance here of the *Alastor* Poet's visionary quest. In this tale, as in the Shelley poem, there is a projection or reproduction of the self; nor is a reunion of the two ultimately possible, for the pursuit ends only with the death of the pursuer. For this reason primarily, the story is a commentary on Romantic alienation, although, like her husband, Mary Shelley is finally quite ambivalent toward the Romantic quest. Frankenstein dies a defeated man, but sublimely, in the style of the Poet.

To go back to Shelley for a moment, it was in the Preface of 1817 [see excerpt above] that he recapitulated the principle of the romance first set down by Walpole: "I have thus endeavored to preserve the truth of the elementary principles of human nature, while I have not scrupled to innovate upon their combinations. The *Iliad,* the tragic poetry of Greece—Shakespeare, in the *Tempest* and *Midsummer Night's Dream*—and most especially Milton, in *Paradise Lost,* conform to this rule. . . ." What he means by "the truth of the elementary principles of human nature" and his innovations on various combinations of same should be clear in the light of his references to the epics and romances: simply, the ordinary and the marvelous. The romance tradition, blending the two, continues right into the nineteenth century and later. However, what is remarkable about this is not so much the continuity of the tradition, but its continual absorption of elements not yet utilized in the early romances. For instance, in *Frankenstein* the main vehicle of Gothic fantasy is no longer the conventional supernatural. Its author, writing in an age of increasing scientism when the old Gothic mysteries had lost much of their appeal, took instead as her theme this same new science whose role M. Krempe had defined as limited to "annihilation" of the old fantasies, and in effect annihilated it as a humane pursuit by demonstrating its possible monstrous results. Despite the many lines of correspondence to the ghosts and devils of the conventional romances, science, with its growing prestige, can generate a totally new species of terror. If scientific man is a kind of God, his scientific method becomes a new supernaturalism, a contemporary witchdoctoring of frightening potential.

However, what is more, oxymoron being a prominent feature of science fiction, contradictory demands are made on the tone and style of the work. To convince his reader, the writer must delineate objects and events in the story very clearly and completely. At the same time, fantasy requires that he surround these objects and events with an atmosphere of wonder and at least the suggestion of the supernatural. For the first, neither Beckford's whimsy and irony, Mrs. Radcliffe's misty landscapes and characterizations, nor Godwin's rhetoric would be appropriate. Instead, Mrs. Shelley borrows the realistic type of scene, event, and character from the by then fully developed orthodox novel of Maria Edgeworth, Jane Austen, and some aspects of Sir Walter Scott. Her description of the De Lacey family, for example, is straight out of the domestic novel. . . . (pp. 83-7)

The second requirement is met as much by ample infusions of the Romantic poets, mainly Wordsworth and Coleridge, as by the conventional Gothicisms. Mary Shelley quotes liberally from "Tintern Abbey" and "The Ancient Mariner," and the Alps, so important to these poets, are there exploited to heighten the feelings of solitude and awe in the two major characters. However, "The Ancient Mariner" is perhaps the most important of these Romantic influences, as we can see from the resemblance that the extensive wanderings of Frankenstein and Walton bear to the Mariner's voyage of atonement. Especially striking in its reference to Coleridge is the final scene:

> Immense and rugged mountains of ice often barred up my passage, and I often heard the thunder of the ground sea which threatened my destruction. But again the frost came and made the paths of the sea secure. . . .
>
> September 9th, the ice began to move, and roarings like thunder were heard at a distance

as the islands split and cracked in every direction. . . .

Here is the Coleridge:

And through the drifts the snowy clifts
Did send a dismal sheen:
Nor shapes of men nor beasts we ken—
The ice was all between.

The ice was here, the ice was there,
The ice was all around:
It cracked and growled, and roared and howled,
Like noises in a swound! . . .

Mrs. Shelley has not fully worked out the symbolic potential of the scene. The term "mountains of ice," nowhere varied or made any more specific, is nowhere strongly referential either; we miss the full sense in it of their dead damp whiteness against the impenetrable night. However, if she has not conquered those particular mountains, others have. Take the way she concludes her tale of Fausto-Promethean defiance—flames that devour the Monster rising to the dark skies above the stark white icebergs—a scene strikingly anticipating Poe who ended his *Arthur Gordon Pym* with just such components as Mrs. Shelley's, but with considerably greater awareness of their possibilities. With Poe, the romance tradition would take on new visual variety and symbolic depth, qualities not lost on other highly gifted romancers such as Hawthorne and Melville, and indeed Dickens. (pp. 87-9)

> *Masao Miyoshi, "The Logic of Passion: Romanticism," in his* The Divided Self: A Perspective on the Literature of the Victorians, *New York University Press, 1969, pp. 47-106.*

WILLIAM A. WALLING   (essay date 1972)

[*In the preface to his full-length critical survey of Shelley's writings, Walling argues that her first three novels—* Frankenstein, Valperga, *and* The Last Man—*"ought to have earned for Mary a higher place in the literature about the fiction of the period than she currently holds." Here, he discusses* Valperga *as a novel of misplaced ambition and delineates the political critique inherent in* The Last Man.]

Mary Shelley, in her second novel [*Valperga*] as well as in her first [*Frankenstein*], is interested in taking up the theme of ambition and exploring the emotional cost it exacts. But if *Frankenstein* may be regarded as a religious and even a philosophical treatment of such a theme, then surely *Valperga,* based on an historical figure of medieval Italy, is a political exploraton of the same basic dilemma: the conflict between intense aspiration (the desire for political power) and the demands of the human heart. In truth, although Mary's criticism of religious orthodoxy is unmistakable in *Valperga* through the character of Beatrice, one of the weaknesses in the construction of the novel as a whole is that the religious elements never really—as they do in *Frankenstein*—become a part of the central theme. Instead, what we find in *Valperga* is that political issues clearly dominate the formal structure, while the religious criticism—despite its vividness—stands to one side as a brilliant but often irrelevant digression. (p. 60)

Valperga deals with a central figure who schemes to bring about "the government of a single person." Quite early in the novel, in fact, when Castruccio is still essentially a boy, Mary makes this intent clear. He has taken up residence with Francis Guinigi, a man who, although once a successful military leader,

has laid "aside the distinctions of society" and has turned to agriculture as a way of life, recognizing, "with lovely humility, . . . the affinity of the meanest peasant to his own noble mind." . . . Castruccio, however, argues with Guinigi, endeavoring to prove to him "that in the present distracted state of mankind, it was better that one man should get the upper hand, to rule the rest." . . . In other words, what Mary presents through Castruccio is the fatal result of the obvious solution to "the present distracted state" of nineteenth-century Europe: the government of each nation by a powerful individual, who is ultimately responsible to no one but himself. (pp. 62-3)

[This] early disputation between Castruccio and Guinigi is also valuable for pointing to Mary's method of organizing her political theme. For what she does is present, as stages in Castruccio's development, a series of dialectic milestones in which Castruccio's colloquist functions somewhat in the fashion of either the good or the bad angel in the old morality plays. Guinigi, for example, is obviously a "good" angel—the first, in fact, that Castruccio encounters—just as Euthanasia is the most important. Alberto Scoto, on the other hand, is the first of Castruccio's "bad" angels, for he introduces Castruccio to the unscrupulous methods of successful power politics. Thus Scoto advises Castruccio, in a Machiavellian passage, "But, having once formed an army, disciplined it, and shewn its temper by success, then is the time to change the arts of war for those of counsel, and to work your way as the mole, shewing no sign of your path, until your triumphant power comes forth where it is least expected." . . . "And in those days," Mary continues by way of summary of Scoto's effect, "the seeds of craft were sown, that, flourishing afterwards, contributed to his advancement to power and glory." . . . (p. 63)

Although Scoto, as the first, is the crucial dark angel in Castruccio's career, Benedetto Pepi, whom Castruccio meets in the Alps while traveling to Italy, is the one receiving the fullest treatment. (pp. 63-4)

Indeed, Pepi, in a striking (although undoubtedly coincidental) similarity to Blake's "The Human Abstract," presents an image of the perdurable nature of human selfishness that seems to insure the perpetution of injustice: "Tyranny is a healthy tree, it strikes a deep root, and each year its branches grow larger and larger, and its shade spreads wider and wider. While liberty is a word, a breath, an air; it will dissipate, and Florence become as slavish as it is now rebellious; did not Rome fall?" . . . As a result, the final stage of Castruccio's moral collapse is indicated by an appropriate reference to his having become indistinguishable from his archtempter: "He now fully subscribed to all the articles of Pepi's political creed, and thought fraud and secret murder fair play, when it thinned the ranks of the enemy." . . . (p. 64)

But, as I have indicated, not only Guinigi but also Euthanasia stands against the malign influences on Castruccio's career. In one of their earliest colloquies, in fact, Euthanasia attempts to rescue Castruccio from the temptation of a self-centered tyranny by suggesting to him that true fulfillment is impossible without a climate of liberty: "The essence of freedom is that clash and struggle which awaken the energies of our nature, and that operation of the elements of our mind, which as it were gives us the force and power that hinder us from degenerating, as they say all things earthly do when not regenerated by change." . . . (pp. 64-5)

And yet, as we know, the nature of Mary's historical material dooms Euthanasia to failure. No matter how well she may argue, no matter how passionately she may champion the cause of liberty—and at times Euthanasia does indeed justify Claire Clairmont's description of her (a "Shelley in female attire")—Castruccio nevertheless continues his downward path. . . . (p. 65)

[With] Euthanasia's failure of persuasion a foregone conclusion, the task which confronted Mary was that of showing how Castruccio's ostensible political success is nothing more than a hollow victory since it is purchased at the cost of his essential humanity—and such a theme inevitably carries us back to the obvious moral of Victor Frankenstein's development. For, like Frankenstein (and, in truth, also like Walton), Castruccio indulges himself "in dreams of . . . distinction" at an early age. . . . Consequently, by the time he becomes an orphan in his seventeeth year and goes to reside with Guinigi, he is already predisposed against the older man's willingness to recognize "the affinity of the meanest peasant" to himself. And his very refusal to acknowledge the principle of equality starts Castruccio not only on the downward path to tyranny but to a condition of increasing emotional deprivation.

For this reason Mary quite clearly places so great an emphasis on "romantic," . . . nonhistorical elements in her narrative. Not once, but twice Castruccio rejects a specific love which is offered to him—first, from Euthanasia; then, from Beatrice. For, while Castruccio persists in his offer to marry Euthanasia, she refuses to accept anyone who is an enemy to liberty, regardless of how deep her love for Castruccio may be. . . . (pp. 65-6)

[The] implicit struggle in Castruccio between his ambitious dreams of power and his love for Euthanasia is given direct expression in the account of the aftereffects of his brief affair with Beatrice: "And love was with him, ever after, the second feeling in his heart, the servant and thrall of his ambition." . . . And the consequences of this triumph of political ambition over the needs of the human heart receive their baldest expression at the end of the novel when, with Euthanasia dead, Castruccio meets again one of the dark angels of his youth, Galeazzo Visconti:

> In recording the events which had passed since their separation, Galeazzo found, that, if he had lost sovereignty and power, Castruccio had lost that which might be considered far more valuable; he had lost his dearest friends. . . . We know nothing of the private communion of these friends; but we may guess that, if Castruccio revealed the sorrows of his heart, Galeazzo might have regretted that, instead of having instigated the ambition, and destroyed the domestic felicity of his friend, he had not taught him other lessons, through which he might have enjoyed that peace, sympathy and happiness, of which he was now for ever deprived. . . .

What we have in *Valperga,* then, is the portrayal of a man who chooses power and personal eminence in preference to love. And, like Victor Frankenstein, Castruccio finds that even the limited achievement of his dream of eminence traps him in a selfhood of exacerbated isolation: like Frankenstein's monster, Castruccio's ambition takes on a murderous autonomy of its own. . . . So it is, that at the end of the novel, with Euthanasia reduced to a captured member of the utterly defeated republican party, she can still assert to the victorious Castruccio the moral point of his ostensibly successful career: that his life is "miserable" and "unworthy"—while Castruccio, driven for the

moment into the clarity of a genuine insight, can do nothing more than agree. . . . In short, in the scheme of *Valperga,* Castruccio, like the Jupiter of *Prometheus Unbound,* is shown to be struggling to retain less than what his victims already possess: the cost of a system of political inequality permeates an entire society, ultimately redounding, in its emotional consequences, upon the tyrant himself. And although analogues drawn from actuality may be less illuminating than ingenious, I doubt if anyone, fresh from reading of the memoirs of Stalin's daughter, Svetlena Alliluyeva, will be inclined to accuse Mary Shelley of naïveté. (pp. 66-7)

• • • • •

For some time it has been recognized by commentators that *The Last Man* . . . represents a creative landmark in Mary Shelley's career—a landmark which has been obscured both by the fame of *Frankenstein* and by her role as Shelley's wife. (p. 72)

The Last Man deserves serious attention in any assessment of Mary Shelley's career. Indeed, although the novel is marred by overwriting and sentimentality (Mary's major literary vices) as well as by its excessive length, *The Last Man* is a book of genuine power. Less readable than *Valperga,* less intense and richly symbolic than *Frankenstein,* it easily surpasses, nonetheless, her three remaining novels and does seem, to me, to merit its current ranking of a firm second place (after *Frankenstein*) by virtue of a greater unity and a more substantial underlying conception than is found in *Valperga.* (p. 73)

For the most part, the suggestive structure of *The Last Man* appears to have been misunderstood. Because more than a third of the novel deals not with the plague at all but with political and romantic elements in republican England, a common criticism is that Mary has provided an unduly tedious introduction to the "real" theme of her book—the plague itself and its far-reaching consequences. Yet such a charge—despite the undoubted tedium of some of the passages dealing with the love relationships—fails to take note of the full implications of *The Last Man.* For, in its deepest import, the novel achieves a striking fusion of the theme of the plague (in the second and third volumes) with the theme of political and social change implicit from the outset in the presentation of England as a republic. Indeed, Mary, who quotes approvingly from Burke's *Reflections on the French Revolution* at least twice in the course of her novel . . . , has produced in *The Last Man* a pervasive criticism of her father's (and, to a degree, of Shelley's) theory of society—a criticism of which Burke himself would have approved.

In Chapter 4 of the first volume, for example, Ryland appears on the scene as the chief opponent of Raymond's early bid for political power. Fully aware that Raymond wishes to overturn the republic and become king, Ryland rises to confront him with a speech that seems to reflect the triumph of many of the ideas advanced by Shelley in his "Philosophical View of Reform":

> Ryland began by praising the present state of the British empire. He recalled past years to their memory; the miserable contentions which in the time of our fathers arose almost to civil war, the abdication of the late king, and the foundation of the republic. He described this republic; shewed how it gave privilege to each individual in the state, to rise to consequence, and even to temporary sovereignty. He com-

An 1831 portrait by S. J. Stump, generally believed to be of Mary Shelley.

pared the royal and republican spirit; shewed how the one tended to enslave the minds of men; while all the institutions of the other served to raise even the meanest among us to something great and good. He shewed how England had become powerful, and its inhabitants valiant and wise, by means of the freedom they enjoyed. . . .

(pp. 88-9)

Yet this presentation of Ryland as the apparent champion of many of Shelley's most prominent political ideas becomes immeasurably more complex in the second volume, once the theme of the plague has been announced. For Ryland, now that Raymond is dead, stands on the very threshold of political power himself; and the policy he intends to pursue if elected lord protector is clearly that of the extension of Shelley's "divine Equality": "The political state of England became agitated as the time drew near when the new Protector was to be elected. This event excited the more interest, since it was the current report that if the popular candidate (Ryland) should be chosen, the question of the abolition of hereditary rank, and other feudal relics, would come under the consideration of parliament." . . . (pp. 89-90)

To Burke, of course, such a proposal as the one attributed to Ryland would have seemed a threat to the very principle of social order. "The power of perpetuating our property in our families," Burke declares in his *Reflections*, "is one of the most valuable . . . circumstances belonging to it, and that which tends the most to the perpetuation of society itself. . . . The possessor of family wealth, and of the distinction which attends hereditary possession . . . are the natural securities for this transmission." And again, in a claim that clearly associates the continuation of what we would today call "culture" with a continuation of the system that Ryland intends to overturn, Burke asserts: "Nothing is more certain, than that our manners, our civilization, and all the good things which are connected with manners, and with civilization, have, in this European world of ours, depended for ages upon two principles; and were indeed the result of both combined; I mean the spirit of a gentleman and the spirit of religion."

Nor is this analogue an idle one, for Burke's argument becomes a part of the texture of Mary's novel as she presents the entire English nation as considering the abolition of rank and title: "The newspapers teemed with nothing else; and in private companies the conversation, however remotely begun, soon verged towards this central point, while voices were lowered and chairs drawn closer. The nobles did not hesitate to express their fear; the other party [that is, the "popular" party] endeavoured to treat the matter lightly." . . . Thus Ryland attempts to dismiss the whole storm of fear and uncertainty with the supremely self-confident rationality of a Jeremy Bentham—or of a William Godwin: "'Shame on the country,' said Ryland, 'to lay so much stress upon words and frippery; it is a question of nothing; of, the new painting of carriage-panels and the embroidery of footmen's coats'." . . . (p. 90)

Yet immediately after this bluff dismissal of aristocratic objections, a long paragraph follows on the prospect of an egalitarian society, a paragraph which presents, ostensibly through Lionel's reflections, the major arguments for and against such an innovation. First, there is the popular party's glowing prediction of what will actually occur in England, despite the widespread fear in the nation that a "democratic style" may introduce a change for the worse:

> Yet could England indeed doff her lordly trappings, and be content with the democratic style of America? Were the pride of ancestry, the patrician spirit, the gentle courtesies and refined pursuits, splendid attributes of rank, to be erased among us? We were told that this would not be the case. . . . We were assured that, when the name and title of Englishman was the sole patent of nobility, we should all be noble; that when no man born under English sway, felt another his superior in rank, courtesy and refinement would become the birth-right of all our countrymen. . . .

But second, and of course counter to this egalitarian argument, runs the Burkean claim of the aristocratic party, which contends that in truth the highest achievements of civilization are at stake: "That party . . . could hardly yet be considered a minority in the kingdom, who extolled the ornament of the column, 'the Corinthian capital of polished society'; they appealed to prejudices without number, to old attachments and young hopes; to the expectation of thousands who might one day become peers; they set up as a scarecrow, the spectre of all that was sordid, mechanic and base in the commercial republic." . . . (pp. 90-1)

And then, with the opening words of the next paragraph, Mary fuses her two themes. "The plague had come to Athens," she writes starkly, exactly as, in the opening sentence of the paragraph directly preceding her description of the egalitarian conflict in England, she had written: "But, though it seemed absurd to calculate upon the arrival of the plague in London, I could not reflect without extreme pain on the desolation this evil would cause in Greece." . . . For, to put it as simply as possible, Mary Shelley, on the deepest symbolic level, surely unaware herself of the full implications of her novel, has created a startlingly pessimistic allegory which identifies egalitarianism with a plague virulent enough to destroy civilization itself.

Nor is this reading in the least a fanciful one. In *Valperga,* Mary made a similar identification, although there, with Shelley still alive, she projected her deepest fears (and they are close to Burke's) onto one of Castruccio's dark angels, Galeazzo Visconti. "The contagion of liberty is dangerous," Galeazzo tells Castruccio: "the Ghibellines [the royalist party] must fall in Lucca, if the Guelphs [the republican party] be not destroyed in Florence. Think you, if your people are allowed free intercourse with this republic, that the plague of liberty will not spread to your state? For no quarantine will eradicate that spot, if once it has entered the soul." . . .

In *The Last Man,* however, Mary Shelley, despondent, psychologically isolated, bitterly resentful over the lack of charity in ordinary humanity . . . produced a novel in which her fears are no longer projected by a minor figure but are incorporated into the very texture of her work.

Symbolically, then, the true subject of *The Last Man* is "the plague of liberty" and its egalitarian consequences. The first volume, with its political concerns, introduces us to an England where the old hierarchies (the monarchy in particular) have broken down; and then, as the novel progresses through its second and third volume, we are presented with the horrified vision of a world from which all social distinctions have vanished and where every man is reduced to the lowest common denominator—that of his most primitive animal interests.

"The race of man had lost in fact all distinctions of rank," we are told as the plague continues to rage across England. . . . Furthermore, with the abandonment of hard and fast hierarchies of labor, the scale of civilized values is reversed, and the most menial abilities rise to the ascendancy. . . . (pp. 91-2)

[This] fusion of the ravages of the plague with the destructive consequences of a thoroughgoing social equality is heightened into genuine, almost Burkean intensity in the opening pages of the third volume. With a nostalgic look backward at a God-centered world, where, paradoxically, man's stature was enlarged through his acceptance of the principle of subordination, Mary writes:

> Once man was a favourite of the Creator, as
> the royal psalmist sang, "God had made him
> a little lower than the angels, and had crowned
> him with glory and honour." . . . Once it was
> so; now is man lord of the creation? Look at
> him—ha! I see plague! She has invested his
> form, is incarnate in his flesh, has entwined
> herself with his being, and blinds his heaven-
> seeking eyes. Lie down, O man, on the flower-
> strown earth; give up all claim to your inher-
> itance, all you can ever possess of it is the small
> cell which the dead require. . . .

For now that all men are reduced to the lowest common denominator, heroic effort is a thing of the past; and intellectual

distinction has dwindled to a low cunning that is useful for nothing more than the preservation of life:

> Plague is the companion of spring, of sunshine,
> and plenty. We no longer struggle with her.
> We have forgotten what we did when she was
> not. Of old navies used to stem the giant ocean-
> waves betwixt Indus and the Pole for slight
> articles of luxury. Men made perilous journies
> to possess themselves of earth's splendid tri-
> fles, gems and gold. Human labour was wasted—
> human life set at nought. Now life is all that
> we covet; that this automaton of flesh should,
> with joints and strings in order, perform its
> functions, that this dwelling of the soul should
> be capable of containing its dweller. Our minds,
> late spread abroad through countless spheres
> and endless combinations of thought, now re-
> trenched themselves behind this wall of flesh,
> eager to preserve its well-being only. We were
> surely sufficiently degraded. . . .

And this overture to the third volume ends with a dying fall that is a palinode to the liberal hopes of an age—a palinode, it must be added, to many of the liberal hopes that Mary herself, on the conscious level of her mind, was to continue to hold almost until her death:

> As the rules of order and pressure of laws were
> lost, some began with hesitation and wonder to
> transgress the accustomed uses of society. Pal-
> aces were deserted, and the poor man dared at
> length, unreproved, intrude into the splended
> apartments, whose very furniture and decora-
> tions were an unknown world to him. . . . We
> were all equal now; magnificent dwellings, lux-
> urious carpets, and beds of down, were af-
> forded to all. Carriages and horses, gardens,
> pictures, statues, and princely libraries, there
> were enough of these even to superfluity; and
> there was nothing to prevent each from assum-
> ing possession of his share. We were all equal
> now; but near at hand was an equality still more
> levelling, a state where beauty and strength,
> and wisdom, would be as vain as riches and
> birth. . . .

For it was only in the last years of her life, as she watched with horror the revolutions of 1848, that Mary allowed into full consciousness the Burkean fears that were hers in 1824-25 during the composition of *The Last Man.* "Strange & fearful events are in progress in Europe," she wrote on June 30, 1848. "Barbarism—countless uncivilized men, long concealed under the varnish of our social system, are breaking out with the force of a volcano & threatening order—law & peace. In Germany the bands of society are entirely broken—no rents are paid— the peasant invades the Chateau—& would take it—were it worth his while." But, as I have tried to show, this horrified reaction of 1848 is only the waking counterpart to the powerful and extended nightmare of *The Last Man,* a nightmare whose deepest symbolic import was concealed from even Mary herself. (pp. 93-4)

• • • • •

Preeminently, it seems to me, [Shelley's] significance rests on her three early novels—*Frankenstein, The Last Man,* and *Valperga*—in that order. Indeed, such a total achievement ought to have earned for Mary a higher place in the literature about the fiction of the period than she currently holds. For, while Scott and Jane Austen are far superior to her, when we descend from these two, past Peacock, into the host of novelists who were Mary's contemporaries in the early nineteenth century, it is difficult to discover—on the basis of the seriousness of conception, the originality and variety of technique, and the relevance to their time and to our own—anything to equal the over-all implications of Mary's three novels. (p. 142)

[Any] study of Mary Shelley must end on a note of regret for her failure to fulfill her early promise. Few novelists have begun with a debut as auspicious as that of *Frankenstein*. No other novelist of her time combined such a promising beginning with so youthful an age. And, when we consider that *Frankenstein* was not an entirely isolated phenomenon in Mary's career, the regret can only grow sharper. For, whatever the final conclusion may be about the unevenness of *Valperga, The Last Man* in its sustained conception is surely a novel with its own independent significance. Briefly, then, the last word on Mary Shelley must be one of regret for her failure to make of her career a more impressive creative whole. And although the reason for the failure can be debated . . . , it is the failure itself which matters. Out of it, in fact, can be found the basis on which Mary Shelley takes her place in English literature as a minor figure. (pp. 142-43)

William A. Walling, in his Mary Shelley, Twayne
Publishers, Inc., 1972, 173 p.

ROBERT KIELY (essay date 1972)

[*Kiely examines and elaborates upon what he considers to be two dominant themes in* Frankenstein: *"the monstrous consequences of egotism" and "the virtue of friendship."*]

Superiority through suffering is a major theme of [*Frankenstein*], a romantic half-tragedy in which the fall from greatness is nearly all fall or, more accurately, where greatness is defined in terms of the personal pain which results from the consciousness of loss which cannot be recalled or comprehended by other men. In unique regret, Frankenstein discovers his true distinction: "I was seized by remorse and the sense of guilt which hurried me away to a hell of intense tortures, such as no language can describe." The failure of language, as always in romantic fiction, is meant to be a sign not of vacuity or of an imaginative limitation of the character or author, but of the singular noncommunicable nature of great experience.

It is unfortunate (though psychologically fitting) that in the popular mind the monster has assumed the name of his creator, because Mary Shelley considered it of some importance that the creature remain unnamed. As Elizabeth Nitchie points out, it was the custom in dramatic performances of *Frankenstein* to represent the monster's part on the playbill with "_____." On first remarking this, Mary Shelley was pleased: "This nameless mode of naming the unnameable is rather good." If the phenomenon itself cannot be named, neither can the feelings it evokes in its maker. No one can know what it is like to be the monster or its "parent." (pp. 158-59)

Mary Shelley spends a great part of her narrative confronting her hero with images which evoke the sublimity of his mental state where ordinary words fail. Frankenstein journeys to Chamonix, where the mountain views elevate him from all "littleness of feeling" and "subdue and tranquilize" his grief though they cannot remove it. Mont Blanc provides him with

a moment of "something like joy," but the Alps, though briefly impressive, are not in the end any more able than words to express or alleviate what Frankenstein feels. Trips up the Rhine, across the sea, even into the Arctic, hint at his unrest, but "imperial Nature," in all her "awful majesty," can no more provide truly adequate images of his misery than she can provide the fulfillment of his ambitious dreams.

At the end of the narrative, Frankenstein accuses himself of over-reaching, but even in doing this, he immodestly compares himself with the prince of overreachers: "Like the archangel who aspired to omnipotence, I am chained in an eternal hell." Rather than looking back on his ambition with disgust, he remembers it with pleasure: "Even now I cannot recollect without passion my reveries while the work was incomplete. I trod heaven in my thoughts, now exulting in my powers, now burning with the idea of their effects." Despite the conventional speeches about the dangers of pride, it becomes more and more evident in the last pages of the novel that Frankenstein, though regretting the *result* of his extraordinary efforts, is not ashamed of having made the effort in the first place. He repeatedly warns Walton, who is engaged in an expedition into the Polar Sea, to content himself with modest ambitions and a quiet life. . . . In his last breath, he begins to warn Walton once more not to make the same mistake he did, but then changes his mind:

> Seek happiness in tranquility and avoid ambition, even if it be only the apparently innocent one of distinguishing yourself in science and discoveries. Yet why do I say this? I have myself been blasted in these hopes, but another may succeed.

That Frankenstein does not die absolutely repentant once again raises the possibility that the monstrous result of his experiment was not the inevitable issue of pride but an accident of circumstance, the result of insufficient knowledge, or an imperfection in nature itself. If one wishes to accept Walton's reverent appraisal of his new friend, it can be said that Frankenstein has the immunity of all scientific and artistic genius from conventional morality, that he is somehow apart from and superior to material circumstances even when he himself seems to have brought them about. (pp. 159-60)

Mary learned her lessons in idealism well, and there is in her narrative a level on which her hero is above reproach. But it must be admitted that there is a mundane side to this fantastic tale. If genius can escape or withdraw from the material universe, ordinary mortals cannot. And however great their admiration for genius may be, they cannot fully separate it from the lesser objects of their perception.

Mary Shelley was a young and impetuous woman when she ran off with the poet; she was also an intelligent woman, but her journals and letters reveal that despite her efforts to form herself after her husband's image, common sense often intruded and made the task difficult. She was never intellectually disloyal to Shelley, yet she admitted that her mind could not follow his to the heights. Her novel, like almost everything else about her life, is an instance of genius observed and admired but not shared. In making her hero the creator of a monster, she does not necessarily mock idealistic ambition, but in making that monster a poor grotesque patchwork, a physical mess of seams and wrinkles, she introduces a consideration of the material universe which challenges and undermines the purity of idealism. In short, the sheer concreteness of the ugly thing which

Frankenstein has created often makes his ambitions and his character—however sympathetically described—seem ridiculous and even insane. The arguments on behalf of idealism and unworldly genius are seriously presented, but the controlling perspective is that of an earthbound woman. (pp. 160-61)

Frankenstein digging about in graveyards and charnel houses, matching eyeballs and sawing bones, is not an inspiring sight. Even less so is the bungled construct of muscles, arteries, and shriveled skin which he had intended as a perfectly proportioned and beautiful being. The gap between the ideal and the real, the ambition and the accomplishment, produces a result as gruesome and absurd as any pseudo-science of the Middle Ages. Still, Mary is not criticizing exalted ambition, but the misapplication of it, the consequences of what Frankenstein himself describes as "unrelaxed and breathless eagerness," a "frantic impulse," a trance-like pursuit of one idea. Through the mouth of her hero, she raises a question which in life she could probably never bring herself to ask her husband: "Is genius forever separate from the reasonable, the reflective, and the probable?" (p. 162)

In describing the way in which Frankenstein's experiment seems most "unnatural," Mary Shelley implies a definition of the natural which is peculiarly feminine in bias. For her, Frankenstein's presumption is not in his attempt to usurp the power of the gods—she quite willingly grants him his "divine" attributes—but in his attempt to usurp the power of women. "A new species would bless me as its creator and source," says Frankenstein in the enthusiasm of his first experiments. "No father could claim the gratitude of his child so completely as I should deserve theirs." He seeks to combine the role of both parents in one, to eliminate the need for woman in the creative act, to make sex unnecessary. At least that would be the net result of his experiment if it were successful, despite the fact that he himself tends to see its consequences in grander and vaguer terms. Thus, while Mary grants her hero the nobility and even the innocence of his intentions, she cannot help but undercut them with her own womanly sense of how things are.

Stripped of rhetoric and ideological decoration, the situation presented is that of a handsome young scientist, engaged to a beautiful woman, who goes off to the mountains alone to create a new human life. When he confesses to Walton that he has "worked hard for nearly two years" to achieve his aim, we may wonder why he does not marry Elizabeth and, with her cooperation, finish the job more quickly and pleasurably. But one must be careful not to imply that Mary's irony is flippant or altogether conscious. Quite to the contrary, her reservations about her hero's presumptuous idealism are so deeply and seriously felt that they produce a symbolic nightmare far more disturbing and gruesome than the monster itself. As soon as the creature begins to show animation and Frankenstein realizes that he has made an abomination, the scientist races to his bedroom, paces feverishly about, and finally falls into a troubled sleep:

> "I slept indeed, but I was disturbed by the wildest dreams. I thought I saw Elizabeth, in the bloom of health, walking in the streets of Ingolstadt. Delighted and surprised, I embraced her; but as I imprinted the first kiss on her lips, they became livid with the hue of death; her features appeared to change, and I thought that I beheld the corpse of my dead mother in my arms; a shroud enveloped her form, and I saw the graveworms crawling in the folds of the

flannel. I started from my sleep with horror . . . (and) beheld the wretch—the miserable monster whom I had created."

In this extraordinary rendition of an Oedipal nightmare, Mary shows, without moral comment, the regressive depths of her hero's mind. Frankenstein's crime against nature is a crime against womanhood, an attempt—however unconscious—to circumvent mature sex. For Mary, this is the supreme symbol of egotism, the ultimate turning away from human society and into the self which must result in desolation. Having moved away from family, friends, and fiancée to perform his "creative" act in isolation, Frankenstein later beholds the monster, in a grotesquely exaggerated re-enactment of his own behavior, "eliminate" his younger brother, his dearest friend, and his beloved Elizabeth.

All the crimes are sins against life in the bloom of youth and beauty, but the murder of the woman is the most effectively presented and, in a way, the most carefully prepared. Frankenstein's fears on his wedding night are presumably due to the monster's threat to pursue him even to his marriage chamber. But the immediate situation and the ambiguity of the language contribute to the impression that the young groom's dread of the monster is mixed with his fear of sexual union as a physical struggle which poses a threat to his independence, integrity, and delicacy of character. Frankenstein describes the event in the following manner:

> "I had been calm during the day: but so soon as night obscured the shapes of objects, a thousand fears arose in my mind. I was anxious and watchful, while my right hand grasped a pistol which was hidden in my bosom; every sound terrified me; but I resolved that I would sell my life dearly, and not shrink from the conflict, until my own life, or that of my adversary, was extinguished.

> "Elizabeth observed my agitation for some time in timid and fearful silence; but there was something in my glance which communicated terror to her, and trembling she asked, 'What is it that agitates you, my dear Victor? What is it you fear?'

> "'Oh! peace, peace, my love,' replied I; 'this night and all will be safe; but this night is dreadful, very dreadful.'

> ". . . I reflected how fearful the combat which I momentarily expected would be to my wife, and I earnestly entreated her to retire, resolving not to join her until I had obtained some knowledge as to the situation of my enemy."

Frankenstein leaves the room, and it is while he is away that his bride is murdered by the monster on her untried marriage bed. The passage is filled with the language of anxiety, phallic inference, and imagery of conflict, yet it is in Frankenstein's absence—not in an eager assertion of his physical presence—that harm comes to Elizabeth. If we take the monster to be one side of Frankenstein's nature, an alter-ego, then we see his physically potent self as brutish, ugly, and destructive, completely unintegrated with his gentle spirit. To depict a radical separation of mind from sexuality is one way to explore an unsatisfactory rapport between the imagination and the natural world. But what is important in the thematic terms of the novel is not the mere existence of the separation, but the fact that physical life is made ugly (indeed, is made to wither and die prematurely) because it is inadequately tended by the mind. The problem is not abuse but neglect.

The importance of the wedding night scene lies in its sexual connotation insofar as that provides the basic and concrete context in which, once again, to exemplify the hero's withdrawal from physical and emotional contact with living human beings. There are earlier instances of his separating himself from his family and from his friend Clerval, even while protesting, as he has with Elizabeth, that he continues to love them in spirit. The outrage dramatized in this novel is not restricted to a specifically sexual offense—nor is it directed against genius or ambition or idealism. The enemy is an egotism which, when carried to the extreme, annihilates all life around it and finally destroys itself.

While the main theme of the novel is the monstrous consequences of egotism, the counter-theme is the virtue of friendship. For, as Frankenstein's crime is seen as a sin against humankind more than against the heavens, it is through human sympathy, rather than divine grace, that it might have been avoided or redeemed. In her treatment of friendship, Mary shows the Coleridgean side of herself. She sees a friend as a balancing and completing agent, one who is sufficiently alike to be able to sympathize and understand, yet sufficiently different to be able to correct, and refine. Above all, the friend, in giving ear to one's dreams and sufferings, provides not only a temporary release from them, but the immediate excuse to order them by putting them into words.

The entire narrative of *Frankenstein* is in the form of three confessions to individuals with whom the speaker has unusually close ties. First, the young explorer Robert Walton writes to his sister in England as he journeys into the Arctic. There he rescues Frankenstein from a shipwreck and listens to his tale, which, in turn, contains a long narrative spoken by the monster to its creator. (pp. 164-67)

Each narrator speaks of the importance of friendship—Walton and the monster because they feel the lack of it, Frankenstein because he has had friends and lost them. In Walton's second letter to his sister, he reports that he has hired a ship and is ready to set sail on his dangerous journey. The one thing that troubles him is that, though he has a well-trained crew, he has no soul companion:

> I have one want which I have never yet been able to satisfy . . . I have no friend . . . When I am glowing with the enthusiasm of success, there will be none to participate in my joy; if I am assailed by disappointment, no one will endeavour to sustain me in dejection . . . I desire the company of a man who could sympathize with me; whose eyes would reply to mine. You may deem me romantic, my dear sister, but I bitterly feel the want of a friend. I have no one near me, gentle yet courageous, possessed of a cultivated as well as of a capacious mind, whose tastes are like my own, to approve or amend my plans. How would such a friend repair the faults of your poor brother!
>
> (pp. 167-68)

Frankenstein condescends to poor Walton even on the subject of friendship. It is too late for him to take up any new ties in

life, he explains, because no man could ever be more to him than Clerval was and no woman more than Elizabeth. (p. 168)

Mary was sufficiently her mother's daughter to assume that a woman, as easily as another man, could be the soul companion, the ideal friend, of a man. She did not regard sexual love as an impediment to ideal friendship, nor, it would seem, as a "small party" of the claims of true love. Elizabeth and Frankenstein almost always address one another as "dear friend," and she and Clerval simply complement different sides of Frankenstein's nature. If it were to come to a choice of one or the other, the novel leaves little doubt that the feminine companion is the more valuable since she can provide both spiritual sympathy and physical affection. It is a great and painful loss for Frankenstein when Clerval is killed, but the death of Elizabeth is the end of everything for him. He dedicates himself to the pursuit and destruction of the monster, follows him to "the everlasting ices of the north" where, surrounded by blankness and waste, he confronts the sterility and uselessness of his life. . . . (pp. 168-69)

An earlier scene of frozen desolation associated with isolation from human—especially feminine—companionship takes place between Frankenstein and the monster on a glacier at the base of Mont Blanc. The monster begs his maker to listen to him and proceeds to explain in detail how he has observed and imitated the ways of man, but is shunned because of his ugliness and is forced to wander over glaciers and hide in caves of ice because these are the only dwellings "man does not grudge." In other words, despite the bizarre details associated with his creation, the monster's lament is much the same as that of the physically presentable Caleb Williams: the world does not see him as he really is. His narrative is punctuated by outcries of loneliness:

> "Everywhere I see bliss, from which I alone am irrevocably excluded."
>
> "When I looked around, I saw and heard of none like me."
>
> "I had never yet seen a being resembling me, or who claimed any intercourse with me. What was I?"
>
> "I am an unfortunate and deserted creature . . . I have no relation or friend upon earth."

The repetition of this theme, with slight variations, continues throughout the monster's narrative. However ludicrous or grotesque it may seem in the concrete, it is nonetheless in keeping with one of the central arguments of the novel that the monster should ask Frankenstein to make him a wife. (pp. 169-70)

The irony of the situation, though heavy-handed, is effective. Having removed himself from human companionship and the sexual means of procreation, Frankenstein brings into being a creature who, though not innately evil, is a torment to himself and to others precisely because he is without companionship and a sexual counterpart. In this respect the monster may well be taken as Frankenstein's alter-ego, his strange and destructive self, which finds no adequate means of communicaton with others, no true resemblances, no reciprocation, a repressed and hidden beast for whom all acceptable forms of human commerce are unavailable and therefore hateful. Frankenstein himself calls the unnameable creature "my own spirit let loose from the grave . . . forced to destroy all that was dear to me."

Mary saw, as did her father, the duality in human nature which is capable of bringing misery and ruin to the most gifted of beings. Her novel is not so pessimistic as *Caleb Williams* nor are the solutions implied in it so optimistic as those outlined in *Political Justice*. Neither her father's trust in system nor her husband's unworldliness seemed satisfactory to her. On the contrary, judging from the events of her novel, both alternatives were too likely to lead to that single-mindedness which, when carried to the extreme, was a kind of insanity. It would seem, in fact, that of all the romantic influences on her mind and work, Shelley's undoubtedly stimulated, but Coleridge's comforted; Shelley's provided confusion and enchantment, Coleridge's provided psychological and moral consolation. The ethereal reveries of her hero are loyal attempts to imitate Shelley, but they are among the most strained and unconvincing passages of the novel. Mary's natural inclination was toward synthesis, integration, a constant effort to find balance, relationship, correspondence, to root all ideals in natural process, and to find in nature the external signs of an ideal region. Her heart is with those, described by Coleridge, "who measuring and sounding the rivers of the vale at the feet of their furthest inaccessible falls have learned, that the sources must be far higher and far inward." Despite his supposedly scientific approach to things, Frankenstein's error is to circumvent an elementary principle of nature in trying to achieve his rather vaguely conceived ambition.

In stressing friendship, and especially heterosexual love, as her "river of the vale," the natural symbol of a higher necessity, Mary presents her own concrete version of the theory of correspondence. We must give her more credit than to think that she supposed the problems of all men—including geniuses—would be solved by marriage to a good woman. What she does mean is that no being truly exists—except in an insane wilderness of its own creation—unless it finds and *accepts* a relationship of mutual dependence with another. The rapport with otherness is both the link with the objective world and the condition for self-delineation. (pp. 170-71)

Mary Shelley's definition of a monster is precisely that being to which nothing corresponds, the product of a genius who tried to exercise its will without reference to other beings. (p. 171)

Frankenstein's first act after creating a new life is to disown it. The problem is not, as in *Caleb Williams,* an ambiguous fascination leading to abuse and immediate and obsessive pursuit. As soon as his dream is realized in concrete form, Frankenstein wants nothing to do with it. Despite his claims to scientific interest, he demonstrates no wish whatever to observe and analyze the imperfect results of his experiment. When he does finally pursue the monster, it is not in order to possess, dominate, or torment it, but to annihilate it. Though there is something ludicrous in the way the monster stumbles upon books and learns to read during his lonely wandering, the thematic consistency of the episode is unmistakable. The monster is most impressed by *Paradise Lost;* he compares himself with Adam before the creation of Eve, but, like a good Romantic, he finds Satan an even "fitter emblem" of his condition. Still, neither emblems, nor words can really help or define him any more than ordinary men can. He can find parallels but no connections and he concludes his encounter with books by envying Satan like all the others, for even he "had his companions."

The two dominant themes of *Frankenstein* never truly harmonize, nor does one succeed effectively in canceling out the other. Surely, the most explicit "moral" theme of the novel—expressed by the author with genuine conviction—is that man discovers and fulfills himself through others and destroys himself alone. Yet played against this, not so much as an argument but as an assumption, is the idea that the genius, even in his failures, is unique, noble, and isolated from other men by divine right.

Frankenstein is neither a pure hymn of praise to Godwin and Shelley nor a simple repudiation of them. Mary's uncertainties are not reflected in parody or burlesque, as Beckford's and Lewis's are in *Vathek* and *The Monk*. Her prose style is solemn, inflated, and imitative, an unhappy combination of Godwin's sentence structure and Shelley's abstract vocabulary. Whatever else she may have thought, Mary obviously did not regard her father or husband as silly. Her reservations about them were deep, complex, and mixed with genuine admiration.

After Shelley's death, Mary considered how best to educate her son, and a friend advised that she teach him to think for himself. Mary is said to have answered, "Oh my God, teach him to think like other people!" If the young wife had been able to speak with the emphatic clarity of the widow, she probably would have had fewer nightmares and *Frankenstein* might never have been written. The book is a bad dream entwined with a moral essay. Like all romantic fiction, it resounds with the fascinating dissonance which usually results from intimate encounters between irrational symbols and reasonable statements. (pp. 171-73)

> Robert Kiely, "'Frankenstein': Mary Wollstonecraft Shelley," in his The Romantic Novel in England, Cambridge, Mass.: Harvard University Press, 1972, pp. 155-73.

ELLEN MOERS   (essay date 1974)

[*In a biographical interpretation of the maternal themes of* Frankenstein, *Moers asserts that the book was largely inspired by Shelley's intense feelings about and experiences of motherhood.*]

Mary Shelley's *Frankenstein,* in 1818, made over the Gothic novel into what today we call science fiction. *Frankenstein* brought a new sophistication to literary terror, and it did so without a heroine, without even an important female victim. Paradoxically, however, no other Gothic work by a woman writer, perhaps no other literary work of any kind by a woman, better repays examination in the light of the sex of its author. For *Frankenstein* is a birth myth, and one that was lodged in the novelist's imagination, I am convinced, by the fact that she was herself a mother.

Much in Mary Shelley's life was remarkable. . . . But nothing so sets her apart from the generality of writers of her own time, and before, and for long afterward, than her early and chaotic experience, at the very time she became an author, with motherhood. Pregnant at sixteen, and almost constantly pregnant throughout the following five years; yet not a secure mother, for she lost most of her babies soon after they were born; and not a lawful mother, for she was not married—not at least when, at the age of eighteen, Mary Godwin began to write *Frankenstein.* So are monsters born.

What in fact has the experience of giving birth to do with women's literature? In the eighteenth and nineteenth centuries very few important women writers, except for Mary Shelley, bore children; most of them, in England and America, were spinsters and virgins. With the coming of Naturalism late in the century, and the lifting of the Victorian taboo against writing about physical sexuality (including pregnancy and labor), the subject of birth was first brought to literature in realistic form by male novelists, from Tolstoy and Zola to William Carlos Williams. (pp. 24-5)

Mary Shelley was a unique case, in literature as in life. She brought birth to fiction not as realism but as Gothic fantasy, and thus contributed to Romanticism a myth of genuine originality. She invented the mad scientist who locks himself in his laboratory and secretly, guiltily, works at creating human life, only to find that he has made a monster. . . .

That is very good horror, but what follows is more horrid still: Frankenstein, the scientist, runs away and abandons the newborn monster, who is and remains nameless. Here, I think, is where Mary Shelley's book is most interesting, most powerful, and most feminine: in the motif of revulsion against newborn life, and the drama of guilt, dread, and flight surrounding birth and its consequences. Most of the novel, roughly two of its three volumes, can be said to deal with the retribution visited upon monster and creator for deficient infant care. *Frankenstein* seems to be distinctly a woman's mythmaking on the subject of birth precisely because its emphasis is not upon what precedes birth, not upon birth itself, but upon what follows birth: the trauma of the afterbirth.

Fear and guilt, depression and anxiety are commonplace reactions to the birth of a baby, and well within the normal range of experience. But more deeply rooted in our cultural mythology, and certainly in our literature, are the happy maternal reactions: ecstasy, a sense of fulfillment, and the rush of nourishing love which sweep over the new mother when she first holds her baby in her arms. . . .

[Mary Shelley] rejoiced at becoming a mother and loved and cherished her babies as long as they lived. But her journal is a chilly and laconic document, mostly concerned with the extraordinary reading program she put herself through at Shelley's side. Her own emphasis on books in the journal has set the tone of most of the discussion of the genesis of *Frankenstein.* (p. 25)

Mary Shelley herself was the first to point to her fortuitous immersion in the romantic and scientific revolutions of her day as the source of *Frankenstein*. Her extreme youth, as well as her sex, has contributed to the generally held opinion that she was not so much an author in her own right as a transparent medium through which passed the ideas of those around her. "All Mrs. Shelley did," writes Mario Praz, "was to provide a passive reflection of some of the wild fantasies which were living in the air about her."

Passive reflections, however, do not produce original works of literature, and *Frankenstein,* if not a great novel, was unquestionably an original one. The major Romantic and minor Gothic tradition to which it *should* have belonged was the literature of the overreacher: the superman who breaks through normal human limitations to defy the rules of society and infringe upon the realm of God. In the Faust story, hypertrophy of the individual will is symbolized by a pact with the devil. Byron's and Balzac's heroes; the rampaging monks of Mat Lewis and E.T.A. Hoffmann; the Wandering Jew and Melmoth the wanderer; the chained and unchained Prometheus: all are overreachers, all are punished by their own excesses—by a surfeit of sensation, of experience, of knowledge, and most typically, by the doom of eternal life.

But Mary Shelley's overreacher is different. Frankenstein's exploration of the forbidden boundaries of human science does not cause the prolongation and extension of his own life, but the creation of a new one. He defies mortality not by living forever, but by giving birth. That this original twist to an old myth should have been the work of a young woman who was also a young mother seems to me, after all, not a very surprising answer to the question that, according to Mary Shelley herself, was asked from the start: "How I, then a young girl, came to think of, and to dilate upon, so very hideous an idea?"

Birth is a hideous thing in *Frankenstein,* even before there is a monster. For Frankenstein's procedure, once he has determined to create new life, is to frequent the vaults and charnel houses and study the human corpse in all its loathsome stages of decay and decomposition. (p. 26)

It is in her journal and her letters that Mary Shelley reveals the workshop of her own creation, where she pieced together the materials for a new species of romantic mythology. They record a horror story of maternity such as literary biography hardly provides again until Sylvia Plath.

As far as I can figure out, she was pregnant, barely pregnant but aware of the fact, when at the age of sixteen she ran off with Shelley in July, 1814. Also pregnant at the same time was Shelley's legal wife Harriet, who gave birth in November to a "son and heir," as Mary noted in her journal. In February, 1815, Mary gave birth to a daughter, illegitimate, premature, and sickly. There is nothing in the journal about domestic help or a nurse in attendance. Mary notes that she breast fed the baby; that Fanny, her half-sister, came to call; that Mrs. Godwin, her stepmother, sent over some linen; that Claire Clairmont, Mrs. Godwin's daughter who had run off with Mary, kept Shelley amused. Bonaparte invaded France, the journal tells us, and Mary took up her incessant reading program: this time, Mme. de Staël's *Corinne*. The baby died in March. "Find my baby dead," Mary wrote. "A miserable day."

In April, 1815, she was pregnant again, about eight weeks after the birth of her first child. In January, 1816, she gave birth to a son: more breast feeding, more reading. In March, Claire Clairmont sought out Lord Byron and managed to get herself pregnant by him within a couple of weeks. This pregnancy would be a subject of embarrassment and strain to Mary and Shelley, and it immediately changed their lives, for Byron left England in April, and Claire, Shelley, Mary, and her infant pursued him to Switzerland in May. There is nothing yet in Mary's journal about a servant, but a good deal about mule travel in the mountains. In June they all settled near Byron on the shores of Lake Geneva.

In June, 1816, also, Mary began *Frankenstein.* And during the year of its writing the following events ran their swift and sinister course: In October, Fanny Imlay, Mary's half-sister, committed suicide after discovering that she was not Godwin's daughter but Mary Wollstonecraft's daughter by her American lover. . . . In early December Mary was pregnant again, which she seems to have sensed almost the day it happened. . . . In mid-December, Harriet Shelley drowned herself in the Serpentine, she was pregnant by someone other than Shelley. In late December Mary married Shelley. In January, 1817, Mary wrote Byron that Claire had borne him a daughter. In May she finished *Frankenstein*, published the following year.

Death and birth were thus as hideously mixed in the life of Mary Shelley as in Frankenstein's "workshop of filthy creation." Who can read without shuddering, and without remembering her myth of the birth of a nameless monster, Mary's journal entry of March 19, 1815, which records the trauma of her loss, when she was seventeen, of her first baby, the little girl who did not live long enough to be given a name. "Dream that my little baby came to life again," Mary wrote; "that it had only been cold, and that we rubbed it before the fire, and it lived. Awake and find no baby. I think about the little thing all day. Not in good spirits." (*"I thought, that if I could bestow animation upon lifeless matter, I might in process of time renew life where death had apparently devoted the body to corruption."*)

So little use has been made of this material by writers about *Frankenstein* that it may be worth emphasizing how important, because how unusual, was Mary Shelley's experience as a woman. The harum-scarum circumstances surrounding her maternity have no parallel until our own time, which in its naïve cerebrations upon family life (and in much else, except genius) resembles the generation of the Shelleys. Mary Godwin sailed into teenage motherhood without any of the financial or social or familial supports that made bearing and rearing children a relaxed experience for the normal middle-class woman of her day (as Jane Austen, for example, described her). She was an unwed mother, responsible for breaking up the marriage of a young woman just as much a mother as she. The father whom she adored broke furiously with her when she eloped; and Mary Wollstonecraft, the mother whose memory she revered, and whose books she was rereading throughout her teenage years, had died in childbirth—died giving birth to Mary herself.

Surely no outside influence need be sought to explain Mary Shelley's fantasy of the newborn as at once monstrous agent

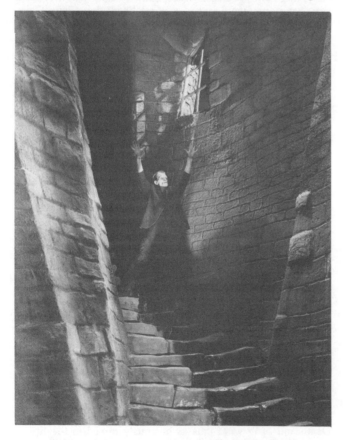

Boris Karloff as the monster, 1931. The Granger Collection, New York.

of destruction and piteous victim of parental abandonment. "I, the miserable and the abandoned," cries the monster at the end of *Frankenstein*, "I am an abortion to be spurned at, and kicked, and trampled on. . . . I have murdered the lovely and the helpless. . . . I have devoted my creator to misery; I have pursued him even to that irremediable ruin."

In the century and a half since its publication, *Frankenstein* has spawned innumerable interpretations among the critics, and among the novelists, playwrights, and filmmakers who have felt its influence. The idea, though not the name, of the robot originated with Mary Shelley's novel, and her title character became a byword for the dangers of scientific knowledge. But the work has also been read as an existential fable; as a commentary on the split between reason and feeling, in both philosophical thought and educational theory; as a parable of the excesses of idealism and genius; as a dramatization of the divided self; as an attack on the stultifying force of social convention.

The versatility of Mary Shelley's myth is due to the brilliance of her mind and the range of her learning, as well as to the influence of the circle in which she moved as a young writer. But *Frankenstein* was most original in its dramatization of dangerous oppositions through the struggle of a creator with monstrous creation. The sources of this Gothic conception, which still has power to "curdle the blood, and quicken the beatings of the heart," were surely the anxieties of a woman who, as daughter, mistress, and mother, was a bearer of death. (pp. 26-8)

Mary Shelley came honestly to grips with the dilemma of a newly created human being, a giant adult male in shape, who must swiftly recapitulate, and without the assistance of his terrified parent, the infantile and adolescent stages of human development. She even faces squarely the monster's sexual needs, for the denouement of the story hangs on his demand that Frankenstein create a female monster partner, and Frankenstein's refusal to do so.

But more than mundane is Mary Shelley's concern with the emotions surrounding the parent-child and child-parent relationship. Here her intention to underline the birth myth in *Frankenstein* becomes most evident, quite apart from biographical evidence about its author. She provides an unusual thickening of the background of the tale with familial fact and fantasy, from the very opening of the story in the letters a brother addresses to his sister of whom he is excessively fond, because they are both orphans. There is Frankenstein's relationship to his doting parents, and his semi-incestuous love for an abandoned orphan girl brought up as his sister. There is the first of the monster's murder victims, Frankenstein's infant brother (precisely drawn, even to his name, after Mary Shelley's baby); and the innocent young girl wrongly executed for the infant's murder, who is also a victim of what Mary Shelley calls that "strange perversity," a mother's hatred. (Justine accepts guilt with docility: "I almost began to think that I was the monster that my confessor said I was. . . .") The abundant material in *Frankenstein* about the abnormal, or monstrous, manifestations of the child-parent tie justifies as much as does its famous monster Mary Shelley's reference to the novel as "my hideous progeny."

What Mary Shelley actually did in *Frankenstein* was to transform the standard Romantic matter of incest, infanticide, and patricide into a phantasmagoria of the nursery. (p. 28)

Ellen Moers, "Female Gothic: The Monster's Mother," in The New York Review of Books, *Vol. XXI, No. 4, March 21, 1974, pp. 24-8.*

JAMES RIEGER (essay date 1974)

[*In his introduction to an edition of* Frankenstein, *Rieger disputes the notion that the novel is either Gothic romance or early science fiction and discusses it as an example of mythic fiction.*]

The complexity of *Frankenstein* becomes apparent as soon as one tries to classify it. The difficulty is the author's rich eclecticism, together with the stylistic inconsistencies and narrative absurdities that are, perhaps, the inescapable converse of that eclecticism. Mary Shelley works so many veins at once that impatient readers have tended to falsify her book by filing it away as late Gothic romance, for example, or early science fiction. Before trying to determine what *Frankenstein* is, let us see what it is not. (pp. xxiv-xxv)

[Gothic romance] shares certain elements with *Frankenstein,* most noticeably an awareness of the deathly and nihilistic components of lust. The reader never learns whether Radcliffe's dark, brooding, and very sexy villains would prefer to rape her heroines or to murder them. Similarly, Frankenstein thinks he is affirming the life force by transfusing it into the stitched-together fragments of various corpses. But the disgusting and homicidal botch that results is a nightmare image, the surface manifestation of the unseen motives that underlie the scientist's "curiosity." It is symbolically appropriate that the monstrous miscreation should cancel the possibility of natural procreation, that he should "be with you on your wedding-night" . . . to break the neck of his maker's bride. The Gothic and Shelleyan perception of the destructive side of sexuality has contemporary analogues in Byron's tragedies and verse romances and in the novels of de Sade.

The Gothic romancers aimed at a middle-class, Protestant, largely female audience, whose education barely extended beyond simple literacy. They exploited the prejudices of this audience against the Catholic south of Europe, which had been feared for centuries as the homeland of Macchiavelli, the Borgia Popes, and Philip of Spain—the source, then, of political trickery, ecclesiastical corruption, poison, and Armadas, together with what we now call polymorphous perversity. Mary Shelley turned this convention around. The lecherous, treacherous Italians and Spaniards depicted by Radcliffe and Lewis yield to Frankenstein's fiancée, Elizabeth Lavenza. In the third edition, Elizabeth's Italy stands for emotional warmth, and her birthplace is the destination of the aborted wedding trip. Conversely, the northward journeys of the two self-proclaimed rationalists, Walton and Frankenstein, are voyages into coldness, darkness, and delusion, though each traveler in his way expects to discover "light" and the innermost secret of life.

Finally, Frankenstein's interest in the occult and the quasi-magical powers he gains through the study of chemistry resemble the diabolical alliances contracted by some Gothic villains and the energy acquired by others through their association with the mystique of Roman Catholic ritual. Lewis's Ambrosio and Radcliffe's Schedoni have taken holy orders, and Frankenstein has enrolled for a degree. The anticlericalism of *The Monk* and *The Italian* and the anti-intellectualism of *Frankenstein* both stem from earlier treatments of the Faust legend, whose central figure has degrees in everything from medicine to theology.

Despite these affinities, *Frankenstein* departs from the Gothic tradition as obviously as it follows it. As its name implies, Gothicism depends on spatial and temporal exoticism. The era is vaguely and unconvincingly medieval in most cases, and the scenery is cultivated, second-hand, "picturesque." Radcliffe's scenic effects, for instance, are explicitly painterly. Mary Shelley's Arctic wastes have a starkness rarely risked by the Gothic romancers, even when they varied picturesqueness with sublimity. And her other major landscapes were drawn from first-hand observation. The symbolism of light and coldness which permeates the description of the Arve glacier, the narrative setting of the second volume, is perhaps obtrusive. Nevertheless, the author had been there with Shelley in July 1816. The scene is concrete and clear, whatever its metaphorical tendency. Above all, it is immediate.

The realistic principle extends to the social context. The center of the novel's centrifugal action is the "republic" of Geneva during the decade of the French Revolution. The Frankensteins are enlightened bourgeois in the birthplace of Rousseau, a city no longer ruled by the theocracy of Calvin. . . . Unlike the rest of Europe in the 1790s, Geneva had neither bishops nor a king. It is upon this emancipated city and its progressive inhabitants—the Frankensteins and the Clervals—that the demonic legacy of the Middle Ages obtrudes in scientific guise. The reversal of the Gothic strategy could not be more complete.

Mary Shelley shared her husband's fascination with the natural sciences. In the 1830s, . . . she would contribute scientific biographies to Lardner's *Cabinet Cyclopedia,* and in her futuristic novel, *The Last Man,* she invented a flying machine. Still, it would be a mistake to call *Frankenstein* a pioneer work of science fiction. Its author knew something of Sir Humphry Davy's chemistry, Erasmus Darwin's botany, and, perhaps, Galvani's physics, but little of this got into her book. Frankenstein's chemistry is switched-on magic, souped-up alchemy, the electrification of Agrippa and Paracelsus. Things simply unknown or undone do not engage his attention; he wants the *forbidden* unknown and undone. He is a criminal magician who employs up-to-date tools. Moreover, the technological plausibility that is essential to science fiction is not even pretended at here. The science-fiction writer says, in effect, since x has been experimentally proven or theoretically postulated, y can be achieved by the following, carefully documented operation. Mary Shelley skips to the outcome and asks, if y had been achieved, by whatever means, what would be the moral consequences? In other words, she skips the science. The terms of her basic question (if that were her only question) would place *Frankenstein* with works that follow the same logic with regard, say, to eternal life or eternal youth: the Struldbrug episode in *Gulliver's Travels,* Godwin's *St. Leon,* Mary Shelley's own **"The Mortal Immortal"** (1834), Tennyson's "Tithonus," and Wilde's *The Picture of Dorian Gray.* (pp. xxv-xxviii)

Like Rousseau and Godwin before her, Mary stresses the role of education in the liberation or enslavement of the personality. She apparently agrees with Locke that the mind is a blank slate at birth, and with the sceptics that sensory evidence can mislead the moral judgment. But *Frankenstein* does not survive as a "novel with a thesis." Rather it comes through to us, in Northrop Frye's words, as "a precursor . . . of the existential thriller, of such a book as Camus's *L'Etranger.*" Its three concentric narrators, geographically, intellectually, and erotically cut off from the rest of mankind, deal with the world by means of a secret: the explorer's "secret of the magnet," the researcher's galvanic secret of life, and the Monster's pure embodiment of these secrets, together with his unique knowledge of what it is like to be born free of history. Each secret reflects the others, or rather, each is an aspect of what Shelley in "Mont Blanc" calls "The secret Strength of things / Which governs thought, and to the infinite dome / Of Heaven is as a law. . . ." By the same token, each narrator finds a mirror-image of himself in one of the others: Walton knows that once he could have possessed Frankenstein as "the brother of my heart," . . . and Frankenstein and the Monster know that their master-slave relationship, in which the balance of power constantly shifts, parodies the love existing between father and son. The attempt to kiss the mirror is thwarted always by the illicit possession of the secret, which withers the heart and condemns its owner to emotional isolation. As Frankenstein puts it, "If the study to which you apply yourself has a tendency to weaken your affections, and to destroy your taste for those simple pleasures in which no alloy can possibly mix, then that study is certainly unlawful, that is to say, not befitting the human mind." . . . (p. xxx)

The moral is Godwinian, as is the imaginative pattern that gives it flesh. Caleb Williams's actions are determined by a ruinous secret, and St. Leon possesses the elixir of life, which destroys him and all around him. Caleb's stricken conscience mirrors Falkland's, and St. Leon's aging mind is at war with his eternally youthful body. As well as foreshadowing the existential hero, Mary Shelley's and Godwin's characters have American cousins in the obsessed and claustrophobic heroes of Brockden Brown, Poe, Hawthorne, and Melville. Brockden Brown acknowledged his debt to Godwin, and it is not fortuitous that Melville read *Frankenstein* in 1849, two years before he published his own tale of a single-minded voyager, Ahab, chasing "round the Norway Maelstrom, and round perdition's flames" his own monstrous secret, "the monomaniac incarnation of all those malicious agencies which some deep men feel eating in them."

All such fiction is mythic, in the same sense that Blake's Prophetic Books and Shelley's *Prometheus Unbound* are myth-poetry. Blake's symbolic personages are fragments of a single, shattered psyche, and the cosmic struggle in Shelley's lyrical drama employs "imagery . . . drawn from the operation of the human mind, or from those external actions by which they are expressed." Psychomachia and theomachia are metaphors of each other, which is to say that the internecine warfare of the gods cannot be distinguished from the mental chaos of their victim and creator. Romantic myth-fiction replaces the fratricidal gods with *Frankenstein*'s ambiguous, magnetic, devouring secret, as later with Melville's "intangible malignity which has been from the beginning." The whiteness of Moby Dick, like that of Mary Shelley's Mont Blanc and Arctic ice-cap, "shadows forth the heartless voids and immensities of the universe . . . a colorless, all-color of atheism from which we shrink." (pp. xxx-xxxi)

> *James Rieger, in an introduction to* Frankenstein; or, The Modern Prometheus: The 1818 Text *by Mary Wollstonecraft Shelley, edited by James Rieger, 1974. Reprint by The University of Chicago Press, 1982, pp. xi-xxxvii.*

GEORGE LEVINE (essay date 1979)

[*An American editor and critic, Levine coedited* The Endurance of "Frankenstein," *the collection of essays from which the following excerpt is drawn. Here, he cites seven of the major im-*plications of the Frankenstein metaphor in contemporary consciousness and outlines their sources in the novel.]

[While] *Frankenstein* is a phenomenon of popular culture, it is so because it has tapped into the center of Western feeling and imagination: we can hear echoes of it, not only in Gothic fiction, science fiction, and fantasies of all sorts, but in far more "respectable" works, written before the glut of popular cinematic distortions. *Frankenstein* has become a metaphor for our own cultural crises, and survives even yet in high literary culture whose professors may have seen Boris Karloff stumbling through the fog, hands outstretched, at least once too often.

Of course, *Frankenstein* is a "minor" novel, radically flawed by its sensationalism, by the inflexibly public and oratorical nature of even its most intimate passages. But it is, arguably, the most important minor novel in English. If we return to the text for a check on Boris Karloff, or, recently, Mel Brooks, or for some further light on Percy Shelley, invariably we find that the book is larger and richer than any of its progeny and too complex to serve as mere background. Even in our dictionaries, "Frankenstein" has become a vital metaphor, peculiarly appropriate to a culture dominated by a consumer technology, neurotically obsessed with "getting in touch" with its authentic self and frightened at what it is discovering: "a work, or agency that proves troublesomely uncontrollable, esp. to its creator." Latent in the metaphor are some of the fundamental dualisms, the social, moral, political and metaphysical crises of Western history since the French Revolution. It may well appear that the metaphorical implications are far more serious than the novel that gave birth to them, but that novel has qualities that allow it to exfoliate as creatively and endlessly as any important myth; if it threatens to lapse into banality and bathos, it yet lives through unforgettable dreamlike images. . . . (pp. 3-4)

Frankenstein's mysterious power derives from a thoroughly earthy, practical, and unideal vision of human nature and possibility. Its modernity lies in its transformation of fantasy and traditional Christian and pagan myths into unremitting secularity, into the myth of mankind as it must work within the limits of the visible, physical world. The novel echoes, for example, with the language and the narrative of *Paradise Lost,* but it is *Paradise Lost* without angels, or devils, or God. . . . The whole narrative of *Frankenstein* is, indeed, acted out in the absence of God. The grand gestures of *Frankenstein* may suggest a world of fantasy that has acquired a profound escapist appeal in modern culture, but they take place in a framework that necessarily makes an ironic commentary on them, even while our sympathies are drawn to dreams of the more than human the narrative will not allow.

This characteristic tension between an impinging, conditional, and time-bound world and a dream of something freer and better makes the central subject matter and form of the nineteenth-century novel and, ironically, of nineteenth-century science as well. The old myths enter nineteenth-century fiction, but they do so in the mode of realism. . . . [Though] it would be absurd to claim Mary Shelley as a direct "influence" on the dominant literary and scientific forms of the century, we can see that in her secularization of the creation myth she invented a metaphor that was irresistible to the culture as a whole. As George Eliot turned to Feuerbach to allow her to transform Christianity into a humanism with all the emotional power of religion, so the novel itself, as a genre, put its faith in a material world of fact that, as Matthew Arnold pointed out, had failed us. In writers as central and various as Feuerbach, Comte, Darwin, Marx, Frazer, and Freud we can find Victor Frankenstein's activity: the attempt to discover in matter what we had previously attributed to spirit, the bestowing *on* matter (or history, or society, or nature) the values once given to God.

This argument puts Mary Shelley in some rather remarkable company, but, of course, the point is not to equate the achievement of her little "ghost story" with that of the great thinkers named. The claim is simply that Mary Shelley did, indeed, create an image, with the authenticity of dream vision, that became prophetic; that the image articulates powerfully the dominant currents of her culture and ours; and that it is for these reasons that *Frankenstein* has survived its own adolescent clumsiness and its later distortions.

The pervasiveness of the Frankenstein metaphor in modern consciousness testifies to the richness and variousness of its implications. The dictionary definition focuses only on the uncontrollable nature of the thing created; but the image of the created Monster, emerging from the isolated workshop of the obsessed but otherwise gentle scientist, unfolds into more possibilities than I can describe.... At the risk of arbitrary exclusions and of belaboring what may seem obvious, I want to outline some of the major implications of the Frankenstein metaphor in contemporary consciousness, and as they have their sources in the novel proper.

1. *Birth and Creation*. In *Frankenstein* we are confronted immediately by the displacement of God and woman from the acts of conception and birth. Where Victor imagines himself embarked on the creation of a new race that would bless him, he behaves, even before his creation proves a monster, as though he is engaged in unnatural, shameful activity. Neither of the two attitudes is entirely undercut by the narrative, even though the dream of the new race is, of course, exploded. The image of Frankenstein in his laboratory is not only of an unnatural act, but also one of an heroic dream, and the novel's insistence, even through Walton and the Monster, on Victor's heroic nature, implies that the creation without God, without woman, need not be taken as an unequivocal evil.

The displacement of woman obviously reflects a fear of birth and Mary Shelley's own ambivalence about childbearing ...; the Monster's presence on the wedding night becomes a permanent image of the horror of sexuality as opposed to the ideal and nonsexual love of the cousins, Victor and Elizabeth. The image of the Monster lurking ominously in the background, with Elizabeth sprawled on the bed, is one of the dominant icons of the film versions. Obviously, the image is profoundly phallic and profoundly violent, an unacceptable alternative to and consequence of the act of conception in the laboratory. Indeed, in the novel itself ... the two scenes precisely echo each other. In both cases, there is an association that runs as constant ground-motif through the novel.

Sexuality and birth, imagination and creation are, in this heavily material world, reverse images of death and destruction. Frankenstein and his creature come to represent, in part, an alternative to the violence of sexuality, on the one hand, and to the sheer spirituality of divine creation, on the other. (pp. 6-9)

2. *The Overreacher*. The aspiration to divine creative activity (akin to Romantic notions of the poet) places Victor Frankenstein in the tradition of Faustian overreachers. Frankenstein the creator is also Frankenstein the modern Prometheus, full of the great Romantic dream—concretized for a moment in the French Revolution—of a rebirth of mankind. True, Victor is seeking a kind of immortality, but, as Ellen Moers points out [see excerpt dated 1974], Mary Shelley works the Faust tradition in an unusual (and, I might again add, secularizing) way by having Victor seek immortality not directly for himself but in the creation of offspring. If we detect the stirrings of selfishness in Victor's desire to have a whole species that would bless him, the text still insists on the profundity of his moral character and the conscious morality of all of his choices save the fatal one. Indeed ..., Frankenstein is removed from direct personal responsibility even for his own ambitions: for the most part he is described as passively consumed by energies larger than himself or as quite literally unconscious and ill when his being conscious might have changed the course of the narrative.

The theme of the overreacher is largely complicated by the evidence that Victor's worst sin is not the creation of the Monster but his refusal to take responsibility for it. It is as though God had withdrawn from his creation. Characteristically, in the secularizing myth, Mary Shelley has imagined the responsibilities of God shifted to mankind. The burden is too great to allow us an easy moral placing of Victor. The theme of the overreacher in this context brings us to the kind of impasse that *Frankenstein* itself reaches in the mutual destruction of creator and created. That is, we see that the ambition is heroic and admirable, yet deadly because humans are incapable of fulfilling their dreams in material reality, or, paradoxically, of bearing the responsibility for them should they succeed. (pp. 9-10)

3. *Rebellion and Moral Isolation*. Obviously, these aspects of the myth are related to "overreaching." Yet it is important to note that they apply not only to Victor but to the Monster as well, whose ambition is really limited to the longing for domestic affection. Victor himself is not quite imagined as a rebel, except perhaps in his pursuit of alchemical knowledge after his father ridicules him for reading Paracelsus. In any case, unlike the Monster, he does not consciously rebel against authority. Yet, "animated by an almost supernatural enthusiasm," Victor takes up an intellectual pursuit (whence did the "principle of life proceed") that places him outside the traditional Christian world, and that ought to make him, like Adam eating the apple, a rebel against God. The context, however, is quietly un-Christian. Victor speaks in a scientific or at least naturalistic language that assumes a natural material answer to what was once a religious and metaphysical question. (pp. 10-11)

The moral isolation into which Victor sinks is, in effect, chosen for him by his obsession. Like Raskolnikov plotting murder, like Dimmesdale guilty of adultery, Victor lives with a secret that we understand, must be kept from public knowledge. Here the residue of metaphysical shame works its effects, but social and psychological explanations offer themselves immediately. In any case, the activity separates Victor from normal life as fully as a direct act of murder would. (p. 11)

The Monster's isolation derives not so much from his actions as from his hideousness. Where Victor moves from domestic bliss to the garret, the Monster leaves the garret to seek that bliss. Victor's revolutionary action causes his isolation; the Monster's isolation causes his revolutionary action. "Believe me, Frankenstein," he says, "I was benevolent; my soul glowed with love and humanity; but am I not alone, miserably alone?" (pp. 11-12)

Despite the apparent moral simplicity of most modern versions of *Frankenstein,* the Frankenstein metaphor implies great ambiguity about where the burden of good and evil rests. Both Victor and the Monster imply resistance to the established order. . . . In early Romantic literature, of course, rebellion is more likely to be a virtue than a sin, and the Monster makes a strong case against social injustice. Even Walton, though warned by Victor, is instinctively convinced of the justice of the Monster's arguments.

The constantly shifting moral perspective of the narrative results from the fact that each of its major figures—Walton, Victor, the Monster—is at once victimizer and victim; and this tradition is even continued in modern movie versions. In novel and films, any singularity is punished by the community, either by forcing isolation or by literal imprisonment. The three major figures and Felix De Lacey variously challenge the established order and acquire dignity by virtue of the challenge and of the punishment that ensues. Thus the novel, which might be taken as a parable of the necessity of limits in an entirely secular world, may also be taken as a parable of the necessity for revolutionary reprisal (at whatever cost) because of the social and political limits that frustrate the noblest elements of the human spirit.

4. *The Unjust Society.* After the execution of the innocent Justine, Elizabeth Lavenza, the vessel of domestic purity, tells Victor that "men appear to me as monsters thirsting for each other's blood." . . . Even if she retracts immediately ("Yet I am certainly unjust"), the notion that the world of men is itself "monstrous" is a constant motif of the novel. Even in the most conventional of the modern Frankenstein films, the motif emerges when, in the obligatory misty night, the villagers turn out as a maddened lynch mob and transform Frankenstein and the Monster into victims of an overwhelming attack on the castle. In almost every film, the townspeople are almost comically banal, the burgomeisters and gendarmerie officious and totally without sensibility. Absurd though these figures may be . . . , they echo the essentially shallow ambitions and dreams of security that fill the background of the novel.

There the motif is handled subtly enough to make the monstrous problematic. Elizabeth's sense that "men are monsters" recurs in the monster's ingenious hectoring of Victor in a fine Godwinian rational discourse. Moreover, the De Lacey story is a continuing narrative of injustice, on all sides. And in his last speech to Walton, the Monster makes clear once more that his own monstrousness is not really different from that of the world that condemns him. . . . The novel has taught us to distrust the evenhandedness of the law that Victor's father praises before Justine is executed; we understand with the Monster that greed is a commonplace of social activity. Not even the family unit—Frankenstein's and the Monster's ideal—escapes the contamination that almost makes rebellion necessary and that makes Victor's escape to his laboratory from Geneva seem psychologically and socially explicable.

5. *The Defects of Domesticity.* The theme of the overreacher and the rebel—the Promethean theme—is the other side of the theme of ideal domesticity. . . . Mary Shelley treats "domestic affection" in such a way as to make it possible to read *Frankenstein* as an attack on the very traditions of bourgeois society it purports to be celebrating. Certainly, as we have seen, "the amiableness of domestic affection" does nothing to satisfy Victor Frankenstein's ambitions, or to prevent the monstrous creation; nor, in the tale of the Monster's wanderings, does it extend to anything outside itself to allow for the domestication

of the Monster's loving energies. "Domestic affection" is, in a way, defined by its exclusion of energy and by its resistance to the larger community. The Monster instinctively believes in the rhetoric of domesticity and the need for community; it is psychologically and dramatically appropriate that he should exhaust himself in the total destruction of ostensibly ideal domesticity when he discovers that he is excluded from it, and that the ideal is false. (pp. 13-14)

6. *The Double.* Almost every critic of *Frankenstein* has noted that Victor and his Monster are doubles. The doubleness even enters some of the popular versions and is un-self-consciously accepted by everyone who casually calls the Monster "Frankenstein." The motif of the *Doppelgänger* was certainly in Mary's mind during the writing, as it was a part of the Gothic tradition in which she wrote; moreover, it is one with which she would have been intimately connected through Shelley himself, as in "Alastor" and "Epipsychidion." So pervasive has been the recognition that the Monster and Frankenstein are two aspects of the same being that the writers in this volume assume rather than argue it. The narrative requires us to see that the doubling extends beyond the two major narrators: Walton is obviously another aspect of Frankenstein, and Clerval yet another; Elizabeth can be paired with Victor's mother, with Justine, and with the unfinished "bride" of the Monster. . . . Such doublings and triplings, with reverberations in and out of the novel in Mary Shelley's own life and in modern psychological theory, suggest again the instability and ambivalence of the book's "meanings."

They point centrally to the way "Frankenstein" as a modern metaphor implies a conception of the divided self, the creator and his work at odds. The civilized man or woman contains within the self a monstrous, destructive, and self-destructive energy. The angel in the house entails a demon outside it, the Monster leering through the window at the horrified Victor and the murdered Elizabeth. Here, in particular, we can watch the specially secularized versions of traditional mythology. The devil and the angel of the morality play are replaced by a modern pre-Freudian psychology that removes the moral issue from the metaphysical context—the traditional concepts of good and evil—and places it entirely within the self. Morality is, as it were, replaced by schizophrenia. Frankenstein's longing for domesticity is echoed in the Monster's (and in Walton's expression of loneliness in the opening pages); Frankenstein's obsession with science is echoed in the Monster's obsession with destruction. The two characters haunt and hunt each other through the novel, each evoking from us sympathy for their sufferings, revulsion from their cruelties.

The echoes force themselves on us with a persistence and intensity that override the mere narrative and even enter into popular versions that are not intrinsically concerned with doubling. The book creates a psychomachia, an internal war that has its own authenticity despite the grotesqueness of the external action. If the characters seem shallow as novelistic figures within the conventions of realism we have come to assume are natural to nineteenth-century fiction, it is partly because they are imagined from the start as incomplete (a notion explored in Peter Brook's essay [see excerpt dated 1979]). They can be seen, indeed, as fragments of a mind in conflict with itself, extremes unreconciled, striving to make themselves whole. Ambition and passivity, hate and love, the need to procreate and the need to destroy are seen, in *Frankenstein,* as symbiotic: the destruction of one is, through various narrative strategies, the destruction of the other.

7. *Technology, Entropy, and the Monstrous.* Perhaps the most obvious and continuing application of the word "Frankenstein" in modern society is to technological advances. This is altogether appropriate to Mary Shelley's original conception of the novel since Victor's discovery of the secret of life is fundamentally scientific; and he talks of his "animation" of the Monster's body as a mere trick of technology. Modern science fiction and modern industry are full of such "animated" beings, the products of computer technology; with the discovery of DNA, biologists even seem on the verge of simulating the natural process of creation of life. But both of these developments are part of the same imagination as Mary Shelley gives us with her Monster: that life is not "spirit" but matter imbued with energy, itself another form of matter.

Martin Tropp has noted that "when Mary Shelley gave her intended 'ghost story' a scientific context, she linked the Gothic concept of the double with technology" [see Additional Bibliography]. Her fears of the creation of life by mere mechanisms, Tropp notes, resulted from her awareness that "technology can never be more than a magnified image of the self." . . . And when that self is engaged in a psychomachia, the result can only be large-scale disaster. In a psychic world of the divided self, in a social world in which domesticity and ambition are seen as incompatible poles, the self expressed in technology can only be what our original dictionary definition tells us, "troublesomely uncontrollable, esp. to its creator," i.e., monstrous. The nightmare quality of the novel depends on this projection of the self into an objectively existing, independent reality over which one necessarily loses control as it acts out one's own monstrous passions. Here all the battery of Freudian equipment comes neatly or, perhaps, explosively into play. All the elements of moral isolation, the grubbing in filthy flesh, the obsessed and inhuman energies that went into the creation of the Monster, can be seen acting themselves out in the destruction they really imply—in the incestuous destructiveness of Victor's ostensibly ideal relation to Elizabeth, in the fraternal hostility buried in his love for poor William, in the hatred of his mother implied in his failure to save Justine (who has adopted Mrs. Frankenstein's very way of life). Such implications are explored in a great deal of criticism of the novel. But the point here is that technology becomes the means by which these buried aspects of the self are enacted. The "work or agency" does not rebel against the creator but actually accomplishes what the creator wants. . . . The uncontrolled technological creation is particularly frightening and obsessively attractive to modern consciousness because it forces a confrontation with our buried selves. It promises to reveal to us our deepest and most powerful desires, and to enact them. The Monster demands our sympathetic engagement while our social consciousness must by an act of will—almost like Walton's when he finds himself irresistibly attracted by the Monster's talk—reject him.

The duality of our relationship to creator and creature is an echo of our relationship to the technology that we worship even as we recognize that it is close to destroying us. Another way to express the duality, in technological terms, is through the idea of entropy. Victor's overreaching is an attempt to create *new* life. He fails to recognize the necessary secular-scientific myth of entropy: that in any closed system, the new energy generated will be less than the energy expended in its creation, and that ultimately the system will run down. It took a great deal of death to make the new life; the making of the Monster is at the expense of all of Victor's immediate world—brother, father, bride, friend. The world of mere matter is both finite

Frankenstein's monster observing the creation of his mate. Illustration by Nino Carbe from the 1932 edition of Frankenstein, *published by World Publishing Company.*

and corrupted. Without the incalculable presence of divine spirit, creation can only entail destruction larger than itself. It is, ultimately, this nightmare image that the Monster represents to our culture. (pp. 15-17)

> George Levine, *"The Ambiguous Heritage of 'Frankenstein',"* in The Endurance of Frankenstein: Essays on Mary Shelley's Novel, *edited by George Levine and U. C. Knoepflmacher, University of California Press, 1979, pp. 3-30.*

PETER BROOKS   (essay date 1979)

[*Brooks analyzes the significance of language in* Frankenstein, *focusing on its importance to the Monster.*]

Mary Shelley's **Frankenstein** continues to solicit and disturb us not only through its creation of a decisive image of Gothic horror, but also by the pathos of a monsterism in doomed dialectic with nature and with culture. It is above all in the question of language, both as explicit theme of the novel and as implicit model of the novel's complex organization, that the problem of the monstrous is played out. We might approach the network of issues dramatized in the novel first through Victor Frankenstein's crucial interview with his monstrous creation, the interview which leads to the Monster's telling his tale to Frankenstein, the story-within-a-story (itself a story-within-a-story, when we consider the role of Robert Walton as initial and ultimate narrator). Following the first murders committed by his Monster—William strangled, Justine judicially done to death through maliciously falsified evidence—Frankenstein seeks solace in the mountains above Chamonix. He penetrates into the "glorious presence-chamber of imperial Nature," climbs to Montanvert and the Mer de Glace, hoping to recapture a remembered effect of "a sublime ecstasy that gave wings to the soul, and allowed it to soar from the obscure world to light and joy." His ascension takes him to a "wonderful and stupendous scene," overlooking the Mer de Glace, facing the "awful majesty" of Mont Blanc; his heart once again opens to joy and he exclaims, in the tones of the Ossianic bard, ''Wandering spirits, if indeed ye wander, and do not rest in your narrow beds; allow me this faint happiness, or take me, as your companion, away from the joys of life.'' . . . Whereupon a superhuman shape comes bounding over the ice. It is, of course, no spirit of the departed, nor any beneficient spirit of nature, but the Monster himself, who has at last tracked down his creator, and will force him into parley. (pp. 205-06)

Frankenstein's initial reaction to the encounter with the Monster consists in curses and an abortive attempt to do battle with him. Still the Monster pleads for a hearing. A hearing that need not be a seeing: when Frankenstein commands, ''Begone! relieve me from the sight of your detested form,'' the Monster responds by placing his huge hands over Frankenstein's eyes: ''Thus I relieve thee, my creator . . . thus I take from thee a sight which you abhor. Still thou canst listen to me, and grant me thy compassion.'' . . . The Monster understands that it is not visual relationship that favors him—indeed, his only favorable reception by a human being has come from a blind man—but rather the auditory, the interlocutory, the relationship of language.

For the Monster is eloquent. From his first words, he shows himself to be a supreme rhetorician of his own situation, one who controls the antitheses and oxymorons that express the pathos of his existence: ''Remember, that I am thy creature; I ought to be thy Adam; but I am rather the fallen angel, whom thou drivest from joy for no misdeed. Everywhere I see bliss, from which I alone am irrevocably excluded. I was benevolent and good; misery made me a fiend. Make me happy, and I shall again be virtuous.'' . . . When we learn of the Monster's self-education—and particularly his three master-texts: *Paradise Lost,* Plutarch's *Lives,* and *Werther*—we understand the sources of his eloquence, and of the conception of a just order of things that animates his plea to his creator. But it is of primary importance to register Mary Shelley's radical and saving decision to stage a deformed and menacing creature who, rather than using grunts and gestures, speaks and reasons with the highest elegance, logic, and persuasiveness. In the Monster's use of language the novel poses its most important questions, for it is language alone that may compensate for a deficient, monstrous nature.

Frankenstein is touched by the Monster's eloquence. When he looks at this ''filthy mass that moved and talked,'' he feels horror and hatred; yet by the end of the Monster's tale he avows: ''His words had a strange effect upon me. I compassionated him.'' . . . Through the medium of language, a first relationship is created. Like Coleridge's Wedding Guest, Frankenstein is compelled to hear out the tale of this cursed being. The force of the compulsion here is no ''glittering eye,'' but the power of language itself to link speaker and listener. (pp. 206-07)

The Monster hence produces a tale, based, like any tale, on the ''narrative contract'' between narrator and narratee. Its very possibility depends on an order of cultural symbolic which implies that network of intersubjective relations from which the Monster protests he has been excluded. The close of his narrative suggests the importance of language as relation. In arguing that Frankenstein create a female monster to be a companion to him, the Monster asserts that only in communication with a similar being can he ''become linked to the chain of existence and events, from which I am now excluded.'' . . . The wish for a *semblable* may itself belong to the imaginary order, as an instance of speculary narcissism and deception. The term *chain,* however, identifies meaning as residing in a

systematic network of relation, in the symbolic order. . . . Exclusion from this chain could be the very definition of monsterism. (p. 208)

Language is also the principal theme of the Monster's story of his life up to this point. His first experience with humankind has laid bare the hopelessness of speculary relationship, its necessary result in alienation and rejection: the shepherd he encounters in a hut flees shrieking from his sight. Retreating into the hovel adjoining the de Lacey cottage, he then begins his education, seeing, but himself unseen. From his hiding place, he discovers that ''these people possessed a method of communicating their experience and feelings to one another by articulate sounds. What particularly impress him are the emotional effects wrought by these sounds, which ''sometimes produced pleasure or pain, smiles or sadness, in the minds and countenances of the beholders. This was indeed a godlike science.''

Mary Shelley's Monster is in many respects an Enlightenment natural man, or noble savage; his first ideas demonstrate the processes of Lockean sensationalism and Hartleyan associationism. His discovery of language implies Rousseau's argument, in the *Essai sur l'origine des langues,* that language springs from passion rather than need: need cannot form the necessary social context for voiced language, since its effect is to scatter men; and need can make do with the barest repertory of visual signs, gestures, imperatives. Passion, on the other hand, brings men together, and the relation of desire calls forth voice. It is hence no accident that what language first reveals to the Monster is human love, and that his rhetorical plea to his creator ends with the demand for a creature whom he might love. (pp. 208-09)

The Monster intuitively grasps that language will be of importance to him because by its very nature it implies the ''chain of existence and events'' within which he seeks a place, defines the interdependency of senders and receivers of messages in that chain, and provides the possibility of emotional effect independent of any designation.

The Monster unerringly discovers language to be on the side of culture rather than nature, and to imply the structures of relation at the basis of culture. The discovery is a vital one, for the side of ''nature'' is irreparably marked by lack, by monsterism. Against the Monster's hearing of the cottagers' language is set his discovery of his own features mirrored in a pool—a sinister parody of Eve's discovery of her fair features in the pool of Eden, on the day of her creation, in Book IV of *Paradise Lost.* In *Frankenstein,* the reflected image convinces the beholder ''that I was in reality the monster that I am.'' . . . This speculary *cogito,* where the Monster witnesses his outward identity as alien to his inner desire, estranged, determined by the view and judgment of the Other, clinches the importance of language as the symbolic order that must compensate for nature. The Monster understands that he must not show himself to the cottagers until he has mastered their language, ''which knowledge might enable me to make them overlook the deformity of my figure.'' . . . (pp. 209-10)

[Language], and especially writing, must appear to the Monster, as it did to Rousseau, ambiguous in effect, like the Promethean gift of fire, so strange in its production of ''opposite effects.'' . . . Yet it remains the necessary compensation, the only hope for linkage to humankind. The Monster will try its effects first on the blind De Lacey. And here the godlike power of the science does reveal itself, as De Lacey responds: ''I am blind, and cannot judge of your countenance, but there is something in your words which persuades me that you are sincere." . . . Mutual sympathy, benefaction, protection, and relation are close to being sealed through language, when Felix, Agatha, and Safie enter and throw the situation brutally back into the speculary order: Agatha faints, Safie flees, and Felix "tore me from his father, to whose knees I clung." . . . The result is Fall. The Monster becomes explicitly satanic—"I, like the arch-fiend, bore a hell within me." . . .

At its completion, the Monster's narrative implies that use of language has failed to gain him entry into the "chain of existence and events," but has rather made him fully aware of his unique and accursed origin. (p. 211)

> *Peter Brooks, " 'Godlike Science/Unhallowed Arts':*
> *Language, Nature, and Monstrosity," in* The Endurance of Frankenstein: Essays on Mary Shelley's
> Novel, *edited by George Levine and U. C. Knoepflmacher, University of California Press, 1979, pp.*
> *205-20.*

THOMAS LIGOTTI   (story date 1985)

[*Ligotti, a contemporary American horror writer, provides an epilogue to* Frankenstein.]

Victor Frankenstein has died on board a ship caught in seas of ice near the North Pole. His body has been sent back to his native Switzerland, where, however, there is no one to receive it. Everyone he ever knew has already died before him. His brother William, his friend Henry, his wife Elizabeth, and his father, Alphonse Frankenstein, among others, are all dead. A minor official in the Genevan civil service comes up with the suggestion to donate the corpse, still very well preserved, to the university at Ingolstadt, where the deceased distinguished himself in scientific studies.

Hans Hoffmann, a prodigy in comparative anatomy at the university at Ingolstadt, is conducting a series of experiments in his apartment. He has assembled, and is quite sure he can vivify, a human being from various body parts he has bought or stolen. To consummate his project, which to his knowledge has never been attempted and would certainly make him famous, he still needs a human brain. He has heard that the body of a former student at the university at Ingolstadt is preserved in the morgue of the medical school. He has heard that the man was a brilliant student. This would be the perfect brain, thinks Hans Hoffmann. Late one night he breaks into the morgue and helps himself.

Well, says Hans Hoffmann on the spectacular evening when the creature first opens its eyes, aren't you a beauty! This is intended ironically, of course; the creature is quite hideous. What Hans Hoffmann now notices is that the creature is gazing around the room, as if expecting to see someone who, for the moment, is absent.

Oh ho, says the scientist, I can see I'm going to have trouble with you. You'll be begging me one of these days to make you a companion, someone of your own kind. Well, look here, says Hans Hoffmann holding a handful of entrails and part of a woman's face. I've already tried to do it, perhaps a little half-heartedly, I admit. It's not the same, making a woman, and I don't have much use for them anyway.

Hans Hoffmann cannot tell whether or not the creature has understood these words. Nevertheless, it has an extremely desolate expression on its face (just possibly due to a few collapsed muscles). Now the creature is staggering around Hans Hoffman's apartment, inadvertantly breaking a number of objects. Finally, it stumbles out the door and into the streets of Ingolstadt. (Good riddance! shouts Hans Hoffmann.)

But as the creature wanders into the darkness, searching for a face it remembers from long ago, it is unaware that the only being left in the entire universe who could possibly offer him any comfort has already incinerated himself on a furious pyre deep in the icy wasteland of the North Pole. (pp. 128-29)

> *Thomas Ligotti, " 'The Agonizing Resurrection of Victor Frankenstein, Citizen of Geneva'," in his* Songs of a Dead Dreamer, *Silver Scarab Press, 1985, pp. 128-29.*

BRIAN W. ALDISS   (essay date 1986)

[*Aldiss is an English novelist, short story writer, critic, and editor who is best known for his science fiction novels and criticism. In this excerpt from his comprehensive history of the genre, Aldiss credits Shelley as the first science fiction author and examines the literary, social, and scientific bases for* Frankenstein.]

Frankenstein: or, The Modern Prometheus was published anonymously on 11th March 1818. . . . The Napoleonic Wars were over; *Savannah* crossed the Atlantic, the first steamship to do so; the early steam locomotives were chuffing along their metal tracks, Boulton's iron foundries going full blast; the Lancashire cotton factories were lit by gas, and gas mains were being laid in London. Telford and McAdam were building roads and bridges, Galvani's followers and Humphry Davy were experimenting with electricity. "So much has been done," exclaimed the soul of Frankenstein, "more, far more, will I achieve!" . . . (p. 36)

[Mary Shelley was the] first writer of science fiction; [she] had imbibed the philosophical ideas of Locke and the scientific ideas of Darwin, Humphry Davy, Joseph Priestley, and others. They helped shape her emotional life and she set about applying her ideas to papers within a loose Gothic structure of suspense and pursuit. (p. 37)

Readers and commentators alike are agreed that *Frankenstein* is Mary Shelley's great original novel. It is hardly surprising. *Frankenstein* is the one novel she wrote during Shelley's lifetime. As he in his poems was opening up new ground, she—caught in the aura of intellectual excitement which existed between them—also ventured into startling new territory. (p. 38)

What exactly is uniquely innovative about *Frankenstein*?

Interest has always centred on the creation of the nameless monster. This is the core of the novel, an experiment that goes wrong—a prescription to be repeated later, more sensationally, in *Amazing Stories* and elsewhere. Frankenstein's is the Faustian dream of unlimited power, but Frankenstein makes no pacts with the devil. "The devil" belongs to a relegated system of belief. Frankenstein's ambitions bear fruit only when he throws away his old reference books from a pre-scientific age and gets down to some research in the laboratory. This is now accepted practice, of course. But what is now accepted practice was, in 1818, a startling perception, a small revolution.

The novel dramatizes the difference between the old age and the new, between an age when things went by rote and one where everything was suddenly called into question. (p. 39)

The Byron-Shelley circle understood themselves to be living in a new age. They felt themselves to be moderns. The study of gases was advanced; much was understood about the composition of the atmosphere; that lightning and electricity were one and the same was already clear—although that it was not a fluid was still not so definite that Mary was unable to use that misconception as a metaphor. Shelley had a microscope while at Oxford, and the study of morbid anatomy was well advanced. Mary lived in a thoroughly Newtonian world, in which natural explanations could be sought for natural phenomena. It is for this reason she sends Victor Frankenstein to Ingolstadt University; it was renowned in its time as a centre for science. Mary knew more of the science of her time than has been generally granted. . . .

Why, then, is so much time spent by Frankenstein with the alchemists, with Cornelius Agrippa and Paracelsus?

One practical answer is that Mary Shelley wished to make it plain that the old authorities who "promised impossibilities and performed nothing" had to go. She had to show that they were useless, outdated, and without merit in a modern age. (p. 40)

As if to dispel any doubts about her aversion to "jiggery-pokery magic", Mary makes it plain that her central marvel shares the essential quality of scientific experiment, rather than the hit-and-miss of legerdermain. She has Frankenstein create life a second time.

Frankenstein agrees to make a female companion for the monster, subject to certain conditions. When his work is almost finished, Frankenstein pauses, thinking of the "race of devils" that might be raised up by the union between his two creatures (a curious moment, this, for science fiction, looking back towards Caliban's snarl to Prospero in *The Tempest*—"I had peopled else the isle with Calibans!"—and forward to the monstrous legions of robots which were to tramp across the pages of the twentieth-century world!). Victor destroys what he has begun, the monster discovers the breach of contract, utters his direst threat—"I shall be with you on your wedding-night"—and disappears.

The rest is a tale of flight and pursuit, punctuated by death and retribution, with everyone's hand turned against the wretched monster. This section contains much of Godwin's thinking, and of his novel, *Caleb Williams,* which, as its preface announced, was a review of "the modes of domestic and unrecorded despotism by which man becomes the destroyer of man."

The influence of Godwin and *Caleb Williams* is very strong. Frankenstein's friend, Clerval, is probably named after Mr Clare, the one good man in *Caleb Williams*—as, in Mary Shelley's later novel, Lord Raymond is named after the Raymond, a kind of eighteenth-century Robin Hood, in her father's novel.

No celestial vengeance here. No devils, no retribution from God. Mankind is left alone, scheming to take over the vacant premises. Like *Caleb Williams, Frankenstein* becomes a story of implacable lay revenge, hatred, judicial blunder, pistols fired from open windows, a thwarted voyage of discovery, exhausting journeys without map or compass. There is nemesis but no promise of afterlife—unless it is the miserable hounded afterlife suffered by the monster. (p. 41)

One enduring attraction of the book is its series of ambiguities, not all of which can have been the intention of an inexperienced novelist. We never see Frankenstein in his laboratory, throwing the fatal switch. That was Boris Karloff. The book tells us only of the creature bending over his master. Again, in the pursuit, pursuer and pursued take turn. In particular, the language of the novel invites us to confuse the main roles. Perhaps we are meant to believe that the creature is Frankenstein's doppelganger, pursuing him to death. Which of them is "restored to animation"? "We . . . restored him to animation . . . As soon as he showed signs of life we wrapped him up in blankets. I often feared that his suffering had deprived him of understanding . . . He is generally melancholy and despairing. . . ."

This is not the monster but Victor, before Victor tells his story to Walton. We have only his word for the story's accuracy, just as, finally, we have only the monster's promises, as he disappears into darkness and distance, that he will destroy himself. The outcome of all the trials (there are four in the book) are unreliable; are we then encouraged to trust our witnesses? (pp. 41-2)

In one of its aspects, *Frankenstein* is a diseased creation myth, prototype of many to come. . . . (p. 42)

Here we confront the more personal side of the novel. The struggle between Victor and his fiend is Oedipal in nature. Like André Gide's Oedipus, the fiend seems to himself to have "welled out of the unknown": "Who was I? What was I? Whence did I come?" it asks itself . . . The muddying of generations and generation reflects the confusion Mary Shelley felt regarding her own involved family situation, surrounded by the half-sisters of both her mother's earlier and her father's later liaisons.

Some critics have read into the more macabre scenes of *Frankenstein* undertones of vampirism (a favourite with Lord Byron) and incest. "I shall be with you on your wedding night," cries the creature to Victor, who is in a sense its mother and father. Sexual tensions move throughout the book. (pp. 42-3)

In referring to *Frankenstein* as a diseased creation myth, I have in mind phrases in the novel with sexual connotations such as "my workshop of filthy creation", used by Frankenstein of his secret work. Mary's experience brought her to see life and death as closely intertwined. The phraseology used to describe her dream [in the 1831 preface; see excerpt above] is significant. She saw "the hideous phantasm of a man stretched out, and then, on the working of some powerful engine, show signs of life, and stir with an uneasy, half vital motion". The vigorous line suggests both a distorted image of her mother dying, in those final restless moments which often tantalizingly suggest recovery rather than its opposite, as well as the stirrings of sexual intercourse, particularly when we recall that "powerful engine" is a term serving in pornography as a synonym for penis. (p. 43)

The last word on *Frankenstein* will never be said. It contains too many seemingly conflicting elements for that. (p. 49)

The Outwardness of science and society is balanced in the novel by an Inwardness which Mary's dream helped her to accommodate. This particular balance is perhaps one of *Frankenstein*'s greatest merits: that its tale of exterior adventure and misfortune is accompanied by—encompassed by—psychological depth. Mary might have claimed for her drama what Shelley said in his Preface to *Prometheus Bound:* "The imagery which I have employed will be found, in many instances, to have been drawn from the operations of the human mind, or from those external actions by which they are expressed."

Love, fear, the cruelty of parents and lovers—such familiar acquaintances are stirred up by the introduction of the central novelty.

Victor's lowly unique creature, outcast from human kind, takes a lofty view of itself and—in contrast with the almost dumb fiend to which the movies have accustomed us—is articulate regarding its sorrows.

Here we are given an educational prescription which looks both backward and forward—to a time when mankind does not judge merely by appearances.

Shelley read *Paradise Lost* aloud to Mary in 1816.

The monster likens himself to Adam in the poem—but how much less fortunate than Adam, for in this case the creator rushes away from "his odious handywork, horror-stricken". The creature's career has something in common with Adam's, with the vital exception of the missing Eve. He is first created, and then brought to full intellectual awareness of the world in which he lives—at which stage, "benevolence and generosity were ever present before me". . . . He then undergoes his version of the Fall, when "the spirit of revenge enkindled in my heart". . . . Now the creature is frequently referred to as "the fiend". In many ways, it becomes less human, more a symbol of inhumanity. "I saw him," says Frankenstein, "descend the mountain with greater speed than the flight of an eagle, and quickly lost him among the undulations of the sea of ice". . . . (pp. 49-50)

The fiend increasingly speaks of itself in Miltonic terms, saying of itself at last, over Victor's corpse, "the fallen angel becomes a malignant devil".

This change in the nature of the monster enables Mary Shelley to bring out two aspects of the struggle which are subordinate to the eschatological theme.

The first aspect is man's confrontation with himself, which the power of creation necessarily entails. The diseased creation myth prefigures Jekyll and Hyde, as Frankenstein struggles with his alter ego; their obsessive pursuit of one another makes sense only in metaphysical terms.

The second aspect is the disintegration of society which follows man's arrogation of power. One perversion of the natural order leads to another. *Frankenstein* is loaded with a sense of corruption, and "the fiend" moves about the world striking where it will, like a disease which, beginning naturally enough in a charnel house, can be isolated and sterilized only on a drift ice flow.

The rejection of a just Heavenly Father, the concern with suffering, the sexual obsessions, have helped preserve *Frankenstein*'s topicality. Not only does it foreshadow our fears about the two-edged triumphs of scientific progress; it is also the first novel to be powered by the evolutionary idea. God, however often called upon, is an absentee landlord. The lodgers have to fight things out between themselves.

Herein lies the force of the novel's sub-title. In Shelley's lyrical drama, *Prometheus Unbound,* mighty Jupiter has chained Prometheus to a rock. Prometheus suffers terrible torture, but is eventually freed when Jupiter is dethroned, to retire into obscurity.

What is mankind to seek, if not God? Answers to this modern conundrum include objectives like knowledge, power, and self-

fulfilment. According to one's reading of the novel, Victor Frankenstein can be understood to seek all three.

The use of this modernized Faust theme is particularly suited to the first real novel of science fiction: Frankenstein is *the* modern predicament, involving the post-Rousseauvian dichotomy between the individual and his society, as well as the encroachment of science on that society, and mankind's dual nature, whose inherited ape curiosity has brought him both success and misery. His great discovery apart, Frankenstein is an over-reacher and victim, staggering through a world where virtues are few (though the fiend *reads* of them). Instead of hope and forgiveness, there remain only the misunderstandings of men and the noxious half life of the monster. Knowledge brings no guarantee of happiness.

For this critic's taste, the Frankenstein theme is more contemporary and more interesting than interstellar travel tales, since it takes us nearer to the enigma of man and thus of life. . . . (pp. 50-1)

Brian W. Aldiss, "On the Origins of Species: Mary Shelley," in his Trillion Year Spree: The History of Science Fiction, *Atheneum, 1986, pp. 25-51.*

ADDITIONAL BIBLIOGRAPHY

Angeli, Helen Rossetti. *Shelley and His Friends in Italy.* London: Methuen & Co., 1911, 326 p.
  A biography detailing the Shelleys' years in Italy.

Bowerbank, Sylvia. "The Social Order vs. the Wretch: Mary Shelley's Contradictory-Mindedness in *Frankenstein.*"*ELH* 46, No. 3 (Fall 1979): 418-31.
  Examines *Frankenstein* from a sociopolitical perspective. According to Bowerbank, the novel reveals the simultaneously radical and conservative attitudes of Shelley and her friends because it "sentimentally defends, and yet skeptically attacks, domestic and social tranquility."

Church, Richard. *Mary Shelley.* 1928. Reprint. Representative Women, edited by Francis Birrell. Folcroft, Pa.: Folcroft Press, 1969, 91 p.
  A reliable early biography containing brief, generally favorable critical comments.

Clifford, Gay. "*Caleb Williams* and *Frankenstein*: First-Person Narratives and 'Things as They Are'." *Genre* 10, No. 4 (Winter 1977): 601-17.
  Outlines the artistic and philosophical viewpoints of the first-person narratives in *Caleb Williams* and *Frankenstein* and compares Shelley's narrative techniques with those of her father.

Cude, Wilfred. "Mary Shelley's Modern Prometheus: A Study in the Ethics of Scientific Creativity." *The Dalhousie Review* 52, No. 2 (Summer 1972): 212-25.
  Regards *Frankenstein* as primarily an exploration through Promethean myth of the ethics of scientific research. According to Cude, Shelley blames modern society for the failure of the "Modern Prometheus" experiment because of society's cruel response to the monster.

Dunn, Richard J. "Narrative Distance in *Frankenstein.*" *Studies in the Novel* VI, No. 4 (Winter 1974): 408-17.
  Asserts that the separate narratives of Captain Walton, the monster, and Dr. Frankenstein create a distancing effect that underscores the common focus of each narrative: "the need for human interrelationship."

Dussinger, John A. "Kinship and Guilt in Mary Shelley's *Frankenstein.*" *Studies in the Novel* VIII, No. 1 (Spring 1976): 38-55.

Proposes that in *Frankenstein* Shelley was depicting not only the dangers of Promethean striving, but also the hazards of denying one's moral responsibility to family and kin.

Fleck, P. D. "Mary Shelley's Notes to Shelley's Poems and *Frankenstein*." *Studies in Romanticism* VI, No. 4 (Summer 1967): 226-54.
Examines Shelley's notes to her husband's poems. According to Fleck, the notes reveal Mary's somewhat hostile attitude toward Percy's romanticism. Fleck also draws a parallel between *Frankenstein* and Percy's poem *Alastor; or, The Spirit of Solitude*.

Florescu, Radu. *In Search of Frankenstein*. New York: Warner Books, 1976, 364 p.
A heavily illustrated, speculative travelogue that documents Florescu's geographical search for the historical origins of *Frankenstein*.

Frank, Frederick S. "Mary Shelley's *Frankenstein*: A Register of Research." *Bulletin of Bibliography* 40, No. 3 (September 1983): 163-88.
A bibliography of twentieth-century research. Individual listings include editions of the novel published between 1950 and 1980, critical biographies of Shelley, bibliographical resources for *Frankenstein*, a listing of critical commentary on *Frankenstein*, and a filmography.

Gardner, Joseph H. "Mary Shelley's Divine Tragedy." *Essays in Literature* IV, No. 2 (Fall 1977): 182-97.
Explores the dichotomy in *Frankenstein* between the characters' quest "for knowledge on the one hand and [their] quest for sympathy and love on the other." Gardner also discusses Shelley's "Miltonic" conception of the justice of God's creation.

Gilbert, Sandra M., and Gubar, Susan. "Horror's Twin: Mary Shelley's Monstrous Eve." In their *The Madwoman in the Attic: The Woman Writer and the Nineteenth-Century Literary Imagination*, pp. 213-47. New Haven: Yale University Press, 1979.
A noted feminist analysis of *Frankenstein*. The critics stress the literary and sexual bases of the novel, which they term a "version of the misogynist story implied in *Paradise Lost*."

Glut, Donald F. *The Frankenstein Legend: A Tribute to Mary Shelley and Boris Karloff*. Metuchen, N.J.: Scarecrow Press, 1973, 372 p.
A heavily illustrated chronicle detailing the development of the *Frankenstein* legend in popular culture. Glut includes chapters on theatrical, film, and television versions of the story, emphasizing Boris Karloff's performances in various *Frankenstein* movies.

Harvey, A. D. "*Frankenstein* and *Caleb Williams*." *Keats-Shelley Journal* XXIX (1980): 21-7.
Traces *Frankenstein*'s structural and thematic debt to *Caleb Williams* and terms both works "novels of pursuit."

Hildebrand, William H. "On Three Prometheuses: Shelley's Two and Mary's One." *The Serif* XI, No. 2 (Summer 1974): 3-11.
Compares and contrasts the theme of Prometheanism in *Frankenstein* with Percy Shelley's use of the same theme in his *Queen Mab* and *Prometheus Unbound*.

Hirsch, Gordon D. "The Monster Was a Lady: On the Psychology of Mary Shelley's *Frankenstein*." *Hartford Studies in Literature* VII, No. 2 (1975): 116-53.
Explores the theme of psychological determinism in *Frankenstein*.

Hume, Robert D. "Gothic Versus Romantic: A Revaluation of the Gothic Novel." *PMLA* 84, No. 2 (March 1969): 282-90.
A brief character analysis of *Frankenstein*'s monster within the context of a discussion of the Gothic novel.

Kaplan, Morton, and Kloss, Robert. "Fantasy of Paternity and the Doppelgänger: Mary Shelley's *Frankenstein*." In their *The Unspoken Motive: A Guide to Psycho-Analytic Literary Criticism*, pp. 119-45. New York: Free Press, 1973.
A psychoanalytic reading tracing the doppelgänger and oedipal motifs in *Frankenstein*.

Ketterer, David. "Mary Shelley and Science Fiction: A Select Bibliography Selectively Annotated." In *Science Fiction Studies* 5, No. 15, Pt. 2 (July 1978): 172-78.
Lists critical works on Shelley, *Frankenstein*, *The Last Man*, and the short story "Roger Dodsworth."

——. *Frankenstein's Creation: The Book, the Monster, and Human Reality*. ELS Monograph Series, edited by Samuel L. Macey, no. 16. Victoria, B.C.: University of Victoria, 1979, 124 p.
Examines the construction of *Frankenstein*.

Koszul, A. Introduction to *Proserpine and Midas*, by Mary Shelley, edited by A. Koszul, pp. v-xxxi. London: Humphrey Milford, 1922.
An overview of Shelley's mythological dramas. Koszul describes the circumstances under which they were written and suggests that the dramas bridge the gap between the fantastical *Frankenstein* and Shelley's other, more pedestrian works.

Levine, George. *The Realistic Imagination: English Fiction from Frankenstein to Lady Chatterley*. Chicago: University of Chicago Press, 1981, 357 p.
Employs *Frankenstein* as a "metaphor for the strategies of realism" in the works of English novelists from Jane Austen to D. H. Lawrence.

——, and Knoepflmacher, U. C., eds. *The Endurance of "Frankenstein": Essays on Mary Shelley's Novel*. Berkeley and Los Angeles: University of California Press, 1974, 341 p.
A collection of essays by twelve contemporary critics covering various aspects of *Frankenstein*, including its literary and biographical sources, language, and adaptations for the theater and cinema. Also included are a brief chronology of Shelley's life, a select bibliography, illustrations, and an introduction by the editors attesting to *Frankenstein*'s growing critical importance.

Lovell, Ernest J., Jr. "Byron and Mary Shelley." *Keats-Shelley Journal* II (January 1953): 36-49.
Details Shelley's relationship with Lord Byron.

Lyles, W. H. *Mary Shelley: An Annotated Bibliography*. New York: Garland Publishing, 1975, 297 p.
A complete bibliography of works by and about Shelley. Appendices include a chronological listing of Shelley's works, an historical essay on "The Legend of George of Frankenstein," a guide to theatrical, film, and television versions of *Frankenstein*, and a list of current selling prices for various books by and about the author.

Marshall, Mrs. Julian. *The Life and Letters of Mary Wollstonecraft Shelley*. 2 vols. London: Richard Bentley & Son, 1889.
An early, essentially noncritical biography that includes many of Shelley's letters and other personal documents.

Massey, Irving. "Singles and Doubles: *Frankenstein*." In his *The Gaping Pig: Literature and Metamorphosis*, pp. 124-37. Berkeley and Los Angeles: University of California Press, 1976.
Examines the theme of dualism in *Frankenstein*.

Mays, Milton A. "*Frankenstein*: Mary Shelley's Black Theodicy." *Southern Humanities Review* III, No. 2 (Spring 1969): 146-53.
Traces the echoes of the *Faust* myth and *Paradise Lost* in *Frankenstein*. The critic posits that the world of *Frankenstein* reveals a "black theodicy" in which "fundamental injustice prevails among men . . . and between men and God."

McCloskey, Frank H. "Mary Shelley's *Frankenstein*." In *The Humanities in the Age of Science: In Honor of Peter Sammartino*, edited by Charles Angoff, pp. 116-138. Rutherford, N.J.: Fairleigh Dickinson University Press, 1968.
Asserts that Shelley's primary intention in *Frankenstein* was to promote Godwin's radical ideas.

Neumann, Bonnie Rayford. *The Lonely Muse: A Critical Biography of Mary Wollstonecraft Shelley*. Salzburg Studies in English Literature: Romantic Reassessment, edited by James Hogg, vol. 85. Salzburg: Universität Salzburg, 1979, 283 p.

A critical biography emphasizing Shelley's sense of personal alienation and tracing that theme in her work. Neumann argues for greater critical recognition of *The Last Man*, which she considers Shelley's "second outstanding work" after *Frankenstein*.

Nitchie, Elizabeth. Introduction to *Mathilda*, by Mary Wollstonecraft Shelley, edited by Elizabeth Nitchie, pp. vii-xv. Chapel Hill: University of North Carolina Press, 1959.

Details the publishing history and autobiographical elements of Shelley's novella. Nitchie comments briefly on the text, stating that while the work is flawed, the heroine Mathilda has a place in "the great tradition of romantic heroines."

Palacio, Jean de. "Mary Shelley and *The Last Man*: A Minor Romantic Theme." *Revue de littérature comparée* XLII, No. 1 (January-March 1968): 37-49.

Compares Shelley's *The Last Man* with literary works on the same theme by her contemporaries Thomas Campbell, Thomas Hood, Edward Bulwer-Lytton, and Jean Batiste de Grainville.

Palmer, D. J., and Dowse, R. E. "*Frankenstein*: A Moral Fable." *The Listener* LXVIII, No. 1743 (23 August 1962): 281-84.

A general discussion of the moral issues raised in *Frankenstein*.

Peck, Walter Edwin. "The Biographical Element in the Novels of Mary Wollstonecraft Shelley." *PMLA* XXXVIII, No. 1 (March 1923): 196-219.

Traces autobiographical elements in *Valperga*, *The Last Man*, and *The Fortunes of Perkin Warbeck*. Peck draws parallels between various fictional characters from these works and the Shelleys, Byron, Claire Clairmont, and other members of their circle.

Pollin, Burton R. "Philosophical and Literary Sources of *Frankenstein*." *Comparative Literature* XVII, No. 2 (Spring 1965): 97-108.

Argues that *Frankenstein* was influenced by such works as Madame di Geulis's *Pygmalion et Galatée*, Ovid's *Metamorphoses*, John Locke's *Essay Concerning Human Understanding*, and *Paradise Lost*. The critic documents Shelley's familiarity with these works with quotes from her diary and letters.

————. "Mary Shelley as the Parvenue." *A Review of English Literature* VIII, No. 3 (July 1967): 9-21.

Explores the biographical bases for Shelley's short story "The Parvenue." According to Pollin, the story derives from Godwin's financial demands on Percy Shelley.

Poovey, Mary. *The Proper Lady and the Woman Writer: Ideology as Style in the Works of Mary Wollstonecraft, Mary Shelley, and Jane Austen*. Women in Culture and Society, edited by Catharine R. Stimpson. Chicago: University of Chicago Press, 1984, 287 p.

Explores the conflict between the bourgeois ideal of the "Proper Lady" and the concept of woman as artist in the works of Shelley, Wollstonecraft, and Austen. Two chapters are devoted to Shelley and *Frankenstein*, which is analyzed chiefly from a biographical standpoint.

Russell, Bertrand. "The Romantic Movement." In his *A History of Western Philosophy and Its Connection with Political and Social Circumstances from the Earliest Times to the Present Day*, pp. 675-83. New York: Simon and Schuster, 1945.

Includes a brief discussion positing that *Frankenstein* "contains what might almost be regarded as an allegorical prophetic history of the development of romanticism."

Small, Christopher. *Ariel Like a Harpy: Shelley, Mary and "Frankenstein."* London: Victor Gollancz, 1972, 352 p.

Explores a broad range of approaches to *Frankenstein*, including biographical, mythical, and philosophical analyses. Small also offers a detailed comparison of the novel and Percy Shelley's *Prometheus Unbound*.

Spark, Muriel. *Child of Light: A Reassessment of Mary Wollstonecraft Shelley*. Hadleigh, Essex: Tower Bridge Publications, 1951, 235 p.

A biographical-critical study. In this, the first serious full-length consideration of Shelley's work, Spark focuses on *Frankenstein*, *The Last Man*, and *Perkin Warbeck*, as well as on Shelley's criticism.

Tannenbaum, Leslie. "From Filthy Type to Truth: Miltonic Myth in *Frankenstein*." *Keats-Shelley Journal* XXVI (1977): 101-113.

Catalogues the parallels between *Paradise Lost* and *Frankenstein* and discusses the presence of Miltonic philosophy throughout the novel.

Twain, Mark. "In Defence of Harriet Shelley: Parts I, II, and III." *The North American Review* CLIX, Nos. 452-54, (July, August, September 1894): 108-19, 240-51, 353-368.

A review of Edward Dowden's *Life of Shelley*. Twain sardonically describes and assesses the controversial events leading to the breakup of Percy Shelley's first marriage.

Robert Louis Stevenson

1850-1894

(Born Robert Lewis Balfour Stevenson) Scottish novelist, short story writer, poet, essayist, dramatist, and prayer writer.

The following entry presents criticism of Stevenson's novel *Strange Case of Dr. Jekyll and Mr. Hyde* (1886). For additional criticism on Stevenson's career and *Dr. Jekyll and Mr. Hyde,* see *NCLC,* Vol. 5.

Dr. Jekyll and Mr. Hyde is one of the most famous tales of English literature; indeed, the kindly and upstanding Dr. Jekyll and his evil alter ego, Mr. Hyde, have become synonymous with the dual aspects of human nature. In this brief novel, Stevenson delineates the moral conflict between the two characters while creating a sinister tale of horror. Its popular appeal was almost instantaneous and continues to this day. However, critics' interpretations of *Dr. Jekyll and Mr. Hyde* have varied widely since its publication, focusing on the novel as either a terrifying melodrama, a moral allegory with Scottish Puritan overtones, or a presentation of Stevenson's own insight into human nature. Despite the diverse readings accorded the novel, most readers agree that in *Dr. Jekyll and Mr. Hyde,* Stevenson achieved a masterpiece of terror and suspense.

Dr. Jekyll and Mr. Hyde appeared near the midpoint of Stevenson's career. Suffering from respiratory ailments all his life, Stevenson was seeking a cure in Europe when he composed the novel in the autumn of 1885. Perhaps because of his failing health, he rejected the lighter tone of his early pieces, especially such books for children as *Kidnapped* and *A Child's Garden of Verses.* Instead, Stevenson wrote *Dr. Jekyll and Mr. Hyde* in a more serious vein, creating an atmosphere of mystery and horror in his later works.

When Stevenson composed *Dr. Jekyll and Mr. Hyde,* his financial situation was poor. He had a family to support, but he seemed unable to create a plot that would attract the reading public. Ironically, the genesis of *Dr. Jekyll and Mr. Hyde* occurred while he was asleep. Afterwards, Stevenson recalled that his wife, Fanny, woke him from a nightmare. Yet when she tried to comfort him, he merely rebuffed her for interrupting his dream: "Why did you awake me? I was dreaming a fine bogey tale." According to Stevenson, he had conjured the idea of Jekyll's personality transformation while asleep, and the rest came quickly to him after he began to write.

Once Stevenson started to record his dream, he found it impossible to stop the composition of his tale; within three days, he had completed the first draft. Fanny, however, disliked his story and objected: "It was merely a story . . . when it should have been a masterpiece." She contended that the tale had no moral implications and was simply sensational. In response to her criticism, Stevenson destroyed the draft, then incorporated her suggestions into a new story, which he completed in three more days. When onlookers commented on the speed of his writing, Stevenson attributed his pace to "Brownies," the tiny creatures in his dreams who worked while he slept.

Despite the complexity of the story's possible meanings, the plot is quite simple. When Henry Jekyll, an honest physician,

swallows a potion that he created in his laboratory, he changes into a horrible creature named Edward Hyde. Jekyll initially is able to control this metamorphosis, but he gradually loses his hold over his own personality, and Hyde comes to dominate Jekyll. After Hyde commits a cold-blooded murder, Jekyll finally emerges, writes a confession of his misdeeds, and kills himself.

Upon completing *Dr. Jekyll and Mr. Hyde,* Stevenson submitted it to the publishers of *Longman's Magazine,* who decided against issuing the work serially, instead printing it in a single volume in a format commonly known as a "shilling shocker." *Dr. Jekyll and Mr. Hyde* was ready for distribution by Christmas 1885, but booksellers were already fully stocked and refused the new piece. When *Dr. Jekyll and Mr. Hyde* finally appeared in January 1886, few copies sold until a glowing anonymous review appeared in the London *Times* (see *NCLC,* Vol. 5). In this article, the critic termed the novel a masterpiece that far surpassed Stevenson's previous works. That review significantly contributed to the popularity of *Dr. Jekyll and Mr. Hyde;* almost overnight, thousands of copies were sold in England. The novel achieved equal success in the United States, where the nature of its moral became a subject of religious dispute. This controversy only made the novel more appealing to Victorian readers, and as the debate increased, more books sold. Londoners interpreted the book as a tale with allegorical overtones and attempted to match the characters with politicians of the era.

While *Dr. Jekyll and Mr. Hyde* was immensely popular with contemporary readers, early critics' reactions varied widely. Almost all acknowledged Stevenson's skill as a writer of suspense, yet many reviewers questioned the work's moral intent, faulting Stevenson's choice of subject matter. Some commentators, however, viewed the novel as a moral allegory on the nature of evil. Stevenson's own remarks are illuminating; he stated that the transformation of Jekyll into Hyde was meant to show that desires, when ignored, become perverted. As the nineteenth-century controversy over the novel's morality waned, the amount of commentary also dwindled. Until the 1930s, the few studies that were published emphasized the novel's moral lesson, while some analyzed the relationship of Jekyll and Hyde as an aspect of that theme. Then, as now, critics have interpreted the pair as a symbol of the classic conflict between the flesh and the spirit. In recent years, scholars have provided psychological readings of *Dr. Jekyll and Mr. Hyde,* discussing the role of the unconscious in Stevenson's composition of the novel, his insight into personality, and his depiction of the divided self. Other modern discussions have focused on the novel's artistic elements, specifically addressing the themes of dualism and the nature of evil and the link between structure and multiple narrative techniques.

Today, *Dr. Jekyll and Mr. Hyde* has been translated into numerous languages and adapted for the stage, screen, and television. Though it is not frequently a subject of critical discussion, the novel is considered to be as popular now as it was during Stevenson's lifetime. Most commentators agree that in *Dr. Jekyll and Mr. Hyde* Stevenson achieved a level of suspenseful prose rivaled only by Edgar Allan Poe. Probably the novel's most enduring legacy is the identification of the names Jekyll and Hyde with the two sides of human nature; their immediate recognition bears testimony to the novel's indelible mark on English literature.

(See also *Dictionary of Literary Biography,* Vol. 18: *Victorian Novelists after 1885.*)

ROBERT LOUIS STEVENSON   (letter date 1886)

[*In the following letter to W. H. Low, an artist and Stevenson's close friend, the author acknowledges the dedication of Low's illustrated edition of John Keats's* Lamia *and sends him the newly published* Dr. Jekyll and Mr. Hyde.]

I send you herewith a Gothic gnome for your Greek nymph; but the gnome is interesting, I think, and he came out of a deep mine, where he guards the fountain of tears. It is not always the time to rejoice. (pp. 381-82)

The gnome's name is *Jekyll & Hyde*; I believe you will find he is likewise quite willing to answer to the name of Low or Stevenson. (p. 382)

> *Robert Louis Stevenson, in a letter to W. H. Low on January 2, 1886, in his* The Letters of Robert Louis Stevenson: 1880-1887, Alps and Highlands— Hyères—Bournemouth, Vol. II, *revised edition, ed-*

ited by Sidney Colvin, 1911. Reprint by Charles Scribner's Sons, 1923, pp. 380-82.

[E. T. COOK]   (essay date 1886)

[*Cook faults the absurdity of the novel's plot.*]

Mr. R. L. Stevenson's proved ability in the invention of exciting stories is by no means at fault in his *Strange Case of Dr. Jekyll and Mr. Hyde.* . . . It is certainly a very strange case, and one which would be extremely difficult to see through from the beginning. It has also the first requisite of such a story—it is extremely clearly narrated, and it holds one's interest. It overshoots the mark, however, by being not merely strange, but impossible, and even absurd when the explanation is given. So good an artist in fanciful mysteries as Mr. Stevenson should have avoided the mistake of a lengthy rationalization which in the nature of things is no rationalization at all. In the effective part of the story two points strike the reader as weak: the first incident which is meant to show the diabolical character of Mr. Hyde is inadequate, and the terms of Dr. Jekyll's will would have been inoperative. Mr. Stevenson has overlooked the fact that a man's will does not come into force until he is dead, and that the fact that he has not been heard of for three months would not enable his executor to carry out his testamentary directions.

> [*E. T. Cook*], *in a review of "Strange Case of Dr. Jekyll and Mr. Hyde," in* The Athenaeum, No. 3038, *January 16, 1886, p. 100.*

JAMES ASHCROFT NOBLE   (essay date 1886)

[*Noble praises the novel and compares it favorably to the works of Nathaniel Hawthorne.*]

The *Strange Case of Dr. Jekyll and Mr. Hyde* is not an orthodox three-volume novel; it is not even a one-volume novel of the ordinary type; it is simply a paper-covered shilling story, belonging, so far as external appearance goes, to a class of literature familiarity with which has bred in the minds of most readers a certain measure of contempt. Appearances, it has been once or twice remarked, are deceitful; and in this case they are very deceitful indeed, for, in spite of the paper cover and the popular price, Mr. Stevenson's story distances so unmistakably its three-volume and one-volume competitors, that its only fitting place is the place of honour. It is, indeed, many years since English fiction has been enriched by any work at once so weirdly imaginative in conception and so faultlessly ingenious in construction as this little tale, which can be read with ease in a couple of hours. . . . [The] story has a much larger and deeper interest than that belonging to a mere skilful narrative. It is a marvellous exploration into the recesses of human nature; and though it is more than possible that Mr. Stevenson wrote with no ethical intent, its impressiveness as a parable is equal to its fascination as a work of art. I do not ignore the many differences between the genius of the author of *The Scarlet Letter* and that of the author of *Dr. Jekyll and Mr. Hyde* when I say that the latter story is worthy of Hawthorne.

> *James Ashcroft Noble, in a review of "Strange Case of Dr. Jekyll and Mr. Hyde," in* The Academy, n.s. *Vol. XXIX, No. 716, January 23, 1886, p. 55.*

THE BOOK BUYER   (essay date 1886)

[*In the following excerpt, the critic praises* Dr. Jekyll and Mr. Hyde, *terming it a masterpiece.*]

The author of the ***New Arabian Nights*** fulfils in ***Dr. Jekyll*** the expectations of the most enthusiastic believers in his powers. His extraordinary hold upon the reader is not kept by mere fantastic *tours de force;* his constructive skill does not consist only in concocting plots which baffle the prophet; even his style, which defies definition, is not the result of any of those artificial factors which well-meaning disciples have tried to see at work in it. Whatever he writes has in it the always indefinable touch of original power, and this has been nowhere shown so forcibly as in the most absorbing, strange, and novel conception of this story.

It is a tale of which no description can be given without letting the reader into the central secret of the plot. The idea of double personality on which it is grounded receives from Mr. Stevenson so new and startling a turn, that from the moment it is caught, one is ''thrilled and possessed,'' as a recent reviewer wrote, by this main motive of the book, until he is in danger of losing sight of the wonderful skill of the details by which he is led on to the *dénouement.* It may be safely promised that the story will be read with such a thrill as no mere ingenuity could produce, and remembered among the few masterpieces of its kind. (pp. 23-4)

> *A review of "Strange Case of Dr. Jekyll and Mr. Hyde," in* The Book Buyer, *n.s. Vol. III, No. 1, February, 1886, pp. 23-4.*

THE CRITIC, NEW YORK   (essay date 1886)

[*This reviewer praises the conception and execution of the novel.*]

[The ***Strange Case of Dr. Jekyll and Mr. Hyde***] is an original and interesting piece of work, combining a French grace of execution with a distinctly Saxon ethical method. It is a bit of art that subserves a high moral purpose. Careless readers will say, in the hackneyed phrase of half-read people, that it 'reminds one of Poe,' but its construction is not that of the author of ''Ligeia'' or ''The Fall of the House of Usher.'' Poe had his method, a legitimate one, in which he won high and lasting success, but it is idle to compare Poe with Hawthorne, merely because both dealt with the abnormal or weird. If ''Ethan Brand'' be at one extreme and one of Poe's best stories at the other, Mr. Stevenson's ***Strange Case*** follows in the Hawthorne line, because it offers both art and ethics, in a remarkable union. We commend it to that celebrated personage, the 'jaded novel-reader,' and still more to those serious people who will read none but noteworthy novels.

> *A review of "Strange Case of Dr. Jekyll and Mr. Hyde," in* The Critic, *New York, Vol. V, February 6, 1886, p. 68.*

FREDERICK W. H. MYERS   (letter date 1886)

[*A poet, classical scholar, and essayist, Myers was also very interested in psychic research. He admired* Dr. Jekyll and Mr.

Hyde *and wrote Stevenson several letters proposing corrections for the novel. In the two letters from February 1886, the initial page references are to the first edition of* Dr. Jekyll and Mr. Hyde, *while the bracketed references are to the South Seas edition of 1925. Stevenson responded in the letter dated March 1, 1886; Myers wrote Stevenson again (see excerpts dated 1886 and 1887), but Stevenson never incorporated any of the revisions suggested by Myers.*]

We have a common friend in Mr. J. A. Symonds, who has often spoken of you to me—and I have often wished that I might have the pleasure of meeting you. The present letter is called forth by the extreme admiration with which I have read and reread your ***Strange Case of Dr. Jekyll and Mr. Hyde.*** I should be afraid to say how high this story seems to me to stand among imaginative productions; and I cannot but hope that it may take a place in our literature as permanent as *Robinson Crusoe.*

But, owing part to the brevity which forms one of the book's merits, partly perhaps to a certain speed in its composition which also reflects itself—especially in the style, there are certain points which I think that you might expand or alter with advantage; and which are well worth the slight trouble involved. These are specially on pages (1st edition)

37 [27]	Nature of crime.
52 [36-7]	Handwriting.
56 [39]	Change in Dr. Lanyon.
83 [54-5]	Condition of room.
103 [66-7]	Metamorphosis in Dr. L's presence.
111 [71-2]	Nature of Metamorphosis.
127 [81]	Same as p. 37 [27].
131 [83-4]	Omission of precaution.
137 [87]	Relationship of consciousness: reason for fear of apprehension.

I think that I would select pp. 121 [77-8], 138 [87-8] as instances of a mastery of language and imagination which it would be hard to parallel in fiction.

I do not know whether you will care to receive any of these suggestions which have occurred to me. But I venture to say that [it] is primarily as the author of this work that you will be known to posterity, and that pains spent on perfecting it will be well repaid. If pushed, I will explain the suggestions which I have thought of. . . . (pp. 213-14)

> *Frederick W. H. Myers, in a letter to Robert Louis Stevenson on February 21, 1886, in* Robert Louis Stevenson: The Critical Heritage, *edited by Paul Maixner, Routledge & Kegan Paul, 1981, pp. 213-14.*

F. W. H. MYERS   (letter date 1886)

[*In the following excerpt, Myers outlines the revisions for the novel that he had proposed in an earlier letter to Stevenson. For additional commentary by Myers, see the excerpts dated 1886 and 1887.*]

p. 6 [7-8]	Quite admirable. Some foolish review (I believe) missed this altogether and saw his act as [?] not sufficiently criminal.

9 [9-10]	After 'in my chambers' are not a few words like '—a grisly time—' needed? One has rather too vague an idea of the group. A word or two as to Hyde's demeanour would be valuable.
19 [16]	Admirable! 22-26 [17-20] Admirable! 33 [24-5] *Admirable!*
35-38 [26-8]	This is the weakest point, to my mind. The cruelty developed from *lust* surely never becomes of just the same quality as the cruelty developed from mere madness [?] and savagery. Hyde would, I think, have simply brushed the baronet aside with a curse, and run on to some long-planned crime. The ground is ticklish, but could you not hint at a projected outrage (not on the baronet) hurried into dangerous haste by his having been long away from Soho and not made the usual preparations? Page 6 [7-8] is the keynote. If you think it needful to avoid a female victim it might be a policeman or some relation of a tacitly-understood victim. No real temptation to make body of baronet jump on roadway (p. 37 [27]). Jekyll was thoroughly civilized, and his degeneration must needs take certain lines only. Have you not sometimes thought of incarnate *evil* rather too vaguely? Hyde is really not a generalized but a specialized fiend. Minor objections. 1) Ambiguity as to house where maid was. Was it in Westminster? How did Baronet need to ask way to post close to Parliament or to his own house? If house is meant to be in a low district how did Baronet come there? 2) Why did Hyde leave the stick? Excitement too *maniacal* to make us thoroughly enter into Hyde.
39-40 [28-9]	Admirable! 42 [30] One would like to hear more of this house. Would Jekyll have sent a picture there? Would he not have concealed the house from his servants? If picture wanted you might try one or two small Jan Steens which he could have taken in a cab.
43 [30-1]	'Other half of stick' Why not thrown away?
45 [32-3]	No obvious reason why Jekyll receives Utterson in *theatre*. (Not important, as he *must* be made to do so, and *need not* give explicit reason.)
52 [36-7]	Here I think you miss a point for want of familiarity with recent psycho-physical discussions. Handwriting in cases of double personality (spontaneous . . . or induced, as in hypnotic cases) *is not* and *cannot be* the same in the two personalities. Hyde's writing might look like Jekyll's done *with the left hand,* or done when partly drunk, or ill: that is the kind of resemblance there might be. Your imagination can make a good point of this.
56 [39]	The effect of shock in Dr. Lanyon might be more specified. At present it seems rather *unreal*. It *might* induce diabetes, if there were previous kidney weakness. Could some slight allusion be made to this on p. 57 [39-40]?
62-65 [43-4]	*Admirable!*
74 [49-50]	Admirable!
83 [54-5]	Surely not a true point—tidiness of room. When had the housemaid been in? Who had removed cinders from under grate? Surely coals were left at door and only the empty coal scuttle put out. Who washed cups? Sugar in tea-cup p. 86 [56] seems to me a false point. Neither J. nor H. would prepare in that minute way for comfort.
99-100 [64-5]	Excellent.
102 [66]	Objections to this page stated later: on page 131 [83-4].
103 [66-7]	Two objections. (1) Style too elevated for Hyde. (Of this further on p. 138 [87-8].) These are not remarks that fit the husky broken voice of Hyde—they are Jekyllian. Surely Hyde's admirable style (p. 24 [19]) should be retained for him. (2) IIc would have been more unwilling to show the transformation. Lanyon should show, I think, more resolve (hint at pistol?) to make him do it.
106-110 [69-71]	Excellent.
111 [71-2]	I suppose the agent must be a drug. But the description of the process surely needs more substance and novelty. For one thing, there must have been a loss of consciousness. (This point admirable when we come to the spontaneous reversions into Hyde during sleep.) The first time the loss of consciousness might last for some hours.
112 [72-3]	*Admirable*—but I think there should be more physical exhaustion the first time. Then he might revive himself by wine placed nearby: his new body would be specially sensitive to stimulants. You perhaps purposely make *few* (but admirable) points as to the new body.
114 [73-4]	Excellent! excellent!
115 [74]	The return to Jekyll should surely be more insisted on—the doubt whether possible, and doubt whether taking drug again might not be *fatal*. A little more too about subsequent shrinkings from the pain etc.—overcome by restless impulse. I don't understand the phrase 'kept awake by ambition.' I thought the stimulus was a different one.
116 [74-5]	We should understand already that he hadn't yet conquered his aversion. Surely the motive for the change was this. And, by the way, I think that it might somewhere be hinted that Jekyll was a good deal more licentious in early life than he avows. I don't want him to be prematurely aged but might there not be something more of flabbiness in his portliness? And some hint of his desiring *variety*? And a word or two more of Utterson's? Or a *thought* of Utterson's? How had Jekyll come across the housekeeper whom he placed in Soho? (What led you to specify Greek street?)

118 [75-6]   Excellent, but needs expansion. 'They soon began to turn towards the monstrous' is almost the only hint in the book of the process by which the thoroughly sympathetic and gently apolaustic Jekyll becomes the ruffianly Hyde. This is one of the great moral nodes of the book, and while I thoroughly admire your rapidity of manner and absence of didactic preoccupation, I nevertheless feel that this is a point on which Jekyll's memory would have dwelt: which he would have insisted on. He would not have liked that his friends should think that he had *fiendish* qualities in him at all to begin with: he would rather have laid all that on the continually expanding desires and insatiable enterprise of Hyde—'That insatiability which is attached to inordinate desires as their bitterest punishment.'

120 [77]   'Sloping my own hand backward': see on p. 52 [36-7]. (Note that Hyde would have to make great effort to simulate Jekyll's signature—be long about it—signature would look odd, but unmistakably Jekyll's.)

121 [77-8]   *This is genius.*

123 [78-9]   Excellent! But correspondingly Jekyll's body should have got flabbier. See also p. 55 [38] where Jekyll, I think, regains vigour and cheerfulness far too rapidly. There should be something deprecative [?] rather than complacent about him after the murder.

124 [79]   An admirable page but 'begun to pamper' might be stronger and we here also begin to note a slight uncertainty in the psychical relationship of the two personalities. Here Hyde is (bandit simile) hardly at all Jekyll; later on (and on p. 120 [77]) he is much more Jekyll and see p. 103 [66-7].

127 [81]   Here I again feel a false note. See on p. 36 [26-7] 'mauled the unresisting body'—no, not an elderly MP's!

129 [82]   'the hands of all men would be raised' Surely the one servant maid and his few acquaintances were not so dangerous. Hyde might have escaped from England easily enough. Why does Jekyll not think of a trip to Brussels?

131 [83-4]   An admirable page! But here one asks why, after the metamorphosis in bed, take the risk of separation from the drug? At any time even before the spontaneous metamorphosis it might have been extremely desirable to change back into Jekyll. If the drug was portable and manageable anywhere he would likely have taken it with him:— and after the murder certainly. Can you suppose that a Bunsen burner or some means of producing intense heat was necessary to effect a chemical combination? Or an electrical machine (which Lanyon also might possess) to assist change of body?

136-138   Genius!
[86-8]

138 [87-8]   But Hyde was in very little danger. Who could identify him? Probably almost any acquaintance that he had could have been bought off. And what chance of their seeing him if he went to an unfamiliar quarter of London? Or why does he not think of Paris or New York? For he is now so psychically separate from Jekyll (and I think something should be said as to growing psychical separation, if you determine to take that line)— he would surely have thought 'I will give up the Jekyll life, which can't really be retained, and will start fresh in New York.' (Even Liverpool would have tempted him, if you say that he was not [?] enough for New York.)

141 [89]   How would it be if Jekyll committed suicide and we were left to infer, from the finding of Hyde's body, that the death-agony had so transformed him?

                                            (pp. 214-19)

F. W. H. Myers, in a letter to Robert Louis Stevenson on February 28, 1886, in Robert Louis Stevenson: The Critical Heritage, *edited by Paul Maixner, Routledge & Kegan Paul, 1981, pp. 214-19.*

ROBERT LOUIS STEVENSON   (letter date 1886)

[*In the following letter, Stevenson thanks Myers for the revisions he proposed (see excerpts dated 1886).*]

I know not how to thank you: this is as handsome as it is clever. With almost every word I agree—much of it I even knew before—much of it, I must confess, would never have been, if I had been able to do what I like, and lay the thing by for the matter of a year. But the wheels of Byles the Butcher drive exceeding swiftly, and *Jekyll* was conceived, written, re-written, re-rewritten, and printed inside ten weeks. Nothing but this white-hot haste would explain the gross error of Hyde's speech at Lanyon's. Your point about the specialised fiend is more subtle, but not less just: I had not seen it.—About the picture, I rather meant that Hyde had brought it himself; and Utterson's hypothesis of the gift . . . an error.—The tidiness of the room, I thought, but I dare say my psychology is here too ingenious to be sound, was due to the dread weariness and horror of the imprisonment. Something has to be done: he would tidy the room. But I dare say it is false.

I shall keep your paper; and if ever my works come to be collected, I will put my back into these suggestions. In the meanwhile, I do truly lack words in which to express my sense of gratitude for the trouble you have taken. The receipt of such a paper is more than a reward for my labours. I have read it with pleasure, and as I say, I hope to use it with profit. (pp. 325-26)

Robert Louis Stevenson, in a letter to F. W. H. Myers on March 1, 1886, in his The Letters of Robert Louis Stevenson: 1880-1887, Alps and Highlands—Hyères—Bournemouth, Vol. II, *revised edition, edited by Sidney Colvin, 1911. Reprint by Charles Scribner's Sons, 1923, pp. 325-26.*

J. A. SYMONDS   (letter date 1886)

[*Symonds was a noted nineteenth-century English critic, poet, historian, and translator. Although primarily remembered for his translations of the Greek poets, Symonds is also known for his aesthetic theory and impressionistic essays. In the following excerpt from a letter to Stevenson, Symonds praises Stevenson's technique but considers the subject of* Dr. Jekyll and Mr. Hyde *too painful to linger over.*]

At last I have read *Dr Jekyll*. It makes me wonder whether a man has the right so to scrutinize "the abysmal deeps of personality." It is indeed a dreadful book, most dreadful because of a certain moral callousness, a want of sympathy, a shutting out of hope. The art is burning and intense. . . . As a piece of literary work, this seems to me the finest you have done—in all that regards style, invention, psychological analysis, exquisite fitting of parts, and admirable employment of motives to realize the abnormal. But it has left such a deeply painful impression on my heart that I do not know how I am ever to turn to it again.

The fact is that, viewed as an allegory, it touches one too closely. Most of us at some epoch of our lives have been upon the verge of developing a Mr Hyde.

Physical and biological Science on a hundred lines is reducing individual freedom to zero, and weakening the sense of responsibility. I doubt whether the artist should lend his genius to this grim argument. Your Dr Jekyll seems to me capable of loosening the last threads of self-control in one who should read it while wavering between his better and worse self. It is like the Cave of Despair in the *Faery Queen*.

I had the great biologist Lauder Brunton with me a fortnight back. He was talking about *Dr Jekyll* and a book by O. W. Holmes [*Elsie Venner*], in [which] atavism is played with. I could see that, though a Christian, he held very feebly to the theory of human liberty; and these two works of fiction interested him, as *Dr Jekyll* does me, upon that point at issue.

I understand now thoroughly how much a sprite you are. Really there is something not quite human in your genius!

The denouement would have been finer, I think, if Dr Jekyll by a last supreme effort of his lucid self had given Mr Hyde up to justice—[which] might have been arranged after the scene in Lanyon's study. Did you ever read Raskolnikow [*Crime and Punishment*]? How fine is that ending! Had you made your hero act thus, you would at least have saved the sense of human dignity. (pp. 120-21)

> *J. A. Symonds, in a letter to Robert Louis Stevenson on March 3, 1886, in his* The Letters of John Addington Symonds: 1885-1893, Vol. III, *edited by Herbert M. Schueller and Robert L. Peters, Wayne State University Press, 1969, pp. 120-22.*

F. W. MYERS   (letter date 1886)

[*In the following letter, Myers suggests more revisions for the novel. For additional commentary by Myers, see the excerpts dated 1886 and 1887.*]

I. Would Hyde have brought a picture? I think—and friends of weight support my view—that such an act would have been altogether unworthy of him. What are the motives which would prompt a person in his situation to that act?

1. There are jaded voluptuaries who seek in a special class of art a substitute or reinforcement for the default of primary stimuli. Mr. Hyde's whole career forbids us to insult him by classing him with these men.

2. There are those who wish for elegant surroundings to allure or overawe the minds of certain persons unaccustomed to luxury or splendour. But does not all that we know of Mr. Hyde teach us that he disdained these modes of adventitious attractions? When he is first presented to us in [*Dr. Jekyll and Mr. Hyde*] as 'stumping along eastward at a good walk' (I have mislaid my copy and must quote from memory) does not this imply the gait of one who aimed at energy but not at grace? And when we read that he was 'very plainly dressed,' don't we know that his means were such that he might have permitted himself without extravagance an elegant costume,—does not this show us the man aiming only at simple convenience, direct sufficiency? not anxious to present himself as personally attractive to others, but relying frankly on a cash nexus, and on that decision of character which would startle—almost terrify into compliance in cases where the blandishments of the irresolute might have been lavished in vain?

3. There are those, again, who surround their more concentrated enjoyments with a halo of mixed estheticism; who even if blameably adventurous in action are gently artistic in repose. Such, no doubt, was Dr. Jekyll: such, no doubt, he *expected* that Mr. Hyde would be. But was he not deceived? Was there not something unlooked for, something Napoleonic, in Hyde's way of pushing aside the aesthetic as well as the moral superfluities of life? Between the conception of some lawless design and its execution do we suppose that Jekyll himself could look at his pictures with tranquil pleasure? Did not his inward state 'suffer with the likeness of an insurrection'? And was not Hyde's permanent state this stabler and intenser reproduction of such absorbed and critical moments in Jekyll's inward history? We do not imagine the young Napoleon as going to concerts or taking a walk in a garden. We imagine him as now plunged in gloomy torpor, now warmly planning crimes to be. I cannot fancy Hyde looking in at picture shops. I cannot think that he ever even left his rooms, except on business. And in these rooms I fancy that there would be a certain look as of lower tenancy supervening [?] on a high-class outfit; a certain admixture of ill-chosen with handsome things; an unhomelike bareness along with provision for ready ease.

II. I have thought of how you could alter the murder with least trouble. Perhaps it might do if the servant maid looked out of the window when the murderous assault had just begun and mentions that there was no one else in the street except 'a shabbily dressed johnny just a-scampering around the street corner.' The girl need never appear again; but Jekyll might speak of the Baronet as having interfered to baulk what (in his way of speaking of Hyde) he would probably call 'an enterprise too hastily conceived.'

III. A very small point. I think that the housekeeper says 'What's he been doing?' If 'now' were added, it might imply that in her view he had already been fortunate in escaping the interference of the Law.

IV. A criticism of Mr. Gladstone's (to whom my sister-in-law took the book while he was forming a ministry [?] which is now, I hope, splitting up more irretrievably than Dr. Jekyll's personality) may introduce my next suggestion. He said that while he much admired and enjoyed the book, he felt that the ethical retransference of Hyde into Jekyll was made too easy a thing;—that he could not fancy so profound and sudden a *backward* change. This, as you perceive, bears out what I ventured to hint as to the progressive effect which the repeated changes must needs operate on the Jekyllian phase. And it suggests, I think, the need of dealing with the subject of community of memory. At first I think such community would be very imperfect; gradually the two memories would fuse into one; and in the last stage you might make an effective contrast of the increasing *fusion* of the two personalities in all except ethical temper, joined with the increasing revulsion in all except ethical temper, joined with the increasing revulsion of Jekyll against the ethical temper of Hyde; a revulsion maintained, no doubt, at great cost of nervous exhaustion—like the prolonged attention needed down an ice-slope which gets steeper and steeper; till the suicide (of Jekyll in my view, not of Hyde) would represent the kind of despairing spring with which the thoroughly exhausted climber leaps to a point where he could not in his right senses have expected to find foothold, misses and falls. (pp. 219-22)

> *F. W. Myers, in a letter to Robert Louis Stevenson on March 17, 1886, in* Robert Louis Stevenson: The Critical Heritage, *edited by Paul Maixner, Routledge & Kegan Paul, 1981, pp. 219-22.*

GERARD MANLEY HOPKINS   (letter date 1886)

[*Hopkins, a Roman Catholic priest, was a nineteenth-century English poet whose work was not published until the twentieth century. Hopkins's poetry is characterized by its striking diction and unusual rhythmic structure. In the following excerpt from a letter to Robert Bridges, Hopkins defends Stevenson's characters against charges of "gross absurdity."*]

Jekyll and Hyde I have read. You speak of 'the gross absurdity' of the interchange. Enough that it is impossible and might perhaps have been a little better masked: it must be connived at, and it gives rise to a fine situation. It is not more impossible than fairies, giants, heathen gods, and lots of things that literature teems with—and none more than yours. You are certainly wrong about Hyde being overdrawn: my Hyde is worse. The trampling scene is perhaps a convention: he was thinking of something unsuitable for fiction.

I can by no means grant that the characters are not characterised, though how deep the springs of their surface action are I am not yet clear. But the superficial touches of character are admirable: how can you be so blind as not to see them? e.g. Utterson frowning, biting the end of his finger, and saying to the butler 'This is a strange tale you tell me, my man, a very strange tale'. And Dr. Lanyon: 'I used to like it, sir [life]; yes, sir, I liked it. Sometimes I think if we knew all' etc. These are worthy of Shakespeare. (p. 238)

> *Gerard Manley Hopkins, in a letter to Robert Bridges on October 28, 1886, in his* The Letters of Gerard Manley Hopkins to Robert Bridges, *edited by Claude Colleer Abbott, Oxford University Press, London, 1935, pp. 235-41.*

ROBERT LOUIS STEVENSON   (letter date 1887)

[*In the following letter, Stevenson discusses his attitudes, and those of his characters, toward sexuality. His comments are later contested by Katharine D. Osbourne (see essay dated 1923).*]

Hyde was the younger of the two. He was not good-looking, however; and not, Great Gods! a mere voluptuary. There is no harm in voluptuaries; and none, with my hand on my heart and in the sight of God, none—no harm whatsoever in what prurient fools call "immorality." The harm was in Jekyll, because he was a hypocrite—not because he was fond of women;

he says so himself; but people are so filled full of folly and inverted lust, that they think of nothing but sexuality. The Hypocrite let out the beast of Hyde—who is no more sexual than another, but who is the essence of cruelty and malice and selfishness and cowardice, and these are the diabolic in man— not this poor wish to love a woman, that they make such a cry about. I know and I dare to say, you know as well as I, that bad and good even to human eyes, has no more connection with what is called dissipation than it has with flying kites. But the sexual field and the business field are the two best fitted for the display of cruelty and cowardice and selfishness. (pp. 129-30)

> *Robert Louis Stevenson, in an extract from a letter to John Paul Bocock in 1887, in* The True Stevenson: A Study in Clarification *by George S. Hellman, Little, Brown, and Company, 1925, pp. 129-30.*

F. W. H. MYERS   (letter date 1887)

[*In the following letter, Myers reminds Stevenson that he has not yet revised the novel. For additional commentary by Myers, see the excerpts dated 1886.*]

I do not want to be importunate, but I cannot but help reminding you that time is going on, and your masterpiece remains (so far as I know) without that final revision, the possible lack of which would be a real misfortune to English literature. The works, even of the most fertile and brilliant authors, which can hope for *permanent* preservation must needs be few. Is it not well worth while to make them as perfect as possible? I have heard the views of many other persons on *Dr. Jekyll and Mr. Hyde* since I last wrote. I have not found any competent person who does not think it your best work, or who did not also feel it contained obvious, and removable, blots.

> *F. W. H. Myers, in a letter to Robert Louis Stevenson on April 17, 1887, in* Robert Louis Stevenson: The Critical Heritage, *edited by Paul Maixner, Routledge & Kegan Paul, 1981, p. 222.*

HENRY JAMES   (essay date 1888)

[*James was an American-born English novelist, short story writer, critic, and essayist of the late nineteenth and early twentieth centuries. The following discussion of Dr. Jekyll and Mr. Hyde is drawn from an overview of Stevenson's writings.*]

Is *Dr. Jekyll and Mr. Hyde* a work of high philosophic intention, or simply the most ingenious and irresponsible of fictions? It has the stamp of a really imaginative production, that we may take it in different ways, but I suppose it would be called the most serious of the author's tales. It deals with the relation of the baser parts of man to his nobler—of the capacity for evil that exists in the most generous natures, and it expresses these things in a fable which is a wonderfully happy invention. The subject is endlessly interesting, and rich in all sorts of provocation, and Mr. Stevenson is to be congratulated on having touched the core of it. I may do him injustice, but it is, however, here, not the profundity of the idea which strikes me so much as the art of the presentation—the extremely successful form. There is a genuine feeling for the perpetual moral question, a fresh sense of the difficulty of being good and the brutishness of being bad, but what there is above all is a singular ability in holding the interest. I confess that that, to my sense, is the most edifying thing in the short, rapid, concentrated story, which is really a masterpiece of concision. There is something almost impertinent in the way . . . in which Mr. Stevenson achieves his best effects without the aid of the ladies, and *Dr. Jekyll* is a capital example of his heartless independence. It is usually supposed that a truly poignant impression cannot be made without them, but in the drama of Mr. Hyde's fatal ascendency they remain altogether in the wing. It is very obvious—I do not say it cynically—that they must have played an important part in his development. The gruesome tone of the tale is, no doubt, deepened by their absence; it is like the late afternoon light of a foggy winter Sunday, when even inanimate objects have a kind of wicked look. I remember few situations in the pages of mystifying fiction more to the purpose than the episode of Mr. Utterson's going to Dr. Jekyll's to confer with the butler, when the doctor is locked up in his laboratory and the old servant, whose sagacity has hitherto encountered successfully the problems of the sideboard and the pantry, confesses that this time he is utterly baffled. The way the two men, at the door of the laboratory, discuss the identity of the mysterious personage inside, who has revealed himself in two or three inhuman glimpses to Poole, has those touches of which irresistible shudders are made. The butler's theory is that his master has been murdered, and that the murderer is in the room, personating him with a sort of clumsy diabolism. "Well, when that masked thing like a monkey jumped from among the chemicals and whipped into the cabinet, it went down my spine like ice." That is the effect upon the reader of most of the story. I say of most rather than all, because the ice rather melts in the sequel, and I have some difficulty in accepting the business of the powders, which seems to me too explicit and explanatory. The powders constitute the machinery of the transformation, and it will probably have struck many readers that this uncanny process would be more conceivable (so far as one may speak of the conceivable in such a case), if the author had not made it so definite. (pp. 877-78)

Henry James, "Robert Louis Stevenson," in The Century, *Vol. XXXV, No. 6, April, 1888, pp. 868-79.*

ROBERT LOUIS STEVENSON (essay date 1888)

[*In the following excerpt from his "A Chapter on Dreams," an essay composed in 1888, Stevenson describes how he transformed dream material into his fiction. He then outlines the method of composition of* Dr. Jekyll and Mr. Hyde, *which he contends was largely subconscious and performed by "Brownies"—the Little People who populate and create his dreams.*]

This honest fellow had long been in the custom of setting himself to sleep with tales, and so had his father before him; but these were irresponsible inventions, told for the teller's pleasure, with no eye to the crass public or the thwart reviewer: tales where a thread might be dropped, or one adventure quitted for another, on fancy's least suggestion. So that the little people who manage man's internal theatre had not as yet received a very rigorous training; and played upon their stage like children who should have slipped into the house and found it empty, rather than like drilled actors performing a set piece to a huge hall of faces. But presently my dreamer began to turn his former amusement of story-telling to (what is called) account; by which I mean that he began to write and sell his tales. Here was he, and here were the little people who did that part of his business, in quite new conditions. The stories must now be trimmed and pared and set upon all fours, they must run from a beginning to an end and fit (after a manner) with the laws of life; the pleasure, in one word, had become a business; and that not only for the dreamer, but for the little people of his theatre.

These understood the change as well as he. When he lay down to prepare himself for sleep, he no longer sought amusement, but printable and profitable tales; and after he had dozed off in his box-seat, his little people continued their evolutions with the same mercantile designs. . . . Often enough the waking is a disappointment: he has been too deep asleep, as I explain the thing; drowsiness has gained his little people, they have gone stumbling and maundering through their parts; and the play, to the awakened mind, is seen to be a tissue of absurdities. And yet how often have these sleepless Brownies done him honest service, and given him, as he sat idly taking his pleasure in the boxes, better tales than he could fashion for himself. (pp. 215-18)

Who are the Little People? They are near connections of the dreamer's, beyond doubt; they share in his financial worries and have an eye to the bank-book; they share plainly in his training; they have plainly learned like him to build the scheme of a considerate story and to arrange emotion in progressive order; only I think they have more talent; and one thing is beyond doubt, they can tell him a story piece by piece, like a serial, and keep him all the while in ignorance of where they aim. Who are they, then? and who is the dreamer?

Well, as regards the dreamer, I can answer that, for he is no less a person than myself;—as I might have told you from the beginning, only that the critics murmur over my consistent egotism;—and as I am positively forced to tell you now, or I could advance but little farther with my story. And for the Little People, what shall I say they are but just my Brownies, God bless them! who do one-half my work for me while I am fast asleep, and in all human likelihood, do the rest for me as well, when I am wide awake and fondly suppose I do it for myself. That part which is done while I am sleeping is the Brownies' part beyond contention; but that which is done when I am up and about is by no means necessarily mine, since all goes to show the Brownies have a hand in it even then. Here is a doubt that much concerns my conscience. For myself— what I call I, my conscience ego, the denizen of the pineal gland unless he has changed his residence since Descartes, the man with the conscience and the variable bank-account, the man with the hat and the boots, and the privilege of voting and not carrying his candidate at the general elections—I am sometimes tempted to suppose he is no story-teller at all, but a creature as matter of fact as any cheesemonger or any cheese, and a realist bemired up to the ears in actuality; so that, by that account, the whole of my published fiction should be the single-handed product of some Brownie, some Familiar, some unseen collaborator, whom I keep locked in a back garret, while I get all the praise and he but a share (which I cannot prevent him getting) of the pudding. I am an excellent adviser, something like Molière's servant; I pull back and I cut down; and I dress the whole in the best words and sentences that I can find and make; I hold the pen, too; and I do the sitting at the table, which is about the worst of it; and when all is done, I make up the manuscript and pay for the registration; so that, on the whole, I have some claim to share, though not so largely as I do, in the profits of our common enterprise.

I can but give an instance or so of what part is done sleeping and what part awake, and leave the reader to share what laurels there are, at his own nod, between myself and my collaborators; and to do this I will first take a book that a number of persons have been polite enough to read, the *Strange Case of Dr. Jekyll and Mr. Hyde.* I had long been trying to write a story on this subject, to find a body, a vehicle, for that strong sense of man's double being which must at times come in upon and overwhelm the mind of every thinking creature. I had even written one, *The Travelling Companion,* which was returned by an editor on the plea that it was a work of genius and indecent, and which I burned the other day on the ground that it was not a work of genius, and that *Jekyll* had supplanted it. Then came one of those financial fluctuations to which (with an elegant modesty) I have hitherto referred in the third person. For two days I went about racking my brains for a plot of any sort; and on the second night I dreamed the scene at the window, and a scene afterwards split in two, in which Hyde, pursued for some crime, took the powder and underwent the change in the presence of his pursuers. All the rest was made awake, and consciously, although I think I can trace in much of it the manner of my Brownies. The meaning of the tale is therefore mine, and had long pre-existed in my garden of Adonis, and tried one body after another in vain; indeed, I do most of the morality, worse luck! and my Brownies have not a rudiment of what we call a conscience. Mine, too, is the setting, mine the characters. All that was given me was the matter of three scenes, and the central idea of a voluntary change becoming involuntary. Will it be thought ungenerous, after I have been so liberally ladling out praise to my unseen collaborators, if I here toss them over, bound hand and foot, into the arena of the critics? For the business of the powders, which so many have censured, is, I am relieved to say, not mine at all but the Brownies'. (pp. 224-28)

> *Robert Louis Stevenson, "A Chapter on Dreams," in his* Across the Plains with Other Memories and Essays, *1892. Reprint by Charles Scribner's Sons, 1923, pp. 206-30.*

REV. W. J. DAWSON   (essay date 1896)

[*Dawson analyzes the "spiritual genius" exhibited in* Dr. Jekyll and Mr. Hyde. *This essay was originally published in the* Young Man *in September 1896.*]

Nowhere does the spiritual genius of Stevenson express itself with such force and fulness as in his *Strange Case of Dr. Jekyll and Mr. Hyde.* . . . Here again we come upon that profound seriousness of soul that underlies all Stevenson's best work; the questioning and philosophic mind groping at the intricate coil of things; the intense imagination of the Celt, fascinated by the grim and subtle mysteries of human nature. The seed-thought of this appalling fable of Dr. Jekyll and Mr. Hyde is familiar enough: it is the ancient Pauline description of a war in our members, so that the thing we would, that we do not; and the thing we would not, that we do. The summary of the whole—it might well form the inscription for the title-page—is that great cry wrung out of the very agonised heart of this internecine conflict, 'O wretched man that I am! who shall deliver me from the body of this death?' We have heard the words many times on the lips of preachers and theologians, but one would certainly have doubted if they were capable of being vitalised by the art of the novelist. . . . A piece of writing like this is a unique achievement in the art of letters. It is really comparable with nothing else; it stands alone. And it is conclusive evidence of that subtlety and force of spiritual genius which gives Stevenson a place apart, and high above all contemporaries, as an interpreter of the deepest things of the human soul. . . .

Stevenson was too modest a man to pose as a thinker; yet a thinker he was, and of great originality and insight. And in the truest sense of the word he was an entirely pious man. He knew what it meant, as he has put it, to go up 'the great bare staircase of his duty, uncheered and undepressed.' In the trials of a life unusually difficult, and pierced by the spear's points of the sharpest limitations, he preserved a splendid and unbroken fortitude. No man ever met life with a higher courage; it is safe to say that a man less courageous would not have lived nearly so long. There are few things more wonderful and admirable than the persistence of his energy; ill and compelled to silence, he still dictates his story in the dumb alphabet, and at his lowest ebb of health makes no complaint. And through all there runs a piety as invincible as his fortitude; a certain gaiety of soul that never deserts him; a faith in the ultimate rightness of destiny which holds him serene amid a sea of troubles. (pp. 219-20)

> *Rev. W. J. Dawson, in an extract in* Stevensoniana, *revised edition, edited by J. A. Hammerton, John Grant, 1910, pp. 217-20.*

LESLIE STEPHEN   (essay date 1902)

[*Stephen is considered one of the most important English critics of the late Victorian and early Edwardian eras. In the following excerpt, Stephen praises Stevenson's novel as a "fine bogey tale."*]

I have always wondered that, after such a proof of his powers of fascination [as *Treasure Island*], Stevenson should only have achieved full recognition by *Dr. Jekyll and Mr. Hyde.* That book, we are told, was also written in a fit of inspiration, suggested by dreaming a 'fine bogey tale.' The public liked it because it became an allegory—a circumstance, I fear, which does not attract me. But considered as a 'bogey tale,' able to revive the old thrill of delicious horror in one who does not care for psychical research, it has the same power of carrying one away by its imaginative intensity. (pp. 233-34)

> *Leslie Stephen, "Robert Louis Stevenson," in his* Studies of a Biographer, *Duckworth and Co., 1902, pp. 206-46.*

KATHARINE D. OSBOURNE   (letter date 1923)

[*Osbourne, the wife of Stevenson's stepson, wrote this letter to George S. Hellman, one of Stevenson's biographers. Here, she attempts to refute a letter by Stevenson (see excerpt dated 1887) in which he examines sexuality in* Dr. Jekyll and Mr. Hyde.]

[There] are two things I want to say now—One regarding the letter you read me of Stevenson's about *Dr. Jekyll and Mr. Hyde.* I do not think it should be taken at full face value. Seldom do any of us write an absolutely truthful letter. They are tempered to suit the recipient. I wish I had noticed the name of the one to whom this letter of Louis Stevenson's was written. If Stevenson had ever thought of its being published or if it had been intended for an understanding public, I think it would have been partly different. We are all things to all men, you know and sometimes Stevenson, not to appear self-righteous to one his heart did not wholly approve, verged from the truth and again did not do himself justice on account of this.

If it were true that hypocrisy and hypocrisy alone was in his mind when writing the story of a dual nature he would have made that point plainer. There was much more in his mind: the constant remembrance of his own love experiences which he did not glory in, but rather realized that could hardly have been different—possessed with his strong temperament, and at the same time he was convinced that no harm was done, since there had been no deception, no destroying of another's happiness. When you see the fragment of autobiography Stevenson began in San Francisco which is to be sent me in your care you will see with what loyalty and gratitude he regarded a woman who had given comfort to a man. I think there is nothing ever written elsewhere that expresses this sublime thought on women. It is chivalry at its highest degree.

Then as to Stevenson's letter about *Dr. Jekyll and Mr. Hyde,* one must set off against it Louis Stevenson's last letter to his cousin Bob. Bob was the one, and he was four years older, that led Louis in the days of adolescence, into many seasons of unrestrained passion. "Bobism" once Lloyd called it in speaking of Louis in those days. In this letter I refer to, Louis's usual desire to be *not censorious* was thrown off. He was speaking not so much to Bob as of conclusions he had come to for himself in reviewing his own life. He was thinking with regret of the waywardness of his youth. He was realizing that this giving way to his passions had had a weakening effect on his own character even if it had not hurt professional prostitutes nor willing women—and he was reviewing the causes which had brought his life to a distressful wasted end as in his depression thus it appeared to him. . . .

He realized that he had been a victim all through, and mainly the victim of public sentiment and ignorance on the public's part of what love and virtue is—and how it is to be hedged about and preserved in its strength, not wasted. . . .

This letter to Bob is of the utmost importance in weighing that part of Louis Stevenson's life which has been left untold, his love nature, and because of this omission makes the chief demand that a new biography be written. (pp. 76-8)

> *Katharine D. Osbourne, in a letter to George S. Hellman on May 28, 1923, in* The True Stevenson: A Study in Clarification *by George S. Hellman, Little, Brown, and Company, 1925, pp. 76-9.*

EDWIN A. McALPIN   (essay date 1928)

[*In the following excerpt, McAlpin discusses the effects of sin in* Dr. Jekyll and Mr. Hyde.]

There is [a] characteristic of sin that prevents it from being considered a mere matter of personal opinion. It is the destroyer of character and also of sound judgment. After a person has yielded to temptation he loses his ability to form correct estimates as to what is right and what is wrong.

Robert Louis Stevenson shows this in *Dr. Jekyll and Mr. Hyde.* Dr. Jekyll possessed a fine intellect, enthusiasm for scientific investigation, and a desire to hold the good opinion of other people. He had also inherited a large fortune. His life gave promise of being both useful and successful. He was honored by his associates and looked up to by all men. He was known for his benevolent disposition and for the efforts he made to relieve those in distress. This respectable and respected man had, as every man has, another side to his nature. He liked to indulge in sensual pleasures.

Dr. Jekyll's investigations included metaphysical as well as medical subjects. These investigations led him to believe that every life was made up of several different personalities held together in one body. He thought it might be possible to find a drug strong enough to dissolve the connecting link and let loose a kind of character other than the one that naturally

controlled the individual's life. He wanted to retain the respect of his professional associates and still indulge his sensual nature. He was torn in two. (pp. 44-5)

The story is made up of the relations and adventures of [the] two different personalities, which dwelt in one body. While he despised the character and activities of Mr. Hyde, Dr. Jekyll enjoyed sensuality too much to give up this obnoxious personality and its indulgences. The dual position seemed a perfectly safe one. When he tired of the excesses and indulgences of Mr. Hyde, he reassumed the person and character of Dr. Jekyll. He did not consider himself a hypocrite. Dr. Jekyll was very sorry for the cruelties of Mr. Hyde, and frequently Dr. Jekyll spent time and money in relieving the distress Mr. Hyde had caused. Once he found it necessary to double the dose before his transformation was completed, but he was deaf to the warning this should have given him. He continued his double life until, one night, in a wild outburst of fury, Mr. Hyde committed a brutal murder. After destroying all evidences of the close connection between Mr. Hyde and Dr. Jekyll he returned to his home and, taking the required dose, was transformed into the respectable and honored Dr. Jekyll. (pp. 46-7)

The story then narrates the efforts Dr. Jekyll made in order to keep from slipping into the features and character of Mr. Hyde. His supply of one of the salts he used to prepare the drug that caused this transformation was becoming exhausted. When he replaced it he discovered the new consignment failed to give results.

It is the old, old story of the good yielding to the evil. Finally the evil reigns supreme.

Under its strange fantasies *Dr. Jekyll and Mr. Hyde* is a good account of the dual elements in personality. Every individual born on this earth has a higher and a lower nature. There are moments when it is comparatively easy to follow the good. At other times it is desperately hard to keep the animal side of life from gaining control. Dr. Jekyll said the drug he used was neither good nor bad, it simply established the mental state that was in ascendance at the moment and made it the controlling power of his life, even to the alteration of his features. For a time a person may be able to live honorably and occasionally indulge in sin, but if a man tries to carry on a dual life, the evil is sure to overcome the good. His moral judgments lose all sense of proportion, and a catastrophe occurs.

In *Dr. Jekyll and Mr. Hyde* Stevenson shows one of the worst characteristics of sin. This is the tendency of evil to overcome and drive out the best elements of character. While the book is only a fantastic tale it is also an allegory of man's struggle against the baser side of life. Unless a person conquers the evil in his nature by unifying his personality on pure and honorable lines, the evil is sure to gain the upper hand and wreck both his individuality and his life. (pp. 48-9)

[Two] truths stand out as danger signals for all who read: first, the innocent must always suffer with the guilty, and second, both character and personality must deteriorate when an individual yields to the subtle influence of sin. We need these warnings. We need the art of the novelist to show us by vivid, startling dramatization that there is no doubt about it: "The wages of sin is death." (p. 49)

> *Edwin A. McAlpin, "Sin and Its Consequences," in his* Old and New Books as Life Teachers, *Doubleday, Doran & Company, Inc., 1928, pp. 36-49.*

G. K. CHESTERTON (essay date 1928)

[Chesterton was one of England's most prominent and colorful men of letters during the early twentieth century. The following excerpt, in which he studies the setting and morality of Dr. Jekyll and Mr. Hyde, *is drawn from his critical biography of Stevenson.]*

It will be realised that I am not, alas, so close a student of Stevensoniana as many who seem to think much less of Stevenson. But it seems to me that the story of [*Dr. Jekyll and Mr. Hyde*], which is presumably presented as happening in London, is all the time very unmistakably happening in Edinburgh. More than one of the characters seem to be pure Scots. Mr. Utterson, the lawyer, is a most unmistakably Scottish lawyer, strictly occupied with Scots Law. No modern English lawyer ever read a book of dry divinity in the evening merely because it was Sunday. Mr. Hyde indeed possesses the cosmopolitan charm that unites all nations; but there is something decidedly Caledonian about Dr. Jekyll; and especially something that calls up that quality in Edinburgh that led an unkind observer (probably from Glasgow) to describe it as "an east-windy, west-endy place." The particular tone about his respectability, and the horror of mixing his reputation with mortal frailty, belongs to the upper middle classes in solid Puritan communities. But what is especially to the point of the present argument, there is a sense in which that Puritanism is expressed even more in Mr. Hyde than in Dr. Jekyll. The sense of the sudden stink of evil, the immediate invitation to step into stark filth, the abruptness of the alternative between that prim and proper pavement and that black and reeking gutter—all this, though doubtless involved in the logic of the tale, is far too frankly and familiarly offered not to have had some basis in observation and reality. It is not thus that the ordinary young pagan, of warmer climes, conceives the alternative of Christ and Aphrodite. His imagination and half his mind are involved in defending the beauty and dignity of the joy of gods and men. It is not so that Stevenson himself came to talk of such things, when he had felt the shadow of old Athens fall on the pagan side of Paris. I allow for all the necessary horror of the conception of Hyde. But this dingy quality does not belong only to the demon antics of Hyde. It is implied, somehow, in every word about the furtive and embarrassed vices of Jekyll. It is the tragedy of a Puritan town; every bit as much as that black legend which Stevenson loved, in which the walking-stick of Major Weir went walking down the street all by itself. I hope to say something in a moment about the very deep and indeed very just and wise morality that is really involved in that ugly tale. I am only remarking here that the atmosphere and setting of it are those of some tale of stiff hypocrisy in a rigid sect or provincial village; it might be a tale of the Middle West savagely dissected in the *Spoon River Anthology*. But the point about it is that the human beauty which makes sin most dangerous hardly appears by a hint; this Belial is never graceful or humane; and in this there seems to me to be something suggestive of the inverted order and ugly contrast with which licence presents itself in a world that has frowned on liberty. It is the utterance of somebody who, in the words of Kipling, knew the worst too young; not necessarily in his own act or by his own fault, but by the nature of a system which saw no difference between the worst and the moderately bad. But whatever form the shock of evil might take, I think it jerked him out of the right development of his romantic nature; and was responsible for much that seemed random or belated in his life.

I do not mean to imply that the morality of the story itself has anything of weakness or morbidity; my opinion is very much the other way. Though the fable may seem mad, the moral is very sane; indeed, the moral is strictly orthodox. The trouble is that most of those who mention it do not know the moral, possibly because they have never read the fable. From time to time those anonymous authorities in the newspapers, who dismiss Stevenson with such languid grace, will say that there is something quite cheap and obvious about the idea that one man is really two men and can be divided into the evil and the good. Unfortunately for them, that does not happen to be the idea. The real stab of the story is not in the discovery that the one man is two men; but in the discovery that the two men are one man. After all the diverse wandering and warring of those two incompatible beings, there was still one man born and only one man buried. Jekyll and Hyde have become a proverb and a joke; only it is a proverb read backwards and a joke that nobody really sees. But it might have occurred to the languid critics, as a part of the joke, that the tale is a tragedy; and that this is only another way of saying that the experiment was a failure. The point of the story is not that a man *can* cut himself off from his conscience, but that he cannot. The surgical operation is fatal in the story. It is an amputation of which both the parts die. Jekyll, even in dying, declares the conclusion of the matter; that the load of man's moral struggle is bound upon him and cannot be thus escaped. The reason is that there can never be equality between the evil and the good. Jekyll and Hyde are not twin brothers. They are rather, as one of them truly remarks, like father and son. After all, Jekyll created Hyde; Hyde would never have created Jekyll; he only destroyed Jekyll. The notion is not so hackneyed as the critics find it, after Stevenson has found it for them thirty years ago. But Jekyll's claim is not that it is the first of such experiments in duality; but rather that it must be the last.

Nor do I necessarily admit the technical clumsiness which some have alleged against the tale, merely because I believe that many of its emotions were first experienced in the crude pain of youth.... That moment in which Jekyll finds his own formula fail him, through an accident he had never foreseen, is simply the supreme moment in every story of a man buying power from hell; the moment when he finds the flaw in the deed. Such a moment comes to Macbeth and Faustus and a hundred others; and the whole point of it is that nothing is really secure, least of all a Satanist security. The moral is that the devil is a liar, and more especially a traitor; that he is more dangerous to his friends than his foes.... [Although] the story ultimately emerged as a gargoyle very carefully graven by a mature master-craftsman, and was moreover a gargoyle of the greatest spiritual edification, eminently suited to be stuck on to the most sacred edifice, my point for the moment is that the stone of which it was made was originally found, I think, by Stevenson as a boy, kicking about the street, not to mention the gutter. In other words, he did not need to leave the respectable metropolis of the north to find the weaknesses of Jekyll and the crimes of Hyde.

I deal with these things in general terms, not merely out of delicacy, but partly out of something that I might almost call impatience or contempt. (pp. 51-6)

Stevenson was not a Catholic: he did not pretend to have remained a Puritan; but he was a highly honourable, responsible and chivalrous Pagan, in a world of Pagans who were most of them considerably less conspicuous for chivalry and honour. I for one, if I may say so, am ready to defend my own standards or to judge other men by theirs. But the Victorian pretence that every well-dressed hero of romance with over five hundred a year is born immune from the temptations which the mightiest saints have rolled themselves in brambles to control—that does not concern me and I shall not discuss it again.

But what does concern me, at this particular stage of the story, is not the question of what Stevenson thought right or wrong when he had become consciously and consistently a Pagan, but the particular way in which right and wrong appeared to him at this crude and groping age when he was still by tradition a Puritan. And I do think there was something tail-foremost, to use one of his own favourite words, in the way in which evil crept into his existence, as it does into everybody else's. He saw the tail of the devil before he saw his horns. Puritanism gave him the key rather to the cellars than the halls of Babylon; and something thus subterranean, suffocating and debased rolls like a smoke over the story of Jekyll and Hyde. (pp. 58-9)

> G. K. Chesterton, in his Robert Louis Stevenson,
> Dodd, Mead & Company, 1928, 211 p.

VLADIMIR NABOKOV   (lecture date 1941-59)

[*A Russian-born American man of letters, Nabokov was a prolific contributor to many literary fields who produced works in both Russian and English and distinguished himself in particular as the author of the novels* Lolita *and* Pale Fire. *Nabokov was fascinated with all aspects of the creative life; in his works he explored the origins of creativity, the relationships of artists to their work, and the nature of invented reality. In the following excerpt, Nabokov analyzes the style and artistic intent of* Dr. Jekyll *and* Mr. Hyde. *This excerpt formed part of a series of lectures given between 1941 and 1959.*]

Dr. Jekyll and Mr. Hyde was written in bed, at Bournemouth on the English Channel, in 1885 in between hemorrhages from the lungs. It was published in January 1886. Dr. Jekyll is a fat, benevolent physician, not without human frailties, who at times by means of a potion projects himself into, or concentrates or precipitates, an evil person of brutal and animal nature taking the name of Hyde, in which character he leads a patchy criminal life of sorts. For a time he is able to revert to his Jekyll personality—there is a down-to-Hyde drug and a back-to-Jekyll drug—but gradually his better nature weakens and finally the back-to-Jekyll potion fails, and he poisons himself when on the verge of exposure. This is the bald plot of the story.

First of all, if you have the Pocket Books edition I have, you will veil the monstrous, abominable, atrocious, criminal, foul, vile, youth-depraving jacket—or better say straitjacket. You will ignore the fact that ham actors under the direction of pork packers have acted in a parody of the book, which parody was then photographed on a film and showed in places called theatres; it seems to me that to call a movie house a theatre is the same as to call an undertaker a mortician.

And now comes my main injunction. Please completely forget, disremember, obliterate, unlearn, consign to oblivion any notion you may have had that **Jekyll and Hyde** is some kind of a mystery story, a detective story, or movie. It is of course quite true that Stevenson's short novel, written in 1885, is one of the ancestors of the modern mystery story. But today's mystery story is the very negation of style, being, at the best, conventional literature. Frankly, I am not one of those college professors who coyly boasts of enjoying detective stories—they are too badly written for my taste and bore me to death. Whereas Stevenson's story is—God bless his pure soul—lame as a detective story. Neither is it a parable nor an allegory, for it would be tasteless as either. It has, however, its own special

enchantment if we regard it as a phenomenon of style. It is not only a good "bogey story," as Stevenson exclaimed when awakening from a dream in which he had visualized it much in the same way I suppose as magic cerebration had granted Coleridge the vision of the most famous of unfinished poems. It is also, and more importantly, "a fable that lies nearer to poetry than to ordinary prose fiction" [according to Stephen Gwynn] and therefore belongs to the same order of art as, for instance, *Madame Bovary* or *Dead Souls*.

There is a delightful winey taste about this book; in fact, a good deal of old mellow wine is drunk in the story: one recalls the wine that Utterson so comfortably sips. This sparkling and comforting draft is very different from the icy pangs caused by the chameleon liquor, the magic reagent that Jekyll brews in his dusty laboratory. Everything is very appetizingly put. Gabriel John Utterson of Gaunt Street mouths his words most roundly; there is an appetizing tang about the chill morning in London, and there is even a certain richness of tone in the description of the horrible sensations Jekyll undergoes during his *hydizations*. Stevenson had to rely on style very much in order to perform the trick, in order to master the two main difficulties confronting him: (1) to make the magic potion a plausible drug based on a chemist's ingredients and (2) to make Jekyll's evil side before and after the hydization a believable evil. (pp. 179-80)

The names Jekyll and Hyde are of Scandinavian origin, and I suspect that Stevenson chose them from the same page of an old book on surnames where I looked them up myself. Hyde comes from the Anglo-Saxon *hyd*, which is the Danish *hide*, "a haven." And Jekyll comes from the Danish name *Jökulle*, which means "an icicle." Not knowing these simple derivations one would be apt to find all kinds of symbolic meanings, especially in Hyde, the most obvious being that Hyde is a kind of hiding place for Dr. Jekyll, in whom the jocular doctor and the killer are combined.

Three important points are completely obliterated by the popular notions about this seldom read book:

1. Is Jekyll good? No, he is a composite being, a mixture of good and bad, a preparation consisting of a ninety-nine percent solution of Jekyllite and one percent of Hyde (or *hydatid* from the Greek "water" which in zoology is a tiny pouch within the body of man and other animals, a pouch containing a limpid fluid with larval tapeworms in it—a delightful arrangement, for the little tapeworms at least. Thus in a sense, Mr. Hyde is Dr. Jekyll's parasite—but I must warn that Stevenson knew nothing of this when he chose the name.) Jekyll's morals are poor from the Victorian point of view. He is a hypocritical creature carefully concealing his little sins. He is vindictive, never forgiving Dr. Lanyon with whom he disagrees in scientific matters. He is foolhardy. Hyde is mingled with him, within him. In this mixture of good and bad in Dr. Jekyll, the bad can be separated as Hyde, who is a precipitate of pure evil, a precipitation in the chemical sense since something of the composite Jekyll remains behind to wonder in horror at Hyde while Hyde is in action.

2. Jekyll is not really transformed into Hyde but projects a concentrate of pure evil that becomes Hyde, who is smaller than Jekyll, a big man, to indicate the larger amount of good that Jekyll possesses.

3. There are really three personalities—Jekyll, Hyde, and a third, the Jekyll residue when Hyde takes over. (pp. 182-83)

Stevenson has set himself a difficult artistic problem, and we wonder very much if he is strong enough to solve it. Let us break it up into the following points:

1. In order to make the fantasy plausible he wishes to have it pass through the minds of matter-of-fact persons, Utterson and Enfield, who even for all their commonplace logic must be affected by something bizarre and nightmarish in Hyde.

2. These two stolid souls must convey to the reader something of the horror of Hyde, but at the same time they, being neither artists nor scientists, unlike Dr. Lanyon, cannot be allowed by the author to notice details.

3. Now if Stevenson makes Enfield and Utterson too commonplace and too plain, they will not be able to express even the vague discomfort Hyde causes them. On the other hand, the reader is curious not only about their reactions but he wishes also to see Hyde's face for himself.

4. But the author himself does not see Hyde's face clearly enough, and could only have it described by Enfield or Utterson in some oblique, imaginative, suggestive way, which, however, would not be a likely manner of expression on the part of these stolid souls.

I suggest that given the situation and the characters, the only way to solve the problem is to have the aspect of Hyde cause in Enfield and Utterson not only a shudder of repulsion but also something else. I suggest that the shock of Hyde's presence brings out the hidden artist in Enfield and the hidden artist in Utterson. Otherwise the bright perceptions that illumine Enfield's story of his journey through the lighted, empty streets before he witnessed Mr. Hyde's assault on the child, and the colorful imaginings of Utterson's dreams after he has heard the story can only be explained by the abrupt intrusion of the author with his own set of artistic values and his own diction and intonation. A curious problem indeed.

There is a further problem. Stevenson gives us the specific, lifelike description of events by humdrum London gentlemen, but contrasting with this are the unspecified, vague, but ominous allusions to pleasures and dreadful vices somewhere behind the scenes. On the one side there is "reality"; on the other, "a nightmare world." If the author really means there to be a sharp contrast between the two, then the story could strike us as a little disappointing. If we are really being told "never mind what the evil was—just believe it was something very bad," then we might feel ourselves cheated and bullied. We could feel cheated by vagueness in the most interesting part of the story just because its setting is so matter of fact and realistic. The question that must be asked of the work is whether Utterson and the fog and the cabs and the pale butler are more "real" than the weird experiments and unmentionable adventures of Jekyll and Hyde. (pp. 192-93)

Vladimir Nabokov, "Robert Louis Stevenson: 'The Strange Case of Dr. Jekyll and Mr. Hyde','' in his Lectures on Literature, *edited by Fredson Bowers, Harcourt Brace Jovanovich, 1980, pp. 179-204.*

RALPH TYMMS (essay date 1949)

[*Tymms discusses the use of the doppelgänger, or literary double, in the novel.*]

In *The Strange Case of Dr. Jekyll and Mr. Hyde,* Stevenson advances from the boundaries of allegory towards the realm of psychological realism; though never does he lose from sight

his point of departure. The basic conception of the *Doppelgänger,* to which he remains true, assumes the moral dualism of man.... Jekyll maintains ... that evil has its right to freedom; and by a magical drug he releases the slumbering monster in his nature, to replace the predominantly good self habitually in control. Jekyll confesses that he had first detected a moral dualism in his nature; but even this (he supposes), if the truth were but known, would not suffice to describe the complexity of man's mind, doubtless 'a mere polity of multifarious, incongruous and independent denizens'. Setting out from his favourite attitude of moral allegory, Stevenson chances on conceptions of dualism closely resembling those of experimental psychologists of his day; and, as Jekyll continues to ponder on the problem of the discordant elements, he concludes that if he could but house each of them in separate identities, each would be freed from the intolerable interference of the other, incongruous, twin. This proves to be true: he succeeds in separating the conflicting selves from the 'agonised womb of consciousness' by the wonder-working drug; it '... had no discriminating action; it was neither diabolical nor divine; it but shook the doors of the prison-house of my disposition; and like the captives of Philippi, that which stood within ran forth'. The evil that lurks within his mind is swift to seize the opportunity, and projects itself in an appropriately hideous bodily form. Under the name of Hyde, it indulges in all the vices and crimes which Jekyll's better self has long resisted; but Hyde is younger and smaller than Jekyll, since, in a lifetime of predominant virtue, the evil self has had less scope for growth and maturity.

Hyde's new freedom progressively strengthens him at the expense of Jekyll's normal self, and Jekyll comes to loathe this horror chained to him—'caged in his flesh', a monster clinging to him ..., in whom he is gradually becoming incorporated, and who, as time goes on, waits for Jekyll's hour of weakness to be born again, even without the help of the drug. Hyde returns Jekyll's hatred, but he is forced to give way to him and to allow Jekyll's habitual self to resume control in body and mind whenever he is himself in danger of capture for the murder he has committed. But in his resentment he plays malicious tricks on his other self, scrawling blasphemies in Jekyll's handwriting on the pages of devotional books, burning his letters, and destroying the portrait of his father. The end of this game of hide-and-seek between the alternating entities comes when Jekyll is unable to keep his own form at all. Hyde has become complete master, and by his very triumph brings about his own ruin; for, in permanently abandoning Jekyll's form, he has involuntarily destroyed his only hope of escape from capture; when he realises that he cannot turn back into Jekyll's wonted form, the monster kills himself, and thereby, Jekyll, too. (pp. 92-3)

Ralph Tymms, "The Double in Post-Romantic Literature," in his Doubles in Literary Psychology, *Bowes & Bowes, 1949, pp. 72-118.*

CHARLES D. ARING (essay date 1960-61)

[*Aring is a neurologist who has written extensively on psychiatry, medical education, and philosophy. In discussing the psychological insights that Stevenson reveals in* Dr. Jekyll and Mr. Hyde, *Aring compares modern perceptions of personality with those of Stevenson's day.*]

Like many another genius, Stevenson was able to share with us the fruits of his fertile mind. These harvests demand inquiring curiosity and critical thought; as wildest dreams they are preludes that may or may not lead to truth. In *The Strange Case of Dr. Jekyll and Mr. Hyde,* Stevenson recovered his dream story and reworked it so provocatively that, like some other writers and poets, he is considered to have been in advance of the great sanitarians of the mind.

Most everybody has heard of Stevenson's tale about the dichotomy resident in each of us. Edward Hyde, the prime mover in the story, is the embodiment of evil; loathsome and ape-like, he evokes hate at first sight, although sighting him is most unusual. Hyde's alter ego, the admirable Dr. Henry Jekyll, is a Fellow of the Royal Society, an eminently successful and respected physician, handsome, wealthy, with a string of degrees attached to his name including, besides the medical, a Doctor of Laws and a Doctorate of Civil Law, all of which, it might be presumed, would have allowed him to know himself. But such was not the case. In 1885, when the story was written, no degree carried with it much hope of enlightenment about the self.

The emergence of the satanic Hyde under the guise of medical research by the good Dr. Jekyll and the eventual loss of control of the former by the latter have become legend. Their destruction was inevitable in those early Darwinian times when the fit survived and there wasn't much to be done about those born less fit. Jekyll's researches into the mind's function are said to be "unscientific balderdash" and Jekyll is "wrong in mind," according to his surgeon friend, Dr. Hastie Lanyon. In retrospect I believe we would term his researches an interesting and needful prelude.

In attempting to find the truth behind these preludes, considerable study has gone into such problems as Stevenson lays before us. We no longer doubt that we are made as Dr. Jekyll and that our behavior is apt to contain Hyde-like vagaries. Human behavior is never quite predictable, mainly because the unseen Hyde, as Stevenson says, "never sleeps and constantly growls for license." While our ability to predict behavior may not have improved since Stevenson's time, we have advanced in our ability to understand the manner in which we have behaved, and in the opportunity to do something about it. "Life can only be understood backward, but it must be lived forward," said Kierkegaard. Stevenson tells us little about Jekyll's history prior to his maturity. We know that he is a prosperous bachelor of fifty and that he was wild when he was young. But as Stevenson had the lawyer Utterson remark in his soliloquy about Jekyll's past, as it bore on his present tribulations, "in the law of God there is no statute of limitations." It would appear, therefore, that Stevenson felt there could be no release from the past, particularly if the past was inadequately considered or vaguely understood.

Stevenson hadn't much use for Hyde, or perhaps it would be more accurate to say that the culture of 1885 had no evident uses for him. In Stevenson's day no better solution for the lively Mr. Hyde was to be had than to do away with him, a method reminiscent of the handling of some of our modern Hydes. Book learning still doesn't cut much of a figure in the presence of the preternatural Hyde. However, convert him into a cadaver and it is remarkable how readily he becomes manageable. Here is the main issue, as a contemporary psychiatrist Bertram D. Lewin has pointed out: some of us prefer to work with a live and even a lively subject; others would have him completely out of the way. There are, of course, intermediate positions between these extremes.

A close examination of the lively Edward Hyde at this later day will reveal that he has many qualities that we could wish for ourselves. He is strong and contemptuous of danger; he can be direct and vigorous; his faculties are sharp; he is completely lacking the dissemblance so crippling to ordinary man. Among his endowments is that of being able to arouse the doctor to do his bidding even in the dead of night, no mean feat in itself. In disaster he maintains a certain equanimity. There is no beating about the bush with Mr. Hyde; you know where you stand with him. Get in his way and he takes steps to go around you or, if necessary, over you—conduct sanctioned in some eminently successful men if we can believe their biographers. Mr. Hyde prefers to be abroad by night, as does the pestilence that walketh in darkness, and as do dreams. Released by the censor, he commits his vigorous predations when the coast is relatively clear, as with the action in dreams. Again like dreams, he is glimpsed by few. He handles troublesome situations forthrightly and with dispatch; this trait is also reminiscent of dream activity.

A patient who has engaged his own Hyde suggests that Stevenson's story should be reworked to indict Jekyll rather than Hyde as the villain. With his personal experience as touchstone, he arrives at the reasonable conclusion that Hyde never had a chance. He was handled as a monster, repressed and in chains, as illustrated in the summary uttered by Jekyll that "my devil

A frontispiece to Dr. Jekyll and Mr. Hyde. *Illustration by W. Stein.*

had long been caged, he came out roaring." As far as the data take us, Hyde seems to be a prime case of character warping. (pp. 70-2)

Jekyll's researches into mind were spectacular but contributed little to an understanding of it. Like some of the flamboyant experiments with mind in our time, they are quite startling, but leave no one the wiser. Jekyll's manipulations are of the order that do things to man rather than with him; they are authoritarian in nature and accordingly ignore or bypass his creative possibilities. Rather than foster more living by knowing, in the sense of Samuel Butler, they encourage helplessness and passivity; one is done for or to, rather than with.

But as is usual, the unknowing victim, Jekyll in this case, readily developed the derivations of his disquiet that we know as symptoms—the same symptoms that have become so ubiquitous in our time. Take insomnia for example: even a doze would suffice to bring the alter-ego Hyde on the scene. By remaining awake one may guard against the evil, the raging hell within. To sleep, then, is to tempt the emergence of all-powerful devils—all-powerful in the proportion that one is weak, or as sickly as Stevenson, or as unknowing as poor Jekyll. As we have learned since, such symptoms as insomnia are a sad substitute for understanding, although the victim usually prefers them to the look within. Symptoms pervert all useful function. Energy is drained into sustaining them, and malfunction, if not disintegration, is the inevitable outcome.

Stevenson goes to some trouble to impress upon us the reaction of the few who had caught glimpses of Hyde: *disgust, loathing* and *fear* are the strong words that he uses. Hyde evoked the desire to kill at first sight, a revulsion not unlike that evinced in even the highest medical circles later in the nineteenth century when glimpses were beginning to be afforded of the unconscious life of man, some of them through dreams. Today it is reasonably said that nothing provokes such fear as one's unconscious. For what other reason is it that we would have inward peace, but will not look within? (pp. 72-3)

Utterson, Jekyll's friend and lawyer, thought that if he could but behold the features of the real Hyde, the mystery of him might lighten, and perhaps be dissipated altogether "as was the habit of mysterious things when well examined." Stevenson is urging us to examine the thing that is dreaded although it occasion disgust, loathing, fear and even murderous impulses—feelings that can be controlled if we will become aware of their nature.

In Stevenson's day the way to health for Jekyll was in dissociation from his alter-ego Hyde, since no other method to unburden the one of the other had been devised. Stevenson noted correctly, to be sure, that the more either was exercised, the stronger it became and assumed the ascendancy. Much that has been said since Stevenson about the constitution of personality, or its reconstituting, has derived largely from fright and ignorance of the manner in which the mind works. (pp. 73-4)

Every authority on behavior—including the Delphic Oracle, Plato, the Bible, Montaigne, Shakespeare, Cervantes, the poets and today's enlightened sociologist and psychiatrist—has reiterated "know thyself" as the best means to achieve Plato's mark of an educated man: that he should be able, and above all that he should always be willing, to see things as they are. . . . Several centuries before Christ, Plato warned about the madness and misery of one who uses the appearance of things as a measure of their reality and makes a mess of it.

It was to this knotty problem that Stevenson addressed himself three-quarters of a century ago, in the working out of his dream fantasy. He had the lawyer Mr. Utterson attempt to lessen the mystery of Hyde by seeking him out and confronting him to try to "know" him. Utterson seemed utterly baffled by the experience. But if we listen carefully to Stevenson's lucid and graceful undertones, we catch hints that his psychological insights were considerably ahead of the times:

> Mr. Hyde was pale and dwarfish, he gave an impression of deformity without any namable malformation, he had a displeasing smile, he had borne himself to the lawyer with a sort of murderous mixture of timidity and boldness, and he spoke with a husky, whispering, and somewhat broken voice: all these were points against him, but not all of these together would explain the hitherto unknown disgust, loathing and fear with which Mr. Utterson regarded him. "There must be something else," said the perplexed gentleman. "There is something more, if I could find a name for it. God bless me, the man seems hardly human! Something troglodytic, shall we say? or can it be the old story of Dr. Fell? or is it the mere radiance of a foul soul that thus transpires through, and transfigures, its clay continent? . . ."

Surely in this day, whenever a Hyde rears an ugly head, the challenge needs to be joined and the thing examined with our very best will, minds, energy and tools to try to learn its meaning. Turning away from it will no longer do; time has run out on this quaint custom. (pp. 75-6)

Despite his eventual solution for the evil and lively Hyde, Stevenson betrays a certain fascination for him. Hyde's spirits were always higher, sharper, more acute than Jekyll's, and it appears that so was his love of life. In their day Jekyll and Hyde were coheirs to death; they were irrevocably oriented toward destruction despite any love for life. Deep, blind, primitive compulsions that bypassed consciousness drew them nearer and nearer to the verge of death. These forces, usually neglected and about which we are therefore unknowing, drag along such persons as Jekyll to premature destruction. Theirs is a drift toward tragedy. Stevenson said of this force ". . . that what was dead and had no shape should usurp the offices of life."

Jekyll was frequently sunk in apathy, almost depression; he had little zest for life and seemed bored by his deadly round. His was, he said, "an aversion to the dryness of a life of study." Today we can better understand Jekyll's method of stimulating his listless spirit, which is described in a line toward the end of the story: "With a transport of glee I mauled the unresisting body [Jekyll's own], tasting delight with every blow. . . ."

While Stevenson had glimmerings that strength, vigor and spirit were on the side of Hyde, he saw no constructive way in which they could be tapped. Indeed, in 1885 there was none. In the late nineteenth century these were waste products buried in the manifest personality, and there was no way to get to them. They were then about as hidden from man as was the force in the atom, and potentially as destructive. Our tools for working these deposits have improved, among them the analysis of dreams, an exquisite although highly subtle instrument.

Stevenson took the tack, perhaps poetic license, perhaps autobiographical and surely timely, that there was no resolution of the problem but death and oblivion. This remains a prevailing breeze, and it hardly matters in what quarter one is standing. Our current Hydes—junior and senior delinquents, beatniks, Communists, obscene literature, and even dreams—too frequently are given the now outmoded treatment of suppression. It is difficult to convey the fact that what is suppressed retains its *full* force. Indeed, suppression may stimulate a swelling of the energy.

We need constantly to be reminded that mystery will lighten and perhaps be dissipated altogether when it is competently examined. This does not guarantee resolution, but it is the starting point of any real investigation motivated by a genuine desire to find out. This requires hard work, even bravery. (pp. 76-7)

The fearful cannot be allowed to restrain our explorations; they would prefer to have us about as circumscribed and restrained as Jekyll sometimes had Hyde. Naturally enough, they are troubled by such manifestations as a searching curiosity or dreams, and they refuse to be responsible for them. They act as though dreams were inspired by alien spirits. They find it impossible to believe that as people become more knowing they become more responsible. Since they have no real faith in themselves, they find everyone untrustworthy. With our uneasy friends, acquiescence in their nostalgic way of life puts their fears temporarily at rest, while an active exploration of the truth arouses their anxiety. They are satisfied with things as they are, with their prerogatives.

There isn't one of the feared, loathed and hated groups or concepts—our Hydes—that does not contain strengths, if we have the curiosity, the wit, the courage and the energy to search them out and to temper them. (pp. 77-8)

So the resolution of the Jekyll-Hyde dilemma is not repression or suicide or death, which in any of their derivations is a quick way out, but rather the cultivation and harvest of the strengths and constructions—the by-products, if you will—of the partial evil. (p. 78)

> *Charles D. Aring, "The Case Becomes Less Strange,"*
> in The American Scholar, *Vol. 30, No. 1, Winter,*
> *1960-61, pp. 67-78.*

MASAO MIYOSHI (essay date 1966)

[*In considering* Dr. Jekyll and Mr. Hyde *as a "story of ideas," Miyoshi analyzes its characters in relation to Victorian society, identifies the literary tradition from which it developed, and addresses the relationship between Jekyll and Hyde.*]

The *Strange Case of Dr. Jekyll and Mr. Hyde* is not exactly a nursery tale, and it is reasonable to expect that, of all the Stevenson stories, that would be the one to get an occasional nod in an article or in the classroom as having something more than entertainment quality, even as having something to do with ideas. Everyone is familiar with its two-men-in-one motif . . . but perhaps not unrelated to this popular status, the book is usually dismissed as crude science fiction or cruder moral allegory. . . . Should *Jekyll and Hyde* be remembered solely or primarily for its author's supposed invention of the dual-personality theme? Is the book too slight for any more conscientious critical effort? I would like to think that . . . *Dr. Jekyll and Mr. Hyde* may be read and studied as a story of ideas, that it will by this means yield insights into certain aspects of the

late Victorian society that was its milieu, and that it will finally suggest something of the literary tradition which fathered it. (p. 471)

In approaching the work, it would be best to envision the world of the story—its men and landscape—before turning to the Jekyll-Hyde relationship itself. To begin with Mr. Utterson, who is evidently a highly respected citizen. The lawyer is always correctly professional and trustworthy, yet there is something furtive and suppressed about him. He is "austere with himself." He never smiles. He is "cold, scanty, and embarrassed in discourse." . . . He claims to like the theater, though he has not been to a play in twenty years. He makes no new friends and socializes only with men he has known well for a very long time. As for his renowned tolerance toward other people's misconduct, this looks suspiciously like the result not of charity but of indifference, though there is the subtlest suggestion of vicarious pleasure. Utterson, too, it turns out, has a past not quite innocent. When it occurs to him that blackmail may be at the root of Hyde's connection with Jekyll, he considers the possibility of a similar threat to himself: "And the lawyer, scared by the thought, brooded a while on his own past, groping in all the corners of memory, lest by chance some Jack-in-the-Box of an old iniquity should leap to light there." . . . When his friend and client Sir Danvers Carew is murdered, the event stirs no deeper emotion in him than worry "lest the good name of another should be sucked down in the eddy of the scandal." . . . (pp. 471-72)

Dr. Hastie Lanyon is, by contrast, an apparently healthy and genial man. Yet he too is shielded from life by an imposing respectability. Estranged from Dr. Jekyll for ten years, Dr. Lanyon is a scientist of "practical usefulness," . . . who sees Jekyll as a man gone wrong with his "scientific heresies." . . . As it happens, when the great Dr. Lanyon confronts a phenomenon which his matter-of-fact science cannot explain, his life is "shaken to its roots." . . . (p. 472)

The important men of the book, then, are all unmarried, barren of ideas, emotionally stifled, joyless. In the city at large the more prosperous business people fix up their homes and shops, yet there is something sleazy about the decor: the houses give an appearance of "coquetry," and the store fronts invite one like "rows of smiling saleswomen.". . . The setting is of a wasteland, but a wasteland hidden by the secure and relatively comfortable respectability of its inhabitants.

In this society of respectables Dr. Jekyll stands out as "the very pink of the proprieties." . . . Although his studies, like those of Faust and Frankenstein before him, tend toward "the mystic and the transcendental," . . . he still manages to maintain a considerable scientific reputation. And yet, despite Jekyll's social role—in fact, because of it—it is Jekyll, rather than Utterson or Lanyon, who brings forth Mr. Hyde.

It will be remembered that, for a period long before the emergence of Mr. Hyde, Dr. Jekyll was "committed to a profound duplicity of life": alongside his "imperious desire" for dignity and reputation, there was that "impatient gaiety of disposition.". . . But for those in the Victorian wasteland, gaiety and respectability are not easily reconciled. Dr. Jekyll, in particular, sees the two as mutually exclusive: a respectable pleasure would be a contradiction in terms. The exacting nature of his ambitions was such that the most unremarkable pleasure resulted in shame. Meanwhile, his Faustian studies, which had already "shed such a strong light on this consciousness of the perennial war among my members,". . . suggested to him a practical means of settling the whole question. (Dr. Jekyll, it should be understood, is incapable of expanding the mere self to the scale of the universe, nor can he hope to unify the antagonists within by a commitment to the betterment of all mankind, both of which Dr. Faust found feasible. Respectable society, of which Jekyll is a member in good standing, would repudiate such spurious modes of self-transcendence. Thus, whereas Faust was irrepressible by definition, Jekyll, the latter-day Faust, must at all costs hold his place as a reputable man and even rise in the establishment if he can.) And so, though pleasure had been suppressed for a long time by the dreary decency that was his life, Dr. Jekyll will enjoy it, after all, in the person of a totally new identity, Edward Hyde.

Hyde, once unleashed, arouses disgust in everyone. Dr. Jekyll's servant, for one, feels "kind of cold and thin" in his marrow after meeting Hyde for the first time . . . , and even the "Sawbones" has the urge to do away with him. To catch sight of Hyde is to be reminded of the hidden *"je"* in each of us, the "troglodytic" . . . animal that only waits for the moment of release. In most societies men agree to curb the *"je"* and are not required to totally suppress it. But in Jekyll's world, the *"je"* must be ruthlessly suppressed—most unequivocally so by the man known as "the very pink of the proprieties," Dr. Henry Jekyll, the most thoroughgoing *"je*-killer" of them all.

Hyde, at once Jekyll's Mephistopheles and his (Frankenstein) monster, looks like the very incarnation of evil, but at the beginning he is in fact merely Jekyll's unrepressed spontaneous existence. Going about in the guise of Mr. Hyde, Dr. Jekyll discovers a new freshness and joy in his life. (pp. 472-73)

But Hyde gradually shows himself dissatisfied with his role as mere "impatient gaiety," and scornful of the rights of others. His "every act and thought [were] centred on self." . . . In fact, his pleasure comes to depend on his torturing others. At this point, the self and society are enemies to the death.

Soon after the episode in which Hyde tramples the child, the Jekyll-Hyde metamorphosis becomes involuntary: the doctor goes to bed Henry Jekyll and awakes as Edward Hyde. The hidden *"je"* released by the social "I" threatens now to overpower it. Yet he believes it is still within his ability to stop this emergence of Mr. Hyde. Resolving to forego the "leaping impulses and secret pleasures," he determines to live once again the life of an "elderly and discontented doctor." . . . Of course, having once allowed his *"je"* the taste of freedom, he finds he cannot long suppress it. Soon Edward Hyde leaps out "roaring" . . . from the cave of Henry Jekyll. When the brutal murder of Sir Danvers Carew is disclosed, Jekyll's remorse is intense, if short-lived, recalling the reaction of countless Gothic villains after indulging their sadism. . . . The next time he goes out it is in the guise of Dr. Henry Jekyll. No wonder, then, that the metamorphosis should have become completely involuntary and the magic drug virtually ineffectual. There are no longer any inner or outer marks to distinguish the two. The merging, however, is in no sense a reconcilement of the Jekyll-Hyde duality. Rather, it signals a return to the starting point of Jekyll's whole experience. Only the annihilation of one of the two selves "reconciles" them: at the end of the story the doctor finally suppresses the *"je"* by murdering Hyde, thereby, of course, becoming a "self-destroyer," . . . a suicide. (p. 473)

Dr. Jekyll bears a close family resemblance to the Gothic romances of the late eighteenth century, a resemblance in respect both to the theme of double personality and their similar wide departure from the realism of the orthodox novel. *The Castle of Otranto, Vathek, The Italian, Caleb Williams, The Monk,* and many other stories feature outrageous villains whose abrupt and inexplicable transformations from a state of uncontrollable passion to that of heartfelt remorse indicate the dual personality in almost as virulent a form as Jekyll's. *Vathek* is cursed by his mother—herself unflaggingly evil—as a "two-headed, four-legged monster." And *Caleb Williams* likens human beings in general to "those twin-births that have two heads indeed, and four hands." This characteristic theme of the romances suggests a central concern of modern writers to document the dualism by examining particularly the disjunct passion and reason which have remained, pretty much throughout the modern period, alien to each other like the two sealed and separate chambers of the Gothic personality. (pp. 474, 479)

Of all the enormous output of the 1890s it is the Stevenson work which, unluckily, has given us a convenient epithet ("Jekyll-and-Hyde") for the post-Freudian with an unhappy double self. Paradoxically, Stevenson was too successful, both in his story-idea and in what has come to be a silly name for it: by that silly name we have been diverted from reading what should have great interest for us. By far the largest part of that interest lies in the vision the book conjures of the late Victorian wasteland, truly a de-Hyde-rated land unfit to sustain a human being simultaneously in an honorable public life and a joyful private one. (p. 480)

Masao Miyoshi, "Dr. Jekyll and the Emergence of Mr. Hyde," in College English, *Vol. 27, No. 6, March, 1966, pp. 470-74, 479-80.*

JOSEPH J. EGAN   (essay date 1966)

[*Egan regards Stevenson's use of artistic elements, including symbolism and narration, as indicative of Stevenson's belief that humanity is capable of both good and evil.*]

[The] idea that Dr. Jekyll himself is both good and evil is the only one supported by the artistic design of the story.

The central pattern of symbolism in *Jekyll and Hyde* is associated with the various dwelling places that figure in the tale to reveal the spiritual condition of their inhabitants. Dr. Jekyll's own home lies in "a square of ancient, handsome houses, now for the most part decayed from their high estate and let in flats and chambers to all sorts . . . of men," . . . and the physician's surroundings thus suggest both the past condition of his soul, when evil was still in check, and its present state of moral debility. We are told that around the corner from this square is a pleasant and respectable bystreet of the London business section: "The street shone out in contrast to its dingy neighborhood, like a fire in a forest; and with its . . . general cleanliness and gayety of note, instantly caught and pleased the eye of the passenger." . . . And yet the attractive scene is marred by the presence of "a certain sinister block of building [that] bore, in every feature, the marks of prolonged and sordid negligence." . . . This structure proves to be the " 'back way to Dr. Jekyll's," . . . by which Mr. Hyde gains access to the physician's home, and in the context of the story becomes symbolic not only of Hyde's depravity but of the tarnished side of all men as well. Like the moral destitution it represents, Hyde's sinister doorway, the appropriate symbol of the "back door" to Henry Jekyll's soul, stands out in contrast to its ostensibly wholesome and orderly surroundings. The London bystreet, then, suggests something of the incongruity in human nature itself, where evil coexists with that which is seemingly most respectable.

The idea of spiritual decay is given further meaning when we discover that this grimy building where Dr. Jekyll performs his secret experiments is called "'Black Mail House'" ..., for evil has indeed come to compromise the good in Henry Jekyll. It is his own frightful inclination towards evil that has brought on the moral ruination of Jekyll, a ruination which cannot long be concealed despite the fact that the doctor's dwelling still wears the deceiving mask of respectability and "a great air of wealth and comfort." ... A more obvious image of corruption is Hyde's filthy residence in Soho, which is guarded by an old woman with "an evil face, smoothed by hypocrisy," ... the fitting companion and familiar for such a creature as Edward Hyde.

Stevenson repeatedly employs the artistic elements in *Jekyll and Hyde* to suggest the spiritual destruction of Dr. Jekyll at the hands of Mr. Hyde. In his "Full Statement of the Case," Dr. Jekyll confesses that he never ceased to believe that evil is "the lethal side of man," ... and the meaning of the story depends on this belief. The blasphemies and profanities which Hyde scribbles on the pages of Jekyll's theological texts are indicative of the attempt of evil to destroy the good in man. Hyde's destruction of the portrait of Jekyll's father is also suggestive of the terrible effects which evil can produce in the human soul. ... Conversely, the son figure, to which Jekyll likens Hyde, is representative of the present imbalance of moral values in the doctor's soul and a total alienation from goodness. When Hyde destroys the portrait of the elder Jekyll, his action is therefore symbolic of the destruction of Henry Jekyll's spiritual integrity by the power of the evil within him.

Several even more vivid examples of the lethal power of evil and its inherent antagonism to all goodness are given in connection with Mr. Hyde's cruelty towards others. Early in the story we are given a description of the terrible way in which Hyde treats the little girl whom he has knocked down: "'Then came the horrible part of the thing; for the man trampled calmly over the child's body and left her screaming on the ground. It sounds nothing to hear, but it was hellish to see. It wasn't like a man; it was like some damned Juggernaut'." ... Hyde's attack on the child, a figure of innocence, represents the assault which his own evil has made upon the soul of Dr. Jekyll. (pp. 28-9)

The murder of Sir Danvers closely parallels the trampling of the little girl; but the meanings of the two events are not quite identical. The child represents an internal state of the innocence of the soul, and it is this inherent goodness which evil first seeks to undermine. Carew, on the other hand, though he remains associated with goodness, is more representative of Henry Jekyll's outer respectability and public reputation, things which, as we have seen, the doctor values very highly. The aspect of the Carew murder most stressed is that the victim was a national figure, a well-known Member of Parliament whose death "'will make a deal of noise'." ... The second assault of Mr. Hyde, then, is directed against Dr. Jekyll's public image, an image which is shattered by the scandal of the doctor's own sinister proclivity towards evil.

A significant relationship exists between the increasing ferocity of Hyde's sadistic attacks on his victims' bodies and the awful growth of his own "energy of life." ... In *The Strange Case of Dr. Jekyll and Mr. Hyde* Edward Hyde is depicted as a vampire who feeds on the very life of his victims, "drinking pleasure with bestial avidity from any degree of torture to another; relentless like a man of stone" ...; and Stevenson uses this vampire image to suggest the way in which indulgence of evil eats away man's capacity for goodness. (pp. 29-30)

Stevenson employs the image of the criminal in relationship to Mr. Hyde in order to give further emphasis to the effect which Hyde has upon Henry Jekyll's spiritual life: "Men have before hired bravos to transact their crimes, while their own person and reputation sat under shelter. I was the first that ever did so for his pleasures.... Hyde was indifferent to Jekyll, or but remembered him as the mountain bandit remembers the cavern in which he conceals himself from pursuit.'... Like a kind of deadly bandit of the soul, Mr. Hyde comes to rob Dr. Jekyll of his goodness and reputation; and yet Hyde is strangely dependent on his victim Jekyll for continued existence.... [He] needs Jekyll as a means of concealing himself from arrest for his crimes, and at the heart of the relationship between Dr. Jekyll and Mr. Hyde is thus the suggestion that in destroying the good, evil comes to destroy itself. When Hyde can no longer change back into Jekyll, he has lost that very thing upon which he preys and has no course left him but the taking of his own life.

But this physical death is suggestive of the spiritual suicide towards which both Jekyll and Hyde have been moving throughout the story, for the indulgence of evil will eventually destroy the whole man and both the good and evil within him.... Mr. Hyde is the figure of the deadly evil which *hides* in the soul of each of us and contains the seeds of our spiritual and psychological destruction; and the name *Jekyll* (*Je* = French, *I; kyll* = *kill*) suggests the self-destroyer.

The death of Dr. Lanyon, brought on by the sight of Hyde's transformation into Jekyll, also symbolizes the perishing of the good in Henry Jekyll. Indeed, Lanyon becomes almost the reflection of Jekyll, and the tragic fates of the two medical men are strikingly similar.... Stevenson thus uses Dr. Lanyon as the counterpart of Henry Jekyll; both were once reasonably good men, but their impetuous inquiry into the nature of evil drove them on to destroy their souls. It is not for nothing, then, that Dr. Lanyon's first name is Hastie, and his physical death suggests the spiritual and psychic death of the man who has too *hastily* called forth the power of evil.

A significant part of the artistic design of *The Strange Case of Dr. Jekyll and Mr. Hyde* is Stevenson's use of three distinct modes of narration in the story. Though the friend and advisor of Dr. Jekyll, Lawyer Utterson is not a medical scientist and he remains to the end only the bewildered onlooker. But his point of view gives way first to that of Dr. Lanyon, who is a party to the hideous secret of transformation, and finally to that of Jekyll himself, who in the last chapter fully exposes the terrible ruination of his soul. The narrative progression of the tale is thus from the outside to within and closely follows the gradual penetration into the troubled mind of Dr. Jekyll.

This narrative thread of *Jekyll and Hyde* is carefully paralleled and reinforced by the skillful use of passageways in the story. A series of doors separate Dr. Jekyll's house from the back courtyard and the laboratory where he conducts his experiments. Just as the narrative movement of the tale brings us ever nearer to the heart of the mystery of Edward Hyde, so too with the opening of each successive door by Mr. Utterson, we move closer and closer towards the innermost depths of Dr. Jekyll's tormented soul, which is itself represented by the sealed cabinet in the upper storey of the laboratory building.

Significantly, the door to this cabinet is covered by red baize, a cheap, coarse material which Dr. Jekyll uses to muffle the sounds of his scientific investigations. The baize itself suggests the "cheapness" of Dr. Jekyll's improper experimentation, and the color red gives additional emphasis to the sinister unholiness of his propensity for evil, for the tincture which helps effect the change into Hyde is "blood-red" in color . . . and at one stage in the process the transformation compound becomes a bright red. . . . The successive changes of the compound's color from red to purple and then to green suggest, in turn, the idea of altered appearance upon which the plot of the story depends. When Utterson and the butler Poole finally smash in the red baize door, their action is symbolic of both the end of the "silence" connected with Henry Jekyll's secret experiments and the exposure of the doctor's spiritual dissolution and the true identity of Edward Hyde.

We also learn that the laboratory building had served its former owner as a dissecting theatre, and it becomes therefore the fit setting for Henry Jekyll's attempts to "dissect" his own personality: "It was the first time that the lawyer [Mr. Utterson] had been received in that part of his friend's quarters; and he eyed the dingy, windowless structure with curiosity, and gazed round with a distasteful sense of strangeness as he crossed the theatre, once crowded with eager students and now lying gaunt and silent, the tables laden with chemical apparatus, the floor strewn with crates and littered with packing straw, and the light falling dimly through the foggy cupola." . . . The shadowy and cluttered aspect of the laboratory suggests the spiritual darkness and disorder in Dr. Jekyll's life, and, significantly, it is in close proximity to these unwholesome surroundings that Henry Jekyll at last disappears forever and that the body of Edward Hyde is found stretched out in the final death agony. And yet in the description of Dr. Jekyll's sealed cabinet, the actual scene of Hyde's suicide, Stevenson calls attention to a quite appropriate irony between apparent order and cheeriness and the hideous double death of good and evil:

> There lay the cabinet before their eyes in the quiet lamplight, a good fire glowing and chattering on the hearth, the kettle singing its thin strain, a drawer or two open, papers neatly set forth on the business table, and nearer the fire, the things laid out for tea: the quietest room, you would have said, and, but for the glazed presses full of chemicals, the most commonplace that night in London.

> Right in the midst there lay the body of a man sorely contorted and still twitching. They drew near on tiptoe, turned it on its back and beheld the face of Edward Hyde. . . .

The tragic irony connected with this description of the cabinet, the image of Jekyll's own soul, suggests the tragic irony of the doctor's fate and points up the incongruities at the heart of human moral life.

Here again Stevenson reinforces the pervading theme of *Jekyll and Hyde*—the idea of the self-contradictory impulses and mingled strains of good and evil within the same man. In his attempt to separate the conflicting elements within his personality, Dr. Jekyll had been prompted by the hope that he need be "no longer exposed to disgrace and penitence by the hands of this extraneous evil." . . . But Dr. Jekyll at last discovers that evil is as essential a part of human nature as good itself and not the "extraneous" factor he had once thought it: "I

have been made to learn that the doom and burthen of our life is bound forever on man's shoulders, and when the attempt is made to cast it off, it but returns upon us with more unfamiliar and more awful pressure." . . . The meaning of *The Strange Case of Dr. Jekyll and Mr. Hyde* and all of the story's artistic design thus continually carry us back to the idea that humanity is, in the end, synonymous with the struggle of good and evil. (pp. 30-2)

> *Joseph J. Egan, "The Relationship of Theme and Art in 'The Strange Case of Dr. Jekyll and Mr. Hyde',"*
> in English Literature in Transition, *Vol. 9, No. 1, 1966, pp. 28-32.*

EDWIN M. EIGNER (essay date 1966)

[*Eigner assesses Stevenson's narrative style and character development in* Dr. Jekyll and Mr. Hyde. *Focusing on the relationship between the two characters, Eigner describes Hyde as a part of Jekyll's personality that the latter unsuccessfully tries to suppress.*]

Stevenson's *Strange Case of Dr. Jekyll and Mr. Hyde* is written from more points of view than any other of his works. It contains two first person narratives, a chapter written in the impersonal style of a newspaper report, and the account of a seemingly uninvolved third person point of view character, Mr. Gabriel Utterson, who sometimes observes Jekyll and Hyde directly and sometimes listens to the stories told by still other characters who have observed them. What the reader who has not looked at the story for some time tends to think of as *Dr. Jekyll and Mr. Hyde* is only the last quarter of it, the part which Jekyll himself recounts.

No doubt this oblique approach to narration added to the suspense and mystery for the work's initial audience. The reader who comes to the story fresh (it is almost impossible to find such a one nowadays) does not know that Jekyll and Hyde are one man until the work is almost three-quarters over, and for this reader the shock is still a potent one. But Stevenson has another and a more serious reason for using all these points of view. The most important focus in the story, as we might expect, will be on Jekyll's attitudes towards his double. Before we come to these reactions, however, Stevenson feels it necessary to present us with a number of other opinions of Hyde, attitudes which should prepare us for Jekyll's and which might furthermore serve us as a standard of comparison.

The first response to Hyde comes from Mr. Richard Enfield, "the well-known man about town," . . . who describes the incident in which Hyde knocks down and tramples the little girl. Enfield takes a loathing to Hyde at first sight. . . . He prides himself as a connoisseur of beauty, and so he finds Hyde's unspecifiable deformity distasteful to the point of nausea. . . . Enfield also provides us with a number of other reactions. He tells, for instance, about the women whom the sight of Hyde turned "as wild as harpies," . . . and about the colorless, "cut-and-dry" Edinburgh apothecary, "about as emotional as a bagpipe," who turned "sick and white with the desire to kill him." . . . (pp. 144-45)

G. J. Utterson of Gaunt Street, to whom Enfield tells this story, is himself something like the unemotional Edinburgh apothecary, and his association with Enfield is really the first *Doppelgänger* relationship the story presents. The two men are distant kinsmen. Nevertheless, they seem to have little in common, for Utterson is "austere with himself" and drinks gin when he is alone "to mortify a taste for vintages." . . . To strengthen his moral fiber, he has for twenty years denied himself the pleasure of going to the theater. Yet Utterson and the *bon vivant* Enfield are fast friends. (pp. 145-46)

The third important, uninvolved narrator reaction comes from Hastie Lanyon, who is a Scottish doctor, like Jekyll himself. Lanyon is a bold and boisterous scientist of the soundest modern principles. He drinks wine when he is alone, instead of gin, but he lacks Utterson's tolerance, and has allowed his friendship with Henry Jekyll to lapse because of the latter's "fanciful" medical theories. "'Such unscientific balderdash,' added the doctor, flushing suddenly purple, 'would have estranged Damon and Pythias'." . . . Edward Hyde fills this scientist with "a disgustful curiosity," . . . and once Lanyon has learned the Jekyll-and-Hyde secret, he rejects Jekyll entirely. (pp. 146-47)

These then are the principal reactions which prepare us for the encounters of Jekyll and Hyde with one another—loathing, disgust, fear, and shocked horror. . . . *Jekyll and Hyde* has developed into a popular myth, one of the very few to come out of the Victorian period, and its meanings have consequently become blurred. . . . The result is that the term Jekyll-and-Hyde, even as used by psychologists, has little reference to Stevenson's work. Most nonexperts, as a matter of my own observation, are rather surprised to learn that the story has a known author, or if they associate Stevenson's name with it, they often assume he took the plot from some well-worn folk legend. (pp. 147-48)

If we have seen the movies, we tend perhaps to regard Jekyll as an essentially good man who looks upon his dangerous experiment as a noble service to mankind. He is a sort of Tennysonian hero, like King Arthur, who strives to free man from the evil in his nature. (p. 149)

This has, indeed, proved to be a very saleable version of the story, but it is hardly fair to saddle Stevenson with it. And it is especially unfair to complain afterwards, as critics oftentimes do, of the story's "slightly too obvious meaning." One such critic [C. Keith], smarting over the insult to his intelligence, explains the moral of *Dr. Jekyll and Mr. Hyde* in the following sarcastic language:

> If you weren't careful, the evil in you would swallow up the good, as the wicked Hyde does Dr. Jekyll. And you'd be lost. So be careful! Nearly as crude as that.

Now there is no suggestion in Stevenson's version of the *Strange Case of Dr. Jekyll and Mr. Hyde* that carelessness was Henry Jekyll's chief fault. On the contrary, according to one of Stevenson's letters, the "harm" was in Jekyll precisely because he was *too* careful, "because he was a hypocrite. . . . The Hypocrite let out the beast of Hyde." (pp. 149-50)

Jekyll, in direct contrast to Stevenson's statement about him, asserts that he "was in no sense a hypocrite," but he means something special by this, something which requires explanation. He means, as he says, that both sides of him "were in dead earnest," . . . that he was not a bad man posing during the day as a good one. He does not mean that he took Sunday afternoon strolls with his *alter ego,* as Utterson and Enfield do. As a matter of fact, he specifically declines an invitation from this engaging pair, who recommend that he take a "quick turn" with them to whip up his "circulation." . . . His one self is deathly ashamed of the other, and the doctor believes,

moreover, that this mortification does him a world of credit. (p. 152)

As for Jekyll's goodness, we have very little evidence for it besides the doctor's own word. There is a period just after Hyde's murder of Sir Danvers when Jekyll goes about actively striving to do good, but this activity is presented almost as though it were contrary to his more general habits. As to his actions prior to this stage, no one in the story will go beyond the author's statement that "he had always been known for his charities." . . . The public nature of his good actions is, in fact, heavily stressed. Enfield calls him "the very pink of the proprieties. . . . One of your fellows who do what they call good." . . . And when Utterson finds a book of Jekyll's which Hyde has disfigured with blasphemies, he describes it as "a pious work for which Jekyll had several times expressed a great esteem." . . . Yet Utterson does not discover any reverent marginalia in *Jekyll's* hands. Neither do we witness Jekyll actually doing any of the good he boasts of and is known for. In a previous draft of the story, obviously intermediate between the destroyed first manuscript and the published version, Stevenson was somewhat more specific in detailing Jekyll's virtues. There Jekyll calls himself "a man of distinction, immersed in toils, open to generous sympathies, never slow to befriend struggling virtue." But even these generalities were not permitted to stand.

Perhaps the problem is simply that Stevenson, here as elsewhere, cannot sufficiently bring himself to believe in positive acts of virtue. The only goodness Stevenson seems capable of rendering in his fiction is the act of renunciation, and sacrifice seems hardly to be Henry Jekyll's strong point. . . . The benevolence in Jekyll seems to stem not from any innate springs of virtue, but, as he admits, from an "imperious desire to carry my head high, and wear a more than commonly grave countenance before the public." . . . As with so many of Stevenson's Lowlanders, the ideal to which Henry Jekyll is committed is not goodness, but mere respectability.

But we should also note that Jekyll is the type of hypocrite who deludes himself along with the world. No doubt he believes that his day-life of negative virtues represents real good, just as he believes that his night-life of sensuous indulgence represents real evil. And these convictions, though Stevenson would have rejected them both, are what lead Henry Jekyll to the recognition of his double nature. (pp. 152-54)

This diagnosis, no matter how mistakenly arrived at, is again a healthy one. It is indeed a truth according to Stevenson's most consistent thought, and it is a truth a man always does well to face. What is unhealthy is the treatment the good doctor prescribes. Jekyll was wrong in attempting to segregate the two sides of his life, and he was even more wrong in glorifying the one side while alternately condemning and indulging the other. His chemical experiment is simply a logical extension of this treatment. . . . Stevenson's Jekyll is at least as much interested in freeing his evil nature from restraint as he is in giving scope to the good in him. . . . According to Jekyll, though, each of the two natures is dear to him, and he sees himself as "radically both." . . . Jekyll, far from wishing to end his double nature, is attempting to make it permanent. He does not mean, at the beginning at least, to reject either of his identities. And when Hyde, the evil nature, appears for the first time, the experiment may be thought of as incomplete, but it should certainly not be considered a failure.

Now that Hyde is out in the open, Jekyll must react to him, and since Jekyll's nature is more distorted by Lowland morality than any of the other narrators'—he lacks the tolerance of Utterson and Enfield and the robustness of Lanyon—we may expect his attitudes to be even more extreme than theirs. . . . Jekyll's reactions are confused and mixed. On the one hand, Jekyll was ''conscious of no repugnance, rather a leap of welcome'' at the appearance of Hyde. ''This, too, was myself. It seemed natural and human.'' . . . As the relationship develops, moreover, he begins to regard Hyde as his own child. Their ages are right for this: Jekyll is fifty, Hyde is in his twenties. And Hyde is the smaller of the two. Like an indulgent father of a scapegrace son, Jekyll writes a check to keep Hyde out of trouble. Later, he even makes Hyde the beneficiary of his will. But while Jekyll is quick enough at first to accept his secret kinship with Hyde and very naturally refers to the latter as ''me,'' he is just as quick to recognize Hyde as wicked, ''tenfold more wicked'' than himself. . . . (pp. 154-56)

Certainly Hyde does not merit the indulgence Jekyll allows him. One wonders also whether at his very first appearance he quite deserves so full a condemnation. I suggest this because it is clear from the incidents which follow that Hyde grows more wicked as the story progresses, and if this is so, he can hardly have been ''pure evil'' at the beginning. It is true that by the end of the story Hyde ''is the essence of cruelty and malice and selfishness and cowardice,'' as we have heard Stevenson say, but at the start he seems perhaps to be something less than this.

No doubt, although the story does not present it, Hyde continues with, and indeed improves upon, Jekyll's voluptuary adventures; but this sort of behavior is pure evil only in the minds of Jekyll and other products of the negative morality from which Stevenson had himself rebelled. And if there is a possibility that Jekyll judges his *alter ego* unjustly, let us re-examine some of the earlier condemnations of Hyde to see whether they too are not excessive in view of the facts.

Hyde's first narrated adventure . . . is described by Richard Enfield. Enfield tells how he saw Hyde and a little girl approaching one another at a street intersection.

> Well, sir, the two ran into one another naturally enough at the corner; and then came the horrible part of the thing; for the man trampled calmly over the child's body and left her screaming on the ground. It sounds nothing to hear; but it was hellish to see. It wasn't like a man; it was like some damned Juggernaut. . . .

This incident shows Hyde as a creature without compassion, but it does not show him as either malicious or cruel. He takes no pleasure, as far as we know, in hurting the child. He tramples ''calmly,'' and the Juggernaut simile underscores the impersonality of his action. Hyde is simply indifferent to the girl's pain. He is, as we might expect after the chemical amputation, a man without a conscience, completely uncivilized.

But Enfield and the other bystanders . . . react to Hyde as though his wickedness were of a more positive nature. (pp. 156-57)

Hyde does not appear purely evil in this adventure, but he does seem to bring out all the cruelty and malice in those who judge him. . . . Enfield, the bystanders, and the other narrators are rejecting a part of themselves when they reject Hyde, and the more strenuously they excise him, the more thoroughly they come to resemble their notion of him, and the more profoundly they are affected by the encounter. . . .

Hyde, of course, is a part of Jekyll, and the harm caused by Jekyll's rejection of him is mirrored in Hyde's own changing nature. At the beginning of their relationship, Hyde was indifferent to Jekyll. (p. 158)

The change in Hyde is a slow one and it must be observed through several of the points of view, but it is, nevertheless, very perceptible and quite extreme. Hyde progresses from conscienceless and impersonal indifference to malicious hatred, from a Juggernaut to a devil. And if he appears sufficiently evil to us at his first appearance in the story, we should remember that Jekyll has been pushing him away from his conscience for more than twenty years. . . . Moreover, the rest of society, as represented by the bystanders and the narrators, with their strong morals or their weak stomachs, have been assisting and encouraging Jekyll in the destructive polarization of his nature. The experiment in the laboratory is only a step in this separation—albeit the most dramatic. There were steps before it, and, tragically, there are steps to follow it.

As the poles widen, Hyde becomes more and more evil. Yet Jekyll continues his dissociation. He decides that Hyde alone is guilty of the nighttime activities, and simultaneously Hyde's crimes ''began to turn toward the monstrous.'' . . . Hyde displays much more than indifference and lack of conscience in his senseless and brutal murder of Sir Danvers Carew. ''Instantly,'' Jekyll writes, ''the spirit of hell awoke in me and raged. With a transport of glee, I mauled the unresisting body, tasting delight from every blow.'' . . . (pp. 158-59)

Nor does the rejection end even here. Indeed, the purpose of Jekyll's next move, his increased performance of benevolent actions and church duties, is to make himself over as much as he can into the direct antithesis of Hyde. (p. 159)

The *Strange Case of Dr. Jekyll and Mr. Hyde* is not an allegory of the evil in man swallowing up the helpless good; rather it is a story of a whole man driving one part of his nature to depravity until the entire ego is destroyed. . . . After the murder of Carew, Jekyll announces that he is ''quite done with'' Hyde . . . , and whereas at the beginning of the relationship he had referred to his *alter ego* in both the first and third person indiscriminately, towards the end of the story he denies Hyde's humanity altogether and cannot bring himself to speak of him as I. (p. 160)

Hyde responds to such treatment with hatred of Jekyll and with increased evil. Near the end he fiendishly destroys Jekyll's papers, and, like the devil in a saint's life, he writes blasphemies in Jekyll's sacred books. . . . But even when Hyde is most wicked, Jekyll cannot be regarded as a victim. The doctor feels he is the tormented one, because he has a conscience, but it is Hyde, after all, who is driven finally to commit suicide out of sheer terror. It is still another case of dog against wolf, and as usual in Stevenson, the dog is by far the more formidable. (pp. 160-61)

In writing such a story of a creature turned diabolic in response to the hatred and rejection afforded him by society and by the man to whom he owes his life, Stevenson must have been aware of similarities to the first important monster story of the century, Mary Shelley's *Frankenstein*. There are several points of strong comparison, the most basic of which is that both works employ *Doppelgänger* to emphasize the duality of human nature. (p. 161)

Another similarity between *Frankenstein* and Stevenson's story is that in both works the hero is excessively self-righteous. We have seen that this was also a part of the intervening tradition as practiced by Hogg, Bulwer, and Dostoyevsky. It figures also in such works as *Les Misérables*, in *The Scarlet Letter*, and in what is perhaps the greatest of the pursuit stories of the century, *Moby Dick*. In *Frankenstein*, as in several of Stevenson's works, the greatest harm comes from two things within the hero's own nature—a delicate sensibility which cannot bear to look at the Monster's ugliness, and an overdeveloped moral conscience which shrinks from the Monster's deeds; in other words, from Enfield and from Utterson. (pp. 162-63)

The emotion in the reader which these works of rejection, pursuit, and mutual destruction aim at is pathos. We are meant to mourn the noble intention and the frantic energy wasted by these rejections of self or of nature. We are probably meant to believe the words of Frankenstein's Monster when he says that his "thoughts were once filled with sublime and transcendent visions of the beauty and the majesty of goodness." (p. 163)

Edward Hyde lacked the Monster's literary education; he had neglected his Milton. He was anyway never an angel. According to Stevenson's theory of duality, though, he was originally not a devil either, but a necessary part of Henry Jekyll's and of every man's character. And he could have been a useful part, as well—not when we first meet him; it was already too late by this time; but years earlier, in the days before Jekyll began to live his double life, channeling all his energy into voluptuary pleasures and all his aspirations into a creed of negative virtues. . . .

Like *Frankenstein* and the other romances of pursuit, the *Strange Case of Dr. Jekyll and Mr. Hyde* is a story of pathetic waste. It is also the story of a weak man—but not weak because he dabbles irresponsibly with evil, as the American play and the American movies would have it. Henry Jekyll's weakness is like that of every other Stevensonian protagonist . . . ; it resides entirely in his tragic inability to accept his own nature. (p. 164)

> *Edwin M. Eigner, in his* Robert Louis Stevenson and Romantic Tradition, *Princeton University Press, 1966, 258 p.*

BARBARA HANNAH   (essay date 1971)

[*In this Jungian analysis, Hannah explores the role of the subconscious in the creation of the novel by relating it to Stevenson's "A Chapter on Dreams" (see excerpt dated 1888). She describes Jekyll's attempts to come to grips with his divided personality, characterizing Stevenson as "a man in tortured flight from himself."*]

Carrying one's cross and carrying one's shadow is only a difference of words—as anyone who has really tried the latter can testify—and Stevenson himself tells us, in *Across the Plains,* how much he suffered from a "strong sense of man's double being which must at times come in upon and overwhelm the mind of every living creature." He puts it more clearly in *The Strange Case of Dr. Jekyll and Mr. Hyde* where he writes that "man is not truly one, but truly two," and that these two are severed into "provinces of good and ill which divide and compound man's dual nature."

It is questionable whether Stevenson realized that this is a problem which can only be solved in one's own individual psyche. (pp. 38-9)

But he had an extraordinary insight into the unconscious—far beyond that of his time—so one cannot doubt that, had he

realized how much can be accomplished by analytic work on oneself, he would have been singularly gifted in this respect. As it was, the objective psyche was known to him under another name, although for many years he regarded its as something not identical with himself but which could help him in his work. What we call the "unconscious" was "the Brownies" to Stevenson and, unlike most creative artists, he gave them full credit for their contributions to his writings. He even says that his Brownies "do one half of my work for me while I am asleep, and in all human likelihood do the rest for me as well, when I am wide awake and fondly suppose I do it for myself." (pp. 39-40)

The Brownies are a modern version of the Cabiri, those creative dwarf gods of antiquity, which we meet again and again in various forms in mythology. Stevenson—although he admits his debt to them most generously—was inclined to take them much too lightly. One doubts whether he realized their full mythological background or anything like their latent power. . . . (p. 40)

After Stevenson had long been trying to find a "story . . . a body, a vehicle" for his "strong sense of man's double being," he tells us that *Jekyll and Hyde* was suggested by a dream. He "dreamed the scene at the window, and a scene afterwards split into two, in which Hyde, pursued for some crime, took the powder and underwent the change in the presence of his pursuers. All the rest was made awake and consciously, although I think I can trace in much of it the manner of my Brownies."

When our totality is left behind us in the unconscious, it is the conscious ego only that takes this one-sided journey. It is in our dreams that we can look for the elements that compensate and enlarge our too narrow consciousness. This dream of Stevenson's not only gave him the outline of the story for which he had been searching so long—a point he was swift to seize upon—but it also offered him an extraordinary insight into his own split and suffering psyche, if only he could have seen the connections. But we will first consider the story as Stevenson wrote it, keeping the dream in mind.

The reader will remember that Stevenson used the second part of his dream, the transformation of Mr. Hyde into Dr. Jekyll, as the main theme of his story. He made an exceedingly exciting tale of it, saving the fact that Jekyll and Hyde were one and the same person for the thrilling denouement at the end. But we are not concerned here with the story as a popular thriller but with the *facts* of the case.

The most fatal fact which was added to the dream by Stevenson or his Brownies in the "conscious waking state" is given at the beginning of the final chapter, "Henry Jekyll's Full Statement of the Case." Jekyll tells us there that he found it hard to reconcile "a certain impatient gaiety of disposition" with his "imperious desire to carry (his) head high, and wear a more than commonly grave countenance before the public." Therefore he concealed his pleasures and soon stood "committed to a profound duplicity of life," thus severing "those provinces of good and ill which divide and compound man's dual nature" with an even "deeper trench than in the majority of men." Jekyll says later:

> It was on the moral side, and in my own person,
> that I learned to recognize the thorough and
> primitive duality of man.

Since his ambition forbade him even to countenance an "impatient gaiety of disposition"—which he says originally was his worst fault—he naturally soon drove the opposites much further apart than is normally the case. But he still realized that "even if I could rightly be said to be either, it was only because I was radically both."

This is a very psychological statement indeed and Dr. Jekyll was near here to a realization of the paradox in every human life which could have led him (and perhaps thus also Stevenson) back towards his original wholeness. However, such a realization would be exceedingly painful and—this is the fatal point—Jekyll began "to dwell with pleasure, as a beloved daydream," on the possibility of escaping this suffering by separating his two natures into two separate identities. Then, he says, "the unjust might go his way, delivered from the aspirations and remorse of his more upright twin; and the just could walk steadfastly and securely on his upward path, doing the good things in which he found his pleasure, and no longer exposed to disgrace and penitence by the hands of this extraneous evil."

It is quite clear that the fatal end of the story was the direct result of an *unwillingness to suffer*. The value of accepting suffering is one of the great contributions of the Christian religion and Louis certainly threw out the baby with the bathwater when he had Dr. Jekyll repudiate it entirely. Reading his life and his letters, one receives the impression that this was also a mistake of Stevenson himself. His nomadic life was, on one side, a legitimate search for health and, on the other, a constant flight from suffering and himself.

It is true that Jekyll admits he was "made to learn that the doom and burthen of our life is bound forever on man's shoulders, and when the attempt is made to cast it off, it but returns upon us with more unfamiliar and more awful pressure," but unfortunately he learned this far too late to avert the complete catastrophe with which the book ends.

In the meantime, having discovered how to compose a powder that would turn the worthy Dr. Jekyll into the infamous Mr. Hyde, he was able for some time to enjoy the emergence into reality of his "beloved day-dream" and to pursue both his good and evil lives, with each life unchecked and undisturbed by its opposite. When he first looked at Hyde in the mirror, he was "conscious of no repugnance, rather of a leap of welcome. *This, too, was myself*. It seemed natural and human." . . . (pp. 43-6)

Though exaggerated and dramatized, for reasons we shall consider later, this is perhaps one of the best descriptions in literature of a man meeting his shadow and recognizing him fully as his own: "This, too, was myself." Dr. Jekyll has an unparalleled opportunity here of taking the first step back toward the original wholeness of man. But this involves suffering, agony indeed, and it is the whole purpose of the experiment to escape any such suffering. So when he discovers that the drug will also change Hyde into Jekyll—in his dream this was the change Stevenson had seen—he merely rejoices in what he feels to be his complete security. (p. 46)

His original recognition when he first saw Hyde, "This, too, was myself," very soon begins to fade. As he indulges his Hyde side, his original "undignified" pleasures become "inherently malign and villainous," Hyde's every act and thought centered on self; drinking pleasure with bestial avidity from any degree of torture to another; relentless like a man of stone." At first Jekyll is somewhat "aghast" but he says that "the situation was apart from ordinary laws, and insidiously relaxed

the grasp of conscience. It was Hyde, after all, and Hyde alone, that was guilty." What has become of his realization: "This, too, was myself"?

It is fear, not conscience, that puts an end to this fool's paradise. The change from Jekyll to Hyde, at first so difficult and painful to bring about, begins to happen involuntarily, even in sleep. The first time this happens, it seems like "the Babylonian finger on the wall." The "beloved day dream" is over and Jekyll feels that he must choose between his two personalities. He chooses Jekyll, though he admits with certain reservations that he is keeping Hyde's clothes and his house in Soho.

His search to escape suffering has thus led Jekyll far from his earlier realization "in his own person" of "the thorough and primitive duality of man." How could he believe that it was possible to choose *one* side of his nature and simply ignore the other? (pp. 46-7)

Experience shows us again and again that the way in which a creative work develops has a strong effect on its creator. One sees this particularly clearly in "active imagination." If someone is able to work out a problem in active imagination, it changes him and makes him more capable of meeting the problems of his own individual life. If Jekyll therefore had profited by his extraordinarily deep insights, such as "If I could rightly be said to be either, it was only because I was radically both," it would undoubtedly have changed the whole course of the story and equally its effect on Stevenson himself.

The reader will remember that Jekyll was "made to learn that the doom and burthen of our life is bound forever on man's shoulders, and when the attempt is made to cast it off, it but returns upon us with more unfamiliar and more awful pressure." The same was true to a great extent in Stevenson's own life. We hear that he was never happy after his life at Hyeres, that is, about two years before he wrote *Jekyll and Hyde*. His health improved a lot in the South Seas, nevertheless one does not get an impression of peace or serenity but rather—till toward the end—of a man in tortured flight from himself. This might have been very different if he had treated Jekyll more seriously, and had perhaps found a solution to the problem of the dual nature of man. Once such a problem has been raised—and no one will deny that Stevenson did raise it—the question will automatically go on haunting the one who asks it.

To return to Stevenson's dream: The transformation which he saw and made the theme of his story was Hyde turning into Jekyll after drinking the powder. Now in the story it is Dr. Jekyll who makes and drinks the powders and thus turns into Hyde. At the end the powder will only work that way. What then did Stevenson (or his Brownies) do to this theme, "awake and consciously," as he calls it himself?

If we were to analyze the dream we would consider the facts often referred to in the story, that Hyde was a smaller man than Jekyll and that his principal characteristic was evil; the latter impressed Stevenson in the dream itself. Since the dreamer was no monster of iniquity—as Stevenson most certainly was not—we could safely assume that Jekyll more nearly represented his usual personality, as it appeared to himself and to his friends, and that Hyde represented a repressed and evil shadow that was yet so intimately connected with him that, in extremity, it could assume his shape. (pp. 48-50)

Hyde, "that thing of darkness," had shown Stevenson that he existed and that something must be done, and urgently, to bring together "the thorough and primitive duality of man." It must be Jekyll, the conscious personality, who integrates the shadow figure—as in the dream—and *not* vice versa. Otherwise the conscious becomes the slave of the autonomous shadow, as is so dramatically illustrated at the end of the story. It was probably not possible at that time for Stevenson to realize . . . that this was essentially his own problem, but he might have taken the situation very differently in the story he made of it. He took it far too lightly. He saw it merely as an opportunity to write a successful thriller in which he made no serious attempt to find a solution, although one feels he might have. (pp. 50-1)

Another point in the dream that he failed to realize was that the transformation took place in public. In the story it is kept a complete secret. This certainly adds to the excitement of the tale but it is disastrous psychologically. The hush-hush politics of the witch is one of his or her most dangerous qualities, and if the secret in *Jekyll and Hyde* had been publicly known the disastrous escape from suffering would not have been possible. Here again Stevenson (or his Brownies) made a dangerous alteration. Yet in another point, Stevenson felt very much bound by his dream. He disliked the use of the powder as too material an agency, but he could not bring himself to change it, for it made such a strong impression on him in the dream. With his pixy-like appearance and his nomadic life, Stevenson was, till almost the end, the typical *puer aeternus* who skimmed the surface of life and hated to be drawn into any real or material situation. Therefore he naturally hated the powder ''as too material an agency.'' But we see that when he was really impressed by a dream motif he was capable of taking it very seriously indeed. In **''A Chapter on Dreams''** he speaks of the help the Brownies gave in writing *Jekyll and Hyde*. . . . (p. 51)

The tragedy of concealing the transformation is, from the psychological point of view, made clearer by another part of his dream, the ''Incident at the Window.'' Mr. Utterson, friend and lawyer of Dr. Jekyll, is out for his usual Sunday walk with Mr. Richard Enfield, his distant kinsman, when the scene occurs. But it should first be pointed out that these two form another pair of opposites in the story, a far more human and less dramatic ego and shadow pair than Jekyll and Hyde, and thus much nearer to the man, Stevenson. Such extremes, as are depicted in Jekyll and Hyde, are entirely beyond our human limitations and enter the archetypal sphere. One could almost say that the infamous Hyde contains all of the qualities that have been left out of our image of God.

The Christian religion, in its conception of the God of Love, has depicted such a summit of the light side that this necessarily casts a correspondingly dark shadow. It may seem blasphemous to speak of Hyde as the image of the archetypal shadow of God in Stevenson's unconscious, yet it is not far from the truth. Nor is this concept very far from the idea of the opposites as they appear in the story of Eden. The serpent, the personification of evil, was even then God's opposite. It ''was more subtle than any beast of the field which the Lord God had made'' and it at once used that subtility *against* the avowed will of the Lord. And since God had ''created man in his own image,'' Adam and Eve immediately came up against their own dual nature in the shape of the serpent who successfully tempted them to disobey the Lord's command.

Mr. Utterson and Mr. Enfield, however, have nothing archetypal about them. Mr. Utterson is the born observer who takes very little active part in life except through his profession and his friendships. He is ''austere with himself'' but has an unusual tolerance for everyone else. He used to say: ''I let my brother go to the devil in his own way'' and thus he was often

''the last good influence in the lives of down-going men.'' Whatever they did ''he never marked a shade of change in his demeanour.'' No one can understand the bond that unites him with Richard Enfield, a ''well-known man about town.'' Their Sunday walks seem to outsiders singularly dull. They say nothing and ''would hail with obvious relief the appearance of a friend. For all that, the two men put the greatest store by these excursions, counted them the chief jewel of each week, and not only set aside occasions of pleasure, but even resisted the calls of business, that they might enjoy them uninterrupted.'' Stevenson, with his extraordinary knowledge of the dual nature of man, has described here two friends, each of whom finds the opposite half of himself in the other in an unsurpassable way.

It is these two men, then, who step into the court of Dr. Jekyll's house one Sunday afternoon and take part in the ''incident at the window'' which Stevenson dreamed. (It is when Jekyll's sufferings are at their height, when the involuntary change into Hyde can no longer be kept at bay and when he is secluded in his laboratory.) They find Dr. Jekyll sitting by an open window ''taking the air with an infinite sadness of mien, like some disconsolate prisoner.'' Refusing to join their walk, Jekyll nevertheless evinces pleasure at the idea of a talk. ''But the words were hardly uttered, before the smile was struck out of his face and succeeded by an expression of such abject terror and despair, as froze the very blood of the two gentlemen below.'' The window is instantly closed and the two friends leave the court: ''They were both pale, and there was an answering horror in their eyes. 'God forgive us, God forgive us,' said Mr. Utterson.'' And they both relapsed into silence. Stevenson's dream continued with the transformation of Mr. Hyde into Dr. Jekyll, so there is no question that he knew what was happening behind that window. Yet in the conscious waking state, he, or his Brownies, kept Mr. Utterson in ignorance till after the death of the Hyde-Jekyll figure. If Utterson had known the facts—with his extraordinary toleration for ''down-going men''—again Stevenson could have ended his story very differently. Utterson begs Jekyll to tell him his secret on many occasions but is always refused.

The dream of the incident at the window gave Stevenson a glimpse of the original wholeness of man. There are four figures: Utterson and Enfield below, the dual figure of Jekyll-Hyde above. The opposites in the latter pair are larger than human; they are more an archetypal pair of opposites. The change, which the dreamer knew was taking place behind the window, was supernatural, and this characterizes the pair as non-human, archetypal symbols, images which man can apprehend but with which he can never identify without disaster.

In such a dream the dreamer could only afford to recognize the human pair as his own personal responsibility. Interestingly enough, Mr. Enfield—the man about town—is exactly the kind of shadow that Jekyll describes at the beginning of his career. He says: ''The worst of my faults was a certain impatient gaiety of disposition, such as has made the happiness of many, but such as I found it hard to reconcile with my imperious desire to carry my head high, and wear a more than commonly grave countenance before the public.'' Yet Stevenson's dream offers an opportunity for reconciling these two figures, provided that Mr. Utterson, the image of the ego, retains his extraordinary tolerance for others and does not try to reject them for false and ambitious purposes. Yes, the dream even predicts success, for, although the friendship between this pair was incomprehensible to others, their meeting was to them ''the chief jewel of each week.''

But if we cannot accept the shadow in its human and bearable form, then we eliminate it and the result is a dangerous vacuum in our immediate neighborhood. If we leave something undone—in this case the attempt to reconcile ego and shadow—we create a vacuum which the unconscious must fill. It is like the pattern of Christ's parable in which the man casts out one devil, presumably his personal shadow with which he ought to come to terms, and then when the house is "swept and garnished"—that is, when a vacuum has been allowed in his most personal sphere—seven devils worse than the first take its place. This is just what happens in *Jekyll and Hyde*. The "impatient gaiety of disposition" is cast out—the house is left swept and garnished—and Mr. Hyde, prototype of the devil himself and quite equal to the seven devils in the parable, takes its place. (pp. 51-5)

> Barbara Hannah, "Robert Louis Stevenson," in her
> Striving towards Wholeness, C. J. Jung Foundation
> for Analytical Psychology, 1971, pp. 38-71.

IRVING MASSEY (essay date 1973)

[*Massey interprets Jekyll as an example of a literary double and attempts to determine the balance of good and evil within his character. This essay originally appeared in* Bulletin of the Midwest Modern Language Association, *Fall, 1973.*]

A common version of the "double" story presents a character who harbors an alien self, or who turns uncontrollably from good to bad. In dealing with [*Dr. Jekyll and Mr. Hyde*], . . . I would like to shift the emphasis from the familiar areas of discussion of the double (such as split personality, or the suppressed natural man) to what one might rather call the discussion of the single. In other words, I would suggest that the problems . . . arise from the unity rather than from the duality of character. (p. 98)

[In] *Jekyll and Hyde,* the evil follows from the good. The two are the same. Jekyll is to begin with a good man. (p. 101)

"Evil" is what is left at the bottom of the pan when we boil down the good-evil choice, which is what is available to the good. Jekyll can hide in Hyde, but where is Hyde to hide? (Or, to put it differently, Jekyll is Jekyll-Hyde, but who is Hyde?) There are no further transformations available to him, and having faced his singleness he cannot forever continue dodging back into the falsehood of duality. It is not because the evil in Jekyll has overwhelmed the good that Hyde can no longer return to the form of Jekyll; it is because our progress or descent toward unity is a one-way process, and the realization of our singleness is something that once learned cannot be forgotten. One by one, the characters in *Jekyll and Hyde*—Lanyon, Utterson, even Poole—must come down to singleness. Hell is the loss of duality, not the victory of evil. Jekyll's suggestion that he could just as easily, by the same mechanical means, have become an angel as a devil . . . remains a barren, unconvincing notion. (pp. 101-02)

The good, then, when it is left without alternatives, must digest inwards into "the bad." Privacy, singleness, is "the bad"; it is an unspeaking, languageless state. The lawyer "Utterson" represents its opposite alternative; for all his taciturnity and his glumness, he is the one who demands speech, an answer. Utterson is Hyde's true double; Jekyll merely mediates between the two. There is a suggestion in the name, "Utterson of Gaunt Street," . . . that he is the extreme, the absolute refusal of what the Jekyll-Hyde dilemma thrusts on us, the contrary aspiration.

"Make a clean breast of this in confidence"; he urges Jekyll; "and I make no doubt I can get you out of it." . . . For him, everything will have to be made explicit, even if only in the spare, precise language that seems to be the ideal of the book and that as such makes him seem the narrator. Utterson is the tragic character in *Jekyll and Hyde*; it is he who is called upon to find his way to a reconciliation with Hyde (not vice versa), through the reading of the posthumous papers that make clear what has happened. His is finally shown to have been the unjustifiable position, and his is the solitary melancholy with which the book ends. (pp. 102-03)

Hyde, in his extreme and ultimate state, is invisible, hidden behind the cabinet door. All that has lately been seen of him is the passing shadow of a small, preternaturally lithe figure flitting through the courtyard. But Hyde, even before his disappearance behind the door, is small, shrivelled; the oversized clothes seem to hang on an emptiness within. He is hardly the embodiment of gross sensual satisfaction; in fact, there is practically nothing in the book that convinces us of his "evil." Like Deacon Brodie in the play of that name, Jekyll is too clean-cut for his admissions of violent criminal behavior through the person of Hyde to be convincing. The scene of Hyde's walking straight on over the body of a small girl whom he most improbably bumps into on the streets late at night, evidently invented to prove how evil Hyde is, is so artificial and unrealistic as to appear merely ridiculous. His two other specified acts of violence are similarly unsatisfactory. In one case . . . , when he is again wandering the streets at night, in a state of intense anxiety, "a woman spoke to him, offering, I think, a box of lights. He smote her in the face, and she fled." In the other . . . , it is an elderly man who asks for directions (again at night); Hyde reacts as if he has been intruded upon, bothered, and clubs him to the ground in what is described as nothing but a fit of absolute exasperation. (p. 104)

In each of these encounters, it is as if Hyde were reacting to an intrusion. He is protecting the inner, silent language from the demands of public communication. People will not realize that he does not have the patience to play their game of sociality, of relatedness, of communication. Sir Danvers Carew wants directions to go to some plausible world, but has no awareness of the real one, which Hyde inhabits (and to which he sends Carew). There may be some sensual satisfaction in Hyde's transgressions, but we see little of it in this book, even though it is talked about a great deal as a justification for his acts of violence. Some clue to the nature of that satisfaction, such as it is, may be derived from another story of Stevenson's, **"Olalla,"** but what we are much more conscious of in *Dr. Jekyll* is our pity for Hyde, our desire to help him and our knowledge that there is no way to get him, or ourselves, out of his dilemma. (p. 105)

Finally all that we hear of Hyde is his odd, light, swinging footstep, his disembodied weeping, then his last words: "for God's sake, have mercy!" For Hyde emerges at that level of our awareness where we are beyond, or below, language. Language is predicated on duality, and . . . on falsehood. The single self cannot communicate; it rests its case on its being; if it is forced to communicate, it communicates with a blow. That blow is all its speech and its refutation of language.

All that really sticks with the reader is one's sorrow for Hyde, not his evil; and by the time that sorrow makes itself felt the book is nearly over, Hyde is hidden from the reader, and soon after is dead. Yet these concluding pages are what matter in the book, not the stage of contrived violence. We learn to identify with Hyde, even to love him. In the end he proves to be less afraid of death than Jekyll had been. Jekyll had admitted that he was glad to have his better impulses "buttressed and guarded by the terrors of the scaffold," . . . and he speculates, on the last page of the book, whether Hyde will or will not "find courage to release himself at the last moment." . . . By that point, we have had the answer. (pp. 105-06)

Irving Massey, "The Third Self: 'Dracula', 'Jekyll and Hyde', 'Lokis'," in his The Gaping Pig: Literature and Metamorphosis, *University of California Press, 1976, pp. 98-114.*

IRVING S. SAPOSNIK (essay date 1974)

[Saposnik offers a detailed analysis of the novel's structural and thematic development, focusing on its presentation of duality.]

Only a careful reading of [*Strange Case of Dr. Jekyll and Mr. Hyde*] reveals its formal complexity and its moral depth. As a narrative, it is the most intricately structured of Stevenson's stories; as a fable, it represents a classic touchstone of Victorian sensibilities. It is clearly difficult today to detail each of the responsive chords which the story struck in the Victorian mind, but its use of duality as both a structural and thematic device suggests that its application goes beyond a simple antithesis of moral opposites or physical components. Present evidence indicates that Victorian man was haunted constantly by an inescapable sense of division. As rational and sensual being, as public and private man, as civilized and bestial creature, he found himself necessarily an actor, playing only that part of himself suitable to the occasion. As both variables grew more predictable, his role became more stylized; and what was initially an occasional practice became a way of life. (pp. 88-9)

The Victorian World

Because the morality of *Dr. Jekyll and Mr. Hyde* lies at the center of the Victorian world, no detail in the story is so vital as its location. Critics, especially G. K. Chesterton [see excerpt dated 1928], have been quick to indicate that the morality is actually more Scottish than English and that the more proper setting for the narrative would have been Edinburgh. Yet although Chesterton and others are right in thinking that Stevenson could no more put aside his Scottish heritage here than he could in other stories, they fail to recognize that only London could serve as the *locus classicus* of Victorian behavior. An enigma composed of multiple layers of being, its confines held virtually all classes of society conducting what were essentially independent lives. (p. 89)

Unlike Edinburgh with its stark division of Old Town and New, London represented that division-within-essential unity which is the very meaning of *Jekyll and Hyde*. As both geographic and symbolic center, London exemplified what Stevenson called it in *New Arabian Nights*, "the great battlefield of mankind." (pp. 89-90)

Of equal importance to a consideration of *Jekyll and Hyde* are the people who inhabit that world and the manner in which they are presented. Critics have often complained that the London of the story is singularly devoid of women. . . . For once it is easy to account for this omission without reference to the bogeyman of Victorian prudery. For better or worse, Victoria's era, despite its monarch, was male-centered; and a story so directed at the essence of its moral behavior is best seen from a male perspective. In addition, . . . an air of fierce austerity pervades the story—a peculiarly masculine breed of asceticism

which, like the London fog, colors the entire surface. It is as if the atmospheric color were itself a symbol of normative rigidity. The men of the story are representative Victorian types, exemplars of a harsh life that is best seen in the somber context of their professional and social conduct.

The four prominent men in the story are gentlemen and, as such, are variations of standard gentlemanly behavior. Three are professional men—two doctors, one lawyer—and the only non/professional, Richard Enfield, is so locked into his role that his description as "the well-known man about town" might as well be a professional designation. The first to be introduced, "Mr. Utterson the lawyer," is characterized immediately by his profession as well as by a somewhat bitter-sweet compound of surface harshness and internal sympathy. Prone to self-mortification in order to stifle temptation, he nonetheless confines his rigorous standard to himself. With others, he is not only tolerant but charitable, as he translates compassion into action. Feigning unconcern, he often remains "the last good influence in the lives of down-going men." Clearly the moral norm of the story, Utterson is introduced first not only because he is Jekyll's confidant (the only one remaining) but because by person and profession he represents the best and worst of Victoria's social beings. Pledged to a code harsh in its application, he has not allowed its pressures to mar his sense of human need. For himself, he has chosen; and he must make his life on that choice; but he judges others with the understanding necessary to human weakness.

As a lawyer, he represents that legality which identifies social behavior as established law, unwritten but binding; as a judge, however, he is a combination of justice and mercy (as his names Gabriel John suggest), tempering rigidity with kindness, self-denial with compassion. His reaction to Hyde must be seen in this context. While Hyde's grim visage seems sufficient to alarm even the most objective observer (witness the Edinburgh apothecary), Hyde's threat to Jekyll's reputation, and possibly his person, makes him even more frightening to Utterson, a partisan in the best sense of the term, and loyal to his friends especially in their adversity. Utterson is the essence of what Stevenson meant in **"Reflections and Remarks on Human Life"** when he said: "It is the business of this life to make excuses for others. . . . Even justice is no right of a man's own, but a thing . . . which he should strive to see rendered to another." . . . (pp. 90-1)

Utterson's walking companion, and the narrator of Hyde's first "crime," Richard Enfield, appears as a strange, yet appropriate, complement to his distant kinsman. Described as "a well-known man about town," his haunts and habits ("I was coming home from some place at the end of the world, about three o'clock of a black winter morning") seem the "other Victorian" side of Utterson's sobriety. Yet even their casual friendship suggests a combination evidently not impossible in the Victorian social world. Their dull but necessary weekly stroll represents a public acknowledgement of a possibility that Henry Jekyll, for one, was unwilling to admit; and it reinforces the belief that the "other Victorians" are very much the Victorians one has always known but only recently grown to understand. (p. 92)

While Utterson and Enfield complement each other's limitations, Lanyon and Jekyll reveal each other's emptiness. Eminent medical men with an initial "bond of common interest," they have severed their bond over what seems a professional quarrel—Jekyll's metaphysical speculations about human identity which Lanyon admits were "too fanciful." Lanyon, however, has made not so much a professional judgement as a personal one; he has refrained from following Jekyll because of cowardice rather than because of conviction. If Jekyll's inquiries were "too fanciful," they were so because Lanyon lacked the courage, though not the curiosity, to follow him; and his horror at the discovery that Hyde and Jekyll are actually one is as much a self-realization as it is a condemnation of his former friend. Lanyon abandoned Jekyll because he was afraid of the temptation to which he finally succumbed, the offer made so perfectly by the serpentine Hyde coaxing the more-than-willing Lanyon to discover "a new province of knowledge and new avenues to fame and power." A friend in name only, his envy of Jekyll works in direct contrast to that which prompts Utterson to loyalty. Like Jekyll, Lanyon's outward manner belies his inner compulsions; but, unlike his colleague, he cannot struggle with their emergence.

Henry Jekyll, however, is nobody's hero. Although his actions are prompted by no single motive, his primary impulse is fear. If Lanyon is afraid to admit vital truths about himself, Jekyll fears these same truths when he discovers them. Dedicated to an ethical rigidity more severe than Utterson's, because solely self-centered, he cannot face the necessary containment of his dual being. However he may attempt to disguise his experiments under scientific objectivity, and his actions under a macabre alter-ego, he is unable to mask his basic selfishness. As he reveals in his final statement (the bare legal term is better than the more sentimental "confession"), he has thrived upon duplicity; and his reputation has been maintained largely upon his successful ability to deceive. Yet he is no ordinary hypocrite, a simple analogue of such other Stevenson characters as Deacon Brodie. Although Jekyll is unable to judge himself accurately, he is right in denying his hypocrisy. Only briefly does he pretend to be someone other than himself. Having recognized his duality, he attempts to isolate his two selves into individual beings and to allow each to go his separate way. Mere disguise is never sufficient for his ambition; and his failure goes beyond hypocrisy, a violation of social honesty, until it touches upon moral transgression, a violation of the physical and metaphysical foundations of human existence. Henry Jekyll is a complex example of his age of anxiety: woefully weighed down by self-deception, cruelly a slave to his own weakness, sadly a disciple of a severe discipline, his is a voice out of "De Profundis," a cry of Victorian man from the depths of his self-imposed underground.

Henry Jekyll's fiction is to identify that underground man as Edward Hyde. The fiction of the story, however, confirms the insoluble duality of his being. Each of the successive narratives strengthens that inherent union of antagonistic forces which Jekyll attempts to deny. In each, the reader learns more about both Jekyll and Hyde. Unlike conventional narratives in which the action usually develops with a continuous depiction of incident, the matter of *Jekyll and Hyde* ends only after the several incidents have been illuminated by subjective comment. For example, the cold objective horror of the maid's description as Hyde pounces upon the unsuspecting Sir Danvers Carew is balanced by the tormented narratives of a pitiful Lanyon and a compulsive Jekyll. The measure of this story is thus not only in its characters' actions but in their narrations of those actions. Nothing in the story is as singly frightening as Henry Jekyll's final narrative, for in it the reader learns most about the distorted mind which released an unwilling Hyde.

The Narrative Voices

The three separable narrative voices—Enfield, Lanyon, Jekyll—are placed in successive order so that they add increasing

Hyde stepping over the child's body. Illustration by W. Stein.

rhetorical and psychological dimension to the events they describe. In contrast to other multiple narratives whose several perspectives often raise questions of subjective truth and moral ambiguity, these individual narratives in *Jekyll and Hyde* provide a linear regularity of information—an incremental catalogue of attitudes toward Hyde's repulsiveness and Jekyll's decline. Enfield's narrative is the briefest since it describes Hyde's trampling a little girl; and the salient items in it are Enfield's unsuccessful attempts at objectivity and the horrified reactions of the other spectators. To Enfield, it is not the collision itself which is of primary importance but Hyde's casual indifference to the screaming agonies of his victim. Hyde violates a norm of respectable behavior, and his subsequent offer of monetary retribution is nothing more than automatic. Enfield's description, therefore, accentuates Hyde's mechanical regularity in contrast to the human concern which a gentleman should display (does Enfield recognize the artificiality of convention?). Thus, objective as he would be by first describing Hyde as a little man with a stumping gait, his rising gorge forces his language toward the metaphors of "hellish," "damned Juggernaut," and "Satan."

Enfield, however, is reacting to an action which he had personally witnessed. More surprising is the reaction of the hate-filled crowd that gathers around the cornered Hyde, for the people respond not to the trampling but to Hyde's physical repulsiveness. Of these, none is more representative than the doctor who comes to attend the child. A cut-and-dry Edinburgh apothecary, the most general of general practitioners, "about as emotional as a bagpipe," he cannot mask a fierce desire to kill Hyde even as he looks at him. The first of the story's three doctors, he represents what might be regarded as the normative medical mind. Placed here as an effective contrast to his more ambitious colleagues Lanyon and Jekyll, the apothecary's immediate, physical loathing foreshadows the later revelation that Hyde is more than a stunted figure of a man, that he is in truth an amoral abstraction.

Lanyon's and Jekyll's narratives follow immediately upon each other, and both are voices from the grave. As Enfield's narrative is meant as an introduction to the dual existence of Jekyll-Hyde, their narratives occur appropriately after that existence has been concluded. Before either may comment, it is necessary that Hyde emerge with uncontrollable suddenness and commit a murder from which there is no escape but death. By the time of Lanyon's narrative, the reader knows that the Hyde whose misdeeds he has been following has killed himself; but he only suspects that Henry Jekyll has also died. Lanyon's narrative is the first to reveal the truth about the Jekyll-Hyde relationship at the same time that it confirms the grim dominance of Hyde and his magnetic "glittering eye." The whole substance of his narrative is meant to carry Hyde beyond the automatic and rather innocent actions of the Enfield narrative so that he may now be seen as truly diabolical. If Enfield's Hyde was a Juggernaut, Lanyon's is a cunning tempter ruthlessly proud of his ability.

Only after the reader has experienced the revelation of Lanyon's narrative does Stevenson permit him Jekyll's "Full Statement," one which should be read not simply as an appropriate conclusion to the narrative action but as the culmination of the multiple-narrative technique. More than the other narratives, it attempts to present some insight into the narrator's psychology at the same time that it chronicles the process of his destruction. It thus proceeds in two complementary directions: a progressive exposition of events verifiable by their previous occurrence, and an explanation of those events necessarily ambiguous since they are offered by a man incapable of self-judgment. Indeed, the structure of Jekyll's statement is directed toward an often inadvertent self-revelation which proves conclusively that his selfishness and moral cowardice released the horrible personification of his hidden drives. This is not to say that Jekyll is a fiend; he is one no more so than Hyde. Yet, with increasing evidence, he incriminates himself as the guilty party in an indivisible relationship.

Jekyll also details the legitimate scientific concerns which prompted his experiment. His error, however, is that he used these as excuses; but the reader can view them only as explanations. Because of his self-delusion, Jekyll remains unaware of the true results of his experiment; until the end, he believes that Hyde "concerns another than myself." Never able to see beyond his initial deception, he learns little about himself or about the essential failure of his experiment, and remains convinced that the incompatible parts of his being can be separated if the pure powder were available. This conviction, as much as anything else, is Henry Jekyll's tragedy. He is so enmeshed in his self-woven net of duplicity that he cannot identify the two entities whose separation he hopes to achieve. By seeing Hyde as another being rather than as part of himself, he is forced to deny the most significant result of his experiment

and indeed of his entire story: the inescapable conclusion that man must dwell in uncomfortable but necessary harmony with his multiple selves. The final suicide is thus fittingly a dual effort: though the hand that administers the poison is Edward Hyde's, Henry Jekyll forces the action. (pp. 95-6)

Stevenson's fictional abilities are further evidenced by his successful insertion of thematic contrasts into the narrative structure itself. The topography of *Jekyll and Hyde* may be seen as a study in symbolic location, a carefully worked out series of contrasts between exterior modes and interior realities. Like much of Victorian life and letters, most of the story's action is physically internalized behind four walls. (p. 96)

The Symbolic Structure

While the structure of *Jekyll and Hyde* is predicated upon a contrast between exterior and interior, the contrast is never allowed to remain static. The actions that occur in each represent an intriguing paradox: in the exterior, social ambles and foul crimes; in the interior, elegant drawing rooms and secreted laboratories. Each division contains two opposing elements which combine to characterize the individual locale, but both locations in their necessary union represent the social cosmos. The result is a social bond no less indivisible than the moral bond which Jekyll attempts unsuccessfully to sever. The central metaphor is Jekyll's house, with its sinister rear entrance through which Hyde passes and its handsome front "which wore a great air of wealth and comfort": the two faces of Jekyll contained in one inseparable dwelling.

The paradox is continued as the action of *Jekyll and Hyde* becomes internalized. The two final subjective accounts solidify this process on a psychological level, and the action itself leads farther and farther into the interior of Jekyll's house. Although the reader's first views of the house are external, the action soon directs him to the hall, then to the study, and finally to the ominous experiments behind the closed door of the former dissection laboratory. As Poole and Utterson break down the last barrier to Jekyll's secret, they literally and metaphorically destroy his one remaining refuge; by invading his physical sanctuary, they force him into a psychological admission whose only possibility is death. Stevenson's skillful juggling of literal and metaphoric—his ability to suggest the symbolic significance of commonplace reality—is undoubtedly the chief difference between the original bogey story to which his wife, Fanny, objected and the classic fable which *Jekyll and Hyde* has become. Clearly, the most telling evidence of this skill is his ability to select highly suggestive scenery and to allow its multiple suggestions to form the several layers of his narrative.

For reader and nonreader alike, the crucial item of thematic significance has been Edward Hyde. Unquestionably the dominant character, his role in the narrative is often considered the fictional mechanism by which the moral truths are driven home. Surely such a reading is partial, for it fails to approach the story as a total construct and thus commits the sin of facile separation only a trifle less grievous than Jekyll's. Yet Hyde's identity, both physical and moral, is the pervasive mystery whose elusiveness and final revelation unites the fictional and moral concerns. Without Jekyll, there could never have been a Hyde; without Hyde, one can never fully know Jekyll. Thus an ability to understand their relationship rests on an ability to identify what Hyde represents. To begin negatively, he is not the antithetical evil to Jekyll's good nor is he evil at all. His cruelty derives from his association with Jekyll, not from any inherent motivation toward destruction. True, he is compulsive (as is Jekyll), a veritable Juggernaut proceeding on his mechanical way; but this characteristic is primarily found in his initial movements when Jekyll's desires first spring him from his lair. One of the more fascinating developments in the story is Hyde's growing malice—his increasing premeditation as he becomes more and more a mortal. (pp. 97-8)

The legendary Hyde is obviously a difficult opponent. There is clearly something consolatory about equating Hyde with illicit sex; it localizes one's impulses and allows indulgences within the proprieties. Stevenson's Hyde, on the other hand, though less formidable, is more substantial. His substantiality increases, in fact, in direct proportion to his recognition as the essence of man's natural vitality. The key word is *natural*, for it governs the entire amoral world from which Hyde emerges. As the mirror of Jekyll's inner compulsions, he represents that shadow side of man which civilization has striven to submerge: he is a creature of primitive sensibilities loosed upon a world bent on denying him. A reminder of the barbarism which underlies civilization, he is a necessary component of human psychology which most would prefer to leave unrealized.

As an essential life force, Hyde's proper role is to act in harmony with the other parts of man's being. (pp. 98-9)

Throughout his writings Stevenson dwells upon the inescapable burden which any relationship between the barbaric and the civilized produces. Painfully aware of the difficulties their conjunction necessitates, he continues to affirm their vital correspondence. (p. 99)

In his fiction in particular Stevenson develops this double strain of being; there he illustrates the inevitable conflict between natural urges and societal pressures, and there he presents the tragedy of those who surrender themselves to either.

Jekyll surrenders to his society. "The harm [that] was in Jekyll" was in large part the harm of Victoria's England; and his unwillingness to acknowledge his kinship with Edward Hyde may be likened to everyone else's intense hatred of his moral twin. The universal hatred directed at Hyde both in and out of the story is a striking verification of the extent to which Victorian England feared what he represented. Jekyll's repugnance is scarcely his alone, and his actions are predicated upon a social ethic only slightly less distorted than his moral myopia. Victorian anxieties contributed greatly to *Jekyll and Hyde*'s success. The fictional paradox revealed the social paradox; Jekyll's dilemma spoke for more of his countrymen than many were willing to admit.

If Jekyll's fears are taken as a barometer of Victorian anxieties, his relationship to Hyde becomes apparent. While Jekyll represents a man "in the pink of the proprieties," Hyde is the brutal embodiment of the moral, social, political, and economic threats which shook the uncertain Victorian world. In his moral role, he exemplifies the impossibility of any successful separation of man's natural being. A metaphysical impulse in a postlapsarian world, any attempted return to Eden (he proves) must be made at the cost of one's life. Likewise, his social identity cautions the attempted imposition of a new Manicheanism based upon a dichotomy between external and internal behavior. (pp. 99-100)

As political and economic man, Hyde's role is more subtle. The inevitability of his brute power, his unceasing energy, no doubt recalled to many the threatening forces which were beating upon the solid doors of their comfortable homes. Hidden in them as he was, Victorian man could not for long confine himself beneath the domestic covers. He feared "the armies of the night," the troops of the new politics and the new economics that were massing for the onslaught. (p. 100)

Hyde is usually described in metaphors because essentially that is what he is: a metaphor of uncontrolled appetites, an amoral abstraction driven by a compelling will unrestrained by any moral halter. Such a creature is, of necessity, only figuratively describable; for his deformity is moral rather than physical. Purposely left vague, he is best described as Jekyll-deformed—dwarfish, stumping, ape-like—a frightening parody of a man unable to exist on the surface. He and Jekyll are inextricably joined because one without the other cannot function in society. As Hyde is Jekyll's initial disguise, so Jekyll is Hyde's refuge after the Carew murder. If Jekyll reflects respectability, then Hyde is his image "through the looking glass."

Hyde's literal power ends with his suicide, but his metaphorical power is seemingly infinite. Many things to his contemporaries, he has grown beyond Stevenson's story in an age of automatic Freudian response. As Hyde has grown, Jekyll has been overshadowed so that his role has shifted from culprit to victim. Accordingly, the original fable has assumed a meaning neither significant for the nineteenth century nor substantial for the twentieth. The time has come for Jekyll and Hyde to be put back together again. (p. 101)

> *Irving S. Saposnik, in his* Robert Louis Stevenson, *Twayne Publishers, Inc., 1974, 164 p.*

JULIA BRIGGS (essay date 1977)

[*Briggs discusses the circumstances surrounding the composition of the novel.*]

The Strange Case of Dr. Jekyll and Mr. Hyde . . . is now the most moralized allegory of duality, but the original version was very different. The first draft, written at high speed during one of Stevenson's recurrent attacks of tuberculosis, was apparently simply a narrative of the transformation; according to his stepson, Lloyd Osbourne, 'a magnificent bit of sensationalism'. It was Stevenson's wife Fanny who told him that he had left out the most important part, 'the morality, worse luck!' Stevenson threw the manuscript on the fire in a fury, but rewrote it in the next two days, in spite of a high temperature. The initial idea for the story had come to him in a nightmare, as he relates in **"A Chapter on Dreams"** [see excerpt dated 1888], his account of the independent and creative activity of the brain in sleep. The 'Brownies' of this essay, the imaginative impulses of the sleeping mind, stand in a strange, ambiguous relation to their author. They work for him, and yet they are a little frightening. They 'have not a rudiment of what we call conscience', and are 'somewhat fantastic, like their stories hot and hot, full of passion and the picturesque, alive with animating incident; and', he continues, 'they have no prejudice against the supernatural'.

The irrational, amoral Brownies, voices of nightmare and delirium, at times appear to set up a dialogue with Stevenson's more repressive conscious mind, and their conflict may well have given rise to the sensation of being 'two people at once' which inspired *Jekyll and Hyde*. . . . The sinister intimacy between the feverish subversive Brownies and Stevenson's conscious mind is not unlike that of Jekyll and Hyde, and it may also be relevant that the change from Jekyll into Hyde is first made spontaneously in sleep. In a moment that anticipates the horrible revelation of Kafka's *Metamorphosis*, Jekyll wakes to find the hand of Hyde lying on his counterpane. Later the same thing happens in public in Regent's Park, and finally, 'if I slept, or even dozed for a moment in my chair, it was always as Hyde that I awakened'. This suggests that the evil of Hyde is at its zenith when Jekyll is asleep, and he awakens as if from a nightmare whose evil influence he cannot cast off. In Jekyll's case—and perhaps in Stevenson's, in a less literal sense—the sleep of reason may be said to have brought forth monsters. (pp. 66-7)

At the outset of the story Jekyll condones Hyde and finds it useful to be able to indulge in 'such irregularities as I was guilty of' at night and in a different guise, while possessing a grave and authoritative mien during the day. As Jekyll asserts in his "Final Statement", 'all men in life . . . are commingled out of good and evil', but it would be wonderfully convenient to be able to isolate one's evil propensities and indulge them as a different person. Edward Hyde is a kind of psychological scapegoat, so utterly wicked that the respectable Jekyll can feel quite dissociated from him, as if his crimes were really someone else's, yet he can share in Hyde's sensual gratifications. Stevenson's allegory is never so naïve as to suggest that Jekyll was ever a genuinely virtuous man. Like so many outwardly respectable Victorians, pillars of their society, he was a man who harboured the desires of Hyde, and had originally hoped to use Hyde as a convenience. Although Hyde was at first younger and not nearly so well developed as the doctor, he grows, and finally the convenience *becomes* him—Jekyll begins to revert to Hyde spontaneously. (pp. 67-8)

Stevenson's frequent attacks of fever, with their accompanying delirium and nightmares, probably made him unusually aware of the activities of the unconscious, at the same time enabling him to take a confidently detached view of them as merely 'the voice of the fever'. Indeed he went further, deliberately exploiting the promising raw material they provided in stories such as *Jekyll,* or his short story of a werewolf, **"Olalla"**. His particular balance of introspection and comparative psychological stability enabled him to write freely and perceptively of the disturbing dualities in man. (p. 68)

One of the practical problems Stevenson set for himself, and did not entirely solve, was how to present an embodiment of pure evil. How is such a being to be depicted so that his behaviour is distinguished from that of the man of average immorality? There are hints of Jekyll's earlier indulgences in Soho, of Hyde's 'strange companions', but Hyde's evil is primarily reduced to two events: walking over a child and the murder of Sir Danvers Carew, both *actes gratuits,* yet both demonstrating a total lack of that 'cunning' which Stevenson several times claims to be characteristic of Hyde's smile. Viewed from a psychological standpoint, he seems anxious to provoke punishment, rather than to administer it. Perhaps the twentieth century, which combines more searching attitudes towards apparently motiveless violence with more obvious contemporary examples of it, tends to be hypercritical of fictional portrayals of evil. The atrocities performed in our times by supposedly civilized men make Hyde's murders look like schoolboy pranks. But here is a genuine artistic problem which, though perhaps appreciated by Wilde, was not resolved until, ten years later, Henry James wrote *The Turn of the Screw.* Faced with the same difficulty, Stevenson's disciple Arthur Machen resorted to references to 'unspeakable' or 'unutterable' orgies, and allusions to Greek mysteries and Sabbaths, which combine sensationalism with evasiveness. His identification of evil with sexual licence is banal and commonplace in comparison with the motiveless malignity of Edward Hyde. (pp. 69-70)

Julia Briggs, "A Scientific Spirit: Mesmerism, Drugs and Psychic Doctors," in her Night Visitors: The Rise and Fall of the English Ghost Story, *Faber & Faber, 1977, pp. 52-75.*

ROSEMARY JACKSON   (essay date 1981)

[*Jackson assesses the moral intent of the novel and the repressed elements in the characters' personalities.*]

[A] famous parable of dualism, *The Strange Case of Dr Jekyll and Mr Hyde* . . . is usually seen as the clearest allegory of Victorian hypocrisy and repression: 'Behind its latterday Gothick lies a very profound and epoch-revealing truth.' The other side of the human returns to act out latent libidinal drives concealed by the social ego. (Je-kyll—I kill—his very name has within it his real nature as murderer, embodied in Hyde— what is hidden.) This exemplifies Freud's theory of fantastic narrative as telling of a return of the repressed: Hyde is able to fulfil Jekyll's desires to steal, love, be violent. . . . [But] Stevenson's is much more than an allegory of good and evil at war with one another. The text itself draws attention to 'evil' as a relative moral category, as a notion imposed upon natural disorder. Jekyll, conducting his 'experiment while under the empire', is drawn towards the world on the other side of the mirror because it offers him an infinite number of 'selves'. . . . Good-evil dichotomies are preceded by an a-moral condition, one which echoes Sade's ideal of undifferentiation, his 'universal prostitution of all beings'. Jekyll is attracted to this ideal as his original, undivided nature. (pp. 114-15)

Hyde is originally a nameless, shapeless thing, without identity, smaller than Jekyll, dwarflike, *within* his parent's form. He is 'hardly human! Something troglodytic, shall we say? . . . Like a man restored from death . . . he gave an impression of deformity without any nameable malformation'. . . . The lawyer, Utterson, reads into Hyde's face 'Satan's signature' and Jekyll refers to him as 'that child of hell', though initially Hyde was 'neither diabolical nor divine', but prior to human concepts of good and evil. Hyde introduces absolute otherness, 'a sense of unreality', an a-morality beneath moral structures. 'As for the moral turpitude that man *unveiled* to me . . . I cannot dwell on it without a sense of horror.' Hyde threatens late Victorian London with his horrid laughter, theft, sexuality, criminality: he breaks every social taboo. What most frightens Jekyll is Hyde's distance from the human, his non-human origins, i.e. his link with the inorganic, which comes to be categorized as demonic in an 'evil' sense:

> he thought of Hyde, for all his energy of life, as of something not only hellish but inorganic. This was the shocking thing; that the slime of the pit seemed to utter cries and voices; that the amorphous dust gesticulated and sinned; that what was dead, and had no shape, should usurp the office of life. And this again, that that insurgent horror was knit to him closer than a wife, closer than an eye . . . (it) prevailed against him, and deposed him out of life. . . .

Once this inorganicism is recognized, the text has to evolve strategies to contain and exclude it. *Dr Jekyll and Mr Hyde* develops in the pattern of the detective novel 'hunting down' anti-social energies, neutralizing desire. The relation of Jekyll to Hyde is also one of father to son. 'Jekyll had more than a father's interest; Hyde had more than a son's indifference.' Like other fantasies, this one repeats the Oedipal drama of father-son conflict and finally rewrites the victory of the first. (pp. 115-16)

> *Rosemary Jackson, "Gothic Tales and Novels," in her* Fantasy: The Literature of Subversion, *Methuen, 1981, pp. 95-122.*

ADDITIONAL BIBLIOGRAPHY

Aldington, Richard. *Portrait of a Rebel: The Life and Work of Robert Louis Stevenson.* London: Evans Brothers, 1957, 245 p.
An intimate portrait of Stevenson that presents information regarding the composition of *Dr. Jekyll and Mr. Hyde.*

Elwin, Malcolm. *The Strange Case of Robert Louis Stevenson.* London: Macdonald, 1950, 256 p.
A biographical study that contains scattered critical references to *Dr. Jekyll and Mr. Hyde.*

Geduld, Harry M., ed. *The Definitive "Dr. Jekyll and Mr. Hyde" Companion.* New York: Garland Publishing, 1983, 219 p.
A collection of essays about the novel, including reviews of the theatrical and cinematic renditions.

Gwynn, Stephen. *Robert Louis Stevenson.* London: Macmillan and Co., 1939, 267 p.
A biography that includes a section on the circumstances surrounding the composition of the novel.

Jefford, Andrew. "Dr. Jekyll and Professor Nabokov: Reading a Reading." In *Robert Louis Stevenson,* edited by Andrew Noble, pp. 47-72. London: Vision Press, 1983.
An analysis of Nabokov's discussion of the novel (see excerpt dated 1941-48).

Kanzer, Mark. "The Self-Analytic Literature of Robert Louis Stevenson." In *Psychoanalysis and Culture: Essays in Honor of Géza Róheim,* edited by George B. Wilbur and Warner Muensterberger, pp. 425-35. New York: International Universities Press, 1951.
Discusses the role of the unconscious in Stevenson's composition of the novel.

Kiely, Robert. *Robert Louis Stevenson and the Fiction of Adventure.* Cambridge: Harvard University Press, 1964, 285 p.
A discussion of Stevenson's adventure fiction, with several references to *Dr. Jekyll and Mr. Hyde.*

Leaf, Munro. *"The Strange Case of Dr. Jekyll and Mr. Hyde." The American Magazine* CXXXI, No. 5 (May 1941): 104.
A brief parody of the novel.

Schultz, Myron G. "The 'Strange Case' of Robert Louis Stevenson." *The Journal of the American Medical Association* 216, No. 1 (5 April 1971): 90-4.
Suggests that Stevenson may have written the novel under the influence of cocaine.

Sontag, Susan. "Doctor Jekyll." In her *I, Etcetera,* pp. 187-230. New York: Farrar, Straus, Giroux, 1978.
Recreates the novel in the vernacular of the late 1970s.

Thomas, Ronald. "In the Company of Strangers: Absent Voices in Stevenson's *Dr. Jekyll and Mr. Hyde* and Beckett's *Company." Modern Fiction Studies* 32, No. 2 (Summer 1986): 157-73.
Interprets *Dr. Jekyll and Mr. Hyde* as an example of the evolution of the modern novel.

Robert Smith Surtees

1805-1864

(Also wrote under pseudonyms of John Jorrocks, The Yorkshireman, and Nim South) English novelist, sketch and manual writer, and autobiographer.

A minor Victorian author, Surtees is recognized as the best sporting novelist in the English language. In a series of works that deal primarily with fox-hunting, he elaborately described mid-nineteenth-century English country life, recording in precise detail his characters' manners and speech and such everyday aspects of their lives as their clothing, meals, and hairstyles. Surtees mercilessly exposed the hypocrisy and social pretensions of the middle and upper classes, yet his satire is balanced by his raucous humor; indeed, he is particularly praised for his vivid, exuberant style and comic characters, most notably John Jorrocks, the vulgar, self-confident, and outspoken Cockney grocer turned huntsman whom he immortalized in *Jorrocks's Jaunts and Jollities, Handley Cross,* and *Hillingdon Hall.* Since the nineteenth century, Surtees' admirers have argued that his works are of interest to both hunting fans and general readers. Nevertheless, his reputation as a sporting novelist has limited his audience and contributed to his critical neglect. While modern commentators debate the literary merits of Surtees' works, they unanimously stress their value as social histories.

Surtees developed a passion for fox-hunting early in life. He was raised at Hamsterley Hall, a country estate near Durham, England, and spent much of his boyhood hunting. A second son, Surtees had no prospect of inheriting the family estate, and he decided to pursue a law career. Although he qualified as a solicitor in 1828, he never practiced law assiduously, preferring to devote most of his time to hunting. Having, as he expressed it, "a taste for scribbling," he began contributing hunting stories under the pseudonym Nim South to the *Sporting Magazine* in 1830. The following year was important for several reasons, including the publication of his first book. *The Horseman's Manual,* a practical guide to the sale and purchase of horses, was the only work to which Surtees signed his name; indeed, numerous critics have questioned why he insisted on remaining anonymous. In addition, his older brother died of smallpox, leaving him heir to the family fortune and Hamsterley Hall. Surtees' improved finances influenced his decision to join Rudolph Ackermann in 1831 in founding the London-based *New Sporting Magazine,* which he edited from its inception until 1836 and which featured many of his stories. After his father's death in 1838, Surtees returned to Hamsterley Hall, where he lived as a country gentleman, hunting, managing his estate, and holding a number of positions of responsibility in Durham County, including sheriff and justice of the peace. He also continued to write, publishing several novels as well as *The Analysis of the Hunting Field,* a collection of sporting sketches that commemorate the 1845-46 hunting season. Surtees was working on an autobiography that he intended to call *Sporting and Social Recollections* when he died of a heart attack in 1864.

Among Surtees' most significant contributions to the *New Sporting Magazine* is a series of sketches that appeared in the periodical between July 1831 and September 1834. In these

sketches, he first recorded the farcical adventures of the now-famous Jorrocks, whose boisterous enthusiasm for fox-hunting has prompted critics to label him the "Falstaff of the chase." In 1838, the Jorrocks stories were published in book form as *Jorrocks's Jaunts and Jollities.* The genre of this work has been debated by critics: while some liken the volume to a picaresque novel, most term it a collection of sketches. On its appearance, *Jorrocks's Jaunts and Jollities* was overshadowed by Charles Dickens's *Pickwick Papers,* which many critics believe was patterned after Surtees' sketches. Surtees further described Jorrocks's exploits in his next two works, *Handley Cross* and *Hillingdon Hall.* In these novels, Jorrocks is accompanied by James Pigg, a hard-riding, hard-drinking huntsman who is praised as one of Surtees' most delightful characters. Neither *Handley Cross* nor *Hillingdon Hall* was popular: modern critics speculate that Surtees offended a large segment of his audience by ridiculing those who viewed fox-hunting as a fashionable sport for the wealthy. In fact, only Jorrocks and Pigg escaped the author's derision for, like Surtees himself, they hunted for the sheer sport of it.

Surtees achieved his greatest popular success with *Mr. Sponge's Sporting Tour,* which originally appeared serially in the *New Monthly Magazine* in 1849-51. The title character of this novel travels throughout the English countryside "sponging" on unsuspecting families who supply him with free room and board;

according to Surtees, Soapey Sponge's "dexterity in getting into people's houses was only equaled by the difficulty of getting him out again." Sponge is a rogue but, like Jorrocks and Pigg, he is redeemed in Surtees' eyes by his genuine fondness for hunting. *Sponge* was the first of Surtees' works to be illustrated by the famous sporting caricaturist John Leech, whose drawings for it and Surtees' later novels have attracted almost as much attention as the texts. Following the success of *Sponge,* Surtees issued an expanded edition of *Handley Cross* that sold much better than the original version and is now considered by most critics to be his best work. In addition, Surtees contracted with William Harrison Ainsworth, the editor of the *New Monthly Magazine,* to publish another novel— *Young Tom Hall*—in the periodical. Only a few installments of the work had appeared when Surtees, learning that Ainsworth had revealed him as the author, abruptly quit writing it. Although he never finished *Young Tom Hall,* Surtees used some of its characters and incidents in his next two novels, *Ask Mamma* and *Plain or Ringlets?* Two of his least popular works, *Ask Mamma* and *Plain or Ringlets?* marked a departure for the author by focusing on nonhunting aspects of country society. Surtees returned to more familiar themes in his last novel, the posthumously published *Mr. Facey Romford's Hounds,* which is a sequel to *Sponge.*

Surtees has never attracted a large following among readers or critics. The greatest reason for this, commentators note, is his reputation as the classic novelist of fox-hunting. Pigeonholed as a sporting writer since the nineteenth century, Surtees remains today, in the words of Alex Hamilton, "the darling of a specialist readership," applauded by hunting enthusiasts but virtually ignored by the literary establishment and the general public. Twentieth-century critics point out that other factors have also adversely affected Surtees' fame. Among these is the widespread notion that the original illustrations to his works— those by Leech as well as those by Henry Alken and Hablot K. Browne (Phiz)—constitute their sole source of appeal. Another factor cited is the author's penchant for anonymity, which has led many commentators to believe that because Surtees viewed writing as a hobby rather than a serious profession, he does not deserve critical attention. As John Shand explains, these critics have disregarded Surtees because "he was not a literary gentleman with an odd taste for hunting, but a hunting gentleman with an odd gift for writing."

Although a number of Surtees' famous contemporaries, including William Makepeace Thackeray and William Morris, avidly read his works, very few reviews appeared in the nineteenth century. By the early 1930s, the amount of Surtees criticism still remained so slight that Frederick Watson was able to write, "because of the nature rather than the quality of his work, Robert Surtees has been allowed a sanctuary from critical discussion." Since that time, a small but admiring group of commentators has attempted to reverse the trend toward classifying Surtees as a sporting novelist by urging that his works possess merits beyond their value as hunting stories. Among these merits are Surtees' host of comic characters and what Virginia Woolf called his "slapdash, gentlemanly" style. A number of critics have attributed the appeal of Surtees' characters to their racy, colloquial speech. Jorrocks, who is especially praised in this respect, is perhaps best known for his invective and for his countless witty sayings, including his often-quoted definition of hunting: "the sport of kings, the image of war without its guilt, and only five-and-twenty per cent. of its danger." In commending Surtees' style, critics have also noted his particularly terse and exciting descriptions

of the hunt. Yet not all twentieth-century commentary on Surtees' artistry has been positive. Many critics have faulted his loosely constructed, episodic plots, while others have censured his overuse of clichés and catch phrases. Still others have objected to his harsh treatment of women, pointing out that Lucy Glitters, who appears in *Sponge* and *Mr. Facey Romford's Hounds,* is his only female character who is not a greedy, conniving shrew. While the artistic worth of Surtees' novels continues to be a subject of controversy, critics have reached a consensus on at least one aspect of his writings: their unflinching realism. Commentators rarely fail to point out that Surtees painted a truthful and uncomplimentary picture of English country life during the mid-nineteenth century. The endless eating and drinking, filthy stables, fashionable inns, and exclusive hunt parties—all, critics agree, are presented in graphic detail, rendering Surtees' works indispensable social documents that recreate a limited but significant phase of nineteenth-century life ignored by most novelists of his day. Although the history of Surtees' reputation indicates that he may never be widely read or granted a large amount of critical attention, recent commentary suggests that he will continue to be admired for his lively humor, memorable characters, and remarkably accurate depiction of one aspect of Victorian life.

(See also *Dictionary of Literary Biography,* Vol. 21: *Victorian Novelists Before 1885.*)

*PRINCIPAL WORKS

The Horseman's Manual: Being a Treatise on Soundness, the Law of Warranty, and Generally on the Laws Relating to Horses (manual) 1831
Jorrocks's Jaunts and Jollities; or, The Hunting, Shooting, Racing, Driving, Sailing, Eating, Eccentric, and Extravagant Exploits of That Renowned Sporting Citizen, Mr. John Jorrocks, of St. Botolph Lane and Great Coram Street (sketches) 1838
Handley Cross; or, The Spa Hunt (novel) 1843; also published as *Handley Cross; or, Mr. Jorrocks's Hunt* [enlarged edition], 1854
Hillingdon Hall; or, The Cockney Squire (novel) 1845
The Analysis of the Hunting Field: Being a Series of Sketches of the Principal Characters That Compose One, the Whole Forming a Slight Souvenir of the Season 1845-6 (sketches) 1846
Hawbuck Grange; or, The Sporting Adventures of Thomas Scott, Esq. (novel) 1847
Mr. Sponge's Sporting Tour (novel) 1853
Ask Mamma; or, The Richest Commoner in England (novel) 1858
Plain or Ringlets? (novel) 1860
Mr. Facey Romford's Hounds (novel) 1865
**Robert Smith Surtees (Creator of "Jorrocks")* (unfinished autobiography) 1924
Young Tom Hall: His Heart-Aches and Horses (unfinished novel) 1926
The Novels of R. S. Surtees. 10 vols. (novels) 1929-30

*Many of Surtees' works were originally published serially in periodicals.

**This work is comprised of Surtees' memoirs, also known as *Sporting and Social Recollections,* and commentary by E. D. Cuming.

JOHN GIBSON LOCKHART (letter date 1836)

[*Lockhart wrote several novels, but his fame rests on his biography of Sir Walter Scott and his critical contributions to* Blackwood's Edinburgh Magazine *and the* Quarterly Review, *which he edited from 1825 to 1853. Critics speculate that this encouraging letter from Lockhart inspired Surtees to write* Handley Cross.]

I believe you are the creator of Jorrocks, who has always delighted me. Do get some cousin of his in the horsey (?) line, and throw the materials into light dramatic form.

> John Gibson Lockhart, *in an extract from a letter to Robert Smith Surtees on July 8, 1836, in* Robert Smith Surtees (Creator of ''Jorrocks''): 1803-1864 *by Robert Smith Surtees and E. D. Cuming, Charles Scribner's Sons, 1924, p. 211.*

FRASER'S MAGAZINE (essay date 1838)

[*In this review of* Jorrocks's Jaunts and Jollities, *the anonymous critic prefers Jorrocks to Dickens's Pickwick.*]

The essays now published under the title of *Jorrocks's Jaunts and Jollities* were the first to lead the way in the . . . [school of sporting] fiction. In these, Mr. Jorrocks, a rich sporting grocer, is the chief character; and competent and unprejudiced judges incline to the opinion, that the idea of the popular character of *Pickwick* was derived from the hero of the Surrey hunt. Pickwick is an excellent character, with the assistance of Sam Weller; but, viewed singly, Jorrocks, in our opinion, is the better of the two. He has all Pickwick's good-natured simplicity, without his lethargic slowness. No man, be he sportsman or otherwise, can read Mr. Jorrocks's adventures—hunting, shooting, racing, driving, &c.—without feeling that the hero is a sportsman; while, despite the title and the wrapper, headed by a man shooting with the gun from the wrong shoulder, no one can accuse any of the members of the Pickwick Club of any pretensions to the name. . . .

The first scene [in *Jorrocks's Jaunts and Jollities*], ''Swell and the Surrey,'' is a parody on Nimrod's article in the *Quarterly*, in which ''Snob,'' or the provincial gentleman on the good little bay horse, makes his appearance among the dandified Meltonians. In lieu of Snob, we have a Melton swell appearing among the Surrey men, astonishing them equally by the cut of his coat and the cut of his nag; who, after a brilliant day among the flints, goes away, thoroughly disgusted with the country. Next, Mr. Jorrocks mounts his Yorkshire friend, to see their ''brilliant 'ounds;'' and the start out of London, in the fog, is, we think, one of the most ludicrous scenes in the book, heightened not a little by Phiz's excellent illustration of Mr. Jorrocks bumping away with the mail-coach lamp strapped to his back. (p. 482)

The scene in the hunting stables at Croydon, where Mr. Jorrocks shews off the nags to his friend, is true to nature; and the meet of the hounds, the find below hill, with the runs up and down, Mr. Jorrocks's tumble into the unsavoury cesspool, with the brilliant finish of the brushless fox, are all done in a style that conveys the very scene to the mind. (p. 484)

Mr. Jorrocks's other adventures embrace nearly all sorts of sporting,—stag-hunting, racing, sailing, driving, &c., in England and France; but each sketch is done in a style to interest the general reader, as well as the lover of the particular amusement. The scene at Newmarket, where the honest grocer joins a party of blacklegs at the White Hart, conveys a better idea of the doings of that noted spot than any we have ever read; and his adventures in France are full of fun. (p. 488)

> ''Sporting Literature,'' *in* Fraser's Magazine, *Vol. XVIII, No. CVI, October, 1838, pp. 481-88.*

[JOHN GIBSON LOCKHART] (essay date 1843)

[*In this favorable review of* Handley Cross, *Lockhart defends the originality of Jorrocks and predicts a bright future for Surtees as a novelist.*]

Many hasty critics accused the author of *Jorrocks's Jaunts and Jollities* . . . of plagiarizing Pickwick and Co., regardless of the preface, which stated that the chapters 'were reprinted from the *New Sporting Magazine,* wherein they had appeared between the years 1831 and 1834,' long before Mr. Dickens emerged into public notice. We will venture to say that the sire of Jorrocks would no more think of such a thing as filching another man's style than would the more prolific 'Boz.' How far the popularity of *The Jaunts* may have induced certain publishers to wish for a Cockney sportsman of their own is another matter: but the dialect of Jorrocks was and is his own; and we must equally disclaim, on the part of our independent friend, as respects character, all clanship or sympathy with the soft Mr Pickwick. Jorrocks is a sportsman to the backbone. (p. 397)

In [*Handley Cross*] the character of the sporting grocer is brought out in still more perfect developement than in [*Jorrocks's Jaunts and Jollities*]. . . . [Our] author, though a crack sportsman, is quite awake upon a variety of subjects besides. (pp. 397-98)

[Jorrocks's historian] is a writer of no common promise. On this occasion Mr. Surtees has not thought proper to trouble himself with much complication of plot; but the easy style in which he arranges and draws out his characters satisfies us that he might, if he pleased, take a high place among our modern novelists. He has a world of knowledge of life and manners beyond what most of those now in vogue can pretend to; and a gentleman-like tone and spirit, perhaps even rarer among them. We advise him to try his hand—and that before he loses the high spirits of youth;—but he must, in so doing, by all means curb his propensity to caricature. (p. 411)

> [John Gibson Lockhart], *in a review of ''Handley Cross; or, The Spa-Hunt,'' in* The Quarterly Review, *Vol. LXXI, No. CXLII, March, 1843, pp. 392-411.*

ROBERT SMITH SURTEES (essay date 1847)

[*In the following extract from* Hawbuck Grange, *Surtees offers a tongue-in-cheek judgment of his works and the profession of writing.*]

''What queer books you write!'' observed our excellent but rather matter-of-fact friend, Sylvanus Bluff, the other day, who seeing us doubling up a sheet of paper in a rather unceremonious way, concluded we were at what he calls our ''old tricks.'' ''I buy all your books,'' added he with a solemn shake of the head, as though we were beggaring him—''I bought your *Jorrocks, Jaunts, and Jollities,* I bought *Handley Cross, or the Spa Hunt,* I bought *Hillingdon Hall, or the Cockney Squire;* but I don't *understand* them. I don't see the *wit* of them. *I* don't see

Surtees' home, Hamsterley Hall.

the *use* of them. *I* wonder you don't write something useful. I should think now," added he seriously, "you could do something better. I should say now you would be quite equal to writing a dictionary, or a book upon draining, and those would be really useful works, and your friends would get something for their money."

Gentle reader! we plead guilty to the charge of writing most egregious nonsense. Nay, we are sometimes surprised how such stuff can ever enter our head, astonished that we should be weak enough to commit it to paper, amazed that there should be publishers rash enough to print it, and lost in utter bewilderment that there should be good, honest, sane, nay sensible folks, not only idle enough to read it, but, oh wonder! of all wonders! extravagant enough to part with their good current coin to buy it!

And talking of friends buying our books out of politeness, we may here avail ourself of the opportunity to say that there is nothing we dislike more; nay, so great is our objection, that if we knew any honest, mistaken man about to commit such an absurdity, we would absolutely forestall our own market by offering him a copy. At least we *think* we would.

We don't know why any one should do so, we are sure, for neither by name, dedication, or date, do we ever provoke so

suicidal an act. We may say, with our excellent friend Peter Morris, that "if putting our Christian name and surname at the beginning of a book were necessary conditions to the dignity of authorship, we should never be one while we live." Like Peter, "we want nerves for this." We rejoice in the privilege of writing and printing *incognito,* and think with him that it is the "finest discovery" that ever was made. Peter, to be sure, got bolder with age, but then he felt that he was "somebody."

Writing, we imagine, is something like snuffing or smoking—men get into the way of it, and can't well leave it off. Like smoking, it serves to beguile an idle hour. Individually speaking, writing makes us tolerably independent, both of the world and the weather. We are never regularly high and dry for want of a companion so long as we can get pen, ink, and paper; and though we should not like to back ourself against such a winter as the last (1846-7), yet writing enables us to contend with a tolerable amount of bad weather. An author has pretty much the same pleasure in seeing his ugly cramped hand turned into neat print that a traveller has in receiving five-and-twenty francs for a sovereign on landing in France. Revising is something like returning to the realities of English money again. But we are getting into the mysteries of authorship. (pp. 222-23)

Robert Smith Surtees, "The Season 1846-7," in his Hawbuck Grange; or, The Sporting Adventures of Thomas Scott, Esq., *1847. Reprint by Methuen & Co. Ltd., 1913, pp. 222-29.*

W. M. THACKERAY   (letter date 1849)

[*A famed Victorian author, Thackeray is best known for his satiric sketches and novels of upper- and middle-class English life. Thackeray and Surtees began corresponding early in 1849 and became close friends shortly thereafter. In his first letter to Thackeray, Surtees asked him to illustrate* Sponge; *Thackeray's response is excerpted below.*]

I was very much flattered by your proposal to illustrate [*Sponge*], but I only draw for my own books, and indeed am not strong enough as an artist to make designs for anybody else's stories. You would find my pictures anything but comical, and I have not the slightest idea how to draw a horse, a dog, or a sporting scene of any sort. My friend Leech, I should think, would be your man—he is of a sporting turn, and to my mind draws a horse excellently. . . .

Mr Jorrocks has long been a dear and intimate friend of mine. I stole from him years ago, having to describe a hunting scene with which I was quite unfamiliar. . . .

> *W. M. Thackeray, in a letter to Robert Smith Surtees in May, 1849, in* Robert Smith Surtees (Creator of "Jorrocks"): 1803-1864 *by Robert Smith Surtees and E. D. Cuming, Charles Scribner's Sons, 1924, p. 245.*

W. M. THACKERAY   (letter date 1852)

[*In this excerpt from a letter to Surtees, Thackeray praises two installments of* Sponge.]

This is not to thank you for the grouse, but for the last two numbers of **Soapey Sponge:** they are capital, and the Flat Hats delightful; those fellows in spectacles divine; and Scamperdale's character perfectly odious and admirable.

> *W. M. Thackeray, in a letter to Robert Smith Surtees in April? 1852, in* Robert Smith Surtees (Creator of "Jorrocks"): 1803-1864 *by Robert Smith Surtees and E. D. Cuming, Charles Scribner's Sons, 1924, p. 260.*

ROBERT SMITH SURTEES   (essay date 1854)

[*Critics who fault the incoherent structure of Surtees' works frequently note that he acknowledged this weakness in both his preface to the 1854 edition of* Handley Cross *and his preface to* Ask Mamma *(see excerpts below).*]

Mr. Jorrocks, having for many years maintained his popularity, it is believed that, with the aid of the illustrious Leech, he is now destined for longevity.

The Author, in the present edition, not being tied to space or quantity, has had a better opportunity of developing his sporting hero than before.

The reader will have the kindness to bear in mind, that the work merely professes to be a tale, and does not aspire to the dignity of a novel.

> *Robert Smith Surtees, in a preface to his* Handley Cross, *second edition, Methuen & Co. Ltd., 1854, p. i.*

ROBERT SMITH SURTEES   (essay date 1858)

[*Surtees' preface to* Ask Mamma *is reprinted below.*]

It may be a recommendation to the lover of light literature to be told, that the following story does not involve the complication of a plot. It is a mere continuous narrative of an almost every day exaggeration, interspersed with sporting scenes and excellent illustrations by Leech.

> *Robert Smith Surtees, in a preface to* "Ask Mamma"; *or, The Richest Commoner in England,* Bradbury, Agnew, & Co., 1858, p. i.

ROBERT SMITH SURTEES   (essay date 1864?)

[*In the following excerpt, Surtees recalls the inception of his literary career. This piece was composed during the last months of Surtees' life and was intended to form part of his unfinished* Sporting and Social Recollections.]

I had always had a taste for scribbling, and thus it happened that I endeavoured to beguile the dead winter of 1829 by writing a semi-sporting novel. Up to that time no one had ever essayed anything in the sporting line that he was not prepared to swear to. (p. 60)

I had got about two-thirds through my work when I showed it to a couple of friends, and these so laughed it to scorn that I put it on the fire, and half resolved to abandon the pursuit of letters for the future. I had, however, kept a hunting journal, and after a time, not being quite satisfied with the verdict of those two friends, and having passed for a good theme-writer at school, I determined to try my hand at facts, and take the opinion of one of those best of critics, a publisher. To this end I sketched out some papers, and, Nimrod being then at variance with the proprietors, I offered them to the editor of what, for the sake of distinction, I will now call the "Old" *Sporting Magazine*. The bait took, and I presently found myself installed as first fiddle in the hunting line. A friend of mine having adopted the signature "Nim North," I took that of "Nim South" for my hunting contributions. I wrote on other subjects over other signatures, however. (pp. 60-1)

> *Robert Smith Surtees, "First Literary Efforts: The 'New Sporting Magazine' and 'The Horseman's Manual'," in* Robert Smith Surtees (Creator of "Jorrocks"): 1803-1864 *by Robert Smith Surtees and E. D. Cuming, Charles Scribner's Sons, 1924, pp. 60-72.*

THE NATION   (essay date 1888)

[*This anonymous critic reviews an 1888 edition of* Hillingdon Hall, *labeling it a "second-rate" novel that has not stood the test of time.*]

It is scarcely probable that the individual exists to-day who could read through **Hillingdon Hall, or The Cockney Squire.** Any interest in this reprint of a novel written forty-four years ago is of the kind attached to literary curiosities. It is a truism to say that posterity is the infallible judge of literary greatness, but if any one should desire personally to test the truth of that truism, let him compare *Pickwick* and **Hillingdon Hall,** Weller and Jorrocks. If that doubting person should also wish to satisfy himself that the general readableness of our second-rate novels is some compensation for our paucity of first-rate, let him select **Hillingdon Hall** first among a bundle of the second-rates of the first half of our century. It appears from the illustrations of the novel that humor, expressed by pictorial art not of the highest excellence, retains the power to amuse longer than that of inferior literary art. The Flathers and Jorrocks, the Marquis of Bray and the Duchess of Donkeyton, are to us caricature of an insufferably dull kind; but it is just as easy to laugh at Wildrake's pictures of "The Guests Departing from Donkeyton Castle" and "The Surprise," as it was the day they were drawn. (p. 275)

> *A review of "Hillingdon Hall; or, The Cockney Squire," in* The Nation, *Vol. XLVII, No. 1214, October 4, 1888, pp. 273-75.*

THEODORE ROOSEVELT   (letter date 1906)

[*Roosevelt was active in American politics during the late nineteenth and early twentieth centuries, serving as assistant secretary of the navy and vice-president of the United States before succeeding William McKinley as president in 1901. The following excerpt, drawn from a letter Roosevelt wrote to an English admirer of Surtees, reveals that both he and his wife were devotees of the author.*]

Yes, Mrs Roosevelt and I are both as fond as you are of the immortal *Soapey Sponge,* but I shall be very grateful if you will send me that copy, because the only copy we have in the house is one Mrs Roosevelt inherited from her father. It is a rather cheap American edition, though with the Leech pictures, and we have read it until it has practically tumbled to pieces. (pp. 270-71)

> *Theodore Roosevelt, in an extract from a letter written January 22, 1906, in* Robert Smith Surtees: A Critical Study *by Frederick Watson, George G. Harrap & Co. Ltd., 1933, pp. 270-71.*

MOIRA O'NEILL   (essay date 1913)

[*Arguing that literary critics have unjustly neglected Surtees' works, O'Neill enthusiastically praises both their authenticity and their artistic value.*]

Those who do not read the novels of Surtees never think of him at all. Those who do read the novels of Surtees never forget him, and never can cease to read them. It becomes a habit, like playing Patience; a habit to be taken up every winter, with the warm waistcoats, and laid down every spring, about the time that warm waistcoats get uncomfortable.

But why is it that Surtees has not been given his proper place in literature? That is simply because literary men are, as a crowd, unsportsmanlike. They cannot see that Surtees is great because there is nothing in them that responds to him. Even Lindsay Gordon and Whyte Melville have had more justice done to them; for both those gentlemen wrote verse, strayed a good deal in regions of romance, and generally speaking spread their wings. But Surtees strictly excluded romance from his field of vision. If he had wings he kept them as carefully concealed from the public as he kept his novels from the sight of his daughters; who confessed to a stranger that they had never read them, "because papa said there was nothing worse for young people than reading bad literature."

Sometimes the world accepts a man's verdict on himself, though ironically spoken, as we know. But if the literary world has been foolish enough to overlook Surtees, the ordinary world, which after all has more people in it, has shown better sense. What books are taken oftener from the shelves in the smoking-room than those thick volumes in cheerful red, **Handley Cross** and **Mr Sponge's Sporting Tour?**—How quickly the happy reader gets absorbed in either of these, growing quieter and lying flatter on his shoulders in the chair, till that moment arrives when his heels begin to drum on the floor, and he utters ecstatic noises. . . .

Now it is a great thing to have added to the gaiety of the nation, as some wise man remarked. Surtees has done this, and more too. He has seen and recorded a side of life which for some good reason is concealed from nearly all the fine writers on human nature. With very few exceptions—Sir Walter Scott is one—they have ignored or misrepresented, but more often simply ignored, that instinct for sport which is deeply rooted in the heart of man. (p. 535)

Now, what we all feel about Surtees is that being a natural man himself, he understood the nature of sport and the hearts of sportsmen as no one ever yet has understood them. A man who will hunt with hounds if he can, and if he can't do that will hunt with ferrets, and if he can't do that will hunt a rat in a rickyard rather than not hunt at all,—that is the kind of sportsman whom Surtees honoured.

He knew every kind of M.F.H. [Master of Foxhounds] that exists—the hereditary M.F.H. like Lord Scamperdale, the rich *parvenu* M.F.H. like Mr Puffington, the adventurer M.F.H. like Mr Facey Romford, that fine sportsman who "could kill a fox with any one," the useless young M.F.H. like Mr Waffles, and the eccentric and joyous M.F.H. like the immortal grocer, Mr Jorrocks. All these are finished portraits in his long picture-gallery; and there is many a thumb-nail sketch besides. . . . (p. 536)

It is the spirit of the thing that we get from Surtees, not a mere surface picture. Many a writer of sporting novels can give a rattling account of a run, lively and truthful enough as far as it goes. But how few have the accurate, *inner* knowledge of hunting that he had, the science and the sympathy combined!

He shows us everything, even the little, warm, dry corner in the cover where the fox is lying private. He makes us hear everything, from the slight crackle of snapping twigs and the stamp of an impatient horse's hoof, to the light whimper of the first hound, the challenge, the full chorus, and the ringing melody that "makes horses jump and plunge with delight, while their riders funk or rejoice according to the stuff of which they are made."

Then the run itself! He has written of every kind of run, in every sort of country, upon every kind of horse that the experience of ten ordinary men would include. . . . We have read them all ten times over, and shall probably read them half as often again. They have life and breath in them, they have sense and speed, and the very sound and smell and excitement of a wintry day in a hunting country. Surely this is no mean achievement for any writer. It is certain that literary merit was the very last thing Surtees would have claimed for his sporting chronicles, and yet literary merit they undoubtedly have. The language is graphic and terse, the narration is swift, the characters original and varied, and the incidents simply imperishable. He confined himself to sporting novels; had he chosen to write political novels instead, they would probably have been highly successful. His gift of cynicism would have been very useful in the political atmosphere. (p. 537)

The wisest writers are those who know their limits best. Miss Austen, that perfect artist, was a strictly limited person, and recognised her limits with a smile, to the immense advantage of her readers. Surtees did the same. He had an extraordinary power of accurate observation; he used that, and kept his imagination always well under the control of his own caustic humour. The result was a perfect realism, which in some ways almost equals the realism of Defoe. He had Defoe's command of detail, too, and his memory must have been one of the most remarkable organs ever possessed by a writer. He never fails to describe with precision the dress of every character presented. . . .

He could describe ladies' dresses . . .—a rare accomplishment,—as well as their curls and their eyebrows. Farther than that he did not go, or at least only on the strictly conventional lines fashionable in his day; when it was an article of faith with men that all women were jealous of each others' good looks, and all wildly anxious to marry the first marriageable man who came in their way. Since even Thackeray clung to these hoary superstitions, it is not surprising that Surtees went easily along with him. Women and sentiment were really out of his line, but he could be immensely amusing about their views of sport. . . . (p. 538)

For all his sarcasms Surtees knew quite well that there is such a thing as a sportswoman. Mrs Somerville, *née* Lucy Glitters, with her light hands, her pluck, and her determination to enjoy herself, was a prototype of a class that has swelled enormously in numbers since **Mr Romford's Hounds** was written; but she was rather a solitary figure in her day. (p. 539)

[Surtees] saw men and things in a remarkably dry light, and reported them precisely as he saw them. He was convinced that nearly half the people in the world were imposing on the other half, and his amusement at the spectacle was much greater than his disgust. This was fortunate for his readers; for what would become of the fun of the thing if Surtees had taken a high moral tone in recounting the sale of that redoubtable horse Hercules by Mr Buckram, the dealer, to Sponge, by Sponge to the helpless Waffles, by Waffles back to Buckram, and by Buckram back to Sponge, with the additional imaginary episode of Lord Bullfrog in a highborn rage? As it is, when Sponge receives the final £250 from the deluded Waffles, we rather sympathise with his comment on the whole transaction.

> *Con*found it! I don't do myself justice. *I'm too much of a gentleman!* I should have had five 'under'd—such an ass as Waffles deserves to be done!

This is exactly the spirit in which we desire to read of such transactions. A little more cleverness, and they would be too sordid to be amusing; a little more cynicism, and they would cease to be realistic. Surtees had the happy knack of telling things easily, as one light-hearted gentleman might to another after dinner, in an hour when the moral sense is not exactly clamorous, and laughter comes naturally. But his ease is masterly all the same. A hundred little, quick, incisive touches show the artist, and there is no repetition.

How many pictures of huntsmen has he given us, and all are distinct portraits! Jack Frostyface is not a bit like Tom Towler, and old Lotherington is not a bit like Watchorn or Dick Bragg. (pp. 539-40)

[When] it comes to James Pigg, comparisons fail. The man from Canny Newcassel is unique. His simplicity and his shrewdness, his honesty and his lying, his obstinacy, his intrepid courage, his taste for "brandy and 'baccy," and his

over-mastering passion for hunting—none of these qualities are so very exceptional in themselves; yet their combination in Pigg is a masterpiece of originality. Jorrocks himself is less remarkable than Pigg. He sometimes reminds us of other fat men in other fields of literature, and very fat men are always declining towards farce. But Pigg reminds us of no one, and he is in the purest vein of comedy.

Surtees was, in fact, a fine comedian. One incident alone would prove this—the death of Jack Spraggon. Almost any other writer would have made this melodramatic, or else have allowed it to be repulsive. But the creator of Lord Scamperdale and Jack Spraggon was equal to the occasion. One never recognises the born comedian so clearly as on the border of a tragedy.

Like all comedians, he loves a crowd. His pages fairly hum with the numbers of people he introduces, and yet there is no confusion; in this point he is nearly the equal of Thackeray. His minor characters are so cleverly sketched in that we know them intimately. (pp. 540-41)

He understood rich Mr Joseph Large and his natural timidity just as well as he understood poor young Charley Stobbs and his natural courage. It takes all sorts to make a world, he thought, just as the old proverb says; and the hunting-world is as diverse in its way as the social or the political.

But Surtees, for all his dry humour, had the true passion of the chase at heart as surely as John Jorrocks had it. And this was why he immortalised John Jorrocks. (p. 541)

It was not very long ago that there appeared in a leading weekly paper extracts from **Handley Cross** and **Mr Sponge's Sporting Tour**. They were, of course, edited in the explanatory American fashion now usual, which consists principally in curtailment and skipping, and the inference was unavoidable that the works themselves were supposed to have passed completely out of knowledge, as being too lengthy in their original form for modern perusal. *If* this be so indeed, then Surtees is in the same case with Dickens, and even with Sir Walter Scott; and we, his loyal admirers, may safely leave him in their excellent company.

But the balance of the evidence seems rather to show that the editor of the leading weekly paper was labouring under a delusion. (p. 542)

> Moira O'Neill, ''Some Novels by Surtees,'' in Blackwood's Magazine, *Vol. CXCIII, No. MCLXX, April, 1913, pp. 535-42.*

RUDYARD KIPLING (essay date 1913)

[*Kipling was a popular English writer who is now generally accepted as one of the masters of the short story form. The following excerpt is drawn from his short story '''My Son's Wife','' which was first published in 1913. In this passage, the story's main character, the London aesthete Frankwell Midmore, stumbles upon a number of Surtees' novels in the library of a country estate.*]

At last [Midmore] was driven to paw over a few score books in a panelled room called the library, and realised with horror what the late Colonel Werf's mind must have been in its prime. The volumes smelt of a dead world as strongly as they did of mildew. He opened and thrust them back, one after another, till crude coloured illustrations of men on horses held his eye. He began at random and read a little, moved into the drawing-

A Leech illustration of Jorrocks giving a lecture on hunting.

room with the volume, and settled down by the fire still reading. It was a foul world into which he peeped for the first time—a heavy-eating, hard-drinking hell of horsecopers, swindlers, matchmaking mothers, economically dependent virgins selling themselves blushingly for cash and lands: Jews, tradesmen, and an ill-considered spawn of Dickens-and-horsedung characters (I give Midmore's own criticism), but he read on, fascinated, and behold, from the pages leaped, as it were, the brother to the red-eyed man of the brook, bellowing at a landlord (here Midmore realised that *he* was that very animal) for new barns; and another man who, like himself again, objected to hoof-marks on gravel. Outrageous as thought and conception were, the stuff seemed to have the rudiments of observation. He dug out other volumes by the same author, till Rhoda came in with a silver candlestick.

'Rhoda,' said he, 'did you ever hear about a character called James Pigg—and Batsey?'

'Why, o' course,' said she. 'The Colonel used to come into the kitchen in 'is dressin'-gown an' read us all those Jorrockses.'

'Oh, Lord!' said Midmore, and went to bed with a book called **Handley Cross** under his arm, and a lonelier Columbus into a stranger world the wet-ringed moon never looked upon. (pp. 348-49)

> Rudyard Kipling, "'My Son's Wife'," in his A Diversity of Creatures, *1917. Reprint by Doubleday, Page & Company, 1926, pp. 335-78.*

THE TIMES LITERARY SUPPLEMENT   (essay date 1916)

[This anonymous critic ranks Surtees' novels in order of merit and briefly describes his artistic method.]

During the fifty years and more which have elapsed [since his death], the books to which Surtees owes his fame have enjoyed a popularity which has never shown any sign of decay. They do not appeal to everybody, but by those who care for them at all they are at the present time esteemed as highly as ever. It is hardly necessary to say that many people are led to read Surtees by their interest in fox hunting. This to a great extent accounts for the steadiness of his popularity. But there are many other readers who appreciate his work quite as much, though their knowledge of hunting hardly extends beyond what they have learnt from him. . . .

In one respect Surtees holds a fortunate position—namely, that there has never been any sham reverence for him. He has never attracted much of the attention of professional literary critics. Very little has been written about him; he is quoted, but that is nearly all. There is no stereotyped view as to his place in literature. . . . To read Surtees has never been regarded by anyone as a duty. Those who liked his books have read them, and to many people almost every page is familiar. Those who have found that they did not care for them have felt no scruple about leaving them alone. . . .

It is characteristic of Surtees that he wrote about nothing outside the range of his own personal knowledge. He was a man of mature experience of the world before he did any of his important work. Dickens was 24 when *Pickwick* was being issued; Surtees was 40 when the first edition of **Handley Cross** appeared, and this was subsequently greatly altered, the alterations including omissions, as well as revision and large additions. All his work which really counts at all appeared, in the form in which we now have it, after he was fifty. . . .

The question which is the best of Surtees's books is not an unreasonable one, for several of them are in some respects better than *Handley Cross,* and as amusing. It seems clear, however, that the answer which has been given by popular acclamation, in favour of *Handley Cross,* must be accepted. Mr. Jorrocks and James Pigg, as they appear here, have taken the popular imagination by storm, while the true touch with which the sport of fox-hunting is handled overrides any absurdities of detail. It is a great achievement for any writer to have created characters which have taken such a hold on the minds of so many generations of readers. What everybody means by "Jorrocks" is simply the Jorrocks of *Handley Cross;* his appearances in other books are negligible in the public eye. Thus *Handley Cross* contains Surtees's most important literary effort, besides, of course, other things which we could not spare; and it is full of the shrewd wit and wisdom of a man of the world. It has obvious defects; it grew as a patchwork; some passages seem rather irrelevant, and some are too farcical; but it is on the whole the successful result of very good, careful work. Some of the work spent upon it can be traced in detail by noting the changes made in revision. We can compare the first draft of **"The Benighted Sportsman"** in the *New Sporting Magazine* with the chapter about Stobbs's adventure as we now have it, or some of the chapters of the first edition with their final form; and in doing so we constantly note the sound judgment with which exuberance was pruned, and the skill with which passages rewritten were amplified. . . .

It is not very easy to separate the three books which stand next in order of merit—namely, *Mr. Sponge's Sporting Tour, Plain or Ringlets?* and *Mr. Romford's Hounds.* They are all admirable, and have more finish as compositions than *Handley Cross.* On the whole we give the preference to *Mr. Romford's Hounds*—partly because it has the best story. In all we have examples of genuine enthusiasm for hunting, as shown in various forms. There is no topic on which Surtees is happier. He has all the buoyancy of mind which just suits it, and he knows too much to be tempted to exaggerate here, whatever he may do elsewhere. It is at home or out visiting that Lord Scamperdale and Jack Spraggon and Mr. Romford sometimes appear in absurd situations, not often out hunting. Moreover, he restrains himself from giving us too much of it. He is mainly concerned with people who, if they go out hunting at all, as many of them do, represent aspects of it other than that of genuine enthusiasm.

There remain three books belonging to a period earlier than that of Surtees's best work. *Hawbuck Grange* is a series of admirable sketches . . . in which perhaps Mr. Trumper is the most enduring character. *Jorrocks's Jaunts and Jollities,* the earliest of all, has the distinction of being the work which first established Surtees's reputation. . . . It contains some clever parody of other writers. . . . The third book is *Hillingdon Hall.* . . . [This] book is not worth reading. The leading topic is a poor one, and the story is elaborated by the introduction of hopelessly stupid people, like Emma Flather and the Marquis, for whom he cannot have cared at all.

Surtees is a standing protest against the view, which we sometimes meet with, that true humour is inseparable from pathos. Surtees's humour throws any amount of light on human nature, but to connect it with pathos would be absurd. We can recall a few examples of pathos in his writings, but not enough for the fingers of one hand. Surtees's methods are to a great extent independent of the ordinary appliances of a novelist. He gives his characters definite parts to play, sometimes giving them fantastic names to fit their parts, and generally makes them act their parts as strictly as if they were in the *Pilgrim's Progress.* There are no searchings of heart, there is no repentance, there is hardly any development of a character into anything different from what is more or less indicated for him when he is introduced. Apparent exceptions to this are generally only partial and superficial. It is true that Mr. Sponge proposes to Lucy Glitters and marries her, thus abandoning his purpose of fortune-hunting; but this is due to a sudden impulse, and is a way of winding up his career. Mr. Romford has more in him than could have been imagined when he is first introduced, but this is doubtless an accident. Probably the author had no idea of ever making him play any very important part when he introduced him in *Mr. Sponge's Sporting Tour,* and had not even settled what his name was to be. Lucy is, perhaps, an exception; and when in the end she bursts into tears, we have the nearest approach to tragedy that Surtees admits. Again, we have no love affairs which excite any real interest. Stobbs will, of course, marry Belinda: there has been no question about this from the beginning of their acquaintance. We are interested in Rosa, and would gladly see her marry Lord Marchhare; they would suit each other very well, and she would enjoy being a duchess. But, of course, there is no chance of this. The only question is whether the bargain is to be made with Jasper Goldspink or with Mr. Bunting, who are both muffs; and the interest in this is so slight as to fit very well with the parallel question, "plain or ringlets." It is only a thread to hang the story on. There is only one book, namely, *Mr. Romford's Hounds,* in which the story as a whole is very important and excites much interest. Often we have scenes which, with a little explanation, might fairly well stand alone. The method of telling varies according to the mood of the author. Often it shows careful craftsmanship, occasionally it is rather random, and sometimes it is too farcical, but it is hardly ever dull. A not uncommon feature of it is caricature.

Surtees's use of caricature deserves a little attention, though to discuss it is rather like giving a ponderous explanation of a pun. There seem to be some people who take it amiss. We have seen a review of *Handley Cross* in which the writer objected to the misspellings and misplacements of h's in Mr. Jorrocks's letters. Here was a man who was a successful merchant in the City; it must be wrong to make him write so grotesquely. It is, of course, a case of caricature. Surtees did not mean that Jorrocks could not spell better. He was not concerned with such a detail; all that he was concerned with was to give, on the whole, a true impression of the man. He cannot tell everything, so he exaggerates some features. Take a simpler example. One of his lawyers writes a letter in which he reports a bargain made for 1,000 pounds. Surtees, who is always ready for a passing jest at the expense of lawyers, makes him write "one thousand pounds, be the same more or less." He does not mean that an actual lawyer could actually write this; but with a touch of his pen we get the effect of a thick-headed lawyer who would write needless, though less amusing, verbiage. A *Quarterly Review*er, in March, 1843, in an appreciative review of the first edition of *Handley Cross* [see excerpt dated 1843], solemnly warned the author to curb his propensity to caricature. He might as well have talked to the winds. Surtees always has this weapon at hand, and we are content with the way he uses it when he needs it.

Surtees will always find grateful readers among those who regard some crudity of form as negligible compared with insight; who appreciate humour, and do not particularly want to have their feelings harrowed; and who like to feel about a writer with whom they are on intimate terms that he is a man of sturdy common sense. If a time should ever come when fox-hunting is dead, we do not doubt that it will be found that Surtees has survived.

"The Novels of Surtees," in The Times Literary Supplement, *No. 780, December 28, 1916, p. 632.*

FRANK J. WILSTACH   (essay date 1922)

[*In this enthusiastic defense of Surtees' works, Wilstach responds to claims made by the author's detractors.*]

Robert Smith Surtees, a contemporary of Dickens and Thackeray, is one of the maddening puzzles of literature. Considered by some as being the greatest fictioneer humorist of his time, he is practically unknown to the general reader.

His reputation has doubtless suffered in consequence of his stories being designated as "sporting novels," and, furthermore, the extraordinary illustrations by Leech, Alken and others have served, in some minds, to becloud the splendors of the tales themselves.

These novels treat of English country life, with fleeting glimpses of London. Incidental to the stories are shooting, hunting, horse racing and other sports, along with jocund and often hilarious accounts of dinners, dances, flirtations, picnics and cattle shows.

Other novels of the period treating of country life, such as J. G. Whyte Melville's *Market Harborough* and Anthony Trollope's *Framley Parsonage,* have brisk huntings of fox—only this, Surtees's hunts, even to one unacquainted with the fox and the hounds, are as exciting as a chase after a burglar. . . .

Having become acquainted with Mr. Soapey Sponge, it is with the risk of being set down as a dizzard, a doodle or a blockhead that I do unblushingly declare that Surtees is altogether the most amusing and delectable story-teller that the Victorian or any other age has produced. . . .

The review of his life which appears in the *Dictionary of National Biography* was written by Thomas Seccombe [see Additional Bibliography]. . . .

The one statement by Mr. Seccombe which seems utterly absurd is this: "Without the original illustrations these works have very small interest." This exasperating statement by Seccombe is sufficient to make the Surteesian howl with rage!

John Leech was a hard-working artist. He illustrated a vast array of books, and, curiously, despite the unquestioned worth of his artistry, none of these, except the novels of Surtees, are held at purse-defying figures. To say that his illustrations to the five Surtees novels are responsible for their popularity, is, to this chronicler, as preposterous as to say that Cruikshank's illustrations for *Oliver Twist* were accountable for the popularity of that novel. . . .

Stanley K. Wilson, an out-and-out detractor of Surtees, lately, in parroting Seccombe, stated that "R. S. Surtees would have died long back, but for the famous Leech illustrations." In point of fact, the Leech plates, instead of being responsible for the life of Surtees's novels, are mainly the cause of his not being generally read.

The point is justly made that the owners of the Leech plates, hand-colored, have kept up the fiction that the books would not be acceptable without them, and were their chief charm. The Surteesians hotly protest against any such notion, contending that the high cost of reproducing these illustrations has served to preclude the making of popular-priced editions, and so has been the means of destroying any chance Surtees might have had of gaining a wide popularity. And when you come to examine the prices in the bookseller's catalogues it is disclosed that the books which were illustrated by other artists than Leech, to whom Seccombe and Wilson attribute his popularity, are held at higher figures. And the most curious thing of all is the price asked for the *Horseman's Manual.* This is without any illustrations whatever, and can be had only at a figure above what one can buy a set of the first editions of the five novels illustrated by Leech. . . .

Mr. Wilson makes another statement which arouses the Surteesians to rage, i. e., that Surtees's novels are marred by "inane pun-making." In point of actual fact Surtees was not infected with the great literary plague of his time—the rhetorical black death—pun-making! John Jorrocks may have been guilty of this crime in a slight degree, but nowhere else in these voluminous volumes is a single pun to be found. William Congreve is not denounced as a punster because he gives his characters such names as Heartwell, Vainlove, Fondlewife, Setter, Maskwell, Careless, Scandal, Tattle, Waitwell. Surely, a name which designates the character and physical peculiarities of a person can hardly be called a pun. Most of Surtees's characters are named after the manner of Congreve and the Restorationists. We, therefore, have Soapey Sponge, the Duke of Donkeyton; Fizzler, the confectioner; Lord Lovetin, Johnny O'Dicey, Captain Doleful, Waffles, Sir Harry Scamperdale, Captain Greatgun, Sir Moses Mainchance, Sir Giles Nabem, Earle of Coarsegab, Duke of Dazzzleton, Mr. Spareneck and Lady Scattercash. . . .

While John Jorrocks is undoubtedly Surtees's greatest character, the two books, *Mr. Sponge's Sporting Tour* and *Mr. Facey Romford's Hounds,* contain the best work of the novelist. Mr. Soapey Sponge does not belie his name, for as Surtees said: "His dexterity in getting into people's houses was only equaled by the difficulty of getting him out again." If Surtees had written nothing else than these two novels he would be entitled to a high place as an English fictioneer. . . .

Those who have written slightingly of Surtees have been those, evidently, who haven't read him. He was not given to circumlocutions or battalogias. He was full up to the chin with bounce and gusto, and there are those who insist upon comparing him to Thackeray and Dickens. This, of course, is an idle pastime. (p. 13)

Finally, by way of protest, in [regard to] Seccombe and Wilson's pestiferous assaults, a procession of the Surteesians on Fifth Avenue has been suggested. Robert H. Davis would jump at the chance to lead the parade on horseback, made up as the renowned John Jorrocks. Then would come a gay cavalcade: Marjorie Rambeau as Lady Scattercash, Henry L. Mencken as Lord Bullfrog, Josephine Drake as Lucy Sparkle, Al Jolson as Waffles, De Wolf Hopper as the Duke of Tergiversation, &c., followed by Simeon Ford in a carriage, representing the author. Then would come Benjamin de Casseres leading the much esteemed Tom Smith, made up as an anti-Surteesian.

Such a demonstration would serve to remove quite a number of bloodclots from the brain of literature, suffered in these parts. Tally-ho! (p. 26)

Frank J. Wilstach, ''Surtees and Charles Dickens,'' in The New York Times Book Review, *July 23, 1922, pp. 13, 26.*

VIRGINIA WOOLF   (essay date 1925)

[*A British novelist, essayist, and short story writer, Woolf is one of the most prominent literary figures of the twentieth century. In the excerpt below, she comments upon how the works of Surtees, Nimrod, Peter Beckford, and Charles St. John influenced the prose style of later English writers.*]

[The] English sporting writers, Beckford, St. John, Surtees, Nimrod, make no mean reading. In their slapdash, gentlemanly way they have ridden their pens as boldly as they have ridden their horses. They have had their effect upon the language. This riding and tumbling, this being blown upon and rained upon and splashed from head to heels with mud, have worked themselves into the very texture of English prose and given it that leap and dash, that stripping of images from flying hedge and tossing tree which distinguish it not indeed above the French but so emphatically from it. (p. 135)

Virginia Woolf, ''Jack Mytton,'' in her The Common Reader, *Harcourt Brace Jovanovich, 1925, pp. 134-40.*

S. M. ELLIS   (essay date 1927)

[*Ellis welcomes the first book publication of* Young Tom Hall.]

It is curious that for seventy-four years an excellent story [*Young Tom Hall*] by R. S. Surtees should have remained unpublished in book form, its existence in the pages of *The New Monthly Magazine* either forgotten or unknown. There is an ever increasing fame and value for the works of Surtees which makes this omission the stranger. The admirers of Surtees are principally to be found among the leisured and monied classes who enjoy hunting scenes and sporting life in the country: I doubt if there is any demand for Surtees in the public libraries of large towns, or if even thirty per centum of the readers of other Victorian novelists know aught of Jorrocks and Soapey Sponge, the two outstanding creations of this author. . . .

[*Young Tom Hall*] is a most entertaining work in Surtees's characteristic vein, being the adventures of a loutish youth, son of a provincial banker and wool-stapler, in search of social uprise and a wife by means of sporting and military endeavours. Here, once again, are the mischances of an embryo sportsman, the amusing scenes of rural entertainments, and a fine description of a hunting day (''At Silverspring Firs''). There is a good deal of caricature of course. The presentation of Colonel Blunt and the officers of the Heavysteeds, a gross collection of guzzling blackguards with no notions of honour in the sale of a horse or in any other matter, can scarcely be accepted as a correct picture of the officers in a dragoon regiment of that period. But Surtees's gift of satirical observation is at its best in his inimitable pictures here of the ''Thé Dansante'' and ''The Hunt Breakfast,'' for example.

This abortive and long-lost child, now clothed in uniform scarlet cloth, must be placed beside his eight fine brethren upon the shelves of every ''gentleman's library,'' as the booksellers and auctioneers would say.

S. M. Ellis, ''A Forgotten Surtees Novel,'' in The Bookman, *New York, Vol. LXXI, No. 426, March, 1927, p. 324.*

SIEGFRIED SASSOON   (essay date 1928)

[*Sassoon's autobiographical novel* Memoirs of a Fox-Hunting Man, *excerpted below, recounts the life of the Sassoon persona, a prosperous country squire named George Sherston. In this passage, Sherston describes how he and his friend Stephen Colwood were influenced by Surtees' works.* Memoirs of a Fox-Hunting Man *was first published in 1928.*]

In describing my friendship with Stephen I am faced by a difficulty which usually arises when one attempts to reproduce the conversational oddities of people who are on easy terms. We adopted and matured a specialized jargon drawn almost exclusively from characters in the novels of Surtees; since we knew these almost by heart, they provided us with something like a dialect of our own, and in our care-free moments we exchanged remarks in the mid-Victorian language of such character-parts as Mr. Romford, Major Yammerton, and Sir Moses Mainchance, while Mr. Jorrocks was an all-pervading influence. In our Surtees obsession we went so far that we almost identified ourselves with certain characters on appropriate occasions. One favourite rôle which Stephen facetiously imposed on me was that of a young gentleman named Billy Pringle who, in the novel which he adorns, is reputed to be very rich. My £600 a year was thus magnified to an imaginary £10,000, and he never wearied of referring to me as 'the richest commoner in England.' The stress was laid on my great wealth and we never troubled to remember that the Mr. Pringle of the novel was a dandified muff and 'only half a gentleman.' I cannot remember that I ever succeeded in finding a consistent rôle for Stephen, but I took the Surtees game for granted from the beginning, and our adaptation of the Ringwell Hunt to the world created by that observant novelist was simplified by the fact that a large proportion of the Ringwell subscribers might have stepped straight out of his pages. (pp. 153-54)

Siegfried Sassoon, ''At the Rectory,'' in his The Memoirs of George Sherston: Memoirs of a Fox-Hunting Man, *Vol. 1,* The Literary Guild of America, Inc., *1937, pp. 152-86.*

[BONAMY DOBRÉE]   (essay date 1930)

[*Dobrée delineates the reasons for Surtees' enduring popularity, citing his vivid characterization, lively yet satiric humor, knowledge of hunting, comic imagination, and vigorous prose.*]

There is . . . no single reason [for the persistence of Surtees]. If we take Surtees's writings as a hunting country and try to pursue the fox of his popularity through it, it is not at all certain that we shall make him ''cry capevi.'' It is a large country, some of it fair and free enough, with no unjumpable fences: but some of it is woodland with, it must be confessed, not a few boggy rides, not unlike those in that ''incorrigible mountain,'' that ''unpardonable wilderness,'' Pinch-me-near Forest. We shall often be in danger of changing foxes, and if we do not keep the pack of our ideas well in hand we may even riot after hare. It would be a woe-begone critic who would have to confess himself in the end a mere currant-jelly man.

How impossible it is, thinking of Surtees, not to drop into his jargon; and there at once is another bit of the secret: it is by very vivid if often repeated catch phrases that he imparts a certain kind of life to his characters. For these, with a few exceptions, are of the nature of ''humours,'' and ''dash my vig!'' is only a variant of swearing by Pharaoh's foot. The lively catch phrase and the ''humour,'' these together account for a degree of vitality; for the humour, if skilfully enough

One of Henry Alken's illustrations for Jorrock's Jaunts and Jollities.

contrived, constantly reminds us of people we know, if we happen to come into contact with the circles from which they were drawn. Those who are not lucky enough to hunt and meet the squire of Hawbuck Grange may yet meet Admiration Jack at whatever watering-place they idle away their health in; just as the traveller abroad must keep very much to himself if he does not run across Sir Politick Would be. Not, of course, that Surtees's mind is as probing or as general as Jonson's, nor has he the same giant's capacity for creating his butts; in short, to compare them as writers would be ridiculous; but we shall not quite see what Surtees was after if we altogether forget the older comic traditions.

The object in writing is not to be confused with the impulse to write, at all events in a minor author like Surtees. His object, one need not question, was to give the average hawbuck something to read besides "Bell's Life," the local paper, and the Post Office Directory, which was the only literature, apparently, to be found in many houses. Himself a man of considerable reading, who could quote the poets, or rather misquote them with a happy familiarity, he did not see why even Soapey Sponge should have to spend an off day in reading nothing but "Mogg's Cab Fares." His books, therefore, would have to be of the lightest, with nothing to strain the mind or make more demands on the attention than a tired fox-hunter would be willing to give, or a disgruntled one cheated of a day with hounds by a black frost. Thus he boldly informed anyone who cared to read the preface to *Ask Mamma:*

> It may be a recommendation to the lover of light literature to be told that the following story does not involve the complication of a plot. It

is a mere continuous narrative of an almost everyday exaggeration, interspersed with sporting scenes and excellent illustrations by Leech [see excerpt dated 1858].

That is a fair description of all Surtees's novels, except that he is not, perhaps, quite fair to himself, since his stories have a certain structure; they have a beginning and an end, even though the middle is elastic and episodic; they are not just separate sketches like the *Jaunts and Jollities;* they have, besides, a hero of recognizable character or humour to bind the episodes together.

Surtees is not an author whom one reads for the sake of intimacy with a charming or profound personality, though the man is engaging enough. . . . [His] impulse to write was a direct reaction to his delight in life; being pleased with it, he wanted to talk about it. And, having once started, it was difficult to stop. . . . So he rambles on, telling us of the joys of fox-hunting, or of the minor ones of hare-hunting, describing odd characters, inveighing against the racing which has become a mere betting match, and against the battue which is slaughter without sport; reviling bad farmers and bad landlords; grumbling at the villainous discomforts and still more villainous charges of country inns, the coldness and robbery of town hotels, and thence praising the development of clubs which give the country squire a home from home. Great also are the feasts, deep and potent the libations which revive the heroes of that Homeric age of hunting; for whatever Surtees may be talking about, the adventures of the chase are the background, where they are not the immediate theme. And, after all, he lived in the glorious age of which his friend Nimrod (Apperley) wrote, which Scrutator (Horlock) knew, when Osbaldestone, the Squire *par excellence,* was alive; when the names of Warde and Assheton Smith were to be conjured with, and the hunt could still attract good painters. It was the age, again, of eccentrics, when the name of Tom Mytton was a household word, and jailbirds would palm themselves off as captains in great houses.

It was just this eccentricity, this "excess," which gave material to the man whose comic vein ran in the mould of the humours. But his humours are nearly all what he called "snobs"—namely, to follow Thackeray's definition, as no doubt he himself did, those who "meanly admire mean things." For him the snob is not so much the man who looks down upon others as it is for us, but those who are like Mr. Sponge, "wishing to be gentlemen without knowing how," thinking that all that is needed is a tolerable amount of cash, an intolerable deal of splash, and a capacity for bullying the under-dog—just as Miss Rosa, too well bred ever to show that she enjoyed anything, thought nothing of working the unfortunate milliner all night so that she might appear in a new bonnet at the next day's picnic. Nearly all his characters are people trying to make a show and to rise in the world by dishonourable means—Soapey Sponge, Facey Romford, the A.D.C. at Handley Cross, who by the ingenious initial disguised the fact that he was only the Assistant Drains Commissioner—and a dozen others, even Jorrocks himself in the Hillingdon Hall stage. Or else they are people of reasonably good position trying meanly to improve it, or to keep it up by mercenary marriages—Jawleyford, Admiration Jack, Captain Miserrimus Doleful—and again a dozen others. There are few likeable people; and they, as a rule, are very minor characters, such as Charley Stobbs, the only exception of full-length size being Thomas Scott, the owner of Hawbuck Grange, a charming, sensible, modest person, who loved hunting for hunting's sake, and not for the glamour, nor the hard riding, nor the appetite, nor the opportunities for horse-coping. A real love of hunting, of course, redeemed anyone for Surtees, as it does Jorrocks, or Lord Scamperdale, or Facey Romford; a pretended love would damn an angel, as it does those who are by no means angels—the Duke of Tergiversation, Jack Bunting, Puff:, the richest commoner in England, and so on. But just occasionally the real "humour" is invented for its own sake, as the altogether delightful, wheezing, puffing, bellows-to-mend Jogglebury Crowdey, consumed by his passion for cutting walkingsticks from hedges, and carving them in likenesses of famous men to provide fortunes for his children. And, of course, there is Pigg.

But in the main, as a result of his satirical bent, for Surtees had taken the Becky Sharp leaf out of *Vanity Fair,* most of his people are unlovable. One loves Pickwick, who owed his birth to Jorrocks, as one does not love Jorrocks; and that is because Pickwick is a lineal descendant of Uncle Toby, whereas Jorrocks derives rather from Commodore Trunnion. Perhaps it is necessary to be a trifle sentimental to make a lovable character, and there is nothing sentimental in Surtees; there is, indeed, no sentiment. Or, failing sentimentality, some quality of subtlety is necessary—something of the subtlety, shall we say, of Becky Sharp as opposed to the hard surface of Lucy Glitters, who is all on the outside, not having had the advantage of an education at the Pinkerton Academy. All Surtees's girls are nasty little monkeys, without heart or passion, however pretty they may be, except Jorrocks's niece, Belinda: all his women aspire meanly after mean things. Then what is there in Surtees which makes us read him? In what channel does the stream of his vitality run? For it is that in the last resort which makes us take down any book from our shelves.

His fame really rests upon *Handley Cross.* *Sponge* is entertaining, certainly, it has something of the creative vigour of the master work; *Ask Mamma* perhaps comes next, coupled with *Facey Romford; Hawbuck Grange* is a treasure to the hunting man; *Plain or Ringlets* is interesting as a light on manners, and does at least contain that brilliant comic invention, the Jug. *Hillingdon Hall* is a slough of dullness, for, apart from hunting, Surtees could make little of Jorrocks. In fact, the more hunting, the more fun. And here, perhaps, is another clue to his persistence: he knew more about hunting than any other novelist of the nineteenth century.... With Surtees ... we are let into the secrets of the stable and the kennel; we know, for instance, that Jorrocks hunted a mixed pack, what he fed his hounds on, and how he made up his entry. By inference, or rather by caricature, he tells us what a good horse, a good pack, a good huntsman, a good anything down to a good pair of boots ought to be like: he has as much information to give us as Beckford and Nimrod combined, and a beginner can learn as much from Mr. Jorrocks's sporting "lectors"—supported equally though they were by Beckford and brandy—as from, say, Lord Willoughby de Broke's *Hunting the Fox,* provided, of course, that he is sharp enough to see when Surtees is fooling and when he is not. And, besides, he rubs in the important lesson that hunting is to be pursued for the sport, to see hounds, and not for any extraneous reason of snobbery, showing off, hard riding, or other irrelevance.... There is nothing of the cut 'em down spirit about Surtees: he would ride if need be, but he would always think of his horse. The psychologist might perhaps scent disappointment, and behold the wish-fulfilment illustrated in the run in which Soapey Sponge took the horn from the huntsman and killed the fox single-handed; or when, on New Year's Day, in a hard frost, his tremendous gallop enabled him to catch the fox and Lucy Glitters at one and the same time; but even the most sober riders may be guilty of dreams. Nor was Surtees a snob, even in hunting, in the way that Nimrod was; he despised the carted stag variety, it is true, for "When you've caught the stag, you're no better off than ye were afore," as Jimmy observed to Mr. Romford; but he was friends with the currant-jelly men: the excellent Major Yammerton is not held up to ridicule, and one of the best descriptions of a hunt is that of the hare with the Goose and Dumpling folk in *Hawbuck Grange.*

Yet with all these qualities, to which must be added his observant eye—there is no excuse for a reader not to know how any one of the characters was dressed on any occasion—we have probably been rioting after hare; and the fox of his popularity is the creative capacity, the *vis comica,* and the gift for racy language which inform *Handley Cross.* Jorrocks is without doubt an imaginative creation; he is of the race of immortal and divine fat men. In a sense he is the Falstaff of the chase; for he is something of a fairy, with a superb gift for variegated invective—though perhaps Lord Scamperdale beats him here—and unanswerable repartee. Like Dr. Johnson, he was called a bear, and scorned your clarety wines. He may not be so gentle as Mr. Pickwick, but he is almost as gullible, which is to say that he has something about him of the heavenly simpleton which is the mark of the great comic character. We do a little love Jorrocks, and are sorry when his wife bundles him into a lunatic asylum. James Pigg, again, is a creation whom Tom Jones surely is not ashamed to be seen with in Hades, perhaps even walking with him hand in hand, "like the sign of the Mutual Insurance hoffice," as the M.F.H. would say.

And if Surtees is often boisterously burlesque, and in this he is not as bad as Smollett, he can be sly as well; he has some delicious pieces of cool irony, while his *à pédant pédant et demi* treatment of Nimrod as Pomponius Ego is real though friendly satire. . . . *Handley Cross,* undoubtedly, is more various than any other of Surtees's books, and rises to greater comic heights. The scene where the genial madman entertains Charley Stobbs at breakfast after the Ongar Park run, finally clapping his saucer on his head and throwing his cup through the window-pane, has a flavour of Borrow, and all the actual hunting scenes have the wisdom of Beckford added to a discriminating observation. He also has something of the genius needed to make the great comic phrase which reveals the aspirations and weaknesses of humanity. "What a huntsman I should be if it weren't for the leaps!": most of us say that in one connexion or another. Most delicious of all, perhaps, is Jorrocks's sigh as he pounded along all elbows and legs, rib-roasting Arterxerxes, on the great Cat and Custard Pot day; "How I wish I was a heagle!" That is as profound, if not as touching as "'I wish, Trim,' said my uncle Toby, 'that I was in bed.'"

Thus, although for many the main interest of *Handley Cross* lies in the talk of horses and hounds, it is not only to those that have "the bump of Fox-un-ta-tiveness werry strongly dewelloped" that the book appeals. For there is the little world of the watering place, with its rival doctors Roger Swizzle and Sebastian Mello, with the preposterous Mrs. Barnington, and the mournful Master of the Ceremonies, done with great zest and an eye for the absurd; and there is that very Dickensian glimpse of seamy London life, with its dingy lawyers' offices, which Surtees knew at first hand; and the strange, sinister figure of Mr. William Bowker, hatching great schemes in the murk of his tobacco shop, and patronizing dog-fights. Surtees, one feels it at every point, had more than the mere novelist's eye which suffices the second-rate novelist; he had the knowledge which comes from an active interest in the doings of men. His range was limited, his apprehensions were not profound, he had no peculiar sensibility, he was, no doubt, rather too complacent; but the whiff of good strong country air is with him wherever he goes. He took a vast delight in life, its ins and outs, its queer characters, its shifts and changes, its unexpectedness.

And this brings us to the last of his claims to popularity, his joyful use of words; for after all it is for their words we read authors as much as for what they have to tell us. Idiom is the salt which keeps fresh the meat which might otherwise have lost its savour. Surtees is full of phrases, not unforgettable, certainly, but which make their mark so that we remember them with a smile when we meet them again—there is, to give one instance, "the tremendous discharge of popularity" which greeted Major Yammerton's speech at Lord Ladythorne's hunt breakfast. But it is rather the vigour, the brio, of the tumbling flow of words which carries us on, whether he is describing a meet or a meal, a dance or a journey; all the clash and clatter is there. He is careless in his writing, no doubt, repeating phrases such as "Third time is killing time"; every comfortable house he describes is "replete" with luxury; the horse "like Gil Blas' mule—all faults," is his veritable King Charles's head. But what does that matter when Lord Scamperdale enlarges the scope of the language in a way that our armies in Flanders would have delighted in; and when Mr. Jorrocks says "Jest put 'em on to me Charley, whilst I make one o' Mr. Craven Smith's all-round-my-'at casts, for that beggar Binjamin's of no more use with a pack of 'ounds than a hopera box

would be to a cow, or a frilled shirt to a pig"? And what could be more ludicrous than the master's concluding a panegyric of himself as a huntsman with a quotation from Cato: "It's not for mortals to command success"?

And even if the words do not linger in the "mind's memory"—there is a Jorrocks's phrase again!—it is they which give vividness to the figures they describe. In the general atmosphere of bustle and movement the figures stand out, and not altogether as puppets. One would recognize them anywhere by their looks alone (for who would fail to greet Sir Harry Scattercash with his strings all flying?); or by their gestures (cannot you hear Mr. Benjamin Buckram letting the coins slide down his pocket, one by one, or in an avalanche?); and one would recognize their horses, for who would not be ashamed to see Arterxerxes or Multum-in-Parvo go by without knowing them by name? But in letting the mind wander over the novels it is detached scenes or gestures that we see, phrases that we hear: Mr. Jorrocks dashes his vig and dances with glee about the fox's corpse; or he is floundering through Pinch-me-Near Forest; or drowning in the bath at Ongar Park: Soapey Sponge canons into Lord Scamperdale, who screams out "Just because you think I'm a Lord and can't swear or use coarse words," before launching out into one of his most lurid torrents; Facey Romford gets his hounds round him with the help of his pretended sister, the late Lucy Glitters; Mr. Jogglebury Crowdey wheezes where the verbs ought to be, and Sir Harry replaces his nouns with a hiccup; that good sportsman Mr. Jovey Jessop gives the office of Jug to his friend Boyston, who is thereby empowered to drink all that his patron cannot hold; Binjamin sticks his fingers into the marmeylad; old Sivin-and-four's-Ilivin the banker counts his bills; Gabriel Junks the peacock prophesies the weather: Mr. Jorrocks in the ecstasy of his fox-hunting dreams kicks his wife out of bed; and over all of them hovers the airy spirit of James Pigg, that racy *lusus naturae,* or loose 'un by nature, invoking Canninewcassel and his cousin Deavilboger, and keeping the tambourine a-rowling while he offers you a gob of tobacco.

Whether or not we have rolled the fox over, or have run him to earth, or have lost the scent completely, there can be no doubt that Surtees is still popular. . . . (pp. 257-58)

> [*Bonamy Dobrée*], *"Robert Smith Surtees," in* The Times Literary Supplement, *No. 1469, March 27, 1930, pp. 257-58.*

W. L. RENWICK   (essay date 1932)

[*In the following extract from an imaginary conversation between two literati named Aelius and Barbarus, Renwick illustrates the ongoing critical debate over the value of reading Surtees' works.*]

[*Ael.*] Nobody, I fancy, reads Surtees, except the sporting illiterates of the Counties, who read nothing else but *The Field,* and perhaps *The Autocar.*

Bar. Don't be uppish. Surtees was good enough for Thackeray and John Gibson Lockhart and William Morris, and lots more of your intellectual as well as your social superiors. Your brilliant youth who convulses his coterie with his subtleties and audacities may be a significant and even an important phenomenon, but the man whose work is read with delight, during three generations, by the multitude of the non-literary, can hardly be brushed aside; and he may have more influence on the world at large. . . . And you have enjoyed Surtees yourself: haven't you now?

Ael. Yes, when I read him long ago, but one reads so uncritically at that age.

Bar. Don't we lose as well as gain by academic habits of reading? Come now, what do you object to in him?

Ael. For one obvious thing, his style. Half his writing moves on eighteenth-century stilts, and shaky ones at that, and the other half is mere vulgar rambling, full of the facetious topical jauntiness of the sporting journalist. It dates so badly, and it's so slovenly.

Bar. I grant you both, within reason. He wasn't fastidious by nature or by training, and he lacked a fastidious audience. But isn't there a third kind in him? Doesn't he sometimes forget both the genteel and the knowing mannerisms when he describes a horse or a hunt, and write clearly and forcibly as he gets excited? Look at bits of *Soapy Sponge* or *Facey Romford*— or for that matter Mr. Jorrocks's own discourses—how he crashes on, over hedge and ditch, sometimes nearly bogged in a complicated series of subordinate clauses, scratched and torn by unrelated participles, sometimes nearly unhorsed trying to take a bit of description faster than the difficult place will allow, but stretching out as the going gets clearer, and coming in at the death with a whoop, and enjoying every minute of it. (pp. 77-8)

Ael. But allowing that he could write excited prose, think of the construction, or lack of construction, in his so-called novels. The merest picaresque.

Bar. There's a good deal to be said for the picaresque. It's better than a collection of the short stories we used to be so precious about, and more difficult. And isn't life rather picaresque? Suppose you write down your adventures in the War, from your first disastrous interview with a Regular adjutant to what happened the night you were demobilized—won't the result be picaresque?

Ael. Don't make me out a Lazarillo de Tormes. I was a perfectly respectable if entirely undistinguished junior officer of His Majesty's Land Forces, trusty and well-beloved. But even if I agreed, life isn't literature, memoirs aren't novels, and a novel should have some sort of construction about it.

Bar. I suppose so, though I'm tired of young men's novels that are hugely praised because the bones show through. Surtees always did retain something of the monthly journalist of *The New Sporting Magazine*. All his books are *Jaunts and Jollities*. But we must take what the gods give. His plots haven't the interest of logical relation, or of the working-out of a theme; but they have other virtues. In the picaresque, all the more weight is thrown on incident, because the other interests are discarded; the incidents must be vivid and exciting and real: and those of Surtees are, very, very often. That's something. And in his later works at least, Surtees has the other necessary virtue: ingenuity in the linking-up of his incidents, in devising neat turns and transitions of narrative. Look at *Mr. Facey Romford's Hounds* again, and you'll see how he solved the problem (as the young men from Oxford would say) of showing two different sorts of mastership in one book, by making the same lady and the same horse the cause of Mr. Romford's losing one pack and getting into touch with the other. Surtees is like Spenser in that.

Ael. Congruous comparison!

Bar. I'm full of congruous comparisons. Haven't you noticed that? It's what I call Criticism. Smollett, then, if you jib at Spenser. The Smollett mark is plain to see. You'll notice that Smollett and all his heirs, from Dickens down through Mr. Wells to Mr. Sinclair Lewis, have this about them, that their men have to think about their bread and butter. The Psychological Analysts always omit the two things that make most difference to a man, his job and his current account. . . . However, we were discussing Surtees, not . . . the psychological complications of Daily Bread. There's another mark of the Smollett clan, that the adventures happen among strangers. The hero is usually sent travelling, and is never at home living what you would call a normal social life.

Ael. And a good job too, so far as Surtees is concerned. As a social novelist he is as low as can be, a coarsened caricature of the worst of his friend Thackeray. I grant you he was a man's man. Drawing-rooms aren't his natural habitat. But though his men are usually understandable, he has that hateful common pose of his time, that semi-cynical and wholly patronizing tone about women, the tone of the Regency rake with the edge off. Except for one or two Sporting Females, his women may be classified as the shrewish or the cuddlesome, and I detest both— and the Sporting Female too, for that matter.

Bar. Let us say that he ignored the more subtle and complex movements of human machinery. But isn't this knowledge-of-the-world-my-boy business, like the monstrous eating and still more monstrous drinking, at least in part a question of Fashion—literary Fashion as much as social? We must always remember to allow for Fashion and Snobbery in literature as well as in clothes and manners and surgery. It is true, though, that the social value, the criticism of life, in Surtees, is limited pretty strictly to the one standard—I won't say the only one he knew, for that would obviously be wrong, but the one he allowed to appear in his books—the standard of the gentleman sportsman.

Ael. I groan. I'm weary of sportsmanship. You remember the lectures they used to inflict on us behind the Line, holding up The Sportsmanship Of The English Public Schoolboy as a shining ideal for honest journeymen soldiers to adore as an ikon? . . . The English Public Schoolboy is dead already, thank goodness, except perhaps in Kenya.

Bar. I'm very much with you. . . . You can talk about Sportsmanship, because it's vague, unintellectual, adolescent, and lazy, and therefore suits the English. But you'll notice I said 'gentleman sportsman'. 'Gentleman' is deader than Public Schoolboy and that's not so lucky. The English have lost all that was valuable in their snobbery and kept the rest. But Surtees had his double standard, and kept his values separate, and that is where he is so superior to the prize-givers and the Indian Army Majors we suffered under. And he meant to make it clear; like every other writer of importance, he regarded his work as instructive as well as recreative—like Sir Philip Sidney, Said He, using another congruous comparison. Because Mr. Facey Romford is a fine horseman and a clever huntsman, scrupulously fair to his horses, his hounds, his foxes, and his field, it does not follow that he is by any means a fine character in other ways; and on the other hand, because Mr. Soapy Sponge is a trifle indelicate in financial affairs, his creator, who made him for the purpose of showing up a shady type of young man, does not deny him certain qualities in the field and even out of it. Indeed, much of his moral and worldly-wise instruction proceeds out of the mouth of his somewhat dubious characters, just as his sporting instruction comes from the entirely comic one of Jorrocks. That makes it the more telling, and also shows his appreciation of the fact that the least admirable of men of this world usually has his code—the good things he will always do, and the evil things he is not fool or blackguard enough to do. He preached sport in itself and for its own sake, which is where the Public School moralists go wrong, for they extend Sportsmanship into fields where it doesn't belong. . . . (pp. 78-81)

Ael. But we were talking books, and it's late at night for moral philosophy. Take it that Surtees showed one virtue in action, and had a deal of the wisdom of the billiard-room. That's a small field and a low one.

Bar. Is there any 'high' and 'low' in art?

Ael. There is in life, anyhow—we seem to be changing places—and, with all deference to Signor Croce, the artist is concerned with life. And unfortunately the horse is usually to be found in lowish surrounding, among Gentlemen Who Always Pay, and most ignoble knaves.

Bar. But not Surtees. He hated all that business. What would *The Sporting and Dramatic,* not to mention *The Daily Herald,* do with a journalist whose only sign of interest, when he was 'covering' Goodwood, was the remark, 'Was much gratified by the scenery'? His recognition of the mixed character was not merely weak tolerance. There were things and people Surtees could not stand: gamblers, dilettante sportsmen whose heart was not in the game, jealous sportsmen, dishonest grooms, and quasi-amateurs who lived by what they pretended was their recreation—he hated them as he hated dirty land and neglected drains, and all the minor dishonesties and slacknesses and insincerities. It is this that makes him so sound, in spite of the drunkennesses and the practical jokes our modern manners dislike. Even at that, he wrote of *The New Sporting Magazine*—here it is in Mr. Cuming's Life of him—'We had expressly stated in our prospectus that Prize-fighting, Bull-baiting, and Cock-fighting were low and demoralizing pursuits, and all reference thereto was to be excluded from our pages.' His idea of sportsmanship is perfectly sound: sport must be free from brutality, an end in itself, with enjoyment as its only reward—he always deprecated the competitive element, as you'll see in the end of *Soapy Sponge*—and he recognized its limitations.

Ael. I've already granted you all that. But it's no great contribution to literature.

Bar. It's a contribution, anyhow. Set Surtees alongside of Thackeray and Dickens and he appears as a very minor novelist, but he is not obscured by them, or superseded by them, as Scott, for instance, superseded the Clara Reeves and obscures the Harrison Ainsworths. In his minor class Marryat is a better artist, but Marryat and Surtees do not compete. Must we always be putting writers into a scale of merit? Isn't it more useful sometimes to place them side by side, to see how they fit into each other, what country they cover and whether they overlap? Then, if we must, we can begin classifying according to value. If we take England of the 30's to the 50's—England growing out of the Regency into the Victorian Age—we have Thackeray for middle-class society and journalism; Thomas Love Peacock for literature, finance, ideas; Dickens for the poor and the law; Charlotte Brontë for the Industrial Revolution and Emily for the moorlands; Marryat for the sea, and Surtees for the hunting and farming folk.

Ael. It had been done before. What about Addison's Tory Foxhunter, and Squire Western, and the Osbaldestones? And what about the Border sports in *Guy Mannering?*

Bar. These are all barbarians, looked at from the outside by civilized writers; and as for *Guy Mannering,* Scott had no part in the scientific study of sport that had been interesting English country gentlemen for a generation. Surtees knew it all from the inside; he ranges with Beckford and Colonel Hawker as well as with Smollett and Marryat. And as the mouthpiece of a great and worthy company, their ideas and their interests, he is, recognizably at the first glance, authentic.

Ael. He may have been inside all that, but his characters don't look like it. What was Carlyle's phrase about Scott—that he described people from the outside and not from the inside?

Bar. I think nane the mair o' Tam for that. Any artist is free to choose his own way of doing things, and why not the natural way? We only do see the outsides of people at first, and then, gradually if at all, their appearance, actions, idiosyncrasies, tics and tricks, enable us to build up some idea of what they are like inside. Why should not a novelist present his people in the same way? It was Chaucer's way, and Surtees, like Chaucer, like every writer who writes like a man of the world and not like a scientist or a theorist, differentiates people first by their clothes, their faces, their tricks of speech, their favourite songs and stories, and so they are all recognizable and consistent, in a human natural sort of way, without becoming abstractions.

Ael. But what are these people? They mean nothing to the great movements of thought of their time or ours. Think of all that happened in Surtees's time, and how little reflection of it there is in his books.

Bar. My dear *Aelius,* remember that most people are oblivious of the great movements of their time. Surely you are old enough to avoid the error of thinking of England in the nineteenth century as inhabited exclusively by Byrons and Shelleys and their victims—so many Castlereaghs—succeeded by a generation of George Eliots and Darwins and Newmans.

Ael. They are the ones who matter; the rest are dead.

Bar. More's the pity, perhaps: we over-concentrate on the picturesque. But anyhow they were alive, and are you, as a democrat, arguing that the majority is negligible? Take a simple case in Surtees: the railway expansion of his time, and its very important social implications—you could make a nice little sketch of social history out of "The Railways in Literature". You could show how Thackeray found them vulgar, but amusing for the opportunities they gave of snap-shotting people; how they provided Dickens with an arabesque paragraph; how in Peacock's eyes they were the excuse for wild, stupid gambling and cheating. You would have to bring in Surtees, and there you would find they were an abomination because they dirtied the countryside, but at the same time a convenience to a man who wanted to get out of town to hunt, or across country to see a horse. His attitude is quite simple and natural: if people go and build railways for our convenience, we'll use them when it suits our convenience. Not very politically-economical and all that sort of thing, but isn't it how we all regard the railways? There is always a majority of decent ordinary folk, who take things as they come; it is something to be their interpreter.

Ael. And it has the advantage that there's not much to interpret. You're doing your best, but really, is there anything in Surtees but descriptions of hunting?

Bar. Even if there were nothing else, there we get at his real value. It's more complicated than it looks. First of all notice

Mr. Jorrocks (loq.) "Come hup! I say—You ugly Beast!"

Jorrocks uttering one of his most famous sayings during a hunt in Handley Cross, *illustrated by Leech.*

that when Surtees gets into the country he's in his own element. His young ladies may be insipid, stupid, rapacious; his horses are interesting and sensible individuals. There is nothing factitious about him now, nothing pumped-up, like Wilde, or palpably got up for the occasion, like Sinclair Lewis in *Martin Arrowsmith*. He knew what he was talking about, and once he leaves the attempt at social satire and arrives in his own province—I should say his own *country*—he is absolutely sincere, unconstrained, and therefore admirable. Now he draws on his own experience, from the early journalistic days when he visited famous hunts with a critical eye, to his later life as a dignified squire with the North Riding, the Slaley, and Lord Elcho's. In the country, among horses and hounds, he is back at home—either in the country of his youth round London, or in the North. People argue whether 'Handley Cross' is Leamington or Shotley Bridge; it's probably both. 'Rosebery Rocks' is Brighton. But when it is not Surrey it's Northumberland and Durham and North Yorkshire. The dialect of his countrymen is always the one familiar to him since childhood. . . . And when he describes a run, the names are made on familiar patterns; wouldn't you look up Tomlinson's *Guide to Northumberland* if some one asked you where are *Corsenside Lane, Howell Burn, Winforth Rig, Birdshope, Kidland Hill?* I've just picked them out of *Handley Cross* here. He remembers days above Slaley, or round Belford, and he plays with names just as Milton did.

Ael. More congruous comparisons!

Bar. And good ones. Surtees uses a name to give flavour and definition to a phrase, just as, I insist, Milton did. Milton liked geography, and Surtees had the huntsman's sense of topography. Mr. Jorrocks may be lost, but his creator never is. Each pack has its country, and though it may be pieced together from different places, the country has definite shape, features, and directions. It may not be possible to follow a point on the Ordnance Survey map, as you might follow one by *The Field*'s report, but that is only because the map happens not to exist, not because the run takes place across a cloudland or because it is only a series of snapshots. That's more difficult than it sounds, creating an imaginary stretch of country that is convincing, and doing it without elaborate set description and without a map—though maps are delectable things and an ornament to any book—and making the reader gradually acquainted with it, so that he instinctively orientates himself as he reads: that's a triumph. And it isn't enough to be there—a man must see, notice, be keen in wits and senses, to convey the lie of ground and the character of country as Surtees does. You feel the same thing in his weather. There's more English weather in Surtees than anywhere I know, except England. Sometimes he sets himself to describe a particular day, but it's there all the time. The wind of The World Turned Upside Down Day in *Handley Cross* is elaborately described—though not fancifully as Dickens would have done it—but it is usually something so simple and telling that I could scarcely pick it out for you. Here's a scrap in *Mr. Sponge's Sporting Tour:*

> Who does not know the chilling feel of an English spring, or rather of a day at the turn of the year before there is any spring? Our gala-day was a perfect specimen of the order—a white frost, succeeded by a bright sun, with an east wind, warming one side of the face and starving the other. It was neither a day for fishing, nor hunting, nor coursing, nor anything but farming. The country, save where there were a few lingering patches of turnips, was all one dingy drab, with abundant scalds on the undrained fallows. The grass was more like hemp than anything else. The very rushes were yellow and sickly.

That's the North: and so simply done, no fine writing, no arabesque, no pumping-up: just the farmer's eye and the feel on your skin. Don't tell me that man couldn't write. And when we remember that this is the prologue to the description of a steeple-chase, a thing Surtees loathed and despised, don't tell me he knew nothing about the art of ironical planning.

Ael. Suppose I grant the authenticity of his horses and hunts and coverts and so on. I'm told hunting-folk swear by him. Then I ask, what is that to you? You admit yourself that he is a very minor novelist, and good only in the hunting-field. Do you then have three days a week and a bye-day with the Tynedale or the Braes of Derwent?

Bar. Not by quite a bit. The only times I ever got across a horse were when my Colonel said I jolly well had to. But don't you see? That's just it! I don't hunt; I don't even ride on the Town Moor: and I read Surtees with something warmer than mere pleasure.

Ael. Isn't it Mr. Birrell who describes the gentle lady at the dinner-party lamenting the decadence of the prize-fighters of England? She was bemused with Borrow; you seem to be bemused with Surtees. There was more excuse for her.

Bar. Perhaps; but the cause is the same. Borrow and Surtees have the one great and essential gift—enthusiasm, gusto, zest—call it what you like. The real gusto that is fed on experience, on the beef of life and not the red peppers and cocktails. . . . And you'll notice a queer thing: with all our English sportiveness, there's mighty little of this enthusiasm for sport in creative literature. . . . You golf—I've heard you bragging about your approach at the ninth and so on—now golf has the great advantage of being a primitive game, in which you employ skill to defeat distance, weather, and vegetation; and the employment of skill is the sheerest of joys, and, if the spiritualistic aestheticians would only believe it, a main element in art. But you also fish, which is the saving of you. Now tell me: isn't the thrill of holing a long putt quite different from the thrill of playing a lively trout?

Ael. Ye-es, yes. But where does that get us to?

Bar. This. England being a badly over-populated country, the English exercise themselves in artificial ball games, played within certain arbitrary rules devised merely to enforce a certain appropriate kind of skill, and no other. . . . So the English idea of sportsmanship is, two sides or two men or two young ladies—known to every cheap reporter by their Christian names—playing a game according to the rules. In fishing and hunting you play according to nature. . . . [My] point is this, that in life and in literature, wherein life is the quarry, you are dealing with nature, not playing an artificial game according to arbitrary and universally understood rules. That's why 'cricket' emasculated English foreign policy and sent you and me into the Line, and that's why so many modern novelists are dull. They are eternally thinking of the rules of the game, and there aren't any. So one page of St. John's *Wild Sports in the Highlands* makes *Point-Counter-Point* look like a six-cylinder motor-engine decorated with lip-stick, and so Surtees in the hunting-field, being natural, is full of that peculiar thrill you get from rising and playing a good fish, but don't get from holing the longest of putts. And it's got to be there, whether you are stalking deer on the hill or character in a pub—the thing that's so much needed just now, that's so difficult to communicate and yet can be communicated so subtly and so completely—the thing Smollett had, the love of the spectacle of life, even if it were only two blackguards kicking one another—the thing Jane Austen had, though it were only a lady and gentleman conversing over breakfast—the thing all the great ones had—gusto, enthusiasm, infectious zest for just being.

Ael. You were Crocean and are now Tolstoyan—the infection theory.

Bar. Infection fact—only don't think it accounts for everything—and Tolstoy had it too. Experience and gusto: there's the formula for the novel, though it's no good to the American University Courses or the coteries on the *terrasse* of the Rotonde.

Ael. Then I'm to tell all my young literary friends to study Surtees and be saved?

Bar. Yes. And Henry James. And Marcel Proust. And Thackeray and Stendhal and Sterne and Fielding and a whole lot more. And have them observe that all these great ones have beef on their bones.

It is late, and we may leave them arguing. (pp. 81-9)

> W. L. Renwick, "Jorrocks: A Conversation," in Essays and Studies by Members of the English Association, Vol XVII, edited by W. H. Hadow, Oxford at the Clarendon Press, Oxford, 1932, pp. 76-89.

ANTHONY STEEL (essay date 1933)

[*Steel's* Jorrocks's England *is a sociological study of mid-Victorian life based on Surtees' works. In his introduction, excerpted below, Steel argues that Surtees' writings provide valuable insight into the social customs of his day.*]

Most people who write books, historians, literary authorities, or what not, have not even read [Surtees], or else have had the edge taken off their appetite by beginning in chronological order with the work which should be read last—namely, *Jorrocks's Jaunts and Jollities.* There are in fact large numbers of people who will not read Surtees because they do not hunt, care nothing for hunting, and yet—this is the odd thing—profess an interest in the middle-class life and literature of England during the nineteenth century. As if, in any case, Surtees meant hunting and nothing more! (pp. 1-2)

There is, however, a persistent delusion that Surtees writes about nothing but hunting, that his characters are practically always on the hunting-field, and away from it do not exist. Actually, his is a wider England, an England in which hunting is only one of many activities not all concerned with sport. This England included not only the upper, but most of the middle, classes in both town and country; that is, outside the great industrial areas. If it is first and foremost Jorrocks's England, it is still no inconsiderable part of the real England: politically speaking, it represents a fair proportion of the England which votes between 1832 and 1867. Surtees lived through this period—he died in 1864—and his writing life almost exactly coincided with it. Within his limits he was an interested and a close and accurate observer. He represents the view of the squire, the county magistrate, the farmer; he is acquainted with, and describes very fully, middle-class life in general, both in London and the provinces—very fully because, though he was emphatically not writing for posterity, he was definitely satirizing his daily life for the amusement of people who shared it with him.

His limits are immediately obvious. He is not interested in religion, or in economic development in the technical sense, except perhaps in agriculture; he is not deeply interested in social problems, in foreign or imperial affairs of any kind, or even in Scotland, Wales or Ireland, or in education or literature to any great extent, or in politics or administration as such, except where they directly and personally concern him, or in science, art or architecture at all, or in the Court or in high society, except in so far as the latter unbends towards the middle classes in the shires, usually for political purposes.

On the other hand, he *is* deeply interested in farming and in the means of communicating with others and of getting about England, and he is interested, more superficially, in the Law and in professional life. In sport his sphere is narrower than is sometimes supposed. He has little use for games of any kind, for racing, which he attacks, or for coursing, and Heaven knows what he would have thought of electric hares: he barely admires horsemanship as such—Jorrocks's riding is consistently made fun of—and he goes out of his way to attack it when practised in steeplechases as an end in itself. He tolerates shooting and harriers, but hardly mentions fishing. He is essentially a landsman, and pays not the least attention to the current cant about the inborn and necessary interest of every native Englishman in the sea: yachting, travel by water and the navy are all practically ignored, and even steamboats have quite evidently none of the fascination for him possessed by railways. He goes out of his way to ridicule the army, but seldom bothers about sailors to any great degree; thus though one or two caricatures of naval men are introduced into his hunting-fields, they are far outnumbered by his ludicrous soldiers, yeomanry and militia. Watching, and hearing, hounds work is in effect the essence of his sporting life, and comprises practically everything that hunting means to him. It is true he has an eye for country, not only in the hunting sense: he was evidently influenced by natural surroundings, and attempts a rather self-conscious, but not unhappy, landscape on more than one occasion. Again, when he is not thinking about a formal representation, he is full of pleasant tributes to the countryside. But this sort of thing, except in a master's hand, is apt to border on the sentimental, and sentimentality and prudery, those alleged traits of the well-to-do Victorians, were alike anathema to him. If such are his limitations, what is there left? There is more than might be supposed.

After all, farming, travelling even within England, and middle-class life in general, are considerable subjects in themselves, especially when we remember that they were all undergoing rapid and far-reaching changes in Surtees' day, changes which he was fully conscious of and eagerly describes. 'Farming' includes such topics as the formation of agricultural associations, anti-Corn-Law activities, drainage, game-laws, land-agents, tenants and land-owners, manures, soils, stock-breeding and forestry, though curiously little about technical improvements; 'travelling', besides railways, memories of coaching and detailed descriptions of every kind of horse vehicle from phaetons to omnibuses, such things as inns, canals, caravans, roads, posts, the electric telegraph and turn-pike gates. Other topics which absorb him at times are business affairs, from the point of view of the investor, the private banker and the tradesman, trivial things in everyday use from food to furniture and costume, male as much as female, while even children's fashions and hairdressing are not neglected. More than any other Victorian novelist Surtees tells us in lavish detail in what sort of houses his characters lived, how they furnished them, what they wore and used and ate and drank from day to day; and we have come near to forgetting in the process of time how immensely varied all these things were three generations ago. Surtees was more observant: it was, in fact, precisely their oddity and variety which astonished him—a rare gift in a contemporary—and impelled him to record them. He is full of formidable interiors, town and country, haunted by the grotesque fashions of the time, and balanced precariously in the half-light of guttering candles between the extremes of heat and cold.

Another topic on which he has much to say is always of interest, that of servants, and the prevalent illusion that here too the nineteenth century witnessed a golden age is immediately dispelled. He writes a good deal of women in general and their place in everyday life, says something about doctors and diseases, and a good deal about watering-places, inland and marine, together with their curious society.

However, all this is anticipating. It is probably clear enough by now that Surtees' characters are, or so it is claimed, presented as human beings, with all the multifarious activities of human beings; that Surtees in short would have found the 'hunting man', pure and simple, as unreal an abstraction as we ourselves have been taught to find the 'economic man' of his contemporaries. Of course his portraits are caricatured, for even in his chosen field Surtees does not adequately describe the best establishments of his day, but embroiders richly upon eccentricities. His strongly drawn studies, touched with just that element of exaggeration which makes them easy to identify, will persist as long as human nature, no matter how surrounded or employed, but in the novels they are put through the tricks of a circus, the better to exhibit their quality, while the paraphernalia and background of their extraordinary careers are sometimes almost equally distorted, and in any case wholly strange.

But how the people live! They swarm out from his pages in a boisterous, unruly crowd, until it is almost difficult to distinguish faces among them, though one can always hear the great voices of Jorrocks and James Pigg bellowing above the rest. They *were* the substantial, semi-barbarous middle classes of that day; that is why they are still recognizable in the living bodies of their descendants. At all times since their original creation the great mass of the inarticulate masculine and prosperous have seen, if not themselves, at least their friends, acquaintances and relations mirrored in these books. That is why it is not only interesting but important to study them, and not only their own selves, but, always allowing for the element of exaggeration, their interests and activities, and the way in which they lived. (pp. 2-6)

Jorrocks's England, though one England out of many, is perhaps uniquely unfortunate in having been overlaid and crusted with a mass of different associations and predominantly alien memories. What was built on it is no doubt more important, for the house is of greater interest than the foundations, and moreover only one small corner of the Victorian mansion rests upon it; yet in order to appreciate a building we must know something of the ground-plan after all. . . . [In] the novels of Surtees lying ready to our hands, there is the sketch we need, a picture which, with all its faults of violence and exaggeration, has attracted kindred spirits since it was first executed, and yet has come to represent a reality which is increasingly strange to us. We shall find it sturdily insular, immensely English; though it is not an aggressive nationalism. Few writers, indeed, have been more essentially pacific than Surtees: the budding 'Jingoism' of the Crimean War—to anticipate a convenient term by twenty years—was utterly repugnant to him, if only through its lack of humour, though his objections went deeper than that, and it finds no place in his work. Still, beneath all his apparent cynicism this quiet country magistrate conceals the usual vein of English sentiment, and can admire with anyone, for all his hatred of militarism, the 'hobbling, frosty-pated, wound-scarred, old cocks of the Peninsula'. (pp. 7-8)

> *Anthony Steel, in his* Jorrocks's England, *E. P. Dutton and Company Inc. Publishers, 1933, 303 p.*

FREDERICK WATSON   (essay date 1933)

[*Arguing that Surtees deserves serious critical attention, Watson analyzes what he considers to be the three most important aspects of his art: his satire, comic characters, and energetic, colloquial style.*]

In a review of a recent edition of Surtees' novels a discerning critic reflected upon the great good fortune of this novelist in evading so unobtrusively, and yet over so long a period, both the enthusiasm and patronage of the superior person. He has not throughout the last eighty years suffered from sham reverence. He is a remarkable, almost a solitary, example of a writer of definite quality who has been permitted to reach an established position without the benediction of indiscriminating applause or the condemnation of academic criticism. (p. 255)

[Between] the publication of *Jorrocks's Jaunts and Jollities* in 1838 and his death in 1864 the success of Surtees, both among fox-hunters and the general public, was so moderate that, although his books survived, their prospects were not encouraging. In a word, Surtees' place in literature could hardly have been regarded seriously until the eighties. Fifty years later the most obvious claim to the qualities of permanence lies in the rugged fact that no author continues to live unless his work is removed beyond the ephemeral, and possesses at least sincerity and imagination. And yet there are admittedly signs of permanent attainment.

There comes a time in the career of a novelist exceptionally gifted—that is, gifted in the creation of character—when the man in the street includes the figures of his fiction in his own family circle. Dickens is the classic example. It is sometimes a little difficult to believe Micawber—that refuge of political controversy—never existed, or Sherlock Holmes—to take a

Leech's rendition of James Pigg crashing into the melon frame, from Handley Cross.

less effulgent modern instance—was unknown in Baker Street. Fame of this character is perhaps the best tribute to an author, because it is the unconscious recognition of common life. So when, in 1864, Whyte-Melville wrote to Colonel Anstruther Thomson and said as an aside, "The longer I live the more cause I have to agree with Mr Jorrocks 'that all time is wasted that is not spent in hunting,'" he took it for granted that Jorrocks was a commonplace to his correspondent, which makes the year 1864 something of a landmark in Surtees' progress.

But it still remains that Surtees' smooth passage down the years may be claimed as fortunate. Where the books of others of equal or greater merit have departed, why is it that his novels have triumphed over changes in fashion and thought, during crises and wars, and taken an unexpected place among standard fiction? . . . Surtees was not a best-seller, even with a hunting public. But that does not mean his preservation has not been dependent throughout good and bad spells upon a public which, from father to son, has come to regard him as its particular classic. Upon that there can be no argument. Just as Scott is admired by the intelligent reader, and also read as a kind of patriotic duty by every Scotsman, so, in a much lesser degree, Surtees has been bought and read as a matter of course wherever hounds are followed. So it will be as long as fox-hunting exists. (pp. 255-56)

It is a great advantage for any man to write about a subject, whether it is a science or a sport, which suffers little change, and he would be a rash prophet who would wager that *Handley Cross* will not be read in A.D. 2000. But if this steadfast public which comes to few authors over a century may be admitted to have kept Surtees' books in circulation it still remains, as a secondary problem, to be discussed whether his novels can be judged by ambitious critical standards or whether they have been justly dismissed as 'merely sporting.'

A critical estimate of Surtees' novels must concentrate in the end upon three distinct qualifications for serious attention. He was a satirist, if not upon his great level, at least quite worthy of Thackeray's unqualified praise; he was a creator of genuine comic characters; and he wrote with an infectious enthusiasm which is so rare that it has gone far to give him a special niche in English literature. Let us take these points in their sequence.

"Wit, my lords," wrote Lord Chesterfield, "is a sort of property; it is the property of those that have it, and too often the only property." So it was with Surtees, and, to do him justice, he recognized the severe limitations of satire, and as he could only write with original genius about ignoble people he proceeded to do so with hardly a false step.

He was lacking in practically all the most attractive and humane qualities of a great and successful writer. He was destitute of romance, sentiment, and reverence. He hit one nail on the head, and that nail was satirical comedy. It is an attitude of art more unpopular than any other because it is cold, uncomfortable, and narrow. But, as Surtees knew and said with truth, "Most men take a pleasure in satire when it is not aimed at themselves." He, like Thackeray, to whom he came nearest in his attitude, wrote with fine scorn of parasites, toadies, vulgarians, and snobs, but, unlike Thackeray, he resisted the prevalent habit of preaching. To him the humanities in fiction came very hardly, and as an artist he shrank from following current demands to the weakening of his limited genius.

Surtees in that *genre* had modelled his attitude and style upon Fielding. Both exposed weakness and knavery, both wrote with meticulous observation and even temperature. Neither suc-

ceeded in portraying women (unless one includes Amelia), and when Thackeray wrote of the greater man's genius that it was "wonderfully wise and detective; it flashes upon a rogue and lightens up a rascal like a policeman's lantern," he might, upon a lesser stage, have included the author of *Mr Sponge's Sporting Tour.* This imperturbable loyalty of Surtees to realism is so significant that it calls for elaboration. It is known that Thackeray loved old Jorrocks, treasured Sponge, and said so. But the author of *Vanity Fair* could not exclude sentiment, and he abandoned the narrow path of satire. "Oh for a little manly, honest, God-relying simplicity—cheerful, unaffected, and humble," he had prayed. But Surtees did not kneel with him. Instead, he created Scamperdale and Spraggon, in whom there is nothing simple or humble, but a great deal of beer and beef with the elementary school left out.

In his character-sketch of "Captain Rook and Mr Pigeon," which in itself sounds like a chapter out of Surtees, Thackeray has commented, "Wherever shines the sun, you are sure to find folly basking in it. Knavery is the shadow at folly's heels." If Surtees preferred the shadow, instead of the footlights, of the human scene one may regret it, but there is no justification whatever for assuming that knavery is not as interesting or as prevalent as honesty. To-day the presentation of types entirely relieved of any beauty of life or character is applauded rather than denounced. Realism is all the rage, and the occupants of the Surtees gallery are, as a consequence, treated as human beings, however conscienceless. The refusal to believe in crude, savage, and vulgar people has given place to an unbiased appreciation of the art by which even curiosities of life may become classics of literature. What is more, the wider knowledge of all classes of men has compelled or persuaded the modern reader to realize that the 'nasty people' of Surtees were, like the giraffe, only astonishing so long as people preferred to deny their existence. Today it is no longer rather shocking to discover that peasants are not as simple as a pastoral idyll, that farmers, like commercial travellers, are not confirmed ascetics, and that a squire may be a Scamperdale and still remain a most accurate portrait. (pp. 257-59)

It is . . . likely that Surtees' acceptance of the stoical was drawn from his own temperament and times rather than from any preference for brutality. "One thing is quite certain," he wrote, "you can't buy experience with another man's money," and if his people were 'nasty' or 'inhuman' that does not mean they were not genuine.

It is much the same with his satire. Here was the man himself directing his keen, ruthless gaze in search of what suited his narrow path. Remote, inscrutable, taciturn—he has left more than a tradition for a nature unkindly, cold, and uncompanionable. Like man, like satire, one may presume. But even then, had Surtees been small-minded or merely a snarling, jaundiced fellow, he could have claimed no place in literature. His people may, with a few exceptions, be singularly relieved of idealism, but they are not savage caricatures. Mr Sponge could be no other than Mr Sponge, and, given the splendid opportunities of old Heartycheer, he could hardly be drawn like a rural dean. Surtees drew the line, not merely somewhere, but rigidly on the safe side of humanity, which is more than could be said of some of his successors. In his novels are no blasphemies, seductions, scenes of cruelty, or passages sneering at what is good or beautiful or sacred to simple people. If his place in literature may be counted among the satirists it is because his satire is removed from personal spite, and not cheapened by the consistent posturing of the professional cynic.

He was, in fact, a gentleman in his traditional sense of the decencies, and when one says that it is no less important to remember he was also a democrat in his hatred of injustice. To read his remarkable letter to *The Times* appealing for mercy for the inmates of Southwark Workhouse is to grasp this profound truth—that the satirist upon occasions differs from the sentimentalist only in his line of approach. When Jorrocks remarked, "He is the best poor man's friend wot gives him a good day's pay for a good day's work," he would not have brought down the house, but it would be impossible to mistake his shrewd compassion.

Surtees cherished, like Jane Austen, not a little of the traditional old maid in his spiteful conclusions, his meticulous eye for detail, his reverence for propriety, and his shrewish hesitancy regarding human motives. Not only did human passion fail to move him, but he actually suspected its complications and prophesied its catastrophes. He employed the same petty preference for surface values, the same bloodless contempt for human frailties, the same eye at the wrong end of the telescope, as the author of *Pride and Prejudice*. Upon women, for instance, no disappointed female could have written with greater venom and cattishness. But, whether he describes their tawdry garments or their tarnished ideals, his eye is alert with the bland serenity of the cynic, not with the savage rancour of disappointment. To Surtees the race of women was united in one brave adventure, which was the pursuit of man. But if he found it impossible to approach them in the spirit of sanctity his malice was not vindictive. If the attitude was ridiculously overdone it was also infinitely more amusing than one of undiluted reverence. But the point to remember is that it was selective choice, not prejudice, which guided him. (pp. 260-62)

If satire grew upon Surtees in the middle years humour carried him with triumph in his London days, and it is his humour which has established his fame. But, in contradiction of the popular view that humour, to be supreme, must include pathos, the comedy of Surtees is innocent of sentiment. And here again the shadow of disapproval fell, and has not altogether been lifted.

If the comedy of his characters, like that of the immortal sea captains of Mr Jacobs, was an example of the highest standard of humour untouched by pathos, it was not, for that reason, artificial, or merely a clever juggling with phrases, or a succession of farcical situations. "All his fun," wrote Mr Harold Child with truth, "is rooted in human nature" [see Additional Bibliography], and in Surtees' comic characters . . . when they make one laugh it is not by what happens to them but simply by their own rich personalities.

To advance the point a step farther, Surtees' humour—especially in *Jorrocks's Jaunts and Jollities* and *Handley Cross*—is, like that of Dickens, inseparable from the creation of comic characters—not merely one or two great personages upon a big scale, but a gallery of those minor figures which so definitely establish an author's place in fiction. To quote Mr Child once more, "In the invention of comic characters and speech Surtees comes second only to Dickens." Even then what is the final test in such things? John Galsworthy acutely observed, "In those few character creations which endure is a quality which can best, perhaps, be described as homespun yet vital," and concluded, "If one had to give the palm to a single factor in the creation of character it would be to sly, dry humour." Few novelists have exercised so successfully the "sly, dry humour" as Robert Surtees in *Handley Cross,* and who—unless it were Baillie Nicol Jarvie—ever kept the comic within the bounds

of caricature and the homespun as vital and yet as overwhelming as old John Jorrocks?

"Comic characters and speech"—if the unities of personality and dialogue are accepted as a test of creative genius few authors have possessed the power of making their characters live as Jorrocks and Pigg and Sponge lived. But fewer still can create subsidiary people who, within a page, possess sharpness of outline and economy of detail like etchings in process—or at least silhouettes.

In his ironical faculty for dialogue Surtees is relieved of much of the sustained tedium and affectation of some Victorian writers. His joy in words is a sure symptom of natural inspiration. (pp. 262-63)

This joy in words is neither common nor trivial. Half of the pure gold of Jorrocks is the manner in which his problems are, as it were, dramatized by his grotesque similes. "Jest put 'em on to me, Charley," he says, with his customary optimism, "whilst I make one o' Mr Craven Smith's patent all-round-my-'at casts, for that beggar Binjamin's of no more use with a pack of 'ounds than a hopera-box would be to a cow, or a frilled shirt to a pig." And other examples are "sellin' small coals from a donkey-cart out of a quart pot," and "frightenin' rats from a barn wi' the bagpipes at a 'alfpenny a day, and findin' yoursel'."

Taking him all in all, Jorrocks seldom disappoints. Even in *Hillingdon Hall* he convinces one that, whatever happens, it will not be his fault if he is a bore—or is bored. Even his artless complacency is not prosy: "Wot a many things are wantin' to 'unt a country plisantly!" he says, which is true, but a normal observation. Then he adds conclusively, "Things that would never enter the 'ead of a sailor," and leaves one with that sense of surprise which the experts say is half the art of fiction.

This gift of creating comic characters who are not simply diverting but also convincing reached its highest level in Jorrocks. But what of Pigg? He remains the classic huntsman. Or what of Sponge? Never does that quiet and cynical man for an instant say or do anything which does not satisfy our sense of his consistency, however much it may wound our hopes of his conversion. Or old Scamperdale? Or Facey Romford? All these are living people, not caricatures. But are his minor characters less successful? When Lockhart reviewed *Handley Cross* in *The Quarterly Review* he concluded with a warning note that the author must be careful of caricaturing [see excerpt dated 1843]. But if the fun is perhaps a little near the grotesque at times these lesser lights still shine bravely enough. One will not easily forget Jogglebury Crowdey with his carved sticks, and Colonel Blunt, that priceless officer, surely the best representative of the second-rate Victorian C.O. in fiction, and what of the "Jug," that delightful but intemperate gentleman in charge of all the precious children at the Hunt?

Surtees' economy in words was masterly in throwing a minor character on his screen. When one meets Mr Cucumber, the gentleman's gentleman, one knows as much about him as most novelists can express in a full-blown novel. And what about Mr Wotherspoon, most tireless of after-dinner speakers, and the lunatic fox-hunter host encountered by Charley Stobbs?

But the final test must always return to Jorrocks. To those who see nothing beyond vulgarity in *Handley Cross* the novels of Surtees must remain a mystery. But it is not a mystery to be explained away by contempt or liable to expire through critical neglect. Jorrocks lives by personality. He may be a number of things, but he remains a character for ever inseparably associated with a conservative sport. (pp. 264-65)

To the present century Surtees remains the classic novelist on fox-hunting. But his net has, in these days of less stringent moralities, drawn in a substantial body of readers who know nothing whatever about horses or hounds. He was—and here we are on solid ground—intensely *national*. Few novelists—unless it be Trollope or Kingsley—have been so representative of the English temperament. He possessed a second great attraction to the ordinary reader in the colloquial ease of his style, which, if it is not suitable for a text-book on literature, is hard to beat in an armchair on holiday.

Surtees will never be translated into Russian, but wherever the Anglo-Saxon lights his pipe and with an uncritical finger skips an occasional page (or even chapter) the creator of Mr Sponge—*Mr Sponge's Sporting Tour* is perhaps the best book for beginners—will beguile an idle hour—so long as that fleeting joy is permitted the modern citizen. What he possessed was the English fibre of Cobbett—most authentic of countrymen. (pp. 266-67)

Surtees is free from affectation, false sentiment, and long stretches of description. He stands the test of time surprisingly well even against the later Victorian humorists. If the standards of nineteenth-century comedy are examined in the adventures of Mr Briggs or the lectures of Mrs Caudle, it will be observed that the Victorians laughed more heartily at incompetence or henpecking than we are able to do to-day. Their sense of superiority and gentility is extremely dated. Victorian humour, like the furniture of the period, is solid, unavoidable, and depressing. It oozes snobbery, parochialism, and a careful elimination of the lower orders. Just as *The Innocents Abroad* of Mark Twain is almost painful in its revelation of the abysmal legend of American superiority, so Victorian humour was most successful when it was most condescending. The modern humorist prefers not merely to find laughter in the most unexpected surroundings of which the Victorian pretended a bland ignorance, but sympathizes, as do Mr H. G. Wells and Arnold Bennett, with the futility, or incompetence, or absurd aspirations of his characters.

Surtees comes very close to this attitude. He was spared 'gentility,' jingoism, and contemporary standards of literature. A single instance may be noted in the occasion when old Jorrocks dined with the Duke of Donkeyton.

> "Pray, Mr Jorrocks, who was your mother?" inquired his Grace, after he had bowed and drunk off his wine.
>
> "Please, your Greece, my mother was a washer-woman."
>
> "*A washer-woman, indeed!*" exclaimed his Grace—"That's very odd—I like washer-women—nice, clean, wholesome people.—I wish my mother had been a washer-woman."

In other words, Surtees treated Jorrocks as Mr Wells treated Mr Polly, or Arnold Bennett "The Card," without that class consciousness which was so prominent a weakness of the Victorian humorist. Possibly, just as the Lord in the Prologue to *Faust* preferred a knave to a bore, the obvious faults in *Handley Cross* are swallowed with good grace.

That Surtees has none of the compact technique of the modern novelist is never in doubt; that he meanders and does not cross his literary *t*'s is only too apparent. To many he must appear hopelessly old-fashioned and slovenly. There is, for example, a great objection to his laboured efforts, so popular a century ago, to make the characters fit their peculiarities. Such names as "Scattercash," "Seedeybuck," or "Heartycheer" are admittedly rather overdoing it, while "Lord Lionel Lazytongs," son of the "Marquis of Fender and Fireirons," is nothing short of deplorable. And yet there is even to-day something rather attractive in such manufactured names when they are not hopelessly exaggerated. One would require to be very critical to refuse to read the story of Mr Sponge because of this weakness. There seems also to be a kind of tradition for baptizing sporting characters with spectacular signatures, and from Surtees to Mr A. P. Herbert, in *Tantivy Towers,* the custom endures. There is probably a temptation to label comic characters with grotesque but descriptive names. . . . Despite such obvious crudities Surtees' perspective is more in sympathy with the present age than the one in which he lived, and possibly for that reason his characters have ceased to shock, and continue to amuse. (pp. 267-69)

[The] reader to-day prefers characters to speak naturally and behave naturally. To bore is the crowning sin in a novelist, and one must allow that Surtees, in his most familiar novels, makes bracing reading. Whether his characters are the kind of people we would remember in our wills is no longer an angle of criticism. When Thackeray, in referring to *Mr Sponge's Sporting Tour,* calls "those fellows in spectacles divine, and Scamperdale's character perfectly odious and admirable" [see excerpt dated 1852], he expresses exactly our own feeling. "Odious and admirable"—those three words explain a good deal of the attraction of Surtees' portrait gallery. There is—to go a step farther—an attractive neutral quality in Romford and Sponge. They neither alarm, depress, nor unduly convulse with laughter. And it is, as a consequence, not a little interesting to see how surely and inevitably Surtees has passed from the covertside to the city. Some of the most inveterate enthusiasts for his novels are, in my experience, men who have never been on a horse, and, I suspect, have never seen a hound. This interesting state of affairs is comparatively recent, and is still making surprising converts. (p. 270)

But one question still remains to answer. What is it in Surtees' more popular novels which still attracts the ordinary reader? It would seem to be, at least in *Handley Cross,* a kind of literary infection. It is, one may suggest, the genius not only for creating comic characters like Jorrocks, but for enabling the reader to partake of their exuberance, share their adventures, and echo their tremendous gusts of laughter. Surtees possessed imaginative energy. Not only do his characters live, but, what is just as important, they *revel* in the fact, and this zest for life, whether in the hunting-field or in the dealer's yard, whether in a horse or in a host, is really what matters in the end. Let it be allowed his style was slovenly, his construction wooden, his characters vulgar. What remains is Surtees himself. He had the saving grace of making human life a world of astonishing encounters with quite astonishing people. (p. 271)

> *Frederick Watson, in his* Robert Smith Surtees: A Critical Study, *George G. Harrap & Co. Ltd., 1933, 291 p.*

JOHN MOORE (essay date 1935)

[*Moore dismisses Surtees' characters as humorless and vulgar.*]

A Leech illustration of Jorrocks and his wife at a hunt ball, from Handley Cross.

I must confess that I have never found Surtees very funny; perhaps he was quoted at me too much in my youth. His gallery of genial rascals, crooks, and cadgers seems to me to be singularly unattractive. These rogues are gross without greatness; they are like the characters in *Pickwick Papers* would be if Dickens were stripped of his all-pervading humanity. Moreover, they have none of the vitality with which Dickens animated his people; the only distinctive thing they possess is a certain pungency of speech. Mr. Soapy Sponge, Mr. Facey Romford, Mr. Jorrocks, and James Pigg: what a hideous scarecrow crew they are! A dismal sort of drunkenness, and a petty sort of dalliance with housekeepers and the like, compose their mean pleasures, and for the rest they cadge, cheat, lie, and swindle in a wholly vulgar and unimaginative way. Their antics are no more humorous than those of the horrible people in Rowlandson's cartoons, of which—far more than of John Leach's excellent drawings—they always somehow remind me. (p. 95)

> *John Moore, "The Hunting Men," in his* Country
> Men, *1935. Reprint by Books for Libraries Press,*
> *1969; distributed by Arno Press, Inc., pp. 76-107.*

EDWARD WAGENKNECHT   (essay date 1943)

> [*Arguing that Surtees' characters are an important contribution
> to English literature, Wagenknecht proclaims that the author "seems
> due for a revival."*]

For many years, the novels of Robert Smith Surtees—expensively printed, with hand-colored illustrations, and handsomely bound in the sportsman's favorite red—have been an indispensable part of every hunting gentleman's library. This cir-

cumstance, placing as it were the stamp of a too narrow specialization upon him, has probably contributed adversely to Surtees's fame as a novelist. It is not his ability to describe the "run" that gives him his place in the history of the English novel; it is rather his ability to create characters like John Jorrocks. And Jorrocks may be enjoyed even by those (like the present writer) who are so far from relishing hunting that they take up toward it the attitude of such Englishmen as John Galsworthy and Thomas Hardy. (p. 197)

Except for *Romford,* which does make some approach to an organized plot, one episode follows another in Surtees's books, and nobody cares particularly whether all the material is brought to bear on a central theme or not. In *Ask Mamma,* Miss de Glancey is introduced as if she were to play an important role; then she is simply dropped. When the terrible Mrs. Jorrocks is not needed, she disappears from *Hillingdon Hall*; on her brief reappearance, the reader finds himself wondering how in the world Jorrocks was able to get away from her for so long, and how he was able to manage so many activities without her. When the Anti-Corn Law League needs a candidate, Mr. Bowker is reintroduced from a former novel, with no particular regard paid to the consistency of his characterization.

The trial scene in *Pickwick* would seem clearly to show the influence of Jorrocks's trial for the killing of Old Tom, the hare—they get him for poaching when it is determined by foot-rule that the length of his great toe was across the line of Squire Cheatum's estate when he fired the fatal shot—and it must be admitted that even with Dickens's immortal bravura piece in mind, Surtees's dialogue is very amusing. There are those who believe that the general idea of *The Pickwick Papers* was suggested to its publishers, Chapman and Hall, by the success of *Jorrocks*. Both Dickens and Surtees go back to Smollett; one feels the influence more strongly in the older writer because his tone is predominantly farcical throughout his work, not merely in his first novel, as Dickens's is, and also because he comes closer to an eighteenth-century outlook. He lacks Smollett's brutality, to be sure, and Smollett's appetite for dirt, but he is as far from Dickens's intense Victorian earnestness as he is from his sentimentalism.

Jorrocks is a savage compared to Pickwick, yet there are many points of resemblance between them. Don Quixote had his Sancho Panza; Pickwick has his Sam Weller; Jorrocks has his huntsman, James Pigg. Jorrocks is not often so innocent as either of these other worthies (though once Pigg saves him from everlasting disgrace by yanking him out of a temperance procession into which he had strayed!), but what Frederick Watson calls ''the contrast between the dry-tongued, uncouth, hard-riding northerner and the voluble, enthusiastic, but timorous cockney'' is consistently maintained. Like Pickwick, the character changes notably; the buffoon of the *Jaunts and Jollities,* who loses his pants on the beach at Margate, is hardly the same man who gives those masterly ''lectors'' on hunting, and whom Surtees uses as the mouthpiece of his own ideas on agriculture and the Corn Laws. Mr. Pickwick in the pound is not a very pretty sight, but Pickwick is abstemious compared to Jorrocks, and his adventure with the lady in curl-papers is mild indeed compared to Jorrocks's Parisian sojourn with the Countess ''Benwolio,'' or even his flirtations with Mrs. Markham and Mrs. Flather.

This does not mean that Jorrocks is necessarily the lesser achievement. He has the peculiar kind of vulgarity that is one of the glories of English literature, the vulgarity which first appeared notably in the Wife of Bath, and which reached its apotheosis in Falstaff. . . . With all his faults, Jorrocks has a refreshing freedom from meanness—his humanity as a magistrate is notable—yet I suppose many readers must be surprised to find themselves thinking of him so kindly as they do. No doubt his marvelous vitality has much to do with it, and so does his marvelous lingo.

''I'm a Post Hoffice Directory, not a Peerage, man,'' he cries. ''Where I dine I sleep and where I sleep I breakfast.'' Muttonbroth reminds him of ''a cold in the 'ead,'' and he calls French macaroni soup ''water with worms in it.'' He refuses mince because he likes to chew his own meat, and he requires ''a good fruity wine; a wine with a grip o' the gob, that leaves a mark on the side o' the glass.'' So enthusiastic is his love of hunting that he hunts in his sleep. ''No man is fit to be called a sportsman,'' he declares in a public address, ''wot doesn't kick his wife out of bed on a haverage once in three weeks!'' His definition of hunting is famous—''the sport of kings, the image of war without its guilt, and only five-and-twenty per cent. of its danger.'' And his ''COME HUP! I say, YOU HUGLY BEAST!'' is still heard and understood among hunting Englishmen.

Surtees has many vivid characters besides Pigg and Jorrocks, but the best of them are surely those two ''dead beats,'' Soapey Sponge and Facey Romford. By 1852 Surtees found it convenient to perform the conventional genuflexion before Mrs. Grundy; he created Soapey, he tells us, ''to put the rising generation on their guard against specious, promiscuous acquaintance, and [train] them on to the noble sport of hunting, to the exclusion of its mercenary, illegitimate off-shoots.'' There can be no question as to the sincerity of Surtees's op-

position to the ''low and demoralising pursuits'' of ''Prizefighting, Bull-baiting, and Cock-fighting''—he would not so much as allow them to be treated in his magazines—but he did not create Soapey as a horrible example. He might even have agreed with Mr. Watson's enthusiastic defense of that engaging rogue. The brutal ending of *Mr. Sponge's Sporting Tour*—the death of Jack Spraggon in a steeplechase—disturbs many readers, and the Defoe-like unemotionalism of Surtees's description is generally attributed to his own coldness of temperament. No doubt this element enters in, but it should not be forgotten that he has a point to make against racing.

It is in the *Sponge* books too that we get Lucy Glitters, whom Sponge marries, then deserts, when the cigar and betting rooms they establish are not going too well, and who is probably Romford's mistress, as well as his partner in the business alliance they set up. In general, Surtees is very cruel to women: an especially flagrant example is the marriage of the heroine's mother in *Plain or Ringlets?* to ''the Jug'' who does Jovey Jessup's drinking for him. Except for Jorrocks's niece, Belinda, who is too much of a lay-figure to count—and even Belinda ''pets'' mildly!—almost all Surtees's women, young and old, are selfish, spiteful, or shrewish. We are told specifically when we first meet Lucy Glitters that the ex-actress is only moderately virtuous, yet we are made to like her, and we feel that Surtees liked her also.

Though Surtees pays little attention to what may be called the intellectual life of his day, it must not be supposed that he was interested only in sport; he reflects his age, indeed, in so many aspects that a whole book has been devoted to the subject. He was deeply concerned over the agricultural problem, and *Hillingdon Hall* is one of the few books in which the modern reader may still find a statement of the case in favor of the Corn Laws. Surtees never rebelled against his age as Dickens did, but he was too intelligent to be entirely conventional; it has been argued that one reason why his hunting books were less immediately popular than Whyte-Melville's was that Jorrocks was not the early Victorian notion of what an M.F.H. ought to be. Huntsmen were not too comfortable under Surtees's chaffing; he did not quite hew to the ''party line.''

Surtees is one of the few English novelists who have never been ''boomed.'' Lockhart, Thackeray, . . . Kipling, Theodore Roosevelt [see excerpts by Lockhart dated 1836 and 1843, by Thackeray dated 1849 and 1852, by Kipling dated 1913, and by Roosevelt dated 1906]—these are among the few famous men who have expressed enthusiasm for him; yet he has safely come through his first hundred years. Both Kipling and Wingfield-Stratford have been horrified by the coarseness of the world he pictures; unfortunately we have plenty of testimony that the picture was only too true. . . . [Because] of his historic importance and his own creative powers, he now seems due for a revival, and there are some signs that he may get it. That it will reach the extent of the Trollope revival is doubtful, however, nor can one believe that such ill-considered judgments as André Maurois's statement that Jorrocks is the *chef d'oeuvre* of the English novel will contribute to it notably. Nevertheless it is high time Surtees was rescued from the stables. (pp. 198-202)

Edward Wagenknecht, ''From Scott to Dickens,'' in his Cavalcade of the English Novel: From Elizabeth to George VI, *Holt, Rinehart and Winston, 1943, pp. 173-212.*

JOHN SHAND (essay date 1945)

[*Shand speculates on the reasons for Surtees' popular and critical neglect, incorporating a defense of the author's works into his discussion.*]

Surtees has never been popular, nor is he ever likely to be. His main subject was sport, which does not attract the intellectual reader; he was a satirist and a cynic, and satire and cynicism are not enjoyed by the general English public. It is true that there is a national love of sport, and a select audience for satiric writing. But Surtees did not write of sport in a way to tickle the multitude, and chose the wrong subject to please the few who would enjoy his humor. He fell between two audiences, pleasing neither the barbarians of Horseback Hall nor the cultured of Heartbreak House.

Like his own Facey Romford, Surtees was "not a man of much blandishment." He wrote in a "take it or leave it" style; and as his satiric strokes were often sharp enough to hurt, most readers chose to leave it. He did not choose his words with conscious care; but he expressed himself in a clear, colloquial English that leaves the reader in no doubt of his meaning and reflects his tart, taciturn personality; and for his comic characters, especially for Jorrocks, he found a torrent of racy, exuberant speech.

Readers who flatter themselves that they know something about English fiction are likely to nod agreeably (if vaguely) at mention of Jorrocks; but it cannot be assumed that they have read even *Handley Cross,* in which the Cockney foxhunter is developed with superb vigor and vivacity from the first faint sketches in *Jorrocks's Jaunts and Jollities*—a book that preceded and probably suggested the writing of *The Pickwick Papers. Handley Cross* is an ill-constructed masterpiece that lives only (but lives decidedly) because of Jorrocks and James Pigg; and it peters out in a couple of law trial scenes that are dismally unfunny and, when contrasted with the magical comedy of Bardell versus Pickwick, seem painfully inept.

But Surtees's novels as a whole, filled as they are with amusing characters and sardonic pictures of the Victorian scene, continue to be ignored by the critical mandarins—probably because he is pigeon-holed as a sporting writer. Art connoisseurs long disdained English sporting pictures for the same reason. Surtees is also something of a "sport" among novelists as well as a novelist of sport. That may be another reason why he is neglected by the literary fancy. For he was not a literary gentleman with an odd taste for hunting, but a hunting gentleman with an odd gift for writing. It is this that gives to his tales an individual flavor and a valuable authenticity. (p. 91)

It is easy to understand why Surtees's novels failed to attract that important body of novel readers, the women of the English—of the Victorian English—middle class. They did not attract Surtees. He viewed them positively with distaste. He disliked their manners, despised their affectations, and laughed at their pretensions to gentility. His attitude towards them could not be better expressed than in the words of "Independent Jimmy," a delightful Tyneside character in *Mr. Romford's Hounds,* who drives a bus, delivers parcels, and knows all the gossip of the country. He is acidly giving an account of a local nabob who has just bought the old squire's house and set up for a gentleman, and Jimmy, in the peculiar dialect of Tyneside, thus continues:—

> As to the darter . . . she's just the impittantest, sarciest gal i' the world, arlways tossin' aboot and givin' gob. Noo, there's the Ladies Rosebud, Lord Flowerdew's darters, when ar gans to the Castle, for any body there, they speak quite civil and plizant; 'Good morning, Jimmy! How do ye do, Jimmy? Hoo are all the little Jimmys?' ("for ar ha' thorteen on 'em," added Jimmy, parenthetically) and so on, while this sarcy thing taks had of her stickin'-out claes, and cries, 'Now, man! get out of the way, man; see, man! look, man! mind, man!' just as if I were a twoad. . . . Sink, but ar often wonders who these sort o' fondies think they impose upon. It can't be the likes o' me . . . for we know all about them; it can't be the gentlefolks, for they'll ha' nout to say to them. It mun just be their arn silly sels.

This touches home. And though these "fondies" no longer wear crinolines, they are otherwise not much altered, and one is still permitted to wonder whom they think they impose upon.

Women readers—indeed, most readers—also prefer a novel to have a story. Surtees never bothered himself much about a plot. This was a fault; but he laughed at love, which was fatal. It was perhaps only a misfortune that he lacked sentiment; but he failed to be sentimental, and that was not to be forgiven. His men (except for one ancient nobleman) never attempt seduction. They can hardly be said to fall in love. His women quite lack romance. The Victorian virgin and her matchmaking mama he depicts entirely without reverence. The one woman in his fiction for whom he exhibits any admiration (and to emphasize his interest in her he brings her into two of his best novels) is an actress from the minor London theaters, and only "tolerably virtuous." The one love scene that has a touch of passion (and it has an oddly convincing quality) is that between her and that rogue, Soapey Sponge.

Generally, Surtees shows his couples courting strictly with a view to a profitable alliance, and if they look foolish, they act with prudence; if one eye fills with feeling, calculation stares from the other, and the lawyer must consent before the priest is asked to bless. "Oh, you needn't be afraid of me, Mr. Ballivant! You needn't be afraid of me, I'm not one of the sentimental sort," remarks Miss Rosa, the heroine of *Plain or Ringlets?* when after a grand inquisition on the hero's funds and property the family attorney advises her mother "to keep Miss back a little for the present"—as if Miss were a good horse whose sale could await a better bid.

This is typical, and shows clearly how Surtees offended every canon of the circulating library. He sees the women as snobs and tuft-hunters of the first degree, and he describes what he sees with masculine vigor and almost feminine relish for detail.

If Surtees offended women readers, surely he pleased the foxhunters of his day? Doubtless he delighted some of them; but as many in proportion ride to hounds because it is the thing to do as go to the opera or travel abroad, and Surtees spared them not. As a foxhunter himself who delighted in the sport, Surtees saw nothing to ridicule in Jorrocks, the Cockney grocer whose passion was hunting. Jorrocks is comical enough, to be sure, but he holds his own in any company because his enjoyment in hunting foxes is as genuine as his love of money, because he hunts for fun, and because he is completely lacking in a sense of reverence for his social superiors. He is completely at home with everybody because he sees no reason why everybody should not feel at home with him.

Surtees reserved his sarcasm for the pretentious Jawleyford, the dandy Puffington, and all that sort of gentry who attend the meet only to speak to his lordship or to show off to the ladies. Surtees with tactless clarity showed his preference for Sponge and Romford, who cheated in order to hunt, to the respectable snobs and toadies whose very presence in the hunting field was a cheat.

As for the earnest intellectual readers of his day, it was hopeless to expect them to approve a writer who had no gospel to preach, who showed no zeal to reform the world, and in whom the pleasures of the chase, the courage of a rider, the cunning of a fox, the sagacity of hounds, obviously raised a warmth of feeling that strongly contrasted with his cynical attitude toward society. Society, indeed, only engaged his unloving attention. Surtees had sharp eyes for faults and follies. He reports details of dress, manners, meals, speech, furniture, transportation, so minutely that his descriptions are sometimes tedious for casual reading, though probably of enormous interest to the social historian.

But though Surtees disliked much of what he observed, he had too much vitality merely to yawn; and as he is never bored, he is not often dull reading. If he has no taste for the ideal, he at least enjoys the real without bitterness. If he does not see his fellows as angels walking, he does not in disappointment call them devils. If his lovers never believe the world well lost for love, it is also true that they do not believe the world well lost for any consideration. The way of the world perfectly suits all his characters. They are completely selfish, and they view unselfishness in others with high suspicion. They adore riches and despise poverty. Altogether they imitate humanity pretty closely.

Being country born and bred, Surtees views field and forest with the practical eyes of a farmer. He is quite unable to be "enthusymusy" about scenery. He takes for granted the enjoyment of fresh air and good food and the changing beauties of the seasons, and leaves to Jorrocks such a truly Cockney cry as: "Dash it, wot a mornin' it is! Wot a many delicious moments one loses by smooterin' i' bed!" It is true that when the scene shifts occasionally to London or to a holiday town, Surtees seems also perfectly at home—his London episodes are particularly amusing; but he is at his best in the country, and views its inhabitants with the penetrating knowledge of an old friend. He is "country," too, in his solid, stolid good sense, his stoical acceptance of things as they are. He never attempts pathos; neither is he ever maudlin. His characters are interested only in everyday matters. As in life, though not in fiction, money is an object of anxious solicitude. Dress is also a serious problem, and an essay on Victorian costume might be written from Surtees's exact descriptions.

Such scenes as that of the Duke of Tergiversation's ball (in *Plain or Ringlets?*) are a panorama of rural society. A shrewd sardonic pen traces all the social reverberations created by this grand local spectacle. The delicious comedy of the ducal couple drawing up the list of guests is accompanied by that of some receiving the coveted cards. The Duke and Duchess are seen including or excluding guests with all the calculation of politicians forming a government; and the complex diplomacy needed to get all the right people into the castle ballroom is balanced by that which goes on in the kitchen to get them fed. The butler must patronize the local shops if the castle credit is still good; if not, the London tradesmen—"terribly obnoxious to the influence of rank"—can always be tapped.

The fuss and bother of the guests is equally good fun. The pleasure of being invited (and of knowing who is not invited) is countered by the expense and fatigue of finding dress and carriage suited to the occasion, and the disgust of discovering that the castle has asked neighbors who ought to have been left out. (Surtees acidly observes that the ducal ball would be excessively exclusive if the guests could issue the invitations.) And at the ball itself, the spectacle of the Duchess "measuring affability" is not less amusing because her star guest is not the Italian prince she supposes him to be, but a dancing master. (pp. 92-4)

[It] is difficult for an admirer of Surtees not to believe that a far larger audience would enjoy his books if they were better known, and it is difficult not to accuse the critics—who so thoroughly omit to recommend them—as guilty of dereliction of duty. (p. 94)

[In] *The English Novel* [Saintsbury] gave Surtees a curt "nearly always readable—and sometimes very amusing—even to those who are not exactly Nimrods" [see Additional Bibliography]. Faint praise—fainter, indeed, than at first it seems, for Saintsbury compares Surtees to his disadvantage with Kingsley's sporting novel, *Yeast,* which he praises for its "most fascinating and real heroine" and its "accurate and real dialogue."

But Saintsbury's brief tribute might pass had he not added . . . just those few words that made him put his foot in it. In contrast to Kingsley's "real heroine" and "real dialogue," he remarks that Surtees's "characters and manners have the old artificial-picaresque quality only"—an observation that makes one wonder if even dimly he appreciated the astonishing reality of Sponge and Romford, and of many other of Surtees's characters, and the fidelity with which he records "manners." Jorrocks and Pigg are another matter: they are "artificial," as all great comic (or tragic) characters are "artificial."

But Sponge and Romford, though amusing, are not in the technical sense comic characters; they are perfectly ordinary masculine creatures boldly and vigorously drawn. They are exceedingly life-like portraits of men moderately "on the make" who see their fellows as much like themselves—"anxious to look after Number One." (pp. 94-5)

Sponge and Romford are "real" because their creator had an enormous preference for what was true to life to what was likely to be popular; and they are likable because—perhaps in spite of himself—Surtees could not help making them excellent sportsmen as well as superb critics, by implication, of social hypocrisy.

Surtees in his own day was inevitably over-shadowed by the genius of Dickens. Where he resembled Dickens, the odds were heavily against him; and where he differed, it was a difference that did not attract Victorian taste. There was a touch of the raffish Regency in him that was not likely to appeal to the respectable reader, and a masculine attitude toward life that would have been better appreciated by the age of Fielding and Smollett. A comparison between the tours of Sponge and Romford and those of Pickwick and Weller would suggest, perhaps, that the books resembled each other only in the seeming ability of their authors to continue the stories indefinitely: they end only because an end must be made.

While the people in *Pickwick* are all transfigured by the golden radiance of good humor, so that Stiggins and Jingle, even Dodson and Fogg, delight no less than Pickwick and the Wellers, in Surtees one is reminded how Stiggins and Jingle and

A Leech illustration of Lucy Glitters leading a hunt, from Mr. Sponge.

Dodson and Fogg would appear in the cold light of day. Compare Sponge going out shooting with Jogglebury Crowdey, with Winkle exhibiting his supposed prowess at Dingley Dell. The scene in Dickens is farce divinely genial; the scene in Surtees, equally ludicrous and not less well written, is farce humanly ungenial.

Winkle is a gorgeous lunatic; Crowdey is as Winkle would look to a real sportsman seriously out for game. The pompous Crowdey, with his undisciplined spaniel anywhere but at heel, who cannot hit a haystack except by accident, is seen through the cold, jeering eyes of an expert shot, who is at once spitefully amused by the absurd spectacle and intensely irritated that he is wasting his time with a fool. It is farce decidedly less pleasant than that of Dickens, but it is excellent fooling, and some palates will always relish its pungent flavor. (p. 95)

John Shand, "Squire Surtees," in The Atlantic Monthly, *Vol. 175, No. 1, January, 1945, pp. 91-6.*

LEONARD COOPER   (essay date 1952)

[*Cooper holds that Surtees was "a stylist of high order," particularly praising his handling of dialogue.*]

In his *Art of Writing* Sir A. T. Quiller-Couch lays down four requirements for a good English style. It must, he says, be accurate, perspicuous, persuasive and appropriate: and measured by these standards Surtees may fairly lay claim to be a stylist of high order. If he fails at all it is in accuracy—that is in precision of grammar and nicety in the use of words. Mrs. Woolf calls his style "Gentlemanly and slapdash" [see excerpt

dated 1925] and there can hardly be a better description. He was certainly careless in construction and more than a little slipshod in his diction in those parts of the book which obviously interested him least. His gravest fault in style is a habit of using over and over again a cliché, either borrowed or of his own invention, and an occasional facetious turn of phrase which seems to come from habit rather than from thought. Someone in his youth must have told him about the sailor who said that he had had "beef, mutton and cheese—all the delicacies of the season" and this not very amusing conceit appears in all the books and more than once in several of them. His use of the catch-phrase, "we beg pardon," is even more frequent and quite as irritating. He writes of "Lucy Glitters—we beg pardon Mrs. Somerville," or "the kind of man—we beg pardon gentleman," as often as he uses his other favourite catch-phrase, "the order of the day." "Munch, crunch, munch was then the order of the day," is his usual descriptive phrase for a dinner or a hunt-breakfast and "Jog, jog, bump, bump, trot trot, was then the order of the day," serves for the field moving off from the meet.

He has, too, a persistent habit of describing any noise made by a man or an animal by an onomatopoeic word and repeating the word as often as the noise occurs and as long as it sounds. Horns always go "toot-toot," cats "mew-mew," and the wind "shoosh." And no character in the book can sneeze, cough, hiccup, smoke or make any kind of noise without its being painstakingly recorded. It is his most persistent and most wearisome habit, but scarcely less persistent is his fondness for calling his characters by names that personify their leading qualities—Sir Harry Scattercash, Mr. Bottleends the butler, Mr. Fleeceall the lawyer and their fellows. But it was the convention of the time and he adopted it—and having adopted it, rode it to death as he was apt to ride his conceits. He carried it to far greater lengths than did his contemporaries though they nearly all indulged in the same practice. (pp. 163-64)

Laboured and verbose as his descriptions are, there is no excuse for any reader of Surtees not knowing exactly what his characters looked like, or how they dressed. His descriptions of clothing are as accurate and detailed as his descriptions of persons. And his persuasiveness, his ability to make his readers see with his own eyes, is never more in evidence than when hounds are running. (p. 165)

No higher tribute can be paid to Surtees' persuasiveness than the fact that his hunting runs can be and are read with enjoyment by men who have never ridden to hounds nor even laid leg across a horse. Such runs as those with the Goose and Dumpling Hounds in **Hawbuck Grange,** the "Cat and Custard-Pot" day in **Handley Cross,** or the Calderlaw Common run with Mr. Facey Romford and the Heavyside Hunt are first-rate pieces of descriptive writing. To the hunting man there is the interest of seeing hounds work, the check and the cast, the final run into view. To the horseman there is the varied delight in the performance of the different horses, the chances of rail and water—a slower more detailed description than the whirlwind steeplechases of Nimrod and Whyte-Melville. But for the great mass of us who are neither hunting men nor horsemen there is the outstanding attraction of the fact that never throughout the run does Surtees lose sight of the men who follow the hounds.

It is noticeable, too, how his style alters when hounds are running, to match the speed and rhythm of the hunt. It becomes crisper and terser, the dialogue is in curt sentences, jerked out by breathless and excited men. Diffuse and verbose as he sometimes is in the less active parts of his writing, he prunes it of all but the barest necessities when the action calls for it. His style is in fact in the fullest sense what Quiller-Couch calls "appropriate." In the inn and the dining-room he is long-winded enough. But when the hounds break out of cover he rides his pen, in Mrs. Woolf's phrase, as gallantly as he rode his horse. "Slapdash and gentlemanly" she calls his style: and hunting is after all a slapdash and gentlemanly occupation.

The real strength of Surtees' style is in his dialogue and it is not too much to say that in this department of his art he surpassed his great contemporaries by as much as he came short of them in other ways. The great Victorians, with all their merits, were as a rule indifferent writers of dialogue. They seemed to ignore the fundamental fact that men and women in ordinary conversation do not talk coherent prose. Their characters could hardly say good-morning to each other without making a speech about it. (pp. 165-66)

But Surtees really did know how people talked. From the earliest discussion at the meet in the **Jaunts and Jollities** to the last talk in **Facey Romford** the books are crammed with dialogue of the very best sort—crisp, accurate, colloquial, amusing and above all natural. So many of the Victorians seem to have written not so much what their characters said as what they ought to have said. Their speech conveys their meaning clearly enough, but conveys it in the accents of the study, the lecture-room or the pulpit. They were hindered—as Surtees was never hindered—by the fact that the characters were bursting with the highest and most creditable of emotions and while their

reactions to the emotions are true and in character their expression of them is at its worst nothing but *oratio obliqua* enclosed in inverted commas. Few of Surtees' characters were troubled by creditable emotions, but still fewer of them are guilty of falseness of expression. He was usually writing comic dialogue which does not lend itself to pomposity except for the purpose of mocking it. (pp. 167-68)

There is no exaggeration in Surtees' dialogue, which is often at its best in the quieter passages. He is not obliged to force the comic relief since there is nothing in the books that needs relief, and so it follows that his characters are talking in their normal accents and at their normal level. There is no virtuosity in the dialogue itself. With the exception of Mr. Jorrocks, who was a humorist in word as well as in deed, there is hardly a character whose speech is worth quoting as purely humorous dialogue. It is too natural, too life-like. It is always the speech of characters, humorous in themselves, who have no need of verbal fireworks. (p. 168)

Whatever Surtees' faults as a stylist may have been he was never at a loss in reporting conversation. His accurate ear, his dislike of exaggeration and his keen sense of humour all helped him. They helped him to avoid the pitfalls that so many of his contemporaries fell into. His characters talk neither coherent prose nor over-forced comedy. They talk like the real people that they are. (p. 172)

Leonard Cooper, in his R. S. Surtees, *Arthur Barker Ltd., 1952, 180 p.*

JOYCE CARY   (essay date 1957)

[Cary contends that Surtees' greatest strengths as a novelist—his objectivity and candor—are best displayed in Sponge. *This essay was written in April 1957.]*

The special quality of Surtees seems to be quite ignored. I dare say this is because people think of him as a writer only for hunting fanatics, and, in fact, **Handley Cross,** with all the adventures of John Jorrocks, is a boring work. It was Surtees's *Pickwick* thrown together without any conception of form and with not a trace of Dickens's genius for humorous character.

Dickens's wildest grotesques live in their own right; we do not feel that Dickens has invented them; we shouldn't be surprised to meet them anywhere. Jorrocks is a mere invention and in a vein of humour completely dead; that mid-Victorian humour which astonishes us in mid-Victorian *Punch.* Who now could read *Mrs. Caudle's Curtain Lectures,* so famous in those days? Jorrocks is in the same style. Even that episode, so often quoted, where he is carousing with Pigg, the huntsman, and, fearing a frost, asks him what the weather is like, has gone flat. Pigg opens the cupboard door in mistake for the shutter and answers, 'Hellish dark, and smells of cheese'. It won't really bear repetition, as you see.

But Surtees after Jorrocks, like Dickens after Pickwick, did acquire a form, and **Mr. Sponge's Sporting Tour** is a masterpiece in its own way.... What is remarkable is the portrait not only of Sponge, but of the whole society in which he moves.

It is an extraordinarily tough society, without any of that self-consciousness which belongs to Hemingway's heroes. The men are tough as a matter of course, yet they are by no means cut to pattern. Look at that sporting nobleman Lord Scamperdale, Master of the Flat Hat Hunt, and his toady Jack Spraggon. Scamperdale is exceedingly tough. One realizes in him one puzzling feature of the Regency—how men of fine manner and classical education could also be thugs, going out to beat up aged watchmen for a joke. (p. vii)

Surtees's England is a century away from us; its peasantry are real peasantry and he describes them with the same fearless honesty that he brings to all his writing. He called them usually 'Chaw-bacons'. They are a poverty-stricken and brutalized race; he had no idea of romanticizing his moujiks. You see them as Goncharov saw his Zahar and Gogol his Petrushka, those two valet-serfs.

I don't know anybody except Surtees who gives this picture, or makes us feel so strongly what a good thing it is that in England we don't any more have a peasantry. Surtees does this without any political motive; he is not a propagandist; we trust him absolutely. Of course, he gives his own picture; he can't do anything else. *Mr. Sponge* is contemporary with Trollope's *The Warden,* and what different pictures it gives of a different England; all authentic to a feeling of the time and all complementary when we allow for the writer's purpose and preoccupation.

Surtees is brilliant not only with touts, lags, and shysters, he is a master at the snob and the climber. His social parasites are inferior only to Thackeray's. In one respect he can be better than Thackeray. Thackeray's Lord Steyne in *Vanity Fair* is a common cad; compare him with Disraeli's Monmouth in *Coningsby.* . . . [Monmouth] is as arrogant and selfish as you like, a complete egotist, but he has the grand style; he is not a vulgarian, and Surtees's Lord Scamperdale in his quite different surroundings has the same quality. He is a simple country squire without any of Monmouth's magnificence, but he is still as different from Steyne as that authentic nobleman. He is a tough, but he does not smell of the gutter.

Probably Surtees owes this success to that observant eye and candour of speech which is his chief force as a writer. He has no cant of any kind; he is sucking up to nobody and no class. He has his moral standards, but he is not trying to preach them; there is none of that sense that we have, even in Trollope, of the moralizer. Trollope's world and Trollope's moralizing were also typical of the time, but Surtees has in pre-eminence that quality—which belongs also to Michael Scott, the author of *Tom Cringle's Log* and another neglected master, not to speak of Gogol—of the *describer.* He writes of what he sees and knows, with a reckless sincerity especially refreshing in these self-conscious times.

I should think it would be almost impossible to read *Sponge* aloud; every second sentence has a broken back or tail, and the grammar is a mine of howlers. Neither does the man get on with the work. He stops at every corner, looks over every hedge. He will take half a page to tell you what some minor character is wearing, what he ate for breakfast. But this is just the charm of the work. (pp. viii-ix)

[There] are two kinds of novelists whose lack of form allows them a great deal of detail which is very close to reporting—which often, if we knew it, is almost certainly from direct observation. One is the slack novelist, filling out a chapter when he has run short of invention. Sergeant Bumptious in *Handley Cross* is such a piece of observation. And for me at least, he is better than Dickens's Buzfuz, founded on the same real person, a certain Sergeant Bompos, renowned for bombast. Bumptious is a rougher sketch of a cruder man, but he jumps out of the page and the scene while Buzfuz stays where he is put, as a comic character.

The other kind of novelist who achieves real life is the picaresque—Le Sage, Gogol, *Gil Blas* and *Dead Souls* are full of people so real that if you put them into a novel of formal construction it would have to be built round them. As secondary characters, if you fitted them in at all, they would steal the stage.

Surtees is not only a slack novelist, in *Sponge* he is also picaresque. He's licensed to stop anywhere and describe anything, or anyone, from a country house bedroom about 1850, with half a dozen different kinds of bath, to a spa dandy and his waistcoats. I defy any writer to beat Surtees on clothes. He gives us not only cut and colour, but fabric and quality, the very sewing. He takes a page to give us Sponge's hunting coat, with lapped seams on the outside, and it's not a word too much. That coat is more real to us than our own for the good reason that it is not only an historic coat, but a moral coat. It expresses Surtees's moral idea, his hatred of sham, pretension, the shoddy in man or clothes, with a force all the more telling in that he is probably quite unaware of it. His eye is on the coat, which certainly existed, and even the fact that he likes it has to be inferred.

Like the true picaresque, he does not deal much in admiration. Sponge is a swindler without a single redeeming virtue except perhaps his clothes and his nerve. Surtees gave him the clothes as the proper equipment of a swell mobsman and also a superb horseman. He could not bear to dress such a horseman in anything but the best. But the clothes are almost the only virtue he allows him and only Surtees would think of clothes as a virtue. Even Sponge's courage is the worst of its kind, the desperate gamble of a con-man. He is not only a crook but a mean crook who will cheat a servant. Among Surtees's gallery of lags, touts and shysters he is surpassed only by Facey Romford in *Mr. Facey Romford's Hounds,* who is an oaf as well as a crook and does not wash.

In this respect Gil Blas, even Gogol's Chichikov, is inferior to Sponge. He is done, in Henry James's phrase, to a turn. And this is Surtees's great virtue as a novelist. He never softens to a man; he never tries to catch a reader's sympathy for his worst, his meanest hero. He is objective to the last, like Flaubert, like Proust, and very unlike the later Thackeray.

It is again typical of the picaresque writer that his dialogue is so good. He is in no hurry to make it serve any purpose except the revelation of character. All Surtees is full of good dialogue in its special kind, like reported talk. Scamperdale and Spraggon are at their best in their smallest talk; it is as though we overheard them. We feel the very stuffiness of Scamperdale's den in their yawns and starts.

Surtees was himself a country squire from the deep North, the M.F.H. of a scratch pack. He had all the prejudices of his kind. He hated the fashionable places and people and smart society, he was suspicious of any kind of cleverness. He was prickly and hard, he had little compassion except for dogs and horses. He is pitiless to his victims. When Sponge and Spraggon unite to swindle and bully a wretched youth called Pacey, he records every detail of the latter's humiliation with the zest of loathing. Pacey was silly and weak and so despicable to him. Surtees prefers crooks to fools, because they are hard, because, as he thinks, they have no illusions.

Sponge is not a book for the sentimentalist, but for the man who likes to understand something of human nature in both its strength and weakness, especially in its power of creating, each man for himself, a complete ideal world, social and moral, and living in it.

Of Surtees's other novels **Mr. Facey Romford's Hounds** is not much inferior to **Sponge,** and Sponge reappears in it. The rest are tedious and flat to the general reader. To the social historian, on the other hand, they are of unique value. **Ask Mamma** and **Plain or Ringlets?** record mid-Victorian life as seen by a highly critical contemporary eye at a time when all the other novelists, even Thackeray, were sentimentalizing it.

Surtees lived through the biggest social revolution in [England] between 1066 and 1938. He was born into the Regency, Pierce Egan's London and the horse age; he describes the three days' journey from his home in Durham to London. He lived to see the railways everywhere, to travel as fast and easily as we do now, and to know a society for whom the Regency buck was not only a brute, but, more significantly, an aberration, a monster.

In Surtees's eyes probably the most striking change was the beginning of the family holiday for the middle class; tens of thousands on the move instead of the few hundred who alone, before the railway age and the excursion train, had been able to afford to travel farther than the county town or the village fair. He records the more superficial consequences: spas crowded with husband-hunting girls and city fops, town-bred rich men playing squire and sportsman, usually, he tells us, with a typical twist of prejudice, in the wrong clothes.

What struck him was not only the complete change in the character of fashionable seaside places like Brighton, but in the manners of the visitors. The place set out to cater for the crowd, and the visitors had quite other notions of amusement than the Regency bucks and their Harriet Wilsons, for whom the seaside was simply an Alsatia in which they could live openly with mistresses who had to be more discreetly entertained in London.

Surtees had not loved the bucks, but he still more detested the mobs, which seemed to him all that was vulgar. No doubt they were. Newly prosperous and newly emancipated people usually are so. They keep the competitive habit of mind which has brought them up in the world and think of society in terms of rivalry. Especially on holiday among strangers they set out to impress. In these mid-century years leading up to the Great Exhibition all industry was booming and the whole country was full of new rich. Surtees describes them, in mass and in detail, with the particularity of his disgust. But he also jibes at the smart gentry, and in their despite makes a hero of the grocer Jorrocks. (pp. ix-xii)

Mr. Sponge's Sporting Tour is solid Surtees; he comes through in every line. The reason is that he has no idea of striking any kind of attitude. He has no self-consciousness, as man or writer. He is not afraid of anybody and rolls no logs. To read him is to escape for an hour or two from eyewash and cant into an atmosphere as brisk as one of his hunting mornings, sharp and raw, highly unflattering to everything in sight, faces, hedges, trees, nibbled pasture and greasy plough, but thoroughly bracing. (p. xii)

> *Joyce Cary, in an introduction to* Mr. Sponge's Sporting Tour *by R. S. Surtees, Oxford University Press, London, 1958, pp. vii-xii.*

V. S. PRITCHETT (essay date 1964)

[*Pritchett, a modern British writer, is respected for his mastery of the short story and for what critics describe as his judicious,*

A portrait of Surtees.

reliable, and insightful literary criticism. In the excerpt below, he interprets Surtees' works as a protest against the snobbishness of the rising middle class in mid-Victorian England.]

Robert Surtees is a sport, in both senses of the term, who flashes in and out of the English novel, excites hope and reduces the critical factions to silence. He has all the dash, all the partiality and all the prospect of an amateur. There is a rush of air, a shower of rain drops from the branches, a burst of thundering mud, a crashing of hazel, the sight of a pink coat and, as far as the English novel is concerned, he has gone. In that brief appearance he has made the genial suggestion that all the other English novelists have been mistaken; they have missed the basic fact in English life—that we are religious, that our religion is violent sport. The unwritten life of a large proportion of the characters in English fiction is passed in playing or watching games in the open air; nature is being worshipped with the senses and the muscles. We are either bemused by fresh air or are daydreaming of some lazy, cunning and exhausting animal life in the open. In that condition, our hourly and sedentary habit of worry as a substitute for thought vanishes and we become people in love. It takes an amateur, like Surtees, to see an obvious thing like this and to exaggerate so that the part becomes the whole of English life. He was a north country squire, an excellent sporting journalist, but handsomely innocent of the future of hunting in England. He really thought that the Industrial Revolution would make the sport democratic! His assumption is that English violence can be appeased only by the horse. He is the final authority on our horse civilization, and Jorrocks is a sort of Don Quixote of the last phase of a brutal chivalry. (pp. 88-9)

It is natural that hunting people should admire Surtees. It is not surprising that serious literary critics should admire him also. He creates a complete world. It is the world which Fielding's and Thackeray's people knew in their off-stage lives. It has no relation with the feeble subculture of horse lovers, pony worshippers, or with the gentility of the jodphur that spread over England as the coach gave way to the railway, provoking the cult of the New Forest pony. The natural democrats of England live in the north and, though Surtees was a Tory squire, he sincerely believed that the horse was an insurance against the new, snobbish exclusiveness of the shot-up Victorian middle class. He imagined, as so many have done before, that class revolutions will not become snobbish and exclusive. Happy pastoral delusion! Surtees did not foresee either the hardness or the sentimentality of the coming urban England. Or, perhaps, he half guessed it. For the point about Jorrocks is that he is (1) not a horse lover but a fox lover, (2) that he rides, buys and sells horses, (3) that he has not an aitch to his name. He is, boldly, incontrovertibly, aggressively, in mid-nineteenth-century—a grocer. His fame is that he is not merely a sportsman, but a Cockney sportsman. He has all the trading sharpness and romanticism of a man who sells tea. Surtees is content (purposefully content) with this reality. Jorrocks is as vulgar as Keats; and, as a northerner and a gentleman, Surtees refuses to accept the improved accents of the new rich in the south. He exploits the rewards our class system offers to our literature. We are continually supplying a number of vulgar geniuses who stand out against the new snobberies which the Puritan streak in us is liable to create; and, in the case of Surtees, there is the anomaly that a Tory squire provides the vulgar protest. The heir of Jorrocks is Mr. Polly. Both are native protests against the mean and successful revolutions that deny the instincts of genial, sincere and natural men.

Surtees owes a lot to the low side of Thackeray and does seamy society a good deal better. His dialogue is as quick and true as the master's. He extends a robust and native tradition: the masculine strain of English comic writing. This comedy is broad and extraverted. It grins at the pleasures and pains of the human animal—if it is male—and has little time for the female. Occasionally Surtees sees a tolerable female, but very rarely. We need not suppose that he agreed with Jorrocks that a man ought to kick his wife out of bed three times a month, but we suspect this was only because he regarded the act wistfully as an ideal unfortunately unattainable. The fact is that our comic extraverts are like Mr. Sponge and bring a horse-dealer's eye to the consideration of women—"fifteen two and a half is plenty of height" for them. In its male world, the comic tradition likes the misfortunes of the body, the bruises, the black eyes, the drinking sessions, the gorging at table; prefers the low to the refined, the masterful and unreasonable to the sensitive and considerate. There is a strong regard for the impossible element in human character, for the eccentric and the obsessed. The brutes have their engaging moments. (They give the right kind of girls half a dozen smacking kisses.) But their transcendent emotions emerge in another direction. Jorrocks will quarrel with his huntsman, Pigg, but be reconciled, to the point of embracing him, at the kill. These people are dedicated. They will suffer anything, from drowning upwards, for their sport. They will experience an ecstasy which goes beyond the animal into the poetic. And, in the meantime, they will rollick. Thoroughly non-Puritan, they understand that

the life of animal pleasure is the life of animal dismay and they accept it. What these writers in the masculine comic tradition dwell on is the variety of human character. They know that action brings this out and, with a kind of mercy, they will forgive anything so long as action, not introspection, has revealed it. (pp. 89-91)

On the one hand, Surtees was a man of the eighteenth century—hence Thackeray's understanding of him; on the other, he was an amateur who dealt almost entirely with background figures, the great Jorrocks excepted. He was deeply knowing about English sporting life, the squirearchy and the law, but he did not construct the melodramas and elaborate plots of the other Victorian novelists, nor did he issue their moralizings. He often excelled them in the recording of ordinary speech and day-to-day incident. He is fresher than the masters, but he is artless. A good deal of his humor is the humor of shrewd sayings which, later on, we find in Kipling. His original contribution is in the field of invective. Surtees has a truly Elizabethan power of denunciation. Here is Jorrocks loosing off to his servant:

> "Come hup, you snivellin', drivellin' son of a
> lucifer-match maker," he roars out to Ben who
> is coming lagging along in his master's wake. . . .
> "Come hup, I say, ye miserable, road-ridin',
> dish-lickin' cub! And give me that quad, for
> you're a disgrace to a saddle, and only fit to
> toast muffins for a young ladies' boarding school.
> Come hup, you preter-pluperfect tense of 'um-
> bugs. . . . Come on, ye miserable, useless son
> of a lily-livered besom-maker. Rot ye, I'll bind
> ye 'prentice to a salmon-pickler."

This is all the more splendid because Jorrocks keeps to the "'ard road" as much as possible, and can't bear taking a fence. He is eloquent, perhaps because he is as cowardly as Falstaff and yet as sincere in his passion. He knows what he wants to be. His is the eloquence of romance. And this is where we come to the Dickensian aspect of Surtees, too. Dickens has several degrees of comic observation. There is the rudimentary Dickens of caricature, of the single trait or phrase turned into the whole man. And there is the Dickens where this is elaborated into soliloquy, in which the character is represented by his fantasy life. Like the rudimentary Dickens, Surtees has the feeling for caricature. *Handley Cross, Facey Romford's Hounds* and *Mr. Sponge's Tours* are packed with minor eccentrics of the field, the fancy and the law; but in Jorrocks, Surtees enters upon the more complex study of people who live out the comic orgy. "By 'eavens, it's sublime," says Jorrocks, watching the hounds stream over a hundred acres of pasture below him. "'Ow they go, screechin' and towlin' along just like a pock-etful o' marbles . . . 'Ow I wish I was a heagle." A "heagle" he is, in that moment; sublimity is his condition. He has shrewdly built up his pack, he has given his uproarious lectures, he has had his vulgar adventures in country houses; he has got the better of his betters and has outdone the new rich in vulgarity—making among other things that immortal remark about mince: "I like to chew my own meat"—he has disgraced Mrs. Jorrocks, but he has pursued an obsession utterly so that it has no more to teach him, beyond the fact that it has damaged his credit among the unimaginative in the City. Fortunately, Surtees has given him power of speech. Jorrocks is never at a loss for repartee or for metaphor. He is remarkable in his duels with Pigg, and the only pity is that Pigg's dialect is nearly incomprehensible. But Pigg and his master are well matched.

They battle like theologians about the true business of life: the pursuit of foxes.

Surtees is a specialist. But he is, to an important extent, outside his speciality. He had strong views about sport. He hated the drunkenness of sporting society and the old squirearchy. He hoped the new age would bring in something better. He was hostile to the literary conventions. His parodies of *Nimrod* show him as an opponent of literary snobbery. He disliked the obsequious regime of servants and the rogueries of the stable, the auctions and the law. It is odd that one so saturated in his world should have seen it all with so fresh an eye. Perhaps he had that morbidity of eye which is given to some men at the end of a period, when they can see things with the detachment which considerable art demands. He was too much the gentleman and amateur to construct a great novel; but he was independent enough and sufficiently instructed by obsession to create in Jorrocks a huge character who could go off and live an episodic life of his own. The Victorians were shy of Surtees's honesty. They were moving away from the notion that there was a level on which all Englishmen could be united. They were building the split culture of our time. Surtees was trying to save England on the acres of Handley Cross. (pp. 91-3)

> *V. S. Pritchett, "The Brutal Chivalry," in his* The Living Novel & Later Appreciations, *revised edition, Random House, 1964, pp. 88-93.*

CHARLES ALVA HOYT   (essay date 1967)

[*Deeming Surtees the best sporting writer in the English language, Hoyt argues that his subject matter has been both "a bane and a blessing" to his reputation. Hoyt also delineates the strengths and weaknesses of Surtees' art, focusing on his characterization.*]

Robert Smith Surtees is a neglected author to whom our century might very well look both for entertainment and instruction. To be sure Surtees . . . is a minor novelist, in the most accepted sense of the term: he is a specialist, a sporting writer, and the best in our language. Unfortunately that is where many of the anthologies leave him, on the tips of the tongues of doctoral candidates, from which bad eminence he is let fall, from time to time, into discussion.

Even these excursions must be rare for him today; young scholars on the prowl want material of greater "significance." And yet they would do well to remember Louis Kronenberger's description of Don Juan's adventures in England: "a stiff ride with the hounds after hypocrites and snobs; a long day on the moors bagging philistines and pharisees; a large coaching party clattering at the heels of politics." As Kronenberger suggests, sport to the British is not idle amusement, but their way of life. A British sporting writer then, if he is a good one, will have a great deal to say about his time. Surtees was the best, and his opinions of nineteenth-century British society are both wise and diverting: vigorous, unsparing, almost always highly critical. His irony is intense, his indignation warm, although he frequently melts into long passages of sheer fun, and nonsense, that sole delight among Victorian virtues. For these and other reasons he remains easy to read; I find him one of the most congenial of the nineteenth-century novelists.

His deficiencies are almost entirely in technique, and even there confined to few, if important, considerations. His style is rich, anecdotal, Dickensian. In his pervasive irony, however, he more resembles Thackeray, with whom he corresponded and sometimes consulted about his books. But even more than Thackeray he is ever the satirist, a fact which our textbooks too often ignore, although it was understood perfectly in his day. (pp. 59-60)

Surtees' chosen subject matter is at once a bane and a blessing: it requires a special knowledge and a special style, both of which I now propose to take up.

All of Surtees' novels are focussed squarely upon hunting, although some spend longer than others in coming to the subject, and some wander freely from it. I think we may set it down as an axiom that the more the books have to do with hunting, the better they are. It is not because Surtees is knowledgeable only upon the one subject, but, apparently, that he is happiest there. The young man who left the law to follow the hounds all over England, who resisted respectability for five years from his editor's desk, had but one great love in life. "'Untin is the foremost passion of my 'eart! compared with it all others are flat and unprofitable (cheers and laughter). It's not never of no manner of use 'umbuggin the matter, but there's no sport fit to hold the candle to fox-'untin'." Thus his alter ego, Jorrocks (**Handley Cross** . . .), the one major character in his fiction to whom we may say that he gave his wholehearted approval. (p. 64)

Surtees was one of the keenest foxhunters of a generation of eager sportsmen. In the course of his profession as touring writer he made himself familiar with every hunting country in England, just as a seasoned sportswriter today knows every city in the league. But much more than baseball is the American game, fox hunting was the sport of the ruling class in nineteenth-century England. It was in fact participated in by members of all classes, from the notorious hunting tailors and grocers of Surrey (Jorrocks was one such), representative of the middle class on the way up, to the sturdy farmers over whose fields the sport was pursued, and the common laborers themselves who frequently followed the hounds on foot. The foxhunter, as appears over and over again in the novels, was welcome everywhere. (pp. 64-5)

But just that strength of subject matter has proven Surtees' downfall in our day, when fox hunting is known to few and practiced by even fewer. If the popularity of the sport insured the hunting novelist a wide audience in the nineteenth century, whatever his faults, so its decay in the twentieth serves to keep him in obscurity in spite of his virtues.

So much for the special knowledge required; there is a similar difficulty involved with the special style. All arts have their mysteries, one of which is a sacred language. The sacred language attached to a lost art is rough going, and that is Surtees' problem in a nutshell. But here too is a positive side: there is such a thing as the fertile cliché. It exists on the outward circumference of style, where it is not only unavoidable but useful, comfortable, and reassuring. Anyone who enjoys baseball, or Baroque music, or literary criticism, must know what I mean. If Surtees suffers from the restrictions of his special language, he also enjoys the stability, security, and comfort it imparts to his style. Consider the following passage, chosen practically at random, and from one of the lesser works:

> Mr. Boggledike was again to be seen standing erect in his stirrups, yoiking and coaxing his hounds into Crashington Gorse. There was Dicky, cap-in-hand, in the centre ride, exhorting the young hounds to dive into the strong sea of gorse. "Y-o-o-icks! wind him! y-o-o-icks!

pash him up!'' cheered the veteran, now turning his horse across to enforce the request. There was his lordship at the high corner as usual, ensconced among the clump of weatherbeaten blackthorns—thorns that had neither advanced nor receded a single inch since he first knew them,—his eagle eye fixed on the narrow fern and coarse grass-covered dell down which Reynard generally stole. There was Harry Swan at one corner to head the fox back from the beans, and Tom Speed at the other to welcome him away over the corn-garnered open. And now the whimper of old sure-finding Harbinger, backed by the sharp ''yap'' of the terrier, proclaims that our friend is at home, and presently a perfect hurricane of melody bursts from the agitated gorse,—every hound is in the paroxysm of excitement, and there are five-and-twenty couple of them, fifty musicians in the whole! ''*Tally-ho!* there he goes across the ride!''

''*Cub!*'' cries his lordship.

''*Cub!*'' responded Dicky.

''*Crack!*'' sounds the whip.—

(*Ask Mamma* . . .)

And so ''the whole infuriated phalanx dashed across the ride,'' and off they go, out of our sight. The passage does not present any particularly interesting or unusual character, like Soapey Sponge or Jorrocks' huntsman, James Pigg. It varies in no important particulars from a thousand others in the sporting literature of the time: the technical terms, the affectionate Victorian circumlocutions—''our friend is at home''—''the veteran''—and the cast, as closely prescribed as in an Oriental drama: the Squire, the field, huntsmen, rustics, horses, hounds, fox.

The technical terms, unlike those of some crafts, are easy to master, and the circumlocutions and other assorted gewgaws of Victorian expression may as well seem quaint and charming to us as offensive, now that we have condemned them so utterly in our own fiction. As for the classic situation and its cast, I welcome them with the same affection that I might show a favorite piece of Baroque woodwind music. Indeed the whole passage seems to me like nothing as much as the imperative opening blast of a quartet by K. P. E. Bach, pregnant with good things to come, things which lose none of their value because one knows what they are to be.

Special pleas to one side, it becomes necessary to attempt some evaluation of Surtees' accomplishment as novelist. And immediately it must be said that he is deficient in one vitally important area—design. His weakness is the more noticeable, appearing as it does against the great strengths of many of his contemporaries, who surely have never been surpassed as systematic observers of human life. With Surtees, however, it is otherwise: he grasps situations with incisive wit and draws individuals brilliantly; but in the managing of large movements or character development he is rarely successful. *Ask Mamma,* for example, is very unsure in direction from the start, and *Hawbuck Grange* is little better than a pastiche of anecdotal fragments. In many of his better books, too, he is forced to take hold of the plot from time to time and wrench it into the direction in which he wishes it to go. The death of Jack Spraggon at the end of *Mr. Sponge's Sporting Tour* serves no purpose whatever that I can see, save to get him out of the way; similarly

the sudden good fortune that descends upon the hero of *Plain or Ringlets* seems nothing more than a last desperate measure to punish the mercenary women who have been misusing him.

Of these weaknesses Surtees himself was aware. In the preface to *Handley Cross* he says, ''The reader will have the kindness to bear in mind, that the work merely professes to be a tale, and does not aspire to the dignity of a novel'' [see excerpt dated 1854]. There is sarcasm there, perhaps, but self-knowledge as well. Before *Ask Mamma,* he writes, ''It may be a recommendation to the lover of light literature to be told, that the following story does not involve the complication of a plot'' [see excerpt dated 1858]. Certainly Surtees tended to counteract his weakness by slipping into the picaresque, which he does with great success in *Mr. Sponge's Sporting Tour.* ''Soapey'' Sponge, a delightful fraud and confidence man, but a keen sportsman, methodically works his way through one unsuspecting family after another on his tour, playing upon his well-to-do hosts' and hostesses' crassness and greed. Similarly, the movements of the hunt give a picaresque flavor to *Handley Cross* as well as to *Mr. Romford's Hounds,* whose hero, ''Facey'' Romford, is like Sponge a confidence man who fattens on the cupidity of his victims.

Subtlety, then, and sophisticated development, of plot, theme, or character, is not to be found here. But what a great deal else is! First of all, the wit and humor, the continuous crackle of exploded pretensions and hypocrises. Surtees has the columnist's feeling for situation. His perception may lack depth or scope, but the reader may supply these for himself if the author has but caught the situation accurately. At times Surtees apprehends it perfectly. (pp. 65-8)

[Surtees' characters] are all either wolves or sheep. There are, however, some exceptions; and exceptions do not make rules; they break them. The half-dozen lovable characters in Surtees' fiction, with all their faults, atone for whole legions of his mutton-headed squires, thieving servants, and rotten society women.

One of the most endearing characteristics of Surtees is that he loves a good rascal. Both Soapey Sponge and Facey Romford are crooks; they make a handsome living cheating respectable people. Yet he gives them nerve and stamina and flair—hunters' virtues. If they live on other people's money, they live with style. They are no Robin Hoods, however. Facey is in fact a considerable skinflint, as far as his own limited funds are concerned, and he is callous, insensitive, crude and ignorant to boot. Soapey is selfish, irresponsible, tactless and impertinent. Yet they can ride, and will ride, and nothing can stop them. Like their creator, they esteem nothing so much as fox hunting.

These men are at the head of Surtees' list of rogues. He has many, many more. A good Surtees novel begins with a hunt and a ball, a banquet and a by-day, and ends with a marriage, an election, or a bankruptcy. In between we have seen hunt society in action: the men trying to sell each other horses; the women, their daughters. This society, as I have suggested, is conceived of by Surtees and his time as including practically everybody. There are rich families looking for titles, titled families looking for riches; poor boys trying to pass themselves off as Earls, and poor girls posing as heiresses. The rich are too often proud, and the poor either envious or craven.

All these dinner parties and dances are in reality fine dressing for a primitive and rather ugly business: buying and selling innocent flesh, and it is a clear case of *caveat emptor.* The buyer is, in fact, almost always cheated, Surtees seems to say, because he has tried to purchase with money that which he should have sought out with an honest heart. If this statement makes Surtees a moralist, so be it. There is no other explanation for his constant attack on Victorian morality.

For it is the "respectable people" who lose, time and again, in every novel. Who wins? Jorrocks, but he is a presumptuous cockney and an unashamed bourgeois, a tea merchant held in disdain by the wealthy Mrs. Barnington and her set. Soapey Sponge and Facey Romford escape to Australia with whole skins and a bit of money after having led the gentry a pretty dance. But old Goldspink, the prosperous banker of *Ask Mamma,* is ruined in business in spite of all his cleverness.

These greedy respectable people are the legitimate prey of frauds, whether professionals like Soapey and Facey, or amateurs like "Fine Billy" Pringle, a harmless simpleton, the hero of *Ask Mamma,* who has somehow acquired a reputation as "the richest commoner in England." Of course he has next to nothing, but he lives very well at the expense of all the greedy mammas who would rather be humbugged ten times over than lose a good prospect to a rival.

Then there are the exotic frauds, like Prince Pirouetteza, the son of a Florentine dancing master, who turns up in *Plain or Ringlets* as house guest of the great Duke of Tergiversation, or Sir Moses Mainchance of *Ask Mamma,* the stock villainous Jew of fiction, wealthy and crass. Sir Moses, however, with the advent of his baronetcy, has embraced the principles of the Church of England. (pp. 72-3)

Then there are *nouveaux riches* like Willy Watkins of *Mr. Romford's Hounds,* "a good-looking fellow without any brains," who has fallen into money somehow in the never-never land Australia, and returned home with a horror of a wife, the sort "who would push her way if she could." There is a marriageable daughter, Cassandra Cleopatra, descended on her father's side of ne'er-do-wells, and on her mother's of deported felons. The Watkins family carries on a duel for honors with Mr. and Mrs. Hazey of a landed family of dubious character. And there are mountebanks and quack doctors—Sebastian Mello, the fastidious fraud of *Handley Cross*—and common cardsharpers—Johnny O'Dicey of *Plain or Ringlets*—all the jackals and kites who lurk at the edges of society. But we have had enough of them.

Truly good men and women are rare in Surtees, as in life, but worth the search. The parade of his characters in their ceaseless vanity reminds one of Hieronymus Bosch's painting, "The Hay Wain." There all mankind is represented as struggling forward in foolish dispute over an enormous load of straw which is rolling them straight to Hell, while far above all the scuffling and shouting two lovers dally, on top of the world as it were, protected from its nonsense by the purity of their emotion. Just so Surtees exempts from his indictment the honest sportsman, the rare man who forsakes worldliness for love. Such a one is Jovey Jessup; several times referred to in the canon, and fully portrayed in *Plain or Ringlets*: "a thorough sportsman and a hearty hospitable fellow." He keeps two cooks, "an Englishman to cook his beefsteak for breakfast, and a Frenchman to send up the fricandeau, etc., for dinner." When his digestion is threatened because of his unceasing dinners and drinking bouts, he does not become a recluse, but rather takes on a fellow to do his drinking for him, a Mr. Boyston who is thereafter known as Jovey Jessup's Jug.

Delightful as these two are, they are eclipsed by Jorrocks and his famous Scotch huntsman, James Pigg ("dinna call me a Scotchman, and keep thy bit bowdekite quiet—ar'll manish matters"). (pp. 74-5)

Hunting, hunting, is Jorrocks' life, but not his only life. Like other great men he plays many parts. Hunting is undoubtedly his preferred role, but Surtees brings him on so that we see him from every side of his imposing personality. In the early sketches we know him as a great merchant of London, an eccentric, already famous as a fox hunting enthusiast. *Handley Cross* brings him down to the country and into country society, as a Master of Fox Hounds—the apex of his ambition. Finally, in *Hillingdon Hall,* he buys an estate and establishes himself as a squire—Justice of the Peace and all. The book ends with his winning an election over the Marquis of Bray by two votes and going into Parliament.

It is Dick Whittington all over again. And indeed Jorrocks is precisely of that tradition, a tradition as honorable and old as London itself. He is the heir to those prosperous city merchants of the old drama, the "flat-caps" of Shakespeare's day who held firm to their principles although scorned by sprigs of quality. . . . Their liberality, their geniality, their prudence and good sense were at the heart of English prosperity, and the old playwrights knew it. Jorrocks is just such another. He has not an ounce of pretense or sham about him; when snobs patronize him by adding an order for tea to their correspondence about fox hunting, he dutifully fills the order before telling them to go to the devil. (pp. 76-7)

It seems to me that it is very much to Surtees' credit that he made this man the central figure of his fiction. . . . Although he has a good deal of fun with Jorrocks, he never patronizes him, no, nor betrays him, either. Whatever Surtees may have lacked as a novelist, it was not what is popularly called *class*.

And thus it is possible to say that he was not entirely disillusioned with his country either, for although he looked unflinchingly at its faults, he believed that in it a man like Jorrocks might still rise from a grocer's apprenticeship to great wealth, popularity in the highest circles, and finally to parliament. The parallels are by no means exact, but Surtees put a great deal of himself into Jorrocks: both were men absolutely devoted. This honest, unpretentious devotion, in both cases, justified and dignified its subject, and incidentally led both men, if we may judge by what Surtees' friends have written of him, away from shallowness and vanity into lives of decency, happiness, and merit. (pp. 77-8)

> *Charles Alva Hoyt, "Robert Smith Surtees," in* Minor British Novelists, *edited by Charles Alva Hoyt, Southern Illinois University Press, 1967, pp. 59-78.*

ALEX HAMILTON   (essay date 1968)

[*In his introduction to* Jorrocks, *Hamilton praises Surtees' creative powers yet suggests that he remains a minor figure among nineteenth-century English novelists because he never fully developed his literary talents.*]

The intransigence of Surtees's sporting heroes lies midway between the utter recklessness known as 'bottom' of eighteenth-century bloods, and the baying for broken glass of Evelyn Waugh's bloody-minded aristocrats. Which is not to say that Surtees would have had patience with either of these terrible manifestations of the petted English male ego—he is saved from the worst excesses of the squirearchy by his lack of com-

Mr. Sponge at Jawleyford Court, illustrated by Leech.

petitive spirit. He might have been disturbed by the threats to the landed interest, as evinced in the move to repeal the Corn Laws—indeed he never wholly repudiated the suggestions of friends that he should involve himself directly in the battle at Westminster—but at the worst he imagined the corruption of a way of living: the prospect of total dispossession can never have occurred to him. And that maudlin sense of not being wanted by the State which crept throughout contemporary Romantic European literature was as remote from him and his concerns as today J. B. Priestley is from the flower people. Somewhere here one must begin to look for the explanation of his finally disappointing his admirers, for with all his exuberance, comic invention, wonderful ear, instinctive sense of an audience and vast experience of the sheer friction caused by the irregularities of character, with everything that should have given him parity on the shelf with Dickens, there is no growth. He never got his whole weight behind his literary talent. He is the darling of a specialist readership, but even within the narrow scope of the English nineteenth-century novel, he remains a minor figure.

The very manner of his first entry on to the literary scene already whispers both the charm of his personality and his ambivalence towards the matter of exploiting it. Tucked in towards the end of the third number of *The New Sporting Magazine,* published in July 1831, which Surtees himself founded and edited, appears a sketch entitled **"A Day with the Surrey,"** by 'A Yorkshireman'. The Yorkshireman hasn't trotted five paragraphs before he's notched a specimen for *The Oxford Dictionary of Quotations*: 'Every man shouting in proportion

to the amount of his subscription', and for thirty-three more years this eccentric, obsessed fellow plied his own lonely covert of literature, sparking off quotable stuff from horses and dogs and the retinue who follow, to borrow another quotation, 'the sport of kings'. . . . Everything Surtees wrote was for magazine publication, usually in serialized form, with the result that his works have the flavour of social occasions, and the difference between one and another is as much, or as little, as that between dancing with one partner all evening, and playing the field. (pp. vii-viii)

The coherence of Surtees's fictional world is established by the unquestioned assumption of every character in it that, while breath can be drawn, he must somehow keep up the pace. If the reader cannot see the presence of this human motive as proper to contriving the death of a fox, the vitality of Surtees's writing will seem to him spurious and even offensive. If he accepts it, he has a mount which will take the obstacles (a certain repetitiousness, plus a mass of arch allusiveness to points of reference rubbed out by time) and hack along comfortably through the barren country. 'Horses and intellects go a racing pace' wrote a Regency versifier—the fork in the road which would take one to the gymkhana and the other to the railway station lay still some way ahead. In Surtees's time horses and intellects were, if not symbiotic, at least at ease with one another. (pp. ix-x)

The Surtees hunting world binds together in good fellowship (whose only prescription is that if they drink water it is 'for the purpose of bringing their stomachs round to stand something stronger') an astonishing variety of characters, and it is exclusive of only one important (which some may think fatal) element: women. (p. xi)

In Jorrocks's view women exist to be kicked out of bed a couple of times a month, and to have the leg of mutton done to a turn at five o'clock sharp. But there is no use in repining over missed opportunities in Surtees's work—he has to be seen like one of those touchy, eccentric innkeepers who are so fond of their own cooking that they serve dinner without ever thinking to offer their guests any choice from a menu. (p. xii)

[Surtees's published works do] not make a very long list of titles, but still it is enough to evoke from those who have read the books an echo of the criticism made by the *Morning Post* of his redoubtable rival, Nimrod, when it printed the opinion that his style was so excellent it was a pity he did not interest himself in something more important than sport. But of course not a few million Englishmen since, confronted with this comment, would instantly have retorted that Nimrod and Surtees alike could at least see what was in front of their noses, unlike most pen-pushers, and that there is nothing more important than sport. It is in this particular, his emphasis on an activity which gives no obvious rewards to the participant, that Surtees really claims gratitude for a valuable insight. He wrote eight novels, all but two of which (*Plain or Ringlets?* and *Ask Mamma,* which spread the jollifications as far as general Victorian amusements, and weddings) are ramifications of the interests expressed in his first novel. *Handley Cross* and *Mr Sponge's Sporting Tour* . . . are undoubtedly the big ones, and one cannot help regretting the fact that he died in 1864 at a time when he was planning one more on this scale, with the modest title of *Sporting and Social Recollections.* (pp. xiv-xv)

One of the anomalies of English literature is the little attention that has been given to sportsmen as heroes. Of late some investigations into the possibilities have been made by novelists, who have returned with strong stories and dismal conclusions about their subjects. They may seem to indicate that Surtees's hopes were misplaced—there is no release from pettiness in a sporting life. It appears the pressures move naturally away from democratization of the athlete. But it is always worth keeping Surtees in mind when making such forays. What he is saying through Jorrocks is that the sportsman may be oddly shaped, the rhythm of his life matched to a metronome in his guts, the weather may be terrible, the terrain dotted with hostile figures, the mount be a spavined nag, and the fox when found turn out to be a rabbit, but that if he has had a run at all the day has been worth while, and in the midst of rueful contemplation of disaster the participants know something screened from the onlooker—things may turn out better tomorrow and today's experience will then add immeasurable spice to the triumph. (p. xv)

> Alex Hamilton, in an introduction to Jorrocks' Jaunts
> and Jollities *by Robert Smith Surtees, edited by Herbert Van Thal, Cassell, 1968, pp. vii-xv.*

BONNIE RAYFORD NEUMANN　(essay date 1978)

[*In this analysis of* Hawbuck Grange, Young Tom Hall, Ask Mamma, Plain or Ringlets?, *and* Mr. Facey Romford's Hounds, *Neumann traces the development of Surtees' art, examining how he experimented with plot, structure, narration, characterization, and theme.*]

"To beguile an idle hour" must have been Surtees's primary reason for writing [*Hawbuck Grange* (see excerpt dated 1847)];

his secondary reason was to provide a kind of memorial to November 1846, "the worst hunting November that perhaps ever was known." . . .

Certainly to write a successful novel covering only one month's time would require a great deal of skill and planning. One would expect to find a strong central character in whom the reader is truly interested, a plot of some complexity that can be developed quickly and concisely and brought soon to a climax, a cast of supporting characters who are easily identifiable and essential to the story, a careful control of time, including a discriminating use of flashbacks. *Hawbuck Grange* has none of these. (p. 80)

It is intriguing to speculate why, after three novels bursting with Jorrocks, Surtees created Tom Scott as the hero of his fourth book. Perhaps he merely desired a change; perhaps he wanted to find out if he could write successfully about another kind of person, far different not only from Jorrocks but also from all the minor characters in his earlier novels. Or perhaps he was reacting to outside influences—none of the earlier novels had been particularly successful, and . . . he might have hoped a Tom Scott would prove more to the public's liking. (pp. 80-1)

"Surtees apparently decided to have a normal human being for a hero for once," writes Cooper, but if Tom Scott is "normal," then the majority of the human race must be very dull. Siegfried Sassoon goes even further. "I have a special affection for Thomas Scott," he writes, "since he is one of the few unquestionably likeable characters in Surtees, charming, sensible and modest, and—in my opinion—the nearest to a self-portrait in his works." The very fact that *Hawbuck Grange* exists at all is sufficient refutation of Sassoon's identification of a self-portrait—Tom Scott lacks both imagination and ambition to undertake a novel, except perhaps in fireside musings, and to complete not one but eight novels and several other works besides is entirely beyond his capacity. Besides, Surtees—with his wife and three children, his financially successful country estate, his numerous positions of responsibility in his community, his political involvement and local lectures, his fighting on behalf of his poorer neighbors and inmates of workhouses, his connections with the literary world—was actively and intimately involved with life. Poor Tom Scott could not even manage to get himself married! . . . Surtees was *not* a Tom Scott, and the world is a much happier place for it. (p. 81)

Fortunately *Hawbuck Grange* has more to offer than one main character; it is essentially a collection of hunting episodes. . . . It is primarily the framework for these sketches that is weak, for once Surtees is in the middle of a chase his writing is every bit as good as it was in *Handley Cross.* (p. 84)

Good and numerous as the hunting scenes are, however, they cannot, unsupported, carry the novel, and *Hawbuck Grange* has little more to offer. In fact its defects quite overshadow its good points. For one thing, Surtees carried further in this novel his experiment in author-intrusion which he started in *Hillingdon Hall.* Perhaps he had Sterne's *Tristram Shandy* in mind as a model; unfortunately, he lacked Sterne's genius, and the result is complete confusion between Tom Scott's story and the author's digressions, between the third person and the first, between the present and the past. Sometimes these digressions are meant to be educational, as when he points out that "good farming is certainly a great promoter of hunting" . . . , or "wet is not indispensable to scent" . . . , or "a horse's coat furnishes a pretty good criterion of the state of the atmosphere'' . . . , or even when he insists that ''there is nothing makes a person look so queer as an extremely long frock or greatcoat.'' . . . Other times he pauses to carry on a conversation with the reader, much in imitation of Sterne. Chapter nine, for example, begins in this distracting way: '' 'WHO-OOP!' 'Who-oop! That's a queer way of beginning a chapter, Mr. Author!' 'So it is, Mr. Reader, but you'll have a good many more of them before you are done'.'' . . . Sterne's great antinovel is composed entirely of such literary devices; unfortunately Surtees's few sorry attempts irritate the reader rather than amuse him. (pp. 85-6)

. . . . .

Surtees never finished [*Young Tom Hall*]. He couldn't bring himself to abandon it altogether though, and he tried to restore it in bits and pieces by using many of the same characters and incidents in his next two novels. Such patchwork is seldom successful, however, and in *Ask Mamma* and *Plain or Ringlets* it is extremely disappointing. *Tom Hall* was on its way to being one of Surtees's best novels; those two which succeeded it and were made up in part from it are among his worst.

Young Tom Hall is something of a departure for Surtees, for in it one sees him gradually drawing away from the hunting field and focusing his attention more and more on the non-hunting element of country society. His next two novels continue the trend and can be appropriately classified, as they are by Ms. Hallgarth, ''fashionable parodies'' as opposed to sporting fiction. The most noticeable difference between the two types of novels is the difference in their main characters, for rather than being true and enthusiastic sportsmen, these men use the hunting field merely to gain social advantage. In fact, of the four heroes in these three books, two of them, Tom Hall and Billy Pringle, genuinely hate to hunt, a third, Jack Bunting, knows virtually nothing about the sport in the beginning but gradually becomes initiated and enthusiastic before the end of the novel, and a fourth, Jasper Goldspink, never hunts at all! (pp. 103-04)

[*Young Tom Hall*] is fast-moving and genuinely interesting. The male characters are all types new to Surtees, and he obviously enjoyed them. All his characters here carry that distinguishing Surtees mark of individuality, of somehow being larger than life, more real than real people. The novel abounds with jovial humor of the kind found in the early Jorrocks books and in *Mr. Sponge*. His satire, although of a slightly different focus, is good-natured and well-balanced between standard Surtees sporting types such as Lord Heartycheer and new satirical subjects such as old ''sivin and four's elivin'' Hall and the Heavysteed Dragoons. . . . Tom has one advantage that Surtees's next few heroes do not have—he is a completely sympathetic character. As physically unattractive and slow-minded as he is, he is the one innocent, unambitious person in the novel, and for that reason alone the reader is entirely on his side.

Altogether, *Young Tom Hall* is a novel which the reader does not like to see interrupted; he really wants to find out what happens to Tom Hall and his engagement to Angelina and his new flirtation with Laura Guineafowle and to Angelina's ''second string,'' the little soldier called ''Jug.'' He has not yet begun to tire of any of them. Sincerely wishing to know how a novel ends is perhaps the highest tribute a reader can pay to an author, but in this case he is doomed to frustration, for the

next two books, far from carrying on either the story or the fun of *Young Tom Hall,* are very sorry affairs indeed.

. . . . .

Ask Mamma is an obvious offshoot from the preceding novel; Lord Heartycheer reappears as Lord Ladythorne, still seventy years old and still hunting both fox and young ladies; Dicky Thorndyke becomes Dicky Boggledyke, huntsman to his Lordship in fields both of sport and of romantic conquest; Major Guineafowle is Major Yammerton, still hunting hare ''five and twenty years without a subscription''; Angelina Blunt reappears as the international coquette Miss de Glancey. . . . (pp. 108-09)

Most interesting, however, are the similarities and differences between the heroes of the two novels, for although Billy Pringle is obviously based on Tom Hall, the two men appear to the reader as entirely different persons, and the novels succeed or fail to the extent that these characters capture the reader's interest and concern. Just as old Tom Hall balances his accounts and declares that ''our Tom shall be a gent!'' so old William Pringle exclaims, ''Our Billy shall be a gent!'' Old Hall's definition of a gentleman, ''a man with plenty of money and nothing to do,'' applies as well to Billy as it does to Tom. Billy, just as much as Tom, lacks any self-motivation, any direction except that imposed on him by others. In fact, the only basic difference between the two characters is their size, for Billy Pringle is slender rather than fat, handsome in a pampered way rather than grotesque, and from that change in the physical appearance of the main character arises a vast difference in the reader's acceptance and interpretation of him. For instance, when Tom affects the ''swell'' he is completely ludicrous. No matter how showy his clothes or tight his new hunting boots, the reader always sees him as he is first introduced, ''disporting himself on three chairs in the bay-windowed coffee-room of the Salutation Inn.'' As a ''round, fat, humming-top-shaped'' man ''upon whose plump limbs the flesh wobbled and trembled'' as he walks, Tom Hall is a perfect victim—the reader sympathizes with him because he has known and sympathized with fat people in real life. While it is true that the stereotype of the naive fat boy is offensive and even cruel, nevertheless it is this very stereotyping that saves Tom as a character, for the reader can accept him and even approve of him on the one-dimensional basis in which he is presented. But take away Tom's size and one has Billy Pringle, a very sad main character indeed.

While Tom is a reluctant social climber, his financial condition, parents, and friends urging the role upon him, Billy Pringle is a ''swell'' of the first order. Whereas Tom's actions, however absurd, have an air of naturalness about them, Billy is Paris-trained to play the snob. Another difference between them is that while Tom's money is real, Billy's is primarily a matter of reputation. Billy's entire character is a vast pretense, and the reader dislikes him immediately. (pp. 109-10)

This sadly disappointing character Billy Pringle is symbolic of the inferiority of *Ask Mamma* to Surtees's earlier works, including *Young Tom Hall.* For one thing, the satire here has a different flavor. Watson calls it ''bleak,'' Hallgarth says it has a ''bitterness'' of tone, and Cooper states that the novel has ''little geniality.'' The new direction of Surtees's satire was already obvious in *Tom Hall,* but in that novel Surtees retains enough of his former successful character types and humorous situations to make a good novel. Here the satire is more limited, more clichéd, and often preachy. The primary difference, again, lies in the differences between main characters, for Tom Hall provides *Young Tom Hall* with a center of focus that *Ask Mamma* lacks. The reader cares about Tom, and this quality of caring raises him above the mere caricature, the butt of laughter, the

Guests dancing the polka at the hunt ball in Ask Mamma, *illustrated by Leech.*

pawn of satire. Although he is far from being a Jorrocks or a Sponge, he is sufficiently honest and natural to represent Surtees's satiric norm; he is the center of consciousness with which the reader identifies to watch and laugh at the absurdities around him. Such is not the case with Billy Pringle. If anything, Billy epitomizes everything Surtees could not stand, and, because he is allowed no redeeming characteristics, the reader cannot stand him either. Consequently he becomes the object of satire rather than the satirical norm, and the soul of the novel is gone; there is no chink in the satirical armor through which the reader can enter and view Surtees's world from inside. There is no John Jorrocks to laugh with, no Soapey Sponge to connive with, no Tom Hall to cheer for. The reader is kept emotionally outside the action while the *nouveau-riche* world of "swells" and hypocrites and social climbers and jealous, possessive, self-satisfied, petty people, led by Billy Pringle himself, are paraded before him. The parade, from this distance, soon becomes obvious, repetitious, and dull. One gets the feeling that Surtees himself did not enjoy it anymore. (p. 112)

But the greatest part of the problem with this novel lies with Surtees—never before had he written with such hesitation, such insecurity. One can find whole chapters that add nothing whatever to the book: "The Major's Stud," "Cards for a Spread," "Commerce and Agriculture." On the occasion of Lord Ladythorne's hunt breakfast, the kind of scene in which Surtees usually excels, he deadens it with entirely too much detail; instead of highlighting the most interesting aspects, he describes *every* guest, *every* costume, *every* serving dish, *every* particle of food, *every* bit of conversation within the hearing of Billy or Ladythorne. . . . Even the best-intentioned reader finds himself skimming and flipping pages.

Worse yet are Surtees's constant, irritating intrusions into the novel with tidbits of irrelevant information. One could make an extensive list of such things: "Posterity will know nothing of the misery their forefathers underwent in the travelling way" . . . ; "Some people can eat at any time, but to a well-regulated appetite, having to undergo even the semblance of an additional meal is inconvenient"; . . . "Let any man of forty look at his tailor's bill when he was twenty, and see what a liberality of innocence it displays" . . . and so on and on and on. Surtees had already experimented with this technique . . . in *Hawbuck Grange;* here it gets entirely out of control. (pp. 117-18)

It is impossible to ascertain for sure just what happened to Surtees in [*Ask Mamma* and *Plain or Ringlets*], although most critics put the blame for their lack of success on the interruption of *Young Tom Hall.* There Surtees had a fine novel underway; when he was abruptly forced to abandon it, he floundered. If he could have brought himself to finish it, even with its greatly reduced chance of publication, he might have avoided this inspirational hiatus. As it was, instead of waiting for a new idea, he grabbed at what he had—a character here, a scene there—and tried to lump them together into some kind of whole, losing sight in the process of both his satirical direction and his reader. The effort was fruitless. Not only does the novel fail, but so does something else—Surtees's heretofore excellent critical judgment, for he plunged immediately into another such novel, salvaging what he could of the rest of *Young Tom Hall.*

. . . . .

Plain or Ringlets is unique among Surtees's works for one reason—of the three main characters, characters who among them provide the novel's points-of-view, one is a woman, Miss Rosa McDermott of Privett Grove. While it is true that in other works Surtees may present a woman in an important role, Mrs. Flather in *Hillingdon Hall,* for example, or Lucy Glitters Sponge in *Mr. Romford's Hounds,* such women are still completely dominated in literary terms by the novels' heroes, John Jorrocks and Facey Romford. Such is not the case in *Plain or Ringlets,* where Rosa plays an equal part with Jasper Goldspink and Jack Bunting, the other two corners of the love-triangle. None of the three is a pleasing character; in fact, to characterize their relationship as a "love-triangle" is misleading, for the only real love they are capable of feeling is for themselves or for someone else's money. Rosa speaks for all three when, warned by her lawyer not to marry hastily, she laughs, "Oh, you needn't be afraid of me, Mr. Ballivant! You needn't be afraid of me, I'm not one of the sentimental sort." This novel, like its predecessor, is constructed of bits and pieces of *Young Tom Hall* carelessly thrown together with picnics and regattas and races and grand balls.... Here Surtees moves even farther from the sporting toward the social novel, for all the interest here centers around the marriage market, around the question of who will end up married to whom. Again Surtees makes the mistake of presenting no sympathetic character, no satirical norm against which to measure the absurdities of the rest of society. In fact, his main characters here are perfect examples of those kinds of people whom Surtees himself most disliked. (pp. 118-19)

Although *Plain or Ringlets* is not a successful novel, it is, however, an extremely important source of social history and of information about the ideas and feelings of Surtees. Instead of those irritating one and two sentence digressions that permeated *Ask Mamma,* in this novel Surtees devotes entire chapters to discussing various aspects of Victorian life, frequently comparing what he sees around him with conditions he knew as a young man. (p. 124)

. . . . .

Although *Handley Cross* and *Mr. Sponge's Sporting Tour* have always been Surtees's most popular books, *Mr. Romford's Hounds* is in many ways a better novel, most obviously because it has two features which all Surtees's earlier novels lack: a new, more human hero, and Surtees's *only* fully drawn, realistic female character.

Although Facey Romford is another of Surtees's great hero-villains, he is neither so arrogant as John Jorrocks nor so self-assertive as Soapey Sponge. While it is true that he takes advantage of the coincidence concerning his name and trades upon the borrowed Romford crest, he never actually *tells* anyone he is the other Romford—he simply lets other people draw the wrong conclusions and does nothing to correct them. As Surtees insists, when a wealthy bachelor, a man who is a fine huntsman and giver of grand parties, is in question, people are every bit as willing to be deceived as Facey is to deceive them. He never pushes himself into people's homes, as Sponge does, or takes advantage of their friendship, as Jorrocks tends to do. Even the questionable horse deals in which he participates are not initiated by him; he merely accepts the offers other people make. If those offers happen to be ridiculous, they are not his responsibility. He simply wants to be able to live comfortably, lamb chops and batter pudding constituting his favorite meal. He has no social pretension; he rents Beldon Hall unseen simply because it is available, and his first sight of so much grandeur genuinely dismays him. (pp. 134-35)

Unlike Soapey Sponge, who hunts primarily to show off a horse he wants to sell, Facey lives to hunt, and the social and economic responsibilities incumbent on a master of hounds are simply to be endured. He would much rather stay at home in the evening with his pipe and a bottle of Lovetin's gin than face a dinner party; in fact, if it were not for Lucy's nagging he probably would never have gone out at all. (p. 135)

Facey has little in common with Jorrocks and even less with that pushier version of Jorrocks, Soapey Sponge. He would rather die than deliver a "sporting lector," rather leave the country than impose himself on a Duke of Donkeyton. The very idea of running for public office would give him nightmares. He values his privacy much too dearly to surrender it to the Puffingtons, Crowdeys, and Scattercashs of the world, even in exchange for free room and board. On the other hand he is certainly a far cry from the innoculous Tom Scott, the dumb Billy Pringle, or the dandy Jack Bunting. He is a new kind of hero for Surtees, an individual, a believable human being, more low-key than Jorrocks and more likable than Sponge, further from a stereotype than any he had yet produced. (p. 136)

[Surtees's] treatment of women as characters in his novels has earned him severe criticism from every person who has written about his work. Not until Lucy Glitters in *Mr. Romford* did Surtees create a woman character in any depth; even more serious, not until Lucy Glitters did Surtees present or even mention women for any purpose other than to demean them or to laugh at them. (p. 138)

Surtees certainly fell victim over and over again to the most degrading of female stereotypes, for all of his women except Lucy Glitters Sponge are two-dimensional and easily categorized. Among his major female characters there are just two types—the marriage-minded "mamma" trying to sell her offspring to the highest bidder (Mrs. Flather, Mrs. Trotter, Mrs. McDermott, and Mrs. Jorrocks with her niece Belinda, as well as that most famous mother of all, Mrs. Pringle) and the marriageable daughter who is perfectly willing to be sold for the best settlement (Emma Flather, Angelina Blunt, Rosa McDermott, Cassandra Cleopatra Watkins, Anna Maria Hazey). Although these are obviously stereotypes, at least Surtees allows them to play conspicuous roles in his works; all his other women are not only stereotypes but also so constricted in their presentation that they never rise above a caricature. Women servants are dirty, lazy thieves. Young girls, while sometimes physically attractive, are always superficial and fickle with minds obsessed with marriage and clothes; in fact, they are never allowed to think one thought not directly connected with those two subjects. Once the girls are married they turn into shrews just like their mothers.

Women are, in other words, a nuisance. They perpetuate conversation at the dinner table when the men want to stuff themselves in peace and quiet; they wear crinolines and hoop-skirts that fill up the inside of a carriage, leaving no room for the men; they insist on having a new dress once in a while. Only one male character, the Marquis of Bray in *Hillingdon Hall,* does not breathe a sigh of relief when the women retire to the drawing room after dinner—in fact, "not being a great man for his liquor" he actually sneaks away from the table and joins them! But then Surtees makes clear that there is some question about the Marquis's masculinity anyway, referring to him as "the butterfly Marquis" and asserting that "Nature meant the Marquis for a girl, and a very pretty one he would have made." After all, no one "of the breeches, at least *le-*

gitimately of the breeches,'' would have acted in such a manner.

It would not be valid to argue that Surtees was writing satire and was, therefore, just as hard on the men. He was not. While it is true that many of his male characters are obviously satirical caricature or ''humour'' characters, even they show more variety and more believable human qualities than do any of his women. In fact, all characters with any imagination, any integrity, any sensitivity, even any intelligence, are men. . . . It would not be surprising if all Surtees's female readers, after such a display as this, would agree with Lucy who ''often said that the only thing that reconciled her to being a woman was, that she could not by any possibility have to marry one.'' . . . (pp. 139-40)

Then suddenly, with this kind of record in the presentation of women, Surtees, in his last novel, came up with a Lucy Glitters Sponge Somerville Sponge. What a delight and what a relief! She is everything the most ardent feminist of today could ask for. She is strong, independent, and hard-working. When the cigar store is in jeopardy and her husband completely irresponsible she goes on trying to make it work. When Sponge runs off the quietly salvages what she can for herself and retires to suffer in private whatever feelings of anger or sense of loss may assail her. She is beautiful and proud of her beauty in the best sense—she dresses well because it makes her feel good about herself; she accepts admiration gracefully but never demands it. She is genuinely fond of Facey and manages, because of her attachment and endless patience, to civilize him. She supports her mother and entertains her friends in style. She is aware of all the stereotypes usually associated with her sex and uses them, sometimes necessarily and sometimes for fun—she can be the coquette or the little girl or the nagging wife or the dumb blonde when assuming those roles will get her what she wants or protect herself or Facey from exposure. Underneath that pretty, feminine exterior she is as intelligent, independent, and tough-minded as any person can be. (p. 140)

All things considered, *Mr. Romford's Hounds,* Surtees's last book, is also his best. It has more structure, more plot, than any of the others. It has genuine suspense created by the assumption of false identities which the reader knows will have to be uncovered. Its hunting scenes have all the color and excitement of those of *Handley Cross* and the ''wheeling and dealing,'' if less prominent, is every bit as clever as in *Mr. Sponge.* Those intimate details of Victorian life, from the discomforts of the ''melon-frame'' buggy to the dingy bedrooms, from the elaborate dinners to the smoky candles, from the glorious dress to the filthy servants, were never better represented. In contrast to the last three novels particularly, the humor has lost its bitterness and the satire its maliciousness. Facey Romford and Lucy Glitters outshine all Surtees's earlier characters. Perhaps his turning from fiction to autobiography was evidence of his own satisfaction, his recognition that he had reached a plateau, that all those characters and methods that he had been experimenting with over the last thirty-three years, ever since the first Jorrocks story appeared in the *New Sporting Magazine,* had finally come together and worked just right. (pp. 141-42)

Bonnie Rayford Neumann, in her Robert Smith Surtees, *Twayne Publishers, 1978, 165 p.*

One of Leech's illustrations for Mr. Facey Romford's Hounds.

VIRGINIA BLAIN (essay date 1981)

[In her introduction to Sponge, *excerpted below, Blain explains how Surtees "is truly unique" among the minor novelists of the Victorian era.]*

Surtees's claim to our consideration does not rest upon his membership [in] a peculiarly English club, the sporting writers, but springs from his unusual ability to bridge the distance between that exclusive set and the larger world of mid-nineteenth century fiction. In *Mr. Sponge's Sporting Tour* Surtees united two literary traditions which had otherwise remained distinct; sporting writing on the one hand, and the satiric comedy of manners on the other. In this way he created a "kind" of novel that was quite unique.

Although his name has from time to time been linked for comparison with Trollope and Dickens, the writer with whom Surtees had most in common was Thackeray. . . . (p. ix)

Mr. Sponge's Sporting Tour is far from being an imitation of *Vanity Fair*, although that novel certainly provided a model of the anti-romanticism which characterized Surtees's own outlook. Surtees does have faults as a writer, but lack of originality is not one of them, and he is in many ways more tough-minded than Thackeray. No one could accuse him of sentimentality: he views the world through a shrewdly observant eye, mercilessly exposing affectation and hypocrisy, and extracting the most extraordinary amounts of information with a glance which apparently embraces only the surface. Nuances of dress are unerringly described in such a way as to pinpoint not only a character's sartorial habits and social class, but his or her personal history, moral standpoint and personality.

Because he was writing chiefly to amuse, he was careful to avoid "the inner chambers of the heart" in his own work and of course this limits his depth. But his range takes us far afield, and it is refreshing as well as instructive to be given such a knowledgeable "tour" of many important but too often neglected aspects of English rural society in the mid-nineteenth century. How did landowners, great and small, occupy themselves during a bleak country winter, for instance? Mr Sponge may indeed be a "characterless character" in more senses than the moral one, but the story of his progress in the gentle art of sponging provides his creator with unlimited opportunities for answering questions like this, and at the same time exposing pretensions and follies across all classes. Lord Scamperdale, the fox-hunting fanatic with such a splendid line in sub-blasphemy ("because I'm a lord and can't swear"), is treated with just as much ironic detachment and good-humoured mockery as Peter Leather, the intrepid groom who looks after Mr Sponge's alarming set of hired horses. One of Surtees's great advantages as a satirist of snobbery was that he feared nobody, neither the labourer nor the lord, with the result that, unusually among his contemporaries, he was never tempted to flatter or vilify either on the basis of class alone.

This characteristic disregard for his readers' prejudices certainly lowered his reputation in genteel circles. . . . It is not difficult to see why certain sections of the sporting public were offended by Surtees. One has only to glance at the novels of "serious" sporting writers, such as Nimrod (Charles Apperley), John Mills, or K. W. Horlock, to realize that flattery of the landed classes was one of their chief purposes. They described fox-hunting not only as an idyllic pastime, but also in terms of its moral advantages in sorting out the manly and noble from the cowards and the tradesmen. At the same time, they would protest that fox-hunting was a nonexclusive sport,

which could be enjoyed regardless of rank or wealth. Ironically enough, as Raymond Carr has pointed out, its "social glamour . . . and its attractions for the fortune hunter and the snob depended on its status as the aristocratic sport *par excellence*."

Surtees was a realist, in a way that his fellows were not, and he could see such ironies very clearly and exploit them in his fiction. So he presented an unwelcome threat to their complacent double-vision by creating such an underbred character as Mr Sponge and allowing him to appear as a bold and expert rider who is generally up at the finish: a position they would have reserved for a *true* gentleman. (pp. x-xi)

[Although] Surtees had a predilection for sporting eccentrics, and although he liked to tease the morally earnest and the socially pretentious, none the less he was at heart a traditionalist too. He believed that the class system was natural, that hereditary wealth and privilege were right, and that hereditary landowners should govern the country. Given the society in which he grew up as one of the privileged, it would indeed be extraordinary if he had not. But when confronted with signs of erosion in the power of the landed classes, it never occurred to him to wall his park and beat his breast, or to close his eyes and find security in complacency. He foresaw that these reactions would only hasten the disappearance of traditional values, and he ridiculed the self-delusions, the shams and vanities, of the landed gentry, because he felt that the only way it could survive was by facing reality and, paradoxically, earning the superiority it was entitled to. His deep-seated belief, shared with the more "serious" sporting writers, that field sports had an essential part to play in ensuring the continuity of the basic pattern of English country life, was complementary to his concern for the increasingly threatened ideal of the true country gentleman.

Moreover, fox-hunting was a rural custom still full of life, and this was another of its attractions for Surtees. True, it was a sport with a particularly strong mystique, a set of unwritten rules for behaviour and dress. Yet once the sherry had been downed and the girths tightened, there it was: man (or, more rarely, woman) confronted by Nature, in the form of horseflesh, mud, thorns, ditches and his own inner self. . . . Nobody but the huntsman in charge of the hounds ever cares whether a fox is actually killed at the end of it all; usually very few even see the finish. For Surtees as novelist the hunting field presented rich opportunities for observing character in action, and this is its chief interest in *Mr. Sponge*. There was a "glorious ideal" of fox-hunting, and Surtees had his share of belief in it, but the clash of the real against such an ideal seemed to him a much more entertaining subject for fiction than the dreary recitation of the latter. He was right, of course, and this is why his competitors, who set themselves up as "high priests" of fox-hunting, are seldom read today, even by devotees of the sport. It is ironic that it was Surtees the demythologizer who should have carried on the myth to later generations. (pp. xii-xiii)

[The secret nature of Surtees's authorship] meant that it retained for him the flavour of a hobby; he never quite took it seriously. Had his material circumstances been less easy, and had he been forced, like Dickens and Thackeray, to earn his living by his pen, his writing might have been the better for it. For even at his best he is uneven, and it is often the air of determined amateurishness which prevents a polished achievement. He responded well to the pressure of a more discriminating audience when it was put upon him, but this happened all too rarely.

In fact the most important instance occurred with *Mr. Sponge's Sporting Tour.* It was only then, with his fourth novel, that Surtees wrote for serial publication in a family magazine with literary pretensions (*The New Monthly,* edited at this time by Harrison Ainsworth), instead of a sporting magazine, whose readers' only demand was for plenty of hunting scenes. So *Mr. Sponge* was written with rather more care than its predecessors. . . . *Mr. Sponge* marked a turning point in Surtees's career in more ways than one. Not only was it his first popular success, it also led to his finding an ideal medium of publication. More importantly, though, it is the book in which he really found his feet as a writer of comic social satire, and it is considered by many to be his best work.

In some ways, however, it is not a novel at all. There is no plot to speak of, and almost no characterization in the conventional sense. But there is an eventful narrative, and there are some splendid caricatures, and they are linked together in so lively a manner that the total effect far surpasses that of many books with more pretensions to be termed novels. The caricatures of Lord Scamperdale, Mr Jawleyford and Mr Jogglebury Crowdey are delightfully vivid and far more alive than many a Forsterian "round" job. We even feel we know well 'Ercles and Parvo, Mr Sponge's profitably iniquitous horses, so zestfully are they presented. Of course in chronicling the progress of a rogue, Surtees is closer to the picaresque mode of the eighteenth century than to the bulk of Victorian novels. It might be possible to regard him simply as a "left-over" eighteenth-century writer stranded in the middle of the nineteenth century, were it not for the fact that he was so very much involved in his Present, even to the extent of updating his topical allusions when revising.

In relying on the progress of Mr Sponge's peregrinations to give the story movement. Surtees ignored both romance and social mobility as material for a real plot. But then upward social mobility, which can perhaps be said to provide the "archeplot" for mid-Victorian novels, did not involve Surtees at a sufficiently deep level. He himself was not placed ambiguously enough in the class system to conceive a great plot based upon it, like that, for instance, of *Our Mutual Friend,* even had he had Dickens's talent. His social rank was unquestioned, and he could only view others' struggles up the ladder from a secure height. That is not to say that he thought those at the top necessarily deserved their places any more than those below: Jawleyford of Jawleyford Court, for instance, bleeding his estate dry to feed his preposterous vanity, is a disgrace as a country gentleman despite his ancestral portraits. That Jawleyford's equally vain daughters marry respectively a stingy ageing aristocrat with homosexual tendencies and a pompous spendthrift parvenu with no sexual tendencies, is matter for amusement; that his tenant farmers are wretchedly oppressed through their landlord's irresponsibility is cause for real concern. None the less, for a writer of this period the tone of the whole is remarkably detached, and so far from being moralistic as to appear almost amoral.

Surtees's anti-romanticism emerges strongly in his depiction of women. Emily and Amelia Jawleyford, entering the drawing-room "in the full fervour of sisterly animosity"; Mrs Jog Crowdey, nagging her family into misery in order to try to ensnare a "rich godpapa" for Gustavus James; the decadent Lady Scattercash, totally indifferent to her husband's mental and physical collapse: these are all women seen in terms of narrow female roles, bogged down in pettiness and vanity. Even the "heroine", Lucy Glitters (late of Astley's Amphi-

theatre), though pretty and good-natured, is a fortune-hunter and possibly a prostitute. Her fortune-hunting matches her with the "hero", and it provides a neat ironic ending for Lucy and Sponge to betroth themselves, each believing the other to be rich. Whether each believed the other to be virtuous as well is not at issue; here again Surtees was more down-to-earth than many of his contemporaries, in depicting a loose woman making a happy marriage rather than dying in degradation. (pp. xiii-xv)

The chief strengths of Surtees's writing lie in his humour, in the combination of his remarkable acuteness of observation with his unusual viewpoint, and in his vigour of style. He is not, however, in any sense a stylist: his syntax is often awry and his locutions ugly, he rarely baulks at a cliché and he is far too repetitive. And yet, at its best, his writing transmits enormous energy, and he displays an extraordinary vitality in his imaginative engagement with his material. His language is remarkable not for any careful professionalism, but for an earthy, sinewy strength, and he can thank his native north country for its gift of some powerfully expressive words: sloggering, scrimmaging, spurlinged, slumpey, smatch, for example. Such words are not self-consciously introduced to provide local colour, they are employed perfectly naturally in contexts where they perform very effectively.

This strongly individual use of language underlines Surtees's originality as a writer. In his avoidance of moralizing, of thematic seriousness, of complexity of structure, and even of plot, he shows himself to be in many ways an anti-novelist rather than a novelist. He cannot be numbered among the great writers, but he is truly unique, and important because so different from what is too often glibly assumed to be the typical minor author of the Victorian age. (pp. xv-xvi)

> *Virginia Blain, in an introduction to* Mr. Sponge's Sporting Tour *by R. S. Surtees, edited by Virginia Blain, Batsford Academic and Educational Ltd., 1981, pp. ix-xvi.*

ADDITIONAL BIBLIOGRAPHY

Allen, Walter. "The Early Victorians." In his *The English Novel: A Short Critical History,* pp. 153-252. New York: E. P. Dutton & Co., 1954.
> Includes an appreciation of Surtees' humor and knowledge of fox-hunting.

Baker, Ernest A. "The Predecessors of Dickens." In his *The History of the English Novel: The Age of Dickens and Thackeray,* pp. 203-36. London: H. F. & G. Witherby, 1936.
> Examines Surtees' realism and its effect upon his characters and plots.

Bell, Quentin. "Surtees." *The New Statesman and Nation* XIX, n.s. No. 472 (9 March 1940): 335.
> Attempts to convince the reading public that Surtees' works deserve attention.

Bovill, E. W. *The England of Nimrod and Surtees, 1815-1854.* London: Oxford University Press, 1959, 188 p.
> A social history based on the works of Surtees and Nimrod. Bovill studies two developments in England during the first half of the nineteenth century: the rise of the stagecoach system and the evolution of fox-hunting into a national sport.

Burn, W. L. "Surtees and Trollope." *Blackwood's Magazine* 261, No. 1578 (April 1947): 301-07.

Compares the works of Surtees and Anthony Trollope, focusing on the authors' attitudes toward women, professional success, and country life.

Carr, Raymond. "Foes of the Fox." *The Times Literary Supplement,* No. 4127 (7 May 1982): 503.
Welcomes the publication of two new editions of *Sponge.*

Child, Harold. "Caricature and the Literature of Sport: *Punch.*" In *The Cambridge History of English Literature,* edited by Sir A. W. Ward and A. R. Waller. Vol. XIV, *The Nineteenth Century,* pt. III, pp. 234-64. New York: G. P. Putnam's Sons, 1917.
Maintains that Surtees ranks second only to Dickens "in the invention of comic character and speech."

Collison, Robert L. "R. S. Surtees: Satirist and Sociologist." *Nineteenth-Century Fiction* VII, No. 3 (December 1952): 202-07.
Holds that Surtees' works are "invaluable" social documents of life in mid-Victorian England.

——. *A Jorrocks Handbook: A Centenary Dictionary of the Characters, Places, Situations, and Allusions Which Occur in the Jorrocks Novels and in the Short Stories by Robert Smith Surtees.* London: Coole Book Service, 1964, 162 p.
A guide to the people, places, and contemporary allusions in *Jorrocks, Handley Cross,* and *Hillingdon Hall.*

Cone, Carl B. "The Genesis of John Jorrocks, Fox-'unter." *The Kentucky Review* III, No. 3 (1982): 20-7.
States that Jorrocks made his first appearance as an unnamed Cockney hunter in a sketch by Surtees published in the August 1830 number of the *Sporting Magazine.*

Darton, F. J. Harvey. "The Age of Jorrocks." In his *From Surtees to Sassoon: Some English Contrasts (1838-1928),* pp. 3-32. 1931. Reprint. Folcroft, Penn.: Folcroft Library Editions, 1977.
Describes how Surtees created characters whose appeal is timeless.

Ellis, Stewart M. "R. S. Surtees." In his *Mainly Victorian,* pp. 95-102. London: Hutchinson & Co., 1925.
A brief biographical sketch and overview of Surtees' writings. Ellis's discussion of the novels focuses on their illustrations.

Engel, Elliot, and King, Margaret F. "Subgenres of the Novel from 1830 to 1837." In their *The Victorian Novel Before Victoria: British Fiction during the Reign of William IV, 1830-37,* pp. 87-134. Macmillan Studies in Victorian Literature. London: Macmillan, 1984.
Studies *Jorrocks* in relation to the comic novels written by Dickens and Theodore Hook between 1830 and 1837.

Gladstone, Hugh S. "Bibliographical Notes." In *Shooting with Surtees,* by Robert Smith Surtees, edited by Hugh S. Gladstone, pp. 203-09. New York: Frederick A. Stokes Co., Publishers, 1928.
A bibliography of Surtees' works that details their publication history.

Johnston-Jones, David R. *"The Deathless Train": The Life and Work of Robert Smith Surtees.* Salzburg Studies in English Literature: Romantic Reassessment, edited by James Hogg, no. 36. Salzburg: Universität Salzburg, 1974, 183 p.
An analysis "from an aesthetic standpoint" of Surtees' contribution to literature, with separate chapters on characterization, humor, style, and construction. Johnston-Jones quotes liberally from Surtees' works and from earlier critical estimates of the author.

Newton, A. Edward. "Jack Jorrocks." In his *End Papers: Literary Recreations,* pp. 111-20. Boston: Little, Brown, and Co., 1933.
Describes the genesis of Jorrocks and attributes the character's immortality to his wit and humor.

Noakes, Aubrey. *Horses, Hounds and Humans: Being the Dramatized Story of R. S. Surtees.* London: Oldbourne, 1957, 183 p.
Combines biographical information with descriptions of Surtees' characters and plots.

O'Neill, Moira. "The Author of 'Jorrocks'." *Blackwood's Magazine* CCXV, No. MCCCIV (June 1924): 857-68.
A biographical portrait.

Pope-Hennessy, Una. "Hamsterley and Jorrocks." In *Durham Company,* pp. 189-223. London: Chatto & Windus, 1941.
Covers various aspects of Surtees' life and career, with particular emphasis on the relationship between his art and that of Dickens.

Ray, Cyril. Introduction to *Robert Smith Surtees: Scenes and Characters,* by Robert Smith Surtees, edited by Cyril Ray, pp. 7-13. Falcon Prose Classics, edited by Leonard Russell. London: Falcon Press, 1948.
An introduction to a collection of extracts from Surtees' works. Ray maintains that Jorrocks is Surtees' greatest character, but regards *Sponge* as his most polished work.

——. "A Master of Life." *The Spectator* 201, No. 6801 (31 October 1958): 573-74.
A favorable review of *Sponge.* Ray summarizes the novel's plot and praises Surtees' "eye for character."

Rendall, Vernon. "Surtees for Christmas." *The Saturday Review* 142, No. 3710 (4 December 1926): 667-68.
Considers Surtees' novels superior to most contemporary literature.

Rivers, W. C. "The Place of R. S. Surtees." *The London Mercury* X, No. 59 (September 1924): 605-13.
A survey of Surtees' works that focuses on two aspects of *Handley Cross*: its characters and its value as a historical document of the Victorian age.

Saintsbury, George. "The Mid-Victorian Novel." In his *The English Novel,* pp. 237-72. The Channels of English Literature, edited by Oliphant Smeaton. London: J. M. Dent & Sons, 1924.
Contains a survey of English sporting novels in which Surtees receives brief attention.

Sassoon, Siegfried. Introduction to *Hillingdon Hall; or, The Cockney Squire,* by Robert Smith Surtees, pp. ix-xiii. New York: William Farquhar Payson, 1933(?).
Argues that *Hillingdon Hall* has been undeservedly labeled Surtees' dullest novel.

Schachterle, Lance. "The Serial Publication of R. S. Surtees's *Jorrocks's Jaunts and Jollities.*" *Victorian Periodicals Newsletter,* No. 20 (June 1973): 8-13.
Compares the book version of *Jorrocks* with the serialized episodes.

[Seccombe, Thomas]. In *The Dictionary of National Biography: From the Earliest Times to 1900,* Vol. XIX, edited by Sir Sidney Lee, pp. 174-75. London: Oxford University Press, 1949-50.
Briefly reviews Surtees' life and career. Critics frequently discuss Seccombe's assertion that the interest of Surtees' novels derives almost exclusively from their illustrations. Seccombe's remarks were first published in 1898-99.

Welcome, John. *The Sporting World of R. S. Surtees.* Oxford: Oxford University Press, 1982, 203 p.
In Welcome's words, "a comprehensive life, placing [Surtees] in the sporting, literary, and social context of his time."

Weygandt, Cornelius. "The Fellows of Scott and the Earlier Victorians." In his *A Century of the English Novel,* pp. 122-71. New York: Century Co., 1925.
Emphasizes Surtees' nationalism.

William Makepeace Thackeray

1811-1863

(Also wrote under pseudonyms of Michael Angelo Titmarsh, Samuel Titmarsh, George Savage Fitz-boodle, Mr. Snob, Yellowplush, Ikey Solomons, The Fat Contributor, and Jeames de la Pluche, among others) English novelist, essayist, short story, fairy tale, and sketch writer, poet, critic, and editor.

The following entry presents criticism of Thackeray's novel *Vanity Fair: A Novel without a Hero* (1848). For additional information on Thackeray's career and *Vanity Fair*, see *NCLC*, Vol. 5.

Vanity Fair is considered one of the great novels of the nineteenth century. For its multitude of successfully realized major and minor characters, and for its vivid panorama of middle- and upper-class English society, it is often compared with such sweeping masterpieces as Leo Tolstoy's *War and Peace* and Honoré de Balzac's *La comédie humaine*. Conceived by Thackeray as a "novel without a hero," *Vanity Fair* challenged many of the conventions of early Victorian fiction with its unprecedentedly realistic approach to characterization and its frankly satirical and often pessimistic view of the human condition. Today, scholars regard Thackeray's innovations as a milestone in the development of realism in English fiction. Critics particularly praise his ability to create complex human characters, among them Becky Sharp, the energetic, attractive, and controversial anti-heroine around whom much of *Vanity Fair* revolves. While many of the novel's early readers found it cynical in tone and harsh in its revelation of human weakness, *Vanity Fair* nevertheless captivated its contemporary audience and has remained a favorite of both critics and the reading public.

Generally regarded as Thackeray's finest work, *Vanity Fair* was also his first great success as an author. Prior to its publication, he had established himself in London literary circles as a minor satirist and magazine writer working under a variety of humorous pseudonyms. His output consisted of numerous essays and reviews, several collections of comic sketches, and a number of novels. While nearly all critics consider *Vanity Fair* an enormous artistic advance for Thackeray, they have also emphasized that the novel owes much of its satirical brilliance and epic scope to the years he spent as a comic sketch writer and author of vivid travel pieces. The series of satiric portraits entitled *The Snobs of England, by One of Themselves* that Thackeray published in *Punch* magazine from 1846 to 1847 is considered of particular importance because it forms a comprehensive gallery of the types of individuals whose acquisitiveness, social affectations, and selfishness the novelist was shortly to attack in a more subtle and far-reaching fashion in *Vanity Fair*.

Scholars disagree over precisely when Thackeray began work on *Vanity Fair*, but they generally believe it to have been in either late 1844 or early the following year. During 1845 he submitted a version of the novel's initial chapters to various publishers, all of whom refused the manuscript. By the beginning of 1846, however, the London firm of Bradbury and Evans had accepted the work for publication in monthly installments—under the title *The Novel without a Hero: Pen and Pencil Sketches of English Society*. Although the book was originally scheduled to begin appearing in May 1846, Thackeray set it aside until the following autumn, when he gave it the name by which it is known today. Thackeray later told an acquaintance that while searching for a better title for his work, the phrase "Vanity Fair" had suddenly occurred to him in the middle of the night, upon which, according to the novelist, he "jumped out of bed and ran three times around my room, uttering as I went, 'Vanity Fair, Vanity Fair, Vanity Fair'." The source for the title lay in John Bunyan's prose allegory *The Pilgrim's Progress*, in which Bunyan portrays Vanity Fair as a wicked place where worldly pleasures are sold. Scholars believe that the moral allegory and unified concept suggested by his new title inspired Thackeray to revise the relatively loose and unstructured chapters of his novel into a narrative possessing greater cohesiveness and artistic purpose than any of his previous writings. The author himself realized that his new work outshone his earlier efforts: in December 1846, he wrote to a friend, "*Vanity Fair* may make me." The first number of *Vanity Fair: Pen and Pencil Sketches of English Society*, featuring Thackeray's own illustrations and published under his real name, appeared in January 1847. The novel ran in nineteen monthly parts through July 1848, when it was published in book form with the new subtitle *A Novel without a Hero*.

Both socially and geographically, *Vanity Fair* covers a wide expanse of early nineteenth-century Europe. Ranging from the streets of Mayfair in London through provincial towns on the Continent, the novel traces the fortunes of two women—Becky and her friend Amelia Sedley—from their boarding school days through marriage, motherhood, wealth, poverty, social prominence, and social ostracism. Amelia, the good-natured but weak and sentimental daughter of wealthy parents, forms a sharp contrast with the heartless Becky, who, though of humble origin, possesses cleverness, ruthless ambition, and an ability to please that allows her to manipulate others. After Amelia's first husband, the selfish dandy George Osborne, dies in the Battle of Waterloo, she ignores the attentions of William Dobbin, whom Thackeray portrays as the only truly noble character in the novel. In the meantime, Becky and her husband, the rakish cavalry officer Rawdon Crawley, establish themselves in London and, under Becky's shrewd direction, attempt to "live well on nothing a year" by borrowing, swindling, and keeping up the appearance of wealth. Eventually, however, Becky's schemes backfire, and she is temporarily forced to flee in disgrace to the Continent. After years of patient waiting and unselfish devotion by Dobbin, Amelia consents to marry him, but only after he realizes that she is perhaps not quite worthy of him. Their union is happy yet falls short of what both had hoped for from life, and the novel ends with the famous exclamation: "Ah! *Vanitas Vanitatum!* which of us is happy in this world? Which of us has his desire? or, having it, is satisfied?"

Although the stories of Becky and Amelia form the central plot of *Vanity Fair,* Thackeray also uses the often-connected events of their lives to expose the corruption, greed, hypocrisy, and pernicious snobbery of almost the entire range of English society, from the servant classes to the aristocracy. The novelist declared in a letter that he intended to portray an entire "set of people living without God in the world." As Becky and Amelia's lives intersect at regular intervals throughout *Vanity Fair,* their stories are caught up in those of a vast array of authentically portrayed secondary characters, including the debauched Lord Steyne, Becky's crude and miserly father-in-law Sir Pitt Crawley, and Jos Sedley, Amelia's gluttonous and weak-willed brother.

While many of *Vanity Fair's* early critics expressed regret that Thackeray had chosen to delve so zealously—and without exception—into the selfish motivations and vain pretensions of his characters, his wide-ranging assaults on sham and hypocrisy met with an appreciative audience. By the time the work had run through half of its scheduled numbers, reviewers had already begun to acclaim it as a highly original and important contribution to the English novel, and Thackeray quickly found himself a famous author. Among the most influential of the early reviews was that of Abraham Hayward in the powerful *Edinburgh Review* (see *NCLC,* Vol. 5). Praising Thackeray's "entire freedom from mannerism and affectation both in style and sentiment," Hayward focused on those aspects of *Vanity Fair* that separated it from current fiction. Along with Hayward, a large proportion of the novel's initial critics recognized that Thackeray had transcended many of the hackneyed conventions prevalent in early Victorian fiction. Foremost among the features of *Vanity Fair* that set it apart from the works of Thackeray's contemporaries was his ability and willingness to reveal both the negative and positive attributes of all his characters, an innovative practice in an era when idealized and simplistic characters were common. Thackeray's calculated avoidance of hero worship and his refusal to distinguish be-

tween good and bad characters bothered many readers, however. Such early critics as George Henry Lewes (see *NCLC,* Vol. 5) and John Forster were among those who remarked upon the extraordinary verisimilitude of the novel's men and women, but both writers faulted Thackeray's overly pessimistic view of human nature. The related question as to why Thackeray had chosen to make Becky such a compelling personality and Amelia such an insipid one also disturbed many early reviewers. Several commentators echoed Lewes in asserting that by depicting evil as attractive and virtue as drab and dull, the author had "erred both against art and nature." Despite the widespread sentiment among early critics that in striving to make his characters real Thackeray had occasionally overemphasized their faults, most contemporary commentary on *Vanity Fair* followed Hayward's example in extolling the elegant simplicity of the novel's style and the unprecedented veracity of its portraiture. After Thackeray's death in 1863, little significant criticism of *Vanity Fair* appeared during the remainder of the nineteenth century.

In the twentieth century, scholars have taken a broad range of approaches to *Vanity Fair.* Among the most frequently discussed aspects of the novel have been its narrative technique, characterization, structure, and major themes. Thackeray's narrative technique in *Vanity Fair* and a range of associated topics, including his dramatic method, handling of time, prose style, shifting perspective, and relationship with his characters, have been the subject of extensive critical debate. Writing in the 1920s, Percy Lubbock explored Thackeray's use of dramatic presentation as a means of narrative expression, praising the author's use of broad retrospection, but faulting his inability to portray the small dramatic moment (see *NCLC,* Vol. 5). John A. Lester, Jr., in a highly influential article written in the mid-1950s, investigated Thackeray's skillful manipulation of chronology in *Vanity Fair,* focusing on the novelist's use of sudden movements back and forward in time to lend his story impact and poignancy (see *NCLC,* Vol. 5). Important analyses of style in *Vanity Fair* include those by G. Armour Craig, who explored the contrast between Thackeray's familiar addresses to the reader and his detached silence about many of the novel's crucial episodes, and John Loofbourow, who examined Thackeray's "flexible, allusive prose" in relation to the development of narrative technique in the English novel.

Thackeray's use of a multiple narrative perspective and his seemingly ambiguous attitude toward his characters have been the focus of many modern discussions of narrative technique in *Vanity Fair.* Numerous critics have attempted to understand Thackeray's regular shifts from an omniscient narrator to a narrator who plays a part in the world he is describing. While some critics, including Russell A. Fraser, have charged that this practice creates confusion and inconsistency, others, among them Juliet McMaster (see *NCLC,* Vol. 5) and Wolfgang Iser, have argued that the lack of a single point of view in the novel contributes to its realism and lends it historical importance as a highly innovative work whose ambiguities place it on the boundary of modern fiction. Closely associated with the issue of Thackeray's uncertain point of view is his handling of Amelia and Becky. Many critics have debated Thackeray's intentions in allowing Becky to eclipse Amelia, questioning why he portrayed Becky as appealing despite her palpably vicious character and her (apparent) capacity for murder. Although a few commentators asserted that Becky was not in fact an attractive figure at all, others sought for clues to her despicable but alluring personality in the riddle of Thackeray's complex attitudes toward women. While the diversity of recent commentary suggests that Thackeray's characterization of Becky and Amelia will continue to be the subject of controversy for some time to come, critics agree that Becky is one of the most memorable characters in English literature.

In analyzing the structure of *Vanity Fair*, twentieth-century scholars have voiced opposing opinions: some have reiterated what Robert Bell had argued in 1848—that the *Novel without a Hero* was "a novel without a plan" (see *NCLC*, Vol. 5)—while others have agreed with David Cecil's assertion in 1934 that "the structural scheme of *Vanity Fair* is Thackeray's greatest technical achievement" (see *NCLC*, Vol. 5). Charles Whibley and Joseph Warren Beach (see *NCLC*, Vol. 5) fall into the group of commentators who found the novel deficient in structural integrity. Writing in the early years of the twentieth century, both Whibley and Beach stressed the negative effects of serial publication on the design of the novel. Conversely, a number of more recent scholars, including Myron Taube and Edgar F. Harden, have perceived a conscious design beneath the surface of *Vanity Fair*. While Taube posited that the novel derives its structure from a series of contrasting characters and situations, Harden argued that the work's unity results from thematic parallels between its monthly parts.

The epic scale of *Vanity Fair* has brought forth a broad spectrum of commentary on what various critics have seen as its central thematic concerns. Although in the nineteenth century such critics as Bell could assert without controversy that the subject of the novel was the "Vanity Fair of the vulgar great"—the slavish pursuit of wealth and fashion by the middle class—scholars in the twentieth century have examined in greater detail the extensive range of *Vanity Fair*'s moral and social concerns. Thus, Joseph E. Baker explored the relationship between Thackeray's concept of Vanity Fair and similar ideas in the works of Bunyan, St. Augustine, and Plato; and A. E. Dyson, in a prominent study of Thackeray's social criticism, investigated the novelist's vision of the effect of Vanity Fair upon individual morality (see *NCLC*, Vol. 5). Critics have also dealt with such themes as the pursuit of love and wealth in *Vanity Fair*, Thackeray's use of the theme of art versus nature, and his portrayal of history.

In assessing Thackeray's accomplishment in *Vanity Fair*, Gordon N. Ray has stated that the novel "was quite as revolutionary a book in the development of Victorian fiction as *Ulysses* has proved to be in the development of modern fiction." In addition to the novel's historical importance, modern scholars have emphasized the enduring relevance of its brilliantly conceived attacks on human greed, corruption, and pretension. For both the vitality of its legion of characters and the monumental achievement inherent in its panoramic vision of English society, critics rank *Vanity Fair* as one of the most important novels of the Victorian era.

(See also *Dictionary of Literary Biography*, Vol. 21: *Victorian Novelists Before 1885*.)

WILLIAM MAKEPEACE THACKERAY   (letter date 1847)

[*In the following excerpt from a letter to his mother, Thackeray responds to the suggestion that Amelia and the other characters in* Vanity Fair *are selfish and unattractive.*]

Of course you are quite right about *Vanity Fair* and Amelia being selfish. . . . My object is not to make a perfect character or anything like it. Dont you see how odious all the people are in the book (with exception of Dobbin)—behind whom all there lies a dark moral I hope. What I want is to make a set of people living without God in the world (only that is a cant phrase) greedy pompous mean perfectly self-satisfied for the most part and at ease about their superior virtue. Dobbin & poor Briggs are the only 2 people with real humility as yet. Amelia's is to come, when her scoundrel of a husband is well dead with a ball in his odious bowels; when she has had sufferings, a child, and a religion—But she has at present a quality above most people whizz: LOVE—by [which] she shall be saved. (p. 309)

> *William Makepeace Thackeray, in a letter to Mrs. Carmichael-Smyth on July 2, 1847, in his* The Letters and Private Papers of William Makepeace Thackeray: 1841-1851, Vol. II, *edited by Gordon N. Ray, Cambridge, Mass.: Harvard University Press, 1945, pp. 308-11.*

WILLIAM MAKEPEACE THACKERAY   (letter date 1848)

[*In the following excerpt from a letter to the noted critic George Henry Lewes, Thackeray explains a passage from* Vanity Fair *that Lewes had recently discussed in the* Morning Chronicle *(see excerpt by Lewes dated 1848 in* NCLC, *Vol. 5).*]

I have just read your notice in the *Chronicle* (I conclude it is a friend who has penned it) and am much affected by the friendliness of the sympathy, and by the kindness of the reproof of the critic.

That passage [which] you quote bears very hardly upon the poor alderman certainly: but I don't mean that the man deprived of turtle would as a consequence steal bread: only that he in the possession of luxuries and riding through life respectably in a gig, should be very chary of despising poor Lazarus on foot, & look very humbly and leniently upon the faults of his less fortunate brethren—If Becky had had 5000 a year I have no doubt in my mind that she would have been respectable; increased her fortune advanced her family in the world: laid up treasures for herself in the shape of 3 per cents, social position, reputation &c—like Louis Philippe let us say, or like many a person highly & comfortably placed in the world not guilty of many wrongs of commission, satisfied with himself, never doubting of his merit, and decorously angry at the errors of less lucky men. What satire is so awful as Lead us not into temptation? What is the gospel and life of our Lord (excuse me for mentioning it) but a tremendous Protest against pride and self-righteousness? God forgive us all, I pray, and deliver us from evil.

I am quite aware of the dismal roguery [which] goes all through the *Vanity Fair* story—and God forbid that the world should be like it altogether: though I fear it is more like it than we like to own. But my object is to make every body engaged, engaged in the pursuit of Vanity and I must carry my story through in this dreary minor key, with only occasional hints here & there of better things—of better things [which] it does not become me to preach.

I never scarcely write letters to critics and beg you to excuse me for sending you this. It is only because I have just laid down the paper, and am much moved by the sincere goodwill of my critic. (pp. 353-54)

William Makepeace Thackeray, in a letter to George
Henry Lewes on March 6, 1848, in his The Letters
and Private Papers of William Makepeace Thackeray:
1841-1851, Vol. II, edited by Gordon N. Ray, Cambridge, Mass.: Harvard University Press, 1945, pp.
353-54.

WILLIAM MAKEPEACE THACKERAY (letter date 1848)

*[In the following excerpt from a letter to the duke of Devonshire,
written before the publication of the final chapters of Vanity Fair,
Thackeray provides a humorous account of the fortunes of various
characters subsequent to the close of the novel.]*

My Lord Duke,—Mrs. Rawdon Crawley, whom I saw last
week, and whom I informed of your Grace's desire to have
her portrait, was good enough to permit me to copy a little
drawing made of her "in happier days," she said with a sigh,
by Smee, the Royal Academician.

Mrs. Crawley now lives in a small but very pretty little house
in Belgravia, and is conspicuous for her numerous charities,
which always get into the newspapers, and her unaffected piety.
Many of the most exalted and spotless of her own sex visit
her, and are of opinion that she is a *most injured woman*. There
is no *sort of truth* in the stories regarding Mrs. Crawley and
the late Lord Steyne. The licentious character of that nobleman
alone gave rise to reports from which, alas! the most spotless
life and reputation cannot always defend themselves. The present Sir Rawdon Crawley (who succeeded his late uncle, Sir
Pitt, 1832; Sir Pitt died on the passing of the Reform Bill) does
not see his mother, and his undutifulness is a cause of the
deepest grief to that admirable lady. "If it were not for *higher
things*," she says, how could she have borne up against the
world's calumny, a wicked husband's cruelty and falseness,
and the thanklessness (sharper than a serpent's tooth) of an
adored child? But she has been preserved, mercifully preserved, to bear all these griefs, and awaits her reward *elsewhere*. The italics are Mrs. Crawley's own.

She took the style and title of Lady Crawley for some time
after Sir Pitt's death in 1832; but it turned out that Colonel
Crawley, Governor of Coventry Island, had died of fever three
months before his brother, whereupon Mrs. Rawdon was obliged
to lay down the title which she had prematurely assumed.

The late Jos. Sedley, Esq., of the Bengal Civil Service, left
her two lakhs of rupees, on the interest of which the widow
lives in the practices of piety and benevolence before mentioned. She has lost what little good looks she once possessed,
and wears false hair and teeth (the latter give her rather a ghastly
look when she smiles), and—for a pious woman—is the best-
crinolined lady in Knightsbridge district.

Colonel and Mrs. W. Dobbin live in Hampshire, near Sir R.
Crawley; Lady Jane was godmother to their little girl, and the
ladies are exceedingly attached to each other. The Colonel's
History of the Punjaub is looked for with much anxiety in some
circles.

Captain and Lt.-Colonel G. Sedley-Osborne (he wishes, he
says, to be distinguished from some other branches of the
Osborne family, and is descended by the mother's side from
Sir Charles Sedley) is, I need not say, well, for I saw him in
a most richly embroidered cambric pink shirt with diamond
studs, bowing to your Grace at the last party at Devonshire
House. He is in Parliament; but the property left him by his
Grandfather has, I hear, been a good deal overrated.

He was very sweet upon Miss Crawley, Sir Pitt's daughter,
who married her cousin, the present Baronet, and a good deal
cut up when he was refused. He is not, however, a man to be
permanently cast down by sentimental disappointments. His
chief cause of annoyance at the present moment is that he is
growing bald, but his whiskers are still without a gray hair and
the finest in London.

I think these are the latest particulars relating to a number of
persons about whom your Grace was good enough to express
some interest. I am very glad to be enabled to give this information. . . . (pp. 375-77)

P.S.—Lady O'Dowd is at O'Dowdstown arming. She has just
sent in a letter of adhesion to the Lord-Lieutenant, which has
been acknowledged by his Excellency's private secretary, Mr.
Corry Connellan. Miss Glorvina O'Dowd is thinking of coming
up to the Castle to marry the last-named gentleman.

P.S.2.—The India mail just arrived announces the utter ruin
of the Union Bank of Calcutta, in which all Mrs. Crawley's
money was. Will Fate never cease to persecute that suffering
saint? (p. 377)

William Makepeace Thackeray, in a letter to the duke
of Devonshire on May 1, 1848, in his The Letters
and Private Papers of William Makepeace Thackeray:
1841-1851, Vol. II, edited by Gordon N. Ray, Cambridge, Mass.: Harvard University Press, 1945, pp.
375-77.

WILLIAM MAKEPEACE THACKERAY (essay date 1848)

*[The following preface to Vanity Fair, in which Thackeray de-
scribes himself as the "Manager of the Performance," is often
discussed in studies of the novel's narrative perspective. Dated
by Thackeray June 28, 1848, the preface was first published when
the novel appeared in book form.]*

As the Manager of the Performance sits before the curtain on
the boards, and looks into the Fair, a feeling of profound
melancholy comes over him in his survey of the bustling place.
There is a great quantity of eating and drinking, making love
and jilting, laughing and the contrary, smoking, cheating, fighting, dancing, and fiddling: there are bullies pushing about,
bucks ogling the women, knaves picking pockets, policemen
on the look-out, quacks (*other* quacks, plague take them!)
bawling in front of their booths, and yokels looking up at the
tinselled dancers and poor old rouged tumblers, while the light-
fingered folk are operating upon their pockets behind. Yes,
this is VANITY FAIR; not a moral place certainly; nor a merry
one, though very noisy. Look at the faces of the actors and
buffoons when they come off from their business; and Tom
Fool washing the paint off his cheeks before he sits down to
dinner with his wife and the little Jack Puddings behind the
canvass. The curtain will be up presently, and he will be turning
over head and heels, and crying, "How are you?"

A man with a reflective turn of mind, walking through an
exhibition of this sort, will not be oppressed, I take it, by his
own or other people's hilarity. An episode of humour or kindness touches and amuses him here and there;—a pretty child
looking at a gingerbread stall; a pretty girl blushing whilst her
lover talks to her and chooses her fairing; poor Tom Fool,
yonder behind the waggon, mumbling his bone with the honest
family which lives by his tumbling;—but the general impression is one more melancholy than mirthful. When you come
home, you sit down, in a sober, contemplative, not uncharitable

frame of mind, and apply yourself to your books or your business.

I have no other moral than this to tag to the present story of *Vanity Fair.* Some people consider Fairs immoral altogether, and eschew such, with their servants and families: very likely they are right. But persons who think otherwise, and are of a lazy, or a benevolent, or a sarcastic mood, may perhaps like to step in for half an hour, and look at the performances. There are scenes of all sorts; some dreadful combats, some grand and lofty horse-riding, some scenes of high life, and some of very middling indeed; some love-making for the sentimental, and some light comic business; the whole accompanied by appropriate scenery, and brilliantly illuminated with the Author's own candles.

What more has the Manager of the Performance to say?—To acknowledge the kindness with which it has been received in all the principal towns of England through which the Show has passed, and where it has been most favourably noticed by the respected conductors of the Public Press, and by the Nobility and Gentry. He is proud to think that his Puppets have given satisfaction to the very best company in this empire. The famous little Becky Puppet has been pronounced to be uncommonly flexible in the joints, and lively on the wire: the Amelia Doll, though it has had a smaller circle of admirers, has yet been carved and dressed with the greatest care by the artist; the Dobbin Figure, though apparently clumsy, yet dances in a very amusing and natural manner: the Little Boys' Dance has been liked by some; and please to remark the richly-dressed figure of the Wicked Nobleman, on which no expense has been spared, and which Old Nick will fetch away at the end of this singular performance.

And with this, and a profound bow to his patrons, the Manager retires, and the curtain rises. (pp. 5-6)

> *William Makepeace Thackeray, "Before the Curtain," in his* Vanity Fair: A Novel without a Hero, *edited by George Tillotson and Kathleen Tillotson, Methuen & Co., Limited, 1963, pp. 5-6.*

[JOHN FORSTER]   (essay date 1848)

[*Forster was an English biographer, historian, critic, and journalist who is best known for* The Life of Charles Dickens, *which is considered one of the finest biographies of a literary figure in the English language. In the following excerpt, Forster explores* Vanity Fair's *realistic characters, social satire, and "cynical, sarcastic tone."*]

Laughing at the minute and interminable details, despising the conventional decencies and real indecorums, wearied by the want of all manly passion in Richardson's *Pamela,* that novel of the pattern morality of its day, Fielding at last revenged himself by a burlesque, which was meant to show how compatible the specious virtue of Mrs Pamela might be, with the absence of every virtue except the one by which she gained for a husband the man who had done his best to ruin her. But Fielding had too great an imagination to allow of his filling up one book with a mere parody of another. From Richardson his satire extended to the fashionable world. . . .

Put the fashionable-life manners of our day for the manners in Richardson's novels, and Mr Thackeray's position in the book before us in some respect resembles Fielding's. The task he first set himself, in *Vanity Fair,* would seem to have been to portray or expose, with witty malice, their ideal of fine life in its various grades. But his better genius forced him beyond the narrow limits of a mere ill-natured joke or burlesque, and informed his pages with characters and incidents full of life and reality. If Mr Thackeray falls short of Fielding, much of whose peculiar power and more of whose manner he has inherited or studiously acquired, it is because an equal amount of large cordiality has not raised him entirely above the region of the sneering, into that of simple uncontaminated human affection. His satiric pencil is dipped in deeper colours than that of his prototype. Not Vanity Fair so properly as Rascality Fair is the scene he lays open to our view; and he never wholly escapes from its equivocal associations, scarcely ever lays aside for a whole page his accustomed sneer. His is a less comfortable, an on the whole therefore, let us add, a less true view of society than Fielding's.

Vanity Fair is the work of a mind, at once accomplished and subtle, which has enjoyed opportunities of observing many and varied circles of society. Its author is endowed with penetrating discrimination and just appreciation of character, and with a rare power of graphic delineation. His *genteel* characters (we dislike the word as much as Dr Johnson did *cleverness,* but we have no better at hand) have a reality about them which we do not remember to have met with in any recent work of fiction except *Pelham.* They are drawn from actual life, not from books and fancy; and they are presented by means of brief, decisive, yet always most discriminative, touches. It never is necessary to have recourse to supplementary reflections and associations, to make amends for dimness and indistinctness in the portraiture. This, for the most part, holds true of all Mr Thackeray's characteristic sketches. But there is a tendency to caricature, to select in preference grotesque and unpleasing lineaments even where no exaggeration is indulged, that detracts considerably from the pleasure such high artistic abilities might otherwise afford; and we are seldom permitted to enjoy the appreciation of all gentle and kind things which we continually meet with in the book, without some neighbouring quip or sneer that would seem to show the author ashamed of what he yet cannot help giving way to.

It would be tasking the reader's patience too severely to inflict upon him a dry analysis of a story already familiar to a wide public, and daily attracting more attention. But a brief review of its elements is necessary to a just estimate of its character and value. If the novel is without a hero, it has two heroines. We are introduced to them as they leave their boarding-school, described in a very few pages, but with inimitable humour; and we follow their adventures, conjointly or alternately, till we leave the one in the secure haven of a second and comfortable marriage, and the other in an incipient old age of missionary and philanthropic societies, cognac, and stalls at fancy fairs. In tracing the fortunes of the artistically accomplished, clever, sensible, daring, selfish, and unprincipled Becky, we are led through beggarly scenes tenanted by adventurers, through avowedly rakish and more splendid circles, through those where a conventional tone of decorum prevails; thence, into the squalid resorts of tattered finery and habitual vice which lie beyond; and thence again, into that withered, sapless, and flowerless region where sham penitents find a refuge, who have returned to external decency without reawakening to virtue. In tracing, on the one hand, the fortunes of the good and amiable but somewhat selfish and insipid Amelia, we are led from the vulgar comfort and splendour of the *bourgeoisie* of Vanity Fair, through sudden reverses of bankruptcy; allowed again to emerge into commonplace affluence; and after a short excursion through the stately haunts of poor German princes, are conducted finally to a home of worth and virtue. The relations of the heroines afford a connecting link between those dissimilar routes and the passengers who crowd them. The scene shifts from England to the continent, and the time of action extends from before the battle of Waterloo to the year of grace in which we write. The heroes and heroines of high life and low life, of town life and country life, and of that amphibious life which is neither, pass in succession before us; and all, whether we like and admire them or the contrary, are presented with a startling reality of effect.

It must not be imagined, because we have hinted at Mr Thackeray's inferior power of escaping from the mere satirical and burlesque when compared with Fielding, that there are not many finely-conceived characters in his book,—characters which win upon us by their intrinsic worth, and are all the more dear from the dash of the ridiculous that mingles with their better qualities. The hero (for after all there is a hero in the novel), Dobbin, though perhaps elaborated here and there in too minute detail, is a noble portrait of awkward devoted affection, of unobtrusive talents, and of uncompromising integrity. We love him from the first page to the last; from his gawky beginnings at school, through his inadequate rewards during life, to his doubtful happiness at the close. He is always kind, loving, truthful, heroical-hearted; a gentleman. The ineffable Peggy O'Dowd, too, is always welcome; whether brushing her husband's accoutrements and preparing his cup of coffee while he takes his natural rest before the battle of Waterloo, or plotting and planning to marry the major with Glorvina, or watching tenderly over the sick bed of the desolate Amelia, or breaking off the intrigue between the lieutenant and the surgeon's wife, or quarrelling with all the other ladies of the regiment, or dancing down an interminable succession of military men and civilians in an Irish jig. Nor less is her quiet, submissive, gallant, and good-natured husband worthy of her. The poor curate at Brompton, Miss Clapp, Miss Schwarz, Jemima, Miss Briggs, Lady Jane, and others, are also people we can take to our heart, and in whose society we edify. Perhaps the noblest conception of all, however, is the manner in which the good qualities of the manly but battered old *roué*, Rawdon, ignorant and uneducated except by vice, are developed under the combined influence of paternal affection, adversity, and occasional association with the good.

Still it cannot be denied that it is in those characters where great natural talents and energy are combined with unredeemed depravity that the author puts forth his full powers, and that in the management and contemplation of them he seems absolutely to revel. The Marquis of Steyne is a magnificent picture; his fiendish sagacity, energy, absorbing self-indulgences, and contemptuous tramplings upon everything human and divine, fascinate while they revolt. It is in like manner impossible to escape being charmed with the indomitable buoyancy, self-possession, and *applomb* of the little adventuress, Becky, even while we are conscious of her utter depravity. She commits every conceivable wickedness; dishonours her husband, betrays her friend, degrades and embrutes herself, and finally commits a murder; without in the least losing those smart, good-tempered, sensible manners and ways, which ingratiate her with the reader in spite of all her atrocities. In this we may think the art questionably employed, but it is not to be denied that it *is* very extraordinary art; and it is due to Mr Thackeray to add that he has been careful to explain the blended good and evil in this woman by very curious and impressive early details of the circumstances of her birth and bringing up. Nor is it so much with respect to these exceptional characters that we feel inclined

to complain of the taunting, cynical, sarcastic tone that too much pervades the work, as with respect to a preponderance of unredeemed selfishness in the more common-place as well as the leading characters, such as the Bullocks, Mrs Clapp, the Miss Dobbinses even, and Amelia's mother. We can relish the shrewd egoism of Miss Crawley; can admire, while we tremble at, the terrible intentness of Mrs Bute Crawley, who writes her husband's sermons, drills her daughters, and persecutes with selfish sycophancy till everybody flies from her; we can bow with awe and veneration before Lady Southdown, that miraculous compound of Lady Bountiful and Lady Macbeth; we can triumph completely over such fribblers as Sir Pitt Crawley the second, and Tapeworm; we see what power there is in making young Osborne so heartless, old Osborne so hateful, old Sedley so contemptible; but we feel that the atmosphere of the work is overloaded with these exhalations of human folly and wickedness. We gasp for a more liberal alternation of refreshing breezes of unsophisticated honesty. Fielding, after he has administered a sufficient dose of Blifil's choke-damp, purifies the air by a hearty laugh from Tom Jones. But the stifling ingredients are administered by Mr Thackeray to excess, without the necessary relief.

It is exclusively in an artistical point of view that we offer this criticism. It would be unjust in the extreme to impute an immoral tendency to *Vanity Fair*. Vice and folly are never made alluring in it, though all justice is done to their superficial meretricious charms. Mr Thackeray's moral is true and just. It is the victims of such adventurers as Becky who are made so mainly by their own faults and follies. Unsuspicious virtue and innocence—as in the case of Dobbin and Amelia—have a charm in their own simple integrity that unconsciously baffles her spells. It is the vices of her victims that subject them to her power—whether their vices be inherent, gross, and revolting, as in the case of Sir Pitt Crawley; or superinduced on a naturally better, but ignorant and uneducated nature, as in the case of poor Rawdon; or feeble and degrading, as in that compound of silly vanity and selfishness, Joseph Sedley; or merely insipidly heartless and unthinking, as with young Osborne. But this moral is insisted upon with a pertinacity, and illustrations of it are heaped upon us with a redundant profusion, unalleviated by a sufficient amount of more gratifying images, that seems to us to go beyond the limits of the pleasurable, and consequently of true art.

Notwithstanding this defect, *Vanity Fair* must be admitted to be one of the most original works of real genius that has of late been given to the world. The author contemplates many phases of society from a point of view entirely his own. The very novelty of tone in the book impeded its first success; but it will be daily more justly appreciated; and will take a lasting place in our literature. If we have not scrupled to dwell with force upon what we conceive to be its grave defect, it is because we are convinced that the author is capable of avoiding it in his future works, and of producing characteristic tales less alloyed in their enjoyment, and equal, if not superior, in racy power. (p. 468)

> [*John Forster*], *in a review of "Vanity Fair: A Novel without a Hero," in* The Examiner, *No. 2112, July 22, 1848, pp. 468-70.*

[ROBERT S. RINTOUL]   (essay date 1848)

> [*Rintoul comments on the novel's artistic unity, its lack of attractive characters, and the quality of its illustrations.*]

The completion of Mr. Thackeray's novel of *Vanity Fair* enables us to take a more entire view of the production, and to form a more complete judgment of it as a work of art, than was possible in the course of piecemeal publication in monthly numbers. Our impression from that review is, that the novel is distinguished by the more remarkable qualities which have created the reputation of the author,—his keen perception of the weaknesses, vanities, and humbug of society, the felicitous point with which he displays or the pungent though goodnatured satire with which he exposes them, and the easy, close, and pregnant diction in which he clothes his perceptions; though, possibly, happier specimens of his peculiar excellencies may be found in some of his other works. *Vanity Fair* displays a depth and at times a pathos which we do not remember to have met with in Mr. Thackeray's previous writings; but, considered as a whole, it is rather a succession of connected scenes and characters than a well-constructed story. Both incidents and persons belong more to the sketch than the finished picture. Either from natural bias or long habits of composition, Mr. Thackeray seems to have looked at life by bits rather than as a whole. A half-length here, a whole-length there, a group in another place, a character or a clique with single actions or incidents belonging to them, have been studied, and transferred to paper with a humour, truth, and spirit, that have rarely been equalled. But something more than this is needed for a finished picture of human life. Such things, indeed, are scarcely its entire elements, for they are little more than parts; and so remain till very many such have been compared by the artist—their general laws evolved by this comparison, and the whole animated and fused by the imagination, so as to present the type of a class without loss of individuality. Mr. Thackeray has rarely accomplished this in *Vanity Fair*. There is, indeed, plenty of individuality; the work is full of it. However exceptional, outré, distasteful, or even farcical the characters may be, they have strong particular traits, well supported in the main, and their delineation is always capital: but this peculiarity attaches to the principal characters—that no useful deduction, no available rule of life, can be drawn from their conduct; except in that of the elder Osborne, who points the moral of sordid vanity and a grovelling love of distinction, and points it with effect, as his vices are made the means of his punishment.

It may be said that this largeness is of no consequence, if there be particular or even exceptional nature: which is true as regards sketches, that exhibit a character on one or two occasions and then drop it. Such sketches of passing phases of society do not, however, suffice to form the materials of a fiction: it requires a whole career—the before and after as well as the present. When the characters have no types in nature, or have that obvious weakness or low vice about them that their example conduces to nothing, they tire in a lengthened exhibition, because we have little sympathy with them. *Vanity Fair* is said by its author to be a novel without a hero: which is undoubtedly a truth; but the heroines do not make up for this omission, since one is without a heart, and the other without a head. The author evidently has his misgivings about Amelia Osborne, (née Sedley,) for although she is clearly a favourite, he deems it necessary occasionally to appeal to the reader in favour of her weakness. But there is rarely weakness without vice; and though the extreme attachment of Amelia to a selfish, worthless, neglectful young man, may be forgiven as *so* natural, yet the manner in which she yields to it, and nurses her sentiment to the neglect of her duties, as well as her subsequent shillyshally conduct to her obsequious admirer Major Dobbin, is rather mawkish than interesting.

Rebecca Crawley (formerly Sharpe) is the principal person of the book, with whom nearly all the others are more or less connected: and a very wonderfully-drawn picture she is, as a woman scheming for self-advancement, without either heart or principle, yet with a constitutional vivacity and a readiness to please, that save her from the contempt or disgust she deserves. As a creation or *character,* we know not where Rebecca can be matched in prose fiction: but she is too deficient in morale to excite interest. The want of entirety we have spoken of is visible in Rebecca's finale. The discredit of a separation from her husband, when not followed by public proceedings, might be surmounted; but a demirep who gambles, consorts with blacklegs and all kinds of disreputables, and raises the wind by advertising concerts that she never gives after getting the money for the tickets, could hardly have regained a place in reputable society, although backed by religious hypocrisy. This conclusion, which was quite needless, is not only wrong as wanting in poetical justice, but untrue as a picture of society even in "Vanity Fair."

A similar want of attractive sympathy runs through the male characters, either from grossness, weakness, sordidness, or vice. It may be urged that these defects of *Vanity Fair* are owing to its periodical publication. That has probably induced an occasional but strong sacrifice of consistency in the characters, to produce an immediate effect; and the same necessity of making parts tell may have given rise to some exaggerations

Thackeray's cover for the monthly parts of Vanity Fair.

that would otherwise have been avoided. There are also obvious drawbacks to continuous perusal, such as direct addresses to the reader, and a little of *writing* for the million, which would have been omitted in another mode of publication. But we think all the peculiarites arising from the mode of publication could be got rid of by revision: the defects we speak of lie deeper, and are owing, we think, to a want of imagination and large comprehension of life.

But if, putting *Vanity Fair* aside as a fiction of high art, we look at it as a series of bits from life, it is entitled to the first rank as a set of sketches lifelike and natural. Sir Pitt Crawley—the selfish, low-minded baronet, the coarsest of the coarse old school, who cannot spell, and who living meanly, acting harshly and cruelly, and exercising great shrewdness in money matters, is notwithstanding always a loser—is a capital portrait; and, though exceptional even in his day, (which was the early part of the century,) still might be found in life. His brother, the jovial, fox-hunting, port-drinking rector, is equal to him as a real piece of flesh and blood. The Marquis of Steyne—the roué whom everybody censures, (except the serious,) but all visit when they get an invitation—revives some reminiscences of a similar personage in *Coningsby:* though Thackeray penetrates the pomps and strips off the conventions that rather imposed upon Disraeli. There are numerous other characters, which, if not quite so powerfully painted as these, are quite as truthful individually; but, always excepting Rebecca, the most large and vigorous delineation in the book is old Mr. Osborne. He is a type of a class; he points a moral; and, though sordid, selfish, sullen, half-savage, and meanly subservient to greatness, he obtains a hold on the reader by the force of his will, at least till he turns to a sort of goodness towards the conclusion.

These characters are frequently engaged in scenes that create amusement or exhibit society; and the sketches are intermingled with lively descriptions or shrewd remarks on life. Read as a series of sketches connected with persons whose fortunes serve to introduce them, *Vanity Fair* will furnish a lively and agreeable entertainment. Read as a continuous story, it will perhaps be felt to lack the interest which a story requires, except in the scenes connected with Rawdon Crawley's arrest, release, and subsequent discovery of his wife's liaison with the Marquis of Steyne. (p. 709)

As is usual with works of fiction published periodically, *Vanity Fair* is profusely illustrated with wood-cuts and etchings representing the persons and incidents of the text, by Mr. Thackeray himself. If only of passable or average merit, they would be creditable, as arguing the possession of a double art; but they strike us as exhibiting powers akin to the literary abilities of the author, besides possessing this further quality: the spirit of the scene and the character—the idiosyncracy of the persons—is more thoroughly entered into and presented to the reader than is common with professional artists. (p. 710)

> [*Robert S. Rintoul*], *in a review of "Vanity Fair," in* The Spectator, *Vol. XXI, No. 1047, July 22, 1848, pp. 709-10.*

[GEORGE HENRY LEWES] (essay date 1848)

[*Lewes was one of the most versatile men of letters in the Victorian era. Critics often cite his influence on the novelist George Eliot, to whom he was a companion and mentor, as his principal contribution to English letters, but they also credit him with critical acumen in his literary commentary, most notably in his dramatic criticism. Here, Lewes discusses artistic continuity and propor-*

tion, style, satirical method, characterization, and realism in Vanity Fair. *For additional criticism on* Vanity Fair *by Lewes, see excerpt dated 1848 in* NCLC, *Vol. 5.*]

For some years Mr. Thackeray has been a marked man in letters,—but known rather as an amusing sketcher than as a serious artist. Light playful contributions to periodical literature, and two amusing books of travel, were insufficient to make a reputation; but a reputation he must now be held to have established by his *Vanity Fair.* It is his greatest effort and his greatest success. The strength which lay within him he has here put forth for the first time. The work before us retains traces of the writer's old fault—a fault fostered no doubt by the carelessness and impromptu proper to serial publication—viz. a sort of indifference to the serious claims of literature, a cavalier impertinence of manner as if he were playing with his subject. Nothing could be more impertinent, for instance, than Mr. Thackeray's second number,—in which he relapsed into his old magazine manner, and postponed the continuation of his narrative to imitations of some of his cotemporary writers of fiction. Fit subjects for ridicule such writers may be—but the ridicule is misplaced in the work which Mr. Thackeray had in hand, considered as a work of Art. In the same number he becomes suddenly aware of the discrepancy between the costume of the period in which he has laid his scene and the costume in which he has depicted the characters in his pictorial illustrations. All he does on the discovery is to notify the fact in a note, and flippantly pretend that the real costume was too hideous for his purpose. He has been guilty, however, of the same confusion of periods throughout the work. Sometimes we are in the early part of the present century—at others we are palpably in 1848. Writing from month to month encourages such laches; but for the sake of such a reputation as Mr. Thackeray has now arrived at, it will be well that he should be more upon his guard.

The style of *Vanity Fair* is winning, easy, masculine, felicitous, and humorous. Its pleasant pages are nowhere distorted by rant. The author indulges in no sentimentalities—inflicts no fine writing on his readers. Trusting to the force of truth and humour, he is the *quietest* of contemporary writers,—a merit worth noting in a literary age which has a tendency to mistake spasm for force. The book has abundant faults of its own,—and we shall presently notice some of them; but they are not the faults most current in our literature. The writer is quite free from theatricality. No glare from the footlights is thrown upon human nature, exaggerating and distorting it. He is guiltless too—let us be thankful for such a boon in the sense here intended—of a "purpose." Unfettered by political or social theories, his views of men and classes are not cramped. The rich in his pages are not necessarily vicious—the poor not as a consequence of their poverty virtuous and high-minded. Again—many jesters take advantage of their cap and bells, and adopt as their motto, "Ridentem dicere *falsum* quid vetat." Under the plea that laughter is not a serious thing, and what is laughingly spoken is not to be critically judged, they have sacrificed truth to their joke. No advocate of any cause, however, should be more scrupulously watched than he who laughing teaches. Against the dogmas of the politician, philosopher, or theologian the reader is on his defence. These "come in such a questionable shape" that we *must* examine them. Their seriousness alarms us. We scrutinize proofs and combat conclusions. But the jester is privileged. He throws us off our guard by the smile of his approach, and insinuates conviction by the bribery of laughter. The laughter passes, but the error may remain. It has gained admittance into our unsuspecting minds,—and is left there unsuspected.

It is a much-disputed question, whether or not ridicule be a test of truth? To us the question appears answered by saying that if the ridicule be developed *ab intra* from the argument—not thrown *on* it *ab extra*—it is a test. If a wit descries the latent absurdity grinning under a moral mask, and exposes it, he has confuted the argument; if he himself grins and makes faces *at* the mask, he may excite laughter but has not carried confutation. . . . It is one of Thackeray's peculiar excellencies that he almost always ridicules *ab intra*. An absurdity is stated by him in the quietest and gravest manner, as if he were himself a believer in it like others, and—enforced by such means of self-accumulation as leave it to unmitigated contempt. His irony of this kind is perfect,—but it is a weapon which he uses far too exclusively. He has shown himself, as we have said, a satirist—but not an artist. With himself we exclaim, ''O brother wearers of motley! are there not moments when one grows sick of grinning and tumbling and the jingling of bells?'' There is nothing so sad as a constant smile. Laughter becomes wearisome when too much prolonged,—for it is then a sort of blasphemy against the divine beauty which is in life. Mr. Thackeray grows serious and pathetic at times—but almost as if he were ashamed of it, like a man caught in tears at the theatre.—It is one weakness of the satirist that he is commonly afraid of the ridicule of others!

We have said that Mr. Thackeray is a satirist, not an artist:—and from that characteristic may be deduced many of his deficiencies. For instance, the reader of *Vanity Fair* will have observed that we have in it nothing but scenes and sketches—only glimpses, not views. There is constant succession of description, but no developement of story. The passions are taken at their culminating point, not exhibited in the process of growth; the incidents are seldom transacted before our eyes, but each is taken as a *fait accompli*. Nor is there anything like proportion kept. The writer opens a chapter, and his pen runs on easily, fed by a full and observant mind,—but recording the suggestions of the moment rather than building up the various portions of an edifice already planned and in which each part has its due significance.

Mr. Thackeray is deficient, too, in passion:—a deficiency that sits lightly on a satirist, but is serious in a writer of fiction. He has no command over this quality—apparently but little knowledge of it. The curtain of the tragedy of life has seldom risen before him—or he has looked on its representations with an incurious eye. Altogether, one may say that Mr. Thackeray has not very curiously or patiently observed moral phenomena. Life he has seen both at home and abroad, and he has reflected on what he has seen. We feel that he is painting after Nature: and this conviction it is which makes his work so delightful. Nothing is permanently interesting but truth.

As a consequence of Mr. Thackeray's satirical tendency may be noted the prodigality of vice and folly to be found in his pages—and which affords no true representation of human nature, but only the exaggeration of a feature. It has been made a serious reproach against this writer that he has arrived at such a pitch of misanthropy or doubt as to think, with Chamfort, that an honest man is a variety of the human species. . . . The writer began, no doubt, with the wholesome intention of lashing the vices and follies of Vanity Fair in a more restrictive sense—regarded as one of the social phases: but gradually *all* the districts of society are swept into his Vanity Fair—and there is *nothing good in it*. This is false and unwholesome

teaching. What a mass of scoundrels, blacklegs, fools, and humbugs Mr. Thackeray has crowded together. There is scarcely a good or estimable person in the book and as little of affection as of virtue. Even the heroine Amelia—with whom the writer seems to have been somewhat enamoured (a feeling of which he is likely to have the monopoly)—is thoroughly selfish as well as silly. The one fine exception is Major Dobbin—a sketch not unworthy of the hand that drew 'My Uncle Toby.'

As we have said, Mr. Thackeray's humour is peculiarly his own. He never frames and glazes an idea. The simplest words and in the simplest manner are used to bring out his meaning; and everything seems to flow from him as water from a rock. We may add that when he chooses to be pathetic, a quality of the same kind gives wonderful effect to his pathos. How beautiful is the scene in which Amelia has resolved at length to part from her child! (pp. 794-95)

The character of Becky is amongst the finest creations of modern fiction. She is perfectly unlike any other clever, heartless woman yet drawn. With great art, she is made rather selfish than wicked—though the excess of the selfishness rises to the force and has the effect of wickedness. Profound immorality is made to seem consistent with unfailing good humour. Becky has neither affections, nor passions, nor principles. She uses men as chessmen—and is not check-mated at last. It is very strange that the reader has a sort of liking for her in spite of his better knowledge. The fact is, the author has contrived in a surprising way to represent not only Becky's *mind* but her *manner*. We are in some sort under her spell,—as Rawdon was. To us she is almost as lively, entertaining and good-humoured as she was to those amongst whom she lived. Like Lord Steyne, we may see through her yet covet her society. Her equability of temper is a nice touch:—it belongs to the physiology of such a character. They who have no affections and no principles can be wounded only in their self-love, and may obtain the character of being good-tempered at the cheapest possible cost. The consistency of this remarkable character is maintained to the last. How full yet brief—graphic and suggestive—is the microscopic view of her life after her separation from her husband!— (p. 796)

Next in point of skill to that of Becky is the portrait of Rawdon Crawley—the heavy, stupid, gentlemanly dragoon and blackleg so completely subjugated by his clever little wife. His affection for his child quite whitewashes him. The reader forgets the blackleg in the father. It is worthy of note with what consummate truth this heavy dragoon is made to feel his insignificance by the side of his clever little wife, but how completely paralyzed the adroit little woman is when she stands guilty before her husband:—how silently she obeys him who has hitherto obeyed her,—how she feels that her arts are powerless against his passion. Brute strength long led by mental cunning here reasserts its empire and is undisputed. The whole scene is most masterly.

Jos Sedley is rather a failure:—nor is he consistently drawn. We are introduced to him as a man painfully shy, nervous, and stupid; but as the story proceeds he drops his shyness, and retains only the gluttony and stupidity of his former self. Meant as a decidedly *comic* character, he creates but little mirth.— George Osborne, the vain and foolish young officer, is capitally drawn. Lord Steyne is one of those *telling* exaggerations which make people exclaim, ''How true!'' when their acquaintance with lords is confined to fashionable novels. Though overdone, however, it is an exaggeration by a master; and the descriptions of Gaunt House and its inmates transcend all previous efforts in that style. Old Miss Crawley is capital. Her selfishness, her sagacity, her terrors in ill health, her triumph over the meanness which surrounds her and which she laughs at and profits by, are vividly presented, yet by the simplest strokes. Here is a sentence pregnant with meaning and very characteristic of the author:—"Picture to yourself, oh fair young reader, a worldly, selfish, graceless, thankless, religionless old woman, writhing in pain and fear, and *without her wig!* Picture her to yourself, and ere you be old learn to love and pray!"

Mrs. O'Dowd must not be forgotten. The gallant woman has won the hearts of her regiment,—and of all her readers. How true, homely, affectionate, and wise is the description of her packing up the Major's traps and preparing his coffee for him on the eve of Waterloo!

The vividness with which the whole of the scenes at Brussels stand out before the eye is marvellous when we reflect that the author is not describing the scenes which he himself witnessed, but only painting after the descriptions of others. They imply a fine faculty for historical romance. Nor is it only in this more elaborate painting that Mr. Thackeray has exhibited a constant mastery in the present book. The instances are abundant of meaning conveyed and intensified by a single line of illustration. . . .

Knowledge of life, good humoured satire, penetration into motive, power of characterization, and great truthfulness are qualities in fiction as rare as they are admirable; and no work that has been published for many years past can claim these qualities so largely as *Vanity Fair.* (p. 797)

> [*George Henry Lewes*], *in a review of "Vanity Fair: A Novel without a Hero," in* The Athenaeum, *No. 1085, August 12, 1848, pp. 794-97.*

WILLIAM MAKEPEACE THACKERAY   (letter date 1848)

[*In the following excerpt from a letter to the critic Robert Bell, Thackeray responds to Bell's review of* Vanity Fair *in* Fraser's Magazine *(see excerpt by Bell dated 1848 in NCLC, Vol. 5).*]

Although I have made a rule to myself never to thank critics yet I like to break it continually, and especially in the present instance for what I hope is the excellent article in *Fraser*. It seems to me very just in most points as regards the author: some he questions as usual—If I had put in more fresh air as you call it my object would have been defeated—It is to indicate, in cheerful terms, that we are for the most part an abominably foolish and selfish people "desperately wicked" and all eager after vanities. Everybody is you see in that book,— for instance if I had made Amelia a higher order of woman there would have been no vanity in Dobbins falling in love with her, whereas the impression at present is that he is a fool for his pains that he has married a silly little thing and in fact has found out his error rather a sweet and tender one however, *quia multum amavit* I want to leave everybody dissatisfied and unhappy at the end of the story—we ought all to be with our own and all other stories. Good God dont I see (in that maybe cracked and warped looking glass in which I am always looking) my own weaknesses wickednesses lusts follies short comings? in company let us hope with better qualities about which we will pretermit discourse. We must lift up our voices about these and howl to a congregation of fools: so much at least has been my endeavour. You have all of you taken my misanthropy to task—I wish I could myself: but take the world by a certain standard (you know what I mean) and who dares

talk of having any virtue at all? For instance Forster says [see excerpt dated 1848] After a scene with Blifil, the air is cleared by a laugh of Tom Jones—Why Tom Jones in my holding is as big a rogue as Blifil. Before God he is—I mean the man is selfish according to his nature as Blifil according to his. In fact I've a strong impression that we are most of us not fit for—never mind.

Pathos I hold should be very occasional indeed in humourous works and indicated rather than expressed or expressed very rarely. In the passage where Amelia is represented as trying to separate herself from the boy—She goes upstairs and leaves him with his aunt 'as that poor Lady Jane Grey tried the axe that was to separate her slender life' I say that is a fine image whoever wrote it (& I came on it quite by surprize in a review the other day) that is greatly pathetic I think: it leaves you to make your own sad pictures—We shouldn't do much more than that I think in comic books—In a story written in the pathetic key it would be different & then the comedy perhaps should be occasional. Some day—but a truce to egotistical twaddle. It seems to me such a time ago that **V F** was written that one may talk of it as of some body elses performance. My dear Bell I am very thankful for your friendliness & pleased to have your good opinion. (pp. 423-25)

> *William Makepeace Thackeray, in a letter to Robert Bell on September 3, 1848, in his* The Letters and Private Papers of William Makepeace Thackeray: 1841-1851, *Vol. II, edited by Gordon N. Ray, Cambridge, Mass.: Harvard University Press, 1945, pp. 423-25.*

CHARLES ASTOR BRISTED   (essay date 1848)

[*In the following excerpt, Bristed discusses various aspects of* Vanity Fair, *including the predominance of "disagreeable" characters in the novel, Becky's personality, and Thackeray's satirical intentions.*]

[A comparison of *Vanity Fair* and Thackeray's other writings with the words of Honoré de Balzac] brings to mind a more serious charge than that of occasional conceit or affectation which we have more than once heard urged against [Thackeray]; namely, that his sketches contain too many disagreeable characters. A queer charge this to come from a reading generation which swallows copious illustrated editions of *Les Mystères* and *Le Juif,* and is lenient to the loathsome vulgarities of *Wuthering Heights* and *Wildfell Hall.* But let us draw a distinction or "discriminate a difference," as a transcendentalist acquaintance of ours used to say. If a story is written for mere purposes of amusement, there certainly ought not to be more disagreeable characters introduced than are absolutely necessary for relief and contrast. But the moral and end of a story may often compel the author to bring before us a great number of unpleasant people. In a former volume of this Review the opinion was pretty broadly stated that no eminent novelist writes merely for amusement without some ulterior aim; most decidedly Thackeray does not at any rate. We shall have occasion to refer to this more than once, for it is doing vast injustice to Mr. T. to regard him merely as a provider of temporary fun. He does introduce us to many scamps, and profligates, and hypocrites, but it is to show them up and put us on our guard against them. His bad people are evidently and unmistakably bad; we hate them, and he hates them, too, and doesn't try to make us fall in love with them, like the philosophers of the "Centre of Civilization," who dish you up seraphic poisoners and chaste adulteresses in a way that perplexes and confounds all established ideas of morality. And if he ever does bestow attractive traits on his rogues, it is to expose the worthlessness and emptiness of some things which are to the world attractive—to show that the good things of Vanity Fair are not good *per se,* but may be coincident with much depravity.

Thus Becky Sharpe, as portrayed by his graphic pen, is an object of envy and admiration for her cleverness and accomplishments to many a fine lady. There are plenty of the "upper ten" who would like to be as "smart" as Rebecca. She speaks French like a French woman, and gets up beautiful dresses out of nothing, and makes all the men admire her, and always has a repartee ready, and insinuates herself every where with an irresistible nonchalance. Then comes in the sage moralist, and shows us that a woman may do all these fine things, and yet be ready to lie right and left to every one, and ruin any amount of confiding tradesmen; to sell one man and poison another; to betray her husband and neglect her child. (That last touch is the most hateful one: in our simplicity we hope it is an exaggeration. That a woman should be utterly regardless of her offspring seems an impossibility—in this country, we are proud to say, it *is* an impossibility.) Or if any of his doubtful personages command our temporary respect and sympathy, it is because they are for the time in the right. Rawdon Crawley is not a very lofty character; he frequently comes before us in a position not even respectable; but when he is defending his honor against the old sybarite Lord Steyne, he rises with the occasion: even the guilty wife is forced to admire her husband, as he stands "strong, brave, and victorious." Nor though he

The title page of the first edition of Vanity Fair, *illustrated by Thackeray.*

finds it sometimes necessary to expose hypocrites, does Thackeray delight in the existence of hypocrisy, and love to seek out bad motives for apparently good actions. His charity rather leads him to attribute with a most humane irony pretended wickedness to weakness. Your French writer brings an upright gentleman before the footlights, and grudges you the pleasure of admiring him; he is impatient to carry him off behind the scenes, strip off his Christian garments, and show him to you in private a very fiend. But Thackeray, when he has put into a youth's mouth an atrociously piratical song, is overjoyed to add quietly that he "remembers seeing him awfully sick on board a Greenwich steamer." (pp. 422-23)

Thackeray never sets about a story of any length without having a will and a purpose. And this indeed is a noticeable difference generally existing between the wit and the humorist, that while the former sparkles away without any object beyond his own momentary amusement, the latter has a definite aim, some abuse to attack, some moral to hint. Thackeray attacks abuses, and it is with an honest indignation and simple earnestness that form the distinguishing features of his serious writings. He assaults all manner of social sham, humbug and flunkeyism, and gives it to them in a way that does you good to hear. Against toadyism, affectation and mobbery, he preaches a crusade in the sturdiest Anglo-Saxon. The charge began in the ***Snobs of England;*** it is now followed up in ***Vanity Fair.*** Any one, therefore, who reads the latter book should read the ***Snob Papers*** in *Punch,* by way of introduction to it. Tin-worship and title-worship, and that "praise of men" which your fashionables love more than the "praise of God"—Titmarsh is sworn foe to all these, and wages unrelenting war on them—but with none of that cant which runs all through Jerrold and half through Dickens: he does not make all his poor people angels, nor all his rich people devils, because they are rich. Nor has he any marked prejudice against Christianity in general, or the Christianity of his own church in particular—which we are weak enough to think rather to his credit. Moreover his sledge-hammer invective against fashionable fooleries, is not engendered of or alloyed with any rusticity or inability to appreciate the refinements of civilized life, as a backwoodsman or Down-easter might abuse things he did not comprehend; for Titmarsh has a soul for art and poetry, and good living, and all that is aesthetic and elegant.

Vanity Fair, then, is a satire on English society. The scene indeed is laid thirty years back, but that is of a piece with Juvenal's

> Experiar quid concedatur in illos
> Quorum Flaminia tegitur cinis atque Latina.

It is meant for the present time, as the very illustrations show, in which all the male characters wear the convenient trouser (*Americanice* pantaloons) of our own day, instead of the stiff "tights" which were the habit of that period. In a work of this sort we naturally expect to find many *type-characters*—that is, characters who represent classes of people. Most of these are very good and true. Rawley Crawdon is a capital representative of the uneducated part of the young British officery—profligate and spendthrift, stupid in everything but cards, billiards, and horseflesh, and too illiterate to spell decently; yet withal bold as a lion. It is pleasant to see such a man properly depicted now and then, for the writer who does it is doing his duty to civilization by assailing the old barbarous feudal notion that mere physical courage, which is generally founded on the consciousness of superior physical strength and dexterity, should ride roughshod over moral courage and intellect. And Lord

Steyne is a thorough specimen of the aristocratic old Sybarite. Others had tried their hands at this character before—D'Israeli and that coarsest of fine ladies, Lady Blessington—but none of them have succeeded like Thackeray. And Pitt Crawley is a perfect model of the stiff, slow, respectable *formula* man. And Osborne, Sr., is one of your regular purse-proud cits who measure everything by what it will fetch on 'Change. But some of the portraits are not fair even to Vanity Fair, and that of Sir Pitt, the elder Crawley, seems to us positively unjust. He may be a true sketch from life; rumor has indeed given him a real name and family; but he is too bad to be a type of country baronets, or even of country squires. And though the high-life characters have bitter justice done them in most things, there is one point on which the men are a little wronged: *they swear too much.* Allowing that a fearful amount of profanity prevails among people who ought to know better, there is surely no necessity for its being repeated. We do not want to hear the thing simply because it is true, any more than we wish to see pictures of disgusting and frightful objects, however faithfully to nature they may be painted. But in fact English gentlemen are not so openly profane as Titmarsh represents them.

The book has no hero: it openly professes to have none. But there is a heroine, at least a prominent female character, and she is equal to a dozen ordinary heroines and heroes. Becky Sharpe is an original creation, not the representative of a class, though there are traits about her that remind you of several classes. Any one who has been much in society must have had the fortune or misfortune to meet more than one woman who resembled Becky in some points—ay, even among us simple, unsophisticated, etc., republicans; for in truth if you only leave out a little nonsense about titles, everything in Titmarsh's literary puppet-show will apply point-blank to our own occidental Vanity Fair. There are women as spitefully satirical as Rebecca, making mischief in the most ingenious and graceful ways—fashionable enough that, and not by any means a sin, but on the contrary no small recommendation in Vanity Fair. There are women all in the best society, who flirt with every passable man that comes near them, as Rebecca did; for observe, it is not proved that Mrs. Rawdon Crawley did anything more; her biographer does not give you to understand that she actually "committed herself" with any one—and this is very proper and pleasing in Vanity Fair. There are women who, like Rebecca, have always a plausible lie ready to excuse themselves; and this is an excusable pecadillo in Vanity Fair. There are women who, like Rebecca, look to marriage only as a means of getting a position "in society," and what can be a more flattering homage to Vanity Fair? There are women, like Rebecca, who sponge upon spooneys and get money under false pretences; and the victims may "cut up rough" about it, but the rest of Vanity Fair pass it over as a venial offence and accept their part of the spoil. In short, put together a number of things the practice of which is not only allowable but successful in Vanity Fair, and what a devil of a woman you will make! Such at least is our idea of the *moral* and theory of Rebecca Crawley *née* Sharpe. (pp. 423-25)

It would take too long to follow Becky through her chequered career—her grand catastrophe, her exile, her ultimate partial recovery. Many of our readers were more or less familiar with her before seeing these remarks of ours; and such as are not, must have been tempted ere this to resolve that they will go to the fountain-head for information about her. We have only to observe, before taking leave of her, the skill which her biographer displays in lightly passing over some of the diabolical scenes she is concerned in, such for instance as "her

second appearance in the character of Clytemnestra." Your true artist will produce infinitely more effect by just hinting at a horror, than a second-rate man can work by going into the most elaborate details.

Some notice should be taken of the Osbornes and Sedleys who make up the underplot of the story. We have some suspicion that Thackeray finished up old Osborne, the purse-proud merchant, more carefully than he had intended at first, in opposition to Mr. Dombey, to show *his* view of such a character in opposition to that of Dickens. If such a comparison is challenged, there can be no doubt that so far as verisimilitude and nature are concerned, Mr. Osborne, Sr., has it by long odds. (pp. 429-30)

The loves and fortunes of young Osborne and Amelia Sedley, are designed to carry out still further the attack on what formed one of the strongest topics of denunciation in the *Snob Papers,*—that heartless system (flourishing to perfection in France, but deep-rooted enough in England) which considers matrimony as the union, not of a young man to a young woman, but of *so much to so much.* A splendid theme for indignant declamation, and one in which the satirist is sure to meet with much sympathy from the young of both sexes. But we must remember that the principle of union for love has, like all principles, its limitations. That two young people, long and fondly attached to each other, should be afraid to marry because they would be obliged to drop a little in the social scale, and deny themselves some of the outward luxuries they enjoy separately; that they should sacrifice their hearts to those abominable dictates of fashion which Titmarsh has summed up in his Snob Commandment, "Thou shalt not marry unless thou hast a Brougham and a man-servant;" this is truly matter of indignation and mourning, against which it is not possible to say too much. But we must also protest against the opposite extreme—the inference drawn from an extension of our principle—that love ought to overcome and exclude *all* objections, want of principles and character in the man for instance; or utter want of means on both sides to support a family; or even—what is generally the first thing to be disregarded in such cases—incompatibility of relations and friends. . . . We appeal to your own experience, reader. Of all the *pur sang* love-matches you have known—matches where one or more of the impediments we have mentioned existed—how many have turned out happily? Nay, we appeal to Titmarsh himself and *his own characters in this very book.* Would it not have been a thousand times better for Amelia if she had married Dobbin in the first place? And might not George as well have taken Miss Schwartz as wed Amelia one month and been ready to run away with another woman the next?

We must take leave of Titmarsh; for he is carrying us off into all sorts of digressions. We never were so long filling the same number of pages as we have been on the present occasion, for whenever we opened the book to make an extract we were tempted to read on, on, on—the same things which we had read a dozen times—but there was no resisting. And when we resolutely turned our back to his people, it was only to think, and reason, and argue about them. How many of the hundreds of novels, published every year, leave any impression in your mind or give you one afterthought about any character in them? It is easy to take exceptions to the book—we have taken our share; we might go on to pick out little slips, instances of forgetfulness, as where we are told first that Amelia Sedley is not the heroine, and two or three pages after that she is; or when the climate of Coventry Island is so bad that no office will insure Rawdon's life there, yet in the very same number it is mentioned how much his life-insurance cost him. But, say what you will, the book draws you back to it, over and over again. Farewell then, O Titmarsh! Truly, thou deservest better treatment than we can give thee. Thy book should be written about in a natural, even, continuous, flowing style like thine own, not in our lumbering paragraphs, that blunder out only half of what we mean to say. And do thou, O reader, buy this book if thou hast not bought it; if thou hast, throw it not away into the chiffonier-basket as thou dost many brown-paper-covered volumes; but put it into a good binding and lay it by—not among the works "that no gentleman's library should be without"—but somewhere easy of access; for it is a book to keep and read, and there are many sermons in it. (pp. 430-31)

> Charles Astor Bristed, in a review of "Vanity Fair," in The American Review, n.s. Vol. II, No. IV, October, 1848, pp. 421-31.

THE LONDON REVIEW (essay date 1861)

[*This anonymous reviewer harshly criticizes* Vanity Fair *for its cynical view of life and lack of idealized characters and situations.*]

[In *Vanity Fair*] Thackeray gives us to understand that he writes as a moralist:—

> My kind reader will please to remember, that this history has "Vanity Fair" for a title, and that Vanity Fair is a very vain, wicked, foolish place, full of all sorts of humbugs, and falsenesses, and pretensions.... People there are living and flourishing in the world ... with no reverence except for prosperity, and no eye for anything beyond success ... faithless, hopeless, charityless: let us have at them, dear friends, with might and main.

And how does Thackeray carry out this intention? He makes us almost like Becky Sharp by endowing her with those deservedly popular qualities, tact, wit, good-humour, and good-temper; and by putting her in contact with other persons equally wicked but not equally pleasant, and with one or two worthy people whom he contrives to make ridiculous or contemptible. We are inclined to pardon Becky's wickedness in 'doing' every one she comes across, when every one she comes across so well deserves to be 'done.' Especially has he failed in putting her in contrast with Amelia, that mean-minded whimpering little woman, whose loving temperament never inspires her with one noble sentiment. Becky has at least one element of greatness; she honours even her enemies when they are worthy of honour; while Amelia is incapable of appreciating true merit even in her friends. We pardon her infatuation for George Osborne, that 'selfish humbug, that low-bred cockney-dandy,' as Becky rightly calls him; we pardon it as a delusion of early youth, rivetted by the premature death of her husband on the battle field; but we cannot pardon her low estimate of, and petty tyranny over Dobbin; we cannot even pardon her hasty marriage, bringing, as it was sure to do, ruin on the man she loved. That hard intellectual type of woman-kind which is commonly stigmatized as 'strong-minded,' is frightening authors from the study of qualities essentially womanly. It is woman's vocation to be strong, not in mind, but in noble and generous impulses; that, while her husband and sons know best what is expedient, logical, or wise, she should know best what is true, gallant, and right. *Vanity Fair* is a remarkable book,

brilliant, entertaining, life-like (as far as life is bad and base); but if we plunge beneath the sparkling surface, it is a dreary book. It gives the real, and utterly omits the ideal: it strips away the veil which our love or trust throws over our neighbours' actions, and holds them up in all their possible selfishness and falseness. The blossom of the gay Epicurean is gone, and we are fed to satiety on the Cynic's bitter fruit. Are we so silly as to imagine that there is such a thing as disinterested service and love? (pp. 291-92)

Don't let us trust any one, dear friends. Nor our lovers, lest, while we picture them 'bivouacking, or attending the couch of a wounded comrade, or studying the art of war in their own desolate chamber,' our angel-thoughts happily find the barrack gates shut, and cannot pass through to 'hear the young fellows roaring over their whiskey-punch.' (p. 293)

O what a dreary book! Give us its narrative, its comedy, its brilliant jesting and wit, and let us laugh and be merry; but spare us these reflections, O bitter cynic, if you would not drive us to despair. The grave irony that praises baseness, or the grave censure that condemns it, leaves us equally helpless and hopeless, if you show us no way of escape. When did the bitterness of the fruit ever prevent men from clutching at the fair outside? We want something better, something substantial on which to rest and feed, in the place of this universal negation, this desolate hollowness and barrenness of life. Human nature is bad enough; but while God reigns over the world, and while His Spirit is abroad in it, we rejoice to think that glimmerings of truth and trust and kindness, of faithful service and disinterested love, are ever breaking through the darkness, witnesses of that gracious Presence which offers light and peace to all. (p. 294)

> A review of "Vanity Fair," in The London Review, Vol. XVI, No. XXXII, July, 1861, pp. 291-94.

JAMES HANNAY (essay date 1868)

[*Hannay was a British novelist and journalist who became a close friend of Thackeray. His* Studies on Thackeray, *from which the following excerpt is drawn, was the first full-length critical survey of the novelist's works. In the excerpt below, he discusses such facets of* Vanity Fair *as its drama, satire, and realism.* Studies on Thackeray *was originally published in 1868 in the magazine* Broadway.]

The warmest admirers of Thackeray's earlier tales must, of course, acknowledge that *Vanity Fair* was a prodigious advance upon them. It retains a peculiar charm, though he reached a still higher grade of art in *Esmond* and in *The Newcomes*. There is an animation and a freedom of satire about *Vanity Fair* which has its own delightfulness as distinct from the mellower beauty and sedater humour of its successors. In dramatic effect, and interest of narration, it, perhaps, takes the lead of all; for Thackeray has scarcely anywhere else such situations as that of the Waterloo crisis, or the surprise of Becky by her husband when he escapes from the spunging-house. And how admirably the story develops itself out of such simple elements! How modest the fountains from which spring the stream of story that by-and-by expands into a mirror-like lake, reflecting the character of a whole generation! We have two middle-class families in Russell Square, the son and daughter of which are engaged to each other. The daughter has a school-fellow who goes out as a governess to make her way in the world. The son enters the army, and naturally makes intimate friends at his mess. But by degrees the interest widens and deepens. A whole group of personages is taken in, and their fortunes linked together; the comedy darkens into tragedy, the satire grows more and more thoughtful and intense, and a book, apparently begun as one of mere amusement, closes leaving its reader a livelong theme for emotion and meditation. The change is chiefly due to the development of the character of Becky Sharp; and nothing is more illustrative of Thackeray's genius than the probable, reasonable, and entirely natural and sensible way in which Becky's progress through life is managed. Nobody can lay his finger on an incident in it not likely enough under the conditions, and in perfect keeing with Becky's own character, and that of the people among whom she is thrown. It is this supreme merit of truth which distinguishes Thackeray from mere novelists of the day; heroes of the Photographic school, which deals in common-place realism; and the Fantastic school, which deals in extravagant incident. There are realists and realists. Thackeray paints common life, but not in a common-place manner. There are novelists whose imitation is mechanical rather than creative, and resembles the employment of real water, real horses, &c., on the stage—a vulgarity which attacks art in its very essence. They make their characters twaddle through whole pages, like those in Swift's satirical piece on "Polite Conversation." But though people do undoubtedly twaddle in the actual world, that is not a sufficient reason for making them twaddle in a work of art, which, though bound to be natural, is bound also to show some power of *selection* amongst the products of nature. Thackeray, in *Vanity Fair,* and everywhere else, detests the false, the turgid, the high-flown; and resolutely prefers good low art to the sham high. But there is a medium; and he is never realistic in the sense in which a post-office directory is so. He was, however, for a long time, too veracious for his readers, and even after *Vanity Fair* had appeared, the sweet, kindly little Amelia was attacked as not clever enough for the place which she held in the novel. As if cleverness was either the commonest, or the most desirable quality in a heroine—at least, a heroine that is intended to be loved and married! Through all Thackeray's books, there runs the prevailing doctrine that women—in spite of their little jealousies and other faults—are better than men by dint of their tenderness and affection; and surely these are found every day in women still duller than Amelia is represented as being. It is curious how completely in *Vanity Fair* Thackeray put on the stage his whole company of actors in the comedy of life. Dobbin has a family likeness to Colonel Newcome and Henry Esmond; George Osborne has a strong moral resemblance to Arthur Pendennis; Laura Bell is a cleverer Amelia; and Miss Crawley claims kin both with old Lady Kew and with the Baroness Bernstein, who, as the brilliant Beatrix, had some points in common (under great difference of condition) with Becky Sharp. . . . I do not the least mean that Thackeray repeated himself, or that these are not all distinct individualities. On the contrary, the very fact that they should be both like and unlike, is a proof of the artist's subtlety as of his fidelity to nature. But the resemblances are worth studying by those who would understand his sympathies and antipathies. (pp. 19-24)

James Hannay, in his Studies on Thackeray, *1869. Reprint by Kennikat Press, 1970, 107 p.*

GEORGE AUGUSTUS SALA (essay date 1869)

[*Sala was an English journalist. In the following excerpt, he discusses Thackeray's authentic representation of character and*

incident in Vanity Fair, *focusing on a single episode that he finds inconsistent with the novel's generally realistic portrayal of life.*]

I can with difficulty assume that there are any intelligent persons of the Victorian era who have not read and re-read the wonderful drama of human life, the more wonderful analysis of human vice, weakness, meanness, and folly, called [*Vanity Fair*]. And with much greater difficulty could I deem it possible for any literate person to wander about Brussels, or take that inevitable but sorely disappointing trip to the field of Waterloo itself, without peopling his mind incontinent with all the Thackerayian *dramatis personae,* and all the phases of the Waterloo episode in *Vanity Fair.* In comparison with the astonishing skill with which Thackeray has made out of the great battle—which, in itself, he never describes—an unseen pivot on which turns, from first to last, the whole machinery of his story, the Waterloo chapter in Victor Hugo's *Misérables,* brilliant and graphic and powerful as it is, seems but a clumsy piece of "padding," dragged in by the head and shoulders to fill up a gap. For my part, the last time I went to Waterloo, I found Hougoumont and the Belle Alliance and the Haye Sainte, so many blackened and crumbling booths in Vanity Fair. I should not have been at all surprised to find the names of the Marquis of Steyne and Sir Pitt Crawley in the visitors' book at Mont St. Jean, or to be told by the cicerone at the Cottonian Museum, that yonder battered shako hanging up had belonged to M. le Capitaine Osborne, or that the dinted broadsword hard by had been worn by M. Crawley, *officier aux Gardes, Milor Anglais.*

The highest praise which, as I conceive, can be awarded to a work of fiction is that the circumstances therein narrated may be taken to be the truth, and the personages represented accepted as real people. The *Iliad* is probably a fiction, and *Paradise Lost* is certainly one; yet everybody believes in Nestor, and Thersites, and Ulysses, and Agamemnon; and Abdiel, and Ithuriel, and Raphael the good-natured angel. Even a battle in heaven with real cannon, or the interference of all the deities of Olympus in the petty squabbles of a lot of rascally Greek klephts, do not strike us—so exquisite has been the dexterity of the narrator—as being very out-of-the-way occurrences. The reality, however, of *Vanity Fair* does not demand even the slight concessions which are extorted from the imagination of those who read Homer or Milton. The epic is a plain-clothes one, and we may take it for granted as completely as we take the *Times* newspaper or *Hart's Army-List.* The realistic excellence attained by Mr. Thackeray in his chapters on the Waterloo time is on a par with the excellence attained by Captain Siborne in his model of the battle-field itself. It is excellence of the kind recognised by the horse and the birds, when the first neighed at the painted representation of a horse, and the last pecked at the painted fruit in the old Greek's picture. The old ship-captain who, when the conversation turned on the voyage to Lilliput, declared that he knew Captain Gulliver very well, only that he lived at Wapping and not at Rotherhithe, passed on Swift's immortal satire a criticism analogous to that which might be passed on *Vanity Fair;* and Swift, be it remembered, to his greater praise, was dealing with the most extravagant personages and the most incredible circumstances. (pp. 351-52)

I look upon *Vanity Fair* as a work so artistically perfect, in the very best sense of literary perfection, the art being all but entirely concealed, that I have often asked myself with surprise and bewilderment what the artist could have been thinking of to introduce in this said Waterloo episode an incident which I can but think grossly unreal, improbable, and unnatural. I allude to the proposal made by George Osborne to Becky Sharpe, on the night of the Duchess of Richmond's ball, that she should "fly" with him. I own that George was over head and ears in love with Becky—infatuated, *ensorcelé,* by that baleful little fairy with the green eyes—whom I heard qualified once by a Frenchman who had read the Hachette edition of *La Foire aux Vanités* as *"une incarnation de l'absinthe des plus désastreuses."* I grant that a man who is in love with a woman will stop short of no folly and no absurdity in the avowal of his passion, and that very few considerations of common sense will hinder him from attempting the most desperate deeds to win her. The restraint is less, perhaps, when the object of love happens to be another man's wife; for the passion being *ab initio* a guilty one demands, on the "much more blood" principle in *Macbeth,* more and more criminality as it approaches culmination. But Mr. Thackeray's George Osborne, although a vain, empty-headed coxcomb, was not a raving madman; and no one but a howling lunatic would have asked, circumstanced as George Osborne then was, a woman to "fly" with him. Whither were they to fly? Into Napoleon's lines? To Ostend? The pair would have been stopped on the shore, and George would have been arrested as a deserter, tried by court-martial, and shot. Could they conceal themselves in Brussels? Could they reach Paris? Why, George Osborne was bound by a hundred indissoluble fetters as strong as Acadian steel to Flanders, to Brussels, and to the headquarters and his regiment. He was a captain in the famous British army. He was on active service. The campaign had begun. From hour to hour a deadly conflict might be expected. Was it likely, was it feasible, was it within the range of possibility, that a British officer—a brave one too, notwithstanding all his conceit and ignorance—would desert his colours, would betray his country, would submit to be branded as a rascal and a dastard, in order to "fly" with his friend's wife? Elopements have been heard of before now, I grant. In peaceful times dissolute gentlemen show as little reluctance in levanting with other people's spouses as in deserting their own; but Don Juan does not commit an amorous escapade in front of the enemy. Faublas does not smuggle a marchioness into a post-chaise and abscond with her on the eve of a tremendous battle. That this strangely-improbable incident was of no hasty or careless commission on the part of Mr. Thackeray is clear. It marks a very important point in the story. Subsequent events of the story hinge upon it. The *dénouement* of **Vanity Fair** is affected by it. It is in the first volume that George Osborne makes this preposterous proposal. It is not until the close of the third that Becky, to bring about Amelia's marriage with Dobbin, triumphantly shows her the letter which she has been hoarding for long years—the letter given to her in a bouquet by George on the night of the Duchess of Richmond's ball, and in which the young man had asked her to "fly." The production of this *billet-doux* at length forces George's widow to the conviction that her darling husband was a false-hearted humbug, and, her eyes being opened, she very sensibly marries Major Dobbin.

This passage in **Vanity Fair** has been to me a stumbling-block for years, and over and over again I have asked myself, with increasing perplexity and general discomfiture, how ever this piece of false art could have crept into a wondrously-polished and homogeneous work—how ever the Homer of this prose epic could not merely have nodded, but have sunk for a time into a slumber as deep as Rip Van Winkle's. When I was young I used to bewilder myself almost as desperately in guesses as to the probability of a broken-down, bankrupt, knavish captain of horse—a *roué,* a gamester, a sharper, such as Rawdon Crawley was—being appointed to the governorship of a West

India island; but years and experience, and the attentive study of the *Court Guide* in connection with the *London Gazette,* have mitigated both my perplexity and my incredulity on *that* head. As things go, have gone, and are likely to go, one need not be surprised at the appointment of anybody to anything. I have some hopes of getting the mission to Timbuctoo myself when I am old and broke.

The only tenable hypothesis I can form as to this "flying" matter in **Vanity Fair** is one which may not be very agreeable to English ears. So long, however, as we have the published reports of a Court for Divorce and Matrimonial Causes, we are constrained to admit that the elopement of other women's husbands with other men's wives are not always of the same Platonic nature as that of Mr. Carker with Mrs. Dombey—the oddest wild-goose chase perhaps ever imagined by a novelist. These divorce-court people mean naughtiness, and as a rule commit naughtiness. I cannot help fancying that the acute philosopher who wrote **Vanity Fair** meant in the first instance that George Osborne should avow his adulterous love for Rebecca Crawley, and ask her for a rendezvous. A French novelist of the present century, or an English novelist of the last one—the virtuous Richardson even—would have made no bones at all about the matter. But Mr. Thackeray may have hesitated. He knew that he was appealing to a refined, a "genteel," a fastidious audience—an audience who will listen unblushingly to the grossest scenes of profligacy at the French plays, but who, when it visits the Olympic or the Princess's, expects that

Thackeray's illustration of Becky's departure from Miss Pinkerton's academy.

profligacy shall be wrapped up in cotton-wool, and naughtiness softened down to indiscretion. Half the *vaudevilles* which English playwrights translate for our theatres, and impudently pass off as their own, turn on the illicit love of a young man for a married woman, or *vice versâ;* but in the English translation the criminality involved is generally slurred over by the convenient device of the young gentleman being in possession of certain letters written by the lady before her marriage; at which discreet compromise refined, fastidious, and genteel society rejoices greatly. May not the expediency of a similarly discreet compromise have occurred to the author of *Vanity Fair?* and what would have been more discreet than George's proposal to Becky to "fly" with him? It is a pity that in conceding so much to genteel squeamishness, a very serious blemish should have fallen on an otherwise perfect work of art. (pp. 352-55)

> George Augustus Sala, "On a Certain Passage in 'Vanity Fair'," in Belgravia, Vol. VIII, No. 31, May, 1869, pp. 345-55.

ANTHONY TROLLOPE   (essay date 1879)

[*A prominent Victorian novelist, Trollope is best known for the "Barsetshire Chronicles," a series of novels that realistically and humorously depicts English provincial life. Trollope's Thackeray, from which the following excerpt was drawn, was one of the earliest book-length studies of the novelist and is still a highly regarded work. Here, Trollope responds to Thackeray's detractors on such issues as* Vanity Fair's *moral influence, its apparently cynical outlook on life, and Amelia's suitability as a heroine.*]

It may be as well to speak first of the faults which were attributed to [*Vanity Fair*]. It was said that the good people were all fools, and that the clever people were all knaves. When the critics,—the talking critics as well as the writing critics,—began to discuss *Vanity Fair,* there had already grown up a feeling as to Thackeray as an author—that he was one who had taken up the business of castigating the vices of the world. Scott had dealt with the heroics, whether displayed in his Flora MacIvors or Meg Merrilieses, in his Ivanhoes or Ochiltrees. Miss Edgeworth had been moral; Miss Austen conventional; Bulwer had been poetical and sentimental; Marryat and Lever had been funny and pugnacious, always with a dash of gallantry, displaying funny naval and funny military life; and Dickens had already become great in painting the virtues of the lower orders. But by all these some kind of virtue had been sung, though it might be only the virtue of riding a horse or fighting a duel. Even Eugene Aram and Jack Sheppard, with whom Thackeray found so much fault, were intended to be fine fellows, though they broke into houses and committed murders. The primary object of all those writers was to create an interest by exciting sympathy. . . . With Thackeray it had been altogether different. Alas, alas! the meanness of human wishes; the poorness of human results! That had been his tone. There can be no doubt that the heroic had appeared contemptible to him, as being untrue. . . . Why sing songs that are false? Why tell of Lucy Ashtons and Kate Nicklebys, when pretty girls, let them be ever so beautiful, can be silly and sly? Why pour philosophy out of the mouth of a fashionable young gentleman like Pelham, seeing that young gentlemen of that sort rarely, or we may say never, talk after that fashion? Why make a housebreaker a gallant charming young fellow, the truth being that housebreakers as a rule are as objectionable in their manners as they are in their morals? Thackeray's mind had in truth worked in this way, and he had become a satirist. That had

been all very well for *Fraser* and *Punch;* but when his satire was continued through a long novel, in twenty-four parts, readers,—who do in truth like the heroic better than the wicked,—began to declare that this writer was no novelist, but only a cynic. (pp. 90-2)

[This] special fault was certainly found with *Vanity Fair* at the time. Heroines should not only be beautiful, but should be endowed also with a quasi celestial grace,—grace of dignity, propriety, and reticence. A heroine should hardly want to be married, the arrangement being almost too mundane,—and, should she be brought to consent to undergo such bond, because of its acknowledged utility, it should be at some period so distant as hardly to present itself to the mind as a reality. Eating and drinking should be altogether indifferent to her, and her clothes should be picturesque rather than smart, and that from accident rather than design. Thackeray's Amelia does not at all come up to the description here given. She is proud of having a lover, constantly declaring to herself and to others that he is "the greatest and the best of men,"—whereas the young gentleman is, in truth, a very little man. She is not at all indifferent as to her finery, nor, as we see incidentally, to enjoying her suppers at Vauxhall. She is anxious to be married,—and as soon as possible. A hero too should be dignified and of a noble presence; a man who, though he may be as poor as Nicholas Nickleby, should nevertheless be beautiful on all occasions, and never deficient in readiness, address, or self-assertion. *Vanity Fair* is specially declared by the author to be "a novel without a hero," and therefore we have hardly a right to complain of deficiency of heroic conduct in any of the male characters. But Captain Dobbin does become the hero, and is deficient. Why was he called Dobbin, except to make him ridiculous? Why is he so shamefully ugly, so shy, so awkward? Why was he the son of a grocer? Thackeray in so depicting him was determined to run counter to the recognised taste of novel readers. And then again there was the feeling of another great fault. Let there be the virtuous in a novel and let there be the vicious, the dignified and the undignified, the sublime and the ridiculous,—only let the virtuous, the dignified, and the sublime be in the ascendant. Edith Bellenden, and Lord Evandale, and Morton himself would be too stilted, were they not enlivened by Mause, and Cuddie, and Poundtext. But here, in this novel, the vicious and the absurd have been made to be of more importance than the good and the noble. Becky Sharp and Rawdon Crawley are the real heroine and hero of the story. It is with them that the reader is called upon to interest himself. It is of them that he will think when he is reading the book. It is by them that he will judge the book when he has read it. There was no doubt a feeling with the public that though satire may be very well in its place, it should not be made the backbone of a work so long and so important as this. A short story such as *Catherine* or *Barry Lyndon* might be pronounced to have been called for by the iniquities of an outside world; but this seemed to the readers to have been addressed almost to themselves. Now men and women like to be painted as Titian would paint them, or Raffaelle,—not as Rembrandt, or even Rubens.

Whether the ideal or the real is the best form of a novel may be questioned, but there can be no doubt that as there are novelists who cannot descend from the bright heaven of the imagination to walk with their feet upon the earth, so there are others to whom it is not given to soar among clouds. The reader must please himself, and make his selection if he cannot enjoy both. There are many who are carried into a heaven of pathos by the woes of a Master of Ravenswood, who fail altogether to be touched by the enduring constancy of a Dobbin. There are others,—and I will not say but they may enjoy the keenest delight which literature can give,—who cannot employ their minds on fiction unless it be conveyed in poetry. With Thackeray it was essential that the representations made by him should be, to his own thinking, lifelike. A Dobbin seemed to him to be such a one as might probably be met with in the world, whereas to his thinking a Ravenswood was simply a creature of the imagination. He would have said of such, as we would say of female faces by Raffaelle, that women would like to be like them, but are not like them. Men might like to be like Ravenswood, and women may dream of men so formed and constituted, but such men do not exist. Dobbins do, and therefore Thackeray chose to write of a Dobbin.

So also of the preference given to Becky Sharp and to Rawdon Crawley. Thackeray thought that more can be done by exposing the vices than extolling the virtues of mankind. No doubt he had a more thorough belief in the one than in the other. The Dobbins he did encounter—seldom; the Rawdon Crawleys very often. He saw around him so much that was mean! He was hurt so often by the little vanities of people! It was thus that he was driven to . . . overthoughtfulness about snobs. . . . It thus became natural to him to insist on the thing which he hated with unceasing assiduity, and only to break out now and again into a rapture of love for the true nobility which was dear to him,—as he did with the character of Captain Dobbin.

It must be added to all this that, before he has done with his snob or his knave, he will generally weave in some little trait of humanity by which the sinner shall be relieved from the absolute darkness of utter iniquity. He deals with no Varneys or Deputy-Shepherds, all villany and all lies, because the snobs and knaves he had seen had never been all snob or all knave. Even Shindy probably had some feeling for the poor woman he left at home. Rawdon Crawley loved his wicked wife dearly, and there were moments even with her in which some redeeming trait half reconciles her to the reader.

Such were the faults which were found in *Vanity Fair;* but though the faults were found freely, the book was read by all. Those who are old enough can well remember the effect which it had, and the welcome which was given to the different numbers as they appeared. Though the story is vague and wandering, clearly commenced without any idea of an ending, yet there is something in the telling which makes every portion of it perfect in itself. There are absurdities in it which would not be admitted to anyone who had not a peculiar gift of making even his absurdities delightful. No schoolgirl who ever lived would have thrown back her gift-book, as Rebecca did the "dixonary," out of the carriage window as she was taken away from school. But who does not love that scene with which the novel commences? How could such a girl as Amelia Osborne have got herself into such society as that in which we see her at Vauxhall? But we forgive it all because of the telling. (pp. 92-6)

There is a double story running through the book, the parts of which are but lightly woven together, of which the former tells us the life and adventures of that singular young woman Becky Sharp, and the other the troubles and ultimate success of our noble hero Captain Dobbin. Though it be true that readers prefer, or pretend to prefer, the romantic to the common in their novels, and complain of pages which are defiled with that which is low, yet I find that the absurd, the ludicrous, and even the evil, leave more impression behind them than the grand, the beautiful, or even the good. Dominie Sampson,

Dugald Dalgetty, and Bothwell are, I think, more remembered than Fergus MacIvor, than Ivanhoe himself, or Mr. Butler the minister. It certainly came to pass that, in spite of the critics, Becky Sharp became the first attraction in *Vanity Fair.* When we speak now of *Vanity Fair,* it is always to Becky that our thoughts recur. She has made a position for herself in the world of fiction, and is one of our established personages. (p. 98)

To the end [Becky] is the same,—utterly false, selfish, covetous, and successful. To have made such a woman really in love would have been a mistake. Her husband she likes best,—because he is, or was, her own. But there is no man so foul, so wicked, so unattractive, but that she can fawn over him for money and jewels. There are women to whom nothing is nasty, either in person, language, scenes, actions, or principle,—and Becky is one of them; and yet she is herself attractive. A most wonderful sketch, for the perpetration of which all Thackeray's power of combined indignation and humour was necessary!

The story of Amelia and her two lovers, George Osborne and Captain, or as he came afterwards to be, Major, and Colonel Dobbin, is less interesting, simply because goodness and eulogy are less exciting than wickedness and censure. Amelia is a true, honest-hearted, thoroughly English young woman, who loves her love because he is grand,—to her eyes,—and loving him, loves him with all her heart. Readers have said that she is silly, only because she is not heroic. I do not know that she is more silly than many young ladies whom we who are old have loved in our youth, or than those whom our sons are loving at the present time. Readers complain of Amelia because she is absolutely true to nature. There are no Raffaellistic touches, no added graces, no divine romance. She is feminine all over, and British,—loving, true, thoroughly unselfish, yet with a taste for having things comfortable, forgiving, quite capable of jealousy, but prone to be appeased at once, at the first kiss; quite convinced that her lover, her husband, her children are the people in all the world to whom the greatest consideration is due. Such a one is sure to be the dupe of a Becky Sharp, should a Becky Sharp come in her way,—as is the case with so many sweet Amelias whom we have known. But in a matter of love she is sound enough and sensible enough,—and she is as true as steel. I know no trait in Amelia which a man would be ashamed to find in his own daughter. (pp. 104-05)

The reader as he closes the book has on his mind a strong conviction, the strongest possible conviction, that among men George is as weak and Dobbin as noble as any that he has met in literature; and that among women Amelia is as true and Becky as vile as any he has encountered. Of so much he will be conscious. In addition to this he will unconsciously have found that every page he has read will have been of interest to him. There has been no padding, no longueurs; every bit will have had its weight with him. And he will find too at the end, if he will think of it—though readers, I fear, seldom think much of this in regard to books they have read—that the lesson taught in every page has been good. There may be details of evil painted so as to disgust,—painted almost too plainly,—but none painted so as to allure. (pp. 106-07)

Anthony Trollope, in his Thackeray, *1879. Reprint by Gale Research Company, 1968, 216 p.*

ROBERT LOUIS STEVENSON (essay date 1882)

[*A famous Scottish novelist and essayist, Stevenson wrote some of the nineteenth century's most beloved novels, including* Treasure Island, Doctor Jekyll and Mr. Hyde, *and* Kidnapped. *In the following excerpt, Stevenson stresses the importance in* Vanity Fair *of the scene in chapter fifty-three in which Rawdon strikes Lord Steyne after finding him alone with Becky. Stevenson's comments were written in 1882.*]

If Rawdon Crawley's blow were not delivered, **Vanity Fair** would cease to be a work of art. That scene is the chief ganglion of the tale; and the discharge of energy from Rawdon's fist is the reward and consolation of the reader. (p. 239)

> Robert Louis Stevenson, "A Gossip on Romance," in his Memories and Portraits, 1887. Reprint by Charles Scribner's Sons, 1923, pp. 229-53.

ADOLPHUS ALFRED JACK (essay date 1895)

[*In the following excerpt, Jack initially examines* Vanity Fair *within the context of Thackeray's output as a whole, speculating on the possibility that prototypes for various characters in the novel may exist in the author's previous works. In the second portion of the excerpt, the critic explores the vision of life presented in the novel as well as Thackeray's portrayal of Becky, Rawdon, Amelia, and Dobbin.*]

[**Vanity Fair**] is singularly straightforward. The same attitude is preserved throughout, and that attitude, though severer than, is in all essentials similar to that formerly adopted. There is a greater diversity in the personages of the novel, and more sagacity in the commentary which accompanies the record of their doings than is to be found in any of Thackeray's earlier works. But the figures are such as we should have expected him, when concentrating his faculties, to be able to draw, and the sentiments have nothing surprising in them, coming from the author of **Catherine, The Hoggarty Diamond,** and **The Book of Snobs.** Miss Wirt, the governess of the two Miss Osbornes, was formerly in the service of Major Ponto; Dobbin's fight at Slaughter House School is a repetition of Mr. Frank Berry's; Deuceace, Viscount Cinqbars, and Lord Bareacres flit about in the background, and just as the mother of the heroine of **The Ravenswing** was a ballet-dancer, so Mrs. Sharp is an opera-girl. These are not merely superficial resemblances, but there are others that are still more striking. "The richly-dressed figure of the wicked nobleman" is merely a compound of all those vices which Thackeray had for long pointed out as appertaining especially to the aristocracy. Dennis Haggarty's devotion to a woman unworthy of him gave a hint for Dobbin's; Rawdon Crawley has not the ability of Redmond Barry or of Deuceace, but he has as many of their vices as were compatible with his stupidity; Amelia gave scope for an elaborate study of the virtues of Mary Titmarsh and Caroline Gann; while it is easy to see that Becky is a cleverer Catherine Hayes, moving in a higher rank of society, and amid less melodramatic surroundings. Mr. Sedley in his misfortunes, and Mr. Osborne in his prosperity, are both indebted to the earlier portraiture of the oil-merchant in **A Shabby Genteel Story;** the feelings entertained for Caroline by the Misses Macarthy, and those that characterize the relations of George Osborne's sisters with his *fiancée,* are the same with a difference; while Sir Pitt has as much bluster as Sir George Tufto, and more vulgar arrogance than Lord Crabs.

The origins of George Osborne, Pitt Crawley, and Miss Briggs, it is true, are not so easily traceable; and though Miss Hoggarty's money had been an object of much solicitude to Mr. Brough, she has no other likeness to Miss Crawley. Major O'Dowd and his wife, and the admirably drawn Jos Sedley, are also original. But though these figures give variety to the

canvas, and we are forced to confess that we do not recognize them, they all have a family likeness to the people whom we already knew, and take their places naturally by their sides. Nor is the treatment accorded to these characters unfamiliar. The sub-title of the book is **A Novel without a Hero,** a phrase that, effective as it is, fails to express the meaning of the author. There was nothing to necessitate a flourish in the absence of a hero. Shakespeare wrote plays without a hero:—the interest of one is centred in Lady Macbeth, and in *Twelfth Night* it is Olivia and Viola who arrest our attention; while *The Blithedale Romance* subordinates Miles Coverdale and Hollingsworth to the more commanding personality of Zenobia. Rebecca Sharp takes up as much of the space of **Vanity Fair** as is usually allocated to a heroine, and there was nothing remarkable in giving to a woman the chief position in a tale. The characteristic of **Vanity Fair** is not that it has no hero, but that there is nothing heroic in it, and this it is that differentiates the novel from the works of other writers, and supplies the real reason of its effect upon the public. But this, for Thackeray, was not a new departure; on the contrary, it is this that furnishes the distinct peculiarity of all his earlier tales. **Vanity Fair** came with the novelty of a new sensation, only because they were so little read. But the book itself is the best justification of its success.

In some ways it is the most striking thing that Thackeray ever did. He never surpassed it for quiet observation of character, and for the skill with which he has contrived to make the most unreal and fantastic of its personages appear to live. But it is hard, one-sided, and the peculiarity which made it famous is the most marked of its defects. It has been said that it is an actual transcript from life, but the *Midsummer Night's Dream* is more near to reality. While we read the book, so great is its fascination, we can almost believe it to be true, but as soon as we lay it down, the narrative begins to assume its true form for us, and we see it as it is, from the beginning to the end "one entire impossibility." It is not that the characters are impossible, though some of them are impossible enough. It is not that no woman was ever simply a calculating machine, it is not that no man was ever merely sanctimonious, it is not that no baronet was ever a brutal bully and nothing more, or a peer ever wholly profligate, or a merchant ever made up only of vulgarity and rage, because such people have on rare occasions existed, and may by possibility again. It is not in this that the impossibility consists, but such a collection was never got together in one corner of the world. There are two good people in the book,—Dobbin, who is a simpleton, and Amelia, who is a fool. But these are not the only virtuous inhabitants of the Vanity Fair in which we live. If it were otherwise, if there were no other virtuous inhabitants, a man walking through it would not only "not be oppressed by his own or other people's hilarity" [see Thackeray's preface to **Vanity Fair,** dated 1848], but he would decline, and very properly decline, to walk through it at all. If life were as Thackeray depicts it in **Vanity Fair,** not only would the earth be more sparsely populated than it is, but it would have been impossible for true virtue ever to have manifested itself. Virtue being the product of precept and example, Scott could not have lived, nor the qualities of the Vicar of Wakefield had opportunity to develop. Had the world been peopled with Neros, there would have been no room for Seneca, and were every one a Crawley or a Sharp, Esmond's self-sacrifice or Colonel Newcome's heroism would never have been understood.

In **The Memoirs of Barry Lyndon** the company is worse than in **Vanity Fair,** and **The Memoirs of Barry Lyndon** is a triumph of art but it would have been far from a triumph if we had been asked to take the company there assembled as a fair representation of society. We should have rejected it at once as an imposture, whereas the falsehood underlying *Vanity Fair* is only apparent—and it is a tribute to Thackeray's power—after a careful perusal of the work. But when this fact is allowed, when we turn to look at *Vanity Fair* not as a portrait, not even as a caricature of society, but as a brilliant painting of a section of it, there remains much that is admirable. It is almost as difficult to draw a woman without a heart as a woman without a soul, and the latter has not yet been seriously attempted. Mr. Benson's Dodo is an ingenious and clever study of such a character, but it is only necessary to compare his method with Thackeray's to see why he has failed, and how much he has underrated the gravity of the task. Thackeray devotes all his resources to the creation of Becky Sharp. He was well aware how long a course of observation had to be undertaken before even the broad lines of such a figure could be accurately sketched. And it is this that makes him watch Becky with a solicitude that might deceive the reader into imagining that her creator could not resist occasionally admiring her cleverness and resource. He calls her ''darling,'' it is true; but the epithet is always abusive, never laudatory, and though in a sense she is the darling of his eye, it is only that he knew that, if he was for a moment to lose sight of her, her interest for the reader could not have been sustained. She is hardly ever absent from the stage, and her introduction is so bold that Mr. Trollope thought it must have slipped in by mistake. ''No schoolgirl,'' he writes, ''who ever lived would have thrown back her gift-book as Rebecca did the 'dixonary' out of the carriage-window as she was taken away from school'' [see excerpt dated 1879]. The error is comprehensible, even in so acute a critic, but the facts are quite the other way. No woman so selfish and calculating as Becky afterwards became could have failed to make mistakes of temper and forwardness in her youth. (pp. 75-82)

Her second appearance as Clytemnestra is, however, less to be defended. She had by that time acquired too much experience to risk, even when driven to bay, poisoning Jos Sedley; but the incident is improbable, not impossible, and the same artist who leaves a lingering suspicion that Lord Steyne may, at the last moment, have been baulked of his prey, refrains from deliberately accusing her of murder. The introduction of Sir Pitt Crawley, on the other hand, is caricature, and Mr. Trollope is justified in supposing that it must have been written before any of the other members of the Crawley family had been conceived. And what a family it is; a selfish old woman who has money, a dissolute clergyman, a hypocritical diplomatist, and a dissipated bully. But they all manage to preserve some relation to humanity, and their actions and sentiments are for the most part chronicled with a strange fidelity to life. (pp. 83-4)

For Rawdon Crawley it is difficult to understand Thackeray's admiration. He calls him ''honest Rawdon,'' with real fondness in his voice, and seems to pity him for his connection with his wife. But the man was a drunkard and a cheat long before Becky had anything to do with him; and we are left to supply the occasion of the duel which ended disastrously for Captain Marker. Duelling days were nearly over then, and it is as likely as not that Captain Marker had some serious cause for offence. That Rawdon should experience a passion for a fascinating governess was nothing particularly meritorious. He did not expect to lose money by it, and when he discovered that he had, even he had sense enough to perceive that he owed something to the woman who alone was able to keep him above

water. Besides, the money was never really his, and he was too stupid to appreciate the excellence of his chance. That he should beat an old man who had been intriguing with his wife so openly that every one but he had seen it long before, was no more praiseworthy than the resentment of a thief when his own property is stolen. It is true that there was a pitch of baseness to which he could not bring himself to descend, and he returned the price of Becky's dishonour to Lord Steyne; but he sulkily accepted from the same nobleman the considerable income of a sinecure which he could easily have refused, and for the slight duties of which he was totally unfit. All this was natural enough, but it was no subject for admiration; and though it was human of him to be fond of his son, there was as much merit in the maudlin tears of Redmond Barry, or the pleasure Catherine took in the fine clothes of the adopted son of Mr. Hayes.

It is one thing to treat vice with charity, and quite another to speak of its professors with affection. The same book that spoke of ''honest Rawdon'' could hardly contain a character that would ensure our respect. Amelia fails even to enlist our sympathy. In prosperity she is childish, in adversity she becomes petted and wilful, and Mr. Senior has pointed out that her reluctance to part with her boy is due wholly to a desire that they should not be separated, not to any fear of the prejudicial results for him that might arise from acquaintance with the Osbornes. She is passionately devoted during his life to George Osborne, who half despises her, and after his death she cherishes a romantic attachment to his memory. To Amelia Sedley, however, a large portion of the book is devoted, and it is not to be supposed that she should not occasionally be betrayed into animation. Thackeray's purpose in delineating this character was twofold; he introduced her first as an example of the negative virtues, and afterwards continued the study of her disposition as a foil to that of Becky. He maintains an unswerving determination to keep her as we first met her, a timid, expansive school-girl, with a fund of maudlin sensibility dangerously apt to develop into selfishness. Again and again, in her passages with Dobbin, Thackeray resists the temptation to endow her with a heart, and where one would have expected from the most long-suffering, righteous anger, or an outburst of wronged and passionate love, we find only sobs and protestations, and a page of sentimental reflection. Once or twice she finds her lot too hard, and becomes peevishly unreasonable, as in the scene with Mrs. Sedley and the baby's medicine, or flings out into a momentary burst of irritation. But these passages are for the most part calculated, and have a touch of artifice. They serve to vary the monotony of her characterless virtue, but they give a laboured effect to the portrait. Once only Nature takes the pen from his hand, and allows us to have a peep at the heart of this too real Cinderella. It is the morning after the Duchess of Richmond's ball, when the English officers have left for Waterloo. (p. 85-8)

But Amelia never again rises to this height of womanly indignation, and she sinks back into the spiritless creature whom the worthy and clumsy Dobbin was content to pursue. His devotion is disinterested and noble, but it is expended on so poor an object that it lessens him in our esteem. She was no ''dear lady Disdain,'' whose waywardness increased her attraction, and it is natural and fitting that her knight-errant should be as uninteresting as herself.

Thackeray might have gauged the effect Amelia would have upon the public from the fate he prescibes for Dobbin. Like her, he is a compound of all the negative virtues, though he

An illustration by Thackeray of George lighting his cigar with one of Amelia's letters.

has a warmer heart, and is, as all soldier-heroes, necessarily courageous. But she prefers the memory of her first husband, who, if he had few virtues, had just enough character to commit occasional and ineffectual sins. His approbation was perhaps also the more precious as she was conscious of having partially lost it. As to Dobbin's affection, it was to be had long before it was asked, and always at her command. He is so formally precise that he cannot even blunder into his own happiness, and it is by a subtle touch of irony that he is made to win Amelia at length, not because her sentiments towards him are altered, but because she has discovered that her first husband was unfaithful. "This is what he has asked for every day and hour for eighteen years. This is what he pined after. Here it is—the summit, the end—the last page of the third volume." Well might Thackeray conclude his book with the melancholy question, "Ah, Vanitas Vanitatum! which of us has his desire? or, having it, is satisfied?" (pp. 92-4)

> *Adolphus Alfred Jack, in his* Thackeray: A Study, *1895. Reprint by Kennikat Press, 1970, 196 p.*

HARRY THURSTON PECK (essay date 1909)

[*Peck discusses numerous aspects of* Vanity Fair, *including the various stages in the development of the novel, its lack of heroic characters, and the influence of Thackeray's membership in men's clubs on his philosophy. The critic also uses* Vanity Fair *to compare Thackeray's works with those of Charles Dickens.*]

To set oneself the task of writing about *Vanity Fair* recalls Schopenhauer's famous saying: "Everything has been thought,

everything has been done, everything has been written, everything has been said." It would not be possible, for example, to discover anything in Becky Sharp which had escaped the observation of a host of critics long ago. From Dobbin and Amelia and Lord Steyne, with his buckteeth and great jarring laugh, and old Osborne, and the gluttonous Jos, down to Kirsch, the courier, and the frowsy German students dabbling their blond moustaches in their beer-mugs at Pumpernickel, all the people in the book have been held beneath the microscope since the time when they were first created for us, sixty years ago. There is not one of them that lacks the breath of life; but for this very reason they are too familiar to need interpretation. Like old acquaintances, we have come to know them down to the very last detail. We do not dwell upon their virtues or deplore their vices. We simply accept them as they are and take them quite for granted.

Nevertheless, of the book itself there remains, perhaps, something still to say. The most curious thing about it is the circumstance that, when Thackeray set out to write it, he did not in the least suppose that he was going to produce a masterpiece. He had been scribbling nearly all his life, often for the sheer love of self-expression, and later, after he had lost his fortune, because of the money which his pen would bring him. (pp. 149-50)

Nearly everything he wrote was in a vein of irony or humour. He took nothing very seriously, least of all himself and his own writings. What he actually valued most was his bent for art. This is only another example of what we so often see— the ambition of a gifted man to shine in some sphere other than that for which his native genius fits him. Thackeray really thought himself an artist of the brush and pencil, and he was hurt when Dickens would not employ him as an illustrator for the early books of "Boz." He was pleased that *Punch* would accept and publish his faulty drawings. So Dickens, in his turn, valued more the perfunctory praise which he won in amateur theatricals than he did the true fame which came to him spontaneously as an author.

Finally after having written an immense deal that is hardly worth recalling, and some other things which do not deserve remembrance, Thackeray put forth, on New Year's Day in 1847, the first number of *Vanity Fair,* in a yellow wrapper. He was led to begin a story to appear in parts by the great success which Dickens had won in the same way. But *Vanity Fair* at first seemed likely to be an utter disappointment. When four numbers had been issued, the publishers were so assured of its failure that they proposed to discontinue it. It is probable that Thackeray himself had no great hope. Then, with the fifth number, the tide turned, and all literary London began talking of the story which in spirit and in manner was something genuinely new.

Nevertheless, if it succeeded, it did so almost in its author's own despite. Thackeray had really planned it as a burlesque. If any one will compare the first edition of it with the form in which we have it now, it will be plain enough that the novel was meant to be written in a comic vein. Whole passages that were farcical were afterward eliminated. In one of the earlier chapters, for instance, the author stops the progress of the tale to explain, with a sort of side-wink to the reader, that, had he chosen, he might have written the adventures of Jos and Becky and Amelia in one of two other manners. Thus, he says, he might have promoted all his characters to the peerage; or, on the other hand, he might have copied the Bulwer-Lytton of his time and made them lackeys and roughs and burglars, who patter thieves' argot—"beladle your glumbanions and bimbole your chickeys"—whatever that may mean. He even writes in a little scene as a specimen of what he could do in the latter *genre* had he but chosen. As he went on, however, his "novel without a hero" took strong hold of him. He afterwards confessed that he "wasn't going to write it in that way when he began." He started out to perpetrate a caricature. He ended by producing a finished painting.

The reason why *Vanity Fair* succeeded at the time is to be found in its freshness of manner. The historical romance, which had been so splendidly developed by Scott, had grown stale in the hands of G. P. R. James, Harrison Ainsworth, and a hundred smaller men. The sentimental romance pure and simple had reached the verge of mawkishness with Miss Landon and Bulwer-Lytton. The latter had also led the ranks of writers who revelled in low life and the psychology of crime. Then upon the scene came Thackeray, to give the English-speaking people a novel of manners, of social experiences, of life as men and women of the world beheld it. Every one had become tired of "fine writing," and Thackeray gave them good writing instead—writing that was often half colloquial and still more often wholly so. Men read him with that sense of relief which, in an earlier generation, they had felt in passing from the rhodomontade of Mrs. Radcliffe and her school to the sturdy, vigorous manner of Sir Walter Scott. But Thackeray pushed the easy style a stage farther. He left rhetoric alone and spoke in that level, easy tone which marks the talk of the club smokingroom rather than the library of the professional man of letters. It was sophisticated writing, but still it had the effectiveness of simplicity.

The men and the women who appear in *Vanity Fair* are also, if not themselves sophisticated, at least seen through sophisticated eyes. Thackeray called the book "a novel without a hero." It is just as truly a novel without a heroine, at least in the old sense of that word. There is, indeed, nothing heroic in any of the characters. There is not one of them who is free from vice or folly or from some petty failing. Thackeray himself declared that he meant to make "a set of people living without God in the world" [see excerpt dated 1847]. He did not really do this; yet, none the less, he has created a set of people who are always far below the level on which we can unfeignedly admire them. Amelia Sedley, for example, is almost worse that Becky Sharp. She is quite as selfish, and she has no brains. She can be maudlin over the cockney dandy who married her almost against his will, and she can weep over her little son, who is as selfish as his father was; but she can not understand the loyal love of an honest man. She will use it unscrupulously for her own convenience, and she will give it no reward except at the last, when she is forced to take it because she needs its strong protection. Thackeray never intended to let Dobbin marry Amelia; but he was urged to do so by his readers until at last he yielded, saying pettishly:

> Well, he shall marry her; but when he has got her, he shall not find her worth the having.

What a wonderful panorama of human weakness is unrolled before our eyes in the chapters of *Vanity Fair!* Try to recall one character whom you can admire without reservation. Dobbin, perhaps, stands forth a finer person than the rest. In character and in mind he makes a strong appeal; yet his awkwardness and loutishness of bearing are continually harped upon. Again and again he appears to be entirely ridiculous. His foolish infatuation for Amelia almost makes one's blood boil, it is so utterly unjustified. For the rest, think of the miserly and clown-

ish old baronet, Sir Pitt Crawley; his fox-hunting, hard-drinking parson brother; his graceless, selfish, and bewigged old sister, and his two sons, one a dissolute bully, and the other a feeble prig. Think of Wenham, the smooth pander, of the senile old general just before Waterloo, and of the cowardly and gluttonous Jos Sedley!

It must be confessed that in this maze of living meannesses, Becky Sharp stands out by contrast almost a good woman. At least, she is consistent from beginning to end. If she is selfish, she is thoroughly good-natured. She is fighting for her own hand, but she does so with wit and grace and astounding cleverness. At the last she is willing even to efface herself to help Amelia, although, of course, she does so only after Amelia's environment begins to bore her. When you close the book you rather sympathise with this free-lance of society; for she is a gallant little campaigner, and she has had to deal with persons who are worse than she, or else infinitely stupid. One resents a little the fact that she fooled poor old Miss Briggs, because Miss Briggs was fooled so very easily; but that she fooled George Osborne and the Crawleys, young and old, is only fitting. Her magnificent insolence to Lady Bareacres in the hotel courtyard at Brussels is really delightful. And when she actually fools Lord Steyne our admiration is unqualified. Indeed, as the reader will remember, it extorted admiration from that hardened sinner himself when he found out that Becky had by tears and pitiful pleas got money from him, ostensibly to pay Miss Briggs, and had then kept it for herself.

> "What an accomplished little devil it is!" thought he. "What a splendid actress and manager! She had almost got a second supply out of me the other day, with her coaxing ways. She beats all the women I have ever seen in the course of all my well-spent life. They are babies compared to her. I am a greenhorn myself, and a fool in her hands—an old fool. She is unsurpassable in lies!"
>
> His Lordship's admiration for Becky rose immeasurably at this proof of her cleverness. Getting the money was nothing—but getting double the sum she wanted, and paying nobody—it was a magnificent stroke.

From Thackeray's standpoint, he was, after all, merely stripping off the false pretences, the hypocritical masks, behind which every one must hide himself while in the confines of Vanity Fair. The picture is true to life itself, though it is not true to all of life. In this respect Thackeray is like Maupassant. Every human being whom he draws is drawn with a pitiless realism. Each separate impression is veracious. The only false thing is the tacit assumption that all the world is peopled by such types as we discover in *Vanity Fair,* and that there are none who are wholly pure-minded, generous, and noble.

Thackeray, in his book, has looked at human nature, not face to face and in the open air, but rather through the bay-window of a club. His philosophy is the philosophy of the man who lives in clubs, and who listens to the talk which comes buzzing to the ear in club-room corners. It is talk made up of *risqué* stories, of hinted scandal, of cynical observation and of worldly aphorisms. So far as it goes, it conveys the truth while it looks only at the seamy side of character. It questions motives with a sneer. It dissects and vivisects and analyses with consummate cleverness. It strips away illusions, and pries into hidden meannesses. But it takes no account of another and fairer world in which men are not debauchees, or card-sharps, or tuft-hunters, or snobs and social climbers, but where they believe in right and justice and in God, where they treat women with respect, and where women are deserving of respect. *Vanity Fair* displays for us a microcosm. Its art is microcosmic.

It was not unnatural that Thackeray should view life from this standpoint. He himself was essentially an inhabitant of clubs. The insanity fo his wife had deprived him of a home. He had roamed about in the Bohemia of Paris and the Behemia of London; and the club-window was the nest on which he settled down as other men repose before their firesides. Later, when many homes were open to him, he knew a world which had not forgotten God; and then we find him writing in a nobler vein, quite as rich in observation and richer far in a perception of what is fine and true. *The Newcomes* shows far less the influence of the club *fumoir*. In *Henry Esmond* we breathe the free air of the greater world which reaches beyond Hyde Park and Piccadilly, beyond London, and even beyond England.

The comparison of Thackeray and Dickens is an old, old literary game. As it is often carried on, nothing can be more absurd. . . . Indeed, the two men and their work are not properly comparable at all. They can not, so to speak, be reduced to a common denominator. Yet, in a broad way, some comparison may be instructive. Both of them were intensely English; but Thackeray was an Englishman of London, while Dickens was an Englishman of England; and his imagination, grotesque and strained as it sometimes is, reaches out beyond the sphere of the Particular up into the illimitable spaces of the Universal. His pathos may be at times theatrical. His humour may be often farcical. Yet, in his mightier moments he appeals to something to which every human heart responds. Thackeray, on the other hand, is technically the greater artist. He is the truest realist that England has produced, except his contemporary, Trollope. But in *Vanity Fair* his realism is a realism that is shrunken to a single corner of his country. It is not large enough and broad enough to comprehend the hearts of men and women everywhere. *Vanity Fair* is a wonderful example of urban literature. Yet unless you are a Londoner, unless you are worldly-wise, unless you have yourself a touch of cynicism in your nature, you will not greatly care for Thackeray. To prefer Dickens to him is to show yourself more broadly human. (pp. 150-58)

To the last Thackeray remained the Englishman of London. He never understood the French. His judgments on them are oftentimes absurd. He set Balzac far below such second-rate French authors as Bernard and Reybaud, whom the world has long ago forgotten. He declares that he could not read Dumas "without a risk of lighting upon horrors." He is sometimes still more smug, as when in Athens he sees nothing but its shabbiness, "which beats Ireland." His smugness is equally apparent in the pages of *Vanity Fair*, whenever he breaks off his marvellous portrait-painting to preach sermons, or again as where he spoils a passage of fine pathos with a sort of cynic leer, so that, as Mr. Whibley says, "he seems to snigger amid sobs." It is equally true that he often sobs amid sniggers. He can not be the artist pure and simple—all of one piece, consistent, whole. He is a product of the clubs, and yet one thinks of him, perhaps, as sneaking out of his club to appease his conscience with an evening in a Wesleyan chapel. This would be commendable did he go boldly to the chapel; but he certainly does not do that. He discovers his place of worship in some remote back alley where his fine friends will not see him; and then, returning and sitting once more in his club-window, he will light a fresh cigar and sneer at the devout.

Vanity Fair is one of the greatest books in English literature, but it belongs to purely English literature, and not to the great masterpieces which the whole world owns and to which it gives an unforced admiration. If you can breathe its atmosphere, you will read it over and over to the end of life. Otherwise its author will be to you simply a remarkable English novelist whom Englishmen will always place in the first rank of their fiction-writers. (pp. 160-61)

Harry Thurston Peck, "Thackeray and 'Vanity Fair'," in his Studies in Several Literatures, *Dodd, Mead and Company, 1909, pp. 149-61.*

G. K. CHESTERTON   (essay date 1930)

[*Chesterton was one of England's most prominent and colorful men of letters during the early twentieth century. Although he is best known today as a detective novelist and essayist, he was also an eminent literary critic. Here, Chesterton provides a general introduction to* Vanity Fair, *commenting on its form, narrative style, characters, and philosophy and comparing Thackeray's tone with that of Dickens. Chesterton's remarks were first published in a 1930 edition of* Vanity Fair. *For additional criticism on the novel by Chesterton, see Additional Bibliography.*]

The rising generations, when confronted with *Vanity Fair*, as with the *Iliad*, the *Book of Job* or other works, are fully entitled to be struck, or even repelled, by the appearance of something old-fashioned; so long as they remember that they will not go on rising very long, before they become old-fashioned themselves. But in the matter of the form of fiction, fashions follow each other today with rather bewildering rapidity. *Vanity Fair* might have appeared somewhat formless to some of the old supporters of the classical unities; it might again have appeared somewhat formless to the exact artistry of the school and generation of Stevenson; but even if it were much more formless than it is, it could hardly reach the superb ecstasy of formlessness, which is admired in many of the long realistic novels of today. As a matter of fact, it is far less formless than it looks. The narrative style of the novelist is garrulous and therefore discursive. Indeed the way in which the tale is told is in a rather special sense the manner of gossip. It is gossip not only in being casual and allusive; but also in actually being indirect. Much of the story comes to us by rumour; tales are told by one club man to another club man; we might say by one Thackeray to another Thackeray. He often manages to suggest more than he is prepared to say, by putting up some jolly old snob to say it. The method of gossip has a certain realism; it suggests the same figure seen from many sides; like a single man seen in all the mirrors of the London club. It will at least be well if the younger critic realises that Thackeray's style, which seems to be one of drawling and dawdling irrelevancy, is not an accident but an artistic method, suitable to his special purposes; and that sometimes his very irrelevance is as relevant as a conjurer's patter. In more direct and economical stylists, such as Stevenson, we know what the author thinks of the character; and possibly what the character thinks of the other character whom he marries or murders with a cutlass. In books like *Vanity Fair*, it is very necessary that we should also know what the World thinks of the character; for indeed in *Vanity Fair* the chief character is the World. It would be an exaggeration to say that the World is the villain of the piece; but it may well be said that in this sense it is a novel without a hero. The theme of it is what the old comic dramatist called *The Way of the World*; and a sort of satiric but not too severe judgment on it, for the way in which it treats all its characters, including the comparatively rare heroes and villains. For this purpose it is necessary that the club of Thackeray, like the island of Prospero, should be "full of voices"; and that we should get a general sense of much that is mere talk, or even mere echoes. For instance; I doubt if it would have been possible to convey the historic but rather unique position of the few very great, because very rich, English Dukes or Marquises (who were something quite different from mere nobility or gentry, in the sense in which any squire or soldier might happen to have a title); it would have been impossible to suggest the strange public position of a man like Lord Steyne, without all those scattered allusions to him and momentary glimpses of him, in the distance, on the high places of English social life. That sort of man is Somebody through all the nobodies who never knew him. We should not feel it enough by being suddenly introduced into his presence; we have to feel that this very absence is as impressive as his presence. All this gossip about the great House of Gaunt is deliberate and even delicate, and without it we should not get the distance or the perspective that points to the ultimate scene; or feel the full force of that splendid blow which the obscure and stupid husband struck, leaving the scar which the Lord Steyne carried till his death.

Allowing for this wandering style (which as I say is often artful as well as artless), I repeat that there is a real form in *Vanity Fair,* the lines of which are kept more carefully than in much modern fiction. The pattern or outline of the story consists of the parallel or divergent careers of two girls, who start together from the same school in the first chapter. Vanity Fair, or the fashion of this world that passes away, is tested by its treatment of these two types and tests the types in its turn. One is the celebrated Becky Sharpe, the adventuress with many of the attractions of adventure; courageous, humorous, quick-witted, but under these natural defences somewhat hard and entirely cynical; one of those children of the poor who are born with a curious moral conviction of a right to possess riches and to rob the rich. The other is a more normal young woman of the sort that most would call ordinary; not demanding much from life, but expecting at the best a happiness of the sort called sentimental; and in all her views of existence at the best traditional, and at the worst conventional. I may remark here that I think it was one of Thackeray's real mistakes that he made her hold on such things rather conventional than traditional. Indeed in this case he was too conventional himself. He was so occupied with his contrasted pattern, with the good golden-haired heroine on one side and the wicked red-haired heroine on the other, that he made the golden-haired heroine a great deal less heroic than she might reasonably have been. It is not stating the alternative of vice and virtue fairly to make the vicious person a wit and imply that the virtuous person must be a fool. If he had been less anxious to make her a pathetic figure, she would have been more of a tragic figure.

Indeed, I think one disadvantage about *Vanity Fair,* especially today, is that one or two of these weak exaggerations occur very early in the book: and some greater passages only towards the end. Amelia is made at the very beginning a mere pink and white doll to be a foil to Becky; and if she represents a rather stale and vapid sort of sentimental comedy, her brother, Jos Sedley, represents a rather stale and vulgar sort of sentimental farce. I never could understand, even in youth, why that fat and featureless buck was allowed to sprawl across so much of the opening of the story; and I think it is rather a false note to make Becky deliberately set her cap at him. I imagine Miss Sharpe as already knowing the world well enough not to

waste herself on so socially fourth-rate a figure. It almost seems as if the Sedley family were more unfairly treated by Thackeray than by fortune; since the brother is vulgarised merely that he may be a slightly more vulgar copy of the dandy Osborne; while the sister suffers throughout from that first water-colour sketch of the two schoolgirls, in which Amelia is given all the water and Rebecca all the colour.

But, allowing for this, which I confess to thinking a mistake, we can still trace the clear outline and the largely convincing logic in the contrast of the two heroines. The contrast is of importance, for it involves the chief debates about Thackeray: the sense in which he was wrongly called cynical; the sense in which he may rightly be called sceptical. First of all, any number of idiots doubtless did call him cynical, because the story of these two girls was not what they called a moral tale; by which they meant the grossly immoral tale which tells, in the teeth of Job and Jesus Christ, the lie that the virtuous are rewarded with wealth. It is not, certainly, in that sense, a story of the Idle and Industrious Apprentice. It is certainly not modelled on the disgusting morals of *Pamela or Virtue Rewarded.* But (and this is the important point) neither is it made to enforce the opposite modern moral of "Amelia or Virtue Punished". There are many twisted and poisoned writers today, who would have played out the whole play with the opposite anti-moral purpose; leaving the wicked Becky in the blaze of the candelabra of Gaunt House and the kind Amelia picking up bits of coal, with a smut on her nose. This tragic trick (which was only too attractive to Thomas Hardy) is quite as much of a refusal to see life steadily and see it whole as the opposite artifice of the most artificial happy ending. It is not probable, but improbable, that Becky, with her desperate double or triple life, would have remained the Queen of Society for ever. It is not probable, but improbable, that anyone with the virtues and old connections of Amelia would have found absolutely none of her old friends ready to patch up her life for her. The point is that it is a sort of patching up in both cases. And with that we come near to the real meaning of Thackeray and the real moral of *Vanity Fair.*

The general inference from *Vanity Fair* is that life largely deceives and disappoints *all* people, bad and good; but that there is a difference, and that is (though the stupid optimist could not see it) rather on the side of the good. If we judge even Becky's life by the ambitious flights and flirtations of the beginning she is a ragged and disreputable failure at the end. If we judge Amelia's life by the romantic hopes of her first engagement, she is a stunned and helpless victim at the end. But if we compare the failure of Becky with the failure of Amelia, we see something that is profoundly true and is the chief truth of *Vanity Fair,* though most of the critics have missed it. The simpler, more innocent and more bewildered person is still capable of settling down into some sort of consolation and contentment; whereas she who has hardened herself against scandal or remorse has also hardened herself against hope.

A good novelist always has a philosophy; but a good novel is never a book of philosophy. The moral philosophy of Thackeray unites him rather with the old moralists than with the modern pessimists. He says, as his favourite authors, Solomon and Horace, would say, that life is in a sense vanity. He would never admit, in the sense of modern authors like Zola and Dreiser, that life is also vileness. His view may be called stoic or sceptic or anything else rather than pessimist. But because he was a novelist and a narrative artist, and not merely a man with a theory, it is true that there did appear in his works something of a personal note, not to be explained by any impersonal system. There is, when all is said and done, something which haunts the air and discolours the very scenery of *Vanity Fair* though it has never been satisfactorily stated or explained. It is a vivacious book, passing chiefly through scenes of gaiety and fashion; it is often witty and satirical; it contains a great deal of humorous interlude and comic characterization; some of it, as I have noted, being even too broadly comic. But it is not a *jolly* book; even when it is for the moment a funny book. There really is something about it faintly acid and antagonistic; and that something did belong partly to Thackeray the man, as well as to Thackeray the philosopher. (pp. 56-61)

If we want to understand the *tone* of Thackeray, the thing which is rather subtle and often misunderstood and makes up so much of the atmosphere of *Vanity Fair,* we must look first at something in his life and character, which can really be seen most sharply in contrast with that of Dickens. Dickens was a man who began in poverty and fought his way up to relative riches. Thackeray was a man who began with the reasonable prospect of riches, lost that prospect and had to work under conditions of relative poverty. With all his social type, tastes, and intentions, those of a gentleman of private means, or at least of considerable leisure, he became a hack and hung about Grub Street for a long time, before he had anything resembling the rapid rise and popularity of Dickens. It happened, as most people know, through his being ruined by professional gamblers, with whom he had played cards in his capacity of casual and lordly man of the world. The theme of such a swindle occurs again and again throughout his work. . . . (p. 62)

Now this did really involve a tone, which the comparison with the other novelist may make more clear. Money was a sore subject with Thackeray. But it was not so much a sore as an itch; in the sense that he could not let it alone and was always irritating it anew. Money was not a sore subject with Dickens. What is much more important, *poverty* was not a sore subject with Dickens. It did not really depress him; because he had faced it from the first and triumphed over it long before the end; and for both reasons he was familiar with it and not ashamed of it. Dickens does not describe the poor as merely unhappy, because he remembers being happy when he was young, and even when he was poor. . . . Now it is sometimes said that Thackeray confined all his attention to the rich and to being a mere novelist of society. This is meant for a sneer; but I rather wish for his sake that it were a truth. The truth is that Thackeray often did describe dismal lodgings and dreary privations and even high life below stairs. But what he could not bring himself to believe was that the lodgings were not always dismal; from the point of view of the lodgers. That is where the real difference from Dickens came in; for, much as Dickens suffered in youth, the lodgings had once, for him, really been *home.* . . . To Thackeray they had never been home, but a miserable seedy asylum for a man who had lost the home of his fathers or his equals. Hence it is not so much that Thackeray never looks at mean houses, as that he never looks at them from within; there is written across all that part of his work the title of one of his tales; *A Shabby Genteel Story.* (pp. 62-3)

In the particular case of *Vanity Fair* this tone can be easily caught in the description of the broken fortunes of the Sedleys; Dickens would never have thought that the Sedleys *were* so completely defeated by the Osbornes, merely because they lost a lot of money. But the paradox is that Dickens thought less

of poverty because he had known it, and thought less of money because he had earned it. To have that particular Thackerayan tone, compounded of pity and acrimony, it is necessary to have a certain bitterness; which is the bitterness of the man who has lost money rather than of the man who has failed to gain it. This tone has been called pessimistic or stoical or helpless or a hundred things; it has been called cynical by the old, and sentimental by the young; and it has elements of all these things. But the essential of it, which determines the idea of *Vanity Fair,* is a certain feeling, which no novelist had yet really introduced into the fiction of England; though Balzac had already introduced it into the fiction of France. It would be putting it too simply to call it The Importance of Money. For it is also a particular sense of something ghastly and unnatural about the Importance of Money. It is the cry of somebody who has found out, by falling over it, or breaking it, or losing it, that it is important; and yet cannot reconcile its importance with his own inner dignity and right reason. Hence the metaphor which makes the whole apparent world a sort of show with booths and puppet-theatres: Vanity Fair. In a sense he could not *believe* in this world; as smaller sceptics cannot believe in the other.

For we may say of Thackeray what he said of Swift; that there did remain at the back of his mind, in spite of all apparent scepticism, a noble but rather dark reality that is of the substance of religion. The Victorian Age had made it vague; the tradition of classical scholarship had made it seem almost heathen; but it was there, by the unanswerable test that applies to all the prophets and the saints. Thackeray thought the world *false;* which alone proves the presence of something contrasted with it which is true. Despite the superficial irritability which I have described, and which accounts for some of his lighter and less convincing sneers, it is true that he was too great a man to be godless and that he did not in his heart doubt that the injustices of the earth stand in contrast with a real justice. That is why I say that he stands rather with the ancient moralists than with the modern pessimists. It is true that this phrase also has been used incessantly and invariably wrongly. He himself confessed to a tendency to moralise; and many modern readers will doubtless repeat with far fiercer contempt this charge of moralising. But as a fact, it is not moralising at all. It is not strictly even philosophising. It is repeating old proverbs like the burden of an old song. It is not surprising that people once called it cynical and now call it sentimental. "Oh, it's the old story" is a sentence that can easily be said, both in a cynical and a sentimental tone. Thackeray was penetrated through and through with the conviction that this story is only the old story; and no criticisms can anticipate him on that. But its importance is that, like many old stories, it is in its way a great tragedy; and tragedy is that point when things are left to God and men can do no more. (pp. 63-5)

> *G. K. Chesterton, " 'Vanity Fair'," in his* A Handful of Authors: Essays on Books & Writers, *edited by Dorothy Collins, Sheed and Ward, 1953, pp. 56-65.*

OSBERT SITWELL   (essay date 1935)

[*Sitwell was an English poet, dramatist, novelist, and critic. In the excerpt below, he offers a negative assessment of Thackeray's skills as a novelist in* Vanity Fair, *unfavorably comparing him with Dickens.*]

I have just been re-reading Thackeray's *Vanity Fair,* pondering the problems that its former popularity raises. For undoubtedly at one time it *was* universally read, though I am unaware of the extent to which the book is read to-day, and whether it has maintained its appeal.

I had not opened its pages, though they still remained familiar to me, since I had left school, and was amazed at the inferiority of Thackeray to Dickens as an artist. And, which renders the position so much more peculiar, all the stock criticisms of Dickens, made by those who dislike his novels: that he cannot render the portrait of a lady, that he exaggerates, that he interpolates chunks of his own feelings into the story and addresses the reader in an irritating manner, that he indulges in sticky, slushy sentimentality are all of them, however untrue of him, fully justified if applied instead to Thackeray. In his drawing of character he uses a vulgar exaggeration, as it were; never the superb, the magnificent distortion by means of which Dickens bestows upon some of his characters a quite extraordinary significance, by no other method obtainable. Even the names of Thackeray's supposedly comic characters, when compared with the nomenclature invented by Dickens, prove the truth of this assertion: how weak a name is Lord Tapeworm, how good Sir Leicester Dedlock!

When he tries to depict it, Thackeray can never, it seems, produce any characters that are true to low life, and though this may actually have been of aid to his popularity in such snobbish times as those in which he wrote, it deprives the broad panorama that it was his aim to produce of some of its vigour; that sense of energy and virility which Hogarth and Rowlandson share in English pictorial art with writers such as Smollett and Dickens.... Further, how much more incisive are the low-life pictures of Dickens than the high-life ones of Thackeray, for which he was so celebrated. Even though Sam Weller and his kind indulge in a Cockney lingo which no longer exists and is difficult for us to read, this does not deprive them of their verisimilitude. Their talk is not nearly so extinct as that of Major Dobbin and Mrs Sedley. In addition, it seems to me that Dickens's Vanity-Fair characters, when he attempts that sort of thing, are actually better than Thackeray's; how much more alive, and of their world, are the distorted portraits of Sir Leicester and Lady Dedlock, in *Bleak House,* and of that supreme poor relation, who always has to be so gay and youthful, Miss Volumnia Dedlock, than any which Thackeray achieves in his exaggerated galleries. What a horrible suppressed sycophancy, for example, exhales, all unnoticed by the author, from the portrait of the majestically wicked Lord Steyne; what cringing before money and position, what peeping into forbidden cupboards and furtive gleaning of old letters locked in drawers. And why should Becky Sharp, the only attractive and comprehensible person in the book, be made to drink and intrigue so scandalously, just because she has Bohemian connections and comes of Bohemian stock? How deep an importance does not her creator attach to the fact that her grandmother is discovered in the end as a person who locks up the boxes at the Paris Opera! ... Again, Dickens surely held up a far more accurate and yet amusing mirror to the middle classes than his great contemporary: the image of Amelia's sister-in-law, the unmarried Miss Osborne, fades into nothingness beside that of Mrs Copperfield's sister-in-law, Miss Murdstone. Indeed, it appears as though Thackeray were only successful in his rendering of foreign scenes; for, directly he removes his characters abroad, whether to Waterloo or to a foreign watering-place, they assume a life hitherto lacking altogether in them; whereas Dickens abroad, as in his *Sketches of Italy,* is at his worst.

It is strange, too, to notice the extent to which Thackeray is obsessed by certain antipathies: young cavalry officers, for instance, and above all Members of Parliament. He can hardly allow a chapter in any novel of his to run its course without chucking a literary coconut or a rotten egg at the august body of poor, dead King George IV; poor sport, one would have assumed, and unworthy of an artist of any description; for, whatever the sensual faults of that monarch, he was the only English Prince since Charles I to be endowed with an interest in the arts and literature; the only English Prince since Charles II who liked to be surrounded by people of wit, such as Fox and Sheridan, rather than by the usual court numskulls. (pp. 303-06)

In this respect, then, as in many others, Thackeray appears to have been unjust.

He is at his best, it may be, in his portraits of the British Merchants: that race of stout, top-hatted, iron-whiskered, bullying braggarts who in his time inhabited the squares and streets of Bloomsbury, now the homes of a much more pacific, cultured and mild-accented sect.... But, indeed, his novels suffer greatly from the way in which the scene has changed, even in the last ten years.... Where are the moustachioed young artists, the gorgeous, lisping cavalry officers; where the villainous card-sharpers of good birth; where the club-toadies? ... All are under the heel of industry, commerce and the Slump. The great houses themselves have been pulled down: Lord Steyne's is a museum, Lady Kew's a club. The vast estates in the country have been disposed of, and their heirs pay 16s. 6d. in the pound in income-tax and super-tax. The country houses are only to be visited by those who, having beheld them in the advertisement pages of *Country Life,* have applied for the proper permit.... And yet, though Vanity Fair has changed, though the vulgar have inherited the earth and hypocrisy has been succeeded by an often revolting frankness, nevertheless Thackeray's picture of it is still recognizable. (pp. 306-07)

> *Osbert Sitwell, "Thackeray and 'Vanity Fair'," in his* Penny Foolish: A Book of Tirades & Panegyrics, *1935. Reprint by Books for Libraries Press, Inc., 1967; distributed by Arno Press, Inc., pp. 303-07.*

J.Y.T. GREIG (essay date 1950)

[*Greig focuses on the development of Becky and Amelia as characters, exploring the effect of serial publication and Thackeray's own attitudes toward his heroines on their changing roles within the story. For additional commentary by Greig on* Vanity Fair, *see excerpt dated 1950 in NCLC, Vol. 5.*]

[**Vanity Fair**], in the form in which most of us know it, has a sub-title, *A Novel without a Hero.* This was added only when Bradbury and Evans published the novel as a whole. The serial publication had another sub-title: **Pen and Pencil Sketches of English Society**, a relic, apparently, of earlier and unsuccessful drafts of the story.

Thackeray might have done better to describe the book as *A Novel with two Heroines.* This, at any rate, is how he thought of it as soon as he gave up the idea of a series of articles like the [**Snob Papers**], and began shaping it as a novel. The principle he worked on was a good one—contrast. Becky Sharp and Amelia Sedley were to balance one another; the first being plain in appearance, but clever, witty, resourceful, unscrupulous, dangerous to her associates, and, for a time at least, successful in life, and the second being pretty, simple-minded, gullible, charming in an unobtrusive way, 'pure', of course, tender-hearted, and, for a time at least, unsuccessful in life. They were also to be linked very closely through a plot. Amelia's task was to give Becky her start in life through the homely society of Russell Square, and Becky's was to destroy Amelia's happiness by stealing her first husband, and then, if the novel could be made to end happily, to restore it with casual generosity by presenting her with a second. As the outline of a plot, this was excellent. Fielding could have woven it into a complex and enthralling pattern. Thackeray tried to. He knew, admired, and often imitated his Fielding, from whom, depend upon it, he had learned the importance of the principle of contrast.

Elaborating as he went along, he continued to apply this principle. Round the pair of heroines he grouped other pairs of characters, each member of the pair balancing the other: George Osborne and Rawdon Crawley, old Osborne and old Sedley, old Sir Pitt Crawley and the Marquis of Steyne (both would-be lovers of the naughty heroine), Miss Crawley, with her Regency outlook, and the Evangelical Lady Southdown. But for fear that the pattern should become too formal, he devised cross-groupings: George Osborne and William Dobbin, Rawdon Crawley and his elder brother, Miss Crawley and the covetous Mrs. Bute Crawley, Becky and her sister-in-law (*née* Sheepshanks). Actions, too, he balanced and contrasted: Becky's marriage of convenience with Amelia's marriage for love; Becky's rise to social eminence with Amelia's descent into poverty; Amelia's final complacent and respectable happiness with Becky's restless and disreputable life at foreign spas.

But this, to be sure, is plotting, and although Thackeray could work out a plot in outline, he lacked Fielding's gift of working it out even to its smallest details. Besides, he was tied to serial composition, and being by habit indolent and dilatory, he soon found himself writing hurriedly, trusting very largely to the inspiration of the moment, in order to get his next number delivered to the printers in time. *Vanity Fair* is unified and shapely up to and including the episodes of Brussels and the Battle of Waterloo: for although it contains two heroines, the adventures and sufferings of the one are casually related to the adventures and sufferings of the other. It becomes unified and shapely again after Chapter XLIII (Pumpernickel), and for the same reason. But in between—roughly 300 pages—the plot of the first and last sections of the book is suspended, and the unity of the novel disappears. Two stories now occupy the author's attention alternately. One is centred in Becky, the other in Amelia. They are still built on the principle of contrast, undoubtedly, for Becky's fortunes are steadily rising until the crisis, and Amelia's just as steadily sinking until the return of Dobbin from India; but there is no causal relation between them, and each might very well have been the basis of a separate novel. (pp. 105-06)

I can only conclude that when Thackeray began upon *Vanity Fair* he intended that Amelia should be entangled all along in the meshes of the Becky story, but that after the scenes in Brussels and the death of George Osborne at Waterloo he discovered that he could not keep it up. It was Amelia herself who destroyed the plan. She had gone limp upon his hands. This was something he had not foreseen when he started, because, apparently, it had not occurred to him that the original of Amelia, his own 'poor little wife', had not enough in her to support the role of a major character. And being emotionally tied by his memories of Isabella, he did not know what to do. His first intention, clearly, had been to make Amelia what Mrs. Procter, after reading only seven numbers of the serial,

blandly told Abraham Hayward, the *Edinburgh* reviewer, that she was: 'Charming . . . not an angel, only a good, true, kindhearted girl.' But something had gone wrong. Although Thackeray may well have believed that it was only kindly memories of the 'poor little woman' that he was using for the novel, yet in fact, not being able to stand back and reshape 'emotion recollected in tranquillity', he was mingling these memories with others not so kindly; and, to make matters worse, he was trying to give solidity to the character by importing certain traits from two other women to whom he was emotionally in bondage, his mother and Jane Brookfield. It was all very well to draw on several originals for Becky. His own relationship to these originals was cool, intellectual, properly 'distanced'; and so he could reshape what he borrowed into a coherent and living personality. But the same method would not work when he was borrowing from Isabella, Jane, and his mother, since from none of these could he withdraw to the proper 'distance' for artistic creation. The result was that Amelia became one thing one moment and another another, according to his mood and the real woman he was thinking of. It was well-intentioned nonsense on the part of Mrs. Procter to compare her with Wordsworth's 'Phantom of Delight'—

> A creature not too bright and good
> For human nature's daily food,
> For transient sorrows, simple wiles,
> Praise, blame, love, kisses, tears and smiles—

and laziness or critical incompetence in Hayward to repeat this comparison in the *Edinburgh* [see excerpt dated 1848 in *NCLC*, Vol. 5].

When Thackeray surrendered to the excitement of creation, his unconscious mind often took control. He once told Whitwell Elwin: 'I have no idea where it all comes from. . . . I am often astonished myself to read it after I have got it on paper.' This is as it should be; at any rate, as it seems to be with most of the greater artists, whether men of letters, painters, sculptors, or musicians: they draw from a well that is deeper than conscious memory. Unfortunately, the waters beneath the level of Thackeray's conscious memory were often troubled, and on the present occasion he was troubling them still more by interference at the fully conscious level.

At all events, Thackeray had to make the best of a failure. Prompted by Hayward's article, perhaps, and certainly by what both Mrs. Carmichael-Smyth and Jane Brookfield had to say about Amelia (which was not much more encouraging than Hayward's attack), he recognized that she would not serve his purpose in the way that he had planned. The trouble was, he could not drop her. At the beginning of the novel he had warned his readers in his customary half-serious, half-joking tone to accept Amelia and not Becky as the heroine. Now, he had to gloss this over. After admitting in Chapter XXX, still in the same tone, that the indomitable Becky had become the heroine, he surrendered more and more to the joys of writing about her, with the result that he tended more and more to follow the lead given him by his mother and Jane Brookfield, and depreciate Amelia. Whibley exaggerates when he says that Amelia 'is drawn with a cold contempt' [see excerpt dated 1903 in *NCLC*, Vol. 5]. It was not so bad as that. But contempt became an ever stronger element in Thackeray's attitude as the book progressed. The 'poor panting little soul', 'poor tender heart' of the days before Waterloo turned into 'a namby-pamby milk-and-water affected creature'; at any rate, he allowed Dobbin's sisters to call her that, and did not take any very active steps to prove that they were wrong. Speaking of her letters to Dobbin himself, he admits that they are 'cold, kind, hopeless and selfish', and when he quotes one for the reader's benefit, he makes it about as simpering and factitious as it is possible for a letter to be.

Even when he repents of his harshness to this silly but forlorn creature, and does his best to prove sympathetic, he betrays himself by fustian ('a sainted agony of tears'), or by that tell-tale repetition of the adjective ('an humble humble heart') which is nearly always the symptom of an unresolved conflict in his mind. Most significant of all, he completely changes his attitude towards another character, whom he had first presented as a little ridiculous—Lady Jane Sheepshanks. The name he had given her had to stand. Possibly he regretted that now. But, Amelia having failed, he now used Lady Jane as a foil to Becky.

It is easy, therefore, to believe an anecdote related in the biography of Dean Liddell. When Mrs. Liddell, an excited reader of *Vanity Fair* as a serial, exclaimed, 'O Mr. Thackeray, you must let Dobbin marry Amelia', he is said to have answered: 'Well, he shall, and when he has got her, he will not find her worth having.'

Life influences fiction, obviously. But fiction also influences life. One wonders whether in the course of writing *Vanity Fair* Thackeray had come round to the same conclusion about himself and Isabella Shawe as he now allowed himself to express about Dobbin and Amelia. (pp. 107-10)

An illustration by Thackeray of Dobbin visiting Amelia and her baby after George's death.

In the middle portion of *Vanity Fair* (Brussels to Pumpernickel) Thackeray devotes rather more than a third of the space to Amelia and rather less than two-thirds to Becky. The style in the different sections often turns out very different. Writing of Becky and the Crawleys, his pen moves easily and swiftly, with vigour and felicity of phrase; writing of Amelia and her family, or of Dobbin and his stupid infatuation, it is apt to flag. But it does not always flag. His account of the decay, moral as well as financial, of the Sedleys is in his best sober-sympathetic manner—gentle, unforced, yet concise and penetrating. He portrays the deterioration in Mrs. Sedley relentlessly—it is one of his proper themes—but without the suggestion of personal animus that we are conscious of in his treatment of Mrs. Prior in *Lovel the Widower;* and though he moralizes on the death of Mr. Sedley, he resists the temptation to become sentimental about it.

As for 'the famous little Becky puppet', Thackeray boasts in 'Before the Curtain' that she 'has been pronounced to be uncommonly flexible in the joints, and lively on the wire' [see essay dated 1848]. No one will deny it. Puppet none the less she must often be called. Readers can watch the author's supple fingers as he pulls the wires; they can listen to his voice, ventriloquizing. He has manufactured her. Sometimes we can see the tool marks. Becky, though a masterpiece of skill, has not been quite 'assembled'.

The usual impression that we get of her is of selfish good-nature. She is too self-possessed to be quick-tempered. She is also greedy for admiration. Why then should she box the ears of her child, young Rawdon, when he listens to her singing? It is not in character. The sudden unfair blow is Thackeray's, not hers. He has jerked the wrong wire. He has remembered with a start (for he secretly admires Becky very deeply) that he ought to make her odious, that the book in which she is disporting herself so gaily ought, like the earlier *Catherine,* to be followed 'to edification'; and being always sentimental when it comes to a 'Mother and Child', he brutally ascribes to her an act which is not credible. And he does something similar twice again. When Lord Steyne discovers that his protégée has not paid Briggs with the money he gave her for that purpose, and accuses her good-humouredly of sharp practice, Thackeray again jerks the wrong wire. Becky, he says, was not disconcerted for long; which is right. Then she made up 'another neat plausible circumstantial story':

> 'It was my husband, by threats and the most savage treatment, forced me to ask for that sum about which I deceived you. . . . He took the money. He told me he had paid Miss Briggs; I did not want, I did not dare to doubt him. Pardon the wrong which a desperate man is forced to commit, and pity a miserable miserable woman.' She bursts into tears as she spoke. Persecuted virtue never looked more bewitchingly wretched.

This is not Becky, the resourceful, brazen Becky we have learnt to know. It is a new, melodramatic Becky from the Lyceum Theatre. Fortunately the shocking impersonation is but temporary.

All the same, we can guess at Thackeray's motive here. He is getting very near the crisis in the Becky plot. When the crisis comes, Becky is to behave with unpardonable callousness towards her blundering but affectionate husband. This behaviour must be led up to; otherwise the reader who has watched and delighted in her triumphs at Gaunt House will receive too great a shock when he finds her mean and treacherous.

And yet, puppet though she is, we believe in her. Here is the most infuriating paradox of all in the novelist Thackeray. He can put men and women on their legs and endow them with vitality; and this, after all, is the one essential gift for the novelist. Other powers, as of humour, satire, a comprehensive knowledge of human nature, skill in the handling of words, may be added to him, but without the essential gift he is nothing. And Thackeray was so perverse that he did not seem to value what the gods in their magnanimity had bestowed on him. The miracle of creation once performed, he would set about spoiling it. He had little reverence for his own creations; he would treat them either as a manufactured article, or, when the fancy took him, as a moral emblem. Unlike other gifted novelists, he is not content that the readers shall 'know' his characters; he must be fussing over them, in the hope that they shall 'know about' them. (pp. 110-12)

Whenever, in *Vanity Fair,* Thackeray will trust Becky, she will be herself, unerringly, miraculously vital. It is this vital Becky who puts the puppy George Osborne in his place when he tries to patronize her in Miss Crawley's drawing-room, who takes her revenge on Lady Bareacres, and who exploits her triumphs in the drawing-rooms at Gaunt House.

> 'How cool that woman is!' said one; 'what airs of independence she assumes, where she ought to sit still and be thankful if anyobody speaks to her!' 'What an honest and good-natured soul she is!' said another. 'What an artful little minx!' said a third. They were all right very likely; but Becky went her own way. . . .

They *were* right, all of them. Becky, in contrast to every other woman who appeared in a Thackeray novel (not excluding Beatrix in *Esmond,* who comes nearest to her), shows 'infinite variety'. And yet the essential Becky emerges in a single statement: 'I think I could be a good woman if I had five thousand a year.'

She went on her own way, says Thackeray. Would that he had always allowed her to! He cannot leave well alone. As soon as she has made her statement about five thousand a year, he comments on it:

> And who knows but Rebecca was right in her speculations—and that it was only a question of money and fortune which made the difference between her and an honest woman? If you take temptations into account, who is to say that he is better than his neighbour? A comfortable career of prosperity, if it does not make people honest, at least keeps them so. An alderman coming from a turtle feast. . . .

and so on. Thackeray would not trust his daemon. (pp. 112-13)

J.Y.T. Greig, in his Thackeray: A Reconsideration, *Oxford University Press, London, 1950, 215 p.*

DOROTHY VAN GHENT (essay date 1953)

[*Van Ghent was an American educator and literary critic. In the following study of* Vanity Fair, *she focuses on narrative technique, imagery, and theme, interpreting the novel within the context of English social and literary history. The critic explores both Thack-eray's portrayal of his society and the relationship between* Vanity Fair *and its literary predecessors and contemporaries.*]

Almost exactly a century separates *Tom Jones* from *Vanity Fair;* but with *Vanity Fair,* so far as technical developments in the novel are concerned, it is as if there had been none. We are in the story telling convention of the "omniscient author" sanctioned by Fielding's great example, but with a damaging difference that is due, not so much to an inherent inadequacy of that convention itself, as the spiritual incoherency of another age. It is true that the technique of omniscient authorship can allow a relaxed garrulity—what James called "the terrible fluidity of self-revelation"—for if the author can enter the story in his own voice, there is nothing to keep him from talking. After discussing Becky's adolescent designs on Jos Sedley, and her visions of shawls and necklaces and aristocratic company which she imagines will be the rewards of marriage with Jos, Thackeray comments,

> Charming Alnaschar visions! it is the happy privilege of youth to construct you, and many a fanciful young creature besides Rebecca Sharp has indulged in these delightful day-dreams ere now!

The comment is both inane and distracting—distracting our attention from the tense mental operations of Becky and turning it upon the momentarily flaccid mentality of her author. The effect is one of rather surprised irritation, as it is again when, having described Jos's wardrobe, his pains in dressing, his vanity and shyness, Thackeray remarks,

> If Miss Rebecca can get the better of *him,* and at her first entrance into life, she is a young person of no ordinary cleverness.

What we feel is that two orders of reality are clumsily getting in each other's way: the order of imaginative reality, where Becky lives, and the order of historical reality, where William Makepeace Thackeray lives. The fault becomes more striking in the following unforgivable parenthesis. Jos has just presented Amelia with flowers.

> "Thank you, dear Joseph," said Amelia, quite ready to kiss her brother, if he were so minded. (And I think for a kiss from such a dear creature as Amelia, I would purchase all Mr. Lee's conservatories out of hand.)

The picture of Thackeray himself kissing Amelia pulls Amelia quite out of the created world of *Vanity Fair* and drops her into some shapeless limbo of Thackerayan sentiment where she loses all aesthetic orientation.

Nevertheless, the conventions employed in a work of art cannot fairly be judged by themselves; they can be judged only as instrumental to a vision. The time in which Thackeray wrote was, compared with Fielding's time, itself looser in what we might call cultural composition; its values were less integrated in a common philosophical "style" or tenor of mind. In *Tom Jones,* the convention of the author's appearance in his book as "gregarious eye," stage manager, and moralist, is a strategy that is used with a highly formal regularity of rhythm, and it animates every turn of Fielding's language, as the ironic life of the language. Most important, the convention had benefited by an age's practice of and belief in form, form in manners and rhetoric and politics and philosophy—that is, by an age's coherently structured world view. The set of feelings and ideas of which Fielding acts as vehicle, when he makes his personal appearances in his book, is a set of feelings and ideas with the stamp of spiritual consistency upon them. They do not afflict us with a sense of confused perspectives between the author's person and his work, his opinions and his creation, as do Thackeray's. Whereas Thackeray seems merely to be victimized or tricked by his adopted convention into a clumsy mishandling of perspectives, Fielding manipulates the same convention deliberately to produce displacements of perspective as an organic element of composition. This is not to say that Fielding's creative perceptions are, on the whole, more penetrating and profound than Thackeray's; indeed, Thackeray's seem to reach a good deal deeper into the difficulties, compromises, and darkness of the human estate; but Fielding's have the organizing power to make an ancient oral convention of storytelling an appropriate instrument of his vision, whereas the same convention—actually one that is most sympathetic to Thackeray's gift of easy, perspicacious, ranging talk—becomes a personal convenience for relaxation of aesthetic control, *even a means to counterfeit* his creative vision.

Becky ruminates, "I think I could be a good woman if I had five thousand a year," and adds with a sigh,

> "Heigho! I wish I could exchange my position
> in society, and all my relations, for a snug sum
> in the Three per Cent. Consols."

Here she is as true to herself psychologically as is Moll Flanders; but she is more complex than Moll, and we know perfectly that, at this promising stage in her career, the sigh is only a casual fantasy—arising chiefly out of boredom with the tedious business of cultivating the good graces of people much less intelligent than herself—and that if the "snug sum" were offered, she would not really exchange her prospects for it, for her temperament is not at present to be satisfied with snugness. There are to be pearl necklaces, presentation at court, a *succès fou* at Gaunt House. But Thackeray interprets for us.

> It may, perhaps, have struck her that to have
> been honest and humble, to have done her duty,
> and to have marched straightforward on her
> way, would have brought her as near happiness
> as that path by which she was striving to attain
> it.

This is a doctrine with which, in principle, we have no cause either to agree or disagree; a novel is not made of doctrines and princples, but of concretely imagined life, and whatever moral principle may be honestly adduced from that life must be intrinsic to it, concretely qualitative within it. *Vanity Fair* is strong with life, but in those concretions where it is alive there is nothing to suggest that to be "honest and humble" can possibly bring happiness. Becky is the happiest person in the book; she is alive from beginning to end, alive in intelligence and activity and *joie de vivre*, whether she is throwing Dr. Johnson's dictionary out of a coach window, in superb scorn of the humiliations of the poor, or exercising her adulterous charm on General Tufto, whether she is prancing to court to be made an "honest woman" (in stolen lace), or hiding a cognac bottle in a sordid bed. From Becky's delighted exercise in being alive, we can learn nothing about the happiness to be derived from humble dutifulness. On the other hand, from Amelia's humble dutifulness we can learn nothing that convinces us doctrinally that happiness lies in such a way of life. For it is not only that the brisk gait and vivid allure of Becky's egoistic and aggressive way of life make Amelia look tepid, tear sodden, and compromised: this effect would not

occur if the book were soundly structured, if its compositional center (what James called the "commanding centre" of the composition) were entirely firm and clear.

The actually functioning compositional center of *Vanity Fair* is that node or intersection of extensive social and spiritual relationships constituted by Becky's activities: her relationships with a multitude of individuals—Jos and Amelia and George, old Sir Pitt and Rawdon and Miss Crawley and the Bute Crawleys and the Pitt Crawleys, Lady Bareacres, Lord Steyne, and so on—and, through these individuals, her relationships with large and significant blocks of a civilization: with the middle-class Sedley block, that block which is in the process of physical destruction because of its lack of shrewdness in an acquisitive culture; with the other middle-class Osborne block, that block which has displaced the Sedley block through its own acquisitive shrewdness and through the necessarily accompanying denial of the compassionate and sympathetic human impulses; with the aristocratic Crawley block, in all its complexity of impotence and mad self-destruction, and (in young Sir Pitt, with the "gooseberry eyes") canny self-renovation through connivance with the economy and morality of the dominant middle class; with the ambiguous Steyne block, that is above the economic strife and therefore free of conventional moral concerns, but in its social freedom, "stained" deeply in nerves and blood. (In the names he gives people, Thackeray plays—like many novelists—on punning suggestion, as he does in the name of the crawling Crawleys, "raw-done" Rawdon, Sharp, Steyne, O'Dowd, etc.) This social relationship, concretized through Becky's relationship with individuals, is the hub of the book's meanings, its "compositional center." But beside this violently whirling and excited center is another, a weak and unavailing epicenter, where Amelia weeps and suffers and wins—wins Dobbin and solvency and neighborhood prestige and a good middle-class house with varnished staircases. Organized around the two centers are two plots, which have as little essentially to do with each other as Thackeray's creative imagination had to do with his sentimental, morally fearful reflections. He cannot bear to allow the wonderfully animated vision of Becky's world to speak for itself, for its meaning is too frightening; he must add to it a complementary world—Amelia's—to act as its judge and corrector. One thinks, in comparison, of Balzac, who was writing almost contemporaneously. Balzac was both as skeptical and as sentimental as Thackeray, but he was a passionate rationalist as well, and a much bolder dramatic formalist. In Balzac, the weak and the suffering and the pure in heart do not win. They have no pretensions to effective moral dynamism in the evil Balzacian world, which uses them as illustrative examples of the impotence of an "honest and humble" way of life.

As the convention of the omniscient author allows Thackeray to keep up a maladroit "sound track" of personal interpolations, so it also collaborates with his confusion as to where the compositional center of his book lies; for though the Becky-world and the Amelia-world, having no common motivation, confront each other with closed entrances, so to speak, yet the author is able, by abuse of his rights of omniscience, to move facilely through these closed doors. We assume that, in Thackeray's plan, the compositional center of the book was to be the moral valence between the two worlds. But there is no valence between them, nothing in either to produce a positive effect of significance on the other. The only effect is negative: the Amelia-plot pales into a morally immature fantasy beside the vivid life of the Becky-plot. For Becky is the great morally meaningful figure, the moral symbol, in the book, and beside her there is room and meaning for Amelia only as victim—certainly not as "success figure." The word "moral" . . . needs perhaps a somewhat closer attention here. Becky is not virtuous, and in speaking of her as a morally significant figure, we cannot possibly confuse her moral meaning with the meaning of "virtue." She is a morally meaningful figure because she symbolizes the morality of her world at its greatest intensity and magnitude. The greediness that has only a reduced, personal meaning in Mrs. Bute Crawley, as she nags and blunders at old Miss Crawley's deathbed, acquires, through Becky's far more intelligent and courageous greed—as she encounters international techniques for the satisfaction of greed with her own subtle and knowing and superior techniques—an extensive social meaning. The corruption that, in old Sir Pitt, has meaning at most for the senility of a caste, becomes, in Becky's prostitution and treason and murderousness, the moral meaning of a culture. For Becky's activities are designed with intelligent discrimination and lively intuition, and they are carried through not only with unflagging will power but with joy as well. By representing her world at its highest energetic potential, by alchemizing all its evil but stupid and confused or formless impulses into brilliantly controlled intention, she endows her world with meaning. The meaning is such as to inspire horror; but the very fact that we conceive this horror intellectually and objectively is an acknowledgment of Becky's morally symbolic stature. (pp. 139-44)

The English novel has tended traditionally to symbolize certain phases of personality through the concrete image (Christian as the "man in rags" with a burden on his back; the Philosopher Square standing among Molly's "other female utensils" when the curtain falls in the bedroom; Clarissa, with streaming eyes and disheveled bosom, prostrating herself before Lovelace; Jaggers washing his hands or Miss Havisham beside the rotten bridecake); while the French novel has tended traditionally to a discursive analysis of feeling and motive, as has the French drama. Image and analysis are merely two different ways of mirroring what goes on in the soul. The methods are never exclusive; and we find such significant exceptions to the general tendency as Flaubert's *Madame Bovary,* where the image dominates, and Conrad's *Lord Jim,* where analysis dominates.

Let us illustrate, from **Vanity Fair,** the method of the image and what it is able to imply as to the "deeper layers of personality." Characteristically, in this book, the social concern is paramount. We have spoken of the various "blocks" of this civilization, some slipping into rubble by the crush of the others or by internal decay, some thrusting themselves up by the neighboring defaultment. But governing all the movements is one ethos of aggressive egoism, articulated through the acquisition of cash and though the prestige fantasies born of cash. Becky herself is a member of no particular class and confined to no particular "block." (Significantly, she is the daughter of a Bohemian artist and a French music-hall singer.) She is more mobile than any of the other characters, because of her freedom from caste, an thus is able to enter into a great variety of class relationships: this is the peculiar novelistic virtue of the picara and picaro, and the enduring source of virility of the picaresque form—the protagonist's freedom of movement. Still acting under the same ethos as that governing the whole civilization, Becky is able to represent its tendencies without class pretenses. Thus Becky, like Moll Flanders, though a strongly individualized character, is the type of a whole civilization, a small-scale model of a world, a microcosm in which the social macrocosm is subtilized and intensified and made significant. With this predominantly social bearing of the novel,

the characters—even Becky—tend to be depicted in a relatively "external" way: that is, there is relatively little discussion of the nuances of their feelings and their motivations; they are not self-analytical characters, as characters in French novels tend to be, nor do they spend much time in deliberate analysis of each other; they appear to us physically, in action; and—with some generalized interpretive help from the author himself (whose interpretations, as we have noted, we cannot always trust)—we enter into their motives and states of feeling by our own intuition. Examples are manifold. There is Becky's meeting of George's eyes in the mirror as she and Amelia, Jos and George, are leaving for Vauxhall: a flashing, accidental illumination of his vanity and vulnerability—and though here might be an excellent opportunity for Becky to engage in psychological speculations and deliberations, little of the kind occurs. There is the physical flash, the illumination by image only, and Becky has George's number. And yet later, when George and Amelia, Becky and Rawdon, meet on their honeymoon trips at Brighton, and Becky with almost unconscious slyness encourages George to make love to her, the early image of the meeting of eyes in a mirror plays on the reader's understanding of motivation, as it does again when we see Becky in overt sexual aggressiveness at the Brussels ball. There has been no need of discursive analysis of motive; the image does the work.

Or—another instance of the work of the image—there is Jos, in his obesity and his neckcloths and his gorgeous waistcoats. We should not expect Jos to analyze himself, nor anyone else to have an interest in analyzing what he feels, for he is below the level of what is rationally interesting; and yet, from the physical picture alone, we are made intuitively aware of deeply disturbed "layers of personality" in Jos. He is one of the most complicated psychological portraits in the book (more complicated, for instance, than that of another voluptuary, the Marquis of Steyne, who has more refined opportunities than Jos and a better head), extremely unpleasant, with suggestions of impalpable submerged perversities, pathetic, with a pathos that is at the same time an outrage to our feeling for what is humanly cognizable in pathos—for Jos is a glandularly suffering animal, with the "human" so hidden in his tortured fat that we feel it to be obscene, while we must still recognize it as human. Jos offering his neck to Isidore's razor . . . is a complex image of a kind of fear so muddied, an image of a psychological state so profoundly irrational, that we react to it with an impulse of horrified laughter—the intuitive horror having no other outlet than in a sense of the absurd. At the same time that these physical images of Jos flash to the mind's eye an impression of something deep and possible in individual personality, they are made by Thackeray to represent to the social reason an extremely significant phase of a culture. We see in Jos's obesity the sickness of a culture, the sickness due to spiritual gourmandism, or, in simpler but still metaphorical words, to "overeating"; in his shyness of women, the repressions and abnormalities of a sick culture; in his stupidity and febrile conceit, the intellectual numbing and tubercular euphoria of a culture. Thus the physical image, here, mirrors most fearful depths of the personal and, at the same time, most threatening perspectives of the social life.

We shall cite a few more illustrations of this method of the "image," as Thackeray uses it, keeping in mind its double significance, its significance for personal psychology (the "deeper layers of personality") and its social significance. But in preparation for these particular citations, we should speak of one singularly important theme of **Vanity Fair,** and that is a theme which we shall call the theme of the "fathers." . . .

[In eighteenth-century novels, the "father" appears] in a light that is rather different from the light that is thrown on the "father" in nineteenth-century novels. There is Squire Allworthy, for instance, who, as "father," though he may have his failures of insight, is still an affirmative moral reference in the *Tom Jones* system of values; he is idealized, but this itself is significant of the fact that the "father" still represents a moral ideal. In the eighteenth century, the idea of the "father" was not, on the whole, ambiguous, or suggestive of doubts or deficiencies or culpability—that is, as this idea is reflected in literature. Mr. Harlowe, in *Clarissa*, is the most exceptional example; but even here, the daughter's return to her "Father's house," on the elevated stage of the divine, is an affirmation and sanction of the usual parental-filial relationship of authority and obedience which is esteemed to be universally valid; Mr. Harlowe made a mistake, but so did Clarissa make a mistake; informed by Clarissa's passion, it is to be hoped that no other daughters or fathers will ever make such mistakes. In *Tristram Shandy*, the "father," Walter Shandy, is a freak, yet he is presented only under the aspect of general human freakishness, pleasant and interesting eccentricity, and we are led in no way to think of him in terms of parental culpability; indeed, as "father," he takes his responsibility most enormously—to be the right kind of father and to bring up the right kind of son is his devouring concern; the inquiries and devotions of fatherhood—as to conditions of conception, size of the son's nose, the son's name, his education—form the whole shape of Walter Shandy's mental activities, his very eccentricity. Similarly in Smollett's *Humphry Clinker,* where the "father" (an uncle, in this case) is a querulous hypochondriac, leading his life in a tone of objection to everything, we are "on his side," we object when he objects, with a grain of salt for his elderly fury; and the book has its moral equipoise in the rightness of this "father's" perceptions.

We see, in the notion of the father in eighteenth-century literature, a reflection of social trust: of trust in and reliance upon and devotion to a general social system of values—that coherent "world view " of the eighteenth century that we have spoken of earlier in this essay. For, under our anciently inherited patriarchal organization of the family, an organization that inevitably extended itself into political organization and philosophic organization, the "father-imago" has acquired vast symbolic extension beyond domestic life and into general social life: our "fathers" are not only our individual fathers but all those who have come before us—society as it has determined our conditions of existence and the problems we have to confront. *Vanity Fair,* with its panorama of western European international society as backdrop to the heroine's activities, is full of "fathers," sick fathers, guilty fathers. (pp. 144-48)

It is significant of the vital intuitiveness of Thackeray's *Vanity Fair* that the theme of the "fathers" should have such importance: in this book, an immensely impressive female, herself quite fatherless, manages to articulate in her career the most meaningful social aspects of the "father" theme. We need, in this view of the book, to free ourselves from the narrower Freudian aspects of the theme and to think in terms of Thackeray's broad social perspective, where the "fathers" are such variants as Mr. Sedley, Mr. Osborne, old Sir Pitt, even the Marquis of Steyne: in other words, such variants as to include all the older, authoritative, and determinative aspects of society.

And now, with this general notion of the significance of the theme of parental authority, we can consider what Thackeray

manages to get out of the "image" of old Mr. Osborne and his daughters coming down the stairs, in their evening ritual, to dinner.

> The obedient bell in the lower regions began ringing the announcement of the meal. The tolling over, the head of the family thrust his hands into the great tail-pockets of his great blue coat and brass buttons, and without waiting for a further announcement, strode downstairs alone, scowling over his shoulder at the four females.
>
> "What's the matter now, my dear?" asked one of the other, as they rose and tripped gingerly behind the sire.
>
> "I suppose the funds are falling," whispered Miss Wirt; and so, trembling and in silence, this hushed female company followed their dark leader.

In the lines just before this there is one other, inconspicuous, touch: in the drawing room where they are waiting for dinner is a chronometer "surmounted by a cheerful brass group of the sacrifice of Iphigenia." The depths which are suggested by this picture, but quite as if accidentally, are the depths of Greek tragedy and, still further back, of Freud's dim, subhuman, imagined "primitive horde": the "dark leader" with his "hushed female company," and the ridiculous but furious Victorian clock "cheerfully" symbolizing the whole. Antiquity's dark brooding over the monstrous nature of man is made to take on, in this incidental image of a family's going to dinner, the unwholesomeness and perversity that have been added to

An illustration by Thackeray of Becky and Rawdon with Lord Steyne. Becky is dressed as Clytemnestra.

man's classical monstrosity by "falling funds," a drop in the stock market.

There is the recurrent incident in the hall outside the bedroom where old Miss Crawley is sick, Becky tending her, everyone—including Becky—waiting for and speculating on the "reversionary spoils."

> Captain Rawdon got an extension of leave on his aunt's illness, and remained dutifully at home. He was always in her ante-chamber. (She lay sick in the state bedroom into which you entered by the little blue saloon.) His father was always meeting him there; or if he came down the corridor ever so quietly, his father's door was sure to open, and the hyaena face of the old gentleman to glare out. What was it set one to watch the other so? A generous rivalry, no doubt, as to which should be most attentive to the dear sufferer in the state bedroom. Rebecca used to come out and comfort both of them—or one or the other of them rather.

Short and unemphasized as the passage is (outside of one ironic line, it consists only of an image, the image of Rawdon opening a door and looking into the corridor, of the old man's "hyaena face" instantly looking out from an opposite door, of Becky coming down the hall to "comfort" them), it contains a pregnant and disturbing meaning, both for personal psychology and for social psychology. Later, when Becky will attempt to inform Sir Pitt about her clandestine marriage, but without telling him the name of her husband, he will be uproariously amused; but as soon as she tells him the name—his son, Rawdon—he goes mad with inexplicable fury. We look back mentally to the incidents in the hall outside Miss Crawley's sickroom, where son and father glare at each other, and where Becky comes to comfort them *separately,* holding each in suspense as to her amorous favor. And we look forward also to that horrible line in Becky's letter to Rawdon (after the disclosure to Sir Pitt), where she says, "I might have been somebody's mamma, instead of—Oh, I tremble, I tremble . . ." What is contained here is probably the most excruciatingly primitive father-son battle in literature, with one of the most sensitively feminine but perversely sentimental reflections upon it. How are we to say, in such a case, whether what we are observing is the "deeper layers of personality" or the social scene?

And then there is the description of the turmoil surrounding old Sir Pitt's death. It consists of a succession of images: Miss Horrocks flitting in ribbons through "the halls of their fathers"; again Miss Horrocks

> of the guilty ribbons, with a wild air, trying at the presses and escritoires with a bunch of keys.—

while upstairs they are "trying to bleed" Sir Pitt (the "trying to" suggests unknown but repulsive derangements); the servant girl screaming and making faces at him in private while he whimpers. The cumulation of these images, scattered and casual as they are, makes the face of a gorgon of destiny. The personal and social idea of the "father" (an idea which is inextricably both personal and social) is made the nasty companion of the ribbon-flitting Miss Horrocks; when Sir Pitt gives the family pearls to Lady Jane ("Pretty pearls—never gave 'em to the ironmonger's daughter"), marital relationships, with all they mean for the security created for us by our elders, are referred back retrospectively to Sir Pitt's chronic tipsiness and

Lady Crawley's worsted knitting—an "enormous interminable piece of knitting"—

> She worked that worsted day and night . . . She had not character enough to take to drinking . . . ;

drawers are tried while the "father" is bled; and finally—so great is the prestige of this "father" and baronet—the servant girl has full amplitude to scream obscenities and make faces at him, for he has turned into "a whimpering old idiot put in and out of bed and cleaned and fed like a baby."

The burden of Thackeray's intuition into personal psychology and its social meaning falls on images like these, and they are innumerable in *Vanity Fair.* But the greatness of *Vanity Fair* is not in scattered images, sensitive as these are. They are all gathered up in Becky Sharp. Becky does for Jos, murderously, at the end; and what she does to Jos is only cancerously implicit in himself and the civilization that has made him; she is the darkness—shining obsidianly in an intelligent personality—in old Mr. Osborn's dense sadism against his daughters and his corruption of the meaning of paternal responsibility toward his son; she manipulates the insane father-son conflict between Sir Pitt and Rawdon; and she is the "guilty ribbons" of Miss Horrocks (instead of a servant's ribbons she has a courtesan's pearls) and at the same time the whimpering idiocy of the dying Sir Pitt (paralleling his repulsive attack of mortality, she inflicts a similarly repulsive mortality on Jos)—for she is at once all the imperatively aggressive, insanely euphoric impulses of a morally sick civilization, and an individual condensation of that civilization. We question whether we would understand her at all, or be charmed by her buoyancy or appalled by her destructiveness, if her impulses were not memorabilia of our own and her civilization our heritage. (pp. 149-52)

> *Dorothy Van Ghent, "On 'Vanity Fair'," in her* The English Novel: Form and Function, *Holt, Rinehart and Winston, 1953, pp. 139-52.*

FRANK O'CONNOR [PSEUDONYM OF MICHAEL O'DONOVAN] (essay date 1956)

[O'Connor was an Irish short story writer and man of letters whose critical commentary is distinguished by his insistent probing into the connections between society and the artist as well as his attempt to analyze the creative process of the writer he is examining. In the following excerpt, O'Connor examines Thackeray's portrayal of human instinct and selfishness in Vanity Fair, *commenting also on the novelist's attitudes toward women and motherhood.]*

Vanity Fair is no mere random choice of a title; it expresses the whole meaning of the book. It is a wonderful novel, and a highly original one. Among English novels it comes closest to the Russian ideal of organic form, of a story that tells itself without recourse to invention by virtue of a certain unity of viewpoint and tone. The viewpoint, however, is an exceedingly disillusioned one. The mainspring of all human actions, if we are to believe the author, is self-interest. From the servant girl up to the Princess, the only motive to be distinguished is that of getting something for oneself. Intelligent people recognize this and act accordingly, and those who do not, behave as they do because their self-interest is of a different sort or because they are too stupid to do anything else. "To part with money is a sacrifice beyond almost all men endowed with a sense of order. There is scarcely any man alive who does not think himself meritorious for giving his neighbour five pounds.

Thriftless gives, not from a beneficent pleasure in giving, but from a lazy delight in spending." Virtue, in Thackeray's eyes, is always weak or stupid. "She was a very good woman," he says of Lady Grizzel, "good to the poor, stupid, blameless, unsuspicious." If she had been an out-and-out criminal, he could not have blasted her more effectively.

This means that the contrast Thackeray sets up between instinct and judgment differs widely from that of all other novelists I know of. In Jane Austen the instinct represents the imaginative life, while the judgment represents morality. In Stendhal the instinct is also an aspect of the imagination, though the judgment usually represents irony. In Thackeray it would almost seem as if the instinct always represented some form of weakness, while the judgment represented selfishness. At any rate, it is he who links the two in describing Osborne's behavior after his son, George, is killed at Waterloo.

> Which of us is there can tell how much vanity lurks in our warmest regard for others and how selfish our love is? Old Osborne did not speculate much on the mingled nature of his feelings, and how his instinct and selfishness were combating together.

The thinking here is childish, as Thackeray's thinking so often is; it is the price one has to pay for so disillusioned a viewpoint; and, for what it is worth, the point he is making had been dealt with pretty effectively by Christ in the parable of the Good Samaritan. But it is clear from this, as from many other passages, that he regards instinct as weakness; selfishness, for all that he affects to denounce it, as strength. It was his preoccupation with selfishness which made him so much better a historian of his period than Dickens.

It is also characteristic of the novel that its real heroine, Becky Sharp, is an adventuress and the personification of human selfishness. She is also, by the same token, a prostitute and a murderess, though Thackeray deals gingerly with those aspects of her character while grumbling at the necessity for doing so. At the same time, what makes the book so remarkable is that, whether Thackeray likes it or not, he turns her into the heroine and even, in his shallow way, tries to defend her. "And who knows but Rebecca was right in her speculations, and that it was only a question of money and fortune which made the difference between her and an honest woman?"

Who *does* know? The answer quite obviously is "Thackeray and no one but Thackeray." The mere fact that the question can be asked at all shows that Becky Sharp is something more than a character in a novel. (pp. 115-17)

[Though] she is to a certain extent a character, she is also a point of view, and that point of view is very close to Thackeray's own, at least to that part of it which he would have attributed to his judgment. Becky lives by discovering the weak points of others and flattering their vanity or stimulating their lusts while herself remaining quite cold and, indeed, good-humored about it all. Becky is "bad," but she is also clever.

Now Amelia, her protagonist, is of course "good," but she is also intolerably stupid. And here we come to the most interesting point in Thackeray's moral dilemma. Amelia is also a mother in a sense in which Becky is not a mother at all. There was something about maternity that fascinated Thackeray, apparently because it broke down the crust of egotism and selfishness in a woman and left her vulnerable to circumstances. In an admirable passage of anlaysis, Lord David Cecil

has pointed out the inconsistency of Becky Sharp's boxing her child's ears when she finds him listening to her singing, and argues quite correctly that "people of her temperament neglect their children, but their very selfishness makes them good-natured to them." At the same time, this is not slipshod writing on Thackeray's part, as Cecil believes. It is quite deliberate and considered, and the same attitude is repeated again and again in the latter part of the book. Becky, as one of her lovers informs us, cannot like children "any more than the Devil can like holy water," and again and again we are told flatly that "gentle thoughts and simple pleasures were odious to Mrs. Becky; they discorded with her; she hated people for liking them; she spurned children and children-lovers." This is not carelessness, but a contradiction in Becky's character required by the fact that she is something other than a character, by the fact that she represents a point of view.

Becky is part of the antithesis that racks Thackeray more than any other novelist I know of. Every great writer, of course, has such antitheses; no matter how much of his material he draws from real life, his characters and situations necessarily form masses and contradict one another in ways that ultimately reveal the whole bent of his nature, but few writers are trying to balance such an unstable antithesis as Thackeray. Becky *cannot* like children because she is antithetical to Amelia, who can like nothing else. This was one of the ways his instinct operated, and if he had to have good women, he preferred them as mothers. When dealing with them he sometimes becomes unendurably mawkish, almost obscene.

> As his eyes opened and his mind expanded, under the influence of the outward nature round about him, she taught the child, to the best of her humble power, to acknowledge the Maker of All; and every night and every morning he and she—(in that awful and touching communion which I think must bring a thrill to the heart of every man who witnesses or who remembers it)—the mother and the little boy— prayed to Our Father together, the mother pleading with all her gentle heart, the child lisping after her as she spoke. And each time they prayed God to bless dear papa, as if he were alive and in the room with them.

It is scarcely possible to believe that this was not written with the shadow of a sneer, and, indeed, . . . I wonder if Thackeray could ever be unselfconsciously emotional. But this was as earnest as he could be, because Amelia—as he, Mrs. Brookfield, and her husband all agreed—was inspired by Mrs. Brookfield. He had not concealed the Brookfield relationship from his mother, and she had done her best to console him. This is how he described her to Mrs. Brookfield at the time.

> I look at her character and go down on my knees as it were with wonder and pity. It is Mater Dolorosa, with a heart bleeding with love. Is not that a pretty phrase? I wrote it yesterday in a book, whilst I was thinking about her—and have no shame somehow now in writing thus sentimentally to all the public; though there are very few people in the world to whom I would have the face to talk in this way tete-a-tete.

There is little question but that there was in Thackeray a childish strain that attracted him to women who resembled his mother, women who were soft, stupid, and indulgent. And there is no question but that the mature man in him was attracted to women of a very different type—cold, sensual, calculating women like Becky Sharp, Blanche Amory, and Beatrix Esmond. That is why *Vanity Fair* has the eternal appeal of its originality. It is the only novel written by a man of mature mind which makes a cold-hearted scheming adventuress into a heroine, and does it so successfully that, in spite of ourselves, we are charmed into accepting her point of view. (pp. 118-20)

> Frank O'Connor [*pseudonym of Michael O'Dono-van*], *"Thackeray: 'Vanity Fair',"* in his The Mirror in the Roadway: A Study of the Modern Novel, *Alfred A. Knopf, 1956, pp. 111-24.*

RUSSELL A. FRASER   (essay date 1957)

[Fraser investigates Thackeray's apparently inconsistent and con-fused attitude toward many of the characters in Vanity Fair.]

The world of fashion is depicted in *Vanity Fair*. The world of power is not. Does Meredith's Diana have to do with the Corn Laws? or Kingsley's poet-tailor with Chartism? There is noth-ing of either in Thackeray's novel. What there is, crucially, is presentation of character. Here all depends on success or fail-ure. And whether the one or the other is achieved will depend just as surely on the character of Thackeray himself, for he plays a real part in the action. He is able to write with conviction of the wedding of George and Amelia, because a friend—Captain Dobbin—has detailed it all for him. . . . He can share Amelia's grief at weaning her child, because the same Dr. Pestler who attended her then has become his acquaintance, as well. . . . What goes on behind the front of Lord Steyne's dreary palace he knows, beyond peradventure, so excellent a ferret is that little Tom Eaves, who informs him. . . . And if he can tell of the opera in Pumpernickel, that "little comfort-able ducal town," it is because once from a place in the stalls he has listened to *Fidelio*—and looked hard at Dob and Jos and Amelia and young George in the loge. . . . (p. 137)

Although his conversation with his characters has been thorough and close, it has made him not unnaturally partisan. He will "step down from the platform" to trounce whatever villainy he descries (lest a suspicious reader fail to see where he stands) or, it may be, to laugh in that same reader's sleeve. . . . But if Thackeray, like his master Fielding, is to take upon himself the role of a Chorus, he must speak with fixed purpose from a single point of view. It will not do to deride a fool's piety one moment and to applaud it sententiously the next. Yet this is precisely what is done. Held up to ridicule are the evening prayers, conducted by the unctuous Pitt Crawley, that com-placent possessor "of a mediocrity which ought to have insured any man a success." But though the servants are "subjected" to those devotional exercises, it is somehow "so much the better" that old Sir Pitt, a notorious infidel, is compelled to partake of them, too. . . . This is to have it both ways, to speak, not consciously, impartially, but uneasily, irresolutely, for two points of view, each opposed to the other. It is a flaw in Thackeray's handling of character. And the flaw persists.

Miss Crawley, for example, has been called "the greatest char-acter in the book." Now this is at least a possible judgment. It is possible because Miss Crawley amuses, and is herself amused at the scrambling for her wealth in which all the Craw-leys join. "Imperious, crochety, and perverse," she is like that maternal grandmother of Thackeray's, in whom, if there was something to censure, there was also much to praise. Just because she sees, she is of the reader's party. He gives her his

trust; and how she betrays it! For the very qualities which constitute her strength, her "free notions about religion and morals" . . . , must be pilloried at last. Her final illness must be aggravated by hysteria and "the most dreadful terrors of death"; an "utter cowardice" must take one who, when in health, had quite ignored the future world. . . . It must be so, if poetic justice is to be done. Remorselessly Thackeray de-stroys what he had well created:

> Picture to yourself, O fair young reader, a worldly, selfish, graceless, thankless, religion-less old woman, writhing in pain and fear, and without her wig. Picture her to yourself, and ere you be old, learn to love and pray!

This is a kind of violation.

It is revealing, however, for what it tells of Thackeray himself. So often one hears him named cynic. In his contemporaries his uncanonical wit aroused both awe and distrust; in Charlotte Brontë, both sorrow and anger. "Why," she demanded, "should his mocking tongue so perversely deny the better feelings of his better moods?" The truth is that, mingled with that mockery and as often as not warring with it, is a strain of intense moral fervor. There is that Thackeray who anticipates the famous preface to *Pendennis:* "One is bound to speak the truth as far as one knows it . . . and a deal of disagreeable matter must come out in the course of such an undertaking." . . . And then there is the prig who assailed Bulwer-Lytton for allowing the hero of *Ernest Maltravers* to seduce an innocent girl; the staid Briton who, as Paris correspondent for the *National Standard*, found the realism of the French romantics mere extravagance—and decidedly repulsive: "Clotted blood . . . scattered brains . . . gaping wounds"; the moralist who would not write on Eugène Sue: were not his books numbered among the most immoral in the world? One thinks of Oscar Wilde, censured also for his flippancy: a daring writer and a wicked, but man-ifesting in plays like *Lady Windermere's Fan* and *A oman of No Importance* the same curious and unlucky confus on that marks and goes far to damage Thackeray's handling of char-acter in *Vanity Fair;* the same predilection to run with the hares—engaging creatures, not vowed to convention—and hunt with the hounds—respectability and all its claims and works.

The "Amelia Doll," as she is named in the preface [see essay by Thackeray dated 1848], makes the point well. She is a woman quite impervious to the world of movers and shakers, unless of course that world impinge on her own little circle. Bonaparte she despises, "for it needs not to be said that this soft and gentle creature took her opinions from those people who surrounded her, such fidelity being much too humble-minded to think for itself." . . . "A dear little creature," her tears are expended on a dead canary, or a mouse, or the end of a sentimental novel. . . . When hard times come to try her, her shifts to surmount them are so futile as to constitute a kind of degradation. So gentle is Amelia, so careless of self, that nature marks her for its victim. . . . (pp. 137-40)

The love she bears George Osborne is debasing, after all: for the reader, who sees Osborne plain, is moved first to indig-nation and at last to dismay by Amelia's inveterate blindness. And there is, in that life, such an awful dearth of action, so little assertion of character. "You see," says Thackeray fairly, "it is not much of a life to describe. There is not much of what you call incident in it." . . . Amelia, who has "begun not unprosperously . . . [has] come down to this—to a mean prison and a long, ignoble bondage." Inevitably, there is something of frustration in her story. For neither satisfaction nor enjoyment, wrote Arnold of *Empedocles on Etna,* can be derived from situations "in which the suffering finds no vent in action; in which a continuous state of mental distress is prolonged, unrelieved by incident, hope, or resistance; in which there is everything to be endured, nothing to be done. In such situations there is inevitably something morbid, in the description of them something monotonous." To own that it is so, as Thackeray does, is only to acknowledge but scarcely to meet one's objection. For in Amelia the reader is given not a heroine, really, but a creature forlorn and pathetic who, demanding pity, finds contempt.

And yet her very weakness is pleasing to Thackeray.... So manifest is his sympathy for her "sweet submission and softness" that one is made aware again of that basic split in attitude which runs like a fault through the novel. Henry James mirrors it nicely when, in *Washington Square,* he makes Mrs. Penniman demand of her brother: "'Do you think it better to be clever than good?' 'Good for what?' asked the Doctor. 'You are good for nothing unless you are clever.'" ... And the answer is more than an epigram. Amelia, not clever, is good for precious little. The Thackeray who does not gladly suffer fools, who scorns to make a virtue of incompetence, sees that it is so and passes a judgment so hardy that tiresome critics like Charlotte Brontë cannot bring themselves to forgive him. But there is also that Thackeray whose sensibility yields nothing to Amelia, who finds in her, for all his strictures, "the kind, fresh, smiling, artless, tender little domestic goddess, whom men are inclined to worship." ... It is as if the ingenuous Mrs. Penniman and the mordant Dr. Sloper were one.

Consider the virtuous, vacuous Lady Jane Crawley, née Sheepshanks, she of the "soft dove-like eyes." What an entrance Thackeray affords her: "Her mamma ordered her dresses, her books, her bonnets, and her ideas." ... And yet a transformation, rather too magical to inspire much confidence, is worked. Lady Jane is seen as the prayerful mother (of an unprepossessing Pitt Binkie), as the loyal spouse (of a thoroughly tedious Sir Pitt). She consoles the broken Rawdon, fights for hearth and home against the unprincipled Becky. How attractive has she latterly become, this Sheepshanks. But the transformation doesn't signify. Her end is not in her beginning.

A fervent admirer of Thackeray once wrote, apropos of an article by Kate Field, "It is like the good little books which say that Tom told a lie and broke his leg, whereas Dick spoke the truth and was at once made a lord." The trouble with such fables, Anthony Trollope concludes, is that "There is no evidence of the facts but the statement of the writer." The trouble with Thackeray is that often the facts are too nettlesome. But to state them away is no solution.

Becky Sharp fares as badly as her antagonist, Jane, if it be bad for an artist to lay violent hands on his work. She is no angel; her own word is proof.... Still, so cool and collected is "the indomitable little aide de camp's wife" that Thackeray, his novel half done, claims her for its heroine.... Some thirty chapters later, he will have it so no more. The evil, or rather, the lack of a positive good, that has characterized Becky from the first, fills her creator with a sudden and overwhelming revulsion. In a memorable passage his heroine is metamorphosed. She becomes—as it were, before his eyes—a monster. Once he had been ready even to applaud her, "this siren, singing and smiling, coaxing and cajoling." Now he is undeceived: "Those who like may peep down under waves that are pretty transparent, and see ... [the tail of the monster]

writhing and twirling, diabolically hideous and slimy, flapping amongst bones, or curling round corpses." ... It is not a pretty picture, nor is it quite fair to its subject, who must pay now belatedly for Thackeray's confusion.

But if Becky is treated to something more than just deserts, the author makes good by bestowing upon her, in the fashion of one who gives the devil his due, more care and close surveillance than is granted to any other of his people. And so mettlesome a creature does his scrutiny reveal her that one cannot choose but admire. In a world which entertains "an insuperable repugnance to hearing vice called by its proper name" ..., she refreshes just because she is candid. To the awful Miss Pinkerton she gives a lesson in forthright behavior: "I am here to speak French with the children ... not to teach them music, and save money for you. Give me money, and I will teach them." She blows up cant and the glib shows of false affection that others put on as a matter of course. Again to the friend of the Great Lexicographer: "You took me because I was useful. There is no question of gratitude between us." ... Do others esteem the simpering George Osborne? She penetrates at once beneath his bland manners, his brave dress, and knows him for the coxcomb he is. And when her quondam lover Jos Sedley panics in Brussels on the even of Waterloo, does he, that splendid fat man, soften her heart with his plight? Why, scarcely. She drives a hard bargain, quite without compunction, for the horses that bear Jos away.

Her coolness and pluck suit well her russet yeas and honest kersey noes. The French are rumored to be marching on Brussels, but Becky is far from distraught: "If the worst comes to the worst ... my retreat is secure; and I have a right-hand seat in the barouche." ... A little reflection, and the idea of flight is put away altogether: "Suppose the French do come ... what can they do to a poor officer's widow? Bah! the times of sacks and sieges are over. We shall be let to go home quietly, or I may live pleasantly abroad with a snug little income." ... And when, her realism vindicated, her husband safely returned, that gentleman complains of their unsettled existence, she rounds on him at once with "Ruined! fidd? diddledee! I will get you a good place before that; or"—and her expectations are nothing if not sanguine—"Pitt and his little boy will die, and we will be Sir Rawdon and my lady. While there is life, there is hope, my dear, and I intend to make a man of you yet."... (pp. 140-43)

Becky never quite succeeds in making a man of her husband. Yet what pains she is at to carry forward the task, with what demure assurance does she take it in hand. Let Miss Crawley, her democratic principles utterly cast down by Rawdon's unfortunate marriage, divorce her nephew from favor. There is only a little repining: Becky, for her part, will see that favor not merely resumed but engrossed. So to Rawdon: "You will now, if you please, my dear, sit down at the writing-table and pen me a pretty little letter to Miss Crawley, in which you'll say that you are a good boy, and that sort of thing." ... And Rawdon does write the letter—with much amazement and more misspelling—and the letter is good. But Miss Crawley is not thereby brought round. Becky's great expectations, now of a marriage, now a legacy, are dashed. A venturesome woman, quite as intrepid as the Iron Duke himself, she ought, one would think, to get on. With a nice lack of modesty she owns to herself how much greater is her charm than that of the Creole Miss Schwartz, she of the hundred thousand pounds; how much finer her figure and more compelling her wit than that of the "little pink-faced chit Amelia." ... She is right. And still she fails. Perhaps it is because she is too clever.

An outlander herself, she is able to perceive, with a clarity most disconcerting, the absolute humbug—"nonsense upon stilts," to take a phrase from Jeremy Bentham—of the society into which she has pushed. And she is not content merely to see; she must parody with undisguised pleasure that society's most signal faults. So to Vanity Fair she acts a sentimental child: Mrs. Sedley finds her "all heart" . . . ; Miss Crawley's wretched Briggs wallows delightedly in her studied italics, her transports, her abnegation of self: "the friendless orphan." . . . And Miss Briggs richly merits the destruction that is her reward, for who will commiserate with a woman who must speak of Rawdon Crawley as "the heroic soldier, whose name is inscribed in the annals of his country's glory?" . . . Sentimentality is bought dear by those who luxuriate in it, and this is just. But it does not make against Becky's cruelty. Yet here is a paradox: whatever Becky's dereliction, whatever the rightness of her fall, the reader sympathizes with her. That this should be so is traceable directly to the ambiguity of Thackeray's point of view.

Of the character of Milton's Satan, Shelley has written, he "engenders in the mind a pernicious casuistry which leads us to weigh his faults with his wrongs, and to excuse the former because the latter exceed all measure." Agree or not with Shelley's dictum in terms of *Paradise Lost,* one must concede its applicability here: for Becky, quite as Satan, is "a superior bad angel" . . . , and her wrongs do exceed all measure. Her earliest memories are of the duns and tradesmen who clamor about her father's door; in consequence she is endowed with "the dismal precocity of poverty." . . . No wonder, then, that she becomes "an eagle in the Chiswick dovecot" . . . , avid of despoiling; a picaro, as lacking in scruple as Barry Lyndon, or Jonathan Wild, and as devoted as they to the main chance.

But her most appropriate role is that of a miniature Napoleon who mocks and discomposes, at least for a time, her own time and the sphere which she has made her own. Just so does the Corsican upstart mock the whole of Europe, which is Vanity Fair writ large. He is a poor Italian, and she the luckless daughter of a French opera girl. He makes for himself a marriage with Austria, and she, very nearly, with an English baronet. He fleers at the sacred totem of patriotism: France, he avers, is his mistress, not his mother, as the venerable cliché would insist. So Becky, a hardheaded opportunist, without a trace in her of rodomontade, flouts the claims of honor, family, and religion: when were they ever allies of the poor? She is Napoleon, seizing his crown from the hands of a scandalized and quiet superfluous Pope. She has the same admirable phlegm, the same incisive intellect which understands that the old gods are false gods, and—unforgiveable fault—acts on that understanding. Like Napoleon she is at once the product and nemesis of Vanity Fair.

It is fitting that as her story begins, as she takes leave of Miss Pinkerton's school, she should cry, *"Vive la France! Vive l'Empereur! Vive Bonaparte!"* . . . ; fitting that Rawdon should believe in his wife "as much as the French soldiers in Napoleon." . . . And if Boney is stigmatized as "the wretched upstart and swindler" . . . , so is she styled a "parvenue" . . . , a "little adventurer" . . . , "an imposter." . . . Yet the admiration she commands, as one who has made her own way, is qualified still. For the Thackeray whose ancestry was of the army and the squirearchy, whose education was of Charterhouse and Cambridge, whose unswerving belief in the sanctity of caste had led him to pillory the social climbing of John Henry Skelton, was the Thackeray who sat in judgment on the

Thackeray's illustration of the scene in which Amelia reads the letter George had written Becky before the Battle of Waterloo.

interloper, Becky Sharp. Of course he condemned her. It was, after all, his snobbery and sense of position—and not merely a sense of the absurd—that begot the *Yellowplush Papers.* That this is so is shown by the essentially irrelevant details—phonetic spelling, for example—which he employs to convict his unhappy Charles Jeames Yellowplush. It is rather Thackeray who is convicted. For his criticism of Vanity Fair is based on a misapprehension: it is not really caste he deplores, but those who violate caste. Thus the unthinking and careless anti-Semitism that pervades his work (the rascally narrator of *Catherine* is, inevitably, Ikey Solomons, Junior): the Jew has no status, but is determined to achieve it. He is therefore satirically drawn.

Not, indeed, that those who stay fixed in their orbit win complete approbation: Amelia is one of them, and Amelia is a fool. But Becky is a knave, and perhaps that is worse. Thackeray's essential feeling might fairly be expressed in the proposition: a good man is a dull man, and he who escapes dullness must be of necessity bad. In that earlier work, *The Great Hoggarty Diamond,* there are good people enough, but they are preyed on by the bad. Thus the proposition is illustrated: the bad live by marauding; the good give themselves up to the bad. And this is the whole duty of good people and bad. Becky is bad. Her neglect of her son is a scandal: "poor lonely little benighted boy!" he is one who worships a stone. . . . Her leechlike attachment to the credulous Briggs is only less painful. Her murder of Jos Sedley, in the character of Clytemnestra, completes her degradation. But Thackeray is quits with her at last: as the novel draws to a close, he dooms her to be forever beginning again: "Whenever Becky made a little circle for herself with incredible toils and labour, somebody came and swept it down rudely." . . . Truly, it is hard, as Thackeray says: "very hard; lonely, and disheartening." It is also retribution, the wages of a knave among fools.

But *Vanity Fair* is not the homily that Trollope describes [see excerpt dated 1879]. Tom, who juggles with the truth, is not without charm; Dick, for all his veracity, has only a very modest success. So Amelia is now praised and now derided; Becky, though damned, retains her glamor forever. Yet if Thackeray's handling of his characters seems to a degree arbitrary and uncertain, if there is at times "no evidence of the facts but the statement of the writer," this constitutes a tribute, however perverse, to the world of the nineteenth century. For idealism, no matter how willful, has this fineness about it: only figures of some heroism attempt to gainsay an unpalatable truth, and appeal from it to another, a higher. In a sense those bitter antagonists—Eldon, who fought to preserve a world that had already vanished, and Shelley, who essayed in his verse "beautiful idealisms of moral excellence" that had not yet been seen in the world—are complementary figures, each expressing the great endeavor of his time: to impose on recalcitrant facts an order which, to the mere realist, those facts could not possibly suggest. For the censorship and sour strictures of the one may reflect the same impulse as the lofty visions of the other. The impulse is formal, poetical. From what seems a dance of matter, agitation without purpose or tendency, the nineteenth century deduces—or, more properly, beguiles—a beneficent pattern. Thus Carlyle in *Characteristics:* "Evil, in the widest sense we can give it, is precisely the dark, disordered material out of which man's Freewill has to create an edifice of order and Good." And after Carlyle, Robert Browning. Hence the casuistry, not of Thackeray alone, but of so much nineteenth-century fiction. Is it better to be clever than good? The question is never really answered. (pp. 143-47)

> *Russell A. Fraser, "Pernicious Casuistry: A Study of Character in 'Vanity Fair'," in* Nineteenth-Century Fiction, *Vol. 12, No. 2, September, 1957, pp. 137-47.*

G. ARMOUR CRAIG (lecture date 1958)

[*In the excerpt below, Craig provides a detailed analysis of various aspects of style in* Vanity Fair, *including its language, drama, and shifting narrative perspective.*]

"Among all our novelists his style is the purest, as to my ears it is also the most harmonious. Sometimes it is disfigured by a slight touch of affectation, by little conceits which smell of the oil;—but the language is always lucid." The judgment is Anthony Trollope's and the lucidity he praises is Thackeray's: "The reader, without labour, knows what he means, and knows all that he means." The judgment has been shared by many, perhaps even by Thackeray himself, for he was vigilant in detecting "fine writing" or "claptraps" in the work of others, and for himself he insisted that "this person writing strives to tell the truth. If there is not that, there is nothing." Yet some reconciling is necessary, for the truth is not always lucid and lucidity may not always be quite true.

There is at any rate a passage in chapter 42 of *Vanity Fair* for Trollope's judgment of which the modern reader—at least this

reader—would give a good deal. It describes the life of Jane Osborne keeping house for her father: her sister is now the fashionable Mrs. Frederick Bullock, her brother, disowned by their father for his marriage to Amelia Sedley, has been killed at Waterloo, and Jane now lives in idle spinsterhood in the great glum house in Russell Square.

> It was an awful existence. She had to get up of black winter's mornings to make breakfast for her scowling old father, who would have turned the whole house out of doors if his tea had not been ready at half-past eight. She remained silent opposite to him, listening to the urn hissing, and sitting in tremor while the parent read his paper, and consumed his accustomed portion of muffins and tea. At half-past nine he rose and went to the City, and she was almost free till dinner-time, to make visitations in the kitchen and to scold the servants: to drive abroad and descend upon the tradesmen, who were prodigiously respectful: to leave her cards and her papa's at the great glum respectable houses of their City friends; or to sit alone in the large drawing-room, expecting visitors; and working at a huge piece of worsted by the fire, on the sopha, hard by the great Iphigenia clock, which ticked and tolled with mournful loudness in the dreary room. The great glass over the mantle-piece, faced by the other great console glass at the opposite end of the room, increased and multiplied between them the brown holland bag in which the chandelier hung; until you saw these brown holland bags fading away in endless perspectives, and this apartment of Miss Osborne's seemed the centre of a system of drawing-rooms. When she removed the cordovan leather from the grand piano, and ventured to play a few notes on it, it sounded with a mournful sadness, startling the dismal echoes of the house. . . .

Thackeray's prose is seldom better than this. The passage comes from a paragraph that comments on the difference between Jane Osborne's life and that of her sister: "One can fancy the pangs" with which Jane regularly read about Mrs. Frederick Bullock in the "Morning Post," particularly the account of her presentation at the Drawing-room. The reader, characteristically, is invited to supply from his own observation the sort of vulgar envy that feeds upon accounts of "Fashionable Reunions" in the newspaper and to look down on Jane Osborne's suffering as no more than the deprivation of the snobbish pleasures of elegant society. The passage begins, then, easily enough: "It was an awful existence." And "awful" is at first simply a colloquial affectation. It becomes something more, however, as we move into the account of Jane's routine and ascend from the tremors of the breakfast table to the solitude of the drawing room with its covered chandelier "fading away in endless perspectives": the conversational pitch turns momentarily solemn with the vision of "this apartment of Miss Osborne's" as "the centre of a system of drawing-rooms"—including perhaps even that most august of all such apartments where her sister has been received. It would be hard to find this an example of the "little conceits which smell of the oil," for even here Thackeray does not lose his customary confidential hold upon the reader. The vision is kept close to us by his usual resource: the opposing mirrors "increased and multiplied between them the brown holland bag in which the chandelier hung; until *you* saw these brown holland bags fading away in endless perspectives.'' The ''you'' is no doubt as unobtrusive as an idiom. But it is not inconsistent with Thackeray's constant and fluent address to his reader, an address at its best as easy as idiom. In this very short passage Thackeray has moved from an example of the snobbery he loved to detect to a memorable symbol of the society in which snobbery flourishes. It is a society of endless perspectives, a system of drawing rooms whose center is everywhere, whose circumference is nowhere.

But is this what Thackeray meant? And is it the ''all'' that he meant? Certainly the symbol is not characteristic—it is indeed unique in *Vanity Fair*. Usually, or at any rate perhaps too often, Thackeray renders the barren routines of high life in mock genealogies or in the kind of mildly allegorical guest list that follows this passage. We are told that twice a month the solitary dinners of Mr. and Miss Osborne are shared with ''Old Dr. Gulp and his lady from Bloomsbury Square, . . . old Mr. Frowser the attorney, . . . old Colonel Livermore, . . . old Serjeant Toffy, . . . sometimes old Sir Thomas Coffin.'' *Vanity Fair,* we recall, began as ''Pen and Pencil Sketches of English Society,'' as an extension of *The Book Of Snobs*. Yet Thackeray seems to have felt the need of some larger, more inclusive presiding idea. In the early stages of writing the first few numbers he ''ransacked'' his brain for another title, and ''Vanity Fair,'' he said, came to him suddenly in the middle of the night. It seems to have summed up for him a position from which he could confidently go on with his ''Novel without a Hero,'' but a position of course very different from John Bunyan's. The original Vanity Fair as described by Evangelist is the dwelling place of abominations. But it is after all only one more obstacle on the road to the Celestial City, and all such obstacles are rewards in disguise. ''He that shall die there,'' says Evangelist, ''although his death will be unnatural, and his pain perhaps great, he will yet have the better of his fellow.'' While there are some unnatural and painful deaths in Thackeray's Fair, there seems to be no act of resistance or sacrifice by which anyone can get the better of anyone else, and the irony of the title has no doubt been lively in the minds of many readers. But Evangelist lays down a more poignantly ironical prescription: ''he that will go to the [Celestial] City, and yet not go through this Town [where Vanity Fair is kept], *must* needs *go out of the World*.'' If there is no Celestial City beyond Thackeray's Fair, and if there is no hero determined to fight on to a heavenly peak, it is even more certain that none of Thackeray's characters shall go out of this world. On every page of *Vanity Fair* we find description, exposure, comment, from a position much less elevated and secure than that of an evangelist, yet one from which we do see into an ''all'' as large as a whole society.

Certainly the style of all this commenting and exposing is this-worldly to a degree that would have puzzled Bunyan as much as it has troubled some of his descendants. In the preface to *Pendennis* Thackeray speaks of his work as ''a sort of confidential talk between reader and writer,'' and it was the excess of this conception of himself—''the little earmark by which he is most conspicuous''—that Trollope found ''his most besetting sin in style.'' The ''sin'' is ''a certain affected familiarity'': Thackeray ''indulges too frequently in little confidences with individual readers, in which pretended allusions to himself are frequent. 'What would you do? what would you say now, if you were in such a position?' he asks'' [see excerpt dated 1879 in *NCLC,* Vol. 5]. Yet for Trollope, although this familiarity might breed occasional contempt, it did not finally

compromise the great virtue of Thackeray's lucidity. ''As I have said before, the reader always understands his words without an effort, and receives all that the author has to give.'' But to know what, and to know all, a writer means is to be in his confidence indeed, and it would be a serious lapse of style that this confidence should break down in affectation or something worse.

In ''Before the Curtain,'' the preface he wrote in 1848 for the completed novel [see essay above], Thackeray promises his reader ''no other moral than this tag to the present story,'' that after wandering with him through the Fair, ''When you come home, you sit down, in a sober, contemplative, not uncharitable frame of mind, and apply yourself to your books or your business.'' He raises no literary expectations, he promises no carefully graduated feast of human nature, he does not even excuse himself to those who find all Fairs ''immoral'' and hence refuse to enter this one. The stern moralists may be quite right in withholding their custom, but those ''of a lazy, or a benevolent, or a sarcastic mood, may perhaps like to step in for half an hour and look at the performance.'' This casualness, the queer juxtaposition of ''lazy,'' ''benevolent,'' and ''sarcastic,'' may seem like the very height of good breeding. It does sum up the uncomfortable collocation of responses that any reader must make to some stretches of the novel. But it also promises that this writer will keep us free from violent emotions as we read. It is the guarantee of a special detachment.

Such detachment is often suggested by a coy version of one of Fielding's comic devices. When we witness the departure of Becky and Amelia from Chiswick Mall, the last flurry of farewells is recounted thus: ''Then came the struggle and the parting below. Words refuse to tell it. . . .'' The congregation of servants and pupils, the hugging and kissing and crying are such ''as no pen can depict, and as the tender heart would fain pass over.'' . . . Or, on the morning after the fatal excursion to Vauxhall, Joseph Sedley lies ''groaning in agonies which the pen refuses to describe'' . . . while he suffers the aftermath of rack punch. Becky, disappointed in her attempt to capture Joseph, goes away from the Sedley house to her duties as governess: ''Finally came the parting with Amelia, over which I intend to throw a veil.'' . . . Such mild affectations as these amuse a good deal less than their frequency suggests they should, however obliquely they may glance at sentimental explorations of young female affection or the tract-writer's interest in the heavy repentance of the drunkard. But they are the simplest and the least interesting form of a larger kind of detachment.

About other episodes the narrator is more artfully silent. Perhaps the most interesting is the courtship of Rawdon Crawley, which extends over several chapters and is concealed in the narrative of Becky's ministrations to old Miss Crawley. It will be recalled that the success of Becky's attentions to this lady, the old aunt whose wealth is the object of all the Crawleys' envy and scheming, alarm Mrs. Bute Crawley—whose portrait, incidentally, as well as that of her family and of her husband the Rector, make one wonder that Thackeray could have quarreled with Jerrold's anticlericalism. Mrs. Bute's scheming to secure Miss Crawley's money for her own leads her to warn Rawdon that when his stepmother dies, old Sir Pitt will marry Becky. Rawdon's response sets the level of intrigue exactly:

> ''By Jove, it's too bad,'' thought Rawdon, ''too
> bad, by Jove! I do believe the woman wants
> the poor girl to be ruined, in order that she

shouldn't come into the family as Lady Crawley.'' ...

He proceeds to the recommended seduction, but is outguessed
by the frank and outraged role that Becky adopts when he
"rallie[s] her in his graceful way about this father's attachment." The game goes on, Miss Crawley recovers from her
surfeit under Becky's assiduous care, and shortly news comes
that the meek Lady Crawley is dead. Rawdon and his aunt
discuss the matter while Becky stands by.

> Rebecca said nothing. She seemed by far the
> gravest and most impressed of the family. She
> left the room before Rawdon went away that
> day; but they met by chance below, as he was
> going away after taking leave, and had a parley
> together. . . .

And the next thing we know, old Sir Pitt has come to town
and is down on his knees to ask for the hand of Becky. The
narrator comments:

> In the course of this history we have never seen
> her lose her presence of mind; but she did now,
> and wept some of the most genuine tears that
> ever fell from her eyes. . . .

But what does "genuine" mean here? Or "they met by chance"
in the passage above? Are we to infer that during their "parley"
Becky uses the threat of a proposal from the father to make
sure of the son? Are we to infer that the tears are genuine
because she has planned too well—the threat she has used to
get one husband has turned out to be prophetic, and she might
have had the father? Are they tears of rage? of regret? As we
move on to the next chapter we certainly find no circumstantial
report of when and how Becky and Rawdon are married; instead
there is a good deal of indirect veiling of the scene and refusing
of the pen. "How they were married is not of the slightest
consequence to anybody." Perhaps, it is conjectured, they went
off one afternoon when Becky was presumed to be visiting
Amelia. But the matter is left in uncertainty. On the one hand,
"Who needs to be told, that if a woman has a will, she will
assuredly find a way?" And on the other: "who on earth, after
the daily experience we have, can question the probability of
a gentleman marrying anybody?" . . . (pp. 87-96)

The concealment of the circumstances of the marriage may
appeal to the lazy, may satisfy the benevolent, and it may give
the sarcastic something to work on too. But its most important
effect is that the narration here, clustered about with confidential comments and dismissive questions, sets before us a
way of knowing the world. It is a way so inferential, so dependent upon unfinished implications, that it comes close to
the character of gossip. And a good gossip, while its unfinished
sentences and its discreet and indiscreet omissions may keep
us from the exhilaration of indignation or rhapsody, can suggest
values and insights superior to the vocabulary of the purveyor
or the listener. Here, whatever the meaning of that "by chance"
that modifies the meeting of Becky and Rawdon, or whatever
the meaning of that "genuine" that modifies her tears, we can
only infer that the marriage is the result neither of grand passion
nor of mean seduction. The veiling of the secret here means
that we can only accept Becky's marriage as a convenience.
Even the grossness of Mrs. Bute's plotting is lost in the shadows.

The questions with which Thackeray disposes of this affair—
"Who needs to be told . . . who can question the probabil-

ity . . .''—are of course the most conspicuous earmark of his
detachment in *Vanity Fair*. There is the issue of who made the
first move in Becky's first romance, with the young Reverend
Mr. Crisp who came infatuated to tea at Chiswick Mall: after
a parenthetical cloud of hints and counter-hints the narrator
concludes, "But who can tell you the real truth of the matter?"
. . . Just as when the pen refuses to tell, the implication here
is only coy. But a good many hundred pages later, in what is
called "A Vagabond Chapter" . . . , this kind of coyness can
exasperate. It comes in a passage summarizing Becky's career
after her fall from polite society in London: "When she got
her money she gambled; when she had gambled it she was put
to shifts to live; who knows how or by what means she succeeded? . . . The present historian can give no certain details
regarding the event." . . . The detachment inculcated here is
vast and affluent indeed; it is perhaps matched only by the
elaborate veiling of the circumstances of Joseph Sedley's death.
But the most puzzling questions in the book are those that
comment upon its crucial passage.

Every reader of *Vanity Fair* remembers the "discovery scene"
of chapter 53—the scene in which Becky suffers exposure and
isolation after her husband and Lord Steyne violently clash.
And every student of the novel knows that this scene is a
battleground upon which the judgments of a number of Thackeray's critics have collided. Rawdon, having been freed from
the spunging house, hurries "across the streets and the great
squares of Vanity Fair, and bursts in upon his wife and Lord
Steyne in something less than *flagrante delicto* though ready
for embarrassment."

> Steyne was hanging over the sofa on which
> Becky sate. The wretched woman was in a bril-
> liant full toilette, her arms and all her fingers
> sparkling with bracelets and rings; and the bril-
> liants on her breast which Steyne had given her.
> He had her hand in his, and was bowing over
> it to kiss it, when Becky started up with a faint
> scream as she caught sight of Rawdon's white
> face. At the next instant she tried a smile, a
> horrid smile, as if to welcome her husband; and
> Steyne rose up, grinding his teeth, pale, and
> with fury in his looks. . . .

> There was that in Rawdon's face which caused
> Becky to fling herself before him. "I am in-
> nocent, Rawdon," she said; "before God, I am
> innocent." She clung hold of his coat, of his
> hands; her own were all covered with serpents,
> and rings, and baubles.

> "I am innocent.—Say I am innocent," she said
> to Lord Steyne.

> He thought a trap had been laid for him, and
> was as furious with the wife as with the hus-
> band. "You innocent! Damn you!" he screamed
> out. "You innocent! Why, every trinket you
> have on your body is paid for by me. I have
> given you thousands of pounds which this fel-
> low has spent, and for which he has sold you."
> . . . Lord Steyne seized up his hat, and, with
> flame in his eyes, and looking his enemy fiercely
> in the face, marched upon him, never for a
> moment doubting that the other would give way.

> But Rawdon Crawley springing out, seized him
> by the neckcloth, until Steyne, almost stran-

gled, writhed, and bent under his arm. "You lie, you dog!" said Rawdon. "You lie, you coward and villain!" And he struck the Peer twice over the face with his open hand, and flung him bleeding to the ground. It was all done before Rebecca could interpose. She stood there trembling before him. She admired her husband, strong, brave, and victorious.

"Come here," he said.—She came up at once.

"Take off those things."—She began, trembling, pulling the jewels from her arms, and the rings from her shaking fingers, and held them all in a heap, quivering, and looking up at him. "Throw them down," he said, and she dropped them. He tore the diamond ornament out of her breast, and flung it at Lord Steyne. It cut him on his bald forehead. Steyne wore the scar to his dying day.

(pp. 96-9)

The theatricality of the passage—Becky's clinging and quivering, the serpents and baubles on her hands, Rawdon's springing out and his terse manifesto, the flame in the eyes of the wicked nobleman and the lifelong scar on his head—all such features suggest that the creator of Punch's Prize novelists is once again engaged in something like parody. On the other hand it has been asserted that far from a joke, the scene "is the chief ganglion of the tale; and the discharge of energy from Rawdon's fist [*sic*] is the reward and consolation of the reader" [see excerpt by Robert Louis Stevenson dated 1882]. The most extensive criticism of the scene finds it unprepared for and conveyed by a dramatic technique foreign to Thackeray's genius [see excerpt by Percy Lubbock dated 1921 in *NCLC*, Vol. 5], but this judgment has in turn been disposed of by another critic who finds Thackeray's usual stamp upon it and some other felicities as well. He suggests that one of these is the way in which "Steyne wore the scar" echoes "Steyne wore the star." By the same sort of reasoning we might infer from "He tore the diamond ornament out of her breast" that Becky's heart is surpassing hard; and certainly Thackeray tells us that the battle takes the heart out of her. But the one touch upon which Thackeray himself is known to have commented is Becky's response to the sudden burst of energy from Rawdon: "She stood there trembling before him. She admired her husband, strong, brave, and victorious." Of this observation Thackeray is reported to have said that it was a touch of genius, and it does consort well with his special genius in the rest of the book.

For although the battle seems to be the expression of outraged honor, it is a collision that misses its main issue and prize. As the resistless masses meet, Becky stands off to one side, and although her admiration is unacceptable or even unknown to Rawdon, and although we are told that her life seems so "miserable, lonely, and profitless" after Rawdon has silently departed that she even thinks of suicide, there is still a profound irrelevance in this violent scene. Becky's maid comes upon her in her dejection and asks the question that is in every reader's mind: "*Mon Dieu*, madame, what has happened?" And the "person writing" concludes this crucial chapter with an enlargement of the same question:

What *had* happened? Was she guilty or not? She said not; but who could tell what was truth which came from those lips; or if that corrupt

heart was in this case pure? All her lies and her schemes, all her selfishness and her wiles, all her wit and her genius had come to this bankruptcy. . . .

Becky lies down, the maid goes to the drawing room to gather up the pile of trinkets, and the chapter ends. If Thackeray has not risen to a cruel joke on those readers who find consolation and reward in the discharge of energy from Rawdon, he has at least interrupted their satisfaction.

Lord Steyne's meaning of "guilty"—"He thought a trap had been laid for him" by Becky and Rawdon—is of course quite false, though it corroborates the characterization of Steyne as one experienced in double-dealing. "Guilty" from Rawdon's point of view of course means, as he tells Pitt next day, that "it was a regular plan between that scoundrel and her" to get him out of the way. . . . And Thackeray goes to as great lengths to make it impossible for us to know that this interpretation is true as he does to conceal the timing and motives of Becky's marriage. To see the entangling and displacing of any clear answer, we need only ask "guilty of what?" The usual answer is of course "guilty of adultery" (or guilty of getting ready for it), and Thackeray's silence is commonly attributed to his awareness of the "squeamishness" of his public. Indeed he himself lends real authority to this account of the matter. In 1840, writing on Fielding, he complains that the world no longer tolerates real satire. "The same vice exists now, only we don't speak about it; the same things are done, but we don't call them by their names." And in *Vanity Fair* he complains that he must be silent about some events in Becky's later career because he must satisfy "the moral world, that has, perhaps, no particular objection to vice, but an insuperable repugnance to hearing vice called by its proper name." . . . There may well be evidence in Thackeray's personal history to suggest in addition that he was, perhaps even before the separation from his mad wife, evasive and unclear on the subject of sexual behavior. But however complicated the tensions of Thackeray's own emotional experience, and however rigid the scruples of his audience, the answer to the questions with which he comments on this most important episode cannot be a single "name" or possess any "proper name." For he has led us here, however uneasily, with mingled attitudes of parody and outrage, to a startling though incomplete vision of a new social world, a vision exactly proportioned to the irrelevance of the violence we have witnessed.

The words of the passage that command our moral response are precisely those that most nearly approach parody: Becky responds to a nameless "that" in Rawdon's face by exclaiming "I am innocent." If the reader trained in melodrama scoffs at the response and turns Becky into a consummate villain, he will have some trouble getting through the rest of the novel, and it is likely that he will long since have become exasperated with Thackeray's tone, his silences and implications. The same is true, moreover, of the sentimental reader who throws down the volume and declares that Becky has been monstrously wronged and victimized by wicked men in a bad world. But the reader who says, in effect, "it is impossible to tell whether or of what she is guilty" is exactly in the difficult position of one who accepts Thackeray's narrative as it is given. And what such a reader sees from this position must fill him with wonder if not dismay. For he sees that while he wants to answer these questions, he cannot do so, and he can only conclude that he is looking at a situation before which his moral vocabulary is irrelevant. Becky in her isolation has finally gone out of this

An illustration by Thackeray depicting Amelia and her family's encounter with Becky at a London fair.

world, and it will take a new casuistry to bring her back. Thackeray uses some strong moral words in his comment, it is true: "who could tell what was truth which came from those lips; or if that corrupt heart was in this case pure?" But while we know that Becky has lied heartily to Steyne, and to his hearty admiration, we cannot know that she is lying to Rawdon when she insists on her innocence. Whatever corruption we may have seen, the question this time is in earnest. The qualities named in the final statement, and especially by its last word, tell us where we are: "All her lies and her schemes, all her selfishness and her wiles, all her wit and her genius had come to this bankruptcy." For these are the terms not so much of moral as of financial enterprise, and "this bankruptcy" is the real touch of genius in the passage. Thackeray's questions and his comment express neither indignation nor sympathy. Rather, they bring before us the terrible irresolution of a society in which market values and moral values are discontinuous and separate. And Thackeray will not—he can not—support us as we revolt from such a spectacle.

The ghostly paradigm upon which human nature plays in *Vanity Fair* is the credit economy that in Thackeray's own lifetime finally developed from a money economy. Even the constant gambling in Thackeray's Fair, historically appropriate as it may be to his Regency setting (and much of his own early experience as it may reflect), suggests the unpredictability of the system. Distant though the gambler may be from respectability, his luck is only a little less mysterious than the power his winnings confer upon him. However it may be in the most famous conversation recorded in modern literary history, it is all too true in *Vanity Fair* that rich people are different because they have more money. Thackeray exposed himself to some high-minded

criticism from George Henry Lewes [see excerpt by Lewes dated 1848 in *NCLC*, Vol. 5] when he published the number containing Becky's famous reflection, "I think I could be a good woman if I had five thousand a year." For he had commented, "And who knows but Rebecca was right in her speculations—and that it was only a question of money and fortune which made the difference between her and an honest woman? . . . In its interrogative form the comment is much more precise than the declaration Thackeray wrote to Lewes. The latter called it "detestable" to say that "honesty is only the virtue of abundance." Thackeray replied that he meant "only that he in the possession of luxuries . . . should be very chary of despising poor Lazarus on foot, and look very humbly and leniently upon the faults of his less fortunate brethren" [see excerpt dated March 6, 1848]. This is of course no answer; or if it is, it asks for a curious forbearance towards Becky Sharp. But Thackeray qualifies at once: "I am quite aware of the dismal roguery . . . [which] goes all through the Vanity Fair story—and God forbid that the world should be like it altogether: though I fear it is more like it than we like to own." The likeness to "the world" is in the belief that money is magic and in the frightening awareness, no doubt recently reinforced by the financial crisis of 1847, that no theory had yet been devised to control it. (pp. 99-105)

The first mention of the "guilt" or "innocence" of Becky's relations to Lord Steyne comes in a passage about the "awful kitchen inquisition" of the servants of Vanity Fair. We are told that Raggles, the retired butler of Miss Crawley, who owns the house in Curzon Street where Becky and Rawdon live well on nothing a year, is ruined by his extension of credit to them. But he is the victim of something more than the simple excess of liabilities over assets. The "*Vehmgericht* of the servants'-hall" early pronounces Becky guilty:

> And I shame to say, she would not have got credit had they not believed her to be guilty. It was the sight of the Marquis of Steyne's carriage-lamps at her door, contemplated by Raggles, burning in the blackness of midnight, "that kep him up," as he afterwards said; that, even more than Rebecca's arts and coaxings. . . .

The question of guilt here is quite subordinate to the question of credit, and Raggles is ruined not because he is right about Becky's guilt but because he believes in a strict correlation between Becky's moral and financial status. The last of Raggles is seen at the drunken party of the servants on the morning after the battle; our last glimpse of him is not as he suffers in ruin but as he looks at his fellows "with a wild surprise" upon hearing from Becky that Rawdon "has got a good appointment." . . . It is no wonder that Thackeray should have said in a letter to his mother written during the very month when the "discovery scene" appeared,

> I cant find the end of the question between property and labour. We want something almost equal to a Divine Person to settle it. I mean if there is ever to be an elucidation of the mystery it is to be solved by a preacher of such novelty and authority, as will awaken and convince mankind—but O how and when?

Whatever the fate of the larger question, Thackeray does do some novel preaching upon bankruptcy in one section of *Vanity Fair*. John Sedley, we recall, is ruined in the uncertainties following Napoleon's escape from Elba . . . , and Thackeray's extended portrait of the "business and bustle and mystery of a ruined man" . . . seems at first sight disproportionate. Of course the bankruptcy accounts for the career of Amelia, but not for all of it. For old Osborne, who also emerges from the background just here, is described as behaving towards his former friend Sedley "with savageness and scorn." Our attitude is shaped precisely by Osborne's insisting that as a bankrupt Sedley must be wicked—that he is both out of business and out of the circle of decency. "From a mere sense of consistency, a persecutor is bound to show that the fallen man is a villain—otherwise he, the persecutor, is a wretch himself." . . . And Osborne is characterized more grossly still by his opposition to Amelia for his son, by his insistence that George marry the rich mulatto Miss Schwarz, and by his vast self-righteousness. Osborne is perhaps an inept caricature of the City man who has succumbed completely to the superstitions of money, but he is a new kind of portrait. . . . (pp. 105-07)

In *Vanity Fair* . . . Becky's bankruptcy offers no clearer connection between villainy—or goodness—and loss of credit than does the situation of Old John Sedley that Osborne so ruthlessly categorizes. The thoroughness with which Thackeray has covered his tracks suggests that no single transaction, not even payment by adultery, is at issue here. The kind of credit upon which the Crawleys lived so well in London and Paris is beyond the power of any act or value to overtake, for it is the social version of that system in which the perpetual promise to pay is taken for the perpetual fact of payment. "The truth is, when we say of a gentleman that he lives well on nothing a year, we use the word 'nothing' to signify something unknown." . . . It may be that Rawdon and Becky are "wicked," but their wickedness will not account for their credit as they pursue the fashionable life. Just as the war that so mysteriously yet inevitably ruined John Sedley was, as Thackeray tells us, a lucky accident interrupting the endless double- and triple-dealing among nations . . . , so for Becky an accident interrupts the double-dealing and counter double-dealing of the scramble for social power. The perspectives here are indeed almost endless; they are certainly beyond the limits of innocence or guilt. Even Rawdon, who experiences something like coversion or reform as Becky's career reaches its height, is not quite secure. His one assertion to Becky after the battle is an ironic fulfillment of Steyne's accusation: "You might have spared me a hundred pounds, Becky, out of all this—I have always shared with you." . . . And the last words he speaks in the novel are as ambiguous as any question from the narrator:

> "She has kep money concealed from me these ten years," he said. "She swore, last night only, she had none from Steyne. She knew it was all up, directly I found it. If she's not guilty, Pitt, she's as bad as guilty, and I'll never see her again, never." . . .

It is hardly possible to find the outrage of manly honor in these exactly struck last words. The distinction between "guilty" and "as bad as guilty" would be the final viciousness if it were not the final irrelevance.

But, again, is this what Thackeray means, and is it the *all* that he means? We can believe so only by acknowledging that the easy confidence between reader and writer promised at the beginning has been renounced, for we are here outside the domain of laziness, benevolence, or sarcasm. If the renunciation were the deliberate act of a supreme ironist who turns and rends us for our naive acceptance of his confidential detachment, Thackeray would indeed have created a masterpiece.

But in the crucial scene and in portions of the chapters that lead to it Thackeray has exposed us to violent emotions that no politeness can conceal. The enmity between Little Rawdy and Lord Steyne, for example, is an extension of Becky's neglect of her child that erupts into physical violence: Becky boxes his ears for listening to her on the stairs as she entertains Lord Steyne. . . . The child indeed makes his first speaking appearance in the same chapter as that in which Lord Steyne also first appears, grinning "hideously, his little eyes leering towards Rebecca." . . . The juxtaposition is emphasized when little Rawdon is apostrophized:

> O thou poor lonely little benighted boy! Mother is the name for God in the lips and hearts of little children; and here was one who was worshipping a stone. . . .

The appeal is no mere instance of competing with the creator of little Paul Dombey, as everyone who has read Thackeray's letters to his own mother will know. It is an appeal similar to many others in the narrative of Amelia, although there Thackeray is more characteristically reticent. When Amelia and her mother are reunited after her marriage, though Thackeray begins by referring to "How the floodgates were opened," he adds, "Let us respect Amelia and her mamma whispering and whimpering and laughing and crying in the parlour and the twilight." And when Amelia retreats to meditate in "the little room" with its "little white bed" in her old home, Thackeray desists:

> Have we a right to repeat or to overhear her prayers? These, brother, are secrets, and out of the domain of Vanity Fair, in which our story lies. . . .

Even—especially—if we construe this scene and its secrets as an expression of Amelia's first awareness that she is to be a mother herself, it still involves relationships and sentiments outside the "domain" that Thackeray so thoroughly explored. It is a domain bounded by the "politeness" invoked in that early address to the reader in which the narrator promises "to love and shake by the hand" his "good and kindly" characters, "to laugh confidentially in the reader's sleeve" at the "silly" ones, but "to abuse in the strongest terms that politeness admits of" all those who are "wicked and heartless." . . . Such terms of abuse for the wicked and love for the good are for the most part so polite that we accept them with all the detachment guaranteed by the Manager of the Performance. But the limits of this detachment—its very bankruptcy—can be shown only as we glimpse the howling wilderness outside, where the secrets of private feelings are violently confused with public forces of huge and mysterious dimensions, and where there is neither lucidity nor truth.

What Thackeray does then exhibit within the domain of the Fair is the impossibility of self-knowledge and, in the fullest sense, dramatic change. The most intimate experiences of the self, whether in prayer or in love, in disappointment or in outrage, must be kept outside. Becky's "I am innocent" is no more an articulation of the truth than it is the lucid exposure of a lie. But to put us where we cannot know "What *had* happened" and to face us with the bewildering irrelevance of our polite detachment, Thackeray was driven to an extreme that no style of his could control. He could not be clear without being untruthful, and he could not be truthful without being obscure. He tried to recover himself, it is true, in the subsequent chapters by returning to the conception of Becky that most saves his book. The most interesting feature of her characterization is not that she begins from the ambiguous social position of the orphan and governess—"'I don't trust them governesses, Pinner,' says the Sedley housekeeper with enormous assurance, 'they're neither one thing nor t'other. They give themselves the hairs and hupstarts of ladies, and their wages is no better than you nor me.'" . . . Thackeray is concerned with much more than the favorite Victorian example of social mobility. The greater truth about Becky is that she is a mimic, that she trades on the difference between fantasy and society, between the role and the fact. But the truth of endless mimicry is much too large for the domain of the lucid. It is larger than any drawing room, park, or square of Vanity Fair, and it could be forced in only by an act of violence that darkened lucidity and concealed truth. The casuistry upon which *Vanity Fair* rests is unique, and the responses of many thousands of readers for a hundred years to this much-read book must constitute one of the most erratic subterranean currents of our moral history. (pp. 108-13)

> G. Armour Craig, "On the Style of 'Vanity Fair'," in Style in Prose Fiction: English Institute Essays 1958, *edited by Harold C. Martin, Columbia University Press, 1959, pp. 87-113.*

MYRON TAUBE (essay date 1963)

[*Taube investigates how the structure of* Vanity Fair *derives from Thackeray's use of contrasting characters and situations.*]

The structure of *Vanity Fair* is in many ways unlike that of the typical Victorian novel, whatever that might be. A general criticism of the serial novel has been that "The serial form of publication . . . has undoubtedly been responsible for much overplotting. The Victorian novel in general suffers from too heavy a structure." While this is true of many of the novels of Dickens and Collins, it is not true of *Vanity Fair*. On the contrary, *Vanity Fair* supposedly lacks structure, organization, and plot. It is a "novel without a plan" [see excerpt by Charles Whibley dated 1903 in *NCLC*, Vol. 5]; "like Topsy, [it] just grew." And, of course, the serial form was to blame: "the spasmodic writing of monthly installments prevented good integration." However, while it is true that *Vanity Fair* does not have the heavy structure of a Dickens or Collins novel, it is not true that it lacks structure or organization. Just as Thackeray's unity is new—a unity of theme rather than the traditional unity of plot involving the life of a hero—so is his structure a new kind of structure. In the traditional novel, structure depended on the continuity of action, on the flow of narrative and dramatic action from one climax to the next. But with *Vanity Fair,* the principle of structure changes from the continuity of action to the contrast of characters and the actions they perform.

Little attention has been paid to the influence of serial publication on the shape and structure of the Victorian novel. Kathleen Tillotson has pointed out that "within a single number, the balance is held between varieties of narrative method—summary, description, and presentation—and also between the fortunes of different sets of characters." Each monthly number served as a frame for a limited action which, whether unified or not, had to fit into the unity of the entire novel. Each monthly number of *Vanity Fair* shows that contrast which serves as the structural principle of the novel. Perhaps the most obvious contrast is between the Amelia and Becky stories, which serve as the frame for the entire novel. Both stories are almost congruent triangles, except that they are direct opposites. Becky knows no love; Amelia is all love. Becky, who loves only herself, marries a man who worships her; Amelia worships and marries a man who loves only himself. Becky has admirers about her all the time; Amelia has one constant admirer. In the first number, Amelia is quietly in love with George and Becky is laying her snares for Jos. Eighteen numbers later, Amelia has given up her foolish infatuation for George, and Becky has finally snared Jos. Between these terminal numbers, the plots show contrast in each monthly number. Thus, in the first two numbers, the two girls begin their lives together in the world: they begin their love affairs. The third and fourth members present a series of contrasts between the Crawley household and the Osborne household, developing the characters. In Number V . . . , Becky begins her rise in the world and is thrown out of Miss Crawley's favor of her marriage to Rawdon. Likewise, Mr. Sedley is ruined financially and Amelia is thrown out of favor with Mr. Osborne. The secret marriage of George and Amelia in Number VII is obviously meant to contrast with the secret Becky-Rawdon marriage in the preceding number. Old Osborne's treatment of George in Number VII . . . is meant to contrast with Miss Crawley's treatment of Rawdon. . . : George is left with £2,000, Rawdon with £20.

The eighth and ninth numbers bring the participants together in a series of interwoven contrasts as they prepare for the battle of Waterloo. In Number X, Becky, Bute, and Pitt Crawley compete for Miss Crawley's money. Number XI contrasts the lives of the Rawdon Crawleys and Amelia. The Crawleys live well on nothing a year; Amelia lives poorly on nothing a year. Becky's career is a rising arc; Amelia is sinking deeper and deeper into personal failure and unhappiness. In Number XII. . . , Becky is making ready to be taken back into the bosom of her family and return to the "halls of her ancestors"; at the same time, Georgy's aunt tells her father that she has seen the boy, thus laying the groundwork for Georgy's return to the halls of *his* ancestors. In Number XIII. . . , further contrast is made between Becky's life and Amelia's, between Becky's treatment of her child and Amelia's treatment of hers; between Amelia's response to the news of Dobbin's supposed marriage, and Dobbin's response to the news of Amelia's supposed marriage. In Number XIV. . . , Becky is at the zenith of her career: she is introduced to the king; she receives money from Lord Steyne; and she appears at her first dinner at Gaunt House. On the other hand, Amelia is at her nadir: she surrenders her son to his grandfather. But then Becky's arc turns sharply downward, and Amelia's turns up. In Number XVI . . . , Becky tries to salvage what she can of a life shattered by the too early arrival of her husband, while the pieces of Amelia's life are ready to be put together by the return from India of her future husband. And so their triangles are again contrasted: Becky gives up the love of a now moral husband for a wealthy, powerful admirer, Lord Steyne. Amelia gives up the love of an honest lover, Dobbin, for a rather despicable husband. Ironically, she does it twice—when she marries George, and when she remains faithful to his memory. Herein is what has been called the "likeness within difference of Amelia's stupid fidelity to her husband's memory, and Becky's stupid infidelity to Rawdon." Later, when Dobbin leaves Amelia to rejoin his regiment and return to India, Thackeray comments, "She didn't wish to marry him, but she wished to keep him. She wished to give him nothing, but that he should give her all. It is a bargain not unfrequently levied in love." Kathleen Tillotson notes, "Outside its context, the second of these sentences could be taken as describing Becky."

The last three numbers contrast Amelia's life and the life of the Osbornes; life on the Continent and life in London; Amelia's new life and Becky's failure. The Becky and Amelia stories are finished in such a way that the circle of their lives is closed: Amelia's by her finally finding the man who really loves her, Becky's by her being true to her inner nature and remaining the outsider she always was.

A good deal of negative opinion has been passed over the last three numbers. It has been contended that they are gratuitous. The novel did not "stop when it should. The logical end of the book is Rawdon Crawley's appointment to the Governorship of Coventry Island, and the regathering of the threads—over 150 pages—is a wanton and tedious operation." Strangely, Whibley has hit upon a valid point, but unfortunately, he has the wrong value judgments and the wrong reasons; and to paraphrase T. S. Eliot, the worst critical treason is to make a judgment with the wrong reasons. The fact is that the last three numbers, but particularly the chapters in Pumpernickel, *are* a regathering of the threads. Actually, the concluding chapters of the novel are a coda, a "concluding passage, the function of which is to bring a composition or division to a proper close" (*Webster's New Collegiate Dictionary*). Artistically, structurally, and thematically, the coda is right: it brings the two major melodic lines—the Becky and Amelia stories—together, rounding out both stories, and maintaining the same bittersweet tone that runs through the novel.

My use of a musical term to describe the ending of *Vanity Fair* is not haphazard. I believe that the structure of *Vanity Fair*, which is a much more carefully planned, complex, and sophisticated structure than has hitherto been assumed, can best be understood if analyzed with a musical analogy. Thus, the Amelia and Becky stories are like two contrapuntal melodies, one played in the treble, one in the bass. Filling the space between them, like variations on a musical theme, are the contrasted and related sub-plots. For example, while Becky's pursuit of wealth and Amelia's loss of wealth are a contrast in the major melodic lines, there are variations which elaborate upon and develop the central theme. The Crawleys pursue Miss Crawley's wealth. In Number III. . . , Thackeray gives the background for what he calls "this race for money.". . . First Sir Pitt had tried, but he had failed. . . . Rawdon's favored position made Becky set her snare for him as she had for Jos. But then the Bute Crawleys enter the race. . . . In Number X, the behind the scenes machinations of Pitt Crawley and Lady Southdown and their decision to use Lady Jane as a means of winning over Miss Crawley . . . contrast with the behind the scenes machinations of the Bute Crawleys and their decision to use their son James. . . . A further variation on the pursuit of wealth theme is seen in the rise and fall of the two British business men—old Osborne and old Sedley. Sedley, who had set up Osborne in business, himself fails, and the recipient of his kindness grows to hate him. In Number V are contrasted their attitudes towards each other and the possible marriage of their children. . . . In Number VI, Old Sedley's interview with Dobbin . . . balances Old Osborne's interview with his son. . . . Embittered by life, the two old men live out their lives in disappointment. Their stories are finally brought together in Number XVIII. . . : Old Sedley dies begging his daughter's forgiveness; Osborne dies before a reconciliation is made with Amelia. And one sees the balance and contrast of deaths in the novel: the decline of Miss Crawley in Number X parallels the decline of Old Sedley in Number XI and the decline of Sir Pitt in Number XII. All die helpless and alone, loveless and

beaten by life, and their deaths are variations on the novel's central theme of anti-materialism and salvation through love.

While the Amelia-Becky stories serve as a frame for the novel, they also supply the material which will be expanded upon in variations. Both girls are seen as children and parents, and these roles become a major theme in *Vanity Fair*. Much of *Vanity Fair* is structured about the moral and emotional parent-child relationships of three generations: Old Osborne, George and his sisters, Georgy; the Sedleys, Amelia and Jos, Georgy; Sir Pitt, Pitt and Rawdon, and their children. . . . In each generation there is conflict between parent and child: Sir Pitt loses Becky to Rawdon in a father-son-female triangle that foreshadows the tragedy of *The Brothers Karamazov;* Osborne, whose actions are symbolized by the "chronometer, which was surmounted by a cheerful brass group of the sacrifice of Iphigenia". . . , sacrifices his children on the altar of his selfishness; Amelia fights with her mother and surrenders herself to the power of her son. Moreover, these patterns of conflict are not haphazard: besides being part of the over-all structure of the novel, they are given additional structural meaning by their development within the monthly number.

Thackeray uses the principle of contrast so that his monthly issues will reveal his characters. Using similar relationships and corresponding characters, he develops his variations on the theme. For example, while Becky and Amelia are opposites in many ways, George and Rawdon are cut from the same fabric but with different patterns. George, a would-be gentleman, is a *nouveau riche arrivist;* Rawdon, the military dandy, is the rake about town. Although both are selfish young bucks with similar tastes, attitudes and activities, they are also quite different. George is too selfish to love and dies too early to change. Rawdon, "a perfectly marvelous piece of verisimilitude," shows the effects of time and circumstance. A Samson shorn of his locks (Thackeray uses the image twice in Chapter xvi), the domesticated Rawdon loses his dash and color and becomes "Mrs. Crawley's husband.". . . But Rawdon Crawley, unlike Becky and George, has one commendable quality: he worships his wife and loves his son. . . . In Number XI, Becky leaves Rawdon behind when she goes to England. . . . [Her] complete indifference is in direct contrast with Rawdon's feelings for the boy. While Becky lets the boy cry at night, Rawdon sneaks off to see him. . . . In Chapter xxxviii (as well as xxxv) are the details of Amelia's life with George and her parents, and Amelia's role as a parent is contrasted with her mother's. Thus, Thackeray has created contrasts not only between the Becky and Amelia stories, but within each story: Becky and Rawdon, Amelia and her mother. And Thackeray's judgment of both Becky and Amelia is implicit; the contrast between the two different kinds of mother love is "subtle, because Thackeray is critical both of heartless neglect and passionate possessiveness."

Because Thackeray's interest is in the revelation of character, and because he uses contrast as a formal principle, he very often places his characters in the same or similar situations so that their actions will reveal the differences between their personalities. After all, "what is character but the determination of incident? What is incident but the illustration of character?" To continue the musical analogy, his variations extend to having the same tune played by different instruments in order to reveal the quality of each instrument. For example, both George and Rawdon are disinherited because of imprudent marriages. However, note the differences in the reactions of the men and their wives: When George finds out that he has been cut by his father and left with only £2,000, he reacts violently:

"A pretty way you have managed the affair," said George, looking savagely at William Dobbin. "Look here, Dobbin," and he flung over to the latter his parent's letter. "A beggar, by Jove, and all in consequence of my d--d sentimentality. Why couldn't we have waited? A ball might have done for me in the course of the war, and may still, and how will Emmy be bettered by being left a beggar's widow? It was all your doing. You were never easy until you got me married and ruined. What the deuce am I to do with two thousand pounds? Such a sum won't last two years. I've lost a hundred and forty to Crawley at cards and billiards since I've been down here. A pretty manager of a man's matters *you* are, forsooth."...

When George breaks the news to Amelia, she asks innocently, "Isn't two thousand pounds an immense deal of money, George?" George, of course, "laughed at her *naiveté.*" On the other hand, Rawdon and Becky begin married life with much less money, and with a completely different attitude. While Mrs. Bute Crawley has Miss Crawley in tow and Rawdon is out of Miss Crawley's favor, Rawdon and Becky wait, and Rawdon realizes that Mrs. Bute connived to bring him and Becky together at every opportunity.... Later, when Rawdon, who had expected at least two hundred pounds from his aunt, went for his check, he "came back furious. 'By Jove, Becky,' says he, 'she's only given me twenty pound!' Though it told against themselves, the joke was too good, and Becky burst out laughing at Rawdon's discomfiture."... (pp. 119-27)

But Thackeray's use of contrast and variation is not restricted to different people performing contrasting or similar actions: so skillfully has Thackeray organzied his novel around the principle of contrast that his characters perform actions which contrast not only with the actions of others, but also with similar actions they themselves had performed in time past! Thus, for example, little Georgy is a beginning again of George, and those about him respond to him not only as to a child, but also as though he were George.... [When] Georgy is being made a gentleman, he is made into a carbon copy of his father: "Georgy, after breakfast, would sit in the armchair in the dining-room, and read the *Morning Post,* just like a grown-up man. 'How he *du* dam and swear,' the servants would cry, delighted at his precocity. Those who remembered the Captain his father, declared Master George was his Pa every inch of him. He made the house lively by his activity, his imperiousness, his scolding, and his good-nature." Moreover, Georgy's return affects his grandfather's sense of guilt over his own son, and Georgy has the same mastery—and then some—over his grandfather that his father had:

> In Russell Square everybody was afraid of Mr. Osborne, and Mr. Osborne was afraid of Georgy. The boy's dashing manners, and offhand rattle about books and learning, his likeness to his father (dead unreconciled in Brussels yonder), awed the old gentleman, and gave the young man the mastery. The old man would start at some hereditary feature or tone unconsciously used by the little lad, and fancy that George's father was again before him. He tried by indulgence to the grandson to make up for harshness to the elder George. . . .

"Come children, let us shut up the box": Thackeray's illustration following the last lines of Vanity Fair.

Not only do we see Old Osborne reacting to the past brought back to the present, but Georgy himself re-enacts the same patterns of development of his father, although there are variations. Georgy's little composition on "Selfishness" is, of course, an ironic comment on most of the characters and actions in the novel...; but it is also a contrast to his father's letter written many years before, in which he revealed his own childish selfishness.... And one sees another of Thackeray's little touches of absolute mastery: the father, in a time when the families were on excellent terms, signed his letter "George Sedley Osborne"; the son, because of his grandfather's continual attacks on Old Sedley, signed his composition "George S. Osborne."

In the same way, Amelia and Dobbin relive their relationships from the past. For Amelia, George is a beginning again, too. And Dobbin, who had been the protector and advisor of the older George, becomes the protector and advisor of the young George. And as he had loved Amelia in the past, so does he continue to love her. But the years have made changes, and these changes lead to Dobbin's final break with Amelia. But through it all, we have the feeling that Thackeray, for what may well be the first time in the English novel, is bringing us into the secret areas of man's life in time. For not only do the years pass, etching their lines on the characters, but the characters, deeply involved in time, make a statement that has the objective qualities of a Bennett or James. Thackeray's approach to his characters was, essentially, that of the eighteenth century: he believed in types, he doubted the efficacy of political action for social improvement, and believed in the necessity of satire. But to his eighteenth century approach, he brought an awareness of time and its effects that is more modern than has been hitherto assumed. When he plays tricks with time, so to speak, Thackeray is making a statement about the cyclical nature of life, suggesting that what one is determines what one will do; he also suggests, I think, that what one does is what one is. And since what one is is affected by time, Thackeray shows the same person responding to two similar events, years apart, and revealing in the different responses the changes produced by time. (pp. 128-30)

Thackeray's use of contrast gives to *Vanity Fair* more than just a formal principle: it also gives the novel a certain texture. To continue the musical analogy, the contrasts between sets of characters and actions fill the space between the two melodic lines with a rich-textured series of variations. While the Becky and Amelia melodies serve to frame the novel, the contrasts in between are contrapuntal variations that develop the basic themes. The result is a vertical development that gives increased richness to the novel. By vertical development I mean, continuing the musical analogy, a chord structure. If the Amelia and Becky stories are melodic, or horizontal, development, then the contrasting variations which fill the space between are a chordal, or vertical, development. Serial publication makes this kind of analogy more readily understandable: each month, the reader received only a part of the plot, or melodic line, but the contrasts, or chord pattern, came complete.

Perhaps a final look at one of Thackeray's chapters will explain more clearly what I mean by the vertical or chord structure. In the first chapter of Number IX..., the melody (narrative) moves very little, but the chordal accompaniment (parallel contrasts) is complete. In this chapter, the participants are getting ready for Waterloo. First we see Major O'Dowd preparing for battle. Instead of going to the big ball, he stays home.... At the same time, Rawdon prepares for battle in a scene that reveals his altered character.... [He] goes through his properties, estimating their value for Becky. Finally, to insure Becky as much as possible, "the Captain dressed himself in his oldest and shabbiest uniform and epaulets, leaving the newest behind under his wife's (or it might be his widow's) guardianship. And this famous dandy of Windsor and Hyde Park went off on his campaign with a kit as modest as that of a sergeant, and with something like a prayer on his lips for the woman he was leaving."

Dobbin and Jos also prepare for battle. Jos, who "would have snoozed on until his usual hour of rising in the forenoon," is awakened by Dobbin, who has come to insure Amelia's safety. While Dobbin tries to make Jos promise to take care of his sister, Jos refuses to discuss his bravery, his ability to take care of Amelia, or even the possibility of an English defeat. When Dobbin leaves, he has seen Amelia: "Our gentle-hearted Captain felt a guilty shock as he looked at her. 'Good God,' thought he, 'and is it grief like this I dared to pry into?' And there was no help; no means to soothe and comfort this helpless, speechless misery. He stood for a moment and looked at her, powerless and torn with pity, as a parent regards an infant in pain."

George, too, prepares to go into battle. His parting from his wife took but a moment.... (pp. 131-33)

Thus we see five men with different attitudes and feelings: the business-like seriousness of the professionals—O'Dowd and Rawdon and Dobbin—contrasts with the flamboyance and bravado of the amateurs—Jos and George. The sober Rawdon contrasts with the selfish George; the greatly concerned Dobbin contrasts with the stupidly indifferent Jos. Besides dealing with the officers, the chapter also covers the officers' wives. Mrs. O'Dowd gets set for her husband's departure:

> Mrs. O'Dowd, the good housewife, arrayed in curl papers and a camisole, felt that her duty was to act, and not to sleep, at this juncture. "Time enough for that," she said, "when Mick's gone;" and so she packed his travelling valise ready for the march, brushed his cloak, his cap,

and other warlike habiliments, set them out in order for him; and stowed away in the cloak pockets a light package of portable refreshments. . . .

Mrs. Crawley, too, retains her composure on the departure of her husband. After Rawdon's departure, Becky goes back to bed, and sleeps until ten. She then continued taking stock of her goods: trinkets, a mare, cashmere shawls, watches—one given by George, the other by General Tufto. Becky finds her position not too uncomfortable. . . . Mrs. Osborne, too, prepares for the departure of her husband, but her conduct lacks the experienced calm and resignation of Mrs. O'Dowd or the complete control motivated by self-interest of Mrs. Crawley. Amelia has lost control; she is on the verge of hysteria and emotional collapse. . . . (pp. 133-34)

The time span of the chapter is from the evening to the next morning, but the action, in effect, has been repeated four times. Thus, the horizontal development—the flow of the story, the narrative—has not moved a great deal in time or distance; but there have been variations on the theme of preparation for war, and these variations have given the chapter a certain texture, a certain feeling of simultaneity of action in different places, a certain feeling of interrelationship among all those involved. The men prepare, and the women prepare, and each one responds in a different way, with different emotions and hopes and fears. These contrasts, extended throughout the book, create a certain feeling of depth in time and space and action. They create a sense of the limited possibilities of human existence, for the contrasts and differences are generally touched with irony. These contrasts—or rather, variations on a theme—provide the novel with a formal principle of structure. Within each monthly number and throughout the novel, contrast is the principle Thackeray uses to develop *Vanity Fair*. (p. 135)

> *Myron Taube, "Contrast as a Principle of Structure in 'Vanity Fair'," in* Nineteeth-Century Fiction, Vol. *18, No. 2, September, 1963, pp. 119-35.*

JOHN LOOFBOUROW   (essay date 1964)

[*Loofbourow explores the interrelationship of style, subject matter, and dramatic structure in* Vanity Fair, *examining the novel's "flexible, allusive prose" within the context of the English literary tradition. For additional commentary by Loofbourow on* Vanity Fair, *see excerpt dated 1964 in NCLC, Vol. 5.*]

When in *Vanity Fair* Thackeray fused his early, satiric expressive conventions into an integral narrative form, a new kind of novel was in the making. In earlier fiction, content, form, and style were separate elements; they could be considered individually as subjects in their own right. But in Thackeray's major novels, as in the work of many modern writers, these aspects of fiction are inseparable and the language itself is a creative element. The difference is like the familiar contrast between classic and romantic art.

The classic-romantic antithesis involves a fairly clear distinction between two ways of envisioning the form-style-content relationship—ways that may conveniently be called "illustration" and "expression." In classical or "illustrative" art, it is the writer's subject that is of primary importance; style is only a means of communicating, form a way of organizing, content. The classicist begins by defining his subject; then he selects an appropriate style and plans an effective presentation. In romantic or "expressive" art, the writer's style is part of the content of his work; his words create meaning, and patterns develop in the process—the method is thought of as a continuous act of expression. The antithesis is figurative—in practice no writer can begin without words or continue without a plan. But the disparity implies dissimilar creative methods and the results are as different as Proust from Fielding. So, in the classical, illustrative tradition, Horace's *Ars Poetica* defines style as decorous exposition (*locum teneant sortita decentum*), form as appropriate presentation (*sibi covenientia finge*), and both form and style merely as instruments for conveying rational content (*verbaque provisam rem non invita sequentur*). The proto-romantic Longinus, however, considers the expressive medium to be synonymous with the artistic concept ("the expressiveness of the word is the essence of art").

English fiction before Thackeray was in the illustrative tradition. Eighteenth-century writers—Defoe, Smollett, Fielding—equated the novel's subject with rational content; for these novelists, form was identical with plot, an effective arrangement of the narrative materials; and style was an expository or decorative means of communication rather than a creative medium. If Richardson's structures were less controlled, his style less apposite, it was due to technical insufficiency rather than artistic originality, and Sterne is the exception, as he is to all literary rules. Long after the content of the nineteenth-century novel had become "romantic," the illustrative method continued to control the writing of English fiction; the development of new narrative methods does not date from the break between the early romantic poets and the neoclassical tradition. The technique of the novel remained basically unchanged from Fielding to Thackeray, and a look at some examples will show how far this is true.

Classicism found its superlative exponent in Jane Austen, and *Emma* is its most brilliant example. *Emma*'s dramatic form is synonymous with narrative fact and, consequently, with its literal "plot." The novel's climaxes coincide with three objective incidents: an abortive marriage proposal, a misguided flirtation, and a successful marriage. The first is a typical instance. Emma attempts to make a match for her friend, Harriet, and her efforts result in Mr. Elton's indecorous proposal for her own hand—the event is logically prepared, Emma's mistake is defined, and the objective outcome of her actions is the rational penalty for her behavior. . . . (pp. 73-5)

Emma's plot is exquisitely correlated with dramatic structure, distinct and iridescent as a Platonic idea: form is an appropriate harmony (*convenientia finge*); moral insights (*rem provisam*) are essential themes. Nowhere does the novel's imaginative content supersede its objective structure or transcend its clear, communicative medium; and this is both an advantage and a limitation.

The melodic consonance of Jane Austen's style is an instance of decorous illustration (*sortita decentum*); and the illustrative technique excludes the expressive diversity of modern narrative prose. Like Parian marble, the classical novel's diction is a common medium, varying only in the degree of rhetorical precision and the effectiveness of the embellishments. The writer's exercise of individuality is confined to the choice of subject and the manner of ornamentation; for all their differences in creative vision and decorative detail, Fielding, Smollett, and Jane Austen write the same fundamental rhetoric. It is impossible, among novelists of this period, to find such stylistic contrasts as between Hardy, Virginia Woolf, James Joyce; and English novelists continued to write illustrative prose until the middle of the nineteenth century.

This proposition may seem untenable when it includes the Brontës, whose fiction seems so distant from the novels of the eighteenth century; but an analysis of their prose makes it clear that they were practicing traditional techniques. Even so "romantic" a writer as Emily Brontë was limited to the common diction. Although the Brontës' visionary effects are not truly compatible with the neo classical rhetoric that exquisitely illustrated Jane Austen's luminous insights, at the time they wrote, prose narrative had no other language to express dramatic event, and they adapted, rather than altered, the accepted medium. Thus in *Wuthering Heights,* Emily Brontë represents climaxes of pure emotional content by conventional images of physical action that typify but do not express Heathcliff's agony and Catherine's passion: "He dashed his head against the knotted trunk; and, lifting up his eyes, howled, not like a man, but like a savage beast"; "such senseless, wicked rages! There she lay . . . her hair flying over her shoulders . . . the muscles of her neck and arms standing out."

The point is made clearer by comparing Emily Brontë's language with the eighteenth-century diction of Richardson's *Clarissa,* where the same basic rhetoric is used to describe the very different instance of a prostitute's "squalid" death—the "infamous" Mrs. Sinclair's "wickedness" and "rage": "howling, more like a wolf than a human," "her hair" conventionally "torn," "violence" distending "her muscular features." The common rhetoric's neoclassical abstractions—"savagery," "wickedness," "rage"—preclude the expressive representation of complex emotions, which must be conveyed by the author's or actors' rational comments, as they are in Jane Austen; and when the writer attempts to surmount this restriction, the tradition's invariable equation of subjective experience with generalized behavior ("dashed his head," "lifted his eyes") produces an indecorous but persistently formulaic effect.

In *Vanity Fair,* Thackeray writes another kind of prose; he dispenses with rational analysis, but develops a narrative medium whose expressive images convey the novel's emotional event—Amelia at Waterloo, "her large eyes fixed and without light"; Steyne, "with flame in his eyes," defying retribution. In *Wuthering Heights,* similitudes are confined to explicit comparisons—"My love for Linton is like the foliage in the woods . . . my love for Heathcliff resembles the eternal rocks beneath." In *Vanity Fair,* similes are replaced by metaphors whose suggestive range is amplified by allusion to familiar artistic conventions, as when a sequence of romance motifs culminates in imagery that transforms men to oaks and women to doves: "Oh, thou poor little panting soul! The very finest tree in the whole forest, with the straightest stem, and the strongest arms, and the thickest foliage, wherein you choose to build and coo, may be marked, for what you know, and may be down with a crash ere long."

Thackeray's prose, the crucial factor in his narrative experiment, was an unaccustomed harmony ("Nobody in our day wrote, I should say, with such perfection of style," Carlyle remarked). Among its precursors were the rhythms of Sterne, who brought a conversational flexibility to his narrative style, and the rhetoric of Carlyle, who revived, in prose, the richness of allegorical figuration. Sterne's rhythmic range greatly increased the capacity of the narrative medium to assimilate diverse modes without losing its expressive unity. His stylistic innovation was simple and profound: he put Locke's theory of associated ideas into fictional practice by adapting the informal rhetoric of personal letters or memoirs—cursive punctuations (dots, dashes, parentheses, semicolons, :—, or —!), conversational inflections ("Fy, Mr. Shandy," "O Thomas! Thomas!"), inversions, ellipses and digressions. There are earlier instances of rhythmic complexity—Swift's "Tale of a Tub," for example—but none in which a story is simultaneously developed. "The machinery of my work," Sterne insisted, "is of a species by itself." Digressions are part of his narration, associations are continuous with statement—"In a word, my work is digressive, and it is progressive too,—and at the same time." It was this freedom of rhythmic movement that permitted Thackeray to integrate diverse expressive textures in *Vanity Fair*—and if the rhythmic resources of Sterne's narrative style enabled Thackeray to assimilate allusive modes, Carlyle's figured rhetoric taught him to fuse these allusions into cumulative metaphor. (pp. 77-8)

Sterne and Carlyle are themselves, of course, only particular instances of the complex processes that prefigured the prose of *Vanity Fair*. Sterne's rhythms were imitated by many writers, including the fashionable novelists that Thackeray parodied; Carlyle's metaphors were derived from Goethe and the German romantics, whose work Thackeray knew, as well as from Milton and Donne. But Thackeray's vigorous version of fashionable syncopations is his tribute to *Tristram Shandy;* and *Sartor* is audible in the resonance of his narrative commentary. *Vanity Fair*'s diction combines Sterne's punctuations, inflections, and digressive continuities with satirical modifications of Carlyle's symbolism; and this unprecedented synthesis produces characteristic overtones in passages like the classical-biblical parable that shadows forth Rebecca's fate: "the honest newspaper-fellow . . . can't survive the glare of fashion long. It scorches him up, as the presence of Jupiter in full dress wasted that poor imprudent Semele—a giddy moth of a creature who ruined herself by venturing out of her natural atmosphere. Her myth ought to be taken to heart amongst the Tyburnians, the Belgravians,—her story, and perhaps Becky's too. Ah, ladies!—ask the Reverend Mr. Thurifer if Belgravia is not a sounding brass, and Tyburnia a tinkling cymbal."

Vanity Fair, formed on this flexible, allusive prose, is as different from *Emma* and the "classical" novel as Berlioz is from Mozart. Thackeray's characters are refractions of allusive color rather than instruments of rational insight. They do not think. In *Vanity Fair*, thinking is sometimes an emotional response— "She thought of her long past life, and all the dismal incidents of it"—sometimes a subjective conflict—"how she tries to hide from herself the thought which will return to her, that she ought to part with the boy"—sometimes an intuitive judgment—"He loved her no more, he thought, as he had loved her"—but never intellectual analysis. There is no mutual explication, since the characters never communicate rationally: "poor Amelia . . . had no confidante; indeed, she could never have one: as she would not allow to herself the possibility of yielding." These actors represent not intellect deluded but delusion itself. *Emma*'s characters often make erroneous choices; in *Vanity Fair*, alternatives are unperceived, and the actors retreat unconsciously from the force of facts: "giving way daily before the enemy with whom she had to battle. One truth after another was marshalling itself silently against her, and keeping its ground." Truth is never confronted in *Vanity Fair;* its inhabitants must be pushed blindfolded over the edge of reality. When Amelia decides at last to relinquish her child, it is in a "burst of anguish": "she was conquered. The sentence was passed." Such characters cannot define or respond to objective event—they hardly recognize it.

The result is that *Vanity Fair*'s objective plot-sequence does not control the novel's effective dramatic form. Since the actors respond not to external facts but to inner images represented by allusive motifs and expressive textures, the literal incidents of the novel's "plot" are not correlated with its imaginative events. When Amelia's father loses his fortune, the factual crisis has no effect on dramatic experience. Before the event, distressed by George's negligence, Amelia expects to marry him; after the event, distressed by George's negligence, Amelia marries him. Conversely, when Rawdon dismisses the Marquis of Steyne, Rebecca suffers no literal loss—unlike the social adventuress in *Bleak House*, Lady Dedlock, she has acquired neither wealth nor real prestige; she forfeits nothing but marital security: Rawdon provides her with "a tolerable annuity" and she was always *demi-mondaine*. Again, in the dramatic and central Waterloo episode, literal event is peripheral: malice, jealousy, panic are its subjective phenomena; its only objective incident is dismissed in the last sentence, and is never emotionally or dramatically represented in the narrative context— "Amelia was praying for George, who was lying on his face, dead."

In *Vanity Fair*, factual incident is a convenience for the common reader and the novel's "plot" has no real relationship to dramatic development. Literal event gives no clue to *Vanity Fair*'s expressive tensions; thus, the opposition between Becky's and Amelia's fortunes which is felt as a formal principle does not correspond to their objective experiences. . . . There is no significant literal relationship between the two fortunes. The heroines' dramatic opposition is not an objective antithesis. Amelia's social status fluctates erratically, never illustrating the emotional sequence—her prolonged personified journey from amorous confusion to maternal agony. The imaginative pattern of Rebecca's picaresque dramatic progress is not based on financial facts which are statistically monotonous from her marriage to Rawdon through her liasion with Steyne. And Waterloo, since no objective event is represented, has no place in the literal plot, although it is the artistic center of the novel.

Dramatic event in *Vanity Fair* is a very different thing from dramatic event in illustrative novels. Created by the words themselves, the significance of Thackeray's "events" is found in expressive, metaphorical values, not in objective elements. In earlier fiction, narrative incident was an illustration of logical content; *Emma*'s final love-scene has no expressive importance: it is an affirmation of rational insights: "She had led her friend astray, and it would be a reproach to her for ever; but her judgment was as strong as her feelings, and as strong as it had ever been before, in reprobating any such alliance for him, as most unequal and degrading. Her way was clear, though not quite smooth." In *Vanity Fair*, there are no rational affirmations to illustrate. The final love-scene draws no morals; instead, its allusive textures assemble, in one expressive realization, the successive satiric emblems of Amelia and Dobbin—"fragrant and blooming tenderly in quiet shady places"; "fluttering to Lieutenant George Osborne's heart"; "the prize I had set my life on was not worth the winning":

> The vessel is in port. He has got the prize he has been trying for all his life. The bird has come in at last. There it is with its head on his shoulder, billing and cooing close up to his heart, with soft outstretched fluttering wings. This is what he has asked for every day and hour for eighteen years. This is what he pined after. Here it is—the summit, the end—the last

page of the third volume. Good-bye, Colonel.—God bless you, honest William!—Farewell, dear Amelia.—Grow green again, tender little parasite, round the rugged old oak to which you cling!

The ironic significance of this passage is a purely expressive phenomenon; its textures are a representation of emotional realities, rather than an illustration of rational truths. There is no logical flaw in the premised union—Dobbin is deserving, Amelia is loving, the marriage is appropriate. But dissonance is overt in the writer's satirical allusion to fashionable finales ("the last page of the third volume"), and this central discord governs a sequence of harmonic incongruities. A rhapsody of saccharine infelicities figures the ironic fulfillment of a fantasy: the worthless "prize" of Dobbin's chivalric quest that began with his worship of George, "the summit" of his pilgrimage—"the end"; Amelia's "feeble remnant" of romance that "clings" to its victim, recalling her role, as George's bride, nesting in "the finest tree in the whole forest" ("Grow green again, tender little parasite")—and the subtly sacrilegious image of Amelia's sentimental ecstasy, the "soft outstretched fluttering wings" of dove-like devotion.

Such narrative event begins with words, and words in *Vanity Fair* are no longer illustration. As Thackeray's writing matures, the pastiches of *Catherine* and the **"Legend"** are developed into sustained dramatic metaphor: creative prose ("the expressiveness of the word") becomes the novel's effective content. Like poetry, this prose includes the language of emotional event; and it was the dramatic potential of this new expressive medium that transformed the novels of many English writers after Thackeray. (pp. 78-83)

In *Vanity Fair,* expressive realization of emotional event is the novel's effective drama, as in the satirical mating of Dobbin and Amelia. *Vanity Fair*'s dramatic "form" depends on allusive continuities—sequences of sentiment and romance—rather than on plot progressions. . . . These [sequences], evolved from expressive continuities, correspond more closely to effective form in *Vanity Fair* than analyses of literal event. The novel's opening scenes are filled with subtle discriminations in fashionable sin and sentiment—Amelia's *"Sehnsucht nach der Liebe,"* Rebecca's "Charming Alnaschar visions." At the first intimation of the heroines' future marriages, the arcs of fashionable parody are intersected by opposing tangents of chivalric satire—Amelia's "little tender heart . . . beating, and longing and trusting" to George, Becky's "barbed shaft" quivering in Rawdon's "dull hide." Waterloo, the satiric paradigm of knightly combat, is *Vanity Fair*'s expressive center—a sentimental-chivalric crux: the novel's opposing tangents of romance—Amelia's amorous grail-motifs, Rebecca's magic metaphors—intersect; the heroines' hostilities qualify Amelia's agony, imaged in the blood-red laceration of George's military sash; and Rebecca's victorious visit to her prostrate rival combines picaresque parody (Becky's exploits) with sentimental satire (Amelia's animosity). After the battle, chivalric oppositions are reversed. Rebecca's magical success approaches satirical apotheosis; Amelia's masochism reaches its nadir in the ironies of maternal sacrifice. As Dobbin returns, Amelia's romantic reprieve spans Rebecca's farcical disaster with Steyne; the swift descent of the glittering rogue is crossed by the amorous dove's ascending flight—and the final sequences are suffused with the satirical sentimentality that opened the novel.

Vanity Fair's expressive form is a vast metaphor, an extended figure filled with typifications. If the novel is named from *The*

A sketch by Thackeray in a copy of Vanity Fair *he presented to the artist George Cruikshank.*

Pilgrim's Progress, its allegory begins in Bunyan's "Town . . . wherein should be sold . . . Lusts, Pleasures, and Delights of all sorts"—"Yes, this is Vanity Fair," the novel's prologue announces, "eating and drinking, making love and jilting . . . not a moral place certainly; nor a merry one, though very noisy" [see essay by Thackeray dated 1848]. As Thackeray's actors begin to suffer, their subjective world becomes a dramatic scene, and the novel's symbolic psychology revives the *Psychomachia*'s generic image of inner strife—a *bellum intestinum* that C. S. Lewis calls "the root of all allegory": "The combat, which we describe in a sentence or two, lasted for many weeks in poor Amelia's heart . . . one by one the outworks of the little citadel were taken, in which the poor soul passionately guarded her only love and treasure." But if Thackeray's initial metaphor is borrowed from Bunyan, his personifications ("behind whom all there lies a dark moral I hope" [see excerpt from Thackeray's letter dated 1847]), unlike the simple symbolism of *The Pilgrim's Progress*, are images of contemporary subjective complexities. Amelia is Love, but delusive love; Dobbin's Faith and Charity are colored by George's Hypocrisy; Rebecca, a moral reprobate, is also a type of Fun and Truth, the artist's persona personified. Thackeray's "Love" becomes an ambivalent quality when the novel's semi-Shakespearian commentary mocks the amorous ingenue ("Perhaps some beloved female subscriber has arrayed an ass in the splendour and glory of her imagination . . . and used him as the brilliant fairy Titania did a certain weaver at Athens.") "Of course you are quite right," Thackeray remarks in [the aforementioned] letter, "about Vanity Fair and Amelia being selfish. . . . My object is not to make a perfect character or anything like it.'' In certain satirical perspectives the ambiguity is intensified—as when Amelia's pathetic poses are ironically reflected in Rebecca's insincerities. Allegory becomes a comic anti-masque when Amelia and Rebecca are beatified—when Amelia's thoughts, ''as if they were angels,'' try ''to peep into the barracks where George was''—''the gates were shut, and the sentry allowed no one to pass; so that the poor little white-robed angel could not hear the songs those young fellows were roaring over the whisky-punch.''—and when Rebecca, the students' ''Angel Engländerin,'' sobs out her simulated sufferings at Baden: ''it was quite evident from hearing her, that if ever there was a white-robed angel escaped from heaven to be subject to the infernal machinations and villainy of fiends here below, that spotless being—that miserable unsullied martyr, was present on the bed before Jos—on the bed, sitting on the brandy-bottle.''

Vanity Fair's recension of the allegory of emotional experience is the beginning of a new kind of fiction that includes such disparate exponents as Meredith, Firbank, and Virginia Woolf; it prepares a medium for such a development as *To the Lighthouse*, where drama is interior, experience subjective, fantasy fused with reality in the symbolism of World War I, as it is at Waterloo in *Vanity Fair*. But, unlike Thackeray, Virginia Woolf forces her war-metaphor to function as an objective as well as an emotional event, sacrificing the imaginative suspension of disbelief that is achieved by Thackeray's displacement of literal incident; the symbolic pattern that is sustained in *Vanity Fair* is discredited in *To the Lighthouse* by the intrusion of the realities it symbolizes.

If *Vanity Fair*'s expressive method revived the techniques and typifications of Sidney, Spenser, and *The Pilgrim's Progress,* its content, like Wagner's orchestration, was a radical polyphony. ''I think I see in him an intellect profounder and more unique than his contemporaries have yet recognised,'' Charlotte Brontë wrote. Thackeray's ability to ''scrutinise and expose'' seemed to her ''prophet-like''—''No commentator on his writings has yet found,'' she insisted, ''the terms which rightly characterise his talent.''

An aspect of this insight was Thackeray's expressive representation of psychological relativity (''after looking into a microscope how infinite littleness even is''). The glittering allusive tangents of his prose reflected a sustained ambivalent logic— recognition of the range of possible relationships:

> O philosophic reader . . . a distinct universe walks about under your hat and mine—all things are different to each—the woman we look at has not the same features, the dish we eat from has not the same taste to the one and the other— you and I are but a pair of infinite isolations, with some fellow-islands a little more or less near to us.

In *Vanity Fair,* perceptions like these fuse bits of human anomaly and fragments of shattered idealisms into eccentric images of psychological truth. ''In the passage where Amelia is represented as trying to separate herself from the boy,'' Thackeray wrote to the critic for *Fraser's Magazine,* '' 'as that poor Lady Jane Grey tried the axe that was to separate her slender life' I say that is a fine image whoever wrote it . . . it leaves you to make your own sad pictures'' [see excerpt dated September 3, 1848]. In this sequence, the mother's suffering is mirrored in images that reflect the whole range of her sentimental neurosis—her personified denial of reality and defeat by truth, her

chivalric fetishism, her amorous idolatry. The episode is conceived in several dimensions—the mother's possessiveness, her jealousy of the boy's aunt, her obsessive image of George, the child's ironic indifference—

> terror is haunting her . . . George's picture and dearest memory. . . . The child must go from her—to others—to forget her. Her heart and her treasure—her joy, hope, love, worship— her God, almost! . . . The mother had not been so well pleased, perhaps, had the rival been better looking . . . preparing him for the change . . . He was longing for it.

Amelia's compulsive fantasies—''her God, almost!''—anticipating religious ironies in the novel's final love-scene, discredit the Victorian image of romantic maternity; and the allegory of Vanity Fair is largely concerned with revealing such emotional compulsions in the elements of accepted conventions. George Henry Lewes, who could accept George Eliot's ambiguities, found Thackeray's too unpleasant (''in *Vanity Fair* . . . how little there is to love'') and protested the inclusion of that ''detestable passage,'' rephrased in the prologue to *Esmond,* ''wherein [the author] adds from himself this remark:— 'And who knows but Rebecca was right in her speculations— and that it was only a question of money and fortune which made the difference between her and an honest woman? . . . An alderman . . . will not step out of his carriage to steal . . . *but put him to starve, and see if he will not purloin a loaf.*' [Lewes' italics] Was it carelessness, or deep misanthropy, distorting an otherwise clear judgment, which allowed such a remark to fall?'' [see excerpt dated 1848 in *NCLC,* Vol. 5].

The passage is not personal observation; it is commentary— the rigorous recognition of the relativity of human values that typifies the novel's method. In *Vanity Fair,* the Commentator is a dimension of dissent—''I wonder is it because men are cowards in heart that they admire bravery so much?'' '''Was Rebecca guilty or not?' The Vehmgericht of the servants' hall had pronounced against her''—and, instead of solving dilemmas, asks questions unanswered in the silence at the end: ''Ah! *Vanitas, Vanitatum!* which of us is happy in this world? Which of us has his desire? or, having it, is satisfied?'' (pp. 83-8)

A contingent aspect of Thackeray's insight (his power, Charlotte Brontë put it, ''to penetrate the sepulchre, and reveal charnel relics'') is expressed in *Vanity Fair*'s mock-epic and romance evocations of primitive impulse—an imaginative projection of the hypotheses of contemporary science that became, in *The Newcomes,* a symbolism of creative method:

> Professor Owen or Professor Agassiz takes a fragment of a bone, and builds an enormous forgotten monster out of it, wallowing in primaeval quagmires, tearing down leaves and branches of plants that flourished thousands of years ago, and perhaps may be coal by this time—so the novelist puts this and that together: from the footprint finds the foot; from the foot, the brute who trod on it; from the brute, the plant he browsed on, the marsh in which he swam—and thus, in his humble way a physiologist too, depicts the habits, size, appearance of the beings whereof he has to treat;— traces this slimy reptile through the mud, and describes his habits filthy and rapacious; prods down his butterfly with a pin, and depicts his

beautiful coat and embroidered waistcoat; points out the singular structure of yonder more important animal, the megatherium of his history.

The biological analogy is not a casual conceit; it is a newly recognized aspect of human reality that impinges on *Vanity Fair.* In Spenserian allegory, personification illustrates enduring moral fact: Una's truth, Acrasia's artifice, Guyon's discipline. The figurations of *Vanity Fair,* like Spenser's types, personify moral qualities; but Thackeray's characters express other kinds of reality as well—the survival of primitive fantasy, the persistence of the biological past. His actors are not only victims of romance delusions but types of subconscious compulsions. Primal violence is implicit at chivalric Waterloo. . . . (pp. 89-90)

The novel's heroines exhibit atavistic symptoms: Amelia acts out archaic obsession—"powerless in the hands of her remorseless little enemy"—Rebecca reveals tribal mores—("She admired her husband, strong, brave, and victorious.") Under fashionable fantasies, chivalric visions, amorous mystique, lurks the "forgotten monster" of *Vanity Fair.* The actors indulge involuntary urges—George's blood-lust, Dobbin's self-abasement, Amelia's idolatry—and *Vanity Fair*'s dramatic structure is partly predicated on these emotional compulsions. Mock-epic imagery reinforces romance motif; ritual fetishes coincide (Amelia worshipping the image of George, Rebecca defacing Miss Pinkerton's doll and piercing Amelia's heart); and racial impulse becomes a sustained expressive metaphor— Sir Pitt is a "hyaena face," Rawdon a rutting bull, Dobbin a Caliban, Amelia a "bleeding heart," and Rebecca a "monster's tail," "writhing and twirling, diabolically hideous and slimy."

This does not mean that *Vanity Fair* is a prototype of Conrad or Kafka; Thackeray is far more concerned with the subtleties of civilized society and the images of idealized convention. His novel is, however, a fable—and a fable with modern as well as traditional implications. Its patterns are unprecedented in English fiction; but they are achieved at a sacrifice. In order to project the internal drama of *Vanity Fair,* Thackeray has excluded the dimension of objective reality and conceived his characters primarily as types. (pp. 90-1)

> *John Loofbourow, in his* Thackeray and the Form of Fiction, *Princeton University Press, 1964, 236 p.*

U. C. KNOEPFLMACHER (essay date 1971)

[*Knoepflmacher examines the important role that the pursuit of love and wealth plays in the lives of various characters in* Vanity Fair. *The critic also discusses how Thackeray illustrates the passage of time in the novel.*]

The characters in *Vanity Fair* are moved by either of two impulses: greed (or what the Showman at one point calls "this race for money") or love (or those feelings which the characters mistake for love). Speaking of the auction at the Sedley home, the narrator argues that such public assemblies afford the novelist with an opportunity to "light on the strangest contrasts laughable and tearful." . . . To be sure, the auction provides the Showman with a perfect miniature spectacle which Satire and Sentiment can visit arm in arm together. The narrator can simultaneously expose two different kinds of appetite: the voraciousness of the bargain-hunters who rummage through the belongings of the Sedleys and the hunger of those sentimentalists who rummage through the associations held by these remnants of a lost past.

Money and material goods possess a kind of permanence in *Vanity Fair.* The acquisition or loss of wealth may alter the characters, but the cult of money is unvarying. As long as Dobbin's father runs a modest shop he is looked down upon by the sons of gentlemen, but when his profits rise he is made Alderman Dobbin and knighted. The distance separating the onetime grocer and Mr. Osborne is thus considerably reduced; their sons are no longer as far apart on the social scale as they seemed at Mr. Swishtail's establishment. On the other hand, the bonds that once existed between Osborne and his benefactor, John Sedley, vanish after Sedley's financial ruin.

On visiting Amelia's fallen father, Dobbin admits that his own father and sisters, who would in earlier years have been most grateful to be noticed by Mr. Sedley, now snub him. In turn, the old man scrapes and bows before Dobbin. In a pathetic mixture of abasement and vanity, he alludes to "the worthy alderman, and my lady, your excellent mother" . . . in order to be overheard by a waiter in the shabby coffeehouse. Mr. Sedley blames his collapse on Napoleon, the British government, and the Kings and Emperors of Austria, Russia, and Prussia. His accusation is an attempt to aggrandize himself by obscuring his own imprudence. But his statements also carries a meaning unintended by him: the kings and emperors of this world *are* on a par with him; they too are warring merchants eager to gain economic supremacy. From top to bottom, money determines alliances and attractions. Just as the rival powers who join to fight the returning Napoleon are willing to overcome their contempt of each other, so is old Osborne more than willing to overlook the social ineligibility of an heiress with 200,000 pounds. In the political world, unequal nations consolidate against a common competitor; in the world of society, unequal marriages are made for money, and undesirable relatives are wooed for their fortunes. Mr. Osborne commands his son to marry Miss Swartz before some aristocrat will snatch her away. Conversely, aristocrats like Rawdon feel that it is their duty to take as much "tin" as possible from gambling "city-men." The Bute Crawleys abjectly court Miss Crawley, although they secretly despise her. Miss Crawley, in turn, unfairly accuses Miss Briggs of waiting for her death to receive a legacy; she assumes that her devoted housekeeper is pleading for Rawdon and Becky because of a bribe. To the materially minded, there can be no disinterested attachments.

Nobody understands better the commodity that sentiment can be than Becky Sharp. Her financial gains are always achieved through her exploitation of the affections of others. She wheedles a gift out of Mr. Sedley by tearfully alluding to herself as a penniless orphan; on reaching the street, she wipes her tears and counts her guineas. The one time she weeps in earnest is on discovering that she could have married Sir Pitt, an ailing man with a title and sure income, instead of sharing the increasingly doubtful expectations of his younger son. Becky's obsession with money is contrasted to the naïvete of Amelia who regards two thousand pounds as "an immense deal of money" that will last for a lifetime. Unlike Becky, who thinks that she could be a good woman on five thousand pounds a year, Amelia never even wonders where the funds maintaining her and Georgy are coming from.

Becky's money-mindedness is also contrasted to Rawdon's disregard for his earnings as a gambler. When we first see the couple living on "nothing a year," Becky's indifference to money seems like Rawdon's. Gradually, however, their attitudes prove to be totally dissimilar. In chapter twenty-five Rawdon stops to think about the future. The impending war makes him pity the newly wed Amelia: "I say, what'll Mrs. O. do, when O. goes out with the regiment?" Becky, too, has thought of the possibility of George's departure. But her foresight takes a significantly different shape: "Rawdon, dear—don't you think—you'd better get that—money from Cupid, before he goes?" While cajoling her husband to claim his bill, she is "fixing on a killing bow" to impress the same man whose death she has so calmly considered.

This same contrast is elaborated in "The Girl I Left Behind" . . . , in which Becky's relation to Rawdon is brilliantly juxtaposed to Mrs. O'Dowd's and Amelia's farewells to their respective husbands. The chapter begins with Mrs. O'Dowd's preparations. The woman who wakes up her husband "as soon as the hands of the 'repayther' pointed to half past one" is acutely aware of time. Like Becky, who is the next wife to be described, she also seems to be realistic and unsentimental, devoid of "the fits of tears and hysterics by which more sensitive females exhibited their love." But as soon as we shift to Becky's leave-taking from Rawdon we realize that Mrs. O'Dowd, for all her outward calm, may in fact be closer to the hysterical Amelia. Despite their matter-of-factness, Mrs. O'Dowd's preparations "betokened affection." Not so Becky's. Sentences which would have aptly described Mrs. O'Dowd's stoic refusal to yield to sentimentality become heavily ironic when applied to Becky: "Knowing how useless regrets are, and how the indulgence of sentiment only serves to make people more miserable, Mrs. Rebecca wisely determined to give way to no vain feelings of sorrow, and bore the parting from her husband with quite a Spartan equanimity. Indeed Captain Rawdon himself was much more affected at the leave-taking than the resolute little woman to whom he bade farewell."

Rebecca's good humor grates on the reader as much as it does on Rawdon. Sensing that her manner has "hurt the feelings" of her husband, she mollifies him by "hastily dashing something from her eyes"; but if Rawdon is convinced, the reader is not. There is something moving in Rawdon's sudden metamorphosis from spendthrift into provider: "'Look here,' said he. 'If I drop, let us see what there is for you. I have had a pretty good run of luck here, and here's two hundred and thirty pounds. I have got ten Napoleons in my pocket. That is as much as I shall want; for the General pays everything like a prince; and if I'm hit, why you know I cost nothing. Don't cry, little woman; I may live to vex you yet.'" Becky remains quite unvexed. Rawdon trots off to battle, wearing his oldest and shabbiest uniform, "leaving the newest behind, under his wife's (or it might be his widow's) guardianship," while Becky, who, "as we have said, wisely determined not to give way to unavailing sentimentality," goes back to bed. After her beauty sleep, she resumes Rawdon's "calculations" beyond any plane imagined by him. Rawdon has given her all his earthly belongings down to his coat and duelling pistols. But we now discover that she, unbeknown to him, has stashed away a fortune in "valuables" given to her by other admirers. Satisfied, she concludes that she can easily "begin the world" again. Rummaging through Rawdon's notes, she finds a twenty pound draft on Osborne: "'I will go and get the draft cashed,' she said, 'and pay a visit afterwards to poor little Emmy.'" Becky is a far more astute economist than her husband: whereas his "plan of economy" is an expression of love, her own calculations show only self-interest.

Rawdon does not die on the battlefield; he lives to vex his wife. What is only implicit in "The Girl I Left Behind" finally becomes explicit when Rawdon surprises Becky with Lord Steyne. Earlier, on being imprisoned, he had asked her to pay his debts; her reply—written "in bed"—dwelt on her difficulties in liberating *"mon pauvre prisonnier."* . . . Now, after Rawdon is released by his sister-in-law, he not only discovers Becky with Lord Steyne but also discovers that the nobleman regards him as a pander who has profited from his wife's prostitution. Forcing Becky to open her desk, Rawdon lights on her hoard: "It contained papers, love-letters many years old—all sorts of small trinkets and woman's memoranda. And it contained a pocket-book with bank notes. Some of these were dated ten years back, too, and one was quite a fresh note—a note for a thousand pounds which Lord Steyne had given her." . . . The scene is one of the high points of the novel; its position—at the three-quarter point—shows the extent of Becky's progress. The wife who murders Rawdon's love is closer to the survivor who eagerly cashes Jos Sedley's insurance policy than to the girl who had flung the dictionary at the kind-hearted Miss Jemima in the first chapter of the novel. Her protestation, "I am innocent," seems less and less believable. Her innocence diminishes in proportion to the pain she inflicts. Although we are forced to make our own surmises, it is clear that the girl whose wit once seemed so delightful has become a woman capable of adultery and murder.

But in a sense, Becky *is* "innocent." She has merely carried the outlook of Vanity Fair to its logical extremes. The reader who belongs to a society as acquisitive as her own finds himself yoked to Becky's cruel logic. Even Rawdon's words upon discovering her treasure reinforce the inescapability of material considerations: "You might have spared me a hundred pounds, Becky, out of all of this—I have always shared with you." Morally, Rawdon is far more innocent than his calculating wife, yet even he must express his affection through the values of Vanity Fair. His words confirm Becky's cynicism. Love, gratitude, affection are to her meaningless abstractions by which most men disguise their true values. At the end of the novel, when the insurance company backs down and pays Becky her claim for Jos' policy, the Showman comments laconically: "The money was paid, and her character established." . . . (pp. 71-6)

Becky thrives by disregarding sentiment. She knows that emotions are salable wares in the mart of Vanity Fair. She is logical and clear-eyed. But what of those who are illogical because they are moved by feeling? Rawdon, Amelia, Dobbin, Lady Jane, Miss Briggs go against the grain of Vanity Fair. They do not care for money. Nonetheless, these characters do not escape the ironic treatment accorded to the materialists of Thackeray's world. . . . Thackeray refuses to dispense sweetmeats and sugar plums. His Amelia is not the model of perfection that her namesake was in Fielding's novel. In his more realistic treatment, love, too, can prove to be a crippling vanity.

While Becky disregards all considerations beyond the self, Amelia's love presumably is directed at others. And yet her childlike and naïve obsession with love resembles Becky's adult and cynical obsession with money. Becky the opportunist thinks ahead, aware of change; Amelia the sentimentalist tries to arrest all growth, to deny change. She refuses to admit that her childhood sweetheart has developed into a man unworthy of her devotion; she loves this man all the more when his death allows her to be true to a fixed and unchanging image. Thackeray makes sure to have Amelia disillusioned in George before his death, for he wants us to see that she knows that her husband is not the ideal she had worshiped. Her distortion of George's character after his death is therefore all the more reprehensible. His death is a blessing to her because it allows her to avoid the reality she was about to face and to revert to her former cult.

Amelia's love, like Becky's, thus is self-love. Although, unlike Becky, she is a dutiful mother, she smothers her son and almost ruins Georgy by fashioning him in the image of his snobbish father. Becky's cynicism leads her to deny all bonds; Amelia's love of love results in similar denials. She is uninterested in the European cataclysm which ruins her father; she is too self-pitying to show commiseration for Mr. Sedley's misfortune; she refuses to acknowledge her debts to Dobbin. Like Becky, she takes without offering a return. And, since her self-love involves an act of self-blinding, we almost prefer Becky's frank egotism—almost, until we realize that such empathy can also lead us to empathize with adultery and murder. Still, just as Becky helps the author to satirize the greed that rules Vanity Fair, so does she allow him to puncture Amelia's false love. Becky is cruel in destroying George's memory, yet for once the reader rejoices in her lack of pity: "Why, the man was weary of you, and would have jilted you, but that Dobbin forced him to keep his word. . . . He used to sneer about you to me, time after time; and made love to me the week after he married you." Becky produces the evidence of George's infidelity by forcing Amelia to look at the letter she has kept: "He wrote that to me—wanted me to run away with him—gave it me under your nose, the day before he was shot—and served him right!" . . . (pp. 76-7)

Becky's savagery is necessary. Yet, though we want her to prick Amelia's illusions, we cannot rejoice in the union she makes possible. . . . The union of Dobbin and Amelia is not a triumph. It merely mitigates Dobbin's misery and chastens Amelia's self-love. The marriage is belated. Amelia is not a prize. . . . The matron who now becomes Dobbin's wife is but a shade of the vision to which he had clung over the years. When Dobbin finally admits that he, and not George, had retrieved Amelia's piano, he unwillingly calls attention to the disparity between past and present:

> "Amelia, Amelia," he said, "I did buy it for you. I loved you then as I do now. I must tell you. I think I loved you from the first minute that I saw you, when George brought me to your house, to show me the Amelia whom he was engaged to. You were but a girl in white, with large ringlets; you came down singing—do you remember?—and we went to Vauxhall. Since then I have thought of but one woman in the world, and that was you."
>
> (pp. 77-8)

Dobbin's recollection exposes the vanity of his own love. Though more intelligent than Amelia, though far more aware of the ways of Vanity Fair, he too is guilty of attributing his own emotions to others. In one of the novel's key ironies, this silent lover forces George into marrying Amelia by bringing him a letter from her thanking George for the gift of the piano: "I shall often play upon the piano—your piano. It was like you to send it." Amelia's sentimental words—words which apply to Dobbin and not to George—are exploited by Dobbin in order to move Amelia's reluctant groom. In delivering the message, Dobbin is overcome by emotion: "'George, she is dying,' William Dobbin said,—and could speak no more." . . . Amelia is hardly dying. Unaware of Bonaparte's fall, unconcerned with Mr. Sedley's plight, the girl who mopes in her room is dimly conscious that her father's ruin somehow prevents her from marrying George. Dobbin is using hyperbole for a calculated effect—his exaggeration, like those of Becky Sharp, has the effect of touching his listener. George is infected by his friend's genuine emotion. He writes a note: "Dearest Emmy—dearest love—dearest wife—come to me." He is happy with himself. He will defy his father and marry the poor and virtuous Amelia. But his pose crumbles to pieces after he discovers that his father remains firm. Vindictively, George turns on Dobbin: "A beggar, by Jove, and all in consequence of my d——d sentimentality." . . . (p. 78)

George's remark is as ugly as his sudden disenchantment with his wife. It is permeated by his love of money. His recrimination is just, nonetheless. He has been blinded by Dobbin's sentimentality. Dobbin has muddled things up. He is responsible for a father's disavowal of his son; he has forced Amelia into a marriage saved only by George's death. And why? "Because he loved her so much that he could not bear to see her unhappy: or because his own sufferings of suspense were so unendurable that he was glad to crush them at once—as we hasten a funeral after a death." . . . Love is selfish even in its unselfishness. Had Dobbin been more cruel and less kind (as Becky will be when she finally crushes Amelia's illusions), he could have spared Amelia this unfortunate marriage. What is more, he could have spared himself the years of misery that now await him. In due time, he admits his mistake. Unlike Amelia's recognition, which must be forced on her by Becky, his admission comes unaided: "It was myself I deluded, and persisted in cajoling; had she been worthy of the love I gave her, she would have returned it long ago. It was a fond mistake. Isn't the whole course of life made up of such?" . . .

Dobbin's recognition cannot be altered. Even after he gets his Amelia he can never love her as he had loved her before. She is no longer the girl in white he had sentimentalized as much as she had sentimentalized George Osborne. Resigned, he weds the querulous mother of a teen-age son. His hopefulness must be placed in his own child, who, significantly, is named after another woman, Lady Jane, in a novel where all other children bear the name of their parents. Dobbin is fonder of Janey "than of anything in the world—fonder even than of his 'History of the Punjaub'." . . . Amelia is envious: "Fonder that he is of me," she thinks rightly. Still, the narrator renders her point of view only to insist, in his own voice, that Dobbin remained a model husband: "he never said a word to Amelia, that was not kind and gentle; or thought of a want of hers that he did not try to gratify." . . . (p. 79)

The narrator avoids a final summing up. He refuses to enter Dobbin's inner life. But, as in the concluding description of Becky's charitable activities, what remains unsaid is as important as what is being said. We are not allowed to forget the stoicism of Dobbin's earlier concession in the same chapter: "I have 'geliebt und gelebt' as the girl in Wallenstein says. I am done.—Pay the bills and get me a cigar." . . . The tone of his statement strongly resembles the narrator's parting words in the novel's last paragraph: "Ah! *Vanitas Vanitatum!* Which of us is happy in this world? Which of us has his desire? or, having it, is satisfied?—Come children, let us shut up the box and the puppets, for our play is played out."

Like the narrator and like the ideal reader demanded by the Showman, Dobbin, the man of feeling, must remain a spectator at the perpetual fair of vanities. The man with the horselike name is a Houyhnhnm among the Yahoos. He has lived as an exile during most of the novel; on tasting the fruits enjoyed by others he finds them insufficient. The goal he has maintained so long, Amelia, proves a mere illusion. Though resigned to his present, Dobbin finds comfort in his observation of the past and his trust in a better future. He writes his 'History of the Punjaub' and also hopes that he may benefit from his past mistakes by making Janey a wiser child than her parents. Like the reader of *Vanity Fair,* this observer of life finds meaning through the act of retrospection. Though the search for happiness proves to be futile, the search itself has not been in vain. As in that other treatise on the vanity of human wishes, Dr. Johnson's *Rasselas,* we are left with a conclusion that is no conclusion. The novel's movement is circular. Time, which both perpetuates and annihilates human vanity, is the protagonist of this novel without a hero.

No work before *Vanity Fair* illustrates so extensively and impressively the passage of time. The very bulk of the panoramic novel allows Thackeray to create the impression of the flow of years. The weight of time affects characters and reader alike, modifying their initial assumptions and threatening their security. Becky destroys Amelia's denial of the past by producing George's faded letter; her bills and letters rupture Rawdon's long-held belief in her innocence. Throughout the novel, time-past mocks the illusions of those who would deny change. Miss Briggs still cherishes the "hectic" love letters of a writing master she flirted with twenty-four years ago. The letters remind the spinster not only of the dead man who could have been hers but also of other dead hopes and expectations. Old Osborne looks at the parcel of letters written by George; young Georgy, in his grandfather's house, sees the initials "G.O." scratched upon a windowpane. The initials are his father's; they establish a link between the failings of Amelia's husband and the potential failings of her son. The recovery of the little piano, the reappearance of Jos' picture, the reemergence of Jos' flowery vests and of the scar on Lord Steyne's forehead help to create a rhythm in which the emphasis is less on the continuity that arises from repetition than it is on the disconnectedness between hope and regret, expectation and disappointment. The narrator wishes that this gap were less apparent; sardonically, he implores men to destroy the record of their onetime feelings:

> Perhaps in Vanity Fair there are no better satires than letters. Take a bundle of your dear friend's of ten years back—your dear friend whom you hate now. Look at a file of your sister's: how you clung to each other till you quarrelled about the twenty pound legacy! Get down the round-hand scrawls of your son who has half broken your heart with selfish undutifulness since; or a parcel of your own, breathing endless ardour and love eternal, which were sent back by your mistress when she married the Nabob—your mistress for whom you now care no more than for Queen Elizabeth. Vows, love, promises, confidences, gratitude, how queerly they read after a while! There ought to be a law in Vanity Fair ordering the destruction of every written document (except receipted tradesmen's bills) after a certain brief and proper interval.

(pp. 79-81)

Change is all in Vanity Fair. The passage of time exposes all human vanity. Although time perpetuates the same aspirations from generation to generation, it also modifies them and ends them. The novel's many death scenes are not due to a mawkish

Victorian fascination with such situations, but rather stem from Thackeray's desire to remind the reader that death, the end of life, is the only true vanquisher of vanity. Osborne, aloof and powerful, and Sedley, low and powerless, die on the same day. Miss Crawley's fortune and the elder Sir Pitt's title change hands after their deaths. Alive, they have used these ornaments as a bait; dead, they are soon forgotten.

Becky and Dobbin, antagonists in so many other ways, can be contrasted in relation to their attitude towards time. Becky always lives in the present; she never permits herself "much useless and unseemly sorrow for the irrevocable past." . . . Her reversals only spur her on—the world is forever before her. Immutable because of her very mutability, she posses a chameleonlike ability to adapt herself to new environs. Jos' fortune renovates her; even her features seem youthful again in Thackeray's last illustration. Dobbin, on the other hand, does age. Though he climbs from Lieutenant to Captain to Major and Colonel, his rise in rank and his father's changed social position are equally irrelevant to him. The civilian who faces Becky with such disgust in the last drawing looks more dignified than the awkward Major Sugarplums depicted earlier. But he also looks wearier, more pained. Becky's experiences have increased her flexibility; Dobbin's experiences have increased his rigidity. The spectator who stands outside Becky's booth is incapable of anchoring his ideals in the ever-shifting bustle of the Fair.

Vanity Fair is primarily a satire. In it, the author of a book on *The Four Georges* tries to laugh at the unheroic age of George IV in the same way that Pope had laughed at the age of George II: "Yes, we saw him. Fate cannot deprive us of *that.* Others have seen Napoleon. Some few still exist who have beheld Frederick the Great, Doctor Johnson, Marie Antoinette, &c.— be it our reasonable boast to our children, that we saw George the Good, the Magnificent, the Great." . . . Yet the irony that Thackeray maintains throughout his masterpiece does not really lead to the purgative laughter of a Swift or Pope. Although, strictly speaking, *Vanity Fair* is neither a religious nor a philosophical work, it raises questions about human existence that are not posed in Trollope's comic world of clergymen. Under the guise of laughter, it laments the external and internal barriers which conspire against freedom and depicts a world of flux in which being is pitted against becoming. Unlike the Brontës, Meredith, George Eliot, or Dickens, Thackeray refuses to impose a moral order on the erratic universe he portrays. Instead, he puts his Amelia doll, Becky puppet, and Dobbin figure back into their box, content to have illustrated the contradictions inherent in human nature. (pp. 81-3)

> U. C. Knoepflmacher, "'Vanity Fair': The Bitterness of Retrospection," in his Laughter & Despair: Readings in Ten Novels of the Victorian Era, *University of California Press, 1971, pp. 50-83.*

BARBARA HARDY   (essay date 1972)

[*Hardy provides a detailed discussion of Thackeray's use of the theme of art versus nature in* Vanity Fair. *For additional commentary on* Vanity Fair *by Hardy, see excerpt dated 1972 in* NCLC, *Vol. 5.*]

One of the major implications of the title and main image of *Vanity Fair* is the corruption of nature by greed, deceit and art. Thackeray approves of honesty, sincerity and spontaneity, and criticizes posing and artifice. The critical emphasis varies, falling on heartlessness or hypocrisy or exhibitionism or artful manipulation, and sometimes on all four simultaneously. Everyone knows that the chief performance in *Vanity Fair* is that given by 'the famous little Becky puppet', as Thackeray describes her in the preliminary address, "Before the Curtain" [see essay dated 1848]. At the very beginning of her performance, in Chapter I, "Chiswick Mall", Thackeray does not show Becky's accomplishments as artist, actress and performer, but rather establishes the environment in which performance becomes necessary. He begins his novel with a critique of Becky's environment which certainly goes far to create and explain her histrionic ways: it shows a hierarchy of power, a pecking-order in which Becky is as yet only finding her way, and it very clearly reveals the incompatibility of success—defined as money and power—with nature, heart, sincerity or love. As yet, Becky is only a novice and learner, as befits a character who is on the brink of leaving school. Her performance has scarcely begun, but Thackeray's analysis of performance is already complex.

The school itself is one of those totally assimilated social symbols which exist in full and self-contained particularity in Thackeray's satiric world: schooling, learning, achievement, testimonials, teaching, finishing the course, are metaphors as well as realities, but Thackeray uses the ready-made social symbol very quietly. It is his great gift, here and elsewhere, to work through a plenitude of such unobtrusively significant action, and not only each detail of pedagogy, teaching and learning, but every single aspect of the scene, events and characters, in this first chapter, is morally expressive.

One key to the theme of art and nature is given in the first image, which contrasts the undignified with the dignified. It does so in a way which draws our attention to the narrow formality of the institution which Becky and Amelia are about to leave for the wide world. The fat horses and the fat coachman, the bandy-legged servant and the red nose of Miss Jemima Pinkerton represent the vivid, undignified informal world, while 'the great iron gate of Miss Pinkerton's academy for young ladies' represents dignity and enclosure. The contrast becomes plainer in the first piece of dialogue between Miss Pinkerton and her sister Miss Jemima, who are a contrasting pair in a novel largely organized on the principle of contrast and duality. The contrast emerges as one of style and sensibility, directing our attention to Miss Jemima's natural, informal, good-hearted, outer-directed attention and the formality and arrangement of Miss Pinkerton's artifice:

> 'It is Mrs Sedley's coach, sister,' said Miss Jemima. 'Sambo, the black servant, has just rung the bell; and the coachman has a new red waistcoat.'
>
> 'Have you completed all the necessary preparations incident to Miss Sedley's departure, Miss Jemima?' asked Miss Pinkerton herself. . . .
>
> (pp. 50-1)

Miss Jemima speaks loosely, but has her eye on the colours and particulars of the world outside. Her concreteness is indeed characteristic of Thackeray's descriptions, and throughout the novel his eye is fixed on the solidity and detail of persons, clothing and objects; his presentation of Amelia and Becky, for instance, is marked by this precision, of action and colour. Here, the concreteness makes Miss Jemima interesting, while her sister is less attractive in her dryness and abstraction of style. The Johnsonian lady, Miss Pinkerton, speaks in the grand style; she is presented appropriately by Thackeray in polysyl-

labic, allusive and high-piled grandeur, as he sets the linguistic tone for the ensuing dialogue: 'Miss Pinkerton herself, that majestic lady; the Semiramis of Hammersmith, the friend of Dr Johnson, the correspondent of Mrs Chapone herself.' His grand style acts as a faint burlesque, not pushing its effects, but maintaining grandeur of vocabulary and syntax. The contrast between the sisters becomes explicit when Miss Jemima uses the old word 'bowpot' and is told to say 'bouquet' as more genteel, doing her best in the compromise of 'booky', which is followed up by the big-hearted but undignified simile, 'as big almost as a haystack'. The sisters' styles draw attention to the formality and pedantry of the one and the clumsy and casual artlessness of the other; and throughout Thackeray works in circumlocutions, like 'autograph letter' or 'billet', and in typically Johnsonian figures of sentiments and negation, parallelism and more periodic elaboration, all shown paradigmatically in this model letter:

> MADAM,—After her six years' residence at the Mall, I have the honour and happiness of presenting Miss Amelia Sedley to her parents, as a young lady not unworthy to occupy a fitting position in their polished and refined circle. Those virtues which characterise the young English gentlewoman, those accomplishments which become her birth and station, will not be found wanting in the amiable Miss Sedley, whose *industry* and *obedience* have endeared her to her instructors, and whose delightful sweetness of temper has charmed her *aged* and her *youthful* companions.
>
> In music, in dancing, in orthography, in every variety of embroidery and needle-work, she will be found to have realised her friends' *fondest wishes*. In geography there is still much to be desired; and a careful and undeviating use of the backboard, for four hours daily during the next three years, is recommended as necessary to the acquirement of that dignified *deportment* and *carriage*, so requisite for every young lady of *fashion*.
>
> (pp. 52-3)

What is said is as important as how it is said, but style and value are related. Miss Pinkerton's careful and pedantic 'For whom is this, Miss Jemima?' is answered by the artless and warm-hearted 'For Becky Sharp: she's going too', which undermines the style and the very insistence of Miss Pinkerton's question. Thackeray works through dialogue and through the surrounding narration and description. The humanity of Miss Jemima's unpedantic, unpremeditated natural style matches her spontaneous show of sensibility: she trembles, blushes all over 'her withered face and neck', and her sensibility shows itself in her wasted imaginative identification with Becky, 'it's only two and ninepence and poor Becky will be miserable if she don't get one'. Miss Jemima, like Briggs later on, is much too simple-minded to criticize the grand and acquisitive cold-heartedness around her, but her criticism is implicit in the language and feelings. Predatory Miss Pinkerton is coldly, self-interestedly and manipulatively in control, in giving, speaking, teaching and writing; Miss Jemima is vulgar, loving, giving, artlessly betrayed by feeling and undignified in action and speech, trotting off, ungrandly, 'exceedingly flurried and nervous'. Miss Pinkerton's condolence is a public event: '. . . Once, when poor Miss Birch died of the scarlet fever, was Miss

A facsimile of a page from the manuscript of Vanity Fair.

Pinkerton known to write personally to the parents of her pupils; and it was Jemima's opinion that if anything *could* console Mrs Birch for her daughter's loss, it would be that pious and eloquent composition in which Miss Pinkerton announced the event.'

From the beginning, therefore, Thackeray establishes a contrast between formal showing-off and lack of heart, loving generosity and lack of style. He also establishes, from the beginning, a sense of social hierarchy and power-structure, not unrelated to the style and capacity for feeling. Those who are at the top, in Vanity Fair, get there by art, not heart. The linguistic and moral contrast between the 'superior' and the 'inferior' sister is followed by the contrast between two other ladies in the hierarchy, Becky and Amelia: 'Miss Sedley's papa was a merchant in London, and a man of some wealth; whereas Miss Sharp was an articled pupil, for whom Miss Pinkerton had done, as she thought, quite enough, without conferring upon her at parting the high honour of the Dixonary.' The psychological pecking-order can override the social, as Thackeray demonstrates in the little passage in which Becky makes her 'adieux' in fluent French, unintelligible to Miss Pinkerton, thus inflicting a stylistic victory, appropriately enough, over the Johnsonian mode. This victory is accompanied by a flouting gesture, as Becky refuses to accept one of Miss Pinkerton's fingers: 'In fact, it was a little battle between the young lady and the old one, and the latter was worsted.' One could describe the whole action of the novel in such military terms, and Thackeray uses them freely; he is well aware of ironic parallels between his story and history, and also of the 'unheroic' ap-

propriation of military or heroic terms to everyday strife. In his novels, these skirmishes are fought with social weapons—with words, sentences, wit, foreign languages, gestures, rituals, refusal of ritual, clothes, presents. Thackeray does more than show Becky as victorious, her strength of personality, intelligence, and learning prevailing over her low place in the social order. He creates a contrast between failure and success in artifice and ritual. Miss Pinkerton makes her ridiculous, elaborate gesture, 'she waved one hand, both by way of adieu, and to give Miss Sharp an opportunity of shaking one of the fingers of the hand which was left out for that purpose', and Becky nonchalantly rejects it. Becky's very last gesture, however, is not an act of social aggression against the style of the Hammersmith Semiramis, but a rejection of poor loving styleless Jemima. The throwing of the dictionary is of course a marvellous rejection of style—Johnson, the institution, order, dignity and pretence—but it is not a simple revolutionary gesture which we can applaud. As so often, Becky is on the wrong side, attacking the Establishment only because she is jealous of its advantages. Our sympathies are carefully withdrawn from her as she throws back what is not only a symbol of 'corrupt' style, but a loving present. Miss Jemima's very last speech and action are typically artless, broken and stammered, and her last generous, if silly, act, is accompanied by the words, 'God bless you!' Becky, like Scrooge, rejects a blessing. The rejection marks her entry into the great world.

Thackeray's last sentences emphasize the contrast between the world of school and the great world, as the gates close; he says, formally, 'and so, farewell to Chiswick Mall'. The brilliant close-up of this first scene has established style and theme, the style and theme of nature and art.

There are certain characters in this chapter I have not mentioned, and they too are involved in style and theme. They are the author and his readers, real and imaginary. Before the curtain rises, in "Before the Curtain", Thackeray has presented himself as the Manager of the Performance; he has begun to develop the histrionic significance, as well as the vanity and commerce of Vanity Fair; he has admitted that he is in it for money, and is not without charlatanry: amongst the crowd he singles out 'quacks (*other* quacks, plague take them!)'. The author is, from the beginning, involved in the business of art and acting. As we know, Thackeray originally intended to call the novel 'A Novel without a Hero' and to develop the theme of unheroic drama, rather than that of Vanity Fair. Although there are divergent emphases, the two themes very plainly overlap, and in Thackeray's claim to the unheroic, he uses the convention of the self-conscious artist to make a certain claim for realism. A certain claim: implicit in his insistence that this is art, that these are puppets, that this is illusion and performance, that it is a book, written for money by an author, and read by various readers, is the claim that it is closer to life and nature than some forms of art. The self-conscious claim to realism is made in the description of Amelia's undignified, unheroinelike beauty and sensibility. Another complex claim for heart as against art, it ends with a disarming address to a Reader, Jones, whose taste is 'for the great and heroic in life and novels' and who will underline the author's 'foolish, twaddling, etc.', and add *'quite true'*. But Jones is critically presented as a worldling, reading at his club, and 'rather flushed with his joint of mutton and half-pint of wine', and it seems likely that Thackeray uses him in order to further the claim for simple, unworldly heroines and passions. He does as much as he can to claim that his novel, though a work of art, has a heart, and not simply by making jokes about the wrong kind of heartless, art-seeking (but wine-flushed) reader like Jones, but by deliberately drawing attention to his own sentimentality. Amelia has a heart, cries over silly novels, and dead pets, and attracts heart: in yet another qualification of the pecking-order, even Semiramis gives orders that Amelia should be treated gently, and when Amelia goes she is surrounded by loving, giving, weeping friends. Indeed, Becky is not entirely the victim of the class hierarchy, since Amelia's friends are seen to love her for herself ('kindly, smiling, tender, gentle, generous heart') and perhaps even Miss Pinkerton is not sensitive to her wholly because of her father's income. Though Becky is made to claim, in Chapter 2, "In Which Miss Sharp and Miss Sedley Prepare to Open the Campaign", that Amelia was her only friend, we shall, in retrospect, blame that on Becky's heartlessness rather than on the social hierarchy of the school. Jones's rejection of Amelia is made to be a rejection of sentimentality, and Thackeray lays claim to the sentimental as an index of sensibility: she cries over dead pets, lost friends, and even silly novels. Thackeray makes it awkward for us by linking the three so that we cannot be as selective in our emotional snobbishness as we should like.

Amelia is, as a character and a woman, deliberately sentimental: that is, she is meant to be the sentimental heroine of an unsentimental novel, illustrating the complexity of the heart's excesses. We shall begin by loving her and feeling with her, in her friendship, love, grief, maternal affection, but we shall eventually learn the limitations of sensibility uncontrolled by reason: she will worship her unworthy husband, alive and dead, spoil her son, and make sentimental demands on Dobbin, her

patient lover. The very first chapter prepares us for this aspect of Thackeray's criticism, his refusal to accept unqualified sensibility as a moral norm. Heart like this can be linked with silliness and excess: it is all very well to cry for dead birds but not for silly novels. But the qualification of heart is less conspicuous, at first, than the qualification of art. Only in the misplaced loving gift of Miss Jemima, the rejected dictionary, do we see our first clear instance of sentimentality; it is punished rudely by its exact opposite, hard-heartedness, which also earns its first clear criticism when, biting the hand that feeds, it throws back the dictionary at the silly affectionate old woman. The reader is involved even with her rejection, because Thackeray tells us, drily, that she is not going to appear again:

> . . . Miss Jemima had already whimpered several times at the idea of Amelia's departure; and, but for fear of her sister, would have gone off in downright hysterics, like the heiress (who paid double) of St Kitt's. Such luxury of grief, however, is only allowed to parlour-boarders. Honest Jemima had all the bills, and the washing, and the mending, and the puddings, and the plate and crockery, and the servants to superintend. But why speak about her? It is probable that we shall not hear of her again from this moment to the end of time, and that when the great filigree iron gates are once closed on her, she and her awful sister will never issue therefrom into this little world of history.
>
> (pp. 53-7)

What does this rather odd passage mean? That there are heroines even less heroic than Amelia, who is, once this passage has urged us to reflect, more of a heroine than Miss Jemima? Thackeray seems to mean what he says in the sentence 'Such luxury of grief, however, is only allowed to parlour-boarders'. In a novel which is about the luxury of grief, Thackeray reminds us, in the dismissal of Jemima, of the circumstances that permit grief, in and out of novels. He also claims for his novel a high degree of realism; though it is interesting to distinguish his claim from George Eliot's in the totally tolerant *Adam Bede*, where Lizbeth Bede *is* permitted her 'luxury of grief'. At the same time, he draws our attention to the social interest of his emotional theme: if people like Amelia dwell on grief, devote themselves to worship of dead husband and living son, it is as a luxury. Thus he makes another qualification of heart: sensitivity, as well as art, depends on position and possessions. Thackeray's initial creation of category is uncomfortably blurred. On the one hand we have Miss Pinkerton, the Johnsonian style, the great filigree iron gates, Jones, with his contempt for sentiment, and Becky, able to put down the grand style with fluent French. On the other hand, Amelia, all tolerant and sentimental readers, and Jemima, loving, giving, artless. Between the two worlds, the rejection of the dictionary; yet, beside it, Jemima's blessing and the two-edged admission that Jemima is not promising material for Thackeray's novel.

The realistic effects of the self-conscious reference should be stressed here. Thackeray insists on the illusion, the art, the performance, the drama, the novel, but in such a way—dismissing a character who is not qualified to be a character—that brings the novel very close indeed to life. There are some unpromising materials, he says, that will not come in; and the very mention reminds us of the novelist's selection from life, in a way that is moving and evaluative. At the extreme of art is Thackeray himself; at the extreme of heart is Jemima, who will be left out. The reader is made wary, and perhaps, as Thackeray wished, uncomfortable. If he is attentive, he will not reject Jones, Amelia, Miss Pinkerton or Johnson's dictionary too precipitately.

This first formal and framing scene in Chapter I of *Vanity Fair* makes plain the heroines' initiation into the great world, and the reader's initiation into the world of the novel. In Chapter 8, Thackeray draws our attention, first by direct dramatic presentation, then by complex authorial commentary, to certain crucial differences between Becky's art and his own. In the chapters that bridge the initiation and the very explicit analysis, we have seen Becky beginning her career as an artist in life. She does, in fact, possess some positive artistic talents, chiefly displayed in her entertaining and persuasive performances of miming and singing. In Chapter 8, Thackeray adds a new artistic achievement, epistolary and literary. Becky's letter to Amelia probably takes a glance at epistolary fiction in its feminine effusiveness and self-pity, and its very lack of resemblance to the situations of Pamela and Clarissa. But the chief purpose, as I see it, is to bridge Becky's artistic forte, which is dramatic, and Thackeray's, which is literary.

Becky is given the whole narrative burden, for the space of her letter, of introducing the reader to a new place and several new characters. She is a quite convenient surrogate for Thackeray, being, like him, sharply attentive, witty and satirical, but she is of course not simply a surrogate, and her letter also shows the Becky Sharp traits of false sensibility and predatoriness. Her letters are usually written to get something, directly or indirectly, and this letter is clearly designed to keep a tenuous hook on the Sedleys—'Is your poor brother recovered of his rack-punch?'—and even Amelia, who may be good for another India muslin or pink silk in the future. But the cast-off dresses are still fresh (see Chapter 11 for the hint about their replacements) and Thackeray is free to develop Becky's literary gifts.

Throughout the novel, her letters are important in the furthering of the action and the development of her character. There is the unsuccessful letter dictated to Rawdon and addressed to Miss Crawley, which does not take in the old lady for a minute, since Becky has thought of using short sentences but not of mis-spelling. Moreover, the letter is fatally amusing, and Miss Crawley detects Becky's fundamental style, as well as appreciating it and asking for more. There is the more crucial letter written to Rawdon in the sponging-house, designed to put him off affectionately and humorously, but unable to hide her exhibitionism and self-interest. Its crude ingratiation does not take in Rawdon, who also detects her fundamental style, failing to be amused by Becky's jokes, and disliking them for the first time. But the first letter, in Chapter 8, is a more disengaged venture. It introduces the reader to King's Crawley and to some new and important characters. It is a superb stroke of art, totally and variously eloquent. The very title of the chapter, "Private and Confidential", is expressive of the epistolary gossip of bosom-friends and its frank-mark, "Free.-Pitt Crawley", is informative and ironic—who pays and for what, or who does not pay, is always of interest in Thackeray.

My Dearest, Sweetest Amelia,

With what mingled joy and sorrow do I take up the pen to write to my dearest friend! Oh, what a change between to-day and yesterday! *Now* I am friendless and alone; yesterday I was at home, in the sweet company of a sister, whom I shall ever, *ever* cherish!

I will not tell you in what tears and sadness I passed the fatal night in which I separated from you. *You* went on Tuesday to joy and happiness, with your mother and *your devoted young soldier* by your side; and I thought of you all night, dancing at Perkins's, the prettiest, I am sure, of all the young ladies at the Ball. I was brought by the groom in the old carriage to Sir Pitt Crawley's town house, where, after John the groom had behaved most rudely and insolently to me (alas! 'twas safe to insult poverty and misfortune!), I was given over to Sir P's care, and made to pass the night in an old gloomy bed, and by the side of a horrid gloomy old charwoman, who keeps the house. I did not sleep one single wink the whole night.

Sir Pitt is not what we silly girls, when we used to read Cecilia at Chiswick, imagined a baronet must have been. Anything, indeed, less like Lord Orville cannot be imagined. Fancy an old, stumpy, short, vulgar, and very dirty man, in old clothes and shabby old gaiters, who smokes a horrid pipe, and cooks his own horrid supper in a saucepan. He speaks with a country accent, and swore a great deal at the old charwoman, at the hackney coachman who drove us to the inn where the coach went from, and on which I made the journey *outside for the greater part of the way. . . .*

Half an hour after our arrival, the great dinner-bell was rung, and I came down with my two pupils (they are very thin and insignificant little chits of ten and eight years old). I came down in your *dear* muslin gown (about which that odious Mrs Pinner was so rude, because you gave it me); for I am to be treated as one of the family, except on company days, when the young ladies and I are to dine up-stairs.

Well, the great dinner-bell rang, and we all assembled in the little drawing-room where my Lady Crawley sits. She is the second Lady Crawley, and mother of the young ladies. She was an ironmonger's daughter, and her marriage was thought a great match. She looks as if she had been handsome once, and her eyes are always weeping for the loss of her beauty. She is pale and meagre, and high-shouldered; and has not a word to say for herself, evidently. Her step-son, Mr Crawley, was likewise in the room. He was in full dress, as pompous as an undertaker. He is pale, thin, ugly, silent; he has thin legs, no chest, hay-coloured whiskers, and straw-coloured hair. . . .

A hundred thousand grateful loves to your dear papa and mamma! Is your poor brother recovered of his rack-punch? Oh, dear! Oh, dear! How men should beware of wicked punch!

Ever and ever thine own,

Rebecca

The first thing we notice is the conventional satire on female sensibility. The strongest impression is that of exaggeration and falsity: 'My Dearest, Sweetest Amelia'; or 'With what mingled joy and sorrow do I take up the pen to write to my dearest friend! . . . Now I am friendless and alone. . . .' But these initial emotions of indulgence, envy and self-pity soon give way to the sheer verve of narrative and presentation of character. Thackeray does something simple but clever with Becky's narration; he allows it to overlap slightly with his own narrative in Chapter 10, so that we see a slight discrepancy between what has happened and what Becky presents as happening. Nothing very marked; just a little evidence that Becky is a liar: the detail that she has not slept a wink (when the author has said that she does) and the omission of her attempt to pump the old charwoman with whom she shares a bed. She presents herself as the heroine of a Gothic novel rather than a resilient, unfastidious and predatory opportunist. But what is most striking is the wit and humour of Becky's narrative, achieved at the expense of the characters in her story. The girls are 'very thin and insignificant little chits of ten and eight years old'. Lady Crawley 'looks as if she had been handsome once, and her eyes are always weeping for the loss of her beauty'. Pitt Crawley is 'pompous as an undertaker . . . pale, thin, ugly, silent; he has thin legs, no chest, hay-coloured whiskers, and straw-coloured hair'. Sir Pitt is exposed by his 'dumpy little legs' and rustic accent. The butler is laughed at for his ludicrous French pronunciation (Becky's pride in her French is one of her humourless weaknesses), and Miss Horrocks, described as 'very much over-dressed', flings Becky a look of scorn as 'she plumped down on her knees'.

Such strokes of wit and ridicule may be enjoyed for their own sake, and our critical spirit may be held in check until Thackeray himself stands back to analyse the letter. The contrast between the maidenly gush and the hard-hitting satire is probably clear, but we do not feel strongly critical until Thackeray drily observes that we should. For although he has been using Becky as a narrator, the narration is itself material for satire. It is satire proffered for the reader's enjoyment, then analysed by the satirist.

> Everything considered, I think it is quite as well for our dear Amelia Sedley, in Russell Square, that Miss Sharp and she are parted. Rebecca is a droll funny creature, to be sure; and those descriptions of the poor lady weeping for the loss of her beauty, and the gentleman 'with hay-coloured whiskers and straw-coloured hair', are very smart, doubtless, and show a great knowledge of the world. That she might, when on her knees, have been thinking of something better than Miss Horrocks's ribbons, has possibly struck both of us. But my kind reader will please to remember, that this history has 'Vanity Fair' for a title, and that Vanity Fair is a very vain, wicked, foolish place, full of all sorts of humbugs and falsenesses and pretensions. And while the moralist, who is holding forth on the cover (an accurate portrait of your humble servant), professes to wear neither gown nor bands, but only the very same long-eared livery in which his congregation is arrayed: yet, look you, one is bound to speak the truth as far as one knows it, whether one mounts a cap and bells or a shovel-hat; and a deal of dis-

agreeable matter must come out in the course of such an undertaking.

(pp. 58-63)

This first ironic combination of criticism and defence is Thackeray at his most subtle and disconcerting: we cannot know what he is saying in this first paragraph which neatly balances indictment with justification, and relates Becky to her author. But what does he mean by speaking the truth? Does he refer to his own exposure of Becky? Or does he also include her exposure of the vanity and foolishness of Lady Crawley, Pitt and Miss Horrocks, who are all easily and accurately describable as vain and foolish, 'full of all sorts of humbugs and falsenesses and pretensions'.

Another contrast and symmetrical figure follow: the story of a preacher—a Neapolitan story-teller—who worked himself up into such a 'rage and passion' against 'some of the villains whose wicked deeds he was describing and inventing that the audience could not resist it'. The result of the story-teller's fervour was a good profit: 'the hat went round, and the bajocchi tumbled into it, in the midst of a perfect storm of sympathy'. This anecdote is balanced against that of the Parisian actors who refuse to play villains and prefer to play virtuous characters for a lower payment. He observes: 'I set these two stories one against the other, so that you may see that it is not from mere mercenary motives that the present performer is desirous to show up and trounce his villains; but because he has a sincere hatred of them, which he cannot keep down, and which must find a vent in suitable abuse and bad language.' Not a simple antithesis, it needs careful analysis before we finally conclude that Thackeray is admitting his own lack of pure motivation. After all, he is a performer who gains from the performance, an author earning his living with this serial (later a book) which is paid for by the reader. Thackeray is distinguishing between his satiric stance and Becky's; he is telling us clearly that though a critic, she is subjected to the author's criticism as 'one who has no reverence except for prosperity, and no eye for anything beyond success. Such people there are living and flourishing in the world—Faithless, Hopeless, Charityless; let us have at them, dear friends, with might and main'.

This disclosure criticizes and clarifies Becky's wit and ridicule. While admitting that Thackeray writes for gain, it claims that his satiric mode derives from Faith, Hope and Charity. It invokes lofty and noble moral purpose: he is mercenary but not 'merely' mercenary. If we then look at Thackeray's irony, scorn, wit and ridicule, we see that his satire is not cynical; rather it derives from Hope and Faith in the possibilities of human nature, and has Charity. Thackeray is a master of timing and placing, and follows this criticism of Becky's immoral and eclectic satire and wit by a conspicuously charitable and serious satiric piece in the next chapter. Another instance of symmetry and juxtaposition, it is also an instance of Thackeray's explicitness and clarity. Uncomfortable though he may be as a satirist constantly involving the reader in the satire, he takes no chances with misunderstanding. He is writing a novel about the corruption of nature, and this corruption shows itself here, in Becky, performance, wit and satire. However, as an artist sharing the actions of performance, wit and satire, he is constrained to distinguish between right and wrong wit, right and wrong satire. The distinctions involve an art which has a heart—Hope, Faith, Charity—and an art which is heartless, 'no reverence for anything except for prosperity'. At the same time, he is aware and forced to admit that he is involved in profiting too. The character and the author are fully compared and contrasted. This is extremely rare in English fiction, apart from the earlier and influential case of Fielding who presented, in *Tom Jones,* antithetical images of his own desire for lofty Fame and worldly prosperity—what Thackeray, memorably recalling Fielding's invocation of roast beef, calls 'a little of the Sunday side'.

Chapter 8, then, exposes Becky as a heartless artist practising Thackeray's arts, and implies that Thackeray is more honourable than Becky. Chapter 9 follows with a demonstration, taking a revised look at those characters analysed so heartlessly and artfully by Becky. Sir Pitt, Lady Crawley and Mr Pitt Crawley are all presented afresh, with wit and satire, and with sympathy and charity. Sir Pitt, for whom admittedly little can be said, is shown as first marrying 'under the auspices of his parents', then marrying to please himself. There is feeling in 'He had his pretty Rose, and what more need a man require than to please himself?' What follows is inside information, not mere brilliant superficial wit, and it is much more devastating than Becky's exposure: 'So he used to get drunk every night: to beat his pretty Rose sometimes: to leave her in Hampshire when he went to London for the parliamentary session, without a single friend in the whole world.' An extremely charitable account of pretty Rose herself follows, together with a glance at her limitations and losses: '. . . she had no sort of character, nor talents, nor opinions, nor occupations, nor amusements, nor that vigour of soul and ferocity of temper which often falls to the lot of entirely foolish women. . . . O Vanity Fair—Vanity Fair! This might have been, but for you, a cheery lass:—Peter Butt and Rose, a happy man and wife'.

There is a dignified and sympathetic account of Pitt, his respect for his mother-in-law, his kindness, and then—just in case we were beginning to identify Thackeray's manner of satiric analysis with charity and imagination—a devastating account of his mediocrity, industry and lack of self-knowledge. Thackeray's own wit is disarmingly produced when least expected, as we nod over his ability to see the humanity of these characters with heart and generosity; it is harder than anything achieved by Becky's rather visual ridicule: '. . . yet he failed somehow, in spite of a mediocrity which ought to have insured any man a success. He did not even get the prize poem, which all his friends said he was sure of'. Thackeray is very deliberate in his revision of Becky's satire, even to the extent of commenting when he agrees with her: 'Miss Sharp's accounts of his employment at Queen's Crawley were not caricatures. He subjected the servants there to the devotional exercises before mentioned, in which (and so much the better) he brought his father to join.' The parentheses of course mark, once more, the comment Becky would not be capable of making.

Thackeray's expansion and revision has one last effect. He has a capacity for moral and social diagnosis and generalization which Becky, at least at this stage in her education, utterly lacks. She sees, at school and out of it, how she is at an unfair disadvantage because of her birth and poverty; but later, when she makes the celebrated suggestion that she could be a good woman on five thousand a year, she does not see into the heartlessness of Vanity Fair, having insufficient heart and vision for the enterprise. Her social criticism, even when generalized, is shallow. Thackeray, having like Becky observed Sir Pitt's drunkenness and illiteracy, though more seriously and less amusedly, also sees the criticism of society involved in marking the defects of this dignitary. Becky finds Sir Pitt funny; 'Anything, indeed, less like Lord Orville cannot be imagined,' she comments, in her literary and hypocritically fastidious way. Thackeray replaces this with a moral fervour:

A drawing by Thackeray in a copy of Vanity Fair *he presented to Lady Normanby.*

Vanity Fair—Vanity Fair! Here was a man, who could not spell, and did not care to read—who had the habits and the cunning of a boor: whose aim in life was pettifogging: who never had a taste, or emotion, or enjoyment, but what was sordid and foul; and yet he had rank, and honours, and power, somehow: and was a dignitary of the land, and a pillar of the state. He was high sheriff, and rode in a golden coach. Great ministers and statesmen courted him; and in Vanity Fair he had a higher place than the most brilliant genius or spotless virtue.

(pp. 63-7)

At one stroke, Thackeray candidly admits his own involvement; he makes explicit and dramatic the seriousness, profundity and passion of his satire. Avoiding a simple division of intellect or feeling into art and nature, he creates an art which is as close to nature, and as inclusive and serious, as possible. He also suggests, craftily and dramatically, that social criticism is his aim. (p. 67)

> *Barbara Hardy, in her* The Exposure of Luxury: Radical Themes in Thackeray, *Peter Owen Limited, London, 1972, 190 p.*

WOLFGANG ISER   (essay date 1972)

[*Iser discusses the narrative techniques employed by Thackeray in* Vanity Fair *and their effect upon the relationship between the reader, narrator, and characters. Iser's study was originally published in German in 1972.*]

The author-reader relationship, which was . . . developed by the eighteenth-century novel, has remained a constant feature of narrative prose and is still in evidence even when the author seems to have disappeared and the reader is deliberately excluded from comprehension. While Fielding offers this reassurance to his readers: "I am, indeed, set over them for their own good only, and was created for their use, and not they for mine," Joyce, at the other end of the scale drops only the ironic information that the author has withdrawn behind his work, "paring his fingernails." The reader of modern novels is deprived of the assistance which the eighteenth-century writer had given him in a variety of devices ranging from earnest exhortation to satire and irony. Instead, he is expected to strive for himself to unravel the mysteries of a sometimes strikingly obscure composition. This development reflects the transformation of the very idea of literature, which seems to have ceased to be a means of relaxation and even luxury, making demands now on the capacity of understanding because the world presented seems to have no bearing on what the reader is familiar with. This change did not happen suddenly. The stages of transition are clearly discernible in the nineteenth century, and one of them is virtually a half-way point in the development: the so-called 'realistic' novel. An outstanding example of this is Thackeray's *Vanity Fair.* Here, the author-reader relationship is as different from the eighteenth-century 'dialogue' as it is from the twentieth-century demand that the reader find for himself the key to a many-sided puzzle. In Thackeray, the reader does have to make his own discoveries, but the author provides him with unmistakable clues to guide him in his search.

The first stage in our discussion must be to modify the term 'author'. We should distinguish, as Wayne Booth does in his *Rhetoric of Fiction,* between the man who writes the book (author), the man whose attitudes shape the book (implied author), and the man who communicates directly with the reader (narrator): "The 'implied author' chooses, consciously or unconsciously, what we read; . . . he is the sum of his own choices. . . . This implied author is always distinct from the 'real man'—whatever we may take him to be—who creates a superior version of himself, a 'second self', as he creates his work." The narrator, of course, is not always to be identified with the implied author.

In the novels of the nineteenth century it happens again and again that the narrator moves even further and further away from the implied author by virtue of being an actual character in the story itself. Traces of this kind of narrator are already apparent in Dickens's novels, and in Thackeray's *Vanity Fair* he is a complete character in his own right. It is almost as if the implied author, who devised the story, has to bow to the narrator, who has a deeper insight into all the situations. What the implied author describes is interpreted by the narrator to a degree far beyond what one might normally deduce from the events. One is bound to ask the purpose of this clear though sometimes complex separation between narration and commentary, especially in a 'realistic' novel which is supposed to represent reality as it is. The justification lies in the fact that even a realistic novel cannot encompass total reality. As Arnold Bennett once remarked: "You can't put the whole of a character into a book." If the limitations of the novel are such that one cannot reveal a complete character, it is even more impossible to try to transcribe complete reality. And so even a novel that is called realistic can present no more than particular aspects of a given reality, although the selection must remain implicit in order to cloak the author's ideology.

Thackeray's *Vanity Fair* is also governed by this principle, which is clearly reflected by the different titles of the original

version and the final one. The first, consisting of eight chapters, was called "Pen and Pencil Sketches of English Society," indicating that the reality described was meant primarily as a reproduction of social situations; the final version, "Vanity Fair," is concerned less with depicting social situations than with offering a judgment of them. This quality is commented on by Thackeray himself in a letter written a few years after the publication of *Vanity Fair:* ". . . the Art of Novels is . . . to convey as strongly as possible the sentiment of reality—in a tragedy or a poem or a lofty drama you aim at producing different emotions; the figures moving, and their words sounding, heroically." "Sentiment of reality" implies that the novel does not represent reality itself, but aims rather at producing an idea of how reality can be experienced. Thus *Vanity Fair* not only offers a panorama of contemporary reality but also reveals the way in which the abundance of details has been organized, so that the reader can participate in the organization of events and thus gain the "sentiment of reality." This is the reason why the novel continues to be effective even today, though the social conditions it describes are only of historical interest. If the past has been kept alive, this is primarily due to the structural pattern through which the events are conveyed to the reader: the effect is gained by the interplay between the implied author who arranges the events, and the narrator who comments on them. The reader can only gain real access to the social reality presented by the implied author, when he follows the adjustments of perspective made by the narrator in viewing the events described. In order to ensure that the reader participates in the way desired, the narrator is set up as a kind of authority between him and the events, conveying the impression that understanding can only be achieved through this medium. In the course of the action, the narrator takes on various guises in order to appear as a fully developed character and in order to control the distance from which the reader has to view the scenes unfolded before him.

At the start of the novel, the narrator introduces himself as "Manager of the Performance" [see essay by Thackeray dated 1848], and gives an outline of what the audience is to expect. The ideal visitor to 'Vanity Fair' is described as a "man with a reflective turn of mind"; this is an advance indication of what the reader has to accomplish, if he is to realize the meaning of the proceedings. But at the same time, the Manager promises that he has something for everyone: "Some people consider Fairs immoral altogether, and eschew such, with their servants and families: very likely they are right. But persons who think otherwise, and are of a lazy, or a benevolent, or a sarcastic mood, may perhaps like to step in for half an hour, and look at the performances. There are scenes of all sorts: some dreadful combats, some grand and lofty horse-riding, some scenes of high life, and some of very middling indeed; some love-making for the sentimental, and some light comic business." In this way the Manager tries to entice all different types of visitors to enter his Fair—bearing in mind the fact that such a visit will also have its after-effects. When the reader has been following the narrator for quite some time, he is informed: "This, dear friends and companions, is my amiable object—to walk with you through the Fair, to examine the shops and the shows there; and that we should all come home after the flare, and the noise, and the gaiety, and be perfectly miserable in private." But the reader will only feel miserable after walking through the Fair if, unexpectedly, he has come upon himself in some of the situations, thereby having his attention drawn to his own behavior, which has shone out at him from the mirror of possibilities. The narrator is only pretending to help the reader—in reality he is goading him. His reliability is already reduced by the fact that he is continually donning new masks: at one moment he is an observer of the Fair, like the reader; then he is suddenly blessed with extraordinary knowledge, though he can explain ironically that "novelists have the privilege of knowing everything"; and then, toward the end, he announces that the whole story was not his own at all, but that he overheard it in a conversation. At the beginning of the novel the narrator is presented as Manager of the Performance, and at the end he presents himself as the reporter of a story which fell into his hands purely by chance. The further away he stands from the social reality depicted, the clearer is the outline of the part he is meant to play. But the reader can only view the social panorama in the constantly shifting perspectives which are opened up for him by this Protean narrator. Although he cannot help following the views and interpretations of the narrator, it is essential for him to understand the motivations behind this constant changing of viewpoints, because only the discovery of the motivations can lead to the comprehension of what is intended. Thus the narrator regulates the distance between reader and events, and in doing so brings about the esthetic effect of the story. The reader is given only as much information as will keep him oriented and interested, but the narrator deliberately leaves open the inferences that are to be drawn from this information. Consequently, empty spaces are bound to occur, spurring the reader's imagination to detect the assumption which might have motivated the narrator's attitude. In this way, we get involved because we react to the viewpoints advanced by the narrator. If the narrator is an independent character, clearly separated from the inventor of the story, the tale of the social aspirations of the two girls Becky and Amelia takes on a greater degree of objectivity, and indeed one gains the impression that this social reality is not a mere narration but actually exists. The narrator can then be regarded as a sort of mediator between the reader and the events, with the implication that it is only through him that the social reality can be rendered communicable in the first place.

The narrator's strategy can be seen even more clearly in his relations with the characters in the novel and with the reader's expectations. *Vanity Fair* has as the subtitle, *A Novel without a Hero,* which indicates that the characters are not regarded as representing an ideal, exemplary form of human conduct, as established by the conventions of the eighteenth-century novel. Instead, the reader's interest is divided between two figures who, despite the contrast in their behavior, can under no circumstances be regarded as complementary or even corrective. For Becky, no price is too high for the fulfillment of her social ambitions; her friend Amelia is simple and sentimental. And so right at the beginning we are told:

> As she is not a heroine, there is no need to describe her person; indeed I am afraid that her nose was rather short than otherwise, and her cheeks a great deal too round and red for a heroine; but her face blushed with rosy health, and her lips with the freshest of smiles, and she had a pair of eyes which sparkled with the brightest and honestest good-humour, except indeed when they filled with tears, and that was a great deal too often; for the silly thing would cry over a dead canary-bird; or over a mouse, that the cat haply had seized upon; or over the end of a novel, were it ever so stupid.

The details of such a description serve only to trivialize those features that were so important in the hero or heroine of the traditional novel. These details give the impression that something significant is being said about the person described, but the succession of clichés, from the round red cheeks and sparkling eyes to the soft-hearted sentimentality, achieve their purpose precisely by depriving the character of its representative nature. But if Amelia is deprived of traditional representative qualities and is not to be regarded as the positive counterpart to the unscrupulous, sophisticated Becky, then the novel denies the reader a basic focal point of orientation. He is prevented from sympathizing with the hero—a process which till now had always provided the nineteenth-century reader with his most important means of access to the events described—as typified by the reaction of a reviewer to Charlotte Brontë's *Jane Eyre:* "We took up *Jane Eyre* one winter's evening, somewhat piqued at the extravagant commendations we had heard, and sternly resolved to be as critical as Croker. But as we read on we forgot both commendations and criticism, identified ourselves with Jane in all her troubles, and finally married Mr. Rochester about four in the morning." In contrast, *Vanity Fair* seems bent on breaking any such direct contact with the characters, and indeed the narrator frequently goes out of his way to prevent the reader from putting himself in their place.

This occurs predominantly through the narrator's comments on the particular patterns of behavior developed by Amelia and Becky in critical situations. He reveals the motives behind their utterances, interpolating consequences of which they themselves are not aware, so that these occasions serve to uncover the imbalance of the characters. Often the behavior of the characters is interpreted far beyond the scope of the reactions shown and in the light of knowledge which at best could only have been revealed by the future. In this way the reader is continually placed at a distance from the characters. As Michel Butor once pointed out, in a different context: "If the reader is put in the place of the hero, he must also be put in the hero's immediate present; he cannot know what the hero does not know, and things must appear to him just as they appear to the hero." In *Vanity Fair,* however, the characters are illuminated by a knowledge to which they themselves have no access. They are constantly kept down below the intellectual level of the narrator, whose views offer the reader a far greater stimulus to identification than do the characters themselves. This detachment from the characters is part of the narrator's avowed intention: ". . . as we bring our characters forward, I will ask leave, as a man and a brother, not only to introduce them, but occasionally to step down from the platform, and talk about them: if they are good and kindly, to love them and shake them by the hand; if they are silly, to laugh at them confidentially in the reader's sleeve: if they are wicked and heartless, to abuse them in the strongest terms which politeness admits of." The characters in this novel are completely hedged in by such judgments, and the reader sees all their actions only when they have been refracted by the narrator's own critical evaluations. The immensity of his presence makes it impossible for the reader to live their lives with them, as did the reviewer we have quoted, during his reading of *Jane Eyre.* The actual gap between the characters' actions and the narrator's comments stimulates the reader into forming judgments of his own—thereby bridging the gaps—and gradually adopting the position of critic himself.

It is mainly this intention that shapes the composition of the characters, and there are two dominant techniques to be observed. The first part of the novel reproduces letters which Becky and Amelia write to each other. The letter makes it possible to reveal the most intimate thoughts and feelings to such a degree that the reader can learn from the correspondents themselves just who they are and what makes them 'tick'. A typical example is Becky's long letter telling Amelia all about her new surroundings at the Crawley family's country seat. Becky's impressions end with the spontaneous self-revelation: "I am determined to make myself agreeable." Fitting in with present circumstances remains her guiding principle throughout her quest for social advancement. Such a wish is so totally in keeping with her own character that the maneuvers necessary for its fulfillment constitute for Becky the natural way to behave. Thus we see that in society, self-seeking hypocrisy has become second nature to man. In the letters, however, Becky's self-esteem remains so constant that she is clearly quite unaware of her two-facedness. The obvious naiveté of such self-portraits is bound to provoke the reader into critical reaction, and the heading of the chapter that reproduces Becky's letter is already pointing in this direction, for the unmistakably ironic title is: "Arcadian Simplicity." Thus the self-revelation of the letter actually justifies the narrator for not taking the character as it is, but setting it at a critical distance so that it can be seen through. Elsewhere we read: "Perhaps in Vanity Fair there are no better satires than letters." But the intention of the satire is for the reader himself to uncover, for the narrator never offers him more than ironic clues. The narrator's keen concern to give the impression that he never commits himself to ultimate clarity reveals itself at those times when he accidentally reaches an 'understanding' with his reader, but then remembers that such an exchange of experiences goes beyond the limits of his narrative: ". . . but we are wandering out of the domain of the story."

The second technique designed to rouse the critical faculties of the reader is revealed in Amelia's almost obsessive habit of "building numberless castles in the air . . . which Amelia adorned with all sorts of flower-gardens, rustic walks, country churches, Sunday schools, and the like." This day-dreaming is typical of Amelia, who devises these beautiful visions as an escape from the narrow confines of her social existence. Her whole outlook is governed by expectations that generally arise out of chance events in her life and are therefore subject to fortuitous change as the social situations she gets into. The dependence of these often very sentimental day-dreams on the circumstances of the moment shows not only the fickleness of her behavior but also the disoriented nature of her desires, the fulfillment of which is inevitably frustrated by the apparently superior forces of her environment. The projection of hopes which cannot be realized leads to an attitude which is as characteristic of Amelia as it is of Becky, who for different motives also covers up what she really is, in order to gain the social position she hankers after. Despite the difference in their motives, both Amelia's and Becky's lives are largely governed by illusions, which are shown up for what they are by the fact that whenever they are partially realized, we see how very trivial the aspirations really were. The characters themselves, however, lack this awareness, and this is hardly surprising, as their ambitions or longings are often roused by chance occurrences which are not of sufficient lasting importance to give the characters a true sense of direction. Becky certainly has greater drive in her quest for social advancement, and one would therefore expect a greater degree of continuity in her conduct; but this very ambition requires that she should adapt her conduct to the various demands made by the different strata of society; and this fact in turn shows how malleable and therefore illusory are the conventions of social life. What is presented in Becky's life as continuity should not be confused with the aspirations of the eighteenth-century hero, who went forth in order to find out the truth about himself; here it is the expression of the many-sided sham which is the very attribute of social reality.

When the narrator introduces his characters at the beginning of the novel, he says of Becky: "The famous little Becky Puppet has been pronounced to be uncommonly flexible in the joints, and lively on the wire." As the characters cannot free themselves from their illusions, it is only to be expected that they should take them for unquestionable reality. The reader is made aware of this fact by the attitude of the narrator, who has not only seen through his 'puppets', but also lets them act on a level of consciousness far below his own. This almost overwhelming superiority of the narrator over his characters also puts the reader in a privileged position, though with the unspoken but ever-present condition that he should draw his own conclusions from the extra knowledge imparted to him by the narrator. There is even an allegory of the reader's task at one point in the novel, when Becky is basking in the splendor of a grand social evening:

> The man who brought her refreshment and stood behind her chair, had talked her character over with the large gentleman in motley-coloured clothes at his side. Bon Dieu! it is awful, that servants' inquisition! You see a woman in a great party in a splendid saloon, surrounded by faithful admirers, distributing sparkling glances, dressed to perfection, curled, rouged, smiling and happy:—Discovery walks respectfully up to her, in the shape of a huge powdered man with large calves and a tray of ices—with Calumny (which is as fatal as truth) behind him, in the shape of the hulking fellow carrying the wafer-biscuits, Madam, your secret will be talked over by those men at their club at the public-house to-night. . . . Some people ought to have mutes for servants in Vanity Fair—mutes who could not write. If you are guilty, tremble. That fellow behind your chair may be a Janissary with a bowstring in his plush breeches pocket. If you are not guilty, have a care of appearances: which are as ruinous as guilt.

This little scene contains a change of standpoints typical of the way in which the reader's observations are conditioned throughout this novel. The servants are suddenly transformed into allegorical figures with the function of uncovering what lies hidden beneath the façades of their masters. But the discovery will only turn into calumny from the standpoint of the person affected. The narrator compares the destructive effect of calumny with that of truth and advises his readers to employ mutes, or better still illiterate mutes, as servants, in order to protect themselves against discovery. Then he brings the reader's view even more sharply into focus, finally leaving him to himself with an indissoluble ambiguity: if he feels guilty, because he is pretending to be something he is not, then he must fear those around him as if they were an army of Janissaries. If he has nothing to hide, then the social circle merely demands of him to keep up appearances; but since this is just as ruinous as deliberate hypocrisy, it follows that life in society imposes roles on all concerned, reducing human behavior to the level of play-acting. All the characters in the novel are caught up in this play, as is expressly shown by the narrator's own stage metaphor at the beginning and at the end. The key word for the reader is 'discover', and the narrator continually prods him along the road to discovery, laying a trail of clues for him to follow. The process reveals not only the extent to which Becky and Amelia take their illusions for reality but also—even more strikingly—the extent to which reality itself is illusory, since it is built on the simulated relationships between people. The reader will not fail to notice the gulf between 'illusion' and 'reality', and in realizing it, he is experiencing the esthetic effect of the novel: Thackeray did not set out to create the conventional illusion that involved the reader in the world of the novel as if it were reality; instead, his narrator constantly interrupts the story precisely in order to prevent such an illusion from coming into being. The reader is deliberately stopped from identifying himself with the characters. And as the aim is to prevent him from taking part in the events, he is allowed to be absorbed only to a certain degree and is then jerked back again, so that he is impelled to criticize from the outside. Thus the story of the two girls serves to get the reader involved, while the meaning of the story can only be arrived at by way of the additional manipulations of perspective carried out by the narrator.

This 'split-level' technique conveys a far stronger impression of reality than does the illusion which claims that the world of the novel corresponds to the whole world. For now the reader himself has to discover the true situation, which becomes clearer and clearer to him as he gets to know the characters in their fetters of illusion. In this way, he himself takes an active part in the animation of all the characters' actions, for they seem real to him because he is constantly under obligation to work out all that is wrong with their behavior. In order that his participation should not be allowed to slacken, the individual characters are fitted out with different types and degrees of delusion, and there are even some, like Dobbin, whose actions and feelings might mislead one into taking them for positive counterparts to all the other characters. Such a false assumption is certainly perceived, even if not intended, by the narrator, who toward the end of the novel addresses the reader as follows: "This woman [i.e., Amelia] had a way of tyrannising over Major Dobbin (for the weakest of all people will domineer over somebody), and she ordered him about, and patted him, and made him fetch and carry just as if he was a great Newfoundland dog. . . . This history has been written to very little purpose if the reader has not perceived that the Major was a spooney." What might have seemed like noble-mindedness was in fact the behavior of a nincompoop, and if the reader has only just realized it, then he has not been particularly successful in the process of 'discovering'.

The esthetic effect of *Vanity Fair* depends on activating the reader's critical faculties so that he may recognize the social reality of the novel as a confusing array of sham attitudes, and experience the exposure of this sham as the true reality. Instead of being expressly stated, the criteria for such judgments have to be inferred. They are the blanks which the reader is supposed to fill in, thus bringing his own criticism to bear. In other words, it is his own criticism to bear. In other words, it is his own criticism that constitutes the reality of the book. The novel, then, is not to be viewed as the mere reflection of a social reality, for its true form will only be revealed when the world it presents has, like all images, been refracted and converted by the mind of the reader. *Vanity Fair* aims not at presenting social reality, but at presenting the way in which such reality can be experienced. "To convey as strongly as possible the sentiment of reality" is Thackeray's description of this process, which he regarded as the function of the novel. If the sense of the narrative can only be completed through the cooperation

of the reader (which is allowed for in the text), then the borderline between fiction and reality becomes increasingly hazy, for the reader can scarcely regard his own participation as fictional. He is bound to look on his reactions as something real, and at no time is this conviction disputed. But since his reactions are real, he will lose the feeling that he is judging a world that is only fictional. Indeed, his own judgments will enhance the impression he has that this world is a reality.

How very concerned Thackeray was to confront the reader with a reality he himself considered to be real is clear from the passage already quoted, in which the narrator tells the reader that his object is to walk with him through the Fair and leave him "perfectly miserable" afterward. Thackeray reiterates this intention in a letter written in 1848: "my object . . . is to indicate, in cheerful terms, that we are for the most part an abominably foolish and selfish people . . . all eager after vanities . . . I want to leave everybody dissatisfied and unhappy at the end of the story—we ought all to be with our own and all other stories" [see excerpt dated September 3, 1848]. For this insight to take root in the reader, the fictional world must be made to seem real to him. Since, in addition, the reader is intended to be a critic of this world, the esthetic appeal of the novel lies in the fact that it gives him the opportunity to step back and take a detached look at that which he had regarded as normal human conduct. This detachment, however, is not to be equated with the edification which the moral novel offered to its readers. Leaving the reader perfectly miserable after his reading indicates that such a novel is not going to offer him pictures of another world that will make him forget the sordid nature of this one; the reader is forced, rather, to exercise his own critical faculties in order to relieve his distress by uncovering potential alternatives arising out of the world he has read about. "A man with a reflective turn of mind" is therefore the ideal reader for this novel. (pp. 102-14)

The aspect of the novel which we have discussed so far is the narrator's continual endeavor to stimulate the reader's mind through extensive commentaries on the actions of the characters. This indirect form of guidance is supplemented by a number of remarks relating directly to the expectations and supposed habits of the novel-reader. If the fulfillment of the novel demands a heightened faculty of judgment, it is only natural that the narrator should also compel the reader—at times quite openly—to reflect on his own situation, for without doing so he will be incapable of judging the actions of the characters in the novel. For this process to be effective, the possible reader must be visualized as playing a particular role with particular characteristics, which may vary according to circumstances. And so just as the author divides himself up into the narrator of the story and the commentator on the events in the story, the reader is also stylized to a certain degree, being given attributes which he may either accept or reject. Whatever happens he will be forced to react to those ready-made qualities ascribed to him. In this manner the double role of the author has a parallel in that of the reader, as W. Booth has pointed out in a discussion on the narrator:

> . . . the same distinction must be made between myself as reader and the very often different self who goes about paying bills, repairing leaky faucets, and failing in generosity and wisdom. It is only as I read that I become the self whose beliefs must coincide with the author's. Regardless of my real beliefs and practices, I must subordinate my mind and heart to the book if

I am to enjoy it to the full. The author creates, in short, an image of himself and another image of his reader; he makes his reader, as he makes his second self, and the most successful reading is one in which the created selves, author and reader, can find complete agreement.

Such an agreement can, however, be reached along widely differing lines, for instance through disagreement—i.e., a subtly instituted opposition between reader and narrator—and this is what happens in *Vanity Fair*.

When the narrator pretends to be at one with the reader in evaluating a certain situation, the reverse is usually the case. For instance, he describes an old but rich spinster who is a member of the great Crawley family, into which Becky is going to marry, in fulfillment of her social aspirations:

> Miss Crawley was . . . an object of great respect when she came to Queen's Crawley, for she had a balance at her banker's which would have made her beloved anywhere. What a dignity it gives an old lady, that balance at the banker's! How tenderly we look at her faults if she is a relative (and may every reader have a score of such), what a kind good-natured old creature we find her! . . . How, when she comes to pay us a visit, we generally find an opportunity to let our friends know her station in the world! We say (and with perfect truth) I wish I had Miss MacWhirter's signature to a cheque for five thousand pounds. She wouldn't miss it, says your wife. She is my aunt, say you, in an easy careless way, when your friend asks if Miss MacWhirter is any relative. Your wife is perpetually sending her little testimonies of affection, your little girls work endless worsted baskets, cushions, and footstools for her. What a good fire there is in her room when she comes to pay you a visit, although your wife laces her stays without one! . . . Is it so, or is it not so?

By using the first person plural, the narrator gives the impression that he is viewing through the reader's eyes the many attentions paid to the old lady with the large bank balance; for the reader such conduct is scarcely remarkable—indeed it is more the expression of a certain *savoir vivre*. By identifying himself with this view, the narrator seems to reinforce rather than to oppose this attitude, which is symptomatic of human nature. But in pretending merely to be describing 'natural' reactions, he is in fact seeking to trap the reader into agreeing with him—and as soon as this is accomplished, the reader realizes for himself the extent to which consideration of personal gain shapes the natural impulses of human conduct.

In this way, the difference between the reader and the characters in the novel is eliminated. Instead of just seeing through them, he sees himself reflected in them, so that the superior position which the narrator has given him over the pretences and illusions of the characters now begins to fade. The reader realizes that he is similar to those who are supposed to be the objects of his criticism, and so the self-confrontations that permeate the novel compel him to become aware of his own position in evaluating that of the characters. In order to develop this awareness, the narrator creates situations in which the characters' actions correspond to what the reader is tricked into regarding as natural, subsequently feeling the irresistible urge to detach

himself from the proceedings. And if the reader ignores the discreet summons to observe himself, then his critical attitude toward the characters becomes unintentionally hypocritical, for he forgets to include himself in the judgment. Thackeray did not want to edify his readers, but to leave them miserable, though with the tacit invitation to find ways of changing this condition for themselves.

This predominantly intellectual appeal to the mind of the reader was not always the norm in the realistic novel. In Dickens, for example, emotions are aroused in order to create a premeditated relationship between the reader and the characters. . . . He follows traditional practice insofar as he brings about a total involvement of the reader in the action. In Thackeray things are different. He is concerned with preventing any close liaison between reader and characters. The reader of *Vanity Fair* is in fact forced into a position outside the reality of the novel, though the judgment demanded of him is not without a tension of its own, as he is always in danger of sliding into the action of the novel, thereby suddenly being subjected to the standards of his own criticism. (pp. 114-17)

The reader is constantly forced to think in terms of alternatives, as the only way in which he can avoid the unambiguous and suspect position of the characters is to visualize the possibilities which they have not thought of. While he is working out these alternatives the scope of his own judgment expands, and he is constantly invited to test and weigh the insights he has arrived at as a result of the profusion of situations offered him. The

A photograph of Thackeray near the end of his life. The Granger Collection, New York.

esthetic appeal of such a technique consists in the fact that it allows a certain latitude for the individual character of the reader, but also compels specific reactions—often unobtrusively—without expressly formulating them. By refusing to draw the reader into the illusory reality of the novel, and keeping him at a variable distance from the events, the text gives him the illusion that he can judge the proceedings in accordance with his own point of view. To do this, he has only to be placed in a position that will provoke him to pass judgments, and the less loaded in advance these judgments are by the text, the greater will be the esthetic effect.

The "Manager of the Performance" opens up a whole panorama of views on the reality described, which can be seen from practically every social and human standpoint. The reader is offered a host of different perspectives, and so is almost continually confronted with the problem of how to make them consistent. This is all the more complicated as it is not just a matter of forming a view of the social world described, but of doing so in face of a rich variety of viewpoints offered by the commentator. There can be no doubt that the author wants to induce his reader to assume a critical attitude toward the reality portrayed, but at the same time he gives him the alternative of adopting one of the views offered him, or of developing one of his own. This choice is not without a certain amount of risk. If the reader adopts one of the attitudes suggested by the author, he must automatically exclude the others. If this happens, the impression arises, in this particular novel, that one is looking more at oneself than at the event described. There is an unmistakable narrowness in every standpoint, and in this respect the reflection the reader will see of himself will be anything but complimentary. But if the reader then changes his viewpoint, in order to avoid this narrowness, he will undergo the additional experience of finding that his behavior is very like that of the two girls who are constantly adapting themselves in order to ascend the social scale. All the same, his criticism of the girls appears to be valid. Is it not a reasonable assumption then that the novel was constructed as a means of turning the reader's criticism of social opportunism back upon himself? This is not mentioned specifically in the text, but it happens all the time. Thus, instead of society, the reader finds himself to be the object of criticism.

Thackeray once mentioned casually: "I have said somewhere it is the unwritten part of books that would be the most interesting." It is in the unwritten part of the book that the reader has his place—hovering between the world of the characters and the guiding sovereignty of the "Manager of the Performance." If he comes too close to the characters, he learns the truth of what the narrator told him at the beginning: "The world is a looking-glass, and gives back to every man the reflection of his own face." If he stands back with the narrator to look at things from a distance, he sees through all the activities of the characters. Through the variableness of his own position, the reader experiences the meaning of *Vanity Fair.* Through the characters he undergoes a temporary entanglement in the web of his own illusions, and through the demand for judgment he is enabled to free himself from it and to get a better view of himself and of the world.

And so the story of the two girls and their social aspirations forms only one aspect of the novel, which is continually supplemented by views through different lenses, all of which are trained on the story with the intention of discovering its meaning. The necessity for these different perspectives indicates that the story itself does not reveal direct evidence as to its meaning, so that the factual reality depicted does not represent a total reality. It can only become total through the *manner* in which it is observed. Thus the narrator's commentary, with its often ingenious provocations of the reader, has the effect of an almost independent action running parallel to the story itself. Herein lies the difference between Thackeray and the naturalists of the nineteenth century, who set out to convince their readers that a relevant 'slice of life' was total reality, whereas in fact it only represented an ideological assumption which, for all the accuracy of its details, was a manipulated reality.

In *Vanity Fair* it is not the slice of life, but the means of observing it that constitute the reality, and as these means of observation remain as valid today as they were in the nineteenth century, the novel remains as 'real' now as it was then, even though the social world depicted is only of historical interest. It is in the preoccupation with different perspectives and with the activation of the reader himself that *Vanity Fair* marks a stage of transition between the traditional and what we now call the 'modern' novel. The predominant aim is no longer to create the illusion of an objective outside reality, and the novelist is no longer concerned with projecting his own unambiguous view of the world onto his reader. Instead, his technique is to diversify his vision, in order to compel the reader to view things for himself and discover his own reality. The author has not yet withdrawn "to pare his fingernails," but he has already entered into the shadows and holds his scissors at the ready. (pp. 118-20)

> Wolfgang Iser, *"The Reader as a Component Part of the Realistic Novel: Esthetic Effects in Thackeray's 'Vanity Fair',"* in his The Implied Reader: Patterns of Communication in Prose Fiction from Bunyan to Beckett, *The Johns Hopkins University Press, 1974, pp. 101-20.*

JOHN SUTHERLAND   (essay date 1983)

[*Sutherland examines the concept of* Vanity Fair *as an historical novel. The critic focuses on the role of the novel's historical background and Thackeray's portrayal of events prior to, during, and following the Battle of Waterloo.*]

As Gordon Ray puts it, *Vanity Fair* signals clearly and early the kind of novel Thackeray will not write [see Additional Bibliography, 1955]; that is to say, the kind of novel the majority of his writing and reading contemporaries affect. Throughout *Vanity Fair,* and explicitly in Chapter VI, Thackeray makes the pharisaical assertion that he is not as other novelists are. But, as critics have come round to noticing, this *censor morum literariorum* would often seem to have a dangerously soft spot for his victims. *Vanity Fair,* for all its show of repudiation, frequently conforms to the fiction it purports to chastise. With its 'arsenical' ending (Becky poisoning Jos) *Vanity Fair* is as much of the Newgate genre as Lytton's sensational *Lucretia* (1846). K. J. Hollingsworth, the authority on this early shoot of crime fiction, goes so far as to claim that *Vanity Fair* is the Newgate novel to end Newgate novels [see Additional Bibliography]. So too, Matthew Rosa sees Thackeray's novel as the *summum genus* of silver forkery. It has certainly survived as the greatest of Waterloo novels (who now remembers the multitudinous works of W. H. Maxwell, or Lever's *Charles O'Malley,* the bestselling novel of 1841 which Thackeray put down hilariously with his spoof, **"Phil Fogarty. A Tale of the Fighting Onety-Oneth"**?). Thackeray was loftily contemptuous in his two reviews of *Coningsby,* affecting to find Disraeli's romance of power politics in the 'saloons of the mighty' obnoxious and absurd. (See also **"Codlingsby"**, by the dubiously eminent hand of 'B. de Shrewsbury, Esq.') But who is the arch villain of *Vanity Fair*? Why, Steyne, avowedly based on the Marquis of Hertford, the same aristocrat who modelled for the all-powerful Monmouth in *Coningsby*.

Thackeray, we may say, has a more complex and intimate relationship with the modes of fashionable fiction of the age than his apparently dismissive satirical manner would suggest. Neither is it easy to fix his feelings about the period in which *Vanity Fair* is principally set—the dissolute Regency and reign of George IV. Here, again, we detect in Thackeray mixed feelings of nostalgia and severe moral criticism. But at least we are on firm ground with the age's figurehead. Of all the historical figures whom Thackeray loathed, the bloated 'first gentleman of Europe' was the blackest of beasts. Even Marlborough in *Esmond* is treated with more tenderness than 'the great simulacrum'. Thackeray's ink boils whenever he describes Florizel. He often did describe him. More or less full-length portraits are found in *Punch* (see, particularly, *The Georges, Punch*, 11 October 1845), in *The Snobs of England* (see particularly Chapter II, 'The Snob Royal'), and—most vituperatively—in *The Four Georges* where the fourth lecture is devoted to an hour-long diatribe against the last Hanoverian. Thackeray's theme is simple. The Prince Regent represents the sink of corruption against which the present, Victorian, age is the wholesome reaction:

> He is dead but thirty years, and one asks how a great society could have tolerated him? Would we bear him now? In this quarter of a century, what a silent revolution has been working! how it has separated us from old times and manners! How it has changed men themselves!

In *Vanity Fair,* the fourth George is referred to frequently. He actually appears on stage twice (and speaks once) at the apogee of Becky's career, in the charade scene at Gaunt House and in the Drawing-room presentation in 1827—Becky's moment of glory. On neither occasion can Thackeray, with a satiric attack of commoner's humility, bring himself to describe, nor even name, the 'great personage':

> What were the circumstances of the interview between Rebecca Crawley, *née* Sharp, and her Imperial Master, it does not become such a feeble and inexperienced pen as mine to attempt to relate. The dazzled eyes close before that Magnificent Idea. Loyal respect and decency tell even the imagination not to look too keenly and audaciously about the sacred audience-chamber, but to back away rapidly, silently, and respectfully, making profound bows out of the August Presence. . . .

But while miming loyal blindness at the incandescence of the Hanoverian sun god, Thackeray insinuates his derogatory view of the Prince Regent and his dandified parasites with the namesake Osborne, and George Osborne's very fat friend, Jos. ('William' Dobbin is significantly named for the decent, if maladroit, 'Silly Billy'. One of his first royal edicts on coming to power in 1830 was to restrict the extravagant military uniforms so beloved of the 'padded booby' George. Dobbin embodies that 'change' Thackeray eulogizes in *The Four Georges*.)

Vanity Fair, then, is an historical novel. In particular the middle-class social life of the Regency (i.e. 1811-20) is reconstructed with apparently personal familiarity. Thackeray, however, was born in the year George was declared Regent. He could scarcely have been conscious of Waterloo, four years later. But the victory remained for him, as for many Victorians, the age's great event. Indeed, with the English 'saving revolution' of 1688, the American Revolution of 1776 and the French Revolution of 1789, Waterloo could easily be conceived as the most monumental occurrence in modern history. The close-run thing in Belgium was the foundation of Britain's century of triumph and the spread of imperial red over the world's map. And had the battle been lost, history would probably have delivered a bloody English Revolution, rather than the Reform Bill of 1832. Nor was it just the European balance of power which was rearranged by Waterloo. The victory had profound social consequences; it marked a moment of regeneration for the British aristocracy. Dandyism fell; Brummell was disgraced in 1815—a fall 'as great as Napoleon's' it was said. The Duke of Wellington was himself a 'dandy general' and led an army whose fashionable regiments fought brilliantly. (Hence, of course, the famous 'won on the playing fields of Eton' proverb.) Thackeray's 'silent revolution' can more plausibly be dated from 1815 than from 1830, when George died. Despite his monarchic radiance in mid-1820s *Vanity Fair*, George's last ten years were spent in almost total social eclipse and public unpopularity.

But despite his fascination with Waterloo, and its profound effect on the novel's five main characters and the world they inhabit, Thackeray's treatment of the battle is tantalizing in the highest degree. The suspense builds from Dobbin's 'the regiment's called away' to the Duchess of Richmond's eve of battle ball, from which officers slip out one by one, some to death, some to glory. We arrive to within earshot of the cannonade at Quatre Bras. But then, at the most teasing moment, we are denied satisfaction (which as thrill-seeking and *paying* readers we legitimately demand) by Thackeray's mock-humble and maidenish retraction:

> We do not claim to rank among the military novelists. Our place is with the non-combatants. When the decks are cleared for action we go below and wait meekly. We should only be in the way of the manoeuvres that the gallant fellows are performing overhead. We shall go no farther with the —th than to the city gate. . . .

As a matter of literary record, the reader indignantly retorts that Thackeray is an excellent military novelist. Any number of examples could be given; but for the nearest turn to Chapters IV, V, VI of *Barry Lyndon,* which Thackeray was writing virtually up to the month when he began *Vanity Fair*. This rollicking autobiography of an eighteenth-century soldier of fortune demonstrates the skill which Thackeray disowns, with infuriating modesty, at the start of the ninth number of *Vanity Fair*.

The novelist teases at other similarly exciting moments in the novel's action. He will not, for instance, conduct us into the penetralium of Gaunt House, giving us, instead, serpentine, 'Tomeavesian' gossip. What we crave is reliable eye-witness report of what's going on at this climax of Becky's English campaign. 'Great personages' pop up momentarily on the edge of *Vanity Fair*'s narrative, only to pop down. Thus the Duke of Wellington himself rides past the novel's heroes and heroines in a Brussels public park. It is his sole appearance and what does Thackeray give us? Peggy O'Dowd's chauvinist Hibernian irrelevance: 'the Wellesleys and Moloneys are related; but, of course, poor *I* would never dream of introjucing myself unless his Grace thought proper to remember our family tie.' The Duchess of Richmond's Brussels ball on 15 June—that conjunction of brilliant social glitter and carnage—is famous from at least two other literary presentations. But Thackeray's thinned account keeps off-stage Byron's 'fated Brunswick'; the glamorous hostess; the martial guest of honour and indeed all personages above field rank. *Charles O'Malley*, by contrast, has the hero on the most hob-nobbing terms with the ducal hostess and Commander-in-Chief. The 'great captain' in Lever's narrative actually 'introjuices' himself to the hero ('know your face well; how d'ye do?') with the lack of reserve which suggests that the brash Moloneys and the Wellesleys might indeed be related.

No more than with Thackeray's battlefield reticence can we put this omission down to authorial inadequacy. The depiction of Marlborough in *Esmond*, of Washington in *The Virginians* (and probably the imminent depiction of Paul Jones in the unfinished *Duval*) testify that Thackeray was as capable of rendering the portrait of a military chief as he was a military fight—when he chose to do so. *Vanity Fair*, then, is an historical novel in whose historical fabric there are gaping, but evidently carefully placed, holes. Thackeray gives us Regency London without Brummell, Byron or the Regent (how easy it would have been to send the Osborne-Sedley-Dobbin party to Vauxhall on the festive night of 13 July . . .); the great Brussels ball without grandees; the frontline in 1815 without Waterloo, Wellington or Napoleon; and, later in the novel, Weimar without Goethe. An historical novel, we might call it, without everything conventionally historical.

The artful anticlimaxes in *Vanity Fair*, and particularly the frustrating vacancy around Waterloo, are partly explained by Thackeray's determination to avoid romantic stereotype. Other factors are his ambivalence about British imperial might, and his circumstances while actually composing *Vanity Fair*. To take this last (and probably least) consideration: the novelist was evidently very pressed for time and space during the writing of the middle sections of his narrative. He intended to get the action to the battle at least two numbers earlier than he actually managed. But what with the marriages and all the falling-out between relatives in the 'hundred days' between March and June, *Vanity Fair* was fairly bursting at the seams. Of course, with a narrator as deft as Thackeray, pressure could not have been the deciding factor. In fact, as the Tillotsons point out, Thackeray's gimmick of telling the story of Waterloo indirectly through its domestic repercussions had been aired as early as 1842, during a visit to Charles Lever's house near Dublin. As reported, Thackeray 'seemed much inclined to "laugh at martial might"', although he still held to the idea that "something might be made out of Waterloo", even without the smoke and din of the action being introduced.' In Lever's *Charles O'Malley*, published in 1841, smoke and din is prominent and the hero observes the epic encounter at Napoleon's side.

Silence in the face of Waterloo was probably also encouraged by Thackeray's perplexity when he went to visit the battlefield, a few weeks before embarking on his novel. What he describes (in a **"Little Travels and Roadside Sketches"** piece, published in *Fraser's Magazine*, January 1845) is strikingly like Orwell's painful sense of British greatness, lying underfoot in the mouldering carcasses of the expendable 'natives' whose sweat, suffering and hunger is empire's real foundation. Walking over the place where thousands of uncommemorated private soldiers were cut, blasted or bled to death, Thackeray felt pride—as what Englishman would not. But he also felt ashamed of a

pride so paid for by others' sacrifice. Moreover, the strength of his mixed feelings induced a conviction that here was a place where one ought to be decently quiet, as in a church. . . . (pp. x–xvi)

One cannot know for certain, but I suspect that until he actually came to writing it, Thackeray kept open the important question of how he should treat Waterloo. We know, for instance, that he ordered an early copy of G. R. Gleig's *Story of the Battle of Waterloo* in June 1847. He evidently devoured the book when it arrived. . . . And he must have been struck by one feature in particular. Gleig, at one point, complains at the feeble powers of the 'pen and pencil' (a phrase Thackeray had used in his novel's title) when it comes to describing this battle of battles. Moreover, the most vivacious by far of Gleig's chapters are those dealing with the furious carnival in Brussels before Waterloo, and the stiltedly entitled chapter 'State of Feeling Where the War was not', which records, with lively detail, the wild currents of pessimism and rumour that swept over Brussels during the three days of fighting. Thackeray plundered these sections for *Vanity Fair*'s ninth number. With one notable exception . . . , the stodgier battle chapters seem to have inspired him less. It is possible, too, that having read Gleig, the novelist felt disinclined to compete with the military historian on his own ground.

To summarize. There is no need to retract, nor even to modify the assertion that *Vanity Fair* is an historical novel. But the sense of historical period and the passage of world-shaking events around the characters is conveyed obliquely. Most obviously by the introduction of minor period detail such as seven shilling pieces and hessian boots. Thackeray inserts material of this kind very judiciously—but it is a simple device, equivalent to theatrical 'props'. More complex is the way in which he throws up a London subtly different from that familiar to his 1848 readers. Thus, in Chapter XXII, Dobbin meets George at the old Slaughter's Coffee House (it stood in St. Martin's Lane until 1843) before his furtive marriage cum elopement with Amelia:

> It was about half an hour from twelve when this brief meeting and colloquy took place between the two captains. A coach, into which Captain Osborne's servant put his master's desk and dressing-case, had been in waiting for some time; and into this the two gentlemen hurried under an umbrella, and the valet mounted on the box, cursing the rain and the dampness of the coachman who was steaming beside him. 'We shall find a better trap than this at the chutch-door,' says he; 'that's a comfort.' And the carriage drove on, taking the road down Piccadilly; where Apsley House and St. George's Hospital wore red jackets still, where there were oil-lamps; where Achilles was not yet born; nor the Pimlico arch raised; nor the hideous equestrian monster which pervades it and the neighbourhood;—and so they drove down by Brompton to a certain chapel near the Fulham road there. . . .

Misfortune is predicted in the proverbially unlucky rain which falls on the bride and groom. Other predictions are contained in the urban landscape. This is early 1815. Apsley House, on Hyde Park Corner, was to become the residence of the Duke of Wellington, victor of Waterloo. Wyatt encased it in Bath stone in 1828 ('red coat' means literally 'brick' but also has a military significance here, as does St. George's Hospital, which is to care for Waterloo wounded). Wyatt was also responsible for the heroic statue of Wellington—weighing forty tons—erected at a cost of £30,000 by public subscription, in 1846. This monstrosity, as Thackeray and many of his contemporaries thought, also stood at the south-eastern entrance to the Park. (It figures, in caricature, on the serial cover. . . .) The Achilles statue was subscribed for (£10,000), and inscribed by 'the women of England.' It was also dedicated as a tribute to Wellington, and was raised in 1822. It was cast partly from enemy cannon captured at Waterloo.

This elaboration of scenic detail serves a number of purposes. It emphasizes how London has changed (omnibuses in 1846 serve this part of London; oil-lighting gave way to gas in 1828). More thematically, we feel the marriage threatened by futurity, a futurity centred on Waterloo. These monuments to victory are also, we sense, George's gravestone. Amelia, although she does not know it, will join the 'women of England' in making a widow's sacrificial donation.

In the above example, Thackeray dwarfs a major novelistic event (the marriage of two principal characters) by throwing gigantic historical shadows across their bridal path. Examples can be found where—for artistic effect—he does just the opposite. In the following, the dizzying European crisis of 1813-14 is shrunk by reflection in Amelia's preoccupation about her engagement to George:

> Meanwhile matters went on in Russell Square, Bloomsbury, just as if matters in Europe were not in the least disorganised. The retreat from Leipsic made no difference in the number of meals Mr. Sambo took in the servants' hall; the allies poured into France, and the dinner-bell rang at five o'clock just as usual. I don't think poor Amelia cared anything about Brienne and Montmirail, or was fairly interested in the war until the abdication of the Emperor; when she clapped her hands and said prayers,—oh, how grateful! and flung herself into George Osborne's arms with all her soul, to the astonishment of every body who witnessed the ebullition of sentiment. The fact is, peace was declared . . . Lieutenant Osborne's regiment would not be ordered on service. That was the way in which Miss Amelia reasoned. The fate of Europe was Lieutenant George Osborne to her. His dangers being over, she sang Te Deum. He was her Europe; her emperor: her allied monarchs and august prince regent. He was her sun and moon; and I believe she thought the grand illumination and ball at the Mansion House, given to the sovereigns, were especially in honour of George Osborne. . . .

There are ironies at work here. Amelia's naive perspective is both admirable and—in a very loaded word which Thackeray used about his 'Vanityfairians'—'selfish'. Soon she is to discover that the great convulsions of European history (which will ruin her father and slaughter her husband) are no respecters of girlish romance, however good and worthy the girl.

In the second half of the novel, after Waterloo, the historical background to *Vanity Fair* fades somewhat. As we follow the fortunes of Thackeray's characters over this most troubled of eras, one has the odd impression of social tranquillity. Perhaps,

as he looked back in a spirit of 'De Juventute', that is how it seemed to Thackeray in 1847-8. *Vanity Fair* is blind to Peterloo, corn law riots, industrial revolution, reform agitation. Even the great Bill itself sneaks in only parenthetically with a reference to Sir Pitt's disappointed retirement from public life after 1832. From the 1820s onwards, things gradually melt into the Victorian present. The novel's last numbers feature many fewer historical markers than their early counterparts. Imperceptibly, the historical texture merges if not into the 'now' of 1847-8, then into the Victorian reader's well-remembered yesterday. It is a fine and very moving effect in the novel. (pp. xvi-xx)

> *John Sutherland, in an introduction to* Vanity Fair: A Novel without a Hero *by William Makepeace Thackeray, Oxford University Press, Oxford, 1983, pp. vii-xlvi.*

ADDITIONAL BIBLIOGRAPHY

Baker, Joseph E. "*Vanity Fair* and the Celestial City." *Nineteenth-Century Fiction* 10, No. 2 (September 1955): 89-98.
> Explores the affinity between Thackeray's concept of Vanity Fair and similar ideas in the works of Bunyan, St. Augustine, and Plato.

Blodgett, Harriet. "Necessary Presence: The Rhetoric of the Narrator in *Vanity Fair*." *Nineteenth-Century Fiction* 22, No. 3 (December 1967): 211-23.
> A study of the narrator's rhetoric. Blodgett maintains that "*Vanity Fair* succeeds because of its narrator, not despite him."

Brophy, Brigid. "*Vanity Fair*." In her *Don't Never Forget: Collected Views and Reviews*, pp. 209-16. New York: Holt, Rinehart and Winston, 1967.
> A general introduction to the novel, focusing on its cynicism, historical perspective, and structure.

Carey, John. "*Vanity Fair*." In his *Thackeray: Prodigal Genius*, pp. 177-201. London: Faber & Faber, 1977.
> Discusses Thackeray's attitudes toward and methods of portraying the central characters in *Vanity Fair*. Carey also provides an extended comparison of the novel with *War and Peace*.

Chesterton, G. K. Introduction to *Masters of Literature: Thackeray*, by William Makepeace Thackeray, edited by G. K. Chesterton, pp. ix-xxxii. London: George Bell and Sons, 1909.
> Discusses the question of Thackeray's alleged cynicism in *Vanity Fair* and contrasts Becky's "energy without joy" with Amelia's simple if usually ineffectual goodness.

Cleall, Charles. *A Guide to "Vanity Fair."* Aberdeen: Aberdeen University Press, 1982, 143 p.
> An extended glossary providing definitions of words, names, and phrases in *Vanity Fair* with which the reader is unlikely to be familiar.

Colby, Robert A. "*Vanity Fair*; or, The Mysteries of Mayfair." In his *Thackeray's Canvass of Humanity: An Author and His Public*, pp. 231-73. Columbus: Ohio State University Press, 1979.
> Focuses on the literary and social environment in which Thackeray wrote *Vanity Fair*. Colby discusses both the influence on the novel of contemporary literature and the connection between *Vanity Fair* and Thackeray's writings for *Punch*.

Dooley, D. J. "Thackeray's Use of Vanity Fair." *Studies in English Literature, 1500-1900* XI, No. 4 (Autumn 1971): 701-13.
> Elaborates on Baker's study of Thackeray's use of Vanity Fair (see annotation above). Dooley assigns additional symbolic meanings to the Vanity Fair concept, exploring the religious and literary traditions with which it has been associated.

Drew, Elizabeth. "William Makepeace Thackeray: *Vanity Fair*." In her *The Novel: A Modern Guide to Fifteen English Masterpieces*, pp. 111-26. New York: Dell Publishing Co., A Laurel Edition, 1963.
A general discussion of the novel, touching upon its characters, satire, narrative, and description.

Ennis, Lambert. "At the Summit." In his *Thackeray: The Sentimental Cynic*, pp. 136-72. Evanston, Ill.: Northwestern University Press, 1950.
Describes the circumstances under which Thackeray composed *Vanity Fair* and also speculates upon possible real-life models for the characters in the novel.

Flamm, Dudley. *Thackeray's Critics: An Annotated Bibliography of British and American Criticism, 1836-1901*. Chapel Hill: University of North Carolina Press, 1966, 184 p.
An annotated guide to criticism of Thackeray's works through 1901.

Hagan, John. "*Vanity Fair:* Becky Brought to Book Again." *Studies in the Novel 7*, No. 4 (Winter 1975): 479-506.
Analyzes the problem of Thackeray's attitude toward Becky. Hagan argues that she cannot be seen as a sympathetic character.

Hannah, Donald. "'The Author's Own Candles': The Significance of the Illustrations to *Vanity Fair*." In *Renaissance and Modern Essays Presented to Vivian de Sola Pinto in Celebration of His Seventieth Birthday*, edited by G. R. Hibbard, pp. 119-27. London: Routledge and Kegan Paul, 1966.
Discusses the function of Thackeray's illustrations to *Vanity Fair*.

Harden, Edgar F. "The Fields of Mars in *Vanity Fair*." *Tennessee Studies in Literature* 10 (1965): 123-32.
Argues that warfare, whether it be literal, personal, or social, is the "underlying principle of life permeating all of Vanity Fair."

——. "The Discipline and Significance of Form in *Vanity Fair*." *PMLA* LXXXII, No. 7 (December 1967): 530-41.
Suggests that the structure of *Vanity Fair* derives from a series of thematic parallels running through the monthly parts.

Hollingsworth, Keith. "*Vanity Fair* and 'George de Barnwell'." In his *The Newgate Novel, 1830-1847: Bulwer, Ainsworth, Dickens, and Thackeray*, pp. 202-22. Detroit: Wayne State University Press, 1963.
Analyzes the relationship between *Vanity Fair* and the popular crime fiction of Thackeray's contemporaries.

Johnson, E.D.H. "*Vanity Fair* and *Amelia:* Thackeray in the Perspective of the Eighteenth Century." *Modern Philology* 59, No. 2 (November 1961): 100-13.
Explores the possible influence of Henry Fielding's novel *Amelia* on *Vanity Fair*.

Karl, Frederick R. "Thackeray's *Vanity Fair:* All the World's a Stage." In his *A Reader's Guide to the Nineteenth Century British Novel*, pp. 177-203. New York: Farrar, Straus and Giroux, The Noonday Press, 1965.
Probes the limitations of Thackeray's realism in *Vanity Fair*. Karl maintains that the novelist was unable to transcend a sentimental view of life and lacked a mature sense of tragedy.

Kettle, Arnold. "Thackeray: *Vanity Fair*." In his *An Introduction to the English Novel*. Vol. I, *To George Eliot*, pp. 156-70. Hutchinson's University Library, English Literature, edited by Basil Willey. London: Gainsborough Press, 1951.
Argues that the "artistic motive-force of *Vanity Fair* is Thackeray's vision of bourgeois society and of the personal relationships engendered by that society."

Kronenberger, Louis. "*Vanity Fair*." In his *The Polished Surface: Essays in the Literature of Worldliness*, pp. 201-16. New York: Alfred A. Knopf, 1969.
Examines *Vanity Fair* within the context of a literary tradition devoted to the portrayal and criticism of worldly life.

Mathison, John K. "The German Sections of *Vanity Fair*." *Nineteenth-Century Fiction* 18, No. 3 (December 1963): 235-46.

Asserts that Thackeray utilizes the German episodes of the novel to help clarify his thematic concerns rather than merely to conclude the narrative.

Moler, Kenneth L. "Evelina in Vanity Fair: Becky Sharp and Her Patrician Heroes." *Nineteenth-Century Fiction* 27, No. 2 (September 1972): 171-81.
Explores the possible connection between *Vanity Fair* and a type of eighteenth-century novel represented by Fanny Burney's *Evelina*. Moler argues that Becky interacts with men who are parodies of the virtuous heroes in Burney's novel.

Olmstead, Charles John. *Thackeray and His Twentieth-Century Critics: An Annotated Bibliography, 1900-1975*. New York: Garland Publishing, 1977, 249 p.
An annotated guide to twentieth-century criticism of Thackeray's works.

Paris, Bernard J. "The Psychic Structure of *Vanity Fair*." *Victorian Studies* X, No. 4 (June 1967): 389-410.
A psychological study of the implied author of *Vanity Fair*.

Pollard, Arthur, ed. *Thackeray: "Vanity Fair," A Casebook*. Casebook Series. London: Macmillan Press, 1978, 237 p.
Reprints selected nineteenth- and twentieth-century critical commentary on *Vanity Fair*. Pollard includes essays by such critics as Forster, Bell, Ray, Dyson, and Craig.

Quennell, Peter. "*Vanity Fair*." In his *Casanova in London*, pp. 97-109. New York: Stein and Day, 1971.
A general introduction to *Vanity Fair*. Quennell discusses the genesis of the novel, Thackeray's attitudes toward his female characters, and the differences between Dickens's and Thackeray's approach to literature.

Rawlins, Jack P. "*Vanity Fair:* The Structure of Self-Refutation." In his *Thackeray's Novels: A Fiction that Is True*, pp. 1-35. Berkeley and Los Angeles: University of California Press, 1974.
A three-part essay dealing with the ways in which *Vanity Fair* "can be described as a dramatic action, an apologue, or a satire."

Ray, Gordon N. "*Vanity Fair:* One Version of the Novelist's Responsibility." In *Essays by Divers Hands*, edited by Sir Edward Marsh, New Series, Vol. XXV, pp. 87-101. London: Oxford University Press, 1950.
Explores the origin of Thackeray's conception of his responsibility as a novelist in *Vanity Fair*.

——. *Thackeray: The Uses of Adversity, 1811-1846*. Vol. I; *Thackeray: The Age of Wisdom, 1846-1863*. Vol. II. New York: McGraw-Hill Book Co., 1955, 1958.
The definitive biography.

Sharp, Sister M. Corona. "Sympathetic Mockery: A Study of the Narrator's Character in *Vanity Fair*." *ELH* 29, No. 3 (September 1962): 324-36.
Argues that the narrator of *Vanity Fair* is a "sophisticated ironist" whose character provides the novel's unifying principle.

Sheets, Robin Ann. "Art and Artistry in *Vanity Fair*." *ELH* 42, No. 3 (Fall 1975): 420-32.
Suggests that art is one of the primary themes in *Vanity Fair*. Sheets examines the artistic abilities and attitudes toward art of various characters in the novel, as well as Thackeray's and the narrator's views on the subject.

Shillingsburg, Peter L. "The Printing, Proof-reading, and Publishing of Thackeray's *Vanity Fair:* The First Edition." *Studies in Bibliography* XXXIV (1981): 118-45.
A technical analysis of the various stages in the publishing process that produced the first edition of *Vanity Fair*.

Stevens, Joan. "Thackeray's *Vanity Fair*." *Review of English Literature* 6, No. 1 (January 1965): 19-38.
Argues that Thackeray's illustrations serve an important function in the novel that later publishers of the text have thwarted by omitting the designs or by placing them in inappropriate locations.

Sundell, M. G., ed. *Twentieth-Century Interpretations of "Vanity Fair": A Collection of Critical Essays.* Twentieth-Century Interpretations, edited by Maynard Mack. Englewood Cliffs, N.J.: Prentice-Hall, A Spectrum Book, 1969, 123 p.

    A collection of twentieth-century critical commentary on *Vanity Fair.* Sundell reprints essays by such critics as Van Ghent, Loofbourow, and Dyson.

Sutherland, J. A. "*Vanity Fair:* The Art of Improvisation." In his *Thackeray at Work,* pp. 11-44. London: Athlone Press, 1974.

    A study of Thackeray's compositional methods during the writing of *Vanity Fair.*

Talon, Henri A. "Thackeray's *Vanity Fair* Revisited: Fiction as Truth." In *Of Books and Humankind: Essays and Poems Presented to Bonamy Dobrée,* edited by John Butt, pp. 117-48. London: Routledge and Kegan Paul, 1964.

    A wide-ranging analysis of the novel, focusing on the Vanity Fair motif, the moral and social significance of various characters, and Thackeray's technique of variation and contrast.

Thackeray, William Makepeace. *Vanity Fair: A Novel without a Hero.* Edited by Geoffrey Tillotson and Kathleen Tillotson. London: Methuen & Co., 1963, 680 p.

    An authoritative text of the novel.

Tilford, John E., Jr. "The Degradation of Becky Sharp." *South Atlantic Quarterly* 58, No. 4 (Autumn 1959): 603-08.

    Argues that critics who have seen Becky as the heroine of *Vanity Fair* have failed to take into account Thackeray's consistent portrayal of her as degraded and evil.

Tillotson, Geoffrey, and Tillotson, Kathleen. Introduction to *Vanity Fair: A Novel without a Hero,* by William Makepeace Thackeray, edited by Geoffrey Tillotson and Kathleen Tillotson, pp. v-xxxix. London: Methuen & Co., 1963.

    A general introduction to *Vanity Fair,* focusing on Thackeray's avoidance of "surplus description," his range of subject matter, and his moral commentary.

Tillotson, Geoffrey, and Hawes, Donald, eds. *Thackeray: The Critical Heritage.* The Critical Heritage series, edited by B. C. Southam. London: Routledge & Kegan Paul, 1968, 392 p.

    Includes selected nineteenth-century critical commentary on *Vanity Fair.*

Wheatley, James H. "*Vanity Fair:* Postures of Wisdom" and "*Vanity Fair:* Wisdom and Art." In his *Patterns in Thackeray's Fiction,* pp. 56-75, pp. 75-93. Cambridge: M.I.T. Press, 1969.

    Two chapters, the first focusing on structural perspectives in *Vanity Fair,* the second concerned with Thackeray's concepts of psychology and causation.

Wilkenfeld, Roger B. "'Before the Curtain' and *Vanity Fair.*" *Nineteenth-Century Fiction* 26, No. 3 (December 1971): 307-18.

    A study of Thackeray's preface to *Vanity Fair* (see essay dated 1848).

Wilkinson, Ann Y. "The Tomeavesian Way of Knowing the World: Technique and Meaning in *Vanity Fair.*" *ELH* 32, No. 3 (September 1965): 370-87.

    Explores the important role that the secret knowledge of others plays in *Vanity Fair.*

Appendix

The following is a listing of all sources used in Volume 14 of *Nineteenth-Century Literature Criticism*. Included in this list are all copyright and reprint rights and acknowledgments for those essays for which permission was obtained. Every effort has been made to trace copyright, but if omissions have been made, please let us know.

THE EXCERPTS IN NCLC, VOLUME 14, WERE REPRINTED FROM THE FOLLOWING PERIODICALS:

The Academy, v. XXIX, January 23, 1886; v. LI, February, 1897.

American Literature, v. 26, November, 1954. Copyright © 1955, renewed 1982, Duke University Press, Durham, NC. Reprinted by permission.

The American Review, n.s. v. II, October, 1848.

The American Scholar, v. 30, Winter, 1960-61 for "The Case Becomes Less Strange" by Charles D. Aring. Copyright © 1961 by the author. Reprinted by permission of the author.

The Athenaeum, n. 135, May 29, 1830; n. 263, November 10, 1832; n. 387, March 28, 1835; n. 1085, August 12, 1848; n. 3038, January 16, 1886; n. 3297, January 3, 1891.

The Atlantic Monthly, v. 97, June, 1906; v. 109, May, 1912; v. 116, July, 1915./ v. 175, January, 1945. Copyright 1945, renewed 1972, by The Atlantic Monthly Company, Boston, MA. Reprinted by permission.

Beeton's Christmas Annual, No. 28, November, 1887.

Belgravia, v. VIII, May, 1869.

Blackwood's Edinburgh Magazine, v. II, March, 1818; v. III, July, 1818; v. XII, March, 1823; v. XXVII, May, 1830; v. CXXV, June, 1879; v. CXLVIII, August, 1890; v. CLII, August, 1892.

Blackwood's Magazine, v. CXCIII, April, 1913.

The Book Buyer, v. III, February, 1886.

The Bookman, London, v. XII, October, 1900.

The Bookman, New York, v. XV, May, 1902; v. XXXVII, March, 1913; v. LXXI, March, 1927.

The British Critic, v. IV, July, 1794; n.s. v. IX, April, 1818.

Broadway, n.s. v. I, September-December, 1868.

Bulletin of the Midwest Language Association, v. 6, Fall, 1973 for "The Third Self: 'Dracula', 'Strange Case of Dr. Jekyll and Mr. Hyde', and Merimee's 'Lokis'," by Irving Massey. Copyright © 1973 by The Midwest Modern Language Association. Reprinted by permission of the publisher and the author.

Canadian Literature, n. 1, Summer, 1959 for "A Gentlewoman of Upper Canada" by Carl F. Klinck; n. 51, Winter, 1972 for "Design and Purpose" by R. D. MacDonald; v. 51, Winter, 1972 for "Susanna Moodie and the English Sketch" by Carl Ballstadt. All reprinted by permission of the respective authors.

Catalyst, n. 3, Summer, 1967. © *Catalyst* 1967. Reprinted by permission.

The Century, v. XXIX, February, 1885; v. XXXV, April, 1888.

The Classical Journal, v. 14, December, 1918.

College English, v. 27, March, 1966 for "Dr. Jekyll and the Emergence of Mr. Hyde" by Masao Miyoshi. Copyright © 1966 by the National Council of Teachers of English. Reprinted by permission of the publisher and the author.

The Cornhill Magazine, v. XXXVIII, December, 1878.

The Criterion, v. VIII, July, 1929.

The Critic, New York, v. V, February 6, 1886.

The Critical Review, n.s. v. XXVII, September, 1799.

The Dalhousie Review, v. 39, Spring, 1959 for "The English Gentlefolk in the Backwoods of Canada" by Lloyd M. Scott; v. 54, Autumn, 1974 for "'Secrets of the Prison-House': Mrs. Moodie and the Canadian Imagination" by David Stouck. Both reprinted by permission of the publisher and the respective authors.

The Dial, v. II, October, 1841.

The Edinburgh Literary Journal, n. 84, June 19, 1830.

The Edinburgh Magazine and Literary Miscellany, n.s. v. II, March, 1818.

The Edinburgh Review, v. XL, March, 1824; v. LI, April, 1830; v. LXXXIII, April, 1846; v. XCI, April, 1850.

English Literature in Transition, v. 9, 1966 for "The Relationship of Theme and Art in 'The Strange Case of Dr. Jekyll and Mr. Hyde'" by Joseph J. Egan. Copyright © 1966 *English Literature in Transition*. Reprinted by permission of the publisher and the author.

Enlightenment Essays, v. IV, Spring, 1973. Copyright 1973 by *Enlightenment Essays*. Reprinted by permission.

Essays in Criticism, v. I, October, 1951; v. V, July, 1955.

Essays on Canadian Writing, n. 29, Summer, 1984. © Essays on Canadian Writing Ltd. Reprinted by permission.

The Examiner, n. 2112, July 22, 1848.

The Foreign Quarterly Review, v. I, July, 1827.

The Fortnightly Review, v. XXVI, October 1, 1876; n.s. v. XXXX, August, 1886.

Fraser's Magazine, v. II, November, 1830; v. LVIII, October, 1834; v. XI, May, 1835; v. XVIII, October, 1838.

Harper's New Monthly Magazine, v. LII, March, 1876.

The International Monthly Magazine, v. V, April 1, 1852.

Ironwood, Vol. 24, 1984. Copyright © 1984 by Ironwood Press. Reprinted by permission.

Journal of Canadian Studies/ Revue d'études canadiennes, v. X, August, 1975. Reprinted by permission.

Aldington, Richard. From *Literary Studies and Reviews*. The Dial Press, 1924.

Aldiss, Brian W. From *Trillion Year Spree: The History of Science Fiction*. Atheneum, 1986, Gollancz, 1986. Copyright © 1973, 1986 Brian Aldiss. Reprinted with the permission of Atheneum Publishers, Inc. In Canada by Victor Gollancz Ltd.

Allen, Gay Wilson. From *American Prosody*. American Book Company, 1935.

Amis, Kingsley. From *New Maps of Hell*. Victor Gollancz Ltd., 1960. Copyright © 1960 by Kingsley Amis. Reprinted by permission of Jonathan Clowes Ltd.

Atwood, Margaret. From *The Journals of Susanna Moodie*. Oxford University Press, Canadian Branch, 1970. © Oxford University Press 1970. Reprinted by permission.

Baker, Ray Palmer. From *A History of English-Canadian Literature to the Confederation: Its Relation to the Literature of Great Britain and the United States*. Cambridge, Mass.: Harvard University Press, 1920.

Barrett, Elizabeth, with Richard Hengist Horne. From "Walter Savage Landor," in *A New Spirit of the Age*. Edited by Richard Hengist Horne. Harper & Brothers, 1844.

Birkhead, Edith. From *The Tale of Terror: A Study of the Gothic Romance*. Constable & Company Ltd., 1921.

Blain, Virginia. From an introduction to *Mr. Sponge's Sporting Tour*. By R. S. Surtees, edited by Virginia Blain. Batsford Academic and Educational Ltd., 1981. Introduction and notes © University of Queensland Press, St. Lucia, Queensland 1981. All rights reserved. Reprinted by permission.

Bleiler, E. F. From an introduction to *Monsieur Lecoq*. By Émile Gaboriau, edited by E. F. Bleiler. Dover, 1975. Copyright © 1975 by Dover Publications, Inc. All rights reserved. Reprinted by permission.

Boulton, James T. From *The Language of Politics in the Age of Wilkes and Burke*. Routledge & Kegan Paul, 1963. © James T. Boulton 1963. Reprinted by permission of Routlege & Kegan Paul PLC.

Bradley, William. From *The Early Poems of Walter Savage Landor: A Study of His Development and Debt to Milton*. Bradbury, Agnes & Co., 1914.

Briggs, Julia. From *Night Visitors: The Rise and Fall of the English Ghost Story*. Faber & Faber, 1977. © 1977 by Julia Briggs. Reprinted by permission of Faber & Faber Ltd.

Brooks, Peter. From "Godlike Science/Unhallowed Arts': Language, Nature, and Monstrosity," in *The Endurance of Frankenstein: Essays on Mary Shelley's Novel*. Edited by George Levine and U. C. Knoepflmacher. University of California, 1979. Copyright © 1979 by The Regents of the University of California. Reprinted by permission of the publisher.

Brophy, Brigid, Michael Levey, and Charles Osborne. From *Fifty Works of English and American Literature We Could Do Without*. Stein and Day, 1968. Copyright © 1967 by Brigid Brophy, Michael Levey, Charles Osborne. All rights reserved. Reprinted with permission of Stein and Day Publishers.

Browning, Robert. From a letter in *Robert Browning and Julia Wedgwood: A Broken Friendship as Revealed by Their Letters*. Edited by Richard Curle. Frederick A. Stokes Company, 1937. Copyright, 1937, by Mary Wedgwood and John Murray. Renewed 1965 by Richard Curle.

Bush, Douglas. From *English Poetry: The Main Currents from Chaucer to the Present*. Methuen & Co. Ltd., 1952.

Cary, Joyce. From an introduction to *Mr. Sponge's Sporting Tour*. By R. S. Surtees. Oxford University Press, London, 1958. Reprinted by permission of the Literary Estate of Joyce Cary.

Chandler, Frank Wadleigh. From *The Literature of Roguery, Vol. II*. Houghton, Mifflin and Company, 1907.

Chesterton, G. K. From *Robert Louis Stevenson*. Dodd, Mead, 1928. Copyright, 1928 by Dodd, Mead & Company, Inc. Renewed 1955 by Oliver Chesterton. Reprinted by permission of A. P. Watt Ltd. on behalf of Miss D. E. Collins.

Chesterton, G. K. From *A Handful of Authors: Essays on Books & Writers*. Edited by Dorothy Collins. Sheed and Ward, 1953.

MacMurchy, Archibald. From *Handbook of Canadian Literature (English)*. William Briggs, 1906.

Macy, John. From *The Spirit of American Literature*. Doubleday, Page & Company, 1913. Copyright 1913 by Doubleday & Company, Inc. Copyright renewed 1940 by William M. Rockwell, as literary executor to the Estate of John Macy.

Malthus, T. R. From *An Essay on the Principle of Population; or, A View of Its Past and Present Effects on Human Happiness, Vol. II*. Third edition. J. Johnson, 1806.

McAlpin, Edwin A. From *Old and New Books as Life Teachers*. Doubleday, Doran, & Company, Inc., 1928.

McDougall, Robert L. From "Editor's Introduction," in *Life in the Clearings*. By Susanna Moodie, edited by Robert L. McDougall. Macmillan, 1959. © 1959 The Macmillan Company of Canada Ltd. All rights reserved. Reprinted by permission of the editor.

Mitford, Mary Russell. From *Recollections of a Literary Life; or, Books, Places, and People*. R. Bentley, 1852.

Miyoshi, Masao. From *The Divided Self: A Perspective on the Literature of the Victorians*. New York University Press, 1969. Copyright © 1969 by New York University. Reprinted by permission of the publisher.

Moodie, Susanna. From *Life in the Clearings versus the Bush*. Richard Bentley, 1853.

Moodie, Susanna. From *Roughing It in the Bush; or, Forest Life in Canada*. G. P. Putnam, 1852.

Moore, Helen. From *Mary Wollstonecraft Shelley*. J. B. Lippincott Company, 1886.

Moore, John. From *Country Men*. J. M. Dent & Sons, Ltd., 1935.

Morse, David. From *Romanticism: A Structural Analysis*. Barnes & Noble, 1982. © David Morse 1982. All rights reserved. Reprinted by permission of Barnes & Noble Books, a Division of Littlefield, Adams & Co., Inc.

Murch, A. E. From *The Development of the Detective Novel*. Philosophical Library, 1958. © A. E. Murch 1958. All rights reserved. Reprinted by permission.

Murry, John Middleton. From *Heroes of Thought*. Julian Messner, Inc., 1938. Copyright, 1938 by John Middleton Murry. Renewed © 1966 by Mary Middleton Murry. Reprinted by permission of Julian Messner, a division of Simon & Schuster, Inc.

Myers, F. W. H. From *Dr. Jeykll and Mr. Hyde*. By Robert Louis Stevenson. B. Tauchnitz, 1886.

Myers, Frederick W. H. From a letter in *Robert Louis Stevenson: The Critical Heritage*. Edited by Paul Maixner. Routledge & Kegan Paul, 1981. Copyright © the Estate of Paul Maixner 1981. Reprinted by permission of Routledge & Kegan Paul PLC.

Nabokov, Vladimir. From *Lectures on Literature*. Edited by Fredson Bowers. Harcourt Brace Jovanovich, 1980. Copyright © 1980 by the Estate of Vladimir Nabokov. Reprinted by permission of Harcourt Brace Jovanovich, Inc.

Neumann, Bonnie Rayford. From *Robert Smith Surtees*. Twayne, 1978. Copyright 1978 by Twayne Publishers. All rights reserved. Reprinted with the permission of Twayne Publishers, a division of G. K. Hall & Co., Boston.

Nitchie, Elizabeth. From *Mary Shelley: Author of "Frankenstein."* Rutgers University Press, 1953. Copyright 1953 by the Trustees of Rutgers College in New Jersey. All rights reserved. Reprinted by permission of the publisher.

Norman, Sylva. From "Mary Shelley: Novelist and Dramatist," in *On Shelley*. By Edmund Blunden, Gavin de Beer, and Sylva Norma. Oxford University Press, London, 1938.

Oberndorf, Clarence P. From "Foreword" and "Introduction: Dynamic Psychiatry and Holmes," in *The Psychiatric Novels of Oliver Wendell Holmes*. By Oliver Wendell Holmes, edited by Clarence P. Oberndorf. Columbia University Press, 1943.

O'Connor, Frank. From *The Mirror in the Roadway: A Study of the Modern Novel*. Alfred A. Knopf, 1956.

Osbourne, Katharine D. From a letter in *The True Stevenson: A Study in Clarification*. By George S. Hellman. Little, Brown and Company, 1925.

Ousby, Ian. From *Bloodhounds of Heaven: The Detective in English Fiction from Godwin to Doyle*. Cambridge, Mass.: Harvard University Press, 1976. Copyright © 1976 by the President and Fellows of Harvard College. All rights reserved. Excerpted by permission.

Parrington, Vernon Louis. From *Main Currents in American Thought, an Interpretation of American Literature from the Beginnings to 1920: The Romantic Revolution in America, 1800-1860, Vol. 2*. Harcourt Brace Jovanovich, 1927. Copyright 1927 by Harcourt Brace

Jovanovich, Inc. Renewed 1955 by Vernon L. Parrington, Jr., Louise P. Tucker, and Elizabeth P. Thomas. All rights reserved. Reprinted by permission of the publisher.

Peck, Harry Thurston. From *Studies in Several Literatures*. Dodd, Mead and Company, 1909.

Praz, Mario. From an introduction to *Three Gothic Novels*. Penguin English Library. Edited by Peter Fairclough. Penguin Books, 1968. Introductory essay copyright © Mario Praz, 1968. Reproduced by permission of Penguin Books Ltd.

Pritchett, V. S. From *The Living Novel & Later Appreciations*. Revised edition. Random House, 1964. Copyright © 1975 by V. S. Pritchett. All rights reserved. Reprinted by permission of Literistic, Ltd.

Proudfit, Charles L. From an introduction to *Landor as Critic*. Edited by Charles L. Proudfit. University of Nebraska Press, 1979. Copyright 1979 Charles L. Proudfit. Reprinted by permission of University of Nebraska Press.

Raleigh, Walter. From *On Writing and Writers*. Edited by George Gordon. Edward Arnold & Co., 1926.

Rashley, R. E. From *Poetry in Canada: The First Three Steps*. The Ryerson Press, 1958. Copyright © McGraw-Hill Ryerson Limited, 1958. All rights reserved. Reprinted by permission of the Literary Estate of R. E. Rashley.

Renwick, W. L. From "Jorrocks: A Conversation," in *Essays and Studies by Members of the English Association, Vol. XVII*. Edited by W. H. Hadow. Oxford at the Clarendon Press, Oxford, 1932.

Rhodenizer, V. B. From *A Handbook of Canadian Literature*. Graphic Publishers Limited, 1930.

Rieger, James. From an introduction to *Frankenstein; or, The Modern Prometheus: The 1818 Text*. By Mary Wollstonecraft Shelley, edited by James Rieger. Bobbs-Merrill, 1974, University of Chicago Press, 1982. © 1974, 1982 by James Rieger. All rights reserved. Reprinted by permission of The University of Chicago Press and the Literary Estate of James Rieger.

Roosevelt, Theodore. From an extract from a letter in *Robert Smith Surtees: A Critical Study*. By Frederick Watson. George G. Harrap & Co. Ltd., 1933.

Rossetti, Lucy Madox. From *Mrs. Shelley*. W. H. Allen & Co., 1890.

Saposnik, Irving S. From *Robert Louis Stevenson*. Twayne, 1974. Copyright 1974 by Twayne Publishers. All rights reserved. Reprinted with the permission of Twayne Publishers, a division of G. K. Hall & Co., Boston.

Sassoon, Siegfried. From *Memoirs of a Fox-Hunting Man*. Faber & Gwyer Limited, 1928. Copyright 1929, renewed 1956, by Siegfried Sassoon. Reprinted by permission of Stackpole Books/The K. S. Giniger Co. Inc. In Canada by Faber & Faber Ltd.

Shelley, Mary Wollstonecraft. From *Frankenstein; or, The Modern Prometheus*. H. Colburn and R. Bentley, 1831.

Shelley, Percy Bysshe. From a preface to *Frankenstein; or, The Modern Prometheus*. By Mary Wollstonecraft Shelley. Lackington, Hughes, Harding, etc., 1818.

Shelley, Percy Bysshe. From *The Revolt of Islam*. N.p., 1818.

Shelley, Percy Bysshe. From *The Letters of Percy Bysshe Shelley: Shelley in England, Vol. I*. Edited by Frederick L. Jones. Oxford at the Clarendon Press, Oxford, 1964.

Shields, Carol. From *Susanna Moodie: Voice and Vision*. Borealis Press, 1977. Copyright Borealis Press Limited, 1977. All rights reserved. Reprinted by permission.

Sitwell, Osbert. From *Penny Foolish: A Book of Tirades & Panegyrics*. Macmillan & Company Ltd., 1935.

Steel, Anthony. From *Jorrocks's England*. E. P. Dutton and Company Inc. Publishers, 1933.

Stephen, Leslie. From *Studies of a Biographer*. Duckworth and Co., 1902.

Stevenson, Robert Louis. From *Memories and Portraits*. C. Scribner's Sons, 1887.

Stevenson, Robert Louis. From *Across the Plains with Other Memories and Essays*. Charles Scribner's Sons, 1892.

Stevenson, Robert Louis. From *The Letters of Robert Louis Stevenson: 1880-1887, Alps and Highlands—Hyères—Bournemouth, Vol. II*. Edited by Sidney Colvin. Revised edition. Charles Scribner's Sons, 1911.

Stevenson, Robert Louis. From a letter in *The True Stevenson: A Study in Clarification*. By George S. Hellman. Little, Brown and Company, 1925.

Stewart, R. F. From *... And Always a Detective: Chapters on the History of Detective Fiction*. David & Charles, 1980. © R. F. Stewart 1980. All rights reserved. Reprinted by permission of the author.

Surtees, Robert Smith. From *Hawbuck Grange; or, The Sporting Adventures of Thomas Scott, Esq*. Longmans, Brown, Green & Longman, 1847.

Surtees, Robert Smith. From *Handley Cross*. Second edition. Methuen & Co. Ltd., 1854.

Surtees, Robert Smith. From *"Ask Mamma"; or, The Richest Commoner in England*. Bradbury, Agnew, & Co., 1858.

Surtees, Robert Smith. From "First Literary Efforts: The 'New Sporting Magazine' and 'The Horseman's Manual'," in *Robert Smith Surtees (Creator of "Jorrocks"): 1803-1864*. By Robert Smith Surtees and E. D. Cuming. Charles Scribner's Sons, 1924.

Sutherland, John. From an introduction to *Vanity Fair: A Novel without a Hero*. By William Makepeace Thackeray. Oxford University Press, Oxford, 1983. Introduction, introductory notes, bibliography, and chronology © John Sutherland 1983. All rights reserved. Reprinted by permission of Oxford University Press.

Sutherland, Ronald. From *Second Image: Comparative Studies in Quebec/Canadian Literature*. New Press, 1971. Copyright © 1971 by Ronald Sutherland. Reprinted by permission of Stoddart Publishing Co. Limited.

Swinburne, Algernon Charles. From "Landor," in *The Encyclopaedia Britannica: A Dictionary of Arts, Sciences, and General Literature*. Edited by T. S. Baynes. Ninth edition. A. C. Black, 1882.

Symonds, J A From *The Letters of John Addington Symonds: 1885-1893, Vol. III*. Edited by Herbert M. Schueller and Robert L. Peters. Wayne State University Press, 1969. Copyright © 1969 by Herbert M. Schueller and Robert L. Peters. All rights reserved. Reprinted by permission of the editors.

Thackeray, W. M. From a letter in *Robert Smith Surtees (Creator of 'Jorrocks'): 1803-1864*. By Robert Smith Surtees and E. D. Cuming. Charles Scribner's Sons, 1924.

Thackeray, William Makepeace. From *Vanity Fair: A Novel without a Hero*. Bradbury & Evans, 1848.

Thackeray, William Makepeace. From *The Letters and Private Papers of William Makepeace Thackeray: 1841-1851, Vol. II*. Edited by Gordon N. Ray. Cambridge, Mass.: Harvard University Press, 1945. Copyright, 1945 by Hester Thackeray Ritchie Fuller and the President and Fellows of Harvard College. Renewed 1973 by Belinda Norman Butler and Gordon H. Ray. Reprinted by permission of the Literary Estate of William Makepeace Thackeray.

Thomas, Clara. From "The Strickland Sisters," in *The Clear Spirit: Twenty Canadian Women and Their Times*. Edited by Mary Quayle Innis. University of Toronto Press, 1966. © University of Toronto Press, 1966. Reprinted by permission of the publisher.

Thomson, H. Douglas. From *Masters of Mystery: A Study of the Detective Story*. W. Collins Sons & Co., 1931.

Trollope, Anthony. From *Thackeray*. Macmillan & Co., Limited, 1879.

Tymms, Ralph. From *Doubles in Literary Psychology*. Bowes & Bowes, 1949.

Van Ghent, Dorothy. From *The English Novel: Form and Function*. Holt, Rinehart and Winston, 1953. Copyright 1953, renewed 1981, by Dorothy Van Ghent. Reprinted by permission of the Literary Estate of Dorothy Van Ghent.

Wagenknecht, Edward. From *Cavalcade of the English Novel: From Elizabeth to George VI*. Holt, Rinehart and Winston, 1943. Copyright 1943 by Henry Holt and Company, Inc. Copyright renewed, 1970 by Edward Wagenknecht. Reprinted by permission of the author.

Walling, William A. From *Mary Shelley*. Twayne, 1972. Copyright 1972 by Twayne Publishers. All rights reserved. Reprinted with the permission of Twayne Publishers, a division of G. K. Hall & Co., Boston.

Watson, Frederick. From *Robert Smith Surtees: A Critical Study*. George G. Harrap & Co. Ltd., 1933.

Whitmore, Clara H. From *Woman's Work in English Fiction: From the Restoration to the Mid-Victorian Period*. G. P. Putnam's Sons, 1910.

Woolf, Virginia. From *The Common Reader*. Harcourt Brace Jovanovich, 1925, L. & V. Woolf, 1925. Copyright 1925 by Harcourt Brace Jovanovich, Inc. Renewed 1953 by Leonard Woolf. Reprinted by permission of Harcourt Brace Jovanovich, Inc. In Canada by the Literary Estate of Virginia Woolf and The Hogarth Press.

Cumulative Index to Authors

This index lists all author entries in the Gale Literary Criticism Series and includes cross-references to other Gale sources. For the convenience of the reader, references to the *Yearbook* in the *Contemporary Literary Criticism* series include the page number (in parentheses) after the volume number. References in the index are identified as follows:

AITN: *Authors in the News*, Volumes 1-2
CAAS: *Contemporary Authors Autobiography Series*, Volumes 1-4
CA: *Contemporary Authors* (original series), Volumes 1-118
CANR: *Contemporary Authors New Revision Series*, Volumes 1-18
CAP: *Contemporary Authors Permanent Series*, Volumes 1-2
CA-R: *Contemporary Authors* (revised editions), Volumes 1-44
CLC: *Contemporary Literary Criticism*, Volumes 1-41
CLR: *Children's Literature Review*, Volumes 1-11
DLB: *Dictionary of Literary Biography*, Volumes 1-53
DLB-DS: *Dictionary of Literary Biography Documentary Series*, Volumes 1-4
DLB-Y: *Dictionary of Literary Biography Yearbook*, Volumes 1980-1985
LC: *Literature Criticism from 1400 to 1800*, Volumes 1-4
NCLC: *Nineteenth-Century Literature Criticism*, Volumes 1-14
SAAS: *Something about the Author Autobiography Series*, Volumes 1-2
SATA: *Something about the Author*, Volumes 1-44
TCLC: *Twentieth-Century Literary Criticism*, Volumes 1-22
YABC: *Yesterday's Authors of Books for Children*, Volumes 1-2

Bagnold, Enid 1889-1981.........CLC 25
See also CANR 5
See also CA 5-8R
See also obituary CA 103
See also SATA 1, 25
See also DLB 13

Bagryana, Elisaveta 1893-.........CLC 10

Baillie, Joanna 1762-1851.........NCLC 2

Bainbridge, Beryl
1933-.......CLC 4, 5, 8, 10, 14, 18, 22
See also CA 21-24R
See also DLB 14

Baker, Elliott 1922-................CLC 8
See also CANR 2
See also CA 45-48

Baker, Russell (Wayne) 1925-......CLC 31
See also CANR 11
See also CA 57-60

Bakshi, Ralph 1938-..............CLC 26
See also CA 112

Baldwin, James (Arthur)
1924-......CLC 1, 2, 3, 4, 5, 8, 13, 15,
17
See also CANR 3
See also CA 1-4R
See also SATA 9
See also DLB 2, 7, 33

Ballard, J(ames) G(raham)
1930-................CLC 3, 6, 14, 36
See also CANR 15
See also CA 5-8R
See also DLB 14

Balmont, Konstantin Dmitriyevich
1867-1943.................TCLC 11
See also CA 109

Balzac, Honoré de 1799-1850 ..... NCLC 5

Bambara, Toni Cade 1939- ....CLC 19
See also CA 29-32R
See also DLB 38

Banim, John 1798-1842
See Banim, John and Banim, Michael

Banim, John 1798-1842 and **Banim,
Michael** 1796-1874 .... NCLC 13

Banim, Michael 1796-1874
See Banim, John and Banim, Michael

Banim, Michael 1796-1874 and **Banim,
John** 1798-1842
See Banim, John and Banim, Michael

Banks, Iain 1954-............ CLC 34 (29)

Banks, Lynne Reid 1929-..........CLC 23
See also Reid Banks, Lynne

Banks, Russell 1940-..............CLC 37
See also CA 65-68

Banville, Théodore (Faullain) de
1832-1891.................. NCLC 9

Baraka, Amiri
1934-........CLC 1, 2, 3, 5, 10, 14, 33
See also Baraka, Imamu Amiri
See also Jones, (Everett) LeRoi
See also DLB 5, 7, 16, 38

Baraka, Imamu Amiri
1934-........CLC 1, 2, 3, 5, 10, 14, 33
See also Baraka, Amiri
See also Jones, (Everett) LeRoi
See also DLB 5, 7, 16, 38

Barbey d'Aurevilly, Jules Amédée
1808-1889.................. NCLC 1

Barbusse, Henri 1873-1935 .... TCLC 5
See also CA 105

Barea, Arturo 1897-1957 .... TCLC 14
See also CA 111

Barfoot, Joan 1946-..............CLC 18
See also CA 105

Baring, Maurice 1874-1945 ...... TCLC 8
See also CA 105
See also DLB 34

Barker, George (Granville)
1913-......................CLC 8
See also CANR 7
See also CA 9-12R
See also DLB 20

Barker, Howard 1946- ....CLC 37
See also CA 102
See also DLB 13

Barker, Pat 19??-.................CLC 32

Barnes, Djuna
1892-1982......... CLC 3, 4, 8, 11, 29
See also CANR 16
See also CA 9-12R
See also obituary CA 107
See also DLB 4, 9, 45

Barnes, Peter 1931-.................CLC 5
See also CA 65-68
See also DLB 13

Baroja (y Nessi), Pío
1872-1956................. TCLC 8
See also CA 104

Barondess, Sue K(aufman) 1926-1977
See Kaufman, Sue
See also CANR 1
See also CA 1-4R
See also obituary CA 69-72

Barrett, (Roger) Syd 1946-
See Pink Floyd

Barrett, William (Christopher)
1913-.......................CLC 27
See also CANR 11
See also CA 13-16R

Barrie, (Sir) J(ames) M(atthew)
1860-1937.................. TCLC 2
See also CA 104
See also YABC 1
See also DLB 10

Barrol, Grady 1953-
See Bograd, Larry

Barry, Philip (James Quinn)
1896-1949.................. TCLC 11
See also CA 109
See also DLB 7

Barth, John (Simmons)
1930-......CLC 1, 2, 3, 5, 7, 9, 10, 14,
27
See also CANR 5
See also CA 1-4R
See also DLB 2
See also AITN 1, 2

Barthelme, Donald
1931-...... CLC 1, 2, 3, 5, 6, 8, 13, 23
See also CA 21-24R
See also SATA 7
See also DLB 2
See also DLB-Y 80

Barthelme, Frederick 1943-........CLC 36
See also CA 114
See also DLB-Y 85

Barthes, Roland 1915-1980 ....CLC 24
See also obituary CA 97-100

Bassani, Giorgio 1916- ....CLC 9
See also CA 65-68

Bataille, Georges 1897-1962.......CLC 29
See also CA 101
See also obituary CA 89-92

Baudelaire, Charles
1821-1867................... NCLC 6

Baum, L(yman) Frank
1856-1919................... TCLC 7
See also CA 108
See also SATA 18
See also DLB 22

Baumbach, Jonathan 1933- ..... CLC 6, 23
See also CANR 12
See also CA 13-16R
See also DLB-Y 80

Baxter, James K(eir)
1926-1972................CLC 14
See also CA 77-80

Bayer, Sylvia 1909-1981
See Glassco, John

Beagle, Peter S(oyer) 1939- ....CLC 7
See also CANR 4
See also CA 9-12R
See also DLB-Y 80

Beard, Charles A(ustin)
1874-1948.................. TCLC 15
See also CA 115
See also SATA 18
See also DLB 17

Beardsley, Aubrey 1872-1898 ..... NCLC 6

Beattie, Ann 1947-.......CLC 8, 13, 18, 40
See also CA 81-84
See also DLB-Y 82

Beauvoir, Simone de
1908-1986....... CLC 1, 2, 4, 8, 14, 31
See also CA 9-12R
See also obituary CA 118

Becker, Jurek 1937- .... CLC 7, 19
See also CA 85-88

Becker, Walter 1950-
See Becker, Walter and Fagen, Donald

Becker, Walter 1950- and
Fagen, Donald 1948- ....CLC 26

Beckett, Samuel (Barclay)
1906-......CLC 1, 2, 3, 4, 6, 9, 10, 11,
14, 18, 29
See also CA 5-8R
See also DLB 13, 15

Beckman, Gunnel 1910-...........CLC 26
See also CANR 15
See also CA 33-36R
See also SATA 6

Becque, Henri 1837-1899 .... NCLC 3

Beddoes, Thomas Lovell
1803-1849.................. NCLC 3

Beecher, John 1904-1980 ....CLC 6
See also CANR 8
See also CA 5-8R
See also obituary CA 105
See also AITN 1

Author Index

Chulkov, Mikhail Dmitrievich
  1743-1792......................LC 2

Churchill, Caryl 1938- ....CLC 31
  See also CA 102
  See also DLB 13

Churchill, Charles 1731?-1764 ....LC 3

Chute, Carolyn 1947- .... CLC 39 (37)

Ciardi, John (Anthony)
  1916-1986................. CLC 10, 40
  See also CAAS 2
  See also CANR 5
  See also CA 5-8R
  See also obituary CA 118
  See also SATA 1
  See also DLB 5

Cimino, Michael 1943?- ....CLC 16
  See also CA 105

Clair, René 1898-1981 ....CLC 20
  See also Chomette, René

Clampitt, Amy 19??-..............CLC 32
  See also CA 110

Clare, John 1793-1864 ....NCLC 9

Clark, (Robert) Brian 1932- ......CLC 29
  See also CA 41-44R

Clark, Eleanor 1913-........... CLC 5, 19
  See also CA 9-12R
  See also DLB 6

Clark, John Pepper 1935- ....CLC 38
  See also CANR 16
  See also CA 65-68

Clark, Mavis Thorpe 1912?- ....CLC 12
  See also CANR 8
  See also CA 57-60
  See also SATA 8

Clark, Walter Van Tilburg
  1909-1971...................CLC 28
  See also CA 9-12R
  See also obituary CA 33-36R
  See also SATA 8
  See also DLB 9

Clarke, Arthur C(harles)
  1917-........ CLC 1, 4, 13, 18, 35
  See also CANR 2
  See also CA 1-4R
  See also SATA 13

Clarke, Austin 1896-1974........ CLC 6, 9
  See also CAP 2
  See also CA 29-32
  See also obituary CA 49-52
  See also DLB 10, 20, 53

Clarke, Austin C(hesterfield)
  1934-.......................CLC 8
  See also CA 25-28R

Clarke, Shirley 1925- ....CLC 16

Clash, The........................CLC 30

Claudel, Paul (Louis Charles Marie)
  1868-1955................ TCLC 2, 10
  See also CA 104

Clavell, James (duMaresq)
  1924-..................... CLC 6, 25
  See also CA 25-28R

Cleaver, (Leroy) Eldridge
  1935-......................CLC 30
  See also CANR 16
  See also CA 21-24R

Cleese, John 1939-
  See Monty Python
  See also CA 112, 116

Cleland, John 1709-1789 ....LC 2
  See also DLB 39

Clemens, Samuel Langhorne 1835-1910
  See Twain, Mark
  See also CA 104
  See also YABC 2
  See also DLB 11, 12, 23

Cliff, Jimmy 1948-................CLC 21

Clifton, Lucille 1936- ....CLC 19
  See also CLR 5
  See also CANR 2
  See also CA 49-52
  See also SATA 20
  See also DLB 5, 41

Clutha, Janet Paterson Frame 1924-
  See Frame (Clutha), Janet (Paterson)
  See also CANR 2
  See also CA 1-4R

Coburn, D(onald) L(ee) 1938-......CLC 10
  See also CA 89-92

Cocteau, Jean (Maurice Eugene Clement)
  1889-1963............CLC 1, 8, 15, 16
  See also CAP 2
  See also CA 25-28

Coetzee, J(ohn) M. 1940-...... CLC 23, 33
  See also CA 77-80

Cohen, Arthur A(llen) 1928- .... CLC 7, 31
  See also CANR 1, 17
  See also CA 1-4R
  See also DLB 28

Cohen, Leonard (Norman)
  1934-..................... CLC 3, 38
  See also CANR 14
  See also CA 21-24R
  See also DLB 53

Cohen, Matt 1942-................CLC 19
  See also CA 61-64
  See also DLB 53

Colegate, Isabel 1931-.............CLC 36
  See also CANR 8
  See also CA 17-20R
  See also DLB 14

Coleridge, Samuel Taylor
  1772-1834...................NCLC 9

Colette (Sidonie-Gabrielle)
  1873-1954..............TCLC 1, 5, 16
  See also CA 104

Collier, Christopher 1930-
  See Collier, Christopher and Collier, James
    L(incoln)
  See also CANR 13
  See also CA 33-36R
  See also SATA 16

Collier, Christopher 1930- and
  Collier, James L(incoln)
  1928-.......................CLC 30

Collier, James L(incoln) 1928-
  See Collier, Christopher and Collier, James
    L(incoln)
  See also CLR 3
  See also CANR 4
  See also CA 9-12R
  See also SATA 8

Collier, James L(incoln) 1928- and
  Collier, Christopher 1930-
  See Collier, Christopher and Collier, James
    L(incoln)

Collins, Hunt 1926-
  See Hunter, Evan

Collins, William 1721-1759 ....LC 4

Collins, (William) Wilkie
  1824-1889..................NCLC 1
  See also DLB 18

Colman, George 1909-1981
  See Glassco, John

Colton, James 1923-
  See Hansen, Joseph

Colum, Padraic 1881-1972.........CLC 28
  See also CA 73-76
  See also obituary CA 33-36R
  See also SATA 15
  See also DLB 19

Colvin, James 1939-
  See Moorcock, Michael

Colwin, Laurie 1945- .... CLC 5, 13, 23
  See also CA 89-92
  See also DLB-Y 80

Comfort, Alex(ander) 1920-.........CLC 7
  See also CANR 1
  See also CA 1-4R

Compton-Burnett, Ivy
  1892-1969........... CLC 1, 3, 10, 15,
                                34 (494)
  See also CANR 4
  See also CA 1-4R
  See also obituary CA 25-28R
  See also DLB 36

Comstock, Anthony
  1844-1915.................. TCLC 13
  See also CA 110

Condon, Richard (Thomas)
  1915-.................CLC 4, 6, 8, 10
  See also CAAS 1
  See also CANR 2
  See also CA 1-4R

Connell, Evan S(helby), Jr.
  1924-..................... CLC 4, 6
  See also CAAS 2
  See also CANR 2
  See also CA 1-4R
  See also DLB 2
  See also DLB-Y 81

Connelly, Marc(us Cook)
  1890-1980.....................CLC 7
  See also CA 85-88
  See also obituary CA 102
  See also obituary SATA 25
  See also DLB 7
  See also DLB-Y 80

Conrad, Joseph
  1857-1924..............TCLC 1, 6, 13
  See also CA 104
  See also SATA 27
  See also DLB 10, 34

Conroy, Pat 1945-................CLC 30
  See also CA 85-88
  See also DLB 6
  See also AITN 1

Constant (de Rebecque), (Henri) Benjamin
  1767-1830.................. NCLC 6

Author Index

Gee, Maurice (Gough) 1931- ....CLC 29
See also CA 97-100

Gelbart, Larry (Simon) 1923- ......CLC 21
See also CA 73-76

Gelber, Jack 1932- .... CLC 1, 6, 14
See also CANR 2
See also CA 1-4R
See also DLB 7

Gellhorn, Martha (Ellis) 1908- .....CLC 14
See also CA 77-80
See also DLB-Y 82

Genet, Jean 1910- ..... CLC 1, 2, 5, 10, 14
See also CA 13-16R

Gent, Peter 1942-.................CLC 29
See also CA 89-92
See also DLB-Y 82
See also AITN 1

George, Jean Craighead 1919- .....CLC 35
See also CLR 1
See also CA 5-8R
See also SATA 2

George, Stefan (Anton)
1868-1933................ TCLC 2, 14
See also CA 104

Gerhardi, William (Alexander) 1895-1977
See Gerhardie, William (Alexander)

Gerhardie, William (Alexander)
1895-1977.....................CLC 5
See also CANR 18
See also CA 25-28R
See also obituary CA 73-76
See also DLB 36

Gertler, T(rudy) 1946?- ...... CLC 34 (49)
See also CA 116

Gessner, Friedrike Victoria 1910-1980
See Adamson, Joy(-Friederike Victoria)

Ghelderode, Michel de
1898-1962................. CLC 6, 11
See also CA 85-88

Ghiselin, Brewster 1903- ....CLC 23
See also CANR 13
See also CA 13-16R

Giacosa, Giuseppe 1847-1906 ..... TCLC 7
See also CA 104

Gibbon, Lewis Grassic
1901-1935................... TCLC 4
See also Mitchell, James Leslie

Gibran, (Gibran) Kahlil
1883-1931................ TCLC 1, 9
See also CA 104

Gibson, William 1914- ....CLC 23
See also CANR 9
See also CA 9-12R
See also DLB 7

Gibson, William 1948- ...... CLC 39 (139)

Gide, André (Paul Guillaume)
1869-1951................ TCLC 5, 12
See also CA 104

Gifford, Barry (Colby)
1946-.................. CLC 34 (457)
See also CANR 9
See also CA 65-68

Gilbert, (Sir) W(illiam) S(chwenck)
1836-1911................... TCLC 3
See also CA 104
See also SATA 36

Gilbreth, Ernestine 1908-
See Carey, Ernestine Gilbreth

Gilbreth, Frank B(unker), Jr. 1911-
See Gilbreth, Frank B(unker), Jr. and
Carey, Ernestine Gilbreth
See also CA 9-12R
See also SATA 2

Gilbreth, Frank B(unker), Jr. 1911- and
Carey, Ernestine Gilbreth
1908-.......................CLC 17

Gilchrist, Ellen 1939- .... CLC 34 (164)
See also CA 113, 116

Giles, Molly 1942- .... CLC 39 (64)

Gilliam, Terry (Vance) 1940-
See Monty Python
See also CA 108, 113

Gilliatt, Penelope (Ann Douglass)
1932-............... CLC 2, 10, 13
See also CA 13-16R
See also DLB 14
See also AITN 2

Gilman, Charlotte (Anna) Perkins (Stetson)
1860-1935................... TCLC 9
See also CA 106

Gilmour, David 1944-
See Pink Floyd

Gilroy, Frank D(aniel) 1925-........CLC 2
See also CA 81-84
See also DLB 7

Ginsberg, Allen
1926-.........CLC 1, 2, 3, 4, 6, 13, 36
See also CANR 2
See also CA 1-4R
See also DLB 5, 16
See also AITN 1

Ginzburg, Natalia 1916-........ CLC 5, 11
See also CA 85-88

Giono, Jean 1895-1970........ CLC 4, 11
See also CANR 2
See also CA 45-48
See also obituary CA 29-32R

Giovanni, Nikki 1943-........ CLC 2, 4, 19
See also CLR 6
See also CANR 18
See also CA 29-32R
See also SATA 24
See also DLB 5
See also AITN 1

Giovene, Andrea 1904-.............CLC 7
See also CA 85-88

Gippius, Zinaida (Nikolayevna) 1869-1945
See also Hippius, Zinaida
See also CA 106

Giraudoux, (Hippolyte) Jean
1882-1944................. TCLC 2, 7
See also CA 104

Gironella, José María 1917-........CLC 11
See also CA 101

Gissing, George (Robert)
1857-1903................... TCLC 3
See also CA 105
See also DLB 18

Glanville, Brian (Lester) 1931- ......CLC 6
See also CANR 3
See also CA 5-8R
See also DLB 15
See also SATA 42

Glasgow, Ellen (Anderson Gholson)
1873?-1945................ TCLC 2, 7
See also CA 104
See also DLB 9, 12

Glassco, John 1909-1981 ....CLC 9
See also CANR 15
See also CA 13-16R
See also obituary CA 102

Glasser, Ronald J. 1940?- ....CLC 37

Glissant, Edouard 1928-...........CLC 10

Gloag, Julian 1930-...............CLC 40
See also CANR 10
See also CA 65-68
See also AITN 1

Glück, Louise 1943- .... CLC 7, 22
See also CA 33-36R
See also DLB 5

Godard, Jean-Luc 1930-...........CLC 20
See also CA 93-96

Godwin, Gail 1937-.......CLC 5, 8, 22, 31
See also CANR 15
See also CA 29-32R
See also DLB 6

Godwin, William 1756-1836 ..... NCLC 14
See also DLB 39

Goethe, Johann Wolfgang von
1749-1832.................... NCLC 4

Gogarty, Oliver St. John
1878-1957................. TCLC 15
See also CA 109
See also DLB 15, 19

Gogol, Nikolai (Vasilyevich)
1809-1852.................... NCLC 5

Gökçeli, Yasar Kemal 1923-
See Kemal, Yashar

Gold, Herbert 1924- .... CLC 4, 7, 14
See also CANR 17
See also CA 9-12R
See also DLB 2
See also DLB-Y 81

Goldbarth, Albert 1948-........ CLC 5, 38
See also CANR 6
See also CA 53-56

Goldberg, Anatol 19??-...... CLC 34 (433)

Golding, William (Gerald)
1911-........CLC 1, 2, 3, 8, 10, 17, 27
See also CANR 13
See also CA 5-8R
See also DLB 15

Goldman, Emma 1869-1940 ..... TCLC 13
See also CA 110

Goldman, William (W.) 1931-.......CLC 1
See also CA 9-12R
See also DLB 44

Goldmann, Lucien 1913-1970 ......CLC 24
See also CAP 2
See also CA 25-28

Goldoni, Carlo 1707-1793 .... LC 4

Goldsberry, Steven 1949- ..... CLC 34 (54)

Goldsmith, Oliver 1728?-1774....... LC 2
See also SATA 26
See also DLB 39

Author Index

Author Index

Author Index

Author Index

North, Andrew 1912-
See Norton, Andre

North, Christopher 1785-1854
See Wilson, John

Norton, Alice Mary 1912-
See Norton, Andre
See also CANR 2
See also CA 1-4R
See also SATA 1, 43

Norton, Andre 1912-..............CLC 12
See also Norton, Mary Alice
See also DLB 8

Norway, Nevil Shute 1899-1960
See Shute (Norway), Nevil
See also CA 102
See also obituary CA 93-96

Nossack, Hans Erich 1901-1978 .....CLC 6
See also CA 93-96
See also obituary CA 85-88

Nova, Craig 1945-............. CLC 7, 31
See also CANR 2
See also CA 45-48

Novalis 1772-1801 .... NCLC 13

Nowlan, Alden (Albert) 1933-......CLC 15
See also CANR 5
See also CA 9-12R
See also DLB 53

Noyes, Alfred 1880-1958 .... TCLC 7
See also CA 104
See also DLB 20

Nunn, Kem 19??-............ CLC 34 (94)

Nye, Robert 1939-................CLC 13
See also CA 33-36R
See also SATA 6
See also DLB 14

Nyro, Laura 1947-................CLC 17

Oates, Joyce Carol
1938-.....CLC 1, 2, 3, 6, 9, 11, 15, 19,
33
See also CA 5-8R
See also DLB 2, 5
See also DLB-Y 81
See also AITN 1

O'Brien, Darcy 1939-..............CLC 11
See also CANR 8
See also CA 21-24R

O'Brien, Edna
1932-............. CLC 3, 5, 8, 13, 36
See also CANR 6
See also CA 1-4R
See also DLB 14

O'Brien, Flann
1911-1966......... CLC 1, 4, 5, 7, 10
See also O Nuallain, Brian

O'Brien, Richard 19??-............CLC 17

O'Brien, (William) Tim(othy)
1946-.................. CLC 7, 19, 40
See also CA 85-88
See also DLB-Y 80

O'Casey, Sean
1880-1964........ CLC 1, 5, 9, 11, 15
See also CA 89-92
See also DLB 10

Ochs, Phil 1940-1976 ....CLC 17
See also obituary CA 65-68

O'Connor, Edwin (Greene)
1918-1968...................CLC 14
See also CA 93-96
See also obituary CA 25-28R

O'Connor, (Mary) Flannery
1925-1964...... CLC 1, 2, 3, 6, 10, 13,
15, 21
See also CANR 3
See also CA 1-4R
See also DLB 2
See also DLB-Y 80

O'Connor, Frank
1903-1966............... CLC 14, 23
See also O'Donovan, Michael (John)

O'Dell, Scott 1903- ....CLC 30
See also CLR 1
See also CANR 12
See also CA 61-64
See also SATA 12

Odets, Clifford 1906-1963 ...... CLC 2, 28
See also CA 85-88
See also DLB 7, 26

O'Donovan, Michael (John) 1903-1966
See O'Connor, Frank
See also CA 93-96

Ōe, Kenzaburō 1935- .... CLC 10, 36
See also CA 97-100

O'Faolain, Julia 1932- .... CLC 6, 19
See also CAAS 2
See also CANR 12
See also CA 81-84
See also DLB 14

O'Faoláin, Seán
1900-................CLC 1, 7, 14, 32
See also CANR 12
See also CA 61-64
See also DLB 15

O'Flaherty, Liam
1896-1984............ CLC 5, 34 (355)
See also CA 101
See also obituary CA 113
See also DLB 36
See also DLB-Y 84

O'Grady, Standish (James)
1846-1928................... TCLC 5
See also CA 104

O'Hara Family
See Banim, John and Banim, Michael

O'Hara, Frank
1926-1966............... CLC 2, 5, 13
See also CA 9-12R
See also obituary CA 25-28R
See also DLB 5, 16

O'Hara, John (Henry)
1905-1970......... CLC 1, 2, 3, 6, 11
See also CA 5-8R
See also obituary CA 25-28R
See also DLB 9
See also DLB-DS 2

O'Hehir, Diana 1922-.............CLC 41
See also CA 93-96

Okigbo, Christopher (Ifenayichukwu)
1932-1967...................CLC 25
See also CA 77-80

Olds, Sharon 1942- ...... CLC 32, 39 (186)
See also CANR 18
See also CA 101

Olesha, Yuri (Karlovich)
1899-1960...................CLC 8
See also CA 85-88

Oliphant, Margaret (Oliphant Wilson)
1828-1897................. NCLC 11
See also DLB 18

Oliver, Mary 1935- ...... CLC 19, 34 (246)
See also CANR 9
See also CA 21-24R
See also DLB 5

Olivier, (Baron) Laurence (Kerr)
1907-.......................CLC 20
See also CA 111

Olsen, Tillie 1913-............. CLC 4, 13
See also CANR 1
See also CA 1-4R
See also DLB 28
See also DLB-Y 80

Olson, Charles (John)
1910-1970....... CLC 1, 2, 5, 6, 9, 11,
29
See also CAP 1
See also CA 15-16
See also obituary CA 25-28R
See also DLB 5, 16

Olson, Theodore 1937-
See Olson, Toby

Olson, Toby 1937-................CLC 28
See also CANR 9
See also CA 65-68

Ondaatje, (Philip) Michael
1943-................... CLC 14, 29
See also CA 77-80

Oneal, Elizabeth 1934-
See Oneal, Zibby
See also CA 106
See also SATA 30

Oneal, Zibby 1934-................CLC 30
See also Oneal, Elizabeth

O'Neill, Eugene (Gladstone)
1888-1953................ TCLC 1, 6
See also CA 110
See also AITN 1
See also DLB 7

Onetti, Juan Carlos 1909- ...... CLC 7, 10
See also CA 85-88

O'Nolan, Brian 1911-1966
See O'Brien, Flann

O Nuallain, Brian 1911-1966
See O'Brien, Flann
See also CAP 2
See also CA 21-22
See also obituary CA 25-28R

Oppen, George
1908-1984........CLC 7, 13, 34 (358)
See also CANR 8
See also CA 13-16R
See also obituary CA 113
See also DLB 5

Orlovitz, Gil 1918-1973 ....CLC 22
See also CA 77-80
See also obituary CA 45-48
See also DLB 2, 5

Ortega y Gasset, José
1883-1955................... TCLC 9
See also CA 106

Author Index

Author Index

Valera (y Acalá-Galiano), Juan
    1824-1905................. TCLC 10
    See also CA 106

Valéry, Paul (Ambroise Toussaint Jules)
    1871-1945................ TCLC 4, 15
    See also CA 104

Valle-Inclán (y Montenegro), Ramón (María)
    del 1866-1936 .... TCLC 5
    See also CA 106

Vallejo, César (Abraham)
    1892-1938.................. TCLC 3
    See also CA 105

Van Ash, Cay 1918- .... CLC 34 (118)

Vance, Jack 1916?-................CLC 35
    See also DLB 8

Vance, John Holbrook 1916?-
    See Vance, Jack
    See also CANR 17
    See also CA 29-32R

Van Den Bogarde, Derek (Jules Gaspard
    Ulric) Niven 1921-
    See Bogarde, Dirk
    See also CA 77-80

Vanderhaeghe, Guy 1951- ....CLC 41
    See also CA 113

Van der Post, Laurens (Jan)
    1906-.........................CLC 5
    See also CA 5-8R

Van Doren, Carl (Clinton)
    1885-1950................. TCLC 18
    See also CA 111

Van Doren, Mark
    1894-1972................ CLC 6, 10
    See also CANR 3
    See also CA 1-4R
    See also obituary CA 37-40R
    See also DLB 45

Van Druten, John (William)
    1901-1957................... TCLC 2
    See also CA 104
    See also DLB 10

Van Duyn, Mona 1921- .... CLC 3, 7
    See also CANR 7
    See also CA 9-12R
    See also DLB 5

Van Itallie, Jean-Claude 1936- ......CLC 3
    See also CAAS 2
    See also CANR 1
    See also CA 45-48
    See also DLB 7

Van Peebles, Melvin 1932-...... CLC 2, 20
    See also CA 85-88

Van Vechten, Carl 1880-1964......CLC 33
    See also obituary CA 89-92
    See also DLB 4, 9

Van Vogt, A(lfred) E(lton)
    1912-.........................CLC 1
    See also CA 21-24R
    See also SATA 14
    See also DLB 8

Varda, Agnès 1928-...............CLC 16
    See also CA 116

Vargas Llosa, (Jorge) Mario (Pedro)
    1936-......... CLC 3, 6, 9, 10, 15, 31
    See also CANR 18
    See also CA 73-76

Vassilikos, Vassilis 1933- .... CLC 4, 8
    See also CA 81-84

Verga, Giovanni 1840-1922 .... TCLC 3
    See also CA 104

Verhaeren, Émile (Adolphe Gustave)
    1855-1916.................. TCLC 12
    See also CA 109

Verlaine, Paul (Marie)
    1844-1896................... NCLC 2

Verne, Jules (Gabriel)
    1828-1905.................. TCLC 6
    See also CA 110
    See also SATA 21

Very, Jones 1813-1880 .... NCLC 9
    See also DLB 1

Vian, Boris 1920-1959 .... TCLC 9
    See also CA 106

Viaud, (Louis Marie) Julien 1850-1923
    See Loti, Pierre
    See also CA 107

Vicker, Angus 1916-
    See Felsen, Henry Gregor

Vidal, Eugene Luther, Jr. 1925-
    See Vidal, Gore

Vidal, Gore
    1925-........CLC 2, 4, 6, 8, 10, 22, 33
    See also CANR 13
    See also CA 5-8R
    See also DLB 6
    See also AITN 1

Viereck, Peter (Robert Edwin)
    1916-.........................CLC 4
    See also CANR 1
    See also CA 1-4R
    See also DLB 5

Vigny, Alfred (Victor) de
    1797-1863................... NCLC 7

Villiers de l'Isle Adam, Jean Marie Mathias
    Philippe Auguste, Comte de,
    1838-1889.................. NCLC 3

Vinge, Joan (Carol) D(ennison)
    1948-........................CLC 30
    See also CA 93-96
    See also SATA 36

Visconti, Luchino 1906-1976.......CLC 16
    See also CA 81-84
    See also obituary CA 65-68

Vittorini, Elio 1908-1966 ..... CLC 6, 9, 14
    See also obituary CA 25-28R

Vizinczey, Stephen 1933- ....CLC 40

Vliet, R(ussell) G. 1929-...........CLC 22
    See also CANR 18
    See also CA 37-40R

Voigt, Cynthia 1942-..............CLC 30
    See also CANR 18
    See also CA 106
    See also SATA 33

Voinovich, Vladimir (Nikolaevich)
    1932-.......................CLC 10
    See also CA 81-84

Von Daeniken, Erich 1935-
    See Von Däniken, Erich
    See also CANR 17
    See also CA 37-40R
    See also AITN 1

Von Däniken, Erich 1935-.........CLC 30
    See also Von Daeniken, Erich

Vonnegut, Kurt, Jr.
    1922-......CLC 1, 2, 3, 4, 5, 8, 12, 22,
                              40
    See also CANR 1
    See also CA 1-4R
    See also DLB 2, 8
    See also DLB-Y 80
    See also DLB-DS 3
    See also AITN 1

Vorster, Gordon 1924- ...... CLC 34 (121)

Voznesensky, Andrei 1933- ..... CLC 1, 15
    See also CA 89-92

Waddington, Miriam 1917- ....CLC 28
    See also CANR 12
    See also CA 21-24R

Wagman, Fredrica 1937- ....CLC 7
    See also CA 97-100

Wagner, Richard 1813-1883 ...... NCLC 9

Wagoner, David (Russell)
    1926-.................. CLC 3, 5, 15
    See also CAAS 3
    See also CANR 2
    See also CA 1-4R
    See also SATA 14
    See also DLB 5

Wahlöö, Per 1926-1975 ....CLC 7
    See also CA 61-64

Wahlöö, Peter 1926-1975
    See Wahlöö, Per

Wain, John (Barrington)
    1925-................. CLC 2, 11, 15
    See also CAAS 4
    See also CA 5-8R
    See also DLB 15, 27

Wajda, Andrzej 1926-..............CLC 16
    See also CA 102

Wakefield, Dan 1932-..............CLC 7
    See also CA 21-24R

Wakoski, Diane
    1937-........... CLC 2, 4, 7, 9, 11, 40
    See also CAAS 1
    See also CANR 9
    See also CA 13-16R
    See also DLB 5

Walcott, Derek (Alton)
    1930- .... CLC 2, 4, 9, 14, 25
    See also CA 89-92
    See also DLB-Y 81

Waldman, Anne 1945- ....CLC 7
    See also CA 37-40R
    See also DLB 16

Waldo, Edward Hamilton 1918-
    See Sturgeon, Theodore (Hamilton)

Walker, Alice
    1944-............ CLC 5, 6, 9, 19, 27
    See also CANR 9
    See also CA 37-40R
    See also SATA 31
    See also DLB 6, 33

Walker, David Harry 1911-........CLC 14
    See also CANR 1
    See also CA 1-4R
    See also SATA 8

Author Index

Author Index

Cumulative Index to Nationalities

AMERICAN
Alcott, Amos Bronson 1
Alcott, Louisa May 6
Alger, Jr., Horatio 8
Allston, Washington 2
Bellamy, Edward 4
Bird, Robert Montgomery 1
Brackenridge, Hugh Henry 7
Brown, William Wells 2
Bryant, William Cullen 6
Child, Lydia Maria 6
Cooke, John Esten 5
Cooper, James Fenimore 1
Crockett, David 8
Douglass, Frederick 7
Dunlap, William 2
Dwight, Timothy 13
Emerson, Ralph Waldo 1
Field, Eugene 3
Frederic, Harold 10
Freneau, Philip Morin 1
Fuller, Margaret 5
Hammon, Jupiter 5
Hawthorne, Nathaniel 2, 10
Holmes, Oliver Wendell 14
Irving, Washington 2
Jefferson, Thomas 11
Kennedy, John Pendleton 2
Lanier, Sidney 6
Lazarus, Emma 8
Longfellow, Henry
  Wadsworth 2
Lowell, James Russell 2
Melville, Herman 3, 12
Parkman, Francis 12
Paulding, James Kirke 2
Poe, Edgar Allan 1
Rowson, Susanna Haswell 5
Simms, William Gilmore 3

Stowe, Harriet Beecher 3
Thoreau, Henry David 7
Tyler, Royall 3
Very, Jones 9
Warren, Mercy Otis 13
Whitman, Walt 4
Whittier, John Greenleaf 8

AUSTRALIAN
Kendall, Henry 12

AUSTRIAN
Grillparzer, Franz 1

CANADIAN
Crawford, Isabella
  Valancy 12
Moodie, Susanna 14

DANISH
Andersen, Hans Christian 7
Grundtvig, Nicolai Frederik
  Severin 1

ENGLISH
Ainsworth, William
  Harrison 13
Arnold, Matthew 6
Austen, Jane 1, 13
Bagehot, Walter 10
Beardsley, Aubrey 6
Beddoes, Thomas Lovell 3
Blake, William 13
Borrow, George 9
Brontë, Anne 4
Brontë, Charlotte 3, 8
Browning, Elizabeth Barrett 1
Bulwer-Lytton, Edward 1
Burney, Fanny 12

Byron, George Gordon, Lord
  Byron 2, 12
Carroll, Lewis 2
Clare, John 9
Coleridge, Samuel Taylor 9
Collins, Wilkie 1
Cowper, William 8
De Quincey, Thomas 4
Dickens, Charles 3, 8
Disraeli, Benjamin 2
Eden, Emily 10
Eliot, George 4, 13
FitzGerald, Edward 9
Forster, John 11
Gaskell, Elizabeth Cleghorn 5
Godwin, William 14
Hunt, Leigh 1
Jerrold, Douglas 2
Keats, John 8
Lamb, Charles 10
Landor, Walter Savage 14
Lear, Edward 3
Lewis, Matthew Gregory 11
Marryat, Frederick 3
Mill, John Stuart 11
Mitford, Mary Russell 4
Montagu, Elizabeth 7
Morris, William 4
Pater, Walter 7
Patmore, Coventry Kersey
  Dighton 9
Radcliffe, Ann 6
Reade, Charles 2
Rossetti, Christina Georgina 2
Rossetti, Dante Gabriel 4
Shelley, Mary Wollstonecraft
  Godwin 14
Southey, Robert 8
Surtees, Robert Smith 14

Thackeray, William
  Makepeace 5, 14
Trollope, Anthony 6
Wordsworth, William 12

FRENCH
Balzac, Honoré de 5
Banville, Théodore de 9
Barbey d'Aurevilly, Jules
  Amédée 1
Baudelaire, Charles 6
Becque, Henri 3
Chateaubriand, François René
  de 3
Constant, Benjamin 6
Daudet, Alphonse 1
Dumas, Alexandre (père) 11
Dumas, Alexandre (fils) 9
Flaubert, Gustave 2, 10
Fromentin, Eugène 10
Gaboriau, Émile 14
Gautier, Théophile 1
Goncourt, Edmond de 7
Goncourt, Jules de 7
Hugo, Victor Marie 3, 10
Joubert, Joseph 9
Laclos, Pierre Ambroise
  François Choderlos de 4
Laforgue, Jules 5
Lamartine, Alphonse de 11
Lautréamont, Comte de 12
Mallarmé, Stéphane 4
Maupassant, Guy de 1
Mérimée, Prosper 6
Musset, Alfred de 7
Nerval, Gérard de 1
Rimbaud, Arthur 4
Sade, Donatien Alphonse
  François, Comte de 3

527

Cumulative Index to Critics

Critic Index

Critic Index

Kronenberger, Louis
Pierre Ambroise François
Choderlos de Laclos **4**:336
Richard Brinsley Sheridan
5:376
Anthony Trollope **6**:505

Kropf, C. R.
William Godwin **14**:84

Kropotkin, Prince
Vissarion Grigoryevich Belinski
5:100
Nikolai Alexandrovich
Dobrolyubov **5**:138
Fedor Mikhailovich Dostoevski
2:163
Ivan Alexandrovich Goncharov
1:361
Aleksandr Ivanovich Herzen
10:327
Nikolai Alekseevich Nekrasov
11:401
Alexander Pushkin **3**:426

Krutch, Joseph Wood
Henry David Thoreau **7**:388

Krzyzanowski, Julian
Aleksander Fredro **8**:286, 292
Ignacy Krasicki **8**:406
Zygmunt Krasiński **4**:309
Adam Mickiewicz **3**:392

Kubicek, Earl C.
Eugene Field **3**:212

Kulkarni, H. B.
Herman Melville **12**:304

Kulp-Hill, Kathleen
Rosalía de Castro **3**:103

Kurz, Harry
Alphonse Daudet **1**:244
Lachal, Louis, S. J.
John Banim and Michael
Banim **13**:130

Lacy, John
Thomas Lovell Beddoes **3**:25

Laforgue, Jules
Charles Baudelaire **6**:88

Lalou, René
Jean Marie Mathias Philippe
Auguste, Comte de Villiers
de l'Isle-Adam **3**:586

Lamartine, Alphonse de
Alexandre Dumas (*père*) **11**:56

Lamb, Charles
William Blake **13**:160
John Clare **9**:78
Samuel Taylor Coleridge **9**:147
John Keats **8**:326
William Wordsworth **12**:396

Lamb, George
Charles Robert Maturin **6**:318

Lamm, Martin
Henri Becque **3**:17
Alexandre Dumas (*fils*) **9**:251

Lampert, E.
Vissarion Grigoryevich Belinski
5:110

Lancaster, H. H.
Matthew Arnold **6**:33

Landor, Walter Savage
William Blake **13**:162
John Forster **11**:94
Walter Savage Landor **14**:155,
156, 168

Landre, Louis
Leigh Hunt **1**:420

Lang, Andrew
Théodore de Banville **9**:22
Lewis Carroll **2**:106
Alexandre Dumas (*père*) **11**:74
John Forster **11**:109
William Morris **4**:418
Walter Pater **7**:303
Ann Radcliffe **6**:412
Robert Louis Stevenson **5**:398

Langbaum, Robert
William Wordsworth **12**:470

Langdon-Davies, B. N.
Benjamin Disraeli **2**:149

Langsjoen, Sven V.
Friedrich Gottlieb Klopstock
11:239

Lanier, Sidney
Sidney Lanier **6**:233

Lascelles, Mary
Jane Austen **1**:46; **13**:66

Laski, Harold J.
John Stuart Mill **11**:367
Alexis de Tocqueville **7**:433

Laski, Marghanita
Emily Eden **10**:110

Lasserre, Pierre
Richard Wagner **9**:437

Lathbury, Bertha
Robert Louis Stevenson **5**:393

Lathbury, Daniel Connor
Robert Louis Stevenson **5**:393

Lathrop, G. P.
Nathaniel Hawthorne **2**:307

Lauerwinkel, Baron von
Thomas Moore **6**:382

Lautréamont, Comte de
Comte de Lautréamont **12**:205,
206

Laveleye, Emile de
Edward Bellamy **4**:24

Lavers, Annette
Aubrey Beardsley **6**:144

Lavrin, Janko
Sergei Timofeyvich Aksakov
2:14
Fedor Mikhailovich Dostoevski
2:187; **7**:84
Ivan Alexandrovich Goncharov
1:365
Aleksandr Ivanovich Herzen
10:334
Guy de Maupassant **1**:461
Nikolai Alekseevich Nekrasov
11:420
Alexander Pushkin **3**:444
Arthur Rimbaud **4**:458

Law, Alice
Charles Lamb **10**:419
Christina Georgina Rossetti
2:562

Law, Marie Hamilton
Leigh Hunt **1**:416

Lawrence, D. H.
James Fenimore Cooper **1**:214
Fedor Mikhailovich Dostoevski
2:181
Ralph Waldo Emerson **1**:291
Nathaniel Hawthorne **2**:322
Herman Melville **3**:334; **12**:259
Edgar Allan Poe **1**:504
Walt Whitman **4**:564

Lawrenny, H.
Charles Dickens **3**:160
George Eliot **4**:105

Lazarus, Emma
Eugène Fromentin **10**:227

Lazarus, Josephine
Emma Lazarus **8**:417

Lea, Henry C.
Leigh Hunt **1**:410

Leach, Elsie
Lewis Carroll **2**:119

Lear, Edward
Edward Lear **3**:296

Leary, Lewis
Hugh Henry Brackenridge **7**:50
Philip Morin Freneau **1**:321
Oliver Wendell Holmes **14**:145
Washington Irving **2**:388
Sidney Lanier **6**:267

Leavis, F. R.
Matthew Arnold **6**:56
Samuel Taylor Coleridge **9**:173
Charles Dickens **3**:184
George Eliot **4**:126
John Stuart Mill **11**:370
William Wordsworth **12**:442

Leavis, Q. D.
Jane Austen **1**:50
Charles Dickens **8**:194
Nathaniel Hawthorne **2**:329
Margaret Oliphant **11**:457, 459

Le Breton, André
Pierre Ambroise François
Choderlos de Laclos **4**:325

Lednicki, Wacław
Zygmunt Krasiński **4**:315
Alexander Pushkin **3**:455

Lee, Ernest D.
John Greenleaf Whittier **8**:512

Leeds, William Henry
Alexander Pushkin **3**:414

Le Fanu, J. S.
Joseph Sheridan Le Fanu **9**:298

Lefevre, Carl
George Gordon Byron, Lord
Byron **2**:89

Le Gallienne, Richard
Sidney Lanier **6**:240
Walter Pater **7**:311
Christina Georgina Rossetti
2:558
Robert Louis Stevenson **5**:410,
412, 414

Lehmann, John
Edward Lear **3**:309

Leisy, Ernest E.
John Pendleton Kennedy **2**:433

Lemaître, Georges
Comte de Lautréamont **12**:214

Lemaître, Jules
Joseph Joubert **9**:283

Leonard, William Ellery
William Cullen Bryant **6**:173

Lepelletier, Edmond
Paul Verlaine **2**:622

Leppington, Blanche
Henri Frédéric Amiel **4**:13

Lermontov, M. Yu.
Mikhail Yuryevich Lermontov
5:287

Lerner, Max
Walter Bagehot **10**:34

Lesser, J.
Alphonse Daudet **1**:245

Lester, John A., Jr.
William Makepeace Thackeray
5:489

Lethbridge, Robert
Eugène Fromentin **10**:259

L'Étrangère
Honoré de Balzac **5**:27

Letwin, Shirley Robin
John Stuart Mill **11**:383

Leventhal, A. J.
George Darley **2**:131

Lever, Charles
Joseph Sheridan Le Fanu **9**:299

Levey, Michael
Charlotte Brontë **3**:77
Nathaniel Hawthorne **10**:309
Oliver Wendell Holmes **14**:145
Charles Lamb **10**:430
Herman Melville **12**:303
Anthony Trollope **6**:504
Walt Whitman **4**:603

Levi, Peter, S.J.
John Clare **9**:114

Levin, David
Francis Parkman **12**:359

Levine, George
George Eliot **4**:136, 145
Mary Wollstonecraft Godwin
Shelley **14**:300

Levy, Leonard W.
Thomas Jefferson **11**:196

Lewes, George Henry
Matthew Arnold **6**:31
Jane Austen **13**:55
Honoré de Balzac **5**:33
George Borrow **9**:46
Charlotte Brontë **3**:43
Charles Dickens **3**:161; **8**:159
John Forster **11**:98
Elizabeth Cleghorn Gaskell
5:180, 184
Johann Wolfgang von Goethe
4:181
Victor Hugo **3**:244, 248
Otto Ludwig **4**:346
George Sand **2**:587, 588
William Makepeace Thackeray
5:445; **14**:392

Critic Index

Critic Index

Critic Index

Critic Index